10e

Understanding Management

Richard L. Daft
Vanderbilt University

Dorothy Marcic
Columbia University

CENGAGE
Learning®

Australia • Brazil • Mexico • Singapore • United Kingdom • United States

Understanding Management,
10th Edition

Richard L. Daft and Dorothy Marcic

Vice President, General Manager, Social Science
& Qualitative Business: Erin Joyner

Product Director: Jason Fremder

Senior Product Manager: Scott Person

Content Developer: Katherine Caudill

Product Assistant: Brian Pierce

Marketing Director: Kristen Hurd

Marketing Manager: Emily Horowitz

Marketing Coordinator: Chris Walz

Art and Cover Direction, Production
    Management, and Composition: Lumina
    Datamatics, Inc

Intellectual Property
    Analyst: Diane Garrity
    Project Manager: Sarah Shainwald

Manufacturing Planner: Ron Montgomery

Cover Image: ©luckyraccoon/Shutterstock

Internal Design Images: ©hxdyl/istockphoto.
    com, ©phoelix/Shutterstock, ©LOVEgraphic/
    Shutterstock, ©Andriy Solovyov/
    Shutterstock, ©Jamen Percy/Shutterstock,
    ©Zarya Maxim Alexandrovich/Shutterstock,
    ©Jason Winter/Shutterstock, ©STILLFX/
    Shutterstock, ©GalapagosPhoto/
    Shutterstock

For product information and technology assistance, contact us at
Cengage Learning Customer & Sales Support, 1-800-354-9706

For permission to use material from this text or product,
submit all requests online at **www.cengage.com/permissions**
Further permissions questions can be emailed to
permissionrequest@cengage.com

Library of Congress Control Number: 2015949190

Student Edition:
ISBN: 978-1-305-50221-5

Loose-leaf Edition:
ISBN: 978-1-305-50223-9

Cengage Learning
20 Channel Center Street
Boston, MA 02210
USA

Cengage Learning is a leading provider of customized learning solutions
with employees residing in nearly 40 different countries and sales in more
than 125 countries around the world. Find your local representative at
www.cengage.com.

Cengage Learning products are represented in Canada by
Nelson Education, Ltd.

To learn more about Cengage Learning Solutions, visit **www.cengage.com**

Purchase any of our products at your local college store or at our preferred
online store **www.cengagebrain.com**

Unless otherwise noted all items © Cengage Learning.

Printed in Canada

Print Number: 01   Print Year: 2015

*The old and the new. In memory of my wonderful Aunt Jenylle,
who weathered unbelievable struggles with quiet strength, resilience,
and radiance. And to my grandson, Nelson Williams, who helps me see
the world, and management, through new eyes.*
—DM

The World of Innovative Management

Today's managers and organizations are being buffeted by massive and far-reaching social, technological, and economic changes. Any manager who believed in the myth of stability was rocked out of complacency when, one after another, large financial institutions in the United States began to fail, automakers filed for bankruptcy, the housing market collapsed, European economies faced financial challenges, and a global economic recession took hold and wouldn't let go. Business schools, as well as managers and businesses, are still scrambling to cope with the aftermath, keep up with fast-changing events and evaluate the impact that this volatile period of history will have on organizations in the future. This edition of *Understanding Management* addresses themes and issues that are directly relevant to the current, fast-shifting business environment.

We revised *Understanding Management*, 10th edition, with the goal of helping current and future managers find innovative solutions to the problems that plague today's organizations—whether they are everyday challenges or once-in-a-lifetime crises. The world in which most students will work as managers is undergoing a tremendous upheaval. Ethical turmoil, the need for crisis management skills, e-business, economic recession and rampant unemployment, rapidly changing technologies, globalization, outsourcing, increasing government regulation, social media, global supply chains, the Wall Street meltdown, and other challenges place demands on managers that go beyond the techniques and ideas traditionally taught in management courses. Managing today requires the full breadth of management skills and capabilities. This text provides comprehensive coverage of both traditional management skills and the new competencies needed in a turbulent environment characterized by economic turmoil, political confusion, and general uncertainty.

In the traditional world of work, management's job was to control and limit people, enforce rules and regulations, seek stability and efficiency, design a top-down hierarchy, and achieve bottom-line results. To spur innovation and achieve high performance, however, managers need different skills, particularly in today's tough economy that has caused suffering for many employees. Managers have to find ways to engage workers' hearts and minds, as well as take advantage of their physical labor. The new workplace asks that managers focus on building trust, inspiring commitment, leading change, harnessing people's creativity and enthusiasm, finding shared visions and values, and sharing information and power. Teamwork, collaboration, participation, and learning are guiding principles that help managers and employees maneuver the difficult terrain of today's turbulent business environment. Rather than controlling their employees, managers focus on training them to adapt to new technologies and extraordinary environmental shifts, and thus achieve high performance and total corporate effectiveness.

Our vision for this edition of *Understanding Management* is to present the newest management ideas for turbulent times in a way that is interesting and valuable to students, while retaining the best of traditional management thinking. To achieve this vision, we have included the most recent management concepts and research and have shown the contemporary application of management ideas in organizations. A questionnaire at the beginning of each chapter draws students personally into the topic and gives them some insight into their own management skills. A chapter feature for new managers, called the New Manager Self-Test, gives students personal feedback about what will be expected when they become managers. At the end of each major chapter section, we have added a Remember This feature that provides a quick review of the salient concepts and terms students should remember. Within each chapter, a new feature called Green Power highlights how various organizations are responding to the growing demand for socially and environmentally responsible ways of doing business. Thoughtful or inspiring quotes within each chapter—some from business leaders, others from novelists, philosophers, and everyday people—help students expand their thinking about management issues. The combination of established scholarship, new ideas, and real-life applications gives students a taste of the energy, challenge, and adventure inherent in the dynamic field of management. We have worked with the Cengage Learning staff to provide a textbook that is better than any other at capturing the excitement of organizational management.

We revised *Understanding Management* to provide a book of utmost quality that will create in students both respect for the changing field of management and confidence that they can understand and master it. The textual portion of this book has been enhanced through the engaging, easy-to-understand writing style and the many new in-text examples, boxed items, and short exercises that make the concepts come alive for students. The graphic component has been enhanced with several new and revised exhibits and updated photo essays that illustrate specific management concepts. The photographs provide vivid illustrations and intimate glimpses of management scenes, events, and people. Combined with brief essays that explain how a specific management concept looks and feels, the textual and graphic portions of the textbook help students grasp the often abstract and distant world of management.

Focus on Innovation: New to the 10th Edition

A primary focus for revising the 10th edition has been to relate management concepts and theories to events in today's turbulent environment by bringing in present-day issues that real-life managers face. Sections that are particularly relevant to fast-shifting current events are marked with a "Hot Topic" icon.

Learning Opportunities

The 10th edition includes several innovative pedagogical features to help students understand their own management capabilities and learn what it is like to manage in an organization today. Each chapter begins with an opening questionnaire that directly relates to the topic of the chapter and enables students to see how they respond to situations and challenges typically faced by real-life managers. A New Manager Self-Test in each chapter provides further opportunity for students to understand their management abilities. These short feedback questionnaires, which are all new for this edition, give students insight into how they would function in the real world of management. The Remember This bullet-point summaries at the end of each major chapter section give students a snapshot of the key points and concepts covered in that section. The end-of-chapter questions have been carefully revised to encourage critical thinking and application of chapter concepts. Self-Learning instruments give students a chance to assess their strengths, while Group Learning exercises give students the opportunity to apply concepts while building teamwork skills, and Action Learning activities give students a chance to practice the chapter concepts in an action-research methodology. Ethical dilemmas and all-new end-of-chapter cases help students sharpen their diagnostic skills for management problem solving.

Chapter Content

Within each chapter, many topics have been added or expanded to address the current issues that managers face. Chapter text has been tightened and sharpened to provide greater focus on the key topics that count for management today. The essential elements concerning operations and information technology, subject matter that is frequently covered in other courses, have been combined into an appendix for students who want more information about these topics.

Chapter 1 includes a discussion of some of the high-impact events and changes that have made innovative management so critical to the success of organizations today and into the future. This introductory chapter also talks about making the leap from being an individual contributor in the organization to becoming a new manager and getting work done primarily through the efforts of others. It introduces the skills and competencies needed to manage organizations effectively, including issues such as managing one's time, maintaining appropriate control, and building trust and credibility.

It includes an expanded discussion of the positive and negative aspects of bureaucracy and an updated discussion of the use of the management science approach in recent years. The chapter also examines contemporary management tools for turbulent times. The final part of the chapter looks at managing the technology-driven workplace, including social media programs, customer relationship management, and supply chain management.

Chapter 2 contains an updated view of current issues related to the environment and corporate culture, including a new discussion of organizational ecosystems, the growing importance of the international environment, and trends in the sociocultural environment, including a growing minority population and today's technologically connected consumer. The chapter includes a new discussion of the concept of strategic issues and also describes how managers shape a high-performance culture as an innovative response to a shifting environment.

Chapter 3 takes a thoroughly updated look at the shifting international landscape, including the Arab Spring and the growing clout of China, India, and Brazil, as well as what these changes mean for managers around the world. The chapter includes a new discussion of the importance of a global mind-set and an updated review of the globalization backlash. The chapter also discusses the bottom-of-the-pyramid concept, economic interdependence, and recent challenges brought about by economic difficulties in European Union countries.

Chapter 4 makes the business case for incorporating ethical values in the organization and looks at the role that managers play in creating an ethical organization. The chapter includes an updated discussion of the state of ethical management today, the pressures that can contribute to unethical behavior in organizations, and criteria that managers can use for resolving ethical dilemmas. The chapter considers corporate social responsibility issues as well, including new discussions of challenges in the global supply chain, the concept of a triple bottom line, and stakeholder mapping.

Chapter 5 provides a discussion of the overall planning and goal-setting process, including the use of strategy maps for aligning goals. A new section describes the socially constructed nature of goals and how managers decide which goals to pursue. The chapter also outlines the benefits and limitations of planning and goal setting, includes a new discussion of management by means (MBM), and takes a close look at crisis planning and how to use scenarios. The final section describes innovative approaches to planning, including the use of intelligence teams and business performance dashboards to help managers plan in a fast-changing environment.

It continues its focus on the basics of formulating and implementing strategy, including the elements of strategy and Porter's competitive strategies. It includes a new section on identifying the target customer as one of the components of competitive advantage. In addition, the chapter explains global strategies and the Boston Consulting Group (BCG) matrix. The final section of the chapter provides an updated discussion of how managers effectively execute strategy.

Chapter 6 gives an overview of managerial decision making, including decision-making models, personal decision styles, and an updated discussion of biases that can cloud managers' judgment and lead to bad decisions. The final section looks at innovative group decision making and includes new discussions of evidence-based decision making and the use of after-action reviews.

Chapter 7 discusses basic principles of organizing and describes both traditional and contemporary organizational structures in detail. The chapter includes a discussion of the strengths and weaknesses associated with each structural approach. It also offers a new discussion of relational coordination as a way to enhance horizontal collaboration and coordination and describes contingency factors that shape structure, including strategy and technology.

Chapter 8 focuses on the critical role of managing change and innovation. The chapter includes new discussions of the bottom-up approach to innovation and the use of innovation contests, as well as an expanded discussion of the horizontal linkage model for new product development. It also describes disruptive innovation and reverse (trickle-up) innovation, open innovation, and crowdsourcing. This chapter provides information about product and technology changes, as well as about changing people and culture, and it discusses techniques for implementing change effectively.

Chapter 9 has been revised thoroughly to reflect the shifting role of human resource management (HRM) in today's turbulent economic environment. The chapter includes an updated discussion of the strategic role of HRM in building human capital, a new discussion of employer branding, and expanded sections on the trends toward contingent employment and flexible scheduling. There are also new sections on using social media and internships for recruiting, online checking of job candidates, and a brief discussion of extreme interviewing. The section on training and development has been updated and includes a new discussion of social learning.

It also includes the most recent thinking on organizational diversity issues. The chapter includes a thoroughly updated discussion of demographic changes occurring in the domestic and global workforce and how organizations are responding. It also includes a new section on the importance of a diversity of perspective within organizations, a revised section on the glass ceiling and the "bamboo ceiling," and a new section offering tips for aspiring female and minority managers.

Chapter 10 continues its solid coverage of the basics of understanding individual behavior, including personality, attitudes, perception, and emotions. In addition, the chapter includes a new section on the value and difficulty of self-awareness, techniques for enhancing self-awareness, a new discussion of self-management, and a step-by-step guide to time management. The section on stress management has been enhanced by a new discussion of challenge stress versus threat stress and new sections describing ways both individuals and organizations can combat the harmful effects of too much stress.

Chapter 11 examines contemporary approaches to leadership, including Level 5 leadership, authentic leadership, and servant leadership. The chapter also discusses charismatic and transformational leadership, task versus relationship leadership behaviors, gender differences in leadership, the importance of leaders discovering and honing their strengths, and the role of followers. The section on leadership power has been revised to include the concept of *hard* versus *soft* power.

Chapter 12 covers the foundations of motivation and incorporates a new section on positive versus negative approaches to motivating employees. The chapter also includes new sections on building a thriving workforce and the importance of making progress as a factor contributing to high employee motivation. The sections on empowerment and employee engagement have been updated as well.

Chapter 13 explores the basics of good communication and includes new discussions of asking questions and communicating with candor, a revised section on creating an open communication climate, and an expanded and enriched discussion of communicating to influence and persuade. A new section discusses using social media to enhance communication within the organization and with stakeholders.

Chapter 14 takes a fresh look at the contributions that teams make in organizations. It also acknowledges that work teams are sometimes ineffective and explores the reasons for this, including such problems as free riders and lack of trust. The chapter covers the types of teams and includes a look at using technology effectively in virtual teams. It also discusses how factors such as team diversity, member roles, norms, and team cohesiveness influence effectiveness. There is a revised section on negotiation and managing conflict, including an explanation of task versus relationship conflict.

Chapter 15 provides an overview of financial and quality control, including the feedback control model, Six Sigma, International Organization for Standards (ISO) certification, and use of the balanced scorecard. The chapter includes a new section on zero-based budgeting, a new discussion of quality partnering, and a new step-by-step benchmarking process. The chapter also addresses current concerns about corporate governance, including new government regulations and requirements.

In addition to the topics listed previously, this text integrates coverage of the Internet, social media, and new technology into the various topics covered in each and every chapter.

Organization

The chapter sequence in *Understanding Management* is organized around the management functions of planning, organizing, leading, and controlling. These four functions effectively encompass both management research and the characteristics of the manager's job.

Part One introduces the world of management, including the nature of management, issues related to today's chaotic environment, historical perspectives on management, and the technology-driven workplace.

Part Two examines the environments of management and organizations. This section includes material on the business environment and corporate culture, the global environment, ethics and social responsibility, and the environment of small business and entrepreneurship.

Part Three presents three chapters on planning, including organizational goal setting and planning, strategy formulation and execution, and the decision-making process.

Part Four focuses on organizing processes. These chapters describe dimensions of structural design, the design alternatives that managers can use to achieve strategic objectives, structural designs for promoting innovation and change, the design and use of the human resource function, and how the approach to managing diverse employees is significant to the organizing function.

Part Five is devoted to leadership. The section begins with a chapter on understanding individual behavior, including self-awareness and self-understanding. This foundation paves the way for subsequent discussions of leadership, motivation of employees, communication, and team management.

Part Six describes the controlling function of management, including basic principles of total quality management (TQM), the design of control systems, and the difference between hierarchical and decentralized control.

Innovative Features

A major goal of this book is to offer better ways of using the textbook medium to convey management knowledge to the reader. To this end, the book includes several innovative features that draw students in and help them contemplate, absorb, and comprehend management concepts. South-Western has brought together a team of experts to create and coordinate color photographs, video cases, beautiful artwork, and supplemental materials for the best management textbook and package on the market.

Chapter Outline and Objectives. Each chapter begins with a clear statement of its learning objectives and an outline of its contents. These devices provide an overview of what is to come and also can be used by students to guide their study and test their understanding and retention of important points.

Opening Questionnaire. The text grabs student attention immediately by giving the student a chance to participate in the chapter content actively by completing a short questionnaire related to the topic.

Take Action. At strategic places within the chapter, students are invited to Take a Moment to complete a New Manager Self-Test or end of chapter activity that relates to the concepts being discussed.

New Manager Self-Tests. New Manager Self-Tests in each chapter provides opportunities for self-assessment as a way for students to experience management issues in a personal way. The change from individual performer to new manager is dramatic, and these self-tests, which are all new for the 10th edition, provide insight into what to expect and how students might perform in the world of the new manager.

Green Power. A new feature for this edition is a Green Power box in each chapter that highlights how managers in a specific company are innovatively addressing issues of sustainability and environmental responsibility. Examples of companies spotlighted in the Green Power boxes include Deutsche Post DHL Group, Nike, Acciona, BMW, Waste Management, Inc., Bean and Body, PepsiCo, Fujitsu, The Honest Company, SAP, and Royal DSM.

Concept Connection Photos. A key feature of the book is the use of photographs accompanied by detailed photo essay captions that enhance learning. Each caption highlights and illustrates one or more specific concepts from the text to reinforce student understanding of the concepts. Although the photos are beautiful to look at, they also convey the vividness, immediacy, and concreteness of management events in today's business world.

Contemporary Examples. Every chapter of this book contains several written examples of management incidents. They are placed at strategic points in the chapter and are designed to illustrate the application of concepts to specific companies. These in-text examples—indicated by the title "Innovative Way"—include well-known U.S. and international organizations, including Apple, Four Seasons, Lenovo, Amazon, Nokia, the Central Intelligence Agency (CIA), and Semco, as well as lesser-known companies and not-for-profit organizations including Godrej & Boyce, Strand Brewing Company, Trader Joe's, Hilcorp Energy, Johnson Storage and Moving, and IGN. The 10th edition includes new and updated examples that put students in touch with the real world of organizations so that they can appreciate the value of management concepts.

Benchmarking. A featured box in each chapter addresses a specific topic straight from the field of management that is of special interest to students. These boxes, most of which are new for the 10th edition, may describe a contemporary topic or problem that is relevant to chapter content, or they may contain a diagnostic questionnaire or a special example of how managers handle a problem. The boxes heighten student interest in the subject matter and provide an auxiliary view of management issues not typically available in textbooks.

Video Cases. At the end of each chapter, there is a video case that illustrates the concepts presented in the text. These "On the Job" videos (one per chapter) enhance the classroom experience by giving students the chance to hear from real-world business leaders so they can see the direct application of the management theories they have learned. Companies discussed include Holden Outerware, Living Social Escapes, Camp Bow Wow, and Theo Chocolate. Each video case explores the issues covered in the video, allowing students to synthesize material they've just viewed. The video cases culminate with several questions that can be used to launch classroom discussion or can be assigned as homework. Suggested answers are provided in the Instructor's Manual.

Exhibits. Several exhibits have been added or revised in this edition to enhance student understanding. Many aspects of management are research based, and some concepts tend to be abstract and theoretical. The many exhibits throughout this book enhance students' awareness and understanding of these concepts. These exhibits consolidate key points, indicate relationships among concepts, and visually illustrate concepts. They also make effective use of color to enhance their imagery and appeal.

Remember This. At the end of each major section of a chapter is a Remember This bullet-point summary of the key concepts, ideas, and terms discussed in that section. The Remember This feature gives students an easy way to review the salient points covered in the chapter.

Glossaries. Learning the management vocabulary is essential to understanding contemporary management. This process is facilitated in three ways. First, key concepts are boldfaced and completely defined where they first appear in the text. Second, brief definitions are set out at the end of each major section in the Remember This bullet points for easy review and follow-up. Third, a glossary summarizing all key terms and definitions appears at the end of the book for handy reference.

Discussion Questions. Each chapter closes with discussion questions that will enable students to check their understanding of key issues, to think beyond basic concepts, and to determine areas that require further study.

Learning Exercises. End-of-chapter exercises called "Self-Learning" and "Ethical Dilemma" provide a self-test for students and an opportunity to experience management issues in a personal way. These exercises take the form of questionnaires, scenarios, and activities. The exercises are tied into the chapter through the Take a Moment feature that refers students to the end-of-chapter exercises at the appropriate point in the chapter content.

Group Learning. Group learning exercises at the end of each chapter give students a chance to develop both team and analytical skills. Completing the small-group activities will help students learn to use the resources provided by others in the group, to pool information, and to develop a successful outcome together. The Small Group Breakouts provide experiential learning that leads to deeper understanding and application of chapter concepts.

Action Learning. These exercises are designed to help the students not only apply the chapter concepts, but to include a action-research component to enhance maximum learning capacity.

Case for Critical Analysis. Also appearing at the end of each chapter is a brief but substantive case that offers an opportunity for student analysis and class discussion. These cases are based on real management problems and dilemmas, but the identities of companies and managers have been disguised. These cases, which are all new for the 10th edition, allow students to sharpen their diagnostic skills for management problem solving.

MindTap's Innovative Digital Features

MindTap

Students who purchase the MindTap product for Understanding Management, 10th edition, will enjoy a number of innovative features designed to enhance their learning experience. The e-book has been enriched with interactive figures and animated videos that increase comprehension of the most challenging topics, and the insightful video cases are embedded directly into the end-of-chapter materials. At the beginning of each chapter, students will be asked to take a self-assessment questionnaire that introduces an important topic and shows how it relates to students' current experience. Students will also have ready access to the assignments chosen by the instructor, which may include test-prep quizzes, homework questions, Write Experience essay-writing practice and experiential exercises (online role-play activities and group projects).

New to this edition, the role-play exercises give students opportunities to practice their managerial and communication skills, while group projects encourage them to take a collaborative and fun approach to applying key concepts. All of these learning activities are designed to enable students to Engage, Connect, Perform, and Lead—in short, to learn to "think like managers," with demonstrable skills in critical thinking, analysis, and much more.

Augmenting the entire MindTap experience, robust diagnostic tools powered by Knewton provide students with feedback and personalized study activities based on actual assigned coursework rather than a separate set of quizzes. Using recommendations provided by Knewton, students can focus their efforts on the most important concepts they need to learn at that moment in time, as well as more effectively prepare for exams. Using the MindTap Progress App, instructors can track student proficiency, which will allow them to quickly react to where students are in their learning and make the best use of class time. This creates even more opportunities to train students to "Think and Act Like Managers."

Of Special Interest to Instructors

Instructor's Companion Site. Key instructor ancillaries (Instructor's Manual, Test Bank, and PowerPoint slides) are provided online, giving instructors the ultimate tool for customizing lectures and presentations and assessing students' progress.

- *Instructor's Manual.* Designed to provide support for instructors new to the course, as well as innovative materials for experienced professors, the Instructor's Manual includes Chapter Outlines, annotated learning objectives, Lecture Notes, and sample Lecture Outlines. In addition, the Instructor's Manual includes answers and teaching notes to end-of-chapter materials, including the video cases and the integrative cases.

- ***Test Bank.*** Scrutinized for accuracy, the Test Bank includes more than 3,000 multiple-choice, true/false, completion, short-answer, and essay questions. Each question is identified by difficulty level, Bloom's taxonomy level, and other useful reference points and outcomes.
- ***PowerPoint Lecture Presentation.*** These resources enable instructors to customize their own multimedia classroom presentation. Containing an average of 27 slides per chapter, the package includes figures and tables from the text, as well as outside materials to supplement chapter concepts. The material is organized by chapter and can be modified or expanded for individual classroom use.
- ***Test Bank.*** This edition's Test Bank has been dramatically upgraded to include a wider range of questions across Bloom's taxonomy. True/false, multiple-choice, completion, and short-answer questions test students' knowledge and comprehension; additional multiple-choice questions explore their ability to analyze and apply key concepts; and finally, essay questions challenge their ability to synthesize and evaluate, or to think like managers. All questions are given metadata tags to assist instructors in locating questions by difficulty level, Bloom's level, learning objective, or topic. Instructors can access the Test Bank through our new Cognero system, which allows for electronic editing and creation of tests, or via Microsoft Word documents available at the Instructor Resource Center. Test Banks can also be ingested into all major learning management systems.

To access the additional course materials and companion resources, please visit www.cengagebrain.com. At the CengageBrain.com home page, search for the ISBN of your title (from the back cover of your book) using the search box at the top of the page. This will take you to the product page, where free companion resources can be found. Students can purchase access to these resources for additional fees; please contact your Cengage sales representative for more information.

Acknowledgments

From Richard Daft: Here at Vanderbilt, I want to extend special appreciation to my assistant, Barbara Haselton. Barbara provided excellent support and assistance on a variety of projects that gave me time to write. I also want to acknowledge an intellectual debt to my colleagues, Bruce Barry, Rich Oliver, David Owens, Ty Park, Ranga Ramanujam, Bart Victor, and Tim Vogus. Thanks also to Deans Jim Bradford and Ray Friedman, who have supported my writing projects and maintained a positive scholarly atmosphere in the school.

I'd like to pay special tribute to my longtime editorial associate, Pat Lane. I can't imagine how I would ever complete such a comprehensive revision on my own. Pat provided truly outstanding help throughout every step of writing this edition of *Understanding Management*. She skillfully drafted materials for a wide range of chapter topics, boxes, and cases; researched topics when new sources were lacking; and did an absolutely superb job with the copyedited manuscript and page proofs. Her commitment to this text enabled us to achieve our dream for its excellence.

I also want to acknowledge the love and support from my daughters—Danielle and Amy—who make my life special during our precious time together. Thanks also to B. J. and Kaitlyn and Kaci and Matthew for their warmth and smiles that brighten my life, especially during our time together visiting interesting places.

Richard L. Daft
Nashville, Tennessee

From Dorothy Marcic: There have been numerous people who have given time and support on this project, including my assistants, Allison Greer and Aja Niesenson, along with Joshua Quinn, who helps out when he is not touring around the country doing theatrical productions. Friends and colleagues who gave invaluable support include Bill Franzblau, Janice Maffei, Deb Victoroff, Deborah Savadge, Wendi Momen, Janet Conrad, Jo Ann Tedesco, Patricia McGraw Romano, Kate DeStefano Weisman, Franky Grebacher, Georgia Sauer, Gail Phanuf, Peter Neamann, Victoria Marsick, Marie Volpe, Bob and Debby Rosenfeld, Nick Ritchie, Karen Streets-Anderson, , Andi Seals, Adrienne Corn, Mark and Maxine Rossman, Adrienne Ewing-Roush, Hillary Chapman, Kenneth Ferrone, Lishy Price, Mehr Mansuri, and Shidan Majidi. How can one do such a project without family love and support? My sister, Janet Mittelsteadt, is a true friend; my cousins, Shannon Stordock Hecht, Marilyn Nowak, Michael Shoemaker (the genealogist who has helped me find my own roots), and Katherine Runde (who is so precious); my Aunts Babe and Maxine, who are forever links to the past, as was my beloved Aunt Jenylle, who passed away recently. There is no way to imagine my life without my three beautiful daughters—Roxanne, Solange, and Elizabeth—who have taught me more than all my degrees combined. And, finally, Dick Daft, whose collaboration on this book is greatly satisfying.

Dorothy Marcic
New York, NY

Acknowledgments

We would also like to continue to acknowledge those reviewers who have contributed comments, suggestions, and feedback on this and all previous editions:

David C. Adams
Manhattanville College

David Alexander
Christian Brothers University

Erin M. Alexander
University of Houston–Clear Lake

David Arseneau
Eastern Illinois University

Reginald L Audibert
California State University—Long Beach

Hal Babson
Columbus State Community College

Reuel Barksdale
Columbus State Community College

Gloria Bemben
Finger Lakes Community College

Pat Bernson
County College of Morris

Andy Bertsch
Minot State University

Art Bethke
Northeast Louisiana University

Frank Bosco
Marshall University

Burrell A. Brown
California University of Pennsylvania

Paula Buchanan
Jacksonville State University

Deb Buerkley
Southwest Minnesota State University

Thomas Butte
Humboldt State University

Peter Bycio
Xavier University, Ohio

Diane Caggiano
Fitchburg State College

Douglas E. Cathon
St. Augustine's College

Peggy Cerrito
Augsburg College

Camille Chapman
Greenville Technical College

Bruce Charnov
Hofstra University

Jim Ciminskie
Bay de Noc Community College

Gloria Cockerell
Collin College

Dan Connaughton
University of Florida

Bruce Conwers
Kaskaskia College

Jack Cox
Amberton University

Byron L. David
City College of New York

V. J. Daviero
Pasco Hernando Community College

H. Kristl Davison
University of Mississippi

Richard De Luca
William Paterson University

Robert DeDominic
Montana Tech

Mark DeHainaut
California University of Pennsylvania

Granison Eader
Manor College

Joe J. Eassa, Jr.
Palm Beach Atlantic University

John C. Edwards
East Carolina University

Mary Ann Edwards
College of Mount St. Joseph

Paul Ewell
Bridgewater College

Mary M. Fanning
College of Notre Dame of Maryland

Janice M. Feldbauer
Austin Community College

Merideth Ferguson
Baylor University

Daryl Fortin
Upper Iowa University

Karen Fritz
Bridgewater College

Michael P. Gagnon
New Hampshire Community Technical College

Richard H. Gayor
Antelope Valley College

Dan Geeding
Xavier University, Ohio

James Genseal
Joliet Junior College

Peter Gibson
Becker College

Alexandra Giesler
Augsburg College

Yezdi H. Godiwalla
University of Wisconsin—Whitewater

Carol R. Graham
Western Kentucky University

Gary Greene
Manatee Community College

James Halloran
Wesleyan College

Ken Harris
Indiana University Southeast

Martin Hart
Manchester Community College

Kathy Hastings
Greenville Technical College

Paul Hayes
Coastal Carolina Community College

Dennis Heaton
Maharishi University of Management, Iowa

Stephen R. Hiatt
Catawba College

Jeffrey D. Hines
Davenport College

Bob Hoerber
Westminster College

Betty Hoge
Bridgewater College

James N. Holly
University of Wisconsin–Green Bay

Genelle Jacobson
Ridgewater College

Jody Jones
Oklahoma Christian University

C. Joy Jones
Ohio Valley College

Kathleen Jones
University of North Dakota

Sheryl Kae
Lynchburg College

Jordan J. Kaplan
Long Island University

J. Michael Keenan
Western Michigan University

Jerry Kinard
Western Carolina University

Renee Nelms King
Eastern Illinois University

Gloria Komer
Stark State College

Paula C. Kougl
Western Oregon University

Cynthia Krom
Mount St. Mary College

Sal Kukalis
California State University–Long Beach

Mukta Kulkarni
University of Texas–San Antonio

Donna LaGanga
Tunxis Community College

William B. Lamb
Millsaps College

Ruth D. Lapsley
Lewis-Clark State College

Robert E. Ledman
Morehouse College

George Lehma
Bluffton College

Joyce LeMay
Bethel University

Cynthia Lengnick-Hall
University of Texas–San Antonio

Gilda Lewis
University of Memphis

Janet C. Luke
Georgia Baptist College of Nursing

Jenna Lundburg
Ithaca College

Walter J. MacMillan
Oral Roberts University

Iraj Mahdavi
National University

Myrna P. Mandell
California State University, Northridge

Daniel B. Marin
Louisiana State University

Michael Market
Jacksonville State University

Joan McBee
Southern Oregon University

Wade McCutcheon
East Texas Baptist College

James C. McElroy
Iowa State University

Tom D. McFarland
Tusculum College

Dennis W. Meyers
Texas State Technical College

Alan N. Miller
University of Nevada–Las Vegas

Irene A. Miller
Southern Illinois University

Tom Miller
Concordia University

W J Mitchell
Bladen Community College

Daniel Morrell
Middle Tennessee State University

James L. Moseley
Wayne State University

Micah Mukabi
Essex County College

David W. Murphy
Madisonville Community College

Nora Nurre
Upper Iowa University

Ross O'Brien
Dallas Baptist University

Tomas J. Ogazon
St. Thomas University

Allen Oghenejbo
Mills College

John Okpara
Bloomsburg University

Linda Overstreet
Hillsborough Community College

Acknowledgments

Michael Payne
Milwaukee School of Engineering

Ken Peterson
Metropolitan State University

Lori A. Peterson
Augsburg College

Clifton D. Petty
Drury College

James I. Phillips
Northeastern State University

Marliss Platz
Cankdeska Cikana Community College

Michael Provitera
Barry University

Linda Putchinski
University of Central Florida

Abe Qastin
Lakeland College

Kenneth Radig
Medaille College

Gerald D. Ramsey
Indiana University Southeast

Holly Caldwell Ratwani
Bridgewater College

Barbara Redmond
Briar Cliff College

Tommie Redwine
Clatsop Community College

William Reisel
St. John's University–New York

Barbara Ribbens
Illinois State University

Terry L. Riddle
Central Virginia Community College

Linda Ridley
Hostos Community College

Walter F. Rohrs
Wagner College

Meir Russ
University of Wisconsin–Green Bay

Marcy Satterwhite
Lake Land College

Don Schreiber
Baylor University

Kilmon Shin
Ferris State University

Daniel G. Spencer
University of Kansas

Gary Spokes
Pace University

M. Sprencz
David N. Meyers College

Shanths Srinivas
California State Polytechnic University, Pomona

Barbara Stasek
Pasco Hernando Community College

Jeffrey Stauffer
Ventura College

William A. Stower
Seton Hall University

Mary Studer
Southwestern Michigan College

James Swenson
Moorhead State University, Minnesota

Thomas Sy
California State University–Long Beach

Irwin Talbot
St. Peter's College

Andrew Timothy
Lourdes College

Frank G. Titlow
St. Petersburg Junior College

John Todd
University of Arkansas

Kevin A. Van Dewark
Humphreys College

Linn Van Dyne
Michigan State University

Philip Varca
University of Wyoming

Dennis L. Varin
Southern Oregon University

Gina Vega
Merrimack College

George S. Vozikis
University of Tulsa

Noemy Wachtel
Kean University

Peter Wachtel
Kean University

Bruce C. Walker
Northeast Louisiana University

Kevin Wayne
Rivier College

Mark Weber
University of Minnesota

Emilia S. Westney
Texas Tech University

Rhonda Wetzler
Illinois Central College

Irene Wilder
Jefferson Community College

Stan Williamson
Northeast Louisiana University

Alla L. Wilson
University of Wisconsin–Green Bay

Ignatius Yacomb
Loma Linda University

Imad Jim Zbib
Ramapo College of New Jersey

Vic Zimmerman
Pima Community College

Richard L. Daft, Ph.D., is the Brownlee O. Currey, Jr., Professor of Management in the Owen Graduate School of Management at Vanderbilt University. Professor Daft specializes in the study of organization theory and leadership. Dr. Daft is a fellow of the Academy of Management and has served on the editorial boards of the *Academy of Management Journal, Administrative Science Quarterly,* and *Journal of Management Education.* He was the associate editor-in-chief of *Organization Science* and served for three years as associate editor of *Administrative Science Quarterly.*

Courtesy of the Author

Professor Daft has authored or co-authored more than a dozen books, including *Building Management Skills: An Action-First Approach* (with Dorothy Marcic, South-Western, 2014), *The Executive and the Elephant: A Leader's Guide for Building Inner Excellence* (Jossey-Bass, 2010), *Organization Theory and Design* (South-Western, 2013), *The Leadership Experience* (South-Western, 2011), and *Fusion Leadership: Unlocking the Subtle Forces That Change People and Organizations* (Berrett-Koehler, 2000, with Robert Lengel). He has also written dozens of scholarly articles, papers, and chapters in other books. His work has been published in *Administrative Science Quarterly, Academy of Management Journal, Academy of Management Review, Strategic Management Journal, Journal of Management, Accounting Organizations and Society, Management Science, MIS Quarterly, California Management Review,* and *Organizational Behavior Teaching Review.* In addition, Professor Daft is an active teacher and consultant. He has taught management, leadership, organizational change, organizational theory, and organizational behavior.

Professor Daft has served as associate dean, produced for-profit theatrical productions, and helped manage a start-up enterprise. He has been involved in management development and consulting for many companies and government organizations, including the American Banking Association, Bridgestone, Bell Canada, the National Transportation Research Board, Nortel, the Tennessee Valley Authority (TVA), Pratt & Whitney, State Farm Insurance, Tenneco, the U.S. Air Force, the U.S. Army, J. C. Bradford & Co., Central Parking System, Entergy Sales and Service, Bristol-Myers Squibb, First American National Bank, and the Vanderbilt University Medical Center.

Dorothy Marcic, EdD, MPH, is a professor at Columbia University and former faculty member at Vanderbilt University. Dr. Marcic is also a former Fulbright Scholar at the University of Economics in Prague and the Czech Management Center, where she taught courses and did research in leadership, organizational behavior, and cross-cultural management. She has taught courses at the Monterrey Institute of International Studies and has taught courses or given presentations at the Helsinki School of Economics, Slovenia Management Center, College of Trade in Bulgaria, City University of Slovakia, Landegg Institute in Switzerland, the Swedish Management Association, Technion University in Israel, and the London School of Economics. Other international work includes projects at the Autonomous University in Guadalajara, Mexico, and a training program for the World Health Organization in Guatemala. She has served on the boards of the Organizational Teaching Society, the Health Administration Section of the American Public Health Association, and the Journal of Applied Business Research.

Francois Bonneau

Dr. Marcic has authored 15 books, including *Organizational Behavior: Experiences and Cases* (South-Western Publishing, 6th edition, 2001), *Management International* (West Publishing, 1984), *Women and Men in Organizations* (George Washington University, 1984), and *Managing with the Wisdom of Love: Uncovering Virtue in People and Organizations* (Jossey-Bass, 1997), which was rated one of the top 10 business books of 1997 by *Management General*. Her most recent book is *Love Lift Me Higher (George Ronald, 2011)*. In addition, she has had dozens of articles printed in such publications as *Journal of Management Development, International Quarterly of Community Health Education, Psychological Reports,* and *Executive Development*. She has recently been exploring how to use the arts in the teaching of leadership and has a book, *RESPECT: Women and Popular Music,* which serves as the basis for the musical theater production *Respect: A Musical Journey of Women*. Her newest artistic endeavor is the Off-Broadway *SISTAS: The Musical*.

Professor Marcic has conducted thousands of seminars on various business topics and consulted for executives at AT&T Bell Labs; the governor and cabinet of North Dakota; the U.S. Air Force; Slovak Management Association; Eurotel; Hallmark Corp, Viacom, Czech Ministry of Finance; the Cattaraugus Center; USAA Insurance; State Farm Insurance; and the Salt River–Pima Indian Tribe in Arizona.

Brief Conte

Part 1 Introduction to Management 2

Chapter 1 The World of Innovative Management 2

Part 2 The Environment of Management 60

Contents

Chapter 4

Managing Ethics and Social Responsibility 144

Business Blooper
Lance Armstrong 152
Spotlight on Skills
Unequal Technologies 156
Spotlight on Skills
Gap Inc. 160
Green Power
Ecomagination 162
Director's Toolkit
Cultivating a Service Mind-Set 167
Spotlight on Skills
Google 168
Spotlight on Skills
Michael Woodford, Olympus 169

Part 3 Planning 182

Chapter 5

Planning and Goal Setting 182

Chapter 6

Managerial Decision Making 226

Part 4 Organizing 268

Chapter 7 Designing Organization Structure 268

Spotlight on Skills
Meetup.com 276

Green Power
A New Department 277

Spotlight on Skills
Toyota 280

Spotlight on Skills
Ben Stiller/Red Hour Digital 281

Business Blooper
Carnival Triumph 282

Director's Toolkit
The Bossless Upside-Down Structure 291

Spotlight on Skills
Smart Balance 293

Spotlight on Skills
Microsoft 296

Spotlight on Skills
Southwest Airlines 299

Director's Toolkit
Nasty Gal 303

Chapter 8 Managing Change and Innovation 316

Chapter 9

Managing Human Resources and Diversity   358

Contents

Part 5   Leading   422

Chapter 10   Understanding Individual Behavior 422

Spotlight on Skills
Landon Donovan, U.S. Soccer
Player 427

Green Power
Make it Meaningful 429

Spotlight on Skills
Marissa Mayer, Yahoo, and Richard
Branson, Virgin Group 435

Spotlight on Skills
The Rise of the Introverted
Manager 437

Spotlight on Skills
Hallmark Cards 442

Business Blooper
Zynga 452

Director's Toolkit
Freelancers Union 454

Chapter 11   Leadership   468

Chapter 12

Motivating Employees   514

Chapter 13

Managing Communication 554

Director's Toolkit
Gender Differences in
Communication 562
Spotlight on Skills
Amgen Inc. 568
Business Blooper
Target Canada 573
Spotlight on Skills
Tupperware Nordic 573
Spotlight on Skills
Theater Resources Unlimited 574
Executive Edge
Alex and Ani 582

Chapter 14

Leading Teams 594

Green Power
The Team's the Thing 598
Business Blooper
Toys R Us and Breaking Bad Dolls 600
Spotlight on Skills
Southwestern Aerospace Inc. 602
Director's Toolkit
How to Run a Great Meeting 609
Spotlight on Skills
Spring Company 610
The Executive Edge
Bedlam Theatre Company 616
Spotlight on Skills
McDevitt Street Bovis 617
Director's Toolkit
TEDxPfizerMumbai 618

Part 6   Controlling   636

Chapter 15   Managing Quality and Performance   636

CHAPTER 1

The **World** of **Innovative Management**

LEARNING OUTCOMES

After studying this chapter, you should be able to:

1.1 Describe five management competencies that are becoming crucial in today's fast-paced and rapidly changing world.

1.2 Explain the difference between efficiency and effectiveness and their importance for organizational performance.

1.3 Describe technical, human, and conceptual skills and their relevance for managers.

1.4 Summarize the personal challenges involved in becoming a new manager.

1.5 Define 10 roles that managers perform in organizations.

1.6 Explain the unique characteristics of the manager's role in small businesses and nonprofit organizations.

1.7 Identify and explain major developments in the history of management thought.

1.8 Describe the major components of the classical, humanistic-management perspectives, as well as management science and its current uses.

1.9 Explain the major concepts of systems thinking, the contingency view, and total quality management.

1.10 Name contemporary management tools and some reasons that management trends change over time.

1.11 Describe the management changes brought about by a technology-driven workplace, including the role of social media programs, customer relationship management (CRM), and supply chain management.

R U Ready 2 B a Manager?

Delivered

Before reading this chapter, please circle either "Mostly True" or "Mostly False" for each of the five questions below.

1 I am good at multitasking.

Mostly True	Mostly False

[page 17]

2 I'd be a good manager, because I enjoy telling people what to do.

Mostly True	Mostly False

[page 20]

3 I get easily distracted if I have frequent interruptions in my work.

Mostly True	Mostly False

[page 18]

4 I like to be systematic when solving problems.

Mostly True	Mostly False

[page 28]

5 I have a keen awareness of other people's needs.

Mostly True	Mostly False

[page 34]

NEW MANAGER Self-Test

Are You Ready to Be a Manager?
Manager Achievement

Welcome to the world of management. Are you ready for it? This questionnaire will help you see whether your priorities align with the demands placed on today's managers.

Instructions: Rate each of the following items based on your orientation toward personal achievement. Read each item and, based on how you feel right now, check either Mostly True or Mostly False.

	Mostly True	Mostly False
1. I enjoy the feeling I get from mastering a new skill.	_____	_____
2. Working alone is typically better than working in a group.	_____	_____
3. I like the feeling I get from winning.	_____	_____
4. I like to develop my skills to a high level.	_____	_____
5. I rarely depend on anyone else to get things done.	_____	_____
6. I am frequently the most valuable contributor to a team.	_____	_____
7. I like competitive situations.	_____	_____
8. To get ahead, it is important to be viewed as a winner.	_____	_____

Scoring and Interpretation: Give yourself one point for each Mostly True answer. In this case, a *low score* is better. A high score means a focus on personal achievement separate from others, which is ideal for a specialist or individual contributor. However, a manager is a generalist who gets things done through other people. Spending time building relationships is key. A desire to be an individual winner may cause you to compete with your people rather than develop their skills. You would not succeed as a lone achiever who does not facilitate and coordinate others, which is the primary job of a manager. If you checked 3 or fewer as Mostly True, your basic orientation is good. If you scored 6 or higher, your focus may be on being an individual winner. You will want to shift your perspective to become an excellent manager.

Most people think of Jon Bon Jovi as an aging rock star. What many don't realize is that Bon Jovi is still one of the world's top-selling bands (in terms of both record sales and concert touring) because their lead singer is also a consummate manager. "In the late 1980s," one music historian wrote, "it seemed inconceivable that [the group] would last five years." In 2011, Jon Bon Jovi was ranked No. 2 on *Forbes*'s list of the year's highest-paid musicians.[1] As the group prepared for the launch of its most recent tour in February 2013, Jon Bon Jovi was hidden away in the arena at the Mohegan Sun casino in Uncasville, Connecticut, for days, overseeing nearly 100 people organized into various teams such as lighting, sound, and video. It is an activity that he performs again and again when the band is touring, managing a tightly coordinated operation similar to setting up or readjusting a production line for a manufacturing business. Yet Bon Jovi is also performing other management activities throughout the year—planning and setting goals for the future, organizing tasks and assigning responsibilities, influencing and motivating band members and others, monitoring operations and finances, and networking inside and outside the organization (in perhaps the most prestigious example, he was appointed to President Barack Obama's White House Council for Community Solutions in 2010). *Efficiency* and *effectiveness* are key words in his vocabulary. "Jon is a businessman," said former co-manager David Munns. "He knows how to have a great-quality show, but he also knows how to be efficient with money."[2]

Jon Bon Jovi was smart enough to hire good people who could handle both production activities and the day-to-day minutia that go along with a global music business. However, it took several years to develop and hone his management skills. He assumed top management responsibilities for the band in 1992, about 10 years after founding it, because he had a vision that his professional managers weren't supporting. "Most of my peers wanted to be on the cover of *Circus* [a magazine devoted to rock music that was published from 1966 to 2006]," he said. "I wanted to be on the cover of *Time*."[3]

One particular surprise for many people when they first step into a management role is that they are much less in control of things than they expected to be. The nature of management is to motivate and coordinate others to cope with diverse and far-reaching challenges. Many new managers expect to have power, to be in control, and to be personally responsible for departmental outcomes. However, managers depend on subordinates more than the reverse, and they are evaluated on the work of other people rather than on their own achievements. Managers set up the systems and conditions that help other people perform well.

In the past, many managers exercised tight control over employees. But the field of management is undergoing a revolution that asks managers to do more with less, to engage employees' hearts and minds as well as their physical energy, to see change rather than stability as natural, and to inspire vision and cultural values that allow people to create a truly collaborative and productive workplace. This textbook introduces and explains the process of management and the changing ways of thinking about the world that are critical for managers. By reviewing the actions of some successful and not-so-successful managers, you will learn the fundamentals of management. By the end of this chapter, you will recognize some of the skills that managers use to keep organizations on track, and you will begin to understand how managers can achieve astonishing results through people. By the end of this book, you will understand the fundamental management skills for planning, organizing, leading, and controlling a department or an entire organization.

1.1 Management Competencies for Today's World

Management is the attainment of organizational goals in an effective and efficient manner through planning, organizing, leading, and controlling organizational resources, as Jon Bon Jovi does for his rock band, and as he did as co-owner of the Philadelphia Soul indoor football team in the Arena Football League. You will learn more about these four basic management functions later in this chapter.

There are certain elements of management that are timeless, but environmental shifts also influence the practice of management. In recent years, rapid environmental changes have caused a fundamental transformation in what is required of effective managers.

"I was once a command-and-control guy, but the environment's different today. I think now it's a question of making people feel they're making a contribution."

—Joseph J. Plumeri, Chairman and CEO of Willis Group Holdings

EXHIBIT 1.1 State-of-the-art Management Competencies for Today's World

Management Principle	From Traditional Approach	To New Competencies
Overseeing Work	From Controller	To Enabler
Accomplishing Tasks	From supervising individuals	To leading teams
Managing Relationships	From conflict and competition	To conversation and collaboration
Leading	From autocratic	To dispersed and empowering
Designing	From maintaining stability	To mobilizing for change

Technological advances such as social media and mobile apps, the rise of virtual work, global market forces, the growing threat of cyber crime, and shifting employee and customer expectations have led to a decline in organizational hierarchies and more empowered workers, which calls for a new approach to management that may be quite different from managing in the past.[4] Exhibit 1.1 shows the shift from the traditional management approach to the new management competencies that are essential in today's environment. Instead of being a *controller*, today's effective manager is an *enabler* who helps people do and be their best. Managers help people get what they need, remove obstacles, provide learning opportunities, and offer feedback, coaching, and career guidance. Instead of "management by keeping tabs," they employ an empowering leadership style. Much work is done in teams rather than by individuals, so team leadership skills are crucial. People in many organizations work at scattered locations, so managers can't monitor employee behavior continually. Some organizations are even experimenting with a bossless design that turns management authority and responsibility completely over to employees. Managing relationships based on authentic conversation and collaboration is essential for successful outcomes. Social media is a growing tool for managers to enhance communication and collaboration in support of empowered or bossless work environments. In addition, managers sometimes coordinate the work of people who aren't under their direct control, such as those in partner organizations, and they sometimes even work with competitors. They have to find common ground among people who might have disparate views and agendas and align them to go in the same direction.

Also, as shown in Exhibit 1.1, today's best managers are "future-facing." That is, they design the organization and culture to anticipate threats and opportunities from the environment, challenge the status quo, and promote creativity, learning, adaptation, and innovation. Industries, technologies, economies, governments, and societies are in a constant flux, and managers are responsible for helping their organizations navigate through the unpredictable with flexibility and innovation.[5] Today's world is constantly changing, but "the more unpredictable the environment, the greater the opportunity—if [managers] have the … skills to capitalize on it."[6]

One manager who exemplifies the new management skills and competencies is Vineet Nayar of India's HCL Technologies (HCL), with 80,000 employees and operations in more than 25 countries.

Spotlight on Skills

Vineet Nayar, HCL Technologies LLC

HCL Technologies is a leading global information technology (IT) services and software development company and India's fourth-largest IT services exporter. When Vineet Nayar (currently vice chairman and joint managing director) took over as CEO in 2005, HCL was a traditional, hierarchical, command-and-control workplace, but Nayar shifted the company's mind-set to treat its employees like customers. He is always on the lookout to upgrade management competencies to serve employees and help them do their jobs better. When HCL needed to cut expenses by $100 million due to the global recession, managers asked the employees to come up with ideas for cutting costs without issuing massive layoffs.

Nayar reorganized the whole company on the principle of "employees first, customers second (EFCS)".

He had to start by building trust, so he decided to share financial information with everyone in the company. Then he took a bold step: He created an open online forum where employees could post questions and leaders would answer them. This could expose weaknesses and problems that anyone—including outside customers and competitors—could see. Indeed, it did. "It was clogged with complaints," Nayar says. "It hurt." But interesting things began to happen, too. People were overjoyed that leaders were willing to acknowledge the problems. Some employees took this a step further and felt empowered to offer solutions. The site ultimately was the beginning of a transfer of the power and responsibility for solving problems from top executives to employees themselves. In the new HCL, the job of managers became to serve the employees.[7]

As Nayar learned, applying new management competencies can really pay off. Guided by the EFCS philosophy, HCL's revenues have grown by over 3.6 times, and net income has increased by 91 percent since 2005. But the shift to a new way of managing isn't easy for traditional managers who are accustomed to being "in charge," making all the decisions, and knowing where their subordinates are and what they're doing at every moment. Even more changes and challenges are on the horizon for organizations and managers. This is an exciting and challenging time to be entering the field of management. Throughout this book, you will learn much more about the new workplace, about the new and dynamic roles that managers are playing in the twenty-first century, and about how you can be an effective manager in a complex, ever-changing world.

REMEMBER THIS

- Managers get things done by coordinating and motivating other people.
- Management is often a different experience from what people expect.
- **Management** is defined as the attainment of organizational goals in an effective and efficient manner through planning, organizing, leading, and controlling organizational resources.
- Turbulent environmental forces have caused a significant shift in the competencies required for effective managers.

- Traditional management competencies could include a command-and-control leadership style, a focus on individual tasks, and standardizing procedures to maintain stability.
- New management competencies include the ability to be an enabler rather than a controller, using an empowering leadership style, encouraging collaboration, leading teams, and mobilizing for change and innovation.
- Vineet Nayar, former CEO of India's HCL, illustrates many of the new management competencies.

1.2 The Basic Functions of Management

"Good management is the art of making problems so interesting and their solutions so constructive that everyone wants to get to work and deal with them."

—Paul Hawken, environmentalist, entrepreneur, and author of *Natural Capitalism*

Every day, managers solve difficult problems, turn organizations around, and achieve astonishing performances. To be successful, every organization needs good managers. The famed management theorist Peter Drucker (1909–2005), often credited with creating the modern study of management, summed up the job of the manager by specifying five tasks, as outlined in Exhibit 1.2.[8] In essence, managers set goals, organize activities, motivate and communicate, measure performance, and develop people. These five manager activities apply not only to top executives such as Mark Zuckerberg at Facebook, Alan Mulally at Ford Motor Company, and Ursula Burns at Xerox, but also to the manager of a restaurant in your hometown, the leader of an airport security team, a supervisor at a Web hosting service, or the director of sales and marketing for a local business.

The activities outlined in Exhibit 1.3 fall into four fundamental management functions: planning (setting goals and deciding activities), organizing (organizing activities and people), leading (motivating, communicating with, and developing people), and controlling

EXHIBIT 1.2   What Do Managers Do?

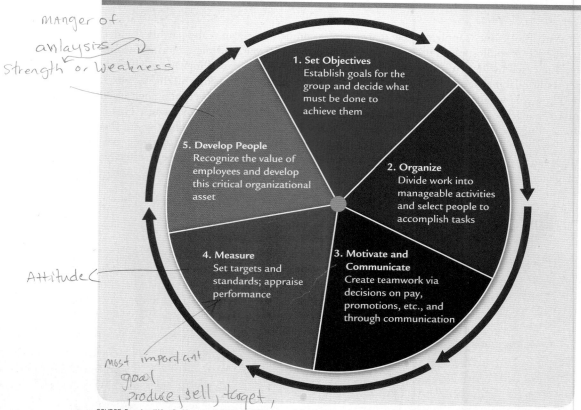

SOURCE: Based on "What Do Managers Do?" *The Wall Street Journal Online*, http://guides.wsj.com/management/developing-a-leadership-style/what-do-managers-do/ (accessed August 11, 2010), article adapted from Alan Murray, *The Wall Street Journal Essential Guide to Management* (New York: Harper Business, 2010).

EXHIBIT 1.3 The Process of Management

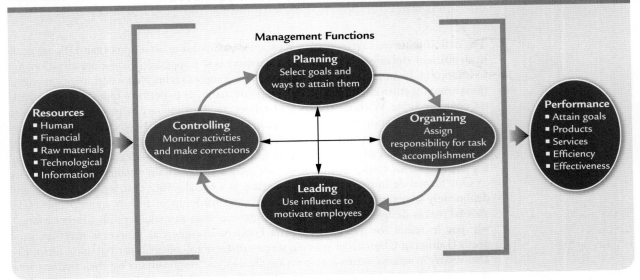

Management Functions

Resources
- Human
- Financial
- Raw materials
- Technological
- Information

Planning
Select goals and ways to attain them

Controlling
Monitor activities and make corrections

Organizing
Assign responsibility for task accomplishment

Leading
Use influence to motivate employees

Performance
- Attain goals
- Products
- Services
- Efficiency
- Effectiveness

(establishing targets and measuring performance). Depending on their job situation, managers perform numerous and varied tasks, but they all can be categorized within these four primary functions.

Exhibit 1.3 illustrates the process of how managers use resources to attain organizational goals through the functions of planning, organizing, leading, and controlling. Chapters of this book are devoted to the multiple activities and skills associated with each function, as well as to the environment, global competitiveness, and ethics that influence how managers perform these functions.

The U.S. Secret Service recently became embroiled in a public relations nightmare, partly due to a breakdown of managerial control. When news broke that members of the security team sent to prepare for President Obama's visit to Cartagena, Colombia, engaged in a night of heavy drinking, visited strip clubs, and brought prostitutes to their hotel rooms, there was a public and legislative uproar. Several agents were fired, and director Mark Sullivan and other managers were called before a Senate subcommittee to explain the breakdown in control. The widespread investigation also brought other allegations of agent misconduct and "morally repugnant behavior" to light. One response from managers has been to create stricter rules of conduct, rules that apply even when agents are off duty.[9]

HOT TOPIC

REMEMBER THIS

- Managers perform a wide variety of activities that fall within four primary management functions.

- The U.S. Secret Service agency prostitution scandal can be traced partly to a breakdown of management control.

1.3 Organizational Performance

The definition of management also encompasses the idea of attaining organizational goals in an efficient and effective manner. Management is so important because organizations are so important. In an industrialized society where complex technologies dominate, organizations bring together knowledge, people, and raw materials to perform tasks that no individual could do alone. Without organizations, how could technology be provided that enables us to share information around the world in an instant; electricity be produced from huge dams and nuclear power plants; and millions of songs, videos, and games be available for our entertainment at any time and place? Organizations pervade our society, and managers are responsible for seeing that resources are used wisely to attain organizational goals.

Our formal definition of an **organization** is a social entity that is goal-directed and deliberately structured. *Social entity* means being made up of two or more people. *Goal directed* means designed to achieve some outcome, such as make a profit (Target Stores), win pay increases for members (United Food & Commercial Workers), meet spiritual needs (Lutheran Church), or provide social satisfaction (college sorority Alpha Delta Pi). *Deliberately structured* means that tasks are divided, and responsibility for their performance is assigned to organization members. This definition applies to all organizations, including both profit and nonprofit ones. Small, offbeat, and nonprofit organizations are more numerous than large, visible corporations—and just as important to society.

Based on our definition of management, the manager's responsibility is to coordinate resources in an effective and efficient manner to accomplish the organization's goals. **Organizational effectiveness** is the degree to which the organization achieves a *stated goal*, or succeeds in accomplishing what it tries to do. Organizational effectiveness means providing a product or service that customers value. Organizational efficiency refers to the amount of resources used to achieve an organizational goal. It is based on how much raw material, money, and people are necessary for producing a given volume of output. *Efficiency* can be defined as the amount of resources used to produce a product or service. Efficiency and effectiveness can both be high in the same organization.

Local Impact

Logistics giant **Deutsche Post DHL Group** has 38 locations in Thailand, where Buddhist teachings about caring for one another lend themselves to helping and teaching the local population. Deutsche Post DHL Group plans for corporate social responsibility with sustainability at the *local* level. By pinpointing local needs and issues, DHL planned site-specific strategies, such as efficient lighting and the reduction of air conditioner demand in Thailand's hot climate, and the installation of global positioning satellite (GPS) systems to minimize fuel consumption.

DHL's commitment to social responsibility is reflected in its three pillars: "Go Green" (climate protection), "Go Help" (disaster relief), and "Go Teach" (education). Each pillar in this corporate plan is indicative of broad goals—such as a 30 percent reduction in CO_2 emissions by 2020—that are customized to fit local needs and cultures. For example, DHL Thailand asks potential business partners to buy into the company's "Go Green" philosophy, reflecting a giant leap in sustainability at the local level.

SOURCE: Based on David Ferguson, "CSR in Asian Logistics: Operationalisation within DHL (Thailand), *Journal of Management Development* 30, 10 (2011): 985–999.

Many managers are using mobile apps to increase efficiency, and in some cases, the apps can enhance effectiveness as well.[10] The current winner in this category is Square, created by Twitter cofounder Jack Dorsey in 2010. Square is revolutionizing small business by enabling any smartphone to become a point-of-sale (POS) terminal that allows the user to accept credit card payments. Millions of small businesses and entrepreneurs in the United States and Canada who once had to turn customers away because they couldn't afford the fees charged by credit card companies can now use Square to process credit cards. Customers get their need to pay with a card met, and businesses get a sale that they might have missed.[11]

All managers have to pay attention to costs, but severe cost cutting to improve efficiency—whether it is by using cutting-edge technology or old-fashioned frugality—can sometimes hurt organizational effectiveness. The ultimate responsibility of managers is to achieve high **performance**, which is the attainment of organizational goals by using resources in an efficient *and* effective manner. Consider the example of Illumination Entertainment, the film production company behind *Dr. Seuss' The Lorax*. Managers continually look for ways to increase efficiency while also meeting the company's goal of producing creative and successful animated films, as described in this chapter's Executive Edge.

So far, Illumination Entertainment has managed to adhere to its efficient, low-cost model while being highly effective in meeting its goals. Compare that to what happened at music company EMI. Weak sales led managers to focus on financial efficiency, which successfully trimmed waste and boosted operating income. However, the efficiencies damaged the company's ability to recruit new artists, who are vital to record companies, and also

THE EXECUTIVE EDGE

Illumination Entertainment

You can't quite make a blockbuster movie on a dime, but Christopher Meledandri is out to prove that strict cost controls and hit animated films aren't mutually exclusive. Most computer-generated animated films cost at least $100 million, with some budgets pushing $150 million. In contrast, Illumination Entertainment made the hit film *Despicable Me* for only $69 million. The budget for *Hop* came in at a mere $63 million. And the company produced its third blockbuster, *Dr. Seuss' The Lorax*, for $70 million—less than the movie earned at the box office on its opening weekend.

Managers at Illumination use many approaches to increase efficiency. For example, when making *Despicable Me*, they decided to eliminate details such as animal fur, which the audience couldn't see on the screen. Other details that were extremely costly to render in computer graphics but that weren't central to the story were also cut, saving the detail work for sets that were used repeatedly. The company paid big bucks for the voice of Steve Carell, but it hired other vocal talent with less star power, a practice that managers follow for all their films. They also seek out first-time directors and young, enthusiastic, less experienced animators, who often cost less than half of what a more experienced artist commands. Organizational details also contribute to efficiency—Meledandri keeps layers of the hierarchy to a minimum so that decisions can be made fast and movies don't languish for years in development, eating up money. Offices are located in a low-rent area behind a cement plant rather than being housed in sumptuous surroundings.

Moviegoing in general is down, but animated family films are hot. And Illumination has had some of the hottest movies going. Peter Chernin, former president of News Corporation, said of Meledandri: "It is rare to find people whose business sense is as strong as their creative sense." Meledandri and his management team are using their business sense to run an efficient operation, and their creative instincts to put money in the right places to produce popular, often critically acclaimed animated films.[12]

led to internal turmoil that caused some longtime acts like the Rolling Stones to leave the label. Thus, the company's overall performance suffered. Managers are struggling to find the right balance between efficiency and effectiveness to get EMI back on the right track.[13]

REMEMBER THIS

- An **organization** is a social entity that is goal-directed and deliberately structured.
- Good management is important because organizations contribute so much to society.
- **Efficiency** pertains to the amount of resources—raw materials, money, and people—used to produce a desired volume of output.
- **Effectiveness** refers to the degree to which the organization achieves a stated goal.

- Some managers are using mobile apps to increase efficiency; one example is Square, used to process credit and debit card payments with a smartphone.
- **Performance** is defined as the organization's ability to attain its goals by using resources in an efficient and effective manner.
- Managers at Illumination Entertainment are concerned both with keeping costs low (efficiency) and producing animated films (such as *The Lorax*) that are critically and financially successful (effectiveness).

1.4 Management Skills

CONCEPT CONNECTION Holding degrees in both physics and economics, entrepreneur Elon Musk certainly possesses his share of **technical skills**. He designed and created the first viable electric car—the Tesla Roadster—as well as the Web-based payment service PayPal and a spacecraft that will enable private citizens to travel to outer space. But it is his stellar **conceptual skills** that allow him to lead the innovative companies that are making these products and services available to people worldwide.

A manager's job requires a range of skills. Although some management theorists propose a long list of skills, the necessary skills for managing a department or an organization can be placed in three categories: conceptual, human, and technical.[14] As illustrated in Exhibit 1.4, the application of these skills changes dramatically when a person is promoted to management. Although the degree of each skill that is required at different levels of an organization may vary, all managers must possess some skill in each of these important areas to perform effectively.

1.4a When Skills Fail

Good management skills are not automatic. Particularly during turbulent times, managers really have to stay on their toes and apply all their skills and competencies in a way that benefits the organization and its stakeholders—employees, customers, investors, the community, and so forth. In recent years, numerous highly publicized examples have shown what happens when managers fail to apply their skills effectively to meet the demands of an uncertain, rapidly changing world.

EXHIBIT 1.4 Relationship of Technical, Human, and Conceptual Skills to Management

Complete the "Self-Learning" on pages 48, which pertains to management skills. Reflect on the strength of your preferences among the three types of skills and the implications for you as a manager.

EXHIBIT 1.5 Google's Rules: Eight Good Behaviors for Managers

To know how to build better managers, Google executives studied performance reviews, feedback surveys, and award nominations to see what qualities made a good manager. Here are the "Eight Good Behaviors" they found, in order of importance:

1. Be a good coach.
2. Empower your team and don't micromanage.
3. Express interest in team members' successes and personal well-being.
4. Don't be a sissy: Be productive and results-oriented.
5. Be a good communicator and listen to your team.
6. Help your employees with career development.
7. Have a clear vision and strategy for the team.
8. Have key technical skills so you can help advise the team.

SOURCE: "Google's Quest to Build a Better Boss," by Adam Bryant, published March 12, 2011, in The New York Times. Courtesy of Google, Inc.

Everyone has flaws and weaknesses, and these shortcomings become most apparent under conditions of rapid change, uncertainty, or crisis.[15] Consider the uproar that resulted in 2013 from the decision of managers at the Internal Revenue Service (IRS) to apply additional screening to tax-exempt applications from conservative Tea Party groups. When a manager for so-called Group 7822, an IRS office that screens and processes thousands of applications a year from organizations seeking tax-exempt status, noticed a growing number of applications from groups identifying themselves as part of the Tea Party, the manager advised workers to flag them and similar groups to see if their purpose was too political to be eligible under the rules for tax exemption. It has long been a practice to give extra scrutiny to certain kinds of groups that present a potential for fraudulent use of tax exempt status, but critics say the agency went too far in how it applied the practice to conservative political organizations, in some cases delaying applications for years. Congressional investigators are probing whether agency activities constituted discrimination against conservative groups, and the full story of what happened and why is still emerging.[16] IRS managers at all levels involved in the decision appear to have needed stronger conceptual skills to prevent this crisis from happening, and higher-level executives had to call upon all their conceptual and human skills to resolve the dilemma and work to restore the public trust.

The numerous ethical and financial scandals of recent years have left people cynical about business and government managers and even less willing to overlook mistakes. Crises and examples of deceit and greed grab the headlines, but many more companies falter or fail less spectacularly. Managers fail to listen to customers, are unable to motivate employees, or can't build a cohesive team. For example, the reputation of Zynga, maker of games like Farmville that were ubiquitous on Facebook for a while, plummeted along with its share price in 2012. Although there were several problems at Zynga, one was that founder and former CEO Mark Pincus had an aggressive style that made it difficult to build a cohesive team. The exodus of key executives left the company floundering, and the company's shares fell 70 percent. Pincus stepped down as CEO in July 2013, and former Xbox executive Don Mattrick took over to try to revive the once-hot game maker.[17] Exhibit 1.6 shows the top 10 factors that cause managers to fail to achieve desired results, based on a survey of managers in U.S. organizations operating in rapidly changing business environments.[18] Notice that many of these factors are due to poor human skills, such as the inability to develop good work relationships, a failure to clarify direction and performance expectations, or an inability to create cooperation and teamwork. The number one reason for manager failure is ineffective communication skills and practices, cited by 81 percent of managers surveyed. Especially in times of uncertainty or crisis, if managers do not communicate effectively, including listening to employees and customers and showing genuine care and concern, organizational performance and reputation suffer.

EXHIBIT 1.6 Top Causes of Manager Failure

1. Ineffective communication skills and practices	81%
2. Poor work relationships/interpersonal skills	78%
3. Person–mismatch	69%
4. Failure to clarify direction or performance expectations	64%
5. Failure to adapt and break old habits	57%
6. Breakdown of delegation and empowerment	56%
7. Lack of personal integrity and trustworthiness	52%
8. Inability to develop cooperation and teamwork	50%
9. Inability to lead/motivate others	47%
10. Poor planning practices/reactionary behavior	45%

SOURCE: Adapted from Clinton O. Longenecker, Mitchell J. Neubert, and Laurence S. Fink, "Causes and Consequences of Managerial Failure in Rapidly Changing Organizations," *Business Horizons* 50 (2007): 145–155, Table 1.

REMEMBER THIS

- Managers have complex jobs that require a range of abilities and skills.
- The two major reasons that managers fail are poor communication and poor interpersonal skills.
- A manager's weaknesses become more apparent during stressful times of uncertainty, change, or crisis.

1.5 What Is a Manager's Job Really Like?

"Despite a proliferation of management gurus, management consultants, and management schools, it remains murky to many of us what managers actually do and why we need them in the first place," wrote Ray Fisman, a Columbia Business School professor.[19] Unless someone has actually performed managerial work, it is hard to understand exactly what managers do on an hour-by-hour, day-to-day basis. One answer to the question of what managers do to plan, organize, lead, and control was provided by Henry Mintzberg, who followed managers around and recorded all their activities.[20] He developed a description of managerial work that included three general characteristics and 10 roles. These characteristics and roles, discussed in detail later in this section, have been supported by other research.[21]

Researchers also have looked at what managers *like* to do. Both male and female managers across five different countries report that they most enjoy activities such as leading others, networking, and leading innovation. Activities that managers like least include controlling subordinates, handling paperwork, and managing time pressures.[22] Many new managers, in particular, find the intense time pressures of management, the load of administrative paperwork, and the challenge of directing others to be quite stressful as they adjust to their new roles and responsibilities. Indeed, the initial leap into management can be one of the scariest moments in a person's career.

1.5a Making the Leap: Becoming a New Manager

Many people who are promoted into a manager position have little idea what the job actually entails and receive little training about how to handle their new role. It's no wonder that, among managers, first-line supervisors tend to experience the most job burnout and attrition.[23]

Making the shift from individual contributor to manager is often tricky. Mark Zuckerberg, whose company, Facebook, went public a week before he turned 28 years old, provides an example. In a sense, the public has been able to watch as Zuckerberg has "grown up" as a manager. He was a strong individual performer in creating the social media platform and forming the company, but he fumbled with day-to-day management, such as interactions with employees and communicating with people both inside and outside Facebook. Zuckerberg was smart enough to hire seasoned managers, including former Google executive Sheryl Sandberg, and cultivate advisors and mentors who have coached him in areas where he is weak. He also shadowed David Graham at the offices of The Post Company (the publisher of *The Washington Post* before it was purchased by Jeff Bezos) for four days to try to learn what it is like to manage a large organization. Now that Facebook is a public company, Zuckerberg is watched more closely than ever to see if he has what it takes to be a manager of a big public corporation.[24]

Harvard professor Linda Hill followed a group of 19 managers over the first year of their managerial careers and found that one key to success is to recognize that becoming a manager involves more than learning a new set of skills. Rather, becoming a manager means a profound transformation in the way people think of themselves, called *personal identity*, which includes letting go of deeply held attitudes and habits and learning new ways of thinking.[25] Exhibit 1.7 outlines the transformation from individual performer to manager. The individual performer is a specialist and a "doer." His or her mind is conditioned to think in terms of performing specific tasks and activities as expertly as possible. The manager, on the other hand, has to be a generalist and learn to coordinate a broad range of activities. Whereas the individual performer strongly identifies with his or her specific tasks, the manager has to identify with the broader organization and industry.

In addition, the individual performer gets things done mostly through his or her own efforts and develops the habit of relying on self rather than others. The manager, though, gets things done through other people. Indeed, one of the most common mistakes that new managers make is wanting to do all the work themselves, rather than delegating to others and developing others' abilities.[26] Hill offers a reminder that, as a manager, you must "be an instrument to get things done in the organization by working with and through others, rather than being the one doing the work."[27]

Another problem for many new managers is that they expect to have greater freedom to do what they think is best for the organization. In reality, though, managers find themselves

EXHIBIT 1.7   Making the Leap from Individual Performer to Manager

From Individual Identity	→	To Manager Identity
Specialist; performs specific tasks		Generalist; coordinates diverse tasks
Gets things done through own efforts		Gets things done through others
An individual actor		A network builder
Works relatively independently		Works in highly interdependent manner

SOURCE: Based on Exhibit 1.1, "Transformation of Identity," in Linda A. Hill, *Becoming a Manager: Mastery of a New Identity*, 2nd ed. (Boston, MA: Harvard Business School Press, 2003), p. 6.

hemmed in by interdependencies. Being a successful manager means thinking in terms of building teams and networks and becoming a motivator and organizer within a highly interdependent system of people and work.[28] Although the distinctions may sound simple in the abstract, they are anything but. In essence, becoming a manager means becoming a new person and viewing oneself in a completely new way.

Many new managers have to make the transformation in a "trial by fire," learning on the job as they go, but organizations are beginning to be more responsive to the need for new manager training. The cost to organizations of losing good employees who can't make the transition is greater than the cost of providing training to help new managers cope, learn, and grow. In addition, some organizations use great care in selecting people for managerial positions, including ensuring that each candidate understands what management involves and really wants to be a manager.

1.5b Manager Activities

Most new managers are unprepared for the variety of activities that managers routinely perform. One of the most interesting findings about managerial activities is how busy managers are and how hectic the average workday can be.

Adventures in Multitasking Managerial activity is characterized by variety, fragmentation, and brevity.[29] The widespread and voluminous nature of a manager's tasks leaves little time for quiet reflection. A recent study by a team from the London School of Economics and Harvard Business School found that the time CEOs spend working alone averages a mere six hours a week. The rest of their time is spent in meetings, on the phone, traveling, and talking with others inside and outside the organization.[30]

Managers shift gears quickly. In his study, Mintzberg found that the average time a top executive spends on any one activity is less than nine minutes, and another survey indicates that some first-line supervisors average one activity every 48 seconds![31] Significant crises are interspersed with trivial events in no predictable sequence. Every manager's job is similar in its diversity and fragmentation to what *Workforce Management* described as a typical day in the life of human resources (HR) manager Kathy Davis:[32]

- 6:55 A.M.—Arrives at work early to begin investigating a complaint of sexual harassment at one of the factories, but as she's walking to her office, she bumps into someone carrying a picket sign that reads "Unfair Hiring! Who Needs HR?" Spends a few minutes talking with the young man, who is a temp that she had let go due to sloppy work.

- 7:10 A.M.—Finds the factory shift supervisor and a security staff member already waiting outside her door to discuss the sexual harassment complaint.

- 7:55 A.M.—Sue, a member of Kathy's team who has just arrived and is unaware of the meeting, interrupts to let Kathy know there is someone picketing in the hallway outside her office and the CEO wants to know what's going on.

- 8:00 A.M.—Alone at last, Kathy calls the CEO and explains the picketing situation, and then she begins her morning routine. Checking voice mail, she finds three messages that she must respond to immediately, and she passes four others to members of her team. She begins checking e-mail but is interrupted again by Sue, who reminds her they have to review the recent HR audit so that the company can respond promptly and avoid penalties.

Read the Director's Toolkit box on page 20 for ideas to improve your time management skills.

- **9:15 A.M.**—As she is reviewing the audit, Kathy gets a call from manager Pete Channing, asking if she's sent the offer letter to a prospective hire. "Don't send it," Pete said, "I've changed my mind." Weeks of interviewing and background checks, and now Pete wants to start over!

- **11:20 A.M.**—Kathy is getting to the end of her critical e-mail list when she hears a commotion outside her door and finds Linda and Sue arguing. "This report IT did for us is full of errors," Linda says, "but Sue says we should let it go." Kathy agrees to take a look at the IT department's report and discovers that there are only a few errors, but they have critical implications.

- **12:25 P.M.**—As she's nearing the end of the IT report, Kathy's e-mail pings an "urgent" message from a supervisor informing her that one of his employees will be absent from work for a few weeks "while a felony morals charge is worked out." This is the first she's heard about it, so she picks up the phone to call the supervisor.

- **1:20 P.M.**—Time for lunch—finally. She grabs a sandwich at a local supermarket and brings one back for the picketer, who thanks her and continues his march.

- **2:00 P.M.**—Meets with CEO Henry Luker to review the audit and IT reports, discuss changes to the company's 401(k) plan, and talk about ideas for reducing turnover.

- **3:00 P.M.**—Rushes back to her office to grab her keys so that she can drive to a meeting with the manufacturing facilities manager, who has asked Kathy to "shadow" him and share ideas about training and skills development.

- **3:15 P.M.**—As she gets out of her car at the facility, Kathy runs into a man who had attended a supervision training course a few months earlier. He tells her that the class really helped him—there are fewer misunderstandings, and the staff seems to respect him more.

- **3:30 P.M.**—Arrives right on time and spends the next couple of hours observing and asking questions, talking to employees to learn about the problems and obstacles they face.

- **5:40 P.M.**—All is quiet back in the HR department, but there's a message from Sue that Kathy has an appointment first thing tomorrow morning with two women who had gotten into a fight in the elevator. Sighing, Kathy returns to her investigation of the sexual harassment complaint that she had begun at 7:00 that morning.

Life on Speed Dial The manager performs a great deal of work at an unrelenting pace.[33] Managers' work is fast-paced and requires great energy. Most top executives routinely work at least 12 hours a day and spend 50 percent or more of their time traveling.[34] Calendars are often booked months in advance, but unexpected disturbances erupt every day. Mintzberg found that the majority of executives' meetings and other contacts are ad hoc, and even scheduled meetings are typically surrounded by other events such as quick phone calls, scanning of e-mail, or spontaneous encounters. During time away from the office, executives catch up on work-related reading, paperwork, phone calls, and e-mail. Technology, such as e-mail, text messaging, cell phones, and laptops, has intensified the pace. Brett Yormark, the National Basketball Association (NBA)'s youngest CEO (he heads the Brooklyn Nets), typically responds to about 60 messages before he even shaves and dresses for the day, and employees are accustomed to getting messages that Yormark has zapped to them in the wee hours of the morning.[35]

The fast pace of a manager's job is illustrated by Michelle Davis, an analytics director at Fair Isaac Corporation (FICO). As a middle manager at this company, best known for calculating consumer credit scores, Davis oversees three direct reports and three other subordinates assigned to her teams. On a typical day, she arrives at work at 6:00 a.m. so she can pick up her children in the early afternoon, and she uses the first hour and a half of quiet time to catch up on messages and respond to urgent requests for data. At 7:30, she has her first meeting, often a conference call with the analytics board of directors. Then Davis leads an hour-long training session for a few dozen staffers on new analytics products, staying longer to answer questions and talk about how clients might use the data. At 10:30 a.m., she checks in with senior members of the product development and product management teams and sorts out various problems. Lunch is a quick stop at the company cafeteria. Then she is on to present a few slides at the monthly lunch-and-learn session. Davis squeezes in an hour or so of hands-on work time before it's back to more meetings. Afternoon meetings often run long, meaning she has to scramble to pick up her three children. While the kids eat snacks and play in the backyard, Davis catches up on e-mail and phone calls. After dinner with her husband, she tries to stay away from work, but admits that she keeps an eye on her text messages until bedtime.[36]

CONCEPT CONNECTION Between the long hours and the high degree of responsibility and stress that is typical of advanced positions, it can be challenging for managers to maintain a healthy balance between their work lives and their personal lives. Oliver Bussmann, chief information officer of UBS, blogged about his rules for finding balance, saying that he puts his family first as his top priority, pays attention to his health and fitness, and takes time to give back to his community in a meaningful way. He feels that these are the keys to success in any career.

TAKE Action!

Can you make a personal transformation from individual performer to manager, accomplishing work by engaging and coordinating other people? Look back at your results on the questionnaire at the beginning of this chapter to see how your priorities align with the demands placed on a manager.

Where Does a Manager Find the Time? With so many responsibilities and so many competing demands on their time, how do managers cope? One manager who was already working 18-hour days five days a week got assigned another project. When the CEO was informed of the problem, he matter-of-factly remarked that by his calculations, she still had "30 more hours Monday through Friday, plus 48 more on the weekend." That is surely an extreme example, but most managers often feel the pressure of too much to do and not enough time to do it.[37] *The Wall Street Journal*'s "Lessons in Leadership" video series asked CEOs of big companies how they managed their time, and it found that many of them carve out time just to think about how to manage their time.[38] Time is a manager's most valuable resource, and one characteristic that identifies successful managers is that they know how to use time effectively to accomplish the important things first and the less important things later.[39] **Time management** refers to using techniques that enable you to get more done in less time and with better results, be more relaxed, and have more time to enjoy your work and your life. New managers in particular often struggle with the

Director's Toolkit

Time Management Tips for New Managers

Becoming a manager is considered by most people to be a positive, forward-looking career move, and indeed, life as a manager offers appealing aspects. However, it also holds many challenges, not the least of which is the increased workload and the difficulty of finding the time to accomplish everything on one's expanded list of duties and responsibilities. The following classic time management techniques can help you eliminate major time-wasters in your daily routines.

- **Keep a To-Do List.** If you don't use any other system for keeping track of your responsibilities and commitments, at the very least you should maintain a to-do list that identifies all the things that you need to do during the day. Although the nature of management means that new responsibilities and shifting priorities occur frequently, it's a fact that people accomplish more with a list than without one.

- **Remember Your ABCs.** This is a highly effective system for prioritizing tasks or activities on your to-do list:

- An "A" item is something highly important. It *must* be done, or you'll face serious consequences.

- A "B" item is a *should do*, but consequences will be minor if you don't get it done.

- "C" items are things that would be nice to get done, but there are no consequences at all if you don't accomplish them.

- "D" items are tasks that you can delegate to someone else.

- **Schedule Your Workday.** Some experts propose that every minute spent in planning saves 10 minutes in execution. Take your to-do list a step further and plan how you will accomplish each task or project you need to handle. Planning to tackle the big tasks first is a good idea because most people are at peak performance early in the day. Save the e-mails and phone calls for less productive times.

- **Do One Thing at a Time.** Multitasking has become the motto of the early twenty-first century, but too much multitasking is a time-waster. Research has shown that multitasking *reduces* rather than enhances productivity. The authors of one study suggest that an inability to focus on one thing at a time could reduce efficiency by 20 to 40 percent. Even for those whose job requires numerous brief activities, the ability to concentrate fully on each one (sometimes called *spotlighting*) saves time. Give each task your full attention, and you'll get more done and get it done better, too.

SOURCES: Based on information in Pamela Dodd and Doug Sundheim, *The 25 Best Time Management Tools & Techniques* (Ann Arbor, MI: Peak Performance Press, Inc., 2005); Brian Tracy, *Eat That Frog: 21 Great Ways to Stop Procrastinating and Get More Done in Less Time* (San Francisco: Berrett-Koehler, 2002); Joshua S. Rubinstein, David E. Meyer, and Jeffrey E. Evans, "Executive Control of Cognitive Processes in Task Switching," *Journal of Experimental Psychology: Human Perception and Performance* 27, no. 4 (August 2001): 763–797; Sue Shellenbarger, "Multitasking Makes You Stupid: Studies Show Pitfalls of Doing Too Much at Once," *The Wall Street Journal* (February 27, 2003): D1; and Ilya Pozin, "Quit Working Late: 8 Tips," *Inc.* (June 26, 2013), http://www.inc.com/ilya-pozin/8-ways-to-leave-work-at-work.html (accessed August 19, 2013).

increased workload, the endless paperwork, the incessant meetings, and the constant interruptions that come with a management job. The Director's Toolkit box offers some tips for time management.

1.5c Manager Roles

Mintzberg's observations and subsequent research indicate that diverse manager activities can be organized into 10 roles.[40] A **role** is a set of expectations for a manager's behavior. Exhibit 1.8 describes activities associated with each of the roles. These roles are divided into three conceptual categories: informational (managing by information), interpersonal (managing through people), and decisional (managing through action).

EXHIBIT 1.8 Ten Manager Roles

Informational

- **Monitor:** Seek and receive information; scan Web, periodicals, reports; maintain personal contacts
- **Disseminator:** Forward information to other organization members; send memos and reports, make phone calls
- **Spokesperson:** Transmit information to outsiders through speeches, reports

Interpersonal

- **Figurehead:** Perform ceremonial and symbolic duties such as greeting visitors, signing legal documents
- **Leader:** Direct and motivate subordinates; train, counsel, and communicate with subordinates
- **Liaison:** Maintain information links inside and outside the organization; use e-mail, phone, meetings

Decisional

- **Entrepreneur:** Initiate improvement projects; identify new ideas, delegate idea responsibility to others
- **Disturbance Handler:** Take corrective action during conflicts or crises; resolve disputes among subordinates
- **Resource Allocator:** Decide who gets resources; schedule, budget, set priorities
- **Negotiator:** Represent team or department's interests; represent department during negotiation of budgets, union contracts, purchases

SOURCE: Adapted from Henry Mintzberg, *The Nature of Managerial Work* (New York: Harper & Row, 1973), pp. 92–93; and Henry Mintzberg, "Managerial Work: Analysis from Observation," *Management Science* 18 (1971), B97–B110.

Each role represents activities that managers undertake to ultimately accomplish the functions of planning, organizing, leading, and controlling. Although it is necessary to separate the components of the manager's job to understand the different roles and activities of a manager, it is important to remember that the real job of management isn't practiced as a set of independent parts; all the roles interact in the real world of management.

Kelly's decisions, such as the surveillance network and revised search practices, have not come without criticism of civil rights violations, but many people credit him with making life in New York City safer and giving foreign investors the confidence to bring hundreds of millions of dollars back to the city.

Spotlight on Skills

New York City Police Department

In the first 178 days of 2013, New York City averaged less than a murder a day. The drop from 202 murders during the first half of 2012 to 154 during the first half of 2013 surprised even police administrators.

Analyzing the findings, Police Commissioner Raymond W. Kelly attributed the decrease partly to changes in how resources are allocated. For example, Kelly increased the number of cops assigned to high-crime neighborhoods and poured resources into a new antigang strategy aimed at preventing retaliatory violence among neighborhood gangs. The strategy relies heavily on closely tracking the activities of gangs and trying to prevent shootings before they happen. Kelly said the initiative led to a 52 percent decline in shootings in one precinct. Another program receiving additional resources is aimed at identifying and monitoring abusive husbands whose behavior seems likely to turn lethal.

Deciding how to allocate resources in the country's biggest police force is similar to the job of a CEO in a midsize *Fortune* 500 company—except that the stakes are much higher because the metrics by which performance is measured have to do with life and death. In addition to fighting everyday crime, the New York Police Department (NYPD) has to battle terrorism. Kelly has put an emphasis on hiring native speakers of languages such as Farsi, Arabic, Urdu, Pashto, and Hindi, and set up a counterterrorism bureau and intelligence division that deploys NYPD cops in foreign cities. He has also invested $100 million in a surveillance network that oversees wide portions of Manhattan and the outer boroughs.[41]

Other factors, such as changing environmental conditions, also may determine which roles are more important for a manager at any given time. Robert Dudley, who took over as CEO of troubled oil giant BP after Tony Hayward was forced out due to mishandling the *Deepwater Horizon* crisis in 2010, found informational roles and decisional roles at the top of his list as he has personally worked to repair relationships with U.S. government officials, mend fences with local communities, carve a path toward restoring the company's reputation, and take steps to prevent such a disastrous event from ever happening again.[42] Managers stay alert to needs both within and outside the organization to determine which roles are most critical at various times. A top manager may regularly put more emphasis on the roles of spokesperson, figurehead, and negotiator, but the emergence of new competitors may require more attention to the monitor role, or a severe decline in employee morale and direction may mean that the CEO has to put more emphasis on the leader role. A marketing manager may focus on interpersonal roles because of the importance of personal contacts in the marketing process, whereas a financial manager may be more likely to emphasize decisional roles such as resource allocator and negotiator. Despite these differences, all managers carry out informational, interpersonal, and decisional roles to meet the needs of the organization.

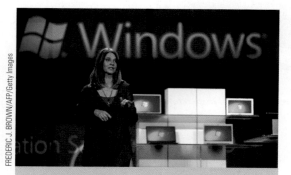

FREDERIC J. BROWN/AFP/Getty Images

CONCEPT CONNECTION As the executive vice president of marketing at Microsoft, Tami Reller plays a number of significant interpersonal roles. She serves as the top **leader** for the company's bevy of marketers on functions like advertising, media usage, and distribution, and she is often Microsoft's **liaison** with the public, providing information about Windows and other products.

REMEMBER THIS

- Becoming a new manager requires a shift in thinking from being an individual performer to playing an interdependent role of coordinating and developing others.
- Because of the interdependent nature of management, new managers often have less freedom and control than they expect to have.
- The job of a manager is highly diverse and fast-paced, so managers need good time-management skills.

- A **role** is a set of expectations for one's behavior.
- Managers at every level perform 10 roles, which are grouped into informational roles, interpersonal roles, and decisional roles.
- As one aspect of his decisional role, New York City police commissioner Raymond W. Kelly allocates resources such as money, technology, and the time of street cops and investigators.

1.6 Managing in Small Businesses and Nonprofit Organizations

Small businesses are growing in importance. Hundreds of small businesses open every month, but the environment for small business today is highly complicated. The Appendix provides detailed information about managing in small businesses and entrepreneurial start-ups.

One interesting finding is that managers in small businesses tend to emphasize roles different from those of managers in large corporations. Managers in small companies often see their most important role as that of spokesperson because they must promote the small, growing company to the outside world. The entrepreneur's role is also critical in small businesses because managers have to be innovative and help their organizations develop new ideas to remain competitive. At LivingSocial, for example, founder and CEO, Tim O'Shaughnessy, spends a lot of his time promoting the rapidly growing daily-deal site and talking with department heads about potential new products and services.[43] Small-business managers tend to rate lower on the leader role and on information-processing roles, compared with their counterparts in large corporations.

Nonprofit organizations also represent a major application of management talent.[44] Organizations such as the Salvation Army, Nature Conservancy, Greater Chicago Food Depository, Girl Scouts, and Cleveland Orchestra all require excellent management. The functions of planning, organizing, leading, and controlling apply to nonprofits just as they do to business organizations, and managers in nonprofit organizations use similar skills and perform similar activities. The primary difference is

CONCEPT CONNECTION Despite having launched and sold several successful start-ups already, San Francisco–based **small business** owner Loïc Le Meur is still a hands-on kind of manager. His daily blog about the blogosphere and the Web in general is read by hundreds of thousands of people worldwide, and he is the chief organizer behind Europe's largest annual tech conference, LeWeb.

WITT/SIPA/Newscom

that managers in businesses direct their activities toward earning money for the company and its owners, whereas managers in nonprofits direct their efforts toward generating some kind of social impact. The characteristics and needs of nonprofit organizations created by this distinction present unique challenges for managers.[45]

Financial resources for government and charity nonprofit organizations typically come from taxes, appropriations, grants, and donations rather than from the sale of products or services to customers. In businesses, managers focus on improving the organization's products and services to increase sales revenues. In nonprofits, however, services are typically provided to nonpaying clients, and a major problem for many organizations is securing a steady stream of funds to continue operating. Nonprofit managers, committed to serving clients with limited resources, must focus on keeping organizational costs as low as possible.[46] Donors generally want their money to go directly to helping clients rather than for overhead costs. If nonprofit managers can't demonstrate a highly efficient use of resources, they might have a hard time securing additional donations or government appropriations. Although the Sarbanes-Oxley Act (the 2002 corporate governance reform law) doesn't apply to nonprofits, for example, many are adopting its guidelines, striving for greater transparency and accountability to boost credibility with constituents and be more competitive when seeking funding.[47]

In addition, some types of nonprofit organizations, such as hospitals and private universities that obtain revenues from selling services to clients, do have to contend with a *bottom line* in the sense of having to generate enough revenues to cover expenses, so managers often struggle with the question of what constitutes results and effectiveness. It is easy to measure revenues compared to expenses, but the metrics of success in nonprofits are typically much more ambiguous. Managers have to measure intangibles such as "improve public health," "upgrade the quality of education," or "increase appreciation for the arts." This intangible nature also makes it more difficult to gauge the performance of employees and managers. An added complication is that managers in some types of nonprofits depend on volunteers and donors who cannot be supervised and controlled in the same way that a business manager deals with employees. Many people who move from the corporate world to a nonprofit are surprised to find that the work hours are often longer and the stress greater than in their previous management jobs.[48]

The roles defined by Mintzberg also apply to nonprofit managers, but they may differ somewhat. We might expect managers in nonprofit organizations to place more emphasis on the roles of spokesperson (to "sell" the organization to donors and the public), leader (to build a mission-driven community of employees and volunteers), and resource allocator (to distribute government resources or grant funds that are often assigned top-down).

Managers in all organizations—large corporations, small businesses, and nonprofit organizations—carefully integrate and adjust the management functions and roles to meet challenges within their own circumstances and keep their organizations healthy.

REMEMBER THIS

- Good management is just as important for small businesses and nonprofit organizations as it is for large corporations.

- Managers in these organizations adjust and integrate the various management functions, activities, and roles to meet the unique challenges they face.

- Managers in small businesses often see their most important roles as being a *spokesperson* for the business and acting as an *entrepreneur*.
- Managers in nonprofit organizations direct their efforts toward generating some kind of social impact rather than toward making money for the organization.
- Managers in nonprofit organizations often struggle with what constitutes effectiveness.

1.7 Innovative Management Thinking for a Changing World

What do managers at India's Tata Group, U.S.-based General Electric (GE), and Africa's M-Pesa mobile money transfer service have in common with eighteenth-century inventor and statesman Benjamin Franklin? The authors of a recent book on innovation say they have all applied a concept called *jugaad* (pronounced joo-gaardh). *Jugaad* is a Hindi word that basically refers to creating something of benefit from limited resources. Benjamin Franklin, the authors say, is a great historical example because he faced scarcity firsthand, but he improvised to create inventions that were for the benefit of the masses.[49]

Management—like most disciplines—loves buzzwords, and *jugaad* is one of the most recent to appear on the radar. *Jugaad* basically refers to an innovation mind-set, used widely by Indian companies, that strives to meet customers' immediate needs quickly and inexpensively. With research and development budgets strained in today's economy, U.S. and other Western managers have quickly picked up on the approach, sometimes calling it *frugal engineering*.[50] Will this be a buzzword that quickly fades from managers' vocabularies, or will it become as ubiquitous in management circles as terms such as total quality or *kaizen*?

Managers are always on the lookout for fresh ideas, innovative management approaches, and new tools and techniques. Management philosophies and organizational forms change over time to meet new needs. The questionnaire at the beginning of this chapter describes two differing philosophies about how people should be managed, and you will learn more about these ideas in this chapter.

If management is always changing, why does history matter to managers? The workplace of today is different from what it was 50 years ago—indeed, from what it was even 10 years ago—yet historical concepts form the backbone of management education.[51] One reason is that a historical perspective provides managers with a broader way of thinking, a way of searching for patterns and determining whether they recur across time periods. It is a way of learning from others' mistakes so as not to repeat them; learning from others' successes so as to repeat them in the appropriate situation; and most of all, learning to understand why things happen to improve organizations in the future. Certain management practices that seem modern, such as open-book management or employee stock ownership, have actually been around for a long time. These techniques have repeatedly gained and lost popularity since the early twentieth century because of shifting historical forces.[52]

This chapter provides a historical overview of the ideas, theories, and management philosophies that have contributed to making the workplace what it is today. The final section of the chapter looks at some recent trends and current approaches that build on this foundation of management understanding. This foundation illustrates that the value of studying management lies not in learning current facts and research, but in developing a perspective that will facilitate the broad, long-term view needed for management success.

NEW MANAGER Self-Test

Are You a New-Style or an Old-Style Manager?[53]
Evolution of Management Thinking

Instructions: The following are various behaviors in which a manager may engage when relating to subordinates. Read each statement carefully and rate each one Mostly True or Mostly False, to reflect the extent to which you would use that behavior.

	Mostly True	Mostly False
1. Supervise my subordinates closely to get better work from them.		
2. Set the goals and objectives for my subordinates and sell them on the merits of my plans.		
3. Set up controls to ensure that my subordinates are getting the job done.		
4. Make sure that my subordinates' work is planned out for them.		
5. Check with my subordinates daily to see if they need any help.		
6. Step in as soon as reports indicate that progress on a job is slipping.		
7. Push my people if necessary in order to meet schedules.		
8. Have frequent meetings to learn from others what is going on.		

Scoring and Interpretation: Add the total number of Mostly True answers and mark your score on the scale below. Theory X tends to be "old-style" management, and Theory Y "new-style," because the styles are based on different assumptions about people. To learn more about these assumptions, you can refer to Exhibit 1.12 and review the assumptions related to Theory X and Theory Y. Strong Theory X assumptions are typically considered inappropriate for today's workplace. Where do you fit on the X–Y scale? Does your score reflect your perception of yourself as a current or future manager?

1.8 Management and Organization

Studying history doesn't mean merely arranging events in chronological order; it means developing an understanding of the impact of societal forces on organizations. Studying history is a way to achieve strategic thinking, see the big picture, and improve conceptual skills. Let's begin by examining how social, political, and economic forces have influenced organizations and the practice of management.[54]

Green Power

Drop Back and Punt

Glenn Rink's great product—popcorn-like sponges for absorbing oil spills—received a cool reception in the 1990s. Corporate skeptics said that traditional skimming of oil off water remained the preferred choice for disaster cleanup. Blocked by resistance to his product, Rink, founder of **Abtech Industries**, followed the historic and time-honored tradition of football teams, which sometimes need to drop back and punt before they can go on offense again.

Rink decided to focus on smaller-scale disasters instead. For more than a decade, Abtech Industries built a reputation for offering low-cost alternatives to address the cleanup needs of cities struggling with a variety of water pollution problems. The strategy paid off. In 2011, a revitalized Abtech, maker of the Smart Sponge Plus, partnered with the huge company Waste Management, Inc. as the exclusive North American distributor to cities, and oil cleanup orders began pouring in. To date, Smart Sponge Plus has been used in more than 15,000 spill locations worldwide.

SOURCE: "Innovation #71: Glenn Rink, Founder of Abtech Industries," *Fast Company* (June 2012): 136 (part of "The 100 Most Creative People in Business 2012," pp. 78–156).

EXHIBIT 1.9   Management Perspectives Over Time

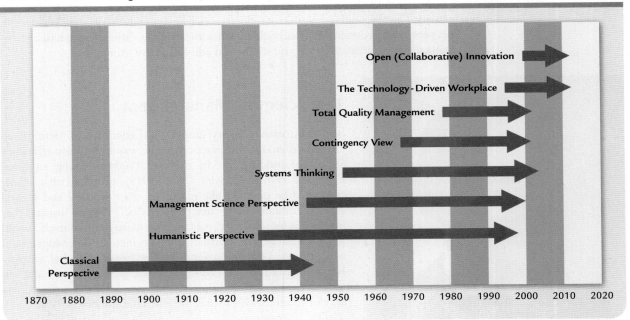

REMEMBER THIS

- Managers are always on the lookout for new techniques and approaches to meet shifting organizational needs.
- Looking at history gives managers a broader perspective for interpreting and responding to current opportunities and problems.

- Management and organizations are shaped by forces in the larger society.

1.9 **Classical Perspective**

The practice of management can be traced to 3000 B.C., to the first government organizations developed by the Sumerians and Egyptians, but the formal study of management is relatively recent.[55] The early study of management as we know it today began with what is now called the **classical perspective**.

The classical perspective on management emerged during the nineteenth and early twentieth centuries. The factory system that began to appear in the 1800s posed challenges that the earlier organizations had not encountered. Problems arose in tooling the plants, organizing managerial structure, training employees (many of them non-English-speaking immigrants), scheduling complex manufacturing operations, and dealing with increased labor dissatisfaction and resulting strikes.

These myriad new problems and the development of large, complex organizations demanded a new approach to coordination and control, and a "new sub-species of economic man—the salaried manager"[56]—was born. Between 1880 and 1920, the number of professional managers in the United States grew from 161,000 to more than 1 million.[57] These professional managers began developing and testing solutions to the mounting challenges of organizing, coordinating, and controlling large numbers of people and increasing worker productivity. Thus began the evolution of modern management with the classical perspective.

This perspective contains three subfields, each with a slightly different emphasis: scientific management, bureaucratic organizations, and administrative principles.[58]

The Granger Collection, New York

CONCEPT CONNECTION
Frederick Winslow Taylor (1856–1915).
Taylor's theory that labor productivity could be improved by scientifically determined management practices earned him the title of "father of scientific management."

1.9a Scientific Management

Scientific management emphasizes scientifically determined jobs and management practices as the way to improve efficiency and labor productivity. In the late 1800s, a young engineer, Frederick Winslow Taylor (1856–1915), proposed that workers "could be retooled like machines, their physical and mental gears recalibrated for better productivity."[59] Taylor insisted that improving productivity meant that management itself would have to change and, further, that the manner of change could be determined only by scientific study; hence, the label *scientific management* emerged. Taylor suggested that decisions based on rules of thumb and tradition be replaced with precise procedures developed after careful study of individual situations.[60]

The scientific management approach is illustrated by the unloading of iron from rail cars and reloading finished steel for the Bethlehem Steel plant in 1898. Taylor calculated that with the correct movements, tools, and sequencing, each man was capable of loading 47.5 tons per day instead of the typical 12.5 tons. He also worked out an incentive system that paid each man $1.85 a day for meeting the new standard, an increase from the previous rate of $1.15. Productivity at Bethlehem Steel shot up overnight.

Although known as the *father of scientific management*, Taylor was not alone in this area. Henry Gantt, an associate of Taylor's, developed the *Gantt chart*, a bar graph that measures planned and completed work along each stage of production by time elapsed.

Two other important pioneers in this area were the husband-and-wife team of Frank B. and Lillian M. Gilbreth. Frank B. Gilbreth (1868–1924) pioneered *time and motion study* and arrived at many of his management techniques independent of Taylor. He stressed efficiency and was known for his quest for the one best way to do work. Although Gilbreth is known for his early work with bricklayers, his work had great impact on medical surgery by drastically reducing the time that patients spent on the operating table. Surgeons were able to save countless lives through the application of time and motion study. Lillian M. Gilbreth (1878–1972) was more interested in the human aspect of work. When her husband died at the age of 56, she had 12 children aged 2 to 19. The undaunted "first lady of management" went right on with her work. She presented a paper in place of her late husband, continued their seminars and consulting, lectured, and eventually became a professor at Purdue University.[61] She pioneered in the field of industrial psychology and made substantial contributions to human resource management.

Exhibit 1.10 shows the basic ideas of scientific management. To use this approach, managers should develop standard methods for doing each job, select workers with the appropriate abilities, train workers in the standard methods, support workers and eliminate interruptions, and provide wage incentives.

CONCEPT CONNECTION Automaker Henry Ford made extensive use of Frederick Taylor's **scientific management** techniques, as illustrated by this assembly of an automobile at a Ford plant circa 1930. Ford replaced workers with machines for heavy lifting and moving autos from one worker to the next. This reduced worker hours and improved efficiency and productivity. Under this system, a Ford car rolled off the assembly line every 10 seconds.

Rue des Archives / The Granger Collection, New York

The ideas of scientific management that began with Taylor dramatically increased productivity across all industries, and they are still important today. Indeed, the idea of engineering work for greater productivity has enjoyed a renaissance in the retail industry. Supermarket chains such as Meijer Inc. and Hannaford, for example, use computerized labor waste elimination systems based on scientific management principles. The system breaks down tasks such as greeting a customer, working the register, scanning

EXHIBIT 1.10   Characteristics of Scientific Management

General Approach

- Developed standard method for performing each job
- Selected workers with appropriate abilities for each job
- Trained workers in standard methods
- Supported workers by planning their work and eliminating interruptions
- Provided wage incentives to workers for increased output

Contributions

- Demonstrated the importance of compensation for performance
- Initiated the careful study of tasks and jobs
- Demonstrated the importance of personnel selection and training

Criticisms

- Did not appreciate the social context of work and higher needs of workers
- Did not acknowledge variance among individuals
- Tended to regard workers as uninformed and ignored their ideas and suggestions

items, and so forth, into quantifiable units and devises standard times to complete each task. Executives say the computerized system has allowed them to staff stores more efficiently because people are routinely monitored by computer and are expected to meet strict standards.[62]

A *Harvard Business Review* article discussing innovations that shaped modern management puts scientific management at the top of its list of 12 influential innovations. Indeed, the ideas of creating a system for maximum efficiency and organizing work for maximum productivity are deeply embedded in our organizations.[63] However, because scientific management ignores the social context and workers' needs, it can lead to increased conflict and clashes between managers and employees. The United Food and Commercial Workers Union, for instance, filed a grievance against Meijer in connection with its cashier performance system. Under such performance management systems, workers often feel exploited—a sharp contrast from the harmony and cooperation that Taylor and his followers had envisioned.

1.9b Bureaucratic Organizations

A systematic approach developed in Europe that looked at the organization as a whole is the **bureaucratic organizations approach**, a subfield within the classical perspective. Max Weber (1864–1920), a German theorist, introduced most of the concepts on bureaucratic organizations.[64]

During the late 1800s, many European organizations were managed on a personal, family-like basis. Employees were loyal to a single individual rather than to the organization or its mission. The dysfunctional consequence of this management practice was that resources were used to realize individual desires rather than organizational goals. Employees in effect owned the organization and used resources for their own gain rather than to serve customers. Weber envisioned organizations that would be managed on an impersonal, rational basis. This form of organization was called a *bureaucracy*. Exhibit 1.11 summarizes the six characteristics of bureaucracy as specified by Weber.

Weber believed that an organization based on rational authority would be more efficient and adaptable to change because continuity is related to formal structure and positions rather than to a particular person, who may leave or die. To Weber, rationality in organizations meant employee selection and advancement based not on whom you know, but rather on competence and technical qualifications, which are assessed by examination or according to specific training and experience. The organization relies on rules and written records for continuity. In addition, rules and procedures are impersonal and applied uniformly to all employees. A clear division of labor arises from distinct definitions of authority and responsibility, legitimized as official duties. Positions are organized in a hierarchy, with each position under the authority of a higher one. The manager gives orders successfully not on the basis of his or her personality, but on the legal power invested in the managerial position.

The term *bureaucracy* has taken on a negative meaning in today's organizations and is associated with endless rules and red tape. We have all been frustrated by waiting in long lines or following seemingly silly procedures. However, the value of bureaucratic principles is still evident in many organizations, such as United Parcel Service (UPS), sometimes nicknamed *Big Brown*.

As this example shows, there are positive as well as negative aspects associated with bureaucratic principles. Weber also struggled with the good and bad sides of bureaucracy.[65] Although he perceived bureaucracy as a threat to basic personal liberties, he recognized it as the most efficient and rational form of organizing. Rules and other bureaucratic procedures

> *"Students would be more likely to have a positive impact on the future of management if they were more engaged with the history and traditions of management— particularly that of a German sociologist [Weber] who died nearly 100 years ago."*
>
> —Stephen Cummings and Todd Bridgman, Victoria University of Wellington, New Zealand

EXHIBIT 1.11   Characteristics of Weberian Bureaucracy

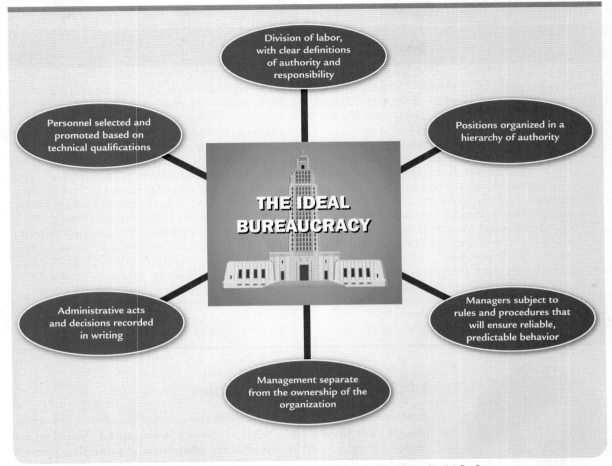

SOURCE: Adapted from Max Weber, *The Theory of Social and Economic Organizations*, ed. and trans. A. M. Henderson and Talcott Parsons (New York: Free Press, 1947), pp. 328–337.

provide a standard way of dealing with employees. Everyone gets equal treatment, and everyone knows what the rules are. Almost every organization needs to have some rules, and rules multiply as organizations grow larger and more complex. Some examples of rules governing employee behavior in a furniture manufacturing company, for example, might include the following:[66]

- Employees must wear protective eye and ear equipment when using machines.

- Employees must carry out any reasonable duty assigned to them, including shop maintenance.

- Employees must maintain an accurate time sheet, showing job and activity.

- The following will be considered causes for dismissal: excessive tardiness or absenteeism, willful damage to equipment, continual careless or unsafe behavior, theft, being under the influence of alcohol or illegal drugs while at work.

Read the Ethical Dilemma on page 50 that pertains to problems with bureaucracy.

Spotlight on Skills

UPS

UPS is the largest package delivery company in the world and a leading global provider of specialized transportation and logistics services. The company operates in more than 200 countries and territories worldwide.

Why has UPS been so successful? One important factor is the concept of bureaucracy. UPS operates according to strict rules and regulations. It teaches drivers an astounding 340 steps for how to deliver a package correctly, such as how to load the truck, how to fasten their seat belts, how to walk, and how to carry their keys. Specific safety rules apply to drivers, loaders, clerks, and managers. Strict dress codes are enforced—clean uniforms (called *browns*), every day, black or brown polished shoes with nonslip soles, no beards, no hair below the collar, no tattoos visible during deliveries, and so on. Before each shift, drivers conduct a "Z-scan," a Z-shaped inspection of the sides and front of their vehicles. Employees are asked to clean off their desks

at the end of each day so they can start fresh the next morning. Managers are given copies of policy books with the expectation that they will use them regularly, and memos on various policies and rules circulate by the hundreds every day.

UPS has a well-defined division of labor. Each plant consists of specialized drivers, loaders, clerks, washers, sorters, and maintenance personnel. UPS thrives on written records, and it has been a leader in using new technology to enhance reliability and efficiency. All drivers have daily worksheets that specify performance goals and work output. Technical qualification is the criterion for hiring and promotion. The UPS policy book says the leader is expected to have the knowledge and capacity to justify the position of leadership. Favoritism is forbidden. The bureaucratic model works just fine at UPS, "the tightest ship in the shipping business."[67]

Mary Parker Follette Foundation and Reading University, UK

●● CONCEPT CONNECTION

Mary Parker Follett (1868–1933). Follett was an early advocate of the **humanistic perspective** on management. Her emphasis on worker participation and shared goals among managers was embraced by many business-people of the day and has been recently "rediscovered" by corporate America.

1.9c Administrative Principles

Another major subfield within the classical perspective is known as the *administrative principles* approach. Whereas scientific management focused on the productivity of the individual worker, the **administrative principles approach** focused on the total organization. The major contributor to this approach was Henri Fayol (1841–1925), a French mining engineer who worked his way up to become head of a large mining group known as Comambault. Pieces of Comambault survive today as part of ArcelorMittal, the world's largest steel and mining company. In his later years, Fayol wrote down his concepts on administration, based largely on his own management experiences.[68]

In his most significant work, *General and Industrial Management*, Fayol discussed 14 general principles of management, several of which are part of management philosophy today. For example:

- *Unity of command.* Each subordinate receives orders from one—and only one—superior.

- *Division of work.* Managerial work and technical work are amenable to specialization to produce more and better work with the same amount of effort.

- *Unity of direction.* Similar activities in an organization should be grouped together under one manager.

- *Scalar chain.* A chain of authority extends from the top to the bottom of the organization and should include every employee.

Fayol felt that these principles could be applied in any organizational setting. He also identified five basic functions or elements of management: *planning, organizing, commanding, coordinating*, and *controlling*. These functions underlie much of the general approach to today's management theory.

The overall classical perspective as an approach to management was very powerful and gave companies fundamental new skills for establishing high productivity and effective treatment of employees. Indeed, the United States surged ahead of the world in management techniques, and other countries, especially Japan, borrowed heavily from American ideas.

REMEMBER THIS

- The study of modern management began in the late nineteenth century with the **classical perspective**, which took a rational, scientific approach to management and sought to turn organizations into efficient operating machines.
- **Scientific management** is a subfield of the classical perspective that emphasizes scientifically determined changes in management practices as the solution to improving labor productivity.
- Frederick Winslow Taylor is known as "the father of scientific management."
- Scientific management is considered one of the most significant innovations influencing modern management.
- Some supermarket chains are using computerized systems based on scientific management principles to schedule employees for maximum efficiency.

- Another subfield of the classical perspective is the **bureaucratic organizations approach**, which emphasizes management on an impersonal, rational basis through elements such as clearly defined authority and responsibility, formal recordkeeping, and separation of management and ownership.
- Max Weber introduced most of the concepts about bureaucratic organizations.
- The **administrative principles approach** is a subfield of the classical perspective that focuses on the total organization rather than the individual worker and delineates the management functions of planning, organizing, commanding, coordinating, and controlling.
- Henri Fayol, a major contributor to the administrative principles approach, outlined 14 general principles of management, several of which are a part of management philosophy today.

1.10 Humanistic Perspective

The **humanistic perspective** on management emphasized the importance of understanding human behaviors, needs, and attitudes in the workplace, as well as social interactions and group processes.[69] There are three primary subfields based on the humanistic perspective: the human relations movement, the human resources perspective, and the behavioral sciences approach.

1.10a Early Advocates

Two early advocates of a more humanistic approach were Mary Parker Follett and Chester Barnard. Mary Parker Follett (1868–1933) was trained in philosophy and political science, but she applied herself in many fields, including social psychology and management. She wrote of the importance of common superordinate goals for reducing conflict in organizations.[70] Her work was popular with businesspeople of her day but was often overlooked by management scholars.[71] Follett's ideas served as a contrast to scientific management and are reemerging as applicable for modern managers dealing with rapid changes in today's global environment. Her approach to leadership stressed the importance of people rather than engineering techniques. She offered the pithy admonition, "Don't hug your blueprints," and analyzed the dynamics of management–organization interactions. Follett addressed issues that are timely today, such as ethics, power, and leading in a way that encourages employees to give their best. The concepts of *empowerment*, facilitating rather than controlling employees, and allowing employees to act depending on the authority of the situation opened new areas for theoretical study by Chester Barnard and others.[72]

Chester I. Barnard (1886–1961) studied economics at Harvard but failed to receive a degree because he did not take a course in laboratory science. He went to work in the statistical department of AT&T, and in 1927, he became president of New Jersey Bell. One of Barnard's significant contributions was the concept of the informal organization. The *informal organization* occurs in all formal organizations and includes cliques, informal networks, and naturally occurring social groupings. Barnard argued that organizations are not machines and stressed that informal relationships are powerful forces that can help the organization if properly managed. Another significant contribution was the *acceptance theory of authority*, which states that people have free will and can choose whether to follow management orders. People typically follow orders because they perceive positive benefit to themselves, but they do have a choice. Managers should treat employees properly because their acceptance of authority may be critical to organization success in important situations.[73]

National Archives

CONCEPT CONNECTION This 1914 photograph shows the initiation of a new arrival at a Nebraska planting camp. This initiation was not part of the formal rules and illustrates the significance of the **informal organization** described by Barnard. Social values and behaviors were powerful forces that could help or hurt the planting organization, depending on how they were managed.

1.10b Human Relations Movement

The **human relations movement** was based on the idea that truly effective control comes from within the individual worker rather than from strict, authoritarian control.[74] This school of thought recognized and directly responded to social pressures for enlightened treatment of employees. The early work on industrial psychology and personnel selection received little attention because of the prominence of scientific management. Then a series of studies at a Chicago electric company, which came to be known as the **Hawthorne studies**, changed all that.

Beginning about 1895, a struggle developed between manufacturers of gas and electric lighting fixtures for control of the residential and industrial market.[75] By 1909, electric lighting had begun to win, but the increasingly efficient electric fixtures used less total power, which was less profitable for the electric companies. The electric companies began a campaign to convince industrial users that they needed more light to get more productivity. When advertising did not work, the industry began using experimental tests to demonstrate their argument. Managers were skeptical about the results, so the Committee on Industrial Lighting (CIL) was set up to run the tests. To further add to the tests' credibility, Thomas Edison was made honorary chairman of the CIL. In one test location—the Hawthorne plant of the Western Electric Company—some interesting events occurred.

The major part of this work involved four experimental and three control groups. In all, five different tests were conducted. These pointed to the importance of factors *other* than illumination in affecting productivity. To examine these factors more carefully, numerous other experiments were conducted.[76] The results of the most famous study, the first Relay Assembly Test Room (RATR) experiment, were extremely controversial. Under the guidance of two Harvard professors, Elton Mayo and Fritz Roethlisberger, the RATR studies lasted nearly six years (May 10, 1927 to May 4, 1933) and involved 24 separate experimental periods. So many factors were changed and so many unforeseen factors uncontrolled that scholars disagree on the factors that truly contributed to the general increase in performance over that time period. Most early interpretations, however, agreed on one point: Money was not the cause of the increased output.[77] It was believed that the factor that best explained increased output was *human relations*. Employees performed better when managers treated them in a positive manner. Recent re-analyses of the experiments have revealed that a number of factors were different for the workers involved, and some suggest that money may well have been the single most important factor.[78] An interview with one of the original participants revealed that just getting into the experimental group meant a huge increase in income.[79]

These new data clearly show that money mattered a great deal at Hawthorne. In addition, worker productivity increased partly as a result of the increased feelings of importance and group pride that employees felt by virtue of being selected for this important project.[80] One unintended contribution of the experiments was a rethinking of field research practices. Researchers and scholars realized that the researcher can influence the outcome of an experiment by being too closely involved with research subjects. This phenomenon has come to be known as the ***Hawthorne effect*** in research methodology. Subjects behaved differently because of the active participation of researchers in the Hawthorne experiments.[81]

Before reading on, take the New Manager Self-Test on page 36. This test will give you feedback about your personal approach to getting things done through others.

From a historical perspective, whether the studies were academically sound is less important than the fact that they stimulated an increased interest in looking at employees as more than extensions of production machinery. The interpretation that employees' output increased when managers treated them in a positive manner started a revolution in worker treatment for improving organizational productivity. Despite flawed methodology or inaccurate conclusions, the findings provided the impetus for the human relations movement. This approach shaped management theory and practice for well over a quarter century, and the belief that human relations is the best area of focus for increasing productivity persists today.

1.10c Human Resources Perspective

The human relations movement initially espoused a *dairy farm* view of management—just as contented cows give more milk, satisfied workers will produce more work. Gradually, views with deeper content began to emerge. The **human resources perspective** maintained an interest in worker participation and considerate leadership but shifted the emphasis to consider the daily tasks that people perform. The human resources perspective combines prescriptions for design of job tasks with theories of motivation.[82] In the human resources view, jobs should be designed so that tasks are not perceived as dehumanizing or demeaning but instead allow workers to use their full potential. Two of the best-known contributors to the human resources perspective were Abraham Maslow and Douglas McGregor.

Western Electric Photographic Services

CONCEPT CONNECTION This is the Relay Room of the Western Electric Hawthorne, Illinois, plant in 1927. Six women worked in this relay assembly test room during the controversial experiments on employee productivity. Professors Mayo and Roethlisberger evaluated conditions such as rest breaks and workday length, physical health, amount of sleep, and diet. Experimental changes were fully discussed with the women and were abandoned if they disapproved. Gradually the researchers began to realize they had created a change in supervisory style and **human relations**, which they believed was the true cause of the increased productivity.

Abraham Maslow (1908–1970), a practicing psychologist, observed that his patients' problems usually stemmed from an inability to satisfy their needs. Thus, he generalized his work and suggested a hierarchy of needs. Maslow's hierarchy started with physiological needs and progressed to safety, belongingness, esteem, and, finally, self-actualization needs. Chapter 12 discusses his ideas in more detail.

Douglas McGregor (1906–1964) had become frustrated with the early simplistic human relations notions while president of Antioch College in Ohio. He challenged both the classical perspective and the early human relations assumptions about human behavior.

NEW MANAGER Self-Test

What's Your Mach?

Instructions: Managers differ in how they view human nature and the tactics that they use to get things done through others. Answer the questions below based on how you view others. Think carefully about each question and be honest about what you feel inside. Please answer whether each item below is Mostly False or Mostly True for you.

	Mostly True	Mostly False
1. Overall, it is better to be humble and honest than to be successful and dishonest.	_____	_____
2. If you trust someone completely, you are asking for trouble.	_____	_____
3. A leader should take action only when it is morally right.	_____	_____
4. A good way to handle people is to tell them what they like to hear.	_____	_____
5. There is no excuse for telling a white lie to someone.	_____	_____
6. It makes sense to flatter important people.	_____	_____
7. Most people who get ahead as leaders have led very moral lives.	_____	_____
8. It is better not to tell people the real reason you did something unless it benefits you to do so.	_____	_____
9. The vast majority of people are brave, good, and kind.	_____	_____
10. It is hard to get to the top without sometimes cutting corners.	_____	_____

Scoring and Interpretation: To compute your Mach score, give yourself one point for each Mostly False answer to items 1, 3, 5, 7, and 9, and one point for each Mostly True answer to items 2, 4, 6, 8, and 10. These items were drawn from the works of Niccoló Machiavelli, an Italian political philosopher who wrote *The Prince* in 1513 to describe how a prince can retain control of his kingdom. Successful management intrigue at the time of Machiavelli was believed to require behaviors that today would be considered ego-centered and manipulative, which is almost the opposite of more enlightened management that arose from the human relations movement. A score of 8–10 points suggests that you have a high Mach score. From 4 to 7 points indicates a moderate score, and 0–3 points would indicate a low Mach score. Having a high Mach score does not mean that the individual is a sinister or vicious person, but it probably means that he or she has a cool detachment, sees life as a game, and is not personally engaged with other people. Discuss your results with other students, and talk about whether you think politicians and top executives would have a high or a low Mach score.

SOURCE: Adapted from R. Christie and F. L. Geis, *Studies in Machiavellianism* (New York: Academic Press, 1970).

EXHIBIT 1.12 Theory X and Theory Y

Assumptions of Theory X
- The average human being has an inherent dislike of work and will avoid it if possible.
- Because of the human characteristic of dislike for work, most people must be coerced, controlled, directed, or threatened with punishment to get them to put forth adequate effort toward the achievement of organizational objectives.
- The average human being prefers to be directed, wishes to avoid responsibility, has relatively little ambition, and wants security above all.

Assumptions of Theory Y
- The expenditure of physical and mental effort in work is as natural as play or rest. The average human being does not inherently dislike work.
- External control and the threat of punishment are not the only means for bringing about effort toward organizational objectives. A person will exercise self-direction and self-control in the service of objectives to which he or she is committed.
- The average human being learns, under proper conditions, not only to accept but to seek responsibility.
- The capacity to exercise a relatively high degree of imagination, ingenuity, and creativity in the solution of organizational problems is widely, not narrowly, distributed in the population.
- Under the conditions of modern industrial life, the intellectual potentialities of the average human being are only partially utilized.

SOURCE: Douglas McGregor, *The Human Side of Enterprise* (New York: McGraw-Hill, 1960), pp. 33–48. (c) McGraw-Hill Companies, Inc.

Based on his experiences as a manager and consultant, his training as a psychologist, and the work of Maslow, McGregor formulated Theory X and Theory Y, which are explained in Exhibit 1.12.[83] McGregor believed that the classical perspective was based on Theory X assumptions about workers. He also felt that a slightly modified version of Theory X fit early human relations ideas. In other words, human relations ideas did not go far enough. McGregor proposed Theory Y as a more realistic view of workers for guiding management thinking.

The point of Theory Y is that organizations can take advantage of the imagination and intellect of all their employees. Employees will exercise self-control and will contribute to organizational goals when given the opportunity. A few companies today still use Theory X management, but many are using Theory Y techniques. Consider how Semco applies Theory Y assumptions to tap into employee creativity and mind power.

For managers like Ricardo Semler, command and control is a thing of the past, with the future belonging to those companies that build leadership throughout the organization. The Theory Y approach has helped Semco succeed in a tough environment. Although few go as far as Semco, other companies are also using Theory Y principles that are more in line with today's emphasis on employee empowerment and involvement.

Look back at your scores on the questionnaire earlier in this chapter related to Theory X and Theory Y. How will your management assumptions about people fit into an organization today?

1.10d Behavioral Sciences Approach

The **behavioral sciences approach** uses scientific methods and draws from sociology, psychology, anthropology, economics, and other disciplines to develop theories about human behavior and interaction in an organizational setting. This approach can be seen in practically every organization. When a company such as Zappos.com conducts research to determine the best set of tests, interviews, and employee profiles to use when selecting new employees, it is using behavioral science techniques. When Best Buy electronics stores train new managers in the techniques of employee motivation, most of the theories and findings are rooted in behavioral science research.

One specific set of management techniques based in the behavioral sciences approach is *organization development* (OD). In the 1970s, OD evolved as a separate field that applied

Spotlight on Skills

Semco

The Brazil-based company Semco's fundamental operating principle is to harness the wisdom of all its employees. It does so by letting people control their work hours, location, and even pay plans. Employees also participate in all organizational decisions, including what businesses Semco should pursue.

Semco leaders believe that economic success requires creating an atmosphere that puts power and control directly in the hands of employees. People can veto any new product idea or business venture. They choose their own leaders and manage themselves to accomplish goals. Information is openly and broadly shared so that everyone knows where they and the company stand. Instead of dictating Semco's

identity and strategy, leaders allow it to be shaped by individual interests and efforts. People are encouraged to seek challenges, explore new ideas and business opportunities, and question the ideas of anyone in the company.

This high level of trust in employees has helped Semco achieve decades of high profitability and growth despite fluctuations in the economy and shifting markets. "At Semco, we don't play by the rules," says Ricardo Semler. Semler, whose father started the company in the 1950s, says it doesn't unnerve him to "step back and see nothing on the company's horizon." He is happy to watch the company and its employees "ramble through their days, running on instinct and opportunity...."[84]

the behavioral sciences to improve the organization's health and effectiveness through its ability to cope with change, improve internal relationships, and increase problem-solving capabilities.[85] The techniques and concepts of OD have since been broadened and expanded to address the increasing complexity of organizations and the environment, and OD is still a vital approach for managers. OD will be discussed in detail in Chapter 8. Other concepts that grew out of the behavioral sciences approach include matrix organizations, self-managed teams, ideas about corporate culture, and management by wandering around. Indeed, the behavioral sciences approach has influenced the majority of tools, techniques, and approaches that managers have applied to organizations since the 1970s.

All the remaining chapters of this book contain research findings and management applications that can be attributed to the behavioral sciences approach.

REMEMBER THIS

- The **humanistic perspective** emphasized understanding human behavior, needs, and attitudes in the workplace.

- Mary Parker Follett and Chester Barnard were early advocates of a more humanistic approach to management.

- Follett emphasized worker participation and empowerment, shared goals, and facilitating rather than controlling employees. Barnard's contributions include the acceptance theory of authority.

- The **human relations movement** stresses the satisfaction of employees' basic needs as the key to increased productivity.

- The **Hawthorne studies** were important in shaping ideas concerning how managers should treat workers.

- The **human resources perspective** suggests that jobs should be designed to meet people's higher-level needs by allowing employees to use their full potential.

- The **behavioral sciences approach** draws from psychology, sociology, and other social sciences to develop theories about human behavior and interaction in an organizational setting.

- Many current management ideas and practices can be traced to the behavioral sciences approach.

1.11 Management Science

World War II caused many management changes. The massive and complicated problems associated with modern global warfare presented managerial decision makers with the need for more sophisticated tools than ever before. **Management science**, also referred to as the *quantitative perspective*, provided a way to address those problems. This view is distinguished for its application of mathematics, statistics, and other quantitative techniques to management decision making and problem solving. During World War II, groups of mathematicians, physicists, and other scientists were formed to solve military problems that frequently involved moving massive amounts of materials and large numbers of people quickly and efficiently. Managers soon saw how quantitative techniques could be applied to large-scale business firms.[86]

Management scholar Peter Drucker's 1946 book *Concept of the Corporation* sparked a dramatic increase in the academic study of business and management. Picking up on techniques developed for the military, scholars began cranking out numerous mathematical tools for corporate managers, such as the application of linear programming for optimizing operations, statistical process control for quality management, and the capital asset pricing model.[87]

These efforts were enhanced with the development and perfection of the computer. Coupled with the growing body of statistical techniques, computers made it possible for managers to collect, store, and process large volumes of data for quantitative decision making, and the quantitative approach is widely used today by managers in a variety of industries. The Walt Disney Company used **quantitative techniques** to develop FASTPASS, a sophisticated computerized system that spares parents the ordeal of standing in long lines for the most popular rides. Disney theme parks have machines that issue coupons with a return time that's been calculated based on the number of people standing in the actual line, the number who have already obtained passes, and each ride's capacity. The next generation of technology, xPass, will let visitors book times for rides before they even leave home.[88] Let's look at three subsets of management science.

Operations research grew directly out of the World War II military groups (called *operational research teams* in Great Britain and *operations research teams* in the United States).[89] It consists of mathematical model building and other applications of quantitative techniques to managerial problems.

Operations management refers to the field of management that specializes in the physical production of goods or services. Operations management specialists use management science to solve manufacturing problems. Some commonly used methods are forecasting, inventory modeling, linear and nonlinear programming, queuing theory, scheduling, simulation, and break-even analysis.

Information technology (IT) is the most recent subfield of management science, which is often reflected in management information systems designed to provide relevant information to managers in a timely and cost-efficient manner. IT has evolved to include intranets and extranets, as well as various software programs that help managers estimate costs, plan and track production, manage projects, allocate resources, or schedule employees. Most of today's organizations have IT specialists who use quantitative techniques to solve complex organizational problems.

However, as events in the mortgage and finance industries show, relying too heavily on quantitative techniques can cause problems for managers. Mortgage companies used quantitative models that showed their investments in subprime mortgages would be okay even if default rates hit historically high proportions. However, the models didn't take into account that no one before in history had thought it made sense to give $500,000 loans to people making minimum wage![90] "Quants" also came to dominate organizational decisions in other financial firms. The term **quants** refers to financial managers and others who base their decisions on complex quantitative analysis, under the assumption that using advanced mathematics and sophisticated computer technology can accurately predict how the market works and help them reap huge profits. The virtually exclusive use of these quantitative models led aggressive traders and managers to take enormous risks. When the market began to go haywire as doubts about subprime mortgages grew, the models went haywire as well. Stocks predicted to go up went down, and vice versa. Events that were predicted to happen only once every 10,000 years happened three days in a row in the market madness. Scott Patterson, a *Wall Street Journal* reporter and author of *The Quants: How a New Breed of Math Whizzes Conquered Wall Street and Nearly Destroyed It,* suggests that the financial crisis that began in 2008 is partly due to the quants' failure to observe market fundamentals, pay attention to human factors, and heed their own intuition.[91]

REMEMBER THIS

- Management science became popular based on its successful application in solving military problems during World War II.
- **Management science**, also called the *quantitative perspective,* uses mathematics, statistical techniques, and computer technology to facilitate management decision making, particularly for complex problems.
- The Walt Disney Company uses management science to solve the problem of long lines for popular rides and attractions at its theme parks.
- Three subsets of management science are operations research, operations management, and information technology.
- **Quants** have come to dominate decision making in financial firms, and the Wall Street meltdown in 2007–2008 shows the danger of relying too heavily on a quantitative approach.
- Management scholar Peter Drucker's classic 1946 book *Concept of the Corporation* sparked a dramatic increase in the academic study of business and management.

1.12 Recent Historical Trends

Despite recent heavy use of management science techniques by some managers, among the approaches that we've discussed so far the humanistic perspective has remained most prevalent from the 1950s until today. The post–World War II period saw the rise of new concepts, along with a continued strong interest in the human aspect of managing, such as team and group dynamics and other ideas that relate to the humanistic perspective. Three new concepts that appeared were systems thinking, the contingency view, and total quality management.

1.12a Systems Thinking

Systems thinking is the ability to see both the distinct elements of a system or situation and the complex and changing interaction among those elements. A **system** is a set of interrelated parts that function as a whole to achieve a common purpose.[92] **Subsystems**

are parts of a system, such as an organization, that depend on one another. Changes in one part of the system (the organization) affect other parts. Managers need to understand the synergy of the whole organization, rather than just the separate elements, and to learn to reinforce or change whole system patterns.[93] **Synergy** means that the whole is greater than the sum of its parts. The organization must be managed as a coordinated whole. Managers who understand subsystem interdependence and synergy are reluctant to make changes that do not recognize subsystem impact on the organization as a whole.

Many people have been trained to solve problems by breaking a complex system, such as an organization, into discrete parts and working to make each part perform as well as possible. However, the success of each piece does not add up to the success of the whole. In fact, sometimes changing one part to make it better actually makes the whole system function less effectively. For example, a small city embarked on a road-building program to solve traffic congestion without whole-systems thinking. With new roads available, more people began moving to the suburbs. Rather than reduce congestion, the solution actually increased traffic congestion, delays, and pollution by enabling suburban sprawl.[94]

It is the *relationship* among the parts that form a whole system—whether a community, an automobile, a nonprofit agency, a human being, or a business organization—that matters. Systems thinking enables managers to look for patterns of movement over time and focus on the qualities of rhythm, flow, direction, shape, and networks of relationships that accomplish the performance of the whole. When managers can see the structures that underlie complex situations, they can facilitate improvement. But doing that requires a focus on the big picture.

An important element of systems thinking is to discern circles of causality. Peter Senge, author of *The Fifth Discipline*, argues that reality is made up of circles rather than straight lines. For example, Exhibit 1.13 shows circles of influence for increasing a retail firm's profits. The events in the circle on the left are caused by the decision to increase advertising; hence the retail firm adds to the advertising budget to aggressively promote its products. The advertising promotions increase sales, which increase profits, which provide money to further increase the advertising budget.

EXHIBIT 1.13 Systems Thinking and Circles of Causality

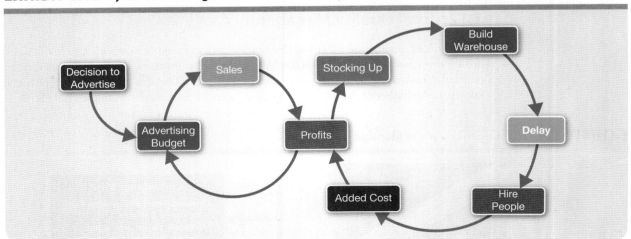

SOURCE: Based on concepts presented in Peter M. Senge, *The Fifth Discipline: The Art and Practice of the Learning Organization* (New York: Doubleday/Currency, 1990).

But another circle of causality is being influenced as well. The decision by marketing managers will have consequences for the operations department. As sales and profits increase, operations will be forced to stock up with greater inventory. Additional inventory will create a need for additional warehouse space. Building a new warehouse will cause a delay in stocking up. After the warehouse is built, new people will be hired, all of which adds to company costs, which will have a negative impact on profits. Thus, understanding all the consequences of their decisions via circles of causality enables company leaders to plan and allocate resources to warehousing as well as to advertising to ensure stable increases in sales and profits. Without understanding system causality, top managers would fail to understand why increasing advertising budgets could cause inventory delays and temporarily reduce profits.

1.12b Contingency View

A second recent extension to management thinking is the **contingency view**. The classical perspective assumed a *universalist* view. Management concepts were thought to be universal; that is, whatever worked in terms of management style, bureaucratic structure, and so on in one organization would work in any other one. In business education, however, an alternative view exists. In this *case* view, each situation is believed to be unique. Principles are not universal, and one learns about management by experiencing a large number of case problem situations. Managers face the task of determining what methods will work in every new situation.

To integrate these views, the contingency view emerged, as illustrated in Exhibit 1.14.[95] Here, neither of the other views is seen as entirely correct. Instead, certain contingencies, or variables, exist for helping managers identify and understand situations. The contingency view tells us that what works in one setting might not work in another. Contingency means that one thing depends on other things and a manager's response to a situation depends on identifying key contingencies in an organizational situation.

One important contingency, for example, is the industry in which the organization operates. The organizational structure that is effective for an Internet company, such as Google, would not be successful for a large auto manufacturer, such as Ford. A management-by-objectives (MBO) system that works well in a manufacturing firm, in turn, might not be right for a school system. When managers learn to identify important patterns and characteristics of their organizations, they can fit solutions to those characteristics.

1.12c Total Quality Management

The theme of quality is another concept that permeates current management thinking. The quality movement is strongly associated with Japanese companies, but these ideas emerged partly as a result of American influence after World War II. The ideas of W. Edwards Deming, known as the "father of the quality movement," were initially scoffed at in the United States,

EXHIBIT 1.14 Contingency View of Management

but the Japanese embraced his theories and modified them to help rebuild their industries into world powers.[96] Japanese companies achieved a significant departure from the American model by gradually shifting from an inspection-oriented approach to quality control toward an approach that emphasized employee involvement in the prevention of quality problems.[97]

During the 1980s and into the 1990s, total quality management (TQM), which focuses on managing the total organization to deliver better quality to customers, moved to the forefront in helping U.S. managers deal with global competition. The approach infuses high-quality values throughout every activity within a company, with frontline workers intimately involved in the process. Four significant elements of quality management are employee involvement, focus on the customer, benchmarking, and continuous improvement, often referred to as *kaizen*.

Employee involvement means that achieving better quality requires companywide participation in quality control. All employees are *focused on the customer*; companies find out what customers want and try to meet their needs and expectations. *Benchmarking* refers to a process whereby companies find out how others do something better than they do and then try to imitate or improve on it. *Continuous improvement* is the implementation of small, incremental improvements in all areas of the organization on an ongoing basis. TQM is not a quick fix, but companies such as GE, Texas Instruments, Procter & Gamble, and DuPont achieved astonishing results in efficiency, quality, and customer satisfaction through TQM.[98] TQM is still an important part of today's organizations, and managers consider benchmarking in particular a highly effective and satisfying management technique.[99]

Hyundai Motor Company

CONCEPT CONNECTION Hyundai Motor Company's rise from 1 percent of the U.S. market in 1999 to about 9 percent of the U.S. market in 2011 shows how commitment to **total quality management (TQM)** can improve a company's products and market position. First, managers increased the quality team from 100 to 865 people and held quality seminars to train employees. Then they **benchmarked** products, using vehicle lifts and high-intensity spotlights to compare against competing brands. Today, Hyundai earns quality ratings comparable to its main competitors, Honda and Toyota.

Some of today's companies pursue highly ambitious quality goals to demonstrate their commitment to improving quality. For example, *Six Sigma*, popularized by Motorola and GE, specifies a goal of no more than 3.4 defects per million parts. However, the term also refers to a broad quality control approach that emphasizes a disciplined and relentless pursuit of higher quality and lower costs. TQM will be discussed in detail in Chapter 15.

REMEMBER THIS

- A **system** is a set of interrelated parts that function as a whole to achieve a common purpose. An organization is a system.

- **Systems thinking** means looking not just at discrete parts of an organizational situation, but also at the continually changing interactions among the parts.

- When managers think systemically and understand subsystem interdependence and synergy, they can get a better handle on managing in a complex environment.

- **Subsystems** are parts of a system that depend on one another for their functioning.

- The concept of **synergy** says that the whole is greater than the sum of its parts. The organization must be managed as a whole.

- The **contingency view** tells managers that what works in one organizational situation might not work in others. Managers can identify important *contingencies* that help guide their decisions regarding the organization.

- The quality movement is associated with Japanese companies, but it emerged partly as a result of American influence after World War II.
- W. Edwards Deming is known as the "father of the quality movement."

- **Total quality management** focuses on managing the total organization to deliver quality to customers.
- Four significant elements of TQM are employee involvement, focus on the customer, benchmarking, and continuous improvement.

1.13 Innovative Management Thinking for a Changing World

All of the ideas and approaches discussed so far in this chapter go into the mix that makes up modern management. Dozens of ideas and techniques in current use can trace their roots to these historical perspectives.[100] In addition, innovative concepts continue to emerge to address new management challenges. Smart managers heed the past but know that they and their organizations have to change with the times. General Motors (GM) was the "ideal" organizational model in a post–World War II environment, but by 2009, it had collapsed into bankruptcy and sought billions of dollars in government aid because managers failed to pay attention as the world changed around them.[101] GM managers assumed that the preeminence of their company would shelter it from change, and they stuck far too long with a strategy, culture, and management approach that were out of tune with the shifting environment.

1.13a Contemporary Management Tools

Recall from the beginning of this chapter our discussion of *jugaad*, an approach to innovation management used in India that many U.S. managers are trying. Management fads and fashions come and go, but managers are always looking for new techniques and approaches that more adequately respond to customer needs and the demands of the environment. A recent survey of European managers reflects that managers pay attention to currently fashionable management concepts. The following table lists the percentage of managers reporting that they were aware of these selected management trends that have been popular over the past decade.[102]

Concept	Awareness Percentage
E-business	99.41
Decentralization	99.12
Customer Relationship Management	97.50
Virtual Organization	91.19
Empowerment	83.41
Reengineering	76.65

Managers especially tend to look for fresh ideas to help them cope during difficult times. For instance, recent challenges such as the tough economy and volatile stock market, environmental and organizational crises, lingering anxieties over war and terrorism, and public suspicion and skepticism resulting from the crisis on Wall Street have left today's executives searching for any management tool—new or old—that can help them get the most out of limited resources. The Spotlight on Skills box lists a wide variety of ideas and techniques used by today's managers. Management idea life cycles have been growing shorter as the pace of change has increased. A study by professors at the University of Louisiana at Lafayette found that, from the 1950s to the 1970s, it typically took more than a decade for interest in a popular management idea to peak. Now, the interval has shrunk to fewer than three years, and some trends come and go even faster.[103]

1.14 Managing the Technology-Driven Workplace

Two popular contemporary tools that have shown some staying power (as reflected in the Spotlight on Skills Box) are customer relationship management and supply chain management. These techniques are related to the shift to a technology-driven workplace. A more recent tool in the technology-driven workplace, social media, is also growing in use and importance.

1.14a Social Media Programs

Companies use social media programs to interact electronically with employees, customers, partners, and other stakeholders. Although only 29 percent of managers surveyed by Bain & Company said their companies used social media programs in 2010, more than half said they planned to use them in 2011.[104] **Social media programs** include company online community pages, social media sites such as Facebook or LinkedIn, microblogging platforms such as Twitter and China's Weibo, and company online forums. One frequent, and controversial, use of social media has been to look into the backgrounds and activities of job candidates. A survey by CareerBuilder found that 37 percent of hiring managers said they had used social media sites to see if job applicants present themselves professionally, to learn more about an applicant's qualifications, or to see if the candidate would be a good fit with the organizational culture.[105] Other uses of social media programs include generating awareness about the company's products and services, sharing ideas and seeking feedback from customers and partners, strengthening relationships among employees, and selling products. One concern for many managers is how to measure the effectiveness of the use of social media programs.

CONCEPT CONNECTION The success and popularity of **social media** tools continues to drive innovation on the Web. In 2012, after an initial launch in France, Muxi: Reddit was founded in 2005, sold to Conde Nast in 2006, went private in 2011 and then raised $50 in funding in 2014 with a total company valuation of $500 million

M4OS Photos/Alamy

1.14b Customer Relationship Management

Unlike social media, many managers have become quite comfortable and adept at using technology for **customer relationship management (CRM)**. CRM systems use the latest information technology to keep in close touch with customers and to collect and manage large amounts of customer data. These systems can

Spotlight on Skills

Management Tools and Trends

Over the history of management, many fashions and fads have appeared. Critics argue that new techniques may not represent permanent solutions. Others feel that managers must adopt new techniques for continuous improvement in a fast-changing world.

In 1993, Bain and Company started a large research project to interview and survey thousands of corporate executives about the 25 most popular management tools and techniques. The most recent list and usage rates for 2010–2011 are shown below. How many of the tools do you know? For more information on specific tools, see Bain's *Management Tools 2011: An Executive's Guide* at www.bain.com/publications/articles/management-tools-2011-executives-guide.aspx.

Popularity. In the 2010–2011 survey, benchmarking held onto the top spot as the most popular tool, reflecting managers' concern with efficiency and cost-cutting in a difficult economy. Mergers and acquisitions have decreased in popularity, with only 35 percent of managers using this technique. Three tools that ranked high in

both use and satisfaction were *strategic planning, mission and vision statements*, and *customer segmentation*, tools that can guide managers' thinking on strategic issues during times of rapid change.

Global Trends. For the first time, firms in emerging markets reported using more tools than those in developed markets. More than half of emerging market executives reported using the *balanced scorecard*. North American managers decreased their use of *outsourcing* and were the largest users of *social media programs*. Managers in Latin American companies used more tools than any other region, but they were the lightest users of *downsizing* and *customer relationship management (CRM)*. Asian companies were the greatest users of *knowledge management*. *Benchmarking* and *change management programs* were top tools for managers in Europe, where acute economic uncertainty continues.

SOURCE: Darrell Rigby and Barbara Bilodeau, "Management Tools and Trends 2011," Bain and Company, Inc., http://www.bain.com/publications/articles/Management-tools-trends-2011.aspx.

Business Blooper

Goldman Sachs

Goldman Sachs was one of the premier investment banks since it began in 1869 and joined the New York Stock Exchange in 1896. For over 100 years it was a symbol of honesty and revolved around team work, humility, and integrity. It wasn't just about the money, which allowed customers to trust the company, but it was about pride in what they were doing to serve clients. But the culture has become one of greed, according to the recently resigned Greg Smith, who lays the blame on CEO Lloyd Blankfein, whose leadership encouraged a culture of profits at all costs, which resulted in advisors telling clients to buy poor stocks the company needed

to unload, or sell customers products that were not good for them, just to earn a profit, and so on. He even heard a number of managing directors refer in an unkind manner to their clients as "muppets." Blankfein did not understand that part of his job was to serve clients. The federal government responded with the first of its high-profile verdicts against Goldman Sachs trader nicknamed "Fabulous Fab Torre."

SOURCE: William E. Bealing, Jr. and Edward Pitingolo, "Same Song, Same Dance: Evidence of Patterns in Securities and Exchange Commission Funding," *Review of Business and Finance Studies* 6(2) (2015): 1–10; Greg Smith

help managers be more accurate in their sales forecasts, coordinate sales and service staff more easily, improve product design and marketing, and act quickly to respond to shifting customer needs and desires. There has been an explosion of interest in CRM. In the Spotlight on Skills box, 58 percent of surveyed managers reported their companies used CRM in 2010, whereas only 35 percent of companies reported using this technique in

EXHIBIT 1.15   Supply Chain for a Retail Organization

SOURCE: Adapted from an exhibit from the Global Supply Chain Games Project, Delft University and the University of Maryland, R. H. Smith School of Business, www.gscg.org:8080/opencms/export/sites/default/gscg/images/supplychain_simple.gif.

2000. Goldman Sachs is one company that could use such techniques, as shown in the Business Blooper box.

Supply Chain Management   **Supply chain management** refers to managing the sequence of suppliers and purchasers, covering all stages of processing from obtaining raw materials to distributing finished goods to consumers.[106] Exhibit 1.15 illustrates a basic supply chain model. A *supply chain* is a network of multiple businesses and individuals that are connected through the flow of products or services.[107] Many organizations manage the supply chain with sophisticated electronic technology. In India, for example, Walmart managers have invested in an efficient supply chain that electronically links farmers and small manufacturers directly to the stores, maximizing value for both ends.[108] Supply chain management will be discussed in detail in the Appendix.

> *"The first rule of any technology used in a business is that automation applied to an efficient operation will magnify the efficiency. The second is that automation applied to an inefficient operation will magnify the inefficiency."*
>
> —Bill Gates, Founder and Chairman of Microsoft

REMEMBER THIS

- Modern management is a lively mix of ideas and techniques from varied historical perspectives, but new concepts continue to emerge.
- Managers tend to look for innovative ideas and approaches particularly during turbulent times.
- Many of today's popular techniques are related to the transition to a technology-driven workplace.
- **Social media programs** include online community pages, social media sites such as Facebook and LinkedIn, microblogging platforms such as Twitter, and company online forums that enable managers to interact electronically with employees, customers, partners, and other stakeholders.

- **Customer relationship management (CRM)** systems use information technology to keep in close touch with customers, collect and manage large amounts of customer data, and provide superior customer value.
- **Supply chain management** refers to managing the sequence of suppliers and purchasers, covering all stages of processing from obtaining raw materials to distributing finished goods to consumers.
- These new approaches require managers to think in fresh ways about managing their relationships with employees, customers, and business partners.

CHAPTER **1** **DISCUSSION QUESTIONS**

1. How do you feel about having management responsibilities in today's world, characterized by uncertainty, ambiguity, and sudden changes or threats from the environment? Describe some skills and competencies that you think are important to managers working in these conditions.

2. Assume that you are a project manager at a biotechnology company, working with managers from research, production, and marketing on a major product modification. You notice that every memo you receive from the marketing manager has been copied to senior management. At every company function, she spends time talking to the big shots. You are also aware that sometimes when you and the other project members are slaving away over the project, she is playing golf with senior managers. What is your evaluation of her behavior? As project manager, what do you do?

3. Jeff Immelt, CEO of GE, tweeted for the first time in September 2012, prompting this response: "@JeffImmelt how come my grandfather got on twitter before you?" Do you think managers should use Twitter and other social media? Can you be an effective manager today without using new media? Why?

4. Think about the highly publicized safety problems at General Motors (GM). One observer said that a goal of efficiency had taken precedence over a goal of quality within this company. Do you think managers can improve both efficiency and effectiveness simultaneously? Discuss. How do you think GM's leaders should respond to the safety situation?

5. You are a bright, hard-working, entry-level manager who fully intends to rise up through the ranks. Your performance evaluation gives you high marks for your technical skills, but low marks when it comes to people skills. Do you think people skills can be learned, or do you need to rethink your career path? If people skills can be learned, how would you go about doing it?

6. A college professor told her students, "The purpose of a management course is to teach students about management, not to teach them to be managers." Do you agree or disagree with this statement? Discuss.

7. The 2010–2011 Bain survey of management tools and trends found that the use of social media programs is growing, but as a tool, social media also has one of the lowest satisfaction ratings. How would you explain this?

8. Can you think of potential drawbacks to retailers using labor-waste elimination systems based on scientific management principles, as described in the text? Despite their being about 100 years old, do you believe scientific management characteristics will ever cease to be a part of organizational life? Discuss.

9. A management professor once said that for successful management, studying the present was most important, studying the past was next, and studying the future was least important. Do you agree? Why?

10. As organizations become more technology-driven, which do you think will become more important—the management of the human element of the organization or the management of technology? Discuss.

SELF-LEARNING

Management Aptitude Questionnaire

Rate each of the following questions according to the following scale:

① I am never like this.
② I am rarely like this.
③ I am sometimes like this.

④ I am often like this.
⑤ I am always like this.

1. When I have a number of tasks or homework to do, I set priorities and organize the work around deadlines.

   1   2   3   4   5

2. Most people would describe me as a good listener.

1   2   3   4   (5)

3. When I am deciding on a particular course of action for myself (such as hobbies to pursue, languages to study, which job to take, or special projects to be involved in), I typically consider the long-term (three years or more) implications of what I would choose to do.

1   (2)   3   4   5

4. I prefer technical or quantitative courses rather than those involving literature, psychology, or sociology.

1   2   (3)   4   5

5. When I have a serious disagreement with someone, I hang in there and talk it out until it is completely resolved.

1   2   3   4   (5)

6. When I have a project or assignment, I really get into the details rather than the "big picture" issues.

1   (2)   3   4   5

7. I would rather sit in front of my computer than spend a lot of time with people.

(1)   2   3   4   5

8. I try to include others in activities or discussions.

1   2   3   (4)   5

9. When I take a course, I relate what I am learning to other courses I took or concepts I learned elsewhere.

1   2   (3)   4   5

10. When somebody makes a mistake, I want to correct the person and let her or him know the proper answer or approach.

1   2   3   (4)   5

11. I think it is better to be efficient with my time when talking with someone, rather than worry about the other person's needs, so that I can get on with my real work.

1   (2)   3   4   5

12. I have a long-term vision of career, family, and other activities and have thought it over carefully.

1   2   3   (4)   5

13. When solving problems, I would much rather analyze some data or statistics than meet with a group of people.

1   (2)   3   4   5

14. When I am working on a group project and someone doesn't pull a fair share of the load, I am more likely to complain to my friends rather than confront the slacker.

(1)   2   3   4   5

15. Talking about ideas or concepts can get me really enthusiastic or excited.

1   2   (3)   4   5

16. The type of management course for which this book is used is really a waste of time.

1   (2)   3   4   5

17. I think it is better to be polite and not hurt people's feelings.

1   2   3   (4)   5

18. Data and things interest me more than people.

(1)   2   3   4   5

Scoring and Interpretation

Subtract your scores for questions 6, 10, 14, and 17 from the number 6, and then add the total points for the following sections:

1, 3, 6, 9, 12, 15 Conceptual skills total score _____
2, 5, 8, 10, 14, 17 Human skills total score _____
4, 7, 11, 13, 16, 18 Technical skills total score _____

These skills are three of the skills needed to be a good manager. Ideally, a manager should be strong (though not necessarily equal) in all three. Anyone noticeably weaker in any of these skills should take courses and read to build up that skill. For further background on the three skills, please refer to the explanation on pages 12–14.

GROUP LEARNING

Your Best and Worst Managers

Step 1. On your own, think of two managers that you have had—the best and the worst. The managers could be anyone who served as an authority figure over you, including an instructor, a boss at work, a manager of a student organization, a leader of a student group, a coach, a volunteer committee in a nonprofit organization, and so on. Think carefully about the specific behaviors that made each manager the best or the worst and write down what that manager did.

The best manager I ever had did the following:

_____

_____

_____

The worst manager I ever had did the following:

_____

_____

_____

Step 2. Divide into groups of four to six members. Each person should share his or her experiences, one at a time. Write on a sheet or whiteboard separate lists of best-manager and worst-manager behaviors.

Step 3. Analyze the two lists. What themes or patterns characterize "best" and "worst" manager behaviors? What are the key differences between the two sets of behaviors?

Step 4. What lessons does your group learn from its analysis? What advice or "words of wisdom" would you give managers to help them be more effective?

ACTION LEARNING

1. Think about some time in your life where you were a leader or had some authority over others. It could have been on a school committee, or as camp counselor, youth coordinator in church/synagogue, yearbook/prom organizer, etc.

2. Either individually, or in a group of two to four, ask yourself the following questions. If you are in a group, someone else can ask you the questions:

   a. Describe some incidents that went really well, where you handled a problem in a satisfying manner.
   b. List some examples when you did not handle problems in a positive manner.
   c. What were the differences between those two types of situations? Was it the type of person you dealt with, the level of your own supervision, the difficulty of the problem, etc.?
   d. What can you learn about your own strengths and weaknesses and a manager from these situations?
   e. What is your best strength as a manager? Can you find a theory in chapter 1 that refers to that strength?
   f. What would you do differently in any of the situations you described, if you had it to do over again?

3. Write a short (two to three pages) paper, comparing situations you encountered. What are the deeper insights you have gained from reflection?

4. Your instructor may ask you to discuss your conclusions in groups, being prepared to share with them the whole class.

ETHICAL DILEMMA

The New Test[109]

The Civil Service Board in a midsize city in Indiana decided that a written exam should be given to all candidates for promotion to supervisor. A written test would assess mental skills and would open access to all personnel who wanted to apply for the position. The board believed a written exam for promotion would be completely fair and objective because it eliminated subjective judgments and personal favoritism regarding a candidate's qualifications.

Maxine Othman, manager of a social service agency, loved to see her employees learn and grow to their full potential. When a rare opening for a supervising clerk occurred, Maxine quickly decided to give Sheryl Hines a shot at the job. Sheryl had been with the agency for 17 years and had shown herself to be a true leader. Sheryl worked hard at becoming a good supervisor, just as she had always worked hard at being a top-notch clerk. She paid attention to the human aspects of employee problems and introduced modern management techniques that strengthened the entire agency. Because of the board's new ruling, Sheryl would have to complete the exam in an open competition—anyone could sign up and take it, even a new employee. The board wanted the candidate with the highest score to get the job but allowed Maxine, as manager of the agency, to have the final say.

Because Sheryl had accepted the provisional opening and proved herself on the job, Maxine was upset that the entire clerical force was deemed qualified to take the test. When the results came back, she was devastated. Sheryl placed 12th in the field of candidates, while one of her newly hired clerks placed first. The Civil Service Board, impressed by the high score, urged Maxine to give the new clerk the permanent supervisory job; however, it was still Maxine's choice. Maxine wonders whether it is fair to base her decision only on the results of a written test. The board was pushing her to honor the objective written test, but could the test really assess fairly who was the right person for the job?

What Would You Do?

1. Ignore the test. Sheryl has proved herself via work experience and deserves the job.

2. Give the job to the candidate with the highest score. You don't need to make enemies on the Civil Service Board, and, although it is a bureaucratic procedure, the test is an objective way to select a permanent placement.

3. Press the board to devise a more comprehensive set of selection criteria—including test results as well as supervisory experience, ability to motivate employees, and knowledge of agency procedures—that can be explained and justified to the board and to employees.

CASE FOR CRITICAL ANALYSIS

SmartStyle Salons

Jamika Westbrook takes pride in her position as salon manager for SmartStyle Salon, one of six local hair salons associated with a large retail store chain located in the Southeast and one of five chain store groups under the Gold Group umbrella. She oversees a staff of 30, including hairdressers, a nail technician, receptionists, shampoo assistants, and a custodian. She enjoys a reputation as a manager who works very hard and takes care of her people. Hairdressers want to work for her.

Following the salon's new-hire policy, Jamika began as a shampoo assistant and quickly became a top hairdresser in the company through a combination of skill, a large and loyal client base, and long hours at work. In 2007, retiring manager Carla Weems handpicked Jamika as her successor, and the board quickly approved.

Initially, the salon, located in a suburban mall, managed a strong, steady increase, holding its position as one of the corporation's top performers. But economic woes hit the area hard, with increases in unemployment, mortgage woes, and foreclosures among current and potential customers. As families sought ways to save, the luxury of regular visits to the hair salon was among the first logical budget cuts. The past year has reflected this economic reality, and Jamika's salon saw a sharp decrease in profits.

Jamika's stomach is in knots as she arrives at the salon on Monday. Scheduled to fly to Atlanta the next morning for a meeting at corporate, she fears potential staffing cuts, but more important, she fears the loss of opportunity to secure her dream job, replacing the retiring manager at Riverwood Mall, the top-performing salon located in an upscale area of the city.

Distracted, Jamika walks past the receptionist, Marianne, who is busily answering the phones. Hanging up the phone, Marianne tells Jamika that Holly and Carol Jean, two popular hairdressers, called in sick, and Jamika now has to reschedule their clients. Jamika had denied their earlier request to travel out of town to attend a concert, and her irritation is obvious. She orders Marianne to call both women and instruct them that, when they return to work, they are to bring a doctor's statement and a copy of any prescriptions that they were given. "They had better be sick!" Jamika shouts as she enters her office, slamming the door more forcefully than she intended. Startled employees and early-morning customers hear the outburst, and, after a momentary pause, they resume their activities and quiet conversation, surprised by the show of managerial anger. Jamika knows she has let Holly and Carol Jean get away with unwarranted absences before and worries that she will do it again. She needs every head of hair that they can style to help the salon's profit.

Jamika takes a deep breath and sits at her desk, turning on the computer and checking e-mails, including one from the group manager reminding her to send the salon's status report in advance of tomorrow's meeting. She buzzes Marianne on the intercom to request final figures for the report on her desk by 1:00 p.m.

Picking up the phone, she calls Sharon, a manager at another SmartStyle salon. "I really lost my cool in front of everyone, but I'm not apologizing," Jamika admits, adding that she wished she had the guts to fire both stylists. "But this is not the day for that drama. I've got that report hanging over my head. I have no idea how to make things look better than they are, but I have to come up with something. Things look pretty dismal."

Sharon assures her that she did the best she could dealing with two "irresponsible" employees. "What will you do if they show up tomorrow with no doctor's statement?"

"I don't know. I hope I scared them enough so that they'll come in with something."

"I know you're worried about the report and the effect it might have on the Riverwood job," Sharon says. "But everyone knows you can't control the economy and its effect on the business. Just focus on the positive. You'll be fine."

At 10:30, as Jamika struggles to put the best possible spin on the report, she is paged to the receptionist desk to speak to an angry customer. "Another interruption," Jamika fumes to herself. Just then, the door opens and top stylist/assistant manager Victoria Boone sticks her head into the office.

"I know you're busy with the report. I'll handle this," she says enthusiastically.

"Thanks," Jamika replies.

No sooner has she handed off the irate client to Victoria than she second-guesses the decision. In addition to her talents as a hairdresser, Victoria had experience as the manager of a successful salon in another city before moving to the area. Recognizing her organizational and people skills, Jamika promoted Victoria to assistant manager soon after her arrival. Now each "I'll handle this" remark by Victoria convinces Jamika that her assistant manager is positioning herself as a potential rival for the Riverwood job. Jamika appreciates her enthusiastic attitude, but she's also trying to limit her opportunities to lead or appear too competent before staff, customers, and company officials. Jamika finds herself wanting to hide Victoria's competence, and she has condescendingly reminded management that Victoria is a "great help to me."

Now, thinking of Victoria's cheerful "I'll handle this," Jamika rises from her desk and marches to the door. *No*, Jamika thinks, *I'll take care of this personally*.

Questions

1. What positive and negative managerial characteristics does Jamika possess?

2. How do these traits help or hinder her potential to get the top position at the Riverwood Mall salon?

3. How do you think Jamika should have handled each of the incidents with Marianne? Holly and Carol Jean? Victoria?

ON THE JOB VIDEO CASES

On the Job: Barcelona Restaurant Group: The Evolution of Management Thinking

Questions

1. In what ways is Barcelona's management approach consistent with modern developments in management thinking?

2. In what ways does Barcelona's management approach run counter to contemporary developments in management thinking?

3. What aspects of restaurant work are especially challenging to wait staff, and how does Barcelona's approach to management help employees overcome the downsides of the job?

THE CLEAN-ENERGY FUTURE IS NOW

As Green Car Journal prepared to publish its much-anticipated "Green Car of the Year" edition for 2012, audiences might have expected a tribute to the Toyota Prius, Nissan Leaf, or another innovation in electric motoring. Instead, the panel of environmental and automotive experts assembled by the magazine made a surprising choice—one that signaled a sea change in green energy. The judges selected the 2012 Honda Civic Natural Gas, an alternative-fuel, partial-zero emissions vehicle that operates solely on compressed natural gas. As the journal noted, not only is the Civic's sticker price of $26,155 more affordable than electric vehicles, and not only does the model possess a driving range and horsepower on par with conventional compacts, but the Civic's alternative fuel costs approximately half the price of gasoline and is sourced almost entirely from abundant reserves in the United States.

Against a backdrop of ubiquitous marketing for electric cars and hybrids, the choice of a natural gas vehicle for Green Car of the Year was an unmistakable nod to a development in green energy that is so immense that it promises to transform the U.S. energy grid and end North American dependence on foreign oil. That development is the discovery of the Marcellus Shale. Located throughout the Appalachian Basin of the eastern United States, the Marcellus Shale is a massive sedimentary rock formation deep beneath the Earth's surface that contains one of the largest methane deposits anywhere in the world. Once thought to possess a modest 1.9 trillion cubic feet of natural gas, this 600-mile-wide black shale formation below Pennsylvania, Ohio, New York, and West Virginia was explored by geologists in 2004 and was found to contain between 168 trillion and 516 trillion cubic feet of natural gas. Combined with other U.S. shale plays, including the Barnett Shale in Texas, the discovery of the Marcellus led the International Energy Agency (IEA) to rank the United States the new number one natural gas producer in the world, edging out resource-rich Russia. In addition, the Marcellus has triggered a green-energy boom known as the Great Shale Gas Rush, which is creating thousands of green jobs, revitalizing the nation's economy, and pointing the way to a clean-energy future.

The breakthrough couldn't have come at a better time. In a highly turbulent business environment shaken by a global recession and new government restrictions on traditional energy, today's business managers struggle to know which energy alternatives are viable, or even affordable. The unexpected bankruptcy of well-funded green-energy darlings Solyndra and Beacon Power further underscore the uncertainty of the alternative energy marketplace. To gain stability for their organizations, managers need solutions that are reliable now, not decades into the future.

Thanks to an abundant supply of affordable natural gas, the green energy future has arrived. According to the U.S. Environmental Protection Agency (EPA) profile on clean energy, natural gas is a clean-burning fuel that generates roughly half the carbon emissions of coal and oil while releasing zero sulfur dioxide or mercury emissions. Given its low price relative to other energy sources, natural gas has game-changing implications for trucking fleets, consumer autos, electric power generation, and commercial heating—not to mention natural gas ovens, clothes dryers, water heaters, and other appliances.

While shale gas is a win-win for business and the environment, its impact on green jobs and the economy is equally important. According to a 2011 IHS Global Insight study, shale gas production—currently 34 percent of all natural gas production in the United States—supported more than 600,000 green jobs in 2010, a number that will increase to 870,000 jobs by 2015. As for the national economy, shale gas contributed $76.9 billion to the U.S. gross domestic product (GDP) in 2010 and is projected to contribute $118.2 billion by 2015. Over the next 25 years, shale gas will raise more than $933 billion in tax revenue for local, state, and federal governments. The news about natural gas is good for average consumers as well. In 2011, property owners in the Marcellus region received $400 million in natural gas royalties—a number that will climb even higher in the next decade. Additionally, individual U.S. consumers can expect $926 in new disposable income per year from cost savings related to natural gas. Combined, this economic activity equates to much-needed relief in hard times.

What does the switch to natural gas mean for industry-leading companies? For automakers like Honda and Volvo, natural gas vehicles have begun making their way into regular assembly-line production. Transport businesses such as UPS are converting fleets from diesel to natural gas as part of the White House's National Clean Fleets Partnership. Transit leaders like Navistar and Clean Energy Fuels have launched strategic partnerships to build America's Natural Gas Highway. Manufacturers such as Westport Innovations have made organizational changes to become leading producers of liquefied and compressed natural gas engines. Utility companies like Dominion are replacing coal-based electricity with gas-fired electric generation. And drillers like Range Resources are finding new ways to improve the quality and safety of natural gas exploration while controlling costs.

There are no limits to the possibilities of the Great Shale Gas Rush. However, it will take visionary leadership and skillful management to deliver on the promise of a truly sustainable clean-energy future.

Integrative Case Questions:

1. What turbulent forces are causing business leaders to rethink their use of energy?

2. Which managers—top managers, middle managers, or first-line managers—would make companywide decisions about energy use? How might the new workplace enable all managers to capitalize on the Great Shale Gas Rush?

3. Which historical management perspectives have particular relevance to the exploration and extraction of natural gas? Explain.

SOURCES: Based on "Honda Civic Natural Gas Is 2012 Green Car of the Year," *Green Car Journal*, November 17, 2011, www.greencar.com/articles/ honda-civic-natural-gas-2012-green-car-year.php (accessed June 7, 2012); Elwin Green, "Natural Gas Locked in the Marcellus Shale Has Companies Rushing to Cash in on Possibilities," *Pittsburgh Post-Gazette*, March 16, 2012, www.post-gazette.com/stories/business/news/naturalgas-locked-in-the-marcellus-shale-has-companies-rushing-to-cash-inon-possibilities-370058 (accessed June 7, 2012); Kevin Begos, "Gas Drillers Generate About $3.5 Billion in Revenues From Marcellus Shale," Associated Press, May 5, 2012, www.timesunion.com/business/article/ AP-Pa-gas-drilling-brought-3-5-billion-in-2011-3536873.php (accessed June 8, 2012); Timothy J. Considine, Robert Watson, and Seth Blumsack, The Pennsylvania Marcellus Natural Gas Industry: Status, Economic Impacts, and Future Potential, John and Willie Leone Family Department of Energy and Mineral Engineering, Penn State University, July 20, 2011, http://marcelluscoalition.org/wp-content/uploads/2011/07/ Final-2011-PA-Marcellus-Economic-Impacts.pdf (accessed June 8, 2012); IHS, "Shale Gas Supports More than 600,000 American Jobs Today; by 2015, Shale Gas Predicted to Support Nearly 870,000 Jobs and Contribute $118.2 Billion to GDP," press release, December 6, 2011, http://press.ihs.com/press-release/energy-power/shale-gas-supportsmore- 600000-american-jobs-today-2015-shale-gas-predict (accessed June 8, 2012); "IEA: U.S. to Overtake Russia as Top Gas Producer," Reuters, Jun 5, 2012, http://af.reuters.com/ article/energyOilNews/ idAFL3E8H45WZ20120605 (accessed June 8, 2012); Environmental Protection Agency, "Clean Energy: Air Emissions," www.epa.gov/cleanenergy/ energy-and-you/affect/air-emissions.html (accessed June 8, 2012); Clifford Krauss, "There's Gas in Those Hills," *The New York Times*, April 8, 2008, www.nytimes.com/2008/04/08/business/08gas.html (accessed June 8, 2012).

ENDNOTES

1. Steven Hyden, "The Winners' History of Rock and Roll, Part 3: Bon Jovi," *Grantland* (January 21, 2013), http://www.grantland.com/story/_/id/8860424/the-winners-history-rock-roll-part-3-bon-jovi (accessed August 15, 2013); Zack O'Malley Greenburg, "The World's Highest-Paid Musicians 2011," *Forbes* (June 15, 2011), http://www.forbes.com/sites/zackomalleygreenburg/2011/06/15/the-worlds-highest-paid-musicians/ (accessed August 14, 2013).

2. Quoted in Zach O'Malley Greenburg, "Jon Bon Jovi: Still Rockin, and Making a Killing," Forbes.com (May 18, 2011), http://www.forbes.com/2011/05/17/celebrity-100-11-jon-bon-jovi-kanye-west-bieber-still-rocking.html (accessed August 13, 2013).

3. This example is based on John Jurgensen, "A Rocker Tunes Up," *Wall Street Journal Online* (February 7, 2013), http://online.wsj.com/article/SB10001424127887323951904578288213834313862.html (accessed August 14, 2013); Greenburg, "Jon Bon Jovi: Still Rockin, and Making a Killing"; and Hyden, "The Winners' History of Rock and Roll, Part 3: Bon Jovi." (The quote from Bon Jovi is from the Greenburg article.)

4. This discussion is based on ideas in Paul J. H. Schoemaker, Steve Krupp, and Samantha Howland, "Strategic Leadership: The Essential Skills," *Harvard Business Review* (January–February 2013): 131–134; Stephen Denning, "Masterclass: The Reinvention of Management," *Strategy & Leadership* 39, no. 2 (2011): 9–17; Julian Birkinshaw and Jules Goddard, "What Is Your Management Model?" *MIT Sloan Management Review* (Winter 2009): 81–90; Paul McDonald, "It's Time for Management Version 2.0: Six Forces Redefining the Future of Modern Management," *Futures* (October 2011): 797ff; and Jeanne C. Meister and Karie Willyerd, "Leadership 2020: Start Preparing People Now," *Leadership Excellence* (July 2010): 5.

5. See Joshua Cooper Ramo, *The Age of the Unthinkable: Why the New World Disorder Constantly Surprises Us and What We Can Do About It* (New York: Little Brown, 2009); and Richard Florida, *The Great Reset: How New Ways of Living and Working Drive Post-Crash Prosperity* (New York: HarperCollins, 2010).

6. Schoemaker, Krupp, and Howland, "Strategic Leadership: The Essential Skills."

7. J. P. Donlon, "What, Put Your Customers Second? Are You Kidding?" (CEO Chronicles), *Chief Executive* (November–December 2010): 14–16; "HCL Technologies CEO, Vineet Nayar, Gets 'Leader in the Digital Age' Award at CeBIT 2011," *Entertainment Close-Up* (March 11, 2011); Birkinshaw and Goddard, "What Is Your Management Model?"; Denning, "Masterclass: The Reinvention of Management"; and Traci L. Fenton, "Inspiring Democracy in the Workplace: From Fear-Based to Freedom-Centered Organizations," *Leader to Leader* (Spring 2012): 57–63.

8. "What Do Managers Do?" *The Wall Street Journal Online*, http://guides.wsj.com/management/developing-a-leadership-style/what-do-managers-do/ (accessed August 11, 2010); article adapted from Alan Murray, *The Wall Street Journal Essential Guide to Management* (New York: Harper Business, 2010).

9. Ed O'Keefe, "Lieberman Calls for Wider Inquiry into Secret Service Scandal," *The Washington Post* (April 23, 2012), A3; Laurie Kellman and Alicia A. Caldwell, "Inquiry Hears of Wider Secret Service Misbehavior," *The Salt Lake Tribune* (May 25, 2012); and "Secret Service Toughens Agent Conduct Rules after Prostitution Scandal: Political Notebook," *The Boston Globe* (April 28, 2012), A8.

10. Anton Troianovski, "Apps: The New Corporate Cost-Cutting Tool," *The Wall Street Journal Online* (March 5, 2013), http://online.wsj.com/article/SB10001424127887324678604578342690461080894.html (accessed August 14, 2013).

11. Ellen McGirt, "05: Square, For Making Magic Out of the Mercantile," *Fast Company* (March 2012), 82–85, 146–147 (part of the section, "The World's 50 Most Innovative Companies").

12. Based on Lauren A. E. Schuker, "Movie Budget Lesson #1: Skip the Fur," *The Wall Street Journal* (July 15, 2010), B1; Brooks Barnes, "Animation Meets Economic Reality," *The New York Times* (April 4, 2011), B1; and Allison Corneau, "*The Lorax* Tops Weekend Box Office," *US Weekly* (March 4, 2012), www.usmagazine.com/entertainment/news/the-lorax-tops-weekend-box-office-201243 (accessed June 12, 2012).

13. Aaron O. Patrick, "EMI Deal Hits a Sour Note," *The Wall Street Journal*, August 15, 2009.

14. Robert L. Katz, "Skills of an Effective Administrator," *Harvard Business Review* 52 (September–October 1974): 90–102.

15. Clinton O. Longenecker, Mitchell J. Neubert, and Laurence S. Fink, "Causes and Consequences of Managerial Failure in Rapidly Changing Organizations," *Business Horizons* 50 (2007): 145–155.

16. Damian Paletta and Dionne Searcey, "Inside IRS Unit under Fire," *The Wall Street Journal* (May 25, 2013), A1; and Nicholas Confessore, David Kocieniewski, and Michael Luo, "Confusion and Staff Troubles Rife at I.R.S. Office in Ohio," *The New York Times* (May 18, 2013), http://www.nytimes.com/2013/05/19/us/politics/at-irs-unprepared-office-seemed-unclear-about-the-rules.html?pagewanted=all&_r=0 (accessed August 15, 2013).

17. Sydney Finkelstein, "The Five Worst CEOs of 2012," *The Washington Post*, December 18, 2012, http://articles.washingtonpost.com/2012-12-18/national/35907884_1_bankia-spanish-banks-rodrigo-rato (accessed December 20, 2012); and Josh Williams, "Why Ex-Xbox Boss Don Mattrick May Be Zynga's Savior," VentureBeat.com, July 10, 2013, http://venturebeat.com/2013/07/10/why-ex-xbox-boss-don-mattrick-may-be-zyngas-savior/ (accessed September 11, 2013).

18. Longenecker, Neubert, and Fink, "Causes and Consequences of Managerial Failure in Rapidly Changing Organizations."

19. Fisman, "In Defense of Middle Management."

20. Henry Mintzberg, *Managing* (San Francisco: Berrett-Kohler Publishers, 2009); Mintzberg, *The Nature of Managerial Work* (New York: Harper & Row, 1973); and Mintzberg, "Rounding Out the Manager's Job," *Sloan Management Review* (Fall 1994): 11–26.

21. Robert E. Kaplan, "Trade Routes: The Manager's Network of Relationships," *Organizational Dynamics* (Spring 1984): 37–52; Rosemary Stewart, "The Nature of Management: A Problem for Management Education," *Journal of Management Studies* 21 (1984): 323–330; John P. Kotter, "What Effective General Managers Really Do," *Harvard Business Review* (November–December 1982): 156–167; and Morgan W. McCall, Jr., Ann M. Morrison, and Robert L. Hannan, "Studies of Managerial Work: Results and Methods," Technical Report No. 9, Center for Creative Leadership, Greensboro, NC, 1978.

22. Alison M. Konrad, Roger Kashlak, Izumi Yoshioka, Robert Waryszak, and Nina Toren, "What Do Managers Like to Do? A Five-Country Study," *Group and Organizational Management* 26, no. 4 (December 2001): 401–433.

23. For a review of the problems faced by first-time managers, see Linda A. Hill and Kent Lineback, "Being the Leader: Observe Three Imperatives," *Leadership Excellence* (November 2012): 15–16; Linda A. Hill, "Becoming the Boss," *Harvard Business Review* (January 2007): 49–56; Loren B. Belker and Gary S. Topchik, *The First-Time Manager: A Practical Guide to the Management of People*, 5th ed. (New York: AMACOM, 2005); J. W. Lorsch and P. F. Mathias, "When Professionals Have to Manage," *Harvard Business Review* (July–August 1987): 78–83; R. A. Webber, *Becoming a Courageous Manager: Overcoming Career Problems of New Managers* (Englewood Cliffs, NJ: Prentice Hall, 1991); D. E. Dougherty, *From Technical Professional to Corporate Manager: A Guide to Career Transition* (New York: Wiley, 1984); J. Falvey, "The Making of a Manager," *Sales and Marketing Management* (March 1989): 42–83; M. K. Badawy, *Developing Managerial Skills in Engineers and Scientists: Succeeding as a Technical Manager* (New York: Van Nostrand Reinhold, 1982); and M. London, *Developing Managers: A Guide to Motivating and Preparing People for Successful Managerial Careers* (San Francisco, CA: Jossey-Bass, 1985).

24. Based on Evelyn Rusli, Nicole Perlroth, and Nick Bilton, "The Hoodie amid the Pinstripes: As Facebook IPO Nears, Is Its Chief up to Running a Public Company?" *International Herald Tribune*, May 14, 2012, 17.

25. This discussion is based on Linda A. Hill, *Becoming a Manager: How New Managers Master the Challenges of Leadership*, 2d ed. (Boston: Harvard Business School Press, 2003), 6–8; and Hill, "Becoming the Boss."

26. See also the "Boss's First Steps" sidebar in Erin White, "Learning to Be the Boss," *The Wall Street Journal*, November 21, 2005, http://online.wsj.com/news/articles/SB113252950779302595 (accessed May 11, 2014); and Belker and Topchik, *The First-Time Manager*.

27. Quoted in Eileen Zimmerman, "Are You Cut Out for Management?" (Career Couch column), *The New York Times*, January 15 2011, www.nytimes.com/2011/01/16/jobs/16career.html (accessed June 14, 2012).

28. Hill and Lineback, "Being the Leader."

29. Mintzberg, *Managing*, 17–41.

30. Study reported in Rachel Emma Silverman, "Where's The Boss? Trapped in a Meeting," *The Wall Street Journal*, February 14, 2012, http://online.wsj.com/article/SB10001424052970204642604577215013504567548.html (accessed June 14, 2012).

31. Mintzberg, *Managing*, pp. 17–41.

32. Based on Allan Halcrow, "A Day in the Life of Kathy Davis: Just Another Day in HR," *Workforce Management* 77, no. 6 (June 1998): 56–62.

33. Mintzberg, *Managing*, pp. 17–41.

34. Carol Hymowitz, "Packed Calendars Rule," *The Asian Wall Street Journal*, June 16, 2009; and "The 18-Hour Day," *The Conference Board Review* (March–April 2008): 20.

35. Adam Shell, "CEO Profile: Casting a Giant (New Jersey) Net," *USA TODAY*, August 25, 2008; Matthew Boyle and Jia Lynn Yang, "All in a Day's Work," *Fortune* (March 20, 2006): 97–104.

36. Korn, "What It's Like Being a Middle Manager Today."

37. Frankki Bevins and Aaron De Smet, "Making Time Management the Organization's Priority," *McKinsey Quarterly* (January 2013), http://www.mckinsey.com/insights/organization/making_time_management_the_organizations_priority (accessed August 19, 2013).

38. "Four CEOs' Tips on Managing Your Time," *The Wall Street Journal*, February 14, 2012, http://online.wsj.com/article/SB10001424052970204883304577221551714492724.html (accessed June 14, 2012).

39. Bevins and De Smet, "Making Time Management the Organization's Priority"; A. Garrett, "Buying Time to Do the Things That Really Matter," *Management Today* (July 2000): 75; and Robert S. Kaplan, "What to Ask the Person in the Mirror," *Harvard Business Review* (January 2007): 86–95.

40. Mintzberg, *Managing*; Lance B. Kurke and Howard E. Aldrich, "Mintzberg Was Right! A Replication and Extension of *The Nature of Managerial Work*," *Management Science* 29 (1983): 975–984; Cynthia M. Pavett and Alan W. Lau, "Managerial Work: The Influence of Hierarchical Level and Functional Specialty," *Academy of Management Journal* 26 (1983): 170–177; and Colin P. Hales, "What Do Managers Do? A Critical Review of the Evidence," *Journal of Management Studies* 23 (1986): 88–115.

41. Joseph Goldstein, "City Homicides Drop Sharply, Again; Police Cite New Antigang Strategy," *The New York Times* (June 28, 2013), http://www.nytimes.com/2013/06/29/nyregion/city-homicides-drop-sharply-again-police-cite-new-antigang-strategy.html?_r=0 (accessed August 19, 2013); and David Whitford, "Does Ray Kelly Have the World's Toughest Job?" *Fortune* (October 29, 2012): 152–160.

42. Guy Chazan and Monica Langley, "Dudley Faces Daunting To-Do List," *The Wall Street Journal Europe*, July 27, 2010.

43. Tim O'Shaughnessy, "The Way I Work: LivingSocial," *Inc.* (March 2012): 104–108.

44. Jean Crawford, "Profiling the Non-Profit Leader of Tomorrow," *Ivey Business Journal* (May–June 2010), www.iveybusinessjournal.com/topics/leadership/-profiling-the-non-profit-leader-of-tomorrow (accessed June 14, 2012).

45. The following discussion is based on Peter F. Drucker, *Managing the Non-Profit Organization: Principles and Practices* (New York: HarperBusiness, 1992); and Thomas Wolf, *Managing a Nonprofit Organization* (New York: Fireside/Simon & Schuster, 1990).

46. Christine W. Letts, William P. Ryan, and Allen Grossman, *High Performance Nonprofit Organizations* (New York: Wiley & Sons, 1999), pp. 30–35.

47. Carol Hymowitz, "In Sarbanes-Oxley Era, Running a Nonprofit Is Only Getting Harder," *The Wall Street Journal*, June 21, 2005; and Bill Birchard, "Nonprofits by the Numbers," *CFO* (June 2005): 50–55.

48. Eilene Zimmerman, "Your True Calling Could Suit a Nonprofit" (interview, Career Couch column), *The New York Times*, April 6, 2008, http://www.nytimes.com/2008/04/06/jobs/06career.html?_r=0 (accessed May 11, 2014).

49. "Q&A: Why the West Needs 'Jugaad' Creativity" (an interview with Navi Radjou, Jaideep Prabhu, and Simone Ahuja), *The Wall Street Journal India Online*, June 6, 2012, http://blogs.wsj.com/indiarealtime/2012/06/06/qa-why-the-west-needs-jugaad-creativity/ (accessed June 19, 2012); and Navi Radjou, Jaideep Prabhu, and Simone Ahuja, *Jugaad Innovation: Think Frugal, Be Flexible, Generate Breakthrough Growth* (San Francisco, CA: Jossey-Bass, 2012).

50. Devita Saraf, "India's Indigenous Genius: Jugaad," *The Wall Street Journal Online*, July 13, 2009, http://online.wsj.com/article/SB124745880685131765.html (accessed June 19, 2012); Nirmalya Kumar and Phanish Puranam," Frugal Engineering: An Emerging Innovation Paradigm," *Ivey Business Journal* (March–April 2012) www.iveybusinessjournal.com/topics/innovation/frugal-engineering-an-emerging-innovation-paradigm (accessed June 19, 2012).

51. M. S. S. el Namaki, "Does the Thinking of Yesterday's Management Gurus Imperil Today's Companies?" *Ivey Business Journal* (March–April 2012), www.iveybusinessjournal.com/topics/strategy/does-the-thinking-of-yesterdays-management-gurus-imperil-todays-companies (accessed June 19, 2012).

52. Eric Abrahamson, "Management Fashion," *Academy of Management Review* 21, no. 1 (January 1996): 254–285. Also see "75 Years of Management Ideas and Practice," a supplement to the *Harvard Business Review* (September–October 1997), for a broad overview of historical trends in management thinking.

53. This questionnaire is from William Pfeiffer and John E. Jones, eds., "Supervisory Attitudes: The X–Y Scale," in The 1972 *Annual Handbook for Group Facilitators* (New York: John Wiley & Sons, 1972), pp. 65–68. The X–Y scale was adapted from an instrument developed by Robert N. Ford of AT&T for in-house manager training.

54. The following discussion is based on Daniel A. Wren, *The Evolution of Management Thought*, 4th ed. (New York: Wiley, 1994).

55. Daniel A. Wren, "Management History: Issues and Ideas for Teaching and Research," *Journal of Management* 13 (1987): 339–350.

56. Business historian Alfred D. Chandler, Jr., quoted in Jerry Useem, "Entrepreneur of the Century," *Inc.* (20th Anniversary Issue, 1999): 159–174.

57. Useem, "Entrepreneur of the Century."

58. The following is based on Wren, *Evolution of Management Thought*, Chapters 4 and 5; and Claude S. George, Jr., *The History of Management Thought* (Englewood Cliffs, NJ:Englewood Cliffs, NJ: Prentice-Hall, 1968), Chapter 4.

59. Cynthia Crossen, "Early Industry Expert Soon Realized a Staff Has Its Own Efficiency," *The Wall Street Journal*, November 6, 2006.

60. Alan Farnham, "The Man Who Changed Work Forever," *Fortune* (July 21, 1997): 114; Charles D. Wrege and Ann Marie Stoka, "Cooke Creates a Classic: The Story Behind F. W. Taylor's Principles of Scientific Management," *Academy of Management Review* (October 1978): 736–749; Robert Kanigel, *The One Best Way: Frederick Winslow Taylor and the Enigma of Efficiency* (New York: Viking, 1997); and "The X and Y Factors: What Goes Around Comes Around," special section in "The New Organisation: A Survey of the Company," *The Economist* (January 21–27, 2006): 17–18.

61. Wren, *Evolution of Management Thought*, 171; and George, *History of Management Thought*, 103–104.

62. Vanessa O'Connell, "Stores Count Seconds to Trim Labor Costs," *The Wall Street Journal*, November 17, 2008; and Vanessa O'Connell, "Retailers Reprogram Workers in Efficiency Push," *The Wall Street Journal*, September 10, 2008.

63. Gary Hamel, "The Why, What, and How of Management Innovation," *Harvard Business Review* (February 2006): 72–84; Peter Coy, "Cog or CoWorker?" *BusinessWeek* (August 20 and 27, 2007): 58–60.

64. Max Weber, *General Economic History*, trans. Frank H. Knight (London: Allen & Unwin, 1927); Max Weber, *The Protestant Ethic and the Spirit of Capitalism*, trans. Talcott Parsons (New York: Scribner, 1930); and Max Weber, *The Theory of Social and Economic Organizations*, ed. and trans. A. M. Henderson and Talcott Parsons (New York: Free Press, 1947).

65. Stephen Cummings and Todd Bridgman, "The Relevant Past: Why the History of Management Should Be Critical to Our Future," *Academy of Management Learning & Education* 10, no. 1 (2011): 77–93.

66. These are based on Paul Downs, "How I Fire People," You're the Boss blog, *The New York Times*, June 4, 2012, http://boss.blogs.nytimes.com/2012/06/04/how-i-fire-people/ (accessed June 20, 2012).

67. Nadira A. Hira, "The Making of a UPS Driver," *Fortune* (November 12, 2007), 118–129; David J. Lynch, "Thanks to Its CEO, UPS Doesn't Just Deliver," *USA Today*, July 24, 2006, www.usatoday.com/money/companies/management/2006-07-23-ups_x.htm?tab1=t2 (accessed July 24, 2006); Kelly Barron, "Logistics in Brown," *Forbes* (January 10, 2000): 78–83; Scott Kirsner, "Venture Vérité: United Parcel Service," *Wired* (September 1999): 83–96; "UPS," *The Atlanta Journal and Constitution*, April 26, 1992; Kathy Goode, Betty Hahn, and Cindy Seibert, "United Parcel Service: The Brown Giant" (unpublished manuscript, Texas A&M University, 1981); and "About UPS," UPS corporate Web site, www.ups.com/content/us/en/about/index.html (accessed June 19, 2012).

68. Henri Fayol, *Industrial and General Administration*, trans. J. A. Coubrough (Geneva: International Management Institute, 1930); Henri Fayol, *General and Industrial Management*, trans. Constance Storrs (London: Pitman and Sons, 1949); and W. J. Arnold et al., *Business-Week, Milestones in Management* (New York: McGraw-Hill, vol. I, 1965; vol. II, 1966).

69. Gregory M. Bounds, Gregory H. Dobbins, and Oscar S. Fowler, *Management: A Total Quality Perspective* (Cincinnati, OH: South-Western Publishing, 1995), pp. 52–53.

70. Mary Parker Follett, *The New State: Group Organization: The Solution of Popular Government* (London: Longmans, Green, 1918); and Mary Parker Follett, *Creative Experience* (London: Longmans, Green, 1924).

71. Henry C. Metcalf and Lyndall Urwick, eds., *Dynamic Administration: The Collected Papers of Mary Parker Follett* (New York: Harper & Row, 1940); Arnold, *Business-Week, Milestones in Management.*

72. Follett, *The New State*; Metcalf and Urwick, *Dynamic Administration* (London: Sir Isaac Pitman, 1941).

73. William B. Wolf, *How to Understand Management: An Introduction to Chester I. Barnard* (Los Angeles: Lucas Brothers, 1968); and David D. Van Fleet, "The Need-Hierarchy and Theories of Authority," *Human Relations* 9 (Spring 1982): 111–118.

74. Curt Tausky, *Work Organizations: Major Theoretical Perspectives* (Itasca, IL: F. E. Peacock, 1978), p. 42.

75. Charles D. Wrege, "Solving Mayo's Mystery: The First Complete Account of the Origin of the Hawthorne Studies—The Forgotten Contributions of Charles E. Snow and Homer Hibarger," paper presented to the Management History Division of the Academy of Management (August 1976).

76. Ronald G. Greenwood, Alfred A. Bolton, and Regina A. Greenwood, "Hawthorne a Half Century Later: Relay Assembly Participants Remember," *Journal of Management* 9 (Fall/Winter 1983): 217–231.

77. F. J. Roethlisberger, W. J. Dickson, and H. A. Wright, *Management and the Worker* (Cambridge, MA: Harvard University Press, 1939).

78. H. M. Parson, "What Happened at Hawthorne?" *Science* 183(1974): 922–932; John G. Adair, "The Hawthorne Effect: A Reconsideration of the Methodological Artifact," *Journal of Applied Psychology* 69, no. 2 (1984): 334–345; and Gordon Diaper, "The Hawthorne Effect: A Fresh Examination," *Educational Studies* 16, no. 3 (1990): 261–268.

79. R. G. Greenwood, A. A. Bolton, and R. A. Greenwood, "Hawthorne a Half Century Later," 219–221.

80. F. J. Roethlisberger and W. J. Dickson, *Management and the Worker.*

81. Ramon J. Aldag and Timothy M. Stearns, *Management*, 2nd ed. (Cincinnati, OH: South-Western Publishing, 1991), pp. 47–48.

82. Tausky, *Work Organizations: Major Theoretical Perspectives*, p. 55.

83. Douglas McGregor, *The Human Side of Enterprise* (New York: McGraw-Hill, 1960), pp. 16–18; Robert A. Cunningham, "Douglas McGregor: A Lasting Impression," *Ivey Business Journal* (October 2011): 5–7.

84. Ricardo Semler, "Out of This World: Doing Things the Semco Way," *Global Business and Organizational Excellence* (July–August 2007): 13–21.

85. Wendell L. French and Cecil H. Bell Jr., "A History of Organizational Development," in Wendell L. French, Cecil H. Bell Jr., and Robert A. Zawacki, *Organization Development and Transformation: Managing Effective Change* (Burr Ridge, IL: Irwin McGraw-Hill, 2000), pp. 20–42.

86. Mansel G. Blackford and K. Austin Kerr, *Business Enterprise in American History* (Boston: Houghton Mifflin, 1986), Chapters 10 and 11; and Alex Groner and the editors of *American Heritage* and *BusinessWeek*, *The American Heritage History of American Business and Industry* (New York: American Heritage Publishing, 1972), Chapter 9.

87. Geoffrey Colvin, "How Alfred P. Sloan, Michael Porter, and Peter Drucker Taught Us All the Art of Management," *Fortune* (March 21, 2005): 83–86.

88. Brooks Barnes, "Disney Technology Tackles a Theme-Park Headache: Lines," *The New York Times*, December 28, 2010, B1; and "Disney Cracks Down on FastPass Enforcement," *Tampa Bay Times*, March 9, 2012, B2.

89. Larry M. Austin and James R. Burns, *Management Science* (New York: Macmillan, 1985).

90. Dan Heath and Chip Heath, "In Defense of Feelings: Why Your Gut Is More Ethical Than Your Brain," *Fast Company* (July–August 2009): 58–59.

91. Scott Patterson, *The Quants: How a New Breed of Math Whizzes Conquered Wall Street and Nearly Destroyed It* (New York: Crown Business, 2010); and Harry Hurt III, "In Practice, Stock Formulas Weren't Perfect," *The New York Times*, February 21, 2010.

92. Ludwig von Bertalanffy et al., "General Systems Theory: A New Approach to Unity of Science," *Human Biology* 23 (December 1951): 302–361; and Kenneth E. Boulding, "General Systems Theory—The Skeleton of Science," *Management Science* 2 (April 1956): 197–208.

93. This section is based on Peter M. Senge, *The Fifth Discipline: The Art and Practice of the Learning Organization* (New York: Doubleday, 1990); John D. Sterman, "Systems Dynamics Modeling: Tools for Learning in a Complex World," *California Management Review* 43, no. 4 (Summer 2001): 8–25; Andrea Gabor, "Seeing Your Company as a System," *Strategy + Business* (Summer 2010), www.strategy-business.com/article/10210?gko=20cca (accessed June 20, 2012); and Ron Zemke, "Systems Thinking," *Training* (February 2001): 40–46.

94. This example is cited in Sterman, "Systems Dynamics Modeling."

95. Fred Luthans, "The Contingency Theory of Management: A Path Out of the Jungle," *Business Horizons* 16 (June 1973): 62–72; and Fremont E. Kast and James E. Rosenzweig, *Contingency Views of Organization and Management* (Chicago: Science Research Associates, 1973).

96. Samuel Greengard, "25 Visionaries Who Shaped Today's Workplace," *Workforce* (January 1997): 50–59; and Ann Harrington, "The Big Ideas," *Fortune* (November 22, 1999): 152–154.

97. Mauro F. Guillen, "The Age of Eclecticism: Current Organizational Trends and the Evolution of Managerial Models," *Sloan Management Review* (Fall 1994): 75–86.

98. Jeremy Main, "How to Steal the Best Ideas Around," *Fortune* (October 19, 1992): 102–106.

99. Darrell Rigby and Barbara Bilodeau, "Management Tools and Trends 2009," Bain & Company Inc., 2009, www.bain.com/management_tools/home.asp (accessed March 10, 2010).

100. Thomas H. Davenport and Laurence Prusak, with Jim Wilson, *What's the Big Idea? Creating and Capitalizing on the Best Management Thinking* (Boston, MA: Harvard Business School Press, 2003); Theodore Kinni, "Have We Run out of Big Ideas?" *Across the Board* (March–April 2003): 16–21, Hamel, "The Why, What, and How of Management Innovation"; and Joyce Thompson Heames and Michael Harvey, "The Evolution of the Concept of the Executive from the 20th-Century Manager to the 21st-Century Global Leader," *Journal of Leadership and Organizational Studies* 13, no. 2 (2006): 29–41.

101. David Hurst, "The New Ecology of Leadership: Revisiting the Foundations of Management," *Ivey Business Journal* (May–June 2012): 1–5; Michael Murphy, "The Race to Failure" (a review of *Crash Course* by Paul Ingrassia, Random House 2010), *The Wall Street Journal*, January 29, 2010, A13.

102. Annick Van Rossem and Kees Van Veen, "Managers' Awareness of Fashionable Management Concepts: An Empirical Study," *European Management Journal* 29 (2011): 206–216.

103. Study reported in Phred Dvorak, "Why Management Trends Quickly Fade Away" (Theory and Practice column), *The Wall Street Journal*, June 26, 2006.

104. Darrell Rigby and Barbara Bilodeau, "Management Tools and Trends 2011," Bain and Company, Inc., www.bain.com/publications/articles/Management-tools-trends-2011.aspx (accessed June 22, 2012).

105. "Survey: 37% Use Social Media to Check Candidates," *Workforce* (April 18, 2012), www.workforce.com/article/20120418/NEWS01/120419964 (accessed June 22, 2012).

106. Definition based on Steven A. Melnyk and David R. Denzler, *Operations Management: A Value-Driven Approach* (Burr Ridge, IL: Richard D. Irwin, 1996): p. 613.

107. The Global Supply Chain Games project, www.gscg.org (accessed July 16, 2008).

108. Eric Bellman and Cecilie Rohwedder, "Western Grocer Modernizes Passage to India's Markets," *The Wall Street Journal*, November 28, 2007.

109. Based on Betty Harrigan, "Career Advice," *Working Woman* (July 1986): 22–24.

CHAPTER 2

The **Environment** and **Corporate Culture**

LEARNING OUTCOMES

After studying this chapter, you should be able to:

2.1 Define an organizational ecosystem and how the general and task environments affect an organization's ability to thrive.

2.2 Explain the strategies managers use to help organizations adapt to an uncertain or turbulent environment.

2.3 Define corporate culture.

2.4 Provide organizational examples of symbols, stories, heroes, slogans, and ceremonies and explain how they relate to corporate culture.

2.5 Describe four types of corporate culture.

2.6 Examine the relationship between culture, corporate values, and business performance.

2.7 Define a cultural leader and explain the tools that a cultural leader uses to create a high-performance culture.

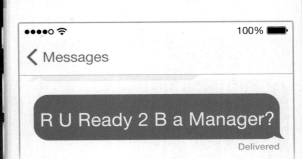

‹ Messages

R U Ready 2 B a Manager?

Delivered

Before reading this chapter, please circle either "Mostly True" or "Mostly False" for each of the five questions below.

1 I think I'd be good for many organizations, because I am very concerned and aware of the natural environment.

Mostly True	Mostly False

[page 71]

2 I feel comfortable with uncertainty around me and am able to adapt quickly to changing situations.

Mostly True	Mostly False

[page 73]

3 When I go into a new organization, such as a campus club, I am good at picking up on its values and norms.

Mostly True	Mostly False

[page 77]

4 I would fit well in an organizational culture that values creativity and risk-taking, as I like being involved in bold ventures.

Mostly True	Mostly False

[page 83]

5 Or, I think I'd do best in a company that values stability and consistency, because I work better with slower change.

Mostly True	Mostly False

[page 85]

"You sometimes feel like you are chasing cats," said Georgetown University Associate Vice President Scott Fleming. He was talking about how hard it is to monitor where the T-shirts, sweatshirts, and other apparel the university's bookstore sales come from. As a result of pressure from student activists and public outrage over recent accidents and worker deaths at overseas textile factories, Georgetown's bookstore remodeled displays so that garments made by Alta Gracia get pride of place ahead of Nike, Adidas, and other big brands. Why? Alta Gracia is the label of a South Carolina company that is carving a

NEW MANAGER Self-Test

Are You Fit for Managerial Uncertainty?[1]

Instructions: Do you approach uncertainty with an open mind? Think back to how you thought or behaved during a time of uncertainty when you were in a formal or informal leadership position. Please answer whether each of the following items was Mostly True or Mostly False in that circumstance.

	Mostly True	Mostly False
1. Enjoyed hearing about new ideas even when trying to meet a deadline.	_____	_____
2. Welcomed unusual viewpoints of others, even if we were working under pressure.	_____	_____
3. Made it a point to attend industry trade shows and company events.	_____	_____
4. Specifically encouraged others to express opposing ideas and arguments.	_____	_____
5. Asked "dumb" questions.	_____	_____
6. Always offered comments on the meaning of data or issues.	_____	_____
7. Expressed a controversial opinion to bosses and peers.	_____	_____
8. Suggested ways of improving my and others' ways of doing things.	_____	_____

Scoring and Interpretation: Give yourself one point for each item that you marked as Mostly True. If you scored less than 5, you might want to start your career as a manager in a stable rather than an unstable environment. A score of 5 or above suggests a higher level of mindfulness and a better fit for a new manager in an organization with an uncertain environment.

In an organization in a highly uncertain environment, everything seems to be changing. In that case, an important quality for a new manager is "mindfulness," which includes the qualities of being open-minded and an independent thinker. In a stable environment, a manager with a closed mind may perform all right because much work can be done in the same old way. In an uncertain environment, even a new manager needs to facilitate new thinking, new ideas, and new ways of working. A high score on the preceding items suggests higher mindfulness and a better fit with an uncertain environment.

niche by paying above-average wages and promoting safe, humane working conditions at its Dominican Republic factory. Georgetown belongs to a nationwide apparel consortium that includes 180 schools that are pressuring the industry by making a commitment to do business with companies with ethical and socially responsible practices. The effect has been small but noticeable. The threat of losing out on the $4 billion market for apparel branded with university logos has gotten the attention of managers at large multinational corporations. "They target young people with their advertising, but they have not respected us enough to realize we won't mindlessly consume their product," said recent Georgetown graduate Natalie Margolis.[2]

Growing concerns over conditions in low-wage overseas factories is a big environmental issue for managers in retail organizations today, as well as for those in manufacturers such as Nike and Apple that use overseas contractors. However, managers face many challenges from both the external and internal environments. This chapter explores in detail components of the external environment and how they affect the organization. The chapter also examines a major part of the organization's internal environment—corporate culture. Corporate culture is both shaped by the external environment and shapes how managers respond to changes in the external environment.

2.1 The External Environment

The external organizational environment includes all elements existing outside the boundary of the organization that have the potential to affect the organization.[3] The environment includes competitors, resources, technology, and economic conditions that influence the organization. It does not include those events so far removed from the organization that their impact is not perceived.

The organization's external environment can be conceptualized further as having two components: task and general environments, as illustrated in Exhibit 2.1.[4] The task environment is closer to the organization and includes the sectors that conduct day-to-day transactions with the organization and directly influence its basic operations and performance.

EXHIBIT 2.1   Dimensions of the Organization's General, Task, and Internal Environments

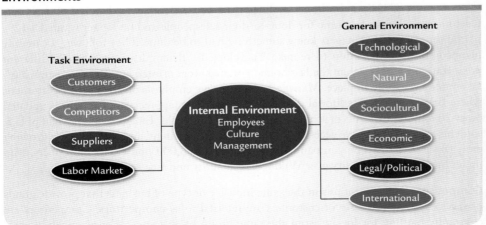

It is generally considered to include competitors, suppliers, customers, and the labor market. Students and suppliers are major elements of the task environment for university bookstores, for example. The general environment affects organizations indirectly. It includes social, economic, legal-political, international, natural, and technological factors that influence all organizations about equally. Changes in federal regulations or an economic recession are part of the organization's general environment, as are shifting social attitudes toward matters such as how and where the products we use are made. These events do not directly change day-to-day operations, but they do affect all organizations eventually.

A new view of the environment argues that organizations are now evolving into business ecosystems. An organizational ecosystem is a system formed by the interaction among a community of organizations in the environment. An ecosystem includes organizations in all the sectors of the task and general environments that provide the resource and information transactions, flows, and linkages necessary for an organization to thrive.[5] For example, Apple's ecosystem includes hundreds of suppliers and millions of customers for the products that it produces across several industries, including consumer electronics, Internet services, mobile phones, personal computers, and entertainment.[6]

The organization also has an internal environment, which includes the elements within the organization's boundaries. The internal environment is composed of current employees, management, and especially corporate culture, which defines employee behavior in the internal environment and how well the organization will adapt to the external environment.

Exhibit 2.1 illustrates the relationship among the task, general, and internal environments. As an open system, the organization draws resources from the external environment and releases goods and services back to it. We will first discuss the two components of the external environment in more detail. Later in the chapter, we examine corporate culture, the key element in the internal environment. Other aspects of the internal environment, such as structure and technology, are covered in later chapters of this book.

2.1a Task Environment

The task environment includes those sectors that have a direct working relationship with the organization, among them customers, competitors, suppliers, and the labor market.

Customers   Those people and organizations in the environment that acquire goods or services from the organization are **customers**. As recipients of the organization's output, customers are important because they determine the organization's success. Organizations have to be responsive to marketplace changes. Consider Encyclopædia Britannica, where sales of the set of 32 bound volumes declined from 100,000 in 1990 to barely 3,000 in 1996. Customers no longer had time for door-to-door salespeople and no longer wanted a 129-pound set of books. Managers knew something had to be done. They followed a carefully planned strategic transition to remake Encyclopædia Britannica into a totally different organization by 2012, when the last bound volumes were printed and the company's digital strategy was fully in place. Managers placed heavy emphasis on their K–12 customers, where Britannica's high editorial quality had always been appreciated. Content is updated every 20 minutes by teams of scholars from around the world. Today, more than half of U.S. students and teachers have access to online Britannica content, and the service is growing even faster overseas. The company also has around 500,000 household subscribers, who prefer quality and credibility over Wikipedia's quantity and free access.[7]

Competitors   Organizations in the same industry or type of business that provide goods or services to the same set of customers are referred to as **competitors**. Competitors are constantly battling for loyalty from the same group of customers. For example, in early

"It is not the strongest of the species that survives, nor the most intelligent that survives. It is the one that is the most adaptable to change."

—Charles Darwin (1809–1882), Naturalist

2013, Samsung became the world leader in smartphone sales, topping Apple in several countries, and the competition has gotten even hotter as Samsung has stepped up the challenge in the U.S. market. The company held its first promotional event for its flagship smartphone, the Galaxy S4, at a packed event at New York's Radio City Music Hall. Apple's iPhone still has strong brand loyalty, but the buzz at the moment is on Samsung's side. A survey found that first-time smartphone buyers preferred Samsung by about a 3-to-1 margin. "This is Samsung's time right now," said Gene Munster, an analyst at Piper Jaffray.[8]

Suppliers   Suppliers provide the raw materials that the organization uses to produce its output. A candy manufacturer, for example, may use suppliers from around the globe for ingredients such as cocoa beans, sugar, and cream. A supply chain is a network of multiple businesses and individuals that are connected through the flow of products or services. For Toyota, the supply chain includes over 500 global parts suppliers organized by a production strategy called *just-in-time* (JIT).[9] JIT improves an organization's return on investment, quality, and efficiency because much less money is invested in idle inventory. In the 1970s, the Japanese taught U.S. companies how to boost profit by keeping inventories lean through JIT. "Instead of months' worth of inventory, there are now days and even hours of inventory," says Jim Lawton, head of supply management solutions at consultant Dun & Bradstreet. Lawton points out that there is a downside, however—one that became dramatically clear after a March 2011 earthquake in Japan: "If supply is disrupted, as in this situation, there's nowhere to get product."[10]

The quake, which triggered massive tsunami waves and caused the second-worst nuclear disaster in history, at the Fukushima power plant along the Pacific coastline, revealed the fragility of today's JIT supply chains. Japanese parts suppliers for the global auto industry were shut down, disrupting production at auto factories around the world. "Even a missing $5 part can stop an assembly line," said a Morgan Stanley representative. Because of this natural disaster, Toyota's production fell by 800,000 vehicles—10 percent of its annual output. Despite the potential for such disruptions, most companies aren't willing to boost inventories to provide a cushion. Even a slight increase in inventory can cost companies millions of dollars.[11]

Hyundai Motor Company

CONCEPT CONNECTION   At the Hyundai Motor Company manufacturing plant in Alabama, auto parts are sourced from nearly 20 **suppliers** located in that same state. While some parts are sourced locally, others come from great distances, and Hyundai deliberately seeks out women- and minority-owned businesses across the globe. The company is committed to maintaining diversity in its **supply chain**.

HOT TOPIC

Labor Market   The labor market represents people in the environment who can be hired to work for the organization. Every organization needs a supply of trained, qualified personnel. Unions, employee associations, and the availability of certain classes of employees can influence the organization's labor market. Labor market forces affecting organizations right now include (1) the growing need for computer-literate knowledge workers; (2) the necessity for continuous investment in human resources through recruitment, education, and training to meet the competitive demands of the borderless world; and (3) the effects of international trading blocs, automation, outsourcing, and shifting facility locations on labor dislocations, creating unused labor pools in some areas and labor shortages in others.

Spotlight on Skills

Costco Wholesale Corporation

Costco Wholesale Corporation, a no-frills, self-service warehouse club, operates an international chain of membership warehouses offering a limited selection of products at reduced prices. Costco's complex environment is illustrated in Exhibit 2.2.

Changes in the various sectors of the general and task environments can create tremendous challenges, especially for organizations operating in complex, rapidly changing industries. Costco Wholesale Corporation, with warehouses throughout the world, is an example of an organization operating in a highly complex environment.

Costco's business model focuses on maintaining its image as a pricing authority, consistently providing the most competitive prices. "Everything we do is to provide goods and services to the customer at a lower price," said Jim Sinegal, cofounder and recently retired CEO. New CEO Craig Jelinek has vowed that a low-price philosophy will continue to guide the company. Costco warehouses are designed to operate efficiently and to communicate value to members. The warehouse decor—high ceilings, metal roofs, exposed trusses—keeps costs low and contributes to the perception that Costco is for serious shoppers seeking serious bargains. Other strategies for keeping prices low include offering only around 4,000 unique products at a time (by contrast, Walmart offers over 100,000) and negotiating low prices with suppliers. Only about 28 percent of sales come from outside the United States, but same store sales in overseas markets have been growing about four times faster than those in the United States. The biggest part of Jelinek's plan is to increase Costco's international presence. In a 2013 interview, he said that the company would open its first locations in France and Spain within the next two years, and that two-thirds of Costco's expansion over the next five years would be international, with a focus on Japan, Taiwan, and South Korea.

Costco's biggest competitive advantage is its loyal workforce. "Costco compensates employees very well—well above the industry in terms of wages and benefits," says R. J. Hottovey, a retail analyst at Morningstar. When the economic downturn worsened in late 2009 and many retailers cut wages and issued layoffs, Costco handed out raises. The happiness and morale of employees is often overlooked in the retail industry, but not at Costco. Thanks to its good treatment of workers, Costco has one of the lowest turnovers in the retail industry (around 5 percent), and since 2009, sales have grown 39 percent and the stock price has doubled.[12]

REMEMBER THIS

- The **organizational environment**, consisting of both task and general environments, includes all elements existing outside the boundary of the organization that have the potential to affect the organization.

- An **organizational ecosystem** includes organizations in all the sectors of the task and general environments that provide the resource and information transactions, flows, and linkages necessary for an organization to thrive.

EXHIBIT 2.2 The External Environment of Costco Wholesale Corporation

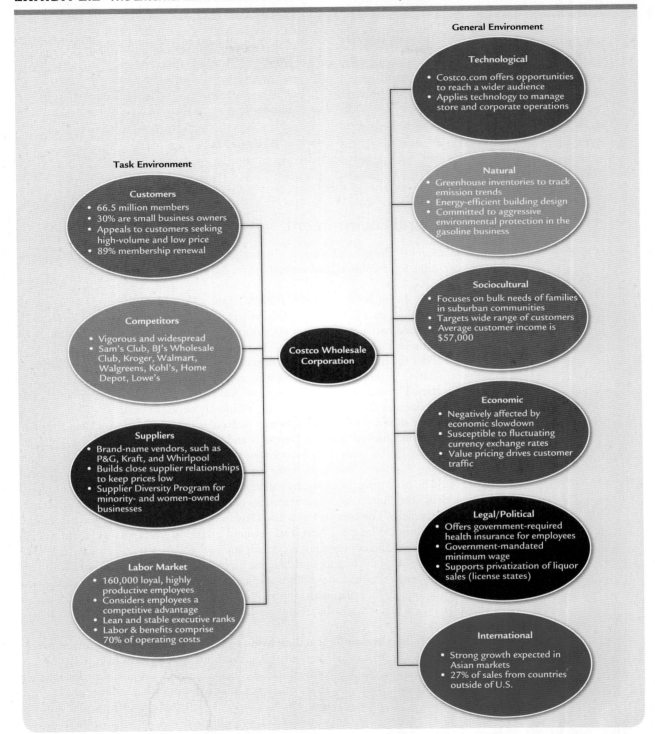

General Environment

Technological
- Costco.com offers opportunities to reach a wider audience
- Applies technology to manage store and corporate operations

Task Environment

Customers
- 66.5 million members
- 30% are small business owners
- Appeals to customers seeking high-volume and low price
- 89% membership renewal

Natural
- Greenhouse inventories to track emission trends
- Energy-efficient building design
- Committed to aggressive environmental protection in the gasoline business

Competitors
- Vigorous and widespread
- Sam's Club, BJ's Wholesale Club, Kroger, Walmart, Walgreens, Kohl's, Home Depot, Lowe's

Costco Wholesale Corporation

Sociocultural
- Focuses on bulk needs of families in suburban communities
- Targets wide range of customers
- Average customer income is $57,000

Economic
- Negatively affected by economic slowdown
- Susceptible to fluctuating currency exchange rates
- Value pricing drives customer traffic

Suppliers
- Brand-name vendors, such as P&G, Kraft, and Whirlpool
- Builds close supplier relationships to keep prices low
- Supplier Diversity Program for minority- and women-owned businesses

Legal/Political
- Offers government-required health insurance for employees
- Government-mandated minimum wage
- Supports privatization of liquor sales (license states)

Labor Market
- 160,000 loyal, highly productive employees
- Considers employees a competitive advantage
- Lean and stable executive ranks
- Labor & benefits comprise 70% of operating costs

International
- Strong growth expected in Asian markets
- 27% of sales from countries outside of U.S.

SOURCES: *Costco Wholesale Annual Report 2012*, Costco Wholesale Corporation Investor Relations Web site, http://phx.corporate-ir.net/phoenix.zhtml?c=83830&p=irol-reportsannual (accessed August 26, 2013); Brad Stone, "Costco CEO Craig Jelinek Leads the Cheapest, Happiest Company in the World," *Bloomberg Businessweek* (June 6, 2013), http://www.businessweek.com/articles/2013-06-06/costco-ceo-craig-jelinek-leads-the-cheapest-happiest-company-in-the-world (accessed August 26, 2013); "Costco Wholesale Corporation," Marketline (April 30, 2012): 3–9; Alaric DeArment, "Costco's Lobbying Changes WA's Liquor Laws: Who Is Next?" *Drug Store News*, (December 12, 2011): 12; and Sharon Edelson, "Costco Keeps Formula as It Expands," *Women's Wear Daily* (January 30, 2012): 1.

- The **general environment** indirectly influences all organizations within an industry and includes five dimensions.
- The **task environment** includes the sectors that conduct day-to-day transactions with the organization and directly influence its basic operations and performance.
- The **internal environment** includes elements within the organization's boundaries, such as employees, management, and corporate culture.

- **Customers** are part of the task environment and include people and organizations that acquire goods or services from the organization.
- **Competitors** are organizations within the same industry or type of business that vie for the same set of customers.
- **Suppliers** provide the raw materials the organization uses to produce its output.
- The **labor market** represents the people available for hire by the organization.

2.1b General Environment

The dimensions of the general environment include international, technological, sociocultural, economic, legal-political, and natural.

International   In his book *The World Is Flat*, Thomas Friedman challenges managers to view global markets as a level playing field where geographical divisions are irrelevant.[13] A flat world, Friedman argues, creates opportunities for companies to expand into global markets and build a global supply chain. As managers expand into global markets, they have to consider the **international dimension** of the external environment, which includes events originating in foreign countries, as well as new opportunities for U.S. companies in other countries. The international environment provides new competitors, customers, and suppliers and shapes social, technological, and economic trends as well.

Consider the mixed results Starbucks experienced as it expanded into European markets. Starbucks fans packed stores in Germany and the United Kingdom, for example, but sales and profits in the company's French stores were disappointing. In fact, after eight years operating 63 stores, Starbucks never turned a profit in France. What international factors could be hindering the company's success in France? First, a sluggish economy and Europe's debt crisis hurt sales. Plus, Starbucks faced high rent and labor costs in France, which eroded profits. The company was also slow to tailor the Starbucks experience to the French café culture. Whereas a New Yorker might grab a paper cup of coffee on the go, the French prefer to linger over a large, ceramic mug of coffee with friends in a café-style environment. To respond to these challenges, Starbucks launched a multimillion-dollar campaign in France that includes an upscale makeover of stores, with more seating and customized beverages and blends that appeal to local tastes.[14] The international environment will be discussed in more detail in the next chapter.

Technological   The **technological dimension** of the general environment includes scientific and technological advancements in a specific industry, as well as in society at large. Advances in technology drive competition and help innovative companies gain market share. However, some industries have failed to adapt to technological shifts and are facing decline. Managers at Fuji got high marks for seeing the trend toward digital cameras and responding faster than Kodak, but even they didn't anticipate or prepare for the wireless revolution. Adding Wi-Fi technology for Internet connectivity is common in many consumer electronics, but for the most part, digital cameras remain stand-alone devices. It's an oversight that is hurting not only Fuji, but also Panasonic, Olympus, Canon, and other camera makers. The number of photos being taken is soaring, but most people are using their smartphones so they can easily share photos on Facebook, Instagram, and other social media. Shipments of compact digital cameras plummeted 42 percent in the first five months of 2013. "It's the classic case of an industry that is unable to adapt," said Christopher Chute, a digital imaging analyst at research firm IDC.[15]

Sociocultural   The **sociocultural dimension** of the general environment represents the demographic characteristics, norms, customs, and values of the general population. Important sociocultural characteristics are geographical distribution and population density, age, and education levels. Today's demographic profiles are the foundation of tomorrow's workforce and consumers. By understanding these profiles and addressing them in the organization's business plans, managers prepare their organizations for long-term success. Smart managers may want to consider how the following sociocultural trends are changing the consumer and business landscape:

1. A new generation of technologically savvy consumers, variously called Gen Z, Re-Gens, the Connected Generation, or simply Post-Millennials, has intimately woven technology into every aspect of their lives. Mobile devices shape the way they communicate, shop, travel, and earn college credits. This generation will make up 40 percent of the population in the United States and Europe by 2020 and will constitute the largest cohort of consumers worldwide. Predictions of what they will value as consumers include brands that are trustworthy and products and companies that show a commitment to environmental, social, and fiscal responsibility.[16]

2. Young people are also leading the trend toward widespread social equality. Polls show that views about social mores and lifestyles are shifting. The percentage saying society should encourage greater tolerance of people with different lifestyles and backgrounds increased from 29 percent in 1999 to 44 percent in 2013. Support for gay marriage increased to 53 percent from 30 percent in 2004, and a number of states already have passed laws allowing same-sex marriage and in 2015 the Supreme court mandated states to approve same-sex marriage.[17] Another poll shows that 57 percent of people support a path to citizenship for illegal immigrants, and 48 percent support the legalization of marijuana.[18]

3. The most recent U.S. census data show that more than half of all babies born in 2011 were members of minority groups, the first time that has happened in U.S. history. Hispanics, African Americans, Asians, and other minorities represented 50.4 percent of births in 2011. The nation's growing diversity has huge implications for business.[19]

Jay Clendenin / Aurora Photos

 CONCEPT CONNECTION   Shrewd home builders are responding to shifts in the sociocultural dimension. Aging baby boomers have been a mainstay of the housing market during the economic downturn, and what they want are smaller houses designed with features to help them stay in their own homes as long as possible. For example, this award-winning Green Lake Residence in Seattle, Washington, designed by Emory Baldwin of ZAI, Inc., offers an efficient, adaptable plan that includes no-step entries and closets stacked on top of each other that can be converted into an elevator shaft if necessary.

Economic   The **economic dimension** represents the general economic health of the country or region in which the organization operates. Consumer purchasing power, the unemployment rate, and interest rates are part of an organization's economic environment. Because organizations today are operating in a global environment, the economic dimension has become exceedingly complex and creates enormous uncertainty for managers.

In the United States, many industries, such as banking, are finding it difficult to make a comeback despite the slowly rebounding economy. KeyCorp, one of the nation's largest banking-based financial services organizations, reports an uneven turnaround, with a mix of both good and bad news. While KeyCorp faces a reduction in total assets, a drop in revenue, and a decline in the profit margin in the lending business, it also reports fewer delinquent loans and strong demand from corporate customers for new loans. With banks stretching from Alaska to Maine, KeyCorp has benefited from geographic diversity because some regions of the United States rebounded faster than others. "As we are in economic recovery … our business model, our size, our geographic diversity is an advantage," said Beth Mooney, KeyCorp's CEO. "Conventional wisdom five years ago would have said differently."[20]

Legal-Political   The **legal-political dimension** includes government regulations at the local, state, and federal levels, as well as political activities designed to influence company behavior. The U.S. political system encourages capitalism, and the government tries not to overregulate business. However, government laws do specify rules of the game. The federal government influences organizations through the Occupational Safety and Health Administration (OSHA), Environmental Protection Agency (EPA), fair trade practices, libel statutes allowing lawsuits against business, consumer protection and privacy legislation, product safety requirements, import and export restrictions, and information and labeling requirements. One of the most recent challenges in the legal-political dimension is the Patient Protection and Affordable Care Act,

Green Power

Reaching Mythical Proportions

In Greek mythology, Nike was the winged goddess of victory. With headquarters in Portland, Oregon—considered one of the world's "greenest" cities—**Nike, Inc**. has a corporate culture centered around a commitment to victory, both on the athletic field and as one of the top 100 most sustainable corporations. Some companies give a nod to sustainability by reducing toxins, but Nike goes further. The company's predictive tool, the Considered Design Index, monitors the total environmental impact of the running shoe production cycle, scoring everything from fabric to reducing waste.

Victory in sustainability also means influencing other companies. Nike CSR staff spearheaded GreenXchange, which brought together companies to explore opportunities, share information, and keep abreast of trends and issues. As Nike's sustainability influence grows, its cultural mantra reflects the winged deity: "There is no finish line for environmental efforts—we can always go further."

SOURCES: Marc J. Epstein, Adriana Rejc Buhovac, and Kristi Yuthas, "Why Nike Kicks Butt in Sustainability," *Organizational Dynamics* 39 (2010): 353–356; and "Sustainable Business at Nike, Inc.," Nike corporate website, http://nikeinc.com/pages/responsibility (accessed July 24, 2012).

sometimes called Obamacare (passed in 2010 and upheld by the Supreme Court as constitutional in 2012 as well as in 2015). The act requires that companies provide health insurance for employees or pay penalties.[21]

Managers in many companies work closely with national lawmakers, educating them about products and services and legislation's impact on their business strategies. Long before its NASDAQ debut in May 2012, for example, Facebook had been quietly befriending the nation's top lawmakers. Managers hired former political aides with access to top leaders in both parties and had them lead training sessions on using Facebook to communicate with voters. In addition, Facebook stepped up its lobbying efforts and set up a political action committee. "It's smart advocacy 101," said Rey Ramsey, CEO of TechNet, an industry group that includes Facebook. What you ultimately want is for a legislator to understand the consequences of their actions."[22]

Ariel Skelley/Blend Images/Getty Images

CONCEPT CONNECTION Whether they are motivated by a desire to preserve natural resources, to impress their customers with their social responsibility, or to comply with new legislation, many companies are looking for ways to treat the **natural environment** better. Some are doing it by switching to renewable energy sources, while others are trying to reduce pollution. Promoting the use of cloth carrying bags like these is just one example of how retailers can help minimize the amount of trash going into the world's landfills.

Natural   In response to pressure from environmental advocates, organizations have become increasingly sensitive to the Earth's diminishing natural resources and the environmental impact of their products and business practices. As a result, the natural dimension of the external environment is growing in importance. The natural dimension includes all elements that occur naturally on Earth, including plants, animals, rocks, and resources such as air, water, and climate. Protection of the natural environment is emerging as a critical policy focus around the world. Governments are increasingly under pressure to explain their performance on pollution control and natural resource management. Nations with the best environmental performance, along with some comparison countries, are listed in Exhibit 2.3. Note that the top performer is Switzerland, which gets most of its power from renewable sources—hydropower and geothermal energy.

The natural dimension is different from other sectors of the general environment because it has no voice of its own. Influence on managers to meet needs in the natural environment may come from other sectors, such as government regulation, consumer concerns, the media, competitors' actions, or even employees.[23] For example, environmental groups advocate various action and policy goals that include reduction and cleanup of pollution, development of renewable energy resources, reduction of greenhouse gases such as carbon dioxide, and sustainable use of scarce resources such as water, land, and air. The oil spill in the Gulf of Mexico in 2010 brought environmental issues to the forefront. Months after a BP-Transocean rig at the *Deepwater Horizon* oil well exploded, hundreds of thousands of gallons of oil were still flowing into open water each day, adding to the millions of gallons already contaminating the water and beaches along the coast of Louisiana, Mississippi, Alabama, and Florida, and threatening the region's fish, birds, turtles, and vegetation. "One of the last pristine, most biologically diverse coastal habitats in the country is about to get wiped out," said Felicia Coleman, who directs the Florida State University Coastal and Marine Laboratory. "And there's not much we can do about it." The effects of the devastating spill are likely to continue for dozens of years.[24]

HOT TOPIC

EXHIBIT 2.3 2012 Environmental Performance Index

Rank	Country	Score
1	Switzerland	76.69
2	Latvia	70.37
3	Norway	69.92
4	Luxembourg	69.2
5	Costa Rica	69.03
6	France	69
7	Austria	68.92
8	Italy	68.9
9	Sweden	68.82
10	United Kingdom	68.82
11	Germany	66.91
12	Slovakia	66.62
13	Iceland	66.28
14	New Zealand	66.05
15	Albania	65.85
37	Canada	58.41
49	United States	56.59
116	China	42.24
125	India	36.23
132	Iraq	25.32

SOURCE: *2012 Environmental Performance Index*, Yale Center for Environmental Law and Policy, Yale University, http://epi.yale.edu/epi2012/rankings; and Center for International Earth Science Information Network, Columbia University.

NOTE: The scores for each country are based on 25 performance indicators covering both environmental public health and ecosystem vitality, such as air pollution and greenhouse gas emissions.

REMEMBER THIS

- The **international dimension** of the external environment represents events originating in foreign countries, as well as opportunities for U.S. companies in other countries.

- The **technological dimension** of the general environment includes scientific and technological advances in society.

- The **sociocultural dimension** includes demographic characteristics, norms, customs, and values of a population within which the organization operates.

- The **economic dimension** represents the general economic health of the country or region in which the organization operates.

- The **legal-political dimension** includes government regulations at the local, state, and federal levels, as well as political activities designed to influence company behavior.

- The **natural dimension** includes all elements that occur naturally on Earth, including plants, animals, rocks, and natural resources such as air, water, and climate.

2.2 The Organization–Environment Relationship

Why do organizations care so much about factors in the external environment? The reason is that the environment creates uncertainty for organization managers, and they must respond by designing the organization to adapt to the environment.

2.2a Environmental Uncertainty

Uncertainty means that managers do not have sufficient information about environmental factors to understand and predict environmental needs and changes.[25] As indicated in Exhibit 2.4, environmental characteristics that influence uncertainty are the number of factors that affect the organization and the extent to which those factors change.

Managers at a large multinational organization like Costco must deal with thousands of factors in the external environment that create uncertainty. When external factors change rapidly, the organization experiences high uncertainty; examples of companies that often face such problems are telecommunications and aerospace firms, computer and electronics companies, and Internet organizations. Consider the uncertainty that Nintendo managers face with a deluge of downloadable inexpensive games for smartphones and tablets. Traditional console game makers like Nintendo are confronting a sea of change in technologies and consumer tastes. In 2012, Nintendo posted the first loss in its history as a video game company.[26]

When an organization deals with only a few external factors and these factors are relatively stable, such as those affecting soft-drink bottlers or food processors, managers experience low uncertainty and can devote less attention to external issues.

Refer to your score on the opening questionnaire to see how well you might adapt as a new manager in an uncertain environment.

EXHIBIT 2.4 The External Environment and Uncertainty

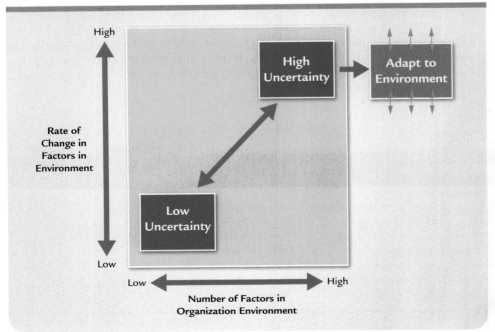

2.2b Adapting to the Environment

Environmental changes may evolve unexpectedly, such as shifting customer tastes for video and computer games or social media sites, or they may occur violently, such as the devastating Japanese earthquake and tsunami in 2011. The level of turbulence created by an environmental shift will determine the type of response that managers must make in order for the organization to survive. Managers continuously scan the business horizon for both subtle and dramatic environmental changes, also called *strategic issues*, and identify those that require strategic responses. But sometimes those conclusions on environmental changes are biased in favor of some natural inclination of the managers, as shown in this chapter's Business Blooper on NBC's *Today Show*.

Strategic issues are "events or forces either inside or outside an organization that are likely to alter its ability to achieve its objectives." As environmental turbulence increases, strategic issues emerge more frequently.[27] Managers use several strategies to adapt to these strategic issues, including business intelligence applications, attempts to influence the environment, creating interorganizational partnerships, and mergers or joint ventures.

Business Intelligence   Organizations depend on information, and companies that most effectively acquire, interpret, disseminate, and use information come out as winners. Managers have learned the importance of not only being aware of what's going on inside the organization, but also getting a handle on what's going on in the external environment. **Boundary spanning** links to and coordinates the organization with key elements in the external environment.[28]

One area of boundary spanning is the use of *business intelligence*, which results from using sophisticated software to search through internal and external data to spot patterns, trends, and relationships that might be significant. The fastest-growing segment of business intelligence is big data analytics. As described earlier in this chapter, *big data analytics* refers to searching and examining massive, complex sets of data to uncover hidden patterns and correlations and make better decisions.[29]

Big data analytics is becoming a driving force in many organizations, with 85 percent of *Fortune* 500 companies reporting in 2012 that they have launched big data initiatives.[30] One of the best-known examples of the use of data analytics among the general population is in the sports world. The popular book *Moneyball: The Art of Winning an Unfair Game*, later made into a movie starring Brad Pitt, tells the story of how the Oakland Athletics general manager Billy Beane built a winning team by analyzing previously ignored player statistics.[31] Today, most sports teams use sophisticated data analytics programs to analyze

Business Blooper

NBC's Today Show

Brought in with much fanfare from ESPN, Jamie Horowitz was named top executive and general manager of the *Today Show* at NBC in September 2014. He put himself at odds immediately with the managers who hired him by suggesting for too many changes too quickly. NBC executives said Mr. Horowitz did not grasp the fine nuances of the "Today" culture. When he was hired, Horowitz was considered as a replacement for the President of NBC News, Deborah Furness, who had actually hired him. Instead, he got fired a mere 10 weeks after he started.

SOURCE: Bill Cartner, "Executive's Aggressive Push to Revamp 'Today' Prompts His Dismissal," November 19, 2014, p. B3.

player statistics. Similarly, businesses use big data analytics to gain insights that can improve performance. Some airlines use a service called RightETA, from PASSUR Aerospace, a provider of decision support technologies for the aviation industry, to eliminate gaps between estimated and actual flight arrival times. PASSUR collects a wide range of multidimensional data and can analyze patterns spanning more than a decade to understand what happens under specific conditions. The company says that enabling airlines to know when planes are going to land and plan accordingly can save several million dollars a year.[32] Banks such as Capital One analyze customers based on credit risk, usage, and multiple other criteria to match customer characteristics with appropriate product offerings. Kaiser Permanente collects petabytes of health data on its 8 million members. Some of that data was used in a study sponsored by the U.S. Food and Drug Administration (FDA) that identified a greater risk of heart attacks among users of the pain medication Vioxx.[33]

Business intelligence and big data analytics are also related to the growing area of boundary spanning known as *competitive intelligence* (CI), which refers to activities to get as much information as possible about one's rivals.[34]

Influence the Environment   Boundary spanning is an increasingly important task in organizations because environmental shifts can happen quickly in today's world. Managers need good information about their customers, competitors, and other elements to make good decisions. Boundary spanning also includes activities that represent the organization's interest in the environment and attempt to influence elements of the external environment.[35] General Electric (GE) spends more than $39 million on political lobbying to influence government officials to take actions that positively affect the company's business performance. GE's political lobbyists span the boundary between the organization and the government, a critical aspect of the external environment.[36]

One currently intense area of lobbying relates to the online sales tax bill in the U.S. Congress. Several states have passed laws requiring that consumers pay the so-called e-sales tax, and in May 2013, the Senate passed the Marketplace Fairness Act (MFA), which gives states the legal authority to compel Internet and catalog retailers, no matter where they are located, to collect such a tax on online purchases. Lobbyists for bricks-and-mortar retailers like Walmart and Target vocally support the bill, which remains in a subcommittee of the House of Representatives, whereas a Web trade association that includes eBay, Overstock.com, and Facebook is fighting it. About 83 percent of small business owners surveyed also oppose the legislation, which they say will make it harder for small retailers to compete with larger companies by forcing them to either raise their online prices or cover the tax themselves. Meanwhile, the giant of online commerce, Amazon, supports this tax, suggesting a shift in the company's strategic direction that includes a greater physical presence in more states. Both sides have ramped up their lobbying efforts.[37]

Interorganizational Partnerships   Organizations often join together to adapt to or influence the environment. With tough global competition, constantly changing technology, and shifting government regulations, few companies can compete effectively unless they join with other firms in various partnerships. Organizations around the world are embedded in complex networks of confusing relationships—collaborating in some markets, competing fiercely in others. The number of corporate alliances has been increasing at a rate of 25 percent annually, and many of those have been between competitors.[38] For example, in the auto industry, General Motors (GM) and Honda compete fiercely, but the two joined together to develop a hydrogen fuel cell that would be shared by both automakers for vehicles they would produce around the end of the decade. Hyundai, Chrysler, and Mitsubishi jointly run the Global Engine Manufacturing Alliance to build four-cylinder engines. Volvo is now owned by Zhejiang Geely Holding Group of China, but it maintains

EXHIBIT 2.5 The Shift to a Partnership Paradigm

From Adversarial Orientation ⟶	To Partnership Orientation
• Suspicion, competition, arm's length	• Trust, value added to both sides
• Price, efficiency, own profits	• Equity, fair dealing, everyone profits
• Information and feedback limited	• E-business links to share information and conduct digital transactions
• Lawsuits to resolve conflict	• Close coordination; virtual teams and people onsite
• Minimal involvement and up-front investment	• Involvement in partner's product design and production
• Short-term contracts	• Long-term contracts
• Contracts limit the relationship	• Business assistance goes beyond the contract

TAKE Action!

Read the "Ethical Dilemma" on page 94, which pertains to CI. Do you have the courage to risk your job by challenging the boss's inappropriate use of confidential information?

an alliance with its previous owner, Ford, to supply engines and certain other components.[39] In a partnership, each organization both supports and depends on the others for success, and perhaps for survival, but that doesn't mean they don't still compete fiercely in certain areas.[40]

Managers in partnering organizations shift from an adversarial orientation to a partnership orientation. The new paradigm, shown in Exhibit 2.5, is based on trust and the ability of partners to work out equitable solutions to conflicts so that everyone profits from the relationship. Managers work to reduce costs and add value to both sides, rather than trying to get all the benefits for their own company. The new model is also characterized by a high level of information sharing, including e-business links for automatic ordering, payments, and other transactions. In addition, person-to-person interaction provides corrective feedback and solves problems. People from other companies may be on site, or they may participate in virtual teams to enable close coordination. Partners are frequently involved in one another's product design and production, and they are committed for the long term. It is not unusual for business partners to help one another, even outside of what is specified in the contract.[41]

Mergers and Joint Ventures   A step beyond strategic partnerships is for companies to become involved in mergers or joint ventures to reduce environmental uncertainty. A frenzy of merger and acquisition activity, both in the United States and internationally, in recent years is an attempt by organizations to cope with the tremendous volatility of the environment.[42] Look at the health care industry, where a sweeping national trend toward joint operating agreements and mergers reflects the tremendous uncertainty in the industry. More than 100 hospital deals took place in 2012, twice the number just three years earlier. Moreover, Gary Ahlquist, a senior partner with Booz & Company, predicts that of the 5,724 hospitals in the United States in 2013, about 1,000 will have new owners within the next seven years.[43]

Michael Loccisano/Getty Images for Heidi Klum/Getty Images

CONCEPT CONNECTION Already the largest drugstore chain in the United States, Walgreens decided to expand its business through a major acquisition. The company paid nearly $400 million to purchase the online health and beauty care product retailer Drugstore.com. **Mergers and acquisitions** are one way organizations adapt to an uncertain environment.

A **merger** occurs when two or more organizations combine to become one. For example, car rental conglomerate Avis Budget Group recently bought Zipcar, the popular car-sharing company based in Cambridge, Massachusetts.[44] A joint venture involves a strategic alliance or program by two or more organizations. A joint venture typically occurs when a project is too complex, expensive, or uncertain for one firm to handle alone. Sikorsky Aircraft and Lockheed Martin, for example, teamed up to bid on a new contract for a fleet of Marine One helicopters. The joint venture would have Sikorsky building the helicopters and Lockheed Martin providing the vast array of specialized systems that each one uses. Although the two companies have previously competed to build presidential helicopters, they joined together to be more competitive against rivals such as Boeing, Bell Helicopters, and Finmeccanica SpA's Agusta Westland.[45] Joint ventures are on the rise as companies strive to keep pace with rapid technological change and compete in the global economy.

REMEMBER THIS

- When external factors change rapidly, the organization experiences high uncertainty.
- **Strategic issues** are events and forces that alter an organization's ability to achieve its goals. As environmental turbulence increases, strategic issues emerge more frequently.
- **Boundary spanning** links to and coordinates the organization with key elements in the external environment.
- **Big data analytics** uses powerful computer technology to search and examine massive, complex sets of data to uncover hidden patterns and correlations so managers can make better decisions.
- **Interorganizational partnerships** reduce boundaries and increase collaboration with other organizations.
- A **merger** occurs when two or more organizations combine to become one.
- A **joint venture** is a strategic alliance or program by two or more organizations.
- Sikorsky Aircraft and Lockheed Martin teamed up to bid on a new contract for Marine One helicopters.

2.3 The Internal Environment: Corporate Culture

The internal environment within which managers work includes corporate culture, production technology, organization structure, and physical facilities. Of these, corporate culture surfaces as being extremely important to competitive advantage. The internal culture must fit the needs of the external environment and company strategy. When this fit occurs, highly committed employees create a high-performance organization that is tough to beat.[46]

Most people don't think about culture; it's just "how we do things around here" or "the way things are here." However, managers have to think about culture. Culture guides how people within the organization interact with one another and how the organization interacts with the external environment, thus playing a significant role in organizational success. Organizational culture has been defined and studied in many and varied ways. For the purposes of this chapter, we define **culture** as the set of key values, beliefs, understandings, and norms shared by members of an organization.[47] The concept of culture helps managers understand the hidden, complex aspects of organizational life. Culture is a pattern of shared values and assumptions about how things are done within the organization. This pattern is learned by members as they cope with external and internal problems and taught to new members as the correct way to perceive, think, and feel.

Although strong corporate cultures are important, they can also sometimes promote negative values and behaviors. When the actions of top leaders are unethical, for instance, the entire culture can become contaminated. Consider what happened at News Corporation, a corporate giant with a lucrative string of media properties all over the world. Rupert Murdoch, chairman and CEO, has been accused of frequently applying unethical, sometimes seedy tactics in his business dealings. In addition, Murdoch has allegedly used "blunt force" spending to silence critics with multimillion dollar payoffs. "Bury your mistakes," Murdoch was fond of saying.[48] But he couldn't bury the scandal that rocked the organization after journalists working for News Corporation newspapers allegedly hacked private voice-mail messages and offered bribes to police in the pursuit of hot scoops. As reported in *The New York Times*, journalists went so far as to hack the voice mail of a murdered 13-year-old girl, Milly Dowler, while she was still listed as missing.[49] As this example illustrates, the values and behaviors of top leaders have the potential to shape significantly the decisions made by employees throughout the organization. Mark Lewis, the lawyer for the family of the murdered girl, pointed out: "This is not just about one individual, but about the culture of an organization."[50]

Culture can be analyzed at two levels, as illustrated in Exhibit 2.6.[51] At the surface level are visible artifacts, which include things such as manner of dress, patterns of behavior, physical symbols, organizational ceremonies, and office layout. Visible artifacts are all the things one can see, hear, and observe by watching members of the organization. At a deeper, less obvious level are values and beliefs, which are not observable but can be discerned from how people explain and justify what they do. Members of the organization hold some values at a conscious level. These values can be interpreted from the stories, language, and symbols that organization members use to represent them.

Some values become so deeply embedded in a culture that members are no longer consciously aware of them. These basic, underlying assumptions and beliefs are the essence of culture and subconsciously guide behavior and decisions. In some organizations, a basic

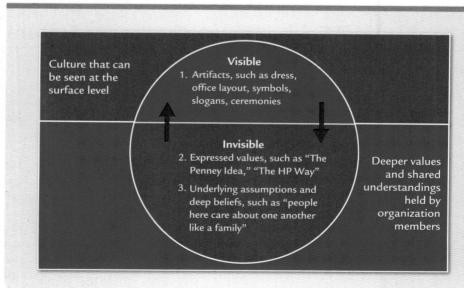

Complete the Group Learning Exercise on page 92 that deals with identifying cultural norms.

EXHIBIT 2.6 Levels of Corporate Culture

Spotlight on Skills

Menlo Innovations

Richard Sheridan, James Goebel, Robert Simms, and Thomas Meloche founded Menlo Innovations to create custom software for organizations, but one of their primary goals was to create a unique culture that embraces the values of equality, teamwork, trust, learning, and fun. Menlo infuses happiness into the often lonely grueling work of software development by making it communal.

At many software companies, developers work alone and are driven to meet rigorous performance goals, but at Menlo, collaboration is valued above anything else. Everyone works in a large, open room with no barriers of any kind to limit communication and information sharing. Employees work in pairs, sharing a single computer and passing the mouse back and forth as they brainstorm ideas and troubleshoot problems. The pairs stay together

for a week and then all switch around to new partners. The variety of partners and tasks helps keep energy high as well as brings fresh perspectives to ever-evolving projects.

Curiosity, willingness to learn, and the ability to "play well with others" are the qualities Menlo wants in its employees. To keep the culture strong, Menlo uses a weird approach to interviewing job candidates. People who apply for jobs are divided into pairs and assigned three exercises, and then evaluated on how effective they are at making the other applicant look good. It's tough for some people to handle—trying to make sure a competitor looks good enough to get the job you want. However, at Menlo, if you can't do that, you won't fit the culture—and fitting the culture is essential. Anyone who says, "I'm right, so let's do it this way" won't last long.[52]

assumption might be that people are essentially lazy and will shirk their duties whenever possible; thus, employees are closely supervised and given little freedom, and colleagues are frequently suspicious of one another. More enlightened organizations operate on the basic assumption that people want to do a good job; in these organizations, employees are given more freedom and responsibility and colleagues trust one another and work cooperatively. At Menlo Innovations, for example, which is part of the trend toward bossless organizations that we discussed earlier in this chapter, the culture promotes trust and collaboration. This chapter's "Director's Toolkit" further describes the bossless trend.

At Menlo, the goal for each person is not to get the right answer, make the right connection, be the smartest, or know the most, but rather to bring out the best in one's partner. The cultural values encourage and support everyone feeling that they are pulling together. An organization's fundamental values are demonstrated through symbols, stories, heroes, slogans, and ceremonies.

2.3a Symbols

A **symbol** is an object, act, or event that conveys meaning to others. Symbols can be considered a rich, nonverbal language that vibrantly conveys the organization's important values concerning how people relate to one another and interact with the environment.[53] At Menlo Innovations, the open workplace is a physical symbol. Mindy Grossman, CEO of HSN Inc., found that sometimes even mundane things can be highly symbolic. When she became CEO, Grossman found a business that was fundamentally broken and employees who were beaten down and uninspired. To fix it, she needed to change the culture. She used physical symbols to give people hope and motivation. One day, Grossman brought in Dumpsters to headquarters and told people to start throwing away all the broken-down furniture and clutter. Then, she had the buildings pressure-washed and painted and bought everyone a new Herman Miller Aeron chair.[54] For employees, these acts symbolized a new company value of caring for employees.

2.3b Stories

A **story** is a narrative based on true events that is repeated frequently and shared among organizational employees. Stories paint pictures that help symbolize the firm's vision and values and help employees personalize and absorb them.[55] A frequently told story at UPS concerns an employee who, without authorization, ordered an extra Boeing 737 to ensure timely delivery of a load of Christmas packages that had been left behind in the holiday rush. As the story goes, rather than punishing the worker, UPS rewarded his initiative. By telling this story, UPS workers communicate that the company stands behind its commitment to worker autonomy and customer service.[56]

Director's Toolkit

The Bossless Workplace

The organizational hierarchy with formal bosses worked well in the past. Then a few leaders began to realize that all the bosses were actually slowing down productivity and stifling employee creativity, thus prompting experiments with the "bossless" workplace.

What are the key success factors of a bossless company?

- **Reduce hierarchies starting from the top down.** Dov Seidman, head of LRN (formerly Legal Research Network), stood in front of 300 employees and ripped up the organization chart, proclaiming that "none of us would report to a boss anymore." Seidman says, "This has to start at the top of any organization." Everyone now reports to the company's mission rather than to other people. The only control is shared values. Twenty teams from around the globe spent six months imagining what a self-governing LRN would look like. Employee councils handle recruiting, performance management, resource allocation, and conflict resolution. People can take as much vacation as they like, so long as it doesn't interfere with their work.

- **Develop a bossless environment that "fits" the organization.** 37Signals, a Chicago software firm, got its start in 1999 and appointed a manager in 2013. Jason Zimdars, the reluctant manager appointee, said that he would rather write code and make things. Disdain for management is true at many newer companies with young employees who need to be creative. "We want people who are doing the work, not managing the work," said Zimdars. Employees are free to overrule the new boss if they feel strongly about green-lighting a creative project.

- **Recruit and hire employees who can adapt to a bossless culture.** Menlo Innovations, founded in

2001, became one of *Inc.* 500's fastest-growing privately held firms in the United States. Menlo's bossless hiring process is called "extreme interviewing," and it bears a striking resemblance to speed dating. Applicants—sometimes as many as five for each open position—are brought into the offices for a series of rapid-fire interviews with a range of current employees. The emphasis is on "kindergarten skills": geniality, curiosity, generosity. Technical proficiency is less important than a candidate's "ability to make [his or her] partner look good." (Sample interview question: "What is the most challenging bug that you helped someone else fix?")

- **Expect bumps in the road with a flat organizational structure.** Retaining highly motivated workers is vital to making a boss-free system work. Most employees take anywhere from six months to a year to adapt, and some leave for more traditional settings. "It's absolutely less efficient upfront" says Terri Kelly, chief executive of W. L. Gore, the maker of Gore-Tex and other materials. "[But] once you have the organization behind it … the buy in and execution happens quickly." One study found that teams of factory workers learned to "encourage and support each other …. They collectively perform the role of a good manager."

SOURCES: Matthew Shaer, "The Boss Stops Here," *New York Magazine* (June 24–July 1, 2013): 26–34; Rachel Emma Silverman, "Who's the Boss? There Isn't One," *The Wall Street Journal Online*, June 19, 2012, http://online.wsj.com/article/SB100014240527023033792 04577474953586383604.html (accessed September 26, 2013); John Southerst, "First We Dump the Bosses," *Canadian Business* (April 1992): 46–51; Rachel Emma Silverman, "Some Tech Firms Ask: Who Needs Managers?" *The Wall Street Journal Online*, August 6, 2013, http://online.wsj.com/article/SB10001424127887323420604578652051466314748.html (accessed August 6, 2013); Dov Seidman, "Letting the Mission Govern a Company," *The New York Times*, June 23, 2012, http://www.nytimes.com/2012/06/24/jobs/a-company-lrn-adopts-collaborative-management.html (accessed June 23, 2012).

2.3c Heroes

A **hero** is a figure who exemplifies the deeds, character, and attributes of a strong culture. Heroes are role models for employees to follow. Heroes with strong legacies may continue to influence a culture even after they are gone. Many people have wondered if the culture that Steve Jobs created at Apple would be sustained after his death in 2011. Jobs exemplified the creativity, innovation, risk-taking, and boundary-breaking thinking that made the company famous.[57] When Jobs's health began to fail, Apple's board began considering replacements who could sustain the fertile culture that Jobs created. They

THE EXECUTIVE EDGE

Chris Rock

Developing a successful comedy routine is no different than inventing and producing a new product, at least if you see how Chris Rock works. He's developed his own process that has become his own organizational "culture." Before a new global tour, Rock starts out by visiting at least 40 small comedy clubs with a yellow note pad that has ideas scribbled. He calls it a boxing training camp. Making sure there is an audience of about 50, he sits quietly until people start to notice him and ask him onstage. Up there, he doesn't do his full "preacher effect" performance, but rather talks and tells jokes in a more conversational style, with his notepad right next to him. In a typical 45-minute set, most of his jokes fall flat and watching it can be awfully painful, as sometimes he rambles, loses his train of thought and keeps referring to his notes. Many audience members sit on their hands, unimpressed. In business, such people are referred to as "active users" and provide the kind of constant criticism needed to improve the material. Rock admits to audiences that some jokes need work and writes on his pad. But during that less-than-an-hour time period, there might be five to ten lines that bring the house down. He builds on these "lightning bolts."

When he's done, he's gone through thousands of ideas and only a few make it in to the final routine. Comedians know that a successful joke has six to seven parts. With such complexity, even stars like Jerry Seinfeld or Rock don't know which combination of ideas is going to work in front of an audience. Even with the amazingly successful *Onion*, the writers propose 600 possibilities for 18 ultimate headlines, or a 3 percent rate.

By the time Rock is ready for an HBO special he's spent six to 12 months testing and retesting his material, including opening, jokes, and transitions. He'll be on stage every night, five to seven nights a week, grinding through every sentence, until the routine is perfectly honed. Rock knows that good ideas don't spring into anyone's mind perfectly formed, but take lots of work. Rock does not see the thousands of failed jokes in the clubs as failures but rather an information in a learning process that ultimately yields gold.

When writing movies, Rock often collaborates, sometimes with Louie C.K., such as with *I Think I Love My Wife*, or he role models Woody Allen's *Stardust Memories*, as he did with 2015's hit *Top Five*, which was produced by Scott Rudin (*Silicon Valley*). Whether with films or standup, Rock knows better than take anything for granted. When people compliment a performance, he'll often say, "Just try staying in show business." But he also knows that "writing is a nerd job." As he says, "There is nothing cool about writing."

SOURCES: Kelefa Sanneh, "The Duke of Doubt," *The New Yorker*, November 10, 2014; "Chris Rock Has Filed for Divorce," *The Brampton Guardian*, December 28, 2014, p. 1; Peter Sims, Little Bets: How Breakthrough Ideas Emerge from Small Discoveries (New York: Simon & Schuster, 2013).

chose Tim Cook, who long had served as second-in-command. Cook is trying to nurture a culture that reflects the values and behaviors of Apple's hero, Steve Jobs. "Apple has a culture of excellence that is, I think, so unique and so special. I'm not going to witness or permit the change of it," he said.[58] Chris Rock holds Woody Allen as one of his heroes and is greatly influenced by Allen's style and work ethic, as shown in this chapter's Executive Edge.

© FashionStock.com/Shutterstock.com

CONCEPT CONNECTION   Around the offices of Tradesy, the high-fashion consignment e-commerce site that blossomed into a $10 million business in just about three years, employees like to tell the story of how Tracy DiNunzio started her business. Desperate for start-up capital, she sold many of her belongings, but when she still didn't have enough to pay the Web developers she was working with, Tracy started renting out her bedroom through the hotel-alternative Web site Airbnb while she slept on her own couch. The story is important to Tradesy because it demonstrates the passion and commitment that is part of the corporate **culture**.

2.3d Slogans

A slogan is a phrase or sentence that succinctly expresses a key corporate value. Many companies use slogans or sayings to convey special meaning to employees. For example, Disney uses the slogan "The happiest place on earth." The Ritz-Carlton adopted the slogan, "Ladies and gentlemen taking care of ladies and gentlemen" to demonstrate its cultural commitment to take care of both employees and customers. "We're in the service business, and service comes only from people. Our promise is to take care of them, and provide a happy place for them to work," said general manager Mark DeCocinis, who manages the Portman Hotel in Shanghai, recipient of the "Best Employer in Asia" award for three consecutive years.[59] Cultural values can also be discerned in written public statements, such as corporate mission statements or other formal statements that express the core values of the organization. At DreamHost, a Web-hosting company where the culture reflects a serious commitment to democracy, the CEO (who was elected by employees), asked a team of workers to draft a mission statement and constitution to guide how the company makes decisions.[60]

2.3e Ceremonies

A **ceremony** is a planned activity at a special event that is conducted for the benefit of an audience. Managers hold ceremonies to provide dramatic examples of company values. Ceremonies are special occasions that reinforce valued accomplishments, create a bond among people by allowing them to share an important event, and anoint and celebrate heroes.[61] In a ceremony to mark its 20th anniversary, Southwest Airlines rolled out a specialty plane called the "Lone Star One," which had the Texas state flag painted on it to signify the company's start in Texas. Later, when the National Basketball Association (NBA) chose Southwest Airlines as the league's official airline, Southwest launched another specialty plane, the "Slam Dunk One," colored blue and orange with a large basketball painted on the nose of the plane. Today, 10 specialty planes celebrate significant milestones in Southwest's history and demonstrate key cultural values.[62]

REMEMBER THIS

- Organizational **culture** is the set of key values, beliefs, understandings, and norms shared by members of an organization.
- A **symbol** is an object, act, or event that conveys meaning to others.
- A **story** is a narrative based on true events and is repeated frequently and shared among organizational employees.
- A **hero** is a figure who exemplifies the deeds, character, and attributes of a strong culture.

- Steve Jobs is a hero at Apple, representing the creativity, risk-taking, and striving for excellence that define the company's culture.
- A **slogan**, such as Disney's "The happiest place on Earth," succinctly expresses a key corporate value.
- Managers hold **ceremonies**, planned activities at special events, to reinforce company values.

2.4 Types of Culture

A big influence on internal corporate culture is the external environment. Cultures can vary widely across organizations; however, organizations within the same industry often reveal similar cultural characteristics because they are operating in similar environments.[63] The internal culture should embody what it takes to succeed in the environment. If the external environment requires extraordinary customer service, the culture should encourage good service; if it calls for careful technical decision making, cultural values should reinforce managerial decision making.

In considering what cultural values are important for the organization, managers consider the external environment, as well as the company's strategy and goals. Studies suggest that the right fit between culture, strategy, and the environment is associated with four categories or types of culture, as illustrated in Exhibit 2.7. These categories are based on two dimensions: (1) the extent to which the external environment requires flexibility or stability and (2) the extent to which a company's strategic focus is internal or external. The four categories associated with these differences are adaptability, achievement, involvement, and consistency.[64]

2.4a Adaptability Culture

The **adaptability culture** emerges in an environment that requires fast response and high-risk decision making. Managers encourage values that support the company's ability to rapidly detect, interpret, and translate signals from the environment into new behaviors. Employees have the autonomy to make decisions and act freely to meet new needs, and responsiveness to customers is highly valued. Managers also actively create change by encouraging and rewarding creativity, experimentation, and risk-taking. When he was 20 years old, Aaron Levie cofounded Box, a company that provides online file storage for businesses, based on the values of an adaptability culture.

EXHIBIT 2.7   Four Types of Corporate Culture

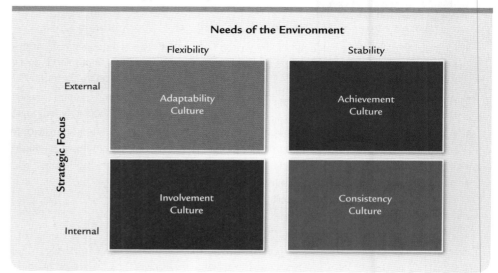

SOURCES: Based on D. R. Denison and A. K. Mishra, "Toward a Theory of Organizational Culture and Effectiveness," *Organization Science* 6, no. 2 (March–April 1995): 204–223; R. Hooijberg and F. Petrock, "On Cultural Change: Using the Competing Values Framework to Help Leaders Execute a Transformational Strategy," *Human Resource Management* 32, no. 1 (1993): 29–50; and R. E. Quinn, *Beyond Rational Management: Mastering the Paradoxes and Competing Demands of High Performance* (San Francisco: Jossey-Bass, 1988).

Spotlight on Skills

Box

Aaron Levie, the young CEO of Box, based in Los Altos, California, is constantly reminding people that they can do things "10 times bigger, 10 times better, and 10 times faster," a core value he calls "10X." Other core values at Box are "Get s— done" and "Take risks. Fail fast."

Levie says his main goals are "to innovate and to disrupt." He adds, "Also, I want to avoid being disrupted." Those goals are reflected in the company's culture, which emphasizes speed, flexibility, and pushing the boundaries. Taking risks is essential for the company to remain competitive, but failing fast means that people can correct mistakes quickly. For a company of 600 people competing with companies that have tens of thousands, speed is crucial. The culture is focused on how much people can get done in as little time as possible. The bar is set very high, and the culture values solving as a team any problem that comes along. No one at Box has a private office, including Levie, and the open floor plan lets people interact and collaborate

continually. The 44 rooms that could be offices serve as conference rooms instead, where people brainstorm and hash out ideas. The glass walls are meant to be written on. People are encouraged to "throw their ideas on the wall." Many of the conference rooms are named after Internet icons.

The fast pace and aggressive goals can mean high pressure, but Box also encourages fun. "We have one of the world's best jugglers and one of the country's best baton twirlers," Levie says. "Circus skills are a pretty important quality around here."[65]

The fun, fast, risk-taking culture at Box has helped the company adapt in a turbulent industry and grow quickly, more than doubling its sales every year since it was founded in 2005. Many technology and Internet-based companies, like Box, use the adaptability type of culture, as do many companies in the marketing, electronics, and cosmetics industries because they must move quickly to respond to rapid changes in the environment.

2.4b Achievement Culture

The **achievement culture** is suited to organizations concerned with serving specific customers in the external environment, but without the intense need for flexibility and rapid change. This results-oriented culture values competitiveness, aggressiveness, personal initiative, cost cutting, and willingness to work long and hard to achieve results. An emphasis on winning and achieving specific ambitious goals is the glue that holds the organization together.[66] Both Oracle and EMC have been criticized for having aggressive, take-no-prisoners cultures, but leaders at the companies make no apologies. Jack Mollen, executive vice president for human resources at EMC, says "Some people might feel it's aggressive, but our people want to be put in jobs where they can work hard, take risks, and get recognized." As for the critics, he adds, "I ask the search firms to name the three hardest companies to recruit [management talent] from, and they say 'Intel, Oracle, and EMC.'"[67]

Would you rather work in an organization with an adaptability, achievement, involvement, or consistency culture? Complete the "New Manager Self-Test" to get an idea of what type of culture you would be most comfortable working in.

2.4c Involvement Culture

The **involvement culture** emphasizes an internal focus on the participation of employees to adapt rapidly to changing needs from the environment. This culture places a high value on meeting the needs of employees, and the organization may be characterized by a caring, family-like atmosphere. Managers emphasize values such as cooperation, consideration of both employees and customers, and avoiding status differences. Four Seasons Hotels and Resorts, for example, has been named one of the "100 Best Companies to Work For" by *Fortune* magazine every year since the survey's inception in 1998. With 86 luxury properties in 35 countries, Four Seasons managers have built a corporate culture that values employees above all other assets. Every location has a committee made up of people from all departments that meets with the general manager each month to discuss workplace concerns. The relentless commitment to employees has sustained Four Seasons during an economic recession that battered many companies in the hospitality industry. Four Seasons clarified its corporate vision to include both being a first-choice ranking among guests and being the best employer.[68]

2.4d Consistency Culture

The final category of culture, the **consistency culture**, uses an internal focus and a consistency orientation for a stable environment. Following the rules and being thrifty are valued, and the culture supports and rewards a methodical, rational, and orderly way of doing things. In today's fast-changing world, few companies operate in a stable environment, and most managers are shifting toward cultures that are more flexible and in tune with changes in the environment. However, Pacific Edge Software (now part of Serena Software) successfully implemented elements of a consistency culture to ensure that all its projects stayed on time and under budget. The husband-and-wife team of Lisa Hjorten and Scott Fuller implanted a culture of order, discipline, and control from the moment they founded the company. The emphasis on order and focus meant that employees could generally go home by 6 p.m. rather than working all night to finish an important project. Although sometimes being careful means being slow, Pacific Edge managed to keep pace with the demands of the external environment.[69]

Each of these four categories of culture can be successful. In addition, organizations usually have values that fall into more than one category. The relative emphasis on various cultural values depends on the needs of the environment and the organization's focus. Managers are responsible for instilling the cultural values the organization needs to be successful in its environment.

REMEMBER THIS

- For an organization to be effective, corporate culture should be aligned with organizational strategy and the needs of the external environment.

- Organizations within the same industry often reveal similar cultural characteristics because they are operating in similar environments.

- The **adaptability culture** is characterized by values that support the company's ability to interpret and translate signals from the environment into new behavior responses.

- An **achievement culture** is a results-oriented culture that values competitiveness, personal initiative, and achievement.

- A culture that places high value on meeting the needs of employees and values cooperation and equality is an **involvement culture**.

- A **consistency culture** values and rewards a methodical, rational, orderly way of doing things.

NEW MANAGER Self-Test

Culture Preference

Instructions: The fit between a new manager and organizational culture can determine success and satisfaction. To understand your culture preference, rank the items here from 1 to 8 based on the strength of your preference (1 = strongest).

1. The organization is very personal, much like an extended family.
2. The organization is dynamic and changing, where people take risks.
3. The organization is achievement-oriented, with the focus on competition and getting jobs done.
4. The organization is stable and structured, with clarity and established procedures.
5. Management style is characterized by teamwork and participation.
6. Management style is characterized by innovation and risk-taking.
7. Management style is characterized by high-performance demands and achievement.
8. Management style is characterized by security and predictability.

Scoring and Interpretation: Each question pertains to one of the four types of culture in Exhibit 2.7. To compute your preference for each type of culture, add together the scores for each set of two questions as follows:

Involvement culture—total for questions 1, 5: _____

Adaptability culture—total for questions 2, 6: _____

Achievement culture—total for questions 3, 7: _____

Consistency culture—total for questions 4, 8: _____

A lower score means a stronger culture preference. You will likely be more comfortable and more effective as a new manager in a corporate culture that is compatible with your personal preferences. A higher score means that the culture would not fit your expectations, and you would have to change your style and preference to be comfortable. Review the text discussion of the four culture types. Do your cultural preference scores seem correct to you? Can you think of companies that fit your culture preference?

SOURCE: Kim S. Cameron and Robert D. Quinn, *Diagnosing and Changing Organizational Culture* (Reading, MA: Addison-Wesley, 1999).

2.5 Shaping Corporate Culture for Innovative Response

Research conducted by a Stanford University professor indicates that the one factor that increases a company's value the most is people and how they are treated.[70] In addition, many top leaders cite organizational culture as their most important mechanism for attracting, motivating, and retaining talented employees, a capability considered the single best predictor of overall organizational excellence.[71] In a survey of Canada's top 500 companies, 82 percent of leaders said that culture has a strong impact on their company's performance.[72] Consider how an "employees first" corporate culture drives stellar financial performance at Southwest Airlines. Profitable every year since 1972, and touting the lowest ratio of complaints per passengers in the industry, Southwest offers industry-leading salaries and benefits, intense career development programs, and a commitment to diversity among its workforce. In addition, Southwest promotes a strong collaborative culture and fosters a good relationship with organized labor.[73] At Southwest, a positive culture that reflects an intense commitment to employees results in a competitive advantage.

Corporate culture plays a key role in creating an organizational climate that enables learning and innovative responses to threats from the external environment, challenging new opportunities, or organizational crises. However, managers realize that they can't focus all their effort on values; they also need a commitment to solid business performance.

2.5a Managing the High-Performance Culture

Companies that succeed in a turbulent world are those in which managers are evaluated and rewarded for paying careful attention to both cultural values *and* business performance. Exhibit 2.8 illustrates four organizational outcomes based on the relative attention that managers pay to cultural values and business results.[74] For example, a company in Quadrant C pays little attention to either values or business results and is unlikely to survive for long. Managers in Quadrant D organizations are highly focused on creating a strong cohesive culture, but they don't tie organizational values directly to goals and desired business results.

When cultural values aren't connected to business performance, they aren't likely to benefit the organization during hard times. The corporate culture at the LEGO Group, with headquarters in Billund, Denmark, nearly doomed the toymaker in the 1990s when sales plummeted as children turned from traditional toys to video games. At that time, LEGO reflected the characteristics found in Quadrant D of Exhibit 2.8. Imagination and creativity, not business performance, were what guided the company. The attitude among employees was, "We're doing great stuff for kids—don't bother us with financial goals." When he became CEO in 2004, Jørgen Vig Knudstorp upended the corporate culture with a new employee motto: "I am here to make money for the company." The shift to bottom-line results had a profound impact, and LEGO has become one of the most successful companies in the toy industry.[75]

Quadrant A represents organizations that are focused primarily on bottom-line results and pay little attention to organizational values. This approach may be profitable in the short run, but the success is difficult to sustain over the long term because the "glue" that holds the organization together—that is, shared cultural values—is missing. Consider how a bottom-line focus at Zynga, the Web's largest social games company, is damaging the organization. Zynga, founded in July 2007 and led until recently by CEO Mark Pincus, met ambitious revenue and profitability goals (which is rare among Internet start-ups),

EXHIBIT 2.8   Combining Culture and Performance

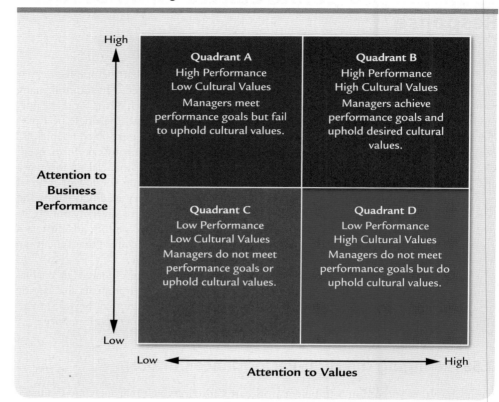

SOURCES: Jeff Rosenthal and Mary Ann Masarech, "High-Performance Cultures: How Values Can Drive Business Results," *Journal of Organizational Excellence* (Spring 2003): 3–18; and Dave Ulrich, Steve Kerr, and Ron Ashkenas, Figure 11-2, GE Leadership Decision Matrix, *The GE Work-Out: How to Implement GE's Revolutionary Method for Busting Bureaucracy and Attacking Organizational Problems—Fast!* (New York: McGraw-Hill, 2002), p. 230.

but the relentless focus on financial performance took a heavy toll. Teams for each game, like FarmVille and CityVille, work under aggressive deadlines and are continuously challenged to meet lofty goals. Managers emphasize performance reports, relentlessly aggregating data, and using the data to demote or fire weak employees. Little attention is paid to cultural values that bind people into a unified whole. Employees began voicing their frustration, complaining about long hours and aggressive deadlines. Former employees describe emotionally charged encounters, including loud outbursts from Pincus, threats from top managers, and moments when colleagues broke down in tears. The company's success likely cannot be sustained without an increased focus on building a more positive culture. Many valued employees have been lured away by competitors in an industry where talent is scarce.[76]

Finally, companies in Quadrant B put high emphasis on both culture and solid business performance as drivers of organizational success. Managers in these organizations align values with the company's day-to-day operations—hiring practices, performance management, budgeting, criteria for promotions and rewards, and so forth. Consider the approach that GE took to accountability and performance management. When he was CEO, Jack Welch helped GE become one of the world's most successful and admired companies. He achieved this by creating a culture in which risk was rewarded and accountability and measurable goals were keys to individual success and company profitability.[77] The company's traditional approach had achieved stellar financial results, but managers motivated people to perform primarily through control, intimidation, and reliance on a small circle of staff. Welch was interested in more than just financial results—he wanted managers to exhibit the following cultural values in addition to "making their numbers":[78]

- Have a passion for excellence and hate bureaucracy

- Be open to ideas from anywhere

- "Live" quality, and drive cost and speed for competitive advantage

Welch knew that for the company to succeed in a rapidly changing world, managers needed to pay careful attention to both cultural values and business performance. Quadrant D organizations represent the **high-performance culture**, a culture that (1) is based on a solid organizational mission or purpose, (2) embodies shared adaptive values that guide decisions and business practices, and (3) encourages individual employee ownership of both bottom-line results and the organization's cultural backbone.[79]

One of the most important things that managers do is create and influence organizational culture to meet strategic goals because culture has a significant impact on performance. In *Corporate Culture and Performance*, John Kotter and James Heskett provided evidence that companies that intentionally managed cultural values outperformed similar companies that did not. Recent research validates that elements of corporate culture are positively correlated with higher financial performance.[80]

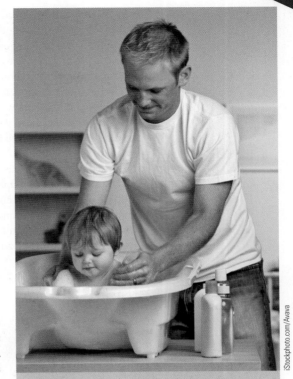

iStockphoto.com/Avava

CONCEPT CONNECTION Johnson & Johnson, makers of a wide range of consumer, health, and prescription products, is considered a **high-performance** workplace. The company has a rich heritage of shared corporate values, and employees are focused on winning by serving their customers. The corporate culture encourages employees to work in teams, think like owners, and remain open to action and change.

2.5b Cultural Leadership

A primary way in which managers shape cultural norms and values to build a high-performance culture is through *cultural leadership*. Managers must *overcommunicate* to ensure that employees understand the new culture values, and they signal these values in actions as well as words.

A **cultural leader** defines and uses signals and symbols to influence corporate culture. The leader clarifies what the new culture should be and crafts a story that inspires people to change. A cultural leader is the "chief marketing officer" for the desired cultural values.[81]

Cultural leaders influence culture in two key areas:

1. *The cultural leader articulates a vision for the organizational culture that employees can believe in.* The leader defines and communicates central values that employees believe in and will rally around. Values are tied to a clear and compelling mission, or core purpose.

2. *The cultural leader heeds the day-to-day activities that reinforce the cultural vision.* The leader makes sure that work procedures and reward systems match and reinforce the values. Actions speak louder than words, so cultural leaders "walk their talk."[82]

"Leaders often treat culture as a happy accident—something that develops organically, driven by personalities. What a mistake. Culture is a critical building block of success."

—Hiroshi Mikitani, founder and CEO of Rakuten

When the culture needs to change, cultural leaders make sure that people understand that the old way of doing things is no longer acceptable. For example, when he was corporate ombudsman at KeySpan Corporation (now part of National Grid), Kenny Moore held a "funeral" for everyone to say goodbye to the company as it once was.[83] Then, managers widely communicate the new cultural values through both words and actions. Values statements that aren't reinforced by management behavior are meaningless, or even harmful, for employees and the organization. Whole Foods founder and CEO John Mackey wants his managers to place more value on creating "a better person, company, and world" than on pursuing personal financial gain. To demonstrate his commitment to this belief, he asked the board of directors to donate all his future stock options to the company's two foundations, the Animal Compassion Foundation and the Whole Planet Foundation.[84]

Cultural leaders also uphold their commitment to values during difficult times or crises. Upholding the cultural values helps organizations weather a crisis and come out stronger on the other side. Creating and maintaining a high-performance culture is not easy in today's turbulent environment and changing workplace, but through their words—and particularly their actions—cultural leaders let everyone in the organization know what really counts.

REMEMBER THIS

- Managers emphasize both values and business results to create a **high-performance culture**.
- Culture enables solid business performance through the alignment of motivated employees with the mission and goals of the company.
- Managers create and sustain adaptive high-performance cultures through cultural leadership.

- **Cultural leaders** define and articulate important values that are tied to a clear and compelling mission, which they communicate widely and uphold through their actions.

CHAPTER 2 DISCUSSION QUESTIONS

1. Surveys reveal dramatic shifts in social attitudes toward issues such as gay marriage and citizenship for illegal immigrants. How do you think these changing attitudes might affect the manager's job over the next few years?

2. Would the task environment for a wireless provider such as U.S. Cellular contain the same elements as that for a government welfare agency? Discuss the similarities and differences.

3. What strategic issues have the potential to create environmental uncertainty in the following four industries: (a) automobile; (b) social media; (c) newspaper; and (d) medical services?

4. Contemporary best-selling management books often argue that customers are the most important element in the external environment. Do you agree? In what company situations might this statement be untrue?

5. What do you see as the primary advantage of using big data analytics—understanding the environment or influencing the environment? Why?

6. Why are interorganizational partnerships so important for today's companies? What elements in the current environment might contribute to either an increase or a decrease in interorganizational collaboration? Discuss.

7. Consider the factors that influence environmental uncertainty (rate of change in factors and number of factors in the environment) that are presented in Exhibit 2.4. Classify each of the following organizations as operating in either (a) a low-uncertainty environment or (b) a high-uncertainty environment: Hyundai, Facebook, a local Subway franchise, FedEx, a cattle ranch in Oklahoma, and McDonald's. Explain your reasoning.

8. Distribution center managers for Anheuser-Busch InBev frequently start the day with a sort of pep rally, reviewing the day's sales targets and motivating people to get out and sell more beer. What does this suggest about the type of culture the company's managers promote?

9. As a manager, how would you use symbols to build an adaptability culture that encourages teamwork and risk-taking? What kinds of symbols could you use to promote the values of an involvement culture?

10. Do you think it is wise for a top executive to fire a manager who is bringing in big sales and profits for the company but not living up to a cultural value of "showing respect for employees"? Explain.

SELF-LEARNING

Working in an Adaptability Culture[85]

Think of a specific full-time job that you have held. Please answer the following questions according to your perception of the *managers above you* in that job. Circle a number on the 1–5 scale based on the extent to which you agree with each statement about the managers above you:

⑤ Strongly agree
④ Agree
③ Neither agree nor disagree
② Disagree
① Strongly disagree

1. Good ideas got serious consideration from management above me.
   1 2 3 4 5

2. Management above me was interested in ideas and suggestions from people at my level in the organization.
   1 2 3 4 5

3. When suggestions were made to management above me, they received a fair evaluation.
   1 2 3 4 5

4. Management did not expect me to challenge or change the status quo.
   1 2 3 4 5

5. Management specifically encouraged me to bring about improvements in my workplace.
   1 2 3 4 5

6. Management above me took action on recommendations made from people at my level.
   1 2 3 4 5

7. Management rewarded me for correcting problems.
   1 2 3 4 5

8. Management clearly expected me to improve work unit procedures and practices.
   1 2 3 4 5

9. I felt free to make recommendations to management above me to change existing practices.
   1 2 3 4 5

10. Good ideas did not get communicated upward because management above me was not very approachable.
    1 2 3 4 5

Scoring and Interpretation

To compute your score: Subtract each of your scores for questions 4 and 10 from the number 6. Using your adjusted scores, add the numbers for all 10 questions to give you the total score. Divide that number by 10 to get your average score: _____.

An adaptability culture is shaped by the values and actions of top and middle managers. When managers actively encourage and welcome change initiatives from below, the organization will be infused with values for change. These 10 questions measure your management's openness to change. A typical average score for management openness to change is about 3. If your average score was 4 or higher, you worked in an organization that expressed strong cultural values of adaptation. If your average score was 2 or below, the company probably did not have an adaptability culture.

Think about this job. Was the level of management openness to change correct for the organization? Why? Compare your scores to those of another student, and take turns describing what it was like working for the managers above you in your jobs. Do you sense a relationship between job satisfaction and your management's openness to change? What specific management characteristics and corporate values explain the openness scores in the two jobs?

GROUP LEARNING

Organizational Culture in the Classroom and Beyond

Step 1. Write down on the table below the norms that you believe to be operating in the following places: (1) in most of your courses, (2) in formal social groups such as fraternities and sororities and (3) in student clubs or school-sponsored organizations. Use your personal experience in each place and consider the norms. Some norms are implicit, so you may have to think carefully to identify them. Other norms may be explicit. Make sure you list *norms* but not *practices*. The difference is that when a norm is broken, there is some negative reaction, or even punishment, while violating a practice carries no negative result.

List norm	Which group or organization is identified with this norm?	What is negative result if norm is violated?

Step 2. After you have developed your lists, divide into groups of four to six students to discuss norms. Each student should share with the group the norms identified for each of the assigned places. Make a list of norms for each place and brainstorm any additional norms that you and fellow group members can think of.

Step 3. Try to group the norms by common themes, and give each group of norms a title. Decide as a group which norms are most important for regulating student behavior in each location. Use the table below.

Name of norm category	List norms in that category	Rate each norm from 1 to 5, with 1 being least important for regulating behavior and 5 most important.	Where does each norm originate? From environment, leader, or other?

Step 4. As a group, analyze the source or origin of each of the more important norms. Does the norm originate in the environment, from a leader, or elsewhere? Can you find any examples of norms that are expressed but not followed, which means that people do not "walk the talk" of the norms?

Step 5. What did you learn about cultural norms that exist in organizations and social groups? How is it helpful to make explicit those aspects of organizational culture that are typically implicit? Who should be responsible for setting norms in your courses or in student social groups and organizations?

ACTION LEARNING

Answer the following questions yourself.

1. Think of a really good work situation you've had (or as member of a student organization) and a really bad one.

2. Consider the types of organizational cultures listed in pages 83–85. Which culture was your best and which was your worst?

3. List aspects of culture that fit you or did not fit.

4. Can you learn anything from this about what you need in a workplace, in order for you to operate at your best?

What was the name of company or organization?	What type of culture was it? Refer to pages 83–85.	Which aspects fit you the best? Or, which aspects were the worst fit?
Best:		
Worst:		

As a group, discuss the following:

1. Where there similarities or differences in what the members found in terms of ideal cultures?

2. If you could design the very ideal culture for your group members, what would it look like?

3. What would the ideal culture look like for people who have different, even opposite, qualities?

ETHICAL DILEMMA

CI Predicament[86]

Miquel Vasquez was proud of his job as a new product manager for a biotechnology start-up, and he loved the high stakes and tough decisions that went along with the job. But as he sat in his den after a long day, he was troubled, struggling over what had happened earlier that day and the information that he now possessed.

Just before lunch, Miquel's boss had handed him a stack of private strategic documents from their closest competitor. It was a CI gold mine—product plans, pricing strategies, partnership agreements, and other documents, most of them clearly marked "proprietary and confidential." When Miquel asked where the documents came from, his boss told him with a touch of pride that he had taken them right off the competing firm's server. "I got into a private section of their intranet and downloaded everything that looked interesting," he said. Later, realizing that Miquel was suspicious, the boss would say only that he had obtained "electronic access" via a colleague and had not personally broken any passwords. Maybe not, Miquel thought to himself, but this situation wouldn't pass the *60 Minutes* test. If word of this acquisition of a competitor's confidential data ever got out to the press, the company's reputation would be ruined.

Miquel didn't feel good about using these materials. He spent the afternoon searching for answers to his dilemma, but found no clear company policies or regulations that offered any guidance. His sense of fair play told him that using the information was unethical, if not downright illegal. What bothered him even more was the knowledge that this kind of thing might happen again. Using this confidential information would certainly give him and his company a competitive advantage, but Miquel wasn't sure that he wanted to work for a firm that would stoop to such tactics.

What Would You Do?

1. Go ahead and use the documents to the company's benefit, but make clear to your boss that you don't want him passing confidential information to you in the future. If he threatens to fire you, threaten to leak the news to the press.

2. Confront your boss privately and let him know that you're uncomfortable with how the documents were obtained and what possession of them says about the company's culture. In addition to the question of the legality of using the information, point out that it is a public relations nightmare waiting to happen.

3. Talk to the company's legal counsel and contact the Strategic and Competitive Intelligence Professionals for guidance. Then, with their opinions and facts to back you up, go to your boss.

CASE FOR CRITICAL ANALYSIS

Not Measuring Up

"I must admit, I'm completely baffled by these scoring results for Cam Leslie," Carole Wheeling said as she and company CEO Ronald Zeitland scrolled through the latest employee surveys for middle management.

For the second year, RTZ Corporation used Wheeling's consulting firm to survey and score managers. An increasingly younger workforce, changing consumer tastes, and technology changes in the industry had caused Zeitland to look more closely at culture and employee satisfaction. The goal of this process was to provide feedback in order to assure continuous improvement across a variety of criteria. The surveys could be used to highlight areas for improvement by showing manager and company strengths and weaknesses, anticipating potential problem areas, providing a barometer for individual job performance, and as a road map for transforming the culture as the company expanded.

From the outset, Zeitland insisted on employee honesty in scoring managers and providing additional comments for the surveys. "We can't change what we don't know," Zeitland instructed employees in meetings two years ago. "This is your opportunity to speak up. We're not looking for gripe sessions. We're looking for constructive analysis and grading for what we do and how we do it. This method assures that everyone is heard. Every survey carries equal weight. Changes are coming to this organization. We want to make those changes as easy and equally beneficial as possible for everyone."

Now, two years into the process, the culture was showing signs of changing and improving.

"The results from last year to this year show overall improvement," Wheeling said. "But for the second year, Cam's survey results are disappointing. In fact, there appears to be a little slippage in some areas."

Zeitland leaned back in his chair, paused, and looked at the survey results on the screen.

"I don't really understand it," Wheeling remarked. "I've talked to Cam. He seems like a nice guy—a hard worker, intelligent, dedicated. He pushes his crew, but he's not a control freak."

"He actually implemented several of the suggestions from last year's survey," Zeitland said. "From all reports and my own observations, Cam has more presence in the department and has increased the number of meetings. He appears to have at least attempted to open up communications. I'm sure he will be as baffled as we are by these new results because he *has* put forth effort."

"Employees mentioned some of these improvements, but it's not altering the scores. Could it merely be a reflection of his personality?" Wheeling asked.

"Well, we have all kinds of personalities throughout management. He's very knowledgeable and very task-oriented. I admit he has a way of relating to people that can be a little standoffish, but I don't think it's always necessary to be slapping everyone on the back and buying them beers at the local pub in order to be liked and respected and …"

"… in order to get high scores?" Wheeling finished his sentence. "Still, the low percentage of 'favorable' scores in relation to 'unfavorable' and even 'neutral'…" her voice trailed off momentarily. "That's the one that gets me. There are so many 'neutral' scores. That's really strange. Don't they have an opinion? I'd love to flesh that one out more. It seems that in a sea of vivid colors, he's beige."

"It's like he's not there," Zeitland said. "The response doesn't tell me that they dislike Cam; they just don't *see* him as their manager."

Wheeling laughed. "Maybe we can wrap him in gauze like the 'Invisible Man,'" she joked.

The joke appeared lost on Zeitland. "That invisibility leaves him disengaged. Look at the comments."

He scrolled down. "Here's a follow-up comment: **Employee Engagement:** *Are you kidding?* And here's another: **Advocacy:** *I don't think and I don't believe anyone here thinks he would go to bat for us.*"

"I know," Wheeling said. "On the other hand, many of their remarks indicate they consider him fair in areas like distribution of workload, and they score him decently in the area of follow-through in achieving company goals. But overall satisfaction and morale levels are low."

"That's what I don't understand," Zeitland commented. "Morale and productivity are normally so strongly linked. Morale in this case is blah, blah, blah, and yet these guys manage to perform right up there with every other division in the company. So they're *doing* it. They just don't like it or find any sense of fulfillment."

"Does Cam?"

"Interesting question," Zeitland agreed.

"So, how do we help Cam improve these scores in the coming year?" Wheeling asked. "What positive steps can he take? I'd at least like to see an up-or-down vote—not all of this neutrality—on his management skills and job performance."

Questions

1. Do you think Zeitland's desire for changes in culture are related to changes in the external environment? Explain.

2. What additional investigation might Wheeling and Zeitland undertake before settling on a plan of action?

3. In which quadrant of Exhibit 2.8 would you place Cam? What are some steps that you would recommend Cam consider to better connect with the employees who report to him?

ON THE JOB
VIDEO CASES

Camp Bow Wow: The Environment and Corporate Culture

Questions

1. What aspects of Camp Bow Wow's corporate culture are visible and conscious? What aspects are invisible and unconscious?

2. Why did Camp Bow Wow have to change its culture when it became a national franchise?

3. What impact does Heidi Ganahl's story have on employees at Camp Bow Wow?

ENDNOTES

1. These questions are based on ideas from R. L. Daft and R. M. Lengel, *Fusion Leadership* (San Francisco: Berrett Koehler, 2000), Chapter 4; B. Bass and B. Avolio, *Multifactor Leadership Questionnaire,* 2nd ed. (Menlo Park, CA: Menlo Park, CA: Mind Garden, Inc., 2004); and Karl E. Weick and Kathleen M. Sutcliffe, *Managing the Unexpected: Assuring High Performance in an Age of Complexity* (San Francisco: Jossey-Bass, 2001).

2. Howard Schneider, "University Logos Become Weapons in Debate over Textile Factory Working Conditions," *The Washington Post* (May 27, 2013), http://articles.washingtonpost.com/2013-05-27/business/39558590_1_university-logos-nike-adidas (accessed August 26, 2013); and Steven Greenhouse, "A Factory Defies Stereotypes, But Can It Thrive?" *The New York Times*, July 18, 2010, BU1.

3. This section is based on Richard L. Daft, *Organization Theory and Design*, 10th ed. (Mason, OH: South-Western, 2010), pp. 140–143.

4. L. J. Bourgeois, "Strategy and Environment: A Conceptual Integration," *Academy of Management Review* 5 (1980): 25–39.

5. James Moore, *The Death of Competition: Leadership and Strategy in the Age of Business Ecosystems* (New York: HarperCollins, 1996).

6. David J. Teece, "Dynamic Capabilities: A Guide for Managers," *Ivey Business Journal* (March/April, 2011), www.iveybusinessjournal.com/topics/strategy/dynamic-capabilities-a-guide-for-managers (accessed June 12, 2012).

7. Jorge Cauz, "How I Did It … Encyclopædia Britannica's President on Killing Off a 244-Year-Old Product," *Harvard Business Review* (March 2013): 39–42.

8. Chuck Jones, "Apple vs. Samsung: Who Could Win the Smartphone War?" *Forbes* (August 20, 2013), http://www.forbes.com/sites/chuckjones/2013/08/20/apple-and-samsung-who-could-win-the-smartphone-war/ (accessed August 26, 2013); and Brian X. Chen and Nick Wingfield, "Samsung Introduces New Galaxy Phone," *The New York Times* (March 14, 2013), http://www.nytimes.com/2013/03/15/technology/samsung-introduces-new-galaxy-phone.html?pagewanted=all&_r=0 (accessed August 26, 2013).

9. Geoff Colvin, "Toyota's Comeback Kid," *Fortune* (February 2, 2012): 73.

10. "Downsides of Just-in-Time Inventory," *Bloomberg Businessweek* (March 28–April 3, 2011): 17–18.

11. Peter Valdes-Dapena, "Japan Earthquake Impact Hits U.S. Auto Plants," *CNNMoney* (March 30, 2011), http://money.cnn.com/2011/03/28/autos/japan_earthquake_autos_outlook/index.htm# (accessed June 13, 2012); and Maxwell Murphy, "Reinforcing the Supply Chain," *The Wall Street Journal*, January 11, 2012, B6.

12. Brad Stone, "Costco CEO Craig Jelinek Leads the Cheapest, Happiest Company in the World," *Bloomberg Businessweek* (June 6, 2013), http://www.businessweek.com/articles/2013-06-06/costco-ceo-craig-jelinek-leads-the-cheapest-happiest-company-in-the-world (accessed August 26, 2013); Sharon Edelson, "Costco Keeps Formula as It Expands," *Women's Wear Daily*, Issue 19 (January 30, 2012):

1; Andria Cheng, "Costco Cracks Taiwan Market," *The Wall Street Journal*, April 2, 2010, B5; and *Costco Wholesale Annual Report 2012,* Costco Wholesale Corporation Investor Relations Web site, http://phx.corporate-ir.net/phoenix.zhtml?c=83830&p=irol-reportsannual (accessed August 26, 2013).

13. Thomas L. Friedman, *The World Is Flat: A Brief History of the Twenty-First Century* (New York: Farrar, Straus, and Giroux, 2005), pp. 3–23.

14. Liz Alderman, "In Europe, Starbucks Adjusts to a Café Culture," *The New York Times,* March 30, 2012.

15. Daisuke Wakabayashi, "The Point-and-Shoot Camera Faces Its Existential Moment," *The Wall Street Journal*, July 30, 2013, http://online.wsj.com/article/SB10001424127887324251504578580263719432252.html (accessed August 26, 2013).

16. "Naming the Next Generation—Speaker Q & A; Tyrus Cukavac, *YPulse* (May 28, 2013), http://www.ypulse.com/post/view/naming-the-next-generation-qa-tyrus-cukavac (accessed August 27, 2013); Roman Friedrich, Michael Peterson, and Alex Koster, "The Rise of Generation C," *Strategy + Business*, Issue 62 (Spring 2011), www.strategy-business.com/article/11110?gko=64e54 (accessed June 25, 2012); and Max Mihelich, "Another Generation Rises: Looking beyond the Millennials," *Workforce* (April 12, 2013), http://www.workforce.com/articles/108-another-generation-rises-looking-beyond-the-millennials (accessed August 22, 2013).

17. *Wall Street Journal* poll, reported in Colleen McCain Nelson, "Poll: Most Women See Bias in the Workplace," *The Wall Street Journal* (April 12, 2013), A4.

18. Peyton M. Craighill and Scott Clement, "Legalize It! The Stark Generational Divide on Pot, Gay Marriage, and Illegal Immigration," *The Washington Post* (November 14, 2012), http://www.washingtonpost.com/blogs/the-fix/wp/2012/11/14/stark-generational-divide-on-gay-marriage-immigration-and-yes-marijuana/ (accessed August 27, 2013).

19. Dennis Cauchon and Paul Overberg, "Census Data Shows Minorities Now a Majority of U.S. Births," *USA Today* (May 17, 2012), www.usatoday.com/news/nation/story/2012-05-17/minority-births-census/55029100/1 (accessed June 12, 2012).

20. Matthias Rieker, "Uneven Economy Hits Banks," *The Wall Street Journal Online* (January 25, 2012), http://online.wsj.com/article/SB10001424052970203718504577180672516174122.html (accessed June 22, 2012).

21. Richard Wolf, Brad Heath, and Chuck Raasch, "How Health Care Law Survived, and What's Next," *USA Today* (June 29, 2012), http://www.usatoday.com/NEWS/usaedition/2012-06-29-still2_CV_U.htm (accessed August 21, 2012).

22. Somini Sengupta, "Facebook Builds Network of Friends in Washington," *The New York Times* (May 18, 2012), www.nytimes.com/2012/05/19/technology/facebook-builds-network-of-friends-in-washington.html?_r=1&emc=eta1 (accessed June 12, 2012).

23. Dror Etzion, "Research on Organizations and the Natural Environment," *Journal of Management* 33 (August 2007): 637–654.

24. Elizabeth Weise and Doyle Rice, "Even the 'Best' Outcome Won't Be Good; The Oil Spill's Potential Toll Is Becoming Clear," *USA Today*, June 9, 2010.

25. Robert B. Duncan, "Characteristics of Organizational Environment and Perceived Environmental Uncertainty," *Administrative Science Quarterly* 17 (1972): 313–327; and Daft, *Organization Theory and Design*, pp. 144–148.

26. Nick Wingfield, "Nintendo Confronts a Changed Video Game World," *The New York Times* (November 24, 2012), http://www.nytimes.com/2012/11/25/technology/nintendos-wii-u-takes-aim-at-a-changed-video-game-world.html?pagewanted=all&_r=0 (accessed November 25, 2012).

27. Bruce E. Perrott, "Strategic Issue Management as Change Catalyst," *Strategy & Leadership* 39, no. 5 (2011): 20–29.

28. Patricia M. Buhler, "Business Intelligence: An Opportunity for Competitive Advantage," *Supervision* 74, no. 3 (March 2013): 8–11; David B. Jemison, "The Importance of Boundary Spanning Roles in Strategic Decision-Making," *Journal of Management Studies* 21 (1984): 131–152; and Marc J. Dollinger, "Environmental Boundary Spanning and Information Processing Effects on Organizational Performance," *Academy of Management Journal* 27 (1984): 351–368.

29. Darrell K. Rigby, *Management Tools 2013: An Executive's Guide* (Bain & Company 2013), http://www.bain.com/Images/MANAGEMENT_TOOLS_2013_An_Executives_guide.pdf (accessed August 27, 2013); Margaret Rouse, "Big Data Analytics," *TechTarget.com* (January 10, 2012), http://searchbusinessanalytics.techtarget.com/definition/big-data-analytics (accessed August 27, 2013); and David Kiron, Renee Boucher Ferguson, and Pamela Kirk Prentice, "From Value to Vision: Reimagining the Possible with Data Analytics," *MIT Sloan Management Review Special Report* (March 5, 2013), http://sloanreview.mit.edu/reports/analytics-innovation/ (accessed August 27, 2013).

30. R. Bean and D. Kiron, "Organizational Alignment Is Key to Big Data Success," *MIT Sloan Management Review* (January 28, 2013), http://sloanreview.mit.edu/article/organizational-alignment-is-key-to-big-data-success/ (accessed August 27, 2013).

31. Michael Lewis, *Moneyball: The Art of Winning an Unfair Game* (New York: W.W. Norton, 2003).

32. Example described in Andrew McAfee and Erik Brynjolfsson, "Big Data: The Management Revolution," *Harvard Business Review* (October 2012): 61–68.

33. Examples reported in Thomas H. Davenport and Jeanne G. Harris, *Competing on Analytics: The New Science of Winning* (Boston: Harvard Business School Press, 2007); and Kiron et al., "From Value to Vision: Reimagining the Possible."

34. Alexander Garrett, "Crash Course in Competitive Intelligence," *Management Today* (May 1, 2011): 18.

35. Jemison, "The Importance of Boundary Spanning Roles in Strategic Decision-Making" and Dollinger, "Environmental Boundary Spanning and Information Processing Effects on Organizational Performance."

36. Sean Lux, T. Russell Crook, and Terry Leap, "Corporate Political Activity: The Good, the Bad, and the Ugly," *Business Horizons* 55, no. 3 (May–June 2012): 307–312.

37. Lisa Wirthman, "Online Sales Tax: What It Could Mean for Entrepreneurs and Small Biz," *Forbes* (August 6, 2013), http://www.forbes.com/sites/northwesternmutual/2013/08/06/online-sales-tax-what-it-could-mean-for-entrepreneurs-and-small-biz-2/print/ (accessed August 27, 2013); Sarah Hurtubise, "Colorado Court Ruling Reignites Online Sales Tax Debate," *The Daily Caller* (August 26, 2013), http://dailycaller.com/2013/08/26/colorado-court-ruling-reignites-online-sales-tax-debate/ (accessed August 27, 2013); and Amrita Jayakumar, "States, Congress Rallying for an e-Sales Tax," *The Washington Post* (July 8, 2012), http://articles.washingtonpost.com/2012-07-08/business/35487298_1_traditional-retailers-sales-tax-online-retailers (accessed August 27, 2013).

38. Jonathan Hughes and Jeff Weiss, "Simple Rules for Making Alliances Work," *Harvard Business Review* (November 2007): 122–131; Howard Muson, "Friend? Foe? Both? The Confusing World of Corporate Alliances," *Across the Board* (March–April 2002): 19–25; and Devi R. Gnyawali and Ravindranath Madhavan, "Cooperative Networks and Competitive Dynamics: A Structural Embeddedness Perspective," *Academy of Management Review* 26, no. 3 (2001): 431–445.

39. Leo Wilkinson, "GM and Honda to Collaborate on Fuel-Cell Technology," *The Telegraph* (July 2, 2013), http://www.telegraph.co.uk/motoring/green-motoring/10155793/GM-and-Honda-to-collaborate-on-fuel-cell-technology.html (accessed August 27, 2013); Katie Merx, "Automakers Interconnected Around World," *Edmonton Journal* April 6, 2007, H14; and Keith Bradsher, "Ford Agrees to Sell Volvo to a Fast-Rising Chinese Company," *The New York Times Online* (March 28, 2010), www.nytimes.com/2010/03/29/business/global/29auto.html (accessed August 1, 2011).

40. Thomas Petzinger, Jr., *The New Pioneers: The Men and Women Who Are Transforming the Workplace and Marketplace* (New York: Simon & Schuster, 1999), pp. 53–54.

41. Stephan M. Wagner and Roman Boutellier, "Capabilities for Managing a Portfolio of Supplier Relationships," *Business Horizons* (November–December 2002): 79–88; Peter Smith Ring and Andrew H. Van de Ven, "Developmental Processes of Corporate Interorganizational Relationships," *Academy of Management Review* 19 (1994): 90–118; Myron Magnet, "The New Golden Rule of Business," *Fortune* (February 21, 1994): 60–64; and Peter Grittner, "Four Elements of Successful Sourcing Strategies," *Management Review* (October 1996): 41–45.

42. Richard L. Daft, "After the Deal: The Art of Fusing Diverse Corporate Cultures into One," paper presented at the Conference on International Corporate Restructuring, Institute of Business Research and Education, Korea University, Seoul, Korea (June 16, 1998).

43. Marsha Mercer, "Merger Mania," *AARP Bulletin* (June 2013): 10–14.

44. Andrew Martin, "Car Sharing Catches on as Zipcar Sells to Avis," *The New York Times* (January 2, 2013).

45. Peter Sanders, "Sikorsky's Business Heads Up," *The Wall Street Journal Online* (April 19, 2010), http://online.wsj.com/article/SB10001424052702304180804575188821353177134.html (accessed April 19, 2010).

46. Yoash Wiener, "Forms of Value Systems: A Focus on Organizational Effectiveness and Culture Change and Maintenance," *Academy of Management Review* 13 (1988): 534–545; V. Lynne Meek, "Organizational Culture: Origins and Weaknesses," *Organization Studies* 9 (1988): 453–473; John J. Sherwood, "Creating Work Cultures with Competitive Advantage," *Organizational Dynamics* (Winter 1988): 5–27; and Andrew D. Brown and Ken Starkey, "The Effect of Organizational Culture on Communication and Information," *Journal of Management Studies* 31, no. 6 (November 1994): 807–828.

47. Joanne Martin, *Organizational Culture: Mapping the Terrain* (Thousand Oaks, CA: Sage Publications, 2002); Ralph H. Kilmann, Mary J. Saxton, and Roy Serpa, "Issues in Understanding and Changing Culture," *California Management Review* 28 (Winter 1986): 87–94; and Linda Smircich, "Concepts of Culture and Organizational Analysis," *Administrative Science Quarterly* 28 (1983): 339–358.

48. David Carr, "Troubles That Money Can't Dispel," *The New York Times Online* (July 17, 2011), www.nytimes.com/2011/07/18/business/media/for-news-corporation-troubles-that-money-cant-dispel.html?pagewanted=all (accessed June 13, 2012).

49. John F. Burns and Jeremy W. Peters, "Two Top Deputies Resign as Crisis Isolates Murdoch," *The New York Times Online* (July 16, 2011), www.hongkong-mart.com/forum/viewtopic.php?f=2&t=367 (accessed June 13, 2012).

50. Carr, "Troubles That Money Can't Dispel."

51. Based on Edgar H. Schein, *Organizational Culture and Leadership*, 2nd ed. (San Francisco: Jossey-Bass, 1992): pp. 3–27.

52. "Core Value: Teamwork," segment in Leigh Buchanan, "2011 Top Small Company Workplaces: Core Values," *Inc.* (June 2011): 60–74; "Our Story," Menlo Innovations Web site, http://www.menloinnovations.com/our-story/history and http://www.menloinnovations.com/our-story/culture (accessed September 12, 2011); and Leigh Buchanan, "Taking Teamwork to the Extreme" in the "Culture" segment of "The Audacious 25: Meet the Scrappiest, Smartest, Most Disruptive Companies of the Year," *Inc.* (May 2013): 54–76 (Menlo profile is on page 76).

53. Michael G. Pratt and Anat Rafaeli, "Symbols as a Language of Organizational Relationships," *Research in Organizational Behavior* 23 (2001): 93–132.

54. Mindy Grossman, "HSN's CEO on Fixing the Shopping Network's Culture," *Harvard Business Review* (December 2011): 43–46.

55. Chip Jarnagin and John W. Slocum, Jr., "Creating Corporate Cultures through Mythopoetic Leadership," *Organizational Dynamics* 36, no. 3 (2007): 288–302.

56. Robert E. Quinn and Gretchen M. Spreitzer, "The Road to Empowerment: Seven Questions Every Leader Should Consider," *Organizational Dynamics* (Autumn 1997): 37–49.

57. Yukari Iwatani Kane and Jessica E. Vascellaro, "Successor Faces Tough Job at Apple," *The Wall Street Journal Online* (August 26, 2011), http://allthingsd.com/20110826/successor-faces-tough-job-at-apple/ (accessed June 13, 2012).

58. Based on an interview with Tim Cook conducted by *The Wall Street Journal*'s Walt Mossberg and Kara Swisher (June 4, 2012), http://online.wsj.com/article/SB10001424052702303552104577436952829794614.html?KEYWORDS=steve+jobs+apple+culture (accessed June 16, 2012).

59. Arthur Yeung, "Setting People up for Success: How the Portman Ritz-Carlton Hotel Gets the Best from Its People," *Human Resource Management* 45, no. 2 (Summer 2006): 267–275.

60. Leigh Buchanan, "Reelect the Boss! Or Not," in the "Culture" segment of "The Audacious 25: Meet the Scrappiest, Smartest, Most Disruptive Companies of the Year," *Inc.* (May 2013): 54–76 (DreamHost profile is on page 76).

61. Harrison M. Trice and Janice M. Beyer, "Studying Organizational Cultures Through Rites and Ceremonials," *Academy of Management Review* 9 (1984): 653–669.

62. PRWeb, "Southwest Airlines Launches New NBA-Themed Specialty Airplane; Slam Dunk One Marks First Southwest Specialty Plane with a Partner in 17 Years," November 3, 2005, www.prweb.com/releases/2005/11/prweb306461.php (accessed February 7, 2008).

63. Jennifer A. Chatman and Karen A. Jehn, "Assessing the Relationship Between Industry Characteristics and Organizational Culture: How Different Can You Be?" *Academy of Management Journal* 37, no. 3 (1994): 522–553.

64. This discussion is based on Paul McDonald and Jeffrey Gandz, "Getting Value from Shared Values," *Organizational Dynamics* 21, no. 3 (Winter 1992): 64–76; and Daniel R. Denison and Aneil K. Mishra, "Toward a Theory of Organizational Culture and Effectiveness," *Organization Science* 6, no. 2 (March–April 1995): 204–223.

65. Aaron Levie, as told to Memon Yaqub, "I'm Obsessed with Speed," *Inc.* (November 2012): 100–103.

66. Robert Hooijberg and Frank Petrock, "On Cultural Change: Using the Competing Values Framework to Help Leaders Execute a Transformational Strategy," *Human Resource Management* 32, no. 1 (1993): 29–50.

67. Dean Foust, "Where Headhunters Fear to Tread," *BusinessWeek* (September 4, 2009): 42–44.

68. Based on *Fortune's* survey results, "100 Best Companies to Work For," http://money.cnn.com/magazines/fortune/best-companies/2013/list/ (accessed August 28, 2013); and Douglas A. Ready and Emily Truelove, "The Power of Collective Ambition," *Harvard Business Review* (December 2011): 94–102.

69. Rekha Balu, "Pacific Edge Projects Itself," *Fast Company* (October 2000): 371–381.

70. Jeffrey Pfeffer, *The Human Equation: Building Profits by Putting People First* (Boston: Harvard Business School Press, 1998).

71. Sanam Islam, "Execs See Link to Bottom Line; Gap Is Closing; More Firms Keen to Be Seen as Best Corporate Culture," *National Post* (November 19, 2008): FP.16; Jeremy Kahn, "What Makes a Company Great?" *Fortune* (October 26, 1998): 218; James C. Collins and Jerry I. Porras, *Built to Last: Successful Habits of Visionary Companies* (New York: HarperBusiness, 1994); and James C. Collins, "Change Is Good—But First Know What Should Never Change," *Fortune* (May 29, 1995): 141.

72. Islam, "Execs See Link to Bottom Line."

73. Based on information in Alison Beard and Richard Hornik, "It's Hard to Be Good," *Harvard Business Review* (November 2011): 88–96.

74. This section is based on Jeff Rosenthal and Mary Ann Masarech, "High-Performance Cultures: How Values Can Drive Business Results," *Journal of Organizational Excellence* (Spring 2003): 3–18.

75. Nelson D. Schwartz, "One Brick at a Time," *Fortune* (June 12, 2006): 45–46; and Nelson D. Schwartz, "Lego's Rebuilds Legacy," *International Herald Tribune* (September 5, 2009).

76. Evelyn M. Ruslie, "Zynga's Tough Culture Risks a Talent Drain," *The New York Times Online* (November 27, 2011), http://dealbook.nytimes.com/2011/11/27/zyngas-tough-culture-risks-a-talent-drain/ (accessed June 18, 2012).

77. This example is based on Dave Ulrich, Steve Kerr, and Ron Ashkenas, *The GE Work-Out* (New York: McGraw-Hill, 2002), pp. 238–230.

78. From Ulrich, Kerr, and Ashkenas, "GE Values," in *The GE Work-Out*, Figure 11-2.

79. Rosenthal and Masarech, "High-Performance Cultures."

80. John P. Kotter and James L. Heskett, *Corporate Culture and Performance* (New York: The Free Press, 1992); Eric Flamholtz and Rangapriya Kannan Narasimhan, "Differential Impact of Cultural Elements on Financial Performance," *European Management Journal* 23, no. 1

(2005): 50–64. Also see J. M. Kouzes and B. Z. Posner, *The Leadership Challenge: How to Keep Getting Extraordinary Things Done in Organizations,* 3d ed. (San Francisco: Jossey-Bass, 2002).

81. Susanne Biro, "Change the Culture," *Leadership Excellence* (April 2013): 4.

82. Rosenthal and Masarech, "High-Performance Cultures"; Patrick Lencioni, "Make Your Values Mean Something," *Harvard Business Review* (July 2002): 113–117; and Thomas J. Peters and Robert H. Waterman, Jr., *In Search of Excellence* (New York: Warner, 1988).

83. Biro, "Change the Culture"; and Linda Tischler, "Kenny Moore Held a Funeral and Everyone Came," *Fast Company* (February 2004), http://www.fastcompany.com/48491/kenny-moore-held-funeral-and-everyone-came (accessed August 28, 2013).

84. Jarnagin and Slocum, "Creating Corporate Cultures Through Mythopoetic Leadership."

85. Based on S. J. Ashford et al., "Out on a Limb: The Role of Context and Impression Management in Issue Selling," *Administrative Science Quarterly* 43 (1998): 23–57; and E. W. Morrison and C. C. Phelps, "Taking Charge at Work: Extrarole Efforts to Initiate Workplace Change," *Academy of Management Journal* 42 (1999): 403–419.

86. Adapted from Kent Weber, "Gold Mine or Fool's Gold?" *Business Ethics* (January–February 2001): 18.

CHAPTER
3

Managing in a **Global** Environment

LEARNING OUTCOMES

After studying this chapter, you should be able to:

3.1 Define globalization and explain how it is creating a borderless world for today's managers.

3.2 Describe a global mind-set and why it has become imperative for companies operating internationally.

3.3 Discuss how the international landscape is changing, including the growing power of China, India, and Brazil.

3.4 Describe the characteristics of a multinational corporation.

3.5 Explain the bottom of the pyramid concept.

3.6 Define outsourcing and the three common market entry strategies: exporting, licensing, and direct investing.

3.7 Indicate how dissimilarities in the economic, sociocultural, and legal-political environments throughout the world can affect business operations.

3.8 Explain why it is important for managers to develop their cultural intelligence.

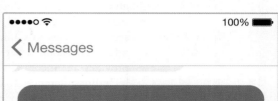

< Messages

R U Ready 2 B a Manager?

Delivered

Before reading this chapter, please circle either "Mostly True" or "Mostly False" for each of the five questions below.

1 I have an ability to understand people from other cultures and to appreciate the differences.

Mostly True	Mostly False

[page 106]

2 I'm good at outsourcing (getting my little sister to do my chores, for example) and bartering, both skills important in international business.

Mostly True	Mostly False

[page 117]

3 I work well individually and as part of a group.

Mostly True	Mostly False

[page 125]

4 When I am solving problems or developing plans, I can think both in short-term and long-term goals.

Mostly True	Mostly False

[page 126]

5 I can easily move within other cultures and adapt to different behavioral norms.

Mostly True	Mostly False

[page 127]

Apple executives recently caved in and did something they initially resisted—they offered an apology to the Chinese government and consumers. Apple has experienced tremendous growth in China, which accounts for a growing percentage of the company's sales and profits, but the company has also been the target of increasing criticism from Chinese government-run media and consumer-rights groups. When a Chinese prime-time television broadcast accused Apple of fudging warranty periods and adopting weaker customer service policies in China, Apple's managers issued a statement saying that the company offers comparable after-sales practices in China as in the rest of the world and that Apple provides an "incomparable user experience." The statement provoked a blistering attack, including references to Apple's "arrogance" and hollow promises. Apple managers realized a little late that what Chinese officials and customers wanted was an apology.

The company said that it would change its customer service policies, replacing defective iPhones with entirely new ones rather than repairing them or replacing components and offering a one-year warranty on any phone that had been replaced. In contrast, the company gives only a 90-day warranty in the United States on a repaired or replaced phone. The apology "should have come earlier," said the official Xinhua news agency, "but it is not too late for [Apple] to rebuild Chinese consumers' trust."[1]

Apple managers certainly hope not. China is the company's second-largest market, after the United States. Marketing and selling goods internationally is a challenge, and managers in most companies believe that winning in China is a new imperative. The country is already a crucial market for many industries, and the potential for growth is huge. In 2012, China accounted for 30 percent of all vehicles sold by General Motors (GM) and 28 percent of those sold by Volkswagen.[2] Brazil, Russia, India, and China (often referred to as BRIC), as well as other emerging economies, are becoming major markets for the products and services of North American firms. At the same time, these regions are growing rapidly as providers of both products and services to the United States, Canada, Europe, and other developed nations. Finding managers with the mind-set needed to succeed in these countries is proving difficult for multinational firms. China, India, and Brazil are expected to see the greatest shortage of executive talent for the next few years.[3]

Every manager today needs to think globally because the whole world is a source of business threats and opportunities. Even managers who spend their entire careers working in their hometowns have to be aware of the international environment and probably interact with people from other cultures. The international dimension is an increasingly important part of the external environment, discussed in Chapter 2. This chapter introduces basic concepts about the global environment and international management. First, we provide an overview of today's borderless world and the global mind-set needed to be effective. Next, we look more closely at the changing international landscape and the growing importance of China, India, and Brazil. Then the chapter discusses multinational corporations (MNCs), considers the globalization backlash, and describes the "bottom of the pyramid (BOP)" concept. We then touch on various strategies and techniques for entering the global arena and take a look at the economic, legal-political, and sociocultural challenges that companies encounter within the global business environment. The chapter also describes how regional trade agreements are reshaping the international business landscape.

3.1 A Borderless World

The reality facing most managers is that isolation from international forces is no longer possible. Organizations in all fields are being reordered around the goal of addressing needs and desires that transcend national boundaries. Consider that the Federal Bureau of Investigation (FBI) now ranks international cybercrime as one of its top

NEW MANAGER Self-Test

Are You Ready to Work Internationally?[4]

Instructions: Are you ready to negotiate a sales contract with someone from another country? Companies, large and small, deal on a global basis. To what extent are you guilty of the behaviors listed here? Please answer each item as "Mostly True" or "Mostly False" for you.

Are You Typically:	*Mostly True*	*Mostly False*
1. Impatient? Do you have a short attention span? Do you want to keep moving to the next topic?	_____	_____
2. A poor listener? Are you uncomfortable with silence? Does your mind think about what you want to say next?	_____	_____
3. Argumentative? Do you enjoy arguing for its own sake?	_____	_____
4. Unfamiliar with cultural specifics in other countries? Do you have limited experience in other countries?	_____	_____
5. Short-term-oriented? Do you place more emphasis on the short term than on the long term in your thinking and planning?	_____	_____
6. "All business"? Do you think that it is a waste of time getting to know someone personally before discussing business?	_____	_____
7. Legalistic to win your point? Do you hold others to an agreement regardless of changing circumstances?	_____	_____
8. Thinking "win/lose" when negotiating? Do you usually try to win a negotiation at the other's expense?	_____	_____

Scoring and Interpretation: American managers often display cross-cultural ignorance during business negotiations compared to their counterparts in other countries. American habits can be disturbing, such as emphasizing areas of disagreement over agreement, spending little time understanding the views and interests of the other side, and adopting an adversarial attitude. Americans often like to leave a negotiation thinking that they won, which can be embarrassing to the other side. For this quiz, a low score shows better international presence. If you answered "Mostly True" to three or fewer questions, then consider yourself ready to assist with an international negotiation. If you scored six or more "Mostly True" responses, you should learn more about other national cultures before participating in international business deals. Try to develop a greater focus on other people's needs and an appreciation for different viewpoints. Be open to compromise and develop empathy for people who are different from you.

priorities because electronic boundaries between countries are virtually nonexistent.[5] "The whole boundary mindset has been obliterated," says John Hering, the executive chairman of Lookout, Inc., a mobile security company with customers in 170 countries using 400 mobile networks around the world. "For many people, this is the only computer they have," he says. "The thought of something bad happening to your phone is untenable."[6]

3.1a Globalization

Business, just like crime, has become a unified, global field. Events, ideas, and trends that influence organizations in one country are likely to influence them in other countries as well. This chapter's "Director's Toolkit" describes how experiments with bosslessness are occurring in companies in multiple countries.

Globalization refers to the extent to which trade and investments, information, social and cultural ideas, and political cooperation flow between countries. One result is that countries, businesses, and people become increasingly interdependent. Japan's Nissan automaker has headquarters in Yokohama, but the chief executive of its luxury Infiniti division has his

Director's Toolkit

Bosslessness Emerges around the Globe

Experimenting with less hierarchy and no bosses is not limited to the United States. Different national cultures create different challenges, but a bossless organization can succeed anywhere.

- **The organization must have a strong values-driven culture.** Semco S.A. is a 3,000-employee industrial equipment manufacturer in São Paulo, Brazil. Ricardo Semler decided to establish a culture built on extreme employee participation and involvement. Employees run the show. Semco has no official structure, no human resources or IT department, not even a fixed CEO (the job rotates). Salaries are public knowledge. Employees elect managers by vote. No promotion is given without letting coworkers have their say. Subordinates anonymously evaluate managers and can vote them out of office. There is no dress code. Employees can change work areas anytime according to their tastes and desires.

- **Bossless environments are especially effective where creativity is essential.** Yoplait, jointly owned by French dairy cooperative Sodiaal and U.S.-based General Mills, has franchises all over the world and a history of relying on self-managing teams to create and launch new flavors and products. In the United States, a group of employees called the Culinary Community of Practice translates emerging ethnic tastes and cuisines into innovative foods made available in stores.

- **Bossless environments increase customer satisfaction.** When CEO Jean-François Zobrist took over FAVI, a 600-person French company that designs and manufactures automotive components, he eliminated the traditional hierarchy. There is no personnel department, no middle management, no time clocks, no employee handbooks. "I told them, 'tomorrow when you come to work, you do not work for me or for a boss. You work for your customer. I don't pay you. They do.'" FAVI hasn't been late with a customer order in 10 years. In the United States, Southwest Airlines allows baggage clerks the freedom to decide how to solve a customer's complaint on the spot, without having to say, "Wait while I consult my boss."

- **Bossless designs may reflect national culture.** Mondragon Corporation in Spain uses a cooperative form of bosslessness. Made up as a collective of many smaller enterprises, the 85,000 employees actually own and direct their respective businesses. Workers choose a managing director and retain power to make all decisions about what to produce and what to do with profits. Top members can earn no more than 6.5 times the lowest-paid member, compared to about 350 times in large U.S. corporations. When times are hard, top people at Mondragon also take the biggest reductions in pay.

SOURCES: Fiona Smith, "Could Your Office Go Lord of the Flies?" *Business Review Weekly*, April 10, 2013, http://www.brw.com.au/p/blogs/fiona_smith/could_your_office_go_lord_of_the_N7PteN1JpXzO8ithUQAjQK (accessed April 10, 2013); "Going Boss-free: Utopia or 'Lord of the Flies'?" Knowledge@Wharton, August 1 2012, http://knowledge.wharton.upenn.edu/article/going-boss-free-utopia-or-lord-of-the-flies/ (accessed September 30, 2013); Peter A. Maresco and Christopher C. York, "Ricardo Semler: Creating Organizational Change Through Employee-Empowered Leadership," Sacred Heart University, http://www.newunionism.net/library/casestudies/SEMCO%20-%20Employee-Powered%20Leadership%20-%20Brazil%20-%202005.pdf (accessed September 30, 2013); Polly LaBarre, "What Does Fulfillment at Work Really Look Like?" *Fortune*, May 1, 2012, http://management.fortune.cnn.com/2012/05/01/happiness-at-work-fulfillment/ (accessed September 30, 2013); Richard Wolff, "Yes, There Is an Alternative to Capitalism: Mondragon Shows the Way," *The Guardian*, June 24, 2012, http://www.theguardian.com/commentisfree/2012/jun/24/alternative-capitalism-mondragon; and Giles Tremlett, "Mondragon: Spain's Giant Cooperative Where Times Are Hard but Few Go Bust," *The Guardian*, March 7, 2013, http://www.theguardian.com/world/2013/mar/07/mondragon-spains-giant-cooperative (accessed September 30, 2013).

office in Hong Kong. The skin, cosmetics, and personal care business of Procter & Gamble (P&G) is based in Singapore.[7] The United States is the largest market for India-based Tata Consultancy Services (TCS) and other India information technology (IT) firms, while the U.S. firm IBM gets most of its tech services revenue from overseas, with sales in India growing 41 percent in one recent quarter.[8] And while Japan's Honda gets 65 percent of the parts for its Accord model from the United States or Canada and assembles the vehicle in Ohio, U.S.-based GM makes the Chevrolet HHR in Mexico with parts that come from all over the world.[9]

Globalization has been on the rise since the 1970s, and most industrialized nations show a high degree of globalization today.[10] The KOF Swiss Economic Institute measures economic, political, and social aspects of globalization and ranks countries on a globalization index. Not surprisingly, the pace of economic globalization slowed in the most recent survey, reflecting the impact of the global financial and economic crisis, but social and political globalization continued its upward trend. Exhibit 3.1 shows how selected countries ranked on the 2013 KOF Index of Globalization (based on the year 2010) compared to their degree of globalization in the mid-1970s. Note that the United States is the least-globalized of the countries shown in the exhibit. Among the 187 countries on the KOF Index, the United States ranks number 34, down from number 27 on the 2011 index. The 10 most globalized countries, according to the KOF Index, are Belgium, Ireland, the Netherlands, Austria, Singapore, Sweden, Denmark, Portugal, Hungary, and Switzerland.[11]

EXHIBIT 3.1 Ranking of Six Countries on the Globalization Index

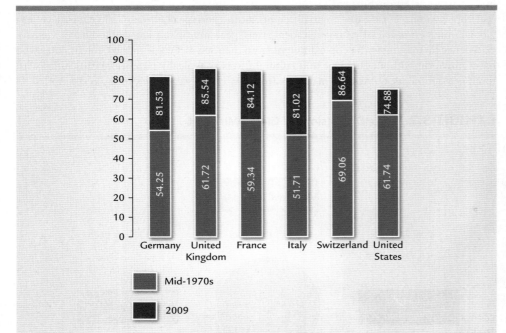

SOURCE: Based on "2013 KOF Index of Globalization," KOF Swiss Economic Institute, http://globalization.kof.ethz.ch/media/filer_public/2013/03/25/rankings_2013.pdf (accessed August 29, 2013); and "KOF Index of Globalization 2013," press release (March 2013).

3.1b Developing a Global Mind-Set

Succeeding on a global level requires more than a desire to go global and a new set of skills and techniques; it requires that managers and organizations develop a *global mind-set*. Managers who can help their companies develop a global perspective, such as Carlos Ghosn, the Brazilian-Lebanese-French CEO of Nissan, or Medtronic CEO Omar Ishrak, a Bangladesh native who was educated in the United Kingdom and worked in the United States for nearly two decades, are in high demand.[12] As more managers find themselves working in foreign countries or working with foreign firms within their own country, they need a mind-set that enables them to navigate through ambiguities and complexities that far exceed anything they encounter within their traditional management responsibilities.[13] A **global mind-set** can be defined as the ability of managers to appreciate and influence individuals, groups, organizations, and systems that represent different social, cultural, political, institutional, intellectual, and psychological characteristics.[14]

A manager with a global mind-set can perceive and respond to many different perspectives at the same time rather than being stuck in a domestic mind-set that sees everything from one's own cultural perspective. Reliance Industries, the largest private-sector company in India, specifically lists "global mind-set" as one of the core competencies for its managers.[15] As illustrated in Exhibit 3.2, a global mind-set requires skills, understanding, and competencies in three dimensions. The *cognitive dimension* means knowing about the global environment and global business, mentally understanding how cultures differ, and having the ability to interpret complex global changes. The *psychological dimension* is the emotional and affective aspect. This includes a liking for diverse ways of thinking and acting, a willingness to take risks, and the energy and self-confidence to deal with the unpredictable and uncertain. The *social dimension* concerns the ability to behave in ways that build trusting relationships with people who are different from oneself.[16]

People who have had exposure to different cultures and speak different languages develop a global mind-set more easily. Global leaders often speak multiple languages and have extensive experience interacting with people different from themselves. People in the United States who have grown up without language and cultural diversity typically have more difficulties with foreign assignments, but willing managers from any country can cultivate a global mind-set.

EXHIBIT 3.2 Three Dimensions of Global Mind-set

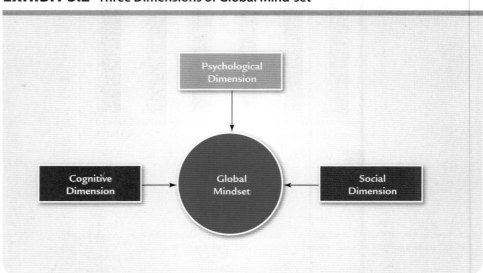

SOURCE: Based on Mansour Javidan and Jennie L. Walker, "A Whole New Global Mindset for Leadership," *People & Strategy* 35, no. 2 (2012): 36–41.

How do people expand their global mind-set? Managers expand globally in two ways—by both thinking and doing.[17] Learning by thinking requires a genuine curiosity about other people and cultures, an interest in and study of world affairs and international business, and the ability to open your mind and appreciate different viewpoints. Learning by doing means cultivating relationships with people across cultural and national boundaries. The rise of social media has opened new opportunities for students as well as managers to create networks of relationships that cross cultural divides. In addition, international travel, foreign study, and learning a foreign language are key activities for developing a global mind-set. For example, Lalit Ahuja, who helped U.S. retailer Target open a second headquarters in India, grew up in that country but traveled to the United States to study and learn about American culture. Alan Boechkmann grew up in the United States but eagerly took overseas job assignments in South Africa and Venezuela.[18] The key is that he immersed himself in those different environments. In the past, many managers who were sent on overseas assignments lived an insular lifestyle that kept them from truly becoming immersed in the foreign culture. "You can lead a true-blue German lifestyle in China," says Siegfried Russwurm, former head of human resources at Siemens (now running the company's industrial sector). "You can live in a gated community with German neighbors. They will tell you where you can find a German baker and butcher."[19] Today, though, the goal for managers who want to succeed is to globalize their thinking.

TAKE Action!

Go to the "Group Learning" on page 135, which pertains to exposure to different cultures and ideas.

"Being outside the United States makes you smarter about global issues. It lets you see the world through a different lens."

—John Rice, vice chairman of General Electric (GE), and president and CEO of Global Growth and Operations

REMEMBER THIS

- Today's companies and managers operate in a borderless world that provides both risks and opportunities.
- **Globalization** refers to the extent to which trade and investments, information, ideas, and political cooperation flow between countries.
- The most globalized countries, according to one ranking, are Belgium, Ireland, the Netherlands, Austria, and Singapore.

- To succeed on a global level requires managers at all levels to have a **global mind-set**, which is the ability to appreciate and influence individuals, groups, organizations, and systems that represent different social, cultural, political, institutional, intellectual, and psychological characteristics.

3.2 The Changing International Landscape

Many companies today are going straight to China or India as a first step into international business. China and India have been the world's fastest-growing economies in recent years. In addition, Brazil is coming on strong as a major player in the international business landscape.

3.2a China, Inc.

For the past several years, foreign companies have invested more in business in China than they spent anywhere else in the world. A market that was of little interest a decade ago has become the one place that nearly every manager is thinking about. China is German car maker BMW's biggest market for its largest and most profitable sedans.[20] That might be one reason Alay Mulally, CEO of U.S.-based Ford Motor Company, spends about a third of his time on matters related to China. Ford was late getting into China and in 2013 had only about 3 percent of the Chinese auto market. Mulally plans to build five additional plants in that country, double the number of dealerships, bring 15 new vehicles to China, and launch the Lincoln brand there in 2014. "Clearly this is going to continue to be the highest rate [of] growth for us," Mulally said. The shift toward putting China at the center of decision making is reflected in a change in meeting times at the U.S. headquarters. "We get up really early, we stay really late," said Mark Fields, Ford's chief operating officer (COO), referring to the practice of holding meetings early in the morning or late in the evening to accommodate managers in China, who are 12 hours ahead.[21]

China, with the fastest-growing middle class in history, is the largest or second-largest market for a variety of products and services, including mobile phones, automobiles, consumer electronics, luxury goods, and Internet use.[22] Coca-Cola's CEO Muhtar Kent predicts that the China division will double its sales of Coke products, helping meet Kent's goal of doubling the company's overall business by 2020. "China will be Coke's largest market," Kent promises. "I can't give you a time, but it will happen."[23]

Yet, as illustrated by the chapter-opening example, doing business in China has never been smooth, and it appears to be getting even tougher. New regulations and government policies are making life hard for foreign companies in all industries. The Coca-Cola Company is training managers at its 40 bottling plants so they can double as public relations ambassadors. Managers in China are encouraged to build relationships with local food-safety regulators and other local officials. Walmart is adding social media staff to spot brewing online controversies in its China business.[24] For Internet companies such as Facebook, Twitter, eBay, and Google, China has sometimes seemed like more a source of trouble and frustration than of new customers.[25] Google closed its Chinese site, Google.cn, in early 2010 because of government restrictions and censorship, although the company later renewed its license to provide limited services in China. Some multinational firms doing business with Chinese organizations, particularly big state-owned companies, have also had problems getting payments on their contracts. "A contract is not an unchangeable bible for Chinese companies,"

When Bentonville Met Beijing

Establishing his business in Bentonville, Arkansas, in 1962, all-American entrepreneur Sam Walton could not have imagined an eventual expansion to over 350 stores and 20,000 suppliers in China. In 2008, Walmart CEO Lee Scott publicly addressed environmental concerns in China and put Walmart's vast resources behind his pledge to make sustainability a priority in the Chinese market. To address waste and pollution, Walmart trained and monitored workers across the Chinese supply chain, from factory and transport to retail stores, and then set environmental standards as a *requirement* for other companies to do business with Walmart. The company also joined forces with China's Institute of Public and Environmental Affairs to map water pollution and wastewater management. The efforts resulted in dramatic drops in water use at many supplier factories. To address mounting food safety concerns among the Chinese, Walmart established the Direct Farm Program, offering local farmers higher incomes for providing safe supplies of fresh food to consumers through the giant retailer.

SOURCE: Orville Schell, "How Walmart Is Changing China—and Vice Versa," *The Atlantic* (December 2011): 80–98.

said Beijing-based lawyer Jingzhou Tao. Chinese managers frequently withhold payments as a tactic in price negotiations. Part of the reason is that these organizations are not just companies, but also political entities. But another reason is cultural differences. "Chinese culture will build a relationship before the contract," said Arthur Bowring, managing director of the Hong Kong Shipowners Association. "The relationship is always something that can be talked about. The contract is just a set of papers that you keep in your bottom drawer."[26]

Despite the problems, China is a market that foreign managers can't afford to ignore. Executives at heavy construction equipment maker Caterpillar say that unless the company can win in China, it risks losing its status as the industry's biggest player. Yet China's fast-growing machinery makers have already begun stealing market share.[27] Competition from domestic companies in other industries is also growing fast. In some industries, local companies have already become market leaders, such as Midea in consumer appliances and 7 Days Inn in budget hotels.[28] One Chinese company that has rapidly become a global leader is Lenovo.

3.2b India, the Service Giant

India, second only to China in population, has taken a different path toward economic development. Whereas China is strong in manufacturing, India is a rising power in software design, services, and precision engineering. Numerous companies see India as a major

Spotlight on Skills

Lenovo

The fastest-growing company in the computer industry is one that most people outside of China hadn't even heard of a few years ago, even after it bought IBM's ThinkPad brand in 2005.

Lenovo is the world's largest PC maker, but it now sells more smartphones and tablets than computers. Lenovo's chairman and CEO, Yang Yuanqing, who started as a salesman and once delivered computers by bicycle, is now China's highest-paid executive. In a conference call with analysts, he said that the company's sales of smartphones more than doubled in the three months that ended June 30, 2013. He declined to comment on the speculation that Lenovo would buy BlackBerry after that company put itself up for sale, but in an interview with *The Wall Street Journal*, Yang made clear that "Lenovo is definitely in a good position to become an important player [in a consolidating industry]. If a target or deal is consistent with Lenovo's strategy, we would take the opportunity." The company has also shown that it isn't afraid of partnerships. Lenovo has quietly started moving into the lucrative enterprise server market through a strategic partnership with EMC. "This is part of our PC-Plus strategy," Yang said.

With its emphasis on quality (its PCs and laptops rank tops for reliability), Lenovo is redefining the perception of the phrase "made in China." Moreover, it is redefining the meaning of a Chinese company, blending the best of Eastern philosophy and culture with the best of Western business and management thinking. The company has headquarters in Beijing, but Yang spends a third of his time at Lenovo's offices in Raleigh, North Carolina. Lenovo's top managers, once almost all Chinese with no international experience, now come from 14 different nations. Most members of the top leadership team speak two or more languages. They live and work in six different cities on three continents. Dan Stone, who was born in Israel, has his office in the United States, while Gerry Smith, born in the United States, works out of Singapore.

Lenovo's top executives know that appreciating and merging Chinese and non-Chinese perspectives is crucial to success. It's an idea that U.S. managers need to be paying attention to. "Chinese people know Americans or the United States more than vice versa," says Lenovo's founder Liu Chuanzhi, who serves as chairman of Lenovo's parent company. "Much more."[29]

Florian Kopp/imagebroker / Alamy

CONCEPT CONNECTION Companies such as Bug Agentes Biologicos, located in Piracicaba, Brazil, reflect the **changing international landscape**. One of *Forbes* magazine's top 50 most innovative companies worldwide, Bug Agentes Biologicos supplies the agriculture industry with predatory insect eggs and parasitoids, which are a natural alternative to harmful agricultural pesticides. Bug sells its products throughout the three largest agricultural producers—the United States, the European Union (EU), and Brazil—and far beyond.

source of technological and scientific brainpower, and the country's large English-speaking population makes it a natural choice for U.S. companies wanting to outsource services. One index lists more than 900 business services companies in India, which employ around 575,000 people.[30]

Some of the fastest-growing industries in India are pharmaceuticals, medical devices, and diagnostics. The country has a large number of highly trained scientists, doctors, and researchers, and U.S. firms Abbott Laboratories and Covidien have both opened research and development centers there. India is also a growing manufacturer of pharmaceuticals and is the world's largest exporter of generic drugs. By 2020, India's pharmaceuticals industry will likely be a global leader, according to a report by PricewaterhouseCoopers (PwC).[31]

3.2c Brazil's Growing Clout

Brazil is another country that is increasingly gaining managers' attention. Although Brazil's economic growth slowed over the past few years, as did all the BRIC countries, it is still one of the fastest-growing emerging economies in the world, with large and growing agricultural, mining, manufacturing, and service sectors.[32] The country's economy, already the seventh largest in the world, is projected to move into fourth place by 2050. The choice of Rio de Janeiro to host the 2016 Summer Olympics is also an indication of Brazil's growing clout in the international arena.

Brazil has a young, vibrant population, the largest in Latin America, and a rapidly growing middle class eager to experience the finer things in life. Consumer spending represents about 60 percent of Brazil's economy, but heavy debt loads have begun to curb consumer spending. The Brazilian government has invested in the development of infrastructure such as highways, ports, and electricity projects, which are creating jobs as well as spurring the development of other businesses. In addition, in 2010, Brazil announced a $22 billion investment in science and technology innovation.

REMEMBER THIS

- Many companies are going straight to China or India as a first step into international business.
- China is strong in manufacturing, whereas India is a major provider of services.
- The Chinese company Lenovo has emerged as the country's first global corporation, with managers coming from 14 different nations, living and working in six cities on three continents.

- Brazil, with its rapidly growing consumer market, is becoming a major player in the shifting international landscape.
- Managers also look to China, India, and Brazil as sources of lower-cost technological and scientific brainpower.

3.3 Multinational Corporations

The size and volume of international businesses are so large that they are hard to comprehend. For example, if revenues were valued at the equivalent of a country's gross domestic product (GDP), the revenue of ExxonMobil is comparable in size to the GDP of Egypt. The revenue of Walmart is comparable to Greece's GDP, that of Toyota to Algeria's GDP, and that of GE to the GDP of Kazakhstan.[33]

A large volume of international business is being carried out by large international businesses that can be thought of as *global corporations, stateless corporations,* or *transnational corporations.* In the business world, these large international firms typically are called *multinational corporations (MNCs),* which have been the subject of enormous attention. In the past 40 years, both the number and the influence of MNCs have grown dramatically. One estimate is that between 1990 and 2003 alone, the number of MNCs increased from 3,000 to 63,000![34] MNCs can move a wealth of assets from country to country and influence national economies, politics, and cultures.

Although the term has no precise definition, a **multinational corporation (MNC)** typically receives more than 25 percent of its total sales revenues from operations outside the parent's home country. During the recent economic slump, the percentage of revenue from foreign operations increased for many multinationals because of stronger sales in developing markets such as China and India. In the third quarter of 2010, revenues for Yum! Brands (including restaurants such as KFC and Pizza Hut) in China surpassed those in the United States for the first time, and by 2012, the company's China business accounted for more than half of the company's $13.6 billion in total revenue, up from 36 percent in 2010.[35] An MNC also has the following distinctive managerial characteristics:

1. An MNC is managed as an integrated worldwide business system in which foreign affiliates act in close alliance and cooperation with one another. Capital, technology, and people are transferred among country affiliates. The MNC can acquire materials and manufacture parts wherever in the world it is most advantageous to do so.

2. An MNC is ultimately controlled by a single management authority that makes key strategic decisions relating to the parent and all affiliates. Although some headquarters are *binational*, such as the Royal Dutch/Shell Group, some centralization of management is required to maintain worldwide integration and profit maximization for the enterprise as a whole.

3. MNC top managers are presumed to exercise a global perspective. They regard the entire world as one market for strategic decisions, resource acquisition, and location of production, advertising, and marketing efficiency.

In a few cases, the MNC management philosophy may differ from that just described. For example, some researchers have distinguished among *ethnocentric companies,* which place emphasis on their home countries; *polycentric companies,* which are oriented toward the markets of individual foreign host countries; and *geocentric companies,* which are truly world-oriented and favor no specific country.[36] The truly global companies that transcend national boundaries are growing in number. These companies no longer see themselves as American, Chinese, or German; they operate globally and serve a global market. Nestlé SA provides a good example. The company gets most of its sales from outside its "home" country of Switzerland, and its 280,000 employees are spread all over the world. CEO Paul Bulcke is Belgian, Chairman, Peter Brabeck-Letmathe was born in Austria,

CONCEPT CONNECTION   The Maharaja Mac and Vegetable Burger served at this McDonald's in New Delhi, India, represent how this **multinational corporation (MNC)** changed its business model by decentralizing its operations. When McDonald's initiated international units, it copied what it did and sold in the United States. Today, though, the fast-food giant seeks local managers who understand the culture and laws of each country. Country managers have the freedom to use different furnishings and develop new products to suit local tastes.

and more than half of the company's managers are non-Swiss. Nestlé has hundreds of brands and has production facilities or other operations in almost every country in the world.[37]

3.3a A Globalization Backlash

The size and power of multinationals, combined with the growth of free trade agreements, which we will discuss later in this chapter, has sparked a backlash over globalization. In a *Fortune* magazine poll, 68 percent of Americans say that other countries benefit the most from free trade, and a 2010 survey by *The Wall Street Journal* and NBC News found that 53 percent of Americans surveyed said that free trade has actually hurt the United States. That figure is up from 46 percent in 2007 and 32 percent in 1999. The sentiment is reflected in other countries such as Germany, France, and even India. "For some reason, everyone thinks they are the loser," said former U.S. trade representative Mickey Kantor.[38]

In the United States, the primary concern has been the loss of jobs as companies expanded their offshoring activities by exporting more and more work overseas. The transfer of jobs such as making shoes, clothing, and toys began decades ago, and in recent years, service and knowledge work have also been outsourced to developing countries. Many American shoppers say they'd be willing to pay higher prices for U.S.-made products to keep jobs from going overseas.[39]

Business leaders, meanwhile, insist that economic benefits of globalization flow back to the U.S. economy in the form of lower prices, expanded markets, and increased profits that can fund innovation.[40] However, another growing trouble spot for managers is how overseas contractors and suppliers treat their employees. Globalization increases the complexity because managers often have a hard time knowing what firms they are actually doing business with. For example, Amazon has distribution centers in Germany, and because of high costs in that country, it often works with third parties to hire and manage thousands of temporary immigrant workers from Poland, Spain, Romania, and other European countries, allowing Amazon to adjust to seasonal needs. The company became embroiled in an ethical quagmire after German public television aired a documentary in which workers said security guards from Hensel European Security Services (HESS) intimidated them, searched them for pilfered food, and spot-checked their cramped living quarters unannounced. The program showed some guards wearing clothing from Thor Steinar, a German fashion label popular with the country's neo-Nazi community. Amazon immediately stopping doing business with HESS, whose executives denied the allegations and said, "We explicitly distance ourselves from any form of political radicalism." Germany's Labor Ministry is also investigating. The relaxing of labor laws in Germany several years ago to allow more temporary workers is being criticized for contributing to the problem of poorly paid, sometimes mistreated workers, but the strongest criticism from labor groups is directed at U.S. companies that they say take advantage of looser labor policies and evade responsibility by turning it over to third parties.[41]

With concerns over jobs and labor practices, the antiglobalization fervor is just getting hotter—and is not likely to dissipate anytime soon. In the end, it is not whether globalization is good or bad, but how business and government managers can work together to ensure that the advantages of a global world are fully and fairly shared.

3.3b Serving the Bottom of the Pyramid

Although large multinational organizations are accused of many negative contributions to society, they also have the resources needed to do good things in the world. One approach that combines business with social responsibility is referred to as *serving the bottom of the pyramid*.

The **bottom of the pyramid (BOP) concept** proposes that corporations can alleviate poverty and other social ills, as well as make significant profits, by selling to the world's poorest people. The term *bottom of the pyramid* refers to the more than 4 billion people who make up the lowest level of the world's economic "pyramid," as defined by per-capita income. These people earn less than U.S. $1,500 a year, with about one-fourth of them earning less than a dollar a day.[42] Traditionally, these people haven't been served by most large businesses because products and services are too expensive, inaccessible, and not suited to their needs; therefore, in many countries, the poor end up paying significantly more than their wealthier counterparts for some basic needs.

A number of leading companies are changing that by adopting BOP business models geared to serving the poorest of the world's consumers. Consider this example from India's Godrej & Boyce.

Joao Silva/The New York Times/Redux

CONCEPT CONNECTION Having dominated almost every market in the world, Coca-Cola has turned its sights on Africa in recent years. The beverage giant sees tremendous potential in countries across the continent, many of whose inhabitants would be considered to be part of the **bottom of the pyramid (BOP)**. The company is working closely with distributors and small business owners to promote its products by offering plenty of incentives and rewards, as well as marketing support.

Spotlight on Skills

Godrej & Boyce

By one estimate, a third of India's food is lost to spoilage, but in 2007, refrigerator market penetration was just 18 percent. Many lower-income people couldn't afford even a basic refrigerator. Another problem, particularly in rural areas, was that electric service was usually unreliable. Godrej & Boyce managers decided it was time to do something about this.

"As a company that made refrigerators for more than 50 years, we asked ourselves why it was that refrigerator penetration was just 18 percent," said G. Sunderraman, vice president of corporate development. The first major insight was that many people not only couldn't afford a refrigerator, but they didn't *need* a large refrigerator that took up too much space in a small house and used a lot of electricity. What they needed was the chotuKool ("The Little Cool"), an innovative appliance introduced by Godrej & Boyce in

2010. The chotuKool, a mini-fridge designed to cool five or six bottles of water and store a few pounds of food, was portable, ran on batteries, and sold for about 3,250 rupees ($69), about 35 percent less than the cheapest refrigerator on the market.

To sell the new product, Godrej & Boyce trained rural villagers as salespeople. The villagers earn a commission of about $3 for each refrigerator sold, and the system reduces Godrej's distribution costs. When asked how many chotuKools the company expected to sell, George Menezes, COO of Godrej Appliances, said, "In three years, probably millions." Godrej & Boyce managers spend a lot of time working directly with consumers and are now testing ideas for other low-cost products aimed at rural markets. "Currently, the rural market accounts for only 10 percent, but it is all set to expand in a huge way," said Menezes.[43]

The U.S. companies are getting in on the BOP act too. P&G researchers are visiting homes in China, Brazil, India, and other developing countries to see how the company can come up with entirely new products and services for consumers living at the bottom of the pyramid. However, P&G is late getting into marketing to the poor. Rival Unilever, for instance, introduced Lifebuoy soap to India more than a century ago, promoting it as the enemy of dirt and disease.[44] Unilever gets more than 55 percent of its sales from developing markets, up from just 20 percent in 1990.[45] "P&G is still very U.S.-centric," says Unilever's CEO, Paul Polman, a Dutchman who is a P&G veteran. "Emerging markets are in the DNA of our company." To try to catch up, P&G's CEO is focusing employees on the mission of "touching and improving more lives, in more parts of the world, more completely." When people feel they are changing lives, "it's almost like you don't have to pay us to do this," said one R&D scientist.[46] Proponents of BOP thinking believe multinational firms can contribute to positive lasting change when the profit motive goes hand in hand with the desire to make a contribution to humankind, as TechSharks does, shown in this chapter's Executive Edge.

THE EXECUTIVE EDGE

Social Entrepreneurship

At age 28, Ahmad Reza Zahedi started TechSharks, a website design business, the fulfillment of a longtime dream after falling in love with computing as a teen, something common among tech entrepreneurs. The best gift he ever got was from his older brother got him a book about learning the computer language Pascal, and he couldn't stop reading it. When he first started TechSharks, he had to educate his clients about the difference between e-mails and websites, between hosting and domains. In 2011, he almost broke even and then doubled his revenue, to $50,000, in 2012. Not sound like much? Consider that Zahedi operates out of Kabul, in a system constantly battling against the Taliban, in a place where the war destroyed the educational system, where adult literacy is 25 percent and one of the world's poorest countries with annual GDP at $600 billion.

Zahedi is part of a worldwide movement of people using business, nonprofits, and technology to create a better, more sustainable world built on peace and justice, and studies confirm that more money is being channeled into such organizations. One of the earliest and largest ventures in this area is Ashoka, started in 1980 by Bill Drayton, who set his sights on identifying leaders around the planet, to help them address local problems through helping with leadership skills, resources, and ideas, so they could become capable ethical change-makers. Back in the 1980s Drayon started by identifying change agents in various countries such as Brazil, India, and Indonesia. He looked for people who went beyond the political activism role and were using innovative ideas and building structures to solve important issues, such as poverty elimination (like Grameen Bank), health care, educational models, or ingenious ideas to improve the environment. Ashoka funds these people and gives them the title of Fellow.

Since then, other organizations are doing similar work. Skoll Foundation funds projects and operates on the principle that "social entrepreneurs excel at togetherness," and that they pursue their goals in a communal way. Echoing Green supports early-stage social entrepreneurs and organizes itself around a core idea that resonates in the whole field: "Social entrepreneurship [has an] inherently hopeful message of individual engagement and efficacy."

SOURCES: Stephen McKay, et al., "The Marketization of Charities in England and Wales," *Voluntas* 26, no. 1 (Feb. 2015), 336–354; For Lemmon: You Say You Want a Revolution, Fast Company, 170, Nov. 2012, 130-134 and 139.

3.4 Getting Started Internationally

Organizations have a couple of ways to become involved internationally. One is to seek cheaper resources such as materials or labor offshore, which is called *offshoring* or *global outsourcing*. Another is to develop markets for finished products or services outside their home countries, which may include exporting, licensing, and direct investing. Exporting, licensing, and direct investing are called market entry strategies because they represent alternative ways to sell products and services in foreign markets. Exhibit 3.3 shows the strategies that companies can use to engage in the international arena, either to acquire resources or to enter new markets.

3.4a Exporting

Over the past three decades, the value of exports has increased from $2 trillion to $18 trillion, with more than half of them now coming from emerging economies.[47] With **exporting**, the company maintains its production facilities within the home nation and transfers its products for sale in foreign countries. Exporting enables a company to market its products in other countries at modest resource cost and with limited risk. Exporting does entail numerous problems based on physical distances, government regulations, foreign currencies, and cultural differences, but it is less expensive than committing the firm's own capital to build plants in host countries. For example, Skooba Designs, a Rochester, New York, manufacturer of carrying cases for laptops, iPads, and other tools, exports to more than 30 countries. Service companies can also export. Netflix is exporting its movie streaming service to customers in Latin America, the United Kingdom, and Ireland, as well as exploring other countries to move into.[48] Hollywood movie studios have long exported films to foreign countries, but they're taking a different approach than in the past.

EXHIBIT 3.3   **Strategies for Entering the International Arena**

Spotlight on Skills

Hollywood Studios

Hollywood films have long been quintessentially American products, and years ago, audiences in Japan or Brazil or South Korea would faithfully go watch movies that were written for and marketed primarily to American audiences. No longer. Local films are giving Hollywood a run for its money. At the same time, audiences are declining in the United States and Canada but growing overseas. Hollywood movies now get about 70 percent of their revenue from abroad, and ticket sales overseas have been the only source of growth since 2010. The 2011 movie *The Smurfs* got 74.7 percent of its box office sales in foreign markets. *Cars 2* wasn't far behind, with 65.8 percent of box office receipts from overseas. A few Hollywood studios have gone as far as making movies specifically for certain foreign markets, and almost all of them are reframing their films to suit foreign tastes. Here are some examples of tactics they are using:

- **Use foreign actors.** For Paramount's *G.I. Joe: The Rise of Cobra* and *G.I. Joe: Retaliation*, Byung-hun Lee, a major Korean movie star, and South African actor Arnold Vosloo were placed in prominent roles.

- **Set the movie in a growing market location.** Several recent films, such as *Rio* and *Fast Five*, have been set in Brazil, which is a rapidly growing market for Hollywood movies. In *The Twilight Saga: Breaking Dawn Part I*, Bella Swan and Edward Cullen spend their honeymoon on a private Brazilian island.

- **Play up foreign brands.** In a recent *Transformers* movie, DreamWorks Studios had a character gulping Shuhua low-lactose milk from China's Yili dairy company.

- **Set the movie in foreign cities.** Pixar's *Cars* didn't do well abroad, so the studio set the sequel in Paris, London, Tokyo, and on the Italian Riviera.

These and other techniques represent a whole new approach to making movies. Rather than trying to lure audiences to their films, studios are targeting their films to the audiences. In addition, managers are increasingly looking for films with global appeal. "I can tell you that no studio is going to make a big, expensive movie that costs $150 million or $200 million unless it has worldwide appeal," said Mark Zoradi, former president of Walt Disney Company's Motion Pictures Group.[49]

3.4b Outsourcing

Global outsourcing, also called *offshoring*, means engaging in the international division of labor so that work activities can be done in countries with the cheapest sources of labor and supplies. Millions of low-level jobs such as textile manufacturing, call center operations, and credit card processing have been outsourced to low-wage countries in recent years. The Internet and plunging telecommunications costs have enabled companies to outsource more and higher-level work as well, such as software development, accounting, or medical services. A patient might have a magnetic resonance imaging (MRI) test performed in Minneapolis and have it read by doctors in India. After the Sarbanes-Oxley Act went into effect, requiring extensive new financial reporting procedures and enhanced oversight, Unisys had a hard time finding enough internal auditors in the United States, so managers outsourced their core auditing practice to China. Large pharmaceutical companies farm out much of their early-stage chemistry research to cheaper labs in China and India.[50]

CONCEPT CONNECTION Throughout the 1970s and 1980s, Kentucky Fried Chicken (now KFC) expanded aggressively across the globe. In Asia, for example, KFC restaurants can be found in China, Japan, Cambodia, Singapore, Taiwan, Malaysia, Vietnam, and Thailand, among other countries. Most of these locations are **franchises**, but some are **joint ventures** also with KFC's parent company, Yum! International.

3.4c Licensing

With **licensing**, a corporation (the licensor) in one country makes certain resources available to companies in another country (the licensee). These resources include technology, managerial skills, and patent or trademark rights. They enable the licensee to produce and market a product or service similar to what the licensor has been producing. Heineken, which has been called the world's first truly global brand of beer, usually begins by exporting to help boost familiarity with its products; if the market looks enticing enough, Heineken then licenses its brands to a local brewer. Licensing offers a business firm relatively easy access to international markets at low cost, but it limits the company's participation in and control over the development of those markets.

One special form of licensing is **franchising**, which occurs when a franchisee buys a complete package of materials and services, including equipment, products, product ingredients, trademark and trade name rights, managerial advice, and a standardized operating system. Whereas with licensing, a licensee generally keeps its own company name, autonomy, and operating systems, a franchise takes the name and systems of the franchisor. The fast-food chains are some of the best-known franchisors. The story is often told of the Japanese child visiting Los Angeles who excitedly pointed out to his parents, "They have McDonald's in America!"

3.4d Direct Investing

A higher level of involvement in international trade is direct investment in facilities in a foreign country. **Direct investing** means that the company is involved in managing the productive assets, which distinguishes it from other entry strategies that permit less managerial control.

Currently, the most popular type of direct investment is to engage in strategic alliances and partnerships. In a **joint venture**, a company shares costs and risks with another firm, typically in the host country, to develop new products, build a manufacturing facility, or set up a sales and distribution network.[51] A partnership is often the fastest, cheapest, and least risky way to get into the global game. For example, Abbott Laboratories teamed up with an Indian drug firm, Biocon Ltd., to develop nutritional supplements and generic drugs tailored to the local market.[52] In addition to joint ventures, the complexity of today's global business environment is causing managers at many companies to develop alliance networks, which are collections of partnerships with various other firms, often across international boundaries.[53]

The other choice is to have a **wholly owned foreign affiliate**, over which the company has complete control. Direct *acquisition* of an affiliate may provide cost savings over exporting by shortening distribution channels and reducing storage and transportation costs. Local managers also have a better understanding of economic, cultural, and political conditions. Chinese companies are increasingly taking a direct acquisition route. In 2012, China's Dalian Wanda Group bought AMC Entertainment, with its 346 multiplex movie theaters, in the largest-ever acquisition by a Chinese company. A Chinese company recently bought the vitamin assets of Inverness Medical to form International Vitamin Corporation. Steven Dai said that buying the U.S. company made sense because the United States has a highly developed vitamin market that "constantly grows every year" and local managers understand the local interests and needs. Kraft Foods bought Cadbury PLC in large part because the firm had established local contacts and distribution networks in emerging markets. Walmart's most successful international ventures have been based on acquiring well-established local companies.[54]

The most costly and risky direct investment is called a **greenfield venture**, which means that a company builds a subsidiary from scratch in a foreign country. The advantage is that the subsidiary is exactly what the company wants and has the potential to be highly profitable. For example, in 2012, Airbus announced plans to build jetliners in its first assembly plant in the United States. By building a huge plant in Alabama and employing American workers, Airbus managers expect to become part of U.S. culture, thereby reducing political opposition to the purchase of the company's airplanes.[55] The disadvantage to this strategy is that the company has to acquire all market knowledge, materials, people, and know-how in a different culture, and mistakes are possible. Another example of a greenfield venture is the Nissan plant in Canton, Mississippi. The plant represents the first auto factory ever built in Mississippi, where the Japanese company had to rely on an untested and largely inexperienced workforce. The logistical and cultural hurdles were so enormous and the risks so high that one Nissan executive later said, "We did what nobody thought was possible."[56]

REMEMBER THIS

- Two major alternatives for engaging in the international arena are to seek cheaper resources via outsourcing and to develop markets outside the home country.

- **Global outsourcing**, sometimes called *offshoring*, means engaging in the international division of labor so as to obtain the cheapest sources of labor and supplies, regardless of country.

- **Market entry strategies** are various tactics that managers use to enter foreign markets.

- **Exporting** is a market-entry strategy in which a company maintains production facilities within its home country and transfers products for sale in foreign countries.

- With a market-entry strategy of **licensing**, a company in one country makes certain resources available to companies in other countries to participate in the production and sale of its products abroad.

- **Franchising** is a form of licensing in which a company provides its foreign franchisees with a complete package of materials and services.

- McDonald's and other U.S. fast food companies have franchises all over the world.

- **Direct investing** is a market-entry strategy in which the organization is directly involved in managing its production facilities in a foreign country.

- Alternatives for direct investing include engaging in joint ventures, acquiring foreign affiliates, and initiating a **greenfield venture**.

- With a **joint venture**, an organization shares costs and risks with another firm in a foreign country to build a facility, develop new products, or set up a sales and distribution network.

- A **wholly owned foreign affiliate** is a foreign subsidiary over which an organization has complete control.

- China's Dalian Wanda Group bought the U.S. company AMC Entertainment as a wholly owned foreign affiliate.

- The most risky type of direct investment is the **greenfield venture**, in which a company builds a subsidiary from scratch in a foreign country.

3.5 The International Business Environment

International management is the management of business operations conducted in more than one country. The fundamental tasks of business management—including the financing, production, and distribution of products and services—do not change in any substantive way when a firm is transacting business across international borders. The basic management functions of planning, organizing, leading, and controlling are the same whether a company operates domestically or internationally. However, managers will experience greater difficulties and risks when performing these management functions on an international scale. Consider the following blunders:

- It took McDonald's more than a year to figure out that Hindus in India do not eat beef because they consider the cow sacred. The company's sales took off only after McDonald's started making burgers sold in India out of lamb.[57]

- When IKEA launched a superstore in Bangkok, managers learned that some of its Swedish product names sound like crude terms for sex when pronounced in Thai.[58]

- In Africa, the labels on bottles show pictures of what is inside so illiterate shoppers can know what they're buying. When a baby-food company showed a picture of an infant on its label, the product didn't sell very well.[59]

- United Airlines discovered that even colors can doom a product. The airline handed out white carnations when it started flying from Hong Kong, only to discover that, to many Asians, such flowers represent death and bad luck.[60]

Some of these examples might seem humorous, but there's nothing funny about them to managers trying to operate in a highly competitive global environment. What should managers of emerging global companies look for to avoid making obvious international mistakes? When they are comparing one country to another, the economic, legal-political, and sociocultural sectors present the greatest difficulties. Key factors to understand in the international environment are summarized in Exhibit 3.4.[61]

EXHIBIT 3.4   Key Factors in the International Environment

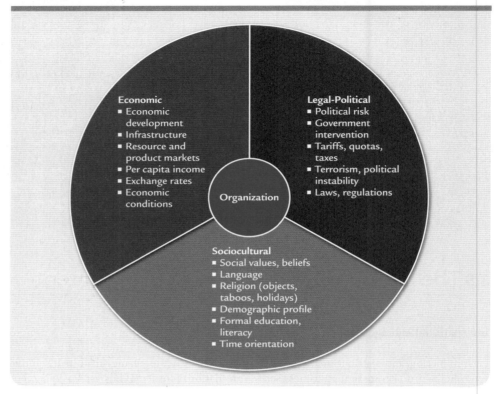

Economic
- Economic development
- Infrastructure
- Resource and product markets
- Per capita income
- Exchange rates
- Economic conditions

Legal-Political
- Political risk
- Government intervention
- Tariffs, quotas, taxes
- Terrorism, political instability
- Laws, regulations

Organization

Sociocultural
- Social values, beliefs
- Language
- Religion (objects, taboos, holidays)
- Demographic profile
- Formal education, literacy
- Time orientation

REMEMBER THIS

- The basic management functions are the same in either a domestic or an international subsidiary, but managers will experience greater difficulties and risks when performing these functions internationally.
- **International management** means managing business operations in more than one country.

- When operating on an international basis, it is important for managers to give considerable thought to economic, legal-political, and sociocultural factors.

Answer the questions in the Self-Learning instrument on page 134 how ready you are to work or travel abroad.

3.6 The Economic Environment

The economic environment represents the economic conditions in the country where the international organization operates. This part of the environment includes factors such as economic development and resource and product markets. In addition, factors such as inflation, interest rates, and economic growth are also part of the international economic environment.

3.6a Economic Development

Economic development differs widely among the countries and regions of the world. Countries can be categorized as either *developing* or *developed*. Developing countries are referred to as *less-developed countries* (LDCs). The criterion traditionally used to classify countries as developed or developing is *per-capita income*, which is the income generated by the nation's production of goods and services divided by total population. The developing countries have low per-capita incomes. LDCs generally are located in Asia, Africa, and South America. Developed countries are generally located in North America, Europe, and Japan. Most international business firms are headquartered in the wealthier, economically advanced countries, but smart managers are investing heavily in less-developed emerging markets. These companies face risks and challenges today, but they stand to reap huge benefits in the future.

Each year, the World Economic Forum analyzes data to gauge how companies are doing in the economic development race and releases its Global Competitiveness Report, which tallies numerous factors that contribute to an economy's competitiveness.[62] The report considers both hard data and perceptions of business leaders around the world and considers government policies, institutions, market size, the sophistication of financial markets, and other factors that drive productivity and thus enable sustained economic growth.

Exhibit 3.5 shows the top 10 countries in the overall ranking for 2011–2012, along with several other countries for comparison. The United States was in first place in 2008–2009, but had fallen to fifth by 2011 and has declined even more since then, dropping to seventh in the 2012–2013 ranking.[63]

TAKE Action!

Read the "Ethical Dilemma" on page 136 that pertains to conducting business in less-developed countries.

EXHIBIT 3.5 Country Competitiveness Comparison, 2011

Country	World Economic Forum Competitiveness Ranking	GDP	Number of People in Labor Force
Switzerland	1	$344,200,000,000	4,899,000
Singapore	2	$318,900,000,000	3,237,000
Sweden	3	$386,600,000,000	5,018,000
Finland	4	$198,200,000,000	2,682,000
United States	5	$15,290,000,000,000	153,600,000
Germany	6	$3,139,000,000,000	43,670,000
Netherlands	7	$713,100,000,000	7,809,000
Denmark	8	$209,200,000,000	2,851,000
Japan	9	$4,497,000,000,000	65,910,000
United Kingdom	10	$2,290,000,000,000	31,720,000
Canada	12	$1,414,000,000,000	18,700,000
Saudi Arabia	17	$691,500,000,000	7,630,000
China	26	$11,440,000,000,000	795,500,000
Kuwait	34	$155,500,000,000	2,227,000
South Africa	50	$562,200,000,000	17,660,000
Brazil	53	$2,324,000,000,000	104,700,000
India	56	$4,515,000,000,000	487,600,000

SOURCE: Based on "The Global Competitiveness Report 2011–2012," World Economic Forum, www3.weforum.org/docs/WEF_GCR_Report_2011-12.pdf (accessed June 27, 2012); *CIA World Factbook 2011*, www.cia.gov/library/publications/the-world-factbook (accessed November 15, 2012).

AP Images/Pavel Rahman

CONCEPT CONNECTION While working as a New York investment banker, Bangladesh native Iqbal Quadir realized that connectivity equals productivity. He also knew his impoverished homeland was one of the least connected places on Earth. That prompted him to collaborate with countryman Muhammad Yunus, Grameen Bank founder and 2006 Nobel Peace Prize winner, to create Village Phone, a program in which entrepreneurs (mostly women) use Grameen Bank microloans to purchase cell phones. "Telephone ladies," such as Monwara Begum (pictured here), then earn the money needed to repay the debt by providing phone service to fellow villagers. Village Phone has resulted in thousands of new small businesses, as well as an improved communication **infrastructure** that makes **economic development** possible.

Note that highly developed countries typically rank higher in the competitiveness index. One important factor in gauging competitiveness is the country's **infrastructure**; that is, the physical facilities, such as highways, airports, utilities, and telephone lines, that support

3.6b Economic Interdependence

One thing that the recent global financial crisis has made abundantly clear is how economically interconnected the world is. Although the recent crisis might seem atypical, savvy international managers realize that their companies will probably be buffeted by similar crises fairly regularly.

For example, most students are probably familiar with the bursting of the dot-com bubble in the early part of this century, which caused a severe drop in the stock market and affected companies around the globe. The Asian financial crisis of 1997–1998 similarly affected firms in North America, Europe, and other parts of the world. More recently, the inability of countries such as Greece, Spain, Ireland, and Italy to make payments on their debt sparked a panic that devalued the euro and threatened the stability of financial markets worldwide.[64]

Recent financial woes have left a number of countries reeling, as reflected in a "misery index" created by a Moody's economist and illustrated in Exhibit 3.6. The misery index adds together a country's unemployment rate and the budget deficit as a percentage of GDP. The 2010 figures suggest significantly greater misery for almost every country compared to the beginning of this century. Iceland and Ireland, two countries hit particularly hard by the recent economic crisis, had a negative misery index in 2000 but registered high scores for misery in 2010. The United States went from a misery score of less than 5 in 2000 to about 21 in 2010.[65]

Another reflection of economic interdependence is the fact that parts, supplies, and labor for many companies come from around the world, which presents managers with new challenges. For example, in late 2011, Honda, Toyota, and other auto plants in the United States, Canada, and Asia had trouble getting the electronics and other parts that they needed from suppliers in Thailand, where historic floods swamped huge industrial sections of the country.[66] Many companies are coming under increasing criticism because of unsafe or inhumane treatment of workers at contract factories in China, Bangladesh, and other low-wage countries. In the first few months of 2010, 10 employees at Foxconn Technologies, a Chinese contract manufacturer that makes electronic products for Apple, Hewlett-Packard (HP), and other U.S. companies, committed suicide. A couple of years later, Foxconn, Apple, and HP were again targets of attack when students at some vocational schools in China said that they were forced to work on the assembly lines. "And they are told they cannot leave, that they must work or they will be dismissed from school," said Debby Chan Sze Wan, representing Students and Scholars against Corporate Misbehavior. Apple has asked for detailed information on its contractors' student workers so it can monitor the issue more carefully. HP, meanwhile, has gone further, issuing specific rules to its Chinese suppliers on how student and other temporary workers must be treated.[67]

EXHIBIT 3.6   How Countries Are Bearing the Economic Crisis: Misery Index, 2010 Compared to 2000

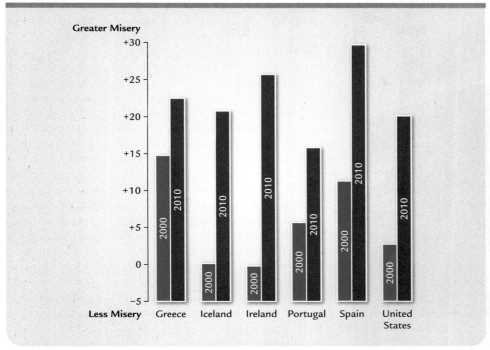

SOURCE: Based on "A New Definition of Misery," *The New York Times* (December 18, 2009), based on data from Moody's; www.nytimes.com/imagepages/ 2009/12/18/business/economy/20091219_CHARTS_GRAPHIC.html (accessed on December 19, 2009).

REMEMBER THIS

- Countries vary widely in terms of **economic development** and are classified as either developed countries or less-developed countries (LDCs).

- **Infrastructure** refers to a country's physical facilities, such as highways, utilities, and airports, which support economic activities.

- The United States has fallen from first to seventh place on a ranking of global competitiveness.

- As recent financial crises in the United States and Europe show, countries are economically interconnected, and financial problems in one area of the world can spread rapidly around the globe.

- International business managers can expect their companies to be affected periodically by economic problems that cross geographical boundaries.

3.7 The Legal-Political Environment

Differing laws and regulations make doing business a challenge for international firms. Host governments have myriad laws concerning libel statutes, consumer protection, information and labeling, employment and safety, and wages. International managers must learn these rules and regulations and abide by them. In addition, managers must deal with unfamiliar

GOH CHAI HIN/AFP/Getty Images

CONCEPT CONNECTION Amway, the U.S.-based network marketing company, spent years patiently negotiating China's **legal-political environment**. In 1998, the Chinese government closed down Amway operations in China because it suspected that the company was either an illegal pyramid scheme or a sinister cult. Amway survived by cultivating relationships with government officials and by departing from its business model. For example, it opened more than 200 retail stores like this one to demonstrate its commitment. In 2006, the Chinese government once again allowed Amway to sell directly to consumers, and the company now earns billions in annual revenue in China.

political systems when they go international, as well as with more government supervision and regulation. Government officials and the general public often view foreign companies as outsiders (or even intruders) and are suspicious of their impact on economic independence and political sovereignty.

Political risk is defined as the risk of loss of assets, earning power, or managerial control due to politically based events or actions by host governments. Although many developing countries today welcome and support foreign firms, political risk is a major concern for international companies, which face a broader and more complex array of threats than ever.[68] The loosening of foreign investment laws in India has paved the way for Walmart to begin opening its first stores in the country, but there is still strong political resistance to the giant U.S. retailer. Further complicating the challenge, small farmers are required to take their harvest to government-run wholesalers. Food in India must go through multiple government channels and middlemen before it can be sold to consumers from retail stores. The country has more than 7,000 government-approved markets, with 413,000 licensed traders, and 214,000 licensed commission agents. The level of bureaucracy, combined with poor infrastructure and others problems, means Walmart and other foreign retailers "need to be prepared to sustain losses in India for years to come," said a retail consultant.[69]

Another frequently cited problem for international companies is **political instability**, which includes riots, revolutions, civil disorders, and frequent changes in government. Political turmoil in Syria, for example, which has occurred off and on ever since the country came into existence following its independence from France in 1946, reignited in mid-2011 as part of the Arab Spring, a revolutionary wave of protests in the Arab world that began in late 2010. By 2013, Syria was embroiled in a bloody civil war, with the United States threatening military action after allegations that the regime of President Bashar al-Assad used chemical weapons against civilians, killing nearly 1,500 people, including 426 children. The wave of protests in the Arab region, affecting not only Syria, but also Tunisia, Egypt, Libya, Yemen, and Bahrain, has created a tumultuous environment for businesses operating in the region. "No president, no government, no police," said Jalila Mezni, owner of Société d'Articles Hygiéniques in Tunisia. "Only complete disorder."[70] Political risk and political instability remain elevated throughout the Arab world, causing problems for both local and foreign organizations. In August 2013, for example, the Syrian Electronic Army (SEA), a group of pro-government computer hackers, disrupted several Western Web sites, including Twitter, *The Washington Post*, and *The New York Times*, which went down twice within a period of two weeks.[71] Zaid Qadoumi, the CEO of Canada's BroadGrain, which has been delivering agricultural commodities to emerging markets and political hot spots since the company was founded, offered extra pay for a crew to deliver a load of wheat to Libya, but advised workers to "cut the ropes and leave" if they believed the situation was too dangerous.[72]

HOT TOPIC

REMEMBER THIS

- Complicated legal and political forces can create huge risks for international managers and organizations.

- **Political risk** refers to a company's risk of loss of assets, earning power, or managerial control due to politically based events or actions by host governments.

- **Political instability** includes events such as riots, revolutions, or government upheavals that can affect the operations of an international company.

- A revolutionary wave of protests in the Arab world that began in late 2010, known as the *Arab Spring*, has created a tumultuous environment for businesses operating in the region.

- Managers must understand and follow the differing laws and regulations in the various countries where they do business.

3.8 The Sociocultural Environment

A nation's culture includes the shared knowledge, beliefs, and values, as well as the common modes of behavior and ways of thinking among members of a society. Cultural factors sometimes can be more perplexing than political and economic factors when working or living in a foreign country.

3.8a Social Values

Many managers fail to realize that the values and behaviors that typically govern how business is done in their own country don't always translate to the rest of the world. American managers in particular are regularly accused of an ethnocentric attitude that assumes their way is the best way. **Ethnocentrism** refers to a natural tendency of people to regard their own culture as superior and to downgrade or dismiss other cultural values. Ethnocentrism can be found in all countries, and strong ethnocentric attitudes within a country make it difficult for foreign firms to operate there.

One way that managers can fight their own ethnocentric tendencies is to understand and appreciate differences in social values.

Hofstede's Value Dimensions   In research that included 116,000 IBM employees in 40 countries, Dutch scientist Geert Hofstede identified four dimensions of national value systems that influence organizational and employee working relationships.[73] Examples of how countries rate on the four dimensions are shown in Exhibit 3.7.

1. *Power distance*. High **power distance** means that people accept inequality in power among institutions, organizations, and people. Low power distance means that people expect equality in power. Countries that value high power distance are Malaysia, India, and the Philippines. Countries that value low power distance are Denmark, Israel, and New Zealand.

2. *Uncertainty avoidance*. High **uncertainty avoidance** means that members of a society feel uncomfortable with uncertainty and ambiguity and thus support beliefs that

EXHIBIT 3.7 Rank Orderings of Ten Countries Along Four Dimensions of National Value Systems

Country	Power Distance[a]	Uncertainty Avoidance[b]	Individualism[c]	Masculinity[d]
Australia	7	7	2	5
Costa Rica	8 (tie)	2 (tie)	10	9
France	3	2 (tie)	4	7
West Germany	8 (tie)	5	5	3
India	2	9	6	6
Japan	5	1	7	1
Mexico	1	4	8	2
Sweden	10	10	3	10
Thailand	4	6	9	8
United States	6	8	1	4

a. 1 = Highest power distance
   10 = Lowest power distance

b. 1 = Highest uncertainty avoidance
   10 = Lowest uncertainty avoidance

c. 1 = Highest individualism
   10 = Lowest individualism

d. 1 = Highest masculinity
   10 = Lowest masculinity

SOURCES: Dorothy Marcic, *Organizational Behavior and Cases*, 4th ed. (St. Paul, MN: West, 1995). Based on two books by Geert Hofstede: *Culture's Consequences* (London: Sage Publications, 1984) and *Cultures and Organizations: Software of the Mind* (New York: McGraw-Hill, 1991).

promise certainty and conformity. Low uncertainty avoidance means that people have great tolerance for the unstructured, the unclear, and the unpredictable. High uncertainty avoidance countries include Greece, Portugal, and Uruguay. Countries with low uncertainty avoidance values include Sweden, Singapore, and Jamaica.

3. *Individualism and collectivism.* **Individualism** reflects a value for a loosely knit social framework in which individuals are expected to take care of themselves. **Collectivism** means a preference for a tightly knit social framework in which individuals look after one another and organizations protect their members' interests. Countries with individualist values include the United States, Canada, and Great Britain. Countries with collectivist values include China, Mexico, and Brazil.

4. *Masculinity/femininity.* **Masculinity** stands for preference for achievement, heroism, assertiveness, work centrality (with resultant high stress), and material success. **Femininity** reflects the values of relationships, cooperation, group decision making, and quality of life. Societies with strong masculine values include Japan, Germany, Italy, and Mexico. Countries with feminine values include Sweden, Costa Rica, Norway, and France. Both men and women subscribe to the dominant value in masculine and feminine cultures.

Hofstede and his colleagues later identified a fifth dimension: long-term orientation versus short-term orientation. **Long-term orientation**, found in China and other Asian countries, includes a greater concern for the future and highly values thrift and perseverance. A **short-term orientation**, found in Russia and West Africa, is more concerned with the past and the present and places a high value on tradition and meeting social obligations.[74] Researchers continue to explore and expand on Hofstede's findings.[75] For example, in the last 30 years, more than 1,400 articles and numerous books were published on individualism and collectivism alone.[76]

Globe Project Value Dimensions   Recent research by the Global Leadership and Organizational Behavior Effectiveness (GLOBE) Project extends Hofstede's assessment and offers a broader understanding for today's managers. The GLOBE Project used data collected from 18,000 managers in 62 countries to identify nine dimensions that explain cultural differences. In addition to the ones identified by Hofstede, the GLOBE project identifies the following characteristics:[77]

1. *Assertiveness.* A high value on assertiveness means that a society encourages toughness, assertiveness, and competitiveness. Low assertiveness means that people value tenderness and concern for others over being competitive.

2. *Future orientation.* Similar to Hofstede's time orientation, this dimension refers to the extent to which a society encourages and rewards planning for the future over short-term results and quick gratification.

3. *Gender differentiation.* This dimension refers to the extent to which a society maximizes gender role differences. In countries with low gender differentiation, such as Denmark, women typically have a higher status and play a larger role in decision making. Countries with high gender differentiation accord men higher social, political, and economic status.

4. *Performance orientation.* A society with a high performance orientation places great emphasis on performance and rewards people for performance improvements and excellence. A low performance orientation means that people pay less attention to performance and more attention to loyalty, belonging, and background.

5. *Humane orientation.* The final dimension refers to the degree to which a society encourages and rewards people for being fair, altruistic, generous, and caring. A country high on humane orientation places great value on helping others and being kind. A country low on this orientation expects people to take care of themselves. Self-enhancement and gratification have high importance.

Exhibit 3.8 gives examples of how some countries rank on these GLOBE dimensions. These dimensions give managers an added tool for identifying and managing cultural

EXHIBIT 3.8   Examples of Country Rankings on Selected GLOBE Value Dimensions

Dimension	Low	Medium	High
Assertiveness	Sweden Switzerland Japan	Egypt Iceland France	Spain United States Germany
Future orientation	Russia Italy Kuwait	Slovenia Australia India	Denmark Canada Singapore
Gender differentiation	Sweden Denmark Poland	Italy Brazil Netherlands	South Korea Egypt China
Performance orientation	Russia Greece Venezuela	Israel England Japan	United States Taiwan Hong Kong
Humane orientation	Germany France Singapore	New Zealand Sweden United States	Indonesia Egypt Iceland

SOURCE: Mansour Javidan and Robert J. House, "Cultural Acumen for the Global Manager: Lessons from Project GLOBE," *Organizational Dynamics* 29, no. 4 (2001): 289–305.

differences. Social values greatly influence organizational functioning and management styles. Consider the difficulty that Emerson Electric managers had when Emerson opened a new manufacturing facility in Suzhou, China. One area in which the American view and the Chinese view differed widely was in terms of time orientation. The American managers favored a short time horizon and quick results, and they viewed their assignments as stepping stones to future career advancement. The Chinese managers, on the other hand, favored a long-term approach, building a system and setting a proper course of action to enable long-term success.[78] Other companies have encountered similar cultural differences. Consider the American concept of self-directed teams, which emphasizes shared power and authority, with team members working on a variety of problems without formal guidelines, rules, and structure. Managers trying to implement teams have had trouble in areas where cultural values support high power distance and a low tolerance for uncertainty, such as Mexico. Many workers in Mexico, as well as in France and Mediterranean countries, expect organizations to be hierarchical. In Russia, people are good at working in groups and like competing as a team rather than on an individual basis. Organizations in Germany and other central European countries typically strive to be impersonal, well-oiled machines. Effective management styles differ in each country, depending on cultural characteristics.[79]

REMEMBER THIS

- Managers working internationally should guard against **ethnocentrism**, which is the natural tendency among people to regard their own culture as superior to others.

- Hofstede's sociocultural value dimensions measure power distance, uncertainty avoidance, individualism–collectivism, and masculinity–femininity.

- **Power distance** is the degree to which people accept inequality in power among institutions, organizations, and people.

- **Uncertainty avoidance** is characterized by people's intolerance for uncertainty and ambiguity and resulting support for beliefs that promise certainty and conformity.

- **Individualism** refers to a preference for a loosely knit social framework in which individuals are expected to take care of themselves.

- **Collectivism** refers to a preference for a tightly knit social framework in which individuals look

after one another and organizations protect their members' interests.

- **Masculinity** is a cultural preference for achievement, heroism, assertiveness, work centrality, and material success.

- **Femininity** is a cultural preference for relationships, cooperation, group decision making, and quality of life.

- Hofstede later identified another dimension: **long-term orientation**, which reflects a greater concern for the future and a high value on thrift and perseverance, versus **short-term orientation**, which reflects a concern with the past and present and a high value on meeting current obligations.

- Additional value dimensions recently identified by the GLOBE Project are assertiveness, future orientation, gender differentiation, performance orientation, and humane orientation.

3.8b Communication Differences

People from some cultures tend to pay more attention to the social context (social setting, nonverbal behavior, social status, etc.) of their verbal communication than Americans do. For example, American managers working in China have discovered that social context is

EXHIBIT 3.9 High-Context and Low-Context Cultures

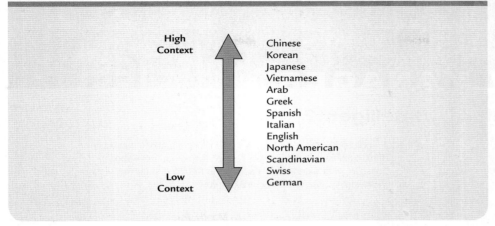

High
Context

Chinese
Korean
Japanese
Vietnamese
Arab
Greek
Spanish
Italian
English
North American
Scandinavian
Swiss
German

Low
Context

SOURCES: Edward T. Hall, *Beyond Culture* (Garden City, NY: Anchor Press/Doubleday, 1976); and J. Kennedy and A. Everest, "Put Diversity in Context," *Personnel Journal* (September 1991): 50–54.

considerably more important in that culture, and they need to learn to suppress their impatience and devote the necessary time to establish personal and social relationships.

Exhibit 3.9 indicates how the emphasis on social context varies among countries. In a **high-context culture**, people are sensitive to circumstances surrounding social exchanges. People use communication primarily to build personal social relationships; meaning is derived from context—setting, status, and nonverbal behavior—more than from explicit words; relationships and trust are more important than business; and the welfare and harmony of the group are valued. In a **low-context culture**, people use communication primarily to exchange facts and information; meaning is derived primarily from words; business transactions are more important than building relationships and trust; and individual welfare and achievement are more important than the group.[80]

To understand how differences in cultural context affect communications, consider the American expression, "The squeaky wheel gets the grease." It means that the loudest person will get the most attention, and attention is assumed to be favorable. Equivalent sayings in China and Japan are "Quacking ducks get shot," and "The nail that sticks up gets hammered down," respectively. In these latter two cultures, standing out as an individual earns *unfavorable* attention. Consider the culture gap when China's Lenovo Group acquired IBM's PC business. In meetings and conference calls, Western executives were frustrated by their Chinese counterparts' reluctance to speak up, while the Chinese managers were irritated by the Americans' propensity to "just talk and talk," as one vice president of human resources put it.[81]

High-context cultures include Asian and Arab countries. Low-context cultures tend to be American and Northern European. Even within North America, cultural subgroups vary in the extent to which context counts, explaining why differences among groups can hinder successful communication. White females, Native Americans, and African Americans all tend to prefer higher context communication than do white males. A high-context interaction requires more time because a relationship has to be developed, and trust and friendship must be established. Furthermore, most male managers and most people doing the hiring in organizations are from low-context cultures, which conflicts with people entering the organization from a background in a higher-context culture.

TAKE Action!

Refer to your score on the questionnaire at the beginning of this chapter, which will give you some insight into whether you lean toward low-context or high-context communications. A higher score indicates low-context behavior, which would be jarring when trying to do business in a high-context culture.

NEW MANAGER Self-Test

Are You Culturally Intelligent?

Instructions: The job of a manager demands a lot, and before long, your activities will include situations that will test your knowledge of and capacity for dealing with people from other national cultures. Are you ready? To find out, think about your experiences in other countries or with people from other countries. To what extent does each of the following statements characterize your behavior? Please answer each of the following items as Mostly True or Mostly False for you.

	Mostly True	Mostly False
1. I plan how I'm going to relate to people from a different culture before I meet them.	_____	_____
2. I understand the religious beliefs of other cultures.	_____	_____
3. I understand the rules for nonverbal behavior in other cultures.	_____	_____
4. I seek out opportunities to interact with people from different cultures.	_____	_____
5. I can handle the stresses of living in a different culture with relative ease.	_____	_____
6. I am confident that I can befriend locals in a culture that is unfamiliar to me.	_____	_____
7. I change my speech style (e.g., accent, tone) when a cross-cultural interaction requires it.	_____	_____
8. I alter my facial expressions and gestures as needed to facilitate a cross-culture interaction.	_____	_____
9. I am quick to change the way that I behave when a cross-culture encounter seems to require it.	_____	_____

Scoring and Interpretation: Each question pertains to one of three aspects of CQ. Questions 1–3 pertain to the head (*cognitive* CQ subscale), questions 4–6 to the heart (*emotional* CQ subscale), and questions 7–9 to behavior (*physical* CQ subscale). If you have sufficient international experience and CQ to have answered "Mostly True" to two of three questions for each subscale or six of nine for all the questions, then consider yourself at a high level of CQ for a new manager. If you scored one or fewer "Mostly True" answers for each subscale or three or fewer for all nine questions, it is time to learn more about other national cultures. Hone your observational skills and learn to pick up on clues about how people from a different country respond to various situations.

SOURCES: Based on P. Christopher Earley and Elaine Mosakowski, "Cultural Intelligence," *Harvard Business Review* (October 2004): 139–146; and Soon Ang et al., "Cultural Intelligence: Its Measurement and Effects on Cultural Judgment and Decision Making, Cultural Adaptation and Task Performance," *Management and Organization Review* 3 (2007): 335–371.

Understanding the subtle contextual differences among cultures requires **cultural intelligence (CQ)**, a person's ability to use reasoning and observation skills to interpret unfamiliar gestures and situations and devise appropriate behavioral responses.[82] Discover the three aspects of cultural intelligence in the "New Manager's Self-Test."

REMEMBER THIS

- A **high-context culture** is one in which people use communication to build personal relationships.

- In a **low-context culture**, people use communication primarily to exchange facts and information.

- The United States is a low-context culture. China is an example of a high-context culture.

- Managers who develop cultural intelligence are more successful in international assignments.

- **Cultural intelligence (CQ)** refers to a person's ability to use reasoning and observation to interpret culturally unfamiliar situations and know how to respond appropriately. The three aspects of CQ are cognitive CQ, emotional CQ, and physical CQ.

3.9 International Trade Alliances

Another highly visible change in the international business environment in recent years has been the development of regional trading alliances and international trade agreements.

Before reading further, find out your level of CQ by completing the "New Manager Self-Test." Does your level of CQ reflect a global mind-set, as described earlier in the chapter?

3.9a GATT and the WTO

The General Agreement on Tariffs and Trade (GATT), signed by 23 nations in 1947, started as a set of rules to ensure nondiscrimination, clear procedures, the negotiation of disputes, and the participation of lesser-developed countries in international trade.[83] GATT sponsored eight rounds of international trade negotiations aimed at reducing trade restrictions. The 1986 to 1994 Uruguay Round (the first to be named for a developing country) involved 125 countries and cut more tariffs than ever before. In addition to lowering tariffs 30 percent from the previous level, it boldly moved the world closer to global free trade by calling for the establishment of the World Trade Organization (WTO) in 1995.

The WTO represents the maturation of GATT into a permanent global institution that can monitor international trade and has legal authority to arbitrate disputes on some 400 trade issues. As of March 2013, 159 countries, including China, Vietnam, and Ukraine, were members of the organization. As a permanent membership organization, the WTO is bringing greater trade liberalization in goods, information, technological developments, and services; stronger enforcement of rules and regulations; and greater power to resolve disputes among trading partners.

3.9b European Union

An alliance begun in 1957 to improve economic and social conditions among its members, the European Economic Community has evolved into the 28-nation European Union (EU) illustrated in Exhibit 3.10. The biggest expansion came in 2004, when the EU welcomed 10 new members from central and eastern Europe.[84]

EXHIBIT 3.10   The Nations of the European Union

The goal of the EU is to create a powerful single-market system for Europe's millions of consumers, allowing people, goods, and services to move freely. The increased competition and economies of scale within Europe enable companies to grow large and efficient, becoming more competitive in the United States and other world markets. Another aspect of European unification is the introduction of the euro. Several member states of the EU have adopted the euro, a single European currency that replaced national currencies in Austria, Belgium, Cyprus, Finland, France, Germany, Greece, Ireland, Italy, Luxembourg, Malta, the Netherlands, Portugal, Slovakia, Slovenia, and Spain.[85]

However, not all has gone smoothly for the integration, particularly since the global recession began. Small but vocal factions in several countries, including the United Kingdom, are arguing that companies and citizens would be better off withdrawing from the eurozone. A January 2013 poll found that a surprising 40 percent of Britons said that they would favor withdrawal.[86] As economic stability varied from country to country, pitting winners against losers, the economic crisis revived national loyalties and cross-border resentments, slowing the move toward a unified and cohesive "European identity." Spain,

Ireland, Portugal, and particularly Greece all have had trouble paying their debts, putting the entire eurozone at risk and leading to a possible breakup of the euro system. Even though government and industries in most of these countries have reversed the downward slide and renewed their competitiveness by cutting spending, raising taxes, and laying off millions of employees, economic uncertainties remain, with some suggestion that Greece might need another bailout. In addition, even though debt is declining in many countries, the numbers of the unemployed are soaring. Moreover, citizens are questioning whether government leaders are telling the truth about the extent of the crisis.[87] Some analysts think a broad breakup of the eurozone is unlikely, but eurozone economies are at a crossroads. Smart managers are rethinking what they would do in the event that a return to national currencies required a rethinking of everything from how to expand operations to how to pick suppliers and pay employees.[88]

3.9c North American Free Trade Agreement (NAFTA)

The North American Free Trade Agreement (NAFTA), which went into effect on January 1, 1994, merged the United States, Canada, and Mexico into a single market. Intended to spur growth and investment, increase exports, and expand jobs in all three nations, NAFTA broke down tariffs and trade restrictions over a 15-year period in a number of key areas. Thus, by 2008, virtually all U.S. industrial exports into Canada and Mexico were duty-free.

Over the first decade of NAFTA, U.S. trade with Mexico increased more than three-fold, while trade with Canada also rose dramatically.[89] Significantly, NAFTA spurred the entry of small businesses into the global arena. Jeff Victor, general manager of Treatment Products, Ltd., which makes car cleaners and waxes, credits NAFTA for his surging export volume. Prior to the pact, Mexican tariffs as high as 20 percent made it impossible for the Chicago-based company to expand its presence south of the border.[90]

However, opinions over the benefits of NAFTA appear to be as divided as they were when talks began, with some people calling it a spectacular success and others referring to it as a dismal failure. In a 2011 survey of managers, only 53 percent of North American managers surveyed said they thought reducing trade barriers and increasing free trade was a positive thing, down from 74 percent in 2003.[91] Although NAFTA has not lived up to its grand expectations, experts stress that it increased trade, investment, and income and continues to enable companies in all three countries to compete more effectively with rival Asian and European firms.[92]

REMEMBER THIS

- Regional trading alliances and international trade agreements are reshaping global business.
- The World Trade Organization (WTO) is a permanent membership organization that monitors trade and has authority to arbitrate disputes among 159 member countries.
- Two important, yet sometimes controversial, regional alliances are the European Union (EU) and the North American Free Trade Agreement (NAFTA).
- The **euro** is a single European currency that has replaced the currencies of 16 EU member nations.

CHAPTER **3**   **DISCUSSION QUESTIONS**

1. What specifically would the experience of living and working in another country contribute to your skills and effectiveness as a manager in your own country?

2. Both China and India are rising economic powers. How might your approach to doing business with China, a communist country, be different from your approach to doing business with India, the world's most populous democracy? In which country would you expect to encounter the most rules? The most bureaucracy?

3. Do you think it is realistic that BOP business practices can have a positive effect on poverty and other social problems in developing countries? Discuss.

4. Somnio, a start-up running shoe company in California, decided to start selling its products around the world from the very beginning. In general terms, name some of the challenges that a start-up company such as Somnio might face internationally.

5. Do you think that it's possible for someone to develop a global mind-set if they never live outside their native country? How might they do that?

6. Should a multinational organization operate as a tightly integrated, worldwide business system, or would it be more effective to let each national subsidiary operate autonomously? Why?

7. Why do you think many people are so frightened by globalization? Based on what is occurring in the world today, do you expect the globalization backlash to grow stronger or weaker over the next decade?

8. Two U.S. companies are competing to take over a large factory in the Czech Republic. One delegation tours the facility and asks questions about how the plant might be run more efficiently. The other delegation focuses on ways to improve working conditions and produce a better product. Which delegation do you think is more likely to succeed with the plant? Why? What information would you want to collect to decide whether to acquire the plant for your company?

9. Which style of communicating do you think would be most beneficial to the long-term success of a U.S. company operating internationally—high-context or low-context communications? Why?

10. How might the social value of low versus high power distance influence how you would lead and motivate employees? What about the value of low versus high performance orientation?

SELF-LEARNING

Rate Your Global Management Potential[93]

A global environment requires that managers learn to deal effectively with people and ideas from a variety of cultures. How well prepared are you to be a global manager? Read the following statements and circle the number on the response scale that most closely reflects how well the statement describes you.

Good Description 10 9 8 7 6 5 4 3 2 1 Poor Description

1. I reach out to people from different cultures.

    10   9   8   7   6   5   4   3   2   1

2. I frequently attend seminars and lectures about other cultures or international topics.

    10   9   8   7   6   5   4   3   2   1

3. I believe female expatriates can be equally as effective as male expatriates.

    10   9   8   7   6   5   4   3   2   1

4. I have a basic knowledge about several countries in addition to my native country.

    10   9   8   7   6   5   4   3   2   1

5. I have good listening and empathy skills.

    10   9   8   7   6   5   4   3   2   1

6. I have spent more than two weeks traveling or working in another country.

10   9   8   7   6   5   4   3   2   1

7. I easily adapt to the different work ethics of students from other cultures when we are involved in a team project.

10   9   8   7   6   5   4   3   2   1

8. I can speak at least one foreign language.

10   9   8   7   6   5   4   3   2   1

9. I know which countries tend to cluster into similar sociocultural and economic groupings.

10   9   8   7   6   5   4   3   2   1

10. I feel capable of assessing different cultures on the basis of power distance, uncertainty avoidance, individualism, and masculinity.

10   9   8   7   6   5   4   3   2   1

Total Score: _____

Scoring and Interpretation

Add up the total points for the ten questions. If you scored 81–100 points, you have a great capacity for developing good global management skills. A score of 61–80 points indicates that you have potential but may lack skills in certain areas, such as language or foreign experience. A score of 60 or less means you need to do some serious work to improve your potential for global management. Regardless of your total score, go back over each item and make a plan of action to increase scores of less than 5 on any question.

GROUP LEARNING

Global Entrepreneurship IQ

1. Which country is the best place to launch a new business?
    a. Great Britain
    b. United States
    c. Canada
    d. Denmark
    e. Singapore

2. Which country improved the most in terms of making it easier for companies to do business?
    a. France
    b. Burundi
    c. Japan
    d. Poland
    e. Serbia

3. Which country implemented the least amount of reforms that would help business operate?
    a. Surinam
    b. Columbia
    c. Vietnam
    d. Rwanda
    e. Croatia

4. Which country has a "one-stop shop" for clearance on construction permits and/or custom, duties, etc.?
    a. Venezuela
    b. Nigeria
    c. Tunisia
    d. Georgia
    e. Egypt

5. Which country in the Middle East has strength of legal institutions and inexpensive procedures for doing business?
    a. Iraq
    b. Iran
    c. Algeria
    d. Saudi Arabia
    e. Lebanon

6. Which country in Latin America has sustained the most business-friendly reforms over time?
    a. Bolivia
    b. Panama
    c. Columbia
    d. Costa Rica
    e. Nicaragua

7. Which country is Europe has brought more economic reforms in the past 20 years and has seen its income increase by the greatest percentage?
    a. Latvia
    b. Greece
    c. Finland
    d. Netherlands
    e. Hungary

8. Which country below as streamlined business processes by as much as 15 days for starting a business and reduced the time it takes for property transfers from 371 days to 25?
    a. Sri Lanka
    b. Rwanda
    c. Argentina
    d. Mexico
    e. France

6. Which country is the most transparent in terms of business practices, government regulations, and corruption?
    a. Algeria
    b. Iran
    c. El Salvador
    d. Sudan
    e. Nigeria

10. Which of the following countries made the most changes to make it easier to start a new business?
    a. Madagascar
    b. Haiti
    c. Mali
    d. Togo
    e. Niger

Source: The World Bank, *Doing Business 2013*, World Bank and International Finance Corporation, 2013.

ACTION LEARNING

Try Being a Minority

1. Singly, or in groups of no more than two, find a place to be a minority, such as a Korean wedding (as long as you are not Korean), an Indian cultural fare, a Black church, an Old Folks home, etc. Do NOT choose something dangerous like a Biker Bar or Inner City club.

2. Go to the place or event and make an effort to talk to at least five people.

3. Write up your experiences in a short paper, answering the following questions:
    a. How did it feel to be the different one?
    b. How did people treat you? Is that how you react to someone who is in a minority situation where you are?
    c. What are the difficulties in being a minority?
    d. What skills do you need in such a situation?
    e. Do you see minorities any different now than you did before this Action Learning?

4. Be prepared to discuss your experiences and conclusions in class.

Source: Adapted from Renate R. Mai-Dalton. From Exchange: *Organizational Behavior Teaching Review*, Vol. 9(3), 1984-85.

ETHICAL DILEMMA

AH Biotech[94]

Dr. Abraham Hassan knew that he couldn't put off the decision any longer. AH Biotech, the Bound Brook, New Jersey-based company started by this psychiatrist-turned-entrepreneur, had developed a novel drug that seemed to promise long-term relief from panic attacks. If it gained approval from the Food and Drug Administration (FDA), it would be the company's first product. It was now time for large-scale clinical trials. But where should AH Biotech conduct those tests?

David Berger, who headed up research and development, was certain he already knew the answer to that question: Albania. "Look, doing these trials in Albania will be quicker, easier, and a lot cheaper than doing them in the States," he pointed out. "What's not to like?"

Dr. Hassan had to concede that Berger's arguments were sound. If they did trials in the United States, AH Biotech would spend considerable time and money advertising for patients and then finding physicians who'd be willing to serve as clinical trial investigators. Rounding up U.S. doctors prepared to take on that job was getting increasingly difficult. They just didn't want to take time out of their busy practices to do the testing, not to mention all the recordkeeping that such a study entailed.

In Albania, it was an entirely different story. It was one of the poorest Eastern European countries—if not *the* poorest—with a just barely functioning health care system. Albanian physicians and patients would practically line up at AH Biotech's doorstep begging to take part. Physicians there could earn much better money as clinical investigators for a U.S. company than they could actually practicing medicine, and patients saw signing up as test subjects as their best chance for receiving any treatment at all, let alone cutting-edge Western medicine. All these factors meant that the company could count on realizing at least a 25 percent savings (maybe even more) by running the tests overseas.

So, what's not to like? As the Egyptian-born CEO of a start-up biotech company with investors and employees hoping for its first marketable drug, there was absolutely nothing not to like. It was when he thought like a U.S.-trained physician that he felt qualms. If he used U.S. test subjects, he knew they'd likely continue to receive the drug until it was approved. At that point, most would have insurance that covered most of the cost of their prescriptions. But he already knew that it wasn't going to make any sense to market the drug in a poor country like Albania, so when the study was over, he'd have to cut off treatment. Sure, he conceded, panic attacks weren't usually fatal. But he knew how debilitating these sudden bouts of feeling completely terrified were—the pounding heart, chest pain, choking sensation, and nausea. The severity and unpredictability of these attacks often made a normal life all but impossible. How could he offer people dramatic relief and then snatch it away?

What Would You Do?

1. Do the clinical trials in Albania. You'll be able to bring the drug to market faster and cheaper, which will be good for AH Biotech's employees and investors and good for the millions of people who suffer from anxiety attacks.

2. Do the clinical trials in the United States. Even though it will certainly be more expensive and time-consuming, you'll feel as if you're living up to the part of the Hippocratic Oath that instructed you to "prescribe regimens for the good of my patients according to my ability and my judgment and never do harm to anyone."

3. Do the clinical trials in Albania, and if the drug is approved, use part of the profits to set up a compassionate use program in Albania, even though setting up a distribution system and training doctors to administer the drug, monitor patients for adverse effects, and track results will entail considerable expense.

CASE FOR CRITICAL ANALYSIS

We Want More Guitars!

Adam Wainwright's early-morning phone call from Valencia, Spain, initially startled his boss, Vincent Fletcher. Adam, a true slave to the latest techno-gadgetry, *never* called. Yet here he was, at 8 a.m. Pacific time, on the phone to the CEO of Fletcher Guitars in Los Angeles.

"What did they do—lose your luggage with all of your toys inside?" Fletcher joked. "Did the plant burn down?"

"No, I just decided to call you on this one. I've been here for a week, looking over operations. Forget the idea of getting any substantial increase in productivity. I don't think these guys are capable of upping production by *ten* guitars per year," Adam complained.

"Isn't that an exaggeration?" Fletcher asked.

There was a momentary silence on the other end of the line. "Adam, did I lose you?"

"No."

"Look, part of our reputation is based on the quality and craftsmanship of the acoustic guitars produced by Dominguez and his workers. This is all high-end stuff," Fletcher said in a voice that always reminded Adam of actor Jason Robards. "Now, with the tremendous rise in the popularity of Latin music, we want to encourage increased production. That's your task, Adam. I shouldn't have to tell you that your success with this assignment could lead to some great opportunities for you."

"I know," Adam paused, carefully weighing his next words. "Salvador and his people do a fabulous job. Just walking through his operation, I have been blown away by the craftsmanship. But the slow pace of work is unbelievably frustrating. These guys act like they are birthing a baby. Everything is so precise, so touchy-feely with every guitar. I used my iPad to create some workflow specs for increased production. Salvador took one look, laughed, and said 'You Americans.'"

Poor Adam, Fletcher thought. *That had to be a major stab in his high-tech heart. Maybe I sent the wrong guy. Nope. He has great potential in management and he has to learn to work through this and deliver.* Fletcher's thoughts were interrupted by Adam's voice, flustered and increasing in volume.

"They go off to lunch and come wandering back in here hours later—*hours,* Fletcher."

"They're Spanish!" Fletcher replied. "So they take two-hour lunches. They work their schedule. It's just not *our* schedule. You may be a lot younger than I am, Adam. But you need to lighten up. Listen, talk to Salvador and see what works for them. They've increased output before and they can do it again. Get this done, Adam. And *e-mail* me."

The international rise in Latin music over the past decade, punctuated by the clear sound and dazzling rhythms of the acoustic guitar, created a sense of urgency for guitar makers around the globe to increase the availability of these classical instruments. Wanting to ride the crest of this musical trend, increase his product offerings, and tap into high-end market sales, Fletcher discovered master craftsman Salvador Dominguez and his Spanish company, Guitarra Dominguez, while attending the prestigious Frankfurt International Fair in 1980.

Salvador liked to tell that among the first sounds he heard following his birth were the words of his father's lullaby, accompanied by an acoustic guitar. As an adult, Salvador combined his lifelong passion for guitars with brilliant craftsmanship, starting his own company in 1976. Located in the Poligono Industrial Fuente del Jarro—Paterna, Valencia, Spain, the company now employed more than 30 craftsmen in the production of acoustic and flamenco instruments. A thin, wiry bundle of energy with graying wavy hair and large eyes with that surprised "Salvador Dalí look," the guitar maker could grasp a piece of wood and, running his hand over the surface, be suddenly transformed into a patient, tender sculptor of sound. To watch this luthier work was almost mesmerizing. Salvador's total silence and habit of leaning his right ear close to the wood as he worked suggested that he was actually *hearing* the music of the instrument as he created it.

Following the phone call to Fletcher, Adam returned to the plant, determined that Salvador would now hear from him.

"Salvador, you do beautiful work. Latin music is one of the hottest trends in music, and musicians are clamoring for the instruments you make. But we can be doing so much more here. There's plenty of room for expansion in this place, and we could nearly double production within the next few years. I have visited companies all over the United States and analyzed their operations. If you will take time to look at the plan I've drawn up, you will clearly see the potential for cranking out more product and meeting the needs of more customers."

"Señor Wainwright. Here in Spain, we do not *crank out product.* We take pride in each creation, and it is important that our methods of craftsmanship remain the same. No two of these instruments are alike."

"Wait. Wait. I'm just saying that there are changes that can be made here that will make this operation more productive. In the States, I see a flow to their operations. Here, we have starts and stops. The Nato mahogany used in many of your acoustic guitar bodies provides a beautiful and unrestricted wood. But Carlos has been off in a corner most of the week, wearing protective gear and experimenting with his notions about the potential tonal qualities of Wenge in acoustic bodies. The bottom line is this: We simply must streamline this operation in order to increase your production."

"No, Señor. *My bottom line* is this: Guitarras Dominguez will not lower *our* standards of craftsmanship to meet *your* plan."

Questions

1. How accurate is Adam Wainwright's analysis of the situation at Guitarras Dominguez? Do you think craftsmanship is incompatible with increasing productivity in this company? Why?

2. What social values are present in Guitarras Dominguez that seem different from U.S. social values (see Exhibits 3.7 and 3.8)? Explain.

3. What do you recommend Adam do to increase production in a business setting that does not seem to value high production?

On the Job: Black Diamond Equipment: Managing in a Global Environment

Questions

1. What evidence do you see of a global mind-set in these managers? List at least three examples of global thinking provided in the video.

2. Referencing the common traits of an MNC described in the text, explain why you think Black Diamond *is* or *is not* a multinational corporation.

3. Describe at least two environmental factors affecting this business, and summarize how the managers are responding to these factors.

ENDNOTES

1. Laurie Burkitt and Paul Mozur, "China Squeezes Western Firms," *The Wall Street Journal*, April 5, 2013, B1.

2. Ibid.

3. Joann S. Lublin, "Hunt Is on for Fresh Executive Talent—Cultural Flexibility in Demand," *The Wall Street Journal*, April 11, 2011, B1.

4. Adapted from Cynthia Barnum and Natasha Wolniansky, "Why Americans Fail at Overseas Negotiations," *Management Review* (October 1989): 54–57.

5. Lolita C. Baldor, "FBI Sends More Agents Abroad to Shield U.S. from Cybercrime; Foreign Hackers Stepping up Their Attacks," *South Florida Sun-Sentinel*, December 10, 2009; and Cassell Bryan-Low, "Criminal Network: To Catch Crooks in Cyberspace, FBI Goes Global," *The Wall Street Journal*, November 21, 2006.

6. Quoted in Ryan Underwood, "Going Global," *Inc.* (March 2011): 96–98.

7. Bettina Wassener, "Living in Asia Appeals to More Company Leaders," *The New York Times*, June 21, 2012, B3; and Emily Glazer, "P&G Unit Bids Goodbye to Cincinnati, Hello to Asia," *The Wall Street Journal*, May 10, 2012, B1.

8. "TCS Can Become India's First Company to Reach $100 Billion in Market Cap: CLSA," *The Economic Times*, August 31, 2013, http://articles.economictimes.indiatimes.com/2013-08-31/news/41619991_1_tcs-market-capitalisation-lakh-crore (accessed September 2, 2013); Steve Hamm, "IBM vs. Tata: Which Is More American?" *BusinessWeek* (May 5, 2008): 28.

9. Chris Woodyard, "The American Car," *USA Today*, February 17, 2009. Woodyard, "The American Car," *USA Today*, February 17, 2009.

10. "KOF Index of Globalization 2013," press release, KOF Swiss Economic Institute (March 2013).

11. "2013 KOF Index of Globalization," KOF Swiss Economic Institute, http://globalization.kof.ethz.ch/media/filer_public/2013/03/25/rankings_2013.pdf (accessed May 13, 2014). *Note:* The 2013 KOF analysis of globalization dimensions is based on the year 2010.

12. Gregory C. Unruh and Ángel Cabrera, "Join the Global Elite," *Harvard Business Review* (May 2013): 135–139.

13. This section is based on Unruh and Cabrera, "Join the Global Elite"; Schon Beechler and Dennis Baltzley, "Creating a Global Mindset," *Chief Learning Officer* (May 29, 2008), http://clomedia.com/articles/view/creating_a_global_mindset/1 (accessed June 26, 2012); Joana S. P. Story and John E. Barbuto, Jr., "Global Mindset: A Construct Clarification and Framework," *Journal of Leadership and Organizational Studies* 18, no. 3 (2011): 377–384; and Stephen L. Cohen, "Effective Global Leadership Requires a Global Mindset," *Industrial and Commercial Training* 42, no. 1 (2010): 3–10.

14. Definition based on Mansour Javidan and Jennie L. Walker, "A Whole New Global Mindset for Leadership," *People & Strategy* 35, no. 2 (2012): 36–41; Mansour Javidan and Mary B. Teagarden, "Conceptualizing and Measuring Global Mindset," *Advances in Global Leadership* 6 (2011): 13–39; and Beechler and Baltzley, "Creating a Global Mindset."

15. Amol Titus, "Competency of Intercultural Management," *The Jakarta Post*, March 11, 2009, www.thejakartapost.com/news/2009/03/11/competency-intercultural-management.html (accessed June 30, 2012).

16. Based on Mansour Javidan and Jennie L. Walker, "A Whole New Global Mindset for Leadership," *People & Strategy* 35, no. 2 (2012): 36–41.

17. This is based on Unruh and Cabrera, "Join the Global Elite."

18. Ibid.

19. Siegfried Russwurm et al., "Developing Your Global Know-How," *Harvard Business Review* (March 2011): 70–75.

20. Bob Davis, "As Global Economy Shifts, Companies Rethink, Retool," *The Wall Street Journal*, November 7, 2010, http://online.wsj.com/article/SB10001424052748704049904575554290932153112.html (accessed June 29, 2012).

21. Mike Ramsey, "Ford's CEO Revs up Auto Maker's China Role," *The Wall Street Journal*, April 16, 2013, B7.

22. George Stalk and David Michael, "What the West Doesn't Get About China," *Harvard Business Review* (June 2011): 25–27; Zoe McKay, "Consumer Spending in China: To Buy or Not to Buy," Forbes.com, June 15, 2012, www.forbes.com/sites/insead/2012/06/15/consumer-spending-in-china-to-buy-or-not-to-buy/ (accessed June 29, 2012); and Adam Davidson, "Come On, China, Buy Our Stuff!" *The New York Times*, January 25, 2012, www.nytimes.com/2012/01/29/magazine/come-on-china-buy-our-stuff.html?pagewanted=all (accessed June 29, 2012).

23. Patricia Sellers, "The New Coke," *Fortune* (May 21, 2012): 140.

24. Laurie Burkitt and Paul Mozur, "Foreign Firms Brace for More Pressure in China," *The Wall Street Journal Online*, April 4, 2013, http://online.wsj.com/news/articles/SB10001424127887323916304578400463208890042 (accessed July 30, 2014).

25. David Barboza and Brad Stone, "A Nation That Trips Up Many," *The New York Times*, January 16, 2010.

26. Andrew Galbraith and Jason Dean, "In China, Some Firms Defy Business Norms," *The Wall Street Journal Online*, September 6, 2011, http://online.wsj.com/-article/SB10001424053111903895904576546381512015722.html (accessed June 29, 2012).

27. Colum Murphy, James T. Areddy, and James R. Hagerty, "Deal Gone Wrong Adds to Caterpillar's Troubles in China," *The Wall Street Journal*, January 21, 2013, http://online.wsj.com/article/SB1000142412788732330110457825574026118404.html (accessed August 29, 2013).

28. Stalk and Michael, "What the West Doesn't Get About China."

29. Eric Pfanner, "Mobile Devices Overtake PC Sales at Lenovo," *The New York Times*, August 15, 2013, http://www.nytimes.com/2013/08/16/business/global/smartphones-and-tablets-outsell-pcs-at-lenovo.html?_r=0 (accessed August 29, 2013); Juro Osawa, "Q&A: Lenovo CEO on Smartphones and BlackBerry," *The Wall Street Journal Online*, August 15, 2013, http://blogs.wsj.com/digits/2013/08/15/qalenovo-ceo-on-smartphones-and-blackberry/ (accessed August 29, 2013); Bien Perez, "Lenovo Making Moves on Enterprise Server Market," *South China Morning Post*, August 29, 2013, http://www.scmp.com/business/china-business/article/1300212/lenovo-making-moves-enterprise-server-market (accessed August 29, 2013); and Chuck Salter, "Lenovo: Protect and Attack," *Fast Company* (December 2011–January 2012): 116–121, 154–155.

30. W. Michael Cox and Richard Alm, "China and India: Two Paths to Economic Power," *Economic Letter*, Federal Reserve Bank of Dallas, August 2008, www.dallasfed.org/research/eclett/2008/el0808.html (accessed July 14, 2010).

31. "Pharmaceuticals," India Brand Equity Foundation, IBEF. org, May 2012, www.ibef.org/industry/pharmaceuticals.aspx (accessed June 29, 2012); and Sushmi Dey, "Indian Pharma Eyes US Generic Gold Rush," *Business Standard*, June 27, 2012, www.business-standard.com/india/news/indian-pharma-eyes-us-generic-gold-rush/478593/ (accessed June 29, 2012).

32. This section is based on "Brazil Economy Grew 0.9% in 2012," *BBC*, March1, 2013, http://www.bbc.co.uk/news/business-21630930 (accessed August 29, 2013); "Brazil GDP Growth Rate," Trading Economics Web site, www.tradingeconomics.com/brazil/gdp-growth (accessed June 29, 2012); "Brazil," *The World Factbook*, Central Intelligence Agency Web site, https://www.cia.gov/library/publications/the-world-factbook/geos/br.html#top (accessed June 29, 2012); Paulo Prada, "For Brazil, It's Finally Tomorrow," *The Wall Street Journal*, March 29, 2010; Melanie Eversley, "Brazil's Olympian Growth," *USA Today*, October 5, 2009; and Liam Denning, "Are Cracks Forming in the BRICs?" *The Wall Street Journal*, February 16, 2010.

33. "Count: *Really* Big Business," *Fast Company* (December 2008–January 2009): 46.

34. Medard Gabel and Henry Bruner, *Global Inc.: An Atlas of the Multinational Corporation* (New York: The New Press, 2003).

35. David E. Bell and Mary L. Shelman, "KFC's Radical Approach to China," *Harvard Business Review* (November 2011): 137–142; and Burkitt and Mozur, "Foreign Firms Brace for More Pressure in China."

36. Howard V. Perlmutter, "The Tortuous Evolution of the Multinational Corporation," *Columbia Journal of World Business* (January–February 1969): 9–18; and Youram Wind, Susan P. Douglas, and Howard V. Perlmutter, "Guidelines for Developing International Marketing Strategies," *Journal of Marketing* (April 1973): 14–23.

37. Deborah Ball, "Boss Talk: Nestlé Focuses on Long Term," *The Wall Street Journal*, November 2, 2009; Transnationale Web site, www.transnationale.org/companies/nestle.php (accessed March 17, 2010); Company Analytics Web site, www.company-analytics.org/company/nestle.php (accessed March 17, 2010); and Nestlé SA Web site, www.nestle.com (accessed March 17, 2010).

38. Sara Murray and Douglas Belkin, "Americans Sour on Trade: Majority Say Free-Trade Pacts Have Hurt U.S.," *The Wall Street Journal*, October 4, 2010; and Nina Easton, "Make the World Go Away," *Fortune* (February 4, 2008): 105–108.

39. Easton, "Make the World Go Away."

40. Michael Schroeder and Timothy Aeppel, "Skilled Workers Sway Politicians with Fervor Against Free Trade," *The Wall Street Journal*, December 10, 2003.

41. Vanessa Fuhrmans, "Amazon Acts on German Controversy; Online Retailer Cuts Ties with Security Firm After a Television Documentary on Working Conditions," *The Wall Street Journal*, February 19, 2013, B3.

42. This discussion is based on C. K. Prahalad, "The Fortune at the Bottom of the Pyramid," *Fast Company* (April 13, 2011), www.fastcompany.com/1746818/ fortune-at-the-bottom-of-the-pyramid-ck-prahalad (accessed June 30, 2012); C. K. Prahalad and S. L. Hart, "The Fortune at the Bottom of the Pyramid," *Strategy + Business* 26 (2002): 54–67; Jakki Mohr, Sanjit Sengupta, and Stanley F. Slater, "Serving Base-of-the-Pyramid Markets: Meeting Real Needs Through a Customized Approach," *Journal of Business Strategy* 33, no. 6 (2012): 4–14; and Scott Johnson, "SC Johnson Builds Business at the Base of the Pyramid," *Global Business and Organizational Excellence* (September–October, 2007): 6–17.

43. Bala Chakravarthy and Sophie Coughlan, "Emerging Market Strategy: Innovating Both Products and Delivery Systems," *Strategy & Leadership* 40, 1 (2012): 27–32; T. V. Mahalingam, "Godrej's Rediscovery of India: They Say They Touch More Consumers than Any Other Indian Company," *Business Today* (July 25, 2010): 58–64; and "Godrej Eyes Youth to Expand Portfolio," *Mail Today*, July 12, 2009.

44. Rob Walker, "Cleaning Up," *New York Times Magazine* (June 10, 2007): 20.

45. Matthew Boyle, "Unilever: Taking on the World, One Stall at a Time," *Bloomberg Businessweek* (January 7–January 13, 2013): 18–20.

46. Boyle, "Unilever: Taking on the World One Stall at a Time"; and Jennifer Reingold, "Can P&G Make Money in Places Where People Earn $2 a Day?" *Fortune* (January 17, 2011): 86–91.

47. Reported in Unruh and Cabrera, "Join the Global Elite."

48. Kate Milani, "Three Best Ways to Export," *The Wall Street Journal Online*, March 15, 2010, http://online.wsj.com/news/articles/SB100014240527487039098045751237830777762888 (accessed July 2, 2014); and Mark Sweney, "Netflix Non-US Losses Hit $100m But Subscribers Increase," *The Guardian*, April 24, 2012, www.guardian.co.uk/media/2012/apr/24/netflix-losses-100m-subscribers-increase (accessed June 27, 2012).

49. Lauren A. E. Schuker, "Plot Change: Foreign Forces Transform Hollywood Films," *The Wall Street Journal*, July 31, 2010, A1; and Nicole Allan, "How to Make a Hollywood Hit," *The Atlantic* (May 2012): 70–71; Miriam Gottfried, "Cinemark's Riveting Screenplay," *The Wall Street Journal*, July 28–29, 2012, B14; and "Made In (But Not For) the U.S.A.," *Fast Company* (July–August 2013): 24.

50. Alison Stein Wellner, "Turning the Tables," *Inc.* (May 2006): 55–59.

51. Kathryn Rudie Harrigan, "Managing Joint Ventures," *Management Review* (February 1987): 24–41; and Therese R. Revesz and Mimi Cauley de Da La Sierra, "Competitive Alliances: Forging Ties Abroad," *Management Review* (March 1987): 57–59.

52. Christopher Weaver, "Abbott Looks to Consumer for Growth," *The Wall Street Journal*, May 2, 2012, http://online.wsj.com/article/SB10001424052702303990604577367760661436198.html (accessed June 28, 2012).

53. Anthony Goerzen, "Managing Alliance Networks: Emerging Practices of Multinational Corporations," *Academy of Management Executive* 19, no. 2 (2005): 94–107.

54. Isabel Zhong, "China's Zealous but Bumpy U.S. Acquisition Spree," *Medill Reports*, Northwestern University, June 14, 2013, http://news.medill.northwestern.edu/chicago/news.aspx?id=223155 (accessed September 30, 2013); Michelle Caruso-Cabrera, "China Boosts U.S. Investment to All-Time High; Seeks More," NBCNews.com, May 22,

2013, http://www.nbcnews.com/business/china-boosts-us-investment-all-time-high-seeks-more-6C10018475 (accessed September 30, 2013); Anjali Cordeiro, "Tang in India and Other Kraft Synergies," *The Wall Street Journal Online*, April 19, 2010, http://online.wsj.com/article/SB10001424052702303348504575184103106388686.html (accessed June 28, 2012); and Tiisetso Motsoeneng and Wendell Roelf, "Wal-Mart Wins Final Go-Ahead for Massmart Deal," Reuters.com, March 9, 2012, www.reuters.com/article/2012/03/09/us-massmart-walmart-idUS-BRE8280KH20120309 (accessed June 27, 2012).

55. Daniel Michaels, Jon Ostrower, and David Pearson, "Airbus's New Push: Made in the U.S.A.," *The Wall Street Journal*, July 2, 2012.

56. G. Pascal Zachary, "Dream Factory," *Business 2.0* (June 2005): 96–102.

57. Jim Holt, "Gone Global?" *Management Review* (March 2000): 13.

58. James Hookway, "IKEA's Products Make Shoppers Blush in Thailand," *The Wall Street Journal*, June 5, 2012, A1.

59. Holt, "Gone Global?"

60. "Slogans Often Lose Something in Translation," *The New Mexican*, July 3, 1994.

61. For a recent overview of various environmental factors influencing firms that operate internationally, see David Conklin, "The Global Environment of Business: New Paradigms for International Management," *Ivey Business Journal* (July–August 2011), www.iveybusinessjournal.com/topics/global-business/the-global-environment-of-business-new-paradigms-for-international-management (accessed June 27, 2012).

62. "The Global Competitiveness Report 2011–2012," World Economic Forum, www3.weforum.org/docs/WEF_GCR_Report_2011-12.pdf (accessed June 27, 2012).

63. "The Global Competitiveness Index 2012–2013, http://www3.weforum.org/docs/CSI/2012-13/GCR_Rankings_2012-13.pdf (accessed August 30, 2013).

64. "European Debt Crisis Fast Facts," *CNN*.com, July 27, 2013, http://www.cnn.com/2013/07/27/world/europe/european-debt-crisis-fast-facts (accessed August 30, 2013).

65. "A New Definition of Misery," *The New York Times*, December 18, 2009 (based on data from *Moody's*), www.nytimes.com/imagepages/2009/12/18/business/economy/20091219_CHARTS_GRAPHIC.html (accessed September 27, 2012).

66. Mike Ramsey and Yoshio Takahashi, "Car Wreck: Honda and Toyota," *The Wall Street Journal Online*, November 1, 2011, http://online.wsj.com/article/SB10001424052970204528204577009044170787650.html (accessed June 29, 2012).

67. Stephanie Wong, John Liu, and Tim Culpan, "Life and Death at the iPad Factory," *Bloomberg Businessweek* (June 7–June 13, 2010): 35–36; Charles Duhigg and Steven Greenhouse, "Apple Supplier in China Pledges Big Labor Changes," *The New York Times*, March 29, 2012, www.nytimes.com/2012/03/30/business/-apple-supplier-in-china-pledges-changes-in-working-conditions.html?pagewanted=all (accessed June 30, 2012); David Barboza and Charles Duhigg, "China Plant Again Faces Labor Issue on iPhones," *The New York Times*, September

10, 2012, http://www.nytimes.com/2012/09/11/technology/foxconn-said-to-use-forced-student-labor-to-make-iphones.html?pagewanted=all&_r=0 (accessed August 30, 2013); and Keith Bradsher and David Barboza, "Hewlett Directs Its Suppliers in China to Limit Student Labor," *The New York Times*, February 7, 2013, http://www.nytimes.com/2013/02/08/business/global/hewlett-packard-joins-push-to-limit-use-of-student-labor-in-china.html (accessed August 30, 2013).

68. Ian Bremmer, "Managing Risk in an Unstable World," *Harvard Business Review* (June 2005): 51–60; Mark Fitzpatrick, "The Definition and Assessment of Political Risk in International Business: A Review of the Literature," *Academy of Management Review* 8 (1983): 249–254; and Jo Jakobsen, "Old Problems Remain, New Ones Crop Up: Political Risk in the 21st Century," *Business Horizons* 53 (2010): 481–490.

69. Amol Sharma and Biman Mukherji, "Bad Roads, Red Tape, Burly Thugs Slow Wal-Mart's Passage in India," *The Wall Street Journal*, January 12, 2013, http://online.wsj.com/article/SB10001424127887323622904578129294224588914.html (accessed January 18, 2013).

70. Alisa Wiersema, "Everything You Need to Know About the Syrian Civil War," *ABC News*, August 31, 2013, http://abcnews.go.com/Politics/syrian-civil-war/story?id=20112311 (accessed September 2, 2013); and quote from Peter Wonacott, "An Entrepreneur Weathers a Tumultuous Arab Spring," *The Wall Street Journal*, January 17, 2012, http://online.wsj.com/article/SB10001424052970203436904577150690233235850.html (accessed June 27, 2012).

71. Suzanne Choney, "New York Times Hacked, Syrian Electronic Army Suspected," *NBC News*, August 28, 2013, http://www.nbcnews.com/technology/new-york-times-hacked-syrian-electronic-armysuspected-8C11016739 (accessed September 2, 2013).

72. Mary Gooderham, "Companies That Go Where Others Fear to Tread," *The Globe and Mail*, June 21, 2012, B7.

73. Geert Hofstede, *Culture's Consequences: International Differences in Work-Related Values* (Beverly Hills, CA: Sage, 1980); G. Hofstede, "The Interaction Between National and Organizational Value Systems," *Journal of Management Studies* 22 (1985): 347–357; and G. Hofstede, *Cultures and Organizations: Software of the Mind* (revised and expanded 2nd ed.) (New York: McGraw-Hill, 2005).

74. Geert Hofstede, "Cultural Constraints in Management Theory," *Academy of Management Executive* 7 (1993): 81–94; and G. Hofstede and M. H. Bond, "The Confucian Connection: From Cultural Roots to Economic Growth," *Organizational Dynamics* 16 (1988): 4–21.

75. Vas Taras, Piers Steel, and Bradley L. Kirkman, "Three Decades of Research on National Culture in the Workplace: Do the Differences Still Make a Difference?" *Organizational Dynamics* 40 (2011): 189–198.

76. For an overview of the research and publications related to Hofstede's dimensions, see "Retrospective: *Culture's Consequences*," a collection of articles focusing on Hofstede's work, in *The Academy of Management Executive* 18, no. 1 (February 2004): 72–93. See also Michele J. Gelfand et al., "Individualism and Collectivism," in *Culture, Leadership, and Organizations: The Globe Study of 62 Societies*, ed. R. J. House et al. (Thousand Oaks, CA: Sage, 2004).

77. Mansour Javidan et al., "In the Eye of the Beholder: Cross-Cultural Lessons from Project GLOBE," *Academy of Management Perspectives* (February 2006): 67–90; Robert J. House et al., eds., *Culture, Leadership, and Organizations: The GLOBE Study of 62 Societies* (Thousand Oaks, CA: Sage Publications, 2004); M. Javidan and R. J. House, "Cultural Acumen for the Global Manager: Lessons from Project GLOBE," *Organizational Dynamics* 29, no. 4 (2001): 289–305; and R. J. House et al., "Understanding Cultures and Implicit Leadership Theories Across the Globe: An Introduction to Project GLOBE," *Journal of World Business* 37 (2002): 3–10.

78. Carlos Sanchez-Runde et al., "Looking Beyond Western Leadership Models: Implications for Global Managers," *Organizational Dynamics* 40 (2011): 207–213.

79. Chantell E. Nicholls, Henry W. Lane, and Mauricio Brehm Brechu, "Taking Self-Managed Teams to Mexico," *Academy of Management Executive* 13, no. 2 (1999): 15–27; Carl F. Fey and Daniel R. Denison, "Organizational Culture and Effectiveness: Can American Theory Be Applied in Russia?" *Organization Science* 14, no. 6 (November–December 2003): 686–706; Ellen F. Jackofsky, John W. Slocum, Jr., and Sara J. -McQuaid, "Cultural Values and the CEO: Alluring Companions?" *Academy of Management Executive* 2 (1988): 39–49.

80. J. Kennedy and A. Everest, "Put Diversity in Context," *Personnel Journal* (September 1991): 50–54.

81. Jane Spencer, "Lenovo Goes Global, But Not Without Strife," *The Wall Street Journal,* November 4, 2008.

82. P. Christopher Earley and Elaine Mosakowski, "Cultural Intelligence," *Harvard Business Review* (October 2004): 139.

83. This discussion is based on "For Richer, for Poorer," *The Economist* (December 1993): 66; Richard Harmsen, "The Uruguay Round: A Boon for the World Economy," *Finance & Development* (March 1995): 24–26; Salil S. Pitroda, "From GATT to WTO: The Institutionalization of World Trade," *Harvard International Review* (Spring 1995): 46–47, 66–67; and the World Trade Organization Web site, http://www.wto.org/english/thewto_e/whatis_e/tif_e/org6_e.htm (accessed March 31, 2013).

84. EUROPA Web site, "The History of the European Union," http://europa.eu/about-eu/eu-history/index_en.htm (accessed July 14, 2010).

85. European Commission Economic and Financial Affairs Web site, http://ec.europa.eu/economy_finance/euro/index_en.htm (accessed March 18, 2010).

86. Reported in Landon Thomas Jr., "In Europe, a Risk-Filled Choice for Britain," *The New York Times,* February 1, 2013, http://www.nytimes.com/2013/02/13/business/global/britains-risk-filled-choice.html?pagewanted=all&_r=0 (accessed September 2, 2013).

87. Jonathan Buck, "Europe's Economy Will Rebound," *Barron's,* July 22, 2013, http://online.barrons.com/article/SB50001424052748704093404578613863100842212.html#articleTabs_article%3D1 (accessed September 2, 2013); Clive Crook, "Opening Remarks: Who Lost the Euro?" part of a "Special Euro Crisis" section, *Bloomberg BusinessWeek* (May 28–June 3, 2012): 10–12; Dalibor Rohac, "The Never-Ending Greek Tragedy," *U.S. News and World Report* (August 30, 2013), http://www.usnews.com/opinion/articles/2013/08/30/greece-shows-the-eurozone-crisis-is-far-from-over (accessed September 2, 2013); Rebecca Clancy, "Rehn: Too Early to Say Eurozone Crisis Is Over," *The Telegraph,* August 29, 2013, http://www.telegraph.co.uk/finance/economics/10273514/Rehn-Too-early-to-say-eurozone-crisis-is-over.html (accessed September 2, 2013); Thomas, "In Europe, a Risk-Filled Choice for Britain"; and Todd Buell, "Germans Believe Politicians Are Lying about Crisis, Says Study," *The Wall Street Journal,* August 15, 2013, http://blogs.wsj.com/eurocrisis/2013/08/15/germans-believe-politicians-are-lying-about-crisis-says-study/ (accessed September 2, 2013).

88. Vanessa Fuhrmans and Dana Cimilluca, "Business Braces for Europe's Worst—Multinationals Scramble to Protect Cash, Revise Contracts, Tighten Payment Terms," *The Wall Street Journal,* June 1, 2012, B1.

89. Tapan Munroe, "NAFTA Still a Work in Progress," *Knight Ridder/Tribune News Service,* January 9, 2004; and J. S. McClenahan, "NAFTA Works," *IW* (January 10, 2000): 5–6.

90. Amy Barrett, "It's a Small (Business) World," *BusinessWeek* (April 17, 1995): 96–101.

91. Darrell Rigby and Barbara Bilodeau, "Management Tools and Trends 2011," Bain & Company, Inc., www.bain.com/publications/articles/Management-tools-trends-2011.aspx (accessed June 22, 2012).

92. Jeffrey Sparshott, "NAFTA Gets Mixed Reviews," *The Washington Times,* December 18, 2003; and Munroe, "NAFTA Still a Work in Progress"; and Amy Borrus, "A Free-Trade Milestone, with Many More Miles to Go," *BusinessWeek* (August 24, 1992): 30–31.

93. Based in part on "How Well Do You Exhibit Good Intercultural Management Skills?" in John W. Newstrom and Keith Davis, *Organizational Behavior: Human Behavior at Work* (Boston, MA: McGraw-Hill Irwin, 2002), pp. 415–416.

94. Based on Gina Kolata, "Companies Facing Ethical Issue as Drugs Are Tested Overseas," *The New York Times,* March 5, 2004; and Julie Schmit, "Costs, Regulations Move More Drug Tests Outside USA," *USA Today,* June 16, 2005.

CHAPTER 4
Managing Ethics and Social Responsibility

CHAPTER OUTLINE

LEARNING OUTCOMES

After studying this chapter, you should be able to:

4.1 Define ethics and explain how ethical behavior relates to behavior governed by law and free choice.

4.2 Discuss why ethics is important for managers and identify recent events that call for a renewed commitment to ethical management.

4.3 Explain the utilitarian, individualism, moral rights, justice, and practical approaches for making ethical decisions.

4.4 Describe the factors that shape a manager's ethical decision making, including levels of moral development.

4.5 Identify important stakeholders for an organization and discuss how managers balance the interests of various stakeholders.

4.6 Explain the philosophy of sustainability, including the triple bottom line, and why organizations are embracing it.

4.7 Define corporate social responsibility and how to evaluate it along economic, legal, ethical, and discretionary criteria.

4.8 Discuss how ethical organizations are created through ethical leadership and organizational structures and systems.

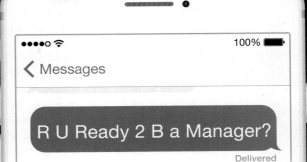

R U Ready 2 B a Manager?

Delivered

Before reading this chapter, please circle either "Mostly True" or "Mostly False" for each of the five questions below.

1 I always strive to do the "right thing," even when it is difficult and I might suffer negative consequences.

| Mostly True | Mostly False |

[page 147]

2 Even if something is legal, I still maintain it is important to make moral decisions.

| Mostly True | Mostly False |

[page 146]

3 When I am faced with a difficult decision, I try to make sure all parties involved are dealt with fairly, rather than merely trying to "win" or gain the most.

| Mostly True | Mostly False |

[page 153]

4 When there is a right and wrong moral dilemma, I don't just act based on what people will find out, or what they will think of me, but rather look to a moral or spiritual principle to follow.

| Mostly True | Mostly False |

[page 155]

5 I am a tireless recycler and I want to work with a company that values the environment.

| Mostly True | Mostly False |

[page 162]

A law professor told *The New York Times* he was "shocked and dismayed." An alumnus said it was "one of the lowest points in Harvard's recent history." Some people, both on campus and off, say the whole incident was blown out of proportion. The incident that they're referring to was the decision of Harvard University administrators to secretly search the e-mail accounts of resident deans to identify the source of media leaks about a cheating scandal on campus. In this scandal, more than 100 students were investigated, and many of them were punished for plagiarism or for copying one another's answers on a take-home test. Administrators said the perusal of resident deans' e-mail accounts, which was limited to a search of subject lines, was handled in a way that was designed to protect the students as well as the deans. "No one's e-mails were opened and the contents of no one's e-mails were searched by human or machine," a statement said. Administrators said they initiated the search because the leak of a confidential memo regarding the cheating scandal led to concerns that other material, including confidential student information, was at risk. The episode has raised privacy concerns and breached the sometimes fragile trust that exists between administrators and faculty and staff. It appears that no policies were broken, but the criticism motivated administrators to create a task force to develop recommendations for how to handle issues of e-mail privacy.[1]

What do you think? Did Harvard administrators do anything wrong? Most organizations allow the monitoring of official workplace e-mail. One faculty member said that the search seemed out of character for Harvard, but that it wasn't really surprising. "I subscribe to the [rule] that I never put anything in e-mail that I wouldn't want published in the *Harvard Crimson*," he said.[2] The dean who authorized the search at Harvard said that although no policies were broken, the way she handled the incident was a mistake. She referred to her 10-year-old son in stressing "how important it is to own up to your mistakes, to apologize, and to make amends. I have to model that behavior for him."[3]

This chapter expands on the ideas about environment, corporate culture, and the international environment discussed in Chapters 2 and 3 to explore the issues of ethical behavior and corporate social responsibility. We first discuss the topic of ethical values, which builds on the idea of corporate culture. We look at the current ethical climate in corporate America, consider the business case for ethics and social responsibility, and examine fundamental approaches that can help managers think through difficult ethical issues. Understanding these ideas will help you build a solid foundation on which to base future decision making. We also examine organizational relationships to the external environment as reflected in corporate social responsibility. The final section of the chapter describes how managers create an ethical organization using codes of ethics and other organizational policies, structures, and systems.

4.1 What Is Managerial Ethics?

Ethics is difficult to define in a precise way. In a general sense, **ethics** is the code of moral principles and values that governs the behaviors of a person or group with respect to what is right or wrong. Ethics sets standards as to what is good or bad in conduct and decision making.[4] An ethical issue is present in a situation when the actions of a person or organization may harm or benefit others.[5]

Ethics can be more clearly understood when compared with behaviors governed by law and by free choice. Exhibit 4.1 illustrates that human behavior falls into three categories. The first is codified law, in which values and standards are written into the legal system and enforceable in the courts. In this area, lawmakers set rules that people and corporations

What Is Your Level of Ethical Maturity?

Instructions: It probably won't happen right away, but soon enough in your duties as a new manager, you will be confronted with a situation that will test the strength of your moral beliefs or your sense of justice. Are you ready? To find out, think about times when you were part of a student or work group. To what extent does each of the following statements characterize your behavior when working with others in a group? Please answer each of the following items as Mostly True or Mostly False for you.

	Mostly True	*Mostly False*
1. I can clearly state the principles and values that guide my actions.		
2. I quickly acknowledge my mistakes and take responsibility for them.		
3. I am able to quickly "forgive and forget" when someone has made a serious mistake that affected me.		
4. When making a difficult decision, I take time to assess my principles and values.		
5. I have a reputation among my friends and coworkers for keeping my word.		
6. I am completely honest and can be trusted to tell the truth.		
7. When someone asks me to keep a confidence, I always do so completely.		
8. I hold others accountable for using ethical practices in their work.		
9. I insist on doing what is fair and ethical even when it is not easy.		
10. My coworkers would say that my behavior is very consistent with my values.		

Scoring and Interpretation: Each of these questions pertains to some aspect of ethical maturity in a group situation, which also reflects a person's level of moral development. Count the number of checks for Mostly True. If you scored 7 or more, congratulations! That behavior suggests you would be near Level 3 in Exhibit 4.3 of the levels of moral development. The postconventional level of development means that you consider principles and values, take personal responsibility, and do not blame others. You may have a highly developed ethical sense. A lower score suggests that you may be at the conventional or even preconventional level. A score below 5 indicates that you may avoid difficult issues or have not been in situations that challenged your ethical values.

Study the specific questions for which you scored Mostly True and Mostly False to learn more about your specific strengths and weaknesses. Think about what influences your ethical behavior and decisions, such as a need for success or approval.

EXHIBIT 4.1 Three Domains of Human Action

| Domain of Codified Law (Legal Standard) | Domain of Ethics (Social Standard) | Domain of Free Choice (Personal Standard) |

Amount of

High   Explicit Control   Low

must follow in a certain way, such as obtaining licenses for cars, paying corporate taxes, or following other local, state, and national laws. For example, federal prosecutors recently uncovered a teacher-test cheating ring in which people paid others to take teacher certification exams for them using false identification. Several people have been indicted on conspiracy charges of wire, mail, and Social Security fraud, and some have already gone to prison for their participation in a scheme that spanned 15 years across three states.[6] Behaviors such as fraud and tax evasion are clearly against the law. The domain of free choice is at the opposite end of the scale and pertains to behavior about which the law has no say and for which an individual or organization enjoys complete freedom. An example is a manager's choice of where to buy a new suit, or an organization's choice of which of two well-qualified candidates to hire for an open position.

Between these domains lies the area of ethics. This domain has no specific laws, yet it does have standards of conduct based on shared principles and values about moral conduct that guide an individual or company. For example, it is not illegal for a manager like Harry Stonecipher, former CEO of Boeing, to have a consensual extramarital affair with a female executive, but his behavior violated Boeing's code of ethical conduct, and Stonecipher was replaced.[7] Numerous other managers have gotten into trouble with the simplified view that decisions are governed by either law or free choice. This view leads people to mistakenly assume that if it's not illegal, it must be ethical, as if there were no third domain.[8] A better option is to recognize the domain of ethics and accept moral values as a powerful force for good that can regulate behaviors both inside and outside organizations.

Bernd Mellmann / Alamy

CONCEPT CONNECTION Each year, the Swiss research firm Covalence looks at the ethical behavior of hundreds of multinational corporations and releases a list of the worst offenders. Around the globe, mining operations like this one often find themselves on the index because their actions can harm the environment and put employees and other stakeholders at risk. Many question the **managerial ethics** of those who decide to put profit ahead of safety.

4.1a Ethical Management Today

Every decade seems to experience its share of scoundrels, but the pervasiveness of ethical lapses during the early 21st century has been astounding. In a recent Gallup poll regarding the perception of business leaders, just 15 percent of respondents rated leaders' honesty and ethical standards as "high" or "very high."[9] More than 75 percent of people surveyed agree with the statement that corporate America's moral compass is "pointing in the wrong direction"; 69 percent say that executives rarely

EXHIBIT 4.2   Four Types of Ethical Manager Behavior

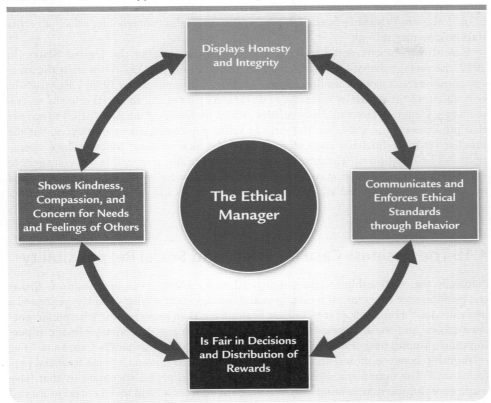

SOURCE: Based on Gary Yukl et al., "An Improved Measure of Ethical Leadership," *Journal of Leadership and Organizational Studies* 20, no. 1 (2013): 38–48.

consider the public good in making decisions; and a whopping 94 percent say that executives make decisions based primarily on advancing their own careers.[10] Another recent survey of Wall Street workers by the law firm Labaton Sucharow shows that those opinions might not be far off the mark. Almost 25 percent of finance professionals say that they would cheat to make $10 million if they could get away with it. Moreover, 52 percent believe that it is likely that their competitors have engaged in illegal or unethical activity.[11]

Managers and organizations engage in unethical behavior for any number of reasons, such as personal ego, greed, or pressures to increase profits or appear successful. Yet managers carry a tremendous responsibility for setting the ethical climate in an organization and can act as role models for ethical behavior.[12] Exhibit 4.2 details the findings from one study that boiled down the range of ethical behaviors to four primary ways in which managers can act to promote a climate in which everyone behaves in an ethical and socially responsible way. Ethical managers display honesty and integrity, communicate and enforce ethical standards through their behavior, are fair in their decisions and the distribution of rewards, and show kindness and concern for others.[13]

Unfortunately, in today's environment, an overemphasis on pleasing shareholders may cause some managers to behave unethically toward customers, employees, and the broader society. Managers are under enormous pressure to meet short-term earnings goals, and some even use accounting gimmicks or other techniques to show returns that meet market expectations rather than ones that reflect true performance. Moreover, most executive

"The bottom line is that when shareholder value capitalism is paramount, the rest of us suffer. CEOs will readily dupe customers, sack employees, and spoil the environment to meet expectations."

—Roger Martin, Dean and Professor at the Rotman School of Management, Toronto compensation plans include hefty stock-based incentives, a practice that sometimes encourages managers to do whatever will increase the share price, even if it hurts the company in the long run. When managers "fall prey to the siren call of shareholder value," all other stakeholders may suffer.[14]

Executive compensation has become a hot-button issue in the United States. In 2012, the average pay of CEOs at large U.S. corporations was 354 times what the average employee was paid, according to one estimate.[15] By contrast, in 1980, CEO pay was only about 42 times that of the average worker. As part of the financial reforms several years ago, Congress directed the Securities and Exchange Commission (SEC) to require that public companies disclose the ratio of CEO pay compared to employees, but the rule has yet to be finalized and enforced, partly because of heavy lobbying by corporations.[16] The question of whether it is ethical and socially responsible for managers to rake in huge sums of money compared to other employees is of growing concern, and in general, the widespread ethical lapses of the past decade have put managers under increasing scrutiny.

4.1b The Business Case for Ethics and Social Responsibility

Naturally, the relationship of ethics and social responsibility to an organization's financial performance concerns both managers and management scholars and has generated a lively debate.[17] Hundreds of studies have been undertaken to determine whether heightened ethical and social responsiveness increases or decreases a company's financial performance. Studies have provided varying results, but they have generally found a positive relationship between ethical and socially responsible behavior and a firm's financial performance.[18] For example, a recent study of the top 100 global corporations that have made a commitment to *sustainability*, weaving environmental and social concerns into all their decisions, had significantly higher sales growth, return on assets, profits, and cash flow from operations in at least some areas of the business.[19] The philosophy of sustainability will be discussed later in this chapter. Another review of the financial performance of large U.S. corporations considered "best corporate citizens" found that they enjoy both superior reputations and superior financial performance.[20] Although results from these studies are not proof, they do provide an indication that using resources for ethics and social responsibility does not hurt companies.[21]

Companies are also making an effort to measure the nonfinancial factors that create value. For example, researchers find that people prefer to work for companies that demonstrate a high level of ethics and social responsibility; thus, these organizations can attract and retain high-quality employees.[22] Customers pay attention too. A study by Walker Research indicates that, price and quality being equal, two-thirds of customers say that they would switch brands to do business with a company that is ethical and socially responsible.[23] Another series of experiments by Remi Trudel and June Cotte of the University of Western Ontario's Ivey School of Business found that consumers were willing to pay slightly more for products they were told had been made using high ethical standards.[24]

© Picture Alliance/Photoshot

CONCEPT CONNECTION Known for its **commitment to sustainability**, the German sports apparel manufacturer Adidas ranked 17th on a recent list of Top 100 Most Sustainable Corporations in the World. Kudos for the company's sustainability efforts may give Adidas a competitive edge over rivals like Nike and Puma because it helps attract new customers and a better quality of employee.

REMEMBER THIS

- Managers face many pressures that can sometimes tempt them to engage in unethical behavior.

- **Ethics** is the code of moral principles and values that governs the behaviors of a person or group with respect to what is right or wrong.

- Just because managers aren't breaking the law doesn't necessarily mean that they are being ethical.

- Ethical managers display honesty and integrity, act in a way that communicates and enforces ethical standards, are fair in their decisions and the distribution of rewards, and show kindness and concern for others.

- Unethical managers seek to serve their own needs and interests at the expense of stakeholders.

- Confidence in business managers and leaders in all walks of life is at an all-time low.

- One hot-button ethical issue concerns excessive executive compensation.

- Companies that are ethical and socially responsible perform as well as—often even better than—those that are not socially responsible.

4.2 Ethical Dilemmas: What Would You Do?

Being ethical is always about making decisions. An **ethical dilemma** arises in a situation concerning right or wrong when values are in conflict.[25] Right and wrong cannot be clearly identified. Ethical issues sometimes can be exceedingly complex and people may hold widely divergent views about the most ethically appropriate or inappropriate actions related to a situation.[26] Consider the issue of competitive intelligence (CI). Companies are increasingly using social media to learn more about their competitors, some even going so far as to "friend" customers or employees of rivals and post seemingly innocuous questions to gather information that can provide them with a competitive advantage.[27] The laws regarding information gathering aren't clear-cut, and neither are opinions regarding the ethics of such tactics. Whereas some people think that any form of corporate spying is wrong, others consider it an acceptable way of learning about the competition.[28]

The individual who must make an ethical choice in an organization is the *moral agent*.[29] Here are some dilemmas that a manager in an organization might face. Think about how you would handle them:

1. You work at a large corporation that requires a terrorist watch list screening for all new customers, which takes approximately 24 hours from the time an order is placed. You can close a lucrative deal with a potential long-term customer if you agree to ship the products overnight, even though that means the required watch list screening will have to be done after the fact.[30]

2. As a sales manager for a major pharmaceuticals company, you've been asked to promote a new drug that costs $2,500 per dose. You've read the reports saying that the drug is only 1 percent more effective than an alternative drug that costs less than $625 per dose. The vice president of sales wants you to promote the $2,500-per-dose drug aggressively. He reminds you that if you don't, lives could be lost that might have been saved with that 1 percent increase in the drug's effectiveness.

Business Blooper

Lance Armstrong

Lance Armstrong was the darling of the sports world. He made cycling in to a sport people were interested in. Photogenic and personable, between 1999 and 2005 he won seven Tour de France races, more than anyone else ever had. Struck down with testicular cancer, he recovered and started a nonprofit, Livestrong, to raise awareness and fund research for that type of cancer. He even had Sheryl Crow as his girlfriend for a while. It all came crashing down in 2013, when Armstrong finally admitted to the doping, on Oprah's couch, he'd been suspected of for years. He not only had lied, but ruined the careers of several people who had been his chief accusers. And he made it difficult for cyclists afterwards.

A month later the U.S. Justice Department joined a whistle-blower suit, claiming Armstrong had defrauded the government (he led the U.S. Postal Service Cycling Team) by $31 million. Not only that, he's lost lucrative endorsement deals from Nike and Anheuser-Busch and been dumped, and his own Livestrong, whose annual income of $48 million is now in jeopardy because of the scandal. Also distancing itself from him is the charity Hope, which he started with Andre Agassi. Armstrong's name was once associated with Hope and now it's been rejected by Hope.

SOURCES: Kerry Gillespie, "Innocent Cyclist Can't Shake Stigma," *The Guelph Mercury*, December 26, 2014, B3; Juliet Macur, "Government Joins Suit Against Armstrong," *New York Times*, February 23, 2013, D1 + D6; Mary Pilon and Andrew W Lehren, "A Scandal Leaves Its Mark," *New York Times*, January 16, 2013, D1–D6.

3. On the train ride from your home in Ipswich to your office in London, your peaceful morning routine is disturbed by neighboring passengers carrying on a loud mobile business meeting. Within minutes, you realize that they are discussing a client that your own firm has been courting. Furthermore, you soon have the time, phone number, and passcode for a conference call that the consultants are having with the client later that day. It isn't your fault that they gave out that information in a public place, but you wonder what you should do with it.[31]

Lance Armstrong lived for years inside an ethical dilemma. Only recently has it come out that he chose to act in the unethical manner, as described in this chapter's Business Blooper box.

These kinds of dilemmas and issues fall squarely in the domain of ethics. How would you handle each of these situations?

REMEMBER THIS

- Ethics is about making choices.
- Most managers encounter ethical dilemmas that are tough to resolve.

- An **ethical dilemma** is a situation in which all alternative choices or behaviors have potentially negative consequences. Right and wrong cannot be clearly distinguished.

4.3 Frameworks for Ethical Decision Making

Most ethical dilemmas involve a conflict between the needs of the part and the whole—the individual versus the organization or the organization versus society as a whole. For example, should a company scrutinize job candidates' or employees' social media postings, which might benefit the organization as a whole but reduce the individual freedom of employees? Or should products that fail to meet tough Food and Drug Administration (FDA) standards be exported to other countries where government standards are lower, benefiting the company but potentially harming world citizens? Sometimes ethical decisions entail a conflict between two groups. For example, should the potential for local health problems resulting from a company's effluents take precedence over the jobs it creates as the town's leading employer?

Managers faced with these kinds of tough ethical choices often benefit from a normative strategy—one based on norms and values—to guide their decision making. Normative ethics uses several approaches to describe values for guiding ethical decision making. Five approaches that are relevant to managers are the utilitarian approach, individualism approach, moral-rights approach, justice approach, and practical approach.[32]

Utilitarian Approach   The **utilitarian approach**, espoused by the nineteenth-century philosophers Jeremy Bentham and John Stuart Mill, holds that moral behavior produces the greatest good for the greatest number. Under this approach, a decision maker is expected to consider the effect of each decision alternative on all parties and select the one that optimizes the benefits for the greatest number of people. The utilitarian ethic is cited as the basis for the recent trend among companies to monitor employee use of the Internet and police personal habits such as alcohol and tobacco consumption, because such behavior affects the entire workplace.[33]

Individualism Approach   The **individualism approach** contends that acts are moral when they promote the individual's best long-term interests.[34] In theory, with everyone pursuing self-direction, the greater good is ultimately served because people learn to accommodate each other in their own long-term interest. Individualism is believed to lead to honesty and integrity because that works best in the long run. Lying and cheating for immediate self-interest just causes business associates to lie and cheat in return. Thus, proponents say, individualism ultimately leads to behavior toward others that fits standards of behavior that people want toward themselves.[35] However, because individualism is easily misinterpreted to support immediate self-gain, it is not popular in the highly organized and group-oriented society of today.

Moral-Rights Approach   The **moral-rights approach** asserts that human beings have fundamental rights and liberties that cannot be taken away by an individual's decision. Thus, an ethically correct decision is one that best maintains the rights of those affected by it. To make ethical decisions, managers need to avoid interfering with the fundamental rights of others, such as the right to privacy, the right of free consent, or the right to freedom of speech. Performing experimental treatments on unconscious trauma patients, for example, might be construed to violate the right to free consent. A decision to monitor employees' nonwork activities violates the right to privacy. The right of free speech would support whistle-blowers who call attention to illegal or inappropriate actions within a company.

Justice Approach   The **justice approach** holds that moral decisions must be based on standards of equity, fairness, and impartiality. Three types of justice are of concern to managers. **Distributive justice** requires that different treatment of people not be based on arbitrary characteristics. For example, men and women should not receive different salaries if they have the same qualifications and are performing the same job. **Procedural justice** requires that rules be administered fairly. Rules

Jim West/Alamy

CONCEPT CONNECTION   Way back when labor unions first began to emerge, proponents took a **moral-rights approach** to ethics in the workplace. They believed that workers had a right to earn a decent living wage and to have some time off from work each week. Some businesses tried to stop people from forming labor unions, so the moral-rights support of the freedom of speech also became an important part of the movement. Union members today still share this same viewpoint.

should be clearly stated and consistently and impartially enforced. **Compensatory justice** argues that individuals should be compensated for the cost of their injuries by the party responsible. The justice approach is closest to the thinking underlying the domain of law in Exhibit 4.1 because it assumes that justice is applied through rules and regulations. Managers are expected to define attributes on which different treatment of employees is acceptable.

Practical Approach   The approaches discussed so far presume to determine what is "right" or good in a moral sense. However, as has been mentioned, ethical issues are frequently not clear-cut, and there are disagreements over what is the ethical choice. The **practical approach** sidesteps debates about what is right, good, or just and bases decisions on prevailing standards of the profession and the larger society, taking the interests of all stakeholders into account.[36] The action of Paula Reid, the manager who set the U.S. Secret Service prostitution scandal in motion by reporting the misconduct of agents in Cartagena, Colombia, was based largely on the practical approach.

Paula Reid, U.S. Secret Service

Put aside the issue of whether it is morally wrong to hire a prostitute, particularly in a country where prostitution is legal in certain areas. The bottom line for Paula Reid is that visits to strip clubs, heavy drinking, and payments to prostitutes are not acceptable behavior for Secret Service agents charged with protecting the President of the United States.

"If every boss was Paula Reid," said a former agent, "the Secret Service would never have a problem. It would be a lot more boring, never a problem." Reid, the new supervising manager for the Miami office, a prestigious division that oversees the South American region, acted swiftly when she received a report of a disturbance at the hotel where agents preparing for President Barack Obama's visit to Cartagena were staying. Based on information from the hotel manager, Reid swiftly rounded up a dozen agents, ordered them out of the country, and notified her superiors that she had found evidence of "egregious misconduct." She acted in spite of a potential internal backlash because she believed that the actions of the agents had both hurt the agency's reputation and damaged its ability to fulfill its protective and investigative missions.

The resulting scandal threw the Secret Service into turmoil and put director Mark Sullivan and other managers on the hot seat. Four of the agents dismissed for engaging in inappropriate conduct have since challenged their dismissals, saying that they are being made scapegoats for behavior that the agency has long tolerated, so long as there is no breach of operational security. Yet, for Reid and others, the "boys will be boys" mentality is not acceptable in today's world. According to former director Ralph Basham, there are many former and current agents who are "deeply ashamed of what these people did."[37]

With the practical approach, a decision would be considered ethical if it is one that would be considered acceptable by the professional community, one that the manager would not hesitate to publicize on the evening news, and one that a person would typically feel comfortable explaining to family and friends. Using the practical approach, managers may combine elements of the utilitarian, moral rights, and justice approaches in their thinking and decision making. For example, one expert on business ethics suggests that managers can ask themselves the following five questions to help resolve ethical dilemmas.[38] Note that these questions cover a variety of the approaches discussed previously.

1. What's in it for me?
2. What decision would lead to the greatest good for the greatest number?
3. What rules, policies, or social norms apply?
4. What are my obligations to others?
5. What will be the long-term impact for myself and important stakeholders?

REMEMBER THIS

- Most ethical dilemmas involve a conflict between the interests of different groups or between the needs of the individual versus the needs of the organization.
- Managers can use various approaches based on norms and values to help them make ethical decisions.
- The **utilitarian approach** to ethical decision making says that the ethical choice is the one that produces the greatest good for the greatest number.
- The **individualism approach** suggests that actions are ethical when they promote the individual's best long-term interests, because with everyone pursuing self-interest, the greater good is ultimately served. This concept is not considered appropriate today because it is easily misused to support one's personal gain at the expense of others.
- Some managers rely on a **moral-rights approach**, which holds that ethical decisions are those that best maintain the fundamental rights of the people affected by them.
- The **justice approach** says that ethical decisions must be based on standards of equity, fairness, and impartiality.
- **Distributive justice** requires that different treatment of individuals not be based on arbitrary characteristics.
- **Procedural justice** holds that rules should be clearly stated and consistently and impartially enforced.
- **Compensatory justice** argues that individuals should be compensated for the cost of their injuries by the party responsible, and individuals should not be held responsible for matters over which they have no control.
- Many managers also use the **practical approach**, which sidesteps debates about what is right, good, or just, and bases decisions on prevailing standards of the profession and the larger society, taking the interests of all stakeholders into account.

4.4 The Individual Manager and Ethical Choices

A recent study found that organizational factors such as an unethical corporate culture and pressure from superiors and colleagues can induce employees to behave unethically. Moreover, when people experience organizational pressure to go against their sense of what is right, they typically become frustrated and emotionally exhausted.[39] Yet there are also personal factors that influence a manager's ability to make ethical decisions. Individuals bring specific personality and behavioral traits to the job. Personal needs, family influence, and religious background all shape a manager's value system. Specific personality characteristics, such as ego strength, self-confidence, and a strong sense of independence, may enable managers to make more ethical choices despite outside pressures and personal risks. For Robert Vito, his sense of entrepreneurship and fair play led to his designing equipment that would help prevent athlete's injuries, a kind of on-the-job safety issue that has caused the U.S. Occupational Safety and Health Administration to threaten the football league with shutdown, as described in the Spotlight on Skills box.

TAKE Action!

Review your responses to the questions at the beginning of this chapter, which will give you some insight into your own level of ethical maturity. A high level of ethical maturity can help managers make ethical choices in the face of opposition or pressure from others.

4.4a The Stages of Moral Development

One important personal factor is the stage of moral development.[40] A simplified version of one model of personal moral development is shown in Exhibit 4.3.

Spotlight on Skills

Unequal Technologies

In 2012 over 3000 retired NFL players and their families sued the National Football League for allegedly covering up information about head injuries and brain disease. Though football is as popular as ever and about 100 million people watch the Super Bowl, football head injuries have been dominating the news.

Robert Vito founded Unequal Technologies in 2008 to supply his patented lightweight bulletproof vests for soldiers and initially got a contract for 10,000 vests for NATO troops. Then in 2010 the company developed a modified vest for Philadelphia Eagles' Michael Vick, who had a sternum injury. Vick wore the Exo Armour and led the Eagles to a strong victory. Before Vito could turn around, the Exo was being worn by NFL players from several teams. In 2011, Vita was asked to use the military technologies to make a helmet to prevent injuries and the company created Concussion-Reduction-Technology,

which was a kind of peel-and-stick method of combining new padding with that already in the helmets. The composite material diffuses the impact throughout the whole helmet before it reaches the skull.

Building on successes, the 24 employees of Unequal were working with 27 of the 32 NFL teams by 2013 and the company is branching out to hockey, lacrosse, and baseball (re-engineering the bats). Its products sell for $40 to $150 and it did $561 million in sales in 2011.

Vito not only wants his business to thrive, but he wants to be part of the solution to head injuries. His next target is amateur sports. "My customer is the mom in Missouri who's buying our products for her kid," says Vito.

SOURCES: Alex Riley, "Head Gear or Baseball Still Evolving," *Tribune Business News*, April 19, 2014; April Joyner, "Military Technology Company Protects NFL Players," *Inc.* magazine, February 1, 2012, 26.

EXHIBIT 4.3   Three Levels of Personal Moral Development

Level 1 Preconventional	Level 2 Conventional	Level 3 Postconventional
Follows rules to avoid punishment. Acts in own interest. Obedience for its own sake.	Lives up to expectations of others. Fulfills duties and obligations of social system. Upholds laws.	Follows self-chosen principles of justice and right. Aware that people hold different values and seeks creative solutions to ethical dilemmas. Balances concern for individual with concern for common good.

← Self-Interest   Societal Expectations   Internal Values →

	Level 1	Level 2	Level 3
Leader Style:	Autocratic/coercive	Guiding/encouraging, team oriented	Transforming or servant leadership
Employee Behavior:	Task accomplishment	Work group collaboration	Empowered employees, full participation

SOURCES: Based on L. Kohlberg, "Moral Stages and Moralization: The Cognitive-Developmental Approach," in *Moral Development and Behavior: Theory, Research, and Social Issues*, ed. T. Lickona (New York: Holt, Rinehart, and Winston, 1976), pp. 31–53; and Jill W. Graham, "Leadership, Moral Development, and Citizenship Behavior," *Business Ethics Quarterly* 5, no. 1 (January 1995): 43–54.

At the *preconventional level*, individuals are concerned with external rewards and punishments and obey authority to avoid detrimental personal consequences. In an organizational context, this level may be associated with managers who use an autocratic or coercive leadership style, with employees oriented toward dependable accomplishment of specific tasks.

At level two, called the *conventional level*, people learn to conform to the expectations of good behavior as defined by colleagues, family, friends, and society. Meeting social and interpersonal obligations is important. Work-group collaboration is the preferred manner of accomplishing organizational goals, and managers use a leadership style that encourages interpersonal relationships and cooperation.

At the *postconventional*, or *principled*, level, individuals are guided by an internal set of values based on universal principles of justice and will even disobey rules or laws that violate these principles. Internal values become more important than the expectations of significant others. One recent example of the postconventional approach was the lifeguard in Hallandale Beach, Florida, who was fired for leaving his assigned zone to help a drowning man even though his supervisor ordered him not to leave his zone and to call 911 instead. "What he did was his own decision," said a manager for the company. "He knew the rules."[41]

The great majority of managers operate at level two, meaning that their ethical thought and behavior is greatly influenced by their superiors and colleagues in the organization or industry. Only about 20 percent of American adults reach the postconventional stage of moral development. People at level three are able to act in an independent, ethical manner regardless of expectations from others inside or outside the organization.

Laura Oda/Oakland Tribune/ZUMA Press/Alamy

CONCEPT CONNECTION   Ahmed Rahim, CEO of Numi Teas in Oakland, California, functions at a **postconventional level** of moral development. Rahim is committed to fair trade practices and to reducing the carbon footprint of his organization on the planet. But this leader has taken things a step further. Partnering with SCS Global Services and other third-party verifiers, Numi Teas has created a proprietary training program that teaches other business leaders how to adopt and verify fair labor practices on a global scale.

4.4b Givers versus Takers

When managers operate from a higher level of development, they may use a form of servant leadership, focusing on the needs of followers and encouraging others to think for themselves. Research has shown that people will work harder and more effectively for people who put others' interests and needs above their own.[42]

Adam Grant, an organizational psychologist at the Wharton School of the University of Pennsylvania, has been observing and studying the differences between "givers" and "takers" since he was an undergraduate student, and he says that changes in society and organizations make self-sacrifice for the sake of a larger purpose an increasingly beneficial characteristic. In one study, Grant found that the single biggest predictor of a team's effectiveness was the amount of help and support that members gave to one another. Grant says that, in the past, takers (people who put their own interests first) could climb to the top over the backs of givers, but that is changing as the nature of work has shifted. For example, Howard Lee, who was heading the South China office for Groupon, received a flood of applications for sales jobs. By searching social media, he could identify that some candidates had a pattern of self-serving behavior. He quickly weeded those out and focused on the applicants who demonstrated a track record as givers.[43]

The shift toward admiring and rewarding givers over takers can bring significant positive changes within organizations. The simple categories of *giver* and *taker* help people understand how they might contribute to or detract from an organization's ethical culture.

Complete the "New Manager Self-Test" on page 158 to see if you have the personal characteristics of a *giver* or a *taker*. What do you think your pattern means for your success and effectiveness as a manager?

NEW MANAGER Self-Test

Are You a Giver or a Taker?

Managers differ in how they view other people and the tactics they use to get things done. Respond to the items here based on how you view yourself and others. Please answer whether each item is Mostly True or Mostly False for you.

	Mostly True	Mostly False
1. My actions meet the needs of others before my own needs.	_____	_____
2. I am always offering a helping hand to those around me.	_____	_____
3. I give away credit and recognition to others.	_____	_____
4. I tend to feel competitive with my coworkers.	_____	_____
5. I often interrupt someone to make my point.	_____	_____
6. I encourage the growth of others, expecting nothing in return.	_____	_____
7. I like to be of service to others.	_____	_____
8. Giving makes me happier than receiving.	_____	_____
9. I reach out to orient new people even though it is not required.	_____	_____

Scoring and Interpretation: Sum questions 1–3 and 6–9 with one point for each Mostly True, and sum questions 4–5 with one point for each Mostly False. Your score pertains to a concept that was introduced by Robert Greenleaf in his book, *Servant Leadership*. Servant leadership means that managers are "givers" and try to place service to others before self-interest, listen as a way to care about others, and nourish others to help them become whole. This approach to management was based on Greenleaf's Quaker beliefs. A score of 7–9 would be considered high on servant or "giving" leadership, and 0–3 would be considered low, which represents a "taker" style of leadership, with a score of 4–6 in the middle range. How do you feel about your score? Are you attracted to the qualities of servant or giving leadership, or would you prefer a different approach to managing others?

SOURCE: Based on Robert Greenleaf, *Servant Leadership: A Journey into the Nature of Legitimate Power and Greatness*, 25th anniversary ed. (New York: Paulist Press, 2002).

REMEMBER THIS

- Organizational pressures can influence people to go against their own sense of right or wrong, and the resulting stress can lead to mental exhaustion and burnout.
- Personality characteristics, family influence, religious background, and other factors influence a manager's ability to make ethical choices.
- One important factor is whether a manager is at a preconventional, conventional, or postconventional level of moral development.
- Most managers operate at a *conventional level*, conforming to standards of behavior expected by society.

- Only about 20 percent of adults reach the *postconventional level* and are able to act in an independent, ethical manner, regardless of the expectations of others.

- Studies show that people work harder and more effectively when managers put the interests of others above their own.

4.5 What Is Corporate Social Responsibility?

There has been an explosion of interest in recent years in the concept of corporate social responsibility.[44] In one sense, the concept of social responsibility, like ethics, is easy to understand: It means distinguishing right from wrong and doing right. It means being a good corporate citizen. The formal definition of **corporate social responsibility (CSR)** is management's obligation to make choices and take actions that will contribute to the welfare and interests of society, not just the organization.[45]

As straightforward as this definition seems, CSR can be a difficult concept to grasp because different people have different beliefs as to which actions improve society's welfare.[46] To make matters worse, social responsibility covers a range of issues, many of which are ambiguous with respect to right or wrong. If a bank deposits the money from a trust fund into a low-interest account for 90 days, from which it makes a substantial profit, is it being a responsible corporate citizen? How about two companies engaging in intense competition? Is it socially responsible for the stronger corporation to drive the weaker one out of business or into a forced merger? Or consider General Motors (GM), Lehman Brothers, Hostess Brands, and the numerous other companies that have declared bankruptcy in recent years—which is perfectly legal—and thus avoided having to meet their mounting financial obligations to suppliers, labor unions, or competitors. These examples contain moral, legal, and economic complexities that make socially responsible behavior hard to define.

4.5a Organizational Stakeholders

One reason for the difficulty of understanding and applying CSR is that managers must confront the question, "Responsibility to whom?" Recall from Chapter 2 that the organization's environment consists of several sectors in both the task and the general environment. From a social responsibility perspective, enlightened organizations view the internal and external environment as a variety of stakeholders.

A **stakeholder** is any group or person within or outside the organization that has some type of investment or interest in the organization's performance and is affected by the organization's actions (employees, customers, shareholders, and so forth). Each stakeholder has a different criterion of responsiveness because it has a different interest in the organization.[47] There is growing interest in a technique called **stakeholder mapping**, which provides a systematic way to identify the expectations, needs, importance, and relative power of various stakeholders, which may change over time.[48] Stakeholder mapping helps managers identify or prioritize the key stakeholders related to a specific issue or project. For instance, Gap Inc., struggling to cope with the turmoil created after the company was targeted by protesters for using contractors that polluted the environment and engaged in child labor practices, decided to use mapping to identify key stakeholders with which the firm could develop deeper, transparent relationships.

Spotlight on Skills

Gap Inc.

When reports surfaced in the fall of 2009 that a contractor in Lesotho, Africa, making clothing for Gap Inc. and other U.S. companies was dumping toxic materials into local landfills and discharging chemicals into the Caledon River, Gap managers swung into action. A similar crisis related to child labor and

unsafe conditions 10 years earlier had resulted in global protests that raged for months and tarnished Gap's reputation, damaged employee morale, and devastated the firm's performance. In contrast, the more recent Lesotho story died down quickly, and Gap came out stronger on the other side.

What happened in those 10 years to make a difference? It's certainly not that the public was less outraged by the stories of poor children being harmed by dangerous chemicals while playing near the river or scavenging through refuse. The result was different this time because Gap managers had carefully cultivated open relationships with labor groups, human rights organizations, trade unions, nongovernmental organizations, and other stakeholders that enabled them to swing into action immediately and take specific steps to solve the problem. In the past, managers' approach would have been to deny responsibility and blame the subcontractor. With the Lesotho incident, though, Gap's top leaders immediately stepped forward to declare the company's commitment to fair and safe conditions and outline the steps it would take. Because of the relationships Gap had developed with numerous stakeholder groups, the company had the support of labor and human rights organizations, which praised managers' commitment and actions.

Gap embarked on the process of engaging with key stakeholders because even though the company had made a strong commitment to social and environmental responsibility since 1992, the previous approach wasn't working. Multimillion-dollar efforts at solving ethical problems in the supply chain had failed. So, managers started by drawing a stakeholder map that listed as many stakeholders as possible, then ranked them by their importance. Starting with mapping gave managers a way to focus their efforts and join with the most influential stakeholders to improve labor practices. It was a long and difficult journey, but the results have been well worth it. The company has received awards and public recognition as a leader in ethics and social responsibility.[49]

The global supply chain is a source of ongoing challenges for managers. As Dan Rees, former director of the Ethical Trading Initiative (ETI) said, "It is not a crime to find child labor in your supply chain. What is important is what you do about it when you find out."[50] Many companies retract their orders and stop doing business with companies that are found to use unsafe or unethical practices. A more recent approach some are taking is to work closely with overseas factories to improve their conditions, which managers say benefits both sides of the equation.[51] By using stakeholder mapping and cultivating open, trust-based relationships with key stakeholders, Gap is trying to ensure that managers are able to do the right thing swiftly, sometimes even turning crises into opportunities.

Exhibit 4.4 illustrates important stakeholders for a large organization such as Gap. Most organizations are influenced by a similar variety of stakeholder groups. Investors and shareholders, employees, customers, and suppliers are considered primary stakeholders, without whom the organization cannot survive. Investors, shareholders, and suppliers'

EXHIBIT 4.4   Major Stakeholders Relevant to Gap, Inc.

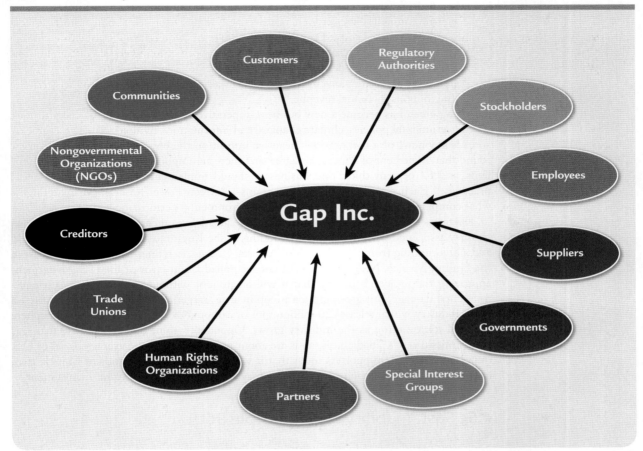

SOURCES: Based on information in D. Wheeler, B. Colbert, and R. E. Freeman, "Focusing on Value: Reconciling Corporate Social Responsibility, Sustainability, and a Stakeholder Approach in a Networked World," *Journal of General Management* 28, no. 3 (Spring 2003): 1–28; J. E. Post, L. E. Preston, and S. Sachs, "Managing the Extended Enterprise: The New Stakeholder View," *California Management Review* 45, no. 1 (Fall 2002): 6–28; and N. Craig Smith, Sean Ansett, and Lior Erex, "How Gap Inc. Engaged with Its Stakeholders," *MIT Sloan Management Review* 52, no. 4 (Summer 2011): 69–76.

interests are served by managerial efficiency—that is, use of resources to achieve profits. Employees expect work satisfaction, pay, and good supervision. Customers are concerned with decisions about the quality, safety, and availability of goods and services. When any primary stakeholder group becomes seriously dissatisfied, the organization's viability is threatened.[52]

Other important stakeholders are the government and the community, which have become increasingly important in recent years. Most corporations exist only under the proper charter and licenses and operate within the limits of safety laws, environmental protection requirements, antitrust regulations, antibribery legislation, and other laws and regulations in the government sector. Government regulations affecting business are increasing because of recent events. The community includes local governments, the natural environment, and the quality of life provided for residents. For many companies such as Gap, trade unions and human rights organizations are highly important stakeholders. Special interest groups may include trade associations, political action committees, professional associations, and consumerists. One special interest group of particular importance today is the green movement.

4.5b The Green Movement

When Jeffrey Immelt, CEO of General Electric (GE), first presented a plan for a "green" business initiative to 35 top GE executives in 2004, they voted it down. But Immelt, in a rare move, overruled them, and Ecomagination was born. Today, GE's Ecomagination is one of the world's most widely recognized corporate green programs. It has not only cut GE's greenhouse gas emissions by 30 percent but also added innovative products that are generating billions in annual revenue.[53]

Going green has become a new business imperative, driven by shifting social attitudes, new governmental policies, climate changes, and information technology (IT) that quickly spreads any news of a corporation's negative impact on the environment. A recent survey found that 90 percent of Americans agree that there are important "green" issues and problems, and 82 percent think that businesses should implement environmentally friendly practices.[54] Each chapter of this text contains a "Green Power" example that highlights what companies are doing to improve their environmental performance.

Energy is an area of growing concern for the green movement, as reflected in the controversy associated with the proposed building of the Keystone XL pipeline, which would add a link running from the oil sands of Alberta, Canada, to refineries on the Texas coast of the Gulf of Mexico. Nearly 6 in 10 Americans polled are in favor of the U.S. government approving the project, believing that it will create jobs without causing significant environmental damage. But green groups are up in arms, targeting Keystone and the entire oil sands industry, which releases 30 million tons of carbon dioxide a year into the atmosphere and will release more as the industry grows. Opponents point out that the "well-to-gas tank" emissions of Canadian oil sands are about twice as high as the average barrel of U.S. imported crude oil. Supporters insist that it is better to tap the oil sands of Canada than to continue helping oil-rich countries that may abuse both people and the environment.[55]

4.5c Sustainability and the Triple Bottom Line

Some corporations are embracing an idea called *sustainability* or *sustainable development*. **Sustainability** refers to economic development that generates wealth and meets the needs of the current generation while preserving the environment and society so that future generations can meet their needs as well.[56] With a philosophy of sustainability, managers weave

Green Power

Ecomagination

The question hovering on the horizon for enlightened CEOs such as GE's Jeff Immelt: *How do we apply technology and sustainability to addressing the economics of scarcity?* Immelt had only to tap into the historical precedent of innovation and imagination set by the creative genius of GE founder Thomas Edison. The result was GE's major commitment to social responsibility through a green technology movement.

Immelt doubled R&D funding to establish new labs and load them with Ph.D.s undertaking innovative sustainability research. The company also created an Ecomagination Advisory Council fueled by "dreaming sessions" that allowed customers and stakeholders to envision the future and the products and services that can improve those futures while providing an innovative business opportunity for GE. Founder Edison must be smiling.

SOURCE: Philip Mirvis, Bradley Googins, and Sylvia Kinnicutt, "Vision, Mission, Values: Guideposts to Sustainability," *Organizational Dynamics* 39 (2010): 316–324.

environmental and social concerns into every strategic decision so that financial goals are achieved in a way that is socially and environmentally responsible. Managers in organizations that embrace sustainability measure their success in terms of a triple bottom line. The term **triple bottom line** refers to measuring an organization's social performance, its environmental performance, and its financial performance. This is sometimes called the three P's: People, Planet, and Profit.[57]

The "People" part of the triple bottom line looks at how socially responsible the organization is in terms of fair labor practices, diversity, supplier relationships, treatment of employees, contributions to the community, and so forth. The "Planet" aspect measures the organization's commitment to environmental sustainability. The third P, of course, looks at the organization's profit, the financial bottom line. Based on the principle that what you measure is what you strive for and achieve, using a triple-bottom-line approach to measuring performance ensures that managers take social and environmental factors into account rather than blindly pursuing profit, no matter the cost to society and the natural environment.

REMEMBER THIS

- **Corporate social responsibility (CSR)** refers to the obligation of organizational managers to make choices and take actions that will enhance the welfare and interests of society, as well as the organization.

- Different stakeholders have different interests in the organization and thus different criteria for social responsiveness.

- The term **stakeholder** refers to any group or person within or outside the organization that has some type of investment or interest in the organization's performance.

- Shareholders, employees, customers, and suppliers are considered primary stakeholders, without whom the organization could not survive.

- Government, the community, and special interest groups are also important stakeholders.

- **Stakeholder mapping** provides a systematic way to identify the expectations, needs, importance, and relative power of various stakeholders.

- The *green movement* is a special interest group of particular importance today.

- **Sustainability** refers to economic development that generates wealth and meets the needs of the current population while preserving society and the environment for the needs of future generations.

- Companies that embrace sustainability measure performance in terms of financial performance, social performance, and environmental performance, referred to as the **triple bottom line**.

- A survey found that 90 percent of Americans agree that there are important "green" issues and problems, and 82 percent think that businesses should implement environmentally friendly practices.

4.6 Evaluating Corporate Social Responsibility

Exhibit 4.5 presents a model for evaluating corporate social performance, which indicates that total corporate social responsibility can be divided into four primary criteria: economic, legal, ethical, and discretionary responsibilities.[58] These four criteria fit together to form the whole of a company's social responsiveness.

EXHIBIT 4.5   Criteria of Corporate Social Performance

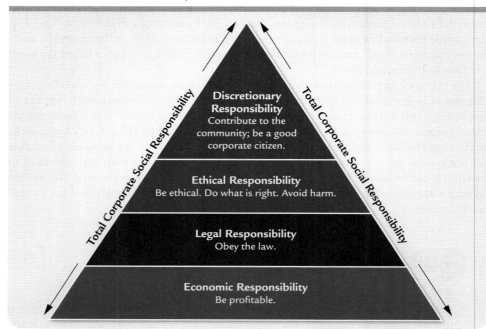

SOURCES: Based on Archie B. Carroll, "A Three-Dimensional Conceptual Model of Corporate Performance," *Academy of Management Review* 4 (1979): 499; A. B. Carroll, "The Pyramid of Corporate Social Responsibility: Toward the Moral Management of Corporate Stakeholders," *Business Horizons* 34 (July–August 1991): 42; and Mark S. Schwartz and Archie B. Carroll, "Corporate Social Responsibility: A Three-Domain Approach," *Business Ethics Quarterly* 13, no. 4 (2003): 503–530.

The first criterion of social responsibility is *economic responsibility*. The business institution is, above all, the basic economic unit of society. Its responsibility is to produce the goods and services that society wants and to maximize profits for its owners and shareholders. Economic responsibility, carried to the extreme, is called the *profit-maximizing view*, advocated by Nobel economist Milton Friedman. This view argues that the corporation should be operated on a profit-oriented basis, with its sole mission to increase its profits so long as it stays within the rules of the game.[59] The purely profit-maximizing view is no longer considered an adequate criterion of social performance in Canada, the United States, and Europe. This approach means that economic gain is the only responsibility, and this can lead companies into trouble, as recent events in the mortgage and finance industries have clearly shown.

Legal responsibility defines what society deems as important with respect to appropriate corporate behavior.[60] That is, businesses are expected to fulfill their economic goals within the framework of legal requirements imposed by local town councils, state legislators, and federal regulatory agencies. Examples of illegal acts by corporations include corporate fraud, intentionally selling defective goods, performing unnecessary repairs or procedures, deliberately misleading consumers, and billing clients for work not done. Organizations that knowingly break the law are poor performers in this category. Both Tyson Foods and Walmart, for example, became embroiled in bribery scandals related to their operations in Mexico. Executives at Walmart de Mexico allegedly paid bribes to local officials and covered up the wrongdoing so that the retailer could corner every edge of the market in that country. Tyson was accused of paying bribes to the wives of veterinarians stationed at its plants as part of an effort to avoid any problems certifying products as suitable for export.[61] Managers at these companies are by no means alone. A 2013 global survey by Transparency International found that more than 25 percent of those surveyed admitted to paying a bribe within the previous 12 months.[62]

Ethical responsibility includes behaviors that are not necessarily codified into law and may not serve the corporation's direct economic interests. As described earlier in this

"For a long time, people believed that the only purpose of industry was to make a profit. They are wrong. Its purpose is to serve the general welfare."

—Henry Ford, Sr. (1863–1947), American Industrialist

chapter, to be *ethical*, organization decision makers should act with equity, fairness, and impartiality, respect the rights of individuals, and provide different treatment of individuals only when relevant to the organization's goals and tasks.[63] *Unethical* behavior occurs when decisions enable an individual or company to gain at the expense of other people or society as a whole. Several well-known companies, including McDonald's, Nickelodeon, General Mills, and Subway, have been accused of unethical behavior by skirting the Children's Online Privacy Protection Act. Since it is illegal to collect e-mail addresses and send marketing materials directly to children, critics say these and other companies use tactics such as getting Web site users to play games and share them with friends, so the site can then target those friends with marketing messages.[64]

Discretionary responsibility is purely voluntary and is guided by a company's desire to make social contributions not mandated by economics, law, or ethics. Discretionary activities include generous philanthropic contributions that offer no payback to the company and are not expected. For example, Procter & Gamble (P&G) provides PUR packets that treat contaminated water and make it safe to drink for victims of natural disasters, such as the Asian tsunami in 2004. The pharmaceutical company Merck discovered a drug (called Mectizan) that will prevent river blindness, a dreadful disease that strikes the poorest of the poor, mostly in African countries. In 1987, realizing those who need the drug could never buy it, Merck pledged to provide it free of charge to anyone who needed it, in perpetuity.[65] Discretionary responsibility is the highest criterion of social responsibility because it goes beyond societal expectations to contribute to the community's welfare.

CONCEPT CONNECTION In the United States, employers have a **legal responsibility** to comply with laws designed to protect workers, such as the health and safety laws enforced by the Occupational Safety and Health Administration (OSHA). For example, companies that run manufacturing plants like this one are required to provide employees with safety goggles, earplugs, hard hats, and other protective gear as needed for various jobs.

© RGtimeline/Shutterstock.com

Discretionary responsibility is related to **organizational virtuousness**, which means that an organization pursues a positive human impact, moral goodness, and unconditional society betterment for its own sake.[66] For example, MAS Holdings, a family-owned apparel manufacturer in Sri Lanka, has made a commitment to contribute to economic development while also improving the lives of employees, their families, and the community. In an era when clothing manufacturers are in the news every week for another ethical, labor relations, or safety violation, MAS Holdings is making news for its owners' belief that businesses have the power to make a positive difference in the lives of employees and the community. MAS, the largest supplier for Victoria's Secret, provides transportation to and from work, free meals, and medical care to all of its 45,000 employees in 28 plants. More than 90 percent of its workers are women, so MAS builds factories in rural areas with easy access so that women can work close to their homes and families.[67]

REMEMBER THIS

- The model for evaluating a company's social performance uses four criteria: economic, legal, ethical, and discretionary.

- Companies may get into trouble when they use economic criteria as their only measure of

responsibility, which is sometimes called the *profit-maximizing* view.

- **Discretionary responsibility** is purely voluntary and is guided by the organization's desire to make

- social contributions not mandated by economics, laws, or ethics.
- Corporations that sent generous donations to Japan following the devastating earthquake and tsunami in 2011 were practicing discretionary responsibility.

- Discretionary responsibility is related to **organizational virtuousness**, which means that an organization pursues a positive human impact, moral goodness, and unconditional society betterment.

Read the "Ethical Dilemma" on page 175, which pertains to legal and ethical responsibilities.

4.7 Managing Company Ethics and Social Responsibility

An expert on the topic of ethics said, "Management is responsible for creating and sustaining conditions in which people are likely to behave themselves."[68] Exhibit 4.6 illustrates ways in which managers create and support an ethical organization. One of the most important steps managers can take is to practice ethical leadership.[69] *Ethical leadership* means that managers are honest and trustworthy, fair in their dealings with employees and customers, and behave ethically in both their personal and professional lives.

Managers and first-line supervisors are important role models for ethical behavior, and they strongly influence the ethical climate in the organization by adhering to high ethical standards in their own behavior and decisions. Moreover, managers are proactive in influencing employees to embody and reflect ethical values.[70] This chapter's "Director's Toolkit" describes an approach that some leading companies are taking to strengthen managers' ethical and socially responsible underpinning.

EXHIBIT 4.6 Building an Ethical Organization

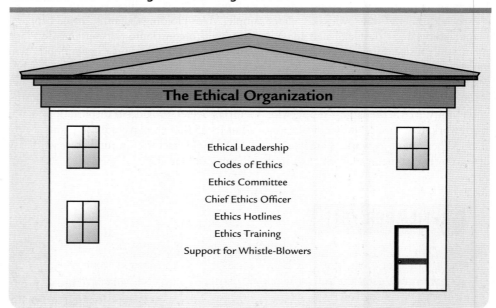

The Ethical Organization

Ethical Leadership
Codes of Ethics
Ethics Committee
Chief Ethics Officer
Ethics Hotlines
Ethics Training
Support for Whistle-Blowers

SOURCE: Adapted from Linda Klebe Treviño, Laura Pincus Hartman, and Michael Brown, "Moral Person and Moral Manager," *California Management Review* 42, no. 4 (Summer 2000): 128–142.

Director's Toolkit

Cultivating a Service Mind-Set

Some of today's best companies are taking a new approach to developing managers—global service programs that place employees with non-profit organizations or small businesses, often in developing countries, to provide free or low-cost technical and managerial assistance. In line with the growing emphasis on sustainability and the triple bottom line, organizations want managers who have a service and sustainability mind-set rather than an attitude of getting all they can for themselves. In one survey, 88 percent of top executives said it was important that future managers have the mind-set and skills to address sustainability issues.

- **Global service programs benefit everyone.** Global service programs have been described as a "win-win-win." It might seem obvious that the non-profit organizations served by these programs benefit, but the companies investing in them and the employees participating in them gain just as much. IBM credits its program with generating about $5 billion in new business. Companies gain greater knowledge of emerging markets, develop social capital and goodwill, and get more well-rounded managers with the service and sustainability mind-set needed in today's world. Participants benefit in numerous ways, including increased self-awareness, new skills, and greater cross-cultural understanding.

- **Many managers view these opportunities as plum assignments.** Laura Benetti of Dow Corning spent four weeks working nine-hour days with rural women in India, helping them learn how to price

and market the garments they made. She and nine colleagues slept in a lodge with limited access to hot water and electricity. "It gives more meaning to your career," said Benetti. Participants in global service also appreciate the opportunity to expand their understanding of global issues. "We all *know* about things like poverty in Africa and corruption and bribery …," said one IBM participant who spent time in Nigeria. "This kind of experience really brings … things to life, you really feel it."

- **How widespread is the trend?** In 2012, at least 27 Fortune 500 companies, including PepsiCo, IBM, FedEx, Dow Corning, and Pfizer, had some type of global service program, up from only six in 2006. Since 2008, IBM has sent more than 1,400 employees to work with projects such as reforming Kenya's postal system or developing ecotourism in Tanzania. Pfizer's program lends employees to nongovernmental organizations (NGOs) to address health care needs in Asia and Africa. The Accenture Development Partnership has been involved in more than 200 projects in 55 countries, where Accenture's professionals work at 50 percent pay for up to six months with organizations such as UNICEF and Freedom from Hunger.

SOURCES: Based on Philip Mirvis, Kevin Thompson, and John Gohring, "Toward Next-Generation Leadership: Global Service," *Leader to Leader* (Spring 2012): 20–26; Matthew Gitsham, "Experiential Learning for Leadership and Sustainability at IBM and HSBC," *Journal of Management Development* 31, no. 3 (2012): 298–307; and Anne Tergesen, "Doing Good to Do Well," *The Wall Street Journal*, January 9, 2012, B7.

Managers can also implement organizational mechanisms to help employees and the company stay on an ethical footing. Some of the primary ones are codes of ethics, ethical structures, and measures to protect whistle-blowers.

4.7a Code of Ethics

A **code of ethics** is a formal statement of a company's values concerning ethics and social issues; it communicates to employees what the company stands for. Codes of ethics tend to exist in two types: principle-based statements and policy-based statements. *Principle-based statements* are designed to affect corporate culture; they define fundamental values and contain general language about company responsibilities, quality of products, and treatment of employees. *Policy-based statements* generally outline the procedures to be used in specific ethical situations. These situations include marketing practices, conflicts of interest, observance of laws, proprietary information, political gifts, and equal opportunities.

Spotlight on Skills

Google

Google is one of the best-known companies in the world, and managers take seriously its reputation for both technological superiority and a commitment to ethics and social responsibility. Google's Code of Conduct starts with these words: "Don't be evil. Googlers generally apply those words to how we serve our users. But 'Don't be evil' is much more than that."

Google uses a well-designed Code of Conduct to put the motto into practice. The code is divided into seven sections, with each subdivided into sections that describe specific values, policies, and expectations. The code also clearly states that employees will be protected if they call attention to ethical violations or misconduct. Here are some excerpts from Google's code:

Serve Our Users

Our users value Google not only because we deliver great products and services, but because we hold ourselves to a higher standard in how we treat users and operate more generally.

Respect Each Other

We are committed to a supportive work environment, where employees have the opportunity to reach their fullest potential. Each Googler is expected to do his or her utmost to create a respectful workplace culture that is free of harassment, intimidation, bias and unlawful discrimination of any kind.

Preserve Confidentiality

We get a lot of press attention around our innovations and our culture, and that's usually fine. However, company information that leaks prematurely into the press or to competitors can hurt our product launches, eliminate our competitive advantage and prove costly in other ways.

Ensure Financial Integrity and Responsibility

Financial integrity and fiscal responsibility are core aspects of corporate professionalism…. The money we spend on behalf of Google is not ours; it's the company's and, ultimately, our shareholders'.

Obey the Law

Google takes its responsibilities to comply with laws and regulations very seriously and each of us is expected to comply with applicable legal requirements and prohibitions.

Conclusion

Google aspires to be a different kind of company. It's impossible to spell out every possible ethical scenario we might face. Instead, we rely on one another's good judgment to uphold a high standard of integrity for ourselves and our company.

And remember … don't be evil, and if you see something that you think isn't right—speak up![71]

General statements of principle are often called *corporate credos*. One good example is Johnson & Johnson's "The Credo." Available in 36 languages, The Credo has guided Johnson & Johnson's managers for more than 60 years in making decisions that honor the company's responsibilities to employees, customers, the community, and stockholders. Another example is Google's *Code of Conduct*. Portions of the Google code are shown in the following example.

Having a strong code of conduct or code of ethics doesn't guarantee that companies won't get into ethical trouble or be challenged by stakeholders on ethical issues. Codes of ethics in and of themselves do little to influence and ensure ethical behavior among employees and managers.[72] However, they are one key element of the organization's ethical framework. Codes of ethics state the values or behaviors expected and those that will not be tolerated. When top management supports and enforces these codes, including rewards for compliance and discipline for violation, ethics codes can boost a company's ethical climate.[73]

4.7b Ethical Structures

Ethical structures represent the various systems, positions, and programs that a company can undertake to encourage and support ethical behavior. An **ethics committee** is a group of executives (and sometimes lower-level employees as well) appointed to oversee company ethics. The committee provides rulings on questionable ethical issues and assumes responsibility for disciplining wrongdoers.

Many companies set up ethics offices with full-time staff to ensure that ethical standards are an integral part of company operations. These offices are headed by a **chief ethics officer**, sometimes called a *chief ethics and compliance officer*, a company executive who oversees all aspects of ethics and legal compliance, including establishing and broadly communicating standards, ethics training, dealing with exceptions or problems, and advising senior managers in the ethical and compliance aspects of decisions.[74] Changing government regulations in the light of accounting irregularities require that large public firms have an individual who is responsible for the ethics and compliance program, and many experts are advising that to be effective, this person should have direct access to the board of directors.[75] Most ethics offices also work as counseling centers to help employees resolve difficult ethical issues. A toll-free confidential *ethics hotline* allows employees to report questionable behavior, as well as seek guidance concerning ethical dilemmas.

4.7c Whistle-Blowing

Employee disclosure of illegal, unethical, or illegitimate practices on the employer's part is called **whistle-blowing**.[76] No organization can rely exclusively on codes of conduct and ethical structures to prevent all unethical behavior. Holding organizations accountable depends to some degree on individuals who are willing to speak up if they detect illegal, dangerous, or unethical activities. Whistle-blowers often report wrongdoing to outsiders, such as regulatory agencies, senators, or newspaper reporters. Some firms have instituted innovative programs and confidential hotlines to encourage and support internal whistle-blowing. For this practice to be an effective ethical safeguard, however, companies must view whistle-blowing as a benefit to the company and make dedicated efforts to encourage and protect whistle-blowers.[77] Michael Woodford, former president and CEO of Olympus, describes what can happen when that isn't the case.

Spotlight on Skills

Michael Woodford, Olympus

Michael Woodford had been with camera maker Olympus for 30 years when he was named president and CEO in early 2011. That appointment turned out to be the beginning of the end of his career with the company.

Woodford soon discovered that unauthorized payments had been made to third parties in an effort to hide significant losses. He went to the board, but they ignored his findings. "I begged them to do what was right. I was the president and I was trying to expose a fraud," he says.

After he went public, Woodford was voted out of his job. He describes what happened next: " I was petrified. You feel your career is slipping away. You fear for your safety ... there were implications of 'anti-social forces,' which means the *yakuza* [Japanese mafia]." Woodford says as painful as the experience was, it was a huge education, and he has no regrets about doing the right thing. The entire board at Olympus eventually resigned, and three senior executives pleaded guilty to fraud.[78]

Complete the Self-Learning Instrument on page 171 that pertains to ethical work environments.

Most whistle-blowers, like Michael Woodford, realize they may suffer financially and emotionally, but they act courageously to do what they think is right.

For people throughout an organization to be willing to "blow the whistle" on unethical or illegal behavior, managers have to *revere* whistle-blowing and make heroes of those who come forward. Unfortunately, the opposite often happens. Consider the situation at Pennsylvania State University. After defensive football coordinator Jerry Sandusky was convicted on 45 counts of child sexual abuse, the courts and the public were astonished to learn that many people supposedly knew about Sandusky's behavior and apparently did nothing beyond talking with him and urging him to get professional help. The fact is that most managers have a natural inclination to protect their colleagues and the organization.[79] Vicky Triponey, vice president of student affairs at Penn State from 2003 to 2007, says she was fired after trying to punish football players for acts of wrongdoing ranging from brutal fights to sexual assault. According to Triponey, Penn State president Graham Spanier told her that she wasn't fitting in with "the Penn State way." Triponey says there was a "blind sense of loyalty—not just at the top, but at all levels. I think people, in order to keep their jobs, have had to turn a blind eye."[80] Indeed, managers want employee loyalty in their organization, and it can be difficult to set aside when unethical activities are discovered.

Penn State managers aren't alone in trying to protect their organization, even at the risk of allowing unethical behavior to continue. The U.S. Office of Special Counsel recently found three air force officials guilty of retaliating against civilian employees who reported the mishandling of the remains of deceased soldiers at Dover Air Force Base, for example. A former executive at Countrywide Financial Corporation says he was bullied and eventually fired after he questioned the company's use of so-called Ninja loans (no income, no job, no assets) at the height of the subprime mortgage craze. And Matthew Lee, a former senior vice president in Lehman Brothers' accounting division, lost his job just weeks after he raised concerns about how the firm was masking risks by temporarily "parking" $50 billion in risky loan assets off its balance sheet.[81]

Unfortunately, many managers still look on whistle-blowers as disgruntled employees who aren't good team players. Yet to maintain high ethical standards, organizations need people who are willing to point out wrongdoing. Managers can be trained to view whistle-blowing as a benefit rather than a threat, and systems can be set up to protect employees who report illegal or unethical activities.

REMEMBER THIS

- Managers are role models. One of the most important ways that managers create ethical and socially responsible organizations is by practicing ethical leadership.
- A **code of ethics** is a formal statement of the organization's values regarding ethics and social issues.
- An **ethics committee** is a group of executives (and sometimes lower-level employees as well) charged with overseeing company ethics by ruling on questionable issues and disciplining violators.
- Some organizations have ethics offices headed by a **chief ethics officer**, a manager who oversees all aspects of ethics and legal compliance.
- Managers who want ethical organizations support **whistle-blowing**, the disclosure by employees of unethical, illegitimate, or illegal practices by the organization.

CHAPTER **4**   **DISCUSSION QUESTIONS**

1. Is it reasonable to expect that managers can measure their social and environmental performance on the same level as they measure financial performance with a triple bottom line? Discuss.

2. In September 2013, Tokyo Electric Power Company (Tepco) reported highly contaminated water leaking from a storage tank at the Fukushima nuclear power plant crippled in a March 2011 earthquake and tsunami. From what you know of the Fukushima disaster, discuss the various stakeholder groups that Tepco should respond to in order to handle this latest crisis.

3. Imagine yourself in a situation of being encouraged by colleagues to inflate your expense account. What factors do you think would influence your decision? Explain.

4. Is it ethical and socially responsible for large corporations to lobby against an SEC rule requiring that they report the ratio of their CEOs' pay compared to that of their average employee, as described in the chapter? Discuss.

5. Managers at some banks and mortgage companies have argued that providing subprime mortgages was based on their desire to give poor people a chance to participate in the American dream of home ownership. What is your opinion of this explanation in terms of ethics and social responsibility?

6. A survey found that 69 percent of MBA students view maximizing shareholder value as the primary responsibility of a company. Do you agree? What do you think this finding suggests about the ethical and socially responsible stance of corporate managers over the next couple of decades?

7. Do you believe that it is ethical for organizational managers to try to get access to and scrutinize the Facebook pages of employees or job applicants? Discuss.

8. Which do you think would be more effective for shaping long-term ethical behavior in an organization: a written code of ethics combined with ethics training, or strong ethical leadership? Which would have more impact on you? Why?

9. The technique of stakeholder mapping lets managers classify which stakeholders they will consider more important and will invest more time to satisfy. Is it appropriate for management to define some stakeholders as more important than others? Should all stakeholders be considered equal?

10. This chapter described studies that show that people work harder and better for managers who put the interests of others above their own. Why might this happen? Do you believe being more of a "giver" than a "taker" will translate into greater career success for these managers? Discuss.

SELF-LEARNING INSTRUMENT

Ethical Work Climates[82]

Think of an organization for which you were employed. Answer the following questions twice: The first time, circle the number that best describes the way things actually were. The second time, answer the questions based on your beliefs about the ideal level that would meet the needs of both individuals and the organization.

Disagree ① ② ③ ④ ⑤ **Agree**

1. What was best for everyone in the company was the major consideration there.

    1   2   3   4   5

2. Our major concern was always what was best for the other person.

    1   2   3   4   5

3. People were expected to comply with the law and professional standards over and above other considerations.

    1   2   3   4   5

4. In the company, the first consideration was whether a decision violated any law.

    1   2   3   4   5

5. It was very important to follow the company's rules and procedures.

   1   2   3   4   5

6. People in the company strictly obeyed the company policies.

   1   2   3   4   5

7. In the company, people were mostly out for themselves.

   1   2   3   4   5

8. People were expected to do anything to further the company's interests, regardless of the consequences.

   1   2   3   4   5

9. In the company, people were guided by their own personal ethics.

   1   2   3   4   5

10. Each person in the company decided for himself or herself what was right and wrong.

   1   2   3   4   5

Scoring and Interpretation

Subtract each of your scores for questions 7 and 8 from the number 6. Then, add up your score for all 10 questions: Actual 5 _____. Ideal 5 _____. These questions measure the dimensions of an organization's ethical climate. Questions 1 and 2 measure caring for people; questions 3 and 4 measure lawfulness; questions 5 and 6 measure adherence to rules; questions 7 and 8 measure emphasis on financial and company performance; and questions 9 and 10 measure individual independence. A total score above 40 indicates a highly positive ethical climate. A score from 30 to 40 indicates an above-average ethical climate. A score from 20 to 30 indicates a below-average ethical climate, and a score below 20 indicates a poor ethical climate. How far from your ideal score was the actual score for your organization? What does that difference mean to you?

Go back over the questions and think about changes that you could have made to improve the ethical climate in the organization. Discuss with other students what you could do as a manager to improve the ethics in future companies for which you work.

GROUP LEARNING

Current Events of an Unethical Type[83]

Step 1. Prior to meeting as a group, each person should find two newspaper or magazine articles from the past several months relating to someone violating business ethics or potentially breaking the law regarding business practices.

Step 2. Summarize the key points of the articles you found.

Step 3. Meet as a group. Have each person share key points from articles with group members.

Step 4. Identify similar themes across the unethical incidents reported in the articles.

What was the source or underlying cause of the unethical behavior? What was the hoped-for outcome? Was an individual or a group involved? Did the accused seem repentant or defensive? Can you identify similar conditions of any kind across incidents? Write the common themes in a list on a sheet of paper or whiteboard.

Step 5. What could you as a manager do to prevent such unethical behavior in your organization? What could you do to fix this kind of problem after it occurred in your organization?

Step 6. Report your findings to the class if asked to do so by your instructor.

Key points from articles	List theme from each article			
Article 1.				
2.				
3.				

Key points from articles	List theme from each article			
4.				
5.				
6.				
7.				
8.				
9.				
10.				

Then fill in these boxes:

List out similar themes

1.

2.

3.

4.

5.

Look at the underlying causes of the unethical behaviors

What were the sources of the underlying causes?

1.

2.

3.

4.

Why did they do it? What was the hoped for outcome?

How often was it a group?

How often an individual?

What were the similar conditions among the various unethical scenarios?

ACTION LEARNING

1. Write down at least three times when you were presented with an ethical dilemma, such as the opportunity to cheat on a test or a paper, being undercharged for something at a store or restaurant, being given "free" food by your friend who was an employee there, taking office sup- plies home for a workplace, using work time for personal activities, etc.

2. As a group of three to six people, choose three of the examples from the group to analyze.

Describe ethical dilemma	What did you do?	What should you have done?	What ethical principal was involved?
1.			
2.			
3.			

3. Each person in the group think of a time that someone behaved UNETHICALLY toward you. Fill out the table that follows.

Describe unethical behavior	How did you react to unethical behavior?	How did it impact your relationship with that person?	What would have been ethical behavior by the other person?

4. In your groups, discuss behaviors and conse- quences in your dilemmas and situations.

5. Why is it important to be ethical?

ETHICAL DILEMMA

Should We Go Beyond the Law?[84]

Nathan Rosillo stared out his office window at the lazy curves and lush, green, flower-lined banks of the Dutch Valley River. He'd grown up near here, and he envisioned the day that his children would enjoy the river as he had as a child. But now his own company might make that a risky proposition.

Nathan is a key product developer at Chem-Tech Corporation, an industry leader. Despite its competitive position, Chem-Tech experienced several quarters of dismal financial performance. Nathan and his team developed a new lubricant product that the company sees as the turning point in its declining fortunes. Top executives are thrilled that they can produce the new product at a significant cost savings because of recent changes in environmental regulations. Regulatory agencies loosened requirements on reducing and recycling wastes, which means that Chem-Tech can now release waste directly into the Dutch Valley River.

Nathan is as eager as anyone to see Chem-Tech survive this economic downturn, but he doesn't think this route is the way to do it. He expressed his opposition regarding the waste dumping to both the plant manager and his direct supervisor, Martin Feldman. Martin has always supported Nathan, but this time was different. The plant manager, too, turned a deaf ear. "We're meeting government standards," he'd said. "It's up to them to protect the water. It's up to us to make a profit and stay in business."

Frustrated and confused, Nathan turned away from the window, his prime office view mocking his inability to protect the river he loved. He knew that the manufacturing vice president was visiting the plant next week. Maybe if he talked with her, she would agree that the decision to dump waste materials in the river was ethically and socially irresponsible. But if she didn't, he would be skating on thin ice. His supervisor had already accused him of not being a team player. Maybe he should just be a passive bystander—after all, the company isn't breaking any laws.

What Would You Do?

1. Talk to the manufacturing vice president and emphasize the responsibility that Chem-Tech has to, as an industry leader, set an example. Present her with a recommendation that Chem-Tech participate in voluntary pollution reduction as a marketing tool, positioning itself as the environmentally friendly choice.

2. Mind your own business and just do your job. The company isn't breaking any laws, and if Chem-Tech's economic situation doesn't improve, a lot of people will be thrown out of work.

3. Call the local environmental advocacy group and get them to stage a protest of the company.

CASE FOR CRITICAL ANALYSIS

Too Much Intelligence?

The rapid growth of Pace Technologies was due in no small part to sales manager Ken Bodine and to the skills of the savvy young sales staff that he had assembled. Bodine prided himself on finding and hiring top grads from two major business schools in the area. In addition to the top salaries offered by Pace, the grads were attracted by Bodine's energy, innovative thinking, and can-do attitude. He was the embodiment of Pace culture—moving fast, ahead of the knowledge curve in high-tech. Pace's sales force consistently stunned the competition with their high performance level.

Among other things, Pace had the reputation for aggressive business intelligence. Competitors found both amusing and frustrating the company's ability

to outmaneuver others and capture accounts. Bodine enjoyed the air of mystery surrounding the Pace organization. Awareness that some competitor sat on the verge of a big sale always stirred Bodine's passion for sales and ignited his desire to "one-up these guys" and grab the sale out from under them.

"If this was a poker game," one board member mused, "Pace would win every hand. It's like Bodine as well as his staff possess the uncanny ability to know the cards your company is holding. He keeps a straight face, a low profile throughout the game, and then suddenly he lays his cards on the table and you're sunk. Here at Pace, we all love it."

A former military intelligence officer, Bodine brought that "sneaky" air into the Pace culture, adding a bit of excitement to the day-to-day business of sales.

"With a great product, great staff, and great business intelligence," Bodine was fond of saying, "you can dominate the market." He wanted everyone—customers, competitors, and the media—to see Pace everywhere. "Every time the competition holds a staff meeting," he said, "the first question should be, 'What's Pace doing?'"

The sales staff was a mirror image of Bodine—younger, but with the same air of invincibility, and very competitive with one another. This, too, Bodine encouraged. A chess player, he enjoyed observing and encouraging the competition within his own sales staff. And seeing the thrill it brought "the boss," ambitious salespeople worked vigorously to prove their competitive worth.

Bodine's latest competitive "match" pitted Cody Rudisell and Ali Sloan in an intellectual and strategic struggle for a coveted assignment to a potential major account with a company that had just expanded into the region. Bodine let it be known that Cody and Ali were being considered for the assignment, and that each could submit a proposal to lure the account to Pace and away from its top rival, Raleigh-Tech.

Both Cody and Ali eagerly grabbed the opportunity to expand their influence within the company and to build their reputations. Putting together their presentations within a short time period meant working long days and late nights. On the evening before the presentations, Cody bounded into Ali's office and dropped a file on her desk. "Top that!" he said.

Ali began thumbing through the file, and as she looked up in startled amazement, Cody slammed his hand on the folder and jerked it from her desk.

"That's like a watershed of Raleigh-Tech's trade secrets," Ali said. "Where did you get that?"

"My secret, sweetie," Cody replied, taking a seat and noisily drumming his fingers on the folder. "With this information, R-T doesn't have a chance. And neither do you."

"You could get into all sorts of trouble," Ali said. "When you lay that on Bodine's ..."

"Bodine's espionage side will love it," Cody interrupted. "This is classic Bodine, classic Pace. You can't tell me that with all of the brilliant moves he's made over the years, Bodine hasn't done the same thing. This is business, cutthroat business, and I may have just topped the master. See you tomorrow."

As he left, Ali sat in stunned silence. "Cutthroat, indeed," she whispered, reaching for the phone. She held the phone for a moment, wondering who she should call. *This is unethical, illegal,* she thought. She hung up the phone. *Should I let him hang himself tomorrow? What if Bodine really does love it? If I call some manager tonight, will everyone see me as a sore loser and a crybaby? Is this really what it takes to win in the big leagues? Is this really the culture of this organization?*

Questions

1. How has Ken Bodine shaped the sales culture at Pace Technologies? Do you consider this culture to be at a preconventional, conventional, or post-conventional level of ethical development? Why?

2. What should Ali Sloan do? What would you actually do if you were in her place? Explain.

3. How might Cody Rudisell's decision differ if he based it on the utilitarian approach vs. individualism approach vs. practical approach to ethical decision making? Which approach does he appear to be using?

ON THE JOB
VIDEO CASES

Theo Chocolate: Managing Ethics and Social Responsibility

Questions

1. What practices at Theo Chocolate reflect the concept of sustainability?

2. What does vice president Debra Music mean when she says that Theo is a "triple bottom line" company? How is this different from any other company?

3. What does the term *fair trade* mean to the leaders at Theo? What happens if fair trade goals conflict with a company's primary responsibility to be profitable?

ENDNOTES

1. Jennifer Levitz, "Harvard Explains Secret Email Search," *The Wall Street Journal*, March 12, 2013, A3; Jena McGregor, "The Harvard Email Controversy," *The Washington Post*, March 12, 2013, http://articles.washingtonpost.com/2013-03-11/national/37615752_1_emails-deans-search (accessed March 12, 2013); Rande Iaboni and Dana Ford, "Harvard College Dean Steps Down after E-mail Scandal," *CNN.com*, May 29, 2013, http://www.cnn.com/2013/05/28/us/massachusetts-harvard-dean (accessed September 3, 2013); and Mary Carmichael and Peter Schworm, "Harvard E-mail Searches Broader Than First Described," *The Boston Globe*, April 2, 2013, http://www.bostonglobe.com/metro/2013/04/02/secret-mail-searches-harvard-cheating-scandal-broader-than-initially-described/uRRdtrde29hWtSSH5wujbO/story.html (accessed September 3, 2013).

2. Levitz, "Harvard Explains Secret Email Search."

3. Carmichael and Schworm, "Harvard E-mail Searches Broader than First Described."

4. Gordon F. Shea, *Practical Ethics* (New York: American Management Association, 1988); and Linda K. Treviño, "Ethical Decision Making in Organizations: A Person-Situation Interactionist Model," *Academy of Management Review* 11 (1986): 601–617.

5. Thomas M. Jones, "Ethical Decision Making by Individuals in Organizations: An Issue-Contingent Model," *Academy of Management Review* 16 (1991): 366–395.

6. Motoko Rich, "2 More Educators in the South Are Charged in Test Cheating," *The New York Times*, June 21, 2013, http://www.nytimes.com/2013/06/22/us/2-more-educators-in-the-south-are-charged-in-test-cheating.html?_r=0 (accessed June 29, 2013).

7. Ashby Jones and Nathan Koppel, "Ethical Lapses Felled Long List of Company Executives," *The Wall Street Journal*, August 7, 2010, http://online.wsj.com/article/SB10001424052748703309704575413842089375632.html (accessed July 2, 2012).

8. Rushworth M. Kidder, "The Three Great Domains of Human Action," *Christian Science Monitor*, January 30, 1990.

9. Gallup Survey results reported in Roger Martin, "The CEO's Ethical Dilemma in the Era of Earnings Management," *Strategy & Leadership* 39, no. 6 (2011): 43–47.

10. Marist College Institute for Public Opinion and Knights of Columbus survey, results reported in Kevin Turner, "Corporate Execs: Nobody Trusts Us; U.S. Lacks Confidence in Business Ethics, Poll Says," *Florida Times Union*, February 27, 2009.

11. Reported in Dan Kadlec, "Gordon Gekko Lives: New Evidence That Greed Is Rampant on Wall Street," *Time*, July 17, 2013, http://business.time.com/2013/07/17/gordon-gekko-lives-new-evidence-that-greed-is-rampant-on-wall-street/ (accessed July 19, 2013).

12. Gary R. Weaver, Linda Klebe Treviño, and Bradley Agle, " 'Somebody I Look Up To': Ethical Role Models in Organizations," *Organizational Dynamics* 34, no. 4 (2005): 313–330.

13. Gary Yukl et al., "An Improved Measure of Ethical Leadership," *Journal of Leadership and Organizational Studies* 20, no. 1 (2013): 38–48.

14. Martin, "The CEO's Ethical Dilemma in the Era of Earnings Management."

15. Reported in Jennifer Liberto, "CEOs Earn 354 Times More than Average Worker," *CNNMoney.com*, April 15, 2013, http://money.cnn.com/2013/04/15/news/economy/ceo-pay-worker/index.html (accessed September 4, 2013).

16. Ibid.

17. Homer H. Johnson, "Does It Pay to Be Good? Social Responsibility and Financial Performance," *Business Horizons* (November–December 2003): 34–40; Jennifer J. Griffin and John F. Mahon, "The Corporate Social Performance and Corporate Financial Performance Debate: Twenty-Five Years of Incomparable Research," *Business and Society* 36, no. 1 (March 1997): 5–31; Bernadette M. Ruf et al., "An Empirical Investigation of the Relationship Between Change in Corporate Social Performance and Financial Performance: A Stakeholder Theory Perspective," *Journal of Business Ethics* 32, no. 2 (July 2001): 143ff; Philip L. Cochran and Robert A. Wood, "Corporate Social Responsibility and Financial Performance," *Academy of Management Journal* 27 (1984): 42–56.

18. Heli Wang, Jaepil Choi, and Jiatao Li, "Too Little or Too Much? Untangling the Relationship Between Corporate Philanthropy and Firm Financial Performance," *Organization Science* 19, no. 1 (January–February 2008): 143–159; Philip L. Cochran, "The Evolution of Corporate Social Responsibility," *Business Horizons* 50 (2007): 449–454; Paul C. Godfrey, "The Relationship Between Corporate Philanthropy and Shareholder Wealth: A Risk Management Perspective," *Academy of Management Review* 30, no. 4 (2005): 777–798; Oliver Falck and Stephan Heblich, "Corporate Social Responsibility: Doing Well by Doing Good," *Business Horizons* 50 (2007): 247–254; J. A. Pearce II and J. P. Doh, "The High Impact of Collaborative Social Initiatives," *MIT Sloan Management Review* (Spring 2005): 31–39; Curtis C. Verschoor and Elizabeth A. Murphy, "The Financial Performance of Large U.S. Firms and Those with Global Prominence: How Do the Best Corporate Citizens Rate?" *Business and Society Review* 107, no. 3 (Fall 2002): 371–381; Johnson, "Does It Pay to Be Good?"; Dale Kurschner, "5 Ways Ethical Business Creates Fatter Profits," *Business Ethics* (March–April 1996): 20–23.

19. Rashid Ameer and Radiah Othman, "Sustainability Practices and Corporate Financial Performance: A Study Based on the Top Global Corporations," *Journal of Business Ethics* 108, no. 1 (June 2012): 61–79.

20. Verschoor and Murphy, "The Financial Performance of Large U.S. Firms."

21. Richard McGill Murphy, "Why Doing Good Is Good For Business," *Fortune* (February 8, 2010): 90–95; Jean B. McGuire, Alison Sundgren, and Thomas Schneeweis, "Corporate Social Responsibility and Firm Financial Performance," *Academy of Management Journal* 31 (1988): 854–872; and Falck and Heblich, "Corporate Social Responsibility: Doing Well by Doing Good."

22. Daniel W. Greening and Daniel B. Turban, "Corporate Social Performance as a Competitive Advantage in Attracting a Quality Workforce," *Business and Society* 39, no. 3 (September 2000): 254–280; and Kate O'Sullivan, "Virtue Rewarded," *CFO* (October 2006): 47–52.

23. "The Socially Correct Corporate Business," in Leslie Holstrom and Simon Brady, " *The Changing Face of Global Business*," a special advertising section, *Fortune* (July 24, 2000): S1–S38.

24. Remi Trudel and June Cotte, "Does Being Ethical Pay?" *The Wall Street Journal*, May 12, 2008.

25. Linda K. Treviño and Katherine A. Nelson, *Managing Business Ethics: Straight Talk About How to Do It Right* (New York: John Wiley & Sons, Inc. 1995), p. 4.

26. Shelby D. Hunt and Jared M. Hansen, "Understanding Ethical Diversity in Organizations," *Organizational Dynamics* 36, no 2 (2007): 202–216.

27. "Socialising for Intelligence," *Computer News Middle East*, November 2, 2011.

28. Justin Scheck, "Accusations of Snooping in Ink-Cartridge Dispute," *The Wall Street Journal Online*, August 11, 2009, http://online.wsj.com/article/SB124995836273921661.html?KEYWORDS=%22Accusations+of+Snooping+in+Ink-Cartridge+Dispute%22 (accessed August 14, 2009).

29. Thomas M. Jones, "Ethical Decision Making by Individuals in Organizations: An Issue-Contingent Model," *Academy of Management Review* 16 (1991): 366–395.

30. Based on a question from a General Electric (GE) employee ethics guide, reported in Kathryn Kranhold, "U.S. Firms Raise Ethics Focus," *The Wall Street Journal*, November 28, 2005.

31. D. Wallis, "Loose Lips Can Sink Trips," *The New York Times*, May 3, 2012, F1.

32. This discussion is based on Gerald F. Cavanagh, Dennis J. Moberg, and Manuel Velasquez, "The Ethics of Organizational Politics," *Academy of Management Review* 6 (1981): 363–374; Justin G. Longenecker, Joseph A. McKinney, and Carlos W. Moore, "Egoism and Independence: Entrepreneurial Ethics," *Organizational Dynamics* (Winter 1988): 64–72; Carolyn Wiley, "The

ABCs of Business Ethics: Definitions, Philosophies, and Implementation," *IM* (February 1995): 22–27; and Mark Mallinger, "Decisive Decision Making: An Exercise Using Ethical Frameworks," *Journal of Management Education* (August 1997): 411–417.

33. Michael J. McCarthy, "Now the Boss Knows Where You're Clicking," and "Virtual Morality: A New Workplace Quandary," *The Wall Street Journal*, October 21, 1999, B1; and Jeffrey L. Seglin, "Who's Snooping on You?" *Business 2.0* (August 8, 2000): 202–203.

34. John Kekes, "Self-Direction: The Core of Ethical Individualism," in *Organizations and Ethical Individualism*, ed. Konstanian Kolenda (New York: Praeger, 1988), pp. 1–18.

35. Tad Tulega, *Beyond the Bottom Line* (New York: Penguin Books, 1987).

36. Bill Lynn, "*Ethics*," Practical Ethics Web site, www.practicalethics.net/ethics.html (accessed March 23, 2010); Richard E. Thompson, "So, Greed's Not Good After All," *Trustee* (January 2003): 28; and Dennis F. Thompson, "*What Is Practical Ethics?*" Harvard University Edmond J. Safra Foundation Center for Ethics Web site, www.ethics.harvard.edu/the-center/what-is-practical-ethics (accessed March 23, 2010).

37. Carol D. Leonnig and David Nakamura, "Official Quickly Corralled Agents," *The Washington Post*, April 22, 2012, A1; David Nakamura, "Out of Public Eye, a Disgusted Secret Service Director," *The Washington Post*, April 26, 2012, A1; and Carol D. Leonnig and David Nakamura, "Four in Secret Service Fight Back," *The Washington Post*, May 23, 2012, A1.

38. Gerard L. Rossy, "Five Questions for Addressing Ethical Dilemmas," *Strategy & Leadership* 39, no. 6 (2011): 35–42.

39. John D. Kammeyer-Mueller, Lauren S. Simon, and Bruce L. Rich, "The Psychic Cost of Doing Wrong: Ethical Conflict, Divestiture Socialization, and Emotional Exhaustion," *Journal of Management* 38, no. 3 (May 2012): 784–808.

40. L. Kohlberg, "Moral Stages and Moralization: The Cognitive-Developmental Approach," in *Moral Development and Behavior: Theory, Research, and Social Issues*, ed. T. Lickona (New York: Holt, Rinehart and Winston, 1976), pp. 31–83; L. Kohlberg, "Stage and Sequence: The Cognitive-Developmental Approach to Socialization," in *Handbook of Socialization Theory and Research*, ed. D. A. Goslin (Chicago: Rand McNally, 1969); Linda K. Treviño, Gary R. Weaver, and Scott J. Reynolds, "Behavioral Ethics in Organizations: A Review," *Journal of Management* 32, no 6 (December 2006): 951–990; and Jill W. Graham, "Leadership, Moral Development, and Citizenship Behavior," *Business Ethics Quarterly* 5, no. 1 (January 1995): 43–54.

41. Ihosvani Rodriguez, "Hallandale Beach Lifeguard Fired After Participating in Beach Rescue," *Sun Sentinel*, July 3, 2012, http://articles.sun-sentinel.com/2012-07-03/news/

fl-hallandale-beach-lifeguards-20120703_1_lifeguard-services-jeff-ellis-beach-rescue (accessed July 9, 2012); and Gilma Avalos and Ari Odzer, "Hallandale Beach Lifeguard Fired for Leaving His Zone to Rescue Drowning Man," *NBCMiami.com*, July 5, 2012, www.nbcmiami.com/news/local/Hallandale-Beach-Lifeguard-Fired-For-Leaving-His-Zone-For-Rescue-161372785.html (accessed July 9, 2012).

42. Studies cited in Adam Grant, "Turning the Tables on Success," *Strategy + Business* (Summer 2013).

43. Adam Grant, "Givers Take All: The Hidden Dimension of Corporate Culture," *McKinsey Quarterly*, Issue 2 (2013): 52–65; and Grant, "Turning the Tables on Success."

44. See Herman Aguinis and Ante Glavas, "What We Know and Don't Know About Corporate Social Responsibility: A Review and Research Agenda," *Journal of Management* 38, no. 4 (July 2012): 932–968; and Archie B. Carroll and Kareem M. Shabana, "The Business Case for Corporate Social Responsibility: A Review of Concepts, Research, and Practice," *International Journal of Management Reviews* 12, no. 1 (March 2010): 85–105.

45. Carroll and Shabana, "The Business Case for Corporate Social Responsibility"; Eugene W. Szwajkowski, "The Myths and Realities of Research on Organizational Misconduct," in *Research in Corporate Social Performance and Policy*, ed. James E. Post (Greenwich, CT: JAI Press, 1986), 9: 103–122; Keith Davis, William C. Frederick, and Robert L. Blostrom, *Business and Society: Concepts and Policy Issues* (New York: McGraw-Hill, 1979).

46. Douglas S. Sherwin, "The Ethical Roots of the Business System," *Harvard Business Review* 61 (November–December 1983): 183–192.

47. Nancy C. Roberts and Paula J. King, "The Stakeholder Audit Goes Public," *Organizational Dynamics* (Winter 1989): 63–79; Thomas Donaldson and Lee E. Preston, "The Stakeholder Theory of The Corporation: Concepts, Evidence, and Implications," *Academy of Management Review* 20, no. 1 (1995): 65–91; and Jeffrey S. Harrison and Caron H. St. John, "Managing and Partnering with External Stakeholders," *Academy of Management Executive* 10, no. 2 (1996): 46–60.

48. R. Mitchell, B. Agle, and D. J. Wood, "Toward a Theory of Stakeholder Identification and Salience: Defining the Principle of Who or What Really Counts," *Academy of Management Review* 22 (1997): 853–886; Virginie Vial, "Taking a Stakeholders' Approach to Corporate Social Responsibility," *Global Business and Organizational Excellence* (September–October 2011): 37–47; and Martijn Poel, Linda Kool, and Annelieke van der Giessen, "How to Decide on the Priorities and Coordination of Information Society Policy? Analytical Framework and Three Case Studies," *Info: The Journal of Policy, Regulation and Strategy for Telecommunications, Information, and Media* 12, no. 6 (2010): 21–39.

49. N. Craig Smith, Sean Ansett, and Lior Erex, "How Gap Inc. Engaged with Its Stakeholders," *MIT Sloan Management Review* 52, no. 4 (Summer 2011): 69–76.

50. Ibid.

51. Jens Hansegard, Tripti Lahiri, and Chritina Passariello, "Retailers' Dilemma: To Ax or Help Fix Bad Factories," *The Wall Street Journal*, May 28, 2011, http://online.wsj.com/article/SB10001424127887323336104578501143973731324.html (accessed September 5, 2013).

52. Max B. E. Clarkson, "A Stakeholder Framework for Analyzing and Evaluating Corporate Social Performance," *Academy of Management Review* 20, no. 1 (1995): 92–117.

53. Rich Kauffeld, Abhishek Malhotra, and Susan Higgins, "Green Is a Strategy," *Strategy + Business* (December 21, 2009).

54. Reported in Dung K. Nguyen and Stanley F. Slater, "Hitting the Sustainability Sweet Spot: Having It All," *Journal of Business Strategy* 31, no. 3 (2010): 5–11.

55. Steven Mufson, "Keystone XL Pipeline Expansion Driven by Oil-Rich Tar Sands in Alberta," *The Washington Post*, June 30, 2012, www.washingtonpost.com/business/economy/keystone-xl-pipeline-expansion-driven-by-oil-rich-tar-sands-in-alberta/2012/06/30/gJQAVe4ZEW_story.html?wpisrc (accessed July 4, 2012).

56. This definition is based on Marc J. Epstein and Marie-Josée Roy, "Improving Sustainability Performance: Specifying, Implementing, and Measuring Key Principles," *Journal of General Management* 29, no. 1 (Autumn 2003): 15–31; World Commission on Economic Development, *Our Common Future* (Oxford: Oxford University Press, 1987); and A. W. Savitz and K. Weber, *The Triple Bottom Line: How Today's Best-run Companies Are Achieving Economic, Social, and Environmental Success* (San Francisco: Jossey-Bass, 2006).

57. This discussion is based on Nguyen and Slater, "Hitting the Sustainability Sweet Spot"; Savitz and Weber, *The Triple Bottom Line*; and "Triple Bottom Line," an article adapted from *The Economist Guide to Management Ideas and Gurus*, by Tim Hindle (London: Profile Books, 2008), *The Economist* (November 17, 2009), www.economist.com/node/14301663 (accessed July 5, 2012). The "people, planet, profit" phrase was first coined in 1994 by John Elkington, founder of a British consulting firm called SustainAbility.

58. Mark S. Schwartz and Archie B. Carroll, "Corporate Social Responsibility: A Three-Domain Approach," *Business Ethics Quarterly* 13, no. 4 (2003): 503–530; and Archie B. Carroll, "A Three-Dimensional Conceptual Model of Corporate Performance," *Academy of Management Review* 4 (1979): 497–505. For a discussion of various models for evaluating corporate social performance, also see Diane L. Swanson, "Addressing a Theoretical Problem by Reorienting the Corporate Social Performance Model," *Academy of Management Review* 20, no. 1 (1995): 43–64.

59. Milton Friedman, *Capitalism and Freedom* (Chicago: University of Chicago Press, 1962), p. 133; and Milton Friedman and Rose Friedman, *Free to Choose* (New York: Harcourt Brace Jovanovich, 1979).

60. Eugene W. Szwajkowski, "Organizational Illegality: Theoretical Integration and Illustrative Application," *Academy of Management Review* 10 (1985): 558–567.

61. David Barstow, "Vast Mexico Bribery Case Hushed up by Walmart after Top-Level Struggle," *The New York Times*, April 21, 2012, www.nytimes.com/2012/04/22/business/at-walmart-in-mexico-a-bribe-inquiry-silenced.html?pagewanted=all (accessed July 6, 2012); and James B. Stewart, "Bribery, but Nobody Was Charged," *The New York Times*, June 24, 2011.

62. Samuel Rubenfeld, "Survey Finds 25% of People Paid Bribes in Last Year," *The Wall Street Journal*, July 9, 2013, http://blogs.wsj.com/riskandcompliance/2013/07/09/survey-finds-one-fourth-of-people-paid-bribes-in-last-year/ (accessed July 16, 2013).

63. David J. Fritzsche and Helmut Becker, "Linking Management Behavior to Ethical Philosophy—An Empirical Investigation," *Academy of Management Journal* 27 (1984): 165–175.

64. Natasha Singer, "Web Sites Accused of Collecting Data on Children," *The New York Times*, August 22, 2012, http://www.nytimes.com/2012/08/22/business/media/web-sites-accused-of-collecting-data-on-children.html?_r=0 (accessed August 22, 2012).

65. These examples are reported in Jakki Mohr, Sanjit Sengupta, and Stanley F. Slater, "Serving Base-of-the-Pyramid Markets: Meeting Real Needs Through a Customized Approach," *Journal of Business Strategy* 33, no. 6 (2012): 4–14.

66. D. Bright, K. Cameron, and A. Caza, "The Amplifying and Buffering Effects of Virtuousness in Downsized Organizations," *Journal of Business Ethics* 64 (2006): 249–269; Mario Fernando and Shamika Almeida, "The Organizational Virtuousness of Strategic Corporate Social Responsibility: A Case Study of the Sri Lankan Family-Owned Enterprise MAS Holdings," *European Management Journal* 30 (2012): 564–576.

67. Fernando and Almeida, "The Organizational Virtuousness of Strategic Corporate Responsibility."

68. Saul W. Gellerman, "Managing Ethics from the Top Down," *Sloan Management Review* (Winter 1989): 73–79.

69. This discussion is based on Linda Klebe Treviño, Laura Pincus Hartman, and Michael Brown, "Moral Person and Moral Manager," *California Management Review* 42, no. 4 (Summer 2000): 128–142; and Mark S. Schwartz, "Developing and Sustaining an Ethical Corporate Culture: The Core Elements," *Business Horizons* 56 (2013): 39–50.

70. Michael E. Brown and Linda K. Treviño, "Ethical Leadership: A Review and Future Directions," *The Leadership Quarterly* 17 (2006): 595–616; Weaver, Treviño, and Agle, " 'Somebody I Look Up To' "; and L. K. Treviño et al., "Managing Ethics and Legal Compliance: What Works and What Hurts?" *California Management Review* 41, no. 2 (Winter 1999): 131–151.

71. "Code of Conduct," Google Investor Relations, April 25, 2012, http://investor.google.com/corporate/code-of-conduct.html (accessed September 28, 2012).

72. M. A. Cleek and S. L. Leonard, "Can Corporate Codes of Ethics Influence Behavior?" *Journal of Business Ethics* 17, no. 6 (1998): 619–630.

73. K. Matthew Gilley, Chris Robertson, and Tim Mazur, "The Bottom-Line Benefits of Ethics Code Commitment," *Business Horizons* 53 (January–February 2010): 31–37; Joseph L. Badaracco and Allen P. Webb, "Business Ethics: A View from the Trenches," *California Management Review* 37, no. 2 (Winter 1995): 8–28; and Ronald B. Morgan, "Self- and Co-Worker Perceptions of Ethics and Their Relationships to Leadership and Salary," *Academy of Management Journal* 36, no. 1 (February 1993): 200–214.

74. Alan Yuspeh, "Do the Right Thing," *CIO* (August 1, 2000): 56–58.

75. Mark S. Schwartz, "Developing and Sustaining an Ethical Corporate Culture: The Core Elements," *Business Horizons* 56 (2013): 39–50.

76. Marcia P. Miceli and Janet P. Near, "The Relationship Among Beliefs, Organizational Positions, and Whistle-Blowing Status: A Discriminant Analysis," *Academy of Management Journal* 27 (1984): 687–705; and Michael T. Rehg et al., "Antecedents and Outcomes of Retaliation Against Whistleblowers: Gender Differences and Power Relationships," *Organization Science* 19, no. 2 (March–April 2008): 221–240.

77. Eugene Garaventa, "*An Enemy of the People* by Henrik Ibsen: The Politics of Whistle-Blowing," *Journal of Management Inquiry* 3, no. 4 (December 1994): 369–374; Marcia P. Miceli and Janet P. Near, "Whistleblowing: Reaping the Benefits," *Academy of Management Executive* 8, no. 3 (1994): 65–74.

78. Robert Jeffery, "Whistleblowers: 'Suddenly I Was the Lead in a John Grisham Novel': How Michael Woodford, The CEO Who Exposed the Olympus Fraud, Gambled His Career on Doing the Right Thing," *People Management* (November 2012): 28–29.

79. Alina Tugent, "Doing the Ethical Thing May Be Right, But It Isn't Automatic," *The New York Times*, November 18, 2011.

80. Jessica Bennett, "Meet Penn State's New Whistleblower, Vicky Triponey," *The Daily Beast*, November 23, 2011, www.thedailybeast.com/articles/2011/11/23/meet-penn-state-s-new-whistleblower-vicky-triponey.html (accessed July 9, 2012).

81. Nicole Gaudiano, "Report: Air Force Whistle-Blowers Targeted," *USA Today*, February 1, 2012, 3A; Gretchen Morgenson, "How a Whistle-Blower Conquered Countrywide," *The New York Times*, February 20, 2011, BU1; and Christine Seib and Alexandra Frean, "Lehman Whistleblower Lost Job a Month After Speaking Out," *The Times*, March 17, 2010, 43.

82. Based on Bart Victor and John B. Cullen, "The Organizational Bases of Ethical Work Climates," *Administrative Science Quarterly* 33 (1988): 101–125.

83. Adapted from Richard L. Daft and Dorothy Marcic, *Understanding Management* (Mason, OH: South-Western, 2008), 134.

84. Adapted from Janet Q. Evans, "What Do You Do: What If Polluting Is Legal?" *Business Ethics* (Fall 2002): 20.

CHAPTER
5

Planning and Goal Setting

LEARNING OUTCOMES

After studying this chapter, you should be able to:

5.1 Define goals and plans and explain the relationship between them.

5.2 Explain the concept of organizational mission and how it influences goal setting and planning.

5.3 Discuss the benefits and limitations of planning.

5.4 Describe contingency planning, scenario building, and crisis planning, and explain the importance of each for today's managers.

5.5 Identify innovative planning approaches that managers use in a fast-changing environment.

5.6 Define the components of strategic management and discuss the three levels of strategy.

5.7 Explain the strategic management process.

5.8 Summarize how SWOT analysis can be used to evaluate a company's strengths, weaknesses, opportunities, and threats.

5.9 Describe Michael Porter's competitive forces and strategies.

5.10 Explain organizational dimensions that managers use to execute strategy.

•••••○ 🛜   100% ▬

< Messages

R U Ready 2 B a Manager?

Delivered

Before reading this chapter, please circle either "Mostly True" or "Mostly False" for each of the five questions below.

1 I want to have a specific goal, or mission, that I can achieve in the next 5–10 years.

| Mostly True | Mostly False |

[page 188]

2 I wish I could figure out what I need to do to achieve the goal in #1, above. In other words, I have to come up with a workable strategy to help me reach my dreams.

| Mostly True | Mostly False |

[page 191]

3 I develop goals for my studying, my work, and my life. These goals help me stay focused and motivated and help me figure out how to allocate my time and money.

| Mostly True | Mostly False |

[page 197]

4 Trying new ways to develop strategy, such as crowdsourcing, appeals to me.

| Mostly True | Mostly False |

[page 210]

5 I have honestly assessed my strengths and weaknesses and I have looked for ways to utilize my strengths in the most effective way possible.

| Mostly True | Mostly False |

[page 210]

Japan's Uniqlo is the biggest apparel chain in Asia, but reaching that goal isn't enough for managers at Fast Retailing Company. Their next goal is to make Uniqlo number one in the United States as well. The company, known for its simple, trendy, inexpensive clothes, has a long way to go, with only seven stores in the United States in mid-2013. Fast Retailing announced opening dates for 10 new stores in October and November of that year and plans to open as many as 20 stores a year over the next eight years. It's all part of CEO Tadashi Yanai's plan for achieving his goal of overtaking Inditex Group (parent of the Zara chain) as the world's biggest apparel chain by 2020. The breakneck pace of growth in Asia, where Uniqlo is still opening an average of two new stores a week, has given managers confidence that Yanai's ambitious goal can be achieved.[1]

One of the primary responsibilities of managers is to set goals for where the organization or department should go in the future and plan how to get it there. Managers in every organization work hard to decide what goals to pursue and how to achieve them. Lack of planning or poor planning can seriously hurt an organization. For example, the nuclear accident at the Fukushima Daiichi nuclear power plant after the earthquake and tsunami in Japan in 2011 has been blamed partly on poor planning. In the fall of 2013, radioactive water was still leaking into the Pacific Ocean from the crippled reactor, bringing fresh criticism of Tokyo Electric Power Company (Tepco). At the time of the accident, Kiyoshi Kurokawa, the chairman of the Fukushima Nuclear Accident Independent Investigation Commission, said: "[This] was a profoundly manmade disaster—that could and should have been foreseen and prevented. And its effect could have been mitigated by a more effective human response."[2] Managers cannot predict the future, nor can they prevent natural disasters such as earthquakes, but proper planning can enable them to respond swiftly and effectively to such unexpected events. At Fukushima, near chaos reigned as communications broke down, the chain of command was confused, and no one seemed to know what to do to maintain safety or to follow up once the accident had occurred.

Of the four management functions—planning, organizing, leading, and controlling—described in Chapter 1, planning is considered the most fundamental. Everything else stems from planning. Yet planning is also the most controversial management function. How do managers plan for the future in a constantly changing environment? The economic, political, and social turmoil of recent years has sparked a renewed interest in organizational planning, particularly planning for crises and unexpected events, yet it also has some managers questioning whether planning is even worthwhile in a world that is in constant flux. Planning cannot read an uncertain future. Planning cannot tame a turbulent environment. A statement by General Colin Powell, former U.S. secretary of state, offers a warning for managers: "No battle plan survives contact with the enemy."[3] Does that mean it is useless for managers to make plans? Of course not. No plan can be perfect, but without plans and goals, organizations and employees flounder. However, good managers understand that plans should grow and change to meet shifting conditions.

In this chapter, we explore the process of planning and consider how managers develop effective plans. Special attention is given to goal setting, for that is where planning starts. Then, we discuss the various types of plans that managers use to help the organization achieve those goals. We also take a look at planning approaches that help managers deal with uncertainty, such as contingency planning, scenario building, and crisis planning. Finally, we examine new approaches to planning that emphasize the involvement of employees (and sometimes other stakeholders) in strategic thinking and execution. The latter part of this chapter will look at strategic planning in depth and examine a number of strategic options that managers can use in a competitive environment. In Chapter 6, we look at management decision making. Appropriate decision-making techniques are crucial to selecting the organization's goals, plans, and strategic options.

NEW MANAGER Self-Test

Does Goal Setting Fit Your Management Style?

Instructions: Are you a good planner? Do you set goals and identify ways to accomplish them? This questionnaire will help you understand how your work habits fit with making plans and setting goals. Answer the following questions as they apply to your work or study habits. Please indicate whether each item is Mostly True or Mostly False for you.

	Mostly True	Mostly False
1. I have clear, specific goals in several areas of my life.	_____	_____
2. I have a definite outcome in life that I want to achieve.	_____	_____
3. I prefer general to specific goals.	_____	_____
4. I work better without specific deadlines.	_____	_____
5. I set aside time each day or week to plan my work.	_____	_____
6. I am clear about the measures that indicate when I have achieved a goal.	_____	_____
7. I work better when I set more challenging goals for myself.	_____	_____
8. I help other people clarify and define their goals.	_____	_____

Scoring and Interpretation: Give yourself one point for each item you marked as Mostly True, except items 3 and 4. For items 3 and 4, give yourself one point for each one that you marked Mostly False. A score of 5 or higher suggests a positive level of goal-setting behavior and good preparation for a new manager role in an organization. If you scored 4 or less, you might want to evaluate and begin to change your goal-setting behavior. An important part of a new manager's job is setting goals, measuring results, and reviewing progress for the department and subordinates.

These questions indicate the extent to which you have already adopted the disciplined use of goals in your life and work. But if you scored low, don't despair. Goal setting can be learned. Most organizations have goal-setting and review systems that managers use. Not everyone thrives under a disciplined goal-setting system, but as a new manager, setting goals and assessing results are tools that will enhance your influence. Research indicates that setting clear, specific, and challenging goals in key areas will produce better performance.

5.1 Goal Setting and Planning Overview

A **goal** is a desired future circumstance or condition that the organization attempts to realize.[4] Goals are important because organizations exist for a purpose, and goals define and state that purpose. A **plan** is a blueprint for goal achievement and specifies the necessary resource allocations, schedules, tasks, and other actions. Goals specify future ends; plans specify today's means. The concept of **planning** usually incorporates both ideas; it means determining the organization's goals and defining the means for achieving them.

5.1a Levels of Goals and Plans

Exhibit 5.1 illustrates the levels of goals and plans in an organization. The planning process starts with a formal mission that defines the basic purpose of the organization, especially for external audiences. The mission is the basis for the strategic (company) level of goals and plans, which in turn shapes the tactical (divisional) level and the operational (departmental) level.[5] That is, a broad higher-level mission, such as "improve the lives of families by providing consumer-preferred paper products for kitchen and bathroom," provides the framework for establishing more specific goals for top managers, such as "improve company profits by 5 percent next year." This might translate into "increase sales by 10 percent next year" for the manager of the Northwest sales division, and an individual salesperson might have a goal of calling on 10 percent more customers.[6] Top managers are typically responsible for establishing *strategic* goals and plans that reflect a commitment to both organizational efficiency and effectiveness, as described in Chapter 1. *Tactical* goals and plans are the responsibility of middle managers, such as the heads of major divisions or functional units. A division manager will formulate tactical plans that focus on the major actions that the division must take to fulfill its part in the strategic plan set by top management. *Operational* plans identify the specific procedures or processes needed at lower levels of the organization, such as individual departments and employees. Frontline managers and supervisors develop operational plans that focus on specific tasks and processes and that help meet tactical and strategic goals. Planning at each level supports the other levels.

EXHIBIT 5.1 Levels of Goals and Plans

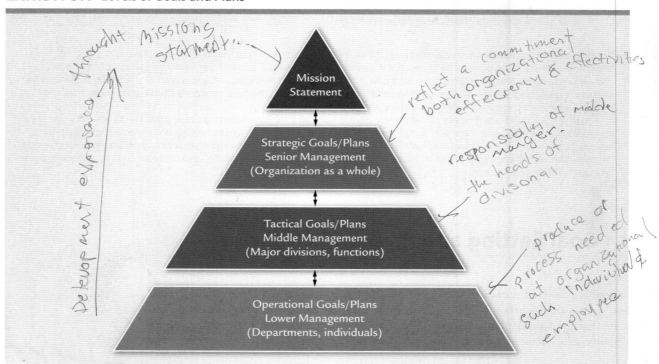

5.1b The Organizational Planning Process

The overall planning process, illustrated in Exhibit 5.2, prevents managers from thinking merely in terms of day-to-day activities. The process begins when managers develop the overall plan for the organization by clearly defining mission and strategic (company-level) goals. Second, they translate the plan into action, which includes defining tactical objectives and plans, developing a strategy map to align goals, formulating contingency and scenario plans, and identifying intelligence teams to analyze major competitive issues. Third, managers lay out the operational factors needed to achieve goals. This involves devising operational goals and plans, selecting the measures and targets that will be used to determine if things are on track, and identifying stretch goals and crisis plans that might need to be put into action. Tools for executing the plan include management-by-objectives (MBO), performance dashboards, single-use plans, and decentralized responsibility. Finally, managers periodically review plans to learn from results and shift plans as needed, starting a new planning cycle.

Mike Fuentes/Bloomberg/Getty Images

CONCEPT CONNECTION From its beginning as a seven-cow farm in New England to its current status as a $350 million organic yogurt business, Stonyfield Farm has incorporated environmental responsibility into its **organizational planning**. Today, every operational plan encompasses Stonyfield's **goal** of carbon-neutral operations.

EXHIBIT 5.2 The Organizational Planning Process

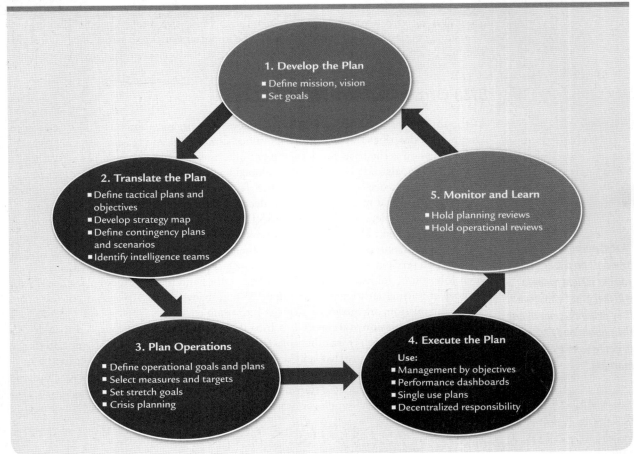

SOURCE: Based on Robert S. Kaplan and David P. Norton, "Mastering the Management System," *Harvard Business Review* (January 2008): 63–77.

REMEMBER THIS

- Planning is the most fundamental of the four management functions.
- A **goal** is a desired future circumstance or condition that the organization wants to realize.
- **Planning** is the act of determining goals and defining the means of achieving them.

- A **plan** is a blueprint specifying the resource allocations, schedules, and other actions necessary for attaining goals.
- Planning helps managers think about the future rather than thinking merely in terms of day-to-day activities.

5.2 Goal Setting in Organizations

The overall planning process begins with a mission statement and goals for the organization as a whole. Goals don't just appear on their own in organizations. Goals are *socially constructed*, which means they are defined by an individual or a group. Managers typically have different ideas about what the goals should be. As A.G. Lafley, CEO of Procter & Gamble, puts it, "Everyone selects and interprets data about the world and comes to a unique conclusion about the best course of action. Each person tends to embrace a single strategic choice as the right answer." Thus, the role of the top executive is to get people thinking as a team and negotiating about which goals are the important ones to pursue.[7] The "Director's Toolkit" describes the process of coalition building that often occurs during goal setting.

5.2a Organizational Mission

At the top of the goal hierarchy is the **mission**—the organization's reason for existence. The mission describes the organization's values, aspirations, and reason for being. A well-defined mission is the basis for development of all subsequent goals and plans. Without a clear mission, goals and plans may be developed haphazardly and not take the organization in the direction it needs to go. One of the defining attributes of successful companies is that they have a clear mission that guides decisions and actions. The mission of Johnson & Johnson, for example, is encapsulated in J&J's Our Credo, which has guided the company since General Robert Wood Johnson wrote it in 1943: "We believe our first responsibility is to the doctors, nurses, and patients, to mothers and fathers, and to all others who use our products and services." The Credo guided managers in handling the Tylenol crisis in 1982, when Johnson & Johnson recalled 31 million bottles and offered free replacements with the goal of putting customers' safety first.[8] When management actions and decisions go against the mission, organizations may get into trouble.

The formal **mission statement** is a broadly stated definition of purpose that distinguishes the organization from others of a similar type. The founders of Holstee, a Brooklyn, New York–based company that sells eco-friendly clothing and accessories, created a mission statement for their company that has inspired people around the world. Holstee's innovative mission statement is shown in Exhibit 5.3. The Holstee mission was written to remind the founders and employees that there is nothing more important than pursuing your passion.

"A real purpose can't just be words on paper.... If you get it right, people will feel great about what they're doing, clear about their goals, and excited to get to work every morning."

— Roy M. Spence Jr., Author of *It's Not What You Sell, It's What You Stand For*

EXHIBIT 5.3   An Innovative Mission Statement: The Holstee Manifesto

Although most corporate mission statements aren't as broad or quite as inspiring as Holstee's, a well-designed mission statement can enhance employee motivation and organizational performance.[9] The content of a mission statement often describes the company's basic business activities and purpose, as well as the values that guide the company. Some mission statements also describe company characteristics such as desired markets and customers, product quality, location of facilities, and attitude toward employees. An example of a short, straightforward mission statement comes from State Farm Insurance:

> State Farm's mission is to help people manage the risks of everyday life, recover from the unexpected, and realize their dreams.

> We are people who make it our business to be like a good neighbor; who built a premier company by selling and keeping promises through our marketing partnership; who bring diverse talents and experiences to our work of serving the State Farm customer.

Our success is built on a foundation of shared values—quality service and relationships, mutual trust, integrity, and financial strength.

Our vision for the future is to be the customer's first and best choice in the products and services we provide. We will continue to be the leader in the insurance industry and we will become a leader in the financial services arena. Our customers' needs will determine our path. Our values will guide us.[10]

Because of mission statements such as that of State Farm, employees as well as customers, suppliers, and stockholders know the company's stated purpose and values.

Director's Toolkit

Who Sets the Goals? Manager versus Coalition

Organizations perform many activities and pursue many goals simultaneously to accomplish an overall mission. But who decides what mission and goals to strive for? Pursuing some goals means that others have to be delayed or set aside, which means managers often disagree about priorities. After China's Zhejiang Geely Holding Group bought Volvo Car Corporation, for example, the Chinese and European managers disagreed strongly. The European managers wanted to continue pursuing goals of providing safe, reliable, family-friendly vehicles for a stable market. The new Chinese owners and managers, on the other hand, wanted to expand aggressively into the super-luxury car market. The goals of the two sides were mutually exclusive, so managers had to negotiate and come to some agreement on which direction the company would take.

Powerful, motivating goals that unite people are typically established not by a single manager, but by a coalition. *Coalitional management* involves building an alliance of people who support a manager's goals and can influence other people to accept and work toward them. Being an effective coalitional manager involves three key steps:

- **Talk to customers and other managers.** Building a coalition requires talking to many people both inside and outside the organization. Coalitional managers solicit the views of employees and key customers. They talk to other managers all across the organization to get a sense of what people care about and learn what challenges and opportunities they face. A manager can learn who believes in and supports a particular direction and goals, and who is opposed to them and the reasons for the opposition.

- **Address conflicts.** Good managers don't let conflicts over goals simmer and detract from goal accomplishment or hurt the organization. At Toyota,

for example, the rash of recent recalls exposed a longstanding internal conflict between managers who wanted to pursue goals of faster growth and higher profit margins and those who believed that rapid growth would strain the company's ability to ensure quality and reliability. Each side is blaming the other for the recent problems, but it is the failure of managers to unite toward a shared goal that is largely to blame.

- **Break down barriers and promote cross-silo cooperation.** A final step is to break down boundaries and get people to cooperate and collaborate across departments, divisions, and levels. When Colin Powell was chairman of the U.S. Joint Chiefs of Staff, he regularly brought together the heads of the Army, Air Force, Navy, and Marines so they could understand one another's viewpoints and come together around key goals. Cross-enterprise understanding and cooperation is essential so that the entire organization will be aligned toward accomplishing desired goals.

As a manager, remember that you will accomplish more and be more effective as part of a coalition than as an individual actor. When there are goals that are highly important to you, take steps to build a coalition to support them. Throw your support behind other managers when appropriate. And remember that building positive relationships, discussion, and negotiation are key skills for good management.

SOURCES: Stephen Friedman and James K. Sebenius, "Organization Transformation: The Quiet Role of Coalitional Leadership," *Ivey Business Journal* (January–February 2009), www.iveybusinessjournal.com/topics/leadership/organizational-transformation-the-quiet-role-of-coalitional-leadership (accessed January 27, 2012); Gerald R. Ferris et al., "Political Skill in Organizations," *Journal of Management* (June 2007): 290–320; Norihiko Shirouzu, "Chinese Begin Volvo Overhaul," *The Wall Street Journal*, June 7, 2011, B1; and Norihiko Shirouzu, "Inside Toyota, Executives Trade Blame Over Debacle," *The Wall Street Journal* (April 14, 2010): A1 .

5.2b Goals and Plans

Strategic goals, sometimes called *official goals*, are broad statements describing where the organization wants to be in the future. These goals pertain to the organization as a whole rather than to specific divisions or departments. Samsung, for example, set a new strategic goal to become a "quality-based" company rather than a "quantity-based" company. The shift in strategic direction, with its focus on creativity and innovation rather than making inexpensive knock-off products, has led to amazing results. Samsung is now a leader in the electronics industry, including threatening Apple in the smartphone market.[11]

Strategic plans define the action steps by which the company intends to attain strategic goals. The strategic plan is the blueprint that defines the organizational activities and resource allocations—in the form of cash, personnel, space, and facilities—required for meeting these targets. Strategic planning tends to be long-term and may define organizational action steps from two to five years in the future. The purpose of strategic plans is to turn organizational goals into realities within that time period. At Unilever, CEO Paul Polman set a strategic goal of doubling the company's revenues by the year 2020.

After strategic goals are formulated, the next step is to define **tactical goals**, which are the results that major divisions and departments within the organization intend to achieve. These goals apply to middle management and describe what major subunits must do for the organization to achieve its overall goals.

As a new manager, what approach will you take to goal setting and planning? Complete the New Manager Self-Test on page 193 to get some insight into your planning approach from the way that you approach studying as a student.

Spotlight on Skills

Unilever

"Our business is not rocket science," said Paul Polman, the first-ever company outsider to lead Unilever. "It's about being a little bit better every day." Polman's strategic plan to achieve the 2020 target of doubling revenues to €80 billion reflects that philosophy of getting a little better every day.

One of the biggest successes has been TRESemmé, which Unilever acquired when it bought Alberto Culver in 2010. The rollout represents Unilever's strategic approach. Managers' goals were to quickly introduce the product into the rapidly growing Brazilian market, but first they had to implement goals for a massive marketing campaign that involved reaching out to 40 big retailers, courting fashion bloggers, and handing out 10 million free samples. Goals for a huge online advertising blitz attracted one million fans to TRESemmé's Brazilian Facebook page in just six months. Sales of the product went from zero to €150 million in the space of a year.

Another part of Polman's strategic plan is to move Unilever into the higher-end personal care market. His initial goal was to send 80 percent of product development employees into the field to see what upscale customers want and to work closely with suppliers, who Polman says now contribute 7 of 10 new product ideas. He's allocated €500 million to a venture

fund with a goal to invest in next-generation products. One example is a Ponds Institute spa in Jakarta, Indonesia, where women shell out about 228,900 rupiah (the equivalent of $20, which is a good deal of money in that country) every two weeks for a "Gold Radiance" facial treatment or other procedures. In addition, the company has continued its goals for the "bottom of the pyramid (BOP)," as described in Chapter 3. Over the past three years, Unilever has accelerated its sales of small packets of Fair & Lovely skin cream, Sunsilk shampoo, and other products that cost about 35 cents a pop. "It's Unilever's moment in the sun," said Deutsche Bank analyst Harold Thompson, pointing out that the company is capturing both ends of the market. While many of its rivals are still struggling in a slow economy, Unilever is thriving. Thanks to effective goals at each level of the company, sales have been steadily increasing, even in recession-wrecked Europe.[12]

Unilever has been operating in developing countries for decades (it's been in India since 1888 and Indonesia since 1933, for example), so managers have an intimate knowledge of these markets. There are two other components to Polman's new strategic goal—to cut the company's carbon footprint in half and to improve the hygiene habits of more than a billion people in developing countries.

Odilon Dimier/PhotoAlto Agency RF Collections/Getty Images

CONCEPT CONNECTION Sustainability has been an ongoing **strategic goal** for NorthTec, a college in western New Zealand. Recently, school administrators and student volunteers worked together to set new tactical goals aimed at achieving greater sustainability. The group studied several specific areas in the school's operation, including electricity use and recycling, and discovered a surprising waste in the amount of photocopying performed on school grounds. The team has set a goal to reduce paper consumption by 15 percent.

Tactical plans are designed to help execute the major strategic plans and to accomplish a specific part of the company's strategy.[13] Tactical plans typically have a shorter time horizon than strategic plans—that is, over the next year or so. The word *tactical* originally comes from the military. In a business or nonprofit organization, tactical plans define what major departments and organizational subunits will do to implement the organization's strategic plan. For example, a tactical goal for Unilever's beauty products division is to develop personalized skin care treatments for the upscale market. Tactical goals and plans help top managers implement their overall strategic plan. Normally, it is the middle manager's job to take the broad strategic plan and identify specific tactical plans.

The results expected from departments, work groups, and individuals are the **operational goals**. They are precise and measurable. "Process 150 sales applications each week," "Achieve 90 percent of deliveries on time," "Reduce overtime by 10 percent next month," and "Develop two new online courses in accounting" are examples of operational goals. An operational goal for Unilever's distribution managers might be to improve on-shelf availability of products by 5 percentage points over the next two years. By keeping its products in stock, Unilever gets more sales and also cements strong relationships with merchants. Walmart and Tesco both recently named Unilever supplier of the year.[14] In the human resources department, an operational goal might be to keep turnover of product development personnel to less than 5 percent a year so that there are longtime employees who have close relationships with suppliers who contribute ideas for new products.

REMEMBER THIS

- Planning starts with the organization's purpose or reason for existence, which is called its **mission**.

- A **mission statement** is a broadly stated definition of the organization's basic business scope and operations that distinguishes it from similar types of organizations.

- Goals begin with broad strategic goals, followed by more specific tactical goals, and then operational goals.

- Plans are defined similarly, with strategic, tactical, and operational plans used to achieve the desired goals.

- **Strategic goals** are broad statements of where the organization wants to be in the future and pertain to the organization as a whole, rather than to specific divisions or departments.

- **Strategic plans** are the action steps by which an organization intends to attain strategic goals.

- The outcomes that major divisions and departments must achieve for the organization to reach its overall goals are called **tactical goals**.

- **Tactical plans** are designed to help execute major strategic plans and to accomplish a specific part of the company's strategy.

- **Operational plans** specify the action steps toward achieving operational goals and support tactical activities.

- Managers at Unilever set a strategic goal to double revenues, to €80 billion, by 2020.

- Goals and plans need to be in alignment so that they are consistent and mutually supportive.

Your Approach to Studying, Part 1

Instructions: Your approach to studying may be a predictor of your planning approach as a new manager. Answer the questions below as they apply to your study behavior. Please answer whether each item below is Mostly True or Mostly False for you.

	Mostly True	Mostly False
1. Before I tackle an assignment, I try to work out the reasoning behind it.	_____	_____
2. When I am reading, I stop occasionally to reflect on what I am trying to get out of it.	_____	_____
3. When I finish my work, I check it through to see if it really meets the assignment.	_____	_____
4. Now and then, I stand back from my studying to think generally how well it is going.	_____	_____
5. I frequently focus on the facts and details because I do not see the overall picture.	_____	_____
6. I write down as much as possible during lectures, because I often am not sure what is really important.	_____	_____
7. I try to relate ideas to other topics or courses whenever possible.	_____	_____
8. When I am working on a topic, I try to see in my own mind how all the ideas fit together.	_____	_____
9. It is important to me to see the bigger picture within which a new concept fits.	_____	_____

Scoring and Interpretation: Give yourself one point for each item you marked as Mostly True except items 5 and 6. For items 5 and 6, give yourself one point for each one you marked Mostly False. An important part of a new manager's job is to plan ahead, which involves grasping the bigger picture. These items measure *metacognitive awareness*, which means to step back and see the bigger picture of one's own learning activities. This same approach enables a manager to step back and see the big picture required for effective planning, monitoring, and evaluating an organization. If you scored 3 or fewer points, you may be caught up in the details of current activities. A score of 7 or above suggests that you see yourself in a bigger picture, which is an approach to studying that very well may reflect a successful planning aptitude.

SOURCES: Adapted from Kristin Backhaus and Joshua P. Liff, "Cognitive Styles and Approaches to Studying in Management Education," *Journal of Management Education* 31 (August 2007): 445–466; and A. Duff, "Learning Styles Measurement: The Revised Approaches to Studying Inventory," *Bristol Business School Teaching and Research Review* 3 (2000): 169–178.

5.3 Operational Planning

Managers use operational goals to direct employees and resources toward achieving specific outcomes that enable the organization to perform efficiently and effectively. One consideration is how to establish effective goals. Then managers use a number of planning approaches, including MBO, single-use plans, and standing plans.

5.3a Criteria for Effective Goals

Research has identified certain factors, shown in Exhibit 5.4, that characterize effective goals. First and foremost, goals need to be *specific and measurable*.[15] When possible, operational goals should be expressed in quantitative terms, such as increasing profits by 2 percent, having zero incomplete sales order forms, or increasing average teacher effectiveness ratings from 3.5 to 3.7. Not all goals can be expressed in numerical terms, but vague goals have little motivating power for employees. By necessity, goals are qualitative as well as quantitative. The important point is that the goals be precisely defined and allow for measurable progress. Effective goals also have a *defined time period* that specifies the date on which goal attainment will be measured. For instance, school administrators might set a deadline for improving teacher effectiveness ratings by the end of the 2015 school term. When a goal involves a two- to three-year time horizon, setting specific dates for achieving parts of it is a good way to keep people on track toward the goal.

Managers should design goals so that they can be translated into measurement of *key result areas*. Goals cannot be set for every aspect of employee behavior or organizational performance; if they were, their sheer number would render them meaningless. Instead, managers establish goals based on the idea of *measurement* and *clarity*. A few carefully chosen goals with clear measures of success can focus organizational attention, energy, and resources more powerfully.[16] The measurements are sometimes referred to as *key performance indicators*. Key performance indicators (KPIs) assess what is important to the organization and how well the organization is progressing toward attaining its strategic goal, so that managers can establish lower-level goals that drive performance toward the overall strategic objective.[17] Managers should set goals that are *challenging but realistic*. When goals are unrealistic, they set employees up for failure and lead to a decrease in employee morale. However, if goals are too easy, employees may not feel motivated. Goals should also be *linked to rewards*. The ultimate impact of goals depends on the extent to which salary increases, promotions, and awards are based on goal achievement. Employees pay attention to what gets noticed and rewarded in the organization.[18]

EXHIBIT 5.4 Characteristics of Effective Goals

Green Power

The Bees Buzz

Moving sustainability beyond fashionable "buzzwords" is a focus of North Carolina–based **Burt's Bees**—makers of personal care products made from natural substances (including, but not limited to, beeswax). Employees at Burt's Bees get down and dirty with the annual companywide Dumpster Dive, sorting through accumulated trash that reached monthly totals of up to 40 tons in one recent year. Employees recommitted to a zero-waste goal, which the company achieved in 2009. With 100 percent employee engagement, Burt's Bees has now focused on achieving a loftier "zero-waste, zero-carbon" goal by 2020.

Sustainability planning and goal-setting at Burt's Bees engages employees in activities such as reducing water use by "steam-cleaning" containers (resulting in a 90 percent water reduction) or extending the paper label on lip balm to eliminate shrink-wrapping (eliminating 900 miles of film). Managerial goals also extend to consumer education through the "Natural Vs." campaign (aimed at clarifying industry terms, such as *natural*). Through all its efforts, Burt's Bees works toward a goal of helping take the "sting" out of environmental problems.

SOURCE: Christopher Marquis and Bobbi Thomason, "Leadership and the First and Last Mile of Sustainability," *Ivey Business Journal*, September–October 2010, www.iveybusinessjournal.com/topics/leadership/leadership-and-the-first-and-last-mile-of-sustainability (accessed August 2, 2012).

5.3b Management-by-Objectives (MBO)

Described by famed management scholar Peter Drucker in his 1954 book *The Practice of Management*, management-by-objectives has remained a popular and compelling method for defining goals and monitoring progress toward achieving them. **Management-by-objectives (MBO)** is a system whereby managers and employees define goals for every department, project, and person and use them to monitor subsequent performance.[19] A model of the essential steps of the MBO system is presented in Exhibit 5.5. Four major activities make MBO successful:[20]

Many companies have used MBO, and most managers think it is an effective management tool. Tim O'Shaughnessy, founder and CEO of LivingSocial, a daily-deal Web site with more than 5,000 employees and 46 million members in 25 countries, uses the principles of MBO to keep the fast-growing business on track. O'Shaughnessy meets regularly with the heads of every department to set goals for items such as sales and membership growth and develop action plans for how to achieve them. Then he is obsessive about tracking metrics to see whether things are on target toward meeting the numbers. Each week, O'Shaughnessy meets with department heads to talk about their key metrics and review their progress. "The more data you gather, the more likely you'll be successful in the long term," he says.[21] Most managers, like O'Shaughnessy, believe that they are better oriented toward goal achievement when MBO is used.

However, like any system, MBO can cause problems when used improperly. For example, an overemphasis on "meeting the goals" can obscure the means that people use to get there. People may cut corners, ignore potential problems, or behave unethically just to meet the targets. In addition, MBO cannot stand alone; it is only a part of effectively managing people to achieve goals. MBO is "like training wheels on a bicycle."[22] It gets you started, but it isn't all you need. In the United States, for example, the implementation of rigorous MBO-type systems in urban police departments and school systems has led to cheating on the numbers, with people lying about their work performance in order to score well on the metrics. The means for achieving goals is just as important as the outcomes. A new systematic approach that has recently emerged is called **management by means (MBM)**, which focuses attention

EXHIBIT 5.5 Model of The MBO Process

Step 1: Set Goals

- Corporate Strategic Goals
- Departmental Goals
- Individual Goals

Step 2: Develop Action Plans

Action Plans

Review Progress

Step 3: Review Progress

Take Corrective Action

Appraise Performance

Step 4: Appraise Overall Performance

on the methods and processes used to achieve goals. A term coined by H. Thomas Johnson and his coauthors in the book *Profit Beyond Measures*, MBM is based on the idea that when managers pursue their activities in the right way, positive outcomes will result. MBM focuses people on considering the means rather than just on reaching the goals.[23]

At Toyota, the recent "sticky accelerator" problem that caused the automaker to recall millions of vehicles has been blamed in part on a breakdown between goals and the methods used to achieve them. Years of aggressive growth goals eventually strained managers' ability to control the means by which the goals were achieved. People had to be hired quickly, with little time for adequate training and development. Therefore, the limited number of highly trained managers and engineers had to do more to keep pace toward the goals. Since the crisis, Toyota has refocused on improving the abilities of managers and employees to use the right means of achieving ambitious goals.[24]

REMEMBER THIS

- Managers formulate goals that are specific and measurable, cover key result areas, are challenging but realistic, have a defined time period, and are linked to rewards.
- **Key performance indicators (KPIs)** are measures that reflect how well lower-level goals are helping the organization progress toward attaining its strategic goal.
- Types of operational planning include management-by-objectives, single-use plans, and standing plans.

- **Management-by-objectives (MBO)** is a method whereby managers and employees define goals for every department, project, and person and use them to monitor subsequent performance. MBO includes the steps of setting goals, developing action plans, reviewing progress, and appraising performance.
- A recent approach that focuses people on the methods and processes used to attain results, rather than on the results themselves, is called **management by means (MBM)**.

5.4 Benefits and Limitations of Planning

Some managers believe that planning ahead is necessary to accomplish anything, whereas others think that planning limits personal and organizational performance. Both opinions have merit because planning can have both advantages and disadvantages.

Research indicates that planning generally positively affects a company's performance.[25] Here are some reasons why:[26]

- *Goals and plans provide a source of motivation and commitment.* Planning can reduce uncertainty for employees and clarify what they should accomplish. The lack of a clear goal hampers motivation because people don't understand what they're working toward.

- *Goals and plans guide resource allocation.* Planning helps managers decide where they need to allocate resources, such as employees, money, and equipment. At Netflix, for example, a goal of having more video offerings online rather than in DVD format means allocating more funds for Internet movie rights and spending more of managers' time developing alliances with other companies.[27]

- *Goals and plans are a guide to action.* Planning focuses attention on specific targets and directs employee efforts toward important outcomes. It helps managers and other employees know what actions they need to take to achieve goals.

- *Goals and plans set a standard of performance.* Because planning and goal setting define desired outcomes, they also establish performance criteria so that managers can measure whether things are on- or off-track. Goals and plans provide a standard of assessment.

Despite these benefits, some researchers also think planning can hurt organizational performance in some ways.[28] Thus, managers should understand the limitations to planning, particularly when the organization is operating in a turbulent environment:

- *Goals and plans can create a false sense of certainty.* Having a plan can give managers a false sense that they know what the future will be like. However, all planning is based on assumptions, and managers can't know what the future holds for their industry or for their competitors, suppliers, and customers.

- *Goals and plans may cause rigidity in a turbulent environment.* A related problem is that planning can lock the organization into specific goals, plans, and time frames, which may no longer be appropriate. Managing under conditions of change and uncertainty requires a degree of flexibility. Managers who believe in "staying the course" will often stick with a faulty plan even when conditions change dramatically.

- *Goals and plans can get in the way of intuition and creativity.* Success often comes from creativity and intuition, which can be hampered by too much routine planning. For example, during the process of setting goals in the MBO process described previously, employees might play it safe to achieve objectives rather than offer creative ideas. Similarly, managers sometimes squelch creative ideas from employees that do not fit with predetermined action plans.[29]

"In preparing for battle, I have always found that plans are useless, but planning is indispensable."
— Dwight D. Eisenhower (1890–1969), U.S. president

5.5 Planning for a Turbulent Environment

Considering the limitations to planning, what are managers to do? One way that managers can gain benefits from planning and control its limitations is by using innovative planning approaches that are in tune with today's turbulent environment. Three approaches that help brace the organization for unexpected—even unimaginable—events are contingency planning, building scenarios, and crisis planning.

5.5a Contingency Planning

When organizations are operating in a highly uncertain environment or dealing with long time horizons, sometimes planning can seem like a waste of time. Indeed, inflexible plans may hinder rather than help an organization's performance in the face of rapid technological, social, economic, or other environmental change. In these cases, managers can develop multiple future alternatives to help them form more adaptive plans.

Contingency plans define company responses to be taken in the case of emergencies, setbacks, or unexpected conditions. To develop contingency plans, managers identify important factors in the environment, such as possible economic downturns, declining markets, increases in cost of supplies, new technological developments, or safety accidents. Managers then forecast a range of alternative responses to the most likely high-impact contingencies, focusing on the worst case.[30] For example, if sales fall 20 percent and prices drop 8 percent, what will the company do? Managers can develop contingency plans that might include layoffs, emergency budgets, new sales efforts, or new markets. A real-life example comes from the airlines, which had to scramble to develop contingency plans after problems in the electrical system of the new Boeing 787 led to the grounding of the entire fleet of 787s. Some routes that had been designed based on the 787, which offered fuel efficiency, long-range capability, and fewer seats to fill than other long-range jets, had to be closed or redesigned when the Federal Aviation Administration (FAA) grounded the new plane. As uncertainty over when the 787 would return to the skies lingered, airline managers began creating contingency plans for what to do if the 787 was out of commission due to this or other problems for months. Should they lease temporary aircraft? Should they substitute larger existing planes from their fleet and sell more seats at a discount to keep traffic moving, or shut down routes altogether? What kind of alternative marketing plans were needed to reassure passengers that the plane would be safe once it was returned to service?[31]

5.5b Building Scenarios

An extension of contingency planning is a forecasting technique known as *scenario building*.[32] **Scenario building** involves looking at current trends and discontinuities and visualizing future possibilities. Rather than looking only at history and thinking about what has been, managers think about what *could be*. The events that cause the most damage to companies are those that no one even conceived of. "Scenarios are meant to expand the range of future possibilities managers should consider and prepare for," says Stephen Millett, author of *Managing the Future*.[33] In today's tumultuous world, traditional planning can't help managers cope with the many shifting and complex variables that might affect their organizations. Lyndon Bird, technical development director at the Business Continuity Institute, emphasizes that broad plans are the answer. In a turbulent and interconnected world, he says, businesses "are going to be interrupted by something and they are probably not going to be able to predict what will happen except that they've got to be able to deal with the consequences."[34]

Managers can't predict the future, but they can rehearse a framework within which future events can be managed. Organizations can be disrupted by any number of events. A recent survey by the Chartered Management Institute and the Business Continuity Institute found that some of the top events that managers might need scenario plans for include extreme weather, loss of IT systems, loss of key employees, loss of access to offices or plants, failure of communications systems, and supply chain disruptions.[35] Some managers use published global scenarios, such as debt problems in Europe, a slowdown in Asia, or global warming to analyze patterns and driving forces that might affect their industry as a starting point for scenario building. This *abbreviated scenario thinking* can give managers a head start on asking "What if…?" leading to increased understanding even before any scenarios are written.[36] Then a broad base of managers mentally rehearses different scenarios based on anticipating the varied changes that could affect the organization. Scenarios are like stories that offer alternative vivid pictures of what the future will be like and how managers will respond. Typically, two to five scenarios are developed for each set of factors, ranging from the most optimistic to the most pessimistic view. For example, if the United States became involved in a military operation in Syria, leaders could create four broad scenarios of what might happen, as they did for Libya a few years ago—two that are positive for the United States and two that could have highly troublesome consequences—and develop plans for how to respond.[37] Similarly, in businesses and other organizations, scenario building forces managers to rehearse mentally what they would do if their best-laid plans collapse.

Robert Giroux/Getty Images

CONCEPT CONNECTION

After several outbreaks of the H1N1 flu revealed the dangers of widespread diseases, Mike Claver, State Farm insurance company's emergency management superintendent, oversaw the development of a thorough **contingency plan** designed to protect State Farm employees during any potential outbreaks in the future. In addition to coordinating with area agencies and encouraging employees to get vaccines, Claver tested the company's ability to function should managers have to ask employees to work at home during an outbreak. More than 1,000 people, about 10 percent of the workforce at the Bloomington, Illinois, headquarters, logged into the company computer network from their homes one August day. Managers used the results of the dry run to fine-tune contingency plans.

TAKE Action!

As a new manager, get in the mind-set of scenario planning. Go to http://www.shell.com/global/future-energy/scenarios.html where Shell Oil publishes the outline of its annual scenario-planning exercise. You might also want to do an Internet search and type in "national intelligence agency scenarios" to find links to reports of global trends and scenario planning done by various organizations.

5.5c Crisis Planning

Many firms also engage in *crisis planning* to enable them to cope with unexpected events that are so sudden and devastating that they have the potential to destroy the organization if managers aren't prepared with a quick and appropriate response. After Hurricane Sandy in October 2012 caused the first multiday shutdown of the U.S. stock market in more than 120 years, managers at NYSE Euronext ramped up their crisis planning to consider "extreme scenarios" and what they would do if the exchange was not able to open or close, considering as one option an all-electronic exchange that could operate without human traders.[38] Companies all along the East Coast, particularly in New York and New Jersey, are still recovering from Hurricane Sandy. Weather events trigger crisis situations

Spotlight on Skills

Western Digital Thailand

Like most large companies, Western Digital has emergency management plans, but the historic floods that inundated industrial areas of Thailand were well beyond what anyone expected. Nevertheless, decisions and actions of managers both before and after the flooding helped Western Digital get up and running just 46 days after the factories were devastated, long before most other companies.

Despite assurances from the government that the dikes protecting industrial estates would hold, Western Digital managers had anticipated what would happen if they failed. A few days before the disaster, they pulled some inventory from the just-in-time (JIT) process at nearby warehouses and moved it to a safer location. The company also had a process in place for speeding up supplier qualification in case new suppliers were needed in an emergency. The crisis budget included funding for smaller suppliers that might need help rebuilding or relocating their production lines. Ultimately, what helped the company most were its strong relationships with employees, customers, suppliers, and other stakeholders.

Even though people's homes were flooded and power was out, more than 500 Western Digital employees, including all of its senior managers, returned to work during the peak flood period. Within a week, operations to recover and restore equipment were underway. Company leaders worked alongside engineers and front-line employees, even taking personal risks by engaging in diving operations. Good relationships with customers meant some agreed to special provisions that deviated from normal contract agreements. Positive relationships with the Thai government meant Western Digital quickly got Thai navy divers dispatched to help with recovery and Royal Thai army soldiers to act as guards and haul heavy equipment.

Communicating with stakeholders was also a priority. Social media was useful for information exchanges among employees and the recovery team. Local managers were kept up to date with the most recent information about flood conditions and recovery efforts but were asked not to talk with reporters. To limit the potential for overreaction and confusion among customers, suppliers, and shareholders, all formal communications were handled by headquarters in the United States.[39]

for organizations worldwide. For example, two of Western Digital's factories in Thailand that produce about a quarter of the world's hard drives were totally paralyzed after historic floods breached the dikes protecting the Bang Pa-In industrial estate in the fall of 2011.

Severe storms like Hurricane Sandy or the floods in Thailand are only one type of crisis organizations might face. Crises have become integral features of the organizational environment. A few of the other recent crises include the mass shooting at Sandy Hook Elementary School in Newtown, Connecticut, that killed 20 children and 6 adults; the earthquake, tsunami, and nuclear disaster in Japan; the collapse of a stage at the Indiana State Fair that killed seven people and injured dozens more; Lance Armstrong's long-delayed admission of using performance-enhancing drugs, which ensnared not only Armstrong but numerous sponsoring organizations; the "pink slime" YouTube video that led to closure of three plants owned by Beef Products, Inc.; the massive BP oil spill in the Gulf of Mexico; and a string of mishaps for the beleaguered Carnival Cruise Lines, including an engine fire on the *Triumph* that kept passengers stranded for nearly a week with no air conditioning, limited food and water, and few working restrooms.

Although crises may vary, a carefully thought-out and coordinated plan can be used to respond to any disaster. In addition, crisis planning reduces the incidence of trouble much like putting a good lock on a door reduces burglaries.[40] Indiana State Fair officials, for example, have been sharply criticized for a lack of planning that probably contributed to the 2011 stage collapse disaster. Because plans were so haphazard, no one

EXHIBIT 5.6 **Essential Stages of Crisis Planning**

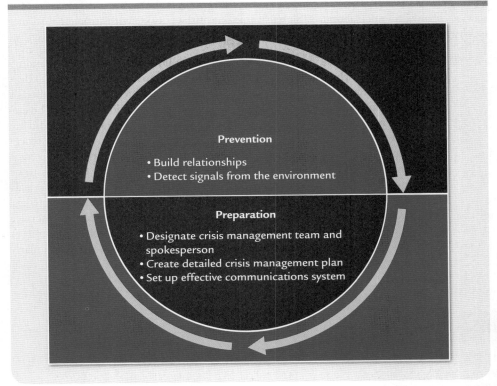

Prevention

- Build relationships
- Detect signals from the environment

Preparation

- Designate crisis management team and spokesperson
- Create detailed crisis management plan
- Set up effective communications system

SOURCE: Based on information in W. Timothy Coombs, *Ongoing Crisis Communication: Planning, Managing, and Responding* (Thousand Oaks, CA: Sage Publications, 1999).

seemed to know who had the authority to delay or cancel the show or what procedures should be followed in case of severe weather. The Indiana Department of Labor fined the state fair commission, as well as Mid-America Sound (which built the stage), and a stagehands union for faulty planning, insufficient inspections, and sloppy construction practices.[41]

Exhibit 5.6 outlines two essential stages of crisis planning.[42]

Crisis prevention. The *crisis prevention* stage involves activities that managers undertake to try to prevent crises from occurring and to detect warning signs of potential crises. A critical part of the prevention stage is building open, trusting relationships with key stakeholders such as employees, customers, suppliers, governments, unions, and the community. By developing favorable relationships, managers can often prevent crises from happening and respond more effectively to those that cannot be avoided.[43]

For example, organizations that have open, trusting relationships with employees and unions may avoid crippling labor strikes. At the software firm 37Signals, managers prevented a crisis by responding quickly and openly when Campfire, a real-time chat tool for small businesses, kept turning off and on unexpectedly. Customers were furious because they used Campfire to run their organizations. Managers immediately began tweeting with customers and posting regular updates on the company's Web site to let people know what was going on and that they were working on the problem. If they didn't understand something, they admitted it. "We responded to every complaint and took the blame every time—even when people went overboard and launched into personal attacks," said Jason Fried of 37Signals. Once the problem was fixed, they gave all customers a free month of service. Thanks to quick action, 37Signals came out of the episode with stronger customer loyalty and goodwill than ever.[44]

- **Crisis preparation.** The *crisis preparation* stage includes all the detailed planning to handle a crisis when it occurs. Three steps in the preparation stage are (1) designating a crisis management team and spokesperson, (2) creating a detailed crisis management plan, and (3) setting up an effective communications system. The crisis management team, for example, is a cross-functional group of people who are designated to swing into action if a crisis occurs. The organization should also designate a spokesperson to be the voice of the company during the crisis.[45] The crisis management plan (CMP) is a detailed, written plan that specifies the steps to be taken, and by whom, if a crisis occurs. The CMP should include the steps for dealing with various types of crises, such as natural disasters like fires or earthquakes; normal accidents like economic crises, industrial accidents, or product and service failures; and abnormal events such as product tampering or acts of terrorism.[46] A key point is that a CMP should be a living, changing document that is regularly reviewed, practiced, and updated as needed.

REMEMBER THIS

- Managers use innovative planning approaches to cope with today's turbulent environment.
- **Contingency planning** identifies important factors in the environment and defines a range of alternative responses to be taken in the case of emergencies, setbacks, or unexpected conditions.
- With **scenario building**, managers look at trends and discontinuities and imagine possible alternative futures to build a framework within which unexpected future events can be managed.
- Scenarios are alternative vivid pictures of what the future might be like.
- Many companies increased their use of contingency and scenario planning because of the global financial crisis and volatile economic conditions.
- Crisis planning involves the two major stages of prevention and preparation.

5.6 Innovative Approaches to Planning

Go to the "Ethical Dilemma" on page 220, which pertains to potential problems with innovative planning approaches.

The process of planning changes over time, like other aspects of managing, to become more in tune with shifts in the environment and employee attitudes. A fresh approach to planning is to involve everyone in the organization, and sometimes outside stakeholders as well, in the planning process. The evolution to a new approach begins with a shift to decentralized planning, which means that planning experts work with managers in major divisions or departments to develop their own goals and plans. Managers throughout the company come up with their own creative solutions to problems and become more committed to following through on the plans. As the environment becomes even more volatile, top executives see the benefits of pushing decentralized planning even further by having planning experts work directly with line managers and front-line employees to develop dynamic plans that meet fast-changing needs.

Spotlight on Skills

Amazon

When Jeff Bezos, CEO of Amazon, first asked engineers in 2004 to create a lightweight, simple e-reader with built-in cellular access, systems engineer Jateen Parekh said, "I thought it was insane. I really did." At the time, nothing like that had ever been tried. But Bezos believed that configuring devices to WiFi networks would be too complicated for many users, and he didn't want people to have to connect to a personal computer. Essentially, he didn't want people to even have to think about the wireless connection. The challenge eventually got Parekh and others fired up.

It took the development group several years, but in 2007, the Kindle was born. It proved to be such a hit that the first batch sold out in just a few hours. Amazon had to scramble to find a key part that had been discontinued by a supplier to get more on the market. "You look at the history of the Kindle, they developed some real skills around the creation of that product. They cut their teeth, so to speak," said Brian Blair, an analyst with Wedge Partners.

Building its own hardware—much less for something that hadn't been done before—was an audacious, high-stakes bet for Amazon at the time, but it paid off. Moreover, making four successive generations of the Kindle e-reader led down the path to the Kindle Fire, which is today the only serious competitor to Apple's iPad.[47]

In a complex and competitive business environment, strategic thinking and execution become the expectation of every employee.[48] Planning comes alive when employees are involved in setting goals and determining the means to reach them. The following sections provide some guidelines for innovative planning.

5.6a Set Stretch Goals for Excellence

Stretch goals are reasonable yet highly ambitious goals that are so clear, compelling, and imaginative that they fire up employees and engender excellence. Stretch goals are typically so far beyond the current levels that people have to be innovative to find ways to reach them. Consider the following example from Amazon.com.

Asking a group of engineers to create the first Kindle e-reader might be considered what James Collins and Jerry Porras have called a *big hairy audacious goal* (*BHAG*). This phrase was first proposed by Collins and Porras in their 1996 article entitled "Building Your Company's Vision."[49] Since then, it has evolved into a term used to describe any goal that is so big, inspiring, and outside the prevailing paradigm that it hits people in the gut and shifts their thinking. At the same time, however, goals must be seen as achievable or employees will be discouraged and demotivated, and some might resort to extreme or unethical measures to meet the targets.[50]

Stretch goals and BHAGs have become extremely important because things move fast. A company that focuses on gradual, incremental improvements in products, processes, or systems will be left behind. Managers can use these goals to compel employees to think in new ways that can lead to bold, innovative breakthroughs.[51]

Dan Krauss/The New York Times/Redux Pictures

CONCEPT CONNECTION Back in 2005, Netflix CEO Reed Hastings announced a **stretch goal** of quadrupling the company's subscriber base to 20 million by 2012. "That's a bit aggressive," he said at the time, "but it's theoretically possible." Fast forward to 2012, and Netflix had not only met this goal but surpassed it, for a total of 30 million subscribers! With success like this, it's no surprise that Hastings has set a new stretch goal of 60 to 90 million subscribers in the future.

- Approaches to planning change with the times. In many companies today, planning is decentralized.
- **Decentralized planning** means that top executives or planning experts work with managers in major divisions or departments to develop their own goals and plans.

- Stretch goals are reasonable yet highly ambitious and compelling goals that energize people and inspire excellence.
- At Amazon, a stretch goal was to build the first Kindle e-reader with built-in cellular access so people didn't have to connect to a PC.

5.7 Strategy

The first part of this chapter provided an overview of the types of goals and plans that organizations use. In this last part of the chapter, we explore strategic management, which is one specific type of planning. First, we define the components of strategic management and discuss the purposes and levels of strategy. Then, we examine several models of strategy formulation at the corporate, business, and functional levels. Finally, we discuss the tools that managers use to execute their strategic plans.

5.8 Thinking Strategically

What does it mean to think strategically? Strategic thinking means to take the long-term view and to see the big picture, including the organization and the competitive environment, and consider how they fit together. Strategic thinking is important for both businesses and nonprofit organizations. In for-profit firms, strategic planning typically pertains to competitive actions in the marketplace. In nonprofit organizations such as the American Red Cross or the Salvation Army, strategic planning pertains to events in the external environment.

Research has shown that strategic thinking and planning positively affect a firm's performance and financial success.[52] Most managers are aware of the importance of strategic planning, as evidenced by a *McKinsey Quarterly* survey. Of responding executives whose companies had no formal strategic planning process, 51 percent said that they were dissatisfied with the company's development of strategy, compared to only 20 percent of those companies that had a formal planning process.[53] CEOs at successful companies make strategic thinking and planning a top management priority. For an organization to succeed, the CEO must be actively involved in making the tough choices and trade-offs that define and support strategy.[54] However, senior executives at today's leading companies want middle- and lower-level managers to think strategically as well. Understanding the strategy concept and the levels of strategy is an important start toward strategic thinking.

The movie rental business sure isn't what it used to be. Remember the local video store? Probably not. Although a few remain, national chains like Blockbuster put most of them out of business years ago. At its peak, Blockbuster had 9,000 video stores and

Spotlight on Skills

What Is Your Strategy Strength?[55]

Instructions: As a new manager, what are your strengths concerning strategy formulation and implementation? To find out, think about *how you handle challenges and issues* in your school or job. Then mark (a) or (b) for each of the following items, depending on which is more descriptive of your behavior. There is no right or wrong answer to these questions. Respond to each item as it best describes how you respond to work situations.

1. When keeping records, I tend to:
   _____ a. Be careful about documentation.
   _____ b. Be haphazard about documentation.

2. If I run a group or a project, I:
   _____ a. Have the general idea and let others figure out how to do the tasks.
   _____ b. Try to figure out specific goals, timelines, and expected outcomes.

3. My thinking style could be more accurately described as:
   _____ a. Linear thinker, going from A to B to C.
   _____ b. Thinking like a grasshopper, hopping from one idea to another.

4. In my office or home, things are:
   _____ a. Here and there, in various piles.
   _____ b. Laid out neatly, or at least in reasonable order.

5. I take pride in developing:
   _____ a. Ways to overcome a barrier to a solution.
   _____ b. New hypotheses about the underlying cause of a problem.

6. I can best help strategy by encouraging:
   _____ a. penness to a wide range of assumptions and ideas.
   _____ b. Thoroughness when implementing new ideas.

7. One of my strengths is:
   _____ a. Commitment to making things work.
   _____ b. Commitment to a dream for the future.

8. I am most effective when I emphasize:
   _____ a. Inventing original solutions.
   _____ b. Making practical improvements.

Scoring and Interpretation: Managers have differing strengths and capabilities when it comes to formulating and implementing strategy. Here's how to determine yours. For *Strategic Formulator* strength, score 1 point for each (a) answer marked for questions 2, 4, 6, and 8, and for each (b) answer marked for questions 1, 3, 5, and 7. For *Strategic Implementer* strength, score 1 point for each (b) answer marked for questions 2, 4, 6, and 8, and for each (a) answer marked for questions 1, 3, 5, and 7. Which of your two scores is higher, and by how much? The higher score indicates your strategy strength.

New managers bring value to strategic management as formulators, implementers, or both. New managers with implementer strengths tend to work within the situation and improve it by making it more efficient and reliable. Managers with the formulator strength push toward out-of-the-box strategies and like to seek dramatic breakthroughs. Both styles are essential to strategic management. Strategic formulators often use their skills in creating whole new strategies and strategic implementers often work with strategic improvements and implementation.

If the difference between your two scores is 2 or less, you have a balanced formulator/implementer style and work well in both arenas. If the difference is 4 or 5 points, you have a moderately strong style and probably work best in the area of your strength. If the difference is 7 or 8 points, you have a distinctive strength and almost certainly would want to work in the area of your strength rather than in the opposite domain.

around 60,000 employees. Then along came Netflix. By the fall of 2013, Blockbuster had only about 350 stores left. That doesn't mean that all is rosy for Netflix, though. Other companies, including Amazon, recognized the opportunities in streaming videos and began taking away customers. One response from Netflix has been to create its own original programming, with shows such as *Orange Is the New Black* and *House of Cards* recently garnering several Emmy awards. The ambitious strategy to be not just a provider but a producer of entertainment is ripe with opportunity but also fraught with risk. Nevertheless, Netflix CEO Reed Hastings knows his company's strategy has to keep evolving to meet the changing technology, growing competition, and shifting entertainment needs of customers.[56]

How important is strategic management? It largely determines which organizations succeed and which ones struggle. Differences in the strategies managers chose and how effectively they executed them help explain why Netflix is thriving and Blockbuster is floundering, how Facebook all but killed MySpace in social networking, and why Apple is beating Microsoft in the world of mobile computing.

Every company is concerned with strategy. In the fast food industry, managers revived Domino's by formulating and aggressively advertising a new pizza recipe that responded to changing consumer tastes. McDonald's has succeeded with a revamped strategy of adding the McCafé line of hot and iced coffee drinks, offering snacks and small dessert items throughout the day, and enhancing its line of products for health-conscious consumers. The KFC chain of Yum! Brands is thriving with an ambitious global strategy, rapidly expanding overseas, particularly in China.[57]

Strategic blunders can hurt a company. For instance, Kodak still hasn't recovered from its managers' failure to plan for the rapid rise of digital photography. A recent article touting the success of a thriving, innovative, adaptive company referred to the firm as the "anti-Kodak." And few people remember when Liz Claiborne was one of the most popular clothing lines around. The company that pioneered career apparel for women has been in decline for years, with managers failing to latch onto a strategy that could keep the clothing line relevant as baby boomers retired and began spending less money on career outfits.[58]

"It's hard to outrun the future if you don't see it coming."
—Gary Hamel, management scholar and author

Complete the Spotlight on Skills test on page 205 to get an idea about your strategic thinking ability.

REMEMBER THIS

- To think strategically means to take the long-term view and see the big picture.

- Managers in all types of organizations, including businesses, nonprofit organizations, and government agencies, have to think about how the organization fits in the environment.

5.9 What Is Strategic Management?

Strategic management refers to the set of decisions and actions used to formulate and execute strategies that will provide a competitively superior fit between the organization and its environment so as to achieve organizational goals.[59] Managers ask questions such as the following: What changes and trends are occurring in the competitive environment? Who are our competitors, and what are their strengths and weaknesses? Who are our customers? What products or services should we offer, and how can we offer them most efficiently? What does the future hold for our industry, and how can we change the rules of the game? Answers to these questions help managers make choices about how to position their organizations in the environment with respect to rival companies.[60] Superior organizational performance is not a matter of luck. It is determined by the choices that managers make.

5.9a Purpose of Strategy

The first step in strategic management is to define an explicit **strategy**, which is the plan of action that describes resource allocation and activities for dealing with the environment, achieving a competitive advantage, and attaining the organization's goals. **Competitive advantage** refers to what sets the organization apart from others and provides it with a distinctive edge for meeting customer or client needs in the marketplace. The essence of formulating strategy is choosing how the organization will be different.[61] Managers make decisions about whether the company will perform different activities or will execute similar activities differently than its rivals do. Strategy necessarily changes over time to fit environmental conditions, but to achieve competitive advantage, companies develop strategies that incorporate the elements illustrated in Exhibit 5.7: target specific customers, focus on core competencies, provide synergy, and create value.[62]

Target Customers   An effective strategy defines the customers and which of their needs are to be served by the company. Managers can define a target market geographically, such as serving people in a certain part of the country; demographically, such as aiming toward people in a certain income bracket or targeting preteen girls; or by a variety of other means. Some firms target people who purchase primarily over the Internet, whereas others aim to serve people who like to shop in small stores with a limited selection of high-quality merchandise. Zipcar managers identify their target customer as anyone who needs to occasionally rent a car by the hour, whereas Hertz identifies its target customer as the business or holiday traveler who needs to rent a car by the day or week while away from home.[63] Volvo's new

EXHIBIT 5.7   The Elements of Competitive Advantage

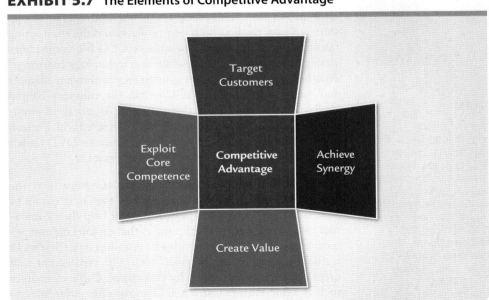

owners and managers are shifting the company's strategy toward a new target customer. Rather than aiming for people who appreciate the brand's reputation for safe, reliable family vehicles, Li Shufu, the company's new Chinese owner, is aiming to expand aggressively into the luxury car market. Volvo is particularly courting the emerging class of rich consumers in China and other overseas markets. Li wants Volvo to offer innovative, electrifying designs that turn heads and win new luxury-minded customers with flashy tastes.[64]

Exploit Core Competencies   A **core competence** is something that the organization does especially well in comparison to its competitors. A core competence represents a competitive advantage because the company acquires expertise that competitors do not have. A core competence may be in the area of superior research and development (R&D), expert technological know-how, process efficiency, or exceptional customer service.[65] Managers at companies such as Family Dollar and Southwest Airlines, for example, focus on a core competence of operational efficiency that enables them to keep costs low. Gaylord Hotels, which has large hotel and conference centers in several states as well as the Opryland complex near Nashville, Tennessee, thrives based on a strategy of offering superior service for large group meetings. Robinson Helicopter succeeds through superior technological know-how for building small, two-seater helicopters used for everything from police patrols in Los Angeles to herding cattle in Australia.[66] In each case, leaders identified what their company does especially well and built strategy around it.

Courtesy of Hayes Diversified Technologies

CONCEPT CONNECTION   When the U.S. Marines needed rugged motorcycles, they looked to manufacturers of on- and off-road bikes. But most motorcycles run on gasoline, which is the wrong fuel for military purposes. Hayes Diversified Technologies had the competitive advantage. After 20 years of building adapted motorcycles for the Marines and the Army Special Forces, Hayes had developed a **core competence** in technology that addresses the fuel limitations faced by the military. Most military machines run on JB8 fuel, a formulation of diesel and kerosene. Hayes Diversified's HDT M1030M1 motorcycle is designed for diesel service, so Hayes readily won the contract.

Build Synergy   When organizational parts interact to produce a joint effect that is greater than the sum of the parts acting alone, **synergy** is achieved. The organization may attain a special advantage with respect to cost, market power, technology, or management skill. When properly managed, synergy can create additional value with existing resources, providing a big boost to the bottom line.[67] Synergy was the motivation for food company Kraft to buy Cadbury and for Yahoo to buy mobile app startups such as Summly, Stamped, and Snip.it, as described in the Appendix. Kraft can use Cadbury's established distribution network in emerging markets to share trucks and store contacts and sell more Kraft products. At Yahoo, buying mobile app start-ups gave the firm both new products and the engineering talent behind them, helping to advance CEO Marissa Mayer's strategy to remake it into a mobile-first technology company.[68] Another way that companies gain synergy is through alliances and partnerships. Leaders at Coinstar, the company behind Redbox movie rentals, take this approach. As rentals of physical videos declined, the Redbox division partnered with Verizon Communications to offer a service that combines DVD rentals and streaming video, benefiting both companies.[69]

Deliver Value   Delivering value to the customer is at the heart of strategy. *Value* can be defined as the combination of benefits received and costs paid. Managers help their companies create value by devising strategies that exploit core competencies and attain synergy. Starbucks introduced the Starbucks Card, which works like a typical retail gift card except that users get benefits like points for free coffee. Cable companies such as Time Warner Cable and Comcast offer *value packages* that provide a combination of basic cable, digital premium channels, video-on-demand, high-speed Internet, and digital phone service for a reduced cost. Some movie theaters are trying to provide greater value by offering "dinner and a movie." In-theater dining provides a more time-efficient way for people to spend a night out, and costs are reasonable compared to eating in a restaurant before or after the film.[70]

Amazon is thriving with a strategy based on targeting customers, exploiting core competencies, building synergy, and providing value.

Spotlight on Skills

Amazon

It's hard to believe that Amazon was once a struggling online bookseller. Today, it is "an existential threat" to every retailer, as Fiona Dias, executive vice president of GSI Commerce, put it. Amazon targets customers who want to find good deals and purchase products conveniently over the Internet. Those customers can find just about anything they want on Amazon.com. They will often pay less for it than they would anywhere else. And if they belong to Amazon Prime, they get free two-day shipping.

Amazon wants to provide "premium products at nonpremium prices." To do that, it has developed an extensive network of third-party merchants—partners with whom it maintains close, mutually beneficial relationships, is constantly honing its operational efficiency, and has created one of the most finely tuned distribution systems around. As if all that weren't enough, along came Prime. For $79 a year, customers got free two-day shipping, as well as free streaming video and other perks (Amazon has since increased the price to $99). Prime allows Amazon to capitalize on its core competencies of wide selection, cost efficiency, and slick distribution. When asked how they decided on the original $79 price tag, a member of the Prime team said it "was never about the $79. It was really about changing people's mentality so they wouldn't shop anywhere else."

Prime was conceived as a way to further cement the loyalty of Amazon's best customers, and it has been more successful than even CEO Jeff Bezos imagined. Amazon Prime, said one recent business article "turns casual shoppers … into Amazon addicts." It provides value to customers, but it also increases sales for Amazon. According to some estimates, customers increase their purchases on the site by about 150 percent after joining Prime. It is credited for helping Amazon's sales zoom 30 percent during the recent recession while other retailers struggled to attract customers.[71]

REMEMBER THIS

- **Strategic management** refers to the set of decisions and actions used to formulate and implement strategies that will provide a competitively superior fit between the organization and its environment so as to achieve organizational goals.

- A **strategy** is the plan of action that describes resource allocation and activities for dealing with the environment, achieving a competitive advantage, and attaining goals.

- **Competitive advantage** refers to what sets the organization apart from others and provides it with a distinctive edge in the marketplace.

- Four elements of competitive advantage are the company's target customer, core competencies, synergy, and value.

- A **core competence** is something that the organization does particularly well in comparison to others.

- Amazon has core competencies of operational efficiency and a superb distribution system.

- **Synergy** exists when the organization's parts interact to produce a joint effect that is greater than the sum of the parts acting alone.

- Kraft bought Cadbury to gain synergy by being able to sell products through Cadbury's established distribution network in emerging markets.

- The heart of strategy is to deliver value to customers.

Spotlight on Skills

Should You Crowdsource Your Strategy?

"Strategy, as we knew it, is dead," said Walt Shill, head of management consulting in North America for Accenture Ltd. This might be an overstatement, but many managers have discovered that they need new approaches to strategy. For one thing, strategies developed by top leaders with little input from people on the front lines can be biased and fail to be embraced by the people who need to carry them out. One new approach that some pioneering companies are taking is to crowdsource their strategy. By opening up the process of strategy formulation to all employees, crowdsourcing adds diversity of thought, gets top executives closer to understanding the implications of their choices, and helps to avoid limited-perspective biases of top managers. Here are a few examples of how companies are doing it:

- **HCL Technologies' My Blueprint.** Top managers at India's HCL Technologies turned the existing strategy planning process, a live meeting called Blueprint that involved a few hundred top executives, into an online platform open to 8,000 employees. Chairman and former CEO Vineet Nayar said managers did more thorough analysis and better planning because they knew that their plans would be reviewed and commented on by employees. One manager credited crowdsourcing for a fivefold increase in sales to an important client over a two-year period. Comments and insights had highlighted a need to reframe the plan away from commoditized applications support and toward new services where HCL had an edge over its larger competitors.

- **Red Hat's Open-Source Strategy.** As the leading provider of open-source software, Red Hat wanted to try an open approach to strategy. Top managers defined an initial set of priorities for exploration and formed teams to explore each one. Teams used wikis and other online tools to generate and organize ideas and gave all employees the opportunity to comment and make suggestions for changes. Leaders say the fresh perspectives spurred "value-creating shifts in direction," including a change in the way the company offered virtualization services for enterprise data centers that led to the acquisition of an external technology provider.

- **3M's "Innovation Live."** 3M Company has long used a "Markets of the Future" process as a crucial aspect of its strategic planning. In the past, this involved a small group of analysts and managers researching megatrends and identifying markets of the future based on them. In 2009, the company reinvigorated the process by inviting all sales, marketing, and R&D employees to a Web-based forum called "Innovation Live." The forum attracted 1,200 participants from 40 countries and generated more than 700 ideas. "The end result was the identification of nine new future markets with an aggregate revenue potential in the tens of billions of dollars." 3M continues to hold "Innovation Live" events.

Crowdsourcing strategy, or "social strategy setting," as it is sometimes called, is a recent trend and creates opportunities for more meaningful participation by employees in strategy formulation and execution.

SOURCES: Walt Shill, quoted in Joann S. Lublin and Dana Mattioli, "Theory & Practice: Strategic Plans Lose Favor," *The Wall Street Journal* (January 25, 2010): B7; and Arne Gast and Michele Zanini, "The Social Side of Strategy," *McKinsey Quarterly*, Issue 2 (2012): 82–93.

5.9b SWOT Analysis

Formulating strategy begins with understanding the circumstances, forces, events, and issues that shape the organization's competitive situation, which requires that managers conduct an audit of both internal and external factors that influence the company's ability to compete.[72] **SWOT analysis** (in which "SWOT" stands for "strengths, weaknesses, opportunities, and threats") includes a careful assessment of the strengths, weaknesses, opportunities, and threats that affect organizational performance. Managers obtain external information about opportunities and threats from a variety of sources, including customers, government reports, professional journals, suppliers, bankers, friends in other organizations, consultants, or association meetings. Many firms contract with special scanning organizations to provide them with newspaper clippings, Internet research, and analyses of relevant domestic and global trends. Others hire competitive intelligence (CI) professionals to scope out competitors, as we discussed in Chapter 2, and use intelligence teams, as described in Chapter 5.

Executives acquire information about internal strengths and weaknesses from a variety of reports, including budgets, financial ratios, profit and loss statements, and surveys of employee attitudes and satisfaction. In addition, managers build an understanding of the company's internal strengths and weaknesses by talking with people at all levels of the hierarchy in frequent face-to-face discussions and meetings.

Go to the Group Learning on page 219, which pertains to SWOT analysis. Before reading further, you might also want to review your strategic strengths as determined by your responses to the questionnaire at the beginning of this chapter.

Internal Strengths and Weaknesses   *Strengths* are positive internal characteristics that the organization can exploit to achieve its strategic performance goals. One strength for interactive video game publisher Activision Blizzard Inc., for example, is a highly creative staff that consistently produces innovative and powerful video game franchises. One of the most recent, Skylanders, created a new genre, combining games and toys that work together. Users place a real collectible toy on a small pedestal device, creating the character in the game. Skylanders generated $1.5 billion in sales for Activision in

EXHIBIT 5.8 **Audit Checklist for Analyzing Organizational Strengths and Weaknesses**

Management and organization	Marketing	Human Resources
Management quality	Distribution channels	Employee experience, education
Staff quality	Market share	Union status
Degree of centralization	Advertising efficiency	Turnover, absenteeism
Organization charts	Customer satisfaction	Work satisfaction
Planning, information, control systems	Product quality	Grievances
	Service reputation	
	Sales force turnover	
Finance	**Production**	**R&D**
Profit margin	Location, resources	Basic applied research
Debt–equity ratio	Machinery obsolescence	Laboratory capabilities
Inventory ratio	Purchasing system	Research programs
Return on investment	Quality control	New-product innovations
Credit rating	Productivity/efficiency	Technology innovations

less than two years.[73] *Weaknesses* are internal characteristics that might inhibit or restrict the organization's performance. Some examples of what managers evaluate to interpret strengths and weaknesses are shown in the audit checklist in Exhibit 5.8. Managers perform an internal audit of specific functions, such as marketing, finance, production, and R&D. Internal analysis also assesses overall organization structure, management competence and quality, and human resource (HR) characteristics. Based on their understanding of these areas, managers can determine their strengths or weaknesses compared with other companies.

External Opportunities and Threats   *Threats* are characteristics of the external environment that may prevent the organization from achieving its strategic goals. One threat to Activision Blizzard is the growing criticism of violent video games in light of mass shootings in the United States by perpetrators who were said to play the games. One recent event of this type was at the Washington Navy Yard in Washington, D.C., in September 2013, when Aaron Alexis, a former navy reservist and current contractor, killed 12 people at the secure military installation.[74] In addition to the children's series Skylanders, Activision publishes the Call of Duty series of war-related shooting games. Alexis reportedly played games (including Call of Duty) for as many as 16 hours at a time. Although evidence suggests that there is no connection between violent video games and real-life violence, the media attention renews the debate with each new tragedy.[75] As another example of an external threat, Intel, whose microprocessors power most PCs, is being hurt by the decline in demand for personal computers as more people turn to tablets and smartphones.[76]

Opportunities are characteristics of the external environment that have the potential to help the organization achieve or exceed its strategic goals. For example, U.S. auto manufacturers have had an unprecedented opportunity to steal customers from Toyota because of the quality, safety, and public relations problems that Toyota has experienced in recent years.[77] German retailer Aldi found an opportunity to expand in the United States because of heated opposition in urban areas to Walmart. Aldi has quietly been setting up small, drugstore-sized shops in cities around the United States, including New York City. "Walmart has sort of become the bad guy that there's a concerted effort against," said Craig Johnson, president of consulting firm Customer Growth Partners. "There's no reason to oppose an Aldi." Because Aldi is a smaller format and has opened only a limited number of stores a year, it was able to slip in under the radar, obtaining space from small landlords while people were focused on fighting Walmart.[78]

Managers evaluate the external environment based on the 10 sectors described in Chapter 2. The task environment sectors are the most relevant to strategic behavior and include the behavior of competitors, customers, suppliers, and the labor supply. The general environment contains those sectors that have an indirect influence on the organization but nevertheless must be understood and incorporated into strategic behavior. The general environment includes technological developments, the economy, legal-political and international events, the natural environment, and sociocultural changes. Additional areas that might reveal opportunities or threats include pressure groups, such as those opposing Walmart's expansion into urban areas, interest groups, creditors, and potentially competitive industries.

A good example of SWOT analysis and how it leads to strategic choices comes from FedEx Corporation.

Spotlight on Skills

FedEx Corporation

FedEx invented the overnight courier services industry in 1973 and is still a leader in the field. In addition, the company offers ground and freight services, logistics solutions, and business support services.

FedEx's greatest *strength* is its strong brand image. The company's name is one of the most recognized in the world and it has been ranked among the top 20 on *Fortune* magazine's list of Most Admired Companies every year since 2001 (it ranked number 8 in 2014). Other strengths include a strong financial performance, with revenues growing 8.6 percent in fiscal year 2012 and operating and net profits also growing substantially. One reason is good decisions made by a strong and experienced management team, which is another strength of the company. A primary weakness is that FedEx is plagued by a number of lawsuits, including several class action suits alleging that employees were forced to work "off the clock" and were not provided with breaks or paid overtime. The company also has substantial unfunded pension obligations, and these are likely to grow due to volatility in financial markets.

One of the biggest external threats to the company is the weak economy and a corresponding drop in demand for FedEx premium-priced services. Domestically, many customers are switching to cheaper ground delivery, and the lucrative international routes have been hurt by customers using "Economy" rather than "Priority" delivery services. Package volume has also declined, dropping 5 percent in the domestic Express business in the first quarter of 2012, for

example, and this seems to be a continuing pattern. Other threats include stiff competition from United Parcel Service (UPS), Deutsche Post DHL Group, Nippon Express, Royal Mail Group, TNT, and Japan Post, especially in the less-than-truckload (LTL) freight business, increasing fuel prices, and the potential adoption of stricter security requirements that could lead to substantial increases in costs. At the same time, though, FedEx sees opportunities in the rapidly recovering North American freight business, as the company's FedEx Ground and FedEx Freight are leading players in that sector. Similarly, FedEx is well positioned to gain from the growing online retail market. The company is one of the leading facilitators of online commerce.

What does SWOT analysis suggest for FedEx? The company unveiled a restructuring plan in late 2012 that plans for $1.7 billion in profitability improvements by the end of fiscal year 2016. The company is making adjustments to its fleet of planes, permanently retiring 24 aircraft at FedEx Express and delaying delivery of 11 Boeing 777 Freighters. The company is also considering options such as rerouting some economy traffic onto slower modes of transportation or consolidating routes to increase profits. At the same time, the company is looking toward growth, acquiring a number of businesses across the globe to boost revenues and geographic presence. These strategic acquisitions give FedEx the chance to expand its services in both developed and emerging markets.[79]

REMEMBER THIS

- **Strategy formulation** is the stage of strategic management that includes the planning and decision making that lead to the establishment of the organization's goals and a specific strategic plan.

- Managers often start with a **SWOT analysis**, an audit or careful examination of *strengths*, *weaknesses*, *opportunities*, and *threats* that affect organizational performance.

- The decline in demand for PCs is a *threat* to Intel. Opposition to the expansion of Walmart provided German retailer Aldi an *opportunity* to gain a foothold in urban areas.

- **Strategy execution** is the stage of strategic management that involves the use of managerial and organizational tools to direct resources toward achieving strategic outcomes.

5.10 Formulating Corporate-Level Strategy

One coherent way to think about portfolio strategy is the BCG matrix. The BCG matrix (named for the Boston Consulting Group, which developed it) is illustrated in Exhibit 5.9. The BCG matrix organizes businesses along two dimensions—business growth rate and market share.[80] *Business growth rate* pertains to how rapidly the entire industry is increasing. *Market share* defines whether a business unit has a larger or smaller share than competitors. The combinations of high and low market share and high and low business growth provide four categories for a corporate portfolio.

The *star* has a large market share in a rapidly growing industry. It is important because it has additional growth potential, and profits should be plowed into this business as investment for future growth and profits. The star is visible and attractive and will generate profits and a positive cash flow even as the industry matures and market growth slows.

The *cash cow* exists in a mature, slow-growth industry but is a dominant business in the industry, with a large market share. Because heavy investments in advertising and plant expansion are no longer required, the corporation earns a positive cash flow. It can milk the cash cow to invest in other, riskier businesses.

The *question mark* exists in a new, rapidly growing industry, but has only a small market share. The question mark business is risky: It could become a star, or it could fail. The

EXHIBIT 5.9 The BCG Matrix

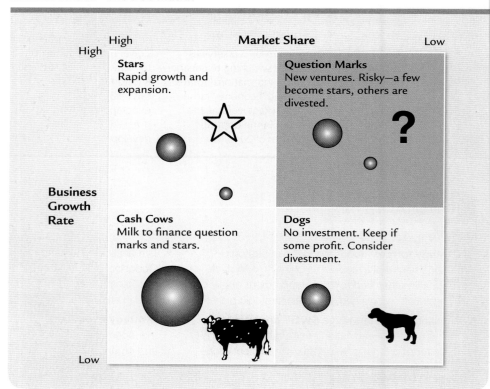

Spotlight on Skills

IBM

IBM used to be primarily a hardware company, but now its strategy is focused primarily on software and services. The company's software for running servers and networks is the biggest *cash cow* in IBM's software portfolio. These software offerings have a large share of a stable market, and IBM is reaping big sales and profits from them.

Database programs that allow firms to store, mine, analyze, and use data have *star* status. IBM has beefed up these programs by incorporating newer technologies that allow for mining social media for customer feedback and managing digital media campaigns.

The company's social business software, a group of programs collectively called "Connections" is a *question mark*. Among other things, Connections software lets companies create corporate versions of Facebook, with user profiles, blogs, and news streaming. IBM hopes social business software will become a billion-dollar business cash cow, but revenue is currently minuscule compared to other offerings.

For now, IBM is using profits from its current cash cows to try to build its question marks and stars. One cash cow, Lotus Notes, a program many people don't even realize still exists, brought in an estimated $1.2 billion in revenue for IBM in one recent year. The problem is that, while Lotus Notes is lucrative, it is declining rather than growing. Managers are considering ways to revive Lotus, but if the business turns into a *dog*, IBM managers will put it out of its misery.[81]

corporation can invest the cash earned from cash cows in question marks with the goal of nurturing them into future stars.

The *dog* is a poor performer. It has only a small share of a slow-growth market. The dog provides little profit for the corporation and may be targeted for divestment or liquidation if turnaround is not possible.

The circles in Exhibit 5.9 represent the business portfolio for a hypothetical corporation. Circle size represents the relative size of each business in the company's portfolio. Most large organizations, such as IBM, have businesses in more than one quadrant, thereby representing different market shares and growth rates.

5.11 Formulating Business-Level Strategy

Now we turn to strategy formulation within the strategic business unit, in which the concern is how to compete. A popular and effective model for formulating strategy is Porter's competitive strategies. Michael E. Porter studied a number of business organizations and proposed that business-level strategies are the result of understanding competitive forces in the company's environment.[82]

5.11a The Competitive Environment

The competitive environment is different for different kinds of businesses. Most large companies have separate business lines and do an industry analysis for each line of business or strategic business unit (SBU). Mars, Inc., for example, operates in six business segments:

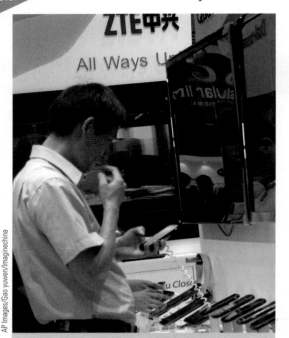

chocolate (Snickers); pet care (Pedigree); gum and confections (Juicy Fruit); food (Uncle Ben's); drinks (FLAVIA); and symbioscience (the Wilson Panel pet DNA kit, used for breed identification). Competitive forces for the chocolate division would be different from those for the symbioscience division, so managers would do a competitive analysis for each business segment, looking at Porter's five forces.

5.11b Porter's Competitive Strategies

To find a competitive edge within the specific business environment, Porter suggests that a company can adopt one of three strategies: differentiation, cost leadership, or focus. The organizational characteristics typically associated with each strategy are summarized in Exhibit 5.10.

Managers should think carefully about which strategy will provide their company with a competitive advantage. Gibson Guitar Corporation, famous in the music world for its innovative, high-quality products, found that switching to a cost leadership strategy to compete against Japanese rivals such as Yamaha and Ibanez actually hurt the company. When managers realized that people wanted Gibson products because of their reputation, not their price, they went back to a differentiation strategy and invested in new technology and marketing.[83]

In his studies, Porter found that some businesses did not consciously adopt one of these three strategies and were stuck with no strategic advantage. Without a strategic advantage, businesses earned below-average profits compared with those that used differentiation, cost leadership, or focus strategies. Similarly, a five-year study of management practices in hundreds of businesses, referred to as the "Evergreen Project," found that a clear strategic direction was a key factor that distinguished winners from losers.[84]

CONCEPT CONNECTION While Americans and Europeans enjoy snapping up the latest—and more expensive—smartphones that feature all kinds of bells and whistles, many cell phone users around the world look for simple, reliable cell phones at affordable prices. And China's ZTE is there to meet their needs. ZTE has employed a **cost leadership strategy**, using efficient production to keep prices low for many of its models. The approach has made the company one of the biggest mobile phone producers in the world.

REMEMBER THIS

- A popular model for formulating business-level strategy is Porter's competitive strategies.

- Managers analyze the competitive environment and adopt one of three types of strategy: differentiation, cost leadership, or focus.

- A **differentiation strategy** is a strategy with which managers seek to distinguish the organization's products and services from those of others in the industry.

- A **cost leadership strategy** is a strategy with which managers aggressively seek efficient facilities, cut costs, and use tight cost controls to be more efficient than others in the industry.

- With a **focus strategy**, managers use either a differentiation or a cost leadership approach, but they concentrate on a specific regional market or buyer group.

EXHIBIT 5.10 Organizational Characteristics of Porter's Competitive Strategies

Broad

Differentiation
- Acts in a flexible, loosely knit way; strong coordination among departments
- Strong capability in basic research
- Creative flair, thinks "out of the box"
- Strong marketing abilities
- Rewards employee innovation
- Corporate reputation for quality or technological leadership

Cost Leadership
- Strong central authority; tight cost controls
- Maintains standard operating procedures
- Easy-to-use manufacturing technologies
- Highly efficient procurement and distribution systems
- Close supervision; finite employee empowerment

Focused Differentiation
- Uses characteristics of differentiation strategy directed at particular target customer
- Values flexibility and customer intimacy
- Pushes empowerment to employees with customer contact

Focused Cost Leadership
- Uses characteristics of cost leadership strategy directed at particular target customer
- Frequent detailed control reports
- Measures cost of providing product or service and maintaining customer loyalty

Narrow

Strategic Target (vertical axis)

Distinctiveness — **Low Costs**

Source of Advantage

SOURCES: Based on Michael E. Porter, *Competitive Strategy: Techniques for Analyzing Industries and Competitors* (New York: Free Press, 1980); Michael Treacy and Fred Wiersema, "How Market Leaders Keep Their Edge," *Fortune* (February 6, 1995): 88–98; and Michael A. Hitt, R. Duane Ireland, and Robert E. Hoskisson, *Strategic Management* (St. Paul, MN: West, 1995), pp. 100–113.

CHAPTER 5   DISCUSSION QUESTIONS

1. What strategic plans could the college or university at which you are taking this management course adopt to compete for students in the marketplace? Would these plans depend on the school's goals?

2. From the information provided in the chapter example, identify how Western Digital Thailand used both the prevention and the preparation stages of crisis planning.

3. A new business venture must develop a comprehensive business plan to borrow money to get started. Companies such as FedEx and Nike say they did not follow the original plan closely. Does that mean that developing the plan was a waste of time for these eventually successful companies?

4. Assume that Southern University decides to do two things: (1) raise its admission standards and (2) initiate a business fair to which local townspeople will be invited. What types of plans might it use to carry out these two activities?

5. LivingSocial started with one "daily deal," a $25 voucher for $50 worth of food at a Washington, D.C., area restaurant. Since then, the company has grown at breakneck speed, has 46 million members in 25 countries, and has acquired a dozen companies that offer related deals and services. Why and how might a company such as LivingSocial want to use scenario building? Discuss.

6. Some people say an organization could never be "prepared" for a disaster such as the shooting at Sandy Hook Elementary School, the Japan nuclear disaster, or the huge BP oil spill in the Gulf of Mexico. Discuss the potential value of crisis planning in situations like these, even if the situations are difficult to plan for.

7. Goals that are overly ambitious can discourage employees and decrease motivation, yet the idea of stretch goals is proposed as a way to get people fired up and motivated. As a manager, how might you decide where to draw the line between a "good" stretch goal and a "bad" one that is unrealistic?

8. Netflix has successfully adapted to a number of challenges in its industry. What do you see as some emerging opportunities and threats for the company?

9. Perform a SWOT analysis for the school or university you attend. Do you think university administrators consider the same factors when devising their strategy?

10. Harley-Davidson, which once boasted that it made "big toys for big boys," is trying to lure more women to the brand to make up for declining sales in a slow economy. How do you think this move will complement or confound the company's differentiation strategy, which has long been based on a macho image?

SELF-LEARNING

Business School Ranking

The dean of the business school at a major university in your state has contacted students in your class to develop a plan for improving its national ranking among business schools. The school recently dropped 10 places in the rankings, and the dean wants to restore the school's perceived luster. The dean provided the following list of variables on which the national ranking is based.

- Written assessment by deans from peer institutions, on a scale of 1 to 5

- Written assessment by recruiters, on a scale of 1 to 5

- Average grade point average (GPA) of incoming students

- Acceptance rate of student applications (a lower percentage is better)

- Average starting salary of the school's most recent graduates

- Percentage of graduates employed on the date of graduation

- Percentage of graduates employed three months after graduation

- Average Scholastic Aptitude Test (SAT; for the undergraduate program) and Graduate Management Admission Test (GMAT; for the MBA program) scores for entering students

The business school has a goal of improving its ranking by 10 places in two years. Brainstorm ideas and develop a 10-point action plan that will list the steps the dean can take to achieve this goal. To develop the plan, think carefully about actions the school might take to improve its ranking on any or all of the measured variables listed above.

After writing down your ideas to develop a plan, meet with a partner to share ideas and discuss the most helpful action steps that will be part of the action plan recommended to the business school dean.

GROUP LEARNING

Apply Your Skills: Small Group Breakout

SWOT Analysis[1]

Step 1. In a group of three to five students, select a local eating establishment for a SWOT analysis. This could be a restaurant, an ice cream store, or a bakery with which your group is familiar.

Step 2. Write a statement of what you perceive to be the business's current strategy.

Step 3. What do you perceive to be the key strengths and weaknesses of this business from a customer's perspective? Make one list for strengths and another list for weaknesses.

Step 4. What do you perceive to be potential opportunities and threats for this business? Make one list for opportunities and another for threats.

Step 5. If the store manager or owner is available, interview the person for his or her perception of strategy strengths, weaknesses, opportunities, and threats. Add new items to your lists.

Step 6. Use your SWOT analysis findings to set a goal of where this business could be in two years in terms of growth, size, new offerings, or expanded customer base. What steps do you recommend to achieve this goal?

Step 7. How did your SWOT analysis help you determine the goal and how to accomplish it during the next two years? What did you learn from this exercise?

[1] Adapted from Richard L. Daft and Dorothy Marcic, *Understanding Management* (Mason, OH: South-Western, 2008), pp. 177–178.

Name of the local restaurant, café, etc.:

Questions to ask	Answers
Key strengths from customer point of view	
Key weaknesses from customer point of view	
Potential opportunities	
Potential threats	
Results of manager interview, if available	
Using your analysis, where do you think this business can be in two years?	
What steps would you recommend for the business to achieve what you have just proposed?	
What did you learn from this exercise?	

ACTION LEARNING

1. Think back to some of the courses you have taken in college or graduate school.

2. List the one in which you feel you did the best and got the best grade, and the one in which you did the worst.

   a. Best   b. Worst

3. What did you do differently in the two classes? Fill out the table below:

	Study strategies and other behaviors that helped	**Strategies and behaviors that did not help**
Name of course		
Best:		
Worst:		

4. What were the differences in what you did in the best course versus the worst one?

5. List down lessons you can learn that will help you in future courses:

   a.   d.
   b.   e.
   c.   f.

ETHICAL DILEMMA

Inspire Learning Corporation[85]

When the idea first occurred to her, it seemed like such a win-win situation. Now she wasn't so sure.

Marge Brygay was a hardworking sales rep for Inspire Learning Corporation, a company intent on becoming the top educational software provider in five years. That newly adopted strategic goal translated into an ambitious, million-dollar sales target for each of Inspire's sales reps. At the beginning of the fiscal year, her share of the sales department's operational goal seemed entirely reasonable to Marge. She believed in Inspire's products. The company had developed innovative, highly regarded math, language, science, and social studies programs for the K–12 market. What set the software apart was a foundation in truly cutting-edge research. Marge had seen for herself how Inspire programs could engage whole classrooms of normally unmotivated kids; the significant rise in scores on those increasingly important standardized tests bore out her subjective impressions.

But now, just days before the end of the year, Marge's sales were $1,000 short of her million-dollar goal. The sale that would have put her comfortably over the top fell through due to last-minute cuts in one large school system's budget. At first, she was nearly overwhelmed with frustration, but then it occurred to her that if she contributed $1,000 to Central High, the inner-city high school in her territory probably most in need of what she had for sale, they could purchase the software and put her over the top.

Her scheme would certainly benefit Central High students. Achieving her sales goal would make Inspire happy, and it wouldn't do her any harm, either professionally or financially. Making the goal would earn her a $10,000 bonus check that would come in handy when the time came to write out that first tuition check for her oldest child, who had just been accepted to a well-known, private university.

Initially, it seemed like the perfect solution all the way around. The more she thought about it, however, the more it didn't quite sit well with her conscience. Time was running out. She needed to decide what to do.

What Would You Do?

1. Donate the $1,000 to Central High, and consider the $10,000 bonus a good return on your investment.

2. Accept the fact that you didn't quite make your sales goal this year. Figure out ways to work smarter next year to increase the odds of achieving your target.

3. Don't make the donation, but investigate whether any other ways are available to help Central High raise the funds that would allow them to purchase the much-needed educational software.

CASE FOR CRITICAL ANALYSIS

Central City Museum

The recently completed new building to house the exhibits and staff of the Central City Museum was located adjacent to the campus of a private university. The new building was financed by the generosity of local donors. The university provided the land and would cover the annual operating expenses with the understanding that the museum would provide a resource for student education. The new governing board would be made up of key donors, as well as selected university administrators and faculty members.

The planning committee of the governing board hired two business students to interview various stakeholders about the future direction of the museum in its new relationship with the university. These interviews were conducted in person, and the interviewees seemed uniformly interested and eager to help. The major questions pertained to the future mission and goals of the museum. Some excerpts from the interviews are listed here:

A major donor: *I think the museum should be a major community resource. My wife and I gave money for the new building with the expectation that the museum would promote visits from the public schools in the area, and particularly serve the inner-city children who don't have access to art exhibits. We don't want the museum to be snobbish or elitist. The focus should definitely be local.*

A university administrator: *The important thing is to have lively contemporary exhibits that will attract both university students and community adults and provide new insight and dialogue about current events. We can bring attention to the museum by having an occasional controversial exhibit, such as on Islamic art, and exhibits that appeal to Hispanics and African*

Americans. This approach would entail bringing in traveling exhibitions from major museums, which would save the administrative costs and overhead of producing our own exhibits.

Head of the art history department: *The key thing is that the museum will not have the artistic resources or the financial resources to serve the community at large. We have a wonderful opportunity to integrate the museum with the academic faculty and make it a teaching institution. It can be a major resource for both undergraduate and graduate students in art education and art history. We can also work with engineering students, architecture students, and liberal arts students. This is a unique opportunity that will distinguish our art history department's teaching mission from others in the country.*

A faculty member in the art history department: *The best use of the museum's relationship with the university is to concentrate on training Ph.D.-level students in art history and to support scholarly research. I strongly urge the museum to focus on graduate education, which would increase the stature of the university nationally. Graduate students would be involved in the design of exhibits that would fit their research. Trying to make the museum popular on campus or in the community will waste our limited resources. Our Ph.D. graduates will be sought after by art history departments throughout the country.*

The reason that you have been given this information from the interviews is that you have been invited to interview for the position of museum director. The previous director retired with the understanding that a new director would be hired upon the completion of fund-raising and construction of the new building. You are thinking about what you would do if you took the job.

Questions

1. What goal or mission for the Central City Museum do you personally prefer? As director, would you try to implement your preferred direction? Explain.

2. How would you resolve the underlying conflicts among key stakeholders about museum direction and goals? What actions would you take?

3. Review Director's Toolkit on coalitions earlier in the chapter on page 190. Do you think that building a coalition and working out stakeholder differences in goal preferences is an important part of a manager's job? Why?

ON THE JOB
VIDEO CASES

Mi Ola Swimwear: Managerial Planning and Goal Setting

Questions

1. Based on how this business owner describes her business, write a one- or two-sentence organizational mission statement for Mi Ola Swimwear.

2. Pick four of the following six categories: strategic goal, strategic plan, tactical goal, tactical plan, operational goal, and operational plan. Then, in the video, find one example to represent each of the four categories you've chosen. Describe your four examples and how they fit their respective categories in your answer.

3. What did you learn about some of the real benefits and limitations of planning by watching this video?

ENDNOTES

1. Mayumi Negishi, Dana Mattioli, and Ryan Dezember, "Japan's Uniqlo Sets Goal: No. 1 in the U.S.," *The Wall Street Journal*, April 12, 2013, B7; Stephanie Clifford, "As U.S. Retailers Retreat, a Japanese Chain Sees an Opening," *The New York Times*, May 22, 2012, http://www.nytimes.com/2012/05/23/business/uniqlo-sees-room-for-growth-in-the-us.html?pagewanted=all&_r=0 (accessed September 12, 2013); and "Uniqlo Announces Opening Dates for Ten New Stores This Fall," Uniqlo press release, September 4, 2013, http://www.uniqlo.com/us/uniqlo-news/2013/uniqlo-announces-opening-dates-for-ten-new-stores-this-fall/ (accessed September 12, 2013).

2. Hiroko Tabuchi, "Inquiry Declares Fukushima Crisis a Man-Made Disaster," *The New York Times*, July 5, 2012, www.nytimes.com/2012/07/06/world/asia/fukushima-nuclear-crisis-a-man-made-disaster-report-says.html (accessed July 19, 2012); and Patrick Kiger, "Fukushima's Radioactive Water Leak: What You Should Know," *National Geographic Daily News*, August 7, 2013, http://news.nationalgeographic.com/news/energy/2013/08/130807-fukushima-radioactive-water-leak/ (accessed September 12, 2013).

3. Quoted in Oren Harari, "Good/Bad News About Strategy," *Management Review* (July 1995): 29–31.

4. Amitai Etzioni, *Modern Organizations* (Englewood Cliffs, NJ: Prentice Hall, 1984), p. 6.

5. Max D. Richards, *Setting Strategic Goals and Objectives*, 2nd ed. (St. Paul, MN: West, 1986).

6. Based on A. G. Lafley and Roger Martin, "Instituting a Company-Wide Strategic Conversation at Procter & Gamble," *Strategy & Leadership* 41, no. 4 (2013): 4–9.

7. Lafley and Martin, "Instituting a Company-Wide Strategic Conversation at Procter & Gamble."

8. Paul Alofs, "Beliefs Creed: It Guides and Inspires," *Leadership Excellence* (August 2012): 20.

9. Mary Klemm, Stuart Sanderson, and George Luffman, "Mission Statements: Selling Corporate Values to Employees," *Long-Range Planning* 24, no. 3 (1991): 73–78; John A. Pearce II and Fred David, "Corporate Mission Statements: The Bottom Line," *Academy of Management Executive* (1987): 109–116; Jerome H. Want, "Corporate Mission: The Intangible Contributor to Performance," *Management Review* (August 1986): 46–50; and Forest R. David and Fred R. David, "It's Time to Redraft Your Mission Statement," *Journal of Business Strategy* (January–February 2003): 11–14.

10. "Tennessee News and Notes from State Farm," State Farm Mutual Automobile Insurance Company, 2004; and "Our Mission, Our Vision, Our Shared Values," State Farm Web site, http://www.statefarm.com/aboutus/company/profile/mission.asp (accessed September 12, 2013).

11. Dongwook Chung, "A Management 180°," *T+D* (July 2013): 56–59.

12. Matthew Boyle, "Unilever: Taking on the World, One Stall at a Time," *Bloomberg Businessweek* (January 7–13, 2013): 18–20.

13. Paul Meising and Joseph Wolfe, "The Art and Science of Planning at the Business Unit Level," *Management Science* 31 (1985): 773–781.

14. Boyle, "Unilever: Taking on the World, One Stall at a Time."

15. Graham Kenny, "From the Stakeholder Viewpoint: Designing Measurable Objectives," *Journal of Business Strategy* 33, no. 6 (2012): 40–46.

16. Sayan Chatterjee, "Core Objectives: Clarity in Designing Strategy," *California Management Review* 47, no. 2 (Winter 2005): 33–49.

17. Jason Piatt, "5 Rules for Selecting the Best KPIs to Drive Operational Improvement," *Industry Week* (November 2012): 30.

18. Edwin A. Locke, Gary P. Latham, and Miriam Erez, "The Determinants of Goal Commitment," *Academy of Management Review* 13 (1988): 23–39.

19. Peter F. Drucker, *The Practice of Management* (New York: Harper & Row, 1954); George S. Odiorne, "MBO: A Backward Glance," *Business Horizons* 21 (October 1978): 14–24; and William F. Roth, "Is Management by Objectives Obsolete?" *Global Business and Organizational Excellence* (May–June 2009): 36–43.

20. Jan P. Muczyk and Bernard C. Reimann, "MBO as a Complement to Effective Leadership," *The Academy of Management Executive* 3 (1989): 131–138; and W. Giegold, *Objective Setting and the MBO Process*, vol. 2 (New York: McGraw-Hill, 1978).

21. Tim O'Shaughnessy, as told to Liz Welch, "The Way I Work: Tim O'Shaughnessy, Living Social," *Inc.* (March 2012): 104–108.

22. This analogy is from Jeffrey K. Liker and Timothy N. Ogden, "The Toyota Recall: Missing the Forest for the Trees," *Ivey Business Journal* (November–December 2011), www.iveybusinessjournal.com/topics/marketing/the-toyota-recall-missing-the-forest-for-the-trees (accessed July 19, 2012).

23. Reylito A. H. Elbo, "MBM: Management by Means, Not Results," *Manila Times*, June 11, 2012, www.manilatimes.net/index.php/business/business-columnist/24633-mbm-management-by-means-not-results (accessed August 8, 2012); and Liker and Ogden, "The Toyota Recall."

24. Liker and Ogden, "The Toyota Recall."

25. C. Chet Miller and Laura B. Cardinal, "Strategic Planning and Firm Performance: A Synthesis of More than Two Decades of Research," *Academy of Management Journal* 37, no. 6 (1994): 1649–1685.

26. These are based on E. A. Locke and G. P. Latham, *A Theory of Goal Setting & Task Performance* (Englewood Cliffs, NJ: Prentice Hall, 1990); Richard L. Daft and Richard M. Steers, *Organizations: A Micro/Macro Approach* (Glenview, IL: Scott, Foresman, 1986), pp. 319–321; Herbert A. Simon, "On the Concept of Organizational Goals," *Administrative Science Quarterly* 9 (1964): 1–22; and Charles B. Saunders and Francis D. Tuggel, "Corporate Goals," *Journal of General Management* 5 (1980): 3–13.

27. Nick Wingfield, "Netflix Boss Plots Life After the DVD," *The Wall Street Journal*, June 23, 2009.

28. These are based on Henry Mintzberg, *The Rise and Fall of Strategic Planning* (New York: Free Press, 1994); H. Mintzberg, "Rethinking Strategic Planning, Part I: Pitfalls and Fallacies," *Long-Range Planning* 27 (1994): 12–21; and H. Mintzberg, "The Pitfalls of Strategic Planning," *California Management Review* 36 (1993): 32–47.

29. Roth, "Is Management by Objectives Obsolete?"

30. Curtis W. Roney, "Planning for Strategic Contingencies," *Business Horizons* (March–April 2003): 35–42; and "Corporate Planning: Drafting a Blueprint for Success," *Small Business Report* (August 1987): 40–44.

31. Doug Cameron, Jeffrey Ng, and Jack Nicas, "Post Jet Grounding, Airlines Scramble to Develop Plan Bs," *The Wall Street Journal*, January 18, 2013, B4; and Gustav Sandstrom, "Norwegian Airlines Encounter Additional Dreamliner Tech Issues," *The Wall Street Journal Online*, September 9, 2013, http://online.wsj.com/article/BT-CO-20130909-701299.html (accessed September 12, 2013).

32. This section is based on Steven Schnaars and Paschalina Ziamou, "The Essentials of Scenario Writing," *Business Horizons* (July–August 2001): 25–31; Peter Cornelius, Alexander Van de Putte, and Mattia Romani, "Three Decades of Scenario Planning in Shell," *California Management Review* 48, no. 1 (Fall 2005): 92–109; Audrey Schriefer and Michael Sales, "Creating Strategic Advantage with Dynamic Scenarios," *Strategy & Leadership* 34, no. 3 (2006): 31–42; William J. Worthington, Jamie D. Collins, and Michael A. Hitt, "Beyond Risk Mitigation: Enhancing Corporate Innovation with Scenario Planning," *Business Horizons* 52 (2009): 441–450; Gill Ringland, "Innovation: Scenarios of Alternative Futures Can Discover New Opportunities for Creativity," *Strategy & Leadership* 36, no. 5 (2008): 22–27; and Stephen M. Millett, "Four Decades of Business Scenarios: What Can Experience Teach?" *Strategy & Leadership* 41, no 1 (1013): 29–33.

33. Millett, "Four Decades of Business Scenarios."

34. Quoted in Claire Churchard, "Tales of the Unexpected," *People Management* (February 2012).

35. Reported in Churchard, "Tales of the Unexpected."

36. Kathleen Wilburn and Ralph Wilburn, "Abbreviated Scenario Thinking," *Business Horizons* 54 (2011): 541–550.

37. Gerald F. Seib, "Four Scenarios for Libya—Some Good and Some Bad," *The Wall Street Journal*, March 29, 2011, http://online.wsj.com/article/SB100014240527487037392045762 28620384027448.html (accessed July 20, 2012).

38. Jacob Bunge, "NYSE Revamps Disaster Plan," *The Wall Street Journal*, March 9, 2013, B1.

39. Lau Chee Wai and Winai Wongsurawat, "Crisis Management: Western Digital's 46-Day Recovery from the 2011 Flood Disaster in Thailand," *Strategy & Leadership* 41, no. 1 (2013): 34–38.

40. Ian Mitroff with Gus Anagnos, *Managing Crises Before They Happen* (New York: AMACOM, 2001); Ian Mitroff and Murat C. Alpaslan, "Preparing for Evil," *Harvard Business Review* (April 2003): 109–115.

41. Jack Nicas, "Faulty Planning, Stage Cited in Fair Collapse," *The Wall Street Journal*, April 12, 2012, http://online.wsj.com/article/SB2000142405270230435660457733 9923897 959492.html (accessed July 20, 2012).

42. The following discussion is based largely on W. Timothy Coombs, *Ongoing Crisis Communication: Planning, Managing, and Responding* (Thousand Oaks, CA: Sage Publications, 1999).

43. Ian I. Mitroff, "Crisis Leadership," *Executive Excellence* (August 2001): 19; Andy Bowen, "Crisis Procedures that Stand the Test of Time," *Public Relations Tactics* (August 2001): 16.

44. Jason Fried, "How to Ride a Storm," *Inc.* (February 2011): 37–39.

45. Christine Pearson, "A Blueprint for Crisis Management," *Ivey Business Journal* (January–February 2002): 69–73.

46. See Mitroff and Alpaslan, "Preparing for Evil," for a discussion of the "wheel of crises" outlining the many different kinds of crises that organizations may face.

47. Brad Stone, "The Omnivore," *Bloomberg Businessweek* (October 3–9, 2011): 58–65.

48. Harari, "Good/Bad News About Strategy."

49. James C. Collins and Jerry I. Porras, "Building Your Company's Vision," *Harvard Business Review* (September–October 1996): 65–77.

50. Steven Kerr and Steffan Landauer, "Using Stretch Goals to Promote Organizational Effectiveness and Personal Growth: General Electric and Goldman Sachs," *Academy of Management Executive* 18, no. 4 (November 2004): 134–138; and Lisa D. Ordóñez et al., "Goals Gone Wild: The Systematic Side Effects of Overprescribing Goal Setting," *Academy of Management Perspectives* (February 2009): 6–16.

51. See Kenneth R. Thompson, Wayne A. Hockwarter, and Nicholas J. Mathys, "Stretch Targets: What Makes Them Effective?" *Academy of Management Executive* 11, no. 3 (August 1997): 48.

52. Chet Miller and Laura B. Cardinal, "Strategic Planning and Firm Performance: A Synthesis of More Than Two Decades of Research," *Academy of Management Journal* 37, no. 6 (1994): 1649–1665.

53. Renée Dye and Olivier Sibony, "How to Improve Strategic Planning," *McKinsey Quarterly*, no. 3 (2007).

54. Keith H. Hammonds, "Michael Porter's Big Ideas," *Fast Company* (March 2001): 150–156.

55. This questionnaire is adapted from Dorothy Marcic and Joe Seltzer, *Organizational Behavior: Experiences and Cases* (Cincinnati, OH: South-Western, 1998), pp. 284–287, and William J. Miller, *Innovation Styles* (Global Creativity Corporation, 1997).

56. Amol Sharma, "Netflix Subscriber Growth Comes Up Shy," *The Wall Street Journal*, July 23, 2013, B1; and Harold Kruger, "Last Area Blockbuster Closing," *Appeal Democrat*, September 13, 2013, http://www.appeal-democrat.com/articles/blockbuster-127611-store-video.html.

57. Bruce Horovitz, "New Pizza Recipe Did Wonders for Domino's Sales," *USA Today*, May 5, 2010, B1; Julie Jargon, "How McDonald's Hit the Spot," *The Wall Street Journal*, December 13, 2011; Paul Lilley, "Weight Watchers Reveals New Partner: McDonald's," *Virginian-Pilot*, March 4, 2010; David E. Bell and Mary Shelman, "KFC's Radical Approach to China," *Harvard Business Review* (November 2011): 137–142.

58. John Bussey, "The Business: The Anti-Kodak: How a U.S. Firm Innovates," *The Wall Street Journal*, January 13, 2012, B1; Rachel Dodes, "Targeting Younger Buyers, Liz Claiborne Hits a Snag," *The Wall Street Journal*, August 16, 2010, A1.

59. Cynthia A. Montgomery, "Strategist-in-Chief," *Leadership Excellence* (July 2012): 12; John E. Prescott, "Environments as Moderators of the Relationship Between Strategy and Performance," *Academy of Management Journal* 29 (1986): 329–346; John A. Pearce II and Richard B. Robinson, Jr., *Strategic Management: Strategy, Formulation, and*

Implementation, 2nd ed. (Homewood, IL: Irwin, 1985); and David J. Teece, "Economic Analysis and Strategic Management," *California Management Review* 26 (Spring 1984): 87–110.

60. Jack Welch, "It's All in the Sauce," excerpt from his book, *Winning*, published in *Fortune* (April 18, 2005): 138–144; and Constantinos Markides, "Strategic Innovation," *Sloan Management Review* (Spring 1997): 9–23.

61. Michael E. Porter, "What Is Strategy?" *Harvard Business Review* (November–December 1996): 61–78.

62. This discussion draws ideas from Ken Favaro, "The Two Levels of Strategy," *Strategy + Business*, April 27, 2012, http://www.strategy-business.com/article/cs00004?gko=8d72a (accessed September 16, 2013); and Ken Favaro with Kasturi Rangan and Evan Hirsh, "Strategy: An Executive's Definition," *Strategy + Business*, March 5, 2012, www.strategy-business.com/article/cs00002?gko=d59c2 (accessed July 24, 2012).

63. Brian Leavy, "Updating a Classic Formula for Strategic Success: Focus, Alignment, Repeatability, and Leadership," *Strategy & Leadership* 41, no. 1 (2013): 18–28.

64. Norihiko Shirouzu, "Chinese Begin Volvo Overhaul," *The Wall Street Journal*, June 7, 2011, B1.

65. Arthur A. Thompson, Jr., and A. J. Strickland III, *Strategic Management: Concepts and Cases*, 6th ed. (Homewood, IL: Irwin, 1992); and Briance Mascarenhas, Alok Baveja, and Mamnoon Jamil, "Dynamics of Core Competencies in Leading Multinational Companies," *California Management Review* 40, no. 4 (Summer 1998): 117–132.

66. "Gaylord Says Hotels Prosper by Becoming Destinations," *The Tennessean*, July 24, 2005; and Chris Woodyard, "Big Dreams for Small Choppers Paid Off," *USA Today*, September 11, 2005.

67. Michael Goold and Andrew Campbell, "Desperately Seeking Synergy," *Harvard Business Review* (September–October 1998): 131–143.

68. Anjali Cordeiro "Boss Talk: Tang in India and Other Kraft Synergies," *The Wall Street Journal Online*, April 19, 2010, http://online.wsj.com/article/SB100014240527023033 48504575184103106388686.html (accessed October 8, 2012); and Sarah Kessler, "Exposing Yahoo's Strategy," *Fast Company* (April 2013), pp. 40, 45.

69. Nick Wingfield, "Thinking Outside the Redbox," *The New York Times*, February 18, 2012, B1.

70. Lauren A. E. Schuker, "Double Feature: Dinner and a Movie—To Upgrade from Dirty Carpets and Tubs of Popcorn, Theater Chains Try Full Menus, Seat-Side Service," *The Wall Street Journal*, January 5, 2011, D1.

71. Brad Stone, "What's in the Box? Instant Gratification," *Bloomberg Businessweek* (November 29–December 5, 2010): 39–40; and S. Levy, "CEO of the Internet: Jeff Bezos Owns the Web in More Ways than You Think," *Wired*, December 2011, www.wired.com/magazine/2011/11/ff_bezos/ (accessed July 24, 2012).

72. Christopher B. Bingham, Kathleen M. Eisenhardt, and Nathan R. Furr, "Which Strategy When?" *MIT Sloan Management Review* (Fall 2011): 71–78.

73. John Kell, "Originality Helps Build Hit Toy Brands," *The Wall Street Journal*, February 10, 2013, http://online.wsj .com/article/SB100014241278873236964045782963018731 93788.html (accessed September 16, 2013); and Jason Hall, " 'Disney Infinity' Versus 'Skylanders,': Can Activision Meet This Challenge?" *The Motley Fool*, September 9, 2013, http://www.fool.com/investing/general/2013/09/09/disney-infinity-versus-skylanders-can-activision-m.aspx (accessed September 16, 2013).

74. Nick Allen, "Aaron Alexis: Washington Navy Yard Gunman 'Obsessed with Violent Video Games,'" *The Telegraph*, September 18, 2013, http://www.telegraph.co.uk/news/worldnews/northamerica/usa/10314585/Aaron-Alexis-Washington-navy-yard-gunman-obsessed-with-violent-video-games.html (accessed September 18, 2013).

75. Jon M. Chang, "How Violent Video Games Fit In with Violent Behavior," *ABC News*, September 18, 2013, http://abcnews.go.com/Technology/navy-yard-shooter-played-military-style-videogames-relevant/story?id=20285169 (accessed September 18, 2013); and Allen, "Aaron Alexis: Washington Navy Yard Gunman 'Obsessed with Violent Video Games.' "

76. Don Clark, "Intel Hurt by PC Shift," *The Wall Street Journal*, January 18, 2013, B3.

77. David Welch, Keith Naughton, and Burt Helm, "Detroit's Big Chance," *Bloomberg Businessweek* (February 22, 2010): 38–44.

78. Stephanie Clifford, "Where Wal-Mart Failed, Aldi Succeeds," *The New York Times*, March 29, 2011, www.nytimes.com/2011/03/30/business/30aldi.html?pagewanted=all (accessed July 26, 2012).

79. Betsy Morris, "FedEx's Path Gets Riskier," *The Wall Street Journal*, December 18, 2012, B1; and "FedEx Corporation SWOT Analysis, MarketLine, February 2013, http://advantage.marketline.com.proxy.library.vanderbilt.edu/Product?pid=3FB515C6-44D5-4A30-BC7E-556271B4A308&view=SWOTAnalysis (accessed September 16, 2013).

80. Thompson and Strickland, *Strategic Management*; and William L. Shanklin and John K. Ryans, Jr., "Is the International Cash Cow Really a Prize Heifer?" *Business Horizons* 24 (1981): 10–16.

81. Spencer E. Ante, "Lotus Notes? It Is Still a $1 Billion IBM Business," *The Wall Street Journal*, January 22, 2013, B1.

82. The following discussion is based on Michael E. Porter, "The Five Competitive Forces That Shape Strategy," *Harvard Business Review* (January 2008): 79–93; Michael E. Porter, *Competitive Strategy* (New York: Free Press, 1980), pp. 36–46; Danny Miller, "Relating Porter's Business Strategies to Environment and Structure: Analysis and Performance Implementations," *Academy of Management Journal* 31 (1988): 280–308; and Michael E. Porter, "From Competitive Advantage to Corporate Strategy," *Harvard Business Review* (May–June 1987): 43–59.

83. Joshua Rosenbaum, "Guitar Maker Looks for a New Key," *The Wall Street Journal*, February 11, 1998.

84. Nitin Nohria, William Joyce, and Bruce Roberson, "What Really Works," *Harvard Business Review* (July 2003): 43–52.

85. Based on Shel Horowitz, "Should Mary Buy Her Own Bonus?" *Business Ethics* (Summer 2005): 34.

CHAPTER
6

Managerial Decision Making

LEARNING OUTCOMES

After studying this chapter, you should be able to:

6.1 Explain why decision making is an important component of good management.

6.2 Compare and contrast programmed and nonprogrammed decisions, and describe the decision characteristics of certainty and uncertainty.

6.3 Compare the ideal, rational model of decision making to the political model of decision making.

6.4 Explain the process by which managers actually make decisions in the real world.

6.5 Summarize the six steps used in managerial decision making.

6.6 Describe four personal decision styles used by managers.

6.7 Identify the biases that frequently cause managers to make bad decisions.

6.8 Explain innovative techniques for decision making, including brainstorming, evidence-based management, and after-action reviews.

Messages

R U Ready 2 B a Manager?

Delivered

Before reading this chapter, please circle either "Mostly True" or "Mostly False" for each of the five questions below.

1 I am good at making decisions when there is certainty and need more help when there is uncertainty. I make both kinds of decisions, not automatically, but with thought and weighing of possible outcomes.

Mostly True — Mostly False
[page 230]

2 When conditions are difficult and priorities conflicting, sometimes you have to make a decision based on "this is the best we can do" and you have to abandon the idea of getting all the needs met.

Mostly True — Mostly False
[page 237]

3 I don't think instincts or intuition can help in the decision-making process.

Mostly True — Mostly False
[page 237]

4 I am good at building coalitions or helping build consensus around a problem and its solution.

Mostly True — Mostly False
[page 238]

5 I try to avoid making bad decisions through being aware that I should not let myself be influenced by (a) justifying past decisions I made, so that I now might look bad; (b) overconfidence; (c) trying to keep things the way they are or the status quo; (d) emotions; or (e) being swayed by initial impressions, rather than digging deeper for more evidence.

Mostly True — Mostly False
[page 248]

"This was bad decisions piled on top of each other," said Gary Brown, the Detroit City Council president pro tem in March 2013, a few months before Detroit became the largest U.S. city ever to file for bankruptcy. True, city managers didn't have much control over the loss of jobs in the auto industry, which had once made Detroit one of the nation's largest and most vibrant cities. However, an in-depth analysis of the mess in Detroit reveals a pattern of bad decisions extending back decades. For example, when Detroit's population and property values declined in the 1960s, city leaders decided to keep adding workers to the payroll. The city didn't make the decision to start seriously downsizing and cutting expenses until the last decade before the bankruptcy. In addition, when temporary prosperity returned after a decline in the 1960s, leaders failed to take advantage of it by investing in new technology that could improve efficiency and productivity. For instance, the team reviewing the city's problems found that in some departments, the records were "basically stuff written on index cards." No one could tell the team how many police officers were patrolling the streets or what the details of the department's budget were. The crisis for Detroit has been years of poor decision making, and there will be no easy fixes. However, leaders and demoralized residents hope that bankruptcy and emergency management will finally lead to the right decisions that can overhaul the out-of-control city systems and services, pay off the overwhelming debts, and give Detroit a fresh start.[1]

Welcome to the world of managerial decision making. Every organization, whether it is General Motors (GM), Apple, the American Red Cross, or the city of Detroit, grows, prospers, or fails as a result of decisions made by its managers. Yet decision making, particularly in relation to complex problems, is not always easy. It is easy to look back and identify flawed decisions, as a team at the *Detroit Free Press* did by examining 10,000 pages of documents covering a period of 50 years and interviewing current and former city leaders and employees. But managers frequently make decisions amid ever-changing factors, unclear information, and conflicting points of view. Managers can sometimes make the wrong decision, even when their intentions are right.

The business world is full of evidence of both good and bad decisions. YouTube was once referred to as "Google's Folly," but decisions made by the video platform's managers have more than justified the $1.65 billion that Google paid for it and turned YouTube into a highly admired company that is redefining the entertainment industry.[2] On the other hand, Caterpillar's decision to purchase China's ERA Mining Machinery Ltd. hasn't worked out so well. After paying $700 million for the deal, Caterpillar managers said less than a year later that they would write down ERA's value as $580 million. The company blamed deliberate accounting misconduct that was designed to overstate profits at the firm's mine-safety equipment unit.[3]

Good decision making is a vital part of good management because decisions determine how the organization solves problems, allocates resources, and accomplishes its goals. This chapter describes decision making in detail. First, we examine decision characteristics. Then we look at decision-making models and the steps that executives should take when making important decisions. The chapter also explores some biases that can cause managers to make bad decisions. Finally, we examine some specific techniques for innovative decision making in today's fast-changing environment.

6.1 Types of Decisions and Problems

A **decision** is a choice made from available alternatives. For example, an accounting manager's selection among Colin, Tasha, and Carlos for the position of junior auditor is a decision. Many people assume that making a choice is the major part of decision making, but it is only a part of it.

NEW MANAGER Self-Test

How Do You Make Decisions?

Instructions: Most of us make decisions automatically, without realizing that people have diverse decision-making behaviors, which they bring to management positions.[4] Think back to how you make decisions in your personal, student, or work life, especially where other people are involved. Please answer whether each of the following items is Mostly True or Mostly False for you.

	Mostly True	Mostly False
1. I like to decide quickly and move on to the next thing.		
2. I would use my authority to make a decision if I'm certain I am right.		
3. I appreciate decisiveness.		
4. There is usually one correct solution to a problem.		
5. I identify everyone who needs to be involved in the decision.		
6. I explicitly seek conflicting perspectives.		
7. I use discussion strategies to reach a solution.		
8. I look for different meanings when faced with a great deal of data.		
9. I take time to reason things through and use systematic logic.		

Scoring and Interpretation: All nine items in the list reflect appropriate decision-making behavior, but items 1–4 are more typical of new managers. Items 5–8 are typical of successful senior-manager decision making. Item 9 is considered part of good decision making at all levels. If you checked Mostly True for three or four of items 1–4 and 9, consider yourself typical of a new manager. If you checked Mostly True for three or four of items 5–8 and 9, you are using behavior consistent with top managers. If you checked a similar number of both sets of items, your behavior is probably flexible and balanced.

New managers typically use a different decision behavior than seasoned executives. The decision behavior of a successful CEO may be almost the opposite of a first-level supervisor. The difference is due partly to the types of decisions and partly to learning what works at each level. New managers often start out with a more directive, decisive, command-oriented behavior to establish their standing and decisiveness and gradually move toward more openness, diversity of viewpoints, and interactions with others as they move up the hierarchy.

Decision making is the process of identifying problems and opportunities and then resolving them. Decision making involves effort both before and after the actual choice. Thus, the decision of whether to select Colin, Tasha, or Carlos requires the accounting manager to ascertain whether a new junior auditor is needed, determine the availability of potential job candidates, interview candidates to acquire necessary information, select one candidate, and follow up with the socialization of the new employee into the organization to ensure the decision's success.

Go to the "Ethical Dilemma" on page 259 which pertains to making nonprogrammed decisions.

6.1a Programmed and Nonprogrammed Decisions

Management decisions typically fall into one of two categories: programmed and nonprogrammed. Programmed decisions involve situations that have occurred often enough to enable decision rules to be developed and applied in the future.[5] Programmed decisions are made in response to recurring organizational problems. The decision to reorder paper and other office supplies when inventories drop to a certain level is a programmed decision. Other programmed decisions concern the types of skills required to fill certain jobs, and selection of freight routes for product deliveries. Once managers formulate decision rules, subordinates and others can make the decision, freeing managers for other tasks. For example, when staffing banquets, many hotels use a rule that specifies having one server per 30 guests for a sit-down function and one server per 20 guests for a buffet.[6]

Nonprogrammed decisions are made in response to situations that are unique, are poorly defined and largely unstructured, and have important consequences for the organization. Perhaps one of the greatest nonprogrammed decisions of all time was Boeing's decision to build the 707. During World War II, the B52 bomber had shown that Boeing had "the right stuff" for building jet aircraft, but no one had considered that the airlines would even be interested in buying jets. Converting to jet technology would be massively expensive for the airlines. Boeing's CEO, Bill Allen, had to decide whether to stick with the defense products that the company knew best or follow his conviction that the real growth would be in the civilian sector. In 1952, he asked Boeing's board to invest $16 million in building the world's first transatlantic commercial jetliner. By the time the 707 rolled off the production line, Boeing had invested $185 million in it—that was $36 million more than Boeing's net worth the previous year. Essentially, Allen was betting the company's future, and it paid off. The 707 changed the course of history for Boeing and altered the course of the entire industry.[7]

Another good example of a nonprogrammed decision comes from Priceline. Many nonprogrammed decisions, such as the ones at Priceline and Boeing, are related to strategic planning because uncertainty is great and decisions are complex. Decisions to develop a new product or service, acquire a company, build a new factory, enter a new geographical

Green Power

Revitalizing Small Farms

PepsiCo executives discovered for themselves that sustainability decisions can be observed and measured in the lives of individuals. Management's decision to launch a pilot project cutting the middleman from the supply chain for Sabritas, its Mexican line of snacks, by initiating direct purchase of corn from 300 small farmers in Mexico brought unimagined benefits.

The decision resulted in visible, measurable outcomes, including lower transportation costs and a stronger relationship with small farmers, who were able to develop pride and a business-like approach to farming. The arrangement with

PepsiCo gave farmers a financial edge in securing much-needed credit for purchasing equipment, fertilizer, and other necessities, resulting in higher crop yields. New levels of financial security also reduced the once-rampant and highly dangerous treks back and forth across the U.S. border that farmers made at great personal risk as they sought ways to support their families. Within three years, PepsiCo's pilot program was expanded to 850 farmers.

SOURCE: Stephanie Strom, "For Pepsi, a Business Decision with Social Benefits," *The New York Times*, February 21, 2011, www.nytimes.com/2011/02/22/business/global/22pepsi.html?pagewanted=all (accessed August 2, 2012).

market, or relocate headquarters to another city are all nonprogrammed decisions.

6.1b Facing Uncertainty and Ambiguity

One primary difference between programmed and nonprogrammed decisions relates to the degree of uncertainty, risk, or ambiguity that managers deal with in making the decision. In a perfect world, managers would have all the information necessary for making decisions. In reality, however, some things are unknowable; thus, some decisions will fail to solve the problem or attain the desired outcome. Managers try to obtain information about decision alternatives that will reduce decision uncertainty. Every decision situation can be organized on a scale according to the availability of information and the possibility of failure. The four positions on the scale are certainty, risk, uncertainty, and ambiguity, as illustrated in Exhibit 6.1. Whereas programmed decisions can be made in situations involving certainty, many situations that managers deal with every day involve at least some degree of uncertainty and require nonprogrammed decision making.

Certainty   **Certainty** means that all the information the decision maker needs is fully available.[8] Managers have information on operating conditions, resource costs, or constraints and each course of action and possible outcome. For example, if a company considers a $10,000 investment in new equipment that it knows for certain will yield $4,000 in cost savings per year over the next five years, managers can calculate a before-tax rate of return of about 40 percent. If managers compare this investment

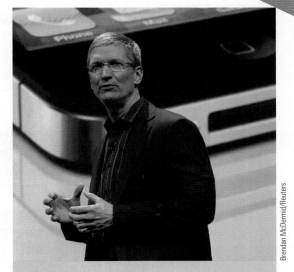

Brendan McDermid/Reuters

CONCEPT CONNECTION Having filled in for Steve Jobs during three medical leaves, COO Tim Cook was ready and able to take the helm of Apple when Jobs had to step down shortly before his death in 2011. The choice of Cook as the new CEO was a **nonprogrammed decision** that had been made well in advance, giving Cook some time to prepare for a seamless transition to his new role. Since then, investors, employees, and customers alike seem impressed with his abilities and generally happy with his performance.

Spotlight on Skills

Priceline

Anyone who has turned on a television in recent years has probably seen William Shatner as the "Priceline Negotiator," the charming but sometimes obnoxious pitchman for the world's leading stand-alone online travel agency. But the brain behind the company's outstanding performance is its low-key CEO, Jeffery Boyd, who took the company from a loss of $19 million in 2002 to a profit of $1.1 billion in 2011.

Boyd's turnaround of Priceline involved a number of nonprogrammed decisions. One early decision was to shut down all the nontravel-related businesses that the Priceline founder had expanded into ("Name your own price" gas fill-ups, insurance, mortgages, and so forth). Then Boyd decided to shift resources from airfares to focus primarily on hotel bookings. The strategic decision to acquire two European hotel reservation sites, the United Kingdom's Active Hotels and Amsterdam-based Booking.com, sent Priceline's growth soaring. "It would be tough to argue that there's been a better acquisition in Internet history," said Thomas White, an analyst at Macquarie Securities, of the Booking.com acquisition. Today, 60 percent of Priceline's revenues come from overseas, where Europeans typically have twice as many vacation days and also take a lot of short "city breaks."

Managers are now focusing on growth opportunities in Asia and South America, so more acquisitions may be in the company's future. The "Priceline Negotiator" plunged off a bridge in a doomed travel bus in a television commercial, but he was later found alive and well, giving people new ways to save money on their business and holiday travel.[9]

EXHIBIT 6.1   Conditions That Affect the Possibility of Decision Failure

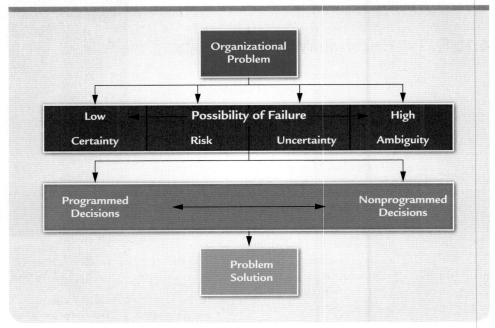

with one that will yield only $3,000 per year in cost savings, they can confidently select the 40 percent return. However, few decisions are certain in the real world. Most contain risk or uncertainty.

CONCEPT CONNECTION   **Uncertainty** is a standard feature in the life of any farmer. Changing weather patterns and unexpected events, like droughts or unseasonable storms, can have devastating effects on crops that no amount of planning can prevent. Yet, despite these unforeseeable situations, farmers must make decisions and continue to operate based on assumptions and expectations.

Risk   **Risk** means that a decision has clear-cut goals and that good information is available, but the future outcomes associated with each alternative are subject to some chance of loss or failure. However, enough information is available to estimate the probability of a successful outcome versus failure.[10] Some financial services managers have become highly risk-averse because of losses that their portfolios sustained during the downturn. The CEO of one financial services firm began calling his portfolio managers the "walking wounded" because they became so afraid to take even ordinary risks with investments. Top executives hired consultants from Decision Strategies International, a firm that helps managers and employees feel more comfortable taking balanced risks. "You can't just avoid all risk, because it will lead to entropy," said Steve Krupp, CEO of Decision Strategies.[11] For specific decisions, managers sometimes use computerized statistical analysis to calculate the probabilities of success or failure for each alternative. For example, executives at fast food chains such as Subway, Wendy's, or McDonald's can analyze potential customer demographics, traffic patterns, supply logistics, and competition, and come up with a reasonably good idea of how successful a restaurant would be in each location being considered.[12]

Uncertainty   **Uncertainty** means that managers know which goals they wish to achieve, but information about alternatives and

Business Blooper

Chevron Ecuador

When Texaco—now Chevron—ceased oil drilling in Ecuador in 1992, it had produced enough oil to become the second largest exporter in Latin America and helped make today's Chevron one of the largest U.S. corporations with annual revenues of $200 billion. During the time the company operated in Ecuador, it is alleged that it dumped 18 billion gallons of toxic waste and left hundreds of open pits of "malignant black sludge." In 1993, a group of indigenous Ecuadorians filed a lawsuit, claiming damages to what is seen as "rain-forest Chernobyl," with high rates of disease and birth defects. Chevron claims it has no responsibility for the damage, saying Texaco's operations were "completely in line with standards of the day." The case has endured on for almost 20 years, with plaintiffs in 2013 being awarded $9.5 billion by the Ecuadorian courts (after U.S. courts said they owed $18 billion). But Chevron is fighting, spending millions of dollars on lawyers, and more millions on improving its PR image, such as images of smiling African women with the caption, "Oil companies should support the communities they're part of." The lead lawyer for Ecuador is not daunted and says this lawsuit is historic, as it is "the first time that a small developing country has had power over a multinational American company." Even so, Chevron won't give up soon. A lobbyist told *Newsweek*, "We can't let little countries screw around with big companies like this." Another Chevron spokesperson said, "We're going to fight this until hell freezes over—and then we'll fight it on the ice." Maybe that's why Greenpeace Switzerland gave Chevron a "Lifetime Award" for the most irresponsible business in the past 10 years.

SOURCES: "French President Links Economics and Security," *Telegraph-Journal*, January 2015, D3; Patrick Radden Keefe, "Reversal of Fortune," *The New Yorker Magazine*, January 9, 2012, pp. 38–49.

future events is incomplete. Factors that may affect a decision, such as price, production costs, volume, or future interest rates, are difficult to analyze and predict. Managers may have to make assumptions from which to forge the decision, even though it will be wrong if the assumptions are incorrect. Former U.S. treasury secretary Robert Rubin defined *uncertainty* as a situation in which even a good decision might produce a bad outcome.[13] Managers face uncertainty every day. Many problems have no clear-cut solution, but managers rely on creativity, judgment, intuition, and experience to craft a response. Chevron acts as if it has no risk in its Ecuadorian fiasco, as shown in this chapter's Business Blooper.

Consider the uncertainty faced by managers in the movie industry. Disney's *Oz the Great and Powerful* cost about $325 million to make and market, but the gamble in putting out a prequel to the beloved 1939 musical *The Wizard of Oz* paid off, bringing in $150 million in revenues on its opening weekend and eventually grossing $495 million. Even though Disney managers did a cost–benefit analysis, there was tremendous uncertainty about how viewers would feel about a new twist on such well-known material.[14] Many films made today don't even break even, which reflects the tremendous uncertainty in the industry. What do people want to see this summer? Will comic book heroes, vampires, or aliens be popular? Will animated films, disaster epics, classics, or romantic comedies attract larger audiences? The interests and preferences of moviegoers are extremely difficult to predict. Moreover, it is hard for managers to understand even after the fact what made a particular movie a hit: Was it because of the storyline, the actors in starring roles, the director, the release time? All of those things? Or none of them? *The Lone Ranger*, another Disney film on a familiar theme (based on a 1950s-era TV show), topped one analyst's list of the 50 biggest box office bombs, even with Johnny Depp starring as Tonto. Despite the uncertainty, managers in the big Hollywood studios make relatively good decisions overall, and one big hit can pay for a lot of flops.[15]

Ambiguity and Conflict   **Ambiguity** is by far the most difficult decision situation. Ambiguity means that the goals to be achieved or the problem to be solved is unclear, alternatives are difficult to define, and information about outcomes is unavailable.[16] Ambiguity is what students would feel if an instructor created student groups and told each group to complete a project, but gave the groups no topic, direction, or guidelines whatsoever. In some situations, managers involved in a decision create ambiguity because they see things differently and disagree about what they want. Managers in different departments often have different priorities and goals for the decision, which can lead to conflicts over decision alternatives.

A highly ambiguous situation can create what is sometimes called a *wicked decision problem*. Wicked decisions are associated with conflicts over goals and decision alternatives, rapidly changing circumstances, fuzzy information, unclear links among decision elements, and the inability to evaluate whether a proposed solution will work. For wicked problems, there often is no "right" answer.[17] Managers have a difficult time coming to grips with the issues and must conjure up reasonable scenarios in the absence of clear information. Retailers such as H&M and Walmart faced a wicked decision problem after a series of deadly fires and a factory collapse in Bangladesh that killed more than 1,100 workers making garments for their stores. The incidents set off public outrage, requiring that retailers respond. Walmart managers eventually decided to publicly blacklist about 250 Bangladesh suppliers found to have safety problems, while H&M managers decided they would stay with their suppliers and help them improve conditions. Neither decision will fix the deeper wicked problem. Almost all apparel and many other consumer goods are made in overseas factories in places like Bangladesh, Cambodia, and Thailand, and safety concerns and poor working conditions exist in many of them. Moreover, the global supply chain is so broad and diffuse that a single product might involve supplies and labor from several countries. Managers have a hard time even determining which factories and suppliers they are really using, and even when they do know, it is difficult to police every aspect of the suppliers' operations.[18]

REMEMBER THIS

- Good decision making is a vital part of good management, but decision making is not easy.
- **Decision making** is the process of identifying problems and opportunities and then resolving them.
- A **decision** is a choice made from available alternatives.
- A **programmed decision** is one made in response to a situation that has occurred often enough to enable managers to develop decision rules that can be applied in the future.
- A **nonprogrammed decision** is one made in response to a situation that is unique, is poorly defined and largely unstructured, and has important consequences for the organization.
- Decisions differ according to the amount of certainty, risk, uncertainty, or ambiguity in the situation.

- **Certainty** is a situation in which all the information the decision maker needs is fully available.
- **Risk** means that a decision has clear-cut goals and good information is available, but the future outcomes associated with each alternative are subject to chance.
- **Uncertainty** occurs when managers know which goals they want to achieve, but information about alternatives and future events is incomplete.
- **Ambiguity** is a condition in which the goals to be achieved or the problem to be solved is unclear, alternatives are difficult to define, and information about outcomes is unavailable.
- Highly ambiguous circumstances can create a wicked decision problem, the most difficult decision situation that managers face.

6.2 Decision-Making Models

The approach that managers use to make decisions usually falls into one of three types—the classical model, the administrative model, or the political model. The choice of model depends on the manager's personal preference, whether the decision is programmed or nonprogrammed, and the degree of uncertainty associated with the decision.

6.2a The Ideal, Rational Model

The **classical model** of decision making is based on rational economic assumptions and manager beliefs about what ideal decision making should be. This model has arisen within the management literature because managers are expected to make decisions that are economically sensible and in the organization's best economic interests. The four assumptions underlying this model are as follows:

- The decision maker operates to accomplish goals that are known and agreed on. Problems are precisely formulated and defined.

- The decision maker strives for conditions of certainty, gathering complete information. All alternatives and the potential results of each are calculated.

- Criteria for evaluating alternatives are known. The decision maker selects the alternative that will maximize the economic return to the organization.

- The decision maker is rational and uses logic to assign values, order preferences, evaluate alternatives, and make the decision that will maximize the attainment of organizational goals.

The classical model of decision making is considered to be **normative**, which means that it defines how a decision maker *should* make decisions. It does not describe how managers actually make decisions so much as it provides guidelines on how to reach an ideal outcome for the organization. The ideal, rational approach of the classical model is often unattainable by real people in real organizations, but the model has value because it helps decision makers be more rational and not rely entirely on personal preference in making decisions. Indeed, a global survey by McKinsey & Company found that when managers incorporate thoughtful analysis into decision making, they get better results. Studying the responses of more than 2,000 executives regarding how their companies made a specific decision, McKinsey concluded that techniques such as detailed analysis, risk assessment, financial models, and considering comparable situations typically contribute to better financial and operational outcomes.[19]

The classical model is most useful when applied to programmed decisions and to decisions characterized by certainty or risk because relevant information is available and probabilities can be calculated. For example, new analytical software programs automate many programmed decisions, such as freezing the account of a customer who has failed to make payments, determining the cell phone service plan that is most appropriate for a particular customer, or sorting insurance claims so that cases are handled most efficiently.[20]

The growth of big data techniques, as described in Chapter 1, has expanded the use of the classical approach. The New York City Police Department uses computerized mapping and analysis of arrest patterns, paydays, sporting events, concerts, rainfall, holidays, and other variables to predict likely crime "hot spots" and decide where to assign officers. Retailers like Target and Kohl's make decisions about what to stock and how to price it based on analysis of sales, economic and demographic data, and so forth.[21] Airlines use automated systems to optimize seat pricing, flight scheduling, and crew assignment decisions.

6.2b How Managers Actually Make Decisions

Another approach to decision making, called the **administrative model,** is considered to be **descriptive,** meaning that it describes how managers actually make decisions in complex situations rather than dictating how they *should* make decisions according to a theoretical ideal. The administrative model recognizes the human and environmental limitations that affect the degree to which managers can pursue a rational decision-making process. In difficult situations, such as those characterized by nonprogrammed decisions, uncertainty, and ambiguity, managers are typically unable to make economically rational decisions even if they want to.[22]

Spotlight on Skills

J. Hilburn Direct Sales

Hil Davis was a 33-year-old Dallas-based investment banker earning $1.4 million per year, but he wanted more. More challenge, more ownership, and a chance to try out his own ideas. After reading that billionaire acquisition guru Warren Buffet said the best investments he ever made, dollar-for-dollar were in direct sales. Direct sales? Like Mary Kay or Tupperware? Intrigued, he read more about direct sales and found that they typically sell low-end products, which forces recruits to force high volume and pressure others to join the team so they can make a percentage off them. But advantages were low capital expenditures, no factory or offices to build, no physical stores, and no up-front costs for customer acquisition. He got two useful insights from his years as an equity researcher: (1) Amazon's marketing directly to consumers cut out expensive middle men, so that customers got lower prices; and (2) direct sales could work in the luxury high-touch service business, so he decided to start a company that makes custom-made shirts, but for less than the $250 they usually go for.

All good ideas, but Davis found many complications along the way. He and his partner, Veeral Rathod, wanted to manufacture shirts in the United States, but the biggest factory could only do 5,000 units a month and they were going to need 20,000. No one at the top manufacturers would return the calls of these "nobodies." They found a place in China that filled an order on spec. The shirts looked and felt good, but then when they washed them a few times, they sagged, making Davis realize

they had used cheap fabric, but had sprayed it to make it look good for a short time. So Davis called one of the best places in Italy and said he had a $1 million order and would rather not have to go to their competitor. A few minutes later he got a call back and negotiated a reasonable deal.

Another problem was correct sizing. Most of the recruits have never worked in retail clothing and made lots of mistakes in measuring the customers, so shirts came back with sleeves too long or collars too tight. David and Rathod knew that they had to do right and offered a money-back guarantee, costing them $75,000 in the first year.

Within five years, though, J. Hilburn became the world's largest and most successful seller of custom dress shirts for men and they currently have a goal of $1 billion in sales. Starting at $89, the shirts are made from the same fabrics as the Armanis of the world. The company still has challenges in training and wants to establish a rating system for the reps, with high-scorers making more commissions. But Davis knows what a gold mine he has with the information garnered. "Just think of the data we have," he says. They know fit preference, measurements, color likes, where they live. "And now think of all the ways we'll be able to mine that data. Nobody has all this. Nobody."

SOURCES: Veeral Rathod, *Apparel*, December 2013, 11; Tom Foster, "Made to Measure," *Inc.*, February 2013, 65–70.

Bounded Rationality and Satisficing   The administrative model of decision making is based on the work of Herbert A. Simon. Simon proposed two concepts that were instrumental in shaping the administrative model: bounded rationality and satisficing. **Bounded rationality** means that people have limits, or boundaries, on how rational they can be. Organizations are incredibly complex, and managers have the time and ability to process only a limited amount of information with which to make decisions.[23] Because managers do not have the time or cognitive ability to process complete information about complex decisions, they must satisfice. **Satisficing** means that decision makers choose the first solution alternative that satisfies minimal decision criteria. Rather than pursuing all alternatives to identify the single solution that will maximize economic returns, managers will opt for the first solution that appears to solve the problem, even if better solutions are presumed to exist. The decision maker cannot justify the time and expense of obtaining complete information.[24] Hil Davis faced overwhelming obstacles finding the best vendor for his start-up, but rather than chase down every possible source, he took a gamble and went after what had seemed an impossible source, as described in the Spotlight on Skills box.

Managers sometimes generate alternatives for complex problems only until they find one that they believe will work. For example, Liz Claiborne managers hired designer Isaac Mizrahi and targeted younger consumers in an effort to revive the flagging brand, but sales and profits continued to decline. Faced with the failure of the new youth-oriented line, a 90 percent cutback in orders from Macy's, high unemployment, a weak economy, and other complex and multifaceted problems, managers weren't sure how to stem the years-long tide of losses and get the company back in the black. They satisficed with a quick decision to form a licensing agreement that will have Liz Claiborne clothing sold exclusively at JC Penney, which will handle all manufacturing and marketing for the brand.[25]

The administrative model relies on assumptions that differ from those of the classical model and focuses on organizational factors that influence individual decisions. According to the administrative model, the following are the assumptions:

- Decision goals often are vague, conflicting, and lack consensus among managers. Managers often are unaware of problems or opportunities that exist in the organization.

- Rational procedures are not always used, and, when they are, they are confined to a simplistic view of the problem that does not capture the complexity of real organizational events.

- Managers' searches for alternatives are limited because of human, information, and resource constraints.

- Most managers settle for a satisficing rather than a maximizing solution, partly because they have limited information and partly because they have only vague criteria for what constitutes a maximizing solution.

Intuition and Quasirationality   Another aspect of administrative decision making is **intuition**. Intuition represents a quick apprehension of a decision situation based on past experience but without conscious thought.[26] Intuitive decision making is not arbitrary or irrational because it is based on years of practice and hands-on experience. Have you ever wondered how the "Intel Inside" logo came to be plastered on virtually every personal computer? Computers are made of various components, and prior to 1991, users had no idea who supplied the microprocessor, just like they had no idea who provided the hard drive or other components. Intel's CEO had a young technical assistant named Dennis Carter, who had two engineering degrees and an MBA, and he believed that Intel's anonymity

James Leynse/Corbis Entertainment/Corbis

"Lots of people hear what I'm doing and think, 'That's a crazy idea!'" says Russell Simmons. The successful entrepreneur, who heads the New York–based media firm Rush Communications, has relied on his **intuition** to build a half-billion-dollar empire on one profitable "crazy idea" after another. It all began with his belief that he could go mainstream with the vibrant rap music he heard in African American neighborhoods. In 1983, he started the pioneering hip-hop Def Jam record label, launching the careers of Beastie Boys, LL Cool J, and Run-DMC, among others. He's since moved on to successful ventures in fashion, media, consumer products, and finance.

Do you tend to analyze things or rely on gut feelings when it comes to making an important decision? Complete the "New Manager Self-Test" on page 239 to find out your predominant approach.

could and should change. CEO Andy Grove had his doubts that a microprocessor could be successfully branded, even though it was the brains of the PC. But because Carter believed in it so strongly, Grove eventually agreed to a test. He gave Carter $500,000, which he used to buy billboards: One had Intel 286 (the company's old chip) inside a circle with a large red X spray painted across it. A week later, another billboard went up with a big bold Intel 386 (the company's new, more powerful chip that no one was buying) inside a circle. The ads worked. Within no time, sales of PCs with the 386 chip shot up. Carter's intuition that Intel's chip—previously an anonymous component—could achieve its own brand identity essentially shifted power in the industry from the PC makers to a key supplier, Intel.[27]

Psychologists and neuroscientists have studied how people make good decisions using their intuition under extreme time pressure and uncertainty.[28] Good intuitive decision making is based on an ability to recognize patterns at lightning speed. When people have a depth of experience and knowledge in a particular area, the right decision often comes quickly and effortlessly as a recognition of information that has been largely forgotten by the conscious mind. This ability can also be seen among soldiers in Iraq, who stopped many roadside bomb attacks based on gut feelings. High-tech gear designed to detect improvised explosive devices, or IEDs, was a supplement rather than a replacement for the ability of the human brain to sense danger and act on it. Soldiers with experience in Iraq subconsciously recognized when something didn't look or feel right. It might be a rock that wasn't there yesterday, a piece of concrete that looked too symmetrical, odd patterns of behavior, or just a different feeling of tension in the air.[29] Similarly, in the business world, managers continuously perceive and process information that they may not consciously be aware of, and their base of knowledge and experience helps them make decisions that may be characterized by uncertainty and ambiguity.

In today's rapidly moving business environment, intuition plays an increasingly important role in decision making. Numerous studies have found that effective managers use a combination of rational analysis and intuition in making complex decisions under time pressure.[30] A new trend in decision making is referred to as quasirationality, which basically means combining intuitive and analytical thought.[31] In many situations, neither analysis nor intuition is sufficient for making a good decision. However, managers may often walk a fine line between two extremes: on the one hand, making arbitrary decisions without careful study, and on the other, relying obsessively on rational analysis. One is not better than the other, and managers need to take a balanced approach by considering both rationality and intuition as important components of effective decision making.[32]

6.2c The Political Model

The third model of decision making is useful for making nonprogrammed decisions when conditions are uncertain, information is limited, and there are manager conflicts about what goals to pursue or what course of action to take. Most organizational decisions involve many managers who are pursuing different goals, and they have to talk with one another to share information and reach an agreement. Managers often engage in coalition building for making complex organizational decisions.[33] A coalition is an informal alliance among managers who support a specific goal. *Coalition building* is the process of forming alliances among managers. In other words, a manager who supports a specific alternative, such as increasing the corporation's growth by acquiring another company, talks informally to other executives and tries to persuade them to support the decision. Without a coalition, a powerful individual or group could derail the decision-making process. Coalition building

NEW MANAGER Self-test

Making Important Decisions

Instructions: How do you make important personal decisions? To find out, think about a time when you made an important career decision or made a large purchase or investment. To what extent does each of the terms below describe how you reached the final decision? Please check five terms below that best describe how you made your final choice.

1. Logic _____

2. Inner knowing _____

3. Data _____

4. Felt sense _____

5. Facts _____

6. Instincts _____

7. Concepts _____

8. Hunch _____

9. Reason _____

10. Feelings _____

Scoring and Interpretation: The odd-numbered items pertain to a linear decision style, and the even-numbered items pertain to a nonlinear decision approach. *Linear* means using logical *rationality* to make decisions; *nonlinear* means using primarily *intuition* to make decisions. Of the five terms you chose, how many represent rationality versus intuition? If all five are either linear or nonlinear, then that is clearly your dominant decision approach. If four terms are either linear or nonlinear, then that approach would be considered your preference. If the terms you chose are mixed (that is, three of one approach and two of the other), you may use a quasirational approach to decision making. The *rational, intuitive,* and *quasirationality* approaches to decision making are described in the text.

SOURCES: Based on Charles M. Vance, Kevin S. Groves, Yongsun Paik, and Herb Kindler, "Understanding and Measuring Linear-Nonlinear Thinking Style for Enhanced Management Education and Professional Practice," *Academy of Management Learning & Education* 6, no. 2 (2007): 167–185; and Mandeep K. Dhami and Mary E. Thomson, "On the Relevance of Cognitive Continuum Theory and Quasirationality for Understanding Management Judgment and Decision Making," *European Management Journal* 30 (2012): 316–326.

gives several managers an opportunity to contribute to decision making, enhancing their commitment to the alternative that is ultimately adopted. Results from the global survey by McKinsey & Company mentioned earlier suggest that coalition building is associated with faster implementation of decisions because managers have developed consensus about which action to pursue.[34] For example, an aerospace company that lost its supply of crucial parts due to the unexpected closing of a key supplier needed swift action to avoid a complete work stoppage. To make sure everyone would support any decisions that were made and implement them quickly, top managers set up a cross-functional team so members from various parts of the organization could identify, evaluate, and debate various options for ensuring that production could continue. The team was ultimately awarded an International Team Excellence silver-level award from the American Society for Quality.[35]

Failing to build a coalition can allow conflict and disagreements to derail a decision, particularly if the opposition builds a powerful coalition of its own. Consider the inability of U.S. Postal Service managers to build an effective coalition among U.S. lawmakers to allow the organization to move into new lines of business.

As a government agency, the U.S. Postal Service is in a bind. Private companies are always lobbying Congress for legislation that supports their interests. For instance, managers at BAE Systems and dozens of its suppliers have launched a lobbying campaign to try to build a coalition among U.S. lawmakers to undo military spending cuts that would reduce production of BAE's line of Bradley fighting vehicles. Supporters in Congress, such as Senator Bob Corker of Tennessee, are helping BAE form a coalition based on the idea of saving local defense industry jobs, even though the Pentagon has suggested suspending the Bradley fleet as one of the best places to cut spending.[36]

The political model closely resembles the real environment in which most managers and decision makers operate. Interviews with CEOs in high-tech industries found that they strived to use some type of rational decision-making process, but the way they actually decided things was through a complex interaction with other managers, subordinates, environmental factors, and organizational events.[37] Decisions are complex and involve many people, information is often ambiguous, and disagreement and conflict over problems and solutions are normal. The political model begins with four basic assumptions:

Spotlight on Skills

U.S. Postal Service

Pity the poor Postal Service. With the volume of traditional mail plummeting, the agency is running out of cash and struggling to stay in business. There are many reasons for the problems at the U.S. Postal Service, but managers have certainly tried over the past decade or more to find new ways to keep the 239-year-old agency relevant for a new age.

For example, in 2000 (long before online bill paying became popular), the Postal Service began operating a secure system that would have enabled it to continue to be the primary way that most Americans paid their monthly bills. The Internet industry, however, formed a coalition to oppose the service, and the U.S. Congress successfully shut it down. It's a pattern that has repeated

itself over and over, with Postal Service managers coming up with a new plan for coping with the decline in traditional mail, only to have powerful private companies lobby against it. In other countries, post offices double as banks or sell insurance or cell phones. A 2010 report from the Postal Service's inspector general said that introducing new products like secure electronic bill payment could add $9.7 billion annually to the agency's revenue. Financial services firms, as well as companies like United Parcel Service (UPS) and FedEx, however, have objected to the agency getting into nonpostal activities, and they have persuaded Congress to agree. Without building a political coalition in Congress, the Postal Service will continue to struggle.[38]

- Organizations are made up of groups with diverse interests, goals, and values. Managers disagree about problem priorities and may not understand or share the goals and interests of other managers.

- Information is ambiguous and incomplete. The attempt to be rational is limited by the complexity of many problems, as well as personal and organizational constraints.

- Managers do not have the time, resources, or mental capacity to identify all dimensions of the problem and process all relevant information. Managers talk to each other and exchange viewpoints to gather information and reduce ambiguity.

- Managers engage in the push and pull of debate to decide goals and discuss alternatives. Decisions are the result of bargaining and discussion among coalition members.

The key dimensions of the classical, administrative, and political models are listed in Exhibit 6.2. Research into decision-making procedures found rational, classical procedures to be associated with high performance for organizations in stable environments. However, administrative and political decision-making procedures and intuition have been associated with high performance in unstable environments in which decisions must be made rapidly and under more difficult conditions.[39]

EXHIBIT 6.2 **Characteristics of Classical, Administrative, and Political Decision-Making Models**

Classical Model	Administrative Model	Political Model
Clear-cut problem and goals	Vague problem and goals	Pluralistic; conflicting goals
Condition of certainty	Condition of uncertainty	Condition of uncertainty or ambiguity
Full information about alternatives and their outcomes	Limited information about alternatives and their outcomes	Inconsistent viewpoints; ambiguous information
Rational choice by individual for maximizing outcomes	Satisficing choice for resolving problem using intuition	Bargaining and discussion among coalition members

REMEMBER THIS

- The ideal, rational approach to decision making, called the **classical model**, is based on the assumption that managers should make logical decisions that are economically sensible and in the organization's best economic interest.

- The classical model is **normative**, meaning that it defines how a manager *should* make logical decisions and provides guidelines for reaching an ideal outcome.

- Software programs based on the classical model are being applied to programmed decisions, such as how to schedule airline crews or how to process insurance claims most efficiently.

- The **administrative model** includes the concepts of *bounded rationality* and *satisficing* and describes how managers make decisions in situations that are characterized by uncertainty and ambiguity.

- The administrative model is **descriptive**, an approach that describes how managers actually make decisions, rather than how they should make decisions according to a theoretical model.

- **Bounded rationality** means that people have the time and cognitive ability to process only a limited amount of information on which to base decisions.
- **Satisficing** means choosing the first alternative that satisfies minimal decision criteria, regardless of whether better solutions are presumed to exist.
- **Intuition** is an aspect of administrative decision making that refers to a quick comprehension of a decision situation based on past experience but without conscious thought.

- Soldiers in Iraq often detected roadside bombs using their intuition.
- A new trend in decision making, **quasirationality**, combines intuitive and analytical thought.
- The political model takes into consideration that many decisions require debate, discussion, and coalition building.
- A **coalition** is an informal alliance among managers who support a specific goal or solution.

6.3 Decision-Making Steps

Whether a decision is programmed or nonprogrammed, and regardless of whether managers choose the classical, administrative, or political model of decision making, six steps typically are associated with effective decision processes. These steps are summarized in Exhibit 6.3.

EXHIBIT 6.3   Six Steps in the Managerial Decision-Making Process

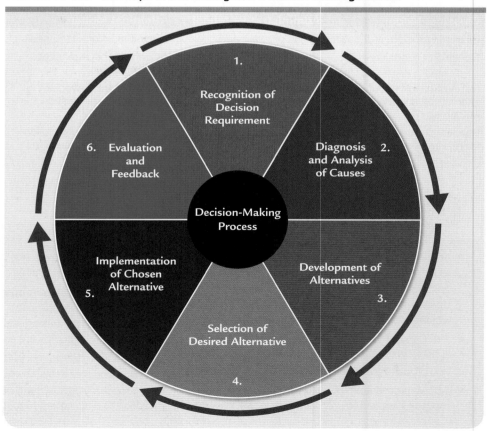

6.3a Recognition of Decision Requirement

Managers confront a decision requirement in the form of either a problem or an opportunity. A **problem** occurs when organizational accomplishment is less than established goals. Some aspect of performance is unsatisfactory. An **opportunity** exists when managers see potential accomplishment that exceeds specified current goals. Managers see the possibility of enhancing performance beyond current levels.

Awareness of a problem or opportunity is the first step in the decision-making sequence, and it requires surveillance of the internal and external environment for issues that merit executive attention.[40] Some information comes from periodic financial reports, performance reports, and other sources that are designed to discover problems before they become too serious. Managers also take advantage of informal sources. They talk to other managers, gather opinions on how things are going, and seek advice on which problems should be tackled or which opportunities embraced.[41] For example, at Google, some managers noticed that employees were eating too many of the free M&Ms scattered in bins around the company, which they thought might conflict with the company's goal of keeping employees not only happy but healthy as well.[42] The company decided to analyze the problem and experiment with ways to get people to eat healthier snacks and drink more water as well as consume the free candy. Recognizing decision requirements is sometimes difficult because it often means integrating bits and pieces of information in novel ways.

6.3b Diagnosis and Analysis of Causes

Once a problem or opportunity comes to a manager's attention, the understanding of the situation should be refined. **Diagnosis** is the step in the decision-making process in which managers analyze underlying causal factors associated with the decision situation.

Many times, the real problem lies hidden behind the problem that managers *think* exists. By looking at a situation from different angles, managers can identify the true problem. In addition, they often discover opportunities that they didn't realize were there.[43] Charles Kepner and Benjamin Tregoe, who conducted extensive studies of manager decision making, recommend that managers ask a series of questions to specify underlying causes, including the following:

- What is the state of disequilibrium affecting us?

- When did it occur?

- Where did it occur?

- How did it occur?

- To whom did it occur?

- What is the urgency of the problem?

- What is the interconnectedness of events?

- What result came from which activity?[44]

Such questions help specify what actually happened and why. Diagnosing a problem can be thought of as peeling an onion layer by layer. Managers cannot solve problems if they don't know about them, or if they are addressing the wrong issues. Some experts

> *"It isn't that they can't see the solution. It's that they can't see the problem."*
>
> —G. K. Chesterton, English Novelist

recommend continually asking "Why?" to get to the root of a problem, a technique some-times called "the **5 Whys**." The 5 Whys is a question-asking method used to explore the root cause underlying a particular problem. The first *why* generally produces a superficial explanation for the problem, and each subsequent *why* probes deeper into the causes of the problem and potential solutions. For example, a consultant met with the CEO of a large accounting and professional services firm, who said that the company's biggest problem was that they didn't have enough qualified people to serve their global clients. The consultant asked *why*. The CEO said that staff members had to spend lots of time passing informa-tion about clients back and forth among themselves. *Why?* Because people have to work together to provide a complete portfolio of services, the CEO said. *Why?* After a couple more *Whys*, the two got down to the real problem, which was not the lack of staff, but inef-ficiency in internal collaboration and communication. The CEO discovered that he might actually be able to *reduce* staff with more effective and efficient systems.[45]

The Group Learning on page 257 will give you a chance to practice a new approach to decision making that focuses on desired outcomes rather than looking at the cause of problems.

6.3c Development of Alternatives

The next stage is to generate possible alternative solutions that will respond to the needs of the situation and correct the underlying causes.

For a programmed decision, feasible alternatives are easy to identify; in fact, they usu-ally are already available within the organization's rules and procedures. Nonprogrammed decisions, however, require developing new courses of action that will meet the company's needs. For decisions made under conditions of high uncertainty, managers may develop only one or two custom solutions that will satisfice for handling the problem. However, studies find that limiting the search for alter-natives is a primary cause of decision failure in organizations.[46]

Decision alternatives can be thought of as tools for reducing the difference between the organization's current and desired performance. Smart managers tap into the knowledge of people throughout the organization, and sometimes even outside the organization, for decision alternatives. Rob McEwen, the chair-man and CEO of Canadian mining group Goldcorp, knew that the company's Red Lake site could be a huge moneymaker. A nearby mine was thriving. The problem was that no one could pin-point where to find the high-grade ore at Red Lake. McEwen cre-ated the Goldcorp Challenge, putting Red Lake's closely guarded topographic data online and offering $575,000 in prize money to anyone who could identify rich drill sites. More than 1,400 techni-cal experts in 50 countries offered alternatives to the problem, and two teams working together in Australia pinpointed locations that have made Red Lake one of the world's richest gold mines.[47]

CONCEPT CONNECTION Reid Carr, founder and CEO of San Diego–based Red Door Interactive, Inc., a firm that manages clients' online presence, involves his staff throughout the decision-making process. Carr believes that when **developing, selecting, and implementing alternatives**, managers should "decide slowly and collaboratively so that you have the best plan produced by those who are tasked with execution. Then, let them execute." Red Door's annual "Start, Stop, and Keep" survey is one way that Carr gathers feedback. It asks employees to suggest which internal processes and practices should be introduced, continued, or discontinued.

6.3d Selection of the Desired Alternative

Once feasible alternatives are developed, one must be selected. In this stage, managers try to select the most promising of several alternative courses of action. The best alternative solution is the one that best fits the overall goals and values of the organiza-tion and achieves the desired results using the fewest resources.[48] Managers want to select the choice with the least amount of risk and uncertainty. Because some risk is inherent for most

Courtesy of Red Door Interactive

EXHIBIT 6.4   Decision Alternatives with Different Levels of Risk

In each of the following situations, which alternative would you choose?	
You're the coach of a college football team and in the final seconds of a game with the team's archrival, you face a choice:	1. Choose a play that has a 95 percent chance of producing a tie score; OR 2. Go for a play that has a 30 percent chance of victory but will lead to certain defeat if it fails.
As president of a Canadian manufacturing company, you face a decision about building a new factory. You can:	1. Build a plant in Canada that has a 90 percent chance of producing a modest return on investment; OR 2. Build a plant in a foreign country that has an unstable political history. This alternative has a 40 percent chance of failing, but the returns will be enormous if it succeeds.
It's your senior year, and it is time to decide your next move. Here are the alternatives you're considering:	1. Go to medical school and become a physician, a career in which you are 80 percent likely to succeed; OR 2. Follow your dreams and be an actor, even though the opportunity for success is only around 20 percent.

nonprogrammed decisions, managers try to gauge the prospects for success. They might rely on their intuition and experience to estimate whether a given course of action is likely to succeed. Basing choices on overall goals and values can also guide the selection of alternatives.

Choosing among alternatives also depends on managers' personality factors and willingness to accept risk and uncertainty. **Risk propensity** is the willingness to undertake risk with the opportunity of gaining an increased payoff. For example, Facebook would never have reached more than a billion users without Mark Zuckerberg's "move fast, break things" mind-set. Motivational posters with that slogan are papered all around the company to prevent delay from too much analysis of alternatives. Rather than running controlled beta versions of new technologies to identify the best alternative, Facebook runs a never-ending series of on-the-fly experiments with real users. Even employees who haven't finished their six-week training program are encouraged to work on the live site. That risky approach means that the whole site crashes occasionally, but Zuckerberg says, "The faster we learn, the better we're going to get to the model of where we should be."[49] The level of risk that a manager is willing to accept will influence the analysis of the costs and benefits to be derived from any decision. Consider the situations in Exhibit 6.4. In each situation, which alternative would you choose? A person with a low risk propensity would tend to take ensured moderate returns by going for a tie score, building a domestic plant, or pursuing a career as a physician. A risk taker would go for the victory, build a plant in a foreign country, or embark on an acting career.

6.3e Implementation of the Chosen Alternative

The **implementation** stage involves the use of managerial, administrative, and persuasive abilities to ensure that the chosen alternative is carried out. This step is similar to the idea of strategy execution described in Chapter 5. The ultimate success of the chosen alternative depends on whether it can be translated into action. Sometimes an alternative never becomes reality because managers lack the resources or energy needed to make things happen, or they have failed to involve people and achieve buy-in for the decision. Successful implementation may require discussion, trust building, and active engagement with people affected by the decision. Communication, motivation, and leadership skills must be used to see that the decision is carried out.[50] When employees see that managers follow up on their decisions by tracking implementation success, they are more committed to positive action.

6.3f Evaluation and Feedback

In the evaluation stage of the decision process, decision makers gather information that tells them how well the decision was implemented and whether it was effective in achieving its goals. The "move fast, break things" approach thrives at Facebook because of rapid feedback. Feedback is important because decision making is an ongoing process. Decision making is not completed when a manager or board of directors votes yes or no. Feedback provides decision makers with information that can precipitate a new decision cycle. The decision may fail, thus generating a new analysis of the problem, evaluation of alternatives, and selection of a new alternative. Many big problems are solved by trying several alternatives in sequence, each providing modest improvement. Feedback is the part of monitoring that assesses whether a new decision needs to be made.

REMEMBER THIS

- Managers face the need to make a decision when they either confront a problem or see an opportunity.
- A **problem** is a situation in which organizational accomplishments have failed to meet established goals.
- An **opportunity** is a situation in which managers see potential organizational accomplishments that exceed current goals.
- The decision-making process typically involves six steps: recognition of the need for a decision, diagnosing causes, developing alternatives, selecting

an alternative, implementing the alternative, and evaluating decision effectiveness.

- **Diagnosis** is the step in which managers analyze underlying causal factors associated with the decision situation.
- Selection of an alternative depends partly on managers' **risk propensity**, or their willingness to undertake risk with the opportunity of gaining an increased payoff.
- The **implementation** step involves using managerial, administrative, and persuasive abilities to translate the chosen alternative into action.

6.4 Personal Decision Framework

Imagine you were a manager at Google, *The New York Times*, an AMC movie theater, or the local public library. How would you go about making important decisions that might shape the future of your department or company? So far in this chapter, we have discussed a number of factors that affect how managers make decisions. For example, decisions may be programmed or nonprogrammed, situations are characterized by various levels of uncertainty,

EXHIBIT 6.5 Personal Decision Framework

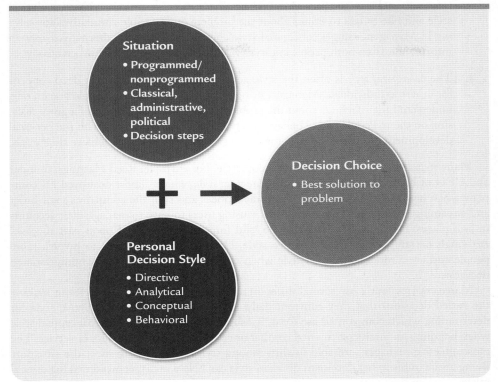

SOURCES: Based on A. J. Rowe, J. D. Boulgaides, and M. R. McGrath, *Managerial Decision Making* (Chicago: Science Research Associates, 1984); and Alan J. Rowe and Richard O. Mason, *Managing with Style: A Guide to Understanding, Assessing, and Improving Your Decision Making* (San Francisco: Jossey-Bass, 1987).

and managers may use the classical, administrative, or political model of decision making. In addition, the decision-making process follows six recognized steps.

However, not all managers go about making decisions in the same way. In fact, significant differences distinguish the ways in which individual managers may approach problems and make decisions concerning them. These differences can be explained by the concept of personal **decision styles**. Exhibit 6.5 illustrates the role of personal styles in the decision-making process. Personal decision styles refer to distinctions among people with respect to how they evaluate problems, generate alternatives, and make choices. Research has identified four major decision styles: directive, analytical, conceptual, and behavioral.[51]

1. The *directive style* is used by people who prefer simple, clear-cut solutions to problems. Managers who use this style often make decisions quickly because they do not like to deal with a lot of information and may consider only one or two alternatives. People who prefer the directive style generally are efficient and rational and prefer to rely on existing rules or procedures for making decisions.

2. Managers with an *analytical style* like to consider complex solutions based on as much data as they can gather. These individuals carefully consider alternatives and often base their decisions on objective, rational data from management control systems and other sources. They search for the best possible decision based on the information available.

3. People who tend toward a *conceptual style* also like to consider a broad amount of information. However, they are more socially oriented than those with an analytical style and like to talk to others about the problem and possible alternatives for solving it. Managers using a conceptual style consider many broad alternatives, rely on information from both people and systems, and like to solve problems creatively.

4. The *behavioral style* is often the style adopted by managers having a deep concern for others as individuals. Managers using this style like to talk to people one on one, understand their feelings about the problem, and consider the effect of a given decision on them. People with a behavioral style usually are concerned with the personal development of others and may make decisions that help others achieve their goals.

Many managers have a dominant decision style. For example, Reed Hastings, founder and CEO of Netflix, seems to prefer the directive style, which almost destroyed his company when he made the quick decision to raise prices and split the company's mail-order and streaming businesses at the same time, causing users to have to manage their accounts in two places. Hastings said later that he "slid into arrogance based upon past success." Although he still often uses a directive style, Hastings has since tried to involve more people and use a more conceptual style when making highly important nonprogrammed decisions.[52]

Managers frequently use several different styles or a combination of styles in making the varied decisions that they confront daily. A manager might use a directive style for determining which company to use for office supplies, yet shift to a more conceptual style when handling an interdepartmental conflict or considering a new product or service. The most effective managers are able to shift among styles as needed to meet the situation. Being aware of his or her dominant decision style can help a manager avoid making critical mistakes when the usual style may be inappropriate to the problem at hand.

REMEMBER THIS

- A manager's personal decision style influences how he or she makes decisions.

- **Decision styles** are differences among people with respect to how they perceive problems and make choices.

- Four major decision styles are directive, analytical, conceptual, and behavioral.

- Most experienced managers use a variety of styles depending on the decision situation.

6.5 Why Do Managers Make Bad Decisions?

To learn more about how you make decisions, go to the Self-Learning on pages 256, which evaluates your personal decision style.

Managers are faced with a relentless demand for decisions, from solving minor problems to implementing major strategic changes. Even the best manager will make mistakes, but managers can increase their percentage of good decisions by understanding some of the factors that cause people to make bad ones. Most bad decisions are errors in judgment that originate in the human mind's limited capacity and in the natural biases managers display during decision making. Answer the questions in the "Director's Toolkit" on page 251 to learn how biases can affect decisions and choices. Are you aware of biases that cloud your judgment when you make decisions and solve problems? Awareness of the following six biases can help managers make more enlightened choices.[53]

1. ***Being influenced by initial impressions.*** When considering decisions, the mind often gives disproportionate weight to the first information that it receives. These initial impressions, statistics, and estimates act as an anchor to our subsequent thoughts and judgments. Anchors can be as simple as a random comment by a colleague or a statistic read in a newspaper. Past events and trends also act as anchors. For example, in business, managers frequently look at the previous year's sales when estimating sales for the coming year. Giving too much weight to the past can lead to poor forecasts and misguided decisions.

2. ***Justifying past decisions.*** Many managers fall into the trap of making choices that justify their past decisions, even if those decisions no longer seem valid. One common example is when a manager continues to pour money into a failing project, hoping to turn things around. This is sometimes referred to as the *sunk cost effect*. Managers often stick with a decision because they've invested a lot of resources in it, even though they'd be better off cutting their losses and moving on.[54] One study of product development found that managers who initiate a new product are much more likely to continue funding it despite evidence that it is failing.[55] Behavioral science research by Daniel Kahneman and others shows that people typically respond more strongly to potential loss, referred to as *loss aversion*, than to expected gain. People hate to lose, so they continue to support a flawed decision in an effort to justify or correct the past.

3. ***Seeing what you want to see.*** People frequently look for information that supports their existing instinct or point of view and avoid information that contradicts it.

This bias affects where managers look for information, as well as how they interpret the information that they find. People tend to give too much weight to supporting information and too little to information that conflicts with their established viewpoints. For example, managers at Tokyo Electric Power Company (Tepco) have been accused of delaying for too long the decision to use seawater to cool nuclear reactors at Fukushima Daiichi following the 2011 Japan earthquake and tsunami. Tepco managers knew that seawater would destroy the reactors, so they gave greater weight to information that supported their decision to delay its use, emphasizing that they were "taking the safety of the whole plant into consideration" in judging the appropriate timing to use seawater in the cool down efforts. Unfortunately, it took an explosion at the plant to convince managers that using seawater was essential to control the overheating of the reactors.[56]

4. ***Perpetuating the status quo.*** Managers may base decisions on what has worked in the past and fail to explore new options, dig for additional information, or investigate new technologies. For example, GM stuck with its strategic decision to offer a multitude of brands long after there was clear evidence that trying to cover the whole range of the auto market was paving the way to disaster. The strategy started to fray in the 1970s with increased competition from Japanese automakers and spikes in oil prices. Yet, as late as February 2008, managers were saying that talk about killing brands was "not a thoughtful discussion." Only bankruptcy and a forced restructuring finally pushed managers to cut GM's brands from eight down to four.[57]

Justin Sullivan/Getty Images

CONCEPT CONNECTION   Despite its phenomenal success, Facebook has been soundly criticized for a number of missteps and mistakes by the organization's leaders, including founder Mark Zuckerberg. Many critics attribute Zuckerberg's lapses in good judgment to his **overconfidence** and the fact that he surrounds himself with board members who may not always question his decisions as thoroughly as they should.

5. ***Being influenced by emotions.*** If you've ever made a decision when you were angry, upset, or even ecstatic, you might already know the danger of being influenced by emotions. A recent study of traders in London investment banks found that effective regulation of emotions was a characteristic of higher-performing traders. Lower-performing traders were less effective in managing and modulating their emotional responses.[58] Another finding is that doctors make less effective decisions when they feel emotions of like or dislike for a patient. If they like a patient, they are less likely to prescribe a painful procedure. If they feel dislike, they may blame the patient for the condition and provide less treatment.[59] Unfortunately, some managers let their emotions influence their decisions on a regular basis. There is some evidence that when people make poor decisions under the influence of strong emotions (such as firing off an angry e-mail message), they tend to continue to make poor decisions because it becomes part of the mind's blueprint for how to behave.[60] Managers make better decisions when—to the extent possible—they take emotions out of the decision-making process.

6. ***Overconfidence.*** Most people overestimate their ability to predict uncertain outcomes. The managers at a fast-food chain were sure that low employee turnover was a key driver of customer satisfaction and store profitability, so they decided to invest in programs to keep employees happy. However, when they analyzed store data, they found that some locations with high turnover were highly profitable, while some with low turnover were struggling.[61] Overconfidence can be particularly dangerous when making risky decisions. Consider how overconfidence contributed to decisions at JPMorgan Chase's chief investment office, made by the so-called London Whale, which led to a multibillion-dollar loss. All banks take risks, but JPMorgan was praised for not taking the kind of outsized risks that many banks took during the mortgage boom—and that contributed to the collapse of the U.S. economy. After the Wall Street crisis, JPMorgan's CEO, Jamie Dimon, was called "the world's most important banker," and his top executives were hailed as a management team that could seemingly do no wrong. The company's chief investment office in London, which was created to protect the bank from volatility caused by complex global financial transactions, gained a reputation for its trading prowess. The unit was a star performer and became a profit center for JPMorgan at a time when industry earnings were under pressure. But managers got overconfident of their ability to spot and manage risks. They began taking larger and larger gambles, including involvement in a highly complicated trading strategy involving derivatives—similar in some ways to the risks that led to the Wall Street crisis. The strategy backfired, eventually causing a loss of almost $6 billion, leading to the firing of several key executives, and damaging the reputation of both the bank and its CEO. Moreover, federal investigators were looking into potential fraud, suspecting that some traders improperly marked their trades to obscure the magnitude of the losses.[62]

Director's Toolkit

Do Biases Influence Your Decision Making?

All of us have biases, but most of us have a hard time see-ing our own. What biases influence your decisions and solutions to problems? Answer the following questions to get an idea of the difficulties and mistakes that likely await you as a new manager.

1. A piece of paper is folded in half, in half again, etc. After 100 folds, how thick will it be? Take your best guess: _____. I am 90 percent sure that the cor-rect answer lies between _____ and _____.

2. Which figure below is most different from the others?

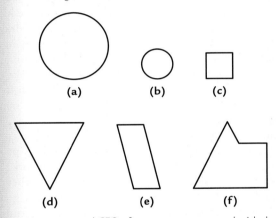

3. As owner and CEO of your company, you decided to invest $100 million to build pilotless drones that cannot be detected by enemy radar. When the project is 90 percent complete, a competing firm begins marketing a completed drone that cannot be detected by radar. In addition, their drone is much faster, smaller, cheaper, and more sophisticated than the drone that your company is developing. The question is: Should you invest the last 10 percent of the research funds to finish your drone? Check one of the following answers.

_____ No; there is no reason to continue spending money on the project.

_____ Yes; after investing $90 million, we might as well finish the project.

4. Give a quick (five-second) estimate of the follow-ing product without actually calculating it:

$8 \times 7 \times 6 \times 5 \times 4 \times 3 \times 2 \times 1 =$ _____.

5. Robert is envious, stubborn, critical, impulsive, industrious, and intelligent. In general, how emo-tional do you think Robert is? (Circle one number.)

Not emotional   1 2 3 4 5 6 7 8 9   Extremely
at all   emotional

6. Which would you choose between the two alter-natives below?

_____ Alternative A: A 50 percent chance of gaining $1,000

_____ Alternative B: A sure gain of $500

Which would you choose between the two alter-natives below?

_____ Alternative C: A 50 percent chance of losing $1,000

_____ Alternative D: A sure loss of $500

After you have specified an answer to each problem, you will find the answers and a description of the potential related bias on page 261.

SOURCES: Questions 1 and 3–6 are from research studies reviewed in Scott Plous, *The Psychology of Judgment and Decision Making* (Philadelphia: Temple University Press, 1993); question 2 is based on an item in the *Creativity in Action Newsletter*, as reported in Arthur B. VanGundy, *Idea Power: Techniques & Resources to Unleash the Creativity in Your Organization* (New York: AMACOM, 1992).

REMEMBER THIS

- Being aware of biases that cloud judgment helps managers avoid decision traps and make better decisions.
- Biases to watch out for include being influenced by initial impressions, trying to correct or justify past flawed decisions, seeing only what you want to see, perpetuating the status quo, being influenced by emotions, and being overconfident.

6.6 Innovative Decision Making

The ability to make fast, widely supported, high-quality decisions on a frequent basis is a critical skill in today's fast-moving organizations.[63] Considering that managers are under pressure to decide quickly, and that biases creep in and cloud judgment, how do managers ever make good decisions? Some innovative techniques can help managers watch out for and avoid mistakes caused by cognitive biases. It is difficult for most managers to see their own biases, but they can build in mechanisms that neutralize or reduce bias-related decision errors at the organizational level.[64]

6.6a Start with Brainstorming

Brainstorming uses a face-to-face interactive group to spontaneously suggest as many ideas as possible for solving a problem. Brainstorming has been found to be highly effective for quickly generating a wide range of alternatives, but it does have some drawbacks.[65] For one thing, people in a group often want to conform to what others are saying. Others may be concerned about pleasing the boss or impressing colleagues. In addition, many creative people simply have social inhibitions that limit their participation or make it difficult to come up with ideas in a group setting. In fact, one study found that when four people are asked to "brainstorm" individually, they typically come up with twice as many ideas as a group of four brainstorming together.

One recent approach, electronic brainstorming, takes advantage of the group approach while overcoming some disadvantages. Electronic brainstorming brings people together in an interactive group over a computer network.[66] One member writes an idea, another reads it and adds other ideas, and so on. Studies show that electronic brainstorming generates about 40 percent more ideas than individuals brainstorming alone, and 25 to 200 percent more ideas than regular brainstorming groups, depending on group size.[67] The approach is anonymous, so it circumvents possible social inhibitions and also allows people to write down their ideas immediately, avoiding the possibility that a good idea might slip away while the person is waiting for a chance to speak in a face-to-face group. Another advantage is that electronic brainstorming can potentially be done with groups made up of employees from around the world, further increasing the diversity of alternatives.

Flying Colours/Digital Vision/Jupiter Images

CONCEPT CONNECTION **Brainstorming** has its share of critics. Some say that it prevents the quiet people from participating, and that a group can be too easily influenced by the emotions of some of the dominant players. In response, a number of brainstorming alternatives have been developed. In fact, some companies bring in certified trainers to teach employees how to use new methods such as the Six Thinking Hats, Lateral Thinking, Nominal Group Technique, Ideation, and more.

6.6b Use Hard Evidence

Using hard evidence can help take emotion out of the decision-making process, keep people from relying on faulty assumptions, and prevent managers from "seeing what they want to see," as described previously. **Evidence-based decision making** means a commitment to make more informed and intelligent decisions based on the best available facts and evidence. It means being alert to potential biases and seeking and examining the evidence with rigor. To keep emotion from clouding their judgment regarding patient care, for example, doctors in the Partners Health Care System incorporate the use of clinical decision support systems based on reams of data about what works and what doesn't.[68] Managers practice evidence-based decision making by being careful and thoughtful rather than carelessly relying on assumptions, past experience, rules of thumb, or intuition.[69] After catastrophic errors in the airline industry where pilots relied solely on their personal experience, many airlines now use a process called crew resource management (CRM) that has revolutionized safety practices. CRM teaches every member of the crew to conduct brief sessions where they update each other about flight status, the current environment, and any impending challenges or safety concerns. Pilots are trained to appropriately act on issues raised by any crew member.[70]

A recent study by Erik Brynjolfsson, an economist at the Sloan School of Management at the Massachusetts Institute of Technology (MIT), supports the idea that organizational decisions can be improved with the use of evidence-based decision making. Brynjolfsson and his colleagues studied 179 large companies and found that the ones that have adopted data-driven decision making achieved productivity that was 5 to 6 percent higher than could be explained by any other factors.[71]

6.6c Engage in Rigorous Debate

Good managers recognize that constructive conflict based on divergent points of view can bring a problem into focus, clarify people's ideas, stimulate creative thinking, limit the role of bias, create a broader understanding of issues and alternatives, and improve decision quality.[72] As described previously, Reed Hastings, CEO of Netflix, is trying to build rigorous debate into the decision-making process to avoid another calamity such as the one that the company experienced following the decision to both increase the price of the service and

Director's Toolkit

Eileen Fisher Inc.

Making women's clothes that are beautiful, elegant, and easy to wear is no simple task, and Eileen Fisher started designing and selling back in the 1980s, basing her clothing on Japanese lines and on the mix-and-match quality of her childhood Catholic school uniforms.

When her company lost its way, in the late 1990s, when she saw both a "need for structure" and "insufficient joy and well-being," she hired Pace University management professor Susan Schor as a consultant, who was later convinced to join the company full-time.

Schor implemented what she'd been teaching: flatter hierarchy and maximum employee engagement. Any meeting was held in a circle, with teams taking on certain tasks. The company facilitated employees taking over as leaders in various situations. For example, a problem needed solving, so all the key people would get in one room (in a circle), with a leader/facilitator, who helped the group ideate/generate ideas, then figure out who will run with which solutions, and who's going to help this solution move forward. It's seen as "holding the space for the team to find." And every employee is encouraged to contribute, regardless of their position or expertise.

Part of Eileen Fisher's ethos is environmental friendliness, and there is a director of sustainability, to keep the company's products and processes green. Fifty percent of its cotton comes from Organic, pesticide-free farms, with nontoxic dyes. It has partnered with organizations such as TakePart, a global entertainment company whose mission is social change and responsible for documentaries such as "An Inconvenient Truth," and "Food Inc."

It's hard to argue with success. Eileen Fisher now has 68 stores, with 60 percent of its sales coming from department stores (such as Bloomingdale's, Neiman Marcus, Nordstrom, etc.), and it has grown to over 1,200 employees with $452 million revenue. Everyone in the company has ownership of the process and the outcomes, as profit-sharing further helps employees remain engaged. Twenty-nine percent of profits are given to the workers. In 2013, each person received about 11 weeks of salary as their profit-sharing bonus. Not bad for a bunch of circles.

SOURCES: Susan Schor, personal communication, February 2015; Company News, Morning Call, January 11, 2015, A8; Janet Malcolm, "Nobody's Looking at You," *The New Yorker*, September 23, 2013, 52–63.

split Netflix into two separate businesses. By using rigorous debate about major decisions, Hastings has gotten Netflix back on the right track—gaining rather than losing customers.[73]

Stimulating rigorous debate can be done in several ways. One way is by ensuring that the group is diverse in terms of age and gender, functional area of expertise, hierarchical level, and experience with the business. Some groups assign a **devil's advocate**, who has the role of challenging the assumptions and assertions made by the group.[74] The devil's advocate may force the group to rethink its approach to the problem and avoid reaching premature conclusions. Jeffrey McKeever, CEO of MicroAge, often plays the devil's advocate, changing his position in the middle of a debate to ensure that other executives don't just go along with his opinions.[75] Still another way to encourage constructive conflict is to use a technique called **point–counterpoint**, which breaks a decision-making group into two subgroups and assigns them different, often competing, responsibilities.[76] The groups then develop and exchange proposals and discuss and debate the various options until they arrive at a common set of understandings and recommendations.

Another way to think of debate might be gentler, with less competition, but still getting widely disparate input. Consider how Eileen Fisher, Inc. makes its decisions, as shown in the Director's Toolkit.

6.6d Avoid Groupthink

It is important for managers to remember that a certain amount of disagreement and conflict is much healthier than blind agreement. Pressures for conformity exist in almost any group, and particularly when people in a group like one another, they tend to avoid anything that might create disharmony. **Groupthink** refers to the tendency of people in groups to suppress contrary opinions. When people slip into groupthink, the desire for harmony outweighs concerns over decision quality. Group members emphasize maintaining unity rather than realistically challenging problems and alternatives. People censor their personal opinions and are reluctant to criticize the opinions of others.[77]

Author and scholar Jerry Harvey coined the related term *Abilene paradox* to illustrate the hidden pressures for conformity that can exist in groups.[78] Harvey tells the story of how members of his extended family sat sweltering on the porch in 104-degree heat in a small town about 50 miles from Abilene, Texas. When someone suggested driving to a café in Abilene, everyone went along with the idea, even though the car was not air conditioned. Everyone was miserable and returned home exhausted and irritable. Later, each person admitted that they hadn't wanted to make the trip and thought it was a ridiculous idea. They only went because they thought the others wanted to go. Because groupthink is such a natural and pervasive challenge to group decision making, some experts recommend using an expert *decision coach* to provide hands-on help and feedback so that people can learn and practice new behaviors rather than revert to the default behavior of suppressing opinions that are contrary to the group.[79]

6.6e Know When to Bail

In a fast-paced environment, good managers encourage risk taking and learning from mistakes, but they also aren't hesitant to pull the plug on something that isn't working. Research has found that managers and organizations often continue to invest time and money in a solution even when there is strong evidence that it is not appropriate. This tendency is referred to as **escalating commitment**. Managers might block or distort negative information because they don't want to be responsible for a bad decision, or they might simply refuse to accept that their solution is wrong.[80] A study in Europe verified that even highly successful managers often miss or ignore warning signals because they become committed to a decision and believe that if they persevere, it will pay off.[81] As companies

"The most dangerous thing is to be successful. You then think every decision is the right one."

—Wong Wai Ming, CFO of Lenovo

face increasing competition, complexity, and change, it is important that managers don't get so attached to their own ideas that they're unwilling to recognize when to move on. According to Stanford University professor Robert Sutton, the key to successful creative decision making is to "fail early, fail often, and pull the plug early."[82]

6.6f Do a Postmortem

To improve decision making, managers need to reflect and learn from every decision they make. When people review the results of their decisions, they learn valuable lessons for how to do things better in the future. A technique that many companies have adopted from the U.S. Army to encourage examination of the evidence and continuous learning is the **after-action review**, a disciplined procedure whereby managers invest time in reviewing the results of decisions on a regular basis and learn from them.[83] After implementation of any significant decision, managers meet to evaluate what worked, what didn't, and how to do things better. Many problems are solved by trial and error. For example, postmortem reviews of decisions regarding attacks from roadside bombs in Iraq led soldiers to suggest the implementation of an overall counterinsurgency strategy rather than relying so much on technology.[84] Numerous business organizations have adopted some form of after-action review. A similar technique emphasized by Lenovo founder Liu Chuanzhi is called *fu pan*, which means "replaying the chessboard." The idea is to review every move to improve the next one. Lenovo managers are trained to apply *fu pan* to everything from a small quick review of a workday incident to a full, in-depth review of a major decision.[85] When managers get prompt feedback on decisions through after-action reviews, it gives them the chance to incorporate new information and greater understanding into their thinking and decision making.

REMEMBER THIS

- Most decisions within organizations are made as part of a group, and whereas managers can't always see their own biases, they can build in mechanisms to prevent bias from influencing major decisions at the organizational level.

- **Brainstorming** is a technique that uses a face-to-face group to spontaneously suggest a broad range of alternatives for making a decision.

- **Electronic brainstorming** brings people together in an interactive group over a computer network, rather than meeting face to face.

- **Evidence-based decision making** is founded on a commitment to examining potential biases, seeking and examining evidence with rigor, and making informed and intelligent decisions based on the best available facts and evidence.

- A **devil's advocate** is a person who is assigned the role of challenging the assumptions and assertions made by the group to prevent premature consensus.

- A group decision-making technique that breaks people into subgroups and assigns them to express competing points of view regarding the decision is called **point–counterpoint**.

- **Groupthink** refers to the tendency of people in groups to suppress contrary opinions in a desire for harmony.

- **Escalating commitment** refers to continuing to invest time and money in a decision despite evidence that it is failing.

- A technique adopted from the U.S. Army, the **after-action review** is a disciplined procedure whereby managers review the results of decisions to evaluate what worked, what didn't, and how to do things better.

- Managers at Lenovo apply a technique called *fu pan*, which means "replaying the chessboard," reviewing every move to improve the next one.

CHAPTER 6 **DISCUSSION QUESTIONS**

1. Aaron Alexis, the former navy reservist who went on a shooting rampage in September 2013 and killed 12 people at the Washington Navy Yard in Washington D.C., had a history of mental instability, but he was carrying a valid security clearance. How would you suggest managers make decisions for issuing or revoking security clearances to prevent this kind of catastrophe?

2. Managers at Gap Inc., formerly one of the top retail chains, are reported to have made a series of decisions that hurt the company: They expanded so rapidly that the chain lost touch with customers; they tried to copy the successful approach of rivals rather than charting their own course; they cut quality to reduce costs; they shifted from one fashion approach to another as each one failed to appeal to customers, and so on. What techniques would you recommend Gap managers use to improve the quality of their decisions?

3. Explain the difference between risk and ambiguity. How might decision making differ for a risky versus an ambiguous situation?

4. Analyze three decisions you made over the past six months. Which of these were programmed and which were nonprogrammed? Which model—the classical, administrative, or political—best describes the approach you took to making each decision?

5. What opportunities and potential problems are posed by the formation of more than one coalition within an organization, each one advocating a different direction or alternative? What steps can you take as a manager to make sure that dueling coalitions result in constructive discussion rather than dissension?

6. Can you think of a bad decision from your own school or work experience, or from recent business or political news stories, that was made in an effort to correct or justify a past decision? As a new manager, how might you resist the urge to choose a decision alternative based on the idea that it might correct or validate a previous decision?

7. Experts advise that most catastrophes in organizations result from a series of small problems or mistakes. As a new, entry-level manager, how might you apply this understanding to help your organization avoid making major mistakes?

8. List some possible advantages and disadvantages to using computer technology for managerial decision making.

9. Can intuition and evidence-based decision making coexist as valid approaches within an organization? How might managers combine their intuition with a rational, data-driven, evidence-based approach?

10. What do you think is your dominant decision style? Is your style compatible with group techniques such as brainstorming and engaging in rigorous debate? Discuss.

SELF LEARNING

What's Your Personal Decision Style?[86]

Read each of the following questions and circle the answer that best describes you. Think about how you typically act in a work or school situation and mark the answer that first comes to mind. There are no right or wrong answers.

1. In performing my job or class work, I look for
   a. Practical results
   b. The best solution
   c. Creative approaches or ideas
   d. Good working conditions

2. I enjoy jobs that
   a. Are technical and well defined
   b. Have a lot of variety
   c. Allow me to be independent and creative
   d. Involve working closely with others

3. The people I most enjoy working with are
   a. Energetic and ambitious
   b. Capable and organized
   c. Open to new ideas
   d. Agreeable and trusting

4. When I have a problem, I usually
   a. Rely on what has worked in the past
   b. Apply careful analysis
   c. Consider a variety of creative approaches
   d. Seek consensus with others

5. I am especially good at
   a. Remembering dates and facts
   b. Solving complex problems
   c. Seeing many possible solutions
   d. Getting along with others

6. When I don't have much time, I
   a. Make decisions and act quickly
   b. Follow established plans or priorities
   c. Take my time and refuse to be pressured
   d. Ask others for guidance and support

7. In social situations, I generally
   a. Talk to others
   b. Think about what's being discussed
   c. Observe
   d. Listen to the conversation

8. Other people consider me
   a. Aggressive
   b. Disciplined
   c. Creative
   d. Supportive

9. What I dislike most is
   a. Not being in control
   b. Doing boring work
   c. Following rules
   d. Being rejected by others

10. The decisions I make are usually
    a. Direct and practical
    b. Systematic or abstract
    c. Broad and flexible
    d. Sensitive to others' needs

Scoring and Interpretation

These questions rate your personal decision style, as described in the text and listed in Exhibit 6.5.

Count the number of *a* answers. They provide your *directive* score.

Count the number of *b* answers for your *analytical* score.

The number of *c* answers is your *conceptual* score.

The number of *d* answers is your *behavioral* score.

What is your dominant decision style? Are you surprised, or does this result reflect the style that you thought you used most often?

GROUP LEARNING

A New Approach to Making Decisions[87]

Managers are typically effective at focusing on problems and diagnosing what is wrong and how to fix it when they have to make a decision. The typical questions that managers might ask themselves include: What is the problem here? What is the cause of this problem? Why is this problem happening to me? What alternatives do I have? What is the best alternative? How do I implement this alternative?

There is a novel approach to decision making, called *outcome-directed thinking*, which some managers have learned to use. It focuses on future outcomes and possibilities rather than on the causes of the problem. People tend to feel more positive emotions, have more creative ideas, and experience more optimism about solving a problem when they focus on desired future outcomes rather than on who or what caused the problem.

Step 1. Think of a problem that you have in your life right now, in which something is not what you would like it to be. It could be any problem that you are having at school, home, or work that you would like to solve. Summarize the problem here in a few words:

_____

_____

_____

Step 2. Now write brief answers to the following questions:

A. What outcome do I really want with respect to this problem? (Your answer equals your desired result about the problem.)

_____

_____

_____

_____

B.   How will I know when I have achieved this future outcome? (What will I see, hear, and feel?)

_____

_____

_____

_____

C.   What resources do I need to pursue this future outcome?

_____

_____

_____

_____

D.   What is the first step I can take to achieve this outcome?

_____

_____

_____

_____

Step 3. In a group of three to five students, take turns sharing your answers to these four questions. In addition, share what you are feeling about your desired outcome for the problem. For example, do you feel that you have created the beginning of a solution that you can implement? In addition, share whether your thinking is more creative and effective by focusing on achieving a desired outcome rather than on the cause of the problem.

ACTION LEARNING

1.   Think about two times when you made decisions, one that had a positive outcome and one that did not turn out so well.

2.   Fill out the following table.

What decision did you have to make?	Decision #1 (positive outcome)	Decision #2 (negative outcome)			
Was the decision programmed or nonprogrammed?					
Was there certainty or uncertainty?					
Did you use your intuition?					
Did you build a coalition?					
Did you engage in any bad decision behaviors, such as defending previous decisions, being too emotional, unduly influenced by initial impressions, etc.?					
Did you explore different alternatives?					
Did you use evidence-based thinking?					
Did you consult a devil's advocate?					

3.   What differences do you see in the two decision-making situations?

4.   What can you learn from this on how to more effectively make decisions in the future?

ETHICAL DILEMMA

The No-Show Consultant[88]

Jeffrey Moses was facing one of the toughest decisions of his short career as a manager with International Consulting. Andrew Carpenter, one of his best consultants, was clearly in trouble, and his problems were affecting his work. International Consulting designs, installs, and implements complex back-office software systems for companies all over the world. About half the consultants work out of the main office, while the rest, including Carpenter, work primarily from home.

This Monday morning, Moses had gotten an irate call from a major New York client saying that Carpenter never showed up at the company's headquarters, where the client had been expecting his new computer system to go live for the first time. In calling around to other customers on the East Coast trying to locate the missing consultant, Moses heard other stories. Carpenter had also missed a few other appointments—all on Monday mornings—but no one had felt the need to report it because he had called to reschedule. In addition, he practically came to blows with an employee who challenged him about the capabilities of the new system, and he inexplicably walked out of one customer's office in the middle of the day, without a word to anyone. Another client reported that the last time he saw Carpenter, he appeared to have a serious hangover. Most of the clients liked Carpenter, but they were concerned that his behavior was increasingly erratic. One client suggested that she would prefer to work with someone else. As for the major New York customer, he preferred that Andrew finish the project rather than a new consultant, but he also demanded that International eat half the $250,000 consultant's fee.

After Moses finally located Carpenter by calling his next-door neighbor, Carpenter confessed that he'd had a "lost weekend" and been too drunk to get on the plane. He then told Moses that his wife had left and taken their two-year-old son with her. He admitted that he had been drinking a little more than usual lately, but insisted that he was getting himself under control and promised no more problems. "I'm really not an alcoholic or anything," he said. "I've just been upset about Brenda leaving, and I let it get out of hand this weekend." Moses told Carpenter that if he would get to New York and complete the project, all would be forgiven.

Now, however, he wondered whether he should really just let things slide. Moses talked to Carpenter's team leader about the situation and was told that the leader was aware of his recent problems but thought everything would smooth itself over. "Consultants with his knowledge, level of skill, and willingness to travel are hard to find. He's well liked among all the customers; he'll get his act together." However, when Moses discussed the problem with Carolyn Walter, vice president of operations, she argued that Carpenter should be dismissed. "You're under no obligation to keep him just because you said you would," she pointed out. "This was a major screw-up, and it's perfectly legal to fire someone for absenteeism. Your calls to customers should make it clear to you that this situation was not a one-time thing. Get rid of him now before things get worse. If you think eating half that $250,000 fee hurts now, just think what could happen if this behavior continues."

What Would You Do?

1. Give Carpenter a month's notice and terminate him. He's known as a good consultant, so he probably won't have any trouble finding a new job, and you'll avoid any further problems associated with his emotional difficulties and his possible alcohol problem.

2. Let it slide. Missing the New York appointment is Carpenter's first big mistake. He says he is getting things under control, and you believe that he should be given a chance to get himself back on track.

3. Let Carpenter know that you care about what he's going through, but insist that he take a short paid leave and get counseling to deal with his emotional difficulties and evaluate the seriousness of his problems with alcohol. If the alcohol abuse continues, require him to attend a treatment program or find another job.

CASE FOR CRITICAL ANALYSIS

The Office

Krista Acklen was the "golden girl" of metropolitan government in a large midwestern city. The top graduate of a local high school, she studied in France and interned at *Vogue* in Paris before returning to the States to get an MBA, and she landed a position with a top New York PR firm. She knew *everyone*, and chatting with or "doing lunch" with the rich and famous was a normal day for Acklen.

The only child of a single mom, Acklen dropped it all and willingly returned to her midwestern hometown when her mother's health declined suddenly. She had barely settled in and established home care for her mother when the mayor's office contacted her with a job proposal. Would Acklen consider a position developing and directing a public arts program for the city? She enthusiastically accepted the job. With her winning connections, drive, and abilities, she quickly expanded her mission to develop a range of arts programs. Donations and grant money poured into programs under her established nonprofit organization developed to support city parks. Headquarters for Acklen and her staff was a comfortable, unused third-floor space in the city library that used to hold books and magazines that were now stored digitally.

Then John Mitchell, director of parks and recreation, summoned her to a meeting "to learn of a decision I have made that will affect your group." Acklen was curious to find out what was going on. Knowing that budget factors recently forced reduction in staff and office space throughout city government, and aware of the importance of dealing carefully with public opinion, as well as the feelings of employees and other stakeholders, Acklen felt that she was prepared for any decision Mitchell might have reached.

She tried to get comfortable in the chair across from Mitchell, who seemed ill at ease. Avoiding small talk, Mitchell said that he intentionally did not discuss the decision in advance because he believed Acklen would object. He would not accept her objections anyway, he indicated, so the decision was final.

"What is the decision?" asked Acklen.

"The mayor wants half of your group's office space for the Greenways project," Mitchell replied, "and I see no alternative except for you to agree. Her idea makes sense, and you must go along."

Acklen felt fury rising in her chest as she stared at Mitchell while thinking, "This people-pleasing, brown-nosing jerk. He will do anything to win the mayor's favor."

The Greenways project, directed by Lisa Todd, had developed a number of beautiful areas throughout the city. In recent years, Greenways had received the bulk of new money and attention from the federal government, and Todd's staff had grown with the additional funding and development projects.

As Acklen regained her composure, she shot back at Mitchell, "Not consulting me on this is unacceptable. I should be part of any decision affecting my staff and program. I could have helped plan a solution that worked for everyone." Mitchell started to speak, but Acklen cut him off. "You have a responsibility to my group, as well as to Mayor Simpson and the other projects of this city. I think you are giving us the shaft as an easy way to please her."

The two argued a while longer, but Mitchell wouldn't budge. Finally, Acklen said, "John, since this was your decision, you should be the one to tell my people. You better come over soon before the word gets out."

"No," Mitchell said, "you are their immediate boss. You have to tell them. That's your job. Where is your team spirit, anyway?"

Acklen returned to her office, seething, and vented about the problem to Joanne Franklin, her most senior employee. "Oh no," Joanne moaned. "We really need all this space. Our program is growing, too."

Acklen agreed, but she explained Mitchell's support of the suggestion from the mayor's office to make additional office space available to Lisa Todd and her staff. Joanne started brainstorming. "I suppose we could pair up in the offices."

Acklen shook her head. "We *are* team players. But John Mitchell and the mayor need to know that this was not handled in a way that shows respect for our employees." After a pause, she continued, "I'm too frazzled to think about it anymore today. Let's talk about this tomorrow."

Questions

1. What mistakes do you think John Mitchell made with the way he solved the problem of limited office space? Explain.

2. What approach would you have used if you were Mitchell? Why?

3. What are Krista Acklen's options for responding to Mitchell's decision? What should she do now? Why?

ANSWERS TO QUESTIONS IN "DIRECTOR'S TOOLKIT"

1. The answer is unbelievably huge: roughly 800,000,000,000,000 times the distance between the Earth and the Sun. Your mind was likely anchored in the thinness of a sheet of paper, thereby leading you to dramatically underestimate the effect of doubling the thickness 100 times. Initial mental anchoring to a low or high point leads to frequent incorrect solutions. How certain did you feel about your answer? This is an example of *overconfidence*, a major cause of manager mistakes.

2. Every figure is different in some way. Figure (a) has the greatest area, (b) has the least area, (c) is the only square, (d) is the only three-sided figure, (e) is most narrow and lopsided, and (f) is least symmetrical and five-sided. Did you stop after finding one correct answer? *Failure to go beyond initial impressions and dig below the surface* often prevents managers from understanding what the real problem is or identifying the correct or best solution.

3. If you checked "yes," you felt the desire to continue investing in a previous decision even when it was failing, which is called *escalating commitment*. This is a mistake that many managers make because they are *emotionally attached* to the previous decision, even one as hopeless as this inadequate drone.

4. The median estimate from students is 2,250. When the numbers are given in reverse order starting with 1×2, etc., the median estimate is 512. The correct answer is 40,320. The *order in which information is presented* makes a difference to a person's solution, and acting quickly produces an answer that is far from correct.

5. When judging people, early information has more impact than later information, called the *primacy effect*. Reversing the word sequence so that *intelligent* and *industrious* come first creates a more favorable impression. Respondents rate Robert more or less emotional depending on the order of the descriptive words. Were you guilty of rating Robert as more emotional because of being *influenced by initial impressions*?

6. Although the options are numerically equivalent, most people choose alternatives B and C. People hate losing more than they enjoy winning, and hence about 80 percent choose a sure small gain (B), and 70 percent will take more risk in the hope of avoiding a loss (C). *Taking emotions out of the process* typically leads to better decisions.

ON THE JOB
VIDEO CASES

Mi Ola Swimwear: Managerial Decision Making

Questions

1. What role does an advisory board play in this business owner's approach to decision making? If you were a business owner, would you want to develop an advisory board?

2. After listening to this entrepreneur's perspective on decision making, how would you categorize her decision-making style? Include at least two examples that support your choice.

3. Customer feedback is an important part of this entrepreneur's decision-making process. Referring to the innovative decision-making techniques described at the end of the chapter, how would you categorize "getting feedback"? Why is feedback valuable in decision making?

ENDNOTES

1. Monica Davey and Mary Williams Walsh, "Billions in Debt, Detroit Tumbles into Insolvency," *The New York Times*, July 18, 2013, http://www.nytimes.com/2013/07/19/us/detroit-files-for-bankruptcy.html?pagewanted=all (accessed September 19, 2013); Nathan Bomey and John Gallagher, "How Detroit Went Broke: The Answers May Surprise You—and Don't Blame Coleman Young," *Detroit Free Press*, September 18, 2013, http://www.freep.com/interactive/article/20130915/NEWS01/130801004/Detroit-Bankruptcy-history-1950-debt-pension-revenue (accessed September 19, 2013); Monica Davey and Mary Williams Walsh, "For Detroit, a Crisis Born of Bad Decisions and Crossed Fingers," *The New York Times*, March 12, 2013, A1.

2. Danielle Sacks, "Blown Away," *Fast Company* (February 2011): 58–65, 104.

3. Colum Murphy, James T. Areddy, and James R. Hagerty, "Deal Gone Wrong Adds to Caterpillar's Troubles in China," *The Wall Street Journal*, January 21, 2013, http://online.wsj.com/article/SB10001424127887323301104578255740261180404.html (accessed August 29, 2013).

4. See Stephen J. Sauer, "Why Bossy Is Better for Rookie Managers," *Harvard Business Review* (May 2012): 30; and Kenneth R. Brousseau et al., "The Seasoned Executive's Decision-Making Style," *Harvard Business Review* (February 2006): 110–121, for a discussion of how decision-making behavior evolves as managers progress in their careers.

5. Herbert A. Simon, *The New Science of Management Decision* (Englewood Cliffs, NJ: Prentice Hall, 1977), p. 47.

6. Paul J. H. Schoemaker and J. Edward Russo, "A Pyramid of Decision Approaches," *California Management Review* (Fall 1993): 9–31.

7. Adam Lashinsky, "Boeing Bets Big On the 707," Segment of "The Greatest Business Decisions of All Time" book excerpt, *Fortune* (October 8, 2012): 178–184.

8. Samuel Eilon, "Structuring Unstructured Decisions," *Omega* 13 (1985): 369–377; and Max H. Bazerman, *Judgment in Managerial Decision Making* (New York: Wiley, 1986).

9. Jon Birger, "How This Man Took Priceline From Dot-Bomb to Highflier," *Fortune* (September 24, 2012): 128–134.

10. James G. March and Zur Shapira, "Managerial Perspectives on Risk and Risk Taking," *Management Science* 33 (1987): 1404–1418; and Inga Skromme Baird and Howard Thomas, "Toward a Contingency Model of Strategic Risk Taking," *Academy of Management Review* 10 (1985): 230–243.

11. Example reported in Leslie Kwoh, "Memo to Staff: Take More Risks" (Theory & Practice column), *The Wall Street Journal*, March 20, 2013, B8.

12. Hugh Courtney, "Decision-Driven Scenarios for Assessing Four Levels of Uncertainty," *Strategy & Leadership* 31, no. 1 (2003): 14–22.

13. Reported in David Leonhardt, "This Fed Chief May Yet Get a Honeymoon," *The New York Times*, August 23, 2006.

14. Brooks Barnes, "'Oz the Great and Powerful' Has Big Opening," *The New York Times*, March 10, 2013, http://artsbeat.blogs.nytimes.com/2013/03/10/oz-the-great-and-powerful-has-big-opening/ (accessed September 20, 2013); and Brooks Barnes, "One More Trip to Land of Oz," *The New York Times*, March 3, 2013, http://www.nytimes.com/2013/03/04/business/media/disney-gambles-on-box-office-wizardry-of-oz.html?pagewanted=all (accessed March 4, 2013).

15. Angie Han, "Four of the 50 Biggest Box Office Bombs Are in Theaters Right Now," *Film* Web site, August 22, 2013, http://www.slashfilm.com/four-of-the-fifty-biggest-box-office-bombs-are-in-theaters-right-now/ (accessed September 20, 2013); and Adam Davidson, "When You Wish Upon 'Ishtar': How Does the Film Industry Actually Make Money?" *The New York Times Magazine* (July 1, 2012): 16–17.

16. Michael Masuch and Perry LaPotin, "Beyond Garbage Cans: An AI Model of Organizational Choice," *Administrative Science Quarterly* 34 (1989): 38–67; and Richard L. Daft and Robert H. Lengel, "Organizational Information Requirements, Media Richness and Structural Design," *Management Science* 32 (1986): 554–571.

17. Peter C. Cairo, David L. Dotlich, and Stephen H. Rhinesmith, "Embracing Ambiguity," *The Conference Board Review* (Summer 2009): 56–61; John C. Camillus, "Strategy as a Wicked Problem," *Harvard Business Review* (May 2008): 98–106; and Richard O. Mason and Ian I. Mitroff, *Challenging Strategic Planning Assumptions* (New York: Wiley Interscience, 1981).

18. Howard Schneider, "University Logos Become Weapons in Debate over Textile Factory Working Conditions," *The Washington Post*, May 27, 2013, http://articles.washingtonpost.com/2013-05-27/business/39558590_1_university-logos-nike-adidas (accessed August 26, 2013); and Jens Hansegard, Tripti Lahiri, and Christina Passariello, "Retailers' Dilemma: To Ax or Help Fix Bad Factories," *The Wall Street Journal*, May 28, 2013, http://online.wsj.com/article/SB10001424127887323336104578501143973731324.html (accessed May 30, 2013).

19. "How Companies Make Good Decisions: McKinsey Global Survey Results," *The McKinsey Quarterly*, January 2009, www.mckinseyquarterly.com (accessed February 3, 2009).

20. Thomas H. Davenport and Jeanne G. Harris, "Automated Decision Making Comes of Age," *MIT Sloan Management Review* (Summer 2005): 83–89; and Stacie McCullough, "On the Front Lines," *CIO* (October 15, 1999): 78–81.

21. These examples are from Steve Lohr, "The Age of Big Data," *The New York Times*, February 12, 2012, SR1.

22. Herbert A. Simon, *The New Science of Management Decision* (New York: Harper & Row, 1960), pp. 5–6; and Amitai Etzioni, "Humble Decision Making," *Harvard Business Review* (July–August 1989): 122–126.

23. James G. March and Herbert A. Simon, *Organizations* (New York: Wiley, 1958).

24. Herbert A. Simon, *Models of Man* (New York: Wiley, 1957), pp. 196–205; and Herbert A. Simon, *Administrative Behavior*, 2nd ed. (New York: Free Press, 1957).

25. Rachel Dodes, "Targeting Younger Buyers, Liz Claiborne Hits a Snag," *The Wall Street Journal*, August 16, 2010, A1.

26. Weston H. Agor, "The Logic of Intuition: How Top Executives Make Important Decisions," *Organizational Dynamics* 14 (Winter 1986): 5–18; and Herbert A. Simon, "Making Management Decisions: The Role of Intuition and Emotion," *Academy of Management Executive* 1 (1987): 57–64. For a recent review of research, see Erik Dane and Michael G. Pratt, "Exploring Intuition and Its Role in Managerial Decision Making," *Academy of Management Review* 32, no. 1 (2007): 33–54.

27. David A. Kaplan, "How Intel Got Consumers to Love Its Chips," segment of "The Greatest Business Decisions of All Time" book excerpt, *Fortune* (October 8, 2012): 178–184.

28. See Gary Klein, *Intuition at Work: Why Developing Your Gut Instincts Will Make You Better at What You Do* (New York: Doubleday, 2002); Kurt Matzler, Franz Bailom, and Todd A. Mooradian, "Intuitive Decision Making," *MIT Sloan Management Review* 49, no. 1 (Fall 2007): 13–15; Malcolm Gladwell, *Blink: The Power of Thinking Without Thinking* (New York: Little Brown, 2005); and Sharon Begley, "Follow Your Intuition: The Unconscious You May Be the Wiser Half," *The Wall Street Journal*, August 30, 2002.

29. Benedict Carey, "Hunches Prove to Be Valuable Assets in Battle," *The New York Times*, July 28, 2009.

30. Jaana Woiceshyn, "Lessons from 'Good Minds': How CEOs Use Intuition, Analysis, and Guiding Principles to Make Strategic Decisions," *Long-Range Planning* 42 (2009): 298–319; Ann Hensman and Eugene Sadler-Smith, "Intuitive Decision Making in Banking and Finance," *European Management Journal* 29 (2011): 51–66; Eugene Sadler-Smith and Erella Shefy, "The Intuitive Executive: Understanding and Applying 'Gut Feel' in Decision-making," *Academy of Management Executive* 18, no. 4 (November 2004): 76–91.

31. Mandeep K. Dhami and Mary E. Thomson, "On the Relevance of Cognitive Continuum Theory and Quasirationality for Understanding Management Judgment and Decision Making," *European Management Journal* 30 (2012): 316–326.

32. Dhami and Thomson, "On the Relevance of Cognitive Continuum Theory"; C. Chet Miller and R. Duane Ireland, "Intuition in Strategic Decision Making: Friend or Foe in the Fast-Paced 21st Century?" *Academy of Management Executive* 19, no. 1 (2005): 19–30; Eric Bonabeau, "Don't Trust Your Gut," *Harvard Business Review* (May 2003): 116ff; Sadler-Smith and Shefy, "The Intuitive Executive"; Simon, "Making Management Decisions"; and Ann Langley, "Between 'Paralysis by Analysis' and 'Extinction by Instinct,'" *Sloan Management Review* (Spring 1995): 63–76.

33. This discussion is based on Stephen Friedman and James K. Sebenius, "Organizational Transformation: The Quiet Role of Coalitional Leadership," *Ivey Business Journal* (January–February 2009): 1ff; Gerald R. Ferris et al., "Political Skill in Organizations," *Journal of Management* (June 2007): 290–320; and William B. Stevenson, Jon L. Pierce, and Lyman W. Porter, "The Concept of 'Coalition' in Organization Theory and Research," *Academy of Management Review* 10 (1985): 256–268.

34. McKinsey Survey, "How Companies Make Good Decisions."

35. Ronald A. Gill, "Quality-Oriented Teamwork Resolves Aerospace Manufacturer's Critical Path Tooling Crisis," *Global Business and Organizational Excellence* (September–October 2012): 34–41.

36. Dion Nissenbaum, "Cut Defense? A Fight Begins," *The Wall Street Journal*, April 23, 2013, B1.

37. George T. Doran and Jack Gunn, "Decision Making in High-Tech Firms: Perspectives of Three Executives," *Business Horizons* (November–December 2002): 7–16.

38. Gill, "Quality-Oriented Teamwork."

39. James W. Fredrickson, "Effects of Decision Motive and Organizational Performance Level on Strategic Decision Processes," *Academy of Management Journal* 28 (1985): 821–843; James W. Fredrickson, "The Comprehensiveness of Strategic Decision Processes: Extension, Observations, Future Directions," *Academy of Management Journal* 27 (1984): 445–466; James W. Dean, Jr., and Mark P. Sharfman, "Procedural Rationality in the Strategic Decision-Making Process," *Journal of Management Studies* 30, no. 4 (July 1993): 587–610; Nandini Rajagopalan, Abdul M. A. Rasheed, and Deepak K. Datta, "Strategic Decision Processes: Critical Review and Future Directions," *Journal of Management* 19, no. 2 (1993): 349–384; and Paul J. H. Schoemaker, "Strategic Decisions in Organizations: Rational and Behavioral Views," *Journal of Management Studies* 30, no. 1 (January 1993): 107–129.

40. Marjorie A. Lyles and Howard Thomas, "Strategic Problem Formulation: Biases and Assumptions Embedded in Alternative Decision-Making Models," *Journal of Management Studies* 25 (1988): 131–145; and Susan E. Jackson and Jane E. Dutton, "Discerning Threats and Opportunities," *Administrative Science Quarterly* 33 (1988): 370–387.

41. Richard L. Daft, Juhani Sormumen, and Don Parks, "Chief Executive Scanning, Environmental Characteristics, and Company Performance: An Empirical Study" (unpublished manuscript, Texas A&M University, 1988).

42. Cecilia Kang, "Google Crunches Data on Munching in Office," *The Washington Post*, September 1, 2013, http://articles.washingtonpost.com/2013-09-01/business/41670762_1_laszlo-bock-last-year-google-data (accessed September 21, 2013).

43. Daniel Burrus and John David Mann, "Whatever Your Problem … That's Not Likely to Be Your Real Problem," *Leadership Excellence* (February 2011): 7–8.

44. Charles H. Kepner and Benjamin B. Tregoe, *The Rational Manager* (New York: McGraw-Hill, 1965).

45. Based on Burrus and Mann, "Whatever Your Problem …"; and Jonathan Taplin, "How To … Turn a Bad idea into a Good Idea," *Fast Company* (February 2013): 20.

46. Paul C. Nutt, "Expanding the Search for Alternatives During Strategic Decision Making," *Academy of Management Executive* 18, no. 4 (2004): 13–28; and P. C. Nutt, "Surprising but True: Half the Decisions in Organizations Fail," *Academy of Management Executive* 13, no. 4 (1999): 75–90.

47. Olivier Leclerc and Mihnea Moldoveanu, "Five Routes to More Innovative Problem Solving," *McKinsey Quarterly* (April 2013), http://www.mckinsey.com/insights/strategy/five_routes_to_more_innovative_problem_solving (accessed May 14, 2013).

48. Peter Mayer, "A Surprisingly Simple Way to Make Better Decisions," *Executive Female* (March–April 1995): 13–14; and Ralph L. Keeney, "Creativity in Decision Making with Value-Focused Thinking," *Sloan Management Review* (Summer 1994): 33–41.

49. Ashlee Vance, "The Making of 1 Billion Users," *Bloomberg Businessweek* (October 4, 2012), http://www.businessweek.com/articles/2012-10-04/facebook-the-making-of-1-billion-users (accessed September 21, 2013).

50. Paul J. H. Schoemaker, Steve Krupp, and Samantha Howland, "Strategic Leadership: The Essential Skills," *Harvard Business Review* (January–February 2013): 131–134; and Mark McNeilly, "Gathering Information for Strategic Decisions, Routinely," *Strategy & Leadership* 30, no. 5 (2002): 29–34.

51. Based on A. J. Rowe, J. D. Boulgaides, and M. R. McGrath, *Managerial Decision Making* (Chicago: Science Research Associates, 1984); and Alan J. Rowe and Richard O. Mason, *Managing with Style: A Guide to Understanding, Assessing, and Improving Your Decision Making* (San Francisco: Jossey-Bass, 1987).

52. James B. Stewart, "Netflix Looks Back on Its Near-Death Spiral," *The New York Times*, April 26, 2013, http://www.nytimes.com/2013/04/27/business/netflix-looks-back-on-its-near-death-spiral.html?pagewanted=all&_r=0 (accessed April 27, 2013).

53. This section is based on John S. Hammond, Ralph L. Keeney, and Howard Raiffa, *Smart Choices: A Practical Guide to Making Better Decisions* (Boston: Harvard Business School Press, 1999); Max H. Bazerman and Dolly Chugh, "Decisions Without Blinders," *Harvard Business Review* (January 2006): 88–97; J. S. Hammond, R. L. Keeney, and H. Raiffa, "The Hidden Traps in Decision Making," *Harvard Business Review* (September–October 1998): 47–58; Oren Harari, "The Thomas Lawson Syndrome," *Management Review* (February 1994): 58–61; Dan Ariely, "Q&A: Why Good CIOs Make Bad Decisions," *CIO* (May 1, 2003): 83–87; Leigh Buchanan, "How to Take Risks in a Time of Anxiety," *Inc.* (May 2003): 76–81; Max H. Bazerman, *Judgment in Managerial Decision Making*, 5th ed. (New York: John Wiley & Sons, 2002).

54. James Surowiecki, "The Financial Page: That Sunk-Cost Feeling," *The New Yorker* (January 21, 2013): 24; and Dustin J. Sleesman et al., "Cleaning Up the Big Muddy: A Meta-Analytic Review of the Determinants of Escalation of Commitment," *Academy of Management Journal* 55, no. 3 (2012): 541–562.

55. J. B. Schmidt and R. J. Calantone, "Escalation of Commitment during New Product Development," *Journal of the Academy of Marketing Science* 30, no. 2 (2002): 103–118.

56. Norihiko Shirouzu, Phred Dvorak, Yuka Hayashi, and Andrew Morse, "Bid to 'Protect Assets' Slowed Reactor Fight," *The Wall Street Journal*, March 19, 2011, http://online.wsj.com/article/SB1000142405274870460850457620 7912642629904.html (accessed August 6, 2012).

57. John D. Stoll, Kevin Helliker, and Neil E. Boudette, "A Saga of Decline and Denial," *The Wall Street Journal*, June 2, 2009.

58. Mark Fenton-O'Creevy et al., "Thinking, Feeling, and Deciding: The influence of Emotions on the Decision Making and Performance of Traders," *Journal of Organizational Behavior* 32 (2011): 1044–1061.

59. Example from Jerome Groopman, *How Doctors Think* (New York: Houghton Mifflin, 2007).

60. Dan Ariely, "The Long-Term Effects of Short-Term Emotions," *Harvard Business Review* (January–February 2010): 38.

61. David Larcker and Brian Tayan study, reported in Michael J. Mauboussin, "The True Measures of Success," *Harvard Business Review* (October 2012): 46–56.

62. Jessica Silver-Greenberg, "New Fraud Inquiry as JPMorgan's Loss Mounts," *The New York Times*, July 13, 2012, http://dealbook.nytimes.com/2012/07/13/jpmorgan-says-traders-obscured-losses-in-first-quarter/ (accessed August 7, 2012); Ben Protess et al., "In JPMorgan Chase Trading Bet, Its Confidence Yields to Loss," *The New York Times*, May 11, 2012, http://dealbook.nytimes.com/2012/05/11/in-jpmorgan-chase-trading-bet-its-confidence-yields-to-loss/ (accessed May 15, 2012); Peter Eavis and Susanne Craig, "The Bet That Blew up for JPMorgan Chase," *The New York Times*, May 11, 2012, http://dealbook.nytimes.com/2012/05/11/the-bet-that-blew-up-for-jpmorgan-chase/ (accessed May 15, 2012); and Jessica Silver-Greenberg and Nelson D. Schwartz, "Red Flags Said to Go Unheeded by Bosses at JPMorgan," *The New York Times*, May 14, 2012, http://dealbook.nytimes.com/2012/05/14/warnings-said-to-go-unheeded-by-chase-bosses/ (accessed May 15, 2012).

63. Kathleen M. Eisenhardt, "Strategy as Strategic Decision Making," *Sloan Management Review* (Spring 1999): 65–72.

64. Daniel Kahneman, Dan Lovallo, and Olivier Sibony, "Before You Make That Big Decision," *Harvard Business Review* (June 2011): 50–60.

65. Josh Hyatt, "Where the Best—and Worst—Ideas Come From" (a brief synopsis of "Idea Generation and the Quality of the Best Idea," by Karen Girotra, Christian Terwiesch, and Karl T. Ulrich), *MIT Sloan Management Review* (Summer 2008): 11–12; and Robert C. Litchfield, "Brainstorming Reconsidered: A Goal-Based View," *Academy of Management Review* 33, no. 3 (2008): 649–668.

66. R. B. Gallupe et al., "Blocking Electronic Brainstorms," *Journal of Applied Psychology* 79 (1994): 77–86; R. B. Gallupe and W. H. Cooper, "Brainstorming Electronically," *Sloan Management Review* (Fall 1993): 27–36; and Alison Stein Wellner, "A Perfect Brainstorm," *Inc.* (October 2003): 31–35.

67. Wellner, "A Perfect Brainstorm"; Gallupe and Cooper, "Brainstorming Electronically."

68. Example from Thomas H. Davenport and Brook Manville, "From the Judgment of Leadership to the Leadership of Judgment: The Fallacy of Heroic Decision Making," *Leader to Leader* (Fall 2012): 26–31.

69. This section is based on Jeffrey Pfeffer and Robert I. Sutton, "Evidence-Based Management," *Harvard Business Review* (January 2006), 62–74; Rosemary Stewart,

Evidence-Based Decision Making (Radcliffe Publishing, 2002); and Joshua Klayman, Richard P. Larrick, and Chip Heath, "Organizational Repairs," *Across the Board* (February 2000), 26–31.

70. Stephen H. Courtright, Greg L. Stewart, and Marcia M. Ward, "Applying Research to Save Lives: Learning from Team Training Approaches in Aviation and Health Care," *Organizational Dynamics* 41 (2012): 291–301.

71. Study by Erik Brynjolfsson, Lorin Hitt, and Heekyung Kim; results reported in Steve Lohr, "The Age of Big Data," *The New York Times*, February 12, 2012, SR1.

72. Sydney Finkelstein, "Think Again: Good Leaders, Bad Decisions," *Leadership Excellence* (June 2009): 7; "Flaws in Strategic Decision Making: McKinsey Global Survey Results," *The McKinsey Quarterly*, January 2009, www.mckinsey.com; Michael A. Roberto, "Making Difficult Decisions in Turbulent Times," *Ivey Business Journal* (May–June 2003): 1–7; Eisenhardt, "Strategy as Strategic Decision Making"; and David A. Garvin and Michael A. Roberto, "What You Don't Know About Making Decisions," *Harvard Business Review* (September 2001): 108–116.

73. Nick Wingfield and Brian Stelter, "A Juggernaut Stumbles," *The New York Times*, October 25, 2011, B1; and Stewart, "Netflix Looks Back on Its Near-Death Spiral."

74. David M. Schweiger and William R. Sandberg, "The Utilization of Individual Capabilities in Group Approaches to Strategic Decision Making," *Strategic Management Journal* 10 (1989): 31–43; "Avoiding Disasters," sidebar in Paul B. Carroll and Chunka Mui, "7 Ways to Fail Big," *Harvard Business Review* (September 2008): 82–91; and "The Devil's Advocate," *Small Business Report* (December 1987): 38–41.

75. Doran and Gunn, "Decision Making in High-Tech Firms."

76. Garvin and Roberto, "What You Don't Know About Making Decisions."

77. Irving L. Janis, *Groupthink: Psychological Studies of Policy Decisions and Fiascoes*, 2nd ed. (Boston: Houghton Mifflin, 1982); and Shlomo Ben-Hur, Nikolas Kinley, and Karsten Jonsen, "Coaching Executive Teams to Better Decisions," *Journal of Management Development* 31, no. 7 (2012): 711–723.

78. Jerry B. Harvey, "The Abilene Paradox: the Management of Agreement," *Organizational Dynamics* (Summer 1988): 17–43.

79. Ben-Hur, et al., "Coaching Executive Teams to Better Decisions."

80. S. Trevis Certo, Brian L. Connelly, and Laszlo Tihanyi, "Managers and Their Not-So-Rational Decisions," *Business Horizons* 51 (2008): 113–119; and Sleesman et al., "Cleaning Up the Big Muddy."

81. Hans Wissema, "Driving Through Red Lights; How Warning Signals Are Missed or Ignored," *Long Range Planning* 35 (2002): 521–539.

82. Ibid.

83. Thomas E. Ricks, "Army Devises System to Decide What Does, Does Not Work," *The Wall Street Journal*, May 23, 1997, A1; David W. Cannon and Jeffrey McCollum, "Army Medical Department Lessons Learned Program Marks 25th Anniversary," *Military Medicine* (November 2011): 1212–1214.

84. Peter Eisler, Blake Morrison, and Tom Vanden Brook, "Strategy That's Making Iraq Safer Was Snubbed for Years," *USA TODAY*, December 19, 2007.

85. Chuck Salter, "Lenovo: Protect and Attack," *Fast Company* (December 2011–January 2012): 116–121, 154–155.

86. Adapted from Rowe and Mason, *Managing with Style*, pp. 40–41.

87. This approach to decision making was developed by Robert P. Bostrom and Victoria K. Clawson of Bostrom and Associates, Columbia, Missouri, and this exercise is based on a write-up appearing in *Inside USAA*, the company newsletter of the United Services Automobile Association (USAA) (September 11, 1996), pp. 8–10; and Victoria K. Clawson and Robert P. Bostrom, "Research-Driven Facilitation Training for Computer-supported Environments," *Group Decision and Negotiation* 5 (1996): 7–29.

88. Based on information in Jeffrey L. Seglin, "The Savior Complex," *Inc.* (February 1999): 67–69; and Nora Johnson, "'He's Been Beating Me,' She Confided," *Business Ethics* (Summer 2001): 21.

PART 3 INTEGRATIVE CASE

Part Three: Planning

Companies Form Strategic Partnership to Build America's Natural Gas Highway

Consumers face a series of important questions when shopping for a new vehicle: Electric or hybrid? Regular or diesel? Powerful or fuel-efficient? Sporty or economical? Yet for eco-minded consumers who seek the ultimate in green motoring, the decision to purchase a vehicle often comes down to one simple question: Where do I fill it up?

Where to refuel is a perplexing issue for buyers of alternative-fuel vehicles. This is because cutting-edge green vehicles lack a nationwide fueling infrastructure. The United States has more than 100,000 standard gas stations, yet few are equipped to fuel vehicles that run on electricity, natural gas, or biofuel. For most consumers, that's a deal-breaker.

Despite the push for cleaner automobiles, today's car buyers find themselves in a Catch-22: an ecologically responsible vehicle might fit in with their needs and desires, but if there is no place to fill up, they can't drive it, so why consider buying one? A similar dilemma exists for fleet purchasers, automakers, and gas station chains: Why purchase or even manufacture alternative-fuel vehicles if there aren't any filling stations? On the other hand, why build filling stations if no one is purchasing or making alternative-fuel vehicles?

Fortunately for consumers and the environment, Clean Energy Fuels Corp. and Navistar International have a plan to solve this chicken-and-egg dilemma. In 2012, the California alternative fuels provider and the Illinois semi-trailer truck giant announced a strategic partnership to build America's Natural Gas Highway, a first-of-its-kind network of natural gas fueling stations across the United States. Slated for completion in 2014, America's Natural Gas Highway will feature 150 liquefied natural gas (LNG) filling stations in major metropolitan areas across the country—San Diego, Los Angeles, and Las Vegas out west; Houston, San Antonio, and Dallas in the Texas Triangle; New York in the east; and major cities in the Midwest and South. Well-placed stations on in-between routes will tie the whole network together, resulting in a coast-to-coast refueling infrastructure for natural gas vehicles.

Top-level planners behind America's Natural Gas Highway say their goal is to offer transport companies a package deal made up of eco-friendly fleets, inexpensive fuel, and reliable fueling stations. "Navistar and Clean Energy have come up with a breakthrough program that offers customers a quicker payback on their investment, plus added fuel cost savings from day one of operation," says Navistar CEO Dan Ustian. "Together, our companies will demonstrate how a natural-gas-integrated vehicle offering the right distribution and fueling solution can be integrated into a fleet's operations to reduce costs and drive efficiencies."

For a natural gas highway to work, effective collaboration must occur between a truck maker, a fuel supplier, a truck stop chain, and a natural gas driller. Navistar and Clean Energy have the first two bases covered: Navistar will sell its best-in-class LNG truck fleets to shippers, along with a mandatory five-year fuel-purchase contract through Clean Energy. News releases indicate that two other companies are included in the plan. Pilot Flying J Travel Centers, the largest network of truck and travel stops, is providing service locations where trucks can refuel. Likewise, Chesapeake Energy, the number-two natural gas driller in the United States, has invested $150 million toward the initial rollout. So Navistar sells natural gas trucks to shippers, Clean Energy supplies the fuel, Pilot Flying J provides the fueling stations, and Chesapeake drills natural gas and provides investment capital.

The plan sounds good on paper, but can it work? Clean Energy CEO Andrew Littlefair says that America's Natural Gas Highway is already well underway. "Clean Energy has already engaged over 100 shippers, private fleets, and for-hire carriers that have shared their operations to qualify for the economic opportunity of operating natural gas trucks. This has helped us in turn plan the first phase of the natural gas fueling highway," Littlefair says. Clean Energy's chief marketing guru, Jim Harger, adds that the financial advantages of the plan are such that transport businesses simply can't refuse. "You get the same lease cost of a diesel truck and get fuel savings too," Harger says. These natural gas fuel savings—approximately $1.50 per gallon compared to gasoline or diesel—have led to a sharp increase in the number of natural gas vehicles (NGVs) on the road in the United States. According to Natural Gas Vehicles for America (NGV America), 135,000 NGVs were in use in 2013, up from 120,000 in 2012.

There are many good reasons to think that America's Natural Gas Highway will succeed. However, executives at Navistar and Clean Energy say that their plan will work for one key reason: Natural gas is the energy of the future and requires no government subsidies. "We remain committed to provide natural gas fuel for transportation because it has genuinely proven to be the cleaner, cheaper domestic alternative fuel choice," says Andrew Littlefair. Navistar's chief agrees, adding that natural gas is both economically sustainable and good for the environment. "The program will allow the industry to transition to natural gas-powered vehicles without relying on government handouts," Ustian says. "This is going to work far differently than any other program in this field for alternative fuels. It can stand on its own and stand very tall, and that's why it's going to be successful."

Questions

1. Why do businesses form strategic partnerships? Does the creation of America's Natural Gas Highway require such a partnership? Why or why not?

2. What opportunities in the external environment may have led Navistar and Clean Energy to formulate their plan for America's Natural Gas Highway?

3. What threats in the external environment could cause this comprehensive natural gas strategy to fail? What can managers do to help ensure that the plan is executed successfully?

SOURCES: Based on Clean Energy Fuels Corp., *America's Natural Gas Highway: The Clean Energy Solution* (Seal Beach, CA: Clean Energy, 2012), http://cleanenergyfuels.com/pdf/CE-OS.ANGH.011212.ff.pdf (accessed July 10, 2012); Shan Li, "Firms Investing to Fuel Demand for Natural Gas Vehicles," *The Los Angeles Times*, January 2, 1014, http://www.latimes.com/business/la-fi-natural-gas-stations-20140103,0,5424680.story (accessed January 8, 2014); John Stodder, "Natural Gas Vehicles Face Chicken-and-Egg Syndrome," *The Daily Reporter*, May 9, 2012, http://dailyreporter.com/2012/05/09/natural-gas-vehicles-face-chicken-and-egg-syndrome/ (accessed July 10, 2012); "Navistar International and Clean Energy Fuels Team on Natural Gas Trucks," *Fleets & Fuels*, February 2, 2012, www.fleetsandfuels.com/fuels/ngvs/2012/02/navistar-clean-energy-team-on-natural-gas-trucks-2012/ (accessed July 10, 2012); James Menzies, "Navistar Partnership with Clean Energy Takes Sting Out of Cost of NG-powered Trucks," *Truck News*, February 3, 2012, www.trucknews.com/news/navistar-partnership-with-clean-energy-takes-sting-out-of-cost-of-ng-powered-trucks/1000876051/ (accessed July 12, 2012); Dave Hurst, "Clean Energy Fuels and Navistar Agreement: More Than Marketing Hype?" Pike Research, May 30, 2012, www.pikeresearch.com/blog/clean-energy-fuels-and-navistar-agreement-more-than-marketing-hype (accessed July 12, 2012); Clean Energy Fuels, "Clean Energy Unveils Backbone Network for America's Natural Gas Highway," press release, January 12, 2012, www.businesswire.com/news/home/20120112005432/en/Clean-Energy-Unveils-Backbone-Network-America's-Natural (accessed July 10, 2012); "Clean Energy Unveils Network Plan for Natural Gas Highway," Trucker News Service, January 16, 2012, www.thetrucker.com/News/Stories/2012/1/16/CleanEnergyunveilsnetworkplanfornaturalgashighway.aspx (accessed July 12, 2012).

CHAPTER
7

Designing Organization Structure

LEARNING OUTCOMES

After studying this chapter, you should be able to:

7.1 Discuss the fundamental characteristics of organizing and explain work specialization, chain of command, span of management, and centralization versus decentralization.

7.2 Describe functional and divisional approaches to structure.

7.3 Explain the matrix approach to structure and its application to both domestic and international organizations.

7.4 Describe the contemporary team and virtual network structures and why they are being adopted by organizations.

7.5 Explain why organizations need coordination across departments and hierarchical levels, and describe mechanisms for achieving coordination.

7.6 Identify how structure can be used to achieve an organization's strategic goals.

7.7 Define production technology and explain how it influences organization structure.

Messages

R U Ready 2 B a Manager?

Delivered

Before reading this chapter, please circle either "Mostly True" or "Mostly False" for each of the five questions below.

1 I am comfortable taking on any authority that is given to me.

| Mostly True | Mostly False |

[page 274]

2 I am able to delegate tasks to other people; In other words, I do not hold on with tight control, or distrust of others.

| Mostly True | Mostly False |

[page 276]

3 I am more capable working in an organization with decentralized power and authority coming more from smaller units rather than from top management.

| Mostly True | Mostly False |

[page 278]

4 I think teams are a waste of time in organizations.

| Mostly True | Mostly False |

[page 289]

5 I believe everyone would prefer to work out of their own home and be part of a virtual work team.

| Mostly True | Mostly False |

[page 294]

Valve Software Corporation is a leader in the video game industry, with *Counter-Strike*, *Half-Life 2*, *Left 4 Dead*, *Portal*, and the wildly popular digital distribution platform *Steam*. In September 2013, the *WhatCulture* online magazine (based in the United Kingdom) ranked Gabe Newell, the cofounder of Valve, on its list of the "five richest tech billionaires who dropped out of university." Newell acts as the CEO of Valve, but the company has been "boss free since 1996," as its Web site proclaims. "It's amazing what creative people can come up with when there's nobody there telling them what to do." Valve's unique organization structure caused a minor media blitz after someone posted the employee handbook online in the spring of 2012, but Valve has been functioning smoothly without bosses since it was founded. Newell and cofounder Mike Harrington, both former Microsoft employees, wanted to create a flat, fast organization that allowed employees maximum flexibility. It sounds like a dream for employees, but many people don't adapt to the "no-structure structure" and leave for more traditional jobs.[1]

Could you work in a company with no bosses, no permanent offices, and no clearly defined structure? Valve is unusual, but as we've seen with examples in previous chapters, many companies are flattening their hierarchies and cutting out layers of management to improve efficiency and be more flexible. Some people thrive in less hierarchical, even bossless, organizations, whereas others have difficulty without a clearly defined vertical structure. New managers in particular are typically more comfortable and more effective working in an organization system that is compatible with their leadership beliefs.

In your career as a manager, you will have to understand and learn to work within a variety of structural configurations. All organizations wrestle with the question of structural design, and reorganization often is necessary to reflect a new strategy, changing market conditions, or innovative technology.

In recent years, many companies have realigned departmental groupings, chains of command, and horizontal coordination mechanisms to attain new strategic goals or to cope with a turbulent environment. Walgreens achieved its "7 by 10" goal (meaning to have 7,000 stores by 2010), so managers shifted from a strategy of expansion to a strategy of providing an exceptional customer experience. To support this new strategy, they added two new positions to the hierarchy. In each of its 30 U.S. markets, Walgreens placed a vice president for markets to move corporate leadership closer to the customer. The second new position, community leader, acts as a mentor to less-experienced store managers to help them provide exceptional service.[2] After the disastrous 2010 explosion and oil spill in the Gulf of Mexico, BP embarked on a major restructuring of its exploration, development, and production operations (referred to as "upstream") to try to make sure that a similar event never happens again. To improve risk management, CEO Robert W. Dudley appointed a dedicated chief executive for all of its upstream operations worldwide. In late 2012, following the appointment of H. Lamar McKay to oversee the operations, Dudley said, "During the past two years, we have successfully introduced a more centralized organization to our upstream, BP's largest organizational change for two decades."[3] Michael Dell created a separate division at his company to focus specifically on products such as mobile phones and other portable devices, the fastest-growing part of the computer industry.[4] Each of these organizations is using fundamental concepts of organizing.

Organizing is the deployment of organizational resources to achieve strategic goals. The deployment of resources is reflected in the organization's division of labor into specific departments and jobs, formal lines of authority, and mechanisms for coordinating diverse organization tasks.

Organizing is important because it follows strategy—the topic of Part 3 of this book. Strategy defines *what* to do; organizing defines *how* to do it. Structure is a powerful tool for reaching strategic goals, and a strategy's success often is determined by its fit with organizational structure. Part 4 of this book explains the variety of organizing principles and concepts used by managers. This chapter covers fundamental concepts that apply to all organizations and departments, including organizing the vertical structure and using mechanisms for horizontal coordination. Chapter 9 discusses how organizations can be structured to facilitate innovation and change. Chapter 9 considers how to use human resources (HR) to the best advantage within the organization's structure.

What Are Your Leadership Beliefs?[5]

Instructions: The fit between a new manager and the organization is often based on personal beliefs about the role of leaders. Things work best when organization design matches a new manager's beliefs about his or her leadership role.

Think about the extent to which each statement reflects your beliefs about a leader's role in an organization. Mark as Mostly True the four statements that are most true for you, and mark as Mostly False the four that are least true for you.

	Mostly True	Mostly False
1. A leader should take charge of the group or organization.	_____	_____
2. The major tasks of a leader are to make and communicate decisions.	_____	_____
3. Group and organization members should be loyal to designated leaders.	_____	_____
4. The responsibility for taking risks lies with the leaders.	_____	_____
5. Leaders should foster discussions among members about the future.	_____	_____
6. Successful leaders make everyone's learning their highest priority.	_____	_____
7. An organization needs to be always changing the way it does things to adapt to a changing world.	_____	_____
8. Everyone in an organization should be responsible for accomplishing organizational goals.	_____	_____

Scoring and Interpretation: Each question pertains to one of two subscales of leadership beliefs. Questions 1–4 reflect position-based leadership beliefs. This is the belief that the most competent and loyal people are placed in positions of leadership, where they assume responsibility and authority for the group or organization. Questions 5–8 reflect nonhierarchical leadership beliefs more consistent with a flat or even a bossless design. This belief is that the group or organization faces a complex system of adaptive challenges, and leaders see their job as facilitating the flow of information among members and their full engagement to respond jointly to those challenges. The subscale for which you checked more items Mostly True may reveal your personal beliefs about position-based versus nonhierarchical leadership.

Position-based beliefs typically work for managers in a traditional vertical hierarchy or mechanistic organization. Nonhierarchical beliefs typically work for managers engaged with horizontal organizing, such as managing teams, projects, and networks, or for cutting-edge bossless organizations.

7.1 Organizing the Vertical Structure

The organizing process leads to the creation of organization structure, which defines how tasks are divided and resources deployed. Organization structure is defined as (1) the set of formal tasks assigned to individuals and departments; (2) formal reporting relationships, including lines of authority, decision responsibility, number of hierarchical levels, and span of managers' control; and (3) the design of systems to ensure effective coordination of employees across departments.[6] Ensuring coordination across departments is just as critical as defining the departments to begin with. Without effective coordination systems, no structure is complete.

The set of formal tasks and formal reporting relationships provides a framework for vertical control of the organization. The characteristics of vertical structure are portrayed in the **organization chart**, which is the visual representation of an organization's structure.

A sample organization chart for a water bottling plant is illustrated in Exhibit 7.1. The plant has four major departments—accounting, HR, production, and marketing. The organization chart delineates the chain of command, indicates departmental tasks and how they fit together, and provides order and logic for the organization. Every employee has an appointed task, line of authority, and decision responsibility. The following sections discuss several important features of vertical structure in more detail.

EXHIBIT 7.1 Organization Chart for a Water Bottling Plant

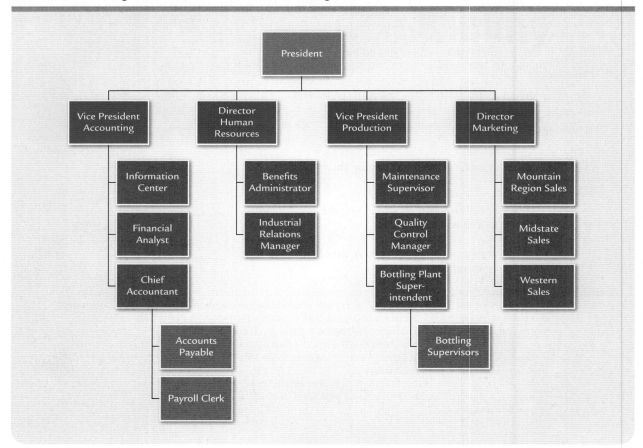

7.1a Work Specialization

Organizations perform a wide variety of tasks. A fundamental principle is that work can be performed more efficiently if employees are allowed to specialize.[7] **Work specialization,** sometimes called *division of labor*, is the degree to which organizational tasks are subdivided into separate jobs. Work specialization in Exhibit 7.1 is illustrated by the separation of production tasks into bottling, quality control, and maintenance. Employees within each department perform only the tasks relevant to their specialized function. When organizations face new strategic issues, managers often create new positions or departments to deal with them. Sony added a new position of chief information security officer (CISO) to its hierarchy after hackers accessed millions of customer files on the supposedly secure Sony network. Many organizations, including Gannett, NBC, Simon & Schuster, Columbia University, and Starbucks, have created chief digital officer (CDO) positions to provide broad leadership for digital-based initiatives, including social business initiatives (as described in Chapter 1). New York City hired its first CDO in 2011, even before many corporations had thought about hiring such executives. At the time, the only other city with a CDO was São Paolo, Brazil.[8] Many organizations didn't even have a chief information officer (CIO) a decade or so ago, but almost every government agency, nonprofit organization, and business firm has a CIO today, and CDOs will likely become just as ubiquitous. In 2009, President Barack Obama appointed Vivek Kundra as the first CIO for the U.S. government.[9]

When work specialization is extensive, employees specialize in a single task. Jobs tend to be small, but they can be performed efficiently. Work specialization is readily visible on an automobile assembly line, where each employee performs the same task over and over again. It would not be efficient to have a single employee build the entire automobile, or even perform a large number of unrelated jobs.

Despite the apparent advantages of specialization, many organizations are moving away from this principle. With too much specialization, employees are isolated and do only a single, boring job. In addition, too much specialization creates separation and hinders the coordination that is essential for organizations to be effective. Many companies are implementing teams and other mechanisms that enhance coordination and provide greater challenge for employees.

REMEMBER THIS

- Managers in every organization face the question about how to organize for maximum efficiency and effectiveness.
- **Organizing** refers to the deployment of organizational resources to achieve strategic goals.
- Organizations such as Simon & Schuster, Starbucks, and the City of New York have created CDO positions to meet changing needs.
- **Organization structure** is defined as the framework in which the organization defines how tasks are divided, resources are deployed, and departments are coordinated.

- An **organization chart** is the visual representation of an organization's structure.
- Fundamental characteristics of vertical organization structure include work specialization, chain of command, span of management, and centralization and decentralization.
- **Work specialization**, sometimes called *division of labor*, is the degree to which organizational tasks are subdivided into individual jobs.

AP Images/Rich Schultz

CONCEPT CONNECTION   Cognizant Technology Solutions Corporation, a U.S.-based outsourcing firm, has an unusual **chain of command** referred to as "two in a box." Originally, project managers supervised company staff in India while living in the United States, where most customers were located. Because spanning that many time zones was difficult, CEO Francisco D'Souza implemented a solution: assign two managers to each project—one in India and one at the client's site. Each is equally responsible for the project's success. The model works because it enhances the company's customer responsiveness, even though it violates the principle of **unity of command**.

An organization's structure is based on authority. As a potential new manager, check out your authority role models by completing the "New Manager Self-Test" on page 275.

7.1b Chain of Command

The **chain of command** is an unbroken line of authority that links all employees in an organization and shows who reports to whom. It is associated with two underlying principles. *Unity of command* means that each employee is held accountable to only one supervisor. The *scalar principle* refers to a clearly defined line of authority in the organization that includes all employees. Authority and responsibility for different tasks should be distinct. All individuals in the organization should know to whom they report, as well as the successive management levels all the way to the top. For example, at Sony, the new CISO reports to the CIO, who reports to the chief transformation officer, who in turn reports to the CEO.[10] In Exhibit 7.1, the payroll clerk reports to the chief accountant, who in turn reports to the vice president, who in turn reports to the company president.

Authority, Responsibility, and Delegation   The chain of command illustrates the authority structure of the organization. **Authority** is the formal and legitimate right of a manager to make decisions, issue orders, and allocate resources to achieve organizationally desired outcomes. Authority is distinguished by three characteristics:[11]

1. Authority is vested in organizational positions, not people. Managers have authority because of the positions they hold, and other people in the same positions would have the same authority.

2. Authority flows down the vertical hierarchy. Positions at the top of the hierarchy are vested with more formal authority than are positions at the bottom.

3. Authority is accepted by subordinates. Although authority flows from the top down, subordinates comply because they believe that managers have a legitimate right to issue orders. The *acceptance theory of authority* argues that a manager has authority only if subordinates choose to accept his or her commands. If subordinates refuse to obey because the order is outside their zone of acceptance, a manager's authority disappears.[12]

Responsibility is the flip side of the authority coin. **Responsibility** is the duty to perform the task or activity as assigned. Typically, managers are assigned authority commensurate with their responsibilities. When managers have responsibility for task outcomes but little authority, the job is possible but difficult. They rely on persuasion and luck. When managers have authority exceeding responsibility, they may become tyrants, using authority to achieve frivolous outcomes.[13]

Accountability is the mechanism through which authority and responsibility are brought into alignment. **Accountability** means that the people with authority and responsibility are subject to reporting and justifying task outcomes to those above them in the chain of command.[14] For organizations to function well, everyone needs to know what they are

NEW MANAGER Self-Test

Authority Role Models

Instructions: Expectations about authority for a new manager are often based on experiences with your first authority figures and role models—Mom and Dad. To understand your authority role models, please answer each of the following items as Mostly True or Mostly False for you. Think about each statement as it applies to the parent or parents who made primary decisions about raising you.

	Mostly True	Mostly False
1. My parent(s) believed that children should get their way in the family as often as the parents do.	_____	_____
2. When a family policy was established, my parent(s) discussed the reasoning behind it with the children.	_____	_____
3. My parent(s) believed that it was for my own good if I was made to conform to what they thought was right.	_____	_____
4. My parent(s) felt that the children should make up our own minds about what we wanted to do, even if they did not agree with us.	_____	_____
5. My parent(s) directed my activities through reasoning and discussion.	_____	_____
6. My parent(s) was clear about who was the boss in the family.	_____	_____
7. My parent(s) allowed me to decide most things for myself without a lot of direction.	_____	_____
8. My parent(s) took the children's opinions into consideration when making family decisions.	_____	_____
9. If I didn't meet parental rules and expectations, I could expect to be punished.	_____	_____

Scoring and Interpretation: Each question pertains to one of three subscales of parental authority. Questions 1, 4, and 7 reflect *permissive* parental authority, questions 2, 5, and 8 indicate *flexible* authority, and questions 3, 6, and 9 indicate *authoritarian* parental authority. The subscale for which you checked more items Mostly True may reveal personal expectations from your early role models that shape your comfort with authority as a new manager. *Authoritarian* expectations typically would fit in a traditional vertical structure with fixed rules and a clear hierarchy of authority (mechanistic organization characteristics). *Flexible* authority expectations typically would fit with horizontal organizing, such as managing teams, projects, and reengineering (organic organization characteristics). Because most organizations thrive on structure, *permissive* expectations may be insufficient to enforce accountability under any structure. How do you think your childhood role models affect your authority expectations? Remember, this questionnaire is just a guide because your current expectations about authority may not directly reflect your childhood experiences.

SOURCE: Adapted from John R. Buri, "Parental Authority Questionnaire," *Journal of Personality and Social Assessment* 57 (1991): 110–119.

accountable for and accept the responsibility and authority for performing it. The British Broadcasting Corporation (BBC) is undergoing structural changes to clarify its chain of command and strengthen management accountability in the wake of a crisis that erupted after the BBC decided not to air a news report about former BBC television personality Jimmy Savile being accused of widespread sexual abuse of children. To make matters worse, the broadcaster got into trouble again by airing a false report that accused a former senior political official of similar offenses. The resulting scandal tarnished the image of the respected broadcaster and left the executive offices of the BBC in turmoil. The director-general resigned after just two months on the job, and two senior executives resigned under pressure while the organization sorted out what went wrong. New director-general Tony Hall emphasized the need to change the culture at the BBC, calling for "greater personal accountability" and a simpler, clearer management structure. Many problems contributed to the crisis, but one was a fuzzy chain of command without clear lines of authority for decision making. After the Savile crisis, the editorial leadership was under extreme pressure, and there was confusion over who had responsibility for the decision to run the story about the senior political official, for instance.[15]

Another important concept related to authority is delegation.[16] Delegation is the process that managers use to transfer authority and responsibility to positions below them in the hierarchy. Most organizations today encourage managers to delegate authority to the lowest possible level to provide maximum flexibility to meet customer needs and adapt to shifts in the environment. Consider how top managers at Meetup.com revived the company by pushing authority and responsibility down to the front lines.

As illustrated by this example, delegating decision making to lower-level managers and employees can be highly motivating and improve speed, flexibility, and creativity. However, many managers find delegation difficult. When managers can't delegate, they undermine the role of their subordinates and prevent people from doing their jobs effectively.

Line and Staff Authority   An important distinction in many organizations is between line authority and staff authority, reflecting whether managers work in line departments or staff departments in the organization's structure. *Line departments* perform tasks that

"I think the most difficult transition for anybody from being a worker bee to a manager is this issue of delegation. What do you give up? How can you have the team do what you would do yourself without you doing it?"

—Tachi Yamada, President of the Bill & Melinda Gates Foundation's Global Health Program

Spotlight on Skills

Meetup.com

Meetup.com is the company known for organizing Howard Dean's presidential campaign in 2004. As an organization that helps other people create organizations, Meetup has been instrumental in setting up local groups for everything from protests to gardening clubs. When Meetup.com went through a period of rapid expansion, top executives implemented a command-and-control structure as a way to regulate and monitor performance. The company even had a "review board" that worked with managers to oversee what employees could and could not do. The trouble was, "productivity went through the floor," says chief technology officer Greg Whalin. One day, a senior manager pulled CEO Scott Heiferman into a conference room and showed him a list of complaints, including "We aren't a creative company" and "I hate the organization chart."

Heiferman decided to go in the opposite direction and push authority and responsibility down to his employees. Now, Meetup's employees have almost total freedom to select the projects they work on and how and when they accomplish them. With the authority and responsibility for setting priorities and making decisions, employee creativity soared. In addition, many people began working harder than ever before. "We got more done in six weeks than in six months last year," said Heiferman.[17]

Green Power

A New Department

SAP created its first-ever chief sustainability officer position in 2009, and Peter Graf, formerly a computer scientist, leads a global team that oversees sustainability initiatives. To change SAP, Graf and his team focused on the top of the hierarchy, educating SAP's board of directors as their first target. Regular e-mails and newsletters to board members defined terminology and answered questions (such as "What does 'offset' mean with regard to sustainability?"). In addition, Graf and his team reminded board members of incidents within SAP's own corporate history, such as the decision by a major German customer to stop ordering SAP software because the company had no sustainability code of conduct.

By the time SAP's board held its next official meeting, members were fully engaged in adopting sustainability policies, speaking with an informed, unified voice as they assisted the new department's efforts to change the sustainability thinking of employees, suppliers, and customers.

SOURCE: Michael S. Hopkins, "How SAP Made the Business Case for Sustainability," *MIT Sloan Management Review* 52, no. 1 (Fall 2010): 69–72.

reflect the organization's primary goal and mission. In a software company, line departments make and sell the product. In an Internet-based company, line departments would be those that develop and manage online offerings and sales. *Staff departments* include all those that provide specialized skills in support of line departments. Staff departments have an advisory relationship with line departments and typically include marketing, labor relations, research, accounting, and HR.

Line authority means that people in management positions have the formal authority to direct and control immediate subordinates. **Staff authority** is narrower and includes the right to advise, recommend, and counsel in the staff specialists' area of expertise. Staff authority is a communication relationship; staff specialists advise managers in technical areas. For example, the finance department of a manufacturing firm would have staff authority to coordinate with line departments about which accounting forms to use to facilitate equipment purchases and standardize payroll services. BP has a new safety department, created in the wake of the BP-Transocean *Deepwater Horizon* oil rig explosion in the Gulf of Mexico that killed 11 crew members and set off an environmental disaster, that advises managers in line departments regarding risk management, agreements with contractors, and other safety-related issues. Unlike many staff specialists, BP's safety unit has broad power to challenge line managers' decisions if it considers them too risky.[18]

To understand the importance of the chain of command and clear lines of authority, responsibility, and delegation, consider the *Deepwater Horizon* oil rig explosion. Activities were so loosely organized that no one seemed to know who was in charge or what their level of authority and responsibility was. When the explosion occurred, confusion reigned. Twenty-three-year-old Andrea Fleytas issued a mayday (distress signal) over the radio when she realized that no one else had done so, but she was chastised for overstepping her authority. One manager said that he didn't call for help because he wasn't sure he had authorization to do so. Still another said that he tried to call to shore but was told that the order needed to come from someone else. Crew members knew that an emergency shutdown needed to be triggered, but there was confusion over who had the authority to give the OK. As fire spread, several minutes passed before people got directions to evacuate. Again, an alarmed Fleytas turned on the public address system and announced that the crew was abandoning the rig. "The scene was very chaotic," said worker Carlos Ramos. "There was no chain of command. Nobody in charge." In the aftermath of the explosion

HOT TOPIC

and oil spill, several federal agencies were also on the hot seat because of loose oversight and confusion over responsibility that led to delays and disagreements that prolonged the suffering of local communities.[19]

7.1c Span of Management

The span of management is the number of employees reporting to a supervisor. Sometimes called the *span of control*, this characteristic of structure determines how closely a supervisor can monitor subordinates. Traditional views of organization design recommended a span of management of about 7 to 10 subordinates per manager. However, many lean organizations today have spans of management as high as 30, 40, and even higher. At PepsiCo, Inc.'s Gamesa cookie operation in Mexico, for instance, employees are trained to keep production running smoothly and are rewarded for quality, teamwork, and productivity. Teams are so productive and efficient that Gamesa factories operate with around 56 subordinates per manager.[20] Research over the past 40 or so years shows that span of management varies widely and that several factors influence the span.[21] Generally, when supervisors must be closely involved with subordinates, the span should be small, and when supervisors need little involvement with subordinates, it can be large. The following list describes the factors that are associated with less supervisor involvement and thus larger spans of control.

Go to the "Ethical Dilemma" on page 309, which pertains to issues of authority, responsibility, and delegation.

- Work performed by subordinates is stable and routine.

- Subordinates perform similar work tasks.

- Subordinates are concentrated in a single location.

- Subordinates are highly trained and need little direction in performing tasks.

- Rules and procedures defining task activities are available.

- Support systems and personnel are available for the manager.

- Little time is required in nonsupervisory activities, such as coordination with other departments or planning.

- Managers' personal preferences and styles favor a large span.

- The average span of control used in an organization determines whether the structure is tall or flat. A **tall structure** has an overall narrow span and more hierarchical levels. A **flat structure** has a wide span, is horizontally dispersed, and has fewer hierarchical levels.

Having too many hierarchical levels and narrow spans of control is a common structural problem for organizations. In a survey conducted for the Conference Board, 72 percent of managers surveyed said that they believed their organizations had too many levels of management.[22] The result may be that routine decisions are made too high in the organization, which pulls higher-level executives away from important, long-range strategic issues and limits the creativity, innovativeness, and accountability of lower-level managers.[23] The trend in recent years has been toward wider spans of control as a way to facilitate delegation.[24]

One recent study found that the span of management for CEOs has doubled over the past two decades, rising from about five to around 10 managers reporting directly to the top executive, with the span of management for those managers also increasing.[25] At the same time, the types of positions in the top team are shifting, with the position of chief operating

EXHIBIT 7.2 **Reorganization to Increase the Span of Management for the President of an International Metals Company**

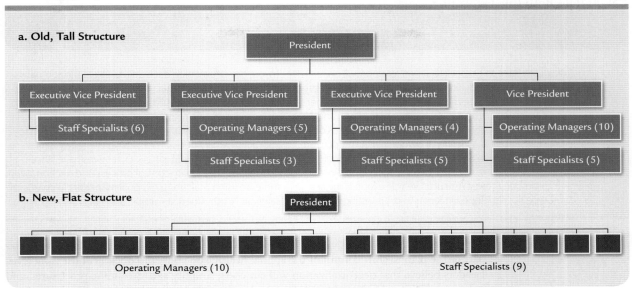

a. Old, Tall Structure

President

Executive Vice President — Staff Specialists (6)

Executive Vice President — Operating Managers (5) / Staff Specialists (3)

Executive Vice President — Operating Managers (4) / Staff Specialists (5)

Vice President — Operating Managers (10) / Staff Specialists (5)

b. New, Flat Structure

President

Operating Managers (10)   Staff Specialists (9)

officer (COO) declining and positions such as CIO or chief marketing officer being added to the top team.[26] A number of factors may influence a top executive's optimum span of control. People who are new to their positions typically want a wider span of control to help them evaluate their executives and learn about more aspects of the business. A CEO who must spend a lot of time interacting directly with customers, partners, or regulators as part of his or her job will need a narrower span of control, allocating more responsibility to direct reports and freeing up more time for external activities, while a CEO involved in a major internal transformation may need a wider span of control to stay on top of what is happening all across the organization.[27] Exhibit 7.2 illustrates how an international metals company was reorganized. The multilevel set of managers shown in panel *a* was replaced with 10 operating managers and nine staff specialists reporting directly to the CEO, as shown in panel *b*. The CEO welcomed this wide span of 19 management subordinates because it fit his style, his management team was top-notch and needed little supervision, and they were all located on the same floor of an office building.

7.1d Centralization and Decentralization

Centralization and decentralization pertain to the hierarchical level at which decisions are made. **Centralization** means that decision authority is located near the top of the organization. With **decentralization**, decision authority is pushed downward to lower organization levels. Organizations may have to experiment to find the correct hierarchical level at which to make decisions. For example, most large school systems are highly centralized. However, a study by William Ouchi found that three large urban school systems that shifted to a decentralized structure (giving school principals and teachers more control over staffing, scheduling, and teaching methods and materials) performed better and more efficiently than centralized systems of similar size.[28] Government leaders in Great Britain hope that the same thing will happen when they decentralize the country's National Health Service (NHS). The system is undergoing the most radical restructuring since it was founded in 1948, with a key

Spotlight on Skills

Toyota

"We didn't have to go back to Japan for approval on everything," said Randy Stephens, the chief engineer at the Toyota Technical Center near Ann Arbor, Michigan, where the new version of the Avalon has been designed and engineered. "We might go back to review the status of the project, but there is a feeling of ownership of this car here."

The new version of the Avalon, designed and engineered in Michigan and built in Kentucky, is being promoted as the company's most American vehicle ever. It is the first prototype not developed in Japan, and it is testing how well

Toyota can decentralize decision making to the company's subsidiaries. Following four years of crisis, Toyota managers have been gradually rebuilding a stronger company, which includes delegating responsibilities more globally.

The company was strongly criticized for its need to coordinate every decision regarding the safety issues and recalls from headquarters. Executives have since overhauled the quality control process and decentralized more decision making to regional managers in charge of safety in North America, Europe, and Asia.[29]

part of the plan to shift control of the annual health care budget to doctors at the local level. Leaders believe that decentralization will cut costs, simplify and streamline procedures, and reduce inefficiency by "putting power in the hands of patients and clinicians."[30]

In the United States and Canada, the trend over the past 30 years has been toward greater decentralization of organizations. Decentralization is believed to relieve the burden on top managers, make greater use of employees' skills and abilities, ensure that decisions are made close to the action by well-informed people, and permit more rapid response to external changes. Stanley McChrystal, former commander of U.S. and North Atlantic Treaty Organization (NATO) forces in Afghanistan, once said, "I learned … that any complex task is best approached by flattening hierarchies. It gets everybody feeling like they're in the inner circle, so that they develop a sense of ownership."[31] Even Japanese companies such as Toyota, which have a strong tradition of centralization, are seeing the power of decentralization for promoting a sense of ownership.

Although many decisions will still rest with executives at headquarters, Toyota has realized that some decisions need to be made close to the action. Regional managers believe that the problems Toyota went through have given top executives the freedom to take risks they might not have taken otherwise.[32]

However, not every organization should decentralize all decisions. Within many companies, there is often a "tug of war between centralization and decentralization," as top executives want to centralize some operations to eliminate duplication while business division managers want to maintain decentralized control.[33] Managers should diagnose the organizational situation and select the decision-making level that will best meet the organization's needs. Factors that typically influence centralization versus decentralization are as follows:

- Greater change and uncertainty in the environment are usually associated with decentralization. A good example of how decentralization can help cope with rapid change and uncertainty occurred following Hurricane Katrina in 2005. Mississippi Power restored power in just 12 days, thanks largely to a decentralized management system that empowered people at the electrical substations to make rapid, on-the-spot decisions.[34] The lightning-quick pace of change in the digital world requires more decentralization, which suits Ben Stiller just fine, as described in the Spotlight on Skills Box.

- The amount of centralization or decentralization should fit the firm's strategy. Google thrived for years with a decentralized approach that allowed creative people to go in their own direction and run their areas as they saw fit. Decentralization

Spotlight on Skills

Ben Stiller/Red Hour Digital

Ben Stiller was at a meeting a while back to try to get him involved in social media, with Facebook and Twitter immediately. Digital strategist Natalie Bruss was trying to show Stiller the benefits of social media when someone else in the room kept asking, "I don't understand, who are the buyers? Who are the buyers?" In the almost four years since his first tweet, Stiller has 4.76 million followers, plus his production company's Red Hour Digital that is producing a Web parody of *The Bachelor* called *Burning Love*, which became a hit for Yahoo and was picked up on E! for a whole year. Red Hour Digital also produced *Stiller and Meara*, in the living room of Stiller's parents, who reprised their old act from the 1960s and 1970s, and was so well-received it ran on Yahoo and later Hulu. Stiller is currently working on an animated series based on *Zoolander,* and other projects.

Though Stiller commands nearly $20 million for a regular movie, he sees the future is digital and has thrown himself into the new media. He loves the freedom and flexibility. As an admitted perfectionist with his films, he works for fluidity in the digital medium, and he has recently partnered with Disney Studios to get a wider reach. An added draw for him is the decentralization that allows him maximum creativity. Gone are the well-covered fights he had with Fox when he was doing *the Ben Stiller Show.* On the Web he can "do what you want to do and have this very pure creative thing." Plus there is synergy with his film work. He was working on *The Secret Life of Walter Mitty* in 2012 and cast someone from one of his web series.

What's unusual about Red Hour Digital is that it began in 2009, when the rest of Hollywood thought YouTube was strictly for amateurs and filmmaker wannabees. Because of his forward thinking, Stiller is a leader and has integrated the new medium into his other work. "Digital is now a pillar of what Ben Stiller does," says WME's Chris Jacquemin.

SOURCES: "CMO Today," *Wall Street Journal*, June 23, 2014, B5; (anonymous) "The Secret (Tech) Life of Ben Stiller," *FastCompany*, April 2013, p. 82; Nicole LaPorte, "The Rebels Saving Hollywood," *FastCompany*, April 2013, 76–86 and 112–113.

---

fit with the strategy of allowing creative people to innovate and respond quickly to consumer needs. As the company grew large, however, it began to lose its focus with the freewheeling approach. Larry Page has brought centralization to Google to fit the strategy of being more consistent and competitive in the post-PC era. Page killed off dozens of nonessential or unsuccessful projects and reorganized the company to focus on key product areas and give top executives more accountability and responsibility for results.[35]

- In times of crisis or risk of company failure, authority may be centralized at the top. Recall our example of how BP has centralized its exploration, development, and production operations so that a single executive is in charge of the upstream operations. Previously, three executives handled the upstream unit, but BP CEO Robert Dudley believed that a strong centralized structure was needed to manage risk.

REMEMBER THIS

- The **chain of command** is an unbroken line of authority that links all individuals in the organization and specifies who reports to whom.

- **Authority** is the formal and legitimate right of a manager to make decisions, issue orders, and allocate resources to achieve outcomes desired by the organization.

- **Responsibility** is the flip side of the authority coin; it refers to the duty to perform the task or activity that one has been assigned.

- **Accountability** means that people with authority and responsibility are subject to reporting and justifying task outcomes to those above them in the chain of command.

- When managers transfer authority and responsibility to positions below them in the hierarchy, it is called **delegation**.

- Managers may have **line authority**, which refers to the formal power to direct and control immediate subordinates, or **staff authority**, which refers to the right to advise, counsel, and recommend in the manager's area of expertise.

- **Span of management**, sometimes called *span of control*, refers to the number of employees reporting to a supervisor.

- A **tall structure** is characterized by an overall narrow span of management and a relatively large number of hierarchical levels.

- A **flat structure** is characterized by an overall broad span of management and relatively few hierarchical levels.

- The trend is toward broader spans of management and greater decentralization.

- **Decentralization** means that decision authority is pushed down to lower organization levels.

- **Centralization** means that decision authority is located near top organization levels.

7.2 Departmentalization

Another fundamental characteristic of organization structure is departmentalization, which is the basis for grouping positions into departments and departments into the total organization. Managers make choices about how to use the chain of command to group people together to perform their work. Five approaches to structural design reflect different uses of the chain of command in departmentalization, as illustrated in Exhibit 7.3. The functional, divisional, and matrix are traditional approaches that rely on the chain of command to define departmental groupings and reporting relationships along the hierarchy. Two innovative approaches are the use of teams and virtual networks, which have emerged to meet changing organizational needs in a turbulent global environment.

The basic difference among structures (illustrated in Exhibit 7.3) is the way in which employees are departmentalized and to whom they report.[36] Each structural approach is described in detail in the following sections.

International Shipping regulation could use a more effective structure, as shown in this chapter's Business Blooper.

Business Blooper

Carnival Triumph

Over 4,000 cruise passengers enduring carpets soaked in sewage and ketchup sandwiches dominated the news for one week in February of 2013. But the Carnival Triumph that got all the attention wasn't the first. The Splendor Cruise with 4,500 passengers in 2010 had a similar fate. In both cases, electrical systems were destroyed when fires broke out below the decks. But even two years after the Splendor debacle, there has been no definitive report on what happened. Because the Splendor is based in the United States, but is registered in Panama, both the Panamanian Maritime Authority and the U.S. Coast Guard have spent most of the time trading drafts of the report back and forth. Evidently no one wanted to take control. Added to the complication is the choice for cruise companies to use valuable space to cram more paying customers on board or use safety equipment. Because no one seems to be in charge of regulations, the companies are choosing more revenue. Hence, a repeat in February of 2013 of the same chaotic conditions as happened in 2010, with the same company. Maybe the new CEO hired after all this mess will end the calamities.

SOURCE: Charisse Jones, "Carnival CEO Steers Cruise Line in New Directions," *USAToday*, January 22, 2015, B6: Barry Meir and John Schwartz, "Giants Dead in the Water," *New York Times*, February 25, 2013, B1 and B4.

EXHIBIT 7.3 Five Approaches to Structural Design

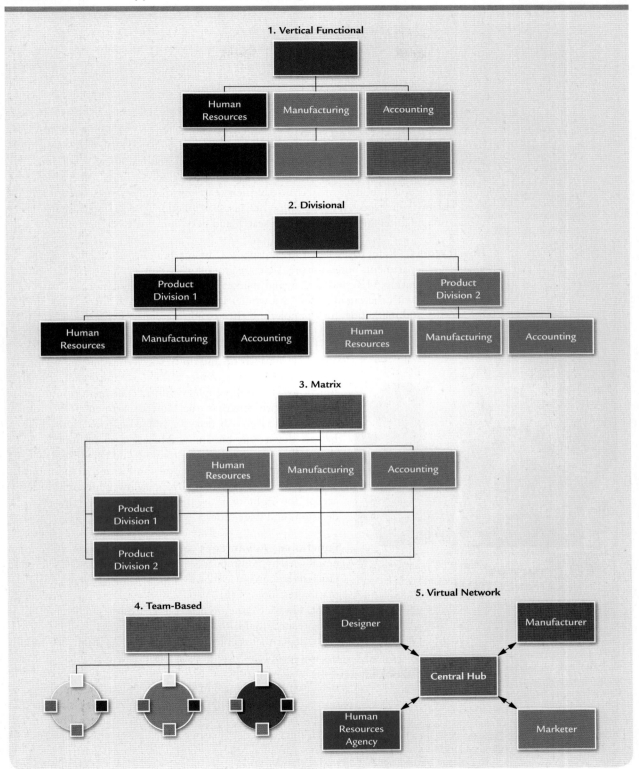

1. Vertical Functional

Human Resources · Manufacturing · Accounting

2. Divisional

Product Division 1 · Product Division 2

Human Resources · Manufacturing · Accounting

Human Resources · Manufacturing · Accounting

3. Matrix

Human Resources · Manufacturing · Accounting

Product Division 1

Product Division 2

4. Team-Based

5. Virtual Network

Designer · Manufacturer

Central Hub

Human Resources Agency · Marketer

7.2a Vertical Functional Approach

In a functional structure, also called a *U-form (unitary structure),* activities are grouped together by common function from the bottom to the top of the organization.[37] The functional structure groups positions into departments based on similar skills, expertise, work activities, and resource use. A functional structure can be thought of as departmentalization by organizational resources because each type of functional activity—accounting, HR, engineering, and manufacturing—represents specific resources for performing the organization's task. People, facilities, and other resources representing a common function are grouped into a single department. One example is Blue Bell Creameries, which relies on in-depth expertise in its various functional departments to produce high-quality ice cream for a limited regional market. The quality control department, for example, tests all incoming ingredients and ensures that only the best go into Blue Bell's ice cream. Quality inspectors also test outgoing products and, because of their years of experience, can detect the slightest deviation from expected quality. Blue Bell also has functional departments such as sales, production, maintenance, distribution, research and development (R&D), and finance.[38]

How It Works   Refer to Exhibit 7.1, on page 272, for an example of a functional structure. The major departments under the president are groupings of similar expertise and resources, such as accounting, HR, production, and marketing. Each of the functional departments is concerned with the organization as a whole. The marketing department is responsible for all sales and marketing, for example, and the accounting department handles financial issues for the entire company.

The functional structure is a strong vertical design. Information flows up and down the vertical hierarchy, and the chain of command converges at the top of the organization. In a functional structure, people within a department communicate primarily with others in the same department to coordinate work and accomplish tasks or implement decisions that are passed down the hierarchy. Managers and employees are compatible because of similar training and expertise. Typically, rules and procedures govern the duties and responsibilities of each employee, and employees at lower hierarchical levels accept the right of those higher in the hierarchy to make decisions and issue orders.

Functional Advantages and Disadvantages   Grouping employees by common task permits economies of scale and efficient resource use. For example, at US Airways, all information technology (IT) people work in the same large department. They have the expertise and skills to handle almost any issue related to IT for the organization. Large, functionally based departments enhance the development of in-depth skills because people work on a variety of related problems and are associated with other experts within their own department. Because the chain of command converges at the top, the functional structure also offers a way to centralize decision making and provide unified direction from top managers. The primary disadvantages reflect barriers that exist across departments. Because people are separated into distinct departments, communication and coordination across functions are often poor,

Blair Gable/Reuters

CONCEPT CONNECTION   A maker of products used for the prevention, diagnosis, and treatment of diseases, the health science company **Nordion Inc.** recently split into two new business units: one called Targeted Therapies and the other, Specialty Isotopes. Nordion's CEO, Steve West, explained that the new **divisional structure** is strategically designed to "take into account the unique product life cycles and the needs of our customers in each of our businesses." Based in Ottawa, Ontario, Canada, Nordion does business in 60 countries around the world.

causing a slow response to environmental changes. Innovation and change require involvement of several departments. Another problem is that decisions involving more than one department may pile up at the top of the organization and be delayed.

7.2b Divisional Approach

In contrast to the functional approach, in which people are grouped by common skills and resources, the **divisional structure** occurs when departments are grouped together based on similar organizational outputs. With a divisional structure, also called an *M-form (multidivisional)* or a *decentralized form*, separate divisions can be organized with responsibility for individual products, services, product groups, major projects or programs, divisions, businesses, or profit centers.[39] The divisional structure is also sometimes called a *product structure*, *program structure*, or *self-contained unit structure*. Each of these terms means essentially the same thing: Diverse departments are brought together to produce a single organizational output, whether it is a product, a program, or service to a single customer.

Most large corporations have separate divisions that perform different tasks, use different technologies, or serve different customers. When a huge organization produces products for different markets, the divisional structure works because each division is an autonomous business. For example, Google has seven product divisions, including YouTube, Chrome and Apps, Android, Knowledge (search), Ad Products, Geo and Commerce, and Google+ (social networking).[40] Walmart uses three major divisions for Walmart Stores, Sam's Club (U.S.), and International Stores. Each of these three large divisions is further subdivided into smaller geographical divisions to better serve customers in different regions.[41]

How It Works   Functional and divisional structures are illustrated in Exhibit 7.4. In a divisional structure, divisions are created as self-contained units, with separate functional departments for each division. For example, in Exhibit 7.4, each functional department

EXHIBIT 7.4 Functional versus Divisional Structures

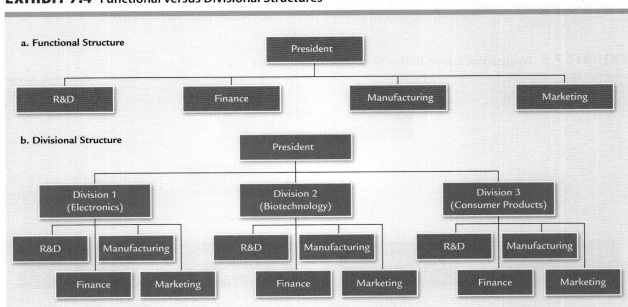

a. Functional Structure

President

R&D | Finance | Manufacturing | Marketing

b. Divisional Structure

President

Division 1 (Electronics) | Division 2 (Biotechnology) | Division 3 (Consumer Products)

R&D | Manufacturing | Finance | Marketing
R&D | Manufacturing | Finance | Marketing
R&D | Manufacturing | Finance | Marketing

resource needed to produce the product is assigned to each division. Whereas in a functional structure, all R&D engineers are grouped together and work on all products, in a divisional structure, separate R&D departments are created within each division. Each department is smaller and focuses on a single product line or customer segment. Departments are duplicated across product lines.

The primary difference between divisional and functional structures is that in a divisional structure, the chain of command from each function converges lower in the hierarchy. In a divisional structure, differences of opinion among R&D, marketing, manufacturing, and finance would be resolved at the divisional level rather than by the president. Thus, the divisional structure encourages decentralization. Decision making is pushed down at least one level in the hierarchy, freeing the president and other top managers for strategic planning. Only if the divisions can't agree, fail to coordinate, or start making decisions that hurt the organization are some decisions pulled back up to the top.

Geographic- or Customer-Based Divisions   An alternative for assigning divisional responsibility is to group company activities by geographic region or customer group. For example, the Internal Revenue Service (IRS) shifted to a structure focused on four distinct taxpayer (customer) groups: individuals, small businesses, corporations, and nonprofit or government agencies.[42] A global geographic structure is illustrated in Exhibit 7.5. In a geographic-based structure, all functions in a specific country or region report to the same division manager. The structure focuses company activities on local market conditions. Competitive advantage may come from the production or sale of a product or service adapted to a given country or region. Walt Disney Company CEO Bob Iger reorganized the Disney Channel into geographic divisions because what appeals to people in different countries varies. Studio executives in Burbank, California, were miffed at the reorganization, but it has paid off. Iger learned that the number one program on Italy's Disney Channel was one that he had never heard of—*Il Mondo di Patty*, an inexpensive, telenovela-style show about an Argentine girl. "It's important that Disney's products are presented in ways that are culturally relevant," Iger said about the geographic reorganization.[43] Large nonprofit organizations such as the National Council of YMCAs, Habitat for Humanity International, and the Girl Scouts of the USA also frequently use a type of geographical structure, with a central headquarters and semiautonomous local units.[44]

EXHIBIT 7.5 **Geographic-Based Global Organization Structure**

Divisional Advantages and Disadvantages   By dividing employees and resources along divisional lines, the organization will be flexible and responsive to change because each unit is small and tuned in to its environment. By having employees working on a single product line, the concern for customers' needs is high. Coordination across functional departments is better because employees are grouped together in a single location and committed to one product line. Great coordination exists within divisions; however, coordination *across* divisions is often poor. Problems can occur when autonomous divisions go in opposite directions. At Google, Larry Page realigned the divisional structure to establish adequate coordination across divisions. "For the first time, someone is thinking across Google products," said Sundar Pichai, who leads the Chrome unit.[45] Another major disadvantage is duplication of resources and the high cost of running separate divisions. Instead of a single research department in which all research people use a single facility, each division may have its own research facility. The organization loses efficiency and economies of scale. In addition, the small size of departments within each division may result in a lack of technical specialization, expertise, and training.

7.2c Matrix Approach

The **matrix approach** combines aspects of both functional and divisional structures simultaneously, in the same part of the organization. The matrix structure evolved as a way to improve horizontal coordination and information sharing.[46] One unique feature of the matrix is that it has dual lines of authority. In Exhibit 7.6, the functional hierarchy of

EXHIBIT 7.6   Dual-Authority Structure in a Matrix Organization

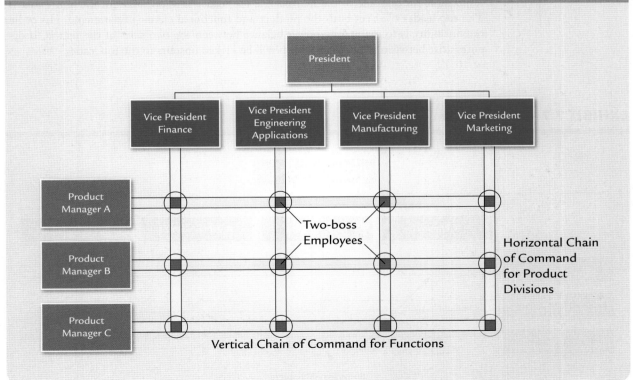

authority runs vertically, and the divisional hierarchy of authority runs horizontally. The vertical structure provides traditional control within functional departments, and the horizontal structure provides coordination across departments. The U.S. operation of Starbucks, for example, uses geographic divisions for Western/Pacific, Northwest/Mountain, Southeast/Plains, and Northeast/Atlantic. Functional departments including finance, marketing, and so forth are centralized and operate as their own vertical units, as well as supporting the horizontal divisions.[47] The matrix structure, therefore, supports a formal chain of command for both functional (vertical) and divisional (horizontal) relationships. As a result of this dual structure, some employees actually report to two supervisors simultaneously.

How It Works   The dual lines of authority make the matrix unique. To see how the matrix works, consider the global matrix structure illustrated in Exhibit 7.7. The two lines of authority are geographic and product. The geographic boss in Germany coordinates all subsidiaries in Germany, and the plastics products boss coordinates the manufacturing and sale of plastics products around the world. Managers of local subsidiary companies in Germany would report to two superiors, both the country boss and the product boss. The dual authority structure violates the unity-of-command concept described earlier in this chapter, but that is necessary to give equal emphasis to both functional and divisional lines of authority. Dual lines of authority can be confusing, but after managers learn to use this structure, the matrix provides excellent coordination simultaneously for each geographic region and each product line.

The success of the matrix structure depends on the abilities of people in key matrix roles. **Two-boss employees**, those who report to two supervisors simultaneously, must resolve conflicting demands from the matrix bosses. They must work with senior managers to reach joint decisions. They need excellent human relations skills with which to confront managers and resolve conflicts. The **matrix boss** is the product or functional boss, who is responsible for one side of the matrix. The top leader is responsible for the entire matrix. The **top leader** oversees both the product and functional chains of command. His or her responsibility is to maintain a power balance between the two sides of the matrix. If disputes arise between them, the problem will be kicked upstairs to the top leader.

EXHIBIT 7.7 Global Matrix Structure

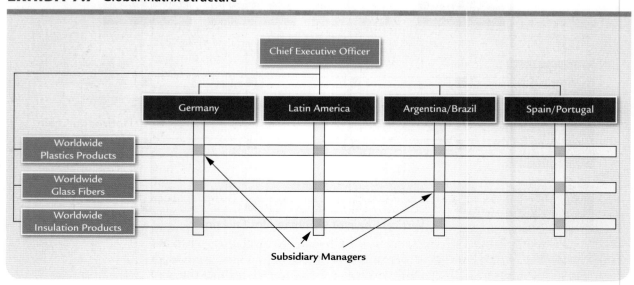

Matrix Advantages and Disadvantages The matrix can be highly effective in a complex, rapidly changing environment in which the organization needs to be flexible, innovative, and adaptable.[48] The conflict and frequent meetings generated by the matrix allow new issues to be raised and resolved. The matrix structure makes efficient use of HR because specialists can be transferred from one division to another. A major problem with the matrix is the confusion and frustration caused by the dual chain of command.[49] Matrix bosses and two-boss employees have difficulty with the dual reporting relationships. The matrix structure also can generate a high level of conflict because it pits divisional against functional goals in a domestic structure, or product line versus country goals in a global structure. Rivalry between the two sides of the matrix can be exceedingly difficult for two-boss employees to manage. This problem leads to the third disadvantage: time lost to meetings and discussions devoted to resolving this conflict. Often the matrix structure leads to more discussion than action because different goals and points of view are being addressed. Managers may spend a great deal of time coordinating meetings and assignments, which takes time away from core work activities.

REMEMBER THIS

- **Departmentalization** is the basis for grouping individual positions into departments and departments into the total organization.

- Three traditional approaches to departmentalization are functional, divisional, and matrix.

- A **functional structure** groups employees into departments based on similar skills, tasks, and use of resources.

- The **divisional structure** groups employees and departments based on similar organizational outputs (products or services), such that each division has a mix of functional skills and tasks.

- An alternative approach to divisional structure is to group employees and departments based on geographic region or customer group.

- The Disney Channel is structured into geographic divisions to better address the interests of children and teens in different parts of the world.

- The **matrix approach** uses both functional and divisional chains of command simultaneously, in the same part of the organization.

- In a matrix structure, some employees, called **two-boss employees**, report to two supervisors simultaneously.

- A **matrix boss** is a functional or product supervisor responsible for one side of the matrix.

- In a matrix structure, the **top leader** oversees both the product and the functional chains of command and is responsible for the entire matrix.

- Each approach to departmentalization has distinct advantages and disadvantages.

7.2d Team Approach

Probably the most widespread trend in departmentalization in recent years has been the implementation of team concepts. The vertical chain of command is a powerful means of control, but passing all decisions up the hierarchy takes too long and keeps responsibility at the top. The team approach gives managers a way to delegate authority, push responsibility to lower levels, and be more flexible and responsive in a complex and competitive global environment. Chapter 14 will discuss teams in detail.

How It Works One approach to using teams in organizations is through cross-functional teams, which consist of employees from various functional departments who are responsible to meet as a team and resolve mutual problems. For example, at Total Attorneys, a

Chicago-based company that provides software and services to small law firms, CEO Ed Scanlan realized that the functional structure, which broke projects down into sequential stages that moved from one department to another, was slowing things down so much that clients' needs had sometimes changed by the time the product was completed. He solved this problem by creating small, cross-functional teams to increase horizontal coordination. Now, designers, coders, and quality-assurance testers work closely together on each project.[50] Cross-functional teams can provide needed horizontal coordination to complement an existing divisional or functional structure. A frequent use of cross-functional teams is for change projects, such as new product or service innovation. Team members typically still report to their functional departments, but they also report to the team, one member of whom may be the leader.

The second approach is to use **permanent teams**, groups of employees who are organized in a way similar to a formal department. Each team brings together employees from all functional areas focused on a specific task or project, such as parts supply and logistics for an automobile plant. Emphasis is on horizontal communication and information sharing because representatives from all functions are coordinating their work and skills to complete a specific organizational task. Authority is pushed down to lower levels, and front-line employees are often given the freedom to make decisions and take action on their own. Team members may share or rotate team leadership. With a **team-based structure**, the entire organization is made up of horizontal teams that coordinate their work and work directly with customers to accomplish the organization's goals. At Whole Foods Market, a team structure is considered a major contributor to the company's success. Each Whole Foods store is made up of eight or so self-directed teams that oversee departments such as fresh produce, prepared foods, dairy, or checkout. Teams are responsible for all key operating decisions, such as product selection, pricing, ordering, hiring, and in-store promotions, and they are accountable for their performance.[51] Teams are related to the "bossless" trend, which is described further in the Director's Toolkit.

© Monkey Business Images/Shutterstock.com

CONCEPT CONNECTION   Hospitals and other health care providers face a great need for **coordination** because medical care needs to be integrated. For instance, collaborative care, like this **cross-functional team** of a nurse, doctor, and dietitian, helps patients with chronic illnesses require fewer emergency department visits. Rush University Medical Center in Chicago started its Virtual Integrated Practice (VIP) project to give physicians in private practice access to teams of physicians, dieticians, pharmacists, and social workers. VIP replicates the collaboration that can occur in a hospital setting by enabling members to share information via e-mail, phone, and fax.

Team Advantages and Disadvantages   The team approach breaks down barriers across departments and improves coordination and cooperation. Team members know one another's problems and compromise rather than blindly pursuing their own goals. The team concept also enables the organization to adapt more quickly to customer requests and environmental changes and speeds decision making because decisions need not go to the top of the hierarchy for approval. Another big advantage is the morale boost. Employees are typically enthusiastic about their involvement in bigger projects rather than narrow departmental tasks. At Lockheed Martin's Missiles and Fire Control division's Pike County Operations in Troy, Alabama, all employees work in self-directed teams that set performance goals and make decisions related to assembling and testing advanced missile systems. Teams at Pike County Operations have contributed to 100 percent on-time delivery with zero customer rejects for the division.[52]

Yet the team approach has disadvantages as well. Employees may be enthusiastic about team participation, but they may also experience conflicts and dual loyalties. A cross-functional

Director's Toolkit

The Bossless Upside-Down Structure

Some companies are finding that command and control structures of the past do not work with today's workforce. Young people are more demanding and are used to being involved via social media and the Internet. So the "bossless" structure is evolving from rigid organization charts to fluid operational and project teams, from narrow job descriptions to dynamic projects with multiple leadership roles, from top-down assignments to bottom-up initiatives by self-organizing teams.

- **How it works in a new company.** At Ciplex, a Web design company, there is no structure. There are no departments. There are no job titles like vice president, executive, or manager. The organization chart is upside down, with customers at the top, employees in the middle, and the higher-ups (called "team support") at the bottom. Flipping the structure promotes a culture where customer satisfaction is top priority. Employees, instead of sitting in department silos, are part of multifunctional teams, and they—not the bosses—solve problems to meet customers' needs.

- **How it works in an existing company.** One of the early bossless experiments was undertaken by Gerry Rich and his team at a Ciba-Geigy agricultural chemical plant in Cambridge, Ontario, Canada. Productivity shot up 20–30 percent after they dumped the bosses. The sacred preserve of the bosses—setting schedules, managing costs, writing job descriptions, interviewing new hires, and making key decisions—was now in the purview of employees. "We've taken away the layers of bureaucracy that smothered incentive," said Rich. A big impact of the reorganization was on former managers, who were now called "advisors." They had to learn new roles of facilitating teamwork, leading training programs,

and helping resolve conflicts. Many left rather than change. The hardest jolt was when a temporary supervisor was needed and former managers had to take their turn filling in along with other employees.

- **How do people progress?** At Valve, a video game developer, there are no promotions because there is no hierarchy. There is no corporate ladder to climb to advance one's career. But employees find it easy to progress in their careers anyway. There are new projects, within which employees grow and learn. For pay increases, employees rank their peers, voting on who they think creates the most value. A flat structure works well for people involved in creative processes and innovation because it allows information to diffuse throughout so that people get exposed to more ideas and diverse thinking.

- **Focus on physical proximity.** At Valve, lawyers sit with engineers and other staff at neighboring desks so that they share knowledge and understand one another's challenges and skills. Valve's Web site says it has been bossless since its founding and has no managers or assigned projects. The 300 employees recruit colleagues to work on projects that they think are worthwhile. Employee desks are mounted on wheels, allowing them to quickly shift to new work areas.

SOURCES: Based on Ilya Pozin, "Why You Need to Flip Your Org Chart," *Inc.*, June 6, 2012, http://www.inc.com/ilya-pozin/why-you-need-to-flip-your-org-chart.html (accessed November 19, 2013); Rachel Emma Silverman, "Who's the Boss? There Isn't One," *The Wall Street Journal*, June 19, 2012, http://online.wsj.com/news/articles/SB10001424052702303 379204577474953586383604 (accessed June 20, 2012); Will Freeman, "Valve's Five Point Guide to 'Bossless Management,'" July 10, 2012, *DEVELOP* Web site: http://www.develop-online.net/news/valve-s-five-point-guide-to-bossless-management/0112454 (accessed July 11, 2012); and J. Southerst, *Canadian Business*, April 1992, 65 (4), 46–51.

team may make different work demands on members than do their department managers, and members who participate in more than one team must resolve these conflicts. A large amount of time is devoted to meetings, thus increasing coordination time. Unless the organization truly needs teams to coordinate complex projects and adapt to the environment, it will lose production efficiency with them. Finally, the team approach may cause too much decentralization.

Senior department managers who traditionally made decisions might feel left out when a team moves ahead on its own. Team members often do not see the big picture of the corporation and may make decisions that are good for their group, but bad for the organization as a whole.

7.2e Virtual Network Approach

The most recent approach to departmentalization extends the idea of horizontal coordination and collaboration beyond the boundaries of the organization. In a variety of industries, vertically integrated, hierarchical organizations are giving way to loosely interconnected groups of companies with permeable boundaries.[53] *Outsourcing*, which means farming out certain activities, such as manufacturing or credit processing, has become a significant trend. British retailer J. Sainsbury, for example, lets Accenture handle its entire IT department. Ohio State University plans to outsource its parking system. And the City of Maywood, California, decided to outsource everything from street maintenance to policing and public safety. The budget for the police department used to be nearly $8 million. Now the city pays about half that to the Los Angeles County Sheriff's Department, and residents say that service has improved.[54] The pharmaceuticals company Pfizer is using an innovative approach that lets some employees pass off certain parts of their jobs to an outsourcing firm in India with a click of a button. Rather than shifting entire functions to contractors, this "personal outsourcing" approach allows people to shift only certain tedious and time-consuming tasks to be handled by the outsourcing partner while they focus on higher-value work.[55]

Some organizations take this networking approach to the extreme to create an innovative structure. The **virtual network structure** means that the firm subcontracts most of its major functions to separate companies and coordinates their activities from a small organization at headquarters.[56] Philip Rosedale, the founder of Linden Labs, created and runs SendLove (formerly called LoveMachine) from his home and coffee shops around San Francisco. SendLove makes software that lets employees send Twitter-like messages to say "Thank you" or "Great job!" When the message is sent, everyone in the company gets a copy, which builds morale, and the basic software is free to companies. The firm has no full-time development staff; instead, it works with a network of freelancers who bid on jobs such as creating new features, fixing glitches, and so forth. Rosedale also contracts out payroll and other administrative tasks.[57]

How It Works The organization may be viewed as a central hub surrounded by a network of outside specialists, sometimes spread all over the world, as illustrated in Exhibit 7.8. Rather than being housed under one roof, services such as accounting, design, manufacturing, and distribution are outsourced to separate organizations that are connected electronically to a central office.[58] Networked computer systems, collaborative software, and the Internet enable organizations to exchange data and information so rapidly and smoothly that a loosely connected network of suppliers, manufacturers, assemblers, and distributors can look and act as one seamless company.

The idea behind networks is that a company can concentrate on what it does best and contract out other activities to companies with distinctive competence in those specific areas, which enables a company to do more with less.[59] The "heart-healthy" food company Smart Balance has been able to innovate and expand rapidly by using a virtual network approach.

With a network structure such as that used at Smart Balance, it is difficult to answer the question "Where is the organization?" in traditional terms. The different organizational parts

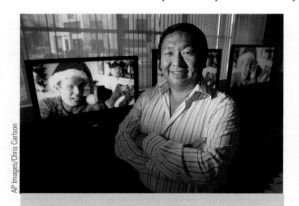

AP Images/Chris Carlson

CONCEPT CONNECTION William Wang, founder of Vizio, Inc., produces competitively priced liquid crystal display (LCD) and plasma televisions using the **virtual network approach**. Wang keeps costs down by running a lean operation, outsourcing manufacturing, R&D, and technical support, and the network approach has paid off. After 10 years in business, the company became the top flat-panel TV brand in the United States and was ranked highest in customer satisfaction.

are drawn together contractually and coordinated electronically, creating a new form of organization. Much like building blocks, parts of the network can be added or taken away to meet changing needs.[60]

EXHIBIT 7.8   Network Approach to Departmentalization

Spotlight on Skills

Smart Balance

Smart Balance has about 67 employees, but nearly 400 people are working for the company. Smart Balance started by making a buttery spread and now has a line of spreads, all-natural peanut butter, nutrient-enhanced milk, cheese, sour cream, popcorn, and other products. Managers credit the virtual network approach for helping the company innovate and expand rapidly.

Smart Balance keeps product development and marketing in-house but uses contractors to do just about everything else, including manufacturing, distribution, sales, IT services, and research and testing. The way that the company got into the milk business shows how the network structure increases speed and flexibility. Peter Dray, vice president of product development, was able to get the help he needed to perfect the product from

contractors. Outside scientists and R&D consultants worked on the formula. The company contracted with a dairy processor to do tests and trial production runs. An outside laboratory assessed nutritional claims, and another company managed consumer taste tests.

Each morning, full-time employees and virtual workers exchange a flurry of e-mail messages and phone calls to update each other on what took place the day before and what needs to happen today. Executives spend much of their time managing relationships. Twice a year, they hold all-company meetings that include permanent staff and contractors. Information is shared widely, and managers make a point of recognizing the contributions of contractors to the company's success, which helps create a sense of unity and commitment.[61]

Virtual Network Advantages and Disadvantages   The biggest advantages to a virtual network approach are flexibility and competitiveness on a global scale. The extreme flexibility of a network approach is illustrated by recent antigovernment protests and the overthrow of leaders in Tunisia and Egypt, for instance.[62] A far-flung collection of groups that share a similar mission and goals but are free to act on their own joined together to mastermind the "Arab Spring" uprisings, much in the same way that terrorist groups have masterminded attacks against the United States and other countries. "Attack any single part of it, and the rest carries on largely untouched," wrote one journalist about the terrorist network. "It cannot be decapitated because the insurgency, for the most part, has no head."[63]

Similarly, today's business organizations can benefit from a flexible network approach that lets them shift resources and respond quickly. A network organization can draw on resources and expertise worldwide to achieve the best quality and price and can sell its products and services worldwide. Flexibility comes from the ability to hire whatever services are needed and to change a few months later without constraints from owning plants, equipment, and facilities. The organization can redefine itself continually to fit new product and market opportunities. This structure is perhaps the leanest of all organization forms because little supervision is required. Large teams of staff specialists and administrators are not needed. A network organization may have only two or three levels of hierarchy, compared with ten or more in traditional organizations.[64]

One of the major disadvantages is lack of hands—on control.[65] Managers do not have all operations under one roof and must rely on contracts, coordination, negotiation, and electronic linkages to hold things together. Each partner in the network necessarily acts in its own self-interest. The weak and ambiguous boundaries create higher uncertainty and greater demands on managers for defining shared goals, managing relationships, keeping people focused and motivated, and coordinating activities so that everything functions as intended. For instance, K'Nex Brands LP, a family-owned toy company near Philadelphia, brought most of the production of its plastic building toys back to its factory in the United States from subcontractors in China to maintain greater control over quality and materials. The safety of toys made in overseas factories has been a growing concern for parents. As wages and transportation costs rose in China, K'Nex managers saw a competitive advantage in bringing production back in-house. Similarly, Walmart, which outsources most of its shipping and receiving, has recently had problems because of claims of poor working conditions and withheld wages at its subcontractors' warehouses clustered around major transportation hubs in Illinois, New Jersey, and California. Walmart managers say that they will begin monitoring subcontractors' U.S. warehouses in the same way that they monitor overseas factories.[66] Customer service and loyalty can also suffer if outsourcing partners fail to perform as expected.[67] Finally, in this type of organization, employee loyalty can weaken. Employees might feel that they can be replaced by contract services. A cohesive corporate culture is less likely to develop, and turnover tends to be higher because emotional commitment between organization and employee is fragile.

Exhibit 7.9 summarizes the major advantages and disadvantages of each type of structure that we have discussed.

EXHIBIT 7.9 Structural Advantages and Disadvantages

Structural Approach	Advantages	Disadvantages
Functional	Efficient use of resources; economies of scale	Poor communication across functional departments
	In-depth skill specialization and development	Slow response to external changes; lagging innovation
	Top manager direction and control	Decisions concentrated at the top of hierarchy, creating delay

Structural Approach	Advantages	Disadvantages
Divisional	Fast response; flexibility in an unstable environment	Duplication of resources across divisions
	Fosters concern for customer needs	Less technical depth and specialization
	Excellent coordination across functional departments	Poor coordination across divisions
Matrix	More efficient use of resources than a single hierarchy	Frustration and confusion from a dual chain of command
	Flexibility, adaptability to a changing environment	High conflict between two sides of the matrix
	Interdisciplinary cooperation; expertise available to all divisions	Many meetings; more discussion than action
Team	Reduced barriers among departments; increased compromise	Dual loyalties and conflict
	Shorter response time; quicker decisions	Time and resources spent on meetings
	Better morale; enthusiasm from employee involvement	Unplanned decentralization
Virtual network	Can draw on expertise worldwide	Lack of control; weak boundaries
	Highly flexible and responsive	Greater demands on managers
	Reduced overhead costs	Weaker employee loyalty

REMEMBER THIS

- Popular contemporary approaches to departmentalization include team and virtual network structures.

- A **cross-functional team** is a group of employees from various functional departments that meet as a team to resolve mutual problems.

- Total Attorneys uses cross-functional teams to improve coordination on software and services projects for small law firms.

- A **permanent team** is a group of employees from all functional areas permanently assigned to focus on a specific task or activity.

- A **team-based structure** is one in which the entire organization is made up of horizontal teams that coordinate their activities and work directly with customers to accomplish organizational goals.

- Whole Foods Market uses a team-based structure.

- With a **virtual network structure**, the organization subcontracts most of its major functions to separate companies and coordinates their activities from a small headquarters organization.

- Both the team and the network approach have distinct advantages and disadvantages.

7.3 Organizing for Horizontal Coordination

One reason for the growing use of teams and networks is that many managers recognize the limits of traditional vertical organization structures in a fast-shifting environment. In general, the trend is toward breaking down barriers between departments, and many companies are moving toward horizontal structures based on work processes rather than departmental functions.[68] However, regardless of the type of structure, every organization needs mechanisms for horizontal integration and coordination. The structure of an organization is not complete without designing the horizontal as well as the vertical dimensions of structure.[69]

7.3a The Need for Coordination

As organizations grow and evolve, two things happen. First, new positions and departments are added to deal with factors in the external environment or with new strategic needs, as described earlier in the chapter. As companies add positions and departments to meet changing needs, they grow more complex, with hundreds of positions and departments performing incredibly diverse activities.

Second, senior managers have to find a way to tie all these departments together. The formal chain of command and the supervision it provides is effective, but it is not enough. The organization needs systems to process information and enable communication among people in different departments and at different levels. **Coordination** refers to the managerial task of adjusting and synchronizing the diverse activities among different individuals and departments. **Collaboration** means a joint effort between people from two or more departments to produce outcomes that meet a common goal or shared purpose and that are typically greater than what any of the individuals or departments could achieve working alone.[70] To understand the value of collaboration, consider the 2011 U.S. mission to raid Osama bin Laden's compound in Pakistan. The raid could not have succeeded without close collaboration between the Central Intelligence Agency (CIA) and the U.S. military. There has traditionally been little interaction between the nation's intelligence officers and its military officers, but the war on terrorism has changed that mindset. During planning for the bin Laden mission, military officers spent every day for months working closely with the CIA team in a remote, secure facility on the CIA campus. "This is the kind of thing that, in the past, people who watched movies thought was possible, but no one in the government thought was possible," one official later said of the collaborative mission.[71]

Collaboration and coordination within business organizations is just as important. Without coordination, a company's left hand will not act in concert with the right, causing problems and conflicts. Coordination is required regardless of whether the organization has a functional, divisional, or team structure. Employees identify with their immediate department or team, taking its interest to heart, and they may not want to compromise and collaborate with other units even for the good of the organization as a whole. Poor

Spotlight on Skills

Microsoft

Microsoft is having a hard time keeping pace with Apple and Google. One big reason is that the company's divisions have long been at war with one another. Steven A. Ballmer, longtime CEO of Microsoft, recently said, "To execute, we've got to move from multiple Microsofts to one Microsoft."

Ballmer and other top executives are implementing a major reorganization that dissolves the existing eight product divisions in favor of four units based on broad themes that the leadership hopes will encourage greater collaboration and teamwork. The goal, said Ballmer, is to organize things so as "to drive a cross-company team for success." Whereas each division once had its own finance and marketing departments, those functions have been centralized to force groups to work more closely together to create complete products where all the hardware, software, and services work together. In a telephone interview, Qi Lu, the head of Bing and Microsoft's other Internet initiatives, said the old structure was similar to baseball, in that it gave individual players opportunities to perform. A better model for the new Microsoft, he says, is football: "You have to huddle before every play."[72]

coordination and collaboration among divisions are blamed for Microsoft's late entry into the profitable smartphone and tablet markets, for instance. Top managers are trying to change that with a massive, but tricky, reorganization.

It remains to be seen if Microsoft's long-feuding divisions can huddle and put the good of the whole above their individual goals. The company's problems have become so worrisome that in early October 2013, three of the top 20 shareholders began lobbying the board to pressure Bill Gates to step down as chairman of the company that he cofounded 38 years earlier.[73] Microsoft will likely use a variety of structural mechanisms, described in the following sections, to encourage greater collaboration across the organization's four broad units and try to put the spark back in the company.

Microsoft is a huge organization, with more than 100,000 employees, which makes coordination even more challenging. The problem of coordination and collaboration is also amplified in the international arena because organizational units are differentiated not only by goals and work activities, but also by geographical distance, time differences, cultural values, and perhaps language. How can managers ensure that needed coordination and collaboration will take place in their company, both domestically and globally? Coordination is the outcome of information and cooperation. Managers can design systems and structures to promote horizontal coordination and collaboration.

Exhibit 7.10 illustrates the evolution of organizational structures, with a growing emphasis on horizontal coordination. Although the vertical functional structure is effective in stable environments, it does not provide the horizontal coordination that is needed in times of rapid change. Innovations such as cross-functional teams, task forces, and project managers work within the vertical structure but provide a means to increase horizontal communication and cooperation. The next stage involves reengineering to structure the organization into teams working on horizontal processes. **Reengineering** refers to the radical redesign of business processes to achieve dramatic improvements in cost, quality, service, and speed. Because the focus of reengineering is on horizontal workflows rather than function, reengineering generally leads to a shift away from a strong vertical structure to one emphasizing stronger horizontal coordination. The vertical hierarchy is flattened, with perhaps only a few senior executives in traditional support functions such as finance and HR.

EXHIBIT 7.10 Evolution of Organization Structures

Traditional Vertical Structure

Cross-Functional Teams and Project Managers

Reengineering to Horizontal Teams

7.3b Task Forces, Teams, and Project Management

A task force is a temporary team or committee designed to solve a problem involving several departments.[74] Task force members represent their departments and share information that enables coordination. For example, at Irving Medical Center, a unit of Kaiser Permanente in California, a task force made up of operating room nurses, surgeons, technicians, housekeeping staff, and others came together to streamline the procedure for performing total-hip and knee-joint replacements, the hospital's costliest and most time-consuming surgeries. The resulting combination of enhanced coordination and reallocated resources meant that the number of these surgeries that could be performed increased from one or two a day up to four a day. Better coordination freed up 188 hours of operating room time a year, reflecting a significant cost savings.[75] In addition to creating task forces, companies also set up *cross-functional teams*, as described previously. A cross-functional team furthers horizontal coordination because participants from several departments meet regularly to solve ongoing problems of common interest.[76] This team is similar to a task force except that it works with continuing rather than temporary problems and might exist for several years. Team members think in terms of working together for the good of the whole rather than just for their own departments.

Companies also use project managers to increase coordination. A **project manager** is a person who is responsible for coordinating the activities of several departments for the completion of a specific project.[77] Project managers might also have titles such as product manager, integrator, program manager, or process owner. The distinctive feature of the project manager position is that the person is not a member of one of the departments being coordinated. Project managers are located outside the departments and have responsibility for coordinating several departments to achieve desired project outcomes. At General Mills, for example, a manager is assigned to each product line, such as Cheerios, Bisquick, and Hamburger Helper. Product managers set budget goals, marketing targets, and strategies and obtain the cooperation from advertising, production, and sales personnel needed for implementing product strategy.

In some organizations, project managers are included on the organization chart, as illustrated in Exhibit 7.11. The project manager is drawn to one side of the chart to indicate authority over the project, but not over the people assigned to it. The *dashed lines* to the project manager indicate responsibility for coordination and communication with assigned team members, but department managers retain line authority over functional employees.

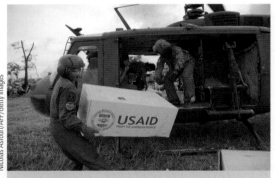

Nicolas Asfouri/AFP/Getty Images

CONCEPT CONNECTION Task forces are a common part of organizational life, from private industry to nonprofits to government operations. After Super Typhoon Haiyan struck the Philippines in November 2013, leaving thousands dead and nearly half a million homeless, various branches of the U.S. military created a task force to help the rescue effort. Made up of members of the U.S. Marines, Navy, State Department, and other agencies, Joint Task Force 505 brought food, water, and other urgently needed relief supplies to the region.

7.3c Relational Coordination

The highest level of horizontal coordination is **relational coordination**, which refers to "frequent, timely, problem-solving communication carried out through [employee] relationships of shared goals, shared knowledge, and mutual respect."[78] Relational coordination isn't a structural device or mechanism such as a project manager, but rather is part of the very fabric and culture of the organization. In an organization with a high

EXHIBIT 7.11   **Example of Project Manager Relationships to Other Departments**

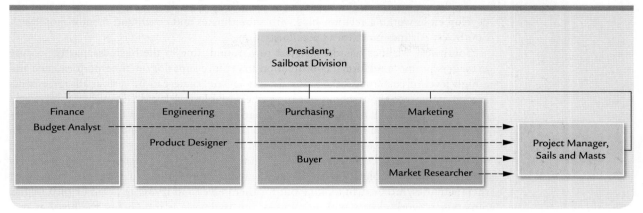

level of relational coordination, people share information freely across departmental boundaries, and people interact on a continuous basis to share knowledge and solve problems. Coordination is carried out through a web of ongoing positive relationships rather than because of formal coordination roles or mechanisms.[79] Employees coordinate directly with each other across units. The desire for relational coordination is reflected in the changing physical environment of many of today's offices. Rather than having people separated into cubicles, companies are using open offices with quiet spaces designed for conversation and impromptu problem solving. Companies including Campbell Soup and Microsoft have hired consultants from office furniture maker Herman Miller to help design common spaces that include "huddle rooms" for meetings of two to four people. Beth Jolly, a Campbell spokesperson, said, "People are collaborating much more" because they aren't "bound by walls or cubes."[80]

Studies have shown that having people work in close proximity to one another does increase collaboration.[81] However, changing the physical environment isn't enough. To build relational coordination into the fabric of the organization, managers invest in training people in the skills needed to interact with one another and resolve cross-departmental conflicts based on shared goals rather than emphasizing goals of their separate departments. People are given freedom from strict work rules so that they have the flexibility to interact

"Management makes the assumption that after it calls you a team, you are a team. But in fact, collaboration requires leadership, commitment, resources, training, and constant reinforcement."

—Michael Beyerlein, Purdue University professor and co-author of *Beyond Teams: Building the Collaborative Organization*

Spotlight on Skills

Southwest Airlines

Airlines face many challenges, but one that they face hundreds of times on a daily basis is getting airplanes loaded and off the ground safely and on time. Flight departure is a highly complex process. It involves numerous employees from various departments—such as ticket agents, pilots, flight attendants, baggage handlers, gate agents, mechanics, ramp agents, fuel attendants, and so forth—performing multiple tasks within a limited time period, under uncertain and ever-changing conditions. If all these groups aren't tightly coordinated, a successful on-time departure is difficult to achieve.

and contribute wherever they are needed, and rewards are based on team efforts and accomplishments. Front-line supervisors typically have smaller spans of control so they can develop close working relationships with subordinates and coach and mentor employees. Southwest Airlines provides a good illustration.

Southwest Airlines has the shortest turnaround time in the business, partly because managers promote relational coordination to achieve superior on-time performance and a high level of customer satisfaction. In any airline, there can be serious disagreements among employees about who is to blame when a flight is delayed, so Southwest managers created what they call *team delay*. Rather than searching for who is to blame when something goes wrong, the team delay is used to point out problems in coordination between various groups. The emphasis on the team focuses everyone on their shared goals of on-time departure, accurate baggage handling, and customer satisfaction. Because delay becomes a team problem, people are motivated to work closely together and coordinate their activities, rather than looking out for themselves and trying to avoid or shift blame. Supervisors work closely with employees, but their role is less "being the boss" as it is facilitating learning and helping people do their jobs. Southwest uses a small supervisory span of control—about one supervisor for every eight or nine front-line employees—so that supervisors have the time to coach and assist employees, who are viewed as internal customers.[82]

By using practices that facilitate relational coordination, Southwest managers ensure that all the departments involved in flight departure are tightly coordinated. When relational coordination is high, people share information and coordinate their activities without having to have bosses or formal mechanisms telling them to do so.

REMEMBER THIS

- In addition to the vertical structure, every organization needs mechanisms for horizontal integration and coordination.
- **Coordination** refers to the managerial task of adjusting and synchronizing the diverse activities among different individuals and departments.
- **Collaboration** means a joint effort between people from two or more departments to produce outcomes that meet a common goal or shared purpose.
- The successful U.S. mission to raid Osama bin Laden's compound in Pakistan was a result of collaboration between the nation's intelligence officers and its military officers.
- As organizations grow, they add new positions, departments, and hierarchical levels, which leads to greater coordination problems.
- Ways to increase horizontal coordination include task forces, teams, project managers, and relational coordination.

- A **task force** is a temporary team or committee formed to solve a specific short-term problem involving several departments.
- A **project manager** is a person responsible for coordinating the activities of several departments for the completion of a specific project.
- Companies often shift to a more horizontal approach after going through **reengineering**, which refers to the radical redesign of business processes to achieve dramatic improvements in cost, quality, service, and speed.
- **Relational coordination** refers to frequent horizontal coordination and communication carried out through ongoing relationships of shared goals, shared knowledge, and mutual respect.
- Southwest Airlines achieves the shortest turnaround time in the airline industry because managers foster relational coordination among the varied people and departments involved in the flight departure process.

7.4 Factors Shaping Structure

Vertical hierarchies continue to thrive because they provide important benefits for organizations. Some degree of vertical hierarchy is often needed to organize a large number
of people effectively to accomplish complex tasks within a coherent framework. Without
a vertical structure, people in a large, global firm wouldn't know what to do. However, in
today's environment, an organization's vertical structure often needs to be balanced with
strong horizontal mechanisms to achieve peak performance.[83]

How do managers know whether to design a structure that emphasizes the formal,
vertical hierarchy or one with an emphasis on horizontal communication and collaboration? The answer lies in the organization's strategic goals and the nature of its technology.
Exhibit 7.12 illustrates that forces affecting organization structure come from both outside and inside the organization. External strategic needs, such as environmental conditions, strategic direction, and organizational goals, create top-down pressure for designing
the organization in such a way as to fit the environment and accomplish strategic goals.
Structural decisions also take into consideration pressures from the bottom up—that is,
from the technology and work processes that are performed to produce the organization's
products and services.

7.4a Structure Follows Strategy

Studies demonstrate that business performance is strongly influenced by how well the
company's structure is aligned with its strategic intent and the needs of the environment,
so managers strive to pick strategies and structures that are congruent.[84] In Chapter 5,
we discussed several strategies that business firms can adopt. Two strategies proposed by
Michael E. Porter are differentiation and cost leadership.[85] With a differentiation strategy,

EXHIBIT 7.12 Factors Affecting Organization Structure

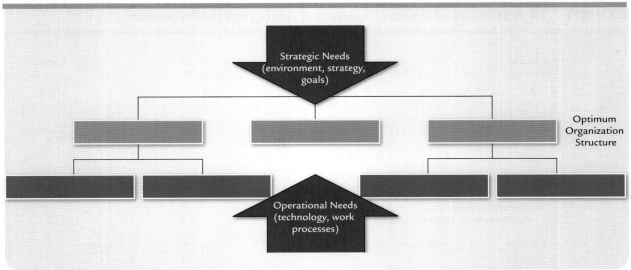

SOURCE: Based on David A. Nadler and Michael L. Tushman, with Mark B. Nadler, *Competing by Design: The Power of Organizational Architecture*
(New York: Oxford University Press, 1997), p. 54.

the organization attempts to develop innovative products unique to the market. With a cost leadership strategy, the organization strives for internal efficiency.

Typically, strategic goals of cost efficiency occur in more stable environments, while goals of innovation and flexibility occur in more uncertain environments. The terms *mechanistic* and *organic* can be used to explain structural responses to strategy and the environment.[86] Goals of efficiency and a stable environment are associated with a mechanistic system. This type of organization typically has a rigid, vertical, centralized structure, with most decisions made at the top. The organization is highly specialized and characterized by rules, procedures, and a clear hierarchy of authority. With goals of innovation and a rapidly changing environment, however, the organization tends to be much looser, free-flowing, and adaptive, using an organic system. The structure is more horizontal, and decision-making authority is decentralized. People at lower levels have more responsibility and authority for solving problems, enabling the organization to be more fluid and adaptable to changes.[87]

Exhibit 7.13 shows a simplified continuum that illustrates how different structural approaches are associated with strategy and the environment. The pure functional structure is appropriate for achieving internal efficiency goals in a stable environment. The vertical functional structure uses task specialization and a strict chain of command to gain efficient use of scarce resources, but it does not enable the organization to be flexible or innovative. In contrast, horizontal teams are appropriate when the primary goal is innovation and the organization needs flexibility to cope with an uncertain environment. Each team is small, is able to be responsive, and has the people and resources necessary for performing its task. The flexible horizontal structure enables organizations to differentiate themselves and respond quickly to the demands of a shifting environment but at the expense of efficient resource use.

Exhibit 7.13 also illustrates how other forms of structure represent intermediate steps on the organization's path to efficiency or innovation. The functional structure with cross-functional teams and project managers provides greater coordination and flexibility than the pure functional structure. The divisional structure promotes differentiation because each division can focus on specific products and customers, although divisions tend to be larger and less flexible than small teams. Exhibit 7.13 does not include all possible

Go to the Self-Learning on page 307, which pertains to organic versus mechanistic structure.

The Group Learning on page 308 will give you a chance to practice organizing to meet strategic needs.

EXHIBIT 7.13   Relationship of Structural Approach to Strategy and the Environment

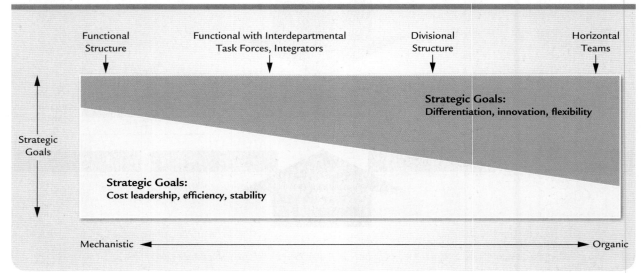

structures, but it illustrates how structures can be used to facilitate the organization's strategic goals. Sophia Amoruso developed structure as she grew her online shopping company, doing things in a unique way that led her to success, as shown in this chapter's Director's Toolkit box.

Director's Toolkit

Nasty Gal

Try starting an Internet business selling vintage clothes at age 22. Challenge the rules at eBay. Don't hire a marketing director and turn down Silicon Valley venture capital four years later. That's the formula for success Sophia Amoruso used to build up her women's clothing site to over $100 million sales. Amoruso, who is now called "The Cinderella of Tech," was 22 and working at a low-wage job checking student IDs, when she started an eBay side venture, NastyGirl (now known as Nasty Gal), selling vintage clothes that she'd found rummaging through Salvation Army and Goodwill bins. There was the Chanel jacket she found for $8 and then sold for $1,000. A former photography student, she did her own photos, captions and shipping, selling about 25 items per week in the early days. She named the site after the "Nasty Girl" album recorded by Betty Davis, former wife of jazz sensation Miles Davis.

Curating her site with funky styles that might include floor-length trench coat, rock t-shirt and blood-red lipstick, she created a loyal following, going up to 60,000 friends on MySpace. But eBay didn't like her links with the other social media player, and Amoruso realized it was a terrible place to start a business, so she launched ShopNastyGirl.com and garnered customers from all over the United States as well as countries from Australia to England. She moved from her family's basement to a

1,700 square foot headquarter in 2007, and outgrew that in eight months.

Her name might have been catnip to young women, but vendors ran the other way. After she realized she couldn't grow fast with only used clothing, she approached Sam Edelman and others, who thought she was some grizzly site. She had to find them at trade shows and show them the company's Web site on her smartphone for them to finally agree to work with her. By 2010, she had created such buzz in Silicon Valley that she was approached by several venture capitalists who wanted to invest in female companies. She turned them all down, not wanting to be a token, or as one of them put it, be part of their "investment thesis." It wasn't until 2012 that Amoruso finally gave up a piece of her business to Index for $9 million capital. By 2015, the company had grown to $100 million in sales. To her credit, she knows the work continues. It's been very charmed, but I'm not willing to rest on my laurels," she said. "It's only going to get harder to keep building from here." By 2015, she realized it was time to hand over the back-breaking CEO work to Sheree Waterson, as she will continue what she does best: brand connecting.

SOURCE: "Briefing Box," *Women's Wear Daily*, January 13, 2015, 7; Nicole Perlroth, "Naughty in Name Only," *New York Times*, March 25, 2013, B1 and B4.

REMEMBER THIS

- Contingency factors of strategic goals, environment, and technology influence the correct structural approach.

- A mechanistic, vertical structure is appropriate for a cost leadership strategy, which typically occurs in a stable environment.

- An organic, horizontal approach is needed for a differentiation strategy and when the organization needs flexibility to cope with an uncertain environment.

7.4b Structure Fits the Technology

Technology includes the knowledge, tools, techniques, and activities used to transform organizational inputs into outputs.[88] Technology includes machinery, employee skills, and work procedures. A useful way to think about technology is as "production activities." The production activities may be to produce Web site content, steel castings, television programs, or computer software. Technologies vary between manufacturing and service organizations.

Woodward's Manufacturing Technology   The most influential research into the relationship between manufacturing technology and organization structure was conducted by Joan Woodward, a British industrial sociologist.[89] She gathered data from 100 British firms to determine whether basic structural characteristics, such as administrative overhead, span of control, and centralization were different across firms. She found that manufacturing firms could be categorized according to three basic types of production technology:

- Small-batch and unit production. Small-batch production firms produce goods in batches of one or a few products designed to customer specification. This technology also is used to make large, one-of-a-kind products, such as computer-controlled machines. Small-batch manufacturing is close to traditional skilled-craft work, because human beings are a large part of the process. Examples of items produced through small-batch manufacturing include custom clothing, special-order machine tools, space capsules, satellites, and submarines.

- Large-batch and mass production. Mass production technology is distinguished by standardized production runs. A large volume of products is produced, and all customers receive the same product. Standard products go into inventory for sale as customers need them. This technology makes greater use of machines than does small-batch production. Machines are designed to do most of the physical work, and employees complement the machinery. Examples of mass production are automobile assembly lines and the large-batch techniques used to produce tobacco products and textiles.

- Continuous process production. In continuous process production, the entire workflow is mechanized in a sophisticated and complex form of production technology. Because the process runs continuously, it has no starting and stopping. Human operators are not part of actual production because machinery does all the work. Human operators simply read dials, fix machines that break down, and manage the production process. Examples of continuous process technologies are chemical plants, distilleries, petroleum refineries, and nuclear power plants.

The difference among the three manufacturing technologies is called technical complexity. **Technical complexity** is the degree to which machinery is involved in the production to the exclusion of people. With a complex technology, employees are hardly needed except to monitor the machines.

The structural characteristics associated with each type of manufacturing technology are illustrated in Exhibit 7.14. Note that centralization is high for mass production and low for small-batch and continuous process. Unlike small-batch and continuous process production, standardized mass-production machinery requires centralized decision making and well-defined rules and procedures. The administrative ratio and the percentage of indirect labor required also increase with technological complexity. Because the production process is nonroutine, closer supervision is needed. More indirect labor, in the form of maintenance people, is required because of the machinery's complexity; thus, the indirect/direct labor

EXHIBIT 7.14 Relationship between Manufacturing Technology and Organization Structure

	Manufacturing Technology		
	Small Batch	Mass Production	Continuous Process
Technical Complexity of Production Technology	Low	Medium	High
Structural Characteristics:			
Centralization	Low	High	Low
Top administrator ratio	Low	Medium	High
Indirect/direct labor ratio	1/9	1/4	1/1
Supervisor span of control	23	48	15
Communication:			
Written (vertical)	Low	High	Low
Verbal (horizontal)	High	Low	High
Overall Structure	Organic	Mechanistic	Organic

SOURCE: Based on Joan Woodward, *Industrial Organizations: Theory and Practice* (London: Oxford University Press, 1965).

ratio is high. Span of control for first-line supervisors is greatest for mass production. On an assembly line, jobs are so routine that a supervisor can handle an average of 48 employees. The number of employees per supervisor in small-batch and continuous process production is lower because closer supervision is needed. Overall, small-batch and continuous process firms have somewhat loose, flexible structures (organic), and mass production firms have tight vertical structures (mechanistic).

Woodward found that the relationship between structure and technology was directly related to company performance. Low-performing firms tended to deviate from the preferred structural form, often adopting a structure appropriate for another type of technology. High-performing organizations had characteristics similar to those listed in Exhibit 7.14.

Service Technology Examples of service organizations include consulting companies, law firms, brokerage houses, airlines, hotels, advertising companies, amusement parks, and educational organizations. In addition, service technology characterizes many departments in large corporations, even manufacturing firms. In a manufacturing company such as Ford Motor Company, the legal, HR, finance, and market research departments all provide service. Thus, the structure and design of these departments reflect their own service technology rather than the manufacturing plant's technology. Service technology can be defined as follows:

- Intangible output. The output of a service firm is intangible. Services are perishable and, unlike physical products, cannot be stored in inventory. The service is either consumed immediately or lost forever. Manufactured products are produced at one point in time and can be stored until sold at another time.

- Direct contact with customers. Employees and customers interact directly to provide and purchase the service. Production and consumption are simultaneous. Service firm employees have direct contact with customers. In a manufacturing firm, technical employees are separated from customers, and hence no direct interactions occur.[90]

One distinct feature of service technology that directly influences structure is the need for employees to be close to the customer.[91] Structural characteristics are similar to those for continuous manufacturing technology, shown in Exhibit 7.14. Service firms tend to be flexible, informal, and decentralized. Horizontal communication is high because employees must share information and resources to serve customers and solve problems. Services also are dispersed; hence each unit is often small and located geographically close to customers. For example, banks, hotels, fast-food franchises, and doctors' offices disperse their facilities into regional and local offices to provide faster and better service to customers.

Some services can be broken down into explicit steps, so that employees can follow set rules and procedures. An interesting example comes from India, where Dr. Devi Shetty runs a hospital that performs open-heart surgery for about 10 percent of the cost charged by hospitals in the United States, without reduced quality, by applying standardized operating procedures and principles of mass production. His approach is in line with a trend toward *lean services* that looks at how to design service work to improve both quality and efficiency. "In healthcare, you can't do one thing and reduce the price," Dr. Shetty says. "We have to do 1,000 small things."[92] When services can be standardized, a tight centralized structure can be effective, but service firms in general tend to be more organic, flexible, and decentralized.

REMEMBER THIS

- Types of technologies include manufacturing and service.
- **Small-batch production** is a type of manufacturing technology that involves the production of goods in batches of one or a few products designed to customer specifications.
- **Mass production** is characterized by long production runs to manufacture a large volume of products with the same specifications.
- **Continuous process production** involves mechanization of the entire workflow and nonstop production, such as in chemical plants or petroleum refineries.
- Small batch and continuous process technologies are associated with a more flexible horizontal structure, whereas a tighter vertical structure is appropriate for mass production.
- Manufacturing technologies differ in terms of **technical complexity**, which refers to the degree to which complex machinery is involved in the production process to the exclusion of people.
- **Service technology** is characterized by intangible outputs and direct contact between employees and customers.
- Examples of service firms include banks, hotels, and law firms.
- Service technologies tend to have more flexible horizontal structures.

CHAPTER 7   DISCUSSION QUESTIONS

1. If you wanted to add a group of big data scientists to a large organization such as PepsiCo, would you centralize the scientists in a central pool at headquarters or decentralize them to separate divisions? Discuss your reasons.

2. How does relational coordination differ from teams and task forces? Do you think that relational coordination seems more valuable for a service technology or a manufacturing technology? Explain your answer.

3. An organizational consultant was heard to say, "Some aspect of functional structure appears in every organization." Do you agree? Explain.

4. Some people argue that the matrix structure should be adopted only as a last resort because the dual chains of command can create more problems than they solve. Discuss. Do you agree or disagree? Why?

5. What is the virtual network approach to structure? Is the use of authority and responsibility different compared to other forms of departmentalization? Explain.

6. The Hay Group published a report that some managers have personalities suited to horizontal relationships, such as project management, that achieve results with little formal authority. Other managers are more suited to operating roles with much formal authority in a vertical structure. What type of structure—functional, matrix, team, or virtual network—do you believe your personality would best fit into? Which structure would be the most challenging for you? Give your reasons.

7. Describe the primary differences between manufacturing and service technology. How do these differences influence the type of structure that will be most effective?

8. Experts say that organizations are becoming increasingly decentralized, with authority, decision-making responsibility, and accountability being pushed farther down into the organization. How will this trend affect what will be asked of you as a new manager?

9. The chapter suggested that structure should be designed to fit strategy. Some theorists argue that strategy should be designed to fit the organization's structure. With which theory do you agree? Explain.

10. Would you expect the structure of a company such as Facebook, which operates almost entirely online, to differ from the structure of a bricks-and-mortar company, such as AT&T, which uses the Internet only for some things, such as customer service and business-to-business transactions? Why or why not?

SELF-LEARNING

Organic versus Mechanistic Organization Structure

Interview an employee at your university, such as a department head or secretary. Have the employee answer the following 13 questions about his or her job and organizational conditions. Then answer the same set of questions for a job that you have held.

Disagree Strongly   1   2   3   4   5   Agree Strongly

1. Your work would be considered routine.

   1   2   3   4   5

2. A clearly known way is established to do the major tasks that you encounter.

   1   2   3   4   5

3. Your work has high variety and frequent exceptions.

   1   2   3   4   5

4. Communications from above consist of information and advice rather than instructions and directions.

   1   2   3   4   5

5. You have the support of peers and your supervisor to do your job well.

   1   2   3   4   5

6. You seldom exchange ideas or information with people doing other kinds of jobs.

   1   2   3   4   5

7. Decisions relevant to your work are made above you and passed down.

   1   2   3   4   5

8. People at your level frequently have to figure out for themselves what their tasks are for each day.

   1   2   3   4   5

9. Lines of authority are clear and precisely defined.

   1   2   3   4   5

10. Leadership tends to be democratic rather than autocratic in style.

    1   2   3   4   5

11. Job descriptions are written and up to date for each job.

    1   2   3   4   5

12. People understand each other's jobs and often do different tasks.

    1   2   3   4   5

13. A manual of policies and procedures is available to use when a problem arises.

    1   2   3   4   5

Scoring and Interpretation

To obtain the total score, subtract the scores for questions 1, 2, 6, 7, 9, 11, and 13 from the number 6 and add up the adjusted scores.

Total Score, Employee: _____

Total Score, You: _____

Compare the total score for a place that you have worked to the score of the university employee that you interviewed. A score of 52 or above suggests that you or the other respondent is working in an organic organization. The score reflects a loose, flexible structure that is often associated with uncertain environments and small-batch or service technology. People working in this structure feel empowered. Many organizations today are moving in the direction of flexible structures and empowerment.

A score of 26 or below suggests a mechanistic structure. This structure uses traditional control and functional specialization, which often occurs in a certain environment, a stable organization, and routine or mass-production technology. People in this structure may feel controlled and constrained.

Discuss the pros and cons of organic versus mechanistic structure. Does the structure of the employee that you interviewed fit the nature of the organization's environment, strategic goals, and technology? How about the structure for your own workplace? How might you redesign the structure to make the work organization more effective?

GROUP LEARNING

Family Business

Step 1. In groups of three to five students, assume that you are a consulting team to a family business. The family has used an inheritance to acquire a medium-sized pharmaceutical company. Last year, sales were down 10 percent from the previous year. Indeed, business has declined over the past three years, even though the pharmaceutical industry has been growing. The family that acquired the business has asked for your help.

Step 2. Your task as a group is to rank the priority of the departmental functions in the order of importance for assigning additional resources to improve business in the future.

Step 3. Individually, rank the following ten functions in order of importance, and make a note of your reasons:

> Distribution
> Manufacturing
> Market research
> New-product development
> Human resources
> Product promotion
> Quality assurance
> Sales
> Legal and governmental affairs
> Office of the comptroller

Step 4. As a group, discuss the order of importance for the ten functions, sharing your reasons for how functional priority should relate to the company's strategic needs.

Step 5. How does the group's reasoning and ranking differ from your original thinking?

Step 6. What did you learn about organization structure and design from this exercise?

ACTION LEARNING

Team Skills

1. Think of three times you have been a member of a work team, with varying levels of success. Complete the following table.

2. Can you see any patterns in the success of the team and some of the characteristics you have identified?

3. Based on what you have learned, how would you recommend structuring a work team?

	Team #1	Team #2	Teams #3
Was there any formal authority in the team? How did that work?			
What was the informal structure?			
How was work divided? What was their specialization?			
Did anyone delegate? How did that work out?			
Over the course of time, did the team get better or did it deteriorate? Why?			

ETHICAL DILEMMA

A Matter of Delegation[93]

Tom Harrington loved his job as an assistant quality control officer for Rockingham Toys. After six months of unemployment, he was anxious to make a good impression on his boss, Frank Golopolus. One of his responsibilities was ensuring that new product lines met federal safety guidelines. Rockingham had made several manufacturing changes over the past year. Golopolus and the rest of the quality control team had been working 60-hour weeks to troubleshoot the new production process.

Harrington was aware of numerous changes in product safety guidelines that he knew would affect the new toys the company was producing. Golopolus was also aware of the guidelines, but he was taking no action to implement them. Harrington wasn't sure whether his boss expected him to implement the new procedures. The ultimate responsibility was his boss's, and Harrington was concerned about moving ahead on his own. To cover for his boss, he continued to avoid the questions that he received from the factory floor, but he was beginning to wonder whether Rockingham would have time to make changes with the Christmas season rapidly approaching.

Harrington felt loyalty to Golopolus for giving him a job and didn't want to alienate him by interfering. However, he was beginning to worry what might happen if he didn't act. Rockingham had a fine product safety reputation and was rarely challenged on matters of quality. Should he question Golopolus about implementing the new safety guidelines?

What Would You Do?

1. Prepare a memo to Golopolus, summarizing the new safety guidelines that affect the Rockingham product line and requesting his authorization for implementation.

2. Mind your own business. Golopolus hasn't said anything about the new guidelines, and you don't want to overstep your authority. You've been unemployed and need this job.

3. Send copies of the reports anonymously to the operations manager, who is Golopolus's boss.

CASE FOR CRITICAL ANALYSIS

Abraham's Grocery Store

The first Abraham's Grocery Store was started in 1967 by Bill Abraham and his sister Doris. They used a small inheritance to start a small grocery store in a suburb of Atlanta, Georgia, and it was immediately successful. The location was good, and both Bill and Doris had winning personalities and a "serve the customer" attitude. Abraham's rapidly growing number of customers enjoyed an abundance of good meats and produce, for which Abraham's became well known.

By 2007, Abraham's had over 200 stores. Company headquarters moved to downtown Atlanta to supervise stores throughout the southeastern United States. There were four regional managers responsible for about 50 stores each. Within each region, there were four districts of 12 to 13 stores each.

Because the stores specialized in excellent meats and produce, there was a separate meat department manager, grocery department manager, and produce department manager within each store. The grocery department manager also served as the store manager, but this person did not have direct authority over the meat department or the produce department. The store meat department manager reported directly to a district meat manager specialist, and the store produce department manager reported directly to a district produce manager specialist. The store manager (who is also the grocery department manager) reported directly to a district store supervisor. This direct line of authority for each store department provided excellent quality control over the meat, produce, and grocery departments within individual stores.

However, there was growing dissatisfaction within the stores. The turnover of store managers was high, mostly because they had no control over the meat and produce departments within their stores. Coordination within stores was terrible, such as when a store manager decided to promote a sale on Coke products as a loss leader. Hundreds of cartons of Coke were brought into the store for the big sale, but the meat and produce department managers would not give up floor space to display Coke cartons. The frustrated store manager insisted that this was no way to run a business and quit on the spot. Many stores experienced conflict rather than cooperation among the meat, produce, and store managers because each was very protective of his or her separate responsibilities.

Doris Abraham asked a consultant for advice. The consultant recommended a reorganization within each store so that the meat, grocery, and produce departments would all report to the store manager. The store manager thus would have complete control over store activities and would be responsible for coordinating across the meat, produce, and grocery departments. The meat department manager in each store would report to the store manager and would also have a dashed-line relationship (communication, coordination) with the district meat specialist. Likewise, each store produce department manager would have a dashed-line relationship with the district produce specialist. The store manager would report directly to the district store supervisor. The district meat and produce specialists would visit individual stores periodically to provide advice and help the store department heads to ensure top quality in the meat, produce, and grocery areas.

The consultant was enthusiastic about the proposed structure. Store managers would have more freedom and responsibility. By assigning responsibility for all store departments to the store manager, the new structure would encourage coordination within stores and give managers the ability to adapt to local tastes and customer needs. The dashed-line relationships would ensure excellent meat, grocery, and produce departments across all stores.

Questions

1. Based on the information available in the case, sketch a picture of the original structure within an Abraham's store and the store managers' relationships with district specialist managers. What type of structure is this? Explain.

2. Based on the information available in the case, sketch a picture of the consultant's recommended structure within the store and the relationship of store department managers with district specialist managers. What type of structure is this? Explain.

3. What are some of the advantages and disadvantages you see for the two types of structures? Which structure do you think will work best for Abraham's? Why?

ON THE JOB
VIDEO CASES

Honest Tea: Designing Organization Structure

Questions

4. What are some of Seth Goldman's responsibilities as "TeaEO" of Honest Tea? Provide at least three detailed examples.

5. How does Goldman's experience as the founder of the company influence his ability to delegate?

6. Referring to Woodward's research on manufacturing technology and structure, how would you categorize Honest Tea's production? In what ways has this probably influenced the company's structure?

ENDNOTES

1. "5 Richest Tech Billionaires Who Dropped Out of University," *WhatCulture*, September 30, 2013, http://www.valvesoftware.com/company/people.html (accessed September 30, 2013); "Our People," Valve Web site, http://www.valvesoftware.com/company/people.html (accessed September 30, 2013); Claire Suddath, "Why There Are No Bosses at Valve," *Bloomberg Businessweek*, April 27, 2012, www.businessweek.com/articles/2012-04-27/why-there-are-no-bosses-at-valve (accessed August 10, 2012); Rachel Emma Silverman, "Who's the Boss? There Isn't One," *The Wall Street Journal*, June 20, 2012, B1; and Alex Hern, "Valve Software: Free Marketeer's Dream, or Nightmare?" *New Statesman*, August 3, 2012, www.newstatesman.com/blogs/economics/2012/08/valve-software-free-marketeers-dream-or-nightmare (accessed August 10, 2012).

2. Mark Wagner and Wayne Orvis, "Changing Structures and Behaviors at Walgreens," *Strategy + Business*, Autumn 2013, http://www.strategy-business.com/article/00195?gko=242ae (accessed October 2, 2013).

3. Julia Werdigier, "BP Appoints New Chief of Production," *The New York Times*, November 24, 2012, B3.

4. Justin Scheck, "Dell Reorganizes, Creating New Mobile Device Division," *The Wall Street Journal*, December 5, 2009, B6.

5. This questionnaire is based on Richard M. Wielkiewicz, "The Leadership Attitudes and Beliefs Scale: An Instrument for Evaluating College Students' Thinking about Leadership and Organizations," *Journal of College Student Development* 41 (May–June 2000): 335–346.

6. John Child, *Organization: A Guide to Problems and Practice*, 2d ed. (London: Harper & Row, 1984).

7. Adam Smith, *The Wealth of Nations* (New York: Modern Library, 1937).

8. David Kiron, Douglas Palmer, and Robert Berkman, "The Executive's Role in Social Business," *MIT Sloan Management Review* (Summer 2013): 83–89; Javier C. Hernandez, "A Digital Matchmaker for the City and Its Public," *The New York Times*, July 31, 2011, MB1.

9. Brian Knowlton, "White House Names First Chief Information Officer," *The New York Times*, March 5, 2009, http://thecaucus.blogs.nytimes.com/2009/03/05/white-house-names-first-chief-information-officer/ (accessed August 13, 2012).

10. John Bussey, "Has Time Come for More CIOs to Start Reporting to the Top?" *The Wall Street Journal*, May 17, 2011, http://online.wsj.com/article/SB10001424052748704281504576327510720752684.html (accessed August 14 2012).

11. This discussion is based on A. J. Grimes, "Authority, Power, Influence, and Social Control: A Theoretical Synthesis," *Academy of Management Review* 3 (1978): 724–735; and W. Graham Astley and Paramjit S. Sachdeva, "Structural Sources of Intraorganizational Power: A Theoretical Synthesis," *Academy of Management Review* 9 (1984): 104–113.

12. C. I. Barnard, *The Functions of the Executive* (Cambridge, MA: Harvard University Press, 1938).

13. Thomas A. Stewart, "CEOs See Clout Shifting," *Fortune* (November 6, 1989): 66.

14. Michael G. O'Loughlin, "What Is Bureaucratic Accountability and How Can We Measure It?" *Administration & Society* 22, no. 3 (November 1990): 275–302; and Brian Dive, "When Is an Organization Too Flat?" *Across the Board* (July–August 2003): 20–23.

15. Jena McGregor, "The BBC and Crisis Management: Why the Second Mistake Can Be Worse than the First," *The Washington Post*, November 13, 2012, http://articles.washingtonpost.com/2012-11-13/national/35503757_1_jimmy-savile-george-entwistle-crisis-management (accessed November 14, 2012); and Matt Chorley and Alasdair Glennie, "BBC Savile Scandal Cost YOU £5 Million: Shocking Report Reveals How Probes into Corporation's Bungled Handling of Crisis Left Taxpayers with Huge Bill," *DailyMail*, July 16, 2013, http://www.dailymail.co.uk/news/article-2365251/BBCs-navel-gazing-Jimmy-Savile-crisis-cost-5million.html#ixzz2gTZOeOHj (accessed September 30, 2013).

16. Carrie R. Leana, "Predictors and Consequences of Delegation," *Academy of Management Journal* 29 (1986): 754–774.

17. Chris Taylor, "Democracy Works," *Fortune Small Business* (May 2009): 40; and Heather Green, "How Meetup Tore up the Rule Book," *BusinessWeek* (June 16, 2008): 88–89.

18. Clifford Kraus and Julia Werdigier, "BP's New Chief, Not Formally in the Role, Is Already Realigning Senior Managers," *The New York Times*, September 30, 2010, B3; and Guy Chazan, "BP's New Chief Puts Emphasis on Safety," *The Wall Street Journal*, September 29, 2010.

19. Ian Urbina, "In Gulf, It Was Unclear Who Was in Charge of Oil Rig," *The New York Times*, June 5, 2010; and Douglas A. Blackmon et al., "There Was 'Nobody in Charge,'" *The Wall Street Journal*, May 27, 2010.

20. George Anders, "Overseeing More Employees—With Fewer Managers" (Theory & Practice column), *The Wall Street Journal*, March 24, 2008.

21. Barbara Davison, "Management Span of Control: How Wide Is Too Wide?" *Journal of Business Strategy* 24, no. 4 (2003): 22–29; Paul D. Collins and Frank Hull, "Technology and Span of Control: Woodward Revisited," *Journal of Management Studies* 23 (March 1986): 143–164; David D. Van Fleet and Arthur G. Bedeian, "A History of the Span of Management," *Academy of Management Review* 2 (1977): 356–372; and C. W. Barkdull, "Span of Control—A Method of Evaluation," *Michigan Business Review* 15 (May 1963): 25–32.

22. Reported in Brian Dive, "Hierarchies for Flow and Profit," *Strategy + Business*, August 26, 2008, www.strategy-business.com/article/08315 (accessed May 25, 2010).

23. Dive, "Hierarchies for Flow and Profit"; and Gary Neilson, Bruce A. Pasternack, and Decio Mendes, "The Four Bases of Organizational DNA," *Strategy + Business* 33 (December 10, 2003): 48–57.

24. Anders, "Overseeing More Employees"; Barbara Davison, "Management Span of Control"; Brian Dive, "When Is an Organization Too Flat?"; Brian Dumaine, "What the Leaders of Tomorrow See," *Fortune* (July 3, 1989): 48–62; and Raghuram G. Rajan and Julie Wulf, "The Flattening Firm: Evidence from Panel Data on the Changing Nature of Corporate Hierarchies," Working Paper, reported in Caroline Ellis, "The Flattening Corporation," *MIT Sloan Management Review* (Summer 2003): 5.

25. Gary L. Neilson and Julie Wulf, "How Many Direct Reports?" *Harvard Business Review* (April 2012): 112–119.

26. Bussey, "Has Time Come for More CIOs to Start Reporting to the Top?"

27. Gary L. Neilson, "Diagnosing Your Top Team's Span of Control," *Strategy + Business Online* (April 9, 2012), http://www.strategy-business.com/article/00107?gko=ce37c (accessed October 1, 2013).

28. William G. Ouchi, "Power to the Principals: Decentralization in Three Large School Districts," *Organization Science* 17, no. 2 (March–April 2006): 298–307.

29. Hiroko Tabuchi and Bill Vlasic, "Battered by Expensive Crises, Toyota Declares a Rebirth," *The New York Times*, January 3, 2013, B1.

30. Sarah Lyall, "Britain Plans to Decentralize Health Care," *The New York Times*, July 24, 2010, www.nytimes.com/2010/07/25/world/europe/25britain.html?pagewanted=all (accessed August 14, 2012).

31. Quoted in Robert D. Kaplan, "Man Versus Afghanistan," *The Atlantic* (April 2010): 60–71.

32. Ibid.

33. Andrew Campbell, Sven Kunisch, and Günter Müller-Stewens, "To Centralize or Not to Centralize?" *McKinsey Quarterly*, June 2011, www.mckinseyquarterly.com/To_centralize_or_not_to_centralize_2815 (accessed August 14, 2012).

34. Dennis Cauchon, "The Little Company That Could," *USA Today*, October 9, 2005, www.usatoday.com/money/companies/management/2005-10-09-mississippi-power-usat_x.htm.

35. Miguel Helft, "Larry Page Looks Ahead," *Fortune* (January 14, 2013): 50–57.

36. The following discussion of structural alternatives draws from Jay R. Galbraith, *Designing Complex Organizations* (Reading, MA: Addison-Wesley, 1973); Jay R. Galbraith, *Organization Design* (Reading, MA: Addison-Wesley, 1977); Jay R. Galbraith, *Designing Dynamic Organizations* (New York: AMACOM, 2002); Robert Duncan, "What Is the Right Organization Structure?" *Organizational Dynamics* (Winter 1979): 59–80; N. Anand and Richard L. Daft, "What Is the Right Organization Design?" *Organizational Dynamics* 36, no. 4 (2007): 329–344; and J. McCann and Jay R. Galbraith, "Interdepartmental Relations," in *Handbook of Organizational Design*, ed. P. Nystrom and W. Starbuck (New York: Oxford University Press, 1981), pp. 60–84.

37. Raymond E. Miles et al., "Designing Organizations to Meet 21st-Century Opportunities and Challenges," *Organizational Dynamics* 39, no. 2 (2010): 93–103.

38. Based on the story of Blue Bell Creameries in Richard L. Daft, *Organization Theory and Design*, 9th ed. (Mason, OH: South-Western, 2007), p. 103.

39. R. E. Miles et al., "Designing Organizations to Meet 21st-Century Opportunities and Challenges."

40. Helft, "Larry Page Looks Ahead."

41. Jaimelynn Hitt, "The Organizational Structure of Starbucks, Unilever, and Wal-Mart" (May 28, 2008), http://voices.yahoo.com/the-organizational-structure-starbucks-unilever-1495147.html (accessed August 15, 2012); Mae Anderson, "Wal-Mart Reorganizes U.S. Operations to Help Spur Growth," *USA Today*, January 28, 2010, www.usatoday.com/money/industries/retail/2010-01-28-walmart-reorganization_N.htm (accessed August 15, 2012); and "Walmart," The Official Board Web site, www.theofficialboard.com/org-chart/wal-mart-stores (accessed August 15, 2012).

42. Eliza Newlin Carney, "Calm in the Storm," *Government Executive* (October 2003): 57–63; and the IRS Web site, www.irs.gov (accessed April 20, 2004).

43. Brooks Barnes, "Is Disney's Chief Having a Cinderella Moment?" *The New York Times*, April 11, 2010, BU1.

44. Maisie O'Flanagan and Lynn K. Taliento, "Nonprofits: Ensuring That Bigger Is Better," *McKinsey Quarterly*, no. 2 (2004): 112ff.

45. Helft, "Larry Page Looks Ahead."

46. The discussion of matrix structure is based on S. H. Appelbaum, D. Nadeau, and M. Cyr, "Performance Evaluation in a Matrix Organization: A Case Study," *Industrial and Commercial Training* 40, no. 5 (2008): 236–241; T. Sy and S. Cote, "Emotional Intelligence: A Key Ability to Succeed in the Matrix Organization," *Journal of Management Development* 23, no. 5 (2004): 439; L. R. Burns, "Matrix Management in Hospitals: Testing Theories of Matrix Structure and Development," *Administrative Science Quarterly* 34 (1989): 349–368; Carol Hymowitz, "Managers Suddenly Have to Answer to a Crowd of Bosses," *The Wall Street Journal*, August 12, 2003; and Stanley M. Davis and Paul R. Lawrence, *Matrix* (Reading, MA: Addison-Wesley, 1977).

47. Howard Schultz, "Starbucks Makes Organizational Changes to Enhance Customer Experience," February 11, 2008, http://news.starbucks.com/article_display.cfm?article_id=66 (accessed August 15, 2012).

48. Robert C. Ford and W. Alan Randolph, "Cross-Functional Structures: A Review and Integration of Matrix Organization and Project Management," *Journal of Management* 18, no. 2 (1992): 267–294; and Thomas Sy and Laura Sue D'Annunzio, "Challenges and Strategies of Matrix Organizations: Top-Level and Mid-Level Managers' Perspectives," *Human Resources Planning* 28, no. 1 (2005): 39–48.

49. These disadvantages are based on Sy and D'Annunzio, "Challenges and Strategies of Matrix Organizations"; and Michael Goold and Andrew Campbell, "Making Matrix Structures Work: Creating Clarity on Unit Roles and Responsibilities," *European Management Journal* 21, no. 3 (June 2003): 351–363.

50. Darren Dahl, "Strategy: Managing Fast, Flexible, and Full of Team Spirit," *Inc.* (May 2009): 95–97.

51. Gary Hamel, "Break Free," *Fortune* (October 1, 2007): 119–126, excerpted from Gary Hamel, *The Future of Management* (Boston: Harvard Business School Press, 2007); and Nick Paumgarten, "Food Fighter: The Whole Foods CEO vs. His Customers" (Profiles column), *The New Yorker* (January 4, 2010): 36.

52. Jill Jusko, "Engaged Teams Keep Lockheed Martin Delivering on Time, Every Time," *IndustryWeek* (January 2013): 26.

53. Melissa A. Schilling and H. Kevin Steensma, "The Use of Modular Organizational Forms: An Industry-Level Analysis," *Academy of Management Journal* 44, no. 6 (December 2001): 1149–1169.

54. Bob Sechler, "Colleges Shedding Non-Core Operations," *The Wall Street Journal*, April 2, 2012, A6; David Streitfeld, "A City Outsources Everything. California's Sky Doesn't Fall," *The New York Times*, July 20, 2010, A1.

55. Jena McGregor, "The Chore Goes Offshore," *BusinessWeek* (March 23 & 30, 2009): 50–51.

56. Raymond E. Miles and Charles C. Snow, "The New Network Firm: A Spherical Structure Built on a Human Investment Philosophy," *Organizational Dynamics* (Spring 1995): 5–18; and Raymond E. Miles et al., "Organizing in the Knowledge Age: Anticipating the Cellular Form," *Academy of Management Executive* 11, no. 4 (1997): 7–24.

57. Darren Dahl, "Want a Job? Let the Bidding Begin; A Radical Take on the Virtual Company," *Inc.* (March 2011), 93–96; and Eric Markowitz, "3 Weird, Game-Changing Ways to Make Employees Happy," *Inc.* May 2012, http://www.inc.com/eric-markowitz/philip-rosedale-second-life-coffee-power-make-emloyees-happy.html (accessed October 2, 2013); and SendLove Web site, http://www.sendlove.us/trial/faq.php.

58. Raymond E. Miles and Charles C. Snow, "Organizations: New Concepts for New Forms," *California Management Review* 28 (Spring 1986): 62–73; and John W. Wilson and Judith H. Dobrzynski, "And Now, the Post-Industrial Corporation," *BusinessWeek* (March 3, 1986): 64–74.

59. N. Anand, "Modular, Virtual, and Hollow Forms of Organization Design," working paper, London Business School (2000); Don Tapscott, "Rethinking Strategy in a Networked World," *Strategy + Business* 24 (Third Quarter 2001): 34–41.

60. Gregory G. Dess et al., "The New Corporate Architecture," *Academy of Management Executive* 9, no. 3 (1995): 7–20.

61. Joann S. Lublin, "Smart Balance Keeps Tight Focus on Creativity" (Theory & Practice Column), *The Wall Street Journal*, June 8, 2009; and Rebecca Reisner, "A Smart Balance of Staff and Contractors," *BusinessWeek Online*, June 16, 2009, www.businessweek.com/managing/content/jun2009/ca20090616_217232.htm (accessed April 30, 2010).

62. Charles Levinson and Margaret Coker, "The Secret Rally That Sparked an Uprising; Cairo Protest Organizers Describe Ruses Used to Gain Foothold Against Police," *The Wall Street Journal Online*, February 11, 2011, http://online.wsj.com/article/SB10001424052748704132204576135882356532702.html (accessed August 16, 2012).

63. Dexter Filkins, "Profusion of Rebel Groups Helps Them Survive in Iraq," *The New York Times*, December 2, 2005, www.nytimes.com/2005/12/02/international/middleeast/02insurgency.html (accessed August 30, 2010).

64. Raymond E. Miles, "Adapting to Technology and Competition: A New Industrial Relations System for the Twenty-First Century," *California Management Review* (Winter 1989): 9–28; and Miles and Snow, "The New Network Firm."

65. These disadvantages are based on Cecily A. Raiborn, Janet B. Butler, and Marc F. Massoud, "Outsourcing Support Functions: Identifying and Managing the Good, the Bad, and the Ugly," *Business Horizons* 52 (2009): 347–356; Dess et al., "The New Corporate Architecture"; Anand and Daft, "What Is the Right Organization Design?"; Henry W. Chesbrough and David J. Teece, "Organizing for Innovation: When Is Virtual Virtuous?" *The Innovative Entrepreneur* (August 2002): 127–134; N. Anand, "Modular, Virtual, and Hollow Forms of Organization Design"; and M. Lynne Markus, Brook Manville, and Carole E. Agres, "What Makes a Virtual Organization Work?" *Sloan Management Review* (Fall 2000): 13–26.

66. James R. Hagerty, "A Toy Maker Comes Home to the U.S.A.," *The Wall Street Journal*, March 11, 2013, B1; Shelly Banjo, "Wal-Mart to Police U.S. Warehouses," *The Wall Street Journal*, December 28, 2012, B4.

67. Steven Pearlstein, "Lifeguard's Ordeal Is Parable about Outsourcing," *The Washington Post*, July 14, 2012, www.washingtonpost.com/business/lifeguards-ordeal-is-parable-about-outsourcing/2012/07/13/gJQAN6TtkW_story.html (accessed August 16, 2012).

68. Laurie P. O'Leary, "Curing the Monday Blues: A U.S. Navy Guide for Structuring Cross-Functional Teams," *National Productivity Review* (Spring 1996): 43–51; and Alan Hurwitz, "Organizational Structures for the 'New World Order,'" *Business Horizons* (May–June 1996): 5–14.

69. Jay Galbraith, Diane Downey, and Amy Kates, "Processes and Lateral Capability," *Designing Dynamic Organizations* (New York: AMACOM, 2002), Chapter 4.

70. Thomas Kayser, "Six Ingredients for Collaborative Partnerships," *Leader to Leader* (Summer 2011): 48–54.

71. Siobhan Gorman and Julian E. Barnes, "Spy, Military Ties Aided bin Laden Raid," *The Wall Street Journal*, May 23, 2011, http://online.wsj.com/article/SB1000142405274870408390457633416017206834.html (accessed May 23, 2011).

72. Nick Wingfield, "Seeking Spark, Microsoft Revamps Its Structure," http://www.nytimes.com/2013/07/12/technology/microsoft-revamps-structure-and-management.html?pagewanted=all (accessed July 11, 2013).

73. Susanna Kim, "Major Microsoft Investors Want Gates Out as Chairman," *ABC News*, October 2, 2013, http://abcnews.go.com/Business/microsoft-shareholders-call-bill-gates-step-chairman/story?id=20443636 (accessed October 2, 2013).

74. William J. Altier, "Task Forces: An Effective Management Tool," *Management Review* (February 1987): 52–57.

75. Example from Paul Adler and Laurence Prusak, "Building a Collaborative Enterprise," *Harvard Business Review* (July–August 2011): 95–101.

76. Henry Mintzberg, *The Structure of Organizations* (Englewood Cliffs, NJ: Prentice Hall, 1979).

77. Paul R. Lawrence and Jay W. Lorsch, "New Managerial Job: The Integrator," *Harvard Business Review* (November–December 1967): 142–151; and Ronald N. Ashkenas and Suzanne C. Francis, "Integration Managers: Special Leaders for Special Times," *Harvard Business Review* (November–December 2000): 108–116.

78. Jody Hoffer Gittell, *The Southwest Airlines Way: Using the Power of Relationships to Achieve High Performance* (New York: McGraw-Hill, 2003).

79. This discussion is based on Jody Hoffer Gittell, "Coordinating Mechanisms in Care Provider Groups: Relational Coordination as a Mediator and Input Uncertainty as a Moderator of Performance Effects," *Management Science* 48, no 11 (November 2002), 1408–1426; J. H. Gittell, "The Power of Relationships," *Sloan Management Review* (Winter 2004), 16–17; and Gittell, *The Southwest Airlines Way.*

80. Ben Kesling and James R. Hagerty, "Say Goodbye to the Office Cubicle," *The Wall Street Journal*, April 2, 2013, B1.

81. University of Michigan study, reported in Rachel Emma Silverman, "The Science of Serendipity in the Workplace," *The Wall Street Journal*, May 1, 2013, B6.

82. Jody Hoffer Gittell, "Paradox of Coordination and Control," *California Management Review* 42, no 3 (Spring 2000): 101–117.

83. Claudio Feser, "Long Live Bureaucracy," *Leader to Leader* (Summer 2012): 57–65; and Harold J. Leavitt, "Why Hierarchies Thrive," *Harvard Business Review* (March 2003): 96–102, discuss the benefits and problems of vertical hierarchies. See Timothy Galpin, Rod Hilpirt, and Bruce Evans, "The Connected Enterprise: Beyond Division of Labor," *Journal of Business Strategy* 28, no. 2 (2007): 38–47, for a discussion of the advantages of horizontal over vertical designs.

84. Eric M. Olson, Stanley F. Slater, and G. Tomas M. Hult, "The Importance of Structure and Process to Strategy Implementation," *Business Horizons* 48 (2005): 47–54; and Dale E. Zand, "Strategic Renewal: How an Organization Realigned Structure with Strategy," *Strategy & Leadership* 37, no. 3 (2009): 23–28.

85. Michael E. Porter, *Competitive Strategy* (New York: Free Press, 1980), pp. 36–46.

86. Tom Burns and G. M. Stalker, *The Management of Innovation* (London: Tavistock, 1961).

87. John A. Coutright, Gail T. Fairhurst, and L. Edna Rogers, "Interaction Patterns in Organic and Mechanistic Systems," *Academy of Management Journal* 32 (1989): 773–802.

88. For more on technology and structure, see Denise M. Rousseau and Robert A. Cooke, "Technology and Structure: The Concrete, Abstract, and Activity Systems of Organizations," *Journal of Management* 10 (1984): 345–361; Charles Perrow, "A Framework for the Comparative Analysis of Organizations," *American Sociological Review* 32 (1967): 194–208; and Denise M. Rousseau, "Assessment of Technology in Organizations: Closed versus Open Systems Approaches," *Academy of Management Review* 4 (1979): 531–542.

89. Joan Woodward, *Industrial Organizations: Theory and Practice* (London: Oxford University Press, 1965); and Joan Woodward, *Management and Technology* (London: Her Majesty's Stationery Office, 1958).

90. Peter K. Mills and Thomas Kurk, "A Preliminary Investigation into the Influence of Customer-Firm Interface on Information Processing and Task Activity in Service Organizations," *Journal of Management* 12 (1986): 91–104; Peter K. Mills and Dennis J. Moberg, "Perspectives on the Technology of Service Operations," *Academy of Management Review* 7 (1982): 467–478; and Roger W. Schmenner, "How Can Service Businesses Survive and Prosper?" *Sloan Management Review* 27 (Spring 1986): 21–32.

91. Richard B. Chase and David A. Tansik, "The Customer Contact Model for Organization Design," *Management Science* 29 (1983): 1037–1050; and Gregory B. Northcraft and Richard B. Chase, "Managing Service Demand at the Point of Delivery," *Academy of Management Review* 10 (1985): 66–75.

92. Geeta Anand, "The Henry Ford of Heart Surgery," *The Wall Street Journal*, November 25, 2009, A16.

93. Based on Doug Wallace, "The Man Who Knew Too Much," *Business Ethics* 2 (March–April 1993): 7–8.

CHAPTER
8

Managing Change and Innovation

CHAPTER OUTLINE

LEARNING OUTCOMES

After studying this chapter, you should be able to:

8.1 Define organizational change and identify some reasons why people frequently resist change.

8.2 Explain disruptive innovation and the ambidextrous approach as possible responses to the forces that drive innovation and change in today's organizations.

8.3 Describe the three innovation strategies that managers implement for changing products and technologies.

8.4 Explain the value of creativity, a bottom-up approach, internal contests, idea incubators, idea champions, and new-venture teams for innovation.

8.5 Describe the horizontal linkage model and how it contributes to successful product and service innovations.

8.6 Explain open innovation and how it is being used by today's organizations.

8.7 Discuss why changes in people and culture are critical to any change process.

8.8 Summarize the organization development (OD) stages of unfreezing, changing, and refreezing, and define large-group interventions.

8.9 Describe force-field analysis and implementation tactics that managers can use to overcome resistance.

●●●●○ 🛜   100% 🔋

‹ Messages

> ## R U Ready 2 B a Manager?
> Delivered

Before reading this chapter, please circle either "Mostly True" or "Mostly False" for each of the five questions below.

1 I think once they figure out a good way to do something, they should just keep doing it.

Mostly True	Mostly False

[page 318]

2 I am very creative.

Mostly True	Mostly False

[page 327]

3 I think being competitive is the best way to innovation.

Mostly True	Mostly False

[page 330]

4 Sometimes managers just want change for the sake of change and it wastes everyone's time.

Mostly True	Mostly False

[page 320]

5 Negotiation is always the best technique for implementing change.

Mostly True	Mostly False

[page 344]

The September 2013 shooting spree at the Washington Navy Yard, which left 12 people dead, is one of the saddest events in the U.S. Navy's recent history. How did a former Navy reservist with a history of mental health issues and a string of arrests for incidents involving firearms gain access to the secure facility and open fire on unsuspecting people? Aaron Alexis was working as a Navy contractor and had a secret security clearance that gave him access to the Yard because of flaws in the security screening process. In the wake of the deadly incident, families of all the victims (as well as the family of Alexis, who had been hearing voices and had sought mental health treatment) called for change. A week after the shooting, Department of Defense officials admitted that some red flags had been missed because of problems with the screening procedures. One significant recommendation for change is that all available police documents be included in reports used for determining eligibility for security clearances, which would have picked up on Alexis's previous incidents involving firearms. The recommendation has been sent to Secretary of Defense Chuck Hagel for approval. Other changes being considered by Navy Secretary Ray Mabus are to require more scrutiny of security applications at top levels and to have senior members, rather than junior officers, handle command security. However, putting any of these changes into practice will require great effort, training, and commitment at all levels to make a difference.[1]

Although this is an extreme example, the military is similar to all organizations in needing to regularly make changes in policies, practices, and operations to address shortcomings, respond to new challenges, or meet shifting needs. Every organization needs to change from time to time. In addition, innovation in products and services is what keeps companies thriving. If organizations don't change and innovate successfully, they die. Consider that only a small number of large companies reach the age of 40, according to a recent study of more than 6 million firms. The ones that survive are ruthless about innovation and change.[2] Every organization sometimes faces the need to change swiftly and dramatically to cope with a changing environment. Consider General Motors (GM). After sinking into bankruptcy and having to be bailed out by the U.S. government just a few years ago, GM amazingly regained its position as the world's largest automaker in 2011 by implementing a combination of management, structure, strategy, and product changes (since then, Toyota has taken over the top spot once again).[3]

In this chapter, we look at how organizations can be designed to respond to the environment through internal change and development. First, we define organizational change, look at some of the reasons why people resist change, and define disruptive innovation and the ambidextrous approach to innovation. Then we examine two key aspects of change in organizations: introducing new products and technologies, and changing people and culture. Finally, we explore some techniques that managers use to implement change.

8.1 Innovation and the Changing Workplace

Organizational change is defined as the adoption of a new idea or behavior by an organization.[4] Sometimes change and innovation are spurred by forces outside the organization, such as when a powerful customer demands annual price cuts, when a key supplier goes out of business, or when new government regulations go into effect. Implementing change is typically one of the most difficult aspects of management. Consider changes associated with implementing the Patient Protection and Affordable Care Act (PPACA), more commonly known as the Affordable Care Act (ACA) or "Obamacare." Open enrollment for individuals in new health insurance marketplaces began October 1, 2013, but by the end of

Do You Have True Grit?[5]

Instructions: Think about typical projects or hobbies that you initiate at home, school, or work. Respond to each of the following items as honestly as possible.

	Mostly True	Mostly False
1. I often set a goal but later choose to pursue a different one.		
2. I have been obsessed with a certain idea or project for a short time but later lose interest.		
3. I have difficulty maintaining my focus on projects that take more than a few months to complete.		
4. New ideas and projects sometimes distract me from previous ones.		
5. I finish whatever I begin.		
6. Setbacks don't discourage me.		
7. I am diligent.		
8. I am a hard worker.		
Total Score		

For items 1–4, give yourself 1 point for each False and 0 points for each True. Reverse this for items 5–8, with 1 point for each True and 0 points for each False.

Scoring and Interpretation: The score on these questions measures your grit, which is defined as your perseverance and passion for long-term goals. Grit is a key trait for change agents who must persevere through resistance and setbacks to succeed with implementation of a significant innovation. The grit score predicted achievement in challenging situations among cadets at West Point and final-round contestants of the Scripps National Spelling Bee. Individuals high in grit do not swerve from their change implementation goals. The grit scale is composed of two parts. Questions 1–4 measure "consistency of interest" and Questions 5–8 measure "perseverance of effort," so you can compare your scores on those two subscales. The average score for a group of students 25–34 was approximately 5 for grit, 2 for consistency of interest, and 3 for perseverance of effort.

the month, only a few people had been able to sign onto the Healthcare.gov Web site, much less sign up for insurance. Technical glitches weren't the only problem that Obama and other leaders encountered, either. Millions of Americans who had believed that they would be able to keep their current individual health insurance plans began receiving cancellation notices because their plans didn't meet the law's requirements. Obama issued an apology, and leaders began meeting with health insurance executives to try to find a solution to the problem of canceled policies.[6]

8.1a Why Do People Resist Change?

Managers and others involved in promoting new ideas have noticed that many people tend to prefer the status quo, which is one reason why change is so difficult. Understanding why people resist change is a good start toward knowing how to help lead needed change in organizations.

Self-Interest   People typically resist a change they believe conflicts with their self-interests. A proposed change in job design, structure, or technology may increase employees' workload, for example, or cause a real or perceived loss of power, prestige, pay, or benefits. Recall our discussion of loss aversion from Chapter 6. *The fear of personal loss is perhaps the biggest obstacle to organizational change.*[7] Many people will do whatever they can to avoid loss. Consider what is happening at Anheuser-Busch, which was acquired by the Belgian company InBev. Managers accustomed to flying first class or on company planes are now required to fly coach. Free beer is a thing of the past, and complimentary tickets to sporting events are few and far between. Once the envy of others in the industry because of their lavish perks, Anheuser-Busch employees are resisting the new managers' wide-ranging changes because they feel that they are losing both financially and in terms of status.[8] Similarly, managers at Houston-based power producer Dynegy resisted the change to an open floor plan for their offices because they viewed their private offices as symbols of their power and prestige in the organization.[9] In addition, they saw the change as a loss of control over their own lives and circumstances, which provoked a strong emotional reaction.

Lack of Understanding and Trust   Employees often distrust the intentions behind a change or do not understand the intended purpose of a change. If previous working relationships with a manager or promoter of an idea have been negative, resistance may occur. When CareFusion Corporation was spun off as a subsidiary of Cardinal Health, CEO David L. Schlotterbeck and other top executives wanted to implement new values of collaboration and teamwork, but lower-level managers were initially suspicious of their intentions. Only when they saw that top leaders were fully committed to the values and honored them in their own behavior did others begin to support the changes.[10]

Uncertainty   *Uncertainty* is lack of information about future events. It represents a fear of the unknown. It is especially threatening for employees who have a low tolerance for change and fear anything out of the ordinary. They do not know how a change will affect them and worry about whether they will be able to meet the demands of a new procedure or technology.[11] Hospitals that have spent millions of dollars adopting electronic medical records are having a hard time getting some doctors to use them. One reason is the uncertainty about how electronic records will change how doctors go about their daily work.[12] Most people have at least some fear of the unknown and are more comfortable dealing with the tried and true.[13] Consider that utility companies installing wireless smart meters in states from Maine to California have faced a strong backlash from customers who say the meters invade their privacy, increase costs, and threaten their health.[14]

"Change hurts. It makes people insecure, confused, and angry. People want things to be the same as they've always been, because that makes life easier. But if you're a leader, you can't let your people hang on to the past."
—Richard Marcinko, former U.S. Navy SEAL, author, and chairman of Red Cell International Corporation

Different Assessments and Goals   Another reason for resistance to change is that people who will be affected by a change or innovation may assess the situation differently from managers or promoters of a new idea. Critics frequently voice legitimate disagreements over the proposed benefits of a change. Managers in each department pursue different goals, and an innovation may detract from performance and goal achievement for some departments. At pharmaceuticals company Pfizer, top executives wanted to implement a computerized system for collecting and processing research trial data, which could cut the cost of new drug development by 40 percent. Research and development (R&D) managers resisted, citing their concern that the automation and standardization of case report forms would hamper their flexibility and creativity.[15]

Apple executives are also currently encountering this type of resistance. Since August 2010, Apple has been the largest U.S. corporation in terms of market valuation. But executives were under pressure to change because of poor working conditions in overseas supplier factories. More than half of the suppliers audited were found to have violated aspects of Apple's code of conduct, and some have broken laws as well. However, there is conflict within the company because although top executives want to improve conditions, some managers argue that a radical overhaul will derail crucial supplier relationships and slow innovation and the delivery of new products.[16]

These reasons for resistance are legitimate in the eyes of employees affected by the change. Managers should not ignore resistance; instead, they should diagnose the reasons and design strategies to gain acceptance by users.[17] Later in the chapter, we will discuss some techniques that managers can use to overcome resistance and smoothly implement change.

The Group Learning on pages 347–350 will give you an idea of how difficult it is to determine who is responsible for change.

8.1b Disruptive Innovation

As we discussed previously, sometimes outside forces compel managers to look for changes, such as creating greater efficiencies in operations or other alterations to keep the organization profitable. Other times, managers within the company see a need for product or service innovation.

Disruptive innovation is becoming a goal for companies that want to remain competitive on a global basis. **Disruptive innovation** refers to innovations in products or services that typically start small and end up completely replacing an existing product or service technology for producers and consumers. Companies that initiate a disruptive innovation typically win big; companies affected by a disruptive technology may be put out of business. DVDs all but wiped out the videotape industry, for example, and now streaming video is threatening DVDs with the same fate. Digital cameras appear to be eliminating the photographic film industry, and the smartphone is threatening the compact digital camera, as we discussed in Chapter 2. People prefer to use their smartphones for snapshots because they can easily share the photos on social networks. Sales of point-and-shoot cameras continue to fall.[18] *Massive, open, online classes (MOOCs)* could become a disruptive innovation to the traditional and expensive classroom-based form of delivering courses for a college education. Coursera, a Mountain View, California, company, has 3.5 million registered users for its 370 mostly free online college courses.[19] A company called Square developed a credit card reader that plugs into a smartphone. This is a disruptive innovation in the trillion-dollar financial services system for credit card payments. Square enabled millions of small businesses that couldn't afford the transaction fees charged by financial companies to begin accepting credit cards.[20] Many disruptive innovations come from small

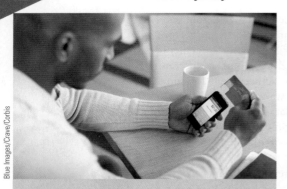

CONCEPT CONNECTION Technological advances in smartphones have paved the way for mobile credit card readers from providers such as Square, Intuit GoPayment, and Merchant Anywhere. This **disruptive innovation** has been a major step forward for small business owners, allowing them to accept credit card payments on the fly and with minimal transaction fees. The mobile readers are especially useful for merchants who sell their wares in outdoor environments, such as flea markets, arts and crafts fairs, and farmer's markets.

entrepreneurial firms like Square and Coursera. Some observers think that companies in emerging markets such as China and India will produce a great percentage of such innovations in the coming years.[21] Godrej & Boyce, for example, created a portable, low-cost, battery-powered refrigerator for India, called the chotuKool, as we described in Chapter 3. Lenovo has introduced LePhone in China as an inexpensive alternative to the iPhone.[22]

This is connected to the trend called **reverse innovation**. Rather than innovating in affluent countries and transferring products to emerging markets, companies such as Lenovo, General Electric (GE), John Deere, Nestlé, Procter & Gamble (P&G), and Xerox are creating innovative, low-cost products for emerging markets and then quickly and inexpensively repackaging them for sale in developed countries. GE Healthcare's team in China created a portable ultrasound machine that sold for less than 15 percent of the cost of the company's high-end machines. GE now sells the product around the world, and it grew to a $278 million global product line within six years. John Deere developed a high-quality, low-cost tractor for farmers in India that is increasingly in demand in the United States among farmers reeling from the recession.[23]

8.1c The Ambidextrous Approach

Change—especially major change such as that associated with disruptive innovation—is not easy, and many organizations struggle with changing successfully. In some cases, employees don't have the desire or motivation to come up with new ideas, or their ideas never get heard by managers who could put them into practice. In other cases, managers learn about good ideas but have trouble getting cooperation from employees for implementation. Successful change requires that organizations be capable of both creating and implementing ideas, which means the organization must learn to be *ambidextrous*.

An **ambidextrous approach** means incorporating structures and processes that are appropriate for both the creative impulse and for the systematic implementation of innovations. For example, a loose, flexible structure and greater employee freedom are excellent for the creation and initiation of ideas; however, these same conditions often make it difficult to implement a change because employees are less likely to comply. With an ambidextrous approach, managers encourage flexibility and freedom to innovate and propose new ideas with creative departments and other mechanisms that we will discuss in this chapter, but they use a more rigid, centralized, and standardized approach for implementing innovations.[24] For example, Mike Lawrie, CEO of the London-based software company Misys, created a separate unit for Misys Open Source Solutions, a venture aimed at creating a potentially disruptive technology in the health care industry. Lawrie wanted creative people to have the time and resources they needed to work on new software that holds the promise of seamless data exchange among hospitals, physicians, insurers, and others involved in the health care system. Implementation of new ideas, where routine and precision is important, occurs within the regular organization.[25] Twenty-eight year-old Nate Morris disrupted the way garbage is handled and has created a successful, growing company, as shown in this chapter's Director's Toolkit.

Director's Toolkit

Rubicon Global

If you think Waste Management is run primarily by Tony Soprano & friends, think again. Nate Morris was 25 when he started Rubicon Global in Walton, Kentucky, being inspired by fellow Kentuckian Colonel Sanders, who started the mega-company KFC from a single, roadside restaurant.

After graduating from George Washington University, he went to graduate school and hoped to go in to politics, but the 2008 crash came, and he knew his prospects were limited. So, he did what he had until then avoided: he went into the family waste management business, even though there was no company to take over. What he learned was that a large percentage of profits was from landfills, so companies were incentivized to create more garbage.

Morris decided it was time for a change and came up with a way to help customers and the environment. He borrowed against his credit cards, started a Web site, reached out to his network, and managed to get in front of the CEO of one of the largest pizza chains." I want your garbage contract," he said, stunning the CEO, who was used to loftier requests. Because of his forthrightness, he got the contract. He figured out that much of the leftover pizza dough could be reprocessed into ethanol. Innovative recycling became his thing. For a supermarket chain, he shredded 40,000 old uniforms for pet bedding; he repurposed used insulated cartons for a different use. One major recycling organization estimates that $11.4 billion worth of recyclable goods get wasted in landfills.

By 2014, Morris had managed to run waste management for a number of *Fortune* 500 companies, including 7-Eleven. He reduces their waste bills by up to 30 percent by not only recycling, but also by being a broker of waste-hauling services. The person he took longest to convince was his mother, who didn't imagine her son would end up as a garbage man. "You could have done that out of high school," she said. Maybe not, if he wanted to run a multimillion dollar company. His mother has since come around.

SOURCE: David Zax, "Dividing and Conquering the Trash," *New York Times*, October 26, 2014, BU1 and BU6

REMEMBER THIS

- Every organization must change and innovate to survive.
- **Organizational change** is defined as the adoption of a new idea or behavior by an organization.
- Many people prefer the status quo and tend to resist change. The biggest obstacle to organizational change is the fear of personal loss.
- Other reasons why people resist change are lack of understanding and trust, uncertainty, and different assessments and goals.

- **Disruptive innovation** refers to innovations in products, services, or processes that radically change competition in an industry, such as the advent of streaming video or online college courses.
- An **ambidextrous approach** means incorporating structures and processes that are appropriate for both the creative impulse and the systematic implementation of innovations.

8.2 Changing Things: New Products and Technologies

Organizations must embrace many types of change. One vital area of innovation is the introduction of new products, services, and technologies. A **product change** is a change in the organization's product or service outputs. Product and service innovation is the primary way in which organizations adapt to changes in markets, technology, and competition.[26] One example of a service innovation is HBO Go, the first comprehensive mobile

Spotlight on Skills

Elkay Manufacturing

The water fountain hasn't changed much in recent decades. Then, a few years ago, managers at Elkay Manufacturing started noticing what they call "the airport dance": people doing a shuffle as they tried to tilt their bottles at the right angle to fill them at the water fountain without splashing water all over themselves.

Elkay began reconsidering the water fountain to create a bottle-filling station instead. Americans have reduced their consumption of soft drinks and also cut their purchases of bottled water. About half of the water people consume these days comes from taps, including drinking fountains. Elkay managers wanted a fountain where people could fill their bottles without ever even touching the fountain, to avoid the concern that many people have about germs. Moreover, they thought that filling a 16-ounce bottle should take less than 10 seconds. Early in the project, one engineer said that wasn't possible. Another engineer, who joined Elkay from an auto parts company, found a way to speed up the flow.

The result was a machine that fills a 16-ounce bottle in about 5 seconds if the water is at room temperature, or a few seconds longer if it goes through refrigeration pipes. The traditional water fountain, by contrast, needed at least 20 seconds.

Elkay isn't the only company that has introduced a bottle-filling station, but the addition of a digital counter on Elkay's first EZH20 model ended up helping "make this thing go viral," said one manager who had originally thought the digital counter was a dumb idea. College students liked tracking how many plastic bottles were being kept out of landfills. Some held intracampus competitions to see who could reuse the most bottles. Incoming freshmen at Muhlenberg College in Allentown, Pennsylvania, which has installed 49 of the new EZH2O stations, receive a free, stainless steel water bottle. The college says sales of bottled water have fallen 90 percent. Students say that's at least 1.4 million plastic bottles that have been kept out of landfills.[27]

television service. In Kenya, where medical care and advice can be a far-off luxury for many people, local telecommunications giant Safaricom introduced a service innovation called Daktari that will connect callers one-on-one with a doctor for a small fee 24 hours a day, 7 days a week.[28] Examples of new products include Nike's Flyknit Racer running shoe, which weighs just 5.6 ounces, SodaStream, the home carbonation seltzer and soda maker, and the Nest home thermostat, which learns its user's patterns and adjusts to save energy.[29] Another "new" product on an old theme is the EZH2O water fountain from Elkay Manufacturing.

Other companies, including Haws Corporation and Oasis International, have also introduced new types of water fountains designed to fill water bottles. Elkay says that its new fountains have been installed in hundreds of colleges and universities and at least 15 airports, including Chicago's O'Hare and New York's LaGuardia.

As this example shows, product and service changes are related to changes in the technology of the organization. A **technology change** is a change in the organization's production process—how the organization does its work. Technology changes are designed to make the production of a product or service more efficient. Hammond's Candies saves hundreds of thousands of dollars a year by implementing technology changes suggested by employees. One example was tweaking a machine gear that reduced the number of employees needed on an assembly line from five to four.[30] Other examples of technology change include the introduction of efficiency-boosting winglets on aircraft at Southwest Airlines, the adoption of automatic mail-sorting machines by the U.S. Postal Service, and the use of biosimulation software to run virtual tests on new drugs at Johnson & Johnson's pharmaceutical research and development department.

Three critical innovation strategies for changing products and technologies are illustrated in Exhibit 8.1.[31] The first strategy, *exploration*, involves designing the organization to encourage creativity and the initiation of new ideas. The strategy of *cooperation* refers to creating conditions and systems to facilitate internal and external coordination and knowledge sharing. Finally, *innovation roles* means that managers put in place processes and structures to ensure that new ideas are carried forward for acceptance and implementation.

TAKE Action!

Assess your creativity by completing the "New Manager Self-Test" on page 327.

EXHIBIT 8.1   Three Innovation Strategies for New Products and Technologies

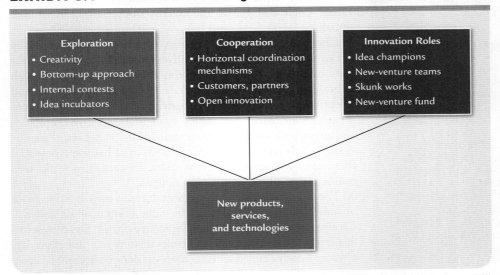

SOURCE: Based on Patrick Reinmoeller and Nicole van Baardwijk, "The Link Between Diversity and Resilience," *MIT Sloan Management Review* (Summer 2005): 61–65.

Green Power

Building a Better Mouse ...

We all have them: old laptops stuffed into closets, computer monitors, hard drives, and printers crammed into the corners of the garage. And who can forget the mouse (five of them, actually, still attached to cords) jammed into a drawer? In a world focused on sustainability, the challenge for managers in the electronics industry is how to change and innovate when the large outer casings for our products won't go away. **Fujitsu** broke this barrier by developing a keyboard made from renewable materials. A year later, using organic materials as a substitute for plastic, the company unveiled a mouse casing that was 100 percent biodegradable. Now, the race is on. Fujitsu's innovations offer a visionary promise that one day, all our electronic devices will be part of the sustainability revolution.

SOURCE: Staff writers, "Fujitsu Unveils 'World's First' Biodegradable Mouse," *Business Green*, January 25, 2011, www.businessgreen.com/bg/news/1939343/fujitsu-unveils-worlds-biodegradable-mouse (accessed January 25, 2011).

Robyn Twomey/Corbis Outline

CONCEPT CONNECTION   Innovative companies such as Intuit want everyone to be coming up with new ideas continually. Managers encourage **creativity** during the **exploration phase** by embracing failure as readily as they do success. "I've had my share of really bad ideas," founder Scott Cook, pictured here with former CEO Steve Bennett, admits. Yet failure can have hidden possibilities. Sticky notes, such as those shown here on Intuit's board, were invented at 3M Corporation based on a failed product—a not-very-sticky adhesive that resulted from a chemist's attempts to create a superglue. The resulting product, Post-it Notes, became one of the best-selling office supplies ever.

8.2a Exploration

Exploration is the stage where ideas for new products and technologies are born. Managers design the organization for exploration by establishing conditions that encourage creativity and allow new ideas to spring forth. Creativity refers to the generation of novel ideas that might meet perceived needs or respond to opportunities for the organization.[32] People noted for their creativity include Edwin Land, who invented the Polaroid camera, and Swiss engineer George de Mestral, who created Velcro after noticing the tiny hooks on some burrs caught on his wool socks. These people saw unique and creative opportunities in familiar situations.

Characteristics of highly creative people are illustrated in the left column of Exhibit 8.2. Creative people often are known for their originality, open-mindedness, curiosity, focused approach to problem solving, persistence, relaxed and playful attitude, and receptiveness to new ideas.[33] Creativity can also be designed into organizations. Most companies want more creative employees and often seek to hire creative individuals. However, the individual is only part of the story, and each of us has some potential for creativity. Managers are responsible for creating a work environment that allows creativity to flourish.[34]

The characteristics of creative organizations correspond to those of individuals, as illustrated in the right column of Exhibit 8.2. Creative organizations are loosely structured. People find themselves in a situation of ambiguity, assignments are vague, territories overlap, tasks are loosely defined, and much work is done by teams. Managers

EXHIBIT 8.2 **Characteristics of Creative People and Organizations**

The Creative Individual

- Persistence
- Commitment
- Focused approach
- Conceptual fluency
- Open-mindedness
- Originality
- Playfulness
- Undisciplined exploration
- Curiosity
- Less authority
- Independence
- Self-confidence

The Creative Organization

- Resources allocated to creative personnel and projects without immediate payoff
- Reward system encourages innovation
- Absolution of peripheral responsibilities
- Open channels of communication
- Contact with outside sources
- Overlapping territories; cross-pollination of ideas across disciplines
- Suggestion systems, brainstorming, freewheeling discussions
- Assigning nonspecialists to problems
- Eccentricity allowed
- Hiring outside your comfort zone
- Freedom to choose and pursue problems
- Not a tight ship, playful culture, doing the impractical
- Freedom to discuss ideas; long time horizon
- Decentralization, loosely defined positions, loose control
- Acceptance of mistakes; rewarding risk-taking
- People encouraged to challenge their bosses

SOURCES: Based on Gary A. Steiner, ed., *The Creative Organization* (Chicago: University of Chicago Press, 1965), pp. 16–18; Rosabeth Moss Kanter, "The Middle Manager as Innovator," *Harvard Business Review* (July–August 1982): 104–105; James Brian Quinn, "Managing Innovation: Controlled Chaos," *Harvard Business Review* (May–June 1985): 73–84; Robert I. Sutton, "The Weird Rules of Creativity," *Harvard Business Review* (September 2001): 94–103; and Bridget Finn, "Playbook: Brainstorming for Better Brainstorming," *Business* 2.0 (April 2005), 109–114.

NEW MANAGER Self-Test

Assess Your Creativity

Instructions: In the following list below, check each adjective that you believe accurately describes your personality. Be very honest with yourself. Check all the words that fit your personality.

1. affected _____

2. capable _____

3. cautious _____

4. clever _____

5. commonplace _____

6. confident _____

7. conservative _____

8. conventional _____

9. egotistical _____

10. dissatisfied _____

11. honest _____

12. humorous _____

13. individualistic _____

14. informal _____

15. insightful _____

16. intelligent _____

17. interests narrow _____

18. interests wide _____

19. inventive _____

20. mannerly _____

21. original _____

22. reflective _____

23. resourceful _____

24. self-confident _____

25. sexy _____

26. snobbish _____

27. sincere _____

28. submissive _____

29. suspicious _____

30. unconventional _____

Scoring and Interpretation: Add 1 point for checking each of the following words: 2, 4, 6, 9, 12, 13, 14, 15, 16, 18, 19, 21, 22, 23, 24, 25, 26, and 30. Subtract 1 point for checking each of the following words: 1, 3, 5, 7, 8, 10, 11, 17, 20, 27, 28, and 29. Score = _____. The highest possible score is +18; the lowest possible score is –12.

Innovation starts with creativity. Your score on this questionnaire reflects your creativity for solving problems and finding novel solutions. The average score for a set of 256 males on this creativity scale was 3.57, and for 126 females was 4.4. A group of 45 male research scientists and a group of 530 male psychology graduate students both had average scores of 6.0, and 124 male architects received an average score of 5.3. A group of 335 female psychology students had an average score of 3.34. If you have a score above 5.0, your personality would be considered above average in creativity. To what extent do you think your score reflects your true creativity? Compare your score to others in your class. Which adjectives were more important for your score compared to other students?

SOURCE: Harrison G. Clough, "A Creative Personality Scale for the Adjective Check List," *Journal of Personality and Social Psychology* 37, no. 8 (1979): 1398–1405.

in creative companies embrace risk and experimentation. They involve employees in a varied range of projects, so that people are not stuck in the rhythm of routine jobs, and they drive out the fear of making mistakes that can inhibit creative thinking.[35] Research shows that successful innovations are often accompanied by a high rate of failure. SurePayroll, a payroll-services company, gives out an annual "Best New Mistake" cash award to encourage people to take creative risks. Similarly, Grey Advertising awards an annual "Heroic Failure" trophy, to reward the "glorious defeats that can make success itself look timid."[36] Creative organizations are those

EXHIBIT 8.3   The World's Most Innovative Companies, 2013

Rank	Company	Reason
1	Nike	Revolutionary new products and a culture of true believers
2	Amazon	Speeding up delivery and the delivery of change
3	Square	Spreading the mobile payments revolution
4	Splunk	Bringing big data to the masses
5	Fab	Evolving into the online destination for design wares
6	Uber	The epitome of a data-driven disruptive startup
7	Sproxil	For sticking it to companies selling fraudulent goods
8	Pinterest	For unlocking our image obsession
9	Safaricom	Bridging a health care gap with telecom
10	Target	For shrinking the big box

SOURCE: "The World's 50 Most Innovative Companies," *Fast Company* (March 2013): 86–156.

that have an internal culture of playfulness, freedom, challenge, and grassroots participation.[37] Exhibit 8.3 shows the world's top 10 innovative companies from the 2013 list in *Fast Company*.

Innovative companies use a bottom-up approach, which means encouraging the flow of ideas from lower levels and making sure that they get heard and acted upon by top executives.[38] Chicago-based software firm 37Signals gave everyone a month off from their regular duties to work on new ideas. For the entire month of June, all nonessential work (which meant everything except customer service and keeping the servers running) was set aside, and people were allowed to work on anything they wanted. Some people worked solo and others formed teams. At the end of the month, top leaders listened to 29 idea presentations, including a new set of tools to manage customer accounts and a new data visualization technique that can help the company better understand how customers use its products. Cofounder Jason Fried says that 37Signals will continue to use the month off for freedom and exploration because it is a great way to get people to come up with new ideas for the business.[39] This chapter's "Director's Toolkit" describes a fun technique that some companies use to get people to come up with creative ideas for solving specific problems.

Some companies also use internal *innovation contests,* which are an increasingly popular way to realize product and service innovations.[40] Mike Hall, CEO of Borrego Solar Systems, holds "innovation challenge" contests on the company intranet to get his shy, introverted engineers to speak up with their ideas for improving the business. Employees vote on their favorites, and the winner takes home a cash prize. One idea that was quickly implemented was using software that enables sales and engineering teams to collaborate.[41] Managers at the accounting and consulting firm PricewaterhouseCoopers (PwC) challenged the stereotype that accountants are boring and unimaginative by sponsoring an *American Idol*–style contest to spur employees to come up with creative ideas.

Just as important as creating ideas is turning them into action. Sadly, research indicates that, on average, a U.S. employee's ideas are implemented only once every six years.[42] "There's nothing worse for morale than when employees feel like their ideas go nowhere," says Larry Bennett, a professor of entrepreneurship.[43] At PwC, all of the final ideas were assigned to a senior "champion," who will help the teams further develop and implement their proposals. Other ideas from the top 20 semifinalists were assigned to an idea incubator group. An idea incubator is a mechanism that provides a safe harbor where ideas from employees throughout the company can be developed without interference from company bureaucracy or politics.[44]

Go to the Self-Learning on page 347, which pertains to creativity in organizations.

Spotlight on Skills

PricewaterhouseCoopers

"We have an average age of 27, but we have roots in tax and assurance," said PricewaterhouseCoopers (PwC) U.S. chairman Bob Moritz. "So how do you make this place feel like a Google or a Facebook? A place that feels leading edge?"

Like other companies, PwC has felt the sting of increased competition and a shaky global economy. Harnessing the creativity of all employees in the search for profitable ideas seemed not only like a good thing to do, but like a business imperative. Mitra Best, PwC's "innovation leader" and a fan of *American Idol*, took ideas from that show, plus ideas from the video-game world of live chats and online discussions, to create PowerPitch, a fun, collaborative competition that would connect and inspire 30,000 PwC employees. Employees loved it. The competition, structured in three stages over a nine-month period, was open to any U.S. employee below the partner level. Each contestant had to recruit a team and pitch either a new service or a radical rethinking of an existing service that could be worth $100 million in

revenue. The winning team would get a $100,000 prize, plus the chance to help implement the new idea.

Nearly 800 proposals were pitched in the first round, and by the grand finale, nearly 60 percent of people in the firm had participated in one way or another—direct participation, voting, comments and suggestions, and so forth. The five finalist teams were flown to PwC headquarters in New York to present their proposals and answer questions from judges in a packed corporate auditorium. Offices around the country held viewing parties, watching the competition via live Webcast. The winning team, led by 25-year-old financial services associate Zachary Capozzi, proposed creating a sophisticated data-mining practice within PwC that uses the sort of analytics that Netflix uses to predict which movies customers are interested in. For clients who don't have that capability in house, the service can be invaluable—and it can be a source of new clients and a big new revenue stream for PwC.[45]

Director's Toolkit

Use Six Thinking Hats for Better Ideas

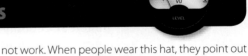

A technique that can promote broader thinking is called Six Thinking Hats, which was developed by Edward de Bono. The model encourages people in a group to combine negative and critical thinking with positive and creative thinking. Participants either literally or figuratively wear a hat to represent a distinct perspective. The wearing of the hats helps individuals step out of their comfort zone and generate creative ideas in a risk-free way. The Six Thinking Hats technique can transform a typical nonproductive meeting into a highly creative problem-solving endeavor. The Six Hats

- **White Hat:** This thinking hat is neutral and concerned with just the objective facts, figures, and information pertaining to a problem.

- **Red Hat:** This hat allows an emotional response to the subject. It is a perspective based on feelings, intuitions, instincts, and hunches.

- **Green Hat:** The green hat is the one that generates new ideas, possibilities, alternatives, and unique solutions for better problem solving.

- **Black Hat:** This is the negative, pessimistic, and critical hat, which focuses on why a suggestion will

not work. When people wear this hat, they point out the flaws and false assumptions in an idea.

- **Yellow Hat:** The yellow hat is the opposite of the black hat. It is optimistic and focuses on the values and benefits of an idea. Its focus is on what will work.

- **Blue Hat:** This hat is concerned with group facilitation. The group leader typically assumes the blue hat role, although any member can wear the blue hat from time to time. Using the Technique

To apply the Six Thinking Hats technique, schedule a specific time during a creative problem-solving meeting when every person in the group wears the same color of hat—that is, takes the same perspective. A time is set aside when everyone uses rational, fact-based thinking (white hat), emotional thinking (red hat), creative thinking (green hat), and so forth. The result is that each perspective (hat) is heard in sequence, and negative views or arguments do not overwhelm creativity. Everyone together has a time to think of good ideas, as well as a time for finding weak points.

SOURCE: Based on Edward de Bono, *Serious Creativity: Using the Power of Lateral Thinking to Create New Ideas* (New York: HarperBusiness, 1992).

REMEMBER THIS

- **A product change** is a change in the organization's products or services, such as the Nike Flyknit Racer running shoe or the Nest home thermostat.
- **Technology change** refers to a change in production processes—how the organization does its work.
- *Exploration* involves designing the organization to encourage creativity and the initiation of new ideas.
- **Creativity** is the generation of novel ideas that may meet perceived needs or respond to opportunities for the organization.

- Software firm 37Signals applied a **bottom-up approach**, giving everyone a month off from their regular duties to come up with creative ideas for new products and services.
- An **idea incubator** is an organizational program that provides a safe harbor where employees can generate and develop ideas without interference from company bureaucracy or politics.

8.2b Cooperation

Ideas for product and technology innovations typically originate at lower levels of the organization and need to flow horizontally across departments. In addition, people and organizations outside the firm can be rich sources of innovative ideas. Lack of innovation is widely recognized as one of the biggest problems facing today's businesses. Consider that 72 percent of top executives surveyed by *BusinessWeek* and the Boston Consulting Group reported that innovation is a top priority, yet almost half said that they are dissatisfied with their results in that area.[46] Thus, many companies are undergoing a transformation in the way they find and use new ideas, focusing on improving both internal and external coordination and cooperation.

Internal Coordination   Successful innovation requires expertise from several departments simultaneously, and failed innovation is often the result of failed cooperation.[47] Recent studies at the Massachusetts Institute of Technology (MIT) suggest that keeping research and manufacturing close together helps companies be more innovative, for instance. GE custom-built a large manufacturing facility in upstate New York to be near its research campus, where a new secret battery technology was being invented. The idea was to knit together design, prototyping, manufacturing, testing, and production for uses of the new battery technology.[48]

Sony, once the epitome of Japanese innovation success, is literally fighting to stay alive because the company hasn't had a hit product in years. To be sure, Sony was battered by one after another disruptive new technology or unexpected competitor, but the biggest problem was that managers were unable to fight back because of poor cooperation within the organization. The company had the technology to create a music player like the iPod long before Apple came out with it (cofounder Akio Morita actually envisioned such a device in the 1980s), but divisions couldn't cooperate to bring the idea to fruition.[49] "Innovation is a team sport," says Drew Boyd, a businessman who speaks about innovation to other companies.[50] Sealy revived its high-end Stearns & Foster line of mattresses by pushing engineers, product designers, and sales and marketing people to work with one another, as well as with customers and outside design firm IDEO. The result was that sales of the Stearns & Foster line broke records. Allen Platek, vice president of new-product development, said the new product revamp was "one of the most fun times of my career."[51]

Companies that successfully innovate usually have the following characteristics:

- People in research and marketing actively work with customers to understand their needs and develop solutions.

- Technical specialists are aware of recent developments and make effective use of new technology.

- A shared new-product development process that is advocated and supported by top management cuts across organizational functions and units.

- Members from key departments—research, manufacturing, marketing—cooperate in the development of the new product or service.

- Each project is guided by a core cross-functional team from beginning to end.[52]

One approach to successful innovation is called the horizontal linkage model, which is illustrated in the center circle of Exhibit 8.4.[53] The model shows that the research, manufacturing, and sales and marketing departments within an organization simultaneously contribute to new products and technologies. People from these departments meet frequently in teams and task forces to share ideas and solve problems. Research people inform marketing of new technical developments to find out whether they will be useful to customers. Marketing people pass customer complaints to research to use in the design of new products and to manufacturing people to develop new ideas for improving production speed and quality. Manufacturing informs other departments whether a product idea can be manufactured within cost limits. Throughout the process, development teams keep in close touch with customers. A study by McKinsey found that 80 percent of successful innovators

EXHIBIT 8.4 Coordination Model for Innovation

CONCEPT CONNECTION   Innovation often requires **internal coordination** because it takes the combined expertise of a number of different team players, each with its own areas of specialization, to come up with a single creative, yet realistic, solution. One successful approach to innovation is the **horizontal linkage model**, which shows the combined importance of the research, manufacturing, sales, and marketing departments simultaneously contributing to new products and technologies.

periodically test and validate customer preferences during development of new products and services.[54] Unfortunately, "new products can take on a life of their own within an organization, becoming so hyped that there's no turning back," wrote Joan Schneider and Julie Hall, coauthors of *The New Launch Plan: 152 Tips, Tactics, and Trends from the Most Memorable New Products.*[55]

The horizontal linkage model is increasingly important in a high-pressure business environment that requires rapidly developing and commercializing products and services. Speed is a pivotal strategic weapon in today's global marketplace.[56] This kind of teamwork is similar to a rugby match, wherein players run together, passing the ball back and forth as they move downfield.[57] Corning used a horizontal linkage model to create a new product for the mobile industry.

By using a horizontal linkage model for new-product development, Corning has been highly effective in rapidly taking products from idea to success in the marketplace. Famous innovation failures—such as Microsoft's Zune music player and the U.S. Mint's Susan B. Anthony dollar, perhaps the most unpopular coin in American history—usually violate the horizontal linkage model.

External Coordination   Exhibit 8.4 also illustrates that organizations look outside their boundaries to find and develop new ideas. Engineers and researchers stay aware of new technological developments. Marketing personnel pay attention to shifting

Spotlight on Skills

Corning, Inc.

Plastic screens on cell phones and tablets are easily scratched and broken, which gave a small team in Corning's specialty materials division an idea: What if they could find a way to make mobile screens out of a superstrong but flexible glass that the company had originally attempted (unsuccessfully) to sell for automobile windshields in the 1960s? Just producing an experimental batch to gauge customer interest would cost as much as $300,000, but managers took the risk because the project had a strong idea champion.

Once the test run was completed and potential customers expressed excitement at the idea, managers had to move quickly. Corning took the project from concept to commercial success in an amazingly short period of time. One reason is that the company had both the right culture and the right systems. Corning divisions and departments know that top managers expect, support, and reward collaboration on promising new product launches. Innovation at Corning is managed

not by lone inventors or small teams in silos, but rather by multidisciplinary groups all across the organization. The company has two units—the Corporate Technology Council and the Growth and Strategy Council—that are charged with overseeing the innovation process and making sure departments effectively cooperate in new product development efforts that are sanctioned by management. Thus, employees from R&D, manufacturing, and sales quickly agreed to serve on the team developing the new glass product.

By the spring of 2013, Corning's new product, called Gorilla Glass, was used on more than 1 billion smartphones and tablets and was a $1 billion-a-year business. Gorilla Glass 2, released in 2012, is up to 20 percent thinner, so companies can make slimmer devices. Version 3 promises to be 40 percent more scratch resistant. As more displays incorporate touch screens, the company keeps innovating. Gorilla Glass landed Corning at Number 36 on *Fast Company's* list of most innovative companies in 2013.[58]

market conditions and customer needs. Some organizations build formal strategic partner-ships, such as alliances and joint ventures, to improve innovation success.

Successful companies often include customers, strategic partners, suppliers, and other outsiders directly in the product and service development process. One of the hottest trends is *open innovation*.[59] In the past, most businesses generated their own ideas in house and then developed, manufactured, marketed, and distributed them, which is a closed innovation approach. Today, however, forward-looking companies are trying a different method. Open innovation means extending the search for and commercialization of new ideas beyond the boundaries of the organization and even beyond the boundaries of the industry, sharing knowledge and resources with other organizations and individuals outside the firm. For example, game maker Rovio extended the commercialization of the Angry Birds brand into books, movies, and toys by letting outsiders license the popular gaming app.[60] Even Apple, which has always been famously "closed" in many ways, found a way to tap into the power of open innovation by allowing anyone to create and market mobile applications for the iPhone in exchange for a share of the revenue generated by the apps.[61] Google looked to filmmakers, videographers, and other creative people when it decided to include original content movies and series on its YouTube, as described in the Spotlight on Skills box.

Spotlight on Skills

Jash/YouTube

Hollywood remembers how the music and newspaper businesses were decimated by technology, and it realizes that 2012 was the first year that more people watched movies on the Internet than in theaters or on DVD. Times have changed. There's a group of "Harvard digital mafia" of 30-ish professionals in start-ups, finance, and publicity who are more proactive and creative in this way. One of these young and brash members is Daniel Kellison, most famous for being a producer for Jimmy Kimmel and also on *Late Night with David Letterman*, where he famously convinced Drew Barrymore to have a wardrobe malfunction and to flash a part of her otherwise-covered anatomy.

When YouTube approached Kellison to be part of their several hundred million dollar project to develop original content that would allow him 100 percent creative control and total ownership, he saw it as the chance of a lifetime. In previous eras (say a few years ago), talent was pursued. Now the current crop of techie kings are after intellectual property (equity) that can be created, owned, and repurposed by the developer. Getting on the ground in this way is seen as the cable-TV opportunity of the twenty-first century. "Folks in the entertainment world realized that equity is how people get rich," says Chris Sacca who recently started a digital entertainment fund.

Kellison is working with comedian Sarah Silverman, who previously had only 40,000 subscribers to her

YouTube channel. Compare this to someone like Jon Elerick, who gets 56 million hits to his comedy videos and has 300,000 subscribers. Seeing a real business opportunity for people like Michael Cera and Silverman who "don't know how to monetize" their work, he helps them find the digital audience through their new "Jash" domain. In fact, Cera was so impressed that he became one of the cofounders of Jash.

Another mover in this direction is Brian Robbins, who watched how his two sons were more enamored of shows and sports games on their laptops than they were on a new large flat-screen TV. That's when Robbins saw the future is *now*. A former actor and producer (*Smallville* and *One Tree Hill*), he's now working in digital and says that it will one day look exactly like cable TV. "I don't know if you know about how ESPN got started but it was, like, these guys in Connecticut." Or, as The Collective digital production founder Michael Green says, "I always think of it like HBO in 1976 or 1977." But one thing Hollywood still has to learn about the YouTube world: It's not just getting hits, but getting people to share, something traditional celebrities such as Sarah Silverman are just starting to learn.

SOURCE: "The Bluths Have Been Busy since 'Arrested Development,' Stl" *St. Louis Post-Dispatch*, September 26, 2014, G17; Nicole LaPorte, "The Rebels Saving Hollywood,," *Fast Company*, April 2013, 76–86, 112–113.

In a study by Booz & Company, 3M was the third most frequently cited innovation leader, right behind Apple and Google. 3M has a track record for developing innovative and successful new products, and managers admit that success depends on open innovation and cross-pollination of ideas. The abrasives division recently introduced an entirely new kind of sandpaper. The division used seven different technologies to create the product, only two of which came from the division. 3M is continually working with employees from universities and other companies, as well as with customers. The company has 30 customer technology centers where technical and marketing employees interact with customers to learn their needs and frustrations.[62]

The Internet has made it possible for companies to tap into ideas from around the world and let hundreds of thousands of people contribute to the innovation process, which is why some approaches to open innovation are referred to as **crowdsourcing**. Fiat introduced the first crowdsourced car, the Mio, in 2010. The automaker launched a Web site asking people to think about what the car of the future should be like, and more than 17,000 people around the world submitted ideas.[63] The most straightforward way to enlist the help of a crowd is with a contest.[64] Since September 2010, more than 16,000 people have participated in online competitions run by the U.S. government at Challenge.gov. In another example, Philips now sells a light-emitting diode (LED) bulb that won a $10-million Department of Energy contest. A current challenge is to get the electronic calendars at Department of Veterans Affairs (VA) hospitals and clinics communicating with one another so that veterans can go to the Web site and make an appointment whenever they need to be seen. After spending a decade and $127 million trying to address the issue, VA officials said they learned that "we needed to look outside rather than internally."[65] The federal government is relatively new to the world of crowdsourcing, but some companies have been using crowdsourcing for years. Tongal used crowdsourcing to create ads for Colgate-Palmolive's Speed Stick "Handle It" campaign. One ad was selected to run during the Super Bowl and was ranked by the Kellogg School of Management's annual review of Super Bowl advertising as number 12 out of 36, outperforming ads by Calvin Klein, Coke, Volkswagen, Toyota, and Pepsi.[66]

Crowdsourcing is also being used to gather creative ideas for solving social problems. After Super Typhoon Haiyan devastated the Philippines, for example, relief agencies had trouble getting health care workers and supplies to some of the most devastated regions. A project called Open Street Map gave hundreds of people a chance to help remotely by identifying where roads and buildings are located and where best to deliver supplies. Having people physically check locations could have taken weeks or months. Similarly, crowdsourced maps were used to identify the location of clinics following the 2010 earthquake in Haiti and to help relief workers set priorities for distribution of food, shelter, and sanitation services following the recent earthquake and tsunami in Japan.[67]

Another approach to innovation in recent years has been to buy start-up companies in order to obtain the innovative products and services, and often the talent behind them as well. This **innovation by acquisition** strategy recognizes that the cutting edge of innovation often happens with young, small, entrepreneurial companies rather than inside the walls of established firms. Google bought Android, and Facebook bought Instagram, to cite just two examples. Hotmail wasn't originally created by Microsoft; rather, it was bought by the firm in 1997. Yahoo has been on a recent acquisition spree, buying a number of start-ups to get new mobile technology.[68] Look at almost any large, successful company today, particularly in fast-moving industries, and you will find examples of innovation by acquisition.

REMEMBER THIS

- Successful product and service innovation depends on cooperation, both within the organization and with customers and others outside the organization.

- Using a **horizontal linkage model** means that several departments, such as marketing, research, and manufacturing, work closely together to develop new products.

- Corning created Gorilla Glass, used for most touch screens, using a horizontal linkage model.

- Some companies, such as 3M and Rovio, creator of the Angry Birds game, extend the search for and commercialization of innovative ideas beyond the boundaries of the organization—a process called **open innovation**.

- **Crowdsourcing**, an open innovation approach used by Fiat, Colgate-Palmolive, and even the U.S. government, taps into ideas from around the world and lets thousands or hundreds of thousands of people participate in the innovation process, usually via the Internet.

- **Innovation by acquisition** means buying start-up companies to get innovative products and services, and usually the talent that created them.

8.2c Innovation Roles

The third aspect of product and technology innovation is creating structural mechanisms to make sure that new ideas are carried forward, accepted, and implemented. Managers can directly influence whether entrepreneurship flourishes in the organization by expressing support of entrepreneurial activities, giving employees a degree of autonomy, and rewarding learning and risk-taking.[69] One important factor is fostering idea champions. The formal definition of an **idea champion** is a person who sees the need for and champions productive change within the organization.

Remember: Change does not occur by itself. Personal energy and effort are required to promote a new idea successfully. When Texas Instruments studied 50 of its new product introductions, a surprising fact emerged: Without exception, every one that failed lacked a zealous champion. By contrast, most of the new products that succeeded had such a champion. Managers made an immediate decision: No new product would be approved unless someone championed it. Similarly, at SRI International, a contract R&D firm, managers use the saying "No champion, no product, no exception."[70] Research confirms that successful new ideas are generally those that are backed by someone who believes in the idea wholeheartedly and is determined to convince others of its value.[71] Recall how the winning proposals at the PwC innovation contest discussed earlier in this chapter were all assigned to a senior champion so that they wouldn't get lost in the everyday shuffle.

Sometimes a new idea is rejected by top managers, but champions are passionately committed to a new idea or product despite rejection by others. For example, Robert Vincent was fired twice by two different division managers at a semiconductor company. Both times, he convinced the president and chairman of the board to reinstate him to continue working on his idea for an airbag sensor that measures acceleration and deceleration. He couldn't get approval for research funding, so Vincent pushed to finish another project in half the time and used the resulting savings to support the new-product development.[72]

Another way to facilitate entrepreneurship is through a **new-venture team**, which is a unit separate from the rest of the organization that is responsible for developing and initiating a major innovation.[73] New-venture teams give free rein to members' creativity because their separate facilities and location unleash people from the restrictions imposed by organizational rules and procedures. These teams typically are small, loosely structured, and flexible, reflecting the characteristics of creative organizations described in Exhibit 8.2. One good example is Nestlé's Nespresso venture, which developed a line of high-quality coffees packaged in individual capsules for use in specially designed coffee machines, similar to Keurig's K-cup system. The team found itself hampered by the large company's rules, structures, and regulations. In addition, the project faced resistance from managers who feared that the new premium line would hurt the existing Nescafé brand. Top managers moved the Nespresso business outside the existing structure so that it could thrive with an entrepreneurial culture and promote innovative ideas.[74] P&G has established several new-business-creation groups that search for and develop breakthrough ideas that cross multiple businesses and divisions. These teams are partly responsible for a dramatic increase in P&G's innovation success rate.[75]

One variation of a new-venture team is called a **skunkworks**,[76] a separate, small, informal, highly autonomous, and often secretive group that focuses on breakthrough ideas for a business. The original skunkworks, which still exists, was created by Lockheed Martin more than 50 years ago. The essence of a skunkworks is that highly talented people are given the time and freedom to let creativity reign.[77] Consider the clandestine Google X lab, which was so hush-hush that until *The New York Times* wrote about it, even many of Google's employees didn't know it existed. Google X is a top-secret lab in an undisclosed location where engineers are working on shoot-for-the-moon ideas like driverless cars, space elevators that can collect information from or haul things into space, and robots that can attend a conference for you while you stay at the office.[78] Similarly, at GM, the location of the skunkworks facility known as Studio X is kept secret even from the automaker's top executives.[79]

A related idea is the **new-venture fund**, which provides resources from which individuals and groups can draw to develop new ideas, products, or businesses. At Pitney Bowes, for example, the New Business Opportunity (NBO) program provides funding for teams to explore potentially lucrative but unproven ideas. The NBO program is intended to generate a pipeline of new businesses for the mail and document management services company. Similarly, Royal Dutch Shell puts 10 percent of its R&D budget into the GameChanger program, which provides seed money for innovation projects that are highly ambitious, radical, or long term and could get lost in the larger product development system.[80] With these programs, the support and assistance of senior managers are often just as important as the funding.[81]

Go to the "Ethical Dilemma" on page 351, which pertains to structural change.

8.3 Changing People and Culture

All successful changes involve changes in people and culture as well. Changes in people and culture pertain to how employees think—changes in mind-set. People change concerns just a few employees, such as sending a handful of middle managers to a training course to improve their leadership skills. Culture change pertains to the organization as a whole, such as when the Internal Revenue Service (IRS) shifted its basic mind-set from an organization focused on collection and compliance to one dedicated to informing, educating, and serving customers (i.e., taxpayers).[82] Large-scale culture change is not easy. Indeed, managers routinely report that changing people and culture is their most difficult job.[83] Consider the situation at GM.

Spotlight on Skills

GM

Leaders at GM have been praised for making tough decisions that led to impressive financial results, bringing out new models that connected with customers, and fixing a myriad of operational and systems issues. "We went from being troubled to being at the top of the heap," said former CEO Dan Akerson. However, there is one area in which Akerson and other leaders admit significant challenges remain: changing the bureaucratic, tradition-bound culture that has crippled GM in the past.

Like leaders in other companies, GM executives are finding that changing culture is the toughest part of leading a turnaround. One of Akerson's goals was to get more women into top jobs, partly because he believed that they can lead the radical culture change the company needs. He's off to a good start. The auto industry in general is male-dominated, and there is no job more associated with machismo than the job of creating and engineering new cars. Who did Akerson pick to be head of product development? A woman—and moreover, the former head of human resources (HR)! Mary Barra, who has held positions in various parts of the company over her 32 years with GM, became the highest-ranking woman in the global auto industry, and she began helping remake the rule-bound, dysfunctional culture from the ground up. Since then, Barra has been promoted to CEO of the company. As head of HR, Barra cut the long list of rules for on-the-job apparel to two words: *Dress appropriately*. With the company's recent safety problems, Barra faces major challenges as the new head of GM, but she can use her position to enact broad changes that cut through red tape and speed decision making.[84]

Two specific tools that managers at GM and other companies can use to smooth the culture change process are training and development programs and organization development (OD). CEO Ron Johnson could have used some expertise in organization change and development in his ultimately unsuccessful overhaul of J.C. Penney, as described in this chapter's Business Blooper box.

Business Blooper J.C. Penney Selling retail clothing and housewares is the same as hawking iPhones, right? That's evidently what the board of J.C. Penney thought when it hired the former head of Apple retail Ron Johnson in 2011. Johnson tried to reverse the company's decline by eliminating company staples: coupons and sales. He also went upscale and started redesigning to get a "store-within-a-store" specialty shops. The result? Sales fell 26 percent in three months and 50 percent in less than a year. But Johnson had his spin machine going, similar to what Steve Jobs did with what his biographer called his "reality distortion field." He told everyone he could turn around his new company the way Apple did when it went from a downturn to spectacular after it opened its retail stores. But Apple had its own innovative products to WOW people, while J.C. Penney relies on a myriad of suppliers. Analysts and Wall Street were not impressed. Investment counselor Margaret Bogenrief said, it was "a ridiculous and condescending move." Finally the board agreed and fired Johnson in April 2013. Thankfully, the company reversed some of the trends. Sales are no longer outlawed and it reintroduced its famous catalog in 2014.

SOURCE: Paul R. La Monica, "Can J.C. Penney and Sears Avoid Radioshack's Fate?" CNN Wire Service, February 10, 2015; Stephanie Clifford, "J.C. Penney Ousts Chief of 17 Months," *New York Times*, April 9, 2013, B1 and B7.

8.3a Training and Development

Training is one of the most frequently used approaches to changing people's mind-sets. A company might offer training programs to large blocks of employees on subjects such as teamwork, diversity, emotional intelligence (EQ), quality circles, communication skills, or participative management.

Successful companies want to provide training and development opportunities for everyone, but they might particularly emphasize training and development for managers, with the idea that the behavior and attitudes of managers will influence people throughout the organization and lead to culture change. For example, by the time that Stephen Helmsley took over as CEO of UnitedHealth Group, the nation's largest health insurer and one of the most powerful companies in the health care industry, the atmosphere within the company was toxic. "We had lots of IQ but not nearly enough EQ," Helmsley said. To encourage more civil, emotionally intelligent, and collaborative behavior, Helmsley sent 8,000 managers to three-day sensitivity training programs to become more aware of their own biases and impact and be more sensitive to other people.[85]

8.3b Organization Development (OD)

Organization development (OD) is a planned, systematic process of change that uses behavioral science knowledge and techniques to improve an organization's health and effectiveness through its ability to adapt to the environment, improve internal relationships, and increase learning and problem-solving capabilities.[86] OD focuses on the human and social aspects of the organization and works to change attitudes and relationships among employees, helping to strengthen the organization's capacity for adaptation and renewal.[87]

OD can help managers address at least three types of current problems:[88]

- Mergers/acquisitions. The disappointing financial results of many mergers and acquisitions are caused by the failure of executives to determine whether the administrative style and corporate culture of the two companies fit. Executives may concentrate on potential synergies in technology, products, marketing, and control systems but fail to recognize that two firms may have widely different values, beliefs, and practices. These differences create stress and anxiety for employees, and these negative emotions affect future performance. Cultural differences should be evaluated during the acquisition process, and OD experts can be used to smooth the integration of two firms.

- Organizational decline/revitalization. Organizations undergoing a period of decline and revitalization experience a variety of problems, including a low level of trust, lack of innovation, high turnover, and high levels of conflict and stress. The period of transition requires the opposite, including confronting stress, creating open communication, and fostering creative innovation to emerge with high levels of productivity. OD techniques can contribute greatly to cultural revitalization by managing conflicts, fostering commitment, and facilitating communication.

- Conflict management. Conflict can occur at any time and place within a healthy organization. For example, a product team for the introduction of a new software package was formed at a computer company. Made of strong-willed individuals, the team made little progress because members could not agree on project goals. At a manufacturing firm, salespeople promised delivery dates to customers that were in conflict with shop supervisor priorities for assembling customer orders.

In a publishing company, two managers disliked each other intensely. They argued at meetings, lobbied politically against each other, and hurt the achievement of both departments. OD efforts can help resolve these kinds of conflicts, as well as conflicts that are related to growing diversity and the global nature of today's organizations.

OD can be used to solve the types of problems just described, as well as many others. However, to be truly valuable to companies and employees, OD practitioners go beyond looking at ways to settle specific problems. Instead, they become involved in broader issues that contribute to improving organizational life, such as encouraging a sense of community, pushing for an organizational climate of openness and trust, and making sure that the company provides employees with opportunities for personal growth and development.[89] One recent study looked at the results of an OD project in a large metropolitan sheriff's department that was plagued by extremely high turnover, low morale, ineffective leadership, and internal conflicts. OD consultants used a variety of activities over a period of four years to solve the crisis threatening the department. It was a long and sometimes difficult process; however, the study not only found that the OD interventions had highly beneficial results, but also that the positive impact lasted over a period of 30 years, right up to the present day.[90]

Fabrice Dimier/Bloomberg /Getty Images

CONCEPT CONNECTION One may not think of GE as an innovative leadership company at the forefront of **organization development (OD)**. At first glance, this multinational corporation may seem quite traditional. However, GE is well known for placing a premium on selecting, developing, and retaining strong leaders at every level of the organization. Along with the company's extensive training and development program, there are many activities at each worksite that provide opportunities for mentoring, volunteering, sports, and social interaction.

OD Activities   OD consultants use a variety of specialized techniques to help meet their goals. Three of the most popular and effective are the following:

- Team-building activities. **Team building** enhances the cohesiveness and success of organizational groups and teams. For example, a series of OD exercises can be used with members of cross-departmental teams to help them learn to act and function as a team. An OD expert can work with team members to increase their communication skills, facilitate their ability to confront one another, and help them accept common goals. A major team building experience at UnitedHealth is the annual broomball tournament held at headquarters in Minnesota. Inaugurated in 2010, the tournament is now a prized tradition held every winter, with 90 teams representing every area of the company participating. This and other OD activities have contributed to a drop in turnover, from 20 percent in 2008 to 8 percent in 2012.[91]

- Survey-feedback activities. **Survey feedback** begins with a questionnaire distributed to employees on values, climate, participation, leadership, and group cohesion within their organization. After the survey is completed, an OD consultant meets with groups of employees to provide feedback about their responses and the problems identified. Employees are engaged in problem solving based on the data.

- Large-group interventions. In recent years, the need for bringing about fundamental organizational change in today's complex, fast-changing world prompted a growing

EXHIBIT 8.5 OD Approaches to Culture Change

	Traditional Organization Development Model	Large-Group Intervention Model
Focus for action:	Specific problem or group	Entire system
Information Source:	Organization	Organization and environment
Distribution:	Limited	Widely shared
Time frame:	Gradual	Fast
Learning:	Individual, small group	Whole organization
Change process:	Incremental change	Rapid transformation

SOURCE: Adapted from Barbara Benedict Bunker and Billie T. Alban, "Conclusion: What Makes Large Group Interventions Effective?" *Journal of Applied Behavioral Science* 28, no. 4 (December 1992): 579–591.

interest in applications of OD techniques to large-group settings.[92] The **large-group intervention** approach brings together participants from all parts of the organization—often including key stakeholders from outside the organization as well—to discuss problems or opportunities and plan for change. A large-group intervention might involve 50 to 500 people and last several days. The idea is to include everyone who has a stake in the change, gather perspectives from all parts of the system, and enable people to create a collective future through sustained, guided dialogue.

Large-group interventions are one of the most popular and fastest-growing OD activities and reflect a significant shift in the approach to organizational change from earlier OD concepts and approaches.[93] Exhibit 8.5 lists the primary differences between the traditional OD model and the large-scale intervention model of organizational change.[94]

In the newer approach, the focus is on the entire system, which takes into account the organization's interaction with its environment. The sources of information for discussion are expanded to include customers, suppliers, community members, and even competitors, and this information is shared widely so that everyone has the same picture of the organization and its environment. The acceleration of change when the entire system is involved can be remarkable. In addition, learning occurs across all parts of the organization simultaneously, rather than by individuals, small groups, or business units alone. The result is that the large-group approach offers greater possibilities for fundamental, radical transformation of the entire culture, whereas the traditional approach creates incremental change in a few individuals or small groups at a time.

REMEMBER THIS

- Often, a manager's toughest job is changing people and culture.
- **People change** refers to a change in the attitudes and behaviors of a few employees.
- **Culture change** is a major shift in the norms, values, and mind-set of the entire organization.
- UnitedHealth sent 8,000 managers to sensitivity training sessions to help them learn to be more

- emotionally intelligent and create a less toxic work environment.
- **Organization development (OD)** is a planned, systematic process of change that uses behavioral science techniques to improve an organization's health and effectiveness through its ability to cope with environmental changes, improve internal relationships, and increase learning and problem-solving capabilities.
- OD can help managers with the task of blending corporate cultures following mergers and acquisitions, as well as with many other people-related problems.

- **Team building** is an OD intervention that enhances cohesiveness by helping groups of people learn to work together as a team.
- With **survey feedback**, OD change agents survey employees to gather their opinions regarding corporate values, leadership, participation, cohesiveness, and other aspects of the organization, then meet with small groups to share the results and brainstorm solutions to problems identified by the results.
- **Large-group intervention** is an OD approach that brings together people from different parts of the organization (and often including outside stakeholders) to discuss problems or opportunities and plan for change.

OD Steps   OD experts acknowledge that changes in corporate culture and human behavior are tough to accomplish and require major effort. The theory underlying OD proposes three distinct stages for achieving behavioral and attitudinal change: (1) unfreezing, (2) changing, and (3) refreezing[95].

The first stage, **unfreezing**, makes people throughout the organization aware of problems and the need for change. This stage creates the motivation for people to change their attitudes and behaviors. Unfreezing may begin when managers present information that shows discrepancies between desired behaviors or performance and the current state of affairs. In addition, managers need to establish a sense of urgency to unfreeze people and create an openness and willingness to change. The **unfreezing stage** is often associated with *diagnosis*, which uses an outside expert called a *change agent*. The change agent is an OD specialist who performs a systematic diagnosis of the organization and identifies work-related problems. He or she gathers and analyzes data through personal interviews, questionnaires, and observations of meetings. The diagnosis helps determine the extent of organizational problems and helps unfreeze managers by making them aware of problems in their behavior.

The second stage, **changing**, occurs when individuals experiment with new behavior and learn new skills to be used in the workplace. This process is sometimes known as *intervention*, during which the change agent implements a specific plan for training managers and employees. The changing stage might involve a number of specific steps.[96] For example, managers put together a coalition of people with the will and power to guide change, create a vision for change that everyone can believe in, and widely communicate the vision and plans for change throughout the company. In addition, successful change involves using emotion as well as logic to persuade people and empowering employees to act on the plan and accomplish the desired changes.

The third stage, **refreezing**, occurs when individuals acquire new attitudes or values and are rewarded for them by the organization. The impact of new behaviors is evaluated and reinforced. The change agent supplies new data that show positive changes in performance. Managers may provide updated data to employees that demonstrate positive changes in individual and organizational performance. Top executives celebrate successes and reward positive behavioral changes. At this stage, changes are institutionalized in the organizational culture, so that employees begin to view the changes as a normal, integral part of how the organization operates. Employees may also participate in refresher courses to maintain and reinforce the new behaviors.

The process of unfreezing-changing-refreezing can be illustrated by efforts of managers at ENSR to create a high-performance, employee-focused culture.

Spotlight on Skills

ENSR

When top executives at ENSR began hearing that high employee turnover was hurting the company's relationships with clients, they knew that something had to be done. ENSR is a full-service environmental services firm with around 3,000 employees in 90 locations around the world. Long-term relationships with clients are the key to ENSR's success.

To attack the turnover problem, managers embarked on a process of changing the culture. To make people aware of the need for change (unfreezing), ENSR's president and CEO traveled with the senior vice president of HR to the largest 50 or so of ENSR's global locations. They held town-hall–style meetings with employees and leadership workshops with ENSR

managers. The changing stage included training. Surveys were conducted to find out what employees considered their primary needs. For example, supervisors were trained in how to help lower-performing employees improve their performance and how to provide greater challenge and rewards to employees who showed high potential for leadership.

Within a few years, new behaviors became the norm. Turnover dropped from 22 percent to only 9 percent, one of the lowest rates in the industry, and employees were recognized and rewarded for meeting high individual and collective goals (refreezing). ENSR continues to attract high-quality employees to fill job openings, which helps to keep the high-performance culture alive.[97]

REMEMBER THIS

- OD practitioners recommend a three-stage approach for changing people's attitudes and behavior.
- **Unfreezing** is the stage in which people are made aware of problems and the need for change.
- Unfreezing requires diagnosing problems, which uses a **change agent**, an OD specialist who contracts with an organization to help managers facilitate change.
- **Changing** is the "intervention" stage of OD, when change agents teach people new behaviors and skills and guide them in using them in the workplace.
- At the **refreezing** stage, people have incorporated new values, attitudes, and behaviors into their everyday work and the changes become institutionalized in the culture.

8.4 Implementing Change

The final step in the change process is *implementation*. A new, creative idea will not benefit the organization until it is in place and being used. Earlier in this chapter, we described some of the reasons that people resist change. Strategies for overcoming resistance and implementing change typically involve three approaches: making people aware of the need for change by creating a sense of urgency, analyzing resistance through the force-field technique, and using selective implementation tactics.

8.4a Create a Sense of Urgency

Many people are not willing to change unless they perceive a problem or a crisis. A crisis or strong need for change lowers resistance. To effectively lead change, managers help people *feel* the need for change rather than just giving them facts and figures. Consider Peter Löscher, the first outsider ever hired as CEO of Siemens, who says, "Never miss the opportunities that come from a good crisis." Löscher stepped in at a very difficult time, with the company facing bribery charges, and he needed to make massive changes in the structure and culture of Siemens. He spent his first 100 days traveling around the world talking with employees about how the bribery scandal had tarnished Siemens's proud heritage.[98] Sometimes, though, there is no obvious crisis. Many organizational problems are subtle, so managers have to recognize and then make others aware of the need for change.[99] A need for change is a disparity between existing and desired performance levels.

8.4b Apply Force-Field Analysis

Force-field analysis grew from the work of Kurt Lewin, who proposed that change was a result of the competition between *driving* and *restraining forces*.[100] Driving forces can be thought of as problems or opportunities that provide motivation for change within the organization. Restraining forces are the various barriers to change, such as a lack of resources, resistance from middle managers, or inadequate employee skills. When a change is introduced, managers should analyze both the forces that drive change (problems and opportunities) and the forces that resist it (barriers to change). By selectively removing forces that restrain change, the driving forces will be strong enough to enable implementation, as illustrated by the move from A to B in Exhibit 8.6. As barriers are reduced or removed, behavior will shift to incorporate the desired changes.

Just-in-time (JIT) inventory control systems schedule materials to arrive at a company just as they are needed on the production line. In an Ohio manufacturing company, management's analysis showed that the driving forces (opportunities) associated with the

EXHIBIT 8.6 Using Force-Field Analysis to Change from Traditional to Just-in-Time Inventory Systems implementation of JIT were (1) the large cost savings from reduced inventories, (2) manpower savings from needing fewer workers to handle inventory, and (3) a quicker, more competitive market response for the company. Restraining forces (barriers) that managers discovered were (1) a freight system that was too slow to deliver inventory on time, (2) a facility layout that emphasized inventory maintenance over new deliveries, (3) worker skills that were inappropriate for handling rapid inventory deployment, and (4) union resistance to loss of jobs. The driving forces were not sufficient to overcome the restraining forces.

To shift the behavior to JIT, managers attacked the barriers. An analysis of the freight system showed that delivery by truck provided the flexibility and quickness needed to schedule inventory arrival at a specific time each day. The problem with facility layout was met by adding four new loading docks. Inappropriate worker skills were improved with a training program to instruct workers in JIT methods and in assembling products with uninspected parts. Union resistance was overcome by agreeing to reassign workers no longer needed for maintaining inventory to jobs in another plant. With the restraining forces reduced, the driving forces were sufficient to allow the JIT system to be implemented.

8.4c Use Implementation Tactics

Managers can use specific tactics to overcome resistance and more smoothly put changes into action. Researchers have studied various methods for dealing with resistance to change. The following five tactics, summarized in Exhibit 8.7, have proven successful.[101]

Top Management Support   One survey found that 80 percent of companies that are successful innovators have top executives who frequently reinforce the importance of innovation both verbally and symbolically.[102] The visible support of top management makes people aware of the importance of the change. For instance, one of the primary correlates of the success of new business ventures is the strong support of top managers, which gives

EXHIBIT 8.7   Tactics for Implementing Change

Approach	When to Use
Top management support	• Change involves multiple departments or reallocation of resources. • Users doubt legitimacy of change.
Communication, education	• Change is technical. • Users need accurate information and analysis to understand change.
Participation	• Users need to feel involved. • Design requires information from others. • Users have power to resist.
Negotiation	• Group has power over implementation. • Group will lose out in the change.
Coercion	• A crisis exists. • Initiators clearly have power. • Other implementation techniques have failed.

SOURCE: Based on J. P. Kotter and L. A. Schlesinger, "Choosing Strategies for Change," *Harvard Business Review* 57 (March–April 1979): 106–114.

the project legitimacy.[103] *Top management support* is especially important when a change involves multiple departments or when resources are being reallocated among departments. Without top management support, changes can get bogged down in squabbling among departments or contradictory orders from lower-level managers.

Communication and Education   *Communication* and *education* are used when solid information about the change is needed by users and others who may resist implementation. Gina Raimondo, the state treasurer of Rhode Island, spent most of a year traveling all over the state to educate the public, union leaders, and legislators about the need for a radical overhaul of the state's pension system. "I would talk to social workers or social-service agencies who … would ask, 'Why should I care about pensions?' And I said, 'Because if you don't, your whatever it is, homeless shelter, is going to lose X thousand dollars of funding,'" she said. Raimondo "conducted a long, relentless, public-education campaign" because she believed reform was essential to keep the state from going broke.[104] Within organizations, education can be especially important when the change involves new technical knowledge or users are unfamiliar with the idea. Managers should also remember that implementing change requires speaking to people's hearts (feelings) as well as to their minds (facts). Emotion is a key component in persuading and influencing others. People are much more likely to change their behavior when they both understand the rational reasons for doing so and see a picture of change that influences their feelings.[105]

Participation   *Participation* involves users and potential resisters in designing the change. This approach is time consuming, but it pays off because users understand and become committed to the change. At Learning Point Associates, which needed to change dramatically to meet new challenges, the change team drew up a comprehensive road map for transformation but had trouble getting the support of most managers. The managers argued that they hadn't been consulted about the plans and didn't feel compelled to participate in implementing them.[106] Research studies have shown that proactively engaging front-line employees in upfront planning and decision making about changes that affect their work results in much smoother implementation.[107] Participation also helps managers determine potential problems and understand the differences in perceptions of change among employees.

Negotiation   Negotiation is a more formal means of achieving cooperation. *Negotiation* uses formal bargaining to win acceptance and approval of a desired change. For example, if the marketing department fears losing power if a new management structure is implemented, top managers may work with marketing to reach a resolution. Companies that have strong unions frequently must formally negotiate change with the unions. The change may become part of the union contract, reflecting the agreement of both parties.

Coercion   *Coercion* means that managers use their formal power to force employees to change. Resisters are told to accept the change or lose rewards (or even their jobs). In most cases, this approach should not be used because employees feel like victims, are angry at change managers, and may even sabotage the changes. However, coercion may be necessary in crisis situations when a rapid response is urgent. For example, at the struggling Chrysler Group, some insiders say that new CEO Sergio Marchionne "injected an element of fear into [Chrysler's] ranks" to get people to change. Several top managers were reassigned or terminated because they wouldn't go along with Marchionne's planned method for returning Chrysler to profitability after it emerged from bankruptcy protection.[108]

Managers can soften resistance and facilitate change and innovation by using smart techniques. By showing support for the change, communicating with employees, providing training, and closely involving employees in the change process, managers can smooth implementation.

REMEMBER THIS

- A **need for change** is a disparity between actual and desired performance.
- Many people aren't willing to change unless they perceive a crisis, so managers need to create a sense of urgency that change is really needed.
- **Force-field analysis** is a technique for determining which forces drive a proposed change and which forces restrain it.

- Driving forces are problems or opportunities that provide motivation to change. Restraining forces are barriers such as a lack of resources or inadequate employee skills.
- The support of top executives is crucial to the successful implementation of a change. In addition, managers use a variety of techniques to smooth the implementation process.

CHAPTER 8   DISCUSSION QUESTIONS

1. Microsoft and Intel are giants of the computer industry. Why do you think that these large companies have had such a hard time competing against disruptive innovations such as mobile computing?

2. A manager of an international chemical company says that few new products in her company have been successful. What would you advise the manager to do to help increase the company's success rate?

3. As a manager, how would you deal with resistance to change when you suspect that employees' fears of job loss are well founded?

4. If you were a manager responsible for floor-cleaning products at a consumer products company, how might you apply crowdsourcing to identify a new product that would meet customer needs?

5. To tap into the experience of battle-tested soldiers, the U.S. Army recently has begun encouraging personnel from all ranks to go online and collaboratively rewrite some of the Army's field manuals in a Wikipedia-like fashion. When the rank and file showed little interest, one retired colonel suggested that top leaders should make soldiers participate. Does coercion seem like a good way to implement this type of change? Discuss.

6. Analyze the driving and restraining forces of a change that you would like to make in your life. Do you believe that understanding force-field analysis can help you more effectively implement a significant change in your own behavior?

7. Why do you think research has shown that idea champions are so essential to the initiation of change? Could they be equally important for implementation?

8. You are a manager, and you believe that the expense reimbursement system for salespeople is far too slow, taking weeks instead of days. How would you go about convincing other managers that this problem needs to be addressed?

9. Do the underlying values of OD differ from assumptions associated with other types of change? Discuss.

10. What do you see as the major advantages and disadvantages of a company moving to open innovation?

SELF-LEARNING

Is Your Company Creative?[109]

An effective way to assess the creative climate of an organization for which you have worked is to fill out the following questionnaire. Answer each question based on your work experience in that firm. Discuss the results with members of your group, and talk about whether changing the firm along the dimensions in the questions would make it more creative.

INSTRUCTIONS: Answer each of the following questions using the five-point scale (*Note:* No rating of 4 is used):

    0 We never do this.
    1 We rarely do this.
    2 We sometimes do this.
    3 We frequently do this.
    5 We always do this.

1. We are encouraged to seek help anywhere inside or outside the organization with new ideas for our work unit.

    0   1   2   3   5

2. Assistance is provided to develop ideas into proposals for management review.

    0   1   2   3   5

3. Our performance reviews encourage risky, creative efforts, ideas, and actions.

    0   1   2   3   5

4. We are encouraged to fill our minds with new information by attending professional meetings and trade fairs, visiting customers, and so on.

    0   1   2   3   5

5. Our meetings are designed to allow people to freewheel, brainstorm, and generate ideas.

    0   1   2   3   5

6. All members contribute ideas during meetings.

    0   1   2   3   5

7. Meetings often involve much spontaneity and humor.

    0   1   2   3   5

8. We discuss how company structure and our actions help or spoil creativity within our work unit.

    0   1   2   3   5

9. During meetings, the chair is rotated among members.

    0   1   2   3   5

10. Everyone in the work unit receives training in creativity techniques and maintaining a creative climate.

    0   1   2   3   5

Scoring and Interpretation

Add up your total score for all 10 questions: _____

To measure how effectively your organization fosters creativity, use the following scale:

Highly effective: 35–50, Moderately effective: 20–34, Moderately ineffective: 10–19, Ineffective: 0–9

GROUP LEARNING

An Ancient Tale

1. Read the introduction and case study and answer the questions.

2. In groups of three to four discuss your answers.

3. Groups report to the whole class and the instructor leads a discussion on the issues raised.

Introduction

To understand, analyze, and improve organizations, we must carefully think through the issue of who is responsible for what activities in different organizational settings. Often we hold responsible someone who has no control over the outcome, or we fail to teach or train someone who could make the vital difference.

To explore this issue, the following exercise could be conducted on either an individual or group basis. It provides an opportunity to see how different individuals assign responsibility for an event. It is also a good opportunity to discuss the concept of organizational boundaries (what is the organization, who is in or out, etc.).

Case Study

You should read the short story and respond quickly to the first three questions. Then take a little more time on questions four through six. The results, criteria, and implications could then be discussed in groups. Long ago in an ancient kingdom there lived a princess who was very young and very beautiful. The princess, recently married, lived in a large and luxurious castle with her husband, a powerful and wealthy lord. The young princess was not content, however, to sit and eat strawberries by herself while her husband took frequent and long journeys to neighboring kingdoms. She felt neglected and soon became quite unhappy. One day, while she was alone in the castle gardens, a handsome vagabond rode out of the forest bordering the castle. He spied the beautiful princess, quickly won her heart, and carried her away with him.

Following a day of dalliance, the young princess found herself ruthlessly abandoned by the vagabond. She then discovered that the only way back to the castle led through the bewitched forest of the wicked sorcerer. Fearing to venture into the forest alone, she sought out her kind and wise godfather. She explained her plight, begged forgiveness of the godfather, and asked his assistance in returning home before her husband returned. The godfather, however, surprised and shocked at her behavior, refused forgiveness and denied her any assistance. Discouraged but still determined, the princess disguised her identity and sought the help of the most noble of all the kingdom's knights. After hearing the sad story, the knight pledged his unfailing aid—for a modest fee. But alas, the princess had no money and the knight rode away to save other damsels.

The beautiful princess had no one else from whom she might seek help, and decided to brave the great peril alone. She followed the safest path she knew, but when she was almost through the forest, the wicked sorcerer spied her and caused her to be devoured by the fire-breathing dragon.

1. Who was inside the organization and who was outside? Where were the boundaries?

2. Who is most responsible for the death of the beautiful princess?

3. Who is next most responsible? Least responsible?

4. What is your criterion for the above decisions?

5. What interventions would you suggest to prevent a recurrence?

6. What are the implications for *organizational development and change?*

Character	Most Responsible	Next Most Responsible	Least Responsible
Princess			
Husband			
Vagabond			
Godfather			
Knight			
Sorcerer			

Check one character in each column.

SOURCE: Adapted from J. B. Ritchie and Paul Thompson. From *Organization and People: Readings, Cases and Exercises in Organizational Behavior.* Copyright 1980 (West Publishing, 1980), pp. 68–70, in Dorothy Marcic, *Organizational Behavior: Experiences and Cases,* 4th ed., pp. 378–79..

Instruction Manual An Ancient Tale[1]

The case study or tale has implications regarding the impact of the organization on the individual, the ability to protect him- or herself in the organization, and how to manage the organization to accomplish objectives which are in the best interest of the organization as well as the participants.

Role-Play Option

If you want to bring life to the case, you could ask students to perform role-plays; to act out, for example, a scene between the Lord and the Princess, between the Princess and the Godfather, or the Princess and the Knight. I have used this with much success in class.

Group Discussion Format

One suggestion is to use a group discussion format for the case as follows:

1. Prior to class, assign members to read the case and answer the questions at the end of the case.

2. Divide class members into groups of four to eight members.

3. Assign each group to discuss the five questions and to arrive at a consensus decision. This should take about 10–20 minutes.

4. With the entire class, have each group report their responses to the questions, noting especially the criteria for making their decisions.

5. After each group has made a presentation, follow the Class Discussion guidelines which follow to highlight the implications of the case for individuals within organizations.

Simulated Court Trial

Another way (optional) of stimulating discussion on "An Ancient Tale" is through the use of a court trial.

1. Prior to the class in which the story will be discussed, assign individuals to play the role of each of the seven characters and "defense attorneys" for each character (Princess, Lord/Husband, Dragon, Vagabond, Sorcerer, Godfather, Knight).

2. Instruct each role player to be prepared to explain in the next session why he/she (or his/

her client) is not responsible for the death of the Princess (who will be brought back from the dead to defend herself).

3. Select an articulate student (or have the instructor) perform the role of prosecuting attorney (have this individual prepare arguments as to why each person should be held responsible for the death of the Princess).

4. On the day of the trial, a jury is selected (volunteers) along with a jury foreman, and the classroom is arranged in the following manner:

Defending Attorneys

Class

Prosecuting Attorney

The trial proceeds in the following manner:

1. The defendant and "defense attorneys" for each character proclaim the defendant's innocence (two minutes per character).

2. After each character proclaims his/her innocence, the prosecutor presents the case for their guilt. The prosecutor will present the case for guilt after each character's defense (two minutes per character).

3. After all the characters have been tried, the jury retires (maximum period–10 minutes) and passes a verdict on each separate defendant. The jury foreman announces the verdict on each character with a brief explanation.

After the trial, discussion follows.

Class Discussion

After the trial or after each group has made their presentation, the following questions can be raised with the entire class.

1. What are the criteria by which we find people responsible for their actions in organizations? Many would argue that the Princess is guilty because individuals must assume personal responsibility for their actions. Others would argue that individuals have responsibilities to perform (the Husband, the Knight, the Godfather) and that when they fail to perform those responsibilities, they are guilty for failures in the organization.

[1]Adapted from *Instructor's Manual for Organization and People*, by Ritchie and Thompson, West Publishing, 1980, pp. 62–64.

2. How likely are individuals in organizations to pass responsibility off onto someone else? The Princess will probably argue her innocence because others in the case (the organization) failed to perform their roles. It is very common in organizations to "pass the buck."

3. If individuals fail to accept responsibility for others (such as the Knight, the Godfather, the Vagabond failing to accept responsibility for the Princess' welfare), what will be the consequences for the individual? For the organization?

4. What are the value issues underlying the jury's decision on guilt? Some will decide that the individual (Princess) is responsible; others will decide that the organizations are responsible. These decisions come from the values held by the jury members.

5. When relating the case to organizational processes, one class made the following analogy: "The Princess is a manager who is not being paid attention to by her manager (the Lord).

The Vagabond (an executive headhunter) calls upon the manager and she leaves the organization in hopes of a more profitable job. The headhunter takes her money (the fee) and leaves her without a job. She turns to some friends in other organizations (the Godfather and Knight), but they give her no help in finding work. Finally, in desperation, she turns to the government (the Sorcerer) agency to help her find work. The government agency places her on welfare (the Dragon) and she loses her desire to work." Ask students to comment on the analogy.

Another frequent occurrence is students blaming the Princess, but when it comes to recommendations for change, they say the Lord has to do things differently. It is important for them to understand that the person who needs to change his behavior is likely the one responsible—since he could have prevented it most.

Another issue here is how responsible the Chief Executive Officer (Husband/Lord) is for what goes on in the lower levels of the organization. Delegation, responsibility, and accountability are important to discuss with this.

ACTION LEARNING

1. Think about two times you had to go through a change. It might have been in your work life, as a student, in your family, with friends. Try to choose two situations that ended differently. In other words, one had a positive outcome, in the long term, and the other one did not have a positive outcome. Fill in the following table below.

	Situation one (positive outcome):	Situation two: (not positive outcome)):
Factors in the situation		
Were you happy with the way things were before the change?		
What was the cause of the change?		
What was your initial reaction to the change?		
Did you find any ways to cope with the change or find something positive? Explain.		
How did authority figures communicate with you?		
How did authority figures handle the situation in general?		
Was there support from other people?		
What was the long-term outcome?		

2. Can you see differences in the way the two situations unfolded in terms of other people's behaviors?

3. Were there differences in your behaviors in the two situations? Why?

4. What would you do differently, if you could go back?

What new insights do you now have about going through change?

ETHICAL DILEMMA

Crowdsourcing[110]

Last year, when Ai-Lan Nguyen told her friend Greg Barnwell that Off the Hook Tees, based in Asheville, North Carolina, was going to experiment with crowdsourcing, he warned her that she wouldn't like the results. Now, as she was about to walk into a meeting to decide whether to adopt this new business model, she was afraid her friend had been right.

Crowdsourcing uses the Internet to invite anyone—professionals and amateurs alike—to perform tasks such as product design that employees usually perform. In exchange, contributors receive recognition—but little or no pay. Ai-Lan, as vice president of operations for Off the Hook, a company specializing in witty T-shirts aimed at young adults, upheld the values of founder Chris Woodhouse, who, like Ai-Lan, was a graphic artist. Before he sold the company, the founder always insisted that T-shirts be well designed by top-notch graphic artists to make sure that each screen print was a work of art. Those graphic artists reported to Ai-Lan.

Over the past 18 months, Off the Hook's sales had been stagnating for the first time in its history. The crowdsourcing experiment was the latest in a series of attempts to jump-start sales growth. Last spring, Off the Hook issued its first open call for T-shirt designs and then posted the entries on the Web so people could vote for their favorites. The top five vote-getters were handed over to the in-house designers, who tweaked the submissions until they met the company's usual quality standards.

When CEO Rob Taylor first announced the company's foray into crowdsourcing, Ai-Lan found herself reassuring the designers that their positions were not in jeopardy. Now Ai-Lan was all but certain she would have to go back on her word. Not only had the crowdsourced shirts sold well, but Rob had put a handful of winning designs directly into production, bypassing the design department altogether. Customers didn't notice the difference.

Ai-Lan concluded that Rob was ready to adopt some form of this Web-based crowdsourcing because it made T-shirt design more responsive to consumer desires. In practical terms, it reduced the uncertainty that surrounded new designs, and it dramatically lowered costs. The people who won the competitions were delighted with the exposure that it gave them.

However, when Ai-Lan looked at the crowdsourced shirts with her graphic artist's eye, she felt that the designs were competent, but none achieved the aesthetic standards attained by her in-house designers. Crowdsourcing essentially replaced training and expertise with public opinion. That made the artist in her uncomfortable.

More distressing, it was beginning to look as if Greg had been right when he'd told her that his working definition of crowdsourcing was "a billion amateurs want your job." It was easy to see that if Off the Hook adopted crowdsourcing, she would be handing out pink slips to most of her design people, longtime employees whose work she admired. "Sure, crowdsourcing costs the company less, but what about the human cost?" Greg asked.

What future course should Ai-Lan argue for at the meeting? And what personal decisions does she face if Off the Hook decides to put the crowd completely in charge when it comes to T-shirt design?

What Would You Do?

1. Go to the meeting and argue for abandoning crowdsourcing for now in favor of maintaining the artistic integrity and values that Off the Hook has always stood for.

2. Accept the reality that because Rob strongly favors crowdsourcing, it's a fait accompli. Be a team player and help work out the details of the new design approach. Prepare to lay off graphic designers as needed.

3. Accept the fact that converting Off the Hook to a crowdsourcing business model is inevitable, but because it violates your own personal values, start looking for a new job elsewhere.

CASE FOR CRITICAL ANALYSIS

Cleaver's Sausage House

Allison Elam, vice president of operations for Cleaver's Sausage House, a maker of fine sausages in Minnesota, was stunned. She felt numb. Just 30 minutes ago, she had been happy and excited about the upcoming meeting, which would decide whether to launch the new material requirements planning (MRP) software system that her department had been planning. Now the meeting was over, and Cleaver's executive committee had not agreed to launch the system.

She thought the go/no-go decision would be just a formality. But David Martin, CFO, expressed a doubt about implementing the system, and things went downhill from there. "I *so* thought he was on board," Elam hissed to herself. Other senior staff then pushed back hard. They warned that the change could be a costly disaster. The vice president of sales doubted whether the MRP system could provide the solid sales forecasts that Cleaver needed. He called MRP "just big corporate BS." He also feared it would result in shortages of raw materials. The director of logistics, Susan Frisch, warned about problems that had erupted at one of her previous employers when a similar system was installed. She related a horror story about customers not getting orders and trucks leaving the plant half-full. Her final comment was, "We are successful. Why upset the apple cart?"

Cleaver CEO Jayden Anderson had hired Elam to take the position vacated by his ailing brother Stefan, who died in late 2009. Elam has been on the job for 10 months, spending much of her time working alone on the MRP project. Stefan had purchased the MRP software prior to his illness, but it had sat unused since then. She sometimes wondered if Stefan would have had an easier time with implementation had he lived to see the project through. Elam was a veteran of big companies such as Heinz and Coca-Cola, and Anderson wanted an outsider like her to bring in new technology to help operations get to the next level. Elam had worked with successful MRP systems in the past, and she had assured Anderson that the new system would overhaul procurement, production, and shipping and would impose much-needed discipline on operations. She estimated that the system would increase annual cash flow by $600,000 and save up to $200,000 annually by reducing waste. This was serious money for a company with only 350 employees.

Elam wondered if the real problem was that implementing the MRP idea would require a radical overhaul of every facet of Cleaver's operations. Making the system work would require at least 25 Cleaver managers and employees to change how they did their jobs. Still angry, Elam thought, "What are the VPs and department heads so scared of?"

Prior to the executive committee meeting, Elam had encountered plenty of obstacles. She was unable to get data from several people to create a mock-up of how the system would work. Some key managers or their direct reports came late to the first and second meetings or simply skipped them, and she had complained about the lack of cooperation to the CEO. It was obvious to Elam that the topic was not a priority for the other VPs and department heads. Anderson's response was to suggest forming a cross-departmental task force to help her. Elam told him, "I believe in this technology, and I will get it done. A task force will just slow me down."

Allison Elam was a pleasant, reserved individual who did not like conflict. She had been mentally unprepared for the executive committee's no-go decision, and she shuddered at the thought that the MRP system might not be adopted at all. She decided to sleep on it for a night or two and then plan a course of action to get this system implemented, both for Cleaver's benefit and for her own conscience.

Questions

1. What do you think are the reasons for people's resistance to the MRP implementation? Explain.

2. What is the value of the task force idea suggested by the CEO as a way to facilitate implementation? Explain.

3. Which implementation tactics do you think Elam should follow? Why?

ON THE JOB
VIDEO CASES

Honest Tea: Managing Change and Innovation

Questions

7. Part of Honest Tea's mission is to convince consumers to make healthier choices by offering innovative products. Based on what you saw in the video, describe at least two "disruptive innovations" this company has made to support this goal.

8. When Honest Tea decided to become a division of Coca-Cola, many employees and customers expressed resistance to that change. Based on what you know about the two companies, why do you think people might have resisted this change?

9. Of the implementation tactics described in the text, which tactics did Honest Tea's leaders most likely use to overcome that resistance?

ENDNOTES

1. Kristina Wong, "Navy Plans Security Changes in Wake of Navy Yard Rampage," *Washington Times*, September 23, 2013, http://www.washingtontimes.com/news/2013/sep/23/navy-plans-security-changes-wake-navy-yard-rampage/ (accessed September 25, 2013); "Navy Wants Security Clearance Changes after Navy Yard Attack," *CrossroadsToday.com*, September 23, 2013, http://www.washingtontimes.com/news/2013/sep/23/navy-plans-security-changes-wake-navy-yard-rampage/ (accessed October 3, 2013); Jim Garamone, "Navy Recommends Security Changes in Wake of Navy Yard Tragedy," Press Release, *America's Navy News Service*, September 23, 2013, http://www.navy.mil/submit/display.asp?story_id=76757 (accessed October 3, 2013); and Dion Nissenbaum, Devlin Barrett, and Siobhan Hughes, "Shooting Exposes Screening Lapses," *The Wall Street Journal*, September 17, 2013, A1.

2. Study by Charles I. Stubbart and Michael B. Knight, reported in Spencer E. Ante, "Avoiding Innovation's Terrible Toll," *The Wall Street Journal*, January 7, 2012, http://online.wsj.com/article/SB10001424052970204331304577144980247499346.html (accessed August 21, 2012).

3. Alex Taylor III, "The New GM: A Report Card," *Fortune* (September 5, 2011): 38–46.

4. Richard L. Daft, "Bureaucratic vs. Nonbureaucratic Structure in the Process of Innovation and Change," in *Perspectives in Organizational Sociology: Theory and Research*, ed. Samuel B. Bacharach (Greenwich, CT: JAI Press, 1982), pp. 129–166.

5. Angela Lee Duckworth and Patrick D. Quinn, "Development and Validation of the Short Grit Scale (Grit-S)," *Journal of Personality Assessment* 91, no. 2 (2009): 166–174.

6. Michael D. Shear and Robert Pear, "Obama Admits Web Site Flaws on Health Law," *The New York Times*, October 21, 2013, http://www.nytimes.com/2013/10/22/us/politics/obama-pushes-health-law-but-concedes-web-site-problems.html?pagewanted=1&_r=0 (accessed October 22, 2013); and "After the Big Obamacare Apology: Where Things Stand," *CNN*, November 8, 2013, http://www.cnn.com/2013/11/08/politics/obama-obamacare-apology/ (accessed November 8, 2013).

7. J. P. Kotter and L. A. Schlesinger, "Choosing Strategies for Change," *Harvard Business Review* 57 (March–April 1979): 106–114.

8. David Kesmodel and Suzanne Vranica, "Unease Brewing at Anheuser as New Owners Slash Costs," *The Wall Street Journal*, April 29, 2009.

9. Joann S. Lublin, "Can a New Culture Fix Troubled Companies?" *The Wall Street Journal*, March 13, 2013, B1.

10. Joann S. Lublin, "Theory & Practice: Firm Offers Blueprint for Makeover in a Spinoff," *The Wall Street Journal*, June 29, 2009.

11. G. Zaltman and Robert B. Duncan, *Strategies for Planned Change* (New York: Wiley Interscience, 1977).

12. Katherine Hobson, "Getting Docs to Use PCs," *The New York Times*, March 15, 2011.

13. Brian J. Hurn, "Management of Change in a Multinational Company," *Industrial and Commercial Training* 44, no. 2 (2012): 41–46.

14. Mark Chediak, "Utilities Try to Tame the Backlash Against Smart Meters," *Bloomberg BusinessWeek*, May 10, 2012, http://www.businessweek.com/articles/2012-05-10/utilities-try-to-tame-the-backlash-against-smart-meters (accessed June 13, 2013).

15. Todd Datz, "No Small Change," *CIO* (February 15, 2004): 66–72.

16. E. S. Browning, Steven Russolillo, and Jessica Vascellaro, "Apple Now Biggest-Ever U.S. Company," *The Wall Street Journal Europe*, August 22, 2012, 24; and Charles Duhigg and David Barboza, "In China, Human Costs Are Built Into an iPad," *The New York Times*, January 25, 2012, www.nytimes.com/2012/01/26/business/ieconomy-apples-ipad-and-the-human-costs-for-workers-in-china.html?pagewanted=all (accessed January 26, 2012).

17. Dorothy Leonard-Barton and Isabelle Deschamps, "Managerial Influence in the Implementation of New Technology," *Management Science* 34 (1988): 1252–1265.

18. Daisuke Wakabayashi, "The Point-and-Shoot Camera Faces Its Existential Moment," *The Wall Street Journal*, July 30, 2013, http://online.wsj.com/article/SB10001424127887324251504578580263719432252.html (accessed August 26, 2013).

19. Melissa A. Korn, "Coursera Defends MOOCs as Road to Learning," *The Wall Street Journal*, May 15, 2013, B5.

20. "05: Square, For Making Magic Out of the Mercantile," in "The World's 50 Most Innovative Companies," *Fast Company* (March 2012): 83–85, 146.

21. David W. Norton and B. Joseph Pine II, "Unique Experiences: Disruptive Innovations Offer Customers More 'Time Well Spent'" *Strategy & Leadership* 37, no. 6 (2009): 4; "The Power to Disrupt," *The Economist* (April 17, 2010): 16; and Constantinos C. Markides, "How Disruptive Will Innovations from Emerging Markets Be?" *MIT Sloan Management Review* (Fall 2012): 23–25.

22.

23. Jeffrey R. Immelt, Vijay Govindarajan, and Chris Trimble, "How GE Is Disrupting Itself," *Harvard Business Review* (October 2009): 3–11; and Navi Radjou, "Polycentric Innovation: A New Mandate for Multinationals," *The Wall Street Journal Online*, November 9, 2009, http://online.wsj.com/article/SB125774328035737917.html (accessed November 13, 2009).

24. For more information on the ambidextrous approach, see R. Duncan, "The Ambidextrous Organization: Designing Dual Structures for Innovation," in *The Management of Organization*, ed. R. H. Killman, L. R. Pondy, and D. Sleven (New York: North Holland, 1976), pp. 167–188; S. Raisch et al., "Organizational Ambidexterity: Balancing Exploitation and Exploration for Sustained Performance," *Organization Science* 20, no. 4 (July–August 2009): 685–695; C. Brooke Dobni, "The Innovation Blueprint," *Business Horizons* (2006): 329–339; Sebastian Raisch and Julian Birkinshaw, "Organizational Ambidexterity: Antecedents, Outcomes, and Moderators," *Journal of Management* 34, no. 3 (June 2008): 375–409; Charles A. O'Reilly III and Michael L. Tushman, "The Ambidextrous Organization," *Harvard Business Review* (April 2004): 74–81; Duane Ireland and Justin W. Webb, "Crossing the Great Divide of Strategic Entrepreneurship: Transitioning Between Exploration and Exploitation," *Business Horizons* 52 (2009): 469–479; and Sebastian Raisch, "Balanced Structures: Designing Organizations for Profitable Growth," *Long Range Planning* 41 (2008): 483–508.

25. Michael L. Tushman, Wendy K. Smith, and Andy Binns, "The Ambidextrous CEO," *Harvard Business Review* (June 2011): 74–80.

26. Glenn Rifkin, "Competing Through Innovation: The Case of Broderbund," *Strategy + Business* 11 (Second Quarter 1998): 48–58; and Deborah Dougherty and Cynthia Hardy, "Sustained Product Innovation in Large, Mature Organizations: Overcoming Innovation-to-Organization Problems," *Academy of Management Journal* 39, no. 5 (1996): 1120–1153.

27. Example from "The World's 50 Most Innovative Companies," *Fast Company* (March 2013): 86–156.

28. Ibid.

29. James R. Hagerty, "With Bottle-Fillers in Mind, the Water Fountain Evolves," *The Wall Street Journal*, March 24, 2013, B1.

30. Example from Teri Evans, "Entrepreneurs Seek to Elicit Workers' Ideas—Contests with Cash Prizes and Other Rewards Stimulate Innovation in Hard Times," *The Wall Street Journal*, December 22, 2009.

31. Adapted from Patrick Reinmoeller and Nicole van Baardwijk, "The Link Between Diversity and Resilience," *MIT Sloan Management Review* (Summer 2005): 61–65.

32. Teresa M. Amabile, "Motivating Creativity in Organizations: On Doing What You Love and Loving What You Do," *California Management Review* 40, no. 1 (Fall 1997): 39–58; Brian Leavy, "Creativity: The New Imperative," *Journal of General Management* 28, no. 1 (Autumn 2002): 70–85; and Timothy A. Matherly and Ronald E. Goldsmith, "The Two Faces of Creativity," *Business Horizons* (September–October 1985): 8.

33. Gordon Vessels, "The Creative Process: An Open-Systems Conceptualization," *Journal of Creative Behavior* 16 (1982): 185–196.

34. Robert J. Sternberg, Linda A. O'Hara, and Todd I. Lubart, "Creativity as Investment," *California Management Review* 40, no. 1 (Fall 1997): 8–21; Amabile, "Motivating Creativity in Organizations"; Leavy, "Creativity: The New Imperative"; and Ken Lizotte, "A Creative State of Mind," *Management Review* (May 1998): 15–17.

35. James Brian Quinn, "Managing Innovation: Controlled Chaos," *Harvard Business Review* 63 (May–June 1985): 73–84; Howard H. Stevenson and David E. Gumpert, "The Heart of Entrepreneurship," *Harvard Business Review* 63 (March–April 1985): 85–94; Marsha Sinetar, "Entrepreneurs, Chaos, and Creativity—Can Creative People Really Survive Large Company Structure?" *Sloan Management Review* 6 (Winter 1985): 57–62; Constantine Andriopoulos, "Six Paradoxes in Managing Creativity: An Embracing Act," *Long Range Planning* 36 (2003): 375–388; and Michael Laff, "Roots of Innovation," *T&D* (July 2009): 35–39.

36. The research studies and examples are reported in Sue Shellenbarger, "Better Ideas Through Failure," *The Wall Street Journal*, September 27, 2011, D1; and "Culture of Creativity," Grey Advertising Web site, http://grey.com/us/culture (accessed May 19, 2014).

37. Cynthia Browne, "Jest for Success," *Moonbeams* (August 1989): 3–5; and Rosabeth Moss Kanter, *The Change Masters* (New York: Simon and Schuster, 1983).

38. J. C. Spender and Bruce Strong, "Who Has Innovative Ideas? Employees." *The Wall Street Journal*, August 23, 2010, R5; Roger L. Martin, "The Innovation Catalysts," *Harvard Business Review* (June 2011): 82–87; and Rachel Emma Silverman, "How to Be Like Apple," *The Wall Street Journal*, August 29, 2011, http://online.wsj.com/article/SB100014 24053111904009304576532842667854706.html (accessed September 16, 2011).

39. Jason Fried, "How to Spark Creativity," *Inc.* (September 2012): 37.

40. Sabrina Adamczyk, Angelika C. Bullinger, and Kathrin M. Möslein, "Innovation Contests: A Review, Classification, and Outlook," *Creativity and Innovation Management* 21, no. 4 (2012): 335–355.

41. Darren Dahl, "Technology: Pipe Up, People! Rounding Up Staff Ideas," *Inc.* (February 2010): 80–81.

42. Reported in Rachel Emma Silverman, "For Bright Ideas, Ask the Staff," *The Wall Street Journal*, October 17, 2011, B7.

43. Dahl, "Technology: Pipe Up, People!"

44. Sherry Eng, "Hatching Schemes," *The Industry Standard* (November 27–December 4, 2000): 174–175.

45. Alison Overholt, "American Idol: Accounting Edition," *Fortune* (October 17, 2011): 100–106.

46. Jena McGregor et al., "The World's Most Innovative Companies," *BusinessWeek* (April 24, 2006): 62ff.

47. James I. Cash, Jr., Michael J. Earl, and Robert Morison, "Teaming Up to Crack Innovation and Enterprise Integration," *Harvard Business Review* (November 2008): 90–100; Barry Jaruzelski, Kevin Dehoff, and Rakesh Bordia, "Money Isn't Everything," *Strategy + Business*, no. 41 (December 5, 2005): 54–67; William L. Shanklin and John K. Ryans, Jr., "Organizing for High-Tech Marketing," *Harvard Business Review* 62 (November–December 1984): 164–171; Arnold O. Putnam, "A Redesign for Engineering," *Harvard Business Review* 63 (May–June 1985): 139–144; and Joan Schneider and Julie Hall, "Why Most Product Launches Fail," *Harvard Business Review* (April 2011): 21–23.

48. Annie Lowrey, "Ideas on an Assembly Line," *The New York Times*, December 14, 2012, B1.

49. Hiroko Tabuchi, "How the Parade Passed Sony By," *The New York Times*, April 15, 2012, BU1.

50. Quoted in Janet Rae-DuPree, "Teamwork, the True Mother of Invention," *The New York Times*, December 7, 2008.

51. Daniel Roberts, "Going to the Mattresses," *Fortune* (September 24, 2012): 28–29.

52. Based on Gloria Barczak and Kenneth B. Kahn, "Identifying New Product Development Best Practice," *Business Horizons* 55 (2012): 293–305; Andrew H. Van de Ven, "Central Problems in the Management of Innovation," *Management Science* 32 (1986): 590–607; Richard L. Daft, *Organization Theory and Design* (Mason, OH: SouthWestern 2010), pp. 424–425; and Science Policy Research Unit, University of Sussex, *Success and Failure in Industrial Innovation* (London: Centre for the Study of Industrial Innovation, 1972).

53. Based on Daft, *Organization Theory and Design*; and Lee Norris Miller, "Debugging Dysfunctional Development," *Industrial Management* (November–December 2011): 10–15.

54. Mike Gordon et al., "The Path to Successful New Products," *McKinsey Quarterly*, January 2010, www.mckinseyquarterly.com/the_path_to_successful_new_products_2489 (accessed February 10, 2012).

55. Reported in Schneider and Hall, "Why Most Product Launches Fail."

56. Erik Brynjolfsson and Michael Schrage, "The New, Faster Face of Innovation," *The Wall Street Journal Online*, August 17, 2009, http://online.wsj.com/article/SB1000142405297 0204830304574130820184260340.html (accessed August 21, 2009).

57. Brian Dumaine, "How Managers Can Succeed Through Speed," *Fortune* (February 13, 1989): 54–59; and George Stalk, Jr., "Time—The Next Source of Competitive Advantage," *Harvard Business Review* (July–August 1988): 41–51.

58. William J. Holstein, "Five Gates to Innovation," *Strategy + Business* (March 1, 2010), www.strategy-business.com/article/00021?gko=0bd39 (accessed September 16, 2011); and "Corning: For Becoming the 800-Pound Gorilla of the Touch Screen Business," segment of "The World's 50 Most Innovative Companies," *Fast Company* (March 2013): 86–156.

59. This discussion of open innovation is based on Henry Chesbrough, "The Era of Open Innovation," *MIT Sloan Management Review* (Spring 2003): 35–41; Ulrich Lichtenthaler, "Open Innovation: Past Research, Current Debates, and Future Directions," *Academy of Management Perspectives* (February 2011): 75–92; Julian Birkinshaw and Susan A. Hill, "Corporate Venturing Units: Vehicles for Strategic Success in the New Europe," *Organizational Dynamics* 34, no. 3 (2005): 247–257; Amy Muller and Liisa Välikangas, "Extending the Boundary of Corporate Innovation," *Strategy & Leadership* 30, no. 3 (2002): 4–9; Navi Radjou, "Networked Innovation Drives Profits," *Industrial Management* (January–February 2005): 14–21; and Henry Chesbrough, "The Logic of Open Innovation: Managing Intellectual Property," *California Management Review* 45, no. 3 (Spring 2003): 33–58.

60. Amy Muller, Nate Hutchins, and Miguel Cardoso Pinto, "Applying Open Innovation Where Your Company Needs It Most," *Strategy & Leadership* 40, no. 2 (2012): 35–42.

61. Farhad Manjoo, "Apple Nation," *Fortune* (July–August 2010): 68–112; and Jorge Rufat-Latre, Amy Muller, and Dave Jones, "Delivering on the Promise of Open Innovation," *Strategy & Leadership* 38, no. 6 (2010): 23–28.

62. Barry Jaruzelski, Richard Holman, and Edward Baker, "3M's Open Innovation," *Strategy + Business*, May 30, 2011, http://www.strategy-business.com/article/00078?gko=121c3 (accessed October 7, 2013).

63. Reported in Muller, Hutchins, and Cardoso Pinto, "Applying Open Innovation."

64. Kevin J. Boudreau and Karim R. Lakhani, "Using the Crowd as an Innovation Partner," *Harvard Business Review* (April 2013): 61–67.

65. Karen Weise, "Solve a Washington Problem, Win a Prize," *Bloomberg BusinessWeek* (June 10, 2013): 34–35.

66. Boudreau and Lakhani, "Using the Crowd as an Innovation Partner."

67. "Crowdsource Mapping Helps Recovery Efforts in Philippines," *Here & Now*, WBUR, November 15, 2013, http://hereandnow.wbur.org/2013/11/15/mapping-effort-philippines (accessed November 18, 2013); Declan Butler, "Crowdsourcing Goes Mainstream in Typhoon Haiyan Response," *Scientific American*, November 20, 2013, http://www.scientificamerican.com/article.cfm?id=crowdsourcing-goes-mainstream-in-typhoon-haiyan-response (accessed November 12, 2013); Steve Lohr, "Online Mapping Shows Potential to Transform Relief Efforts," *The New York Times*, March 28, 2011, www.nytimes.com/2011/03/28/business/28map.html?_r=1 (accessed August 22, 2012); and Tina Rosenberg, "Crowdsourcing a Better World," *The New York Times*, March 28, 2011, http://opinionator.blogs.nytimes.com/2011/03/28/crowdsourcing-a-better-world/ (accessed March 29, 2011).

68. "Innovation Through Acquisition," *The Wall Street Journal*, January 21, 2013, http://online.wsj.com/article/SB10001424127887323468604578245620735086626.html (accessed October 7,

2013); and "Innovation by Acquisition," *Royal Pingdom Web site*, March 10, 2010, http://royal.pingdom.com/2010/03/10/innovation-by-acquisition/ (accessed October 7, 2013).

69. Daniel T. Holt, Matthew W. Rutherford, and Gretchen R. Clohessy, "Corporate Entrepreneurship: An Empirical Look at Individual Characteristics, Context, and Process," *Journal of Leadership and Organizational Studies* 13, no. 4 (2007): 40–54.

70. Curtis R. Carlson and William W. Wilmot, *Innovation: The Five Disciplines for Creating What Customers Want* (New York: Crown Business, 2006).

71. Robert I. Sutton, "The Weird Rules of Creativity," *Harvard Business Review* (September 2001): 94–103; and Julian Birkinshaw and Michael Mol, "How Management Innovation Happens," *MIT Sloan Management Review* (Summer 2006): 81–88.

72. Jane M. Howell, "The Right Stuff: Identifying and Developing Effective Champions of Innovation," *Academy of Management Executive* 19, no. 2 (2005): 108–119.

73. C. K. Bart, "New Venture Units: Use Them Wisely to Manage Innovation," *Sloan Management Review* (Summer 1988): 35–43; Michael Tushman and David Nadler, "Organizing for Innovation," *California Management Review* 28 (Spring 1986): 74–92; Peter F. Drucker, *Innovation and Entrepreneurship* (New York: Harper & Row, 1985); and Henry W. Chesbrough, "Making Sense of Corporate Venture Capital," *Harvard Business Review* 80, no. 3 (March 2002): 90–99.

74. Raisch, "Balanced Structures."

75. Bruce B. Brown and Scott D. Anthony, "How P&G Tripled Its Innovation Success Rate," *Harvard Business Review* (June 2011): 64–72.

76. Christopher Hoenig, "Skunk Works Secrets," *CIO* (July 1, 2000): 74–76; and Tom Peters and Nancy Austin, *A Passion for Excellence: The Leadership Difference* (New York: Random House, 1985).

77. Hoenig, "Skunk Works Secrets."

78. Claire Cain Miller and Nick Bilton, "Google's Lab of Wildest Dreams," *The New York Times*, November 13, 2011, www.nytimes.com/2011/11/14/technology/at-google-x-a-top-secret-lab-dreaming-up-the-future.html?pagewanted=all (accessed November14, 2011).

79. Taylor, "The New GM."

80. David Dobson, "Integrated Innovation at Pitney Bowes," *Strategy + Business Online*, October 26, 2009, www.strategy-business.com/article/09404b?gko=f9661 (accessed December 30, 2009); and Cash et al., "Teaming Up to Crack Innovation and Enterprise Integration."

81. Robert C. Wolcott and Michael J. Lippitz, "The Four Models of Corporate Entrepreneurship," *MIT Sloan Management Review* (Fall 2007): 75–82.

82. E. H. Schein, "Organizational Culture," *American Psychologist* 45 (February 1990): 109–119; Eliza Newlin Carney, "Calm in the Storm," *Government Executive* (October 2003): 57–63.

83. Rosabeth Moss Kanter, "Execution: The Un-Idea," sidebar in Art Kleiner, "Our 10 Most Enduring Ideas," *Strategy + Business*, no. 41 (December 12, 2005): 36–41.

84. Alex Taylor III, "The New GM: A Report Card," *Fortune* (September 5, 2011), pp. 38–46; Alan Murray, "Women in a Man's World: Dan Akerson of General Motors on Changing a Male-Dominated Culture," *The Wall Street Journal*, May 7, 2012, p. B11; Alex Taylor III, "Most Powerful Women: Big

Wheel at GM," *Fortune* (December 24, 2012), p. 22; and Jeff Bennett, "CEO Akerson Sets Goals for a Revitalized GM" (Boss Talk), *The Wall Street Journal*, January 8, 2013, http://online.wsj.com/article/SB100014241278873234825045782298525719 58928.html (accessed June 5, 2013).

85. Shawn Tully, "Can UnitedHealth Really Fix the System?" *Fortune* (May 29, 2013): 187–194.

86. M. Sashkin and W. W. Burke, "Organization Development in the 1980s," *General Management* 13 (1987): 393–417; and Richard Beckhard, "What Is Organization Development?" in *Organization Development and Transformation: Managing Effective Change*, ed. Wendell L. French, Cecil H. Bell, Jr., and Robert A. Zawacki (Burr Ridge, IL: Irwin McGraw-Hill, 2000), pp. 16–19.

87. Wendell L. French and Cecil H. Bell, Jr., "A History of Organization Development," in French, Bell, and Zawacki, *Organization Development and Transformation*, pp. 20–42; and Christopher G. Worley and Ann E. Feyerherm, "Reflections on the Future of Organization Development," *The Journal of Applied Behavioral Science* 39, no. 1 (March 2003): 97–115.

88. Paul F. Buller, "For Successful Strategic Change: Blend OD Practices with Strategic Management," *Organizational Dynamics* (Winter 1988): 42–55; Robert M. Fulmer and Roderick Gilkey, "Blending Corporate Families: Management and Organization Development in a Postmerger Environment," *The Academy of Management Executive* 2 (1988): 275–283; and Worley and Feyerherm, "Reflections on the Future of Organization Development."

89. W. Warner Burke, "The New Agenda for Organization Development," *Organizational Dynamics* (Summer 1997): 7–19.

90. R. Wayne Bass et al., "Sustainable Change in the Public Sector: The Longitudinal Benefits of Organization Development," *The Journal of Applied Behavioral Science* 46, no. 4 (2010): 436–472.

91. Tully, "Can UnitedHealth Really Fix the System?"

92. This discussion is based on Kathleen D. Dannemiller and Robert W. Jacobs, "Changing the Way Organizations Change: A Revolution of Common Sense," *The Journal of Applied Behavioral Science* 28, no. 4 (December 1992): 480–498; and Barbara Benedict Bunker and Billie T. Alban, "Conclusion: What Makes Large Group Interventions Effective?" *Journal of Applied Behavioral Science* 28, no. 4 (December 1992): 570–591.

93. For a recent review of the literature related to large group interventions, see Christopher G. Worley, Susan A. Mohrman, and Jennifer A. Nevitt, "Large Group Interventions: An Empirical Study of Their Composition, Process, and Outcomes," *The Journal of Applied Behavioral Science* 47, no. 4 (2011): 404–431.

94. Bunker and Alban, "Conclusion: What Makes Large Group Interventions Effective?"

95. Kurt Lewin, "Frontiers in Group Dynamics: Concepts, Method, and Reality in Social Science," *Human Relations* 1 (1947): 5–41; and E. F. Huse and T. G. Cummings, *Organization Development and Change*, 3rd ed. (St. Paul, MN: West, 1985).

96. Based on John Kotter's eight-step model of planned change, which is described in John P. Kotter, *Leading Change* (Boston: Harvard Business School Press, 1996), pp. 20–25, and John Kotter, "Leading Change: Why Transformation Efforts Fail," *Harvard Business Review* (March–April, 1995): 59–67.

97. Based on Bob Kelleher, "Employee Engagement Carries ENSR Through Organizational Challenges and Economic Turmoil," *Global Business and Organizational Excellence* 28, no. 3 (March–April 2009): 6–19.

98. Peter Löscher, "How I Did It … The CEO of Siemens on Using a Scandal to Drive Change," *Harvard Business Review* (November 2012), pp. 39–42.

99. Kotter, *Leading Change*, pp. 20–25; and "Leading Change: Why Transformation Efforts Fail."

100. Kurt Lewin, *Field Theory in Social Science: Selected Theoretical Papers* (New York: Harper & Brothers, 1951).

101. Paul C. Nutt, "Tactics of Implementation," *Academy of Management Journal* 29 (1986): 230–261; Kotter and Schlesinger, "Choosing Strategies for Change"; R. L. Daft and S. Becker, *Innovation in Organizations: Innovation Adoption in School Organizations* (New York: Elsevier, 1978); and R. Beckhard, *Organization Development: Strategies and Models* (Reading, MA: Addison-Wesley, 1969).

102. Strategos survey results, reported in Pierre Loewe and Jennifer Dominiquini, "Overcoming the Barriers to Effective Innovation," *Strategy & Leadership* 34, no. 1 (2006): 24–31.

103. Donald F. Kuratko, Jeffrey G. Covin, and Robert P. Garrett, "Corporate Venturing: Insights from Actual Performance," *Business Horizons* 52 (2009): 459–467.

104. Allysia Finley, "The Democrat Who Took On the Unions," *The Wall Street Journal*, March 24, 2012, A13.

105. Gerard H. Seijts and Grace O'Farrell, "Engage the Heart: Appealing to the Emotions Facilitates Change," *Ivey Business Journal* (January–February 2003): 1–5; John P. Kotter and Dan S. Cohen, *The Heart of Change: Real-Life Stories of How People Change Their Organizations* (Boston: Harvard Business School Press, 2002); and Shaul Fox and Yair Amichai-Hamburger, "The Power of Emotional Appeals in Promoting Organizational Change Programs," *Academy of Management Executive* 15, no. 4 (2001): 84–95.

106. Gina Burkhardt and Diane Gerard, "People: The Lever for Changing the Business Model at Learning Point Associates," *Journal of Organizational Excellence* (Autumn 2006): 31–43.

107. Henry Hornstein, "Using a Change Management Approach to Implement IT Programs," *Ivey Business Journal* (January–February 2008); Philip H. Mirvis, Amy L. Sales, and Edward J. Hackett, "The Implementation and Adoption of New Technology in Organizations: The Impact on Work, People, and Culture," *Human Resource Management* 30 (Spring 1991): 113–139; Arthur E. Wallach, "System Changes Begin in the Training Department," *Personnel Journal* 58 (1979): 846–848, 872; and Paul R. Lawrence, "How to Deal with Resistance to Change," *Harvard Business Review* 47 (January–February 1969): 4–12, 166–176.

108. Kate Linebaugh and Jeff Bennett, "Marchionne Upends Chrysler's Ways: CEO Decries Detroit's 'Fanatical' Focus on Market Share," *The Wall Street Journal*, January 12, 2010.

109. Adapted from Edward Glassman, *Creativity Handbook: Idea Triggers and Sparks That Work* (Chapel Hill, NC: LCS Press, 1990).

110. Based on Paul Boutin, "Crowdsourcing: Consumers as Creators," *BusinessWeek Online*, July 13, 2006, www.businessweek.com/innovate/content/jul2006/id20060713_755844.htm (accessed August 30, 2010); Jeff Howe, "The Rise of Crowdsourcing," *Wired*, June 2006, www.wired.com/wired/archive/14.06/crowds.html (accessed August 30, 2010); and Jeff Howe, Crowdsourcing blog, www.crowdsourcing.com (accessed August 30, 2010).

CHAPTER
9

Managing Human Resources and Diversity

LEARNING OUTCOMES

After studying this chapter, you should be able to:

9.1 Explain the strategic role of human resource management.

9.2 Describe federal legislation and societal trends that influence human resource management.

9.3 Explain what the changing social contract between organizations and employees means for workers and human resource managers.

9.4 Show how organizations determine their future staffing needs through human resource planning.

9.5 Describe the tools that managers use to recruit and select employees.

9.6 Describe the pervasive demographic changes occurring in the domestic and global workforces and how corporations are responding.

9.7 Summarize the factors that affect women's opportunities, including the glass ceiling, the opt-out trend, and the female advantage.

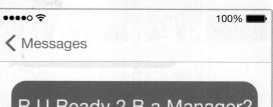

●●●●○ 📶   100% 🔋

‹ Messages

R U Ready 2 B a Manager?

Delivered

Before reading this chapter, please circle either "Mostly True" or "Mostly False" for each of the five questions below.

1 Employees who learn and grow are more valuable to their company.

Mostly True	Mostly False

[page 364]

2 I know that the kind of job security my parents or grandparents had is gone.

Mostly True	Mostly False

[page 368]

3 I know how important it is to behave professionally and do my homework for a job interview.

Mostly True	Mostly False

[page 375]

4 It is easy for me to relate to people from different ethnic backgrounds, social classes, or religions.

Mostly True	Mostly False

[page 391]

5 In some ways, women make better managers than men.

Mostly True	Mostly False

[page 407]

Getting the Right People on the Bus[1]

Instructions: As a new manager, how much emphasis will you give to getting the right people on your team? Find out by answering the following questions based on your expectations and beliefs for handling the people part of your management job. Please answer whether each item is mostly true or mostly false for you.

	Mostly True	Mostly False
1. I will readily fire someone who isn't working out for the interests of the organization.	_____	_____
2. Selecting the right people for a winning business team is as important to me as it is to a winning sports team.	_____	_____
3. I expect to spend 40–60 percent of my management time on issues such as recruiting, developing, and placing people.	_____	_____
4. I will paint a realistic picture of negative job aspects that will help scare off the wrong people for the job.	_____	_____
5. My priority as a manager is first to hire the right people, second to put people in the right positions, and third to decide strategy and vision.	_____	_____
6. With the right people on my team, problems of motivation and supervision will largely go away.	_____	_____
7. I expect that hiring the right people is a lengthy and arduous process.	_____	_____
8. I view firing people as helping them find the place where they belong so that they can find fulfillment.	_____	_____

Scoring and Interpretation: Most new managers are shocked at the large amount of time, effort, and skill required to recruit, place, and retain the right people. In recent years, the importance of "getting the right people on the bus" has been described in popular business books such as Good to Great, by Jim Collins, and Execution: The Discipline of Getting Things Done, by Larry Bossidy and Ram Charan. The right people can make an organization great; the wrong people can be catastrophic.

  Give yourself 1 point for each item you marked as Mostly True. If you scored 4 or less, you may be in for a shock as a new manager. People issues will take up most of your time, and if you don't handle people correctly, your effectiveness will suffer. You should learn how to get the right people on the bus and how to get the wrong people off the bus. The faster you learn these lessons, the better a new manager you will be. A score of 5 or more suggests that you have the right understanding and expectations for becoming a manager and dealing with people on the bus.

Germany is one of Amazon's largest markets outside the United States, and the company has a big human resource (HR) responsibility there, with 8,000 permanent workers at eight distribution centers, along with more than 10,000 temporary workers for seasonal jobs. But the giant online retailer has become the latest symbol of everything that many Germans resent about American-style human resource management (HRM). A series of protests by ver.di, one of the largest labor unions in Germany, has raised the question of whether Amazon will become the latest company to run afoul of German labor laws, which are much tougher than those in the United States. Walmart abandoned Germany in 2006 after a number of setbacks, including a struggle with ver.di. The triggering event for Amazon was a documentary about third-party contractors hired to manage thousands of temporary immigrant workers, as described in 3. The documentary interviewed workers who said that security guards intimidate them, and even went so far as to imply that Amazon uses neo-Nazi thugs to keep workers in line. Amazon immediately stopped doing business with that security company. Amazon already pays above union wages, but ver.di has other complaints. Union officials say that a "big brother" atmosphere prevails at the company. "Everything is measured, everything is calculated, everything is geared toward efficiency," said Heiner Reimann, a spokesman for ver.di. "People want to be treated with respect."[2]

As this example shows, managers have to worry not only about finding and developing the right people, but also meeting the legal requirements and managing public relations in the various countries in which they do business. As business becomes increasingly international, this adds to the complexity of the HR manager's job.

This chapter explores the topic of human resource management in detail. The term **human resource management (HRM)** refers to the design and application of formal systems in an organization to ensure the effective and efficient use of human talent to accomplish organizational goals.[3] This includes activities undertaken to attract, develop, and maintain an effective workforce. Managers have to find the right people, place them in positions where they can be most effective, and develop them so that they contribute to company success.

HRM has shed its old "personnel" image and gained recognition as a vital player in corporate strategy.[4] "Many organizations are looking for their HR leader to be able to understand in great detail the business and the challenges of the business," says Fran Luisi of Charleston Partners, a search firm that specializes in HR managers.[5] The growing clout of the HR function is reflected in the fact that current and former HR managers are increasingly being sought to fill board seats as outside directors at other companies. Hot-button issues such as executive compensation, changing government regulations, and the frequency of mergers and acquisitions make HRM a critical skill for both business and nonprofit organizations.[6] All managers need to be skilled in the basics of HRM.

9.1 The Strategic Role of HRM Is to Drive Organizational Performance

A survey of more than 1,700 CEOs around the world found that *human capital* was cited as the top factor in maintaining competitive success, which reflects the critical role of managing talent. Smart managers know that employees *are* the company—if they don't perform well, the company doesn't stand a chance of succeeding. **Human capital** refers to the economic value of the combined knowledge, experience, skills, and capabilities of employees.[7] Exhibit 9.1 shows the top three factors cited by CEOs in the survey. Human capital ranked far higher than assets such as technology, physical resources, and access to raw materials.[8]

EXHIBIT 9.1 Top Three Factors for Maintaining Competitive Success

Percentage of CEOs reporting these factors as important for competitive success:

Factor	Percentage
Human Capital	71%
Customer Relationships	66%
Product and Service Innovation	52%

SOURCE: "Leading Through Connections: The IBM 2012 Chief Executive Officer Study," reported in Eric Lesser and Carl Hoffman, "Workforce Analytics: Making the Most of a Critical Asset," *Ivey Business Journal,* July–August 2012, www.iveybusinessjournal.com/topics/strategy/workforce-analytics-making-the-most-of-a-critical-asset (accessed August 27, 2012).

9.1a The Strategic Approach

"If each of us hires people who are smaller than we are, we shall become a company of dwarfs. But if each of us hires people who are bigger than we are, we shall become a company of giants."

—David Ogilvy (1911–1999), founder of the Ogilvy & Mather advertising agency

The best HR departments not only support strategic objectives, but also actively pursue an ongoing, integrated plan for furthering the organization's performance.[9] Research has found that effective HRM and the alignment of HR strategies with the organization's strategic direction have a positive impact on performance, including higher employee productivity and stronger financial results.[10]

When Anglo American PLC adopted a strategy to begin digging for iron ore in a remote area of Brazil, the HR department worked to create a pool of well-trained local employees to work the mines for years to come.

The strategic approach to HRM recognizes three key elements. First, all managers are involved in managing HR. Second, employees are viewed as assets. No strategy can be implemented effectively without the right people to put it into action. Employees, not buildings and machinery, give a company its competitive edge. Third, HRM is a matching process, integrating the organization's strategy and goals with the correct approach to managing human capital.[11] Some current strategic issues of particular concern to managers include the following:

- Hiring the right people to become more competitive on a global basis

- Hiring the right people for improving quality, innovation, and customer service

- Knowing the right people to retain after mergers, acquisitions, or downsizing

- Hiring the right people to apply new information technology (IT) for e-business

All of these strategic decisions determine a company's need for skills and employees.

This chapter examines the three primary goals of HRM, as illustrated in Exhibit 9.2. HRM activities and goals do not take place inside a vacuum, but within the context of issues and factors affecting the entire organization, such as globalization, changing technology, the need for rapid innovation, quick shifts in markets and the external environment, societal trends, government regulations, and changes in the organization's culture, structure, strategy, and goals.

The three broad HRM activities outlined in Exhibit 9.2 are to find the right people, manage talent so that people achieve their potential, and maintain the workforce over the long term.[12]

Spotlight on Skills

Anglo American PLC

"There are lots of people in this area who were simply unemployable," said Pedro Borrego, director of HR at the Anglo American operation in Brazil. He was talking about the company's Minas Gerais iron ore mine, located in a town where cows outnumber people almost two to one.

Anglo American (Anglo) is one of the world's largest diversified mining companies, with copper, diamond, iron ore, and other mines all over the world. The company was first drawn to Minas Gerais in 2007 by the region's rich reserves of iron ore, which is one of the key ingredients for making steel. The problem was finding people to work the mines. Managers knew that hiring locally was the key to getting a loyal, stable workforce. In some areas, companies can partner with local colleges to fund a training program, but that wasn't an option here. So Anglo renovated a crumbling grade school and set up its own classes to teach local people everything from welding parts and changing lightbulbs to repairing diesel engines

and operating conveyor belts. More than 20 percent of the workers being trained are women, compared to fewer than 10 percent at mining firms globally, thanks in part to incentives that Anglo is offering to mothers.

The first class of 151 trainees graduated in January 2013, with some hired by Anglo and others hired by contractors. The company plans to train 500 more local people over the next three years. "My parents are farmers, and I wanted to be a teacher," said 22-year-old Vanessa Carvalho Reis. Now she is training to be an operator at a plant where Anglo American will pump iron ore through a series of mixers and crushers to enrich the metal.[13]

Hiring and keeping high-quality employees with the right set of skills is one of the most urgent concerns for today's organizations.[14] By training young people who otherwise would have few options for employment, Anglo is ensuring that it will have a stable, well-trained workforce for years to come.

EXHIBIT 9.2 **Strategic Human Resource Management**

Dick Blume/Syracuse Newspapers/The Image Works

CONCEPT CONNECTION Lowe's 260,000 employees help customers with remodeling, building, and gardening ideas at its 1,830 stores. They cut lumber, blinds, pipe, and chains; thread pipes; assemble items; provide computer project design and landscape garden design; match paint colors; teach how-to clinics; and offer many other services. Managers know that providing superior customer service depends on **human capital**, so they invest in finding the best people and helping them develop and apply their combined knowledge, skills, experience, and talent.

9.1b Building Human Capital to Drive Performance

In many companies, especially those that rely more on employee information, creativity, knowledge, and service rather than on production machinery, success depends on the ability to manage human capital, as described earlier.[15] To build human capital, HRM develops strategies for finding the best people, enhancing their skills and knowledge with training programs and opportunities for personal and professional development, and providing compensation and benefits that support the sharing of knowledge and appropriately reward people for their contributions to the organization.[16]

The importance of human capital for business results is illustrated in Exhibit 9.3, which shows a portion of a framework developed by Accenture and used by software and services company SAP. SAP needed a way to evaluate and revise its human capital processes to shift to a new strategy that called for stronger customer focus and greater individual employee accountability. The idea is to show how investments in human capital contribute to stronger organizational performance and better financial results. The framework begins at the bottom (level 3) by assessing internal processes such as workforce planning, career development, performance appraisal, and so forth. Managers use these activities to increase human capital capabilities that drive higher performance in key areas such as innovation or customer service (level 2). Improvements in key performance areas, in turn, lead to improved business results (level 1).[17]

Green Power

The "You" in Sustainability

"You are our sustainability edge!" is the new slogan to bring employees on board for sustainability. **HSBC** carried employee involvement to a new level by promoting individual projects and action plans through its Climate Champions Program. HSBC paved the way by partnering with powerful environmental organizations, including the Smithsonian Institution, Earthwatch, and the Climate Group. Participants must go through an application process for a 12-month residential program. Working alongside Earthwatch scientists, HSBC employees complete climate-related business projects, gaining skills and developing methods that can be transferred to the workplace. HSBC's Climate Champions program has ignited employee curiosity and excitement. The program tells participants, "You have a voice in sustainability. You own this project. You are our sustainability edge."

SOURCE: Matthew Gitsham, "Experiential Learning for Leadership and Sustainability at IBM and HSBC," *Journal of Management Development* 31, no. 3 (2012): 298–307.

EXHIBIT 9.3 The Role and Value of Human Capital Investments

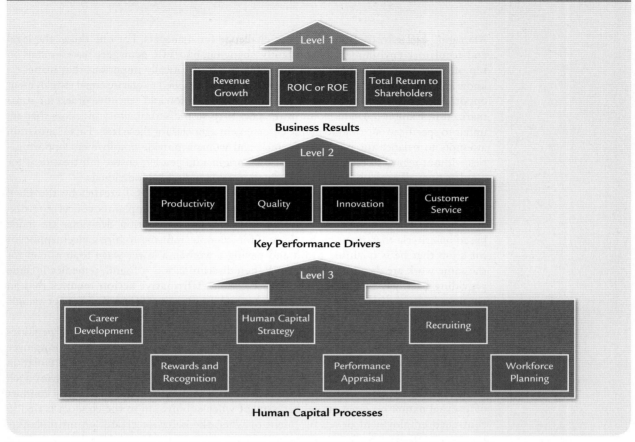

SOURCE: Adapted from Susan Cantrell et al., "Measuring the Value of Human Capital Investments: The SAP Case," Strategy & Leadership 34, no. 2 (2006): 43–52.

REMEMBER THIS

- **Human resource management (HRM)** refers to the design and application of formal systems to ensure the effective and efficient use of human talent to accomplish organizational goals.

- HRM includes activities undertaken to attract, select, develop, and maintain an effective workforce.

- HR managers are vital players in corporate strategy because no strategy can be effective without the right people to put it into action.

- **Human capital** refers to the economic value of the combined knowledge, experience, skills, and capabilities of employees.

- Mining giant Anglo American PLC created its own training facility to develop a pool of skilled, dedicated employees for its Minas Gerais iron ore mine in Brazil.

9.2 The Impact of Federal Legislation on HRM

Managing HR effectively is a complex challenge for managers. For one thing, the legal and regulatory environment is constantly changing, and HR managers have to stay on top of issues that might have legal consequences. It is critically important that managers know and apply a variety of federal laws that have been passed to ensure equal employment opportunity (EEO). Some of the most significant legislation and executive orders are summarized in Exhibit 9.4. The point of the laws is to stop discriminatory practices that are unfair to specific groups and to define enforcement agencies for these laws. EEO legislation attempts to balance the pay given to men and women; provide employment opportunities without regard to race, religion, national origin, and gender; ensure fair treatment for employees of all ages; and avoid discrimination against disabled individuals.

The Equal Employment Opportunity Commission (EEOC) created by the Civil Rights Act of 1964 initiates investigations in response to complaints concerning discrimination. **Discrimination** occurs when hiring and promotion decisions are made based on criteria that are not job-relevant; for example, refusing to hire a black applicant for a job that he is qualified to fill and paying a woman a lower wage than a man for the same work are discriminatory acts. When discrimination is found, remedies include providing back pay and taking affirmative action. **Affirmative action** requires that an employer take positive steps to guarantee equal employment opportunities for people within protected groups.

Failure to comply with EEO legislation can result in substantial fines and penalties for employers. Suits for discriminatory practices can cover a broad range of employee complaints. One issue of growing concern is *sexual harassment,* which is also a violation of Title VII of the Civil Rights Act. The EEOC guidelines specify that behavior such as unwelcome advances, requests for sexual favors, and other verbal and physical conduct of a sexual nature becomes sexual harassment when submission to the conduct is tied to continued employment or advancement or when the behavior creates an intimidating, hostile, or offensive work environment.[18] Changes in the workplace have brought about shifts in the types of complaints being seen. Complaints of sexual harassment by men against both male and female bosses, for example, increased about 5 percent between 1997 and 2010. In addition, there are fewer complaints related to blatant harassment and more related to bosses who make sexually charged comments and send inappropriate e-mail or text messages.[19] Sexual harassment will be discussed in more detail at the end of this chapter.

Exhibit 9.4 also lists major federal laws related to compensation and benefits and health and safety issues. This is only a sampling of the federal laws that HR managers must know and understand. In addition, many states and municipalities have their own laws that relate to HR issues. California, for example, requires that companies with 50 or more employees provide sexual harassment training for all employees every two years.[20] The scope of HR legislation is increasing at federal, state, and municipal levels. In addition, social and technological changes bring new legal challenges. The National Labor Relations Board (NLRB) recently filed suit on behalf of Dawnmarie Souza, who was fired because of a comment she made on Facebook—the NLRB's first (but likely not the last) case involving a firing related to social media.[21] As illustrated by the example about Amazon in the chapter opener, companies operating internationally also have to be aware of laws related to HRM in the various countries in which they do business.

EXHIBIT 9.4 **Major Federal Laws Related to Human Resource Management**

Federal Law	Year	Provisions
Equal Opportunity/ Discrimination Laws		
Civil Rights Act	1991	Provides for possible compensatory and punitive damages, plus traditional back pay, for cases of intentional discrimination brought under Title VII of the 1964 Civil Rights Act. Shifts the burden of proof to the employer.
Americans with Disabilities Act	1990	Prohibits discrimination against qualified individuals by employers on the basis of disability and demands that "reasonable accommodations" be provided for the disabled to allow performance of duties.
Vocational Rehabilitation Act	1973	Prohibits discrimination based on physical or mental disability and requires that employees be informed about affirmative action plans.
Age Discrimination in Employment Act (ADEA)	1967 (amended in 1978 and 1986)	Prohibits age discrimination and restricts mandatory retirement.
Civil Rights Act, Title VII	1964	Prohibits discrimination in employment on the basis of race, religion, color, sex, or national origin.
Compensation/Benefits Laws		
Health Insurance Portability Accountability Act (HIPAA)	1996	Allows employees to switch health insurance plans when changing jobs and get the new coverage regardless of preexisting health conditions; prohibits group plans from dropping a sick employee.
Family and Medical Leave Act (FMLA)	1993	Requires employers to provide up to 12 weeks unpaid leave for childbirth, adoption, or family emergencies.
Equal Pay Act	1963	Prohibits sex differences in pay for substantially equal work.
Health/Safety Laws		
Patient Protection and Affordable Care Act (PPACA)	2010	Imposes a fee on firms with 50 or more employees if the government subsidizes their employees' health care coverage; prevents insurers from denying coverage based on preexisting conditions or charging women more than men.
Consolidated Omnibus Budget Reconciliation Act (COBRA)	1985	Requires continued health insurance coverage (paid by employee) following termination.
Occupational Safety and Health Act (OSHA)	1970	Establishes mandatory safety and health standards in organizations.

REMEMBER THIS

- HR managers have to understand and apply a variety of federal laws that prohibit discrimination, establish safety standards, or require organizations to provide certain benefits.

- **Discrimination** means making hiring and promotion decisions based on criteria that are not job-relevant.

- **Affirmative action** requires that employers take positive steps to guarantee equal employment opportunities for people within protected groups.

- The National Labor Relations Board (NLRB) recently filed suit on behalf of an employee who was fired because of a comment that she made on a social networking site.

9.3 The Changing Nature of Careers

Another current issue is the changing nature of careers and a shift in the relationship between employers and employees.

9.3a The Changing Social Contract

In the old social contract between the organization and the employee, the employee could contribute ability, education, loyalty, and commitment and expect, in return, that the company would provide wages and benefits, work, advancement, and training throughout the employee's working life. Then along came globalization, outsourcing, hypercompetition, and other volatile changes in the environment. Consider the following list found on a bulletin board at a company undergoing major restructuring:

- We can't promise you how long we'll be in business.

- We can't promise you that we won't be acquired.

- We can't promise that there'll be room for promotion.

- We can't promise that your job will exist when you reach retirement age.

- We can't promise that the money will be available for your pension.

- We can't expect your undying loyalty, and we aren't even sure we want it.[22]

The recent economic downturn has accelerated the erosion of the old social contract. Employer-subsidized retirement benefits are in serious decline, for example, with only about 20 percent of employees covered by traditional pension plans today. During the recent recession, many companies suspended their contributions to employee 401(k) plans. Moreover, many organizations that cut benefits say that they don't intend to restore them.[23]

These changes and the bulleted list items reflect a primarily negative view of the new employer-employee relationship, but there are positive aspects as well. In a sense, companies and employees become allies helping one another grow stronger. Employees help the company become more adaptable, while the company helps the employee become more employable.[24] Many young people don't have any desire to stay with one company throughout their careers. They like the expectations of responsibility, learning, growth, and mobility embedded in the new social contract. CEO Reed Hastings of Netflix says of his company: "We're a team; not a family."[25] Workplace expert Lynda Gratton says that building trust is more important than loyalty today, when "serial career monogamy" is the order for many young employees, who are continually evaluating whether their work is meaningful and challenging and fits with their lives.[26]

EXHIBIT 9.5   The Changing Social Contract

	New Contract	Old Contract
Employee	• Employability; personal responsibility • Partner in business improvement • Learning; skill development	• Job security • A cog in the machine • Knowing
Employer	• Creative development opportunities • Lateral career moves; incentive compensation • Challenging assignments • Information and resources; decision-making authority	• Standard training programs • Traditional compensation package • Routine jobs • Limited information and authority

SOURCES: Based on Louisa Wah, "The New Workplace Paradox," *Management Review* (January 1998): 7; and Douglas T. Hall and Jonathan E. Moss, "The New Protean Career Contract: Helping Organizations and Employees Adapt," *Organizational Dynamics* (Winter 1998): 22–37.

Exhibit 9.5 lists some elements of the new social contract. The new contract is based on the concept of employability rather than lifetime employment. Individuals are responsible for developing their own skills and abilities and demonstrating their value to the organization. The employer, in turn, invests in creative training and development opportunities so that people will be more employable when the company no longer needs their services. This means offering challenging work assignments, opportunities to participate in decision making, and access to information and resources. In addition, an important challenge for HRM is revising performance evaluation, compensation, and other practices to be compatible with the new social contract. For example, with the tough economy in recent years, companies have had to lay off thousands of experienced employees. Many organizations, including KPMG International, IBM, Microsoft, and Lockheed Martin, have set up "alumni social networks" so that people who have to be let go can keep in touch with colleagues and the industry.[27] McKinsey & Company has operated an alumni network since the 1960s.[28]

9.3b Innovations in HRM

The field of HRM is constantly changing. Some important HRM issues today are branding the company as an employer of choice, acquiring companies to obtain talent, and addressing the needs of temporary employees and part-time workers.

Branding the Company as an Employer of Choice   You might think with the high unemployment rate currently, companies wouldn't be worried about recruiting good people. But managers are finding that the most skilled and knowledgeable employees are in short supply and great demand.[29] Both small and large companies in a variety of industries are using employer branding to attract desirable job candidates. An employer brand is similar to a product brand, except that rather than promoting a specific product, its aim is to make the organization seem like a highly desirable place to work. Employer-branding campaigns are like marketing campaigns to "sell" the company and attract the best job candidates. At Risk Management Solutions (RMS), HR executive Amelia Merrill used employer branding after she discovered that few people in Silicon Valley where the firm is based had a clue what RMS was. To attract the kind of high-quality technology professionals that RMS needed, Merrill's team began selling the company in the same way that its salespeople sold its services. One step was to rent San Francisco's popular "Bacon Bacon" food truck for a day and set up at a local cloud-computing exposition. Merrill says that branding is having a slow but sure effect on recruiting efforts, as people in the IT industry become more familiar with the company name.[30] However, many large, well-known companies, including

PepsiCo, General Electric (GE), Nokia, AT&T, and Credit Suisse Group, are also using employer branding as companies fight for talent.[31]

Using Temporary and Part-Time Employees   Contingent workers are becoming a larger part of the workforce in both the United States and Europe. **Contingent workers** are people who work for an organization, but not on a permanent or full-time basis. Data from the U.S. Bureau of Labor Statistics suggest that a third, and perhaps up to 40 percent, of American workers are in part-time, contract, or other types of nonstandard positions. "There's been a really fundamental shift in the nature of employment [over the past 20 years]—it's a sea change," said Katherine Stone, a law professor at the University of California, Los Angeles, and a labor specialist.[32] Although many of these people are "involuntary" temporary or part-time workers who lost jobs during the recession, others like the option of working for different companies for short periods of time. For organizations, the primary goal is to access specialized skills for specific projects, enabling the company to maintain flexibility and keep costs low.[33]

In the past, most temporary workers were in clerical and manufacturing positions, but in recent years, demand has grown for contingent professionals, such as accountants and financial analysts, interim managers, IT specialists, product managers, lawyers, and even CEOs. Sometimes called *supertemps*, these are people who are highly skilled and choose to pursue independent careers. Supertemps often do mission-critical work. Ed Trevasani, who loves the freedom and flexibility of contingent work, has served as interim CEO for an international firm, developed a mergers and acquisitions strategy for a global manufacturer, and led the IT selection process for a major insurance company.[34]

Acquiring Start-Ups to Get the Talent   Andrea Vaccari created Glancee as a mobile app to help people find others with similar interests. But just as the company was taking off, he and his cofounders faced a tough decision—accept an acquisition bid from Facebook or go for broke? The problem was that Vaccari was already almost broke, living in a closet at a friend's apartment. The cofounders decided to accept Facebook's offer, even though they knew that it was made primarily to recruit them to work at the larger company.[35] The so-called **acqui-hiring** has become common in the tech world. Established companies such as Facebook, Google, Yahoo, LinkedIn, and Salesforce.com buy early-stage start-ups, often shutting them down, simply to acquire their engineering talent. These deals, ranging from about $3 to $6 million, have increased amid soaring demand for talented software engineers. The strategy makes sense for the larger companies because they get teams of engineers who are accustomed to working together. For entrepreneurs, it's a trade-off. Thinkfuse Inc. cofounder Aydin Ghajar says that being acquired by Salesforce.com was a good outcome for his team. At the time, Ghajar and his four engineers were making below-market salaries and working in a business incubator with about 30 other start-ups. Now they work in a high-rise building with a gym. The Glancee engineers working for Facebook are also doing all right, but Vaccari says that it was agonizing to have to decide whether the company could be "the next big thing" by going it alone. "You will never know if it will be better to continue," he says.

REMEMBER THIS

- The new social contract between employers and employees is based on the notion of employability and personal responsibility rather than lifelong employment by an organization.

- An **employer brand** is similar to a product brand except that it promotes the organization as a great place to work, rather than promoting a specific product or service.

- **Contingent workers** are people who work for an organization, but not on a permanent or full-time basis, including temporary placements, independent contractors, freelancers, and part-time employees.

- It is estimated that up to 40 percent of Americans are in part-time, contract, or other types of non-standard jobs.
- **Acqui-hiring** means buying an early-stage start-up (and usually shutting it down) in order to obtain the creative talent.

9.4 Finding the Right People

Now let's turn to the three broad goals of HRM: finding, developing, and maintaining an effective workforce. The first step in finding the right people is human resource planning, in which managers or HRM professionals predict the need for new employees based on the types of vacancies that exist, as illustrated in Exhibit 9.6. The second step is to use recruiting procedures to communicate with potential applicants. The third step is to select from the applicants those persons believed to be the best potential contributors to the organization. Finally, the new employees are welcomed into the organization.

Underlying the organization's effort to attract employees is a matching model. With the **matching model**, the organization and the individual attempt to match the needs, interests, and values that they offer each other.[36] For example, a small software developer might require long hours from creative, technically skilled employees. In return, it can offer freedom from bureaucracy, tolerance of idiosyncrasies, and potentially high pay. A large

EXHIBIT 9.6 Attracting an Effective Workforce

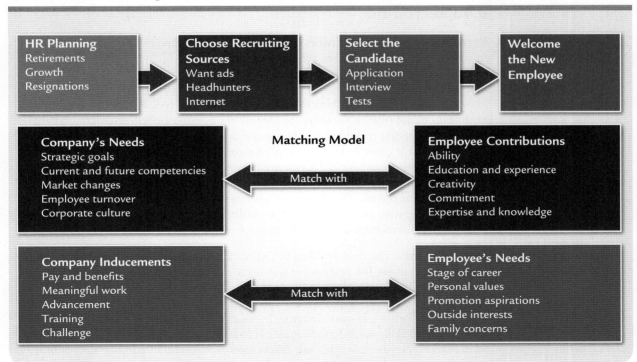

manufacturer can offer employment security and stability, but it might have more rules and regulations and require a greater ability to "get approval from the higher-ups." The individual who would thrive working for the software developer might feel stymied and unhappy working for a large manufacturer. Both the company and the employee are interested in finding a good match.

9.4a Human Resource Planning

Human resource planning is the forecasting of HR needs and the projected matching of individuals with expected vacancies. Human resource planning begins with several big-picture questions:

- What new technologies are emerging, and how will these affect the work system?

- What is the volume of the business likely to be in the next 5 to 10 years?

- What is the turnover rate, and how much, if any, is avoidable?

The responses to these questions are used to formulate specific questions pertaining to HR activities, such as the following:

- What types of engineers will we need, and how many?

- How many administrative personnel will we need to support the additional engineers?

- Can we use temporary, part-time, or virtual workers to handle some tasks?[37]

By anticipating future HR needs, the organization can prepare itself to meet competitive challenges more effectively than organizations that react to problems only as they arise.

9.4b Recruiting

Recruiting is defined as "activities or practices that define the characteristics of applicants to whom selection procedures are ultimately applied."[38] Today, recruiting is sometimes referred to as *talent acquisition* to reflect the importance of the human factor in the organization's success.[39]

Although we frequently think of campus recruiting as a typical recruiting activity, many organizations use *internal recruiting,* or *promote-from-within* policies, to fill their high-level positions.[40] Internal recruiting has two major advantages: It is less costly than an external search, and it generates higher employee commitment, development, and satisfaction because it offers opportunities for career advancement to employees rather than outsiders. Frequently, however, *external recruiting*—recruiting newcomers from outside the organization—is advantageous. Applicants are provided by a variety of outside sources, including advertising, state employment services, online recruiting services, private employment agencies (headhunters), job fairs, and employee referrals.

Assessing Jobs   The basic building blocks of HRM include job analysis, job descriptions, and job specifications. **Job analysis** is a systematic process of gathering and interpreting information about the essential duties, tasks, and responsibilities of a job, as well as about the context within which the job is performed.[41] To perform job analysis, managers or specialists ask about work activities and work flow, the degree of supervision given and received in the job, knowledge and skills needed, performance standards, working conditions, and so forth. The manager then prepares a written **job description**, which is a clear and concise summary of the specific tasks, duties, and responsibilities, and **job specification**, which outlines the knowledge, skills, education, physical abilities, and other characteristics needed to perform the job adequately.

Job analysis helps organizations recruit the right kind of people and match them to appropriate jobs. For example, to enhance internal recruiting, Sara Lee Corporation identified six functional areas and 24 significant skills that it wants its finance executives to develop, such as communication (and under that credibility and presentation style) and planning (which includes profitability analysis and managing budget processes). Managers are tracked on their development and moved into other positions to help them acquire the needed skills.[42]

Realistic Job Previews   Job analysis also enhances recruiting effectiveness by enabling the creation of realistic job previews (RJPs), which give applicants all pertinent and realistic information—positive and negative—about the job and the organization.[43] RJPs contribute to greater employee satisfaction and lower turnover because they facilitate matching individuals, jobs, and organizations. Individuals have a better basis on which to determine their suitability to the organization and "self-select" into or out of positions based on full information.

CONCEPT CONNECTION   For people just entering the medical field, working in a hospital's emergency room (ER) where you can save lives every day may sound exciting and meaningful, but not everyone is cut out to deal with the hectic pace of a typical ER. That's why this hospital asks job applicants to work a shift or two as part of a **realistic job preview (RJP)**. The trial run allows both the applicant and the hospital's staff to determine whether the job candidate is a good fit for this challenging work environment.

Robb Kendrick/Aurora Photos/Alamy

Social Media   Smart managers do much of their recruiting today via the Internet, including social media sites such as LinkedIn, Facebook, and Twitter. Interestingly, a survey by staffing services firm Spherion found that high-achieving young professionals deem a company's social media reputation as important as the job offer when considering which company they want to work for.[44] The British army launched a social media campaign in 2013 to recruit 10,000 new soldiers. Companies in China have become particularly adept at using this approach because traditional online recruiting boards in China attract far too many unqualified candidates to make them valuable. Therefore, managers turn to social media such as Weibo, a Twitter-like messaging service, to build a community of potential candidates.[45] China's Lenovo Group reports finding 70 good candidates during a three-month recruiting surge via social media, including LinkedIn, Weibo, and Tianji, a Chinese professional social networking site.[46]

LinkedIn's 2013 *Global Recruiting Trends Report* surveyed 3,300 talent acquisition managers around the globe and found that HR recruiters are becoming more social, mobile, and data-driven. Recruiters have historically had little data on external candidates, but professional social media can provide recruiters with an immense amount of data, such as work experience, skills, certifications, achievements, connections, and education. For companies that pay for its profile-searching system, for example, LinkedIn has added a service called "People You May Want to Hire." LinkedIn has created algorithms that search through its massive amounts of data and identify candidates with the exact combination of skills, background, expertise, and passion a company might be looking for. LinkedIn's report indicates that 39 percent of recruiters list social and professional networks as their number-one longlasting recruiting trend. The number who named big data analytics as a long-lasting trend increased 8 percentage points since 2012.[47]

Internships   Another popular use of social media is to find people to serve as either paid or unpaid interns at the organization. An internship is an arrangement whereby an intern (usually a high school or college student) exchanges free or low-cost labor for the opportunity to explore whether a particular career is appealing or to gain valuable work experience in a particular field.[48] Companies are increasingly viewing internships as a valuable recruiting tool because they provide a way to "test-drive" a potential employee, as well as allow the intern to evaluate whether the job and the company make a good fit. The old image of the intern as the "gopher" who makes coffee and photocopies has given way to the budding professional who performs meaningful tasks and learns valuable skills. Interns aren't always offered a job with the company, but one career development expert says that internships are more closely tied to permanent hiring today than ever before.[49] Media and online entertainment company IGN takes an innovative approach to recruiting via internships.

Spotlight on Skills

IGN's Code Foo

"Flipping burgers to scrape together enough cash to buy *Portal 2*? Blow our minds while you're here and we'll hire you." That was the recruitment ad for IGN's first Code Foo challenge—a no-résumés-allowed program designed to find exceptional "hackers," the term that IGN's director of engineering prefers when referring to computer programmers and coders. "For serious engineers who really care about their craft, it's a good thing to be a hacker," Tony Ford says.

Applicants to the Code Foo challenge complete an online form in which they submit a statement of passion for IGN and answer questions that test their coding ability. For the 2011 challenge, 75,000 people viewed the application, 104 applied, and 30 were selected to participate. Only half of those had college degrees in a technical field, and some didn't have degrees at all. The 2012 challenge selected 18 participants. Once they were

accepted, the Code Fooers spent six weeks working at IGN, getting paid a small amount while learning coding languages and working on real engineering projects. According to IGN president Roy Bahat, the six weeks was for "teaching them something to see if we could get them to a level where we might actually want to hire them." Adam Passey, for example, spent his summer coding unique features for a hub for mobile games. IGN's engineers were impressed, and Passey was offered a job. He has since been involved in leading the Code Foo challenge.

Although Bahat hoped that the Code Foo experiment would lead to one or two good hires, the company actually extended job offers to eight people the first time around. It was so successful that the company held the challenge again in 2013. As the market for programmers and coders grows more competitive, it's a "guerilla recruitment strategy" that is paying off.[49]

REMEMBER THIS

- Finding the right people starts with **human resource planning**, which refers to the forecasting of HR needs and the projected matching of individuals with anticipated job vacancies.

- The **matching model** is an HR approach in which the organization and the individual attempt to match each other's needs, interests, and values.

- **Recruiting** refers to activities or practices that define the desired characteristics of applicants for specific jobs.

- Many of today's organizations use social media, including Twitter, Weibo, LinkedIn, Tianji, and Facebook, for recruiting.

- **Job analysis** is the systematic process of gathering and interpreting information about the essential duties, tasks, and responsibilities of a job.

- Managers prepare a **job description** for each open position, which is a concise summary of the specific tasks and responsibilities of that job.

- A **job specification** outlines the knowledge, skills, education, physical abilities, and other characteristics needed to perform a specific job adequately.

- Managers use **realistic job previews (RJPs)** in recruiting to give applicants all pertinent and realistic information—both positive and negative—about a job and the organization.

- Internships are an increasingly popular approach to recruiting because they provide a way to "test-drive" a potential employee.

- An **internship** is an arrangement whereby an intern (usually a high school or college student)

exchanges his or her services for the opportunity to gain work experience and see whether a particular career is appealing.

9.4c Selecting

In the **selection** process, employers assess applicants' characteristics in an attempt to determine the "fit" between the job and applicant characteristics. The most frequently used selection devices are the application form, interview, and employment test. In general, the greater the skill requirements and work demands of an open position, the greater the number and variety of selection tools the organization will use.[50]

Refer to the opening questionnaire to test your own preparation as a new manager for recruiting and selecting the right people for your team. Do you have what it takes?

Application Form   The **application form** is used to collect information about the applicant's education, previous job experience, and other background characteristics. Research shows that biographical information inventories can validly predict future job success.[52]

One pitfall to be avoided is the inclusion of questions that are irrelevant to job success. In line with EEO guidelines, the application form should not ask questions that will create an adverse impact on protected groups unless the questions are clearly related to the job.[53] For example, employers should not ask whether the applicant rents or owns his or her own home because (1) an applicant's response might adversely affect his or her chances at the job, (2) minorities and women may be less likely to own a home, and (3) home ownership is probably unrelated to job performance. By contrast, passing the CPA exam is relevant to job performance in a CPA firm; thus, it is appropriate to ask whether an applicant for employment has passed the CPA exam, even if only one-half of all female or minority applicants have done so, versus nine-tenths of white male applicants.

Interview   Some type of *interview* is used as a selection technique in almost every job category in nearly every organization. This is another area where the organization can get into legal trouble if the interviewer asks questions that violate EEO guidelines. Exhibit 9.7 lists some examples of appropriate and inappropriate interview questions.

There is some evidence that the typical interview is not generally a good predictor of job performance. Many companies are bringing in coaches or using training programs to boost managers' interviewing skills because bad hires are costly. Researchers at Harvard Business School found that interviewers who let their own insecurities or biases subconsciously drive the interviewing process can have a worse effect on hiring decisions than if a candidate were simply chosen at random![54] Managers can improve their interviewing skills, and candidates can improve their chances of having a successful interview, by understanding some dos and don'ts related to the interview, as outlined in the "Director's Toolkit."

Managers use a variety of interview approaches to get a more reliable picture of a candidate's suitability for the job. **Structured interviews** use a set of standardized questions that are asked of every applicant so that comparisons can easily be made. These may include *biographical interviews*, which ask about the person's previous life and work experiences; *behavioral interviews*, which ask people to describe how they have performed a certain task or handled a particular problem; and *situational interviews*, which require people to describe how they might handle a hypothetical situation. With a **nondirective interview**, the interviewer asks broad, open-ended questions and permits the applicant to talk freely, with minimal interruption. Nondirective interviews may bring to light information, attitudes, and behavioral characteristics that might be concealed when answering structured questions.

EXHIBIT 9.7 Employment Applications and Interviews: What Can You Ask?

Category	Okay to Ask	Inappropriate or Illegal to Ask
National origin	• The applicant's name • If the applicant has ever worked under a different name	• The origin of the applicant's name • The applicant's ancestry/ethnicity
Race	• Nothing	• Race or color of skin
Disabilities	• Whether the applicant has any disabilities that might inhibit performance on the job	• If the applicant has any physical or mental defects • If the applicant has ever filed a workers' compensation claim
Age	• If the applicant is over 18	• Applicant's specific age • When the applicant graduated from high school
Religion	• Nothing	• The applicant's religious affiliation • What religious holidays the applicant observes
Criminal record	• If applicant has ever been convicted of a crime	• If the applicant has ever been arrested
Marital/family status	• Nothing	• Marital status; number of children or planned children • Childcare arrangements
Education and experience	• Where the applicant went to school • Prior work experience	• When the applicant graduated • Hobbies
Citizenship	• If the applicant has a legal right to work in the United States	• If the applicant is a citizen of another country

SOURCES: Based on "Appropriate and Inappropriate Interview Questions," in George Bohlander, Scott Snell, and Arthur Sherman, *Managing Human Resources*, 12th ed. (Cincinnati, OH: South-Western, 2001), p. 207; and "Guidelines to Lawful and Unlawful Preemployment Inquiries," Appendix E, in Robert L. Mathis and John H. Jackson, *Human Resource Management*, 2nd ed. (Cincinnati, OH: South-Western, 2002), pp. 189–190.

Some organizations put candidates through a series of interviews, each one conducted by a different person and each one probing a different aspect of the candidate. Others use **panel interviews**, in which the candidate meets with several interviewers who take turns asking questions.[55] In addition, some firms are using offbeat approaches, sometimes referred to as *extreme interviewing*, to test job candidates' ability to handle problems, cope with change, think on their feet, and work well with others. Danielle Bemoras found herself in a joint interview with a rival candidate when she applied for a job with *SceneTap*, a digital nightlife guide. Rather than trying to upstage her competitor, Bemoras was respectful and helpful, an approach that won her an internship, followed by a full-time job offer.[56]

Employment Test   **Employment tests** may include cognitive ability tests, physical ability tests, personality inventories, and other assessments. *Cognitive ability tests* measure an applicant's thinking, reasoning, verbal, and mathematical abilities. IQ tests, for example, have been found to be the most consistent predictor of good performance across a variety of jobs because a high IQ shows a candidate's ability to learn.[57] *Physical ability tests* that measure qualities such as strength, energy, and endurance may be used for jobs such as

Director's Toolkit

Ace the Interview

Many of us have experienced job interviews where everything seems to be going well, but then, things take a drastic turn for the worse. Here are some thoughts that can help you ace your next interview—and improve your interviewing skills as a manager.

The Big Three Questions

No matter what questions you are asked in an interview, you can be more effective if you remember that there are really only three essential things that the hiring manager and company want to know:

- **Can you do the job?** The company wants to know your strengths, not just in terms of technical ability, but also your leadership, teamwork, and interpersonal skills. Can you not only handle the tasks and activities of the job exceptionally well, but also interact effectively with your colleagues and contribute to a positive organizational atmosphere?

- **Will you love the job?** Organizations want people who bring enthusiasm and positive energy with them into the workplace every day. The hiring manager wants to be convinced that you're excited about the particular position you're interviewing for, as well as the overall industry, and that you'll thrive on embracing the challenges associated with the job.

- **Can we tolerate working with you?** Believing that you'll be a good fit with the culture is a huge part of the equation when most managers are deciding among job candidates. At LivingSocial, every job candidate is interviewed by a member of the "culture police," a team of people who have a knack for spotting what works and doesn't work with the company's culture. No one gets hired unless the culture police give the okay.

Killer Interview Strategies

- **Do your research.** To answer the Big Three Questions, you have to understand the job you're applying for, know something about the overall industry the company operates in, and have some feeling for the organizational culture. Learn all you can. Find out how the company is structured and managed by looking at its Web site. Tap into your social networking connections, see if there are videos on YouTube, read stories in blogs, and so forth.

- **Turn questions into conversations.** If you've done your research, you'll be able to converse with the interviewer on a peer-to-peer level. If asked, for example, how you would restructure a division, you might politely say something like: "Do you mind if I ask you a couple of questions first? I know there's a plant in Greece. Has the business been affected by the country's economic troubles?" Also, think of a few stories and examples ahead of time that illustrate your skills and strengths, show off your commitment and motivation, and demonstrate how you will fit with the organization. Use them judiciously when you get the chance.

- **Think the way they do.** Again, if you've done your research, you should have some idea of the issues and problems the company faces and the type of questions you might be asked. A company such as Zappos.com will interview in a different way from a company like GE. Imagine that you were a manager with the company, and think up 10 or so questions that you would ask a candidate.

SOURCES: George Brandt, "Top Executive Recruiters Agree There Are Only Three True Job Interview Questions," *Forbes*, April 27, 2011, www.forbes.com/sites/georgebradt/2011/04/27/top-executive-recruiters-agree-there-are-only-three-key-job-interview-questions/ (accessed August 29, 2012); Jennifer Alsever, "How to Get a Job: Show, Don't Tell," *Fortune* (March 19, 2012): 29–31; and LivingSocial example from Darren Dahl, "Hiring: You Get a Job, and You, and You … How to Staff Up in a Hurry," *Inc.* (November 2010): 128–129.

delivery drivers who must lift heavy packages, electric line workers who must climb ladders and carry equipment, and other positions that involve physical tasks. It is essential that these tests assess only cognitive and physical skills that are job related to avoid violating laws against discrimination.

Many companies also use various types of *personality tests* to assess such characteristics as openness to learning, agreeableness, conscientiousness, creativity, and emotional stability. In addition, companies look for personality characteristics that match the needs of the

AP Images/Kelley McCall

CONCEPT CONNECTION

Employment tests range from personality profiles to proficiency testing in specific skills required for a position. For a 911 operator position, an applicant should expect to take tests such as data entry for speed and accuracy, 911 address checking, 911 grid map reading and direction accuracy, 911 memorization, customer service assessment, and a personal characteristics profile. Here, Rick Bias, 911 communications director for Morgan County, Missouri, oversees operations in the Public Service Answer Point Area.

particular job so that there is a good fit. One company found that people who score well in traits such as assertiveness and extroversion typically make good salespeople, so they looked for those traits in testing candidates for new positions.[58] Interestingly, numerous studies show that personality tests are better predictors of future career success than job interviews, letters of recommendation, and educational credentials.[59] Many companies, such as Xerox, are also turning to big data analytics, using computers and software to select the right candidates based on their responses to personality tests and other criteria. After a half-year trial letting big data software pick call center workers, Xerox cut attrition by one-fifth.[60] Another unusual type of test, called a *brain teaser*, is being used by companies that put a premium on innovativeness and problem solving. The answers aren't as important as how the applicant goes about solving the problem. See how you do answering the brain teasers in Exhibit 9.8.

Online Checks   The Internet gives recruiters and hiring managers a new way to search for a candidate's criminal record, credit history, and other indications of honesty, integrity, and stability. Moreover, many companies want to see what a candidate has to say about him or herself on blogs and social networking sites to gauge whether the person would be a good fit with the organization. A survey by Microsoft in 2011 found that 75 percent of U.S. recruiters and HR professionals said that their bosses required them to research job candidates online, and another survey found

EXHIBIT 9.8 Try Your Hand at Some Interview Brain Teasers

How would you answer the following questions in a job interview?

1. How would you fit a stack of pennies as high as the Empire State Building in one room?
2. Why are manhole covers round?
3. How much should you charge to wash all the windows in Seattle?
4. You're shrunk and trapped in a blender that will turn on in 60 seconds. What do you do?
5. A man pushed his car to a hotel and lost his fortune. What happened?

Answers: There might be many solutions to these questions. Here are some that interviewers consider good answers:

1. The Empire State Building has about 110 floors. To fit the stack into one room, break it into one hundred shorter, floor-to-ceiling stacks.
2. A square cover might fall into its hole. If you hold a square manhole cover vertically and turn it a little, it will fall easily into the hole. In contrast, a round cover with a slight recess in the center can never fall in, no matter how it is held.
3. Assuming 10,000 city blocks, 600 windows per block, five minutes per window, and a rate of $20 per hour, about $10 million.
4. Use the measurement marks on the side of the container to climb out.
5. This is an oddball question more than a brain teaser, but one good answer would be: The man was playing Monopoly.

SOURCES: Similar questions are used at companies such as Microsoft, Google, and eBay. Reported in William Poundstone, "The Google Cheat Sheet," *Bloomberg BusinessWeek* (January 9–January 15, 2012): 79; Michael Kaplan, "Job Interview Brainteasers," *Business 2.0* (September 2007): 35–37; and William Poundstone, "Impossible Questions," *Across the Board* (September–October 2003): 44–48.

that 37 percent specifically investigated candidates' social media profiles.[61] In a survey by Adecco Staffing, inappropriate content on their social media sites was the number two reason hiring managers gave for why applicants ages 18 to 32 didn't get jobs (wearing inappropriate attire to job interviews was the top reason).[62] Miranda Shaw, a manager at a leading consulting firm, rejected a candidate whom she had previously been impressed with after she discovered photographs of him drinking and "smokin' blunts" with fraternity brothers on the Facebook page of one of his "friends" who hadn't enabled privacy settings.[63] Other recent college graduates looking for jobs have found doors closed to them because of risqué or teasing photos or vivid comments about drinking, drug use, or sexual exploits.

Online checks are an increasingly murky area for companies. "Social media background checks are a hot item," says attorney Kevin McCormick, "but I'm not a fan." Maryland, Illinois, and California have passed or are considering laws to make it illegal for employers to ask job candidates for their social media passwords, and 10 other states are considering similar legislation.[64] Using social networking as a background check without disclosing the investigation to the candidate can also open organizations to lawsuits. Moreover, because an online search often reveals information such as race, gender, sexual orientation, and so forth, HR managers have to be sure that this information isn't used in a way that could be construed as discriminatory. Because of increasing regulations and closer scrutiny by the courts, 69 percent of companies surveyed by the Society for Human Resource Management in 2013 said that they do not use social media for screening. However, experts say that while HR departments might not be doing it, hiring managers more than likely still are.[65]

REMEMBER THIS

- **Selection** is the process of assessing the skills, abilities, and other attributes of applicants in an attempt to determine the fit between the job and each applicant's characteristics.

- The **application form** is a selection device that collects information about the applicant's education, previous work experience, and other background characteristics.

- A **structured interview** uses a set of standardized questions that are asked of every applicant so that comparisons can be made easily.

- In a **nondirective interview**, the interviewer asks broad, open-ended questions and permits the applicant to talk freely with minimal interruption in an attempt to bring to light information, attitudes, and behavioral characteristics that might be concealed when answering structured questions.

- A **panel interview** is an interview in which the candidate meets with several interviewers who take turns asking questions.

- Some companies are using offbeat approaches, called *extreme interviewing*, to test job candidates' ability to handle problems, cope with change, and work well with others.

- **Employment tests** assess candidates on various factors considered important for the job to be performed; they include cognitive ability tests, physical ability tests, and personality tests.

- One way in which HR managers gauge an applicant's suitability for an open position is by checking what the applicant says on social media sites.

- Maryland was the first state to pass a law making it illegal to ask job applicants for their social networking passwords, and other states have either also done so or are considering it.

9.5 Developing Talent

Following selection, the next goal of HRM is to develop employees into an effective workforce. Key development activities include training and performance appraisal.

Go to the Group Learning on page 411, which pertains to the desired manager competencies at IBM.

9.5a Training and Development

Training and development programs represent a planned effort by an organization to facilitate employees' learning of job-related skills and behaviors.[66] *Training* magazine's most recent "Industry Report" shows that organizations spent some $55.8 billion on formal training programs in 2012, with spending on training payroll increasing and spending on outside products and services decreasing.[67] Exhibit 9.9 shows some frequently used types

EXHIBIT 9.9 Methods of Training and Intended Training Expenditures

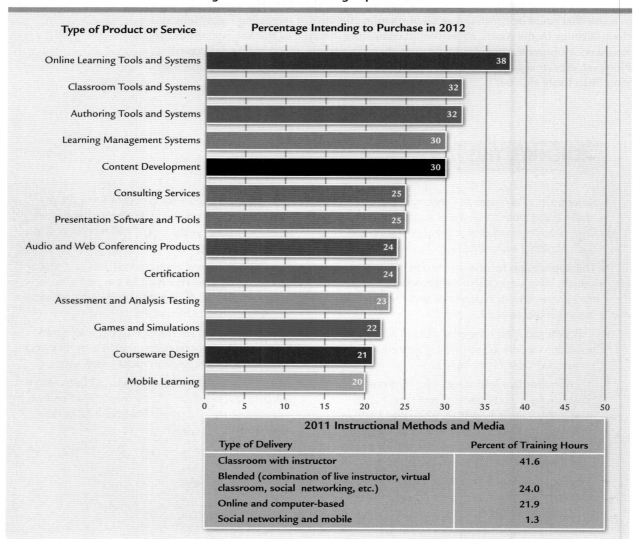

Type of Product or Service	Percentage Intending to Purchase in 2012
Online Learning Tools and Systems	38
Classroom Tools and Systems	32
Authoring Tools and Systems	32
Learning Management Systems	30
Content Development	30
Consulting Services	25
Presentation Software and Tools	25
Audio and Web Conferencing Products	24
Certification	24
Assessment and Analysis Testing	23
Games and Simulations	22
Courseware Design	21
Mobile Learning	20

2011 Instructional Methods and Media	
Type of Delivery	**Percent of Training Hours**
Classroom with instructor	41.6
Blended (combination of live instructor, virtual classroom, social networking, etc.)	24.0
Online and computer-based	21.9
Social networking and mobile	1.3

SOURCE: "2012 Training Industry Report," *Training* (November–December 2012): 20–33.

Spotlight on Skills

Taj Mahal Palace Mumbai

Imagine enjoying yourself at a corporate dinner to welcome the new CEO when terrorists storm the hotel. That's what happened at the Taj Mahal Palace hotel in Mumbai (Taj Mumbai) at the end of a dinner hosted by Hindustan Lever. The Taj Mumbai banquet staff, led by 24-year-old Mallika Jagad, quickly recognized that something was wrong and swung into action, locking the doors and turning off the lights. As the group huddled in the banquet room overnight, staff constantly went around offering water and calming the guests. The next morning, a fire broke out, forcing the group to climb out the windows. Again, the staff calmly evacuated all the guests first. "It was my responsibility," said Jagad. "I may have been the youngest person in the room, but I was still doing my job." Elsewhere in the hotel, similar acts of heroism were going on. At least 11 Taj Mumbai employees died while helping guests escape.

The Taj Mumbai staff gave the term customer service a whole new meaning that night. There were no policy manuals or procedures specifying how employees should behave in such a crisis situation. The actions of the staff were a result of unique hiring, training, and incentive systems that create a culture in which employees always put guests first, even if it means risking their own lives.

At the Taj Mumbai, all employees go through 18 months of training, which includes both classroom and on-the-job training. Classes are taught by incumbent managers, not consultants. Training is designed to impart three kinds of skills: technical skills, so that people can do their specific jobs; grooming, personality, and language skills; and customer service skills, so that employees learn to listen, empathize, and improvise. People are taught to think and be creative rather than rely on strict rules and procedures, and they learn to be customer ambassadors who place guests' interests ahead of the company's interests.[68]

and methods of training. Training conducted by a "stand-and-deliver" instructor in a classroom remains the most popular method of training. Interestingly, this method of training, representing 45.2 percent of training hours reported, increased from the 41.2 percent reported in 2011. Online training methods increased only slightly, and delivering training via social media and mobile devices has declined slightly.

To understand the importance of training, consider the following extreme example. When the Taj Mahal Palace in Mumbai was attacked by terrorists, employees risked their lives to protect guests.

The Taj Group expects managers to lead by example, and every manager goes through 18 months of training similar to lower-level employees. In addition, managers must develop three sets of leadership competencies, and the company hires an external coach to support each manager's development.

Development is sometimes distinguished from training. The general term *training* is typically used to refer to teaching people how to perform tasks related to their present jobs, while *development* means teaching people broader skills that are not only useful in their present jobs but also prepare them for greater responsibilities in future jobs. At farming equipment manufacturer Deere, rising managers get coaching from influential board members, for example, to develop their leadership skills.[69] GE has adopted a new approach to developing managers due to changes in the global competitive environment. Instead of moving its executives around to different divisions every few years so that they gain a broad understanding of the company and develop general management skills, GE is leaving them where they are so that they can gain a deeper understanding of the products and customers of a specific unit. "The world is so complex," says Susan Peters, leader of executive development at GE. "We need people who are pretty deep."[70]

On-the-Job Training (OJT)   The most common type of training is **on-the-job training (OJT)**, where an experienced employee is asked to take a new employee "under his or her wing" and show the newcomer how to perform job duties. OJT has many advantages, such as few out-of-pocket costs for training facilities, materials, or instructor fees and easy transfer of learning back to the job. When implemented well, OJT is considered the fastest and most effective means of facilitating learning in the workplace.[71] One type of OJT involves moving people to various types of jobs within the organization, where they work with experienced employees to learn different tasks. This *cross-training* may place an employee in a new position for as short a time as a few hours or for as long as a year, enabling the individual to develop new skills and giving the organization greater flexibility.

Social Learning   As shown in Exhibit 9.9, many companies report plans to purchase products and services for online and mobile learning in 2013. This reflects an awareness of the importance of social learning, particularly for younger employees. **Social learning** basically means learning informally from others by using social media tools, including mobile technologies, social networking, wikis and blogs, virtual games, and so forth.[72] A simple example might be an employee who asks a question on a blog or in a tweet, seeking advice from colleagues about a process or task. The majority of organizational learning occurs through informal rather than formal channels, so managers are supporting the use of social media technology for learning in day-to-day work. These tools allow people to share information, access knowledge, find resources, and collaborate in a natural way. An IBM survey found that high-performing organizations are 57 percent more likely than other companies to provide employees with collaborative and social media tools.[73]

Corporate Universities   Another popular approach to training and development is the **corporate university**, an in-house training and education facility that offers broad-based learning opportunities for employees—and frequently for customers, suppliers, and strategic partners as well—throughout their careers.[74] One well-known corporate university is Hamburger University, McDonald's worldwide training center. This institution is so well respected that its curriculum is recognized by the American Council on Education, so employees can actually earn college credits. Whereas all management training used to be held in the United States, there are now seven locations of Hamburger University around the world, including in São Paulo, Shanghai, Munich, and Mumbai.[75] Numerous other companies, including FedEx, GE, Intel, Harley-Davidson, Procter & Gamble (P&G), and Capital One, use corporate universities to build human capital.

Nuclear energy company Westinghouse Electric recently invested "tens of millions" of dollars into a corporate university, according to director of talent management Jim Ice, to train current and new employees. Because there hasn't been much nuclear plant construction in the United States since the 1979 Three Mile Island disaster, the company has had to hire people with little or no experience in the nuclear industry and recognized a need for better training.[76]

Promotion from Within   Another way to further employee development is through promotion from within, which helps companies retain and develop valuable people. Promotions provide more challenging assignments, prescribe new responsibilities, and help employees grow by expanding and developing their abilities. The Peebles Hydro hotel in Scotland is passionate about promoting from within as a way to retain good people and give them opportunities for growth. A maid has been promoted to head housekeeper, a wine waitress to restaurant head, and a student worker to deputy manager. The hotel also provides ongoing training in all areas. These techniques, combined with a commitment to job flexibility, helped the hotel retain high-quality workers at a time when others in the tourism and hospitality industry were suffering from a shortage of skilled labor. Staff members with 10, 15, or even 20 years of service aren't uncommon at Hydro.[77]

9.5b Performance Appraisal

Performance appraisal refers to observing and assessing employee performance, recording the assessment, and providing feedback to the employee. During performance appraisal, skillful managers give feedback and praise concerning the acceptable elements of the employee's performance. They also describe performance areas that need improvement. One of the biggest corporate talent management mistakes, according to management expert Ram Charan, is the failure to provide candid performance assessments that focus on development needs.[78] When employees get this feedback, they can use it to improve their performance. Unfortunately, only 3 in 10 employees surveyed believe that their companies' performance review system actually helps to improve performance, indicating a need for improved methods of appraisal and feedback.[79]

The performance appraisal process is widely disliked in organizations, but good performance appraisals are an important part of an overall performance management system that helps retain valued employees by helping them develop their skills, obtain rewards, and advance in the organization.[80] Generally, HRM professionals concentrate on two things to make performance appraisal a positive force in their organizations: (1) the accurate evaluation of performance through the development and application of assessment systems such as rating scales and (2) training managers to use the performance appraisal interview effectively so that managers can provide feedback that will reinforce good performance and motivate employee development. Current thinking is that performance appraisal should be ongoing, not something that is done only once a year as part of a consideration of raises.

Assessing Performance Accurately   Jobs are multidimensional, and therefore performance may be multidimensional as well. A recent trend in performance appraisal is called **360-degree feedback**, a process that uses multiple raters, including self-rating, as a way to increase awareness of strengths and weaknesses and guide employee development. Members of the appraisal group may include supervisors, coworkers, and customers, as well as the individual, thus providing a holistic view of the employee's performance.[81] Some companies use social networking style systems to make 360-degree performance feedback a dynamic, ongoing process. One software program from Rypple, for example, lets people post short, Twitter-style questions about their performance of a particular task and get feedback from managers, peers, or anyone else the user selects. Another system from Accenture has employees post photos, status updates, and two or three weekly goals that can be viewed, followed, and assessed by colleagues.[82]

Another alternative performance-evaluation method is the *performance review ranking system*.[83] This method is increasingly controversial because it essentially evaluates employees by pitting them against one another. As most commonly used, these systems rank employees according to their relative performance: 20 percent would be placed in the top group of performers; 70 percent have to be ranked in the middle; and 10 percent are ranked at the bottom. The bottom tier are given a set period of time to improve their performance, and if they don't improve, they are fired. The idea behind the forced ranking of employees is that everyone will be motivated to improve performance.

The advantages of a performance-ranking system are that it (1) forces reluctant managers to make difficult decisions and identify the best and worst performers; and (2) creates and sustains a high-performance culture in which people continuously improve. The disadvantages are that the system (1) may increase cutthroat competition among employees; (2) discourages collaboration and teamwork; and (3) potentially harms morale. Many companies have dropped the ranking system or modified it so that it doesn't insist on quotas for underperformers.[84]

Performance Evaluation Errors   Although we would like to believe that every manager assesses employees' performance in a careful and bias-free manner, researchers have identified several rating problems.[85] One of the most dangerous is **stereotyping**, which occurs when a rater places an employee into a class or category based on one or a few traits or characteristics—for example, stereotyping an older worker as slower and more difficult to train. Another rating error is the **halo effect**, in which a manager gives an employee the same rating on all dimensions, even if his or her performance is good on some dimensions and poor on others.

Exhibit 9.10 illustrates the behaviorally anchored rating scale (BARS) method for evaluating a production line supervisor. The production supervisor's job can be broken down into several dimensions, such as equipment maintenance, employee training, and work scheduling. A BARS should be developed for each dimension. The dimension in Exhibit 9.10 is work scheduling. Good performance is represented by a 4 or 5 on the scale, and unacceptable performance by a 1 or 2. If a production supervisor's job has eight dimensions, the total performance evaluation will be the sum of the scores for each of eight scales.

REMEMBER THIS

- Training typically refers to teaching people skills needed in their current job, whereas development refers to teaching people broader career skills.
- The most common method of training is **on-the-job-training (OJT)**, in which an experienced employee is asked to teach a new employee how to perform job duties.
- **Social learning** refers to using social media tools to network and learn informally.
- A **corporate university** is an in-house training and development facility that offers broad-based learning opportunities for employees.
- McDonald's Hamburger University has seven management training centers around the world, including one in Shanghai and one in São Paulo.
- **Performance appraisal** is the process of observing and evaluating an employee's performance, recording the assessment, and providing feedback.
- A recent trend is **360-degree feedback**, which uses multiple raters, including self-rating, to appraise employee performance and guide development.
- Performance review ranking systems are increasingly being criticized because they tend to pit employees against one another rather than promoting cooperation and teamwork.
- **Stereotyping** is a performance-evaluation error that occurs when a manager places an employee into a class or category based on one or a few traits or characteristics.
- The **halo effect** occurs when a manager gives an employee the same rating on all dimensions of the job, even though performance may be good on some dimensions and poor on others.
- One way to overcome evaluation errors is to use a **behaviorally anchored rating scale (BARS)**, which is a performance-evaluation technique that relates an employee's performance to specific job-related incidents.

EXHIBIT 9.10 Example of a Behaviorally Anchored Rating Scale

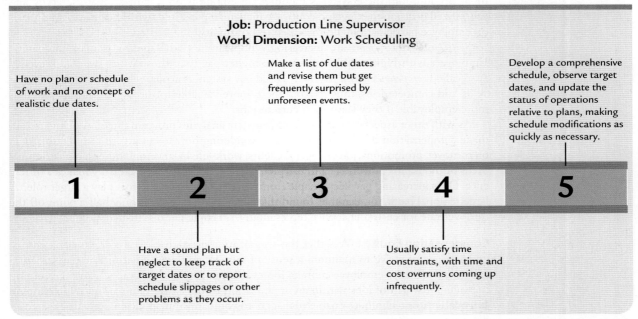

SOURCES: Based on J. P. Campbell et al., "The Development and Evaluation of Behaviorally Based Rating Scales," *Journal of Applied Psychology* 57 (1973): 15–22; and Francine Alexander, "Performance Appraisals," *Small Business Reports* (March 1989): 20–29.

9.6 Maintaining an Effective Workforce

Now we turn to the topic of how managers and HRM professionals maintain a workforce that has been recruited and developed. The maintenance of the current workforce involves compensation, wage and salary systems, benefits, and (occasionally) termination.

9.6a Compensation

The term *compensation* refers to (1) all monetary payments and (2) all goods or commodities used in lieu of money to reward employees.[86] An organization's compensation structure includes wages and salaries and benefits such as health insurance, paid vacations, or employee fitness centers. Developing an effective compensation system is an important part of HRM because it helps to attract and retain talented workers. In addition, a company's compensation system has an impact on strategic performance.[87] HR managers design the pay and benefits systems to fit company strategy and to provide compensation equity.

Wage and Salary Systems Ideally, management's strategy for the organization should be a critical determinant of the features and operations of the pay system.[88] For example, managers may have the goal of maintaining or improving profitability or market share by stimulating employee performance. Thus, they should design and use a merit pay system rather than a system based on other criteria such as seniority. At retailer Macy's, for example, the board increased the sales component of bonuses for senior executives to encourage sales growth. In addition, if Macy's sales increase above the company plan, top executives can earn higher bonuses.[89]

The most common approach to employee compensation is *job-based pay,* which means linking compensation to the specific tasks an employee performs. However, these systems present several problems. For one thing, job-based pay may fail to reward the type of learning behavior needed for the organization to adapt and survive in a turbulent environment. In addition, these systems reinforce an emphasis on organizational hierarchy and centralized decision making and control, which are inconsistent with the growing emphasis on employee participation and increased responsibility.[90]

Skill-based pay systems are increasingly popular in both large and small companies. Employees with higher skill levels receive higher pay than those with lower skill levels.[91] Also called *competency-based pay*, skill-based pay systems encourage people to develop their skills and competencies, thus making them more valuable to the organization, as well as more employable if they leave their current jobs.

As with other aspects of management, big data analytics programs are now being used to make compensation decisions. A company wondering how to cut attrition can gather data on turnover, promotions, job changes, benefits, work–life balance, and other factors for hundreds of thousands of workers and use predictive analytics to see what truly makes a difference. Does increasing pay keep people from leaving, or do other factors play a larger role? A large regional bank, for example, found that increasing pay shaved only half a point off the turnover rate for customer service representatives. People felt dissatisfied, not underpaid.[92]

Compensation Equity   Whether the organization uses job-based pay or skill-based pay, good managers strive to maintain a sense of fairness and equity within the pay structure and thereby fortify employee morale. Job evaluation refers to the process of determining the value or worth of jobs within an organization through an examination of job content. **Job evaluation** techniques enable managers to compare similar and dissimilar jobs and to determine internally equitable pay rates—that is, pay rates that employees believe are fair compared to those for other jobs in the organization.

Organizations also want to make sure that their pay rates are fair compared to other companies. HR managers may obtain **wage and salary surveys** that show what other organizations pay incumbents in jobs that match a sample of "key" jobs selected by the organization. These surveys are available from a number of sources, including the U.S. Bureau of Labor Statistics National Compensation Survey.

Pay-for-Performance   Many of today's organizations develop compensation plans based on a *pay-for-performance standard* to raise productivity and cut labor costs in a competitive global environment. **Pay-for-performance**, also called *incentive pay*, means tying at least part of compensation to employee effort and performance, whether it be through merit-based pay, bonuses, team incentives, or various gain-sharing or profit-sharing plans. With pay-for-performance, incentives are aligned with the behaviors needed to help the organization achieve its strategic goals. Employees have an incentive to make the company more efficient and profitable because if goals are not met, no bonuses are paid.

However, recent years have shown the potential dangers of misdirected pay-for-performance plans. Alan Blinder, Princeton professor of economics and public affairs, points out that a fundamental cause of the 2008–2009 financial crisis in the United States was the "perverse go-for-broke incentives" that rewarded people for taking excessive risks with other people's money.[93] During the financial meltdown, it became clear that people at every level of the financial system were getting rewarded for short-term performance—if things went wrong down the line, it was someone else's problem. Then it all came crashing down. Managers can take care to create pay-for-performance plans that align with the long-term interests of the organization, shareholders, and the broader society.

9.6b Benefits

An effective compensation package requires more than money. Although salary is an important component, benefits are equally important.

Organizations are required by law to provide some benefits, such as Social Security, unemployment compensation, and workers' compensation. Other types of benefits, such as vacations and things such as onsite daycare or educational reimbursements, are not required by law but are provided by organizations to attract and maintain an effective workforce. The benefits packages provided by large companies attempt to meet the needs of all employees. Some companies, particularly in the technology industry where skilled employees are hard to find, offer extremely generous benefit packages. SAS Institute, for example, provides (among other benefits) 90 percent coverage of health insurance premiums, free health care at an onsite medical clinic, an onsite fitness center, unlimited sick days, three weeks annual vacation for entry-level employees, onsite child care, and a work–life center offering services ranging from parenting classes to elder care. Other tech firms such as Google, Yahoo, and Facebook are also using innovative benefits to recruit and retain top talent.[94]

During the recent recession, many employers have cut benefits not required by law, and most say that they don't plan to restore them to prerecession levels.[95] One company, however, is going in the opposite direction. The Cumberland Gulf Group, based in Framingham, Massachusetts, which owns Cumberland Farms convenience stores and the Gulf Oil brand, reclassified an additional 1,500 workers as full time so they would be eligible for company-sponsored health insurance in advance of the Affordable Care Act deadline. "The company has decided to make employee satisfaction and retention a corporate priority," said president and COO Ari Haseotes. The change will cost the company "several million dollars," he says, but managers believe that this will be compensated for by a greater level of employee loyalty and customer satisfaction.[96]

9.6c Rightsizing the Organization

In some cases, organizations have more people than they need and have to let some employees go. **Rightsizing** refers to reducing the company's workforce intentionally to the point where the number of employees is deemed to be right for the company's current situation. Also called *downsizing*, planned reductions in the size of the workforce are a reality for many of today's companies. Although many companies have begun hiring workers again after major layoffs in 2009 and 2010, the unemployment rate in the United States was still hovering at around 7.3 percent in August 2013.[97]

As the term *rightsizing* implies, the goal is to make the company stronger and more competitive by aligning the size of the workforce with the company's current needs. However, some researchers have found that massive cuts often fail to achieve the intended benefits, and in some cases, they significantly harm the organization.[98] Unless HRM departments effectively and humanely manage the rightsizing process, layoffs can lead to decreased morale and performance. Managers can smooth the process by regularly communicating with employees and providing them with as much information as possible, providing assistance to workers who will lose their jobs, and using training and development to help address the emotional needs of remaining employees and enable them to cope with new or additional responsibilities.[99]

9.6d Termination

Despite the best efforts of line managers and HRM professionals, the organization will lose employees. Some will retire, others will depart voluntarily for other jobs, and still others will be forced out through mergers and cutbacks or for poor performance. Sometimes the termination comes too late, after damage has been done, as shown in this chapter's Business Blooper.

Business Blooper

Rutgers University Basketball

A video showing Rutgers basketball coach, Mike Rice, being physically and verbally abusive to players circulated in December 2012 among university officials. Nothing was done until the story hit the news in April 2013, when fingers started pointing. Athletic Director Tim Pernetti said he had wanted to fire Rice but university officials had wanted to involve lawyers and HR. University president Robert L. Barchi blamed Pernetti, who he claimed had only wanted to suspend Rice, while Barchi had wanted to terminate Rice. Two days after Rice was let go in April, a 50-page report by an outside lawyer

surfaced, showing that the university was well aware of Rice's history of abuse, but said that his methods were "permissible training." In the only comment that indicated someone had a sense of responsibility, Pernetti said, after he resigned, "I have admitted my role in, and regret for, that decision, and wish that I had the opportunity to go back and override it for the sake of everyone involved."

SOURCE: Kate Zernike and Steve Eder, "Athletic Director Quits at 'Rutgers as Fallout Grows," *New York Times*, April 5, 2013, A1 & D2.

Joe Songer/Birmingham News/Landov

CONCEPT CONNECTION

Carefully reviewing market needs, new technologies, and future goals helps leaders strategically plan for and proactively assess **rightsizing** of an organization. This rightsizing activity should be a constant part of the management of any organization. Nucor Corporation has taken a very strategic approach to the manufacturing sector since the Great Recession of 2008 that has resulted in 4 percent growth over the past five years.

"I have a hard time looking myself in the mirror if I keep someone around who can't do the job. It is not fair to the other employees, and it certainly is not fair to my customers."

—Jay Goltz, entrepreneur and business speaker

The value of termination for maintaining an effective workforce is twofold. First, employees who are poor performers can be dismissed. Productive employees often resent disruptive, low-performing employees who are allowed to stay with the company and receive pay and benefits comparable to theirs. Second, managers can use exit interviews as a valuable HR tool, regardless of whether the employee leaves voluntarily or is forced out. An **exit interview** is an interview conducted with departing employees to determine why they are leaving the company. The value of the exit interview is to provide an inexpensive way to learn about pockets of dissatisfaction within the organization and hence find ways to reduce future turnover.[100] As John Donahoe, president and CEO of eBay, put it, "when people are leaving, they're often in a very reflective state and … they're also just stunningly direct, because it's like they have nothing to lose." One thing that Donahoe learned from conducting exit interviews at eBay was that midlevel executives were unclear about their responsibility and authority, so he reorganized to clarify lines of decision-making responsibility and authority.[101] The oil services giant Schlumberger includes an exit interview as part of a full-scale investigation of every departure, with the results posted online so that managers all around the company can get insight into problems.[102]

However, in some cases, employees who leave voluntarily are reluctant to air uncomfortable complaints or discuss their real reasons for leaving. Companies such as T-Mobile, Campbell Soup, and Conair found that having people complete an online exit questionnaire yields more open and honest information. When people have negative things to say about managers or the company, the online format is a chance to speak their mind without having to do it in a face-to-face meeting.[103]

9.6e Managing Diversity

When Jürgen Fitschen took over as head of Deutsche Bank AG in 2012, he promised to name a woman to the German bank's executive committee during his tenure. But although Fitschen and his co-CEO named a dozen members to the expanded committee, which ranks one rung below the top-level management board, all were men. "This has to change," Fitschen said. "We want to change this. We're making a big effort internally to create a level playing field for women to make it to the top. But so far, we haven't achieved the desired success." The lack of women at senior positions stretches across the global financial industry, but Germany's Deutsche Bank has become a particular target for criticism. Germany overall has one of the worst records in Europe in terms of females in senior management positions. "It's not that there aren't enough women, but rather that the management boards aren't looking closely enough," said Angela Hornberg, who runs Advance Human Capital, a Frankfurt headhunting firm. "If they really did their homework, they'd find a wonderful talent pool of women."[104]

Other companies, in the United States as well as other countries, also struggle with diversity issues. Nationwide retailer Wet Seal, which caters to a core customer group of 13- to 23-year-olds, has been accused of firing and denying promotions to African Americans because they don't fit the company's brand image. In a discrimination lawsuit, one of the plaintiffs says that after she was fired, she heard a senior vice president tell the district manager that she wanted someone with blond hair and blue eyes.[105] Wet Seal is being accused of being a company where discrimination is "not only tolerated, but required." If true, it is almost stunning that this kind of blatant discrimination still occurs.

Leaders at most companies strive to avoid discriminatory policies and practices that lead to lawsuits. In addition, many companies have learned that valuing and supporting diverse employees pays off. Valuing and supporting diversity is not only the right thing to do ethically and culturally, but it also creates new business opportunities. To capitalize on those opportunities, organizations recognize that workplaces need to reflect the diversity in the marketplace. "Our country's consumer base is so varied," says Shelley Willingham-Hinton, president of the National Organization for Diversity in Sales and Marketing. "I can't think of how a company can succeed without having that kind of diversity with their employees."[106] Forward-thinking managers agree and take steps to attract and retain a workforce that reflects the cultural diversity of the population. They take seriously the fact that there is a link between the diversity of the workforce and financial success in the marketplace. Exhibit 9.11 lists some corporations that are considered leaders in diversity. They make diversity a top priority and actively pursue a corporate culture that values equality and reflects today's multicultural consumer base.

The last half of this chapter describes how the domestic and global workforce is becoming increasingly diverse and how corporations are responding to the challenges and opportunities this presents. We look at the myriad complex issues that managers and employees face in a diverse workplace, including prejudice, stereotypes, discrimination, and ethnocentrism. Factors that specifically affect women—the glass ceiling, the opt-out trend, and the female advantage—are also considered. The chapter concludes by presenting an overview of initiatives taken by corporations to create an environment that welcomes and values a broad spectrum of diversity among its employees.

> "If we don't reflect the global nature of our business in our employees, how can we possibly hope to nderstand our customers?"
>
> —Mark Palmer-Edgecumbe, Google's head of diversity and inclusion

EXHIBIT 9.11   **Examples of Leaders in Corporate Diversity (continues)**

Company	U.S. Employees	Minority Employees (%)
Baptist Health South Florida	13,302	72
Methodist Hospital System	12,152	66
Intercontinental Hotels Group	14,508	65
Four Seasons Hotels & Resorts	12,439	62
Marriott International	108,939	62
Kimpton Hotels & Restaurants	6,996	62

EXHIBIT 9.11   Examples of Leaders in Corporate Diversity (continued)

Company	U.S. Employees	Minority Employees (%)
Scripps Health	12,006	53
Qualcomm	13,353	53
Men's Wearhouse	14,784	52
Cisco	34,847	49
Camden Property Trust	1,678	48
Capital One	27,912	45
Navy Federal Credit Union	7,745	45
Genentech	11,592	45
Children's Healthcare of Atlanta	6,618	44
Whole Foods Market	60,213	43
USAA	23,211	43
Darden Restaurants	169,516	42
Nordstrom	52,431	42
Atlantic Health	7,255	41
Intel	44,209	41

SOURCE: "100 Best Companies to Work For, 2012; Top Companies: Most Diverse," http://archive.fortune.com/magazines/fortune/best-companies/2012/minorities/ (accessed October 14, 2013).

REMEMBER THIS

- **Compensation** refers to all monetary payments and all nonmonetary goods or benefits used to reward employees.
- Managers strive to maintain fairness and equity in the pay system.
- **Job evaluation** is the process of determining the value of jobs within an organization through an examination of job content.
- **Wage and salary surveys** show what other organizations pay incumbents in jobs that match a sample of key jobs selected by the organization.
- **Pay-for-performance**, also called *incentive pay,* means tying at least a portion of compensation to employee effort and performance.
- Benefits make up a large portion of labor costs in the United States.

- During the recession, many organizations have cut benefits that are not required by law.
- **Rightsizing**, also called *downsizing*, refers to reducing the company's workforce intentionally to the point where the number of employees is deemed right for the company's current situation.
- If not managed effectively and humanely, rightsizing can lead to decreased morale and performance.
- An **exit interview** is an interview conducted with departing employees to determine reasons for their departure and learn about potential problems in the organization.
- Campbell Soup Company and some other organizations let people complete an online exit questionnaire so they can express their complaints or ideas freely, without having to talk face-to-face with a manager.

9.7 Diversity in the Workplace

When Brenda Thompson, the director of diversity and leadership education at MGM Resorts International, steps into one of the company's hotel lobbies, she closes her eyes and listens. "It's amazing all the different languages I can hear just standing in the lobbies of any of our hotels," she says. "Our guests come from all over the world, and it really makes us realize the importance of reflecting that diversity in our workplace."[107] The diversity Thompson notices in the lobbies of the MGM Mirage hotels is a small reflection of the cultural diversity in the larger domestic and global workplaces.

Go to the Self-Learning on pages 409, which pertains to your level of tolerance for differences.

9.7a Diversity in Corporate America

Faced with fewer resources, a slow economy, and increased domestic and global competition, managers are searching for ways to set their organizations apart from the competition and create breakthrough innovations. Managers who cultivate a diversified workforce have been shown to improve their organization's chances of success. Diverse teams that perform efficiently add value by combining individuals' strengths, making the whole greater than the sum of its parts.[108]

In the past, when managers thought of diversity, they focused on the "problems" associated with diversity, such as discrimination, bias, affirmative action, and tokenism.[109] Now managers recognize that the differences that people bring to the workplace are valuable.[110] Rather than expecting all employees to adopt similar attitudes and values, managers are learning that these differences enable their companies to compete globally and tap into rich sources of new talent. Although diversity in North America has been a reality for some time, genuine efforts to accept and *manage* diverse people began only in recent years. Exhibit 9.12 lists some interesting milestones in the history of corporate diversity.

Diversity in corporate America has become a key topic in part because of the vast changes occurring in today's workplace. The following statistics illustrate how the workplace is changing and challenging frontline managers who are trying to build cohesive teams:

- Unprecedented generational diversity. Today's workforce is in a state of flux as a blend of four generations presents new management challenges, with people staying healthy and working longer not only in the United States, but in China, Brazil, Russia, and elsewhere.[111] Although most people from the World War II generation have retired, there are still a few members in their late eighties and even nineties in the workplace. According to the Bureau of Labor Statistics, for example, this generation represented about 5 percent of the labor force in the United States, and nearly 7 percent in Canada in 2011. These employees, and the rapidly aging baby boomers, share a "corporate memory" that is invaluable to organizations, but as they stay in the workforce longer, there is little room for Generation X managers wanting to move up the hierarchy. As Gen-X workers move into middle age, they are struggling with reduced guarantees about their financial futures and job security. Meanwhile, Gen-Yers, sometimes called Millennials, are characterized as ambitious, lacking loyalty to one organization, and eager for quick success. Unlike different generations working together in the past, there are strong value differences among employees from different eras today.[112]

EXHIBIT 9.12   Milestones in the History of Corporate Diversity

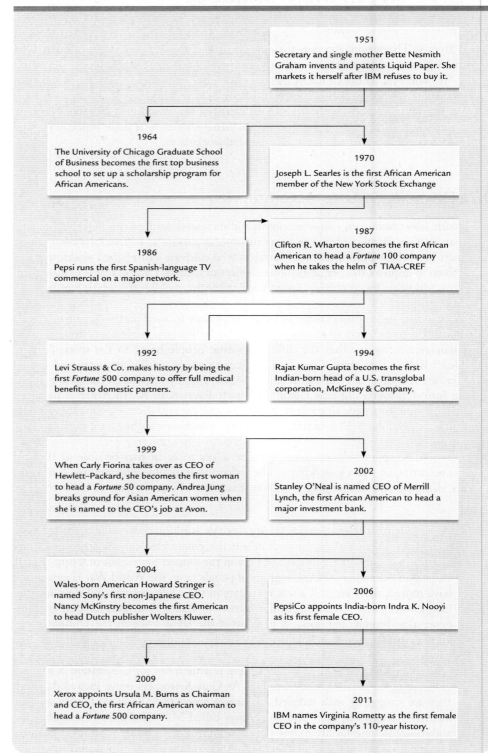

1951
Secretary and single mother Bette Nesmith Graham invents and patents Liquid Paper. She markets it herself after IBM refuses to buy it.

1964
The University of Chicago Graduate School of Business becomes the first top business school to set up a scholarship program for African Americans.

1970
Joseph L. Searles is the first African American member of the New York Stock Exchange

1986
Pepsi runs the first Spanish-language TV commercial on a major network.

1987
Clifton R. Wharton becomes the first African American to head a *Fortune* 100 company when he takes the helm of TIAA-CREF

1992
Levi Strauss & Co. makes history by being the first *Fortune* 500 company to offer full medical benefits to domestic partners.

1994
Rajat Kumar Gupta becomes the first Indian-born head of a U.S. transglobal corporation, McKinsey & Company.

1999
When Carly Fiorina takes over as CEO of Hewlett–Packard, she becomes the first woman to head a *Fortune* 50 company. Andrea Jung breaks ground for Asian American women when she is named to the CEO's job at Avon.

2002
Stanley O'Neal is named CEO of Merrill Lynch, the first African American to head a major investment bank.

2004
Wales-born American Howard Stringer is named Sony's first non-Japanese CEO. Nancy McKinstry becomes the first American to head Dutch publisher Wolters Kluwer.

2006
PepsiCo appoints India-born Indra K. Nooyi as its first female CEO.

2009
Xerox appoints Ursula M. Burns as Chairman and CEO, the first African American woman to head a *Fortune* 500 company.

2011
IBM names Virginia Rometty as the first female CEO in the company's 110-year history.

SOURCES: "Spotlight on Diversity," special advertising section, *MBA Jungle* (March–April 2003): 58–61; and Xerox corporate Web site, www.news.xerox.com.

- Aging workers. Baby boomers continue to affect the workplace as this massive group of workers progresses through its life stages. Baby boomers are continuously bumping up the average age of the workforce. While the number of workers between 25 and 45 years old is expected to decline from 66.9 to 63.7 percent by 2020, the number of workers age 55 years and older will leap from 19.5 to 25.2 percent in the same period.[113]

- Increased diversity. Today's workplace is becoming more diverse as the number of foreign-born workers increases. Foreign-born workers make up 16 percent of the U.S. workforce and are most likely employed in service industries, such as food preparation, cleaning, and maintenance. Of the total number of foreign-born workers, nearly half are Hispanic and 23 percent are Asian.[114] Looking ahead, the number of Hispanic employees will grow the most, increasing 18.6 percent by 2020.[115] Exhibit 9.13 shows the projected changes in employment among different racial and ethnic groups in the United States.

Go to the "Ethical Dilemma" on pages 412, which pertains to religious observances of employees.

- More women workers. Today, women outnumber men in the workplace, and their numbers are projected to grow slightly faster, at 7.4 percent compared to 6.3 percent for men. The good news is that nearly 73 percent of *Fortune* 500 companies now have at least one female executive officer, but women comprise just 14 percent of executive officers, according to Catalyst, a leading advocacy group for women.[116] To accelerate their progress, many corporations have initiated coaching and training programs that prepare women for senior-level positions.

EXHIBIT 9.13   **Projected Changes in U.S. Labor Force, 2012–2022**

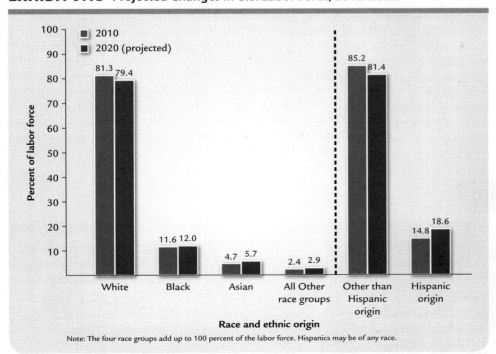

Note: The four race groups add up to 100 percent of the labor force. Hispanics may be of any race.

SOURCE: *Employment Projections: Civilian Labor Force by Age, Sex, Race, and Ethnicity,* Bureau of Labor Statistics, U.S. Department of Labor, Table 3.1, Civilian Labor Force by Age, Sex, Race, and Ethnicity, 1992, 2002, 2012, and Projected 2022, http://www.bls.gov/emp/ep_table_301.htm (accessed May 22, 2014).

These trends underscore the complex nature of today's workforce and the potential pitfalls managers face as they lead diverse teams toward common goals. While many managers recognize the value of multicultural diversity, some simply haven't kept pace with these demographic trends. In fact, as diversity has increased, so have the number of discrimination complaints with the EEOC, which investigates employee claims and sometimes brings lawsuits on behalf of workers. One recent complaint is against Bass Pro Shops, accused of repeatedly refusing to hire nonwhite workers as clerks, cashiers, or managers, and using discriminatory language to explain their reasons. Among other charges in the lawsuit is the allegation that a senior worker in Indiana was seen discarding employment applications, explaining that he could tell by the job seekers' names that they were black. The suit also alleges that the general manager of a Houston store regularly referred to those of Hispanic origin as "Pedro" or "Mexican."[117]

9.7b Diversity on a Global Scale

Managers across the globe wrestle with many of the same diversity challenges as U.S. managers, especially concerning the progression of women into upper management positions. Consider, for example, that in Italy, only 6 percent of the total number of corporate board members are women, 14 percent in Britain, and 2 percent in Germany and India. As mentioned before, 14 percent of all board members in the United States are women.[118] To boost the percentage of women on the corporate boards of European countries, the European Commission is studying whether to introduce quotas across the continent, similar to a recent law in Italy that requires Italian-listed and state-owned companies to ensure that by 2015, one-third of their board members are women. "We needed a shock to the system," said Alessia Mosca, a member of Parliament for the center-left Democratic Party, who coauthored Italy's new "pink quota" law. "The hope is that this will set off cultural change."[119]

Japanese companies have an even greater struggle to bridge the gender gap on corporate boards, where women make up just 1.2 percent of senior executives.[120] In fact, only 65 percent of college-educated Japanese women are employed, many of them in low-paid temp jobs, compared with 80 percent of women in the United States. The reasons for the dearth of women in the Japanese workforce are complex. Part of it relates to tepid economic growth. But over two-thirds of Japanese women leave work after their first child is born, compared to just one-third of U.S. women, often because of insufficient child care and societal expectations.[121]

Cultural norms, such as those that restrict the progression of women in Japan, are intangible, pervasive, and difficult to comprehend. However, it is imperative that managers learn to understand local cultures and deal with them effectively.[122]

REMEMBER THIS

- A workforce that displays characteristics of today's diversified marketplace is an important tool for managers who are striving for success in a highly competitive business environment.

- The U.S. workforce is being transformed by a four-generation workforce, aging baby boomers, an increase in Hispanic and Asian workers, and an increasing number of women employees.

- The progression of women into executive positions continues to be slow in both U.S. and global corporations, but innovative companies are initiating programs to boost women's advancement into higher levels of responsibility.

- To succeed in the global marketplace, managers need to understand other cultures and deal with them effectively.

Green Power

Diversity and Biodiversity

When we were children running up against differing opinions, our grandmothers reminded us, "It takes all kinds to make a world." The preservation of diverse plant and animal life forms also echoes Grandma's words. To promote biodiversity preservation, managers at beverage maker **Bean and Body** use proceeds from the sale of its healthy coffees to sponsor The Bean and Body Protected Grounds Initiative, which works in collaboration with the World Land Trust to buy, protect, and preserve the most threatened areas of the world's rain forests, wetlands, and coastlines. The award-winning

effort meets corporate goals to promote a healthy life-style while taking intentional steps to promote ecological, economic, and social preservation. The Bean and Body initiative works to solve biodiversity problems by helping the farmers whose cultivation of coffee beans affects the environment through groundwater runoff and incursions into rain forests.

SOURCES: Andrew J. Hoffman, "Climate Change as a Cultural and Behavioral Issue: Addressing Barriers and Implementing Solutions," *Organizational Dynamics* 39 (2010): 295–305; and Erin Legg, "Coffee Re-imagined: Bean and Body Emerge as Global Leaders," *Healthy New Age* Web site, July 2010, www.healthynewage.com/blog/bean-and-body-wins-award/ (accessed August 1, 2012).

9.8 Managing Diversity

Managers who want to boost performance and jumpstart innovation agree that diverse teams produce the best results. In one survey of 32 department heads and executives, 84 percent stated that they prefer heterogeneous teams because they lead to multiple viewpoints and more prolific ideas.[123] The following sections describe the characteristics of a diverse workforce and the dividends of cultivating one.

9.8a Diversity and Inclusion

Diversity is defined as all the ways in which people differ.[124] Diversity wasn't always defined this broadly. Decades ago, many companies defined diversity in terms of race, gender, age, lifestyle, and disability. That focus helped create awareness, change mindsets, and create new opportunities for many. Today, companies are embracing a more inclusive definition of diversity that recognizes a spectrum of differences that influence how employees approach work, interact with each other, derive satisfaction from their work, and define who they are as people in the workplace.[125]

Exhibit 9.14 illustrates the difference between the traditional model and the inclusive model of diversity. The dimensions of diversity shown in the traditional model include inborn differences that are immediately observable and include race, gender, age, and physical ability. However, the inclusive model of diversity

AP Images/Manish Swarup

CONCEPT CONNECTION Successful organizations seek a **diverse and inclusive workforce**. Indra Nooyi was named CEO of PepsiCo in 2006 after 12 years with the food and beverage giant, spending most of those years leading its global strategy. Both *Fortune* and *Forbes* magazines named the Indian-born executive one of the most powerful women in the United States. "I am not your normal, nondiverse CEO. I am everything that this company took forth in diversity and inclusion, and it has all come together with me," says Nooyi.

EXHIBIT 9.14   Traditional versus Inclusive Models of Diversity

SOURCE: Based on Anthony Oshiotse and Richard O'Leary, "Corning Creates an Inclusive Culture to Drive Technology Innovation and Performance," *Global Business and Organizational Excellence* 26, no. 3 (March/April 2007): 7–21.

includes *all* the ways in which employees differ, including aspects of diversity that can be acquired or changed throughout one's lifetime. These dimensions may have less impact than those included only in the traditional model, but they nevertheless affect a person's self-definition and worldview and the way the person is viewed by others. Many organizational leaders embrace this more inclusive definition of diversity. "Diversity has to be looked at in its broadest sense," said Wally Parker, former CEO of Key Span Energy (now National Grid). "To me, it's all about recognizing, respecting, and supporting individuals regardless of what makes up that individuality. So, yes, that's race, gender, and sexual orientation. But it's also introverted and extroverted, ethnic backgrounds, cultural upbringing, all those things."[126]

One of the challenges of managing a diverse workforce is creating an environment where all employees feel accepted as members of the team and where their unique talents are appreciated. When managers create a feeling of inclusiveness, employees display more loyalty, cooperation, and trustworthiness. Inclusion is the degree to which an employee feels like an esteemed member of a group in which his or her uniqueness is highly appreciated. Inclusion creates a strong sense of belonging where all people can have their voices heard and appreciated.[127] Consider how a manager of a retail store embraced an employee's unique perspective with positive results. Hal, the manager, supervised an employee, Olivia, who was quiet and seemed to have few innovative ideas. But as Hal discussed marketing strategies for the store with Olivia, he was surprised to learn that she was a highly creative thinker, consistently interjecting novel ideas into the discussion. Over time, Hal realized that this seemingly quiet employee was one of the most creative marketing thinkers he had ever met, and together they created a very successful line of children's outerwear. Hal has become a strong supporter of inclusion and a champion for individuals who operate differently from the norm.[128]

In creating a culture of inclusion, managers may experience times of tension and discord as people with different backgrounds bring different opinions and ideas. Conflicts, anxiety, and misunderstandings may increase. Embracing these differences and using them to improve company performance can be challenging. Managing diversity, a key management skill in today's global economy, means creating a climate in which the potential advantages of diversity for organizational or group performance are maximized, while the potential disadvantages are minimized.[129]

9.8b Diversity of Perspective

You may have heard the expression, "Great minds think alike." But when it comes to achieving breakthrough levels of innovation and performance, the best minds are those that *don't* think alike. Over a 10-year period, for example, DiversityInc.'s top 50 companies for any given year outperformed the Dow Jones Industrial Average by 22 percent and NASDAQ by 28 percent, according to Catalyst. Other studies by McKinsey & Company of executive board diversity in the United States, France, Germany, and the United Kingdom show that companies that rank in the top quartile for diversity had returns on equity that were 53 percent higher, on average, than those for the least diverse companies.[130]

Heterogeneous teams and organizations, made up of individuals with different backgrounds and skill sets, increase the chances of getting a diversity of perspective, which provides a broader and deeper base of ideas, opinions, and experiences for problem solving, creativity, and innovation. Managers who cultivate a diversity of perspective significantly increase the chance of creating hard-to-replicate competitive advantage. By tapping into the strengths of diversity, teams are more likely to experience higher efficiency, better quality, less duplication of effort among team members, and increased innovation and creativity.[131]

According to the results of one study, companies that rate high on creativity and innovation have a higher percentage of women and nonwhite male employees than less innovative companies. Another recent study showed that a team's collective intelligence increases when there are more women members on the team.[132] Moreover, companies with more diverse top leadership teams outperform their peers financially. Researchers analyzed return on equity (ROE) and margins for earnings before interest and taxes (EBIT) for 180 corporations in the United States, France, Germany, and the United Kingdom and found that those with a higher percentage of women and foreign nationals performed significantly better than their peers with less-diverse top teams.[133]

At Reckitt Benckiser, a U.K.-based producer of home, health, and personal care products, no nationality dominates the top leadership team. Two executives are Dutch, one is German, two are British, one is South African, two are Italian, and one is from India. Leaders believe the diversity of the company's workforce is one reason that income increased 17 percent annually, on average, from 1999 to 2010. Recently retired CEO Bart Becht said, "It doesn't matter whether I have a Pakistani, a Chinese person, a Brit, or a Turk, man or woman, sitting in the same room, or whether I have people from sales or something else, so long as I have people with different experiences—because the chance for new ideas is much greater when you have people with different backgrounds."[134]

Christopher J. Morris/Corbis News/Corbis

CONCEPT CONNECTION As part of its award-winning supplier diversity program, San Francisco–based Pacific Gas & Electric (PG&E) spent a record $2.1 billion in 2012, or 38.8 percent of its total procurement funds, on products and services from businesses owned by minorities, women, and service-disabled veterans. Because many of these suppliers are also PG&E customers, the utility's managers don't have to look far to find the **diversity dividend** PG&E reaps from this program.

9.8c Dividends of Workplace Diversity

Managers who build strong, diverse organizations reap numerous dividends, as described here and shown in Exhibit 9.15.[135] The dividends of diversity include the following:

- Better use of employee talent. Companies with the best talent are the ones with the best competitive advantage. Attracting a diverse workforce is not enough;

EXHIBIT 9.15 Dividends of Workplace Diversity

- Better use of employee talent
- Increased understanding of the marketplace
- Enhanced breadth of understanding in leadership positions
- Increased quality of team problem solving
- Reduced costs associated with high turnover, absenteeism, and lawsuits

SOURCE: Gail Robinson and Kathleen Dechant, "Building a Business Case for Diversity," *Academy of Management Executive* 11, no. 3 (1997): 21–31.

companies must also provide career opportunities and advancement for minorities and women to retain them.

- **Increased understanding of the marketplace.** A diverse workforce is better able to anticipate and respond to changing consumer needs. Ford Motor Company realized it could reach its business objectives only if it created a workforce that reflected the multicultural face of the country. So it assembled a workforce made up of 25 percent minorities (18.4 percent are African American) to foster a culture of inclusion, winning it a spot on *Black Enterprise's* "40 Best Companies for Diversity."[136]

- **Enhanced breadth of understanding in leadership positions.** Homogeneous top management teams tend to be myopic in their perspectives. According to Niall FitzGerald of Unilever, "It is important for any business operating in an increasingly complex and rapidly changing environment to deploy a broad range of talents. That provides a breadth of understanding of the world and environment and a fusion of the very best values and different perspectives which make up that world."[137]

- **Increased quality of team problem solving.** Teams with diverse backgrounds bring different perspectives to a discussion that result in more creative ideas and solutions.[138] Although a large percent of Ernst & Young's senior leadership is still male, the company is taking steps to create a more diverse leadership team because it's better for business. "We know you get better solutions when you put a diverse team at the table. People come from different backgrounds and they have different frames of reference. When you put these people together, you get the best solution for our clients," says Billie Williamson, director of flexibility and gender equity strategy at Ernst & Young.[141]

- **Reduced costs associated with high turnover, absenteeism, and lawsuits.** Companies that foster a diverse workforce reduce turnover, absenteeism, and the risk of lawsuits. Because family responsibilities contribute to turnover and absenteeism, many companies now offer child-care and elder-care benefits, flexible work arrangements, telecommuting, and part-time employment to accommodate employee responsibilities at home. Discrimination lawsuits are also a costly side effect of a discriminatory work environment. A racial harassment suit against Lockheed Martin Corporation cost the company $2.5 million, the largest individual racial-discrimination payment obtained by the EEOC.[142]

The most successful organizations appreciate the importance of diversity and know that their biggest asset is their people. Organizations with diverse workforces are better prepared to anticipate strategic surprises, as the Central Intelligence Agency (CIA) discovered.

What attitudes do you have that influence your feelings about diversity in the workplace? Complete the "New Manager Self-Test" on page 400 to see how prepared you are to put stereotypes aside so you can manage effectively.

Spotlight on Skills

Central Intelligence Agency (CIA)

Surprises always catch us off guard. When they happen, we ask ourselves, "Who would have seen that coming?" The surprise attacks in the United States by Islamic terrorists on September 11, 2001, left the nation stunned, especially the CIA officers who were responsible for gathering intelligence about terrorist activities and warning of possible threats. Why didn't the CIA, one of the most influential institutions of the last 60 years, predict these attacks? Why did they have such a hard time getting inside the heads of the Islamic terrorists who crafted a devastating attack on U.S. soil?

When an organization such as the CIA experiences a "strategic surprise"—an unexpected, game-changing event that throws it off course—the results can be devastating. To better anticipate strategic surprises, organizations need a diverse workforce, one that reflects the diversity in the communities they serve. The CIA's workforce has long been largely homogeneous in terms of race, gender, ethnicity, class, and culture. The majority of its agents and analysts have been a tight group of Caucasian, Protestant, liberal-arts-educated American males. Few

have traveled abroad or learned to speak a foreign language. The results of this homogeneity are intelligence failures. Consider the Cuban missile crisis of the early 1960s, where CIA analysts dismissed key intelligence about the Cuban missile buildup because of racist attitudes about Cuban informants. Even up through September 11, 2001, Robert Gates, former CIA director and U.S. secretary of defense, claimed that the CIA was less and less willing to employ "people that are a little different, people who are eccentric, people who don't look good in a suit and tie, people who don't play well in the sandbox with others."[139]

Today's CIA, however, seems to be recognizing the value of a heterogeneous workforce. According to retired general David H. Petraeus, who resigned as CIA director in 2012, "Our key challenge now is to ensure that the CIA's extraordinarily gifted and dedicated workforce is contributing to its full potential. That means we must, at every level, be as inclusive as possible in our composition and in how we make decisions. Intelligence work is teamwork, and we have a duty, in our own teams, to reinforce each day the values of diversity, fairness, respect, and inclusion."[140]

REMEMBER THIS

- **Diversity** is defined as all the ways in which employees differ.

- **Inclusion** is the degree to which an employee feels like an esteemed member of a group in which his or her uniqueness is highly appreciated.

- **Diversity of perspective** is achieved when a manager creates a heterogeneous team made up of individuals with diverse backgrounds and skill sets.

- **Managing diversity**, which means creating a climate in which the potential advantages of diversity

for organizational performance are maximized while the potential disadvantages are minimized, is a key management skill today.

- Corporations that recruit and retain a diverse workforce reap numerous benefits, including improved team problem solving and increased understanding of the marketplace.

- Reckitt Benckiser attributes an increase in sales and income to the diversity of its top management team and workforce.

9.9 Factors Shaping Personal Bias

To reap the benefits of diversity, organizations are seeking managers who will serve as catalysts in the workplace to reduce barriers and eliminate obstacles for women and minorities. To successfully manage a diverse workgroup and create a positive, productive environment for all employees, managers need to start with an understanding of the complex attitudes, opinions, and issues that already exist in the workplace or that employees bring into the workplace. These include several factors that shape personal bias: prejudice, discrimination, stereotypes, and ethnocentrism.

Valuing Workplace Diversity

Instructions: Circle all the words below that you associate with your personal response to the idea of workplace diversity.

Abnormal	Dispute	Oppose
Accommodate	Dissatisfaction	Optimistic
Aggravation	Dread	Partake
Appreciative	Eager	Perplexed
Assist	Gratified	Please
Baseless	Hostile	Reasonable
Belittle	Impractical	Retreat
Beneficial	Irritation	Right
Biased	Join	Suitable
Committed	Just	Sympathetic
Comprehend	Listen	Uneasy
Corrupt	Necessary	Unfounded
Criticize	Noble	Valueless
Dislike	Obstinate	Welcoming

Total Score A _____. Add 1 point for each of the following words circled: Beneficial, Just, Necessary, Noble, Reasonable, Right, Suitable. Subtract 1 point for each of the following words circled: Abnormal, Baseless, Biased, Corrupt, Impractical, Unfounded, Valueless.

Total Score B _____. Add 1 point for each of the following words circled: Appreciative, Committed, Eager, Gratified, Optimistic, Pleased, Sympathetic. Subtract 1 point for each of the following words circled: Aggravation, Dislike, Dissatisfaction, Dread, Irritation, Perplexed, Uneasy.

Total Score C _____. Add 1 point for each of the following words circled: Accommodate, Assist, Comprehend, Join, Listen, Partake, Welcoming. Subtract 1 point for each of the following words circled: Belittle, Criticize, Dispute, Hostile, Obstinate, Oppose, Retreat.

Scoring and Interpretation: Your scores on this questionnaire pertain to your attitudes toward workplace diversity, which are reflected in your personal diversity values. Your score for Part A pertains to your intellectual judgments toward workplace diversity, Part B pertains to your affective (emotional) reaction, and Part C to your behavioral response to diversity. If your scores are near zero, then your attitudes and values toward workplace diversity are neutral. Higher positive scores mean that you hold positive values toward diversity and will likely deal sympathetically with bias in the workplace. Higher negative scores mean you hold negative values toward diversity and may be ill prepared to deal with diversity issues that arise in your role as manager. What experiences have led to your diversity values? How do you think your values will contribute to a career in management for you?

SOURCES: Based on Kenneth P. De Meuse and Todd J. Hostager, "Developing an Instrument for Measuring Attitudes Toward and Perceptions of Workplace Diversity: An Initial Report," *Human Resource Development Quarterly* (Spring 2001): 33–51; and Alfred B. Heilbrun, "Measurement of Masculine and Feminine Sex Role Identities as Independent Dimensions," *Journal of Consulting and Clinical Psychology* 44 (1976): 183–190.

9.9a Workplace Prejudice, Discrimination, and Stereotypes

Prejudice is the tendency to view people who are different as being deficient. If someone acts out their prejudicial attitudes toward people who are the targets of their prejudice, **discrimination** has occurred.[143] Paying a woman less than a man for the same work is gender discrimination. Mistreating people because they have a different ethnicity is ethnic discrimination. Although blatant discrimination is not as widespread as in the past, bias in the workplace often shows up in subtle ways. "I could go to a meeting and offer an opinion, and it was like I didn't even say a word," said Christine Dale. "A guy can offer the same opinion and it's like, 'Oh, that's brilliant.' "[144] A survey by Korn Ferry International found that 59 percent of minority managers surveyed had observed a racially motivated double standard in the delegation of assignments.[145] One interesting recent study found that while talkative men tend to be seen as powerful and competent, talkative women tend to be perceived as less competent and pushy.[146]

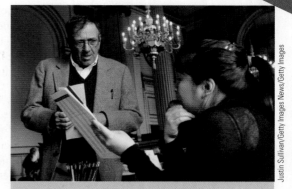

CONCEPT CONNECTION **Age discrimination** has made a difficult situation even more trying for older workers looking for jobs in this economy. In May 2013, for instance, the average duration of unemployment for job seekers over age 55, such as Larry Visakowitz (pictured at a job fair for veterans), hovered around 54 weeks—over one full year. That's 17 weeks longer than the national average. **Stereotypes** that plague older job seekers include the beliefs that they are more expensive, harder to train, more likely to leave, and less productive, adaptable, and technologically adept.

A major component of prejudice is stereotypes, rigid, exaggerated, irrational beliefs associated with a particular group of people.[147] To be successful managing diversity, managers need to eliminate harmful stereotypes from their thinking, shedding any biases that negatively affect the workplace. For example, old stereotypes often bubble up and block women's rise to higher-level positions. These silent but potent beliefs include the perception that women pose a greater risk in senior positions or that working mothers are unable to hold positions requiring extensive travel and stress. Stereotypes also may block the honest feedback women need for improving their performance. If a man makes a bad presentation, his male superiors might slap him on the back and say, "Buddy, what happened? You screwed up, man!" If a woman gives a bad presentation, she may never hear candid feedback. Instead, it may be spoken behind her back: "Wow! She really screwed up."[148]

Managers can learn to *value differences,* which means that they recognize individual differences and see these differences with an appreciative attitude. To facilitate this attitude,

EXHIBIT 9.16   Difference between Stereotyping and Valuing Cultural Differences

Stereotyping	Valuing Cultural Differences
Is based on false assumptions, anecdotal evidence, or impressions without any direct experience with a group	Is based on cultural differences verified by scientific research methods
Assigns negative traits to members of a group	Views cultural differences as positive or neutral
Assumes that all members of a group have the same characteristics	Does not assume that all individuals within a group have the same characteristics
Example: Suzuko Akoi is Asian and is therefore not aggressive by white, male standards.	*Example: As a group, Asians tend to be less aggressive than white, male Americans.*

SOURCE: Adapted from Taylor Cox, Jr., and Ruby L. Beale, *Developing Competency to Manage Diversity: Readings, Cases and Activities* (San Francisco: Berrett-Koehler Publishers, Inc., 1997).

managers can learn about cultural patterns and typical beliefs of groups to help under-stand why people act the way they do. It helps to understand the difference between these two ways of thinking—most notably that stereotyping is a barrier to diversity, but valuing cultural differences facilitates diversity. These two different ways of thinking are listed in Exhibit 9.16 and described here.[149]

- Stereotypes are often based on folklore, media portrayals, and other unreliable sources of information. For example, studies have shown that the traditional stereo-type of a "good" manager is masculine, adopting characteristics such as assertiveness and competitiveness. Interestingly, however, for people who have worked in organi-zations with a high percentage of female managers, that stereotype no longer exists. Those employees often show a stronger preference for feminine characteristics such as caring and compassion.[150] Legitimate cultural differences are backed up by sys-tematic research of real differences, not folklore and supposition.

- Stereotypes contain negative connotations. On the other hand, managers who value diversity view differences as potentially positive or neutral. For example, the obser-vation that Asian males are typically less aggressive does not imply they are inferior or superior to white males—it simply means that there is a difference.

- Stereotypes assume that all members of a group have the same characteristics. Managers who value diversity recognize that individuals within a group of people may or may not share the same characteristics.[151]

Not only should managers rid themselves of stereotypical thinking, they should also recognize the stereotype threat that may jeopardize the performance of at-risk employees. **Stereotype threat** describes the psychological experience of a person who, when engaged in a task, is aware of a stereotype about his or her identity group suggesting that he or she will not perform well on that task.[152] Suppose that you are a member of a minority group presenting complicated market research results to your management team and are anxious about making a good impression. Assume that some members of your audience have a negative stereotype about your identity group. As you ponder this, your anxiety skyrockets and your confidence is shaken. Understandably, your presentation suffers because you are distracted by worries and self-doubt as you invest energy in overcoming the stereotype. The feelings you are experiencing are called *stereotype threat*.

People most affected by stereotype threat are those we consider as disadvantaged in the workplace due to negative stereotypes—racial and ethnic minorities, members of lower socioeconomic classes, women, older people, gay and lesbian individuals, and people with disabilities. Although anxiety about performing a task may be normal, people with stereo-type threat feel an extra scrutiny and worry that their failure will reflect not only on them-selves as individuals, but on the larger group to which they belong. As Beyoncé Knowles said, "It's like you have something to prove, and you don't want to mess it up and be a nega-tive reflection on black women."[153]

9.9b Ethnocentrism

Ethnocentrism is one roadblock for managers trying to recognize, welcome, and encourage dif-ferences among people so that they can develop their unique talents and be effective organiza-tional members. **Ethnocentrism** is the belief that one's own group and culture are inherently superior to other groups and cultures. Ethnocentrism makes it difficult to value diversity. Viewing one's own culture as the best culture is a natural tendency among most people. Moreover, the business world still tends to reflect the values, behaviors, and assumptions based on the expe-riences of a rather homogeneous, white, middle-class, male workforce. Indeed, most theories of management presume that workers share similar values, beliefs, motivations, and attitudes about work and life in general. These theories presume that one set of behaviors best helps an organization to be productive and effective and therefore should be adopted by all employees.[154]

Ethnocentric viewpoints and a standard set of cultural practices produce a **monoculture**, a culture that accepts only one way of doing things and one set of values and beliefs, which can cause problems for minority employees. People of color, women, gay people, the disabled, the elderly, and other diverse employees may feel undue pressure to conform, may be victims of stereotyping attitudes, and may be presumed deficient because they are different. White, heterosexual men, many of whom do not fit the notion of the "ideal" employee, may also feel uncomfortable with the monoculture and resent stereotypes that label white males as racists and sexists. Valuing diversity means ensuring that *all* people are given equal opportunities in the workplace.[155]

The goal for organizations seeking cultural diversity is pluralism rather than a monoculture and ethnorelativism rather than ethnocentrism. **Ethnorelativism** is the belief that groups and subcultures are inherently equal. **Pluralism** means that an organization accommodates several subcultures. Movement toward pluralism seeks to integrate fully into the organization the employees who otherwise would feel isolated and ignored. To promote pluralism in its Mountain View corporate headquarters, chefs at Google's corporate cafeteria ensure that its menu accommodates the different tastes of its ethnically diverse workforce.

How tolerant are you of people who are different from you? Complete the Self-Learning on page 409 to assess your tolerance for diversity.

Spotlight on Skills

Google

Employees in Google's corporate headquarters come from all corners of the world, but they feel a little closer to home when they see familiar foods from their homeland on the cafeteria menu. With a goal of satisfying a diverse, ethnically varied palate, Google's first food guru and chef Charlie Ayers designed menus that reflected his eclectic tastes yet also met the needs of an increasingly diverse workforce. He created his own dishes, searched all types of restaurants for new recipes, and often got some of his best ideas from foreign-born employees. For example, a Filipino accountant offered a recipe for chicken *adobo,* a popular dish from her native country. Scattered around the Googleplex are cafés specializing in Southwestern, Italian, California-Mediterranean, and vegetarian cuisines. And because more and more Googlers originally hail from Asia, employees can find sushi at the Japanese-themed Pacific Café and Thai red curry beef at the East Meets West Café.

Google believes that food can be a tool for supporting an inclusive workplace. The array of menu options gives people a chance to try new things and learn more about their coworkers. And the company knows that when people need a little comfort and familiarity, nothing takes the edge off of working in a foreign country like eating food that reminds you of home.[156]

REMEMBER THIS

- The tendency to view people who are different as being deficient is called **prejudice**.
- **Discrimination** occurs when someone acts out their negative attitudes toward people who are the targets of their prejudice.
- A rigid, exaggerated, irrational belief associated with a particular group of people is called a **stereotype**.

- One stereotype is that talkative women are less capable and pushy, whereas talkative men are viewed as competent and powerful.
- **Stereotype threat** occurs when a person who, when engaged in a task, is aware of a stereotype about his or her identity group suggesting that he or she will not perform well on that task.

- **Ethnocentrism** is the belief that one's own group is inherently superior to other groups.
- A culture that accepts only one way of doing things and one set of values and beliefs is called a **monoculture**.

- **Ethnorelativism** is the belief that groups and subcultures are inherently equal.
- **Pluralism** describes an environment in which the organization accommodates several subcultures, including employees who would otherwise feel isolated and ignored.

9.10 Factors Affecting Women's Careers

Research shows that companies with several senior-level women outperform those without senior-level women both financially and organizationally. One survey of 58,000 employees in over 100 global companies revealed that companies with three or more women in top management are perceived to be more capable, have stronger leadership, and inspire higher employee motivation, among other important organizational characteristics.[157] However, there is evidence that women are stalling at the middle-management level. Women hold 53 percent of entry-level professional positions, but they hold only 37 percent of middle-management positions, 28 percent of vice president and senior managerial roles, and 14 percent of executive positions.[158] In addition, men as a group still have the benefit of higher wages and faster promotions.

Both the glass ceiling and the decision to "opt out" of a high-pressure career have an impact on women's advancement opportunities and pay. Yet women are sometimes favored in leadership roles for demonstrating behaviors and attitudes that help them succeed in the workplace, a factor called "the female advantage."

9.10a The Glass Ceiling

For the first time in U.S. history, women hold a majority of the nation's jobs.[159] As they move up the career ladder, the numbers of men and women are comparable, with women holding 51 percent of all lower- and mid-level managerial and professional jobs.[160] But very few women break through the glass ceiling to reach senior management positions. In fact, only 3.6 percent of *Fortune* 500 companies have a woman CEO.[161] The glass ceiling is an invisible barrier that exists for women and minorities that limits their upward mobility in organizations. They can look up through the ceiling and see top management, but prevailing attitudes and stereotypes are invisible obstacles to their own advancement. As described in the following "Spotlight on Skills," box in addition to societal and institutional barriers, some women believe that mistakes women make in their patterns of communication and power relationships have held them back from achieving higher-level positions.

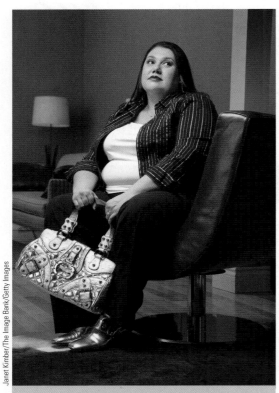

Janet Kimber/The Image Bank/Getty Images

CONCEPT CONNECTION A number of studies conducted around the world in recent years confirm that weight discrimination adds to the **glass ceiling** effect for women. While overweight males are disproportionately represented among CEOs, overweight and obese women are underrepresented. Several years ago, ABC News sent a woman out to interview twice—once appearing to be an individual of normal weight and the second time in padded clothing to appear overweight. She received more job offers as a thin person despite the fact that she handed prospective employers a stronger résumé in her overweight incarnation.

The glass ceiling also impedes the career progress of minorities. In particular, Asian managers bump up against the *bamboo ceiling*, a combination of cultural and organizational barriers that impede Asians' career progress. Today, while Asians are the most educated and make up a good share of the entry-level workforce in certain industries, they make up only 1.5 percent of corporate board members in the United States.[162]

To break through the glass ceiling into senior management roles, top executives suggest female and minority managers follow this advice:

- Be assertive and ask for what you want. Many Asian managers have found themselves stereotyped as "not top manager material" because they are too quiet and unassertive. Women in general are also uncomfortable asking for what they want, for fear of being perceived as too aggressive or too selfish. Sheryl Sandberg, Facebook's chief operating officer, says that 57 percent of men entering the workforce negotiate their salaries, but only 7 percent of women do likewise.[163] In addition, women and minorities need to build their case around things that matter most to their employer—principally, the impact on the bottom line.[164]

> *"The most important factor in determining whether you will succeed isn't your gender, it's you. Be open to opportunity and take risks. In fact, take the worst, the messiest, the most challenging assignment you can find, and then take control."*
>
> —Angela Braly, FORMER WellPoint CEO

Spotlight on Skills

How Women Hold Themselves Back

Sheryl Sandberg, chief operating officer of Facebook, wrote the recent book Lean In to acknowledge that women face tremendous barriers in the workplace, but also to argue that women need to break down the barriers within themselves. She recounts workplace and social science research proving that bias exists, as well as some showing that women hold themselves back. Gender stereotypes, Sandberg says, are so powerfully ingrained in women that they continue to perpetuate them subconsciously. Sandberg is not alone in her belief that women are partly to blame for the fact that "men still run the world." Here are a few of the career sins that some people say women commit.

- They don't take responsibility for their success. Societal norms and stereotypes of how women "should" act in the workplace have been around for decades, but they will change only if women take responsibility for redefining expectations. Too many women, Sandberg says, get caught in the "tiara syndrome," expecting to be rewarded for good work rather than seizing opportunities and asking for what they deserve. Women have to actively "sit at the table" rather than being observers in their own careers.

- They don't display credibility and confidence in their body language. Consultant Carol Kinsey Goman says women tend to physically condense themselves, whereas high-status men expand and take up more space, claiming their turf. Goman also advises against other nonverbal messages that reduce women's authority: (1) tilting the head when listening; (2) waiting your turn; (3) excessive smiling; (4) nodding too much; (5) delicate handshakes; and (6) flirting.

- They seek mentors. Having a mentor can be a powerful benefit to anyone's career, but people should get mentors when they do great work and attract the attention of higher executives who want to help them. "Searching for a mentor has become the professional equivalent of waiting for Prince Charming," Sandberg says. Rather than expecting to get a mentor in order to excel, the logic women should use is, "excel and you will get a mentor."

- They leave before they leave. Women tend to make incremental decisions based on future plans that chip away at their career options. "A law associate might decide not to shoot for partner because someday she hopes to have a family," Sandberg writes. "A sales representative might take a smaller territory or not apply for a management role. Often without even realizing it, the woman stops reaching for new opportunities" because of the long-term future impact. Sandberg pays tribute to women who sideline careers for children, but she emphasizes: "The time to scale back is when a break is needed or a child arrives—not before, and certainly not years in advance."

Things will get better for women when there are more women in high-level positions who can change organizational cultures from within. For that to happen, women have to overcome the inner barriers that are holding them back.

SOURCES: Sheryl Sandberg, *Lean In: Women, Work, and the Will to Lead* (New York: Alfred A. Knopf, 2013); and Carol Kinsey Goman, "Body Language," *Leadership Excellence* (August, 2010): 9.

- Highlight your achievements. Women tend to downplay their accomplishments and insights to avoid being judged as unfeminine. Maggie Wilderotter, CEO of Frontier Communications, recalls making points in boardrooms, then watching the group actively take notes when a man later said the same thing. "When that happened, I'd stop the conversation and say, 'Do you realize I said that 10 minutes ago?'"[165] In addition, modest women and minorities from group-oriented cultures often will not ask for rewards for themselves, but they may ask for rewards for others. White males, on the other hand, typically self-promote their successes. To achieve recognition and credit for their successes, female and minority managers should highlight their achievements and promote their own accomplishments.[166]

9.10b Opt-Out Trend

Some women never hit the glass ceiling because they choose to get off the fast track long before it comes into view. In recent years, an ongoing discussion concerns something referred to as the *opt-out trend*. In a survey of nearly 2,500 women and 653 men, 37 percent of highly qualified women report that they voluntarily left the workforce at some point in their careers, compared to only 24 percent of similarly qualified men.[167]

Quite a debate rages over the reasons for the larger number of women who drop out of mainstream careers. Opt-out proponents say that women are deciding that corporate success isn't worth the price in terms of reduced family and personal time, greater stress, and negative health effects.[168] Anne-Marie Slaughter, a Princeton professor and former top aide to Hillary Clinton, left her prestigious position to spend more time at home with a rebellious teenager. Unable to balance work and family with success, Slaughter challenged the concept that women can "have it all" in a controversial 2012 article in The Atlantic. In the piece, Slaughter said that today's workplace needs to adapt, and women who opt out have no need to apologize. "Women of my generation have clung to the feminist credo we were raised with ... because we are determined not to drop the flag for the next generation," Ms. Slaughter wrote. "But when many members of the younger generation have stopped listening, on the grounds that glibly repeating 'you can have it all' is simply airbrushing reality, it is time to talk."[169]

One school of thought says that women don't want corporate power and status in the same way that men do, and clawing one's way up the corporate ladder has become less appealing. Yet critics argue that this view is just another way to blame women themselves for the dearth of female managers at higher levels.[170] Vanessa Castagna, for example, says that she left J. C. Penney after decades with the company not because she wanted more family or personal time, but because she kept getting passed over for top jobs.[171] Although some women are voluntarily leaving the fast track, many more genuinely want to move up the corporate ladder but find their paths blocked. In a survey by Catalyst of executive women, 55 percent said they aspire to senior leadership levels.[172] In addition, a survey of 103 women voluntarily leaving executive jobs in *Fortune* 1000 companies found that corporate culture was cited as the number-one reason for leaving.[173] The greatest disadvantages of women leaders stem largely from prejudicial attitudes and a heavily male-oriented corporate culture.[174]

Another troublesome issue that could contribute to the opt-out trend is the **queen bee syndrome**, a term that refers to a female boss who not only has no interest in fostering the careers of other women but might even actively undermine them. In a 2011 survey by the American Management Association, 95 percent of 1,000 working women said that they believed they had been undermined by another woman at some point in their careers. A study by the Workplace Bullying Institute reported that female bullies direct their hostilities toward other women 80 percent of the time. However, queen bees may be creatures of circumstances and ingrained corporate cultures. Women are expected to be softer and gentler, yet their hard, more assertive qualities get them rewarded and promoted (and perhaps labeled as queen bees for their lack of sympathy).[175]

9.10c The Female Advantage

Some people think that women might actually be better managers, partly because of a more collaborative, less hierarchical, relationship-oriented approach that is in tune with today's global and multicultural environment.[176] As attitudes and values change with changing generations, the qualities that women seem to possess naturally may lead to a gradual role reversal in organizations. For example, a stunning gender reversal is taking place in U.S. education, with girls taking over almost every leadership role from kindergarten to graduate school. In addition, women of all races and ethnic groups are outpacing men in earning bachelor's and master's degrees. In higher-education institutions in the United States, women make up 58 percent of enrolled students overall.[177] Among 25- to 29-year-olds, 32 percent of women have college degrees, compared to 27 percent of men. Women are rapidly closing the M.D. and Ph.D. gap, and they make up about half of all U.S. law students, half of all undergraduate business majors, and about 30 percent of MBA candidates. Overall, women's participation in both the labor force and civic affairs has steadily increased since the mid-1950s, while men's participation has slowly but steadily declined.[178]

According to James Gabarino, an author and professor of human development at Cornell University, women are "better able to deliver in terms of what modern society requires of people—paying attention, abiding by rules, being verbally competent, and dealing with interpersonal relationships in offices."[179] His observation is supported by the fact that female managers are typically rated higher by subordinates on interpersonal skills, as well as on factors such as task behavior, communication, ability to motivate others, and goal accomplishment.[180] Recent research found a correlation between balanced gender composition in companies (that is, roughly equal male and female representation) and higher organizational performance. Moreover, a study by Catalyst indicates that organizations with the highest percentage of women in top management financially outperform, by about 35 percent, those with the lowest percentage of women in higher-level jobs.[181]

9.10d Increasing Awareness of Sexual Harassment

Although psychological closeness between men and women in the workplace may be a positive experience, sexual harassment is not. It is illegal. As a form of sexual discrimination, sexual harassment in the workplace is a violation of Title VII of the 1964 Civil Rights Act. Sexual harassment in the classroom is a violation of Title VIII of the Education Amendment of 1972. Many companies offer sexual harassment awareness programs that create awareness of what defines sexual harassment and the legal ramifications of violations. The following list categorizes various forms of sexual harassment as defined by one university.

- Generalized. This form involves sexual remarks and actions that are not intended to lead to sexual activity but that are directed toward a coworker based solely on gender and reflect on the entire group.

- Inappropriate/offensive. Though not sexually threatening, the behavior causes discomfort in a coworker, whose reaction in avoiding the harasser may limit his or her freedom and ability to function in the workplace.

- Solicitation with promise of reward. This action treads a fine line as an attempt to "purchase" sex, with the potential for criminal prosecution.

- Coercion with threat of punishment. The harasser coerces a coworker into sexual activity by using the threat of power (through recommendations, grades, promotions, and so on) to jeopardize the victim's career.

- Sexual crimes and misdemeanors. The highest level of sexual harassment, these acts would, if reported to the police, be considered felonies or misdemeanors.[182]

A recent example comes from the city of San Diego, where more than a dozen women accused former mayor Bob Filner of making unwanted sexual advances, including groping, kissing, and making lewd comments. One woman says that Filner asked her to work without panties, told her he wanted to see her naked, and dragged her in a headlock while whispering in her ear. Filner continued to proclaim his innocence and refused for months to resign, agreeing to step down only after the city agreed to pick up some of his legal costs in order to avoid the time and expense of a recall. The scandal left the city in turmoil.[183]

REMEMBER THIS

- Companies that promote women to senior-level positions outperform those without women in these positions, both financially and organizationally.
- The **glass ceiling** is an invisible barrier that separates women and minorities from senior management positions.
- Proponents of the opt-out trend say that some women choose to leave the workforce because they decide success isn't worth it in terms of reduced family and personal time, greater stress, and negative health effects.

- Critics say that opinion is just a way to blame women for the scarcity of female top managers and argue that organizations must change.
- The **queen bee syndrome** refers to a female boss who not only has no interest in fostering the careers of other women but might even actively undermine them.
- Women are likely to be more collaborative, less hierarchical, and more relationship-oriented than men, qualities that prepare them to succeed in today's multicultural work environment.

CHAPTER 9   DISCUSSION QUESTIONS

1. Does it seem like a good idea to let a big data computer program make hiring decisions, as some companies like Xerox are doing, as described in this chapter? What types of positions do you think this might be suitable for? What might be some drawbacks to this approach?

2. Assume that it is the year 2027. In your company, central planning has given way to frontline decision making, and bureaucracy has given way to teamwork. Shop floor workers use handheld devices and robots. A labor shortage currently affects many job openings, and the few applicants that you do attract lack skills to work in teams, make their own production decisions, or use sophisticated technology. As vice president of HRM since 2013, what should you have done to prepare for this situation?

3. Is it wise for managers to evaluate a promising candidate's tweets or postings on social networking sites as grounds for rejection before even interviewing him or her? What might be some ethical and legal issues that managers should consider? Discuss.

4. As HR manager for a small company that makes computer games and software, what are some steps that you might take to create an employer brand?

5. One HR manager recently got a thank-you note on her iPhone that said "Thx 4 the Iview! Wud ♥ to wrk 4 u!!!" The manager had liked the candidate in the interview, but after getting this note, she put him in the reject pile. Do you think it was fair for the manager to reject the candidate so automatically? Should "textspeak" be considered acceptable workplace communication? Discuss.

6. How would you go about deciding whether to use a job-based, skills-based, or pay-for-performance compensation plan for employees in a textile manufacturing plant? For waitstaff in a restaurant? For salespeople in an insurance company?

7. Evaluate your own personal experiences with people from other cultural backgrounds. How well do you think those experiences have prepared you to understand the unique needs and dilemmas of a diverse workforce?

8. Until Sheryl Sandberg was promoted to chief operating officer of Facebook in 2012, its board was composed of only men. Yet a majority of Facebook's 845 million users are women. Given this demographic, explain how Facebook might benefit from increasing the presence of women on its corporate board.

9. Describe employees who are most vulnerable to stereotype threat. Why is it important for managers to understand that some employees may experience stereotype threat?

10. If talkative men are viewed as powerful and competent, why do you think talkative women are seen as less capable and pushy? Do you think this perception would be different in an organization with a large percentage of female managers at top levels?

SELF-LEARNING

How Tolerant Are You?[184]

For each of the following questions, circle the answer that best describes you.

1. Most of your friends:
   a. Are very similar to you
   b. Are very different from you and from each other
   c. Are like you in some respects but different in others

2. When someone does something you disapprove of, you:
   a. Break off the relationship
   b. Tell how you feel but keep in touch
   c. Tell yourself that it doesn't really matter and behave as you always have

3. Which virtue is most important to you?
   a. Kindness
   b. Objectivity
   c. Obedience

4. When it comes to beliefs, you:
   a. Do all you can to make others see things the same way you do
   b. Advance your point of view actively, but stop short of argument
   c. Keep your feelings to yourself

5. Would you hire a person who has had emotional problems?
   a. No
   b. Yes, provided that the person shows evidence of complete recovery
   c. Yes, if the person is suitable for the job

6. Do you voluntarily read material that supports views different from your own?
   a. Never
   b. Sometimes
   c. Often

7. You react to old people with:
   a. Patience
   b. Annoyance
   c. Sometimes a, sometimes b

8. Do you agree with the statement, "What is right and wrong depends upon the time, place, and circumstance"?

   a. Strongly agree
   b. Agree to a point
   c. Strongly disagree

9. Would you marry someone from a different race?

   a. Yes
   b. No
   c. Probably not

10. If someone in your family were homosexual, you would:

    a. View this as a problem and try to change the person to a heterosexual orientation
    b. Accept the person as a homosexual with no change in feelings or treatment
    c. Avoid or reject the person

11. You react to little children with:

    a. Patience
    b. Annoyance
    c. Sometimes *a*, sometimes *b*

12. Other people's personal habits annoy you:

    a. Often
    b. Not at all
    c. Only if extreme

13. If you stay in a household run differently from yours (in terms of cleanliness, manners, meals, and other customs), you:

    a. Adapt readily
    b. Quickly become uncomfortable and irritated
    c. Adjust for a while, but not for long

14. Which statement do you agree with most?

    a. We should avoid judging others because no one can fully understand the motives of another person.
    b. People are responsible for their actions and have to accept the consequences.
    c. Both motives and actions are important when considering questions of right and wrong.

Scoring and Interpretation

Circle your score for each of the answers and total the scores:

1. a = 4; b = 0; c = 2
2. a = 4; b = 2; c = 0
3. a = 0; b = 2; c = 4
4. a = 4; b = 2; c = 0
5. a = 4; b = 2; c = 0
6. a = 4; b = 2; c = 0
7. a = 0; b = 4; c = 2
8. a = 0; b = 2; c = 4
9. a = 0; b = 4; c = 2
10. a = 2; b = 0; c = 4
11. a = 0; b = 4; c = 2
12. a = 4; b = 0; c = 2
13. a = 0; b = 4; c = 2
14. a = 0; b = 4; c = 2

Total Score

0–14: If you score 14 or below, you are a very tolerant person, and dealing with diversity comes easily to you.

15–28: You are basically a tolerant person, and others think of you that way. In general, diversity presents few problems for you; you may be broad-minded in some areas and have less-tolerant ideas in other areas of life, such as attitudes toward older people or male-female social roles.

29–42: You are less tolerant than most people and should work on developing greater tolerance of people different from you. Your low tolerance level could affect your business or personal relationships.

43–56: You have a very low tolerance for diversity. The only people that you are likely to respect are those with beliefs similar to your own. You reflect a level of intolerance that could cause difficulties in today's multicultural business environment.

GROUP LEARNING

Management Competencies[185]

Step 1. An important responsibility of the HR department at many companies is to develop a list of managerial competencies and then to provide training to help managers improve on those competencies. The list below includes desired manager competencies from IBM. Make notes to the right of each competency describing the management behaviors you think would be covered.

Desired competencies	Management behaviors
Collaborative influence	
Developing IBM people and communities	
Earning trust	
Embracing challenge	
Enabling growth	
Passion for IBM's future	
Strategic risk taking	
Thinking horizontal	

Step 2. In groups of three to five students, compare, discuss, and agree upon the expected behaviors for each competency. One student be the recorder and be prepared to report the behaviors to the class.

Step 3. After agreeing upon competency behaviors, each student should take a turn stating the competencies they believe will be easiest and hardest for them to master.

Step 4. Why do you think IBM arrived at this set of competencies? How do you think it might differ from management or leadership competencies for other companies?

Step 5. Outside of class, go online and look up information on IBM's competencies. (Search for "IBM Leadership Competencies.") Are the competencies defined as you expected? Look up competencies for another company as well. Why do you think HR departments in these companies put so much energy into developing a list of desired manager competencies?

ACTION LEARNING

Gender and Management

This exercise will help you to examine the differences in career and family life of male versus female managers.

1. Divide into groups of two. It would be good if you can have a male and a female paired up, but that won't be possible for the whole class. Each of you will interview two managers.

2. Choose two managers to interview personally, one male, one female. They must have been managers at least 15 years and they should be roughly in the same level of position in their own organizations. And they should be close to the same age. The questions to ask are below.

3. After your interviews, get together with your partner and discuss similarities and differences between the male and female managers.

4. Write a report to give to your instructor.

5. Be prepared to talk about your findings in class, without giving any names.

Questions to ask in interview. You may ask other ones, as well. Let the managers know that you are doing a study on gender issues and management for a course. Answers will be kept confidential. No identifying information will be given to the teacher.

Question	Female manager's answer	Male Manager's answer
1. What education do you have?		
2. How did you start your career?		
3. What were your career aspirations when you started out?		
4. What were the obstacles in your career advancement?		
5. Are you married? Children? What ages?		
6. Do women and men make different types of managers?		
7. Is it different now for women than it used to be?		
8. What would you do differently than you did in your career?		
9. What do you wish had been different for you?		

ETHICAL DILEMMA

Sunset Prayers[186]

Frank Piechowski, plant manager for a Minnesota North Woods Appliance Corporation refrigerator plant, just received his instructions from the vice president for manufacturing. He was to hire 40 more temporary workers through Twin Cities Staffing, the local labor agency that North Woods used. Frank already knew from past experience that most, if not all, of the new hires available to work the assembly line would be Muslim Somali refugees, people who had immigrated to Minnesota from their war-torn native country en masse over the past 15 years.

North Woods, like all appliance manufacturers, was trying to survive in a highly competitive, mature industry. Appliance companies were competing mainly on price. The entrance of large chains such as Best Buy and Home Depot only intensified the price wars, not to mention that consumers could easily do comparison shopping before leaving home by logging on to the Internet. The pressure to keep production costs low was considerable.

That's where the Somali workers came in. In an effort to keep labor costs low, North Woods was relying more and more on temporary workers rather than increasing the ranks of permanent employees. Frank was quite pleased with the Somalis already at work on the assembly line. Although few in number, they were responsible, hardworking, and willing to work for the wages that he could afford to pay.

It was the first time this son of Polish immigrants had ever come into contact with Muslims, but so far, it had gone well. Frank had established a good working relationship with the Somalis' spokesperson, Halima Adan, who explained that unlike most Western faiths, Islamic religious practices were inextricably woven into everyday life. As a result of the good rapport they had, together they had worked out ways to accommodate Muslim customs. Frank authorized changes in the plant's cafeteria menu so that the Somali workers had more options that conformed to their dietary restrictions, and he allowed women to wear traditional clothing, so long as they weren't violating safety standards.

After learning that the Somalis would need to perform at least some of the ceremonial washing and prayers they were required to do five times a day during work hours, the plant manager set aside a quiet, clean room where they could observe their 15-minute rituals during their breaks and at sunset. The Maghrib sunset prayers that second-shift workers had to perform were disruptive to a smooth workflow. Compared to their midday and afternoon rituals, the Muslim faithful had considerably less leeway as to when they said the sunset prayers, and of course, the sun set at a slightly different time each day. But so far, they'd all coped.

But what was he going to do about the sunset prayers with an influx of 40 Somali workers that would dramatically increase the number of people who would need to leave the line to pray? Was it time to modify his policy? He knew that Title VII of the Civil Right Act required that he make "reasonable" accommodations to his employees' religious practices unless doing so would impose an "undue hardship" on the employer. Had he reached the point where the accommodations that Halima Adan would probably request crossed the line from reasonable to unreasonable? But if he changed his policy, did he risk alienating his workforce?

What Would You Do?

1. Continue the current policy that leaves it up to the Muslim workers as to when they leave the assembly line to perform their sunset rituals.

2. Try to hire the fewest possible Muslim workers so the work line will be efficient on second shift.

3. Ask the Muslim workers to delay their sunset prayers until a regularly scheduled break occurs, pointing out that North Woods is primarily a place of business, not a house of worship.

CASE FOR CRITICAL ANALYSIS

The Right Way with Employees?

As a senior manager for a global player in automobile production and sales, Kirby Ellis had joined thousands of fellow employees in the excitement surrounding production of the company's new hybrid vehicles.

But barely two years into production, embarrassing component shortages, delivery delays, and a recall of the first models had a ripple effect, presenting the company with mounting concerns. In the confusion, many customers canceled orders and turned to competitors for purchase of the eco-friendly vehicles. Ellis's company was facing a financial downturn.

With three decades of service to the company, Kirby led a contingent of managers intent upon keeping together as much of the company and as many employees as possible.

"We know there will be some necessary cuts," Kirby admitted. "But this company has a long history of sticking by its people. Our first priority should be internal streamlining of how we do things and making sure we have the right people on board."

Many managers liked what they heard from Kirby. He was well respected and had an unequaled reputation for his leadership and collaborative skills and his ability to work with managers, as well as line workers on the factory floors. People marveled at the number of individuals he knew on a personal level throughout the company.

Drew Cunningham influenced a second contingent within the management group. A brash go-getter with a reputation for *fixing* companies in crisis, he proposed across-the-board cuts in employees in order to implement a solution as quickly as possible. He proposed the immediate creation of a forced ranking system in order to identify and get rid of lower-ranking employees.

Kirby raised his hand and rose to his feet in objection. "So we're going to create a system to *fire* ..."

"I didn't say *fire* ..."

"OK, *cut* our own hard-working people? It sounds like some lame government commission," Kirby said. "We've got bright people. This thing simply got worse faster than we thought. We can work with the people we have in setting up more efficient workflow, establishing reasonable deadlines to increase output and ..."

"Kirby, these are not the days of knowing everyone in the plant," Drew said. "You're not throwing out your wife's uncle Harry. We are taking a serious look at what we do, how we do it, and streamlining everything by keeping the right people in the organization and cutting the rest."

Questions

1. What kind of employee social contract is assumed by Kirby and by Drew? Explain.

2. If you were an HR manager at the company, which view would you support? Why?

3. HR departments hire and develop human capital to serve the organization's strategy and drive performance. Which approach—Kirby's or Drew's—is more likely to have a greater positive impact on performance? Discuss.

ON THE JOB VIDEO CASES

Barcelona Restaurant Group: Managing Human Resources

Questions

1. List the three main activities of HRM and identify which activity is examined at length in the video.

2. Of the various steps in Barcelona's employee selection process, the job interview is the briefest. Do you agree with the company's approach to interviewing? Why or why not?

3. Identify Barcelona's three-stage process for matching job applicants with its organizational objectives, and explain how each stage reveals the fit between job applicants and the needs of the restaurant.

ENDNOTES

1. Based on ideas presented in Jim Collins, *Good to Great: Why Some Companies Make the Leap … and Others Don't* (New York: Harper Business, 2001).

2. Jack Ewing, "Germans Scrutinize Amazon's Labor Practices," *The New York Times*, March 4, 2013, B2; and Vanessa Fuhrmans, "Amazon Acts on German Controversy; Online Retailer Cuts Ties with Security Firm After a Television Documentary on Working Conditions," *The Wall Street Journal*, February 19, 2013, B3.

3. Robert L. Mathis and John H. Jackson, *Human Resource Management: Essential Perspectives*, 2nd ed. (Cincinnati, OH: South-Western Publishing, 2002), p. 1.

4. See James C. Wimbush, "Spotlight on Human Resource Management," *Business Horizons* 48 (2005): 463–467; Jonathan Tompkins, "Strategic Human Resources Management in Government: Unresolved Issues," *Public Personnel Management* (Spring 2002): 95–110; Noel M. Tichy, Charles J. Fombrun, and Mary Anne Devanna, "Strategic Human Resource Management," *Sloan Management Review* 23 (Winter 1982): 47–61; Cynthia A. Lengnick-Hall and Mark L. Lengnick-Hall, "Strategic Human Resources Management: A Review of the Literature and a Proposed Typology," *Academy of Management Review* 13 (July 1988): 454–470; Eugene B. McGregor, *Strategic Management of Human Knowledge, Skills, and Abilities* (San Francisco: Jossey-Bass, 1991).

5. Quoted in Erin White, "HR Departments Get New Star Power at Some Firms; Business Executives Now Tapped to Lead as Job Is Rethought" (Theory & Practice column), *The Wall Street Journal*, June 23, 2008.

6. Joann S. Lublin, "HR Executives Suddenly Get Hot" (Theory & Practice column), *The Wall Street Journal*, December 14, 2009.

7. This definition is based on George Bohlander, Scott Snell, and Arthur Sherman, *Managing Human Resources*, 12th ed. (Cincinnati, OH: South-Western, 2001), pp. 13–15.

8. "Leading Through Connections: The IBM 2012 Chief Executive Officer Study," reported in Eric Lesser and Carl Hoffman, "Workforce Analytics: Making the Most of a Critical Asset," *Ivey Business Journal*, July–August 2012, www.iveybusinessjournal.com/topics/strategy/workforce-analytics-making-the-most-of-a-critical-asset (accessed August 27, 2012).

9. P. Wright, G. McMahan, and A. McWilliams, "Human Resources and Sustained Competitive Advantage: A Resource-Based Perspective," *International Journal of Human Resource Management* 5 (1994): 301–326; Tompkins, "Strategic Human Resource Management in Government."

10. Liza Castro Christiansen and Malcolm Higgs, "How the Alignment of Business Strategy and HR Strategy Can Impact Performance," *Journal of General Management* 33, no. 4 (Summer 2008): 13–33; Seema Sanghi, "Building Competencies," *Industrial Management* (May–June 2009): 14–17; B. Becker and M. Huselid, "High Performance Work Systems and Firm Performance: A Synthesis of Research and Managerial Implications," *Research in Personnel and Human Resources Management* 16 (1998): 53–101; S. Ramlall, "Measuring Human Resource Management's Effectiveness in Improving Performance,"

Human Resource Planning 26 (2003): 51; Mark A. Huselid, Susan E. Jackson, and Randall S. Schuler, "Technical and Strategic Human Resource Management Effectiveness as Determinants of Firm Performance," *Academy of Management Journal* 40, no. 1 (1997): 171–188; and John T. Delaney and Mark A. Huselid, "The Impact of Human Resource Management Practices on Perceptions of Organizational Performance," *Academy of Management Journal* 39, no. 4 (1996): 949–969.

11. James N. Baron and David M. Kreps, "Consistent Human Resource Practices," *California Management Review* 41, no. 3 (Spring 1999): 29–53.

12. Cynthia D. Fisher, "Current and Recurrent Challenges in HRM," *Journal of Management* 15 (1989): 157–180.

13. John W. Miller, "Wanted: Miners in Brazil for Anglo American," *The Wall Street Journal*, May 19, 2013, http://online.wsj.com/news/articles/SB10001424127887324582004578461171873348926 (accessed October 9, 2013).

14. Results of a McKinsey Consulting survey, reported in Leigh Branham, "Planning to Become an Employer of Choice," *Journal of Organizational Excellence* (Summer 2005): 57–68.

15. Floyd Kemske, "HR 2008: A Forecast Based on Our Exclusive Study," *Workforce* (January 1998): 46–60.

16. This discussion is based in part on Bohlander, Snell, and Sherman, *Managing Human Resources*, pp. 13–15; and Harry Scarbrough, "Recipe for Success," *People Management* (January 23, 2003): 22–25.

17. Susan Cantrell et al., "Measuring the Value of Human Capital Investments: The SAP Case," *Strategy & Leadership* 34, no. 2 (2006): 43–52.

18. Section 1604.1 of the EEOC Guidelines based on the Civil Rights Act of 1964, Title VII.

19. Reported in Jeff Green, "The Silencing of Sexual Harassment," *Bloomberg BusinessWeek* (November 21–27, 2011): 27–28.

20. Ibid.

21. Melanie Trottman, "For Angry Employees, Legal Cover for Rants," *The Wall Street Journal*, December 2, 2011, http://online.wsj.com/article/SB1000142405297020371070457704982809710332.html (accessed August 27, 2012).

22. Reported in D. T. Hall and P. H. Mirvis, "The New Protean Career: Psychological Success and the Path with a Heart," in D. T. Hall & Associates, *The Career Is Dead—Long Live the Career: A Relational Approach to Careers* (San Francisco: Jossey-Bass, 1995), pp. 15–45.

23. Phred Dvorak and Scott Thurm, "Slump Prods Firms to Seek New Compact with Workers," *The Wall Street Journal*, October 20, 2009.

24. Reid Hoffman, Ben Casnocha, and Chris Yeh, "Tours of Duty: The New Employer-Employee Compact," *Harvard Business Review* (June 2013): 49–58.

25. Ibid.

26. Lynda Gratton, as reported in Phyllis Korkki, "The Shifting Definition of Worker Loyalty," *The New York Times*, April 23, 2011, www.nytimes.com/2011/04/24/jobs/24search.html (accessed August 27, 2012).

27. Stephen Baker, "You're Fired—But Stay in Touch," *BusinessWeek* (May 4, 2009): 54–55.

28. Hoffman, Casnocha, and Yeh, "Tours of Duty: The New Employer-Employee Compact."

29. This discussion is based on Joe Light, "In Hiring, Firms Shine Images," *The Wall Street Journal*, May 16, 2011, B9; and Lauren Weber, "On the Hunt for Tech Hires," *The Wall Street Journal*, April 11, 2012, B6.

30. Weber, "On the Hunt for Tech Hires."

31. . Weber, "On the Hunt for Tech Hires"; and Light, "In Hiring, Firms Shine Images."

32. Statistics and quote from Charles Wilbanks, "Temp Work Raises Long-Term Questions for Economy," *CBS News Money Watch*, March 7, 2013, http://www.cbsnews.com/8301-505143_162-57573141/temp-work-raises-long-term-questions-for-economy/ (accessed October 10, 2013).

33. Motoko Rich, "Weighing Costs, Companies Favor Temporary Help," *The New York Times*, December 19, 2010, www.nytimes.com/2010/12/20/business/economy/20temp.html?pagewanted=all (accessed December 20, 2010).

34. Jody Greenstone Miller and Matt Miller, "The Best Executive and Professional Jobs May No Longer Be Full-Time Gigs," *Harvard Business Review* (May 2012): 51–62.

35. This example and the discussion are based on Sarah E. Needleman, "Start-Ups Get Snapped Up for Their Talent," *The Wall Street Journal*, September 13, 2012, B6.

36. James G. March and Herbert A. Simon, *Organizations* (New York: Wiley, 1958).

37. Dennis J. Kravetz, *The Human Resources Revolution* (San Francisco: Jossey-Bass, 1989).

38. J. W. Boudreau and S. L. Rynes, "Role of Recruitment in Staffing Utility Analysis," *Journal of Applied Psychology* 70 (1985): 354–366.

39. Megan Santosus, "The Human Capital Factor," *CFO-IT* (Fall 2005): 26–27.

40. Brian Dumaine, "The New Art of Hiring Smart," *Fortune* (August 17, 1987): 78–81.

41. This discussion is based on Mathis and Jackson, *Human Resource Management*, Chapter 4, pp. 49–60.

42. Victoria Griffith, "When Only Internal Expertise Will Do," *CFO* (October 1998): 95–96, 102.

43. J. P. Wanous, *Organizational Entry* (Reading, MA: Addison-Wesley, 1980).

44. Paul Shread, "Your Social Media Reputation Can Attract Employees," *Time*, March 1, 2013, http://business.time.com/2013/03/01/your-social-media-reputation-can-attract-employees/ (accessed October 10, 2013).

45. Kate Burrows, "British Army Launches Social Media Recruitment Campaign," *Chartered Management Institute*, May 22, 2013, http://www.managers.org.uk/news/british-army-launches-social-media-recruitment-campaign (accessed October 10, 2013); and Juro Osawa and Paul Mozur, "In China, Recruiting Gets Social," *The Wall Street Journal*, August 1, 2012, B4.

46. Osawa and Mozur, "In China, Recruiting Gets Social."

47. Kristin Burnham, "4 Recruiting Trends for Job Hunters, via LinkedIn," *InformationWeek*, July 17, 2013, http://www.informationweek.com/global-cio/recruiting/4-recruiting-trends-for-job-hunters-via/240158373 (accessed October 10, 2013); and George Anders, "Who Should You Hire? LinkedIn Says: Try Our Algorithm," *Forbes*, April 10, 2013, http://www.forbes.com/sites/georgeanders/2013/04/10/who-should-you-hire-linkedin-says-try-our-algorithm/ (accessed October 10, 2013).

48. Based on "United Nations New York Headquarters Internship Programme," www.un.org/depts/OHRM/sds/internsh/index.htm (accessed August 29, 2012); and Phyllis Korkki, "The Internship as Inside Track," *The New York Times*, March 25, 2011, www.nytimes.com/2011/03/27/jobs/27searches.html (accessed March 27, 2011).

49. "Silicon Valley's New Hiring Strategy," *Fast Company*, October 20, 2011, www.fastcompany.com/1784737/silicon-valleys-new-hiring-strategy (accessed August 29, 2012); Andrea Siedsma, "Alternative Recruiting Strategies Employed by Companies Vying for Top Tech Talent," *Workforce Management*, May 18, 2012, www.workforce.com/article/20120518/NEWS02/120519953/alternative-recruiting-strategies-employed-by-companies-vying-for-top (accessed August 27, 2012); and Adam Passey, "Code Foo 2013," IGN Web site, April 24, 2013, http://www.ign.com/blogs/adampassey-ign/2013/04/24/code-foo-2013 (accessed October 10, 2013).

50. Trudy Steinfeld, as reported in Korrki, "The Internship as Inside Track."

51. Wimbush, "Spotlight on Human Resource Management."

52. Paul W. Thayer, "Somethings Old, Somethings New," *Personnel Psychology* 30, no. 4 (Winter 1977): 513–524.

53. J. Ledvinka, *Federal Regulation of Personnel and Human Resource Management* (Boston: Kent, 1982); and *Civil Rights Act*, Title VII, Section 2000e *et seq.*, U.S. Code 42 (1964).

54. Research reported in Lauren Weber, "Tips on Acing Job Interviews—For Managers," *The Wall Street Journal*, December 5, 2012, B8.

55. Bohlander, Snell, and Sherman, *Managing Human Resources*, p. 202.

56. Tiffany Hsu, "Job Interviewing, to the Extreme," *Los Angeles Times*, February 19, 2012, http://articles.latimes.com/2012/feb/19/business/la-fi-extreme-interviewing-20120219 (accessed February 19, 2012).

57. Reported in Tomas Chamorro-Premuzic and Christopher Steinmetz, "The Perfect Hire," *Scientific American Mind* (July–August 2013): 43–47.

58. Susan Greco, "Sales & Marketing: He Can Close, but How Is His Interpersonal Sensitivity? Testing Sales Recruits," *Inc.* (March 2009): 96–98.

59. Reported in Chamorro-Premuzic and Steinmetz, "The Perfect Hire."

60. Joseph Walker, "Meet the New Boss: Big Data," *The Wall Street Journal*, September 20, 2012, http://online.wsj.com/news/articles/SB10000872396390443890304578006252019616768 (accessed October 10, 2013).

61. Reported in "Should You Check Facebook Before Hiring?" *Washington Post*, January 22, 2011, www.washingtonpost.com/wp-dyn/content/article/2011/01/22/AR2011012203193.html (accessed January 23, 2011); and CareerBuilder survey results reported in "Survey: 37% Use Social Media to Check Candidates," *Workforce Management*, April 18, 2012, www.workforce.com/article/20120418/NEWS01/120419964 (accessed June 19, 2012).

62. Adecco survey, reported in Jenna Goudreau, "Top 5 Interview Mistakes Millennials Make," *Forbes*, September 26, 2012, http://www.forbes.com/sites/jennagoudreau/2012/09/26/top-5-interview-mistakes-millennials-make/ (accessed October 10, 2013).

63. Reported in "Should You Check Facebook Before Hiring?"

64. Quote and information reported in Stephen Bruce, "Social Media Background Checks? 'I'm Not a Fan,'" *HR Policies and Procedures*, March 11, 2013, http://hrdailyadvisor.blr.com/2013/03/11/social-media-background-checks-i-m-not-a-fan/# (accessed October 10, 2013).

65. China Gorman, "Recruiting and Social Networking: SHRM Research Shows a Few Surprises," TLNT.com, May 1, 2013, http://www.tlnt.com/2013/05/01/recruiting-and-social-networking-shrm-research-shows-a-few-surprises/ (accessed October 10, 2013).

66. Bernard Keys and Joseph Wolfe, "Management Education and Development: Current Issues and Emerging Trends," *Journal of Management* 14 (1988): 205–229.

67. "2012 Training Industry Report," *Training* (November–December 2012): 20–33.

68. Rohit Deshpandé and Anjali Raina, "The Ordinary Heroes of the Taj," *Harvard Business Review* (December 2011): 119–123; and "Building an Institution Through Human Values," *Shanmugam's Blog*, January 22, 2012, http://cgshanmugam.wordpress.com/2012/01/22/building-an-institution-through-human-values/ (accessed October 10, 2013).

69. "How Do Great Companies Groom Talent?" *Fortune* (November 21, 2011): 166.

70. Kate Linebaugh, "The New GE Way: Go Deep, Not Wide," *The Wall Street Journal*, March 7, 2012, B1.

71. William J. Rothwell and H. C. Kazanas, *Improving On-the-Job Training: How to Establish and Operate a Comprehensive OJT Program* (San Francisco: Jossey-Bass, 1994).

72. Matt Allen and Jennifer Naughton, "Social Learning: A Call to Action for Learning Professionals," *T+D* (August 2011): 50–55.

73. Reported in Margaret Schweer et al., "Building a Well-Networked Organization," *MIT Sloan Management Review* (Winter 2012): 35–42.

74. Jeanne C. Meister, "The Brave New World of Corporate Education," *The Chronicle of Higher Education* (February 9, 2001): B10; and Meryl Davids Landau, "Corporate Universities Crack Open Their Doors," *The Journal of Business Strategy* (May–June 2000): 18–23.

75. Janet Wiscombe, "McDonald's Corp." *Workforce Management* (November 2010): 38–40.

76. Lauren Weber, "Managing & Careers: Fine-Tuning the Perfect Employee," *The Wall Street Journal*, December 5, 2011, B9.

77. Jim Dow, "Spa Attraction," *People Management* (May 29, 2003): 34–35.

78. "Talent Tutor: Ram Charan's List of Biggest Corporate Talent-Management Mistakes," sidebar in Joann S. Lublin, "Managing & Careers—Boss Talk; Ram Charan: Message to CEOs: Do More to Keep Your Key Employees," *The Wall Street Journal*, December 27, 2010, B5.

79. Survey by HR consulting firm Watson Wyatt, reported in Kelley Holland, "Performance Reviews: Many Need Improvement," *The New York Times*, September 10, 2006.

80. Jesse W. Brogan, "Problem Appraisal Systems," *Industrial Management* (September–October 2012): 24–27; Herman Aquinis, Ryan K. Gottfredson, and Harry Joo, "Using Performance Management to Win the Talent War," *Business Horizons* 55 (2012): 609–616.

81. Kyle Couch, "Talent Management: Build on Four Key Components," *Leadership Excellence* (February 2012): 18; Walter W. Tornow, "Editor's Note: Introduction to Special Issue on 360-Degree Feedback," *Human Resource Management* 32, no. 2–3 (Summer–Fall 1993): 211–219; and Brian O'Reilly, "360 Feedback Can Change Your Life," *Fortune* (October 17, 1994): 93–100.

82. Jena McGregor, "Job Review in 140 Keystrokes," *BusinessWeek* (March 23 & 30, 2009): 58.

83. This discussion is based on Dick Grote, "Forced Ranking: Behind the Scenes," *Across the Board* (November–December 2002): 40–45; Matthew Boyle, "Performance Reviews: Perilous Curves Ahead," *Fortune* (May 28, 2001): 187–188; Carol Hymowitz, "Ranking Systems Gain Popularity but Have Many Staffers Riled," *The Wall Street Journal*, May 15, 2001; and Kris Frieswick, "Truth and Consequences," *CFO* (June 2001): 56–63.

84. "Forced Ranking (Forced Distribution)," *HR Management* Web site, www.humanresources.hrvinet.com/forced-ranking-forced-distribution/ (accessed January 21, 2012); and Leslie Kwoh, "'Rank and Yank' Retains Vocal Fans," *The Wall Street Journal*, January 31, 2012.

85. V. R. Buzzotta, "Improve Your Performance Appraisals," *Management Review* (August 1988): 40–43; and H. J. Bernardin and R. W. Beatty, *Performance Appraisal: Assessing Human Behavior at Work* (Boston: Kent, 1984).

86. Richard I. Henderson, *Compensation Management: Rewarding Performance*, 4th ed. (Reston, VA: Reston, 1985).

87. L. R. Gomez-Mejia, "Structure and Process Diversification, Compensation Strategy, and Firm Performance," *Strategic Management Journal* 13 (1992): 381–397; and E. Montemayor, "Congruence Between Pay Policy and Competitive Strategy in High-Performing Firms," *Journal of Management* 22, no. 6 (1996): 889–908.

88. Renée F. Broderick and George T. Milkovich, "Pay Planning, Organization Strategy, Structure and 'Fit': A Prescriptive Model of Pay," paper presented at the 45th Annual Meeting of the Academy of Management, San Diego (August 1985).

89. Rachel Dodes and Dana Mattioli, "Theory & Practice: Retailers Try on New Sales Tactics," *The Wall Street Journal*, April 19, 2010, B9.

90. E. F. Lawler, III, *Strategic Pay: Aligning Organizational Strategies and Pay Systems* (San Francisco: Jossey-Bass, 1990); and R. J. Greene, "Person-Focused Pay: Should It Replace Job-Based Pay?" *Compensation and Benefits Management* 9, no. 4 (1993): 46–55.

91. L. Wiener, "No New Skills? No Raise," *U.S. News and World Report* (October 26, 1992): 78.

92. Reported in Rachel Emma Silverman, "Big Data Upends the Way Workers Are Paid," *The Wall Street Journal*, September 19, 2012, http://online.wsj.com/news/articles/SB10000872396390444433504577651741900453730 (accessed September 20, 2012).

93. Alan S. Blinder, "Crazy Compensation and the Crisis," *The Wall Street Journal*, May 28, 2009.

94. Janet Wiscombe, "SAS," *Workforce Management* (October 2010): 36–38; Martha Mendoza, "Tech Firms Bumping Up Perks to Recruit, Retain," *USA Today*, April 7, 2013.

95. Joe Walker, "Even with a Recovery, Job Perks May Not Return," *The Wall Street Journal Online*, April 5, 2010, http://online.wsj.com/article/SB10001424052702304017404575165854181296256.html (accessed April 10, 2010).

96. Lauren Weber, "What Makes Employees Stick Around? One Company Has an Answer," *The Wall Street Journal*, June 10, 2013, http://blogs.wsj.com/atwork/2013/06/10/what-makes-employees-stick-around-one-company-has-an-answer/ (accessed October 11, 2013).

97. U.S. Department of Labor, Bureau of Labor Statistics, press release, September 6, 2013, http://www.bls.gov/news.release/pdf/empsit.pdf (accessed October 11, 2013).

98. James R. Morris, Wayne F. Cascio, and Clifford Young, "Downsizing After All These Years: Questions and Answers About Who Did It, How Many Did It, and Who Benefited from It," *Organizational Dynamics* (Winter 1999): 78–86; William McKinley, Carol M. Sanchez, and Allen G. Schick, "Organizational Downsizing: Constraining, Cloning, Learning," *Academy of Management Executive* 9, no. 3 (1995): 32–42; and Brett C. Luthans and Steven M. Sommer, "The Impact of Downsizing on Workplace Attitudes," *Group and Organization Management* 2, no. 1 (1999): 46–70.

99. Effective downsizing techniques are discussed in detail in Bob Nelson, "The Care of the Un-Downsized," *Training and Development* (April 1997): 40–43; Shari Caudron, "Teaching Downsizing Survivors How to Thrive," *Personnel Journal* (January 1996): 38; Joel Brockner, "Managing the Effects of Layoffs on Survivors," *California Management Review* (Winter 1992): 9–28; and Kim S. Cameron, "Strategies for Successful Organizational Downsizing," *Human Resource Management* 33, no. 2 (Summer 1994): 189–211.

100. Scott Westcott, "Goodbye and Good Luck," *Inc.* (April 2006): 40–42.

101. Adam Bryant, "There's No Need to Bat .900" (Corner Office column, an interview with John Donahoe), *The New York Times*, April 5, 2009.

102. Nanette Byrnes, "Star Search," *BusinessWeek* (October 10, 2005): 68–78.

103. Mike Brewster, "No Exit," *Fast Company* (April 2005): 93.

104. Laura Stevens, "Deutsche Bank Lags on Its Gender Pledge," *The Wall Street Journal*, April 29, 2013, C1.

105. Steven Greenhouse, "Lawsuit Claims Race Bias at Wet Seal Retail Chain," *The New York Times*, July 12, 2012, http://www.nytimes.com/2012/07/13/business/wet-seal-accused-of-racial-bias-by-3-ex-managers.html?_r=0 (accessed May 8, 2013).

106. Quoted in Susan Caminiti, "The Diversity Factor," *Fortune* (October 19, 2007): 95–105.

107. Caminiti, "The Diversity Factor."

108. Yair Holtzman and Johan Anderberg, "Diversify Your Teams and Collaborate: Because Great Minds Don't Think Alike," *Journal of Management Development* 30, no. 1 (2011): 75–92.

109. Lynn M. Shore et al., "Inclusion and Diversity in Work Groups: A Review and Model for Future Research," *Journal of Management* 37, no. 4 (July 2011): 1262–1289.

110. Taylor H. Cox, "Managing Cultural Diversity: Implications for Organizational Competitiveness," *Academy of Management Executive* 5, no. 3 (1991): 45–56; and Faye Rice, "How to Make Diversity Pay," *Fortune* (August 8, 1994): 78–86.

111. Rawn Shah, "Working with Five Generations in the Workplace," *Forbes.com*, April 20, 2011, www.forbes.com/sites/rawnshah/2011/04/20/working-with-five-generations-in-the-workplace/ (accessed August 9, 2012); and Jeanne Meister and Karie Willyerd, *The 2020 Workplace* (New York: HarperCollins 2010).

112. "Generations in the Workplace in the United States and Canada," Catalyst.org, May 2012, www.catalyst.org/publication/434/generations-in-the-workplace-in-the-united-states-canada (accessed August 9, 2012); Lisa Beyer et al., "Workforce 90th Anniversary: Workforce Management Looks Back at Workplace History," *Workforce.com*, July 2, 2012, www.workforce.com/article/20120702/WORKFORCE90/120629967/1066/newsletter01 (accessed August 9, 2012); and Shah, "Working with Five Generations in the Workplace."

113. *Occupational Outlook Handbook, Bureau of Labor Statistics*, www.bls.gov/ooh/about/projections-overview.htm#laborforce (accessed June 29, 2012).

114. "Foreign-Born Workers and Labor Force Characteristics: 2011," *United States Labor Department Bureau of Labor Statistics*, www.bls.gov/news.release/pdf/forbrn.pdf (accessed June 29, 2012).

115. *Occupational Outlook Handbook*, Bureau of Labor Statistics.

116. Joann S. Lublin and Kelly Eggers, "More Women Are Primed to Land CEO Roles," *The Wall Street Journal Online*, April 30, 2012, http://online.wsj.com/article/SB10001424052702303990604577368344256435440.html (accessed June 29, 2012).

117. Ann Zimmerman, "U.S. Charges Bass Pro Shops with Racial Bias," *The Wall Street Journal*, September 22, 2011, B1–B2.

118. Giada Zampano, "Italy to Push Pink Quotas," *The Wall Street Journal Online*, June 5, 2012, https://www.google.com/search?sourceid=navclient&aq=0&oq=italy+to+push&ie=UTF-8&rlz=1T4ADRA_enUS426US427&q=italy+to+push+'pink+quotes'&gs_upl=0l0l0l4406l1l1l1l1l1l1l0&aqi=g4&

pbx=1 (accessed July 2, 2012); Katrin Bennhold, "Women Nudged out of German Workforce," *The New York Times Online*, June 28, 2011, www.nytimes.com/2011/06/29/world/europe/29iht-FFgermany29.html?pagewanted=all.

119. Zampano, "Italy to Push Pink Quotas."

120. Mariko Sanchanta, "Japan's Women Reach Job Milestones," *The Wall Street Journal*, July 14, 2010, A15.

121. Hiroka Tabuchi, "Leading in 3-D TV, Breaking Japan's Glass Ceiling," *The New York Times Online*, January 17, 2011, www.nytimes.com/2011/01/18/business/global/18screen.html?pagewanted=all (accessed July 3, 2012).

122. Richard L. Daft, *The Leadership Experience* (Cincinnati, OH: Cengage Learning, 2008), p. 340.

123. Holtzman and Anderberg, "Diversify Your Teams and Collaborate."

124. Michael L. Wheeler, "Diversity: Business Rationale and Strategies," The Conference Board, Report No. 1130-95-RR, 1995, p. 25.

125. Anthony Oshiotse and Richard O'Leary, "Corning Creates an Inclusive Culture to Drive Technology Innovation and Performance," Wiley InterScience, *Global Business and Organizational Excellence* 26, no. 3 (March April 2007): 7–21.

126. "When CEOs Drive Diversity, Everybody Wins," *Chief Executive*, July 2005, www.chiefexecutive.net/ME2/dirmod.asp?sid=&nm=&type=Publishing&mod=Publications%3A%3AArticle&mid=8F3A7027421841978F18BE895F87F791&tier=4&id=201D3B11B9D4419893E78DDA4B7ACDC8 (accessed September 21, 2010).

127. Shore et al., "Inclusion and Diversity in Work Groups."

128. Martin N. Davidson, "The End of Diversity: How Leaders Make Differences Really Matter," *Leader to Leader* (Spring 2012): 51–55.

129. Taylor Cox, Jr., and Ruby L. Beale, *Developing Competency to Manage Diversity* (San Francisco: Berrett-Koehler Publishers, Inc., 1997), p. 2.

130. Reported in Marjorie Derven, "The Competitive Advantage of Diverse Perspectives," *T+D* (August 2013): 45–48.

131. Holtzman and Anderberg, "Diversify Your Teams and Collaborate." Thomas E. Poulin, "The Other Diversity," *PA Times, American Society for Public Administration* (March 2009): 8; and Clayton H. Osborne and Vincent M. Cramer, "Fueling High Performance Through Diversity," *Chief Learning Officer* (November 2005): 22.

132. Anita Woolley and Thomas Malone, "What Makes a Team Smarter? More Women," *Harvard Business Review* (June 2011): 32–33; and Peter Gwynne, "Group Intelligence, Teamwork, and Productivity," *Research-Technology Management* 55, no. 2 (March–April 2012): 7–8

133. Thomas Barta, Markus Kleiner, and Tilo Neumann, "Is There a Payoff from Top-Team Diversity?" *McKinsey Quarterly*, Issue 2 (April 2012): 13–15.

134. Herminia Ibarra and Morten T. Hansen, "Are You a Collaborative Leader?" *Harvard Business Review* (July–August 2011): 69–74.

135. Gail Robinson and Kathleen Dechant, "Building a Business Case for Diversity," *Academy of Management Executive* 11, no. 3 (1997): 21–31.

136. Sonie Alleyne and Nicole Marie Richardson, "The 40 Best Companies for Diversity," *Black Enterprise* 36, no. 12 (July 2006): 15.

137. Robinson and Dechant, "Building a Business Case for Diversity."

138. Ibid.

139. Frederick E. Allen, "Lack of Diversity Paralyzed the CIA. It Can Cripple Your Organization Too," *Forbes*, April 26, 2012, www.forbes.com/sites/frederickallen/2012/04/26/lack-of-diversity-paralyzed-the-cia-it-can-cripple-your-organization-too/ (accessed July 19, 2012).

140. CIA Web site, https://www.cia.gov/careers/diversity/directors-diversity-commitment.html (accessed July 19, 2012).

141. Quoted in Carol Hymowitz, "Coaching Men on Mentoring Women Is Ernst & Young Partner's Mission," *The Wall Street Journal Online*, June 14, 2007, http://online.wsj.com/article/SB118167178575132768search.html (accessed July 9, 2007).

142. Kris Maher, "Lockheed Settles Racial-Discrimination Suit," *The Wall Street Journal*, January 3, 2008.

143. Norma Carr-Ruffino, *Managing Diversity: People Skills for a Multicultural Workplace* (Tucson, AZ: Thomson Executive Press, 1996), p. 92.

144. Quoted in Colleen McCain Nelson, "Poll: Most Women See Bias in the Workplace," *The Wall Street Journal*, April 12, 2013, p. A4.

145. Reported in Roy Harris, "The Illusion of Inclusion," *CFO* (May 2001): 42–50.

146. Studies by Victoria Brescoll, reported in Leslie Kwoh, "News & Trends: Talkative Women Lose at Work, Study Says," *The Wall Street Journal*, May 16, 2012, B8; and in Selena Rezvani, "What's Wrong with Research About Female Bosses," *Washington Post*, June 4, 2013, http://www.washingtonpost.com/blogs/on-leadership/wp/2013/06/04/whats-wrong-with-research-about-female-bosses/ (accessed October 15, 2013).

147. Carr-Ruffino, *Managing Diversity*, pp. 98–99.

148. Based on an interview with PepsiCo chairman and CEO Indra Nooyi, in Rebecca Blumenstein, "View from the Top," *The Wall Street Journal*, April 11, 2011, R9.

149. Cox and Beale, "Developing Competency to Manage Diversity," p. 79.

150. Ibid., pp. 80–81.

151. Ibid.

152. Loriann Roberson and Carol T. Kulik, "Stereotype Threat at Work," *Academy of Management Perspectives* 21, no. 2 (May 2007): 25–27.

153. Ibid., 26.

154. Robert Doktor, Rosalie Tung, and Mary Ann von Glinow, "Future Directions for Management Theory Development," *Academy of Management Review* 16 (1991): 362–365; and Mary Munter, "Cross-Cultural Communication for Managers," *Business Horizons* (May–June 1993): 69–78.

155. Renee Blank and Sandra Slipp, "The White Male: An Endangered Species?" *Management Review* (September 1994): 27–32; Michael S. Kimmel, "What Do Men Want?" *Harvard Business Review* (November–December 1993):

50–63; and Sharon Nelton, "Nurturing Diversity," *Nation's Business* (June 1995): 25–27.

156. Jim Carlton, "Dig In," *The Wall Street Journal,* November 14, 2005; Tony DiRomualdo, "Is Google's Cafeteria a Competitive Weapon?" *Wisconsin Technology Network,* August 30, 2005, http://wistechnology.com/article.php?id=2190 (accessed August 31, 2005); and Marc Ramirez, "Tray Chic: At Work, Cool Cafeterias, Imaginative Menus," *The Seattle Times*, November 21, 2005, http://seattletimes.nwsource.com/html/living/2002634266_cafés21.html?pageid=display-in-thenews.module&pageregion=itnbody (accessed November 22, 2005).

157. Georges Desvaux, Sandrine Devillard-Hoellinger, and Mary C. Meaney, "A Business Case for Women," *The McKinsey Quarterly: The Online Journal of McKinsey & Co.*, September 2008, www.mckinseyquarterly.com/A_business_case_for_women_2192 (accessed June 17, 2010).

158. Joanna Barsh and Lareina Yee, "Changing Companies' Minds About Women," *McKinsey Quarterly Online*, September 2011, www.mckinsey.com/careers/women/~/media/Reports/Women/Changing_companies_minds_about_women.ashx (accessed June 29, 2012).

159. Hanna Rosin, "The End of Men," *The Atlantic*, July/August 2010, www.theatlantic.com/magazine/print/2010/07/the-end-of-men/8135/ (accessed July 9, 2012).

160. Jenny M. Hoobler, Grace Lemmon, and Sandy J. Wayne, "Women's Underrepresentation in Upper Management: New Insights on a Persistent Problem," *Organizational Dynamics* 40 (2011): 151–156.

161. John Bussey, "How Women Can Get Ahead: Advice from Female CEOs," *The Wall Street Journal Online*, May 18, 2012, http://online.wsj.com/article/SB10001424052702303879604577410520511235252.html (accessed July 8, 2012).

162. Jane Hyun, "Leadership Principles for Capitalizing on Culturally Diverse Teams: The Bamboo Ceiling Revisited," *Leader to Leader* (Spring 2012): 14–19.

163. Ken Auletta, "A Woman's Place," *The New Yorker* (July 11 and 18, 2011): 55–63.

164. Peggy Klaus, "Don't Fret. Just Ask for What You Need," *The New York Times*, July 9, 2011, www.nytimes.com/2011/07/10/jobs/10pre.html (accessed July 8, 2012).

165. Quoted in Bussey, "How Women Can Get Ahead: Advice from Female CEOs."

166. Marie-Helene Budworth and Sara L. Mann, "Becoming a Leader: The Challenge of Modesty for Women," *Journal of Management Development* 29, no. 2 (2010): 177–186.

167. Sylvia Ann Hewlett and Carolyn Buck Luce, "Off-Ramps and On-Ramps: Keeping Talented Women on the Road to Success," *Harvard Business Review* (March 2005): 43–54.

168. Lisa Belkin, "The Opt-Out Revolution," *The New York Times Magazine* (October 26, 2002): 43–47, 58.

169. Jodi Kantor, "Elite Women Put a New Spin on an Old Debate," *The New York Times*, June 21, 2012, www.nytimes.com/2012/06/22/us/elite-women-put-a-new-spin-on-work-life-debate.html (accessed July 9, 2012); Anne-Marie Slaughter, "Why Women Still Can't Have It All," *The Atlantic*, July–August 2012, www.theatlantic.com/magazine/archive/2012/07/why-women-still-cant-have-it-all/309020/ (accessed October 15, 2012).

170. C. J. Prince, "Media Myths: The Truth About the Opt-Out Hype," *NAFE Magazine* (Second Quarter 2004): 14–18; Patricia Sellers, "Power: Do Women Really Want It?" *Fortune* (October 13, 2003): 80–100.

171. Jia Lynn Yang, "Goodbye to All That," *Fortune* (November 14, 2005): 169–170.

172. Sheila Wellington, Marcia Brumit Kropf, and Paulette R. Gerkovich, "What's Holding Women Back?" *Harvard Business Review* (June 2003): 18–19.

173. The Leader's Edge/Executive Women Research 2002 survey, reported in "Why Women Leave," *Executive Female* (Summer 2003): 4.

174. Barbara Reinhold, "Smashing Glass Ceilings: Why Women Still Find It Tough to Advance to the Executive Suite," *Journal of Organizational Excellence* (Summer 2005): 43–55; Jory Des Jardins, "I Am Woman (I Think)," *Fast Company* (May 2005): 25–26; and Alice H. Eagly and Linda L. Carli, "The Female Leadership Advantage: An Evaluation of the Evidence," *The Leadership Quarterly* 14 (2003): 807–834.

175. Various studies and surveys reported in Peggy Drexler, "The Tyranny of the Queen Bee," *The Wall Street Journal*, March 2, 2013, C1.

176. Eagly and Carli, "The Female Leadership Advantage"; Reinhold, "Smashing Glass Ceilings"; Sally Helgesen, *The Female Advantage: Women's Ways of Leadership* (New York: Doubleday Currency, 1990); Rochelle Sharpe, "As Leaders, Women Rule: New Studies Find that Female Managers Outshine Their Male Counterparts in Almost Every Measure," *BusinessWeek* (November 20, 2000): 5ff; and Del Jones, "2003: Year of the Woman Among the *Fortune* 500?" *USA TODAY*, December 30, 2003.

177. Tamar Lewin, "At Colleges, Women Are Leaving Men in the Dust," *The New York Times Online,* July 9, 2006, www.nytimes.com/2006/07/09/education/09college.html?_r=1&scp=1&sq=at%20colleges,%20women%20are%20leaving%20men%20in%20the%20dust&st=cse&oref=slogin (accessed March 13, 2008).

178. Michelle Conlin, "The New Gender Gap," *BusinessWeek* (May 26, 2003): 74–82.

179. Quoted in Conlin, "The New Gender Gap."

180. Kathryn M. Bartol, David C. Martin, and Julie A. Kromkowski, "Leadership and the Glass Ceiling: Gender and Ethnic Group Influences on Leader Behaviors at Middle and Executive Managerial Levels," *Journal of Leadership and Organizational Studies* 9, no. 3 (2003): 8–19; Bernard M. Bass and Bruce J. Avolio, "Shatter the Glass Ceiling: Women May Make Better Managers," *Human Resource Management* 33, no. 4 (Winter 1994): 549–560; and Sharpe, "As Leaders, Women Rule."

181. Dwight D. Frink et al., "Gender Demography and Organization Performance: A Two-Study Investigation with Convergence," *Group & Organization Management* 28, no. 1 (March 2003): 127–147; Catalyst research project cited in Reinhold, "Smashing Glass Ceilings."

182. "Sexual Harassment: Vanderbilt University Policy" (Nashville: Vanderbilt University, 1993).

183. Julie Watson and Elliot Spagat, "Bob Filner Resigns: San Diego Mayor Agrees to Step Down Amid Sexual Harassment Scandal," *Associated Press*, August 23, 2013, http://www.huffingtonpost.com/2013/08/23/san-diego-mayor-bob-filner-resigns-sexual-harass_n_3807073.html (accessed October 17, 2013); and Tamara Audi, "San Diego Mayor Bob Filner to Resign amid Sexual-Harassment Scandal," *The Wall Street Journal*, August 23, 2013, http://online.wsj.com/news/articles/SB10001424127887323366550457903142395252220 (accessed October 17, 2013).

184. Adapted from the Tolerance Scale by Maria Heiselman, Naomi Miller, and Bob Schlorman, Northern Kentucky University, 1982. In George Manning, Kent Curtis, and Steve McMillen, *Building Community: The Human Side of Work* (Cincinnati, OH: Thomson Executive Press, 1996), pp. 272–277.

185. Based on Linda Tischler, "IBM's Management Makeover," *Fast Company*, November 1, 2004, www.fastcompany.com/51673/ibms-management-makeover (accessed November 26, 2012); and www.zurich.ibm.com/employment/environment.html (accessed September 13, 2010).

186. Based on Rob Johnson, "30 Muslim Workers Fired for Praying on Job at Dell," *The Tennessean*, March 10, 2005; Anayat Durrani, "Religious Accommodation for Muslim Employees," *Workforce.com*, www.workforce.com/archive/feature/religious-accommodation-muslim-employees/index.php (accessed September 21, 2010); "Questions and Answers About Employer Responsibilities Concerning the Employment of Muslims, Arabs, South Asians, and Sikhs," the U.S. Equal Employment Opportunity Commission, www.eeoc.gov/facts/backlash-employer.html (accessed September 20, 2010); and "2006 Household Appliance Industry Outlook," U.S. Department of Commerce, International Trade Administration, www.ita.doc.gov/td/ocg/outlook06_appliances.pdf (accessed September 21, 2010).

CHAPTER
10 Understanding Individual Behavior

LEARNING OUTCOMES

After studying this chapter, you should be able to:

10.1 Explain why understanding yourself is essential for being a good manager, and describe two methods for enhancing self-awareness.

10.2 Discuss the importance of job satisfaction and trust for effective employee performance.

10.3 Describe the perception process and explain internal and external attributions.

10.4 Define major personality traits and describe how personality can influence workplace behaviors.

10.5 Identify positive and negative emotions and describe how emotions affect behavior.

10.6 Define the four components of emotional intelligence and explain why they are important for today's managers.

10.7 Outline a step-by-step system for managing yourself and your time.

10.8 Explain the difference between challenge stress and threat stress.

10.9 Identify ways individuals and organizations can manage stress to improve employee health, satisfaction, and productivity.

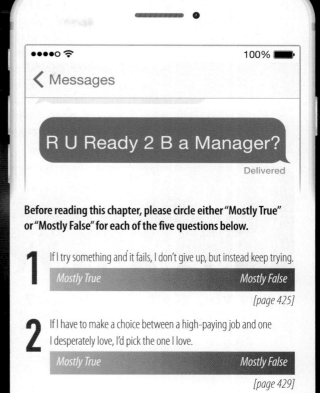

●●●●○ 🛜   100% 🔋

‹ Messages

R U Ready 2 B a Manager?

Delivered

Before reading this chapter, please circle either "Mostly True" or "Mostly False" for each of the five questions below.

1 If I try something and it fails, I don't give up, but instead keep trying.

Mostly True	Mostly False

[page 425]

2 If I have to make a choice between a high-paying job and one I desperately love, I'd pick the one I love.

Mostly True	Mostly False

[page 429]

3 I try and make a distinction between fact and opinion when I am making decisions.

Mostly True	Mostly False

[page 431]

4 I am aware of my personality strengths and I try not to judge people on their "goodness" as being similar to my own personality.

Mostly True	Mostly False

[page 434]

5 If I fail a test, I often think that the teacher was unfair in the grading.

Mostly True	Mostly False

[page 436]

IBM's first female CEO, Virginia M. Rometty, says she learned an important lesson early in her career. Rometty was offered a big job, but she felt that she didn't have enough experience. So she told the recruiter that she needed time to think it over. Later, Rometty's husband asked her, "Do you think a man would have ever answered that question that way?" The lesson that Rometty learned, she says, was that "you have to be very confident, even though you're so self-critical inside about what it is you may or may not know." Managers can accomplish significant results—and advance in their careers—only when they have the self-confidence to take risks and push beyond their comfort zones. Rometty spent 30 years at IBM, rising through the ranks until being named CEO in 2011.[1]

Naturally, when people take risks, they sometimes fail, but many people who have accomplished great outcomes give credit to their previous failures for driving them to

NEW MANAGER Self-Test

Are You Self-Confident?

Instructions: Self-confidence is the foundation for many important behaviors of a new manager. To learn something about your level of self-confidence, answer the following questions. Please answer whether each item is Mostly True or Mostly False for you.

	Mostly True	Mostly False
1. I have lots of confidence in my decisions.	_____	_____
2. I would like to change some things about myself.	_____	_____
3. I am satisfied with my appearance and personality.	_____	_____
4. I would be nervous about meeting important people.	_____	_____
5. I come across as a positive person.	_____	_____
6. I sometimes think of myself as a failure.	_____	_____
7. I am able to do things as well as most people.	_____	_____
8. I find it difficult to believe nice things someone says about me.	_____	_____

Scoring and Interpretation: Many good things come from self-confidence. How self-confident are you? Give yourself one point for each odd-numbered item above marked as Mostly True and one point for each even-numbered item marked Mostly False. If you scored 3 or less, your self-confidence may not be very high. You might want to practice new behavior in problematic areas to develop greater confidence. A score of 6 or above suggests a high level of self-confidence and a solid foundation on which to begin your career as a new manager.

If a new manager lacks self-confidence, he or she is more likely to avoid difficult decisions and confrontations and may tend to overcontrol subordinates, which is called micromanaging. A lack of self-confidence also leads to less sharing of information and less time hiring and developing capable people. Self-confident managers, by contrast, can more easily delegate responsibility, take risks, give credit to others, confront problems, and assert themselves for the good of their team.

succeed. Consider billionaire author J. K. Rowling, whose first *Harry Potter* book was rejected by 12 publishers before Bloomsbury bought it for the equivalent of $4,000. In her 2008 commencement speech to the graduating class at Harvard University, Rowling recounted how setbacks and rejection had not discouraged her, but simply made her stronger.[2] Unlike J. K. Rowling and Virginia Rometty, there are many talented individuals who experience one defeat or discouragement and never try again.[3]

What makes the difference? Psychologists suggest it comes down to a characteristic called *self-efficacy*. It is one of the many ways in which individuals differ, along with their personality traits, attitudes, emotions, and values. **Self-efficacy** is an individual's strong belief that he or she can accomplish a specific task or outcome successfully.[4] Self-efficacy is one dimension of **self-confidence**, which refers to general assurance in one's own ideas, judgment, and capabilities. Personality traits, emotions, and characteristics such as self-confidence and self-efficacy influence how people behave, including how they handle work situations and relate to others.

10.1 Understanding Yourself and Others

Having insight into why people behave the way they do is a part of good management. People bring their individual differences to work each day, and these differences influence how they interpret assignments, whether they like to be told what to do, how they handle challenges, and how they interact with others. By increasing their understanding of individual differences, as described throughout this chapter, managers can learn how to get the best out of each employee and more effectively lead people through workplace challenges. However, the first requirement for being a good manager is understanding oneself. Managers' characteristics and behavior can profoundly affect the workplace and influence employee motivation, morale, and job performance.

10.1a The Value and Difficulty of Knowing Yourself

A survey of 75 members of the Stanford Graduate School of Business's Advisory Council revealed the nearly unanimous answer to a question about the most important capability for leaders to develop: self-awareness.[5] Self-awareness means being aware of the internal aspects of one's nature, such as personality traits, beliefs, emotions, and perceptions, and appreciating how your patterns affect other people. Most management experts agree that a primary characteristic of effective leaders is that they know who they are and what they stand for.[6] When managers deeply understand themselves, they remain grounded and constant. People know what to expect from them. As one employee put it, "... it's like they have a stick down through the center of them that's rooted in the ground."[7]

Yet developing self-awareness is easier said than done. Consider Charlotte Beers, former chairwoman and CEO of Ogilvy & Mather Worldwide, who now conducts seminars for women leaders. When Beers first became a management supervisor, she considered herself to be a friendly, approachable, easygoing leader. She was shocked when a friend told her that one of her colleagues described her management style as "menacing." That comment was devastating to Beers because it was the exact opposite of the way she thought of herself.[8] Many of us, like Beers, might be surprised to find out what others honestly think about us. Most of us don't take the time to think about who we really are or the effect our patterns of thought and behavior have on others. To be a good manager, such self-reflection is essential.

10.1b Enhancing Your Self-Awareness

There are a number of ways that people can increase their understanding of themselves. Two important approaches to enhancing self-awareness, as shown in Exhibit 10.1, are soliciting feedback from others and using self-assessments.

Soliciting Feedback   Just as we use a mirror in the mornings to shave or fix our hair, we can use other people as a mirror to see ourselves more clearly.[9] A manager might consider himself to be patient and understanding, but his employees may see that he is easily irritated and unsympathetic. Francisco D'Souza, CEO of Cognizant Technology Solutions Corporation, worked with a coach who talked to people who worked with and for him. "It was difficult feedback," D'Souza says, "but very enlightening. That helped me identify a couple of my blind spots." Many people have blind spots—attributes about themselves that they are not aware of or don't recognize as problems—which limit their effectiveness and hinder their career success.[10] D'Souza learned that people had confidence in his ability but felt that he was harsh in his criticism. "It made me understand that the weight of my words was a lot heavier than I gave myself credit for, and it led me to be much more thoughtful and measured in how I give feedback," he said.[11] When we go through life without feedback, we're like the balding man who sweeps thin strands of hair across his scalp and thinks

EXHIBIT 10.1   Two Keys to Self-Awareness

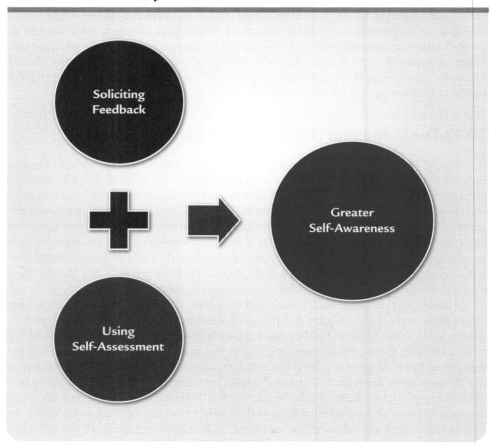

no one notices. Seeking feedback to enhance self-awareness can improve performance and job satisfaction for both managers and employees.[12] We all have illusions about ourselves, so we need help from others to get a clear picture of who we are.

Self-Assessment   Another highly valuable way to increase self-awareness is *self-assessment*, which uses self-inquiry and reflection to gain insights into oneself from the results of scores on self-assessment instruments such as those throughout this text. By completing these assessments as honestly as possible, you can analyze your scores and increase your under-standing of various aspects of yourself. Some managers, including Stuart McClure, who left a job as chief technology officer at McAfee to start information security company Cylance, go through assessment exercises administered by Development Dimensions International (DDI) and other consulting firms to learn about aspects of themselves. McClure learned that he has great strengths in getting things done, but that he tends to take on too much and be impatient when interrupted with people or ideas outside his immediate interest. "I have to slow myself down," he says.[13]

Self-assessment also means regularly reflecting on our thoughts and feelings. Introspection—reflecting on our experiences, examining the effects of our actions and behavior, looking at the consequences for ourselves and others, and asking, "What can I learn?" is a valuable use of time that too many managers overlook. Some people keep a journal, meditate, or just sit quietly and think through their day.[14] Major League Soccer star Landon Donovan used both feedback and introspection to increase his understanding of himself and improve his life and relationships, as described in the following example.

Not everyone wants to engage in therapy, as Landon Donovan did, but forms of intro-spection and feedback can help each of us benefit by learning more about ourselves. When a manager understands himself or herself, the manager is better able to understand and interact effectively with others.

Spotlight on Skills

Landon Donovan, U.S. Soccer Player

At the height of his career, Landon Donovan walked away from the sport he loved. Donovan holds the all-time record for both U.S. goals scored and assists and is just two shy of the MLS career scoring record. When his con-tract with the Los Angeles Galaxy expired at the end of the 2013 season, Donovan said that he needed a break. "I didn't have a specific explanation as to why I needed to get away. But I did have a gut feeling that said, 'You need some time,'" he said. "I was very aware when I left, it could have been the end of my career. But at the end of the day, it was very important for me to do that."

Interestingly, after coming back from his three months off, Donovan began playing the best soccer of his life. Going AWOL might not sound like the best way to improve your career, but "one thing about Landon is he knows what he needs," says Galaxy president Chris Klein, who is also a former teammate. "He's in a place, personally, that I've never seen him in before." He got there by looking inside himself. While others studied the competition, Donovan studied himself. "I play best when I'm happy inside. And that comes from me working on myself," Donovan said. Despite the work he did, Donovan was cut from the U.S. national team for the 2014 World Cup in Brazil, and he later made comments about the team's loss that many interpreted as bitterness and sour grapes. Others thought it was just a reflection of Dono-van's natural tendency to speak his mind.

Spending time in meditation and therapy is nothing new for Donavan. He revealed several years ago that he had been attending therapy sessions and spending long hours in introspective conversations with fam-ily and friends after his poor performance at the 2006 World Cup. Referring to himself at the time of the 2006 competition, Donovan said he was "someone completely unfamiliar." He went on to explain: "Most people don't want to spend time digging deep and finding out why you are the way you are. But I do want to, and I want to embrace it."[15]

REMEMBER THIS

- Individual differences among people, including personality traits, emotions, and characteristics such as self-confidence and self-efficacy influence how people relate to others and behave at work.

- **Self-efficacy** is an individual's strong belief that he or she can successfully accomplish a specific task or outcome.

- J. K. Rowling demonstrated self-efficacy with her belief that she could publish her first book about Harry Potter despite repeated rejections.

- Self-efficacy is related to **self-confidence**, which means general assurance in one's own ideas, judgment, and capabilities.

- Understanding oneself is essential for being a good manager, but self-awareness is not easy to achieve. **Self-awareness** means being conscious of the internal aspects of one's nature, such as personality traits, beliefs, emotions, attitudes, and perceptions, and appreciating how your patterns affect other people.

- Two valuable ways to enhance self-awareness are soliciting feedback and self-assessment, including introspection.

- Soccer player Landon Donovan spent many hours in meditation, therapy, and introspective conversations with family and friends to increase his understanding of himself.

Bill Pugliano/Stringer/Getty Images

CONCEPT CONNECTION   Just how has the recession affected **job satisfaction**? Polls conducted in the United States, such as the Gallup-Healthways Well-Being Index, have shown minor fluctuations in job satisfaction, but the degree of satisfaction generally ranges between 85 and 90 percent. Some economic pundits say that many U.S. employees, like this automobile assembly plant worker, are reluctant to complain and remain thankful for their jobs, given that the unemployment rate reached a peak of 10 percent in 2010 and has remained fairly high ever since.

10.2 Job Satisfaction and Trust

Most managers strive to develop and reinforce positive attitudes among all employees, because people are healthier and more effective when they have positive feelings about their jobs, their coworkers, the company, and the work environment.[16] Two important elements of happy and productive employees are job satisfaction and trust.

10.2a Job Satisfaction

Job satisfaction reflects the degree to which a person finds fulfillment in his or her job. In general, people experience job satisfaction when their work matches their needs and interests, when working conditions and rewards (such as pay) are satisfactory, when they like their coworkers, and when they have positive relationships with supervisors. Take the quiz in Exhibit 10.2 to better understand some of the factors that contribute to job satisfaction.

Many managers believe that job satisfaction is important because they think satisfied employees will do better work. In fact, research shows that the link between satisfaction and performance is generally small and is influenced by other factors.[17] For example, the importance of satisfaction varies according to the amount of control the employee has; an employee doing routine tasks may produce about the same output, no matter how he or

EXHIBIT 10.2   Rate Your Job Satisfaction

Instructions: Think of a job—either a current or previous job—that was important to you, and then answer the following questions with respect to how satisfied you were with that job. Please answer the six questions with a number (1–5) that reflects the extent of your satisfaction.

1 = Very dissatisfied   3 = Neutral   5 = Very satisfied
2 = Dissatisfied   4 = Satisfied

1. Overall, how satisfied are you with your job?	1	2	3	4	5
2. How satisfied are you with the opportunities to learn new things?	1	2	3	4	5
3. How satisfied are you with your boss?	1	2	3	4	5
4. How satisfied are you with the people in your work group?	1	2	3	4	5
5. How satisfied are you with the amount of pay you receive?	1	2	3	4	5
6. How satisfied are you with the advancement that you are making in the organization?	1	2	3	4	5

Scoring and Interpretation: Add up your responses to the six questions to obtain your total score: _____.
The questions represent various aspects of satisfaction that an employee may experience on a job. If your score is 24 or above, you probably feel satisfied with the job. If your score is 12 or below, you probably do not feel satisfied. What is your level of performance in your job, and is your performance related to your level of satisfaction?

SOURCES: These questions were adapted from Daniel R. Denison, *Corporate Culture and Organizational Effectiveness* (New York: John Wiley, 1990); and John D. Cook et al., *The Experience of Work: A Compendium and Review of 249 Measures and Their Use* (San Diego, CA: Academic Press, 1981).

Green Power

Make it Meaningful

The success of a sustainability program often depends on the ability of managers to engage employees. Canada's **LoyaltyOne** management team believes the secret to employee satisfaction lies in doing small things that transform employee thinking and behavior over time. LoyaltyOne's sustainability efforts, including regular town hall meetings, annual environmental fairs, contests, and giveaways, create a participatory culture of fun as the organization moves to fulfill its sustainability goals. Employees are encouraged to build initiatives based on their own concerns. LoyaltyOne provided people with take-home meters to measure their personal power usage, which had greater impact on individual social responsibility than any lecture or position paper. Recognized in 2014 by global consulting firm Aon Hewitt as one of the Best Employers in Canada, LoyaltyOne successfully injects challenge, empowerment, creativity, fun, and "making a difference" into the workplace sustainability experience of each employee.

SOURCES: "Environmental Sustainability and Top Talents," *Cool Choices*, August 4, 2011, www.coolchoicesnetwork.org/2011/08/04/environmental-sustainability-and-top-talents/ (accessed August 1, 2012); and Derek Wong, "Top Talents Attracted to Socially Responsible Companies," *Environmental Leaders: Environmental and Energy Management News*, July 11, 2011, http://www.environmentalleader.com/2011/07/11/top-talents-attracted-to-socially-responsible-companies (accessed August 1, 2012).

she feels about the job. Managers of today's knowledge workers, however, often rely on job satisfaction to keep motivation and enthusiasm high. They can't afford to lose talented, highly skilled employees. Regrettably, a recent survey by the Conference Board found that only 45 percent of U.S. employees say they are satisfied at work, the lowest satisfaction level in the survey's history.[18]

Managers create the environment that determines whether employees have positive or negative feelings toward their jobs.[19]

10.2b Trust

Considering how important trust is in any relationship, it is surprising how little attention many managers devote to building and maintaining trust in the workplace. Trust can make all the difference between an employee who is emotionally committed to the organization and one who is not. **Organizational commitment** refers to an employee's loyalty to and engagement with the organization. An employee with a high degree of organizational commitment is likely to say *we* when talking about the company. Such a person likes being a part of the organization and tries to contribute to its success. Sadly, the most recent Gallup workforce survey places the number of *disengaged* employees in the United States at 70 percent.[20] Another recent survey suggests that commitment and engagement levels around the world are also relatively low.[21]

These results reflect a low level of trust in management, which is an essential component for success in today's chaotic environment. Companies cannot prevent major catastrophes or crises, but by building organizations based on trust, they can be "battle-ready" when crises and catastrophes hit. When Irene Rosenfeld, CEO of Mondelez International, talked about the restructuring of Kraft (the predecessor of Mondelez) at the World Business Forum, she emphasized the effort that managers had made to be "straightforward, open, and honest," even in the midst of plant closings and job cuts. The trust that this fostered, Rosenfeld said, was "a critical part" of the company's ability to move forward.[22]

Various polls in recent years have found that a majority of people don't trust what senior management is telling them. Most people think that managers try to hide things or "spin" them.[23] Only 20 percent of people surveyed by Leadership IQ, a leadership training organization, said that they strongly trust their top management, with 36 percent reporting a moderate trust level, and 44 percent saying that they either distrust or strongly distrust their bosses.[24] In addition, the survey confirms that trust relates to organizational commitment. According to the study, about 32 percent of an employee's desire to stay with a company or leave depends on trust in management. Most of us don't need a poll to tell us that the level of trust in business and government leaders is dismal. From the Enron debacle early in the century, to the scads of Wall Street managers and traders rewarded for unethical behavior with large bonuses during the more recent financial crisis, there are numerous reasons why people mistrust organizational leadership.

Once trust is undermined, everything else tends to unravel. Managers promote trust by being open and honest in their business dealings, keeping employees informed, giving them a say in decisions, providing the necessary training and other resources that enable them to succeed, treating them fairly, and offering rewards that they value. "People in leadership positions simply have not done a good job of earning trust," says Doug Harward, president of Training Industry, Inc. "Employees have a right to expect that their managers are trustworthy and that they will create stable organizations. Too many of our leaders have violated that trust."[25]

REMEMBER THIS

- A positive feeling about one's job is called **job satisfaction**.
- Surveys suggest that job satisfaction levels are at an all-time low.
- **Organizational commitment** refers to loyalty to and engagement with one's work organization.
- Trust is an important component of organizational commitment.
- A survey found that 32 percent of an employee's desire to stay with a company or leave depends on the employee's trust in management.

10.3 Perception and Attributions

Other critical aspects of understanding behavior are perception and attributions, which are a special kind of perception.

10.3a Perception and Perceptual Distortions

Perception is the cognitive process that people use to make sense out of the environment by selecting, organizing, and interpreting information from the environment. Because of individual differences in personality, values, interests, and so forth, people often "see" the same thing in different ways. A class that is boring to one student might be fascinating to another. One student might perceive an assignment to be challenging and stimulating, whereas another might find it a silly waste of time.

We can think of perception as a step-by-step process, as shown in Exhibit 10.3. First, we observe information (sensory data) from the environment through our senses: taste, smell, hearing, sight, and touch. Next, our mind screens the data and will select only the items that we will process further. Third, we organize the selected data into meaningful patterns for interpretation and response. Most differences in perception among people at work are related to how they select and organize sensory data. You can experience differences in perceptual organization by looking at the visuals in Exhibit 10.4. What do you see in part *a* of Exhibit 10.4? Most people see this image as a dog, but others see only a series of unrelated ink blots. Some people will see the figure in part *b* as a beautiful young woman, while others will see an old one. Now look at part *c*. How many blocks do you see—six or seven? Some people have to turn the figure upside down before they can see seven blocks. These visuals illustrate how complex perception is.

Of particular concern in the work environment are **perceptual distortions**, errors in perceptual judgment that arise from inaccuracies in any part of the perception process. One common perceptual error is **stereotyping**, the tendency to assign an individual to a group or broad category (e.g., female, black, elderly; or male, white, disabled) and then to attribute widely held generalizations about the group to the individual. Recall our discussion from Chapter 9 of the inaccurate stereotype that talkative female managers are incompetent. As another example, someone meets a new colleague, sees that he is in a wheelchair, assigns him to the category "physically disabled," and attributes to this colleague generalizations that she believes about people with disabilities, which may include a belief that he is less able than other coworkers. However, the person's inability to walk should not be seen as indicative of lesser abilities in other areas. Stereotyping prevents people from truly knowing those whom they classify in this way. In addition, negative stereotypes prevent talented people from advancing in an organization and fully contributing their talents to the organization's success.

EXHIBIT 10.3 The Perception Process

EXHIBIT 10.4 Perception—What Do You See?

a. Do you see the dog?

b. Old woman or young woman?

c. How many blocks?

EXHIBIT 10.5 How Accurate Is Your Perception?

Instructions: Think about a job that you have held or a project that you have worked on in class or a volunteer organization. With respect to data or information coming to you, rate whether each statement below is Mostly True or Mostly False for you.

	Mostly True	Mostly False
1. I look for inconsistencies and seek explanations for them.		
2. I generate multiple explanations for available information.		
3. I check for omissions, distortions, or exaggerations in available information.		
4. I make it a point to distinguish facts from opinions.		
5. I stay conscious of my own style of approaching problems and how this might affect the way that I process information.		
6. I am well aware of my own biases and values that influence the way I see people.		

Scoring and Interpretation: Your total score is the number of Mostly True answers to all six questions. A score of 5 or 6 suggests that you are conscious of and make attempts to remove distortions from your perception. A score of 3 or 4 indicates that you make a solid effort, and a score of 1 or 2 suggests that you take perception for granted. Look at any individual items where you have marked Mostly False to get an idea of where you might have perceptual weaknesses. What can you do to improve your perception?

SOURCE: Adapted from Patricia M. Fandt, *Management Skills: Practice and Experience* (Minneapolis: West Publishing, 1994), pp. 210–211.

The **halo effect** occurs when the perceiver develops an overall impression of a person or situation based on one characteristic, either favorable or unfavorable. In other words, a halo blinds the perceiver to other characteristics that should be used in generating a more complete assessment. The halo effect can play a significant role in performance appraisal, as we discussed in Chapter 9. For example, a person with an outstanding attendance record may be assessed as responsible, industrious, and highly productive; another person with less-than-average attendance may be assessed as a poor performer. Either assessment may be true, but it is the manager's job to be sure that the assessment is based on complete information about all job-related characteristics, not just the employee's preference for good attendance. How accurate is your perception? Answering the questions in Exhibit 10.5 will give you an idea of whether you allow perceptual distortions to cloud your judgment.

10.3b Attributions: A Special Case of Perception

Among the assessments that people make as part of the perception process are attributions.[26] **Attributions** are judgments about what caused a person's behavior—something about the person or something about the situation. People make attributions as an attempt to understand why others behave as they do. An *internal attribution* says that characteristics of the person led to the behavior. ("Susan missed the deadline because she's careless and lazy.") An *external attribution* says that something about the situation caused the person's behavior. ("Susan missed the deadline because she couldn't get the information she needed in a timely manner.") Understanding attributions is important because attributions influence how a manager will handle a situation. In the case of the missed deadline, a manager who blames it on the employee's personality will view Susan as the problem and might give her unfavorable performance reviews and less attention and support. In contrast, a manager who blames the behavior on the situation might try to prevent such situations in the future, such as by improving horizontal communication mechanisms so people get the information that they need in a timely way.

People often have biases that they apply when making attributions. When evaluating others, we tend to underestimate the influence of external factors and overestimate the influence of internal factors. This tendency is called the **fundamental attribution error**. Consider the case of someone being promoted to CEO. Employees, outsiders, and the media generally focus on the characteristics of the person that allowed him or her to achieve the promotion. In reality, however, the selection of that person might have been heavily influenced by external factors, such as business conditions creating a need for someone with a strong financial or marketing background at that particular time.

Another bias that distorts attributions involves attributions that we make about our own behavior. People tend to overestimate the contribution of internal factors to their successes and overestimate the contribution of external factors to their failures. This tendency, called the **self-serving bias**, means that people give themselves too much credit for what they do well and give external forces too much blame when they fail. Thus, if your manager says that you don't communicate well enough, and you think that your manager doesn't listen well enough, the truth may actually lie somewhere in between.

REMEMBER THIS

- **Perception** is the cognitive process that people use to make sense out of the environment by selecting, organizing, and interpreting information.
- People often see the same thing in different ways.
- **Perceptual distortions** are errors in perceptual judgment that result from inaccuracies in any part of the perception process.
- **Stereotyping** refers to the tendency to assign an individual to a group or broad category and then attribute generalizations about the group to the individual.
- The **halo effect** occurs when a perceiver develops an overall impression of a person or situation based on one characteristic, either favorable or unfavorable.
- **Attributions** are judgments about what caused a person's behavior—either characteristics of the person or of the situation.
- An internal attribution says that characteristics of the individual caused the person to behave in a certain way, whereas an external attribution places the cause on aspects of the situation.
- The **fundamental attribution error** is a tendency to underestimate the influence of external factors on another person's behavior and to overestimate the influence of internal factors.

- The **self-serving bias** is the tendency to overestimate the contribution of internal factors to one's successes and the contribution of external factors to one's failures.

10.4 **Personality and Behavior**

In recent years, many employers have shown a heightened interest in matching people's personalities to the needs of the job and the organization. An individual's **personality** is the set of characteristics that underlie a relatively stable pattern of behavior in response to ideas, objects, or people in the environment. Interestingly, although 71 percent of human resource (HR) professionals surveyed say that personality tests can be useful for predicting job-related behavior and organizational fit, the use of such tests has actually declined in recent years. Only 18 percent reported that their companies use personality tests in hiring and promotion decisions. Part of the reason is that more companies are relying on social media to assess candidates based on what they have to say and show about themselves.[27]

10.4a **Personality Traits**

In common use, people think of personality in terms of traits, the fairly consistent characteristics that a person exhibits. Researchers investigated whether any traits stand up to scientific scrutiny. Although investigators examined thousands of traits over the years, their findings fit into five general dimensions that describe personality. These dimensions, often called the "Big Five" personality factors, are illustrated in Exhibit 10.6.[28]

Each factor may contain a wide range of specific traits. **The Big Five personality** factors describe an individual's extroversion, agreeableness, conscientiousness, emotional stability, and openness to experience:

1. *Extroversion.* The degree to which a person is outgoing, sociable, assertive, and comfortable with interpersonal relationships.

2. *Agreeableness.* The degree to which a person is able to get along with others by being good-natured, likable, cooperative, forgiving, understanding, and trusting.

3. *Conscientiousness.* The degree to which a person is focused on a few goals, thus behaving in ways that are responsible, dependable, persistent, and achievement-oriented.

4. *Emotional stability.* The degree to which a person is calm, enthusiastic, and self-confident, rather than tense, depressed, moody, or insecure.

5. *Openness to experience.* The degree to which a person has a broad range of interests and is imaginative, creative, artistically sensitive, and willing to consider new ideas.

© stefanolunardi/Shutterstock.com

CONCEPT CONNECTION Marriott carefully screens candidates for critical customer service positions, such as this housekeeper at a Marriott Residence Inn in Cleveland, Ohio. One important way that managers determine whether people have the "right stuff" is through **personality testing**. During the application process, candidates answer a series of questions about their beliefs, attitudes, work habits, and how they might handle situations, enabling Marriott to identify people with interests and motivations that are compatible with company values. As managers reevaluate Marriott's mission and goals, the test evolves. Some fear that personality tests have too much influence, determining not just who gets hired, but who gets an interview in the first place.

EXHIBIT 10.6 The Big Five Personality Factors

Instructions: Each individual's collection of personality traits is different; it is what makes us unique. But although each *collection* of traits varies, we all share many common traits. The following phrases describe various traits and behaviors. Rate how accurately each statement describes you on a scale of 1 to 5, with 1 being very inaccurate and 5 very accurate. Describe yourself as you are now, not as you wish to be. There are no right or wrong answers.

                            1   2   3   4   5
              Very Inaccurate   Very Accurate

Extroversion

I am usually the life of the party.	1	2	3	4	5
I feel comfortable around people.	1	2	3	4	5
I am talkative.	1	2	3	4	5

Neuroticism (Low Emotional Stability)

I often feel critical of myself.	1	2	3	4	5
I often envy others.	1	2	3	4	5
I am temperamental.	1	2	3	4	5

Agreeableness

I am kind and sympathetic.	1	2	3	4	5
I have a good word for everyone.	1	2	3	4	5
I never insult people.	1	2	3	4	5

Openness to New Experiences

I am imaginative.	1	2	3	4	5
I prefer to vote for liberal political candidates.	1	2	3	4	5
I really like art.	1	2	3	4	5

Conscientiousness

I am systematic and efficient.	1	2	3	4	5
I pay attention to details.	1	2	3	4	5
I am always prepared for class.	1	2	3	4	5

Which are your most prominent traits? For fun and discussion, compare your responses with those of classmates.

Spotlight on Skills

Marissa Mayer, Yahoo, and Richard Branson, Virgin Group

If you ever watched the YouTube video of Marissa Mayer interviewing Lady Gaga, or saw *Vogue's* take on her 2009 wedding to Zack Bogue, you probably wouldn't think of her as an introvert, but Mayer describes herself as a very shy person by nature. She says that in high school, she was the student who knew all the answers but waited to be called on. Like many introverts, Mayer can overcome her natural tendencies to do things that are important to her.

Another leader who understands that is Richard Branson, who dresses up in silly costumes to publicize the Virgin Group. Branson says that his flamboyant public persona bears little resemblance to his innate personality. "I was a shy and retiring individual who couldn't make speeches and get out there," Branson says of himself prior to founding Virgin. "I had to train myself into becoming more of an extrovert" in order to promote the new company.

Nancy Ancowitz wrote a book called *Self-Promotion for Introverts* because she knew from experience that it is easy for introverted people to get overlooked in the corporate world. Ancowitz worked for years on Wall Street, but she found the days filled with meetings, constant jockeying for attention, and the lack of quiet time to reflect and recharge so draining that she eventually left. However, she learned some valuable lessons before doing so, such as the importance of speaking up more at meetings, making sure her accomplishments were noticed, and building a strong professional network. Ancowitz says that she could have thrived on Wall Street, even as an introvert, if she had wanted it badly enough, but today she works as a consultant helping other introverts learn to raise their visibility to succeed in the business world.[29]

As illustrated in the exhibit, these factors represent a continuum. That is, a person may have a low, moderate, or high degree of each quality. Answer the questions in Exhibit 10.6 to see where you fall on the Big Five scale for each of the factors. Having a moderate-to-high degree of each of the Big Five personality factors is considered desirable for a wide range of employees, but this isn't always a key to success. For example, having an outgoing, sociable personality (extroversion) is considered desirable for managers, but many successful leaders, including Bill Gates, Hillary Clinton, Charles Schwab, and Steven Spielberg, are introverts, people who may become drained by social encounters and need time alone to reflect and recharge their batteries. One study found that four in 10 top executives test out to be introverts.[30] Two other introverts who have found success in high-profile positions are Marisa Mayer and Richard Branson.

In recent years, there has been a growing awareness that introverted people have some qualities that actually might make them better leaders.[31] At Stanford University, for example, Marissa Mayer stood out because of her deep understanding of people and her ability to really listen to them.[32] The Spotlight on Skills that follows describes some benefits of the introverted personality for managers and offers some tips for introverted managers on how to shine despite their lack of natural gregariousness. Introversion or extroversion is simply one aspect of an individual's personality, and each style has both strengths and weaknesses.

Although the quality of extroversion is not as significant as is often presumed, traits of agreeableness seem to be particularly important in today's collaborative organizations. Studies show that people who score high on agreeableness are more likely to get jobs and keep them than are less agreeable people.[33] Although there is also some evidence that people who are *overly* agreeable tend to be promoted less often, the days are over when a hard-driving manager can run roughshod over others to earn a promotion. Executive search firm Korn Ferry International examined data from millions of manager profiles and found that the most successful executives today are team-oriented leaders who gather information and work collaboratively with many different people.[34] Recent research also suggests that traits of conscientiousness are more important than those of extroversion for effective leadership. A study at the Stanford Graduate School of Business found a link between how guilty people feel when they make serious mistakes and how well they perform as leaders. Guilt can be a positive emotion for a leader because it is associated with a heightened sense of responsibility to others, something that certainly could have benefited leaders involved in the recent mortgage and financial crisis![35]

10.4b Attitudes and Behaviors Influenced by Personality

An individual's personality influences his or her work-related attitudes and behaviors. As a new manager, you will have to manage people with a wide variety of personality characteristics. Four areas related to personality that are of particular interest to managers are locus of control, authoritarianism, Machiavellianism, and problem-solving styles.

Locus of Control   Individuals differ in terms of what they tend to accredit as the cause of their success or failure. Locus of control refers to how people perceive the cause of life events—whether they place the primary responsibility within themselves or on outside forces.[36] Some people believe that their own actions strongly influence what happens to them. They feel in control of their own fate. These individuals have a high *internal* locus of control. Other people believe that events in their lives occur because of chance, luck, or outside people and events. They feel more like pawns of their fate. These individuals have a high *external* locus of control.

iStockphoto.com/monkeybusinessimages

CONCEPT CONNECTION   Teach for America sends recent college graduates to teach for two years in low-income schools throughout the United States. What does Teach for America look for when reviewing approximately 45,000 applications for only about 5,000 positions? Founder and CEO Wendy Kopp says a high **internal locus of control** is at the top of her list. Those are the candidates who, when faced with a challenge, respond with optimism and resolve. Says Kopp, "They have the instinct to figure out what they can control and to own it, rather than to blame everyone else in the system."

Spotlight on Skills

The Rise of the Introverted Manager

In today's world of open offices and collaborative work arrangements, being an introverted manager is a challenge, especially in the United States and other cultures that reward people for being outgoing and sociable. Yet experts are beginning to tout the virtues of the introverted manager, as well as offer tips for how introverts can make sure that they don't get lost amid the gregarious leaders around them.

The Upside of Being an Introvert

Some benefits of an introverted personality include the following:

- **They are more cautious and deliberate.** Introverts tend to make more thoughtful decisions. They can become excited by opportunities and potential rewards, but they seem to have a keener awareness of risks than do extroverts, which can help to prevent train wrecks such as those that felled Bear Stearns and Lehmann Brothers.

- **They have a greater ability to listen and take suggestions.** We've all been charmed by charismatic, talkative people who are "working the room" while the introverts are huddled in a corner. Yet new research confirms what many of us suspect: Extroverts tend to be poor listeners! Adam M. Grant, who studies this subject, says that introverted managers can be better bosses in dynamic and unpredictable environments because of their ability to listen, empathize with others, and empower employees to think for themselves.

- **They are more creative.** The most stunningly innovative people in many fields are introverts. Why? Because creativity thrives on solitude. "Without great solitude, no serious work is possible," Picasso said. Steve Jobs was the extrovert behind Apple, but the company would never have come into being without the hard work put in by introverted cofounder Steve Wozniak, who spent long hours working alone to create the company's first computer. "Most inventors and engineers I've met are like me . . . they live in their heads," Wozniak said.

Succeeding as an Introverted Manager

Introverted managers can get overlooked, particularly in large organizations. In addition, introverts are often,

although not always, shy, which makes it harder for them to feel comfortable in the role of a manager. Here are some tips that can help introverts succeed as managers:

- **Stretch your personality.** If you want something badly enough, you can stretch the limits of a naturally introverted personality. Like Richard Branson, who had to train himself to be more extroverted to promote Virgin, managers can stretch beyond their natural tendency toward introversion to achieve an important goal.

- **Let people know who you are.** Introverts like Branson may be able to act more extroverted when they need to, but they will always need quiet time to reflect, process, and recharge their energies. This tendency to need time alone can be misinterpreted. Douglas Conant, who headed Campbell Soup Company for years as a shy, introverted leader, says that he'd give a little talk to new employees and colleagues right off the bat so they didn't think that he was aloof and uninterested in them. "The more transparent I became, the more engaged people became," he says.

- **Mix with people, speak up, and get out there.** If you want to be a manager, and particularly if you want to advance to higher levels, there is no denying that you need to push yourself to get out there and connect with people both within and outside the organization. You will have to speak up at meetings, make presentations, and be more sociable and outgoing at conferences and other professional events. You can behave in more extroverted ways when you need to. Just remember to find alone time to recharge your batteries.

SOURCES: Based on Adam M. Grant, Francesca Gino, and David A. Hoffmann, "The Hidden Advantages of Quiet Bosses," *Harvard Business Review* (December 2010): 28; Susan Cain, "The Rise of the New Groupthink," *The New York Times*, January 15, 2012, SR-1; Bryan Walsh, "The Upside of Being an Introvert (and Why Extroverts Are Overrated)," *Time* (February 6, 2012): 40–45; "How Introverts Can Be Leaders—The Expert: Doug Conant," *Fortune* (May 21, 2012): 56; Joann S. Lublin, "Introverted Execs Find Ways to Shine," *The Wall Street Journal Asia*, April 18, 2011, 31; Jack and Suzy Welch, "The Welchway: Release Your Inner Extrovert," *BusinessWeek* (December 8, 2008): 92; Richard Branson example from Ginka Toegel and Jean-Louis Barsoux, "How to Become a Better Leader," *MIT Sloan Management Review* (Spring 2012): 51–60.

Research on locus of control shows real differences in behavior across a wide range of settings. People with an internal locus of control are easier to motivate because they believe that rewards are the result of their behavior. They are better able to handle complex information and problem solving, are more achievement-oriented, but are also more independent and therefore more difficult to manage. By contrast, people with an external locus of control are harder to motivate, less involved in their jobs, and more likely to blame others when faced with a poor performance evaluation, but they are also more compliant and conforming and, therefore, easier to manage.[37]

Do you believe luck plays an important role in your life, or do you feel that you control your own fate? To find out more about your locus of control, read the instructions and complete the questionnaire in Exhibit 10.7.

Authoritarianism **Authoritarianism** is the belief that power and status differences should exist within the organization.[38] Individuals high in authoritarianism tend to be concerned with power and toughness, obey recognized authority above them, stick to conventional values, critically judge others, and oppose the use of subjective feelings. The degree to which managers possess authoritarianism will influence how they wield and share power. The degree to which employees possess authoritarianism will influence how they react to

EXHIBIT 10.7 Measuring Locus of Control

Your Locus of Control

Instructions: For each of these 10 questions, indicate the extent to which you agree or disagree using the following scale:

1 = Strongly disagree   4 = Neither disagree nor agree   7 = Strongly agree
2 = Disagree   5 = Slightly agree
3 = Slightly disagree   6 = Agree

1. When I get what I want, it is usually because I worked hard for it.	1	2	3	4	5	6	7
2. When I make plans, I am almost certain to make them work.	1	2	3	4	5	6	7
3. I prefer games involving some luck over games requiring pure skill.	1	2	3	4	5	6	7
4. I can learn almost anything if I set my mind to it.	1	2	3	4	5	6	7
5. My major accomplishments are entirely due to my hard work and ability.	1	2	3	4	5	6	7
6. I usually don't set goals because I have a hard time following through on them.	1	2	3	4	5	6	7
7. Competition discourages excellence.	1	2	3	4	5	6	7
8. Often people get ahead just by being lucky.	1	2	3	4	5	6	7
9. On any sort of exam or competition, I like to know how well I do relative to everyone else.	1	2	3	4	5	6	7
10. It's pointless to keep working on something that's too difficult for me.	1	2	3	4	5	6	7

Scoring and Interpretation: To determine your score, reverse the values that you selected for questions 3, 6, 7, 8, and 10 (1 = 7, 2 = 6, 3 = 5, 4 = 4, 5 = 3, 6 = 2, 7 = 1). For example, if you strongly disagree with the statement in question 3, you would have given it a value of 1. Change this value to a 7. Reverse the scores in a similar manner for questions 6, 7, 8, and 10. Now add the point values for all ten questions together.

Your score _____

Researchers using this questionnaire in a study of college students found a mean of 51.8 for men and 52.2 for women, with a standard deviation of 6 for each. The higher your score on this questionnaire, the more you tend to believe that you are generally responsible for what happens to you; in other words, higher scores are associated with internal locus of control. Low scores are associated with external locus of control. Scoring low indicates that you tend to believe that forces beyond your control, such as powerful people, fate, or chance, are responsible for what happens to you.

SOURCES: Adapted from J. M. Burger, *Personality: Theory and Research* (Belmont, CA: Wadsworth, 1986), pp. 400–401, cited in D. Hellriegel, J. W. Slocum, Jr., and R. W. Woodman, *Organizational Behavior*, 6th ed. (St. Paul, MN: West, 1992), pp. 97–100. Original source: D. L. Paulhus, "Sphere-Specific Measures of Perceived Control," *Journal of Personality and Social Psychology*, 44, no. 6 (1983): 1253–1265.

their managers. If a manager and employees differ in their degree of authoritarianism, the manager may have difficulty leading effectively. The trend toward empowerment and shifts in expectations among younger employees for more equitable relationships contribute to a decline in strict authoritarianism in many organizations.

Machiavellianism Another personality dimension that is helpful in understanding work behavior is **Machiavellianism**, which is characterized by the acquisition of power and the manipulation of other people for purely personal gain. Machiavellianism is named after Niccolò Machiavelli, a sixteenth-century Italian political philosopher who wrote *The Prince*, a book for noblemen of the day on how to acquire and use power, in 1513.[39] Psychologists developed instruments to measure a person's Machiavellianism (Mach) orientation.[40] The short quiz in Exhibit 10.8 will give you an idea of how you rate on Machiavellian tendencies. Research shows that high Machs are predisposed to being pragmatic, capable of lying to achieve personal goals, more likely to win in win-lose situations, and more likely to persuade than be persuaded.[41]

EXHIBIT 10.8 What's Your Mach?

Instructions: Managers differ in how they view human nature and the tactics that they use to get things done through others. Answer the questions below based on how you view others. Think carefully about each question and be honest about what you feel inside. Please answer whether each item below is Mostly True or Mostly False for you.

	Mostly True	Mostly False
1. Overall, it is better to be humble and honest than to be successful and dishonest.	_____	_____
2. If you trust someone completely, you are asking for trouble.	_____	_____
3. A leader should take action only when it is morally right.	_____	_____
4. A good way to handle people is to tell them what they like to hear.	_____	_____
5. There is no excuse for telling a white lie to someone.	_____	_____
6. It makes sense to flatter important people.	_____	_____
7. Most people who get ahead as leaders have led very moral lives.	_____	_____
8. It is better not to tell people the real reason that you did something unless it benefits you to do so.	_____	_____
9. The vast majority of people are brave, good, and kind.	_____	_____
10. It is hard to get to the top without sometimes cutting corners.	_____	_____

Scoring and Interpretation: To compute your Mach score, give yourself one point for each Mostly False answer to items 1, 3, 5, 7, and 9, and one point for each Mostly True answer to items 2, 4, 6, 8, and 10. These items were drawn from the works of Machiavelli. Successful management intrigue at the time of Machiavelli was believed to require behaviors that today would be considered ego-centered and manipulative, which is almost the opposite of more enlightened management. A score of 8–10 points suggests that you have a high Mach score, 4–7 points indicate a moderate score, and 0–3 points indicate a low Mach score. Having a high Mach score does not mean that the individual is a sinister or vicious person, but it probably means that he or she has a cool detachment, sees life as a game, and is not personally engaged with other people. Discuss your results with other students, and talk about whether you think politicians and top executives would have a high or a low Mach score.

SOURCE: Adapted from R. Christie and F. L. Geis, *Studies in Machiavellianism* (New York: Academic Press, 1970).

Different situations may require people who demonstrate one or the other type of behavior. In loosely structured situations, high Machs actively take control, while low Machs accept the direction given by others. Low Machs thrive in highly structured situations, while high Machs perform in a detached, disinterested way. High Machs are particularly good in jobs that require bargaining skills or that involve substantial rewards for winning.[42]

REMEMBER THIS

- **Personality** is the set of characteristics that underlie a relatively stable pattern of behavior in response to ideas, objects, or people in the environment.
- The **Big Five personality factors** are dimensions that describe an individual's extroversion, agreeableness, conscientiousness, emotional stability, and openness to experience.
- Marissa Mayer is an example of a leader with an introverted personality who succeeds in a high-profile position.

- **Locus of control** defines whether an individual places the primary responsibility for his successes and failures within himself or on outside forces.
- **Authoritarianism** is the belief that power and status differences should exist within an organization.
- A person high in authoritarianism is typically concerned with power and status, obeys established authority, and sticks to conventional values.
- **Machiavellianism** refers to a tendency to direct one's behavior toward the acquisition of power and the manipulation of other people for personal gain.

10.4c Problem-Solving Styles and the Myers Briggs Type Indicator

"Each of us is meant to have a character all our own, to be what no other can exactly be, and do what no other can exactly do."

—William Ellery Channing (1780–1842), American writer and clergyman

Managers also need to realize that individuals solve problems and make decisions in different ways. One approach to understanding problem-solving styles grew out of the work of psychologist Carl Jung. Jung believed differences resulted from our preferences in how we go about gathering and evaluating information.[43] According to Jung, gathering information and evaluating information are separate activities. People gather information either by *sensation* or *intuition*, but not by both simultaneously. Sensation-type people would rather work with known facts and hard data and prefer routine and order in gathering information. Intuitive-type people would rather look for possibilities than work with facts and prefer solving new problems and using abstract concepts.

Evaluating information involves making judgments about the information that a person has gathered. People evaluate information by *thinking* or *feeling*. These represent the extremes in orientation. Thinking-type individuals base their judgments on impersonal analysis, using reason and logic rather than personal values or emotional aspects of the situation. Feeling-type individuals base their judgments more on personal feelings such as harmony and tend to make decisions that result in approval from others.

According to Jung, only one of the four functions—sensation, intuition, thinking, or feeling—is dominant in an individual. However, the dominant function usually is backed up by one of the functions from the other set of paired opposites. Exhibit 10.9 shows the four problem-solving styles that result from these matchups, as well as occupations that people with each style tend to prefer.

Two additional sets of paired opposites not directly related to problem solving are *introversion–extroversion* and *judging–perceiving*. Introverts gain energy by focusing on personal thoughts and feelings, whereas extroverts gain energy from being around others and

EXHIBIT 10.9   Four Problem-Solving Styles

Personal Style	Action Tendencies	Likely Occupations
Sensation-Thinking	• Emphasizes details, facts, certainty • Is a decisive, applied thinker • Focuses on short-term, realistic goals • Develops rules and regulations for judging performance	• Accounting • Production • Software engineers • Market research • Engineering
Intuitive-Thinking	• Prefers dealing with theoretical or technical problems • Is a creative, progressive, perceptive thinker • Focuses on possibilities using impersonal analysis • Is able to consider a number of options and problems simultaneously	• Systems design • Internet security • Law • Middle/top management • Teaching business, economics
Sensation-Feeling	• Shows concern for current, real-life human problems • Is pragmatic, analytical, methodical, and conscientious • Emphasizes detailed facts about people rather than tasks • Focuses on structuring organizations for the benefit of people	• Directing supervisor • Counseling • Negotiating • Selling • Interviewing
Intuitive-Feeling	• Avoids specifics • Is charismatic, participative, people oriented, and helpful • Focuses on general views, broad themes, and feelings • Decentralizes decision making, develops few rules and regulations	• Public relations • Advertising • Human Resources • Politics • Customer service

interacting with others. On the judging versus perceiving dimension, people with a judging preference favor certainty and closure and tend to make decisions quickly based on available data. Perceiving people, on the other hand, enjoy ambiguity, dislike deadlines, and may change their minds several times as they gather large amounts of data and information to make decisions.

A widely used test that measures how people differ on all four of Jung's sets of paired opposites is the **Myers-Briggs Type Indicator (MBTI™)** assessment. The MBTI™ assessment measures a person's preferences for introversion versus extroversion, sensation versus intuition, thinking versus feeling, and judging versus perceiving. The various combinations of these four preferences result in 16 unique personality types.

Each of these types can have positive and negative consequences for behavior. Based on the limited research that has been done, the two preferences that seem to be most strongly associated with effective management in a variety of organizations and industries are thinking and judging.[44] However, people with other preferences can also be good managers. One advantage of understanding your natural preferences is to maximize your innate strengths and abilities and minimize your weaknesses.

Nearly 200 agencies of the U.S. government, including the Environmental Protection Agency (EPA), the Central Intelligence Agency (CIA), and the Department of Veterans Affairs (VA), have been reported to use the MBTI™ instrument as part of their training programs. Brian Twillman of the EPA says that at least a quarter of the agency's 17,000

Go to the Self-Learning on pages 457, which pertains to evaluating your personality type.

Spotlight on Skills

Hallmark Cards

The value of people understanding and seeing the best in one another is a core part of Hallmark's mission. That's part of what helps the company produce greeting cards that splendidly and succinctly tap into positive human emotions. The mission and core philosophy have remained constant, but the market, workforce, and business environment have changed dramatically in recent years, becoming more global, diverse, and mobile.

To meet the challenges of this new reality, Hallmark executives wanted to develop leaders who can see things from different perspectives, work together for everyone's success, and fully engage and inspire both employees and customers. One approach to creating that new culture was using the MBTI™ to give managers greater self-awareness and insight into how their patterns of thought and behavior affect others. "We tend to place people into 'files' according to our perceptions of them, which are often skewed," said Mary Beth Ebmeyer, HR manager for corporate development.

The MBTI™ has helped leaders understand how easily misunderstandings can occur between people with different preferences. For example, a leader might receive an e-mail message that he considers to be confrontational, whereas the person who sent it might simply be expressing a well-intentioned concern in a way typical of her personality type. Understanding different MBTI™ types has enabled leaders to test their perceptions against reality, as well as helped them better communicate with different types. Moreover, decisions are being made faster because there are fewer misunderstandings among managers.[45]

federal employees have taken the test, and that without it, "there would be a lot of blind spots within the agency."[46] Many corporations, including Hallmark Cards, have also used the MBTI™ to help people better understand themselves and improve their interactions.

By understanding different MBTI™ types, Hallmark leaders can flex their communication style as needed and connect more meaningfully with employees. In addition, being aware of their own MBTI™ type enables leaders to maximize their strengths and minimize their weaknesses. Leaders should remember that each type can have positive and negative consequences for behavior.

Some organizations also use the MBTI™ assessment to help put people in the right jobs, where they will be happiest and make their best contribution to the organization. In one survey, 89 of the *Fortune* 100 companies reported that they have used the test in hiring and promotion decisions.[47]

REMEMBER THIS

- Four problem-solving styles are sensation-thinking, intuitive-thinking, sensation-feeling, and intuitive-feeling.
- The **Myers-Briggs Type Indicator (MBTI™)** assessment measures a person's preferences for introversion versus extroversion, sensation versus intuition, thinking versus feeling, and judging versus perceiving.
- Hallmark Cards used the MBTI™ assessment to increase managers' self-awareness and enable them to understand how their patterns of behavior affect others.

10.5 Emotions

Managers might like to think that people come to work and conduct their jobs in a logical and rational manner, leaving their emotions at home or tucked safely in the car until it's time to go home for the day. Yet people cannot be separated from their emotions, and organizations suffer when managers fail to pay attention to how employees' emotions affect productivity and the work environment.[48] Managers can increase their effectiveness by understanding positive and negative emotions and developing emotional intelligence.

10.5a Positive and Negative Emotions

Although the term is somewhat difficult to define in a precise way, an **emotion** can be thought of as a mental state that arises spontaneously within a person based on interaction with the environment rather than through conscious effort and is often accompanied by physiological changes or sensations. People can experience a wide range of emotions at work, such as happiness, anger, fear, or relief, and these affect their workplace attitudes and behaviors. Researchers have been attempting to understand emotions for thousands of years, and scientific debate continues about how to categorize emotions.[49] One model that is useful for managers, shown in Exhibit 10.10, distinguishes the major positive and negative emotions. Negative emotions

EXHIBIT 10.10   Positive and Negative Emotions

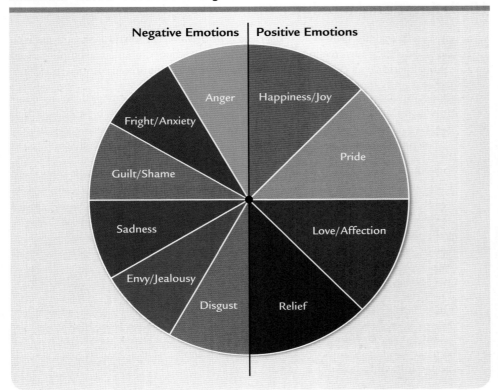

are sparked when a person becomes frustrated in trying to achieve his or her goals, while positive emotions are triggered when people are on track toward achieving goals.

Thus, emotions can be understood as being determined by whether people are getting their needs and goals met. An employee who fails to get a pay raise or is reprimanded by a supervisor would likely experience negative emotions such as sadness, anger, or anxiety, whereas a person who gets a promotion would experience feelings of pride and happiness. Managers can influence whether people experience primarily positive or negative emotions at work. For one thing, the emotional state of the manager influences the entire team or department. Most of us realize that we can "catch" emotions from others. If we're around someone who is happy and enthusiastic, the positive emotions rub off on us. On the other hand, someone who is sad and angry can bring us down. This *emotional contagion*[50] means that managers who express positive emotions such as happiness, enthusiasm, and appreciation trigger positive emotions in employees. Research suggests that nearly all human beings are subject to emotional contagion and will automatically and unconsciously start feeling and displaying the same emotions as those around them.[51] The energy level of the entire organization increases when leaders are optimistic and hopeful rather than angry or depressed. Interesting new research by organization behavior scientists suggests that negative emotions might spread more easily than positive ones. Psychologists have also found that negative people and events have a disproportionately large effect on our emotions and moods.[52]

Good managers pay attention to people's emotions because positive emotions are typically linked to higher productivity and greater effectiveness. A *Gallup Management Journal* survey found that managers, especially front-line supervisors, have a lot to do with whether employees have positive or negative emotions associated with their work lives.[53]

10.5b Emotional Intelligence

In recent years, research in the area of *emotional intelligence* has shown that managers who are in touch with their own feelings and the feelings of others can enhance employee and organizational performance. Emotional intelligence includes four basic components:[54]

- Self-awareness. Being aware of what you are feeling; the basis for all the other components. People who are in touch with their feelings are better able to guide their own lives and actions. A high degree of self-awareness means you can accurately assess your own strengths and limitations and have a healthy sense of self-confidence.

- Self-management. The ability to control disruptive or harmful emotions and balance one's moods so that worry, anxiety, fear, and anger do not cloud thinking and get in the way of what needs to be done. People who are skilled at self-management remain optimistic and hopeful despite setbacks and obstacles. This ability is crucial for pursuing long-term goals. MetLife found that applicants who failed the regular sales aptitude test but scored high on optimism made 21 percent more sales in their first year and 57 percent more in their second year than those who passed the sales test but scored high on pessimism.[55]

- Social awareness. The ability to understand others and practice *empathy*, which means being able to put yourself in someone else's shoes, to recognize what others are feeling without them needing to tell you. People with social awareness are capable of understanding divergent points of view and interacting effectively with many different types of people.

Complete the "New Manager Self-Test" on page 446 to assess your level of positive emotional expression. You might also want to refer back to the questionnaire related to self-confidence at the beginning of this chapter. Self-confidence strongly influences a manager's emotional intelligence.

- Relationship management. The ability to connect to others, build positive relationships, respond to the emotions of others, and influence others. People with relationship management skills know how to listen and communicate clearly, and they treat others with compassion and respect.

Studies show a positive relationship between job performance and a high emotional intelligence quotient (EQ) in a variety of jobs. Numerous organizations, including the U.S. Air Force and Canada Life, use EQ tests to measure things such as self-awareness, ability to empathize, and capacity to build positive relationships.[56] A high EQ seems to be particularly important for jobs such as sales, which require a high degree of social interaction. It is also critical for managers, who are responsible for influencing others and building positive attitudes and relationships in the organization.

Managers with low EQs can undermine employee morale and harm the organization. Tim Armstrong, CEO of AOL, issued a rare apology after he fired Abel Lenz during a conference call with more than 1,000 employees of Patch, the local news service that AOL runs for hundreds of towns. Armstrong had called the meeting to emphasize the direness of the company's circumstances and prepare for a turnaround, but the brutal way he handled the firing left people reeling. One business writer called Armstrong's "tantrum" one of "the most bizarre sequences in AOL history."[57]

Also, consider that 44 percent of people surveyed by the Employment Law Alliance say that they have worked for a manager that they considered an abusive bully.[58] "It's usually the manager or senior executive who's just a complete out-of-control jerk," said Margaret Fiester, operations manager at the Society for Human Resource Management, where she often fields questions about the growing problem of workplace bullying. In Massachusetts, the National Association of Government Executives Local 282 became one of the first unions in the country to include in collective bargaining agreements an antibullying clause calling for "mutual respect." A recent survey found that 56 percent of companies have some kind of antibullying policy, usually as part of an employee handbook or code of conduct.[59] Growing concerns over workplace bullying have prompted enlightened companies to take action that helps managers develop greater emotional intelligence, such as by honing their self-awareness and empathy and enhancing their self-management skills.

REMEMBER THIS

- An **emotion** is a mental state that arises spontaneously, rather than through conscious effort, and is often accompanied by physiological changes.

- People experience both positive emotions of happiness, pride, love, and relief, as well as negative emotions of anger, anxiety, sadness, envy, and disgust.

- The concept of *emotional contagion* suggests that people can "catch" emotions from those around them, so good managers try to express positive emotions at work.

- Recent research suggests that negative emotions might spread more quickly than positive ones.

- Emotional intelligence includes the components of self-awareness, self-management, social awareness, and relationship management.

- The National Association of Government Executives Local 282 became one of the first unions in the country to include an antibullying clause in collective bargaining agreements.

NEW MANAGER Self-Test

Expressed Emotions

Instructions: Think about the feelings that you express to others during your interactions with people during a typical week of school or work activities. Rate each item below based on whether you typically express that emotion often, sometimes, or rarely during a typical week. There are no right or wrong answers, so answer honestly to receive accurate feedback.

	Often	Sometimes	Rarely
1. Enthusiastic	_____	_____	_____
2. Interested	_____	_____	_____
3. Inspired	_____	_____	_____
4. Energetic	_____	_____	_____
5. Proud	_____	_____	_____
6. Attentive	_____	_____	_____
7. Grateful	_____	_____	_____
8. Amused	_____	_____	_____
9. Hopeful	_____	_____	_____
10. Caring	_____	_____	_____

Scoring and Interpretation: Sum items 1–10, giving 3 points for each Often, 2 points for each Sometimes, and 1 point for each Rarely. Total = _____. In fulfilling their roles, managers are often required to display positive emotions in their relationships with employees and customers. Sometimes a manager may display an emotion without really feeling it, which is called *surface acting*. *Deep acting* is when managers generate the actual emotion that needs to be displayed as part of the job. If you have a high score, it probably means that you display authentic positive emotion. If you have a lower score, can you display positive emotions when needed by pretending to feel the emotion or by generating the appropriate emotion from within? Frequent surface acting is related to stress, and frequent deep acting is related to the perceived quality of emotion expression and with job satisfaction. Compare your score with others in your class. Can you express emotions on demand? Do you think emotional expression is related to the self-management aspect of emotional intelligence?

SOURCES: Based on David Watson, Lee Anna Clark, and Auke Tellegen, "Development and Validation of Brief Measures of Positive and Negative Affect: The PANAS Scales," *Journal of Personality and Social Psychology* 54, no. 6 (1988): 1063–1070; Celeste M. Brotheridge and Raymond T. Lee, "Development and Validation of the Emotional Labour Scale," *Journal of Occupational and Organizational Psychology* 76 (2003): 365–379; and Alicia A. Grandey, "When 'The Show Must Go On': Surface Acting and Deep Acting as Determinants of Emotional Exhaustion and Peer-Rated Service Delivery," *Academy of Management Journal* 46, no. 1 (2003): 86–96.

10.6 **Managing Yourself**

Now let's turn to another topic that every manager needs to know about—time management. We introduced the topic of time management in Chapter 1, and there was a Director's Toolkit box in that chapter that outlined some specific time management tips. In this chapter, we talk about a broader self-management system that people can apply to gain control over their hectic schedules. **Self-management** is the ability to engage in self-regulating thoughts and behavior to accomplish all your tasks and handle difficult or challenging situations. Yet all of us have patterns of habit and behavior that may make it hard to manage ourselves toward more efficient behavior. Even the best managers can sometimes find themselves feeling overwhelmed. Many people get stuck and can't take action when they have too much on their minds or too many competing demands on their time. One approach for "getting a grip" when you have too much to do and can't seem to get any of it done is to apply a bottom-up strategy that starts by analyzing the details of what you are actually doing right now, and then building a system to manage all your activities.

10.6a Basic Principles for Self-Management

Three basic principles define how to manage your many big and small commitments effectively so that you can get them accomplished:[60]

1. *Clarity of mind.* The first principle is that if you're carrying too much around in your head, your mind can't be clear. If your mind isn't clear, you can't focus. If you can't focus, you can't get anything done. Thus, anything you consider unfinished needs to be placed in some kind of trusted system *outside* your head.

2. *Clarity of objectives.* Next, you have to be clear about exactly what you need to do and decide the steps to take toward accomplishing it.

3. *An organized system.* Finally, once you've decided the actions that you need to take, you need to keep reminders in a well-organized system.

By building a self-management approach based on these three principles—clarity of mind, clarity of objectives, and a system of organized reminders—you can get unstuck and make measurable progress toward achieving all the things that you need to do.

10.6b A Step-by-Step Guide for Managing Your Time

Many people don't realize that they waste at least an hour of a typical workday simply because they are disorganized.[61] You can gain better control of your life and the many things that you have to do by mastering some simple but powerful steps.[62] Exhibit 10.11 summarizes these five steps, and each is described next.

1. *Empty your head.* In order to clear your mind, you first have to see all the many things weighing on it. The first step, therefore, is to write down on separate scraps of paper all the activities, duties, tasks, or commitments that are demanding part of your attention. The idea is to get everything out of your head and down on paper.
    To organize all this "stuff," combine similar items into various "buckets." There are numerous tools that can serve as your buckets, including computer and wireless devices for electronic note-taking; physical in-baskets for holding mail, memos, and phone slips; notebooks or legal pads for writing down things to do; or digital

EXHIBIT 10.11 Follow These Steps to Get Organized

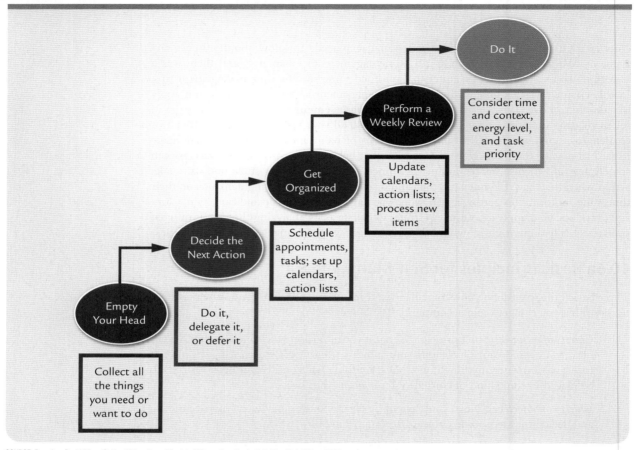

SOURCE: Based on David Allen, *Getting Things Done: The Art of Stress-Free Productivity* (New York: Viking, 2001).

recorders for recording things you need to remember. Keep a notepad or handheld device with you so that you can add new projects or commitments at any time and get them out of your head. Remember to keep the number of buckets to a minimum; otherwise, you'll still feel scattered and overwhelmed.

2. ***Decide the next action.*** For each item in your buckets, decide the real, specific, physical action that you need to take next. If you have a team meeting on Friday to discuss a class project, your next action might be to draft thoughts and ideas that you want to share with the team. Then, you have three options:

   • ***Do it.*** Follow the two-minute rule: If something can be done in less than two minutes, do it now. In some cases, you'll find items in your bucket that require no action and are of no importance. These should be trashed immediately. For items that are of potential use in the future, file in a system for reference material.

   • ***Delegate it.*** Ask yourself if you're the right person to handle a task. If something can be done as well by someone else, delegate it.

   • ***Defer it.*** If something will take longer than two minutes but cannot be delegated to someone else, you'll have to defer it. These things go into an incubation or tickler file, such as an organized "To Do" list, which you will review regularly and perhaps schedule a specific time for their completion.

3. *Get organized.* The third step is to organize all the items that you've deferred. At this stage, schedule any appointments that you identified as "next actions" and record them on whatever calendar you check daily. Also record on your calendar any items that have to be done on a specific day or at a specific time. You can assign yourself a definite date in the future to perform certain tasks that are in your incubation or tickler file.

    For all other items, keep a list of "Next Actions," either on paper on in a portable device that you will have with you at all times so that you can take action when and where you have the time to do so. This can be either on a single list or in categories.

4. *Perform a weekly review.* Once a week, review your complete Next Actions list and your calendar for the coming week. Scan the entire list of outstanding projects and actions needed so that you can make efficient choices about using your time. This weekly review is critical because it keeps your mind from taking back the job of trying to hold and remember everything. The weekly review is also the time to "put your house in order" by collecting, processing, and organizing new items. Thus, during the weekly review, you'll take four actions: (1) collect and process all the new stuff; (2) review your entire system; (3) revise your lists; and (4) get clear, up to date, and complete about what needs to be done next.

5. *Now do it.* Once you have collected, processed, organized, and reviewed your current commitments, you'll have a better sense of what needs to be done, enabling you to make better choices about how to use your time. Your intuition and your understanding of yourself can help you in deciding what to do when.

This approach to self-management can help you get a handle on all the various things that you have to do and approach them in a systematic way with a clear mind. If you follow it, you'll find yourself getting more accomplished with less stress—and with fewer things falling between the cracks. Refer to the time management tips in the "Director's Toolkit" in Chapter 1. You can pick and choose the techniques that work for you and combine them with this overall self-management approach.

REMEMBER THIS

- **Self-management** is the ability to engage in self-regulating thoughts and behavior to accomplish all your tasks and handle difficult or challenging situations.

- Three basic principles for self-management are clarity of mind, clarity of objectives, and an organized system.

- One self-management system is based on five steps: Empty your head; decide the next action; get organized; perform a weekly review; then do what needs to be done.

10.7 Stress and Stress Management

No matter how organized you are, as a manager, you will likely experience stress—your own and that of others—at some time in your career. Formally defined, **stress** is an individual's physiological and emotional response to external stimuli that place physical or psychological demands on the individual and create uncertainty and lack of personal control when important outcomes are at stake.[63] These stimuli, called *stressors,* produce some combination of frustration (the inability to achieve a goal, such as the inability to meet a deadline because of inadequate resources) and anxiety (such as the fear of being disciplined for not meeting deadlines).

Stress levels have gone up in many organizations in recent years, as managers have found themselves dealing with a workforce that is frightened, nervous, and unsure about the future.[64] The number of employees who are irritable, insulting, or discourteous has grown, as people are coping with the stress of job uncertainty, overwhelming debt, tighter access to credit, and increased workloads due to downsizing. In a recent survey, nearly half of U.S. workers reported experiencing yelling and verbal abuse on the job, and another study found that 2–3 percent of people admit to pushing, slapping, or hitting someone at work.[65] "People are trapped; they don't have the same alternative jobs to jump to," said Gary Namie, a social psychologist who cofounded the Workplace Bullying Institute. People "are staying longer in these pressured, stress-filled toxic work environments."[66]

10.7a Challenge Stress and Threat Stress

Stress isn't always negative. Without a certain amount of stress, we would be complacent and accomplish little. Psychologists have long noted this "dual face of stress," and make a distinction between *challenge stress* and *threat stress.* Challenge stress fires you up, whereas threat stress burns you out.[67] As originally proposed by two Harvard researchers, Robert Yerkes and John Dodson, and illustrated in Exhibit 10.12, a certain level of stress challenges you and increases your focus, alertness, efficiency, and productivity.[68] After that point, however, things go downhill quickly, and stress compromises your job performance, your relationships, and even your health. Another interesting finding is that too much stress inhibits learning and flexibility.[69]

EXHIBIT 10.12 The Yerkes–Dodson Stress Curve

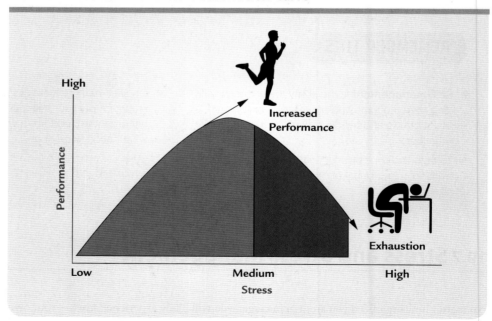

SOURCE: Based on an exhibit by Emeran A. Mayer, M.D., UCLA Center for Neurobiology of Stress.

The point at which things tip over from challenge stress (good) to threat stress (bad) may vary with each individual. Most of us can easily tell when we've gone over the top of the stress curve. We stop feeling productive; experience emotions of anxiety, fear, depression, anger, or a combination; are easily irritated; and may have trouble making decisions. Many people also have physical symptoms, such as headaches, insomnia, or stomach problems. In the United States, an estimated one million people each day don't show up for work because of stress.[70] Similarly, a survey in the United Kingdom found that 68 percent of nonmanual workers and 42 percent of manual workers reported missing work because of stress-related illness.[71] Just as big a problem for organizations as absenteeism is *presenteeism*, which refers to people who go to work but are too stressed and distracted to be productive.[72]

10.7b Type A and Type B Behavior

Researchers observed that some people seem to be more vulnerable than others to the ill effects of stress. From studies of stress-related heart disease, they categorized people as having behavior patterns called Type A and Type B.[73] The **Type A behavior** pattern includes extreme competitiveness, impatience, aggressiveness, and devotion to work. David Sacks, founder and CEO of Yammer, for example, says he is "in a perpetual state of frustration over the product. I want it to be perfect and it's not." He adds, "I think about work constantly, I wish I had an On/Off switch."[74] In contrast, people with a **Type B behavior** pattern exhibit fewer of these behaviors. They consequently experience less conflict with other people and a more balanced, relaxed lifestyle. Type A people tend to experience more stress-related illness than Type B people.

Most Type A individuals, like David Sacks, are high-energy people and may seek positions of power and responsibility. By pacing themselves and learning the control and intelligent use of their natural high-energy tendencies, Type A individuals can be powerful forces for innovation and leadership within their organizations. However, many Type A personalities cause stress-related problems for themselves, and sometimes for those around them as well. At Yammer, Sacks has consciously changed some of his behaviors so that his impatience doesn't cause stress for others. Type B individuals typically live with less stress unless they are in high-stress situations. A number of factors can cause stress in the workplace, even for people who are not naturally prone to high stress.

10.7c Causes of Work Stress

Workplace stress has been skyrocketing worldwide for some years. The number of people in the United States who reported that work is a significant source of stress soared to 69 percent in 2009, and 41 percent say that they typically feel stressed or tense during their workday.[75] Surveys in Canada consistently cite work as the top source of stress for people in that country. In India, growing numbers of young software professionals and call-center workers are falling prey to depression, anxiety, and other mental illnesses because of increasing workplace stress.[76] And the long hours and stressful conditions that have led to suicides among contract manufacturing workers in China have prompted managers at technology firms such as Apple, IBM, Hewlett-Packard, and Toshiba to do some serious soul-searching.[77] "Work conditions can cause mental illness," says psychologist Rodney L. Lowman. "If we put healthy, well-adjusted people in the right foxhole with guns blaring at them, the likelihood of them experiencing depression and anxiety is very high."[78]

Managers can better cope with their own stress and establish ways for the organization to help employees cope if they understand the conditions that tend to produce work stress. Unethical environments and unsafe working conditions, such as those at some contract

Go to the "Ethical Dilemma" on pages 462, which pertains to organizational sources of stress.

Business Blooper

Zynga

Even with policies designed to soothe and take care of employees, sometimes it's not enough. Zynga, of Farmville fame, offers on-site yoga, a health club, a hair salon, free meals, and even a candy room. They thought it was great for employee morale, and they also thought they could afford it. After developing the whole idea of social gaming and convincing tens of millions of Facebook users to sign up, they've been on a losing streak. Set for a public offering the company's valuation was $20 billion. By the time of the offering, in 2012, it went down to $7 billion and is sliding downhill fast. The profits are nowhere in sight, hits are rare and important employees are running away. Right now the big challenge is going mobile, but the question is whether it is too little, too late. "Do I

wish we would have gone all-in on mobile and made a bigger commitment to it earlier?" asks Zynga's founder Mark Pincus. "Yes." The company has been unable to build an adequate network around mobile devices and has come nowhere near success with later apps. The pain of transitioning to mobile was shown in the earnings report in early 2013: Down $311 million and from 2014 to February 2015 the stock dropped 40 percent. It seems that the social gaming company isn't as social as they wish.

SOURCES: Juhi Kulkarni, "Here's Why Zynga Doesn't Deserve a Place in Your Portfolio," Newstex Finance & Accounting Blogs, February 20, 2015; Andre Tartar, "The Tech World's Tactics for Keeping Workers Working," *New York Magazine*, April 22, 2013, p. 18; David Streitfield, "Tested by Mobile, Zynga Aims to Rebuild," *New York Times*, February 6, 2013, B1–B2.

manufacturers, are major stressors, of course. In terms of more typical everyday work stressors, one approach is to think about the stress caused by the demands of job tasks and stress caused by interpersonal pressures and conflicts. But even if a company tries to help workers cope with stress, other conditions may cause a market slide, as shown in this chapter's Business Blooper about Farmville's developer, Zynga.

- **Task demands** are stressors arising from the tasks required of a person holding a particular job. Some kinds of decisions are inherently stressful: those made under time pressure, those that have serious consequences, and those that must be made with incomplete information. For example, emergency room doctors are under tremendous stress as a result of the task demands of their jobs. They regularly have to make quick decisions based on limited information that may determine whether a patient lives or dies. Jobs in which people have to deal with irate customers can also be highly stressful. Turnover among customer service employees can be as high as 300 percent a year in some industries.[79] Almost all jobs, especially those of managers, have some level of stress associated with task demands. Task demands also sometimes cause stress because of **role ambiguity**, which means that people are unclear about what task behaviors are expected of them. In a 2012 survey by the American Psychological Association (APA), 35 percent of respondents cited unclear job expectations as a cause of their workplace stress.[80]

- **Interpersonal demands** are stressors associated with relationships in the organization. Although interpersonal relationships can alleviate stress in some cases, they also can be a source of stress when the group puts pressure on an individual or when conflicts arise between individuals. Managers can resolve many conflicts using techniques that will be discussed in Chapter 14. **Role conflict** occurs when an individual perceives incompatible demands from others. Managers often feel role conflict because the demands of their superiors conflict with those of the employees in their department. They may be expected to support employees and provide them with opportunities to experiment and be creative, while at the same time, top executives are demanding a consistent level of output that leaves little time for creativity and experimentation.

10.7d Innovative Responses to Stress

Organizations that want to challenge their employees and stay competitive will never be stress-free, but healthy workplaces promote the physical and emotional well-being of their employees. Even simple things can change how people feel about their work. John Weaver, a psychologist at Psychology for Business, a management consultancy firm, advised managers at a long-term care facility in Wisconsin that had been flooded. Because of the water damage, the residents and employees had to move into an already occupied facility, and everyone was feeling cramped and annoyed. Pettiness was getting out of hand. Weaver and managers began asking each employee a simple question: *Why do you do this work?* "As they thought about the question," Weaver says, "you could see their attitude change. They could see the reasons why they needed to work together to put aside difficulties and compromise, and residents were treated better."[81]

What You Can Do to Combat Stress   Scientist and stress researcher Hans Selye said, "It's not stress that kills us, it is our reaction to it." Exhibit 10.13 lists 10 ways to stress-proof your day. A variety of techniques can help individuals avoid or manage the harmful effects of stress.

- ***Seek and destroy key sources of stress.*** A recent study found that the most beneficial stress management competency is *prevention*.[82] None of us can eliminate all the potential sources of stress from our lives, but we can avoid some of them and manage others. Take some time each

CONCEPT CONNECTION   Many companies help employees **manage stress** by offering discounts to local gyms, although a fairly recent workplace trend enables employees to work out while they work. Treadmill desks have shelves where employees can park their laptops and plug in their mobile phones so they can review documents, do online research, and hold meetings as they rack up the miles. Employees who've made use of these multitasking opportunities report that they have more energy, feel less stressed, and have lost weight thanks to these treadmill desks.

Mango Productions/Comet/Corbis

EXHIBIT 10.13   Ten Ways to Stress-Proof Your Day

Most people can find plenty of ways at work to get stressed out. Here are 10 steps that can help you de-pressurize:

1. Reframe a negative experience. If you left your laptop for a meeting in the car, for example, interpret it as a chance to compose your thoughts on the walk to retrieve it.
2. Attend a meeting in another department, just out of interest, to see what they're doing.
3. Notice at least one good thing about someone you don't like very well.
4. Find a quiet place where you can sit undisturbed and be alone with yourself, even if it's just for a few minutes.
5. Do something nice for someone—studies show that it can make you happier and calmer.
6. If you encounter a problem in your work or personal life, think of it as a challenge and an opportunity to learn.
7. Notice at least one good thing that you experience each day.
8. Make a list of achievable goals for the week and aim to mark one off your list each day.
9. Every day when you wake up, express gratitude for the new day and another chance to make a difference in the world.
10. Get enough sleep each night. If you don't, take a nap!

SOURCES: Based on "8 Steps to Stress-Proof Your Day," sidebar in Thea Singer, "The Perfect Amount of Stress," *Psychology Today* (March–April 2012): 78–85; "A New Kind of 'To Do' List," sidebar in Betty Shotton, "Awe: A Doorway to Breakthroughs, Insight, and Innovation," *Leader to Leader* (Spring 2013): 7–12; and Ruth Mantell, "How to Lower Your Workplace Stress," *The Wall Street Journal*, January 15, 2012, http://online.wsj.com/news/articles/SB10001424052970204257504577152502470874464 (accessed October 18, 2013).

day to identify stressors in your life and find ways to eliminate or reduce them. Being well organized, planning ahead, and using the various time-management techniques we've discussed in this chapter, such as emptying your head of all the pressures weighing on you, are highly effective ways to manage and prevent stress. One source of stress for some workers, especially freelancers, has been lack of health insurance. Sara Horowitz is on a mission to help prevent this type of stress, as described in this chapter's Director's Toolkit box.

- ***Find meaning and support.*** You are much more likely to experience ill effects from stress if you're working in a job that has no meaning for you and if you feel alone in life. The *buffering hypothesis* says that a perceived high degree of social support from family and friends protects one from the potentially adverse effects of stressful events.[83] That is, if you feel like you have a lot of support, you're less susceptible to the negative effects of bad stress.

- ***Meditate and manage your energy.*** Meditation is a way to both prevent and alleviate harmful stress responses. Some people meditate every morning or evening

Director's Toolkit

Freelancers Union

Being an independent worker has the advantages of being able to set our own hours, to take off for a yoga class, and schedule your own vacation time, but it also usually means you don't have health insurance. Sara Horowitz is on a mission to change that. After being hired by a law firm as an "independent contractor" she faced the realities of work with no benefits. Considering that her father was a labor attorney and her grandfather a leader in the International Ladies' Garment Workers Union, it's not surprising she started her own organization, The Freelancers Union. But whereas her paterfamilias organized strikes, she realized times have changed. Independent employees now number 20 million. Their most burning issue, Horowitz found, was lack of health insurance (though that has eased up since Obamacare). So she provided it to what is now over 200,000 members including graphic designers, accountants, lawyers, consultants, writers, web designers and sellers on Etsy. That might not sound like much, until you consider that the United Auto Workers currently has 380,000 members. Another problem is how to get work. Horowitz thinks Work Market and others like it are part of the solution, for they offer leads without cost to the freelancer and they help with one of the big frustrations: getting paid. Work Market kicks companies off their site if they don't follow through with the money.

On a typical day, Horowitz meets with a group of union members to talk about the health clinic and met in the clinic's Yoga and Meditation Studio. People liked the on-site nutritionist and acupuncturist and the fact that the average wait to see a doctor is just 10 minutes. The clinic is free to anyone who has signed up for the insurance, where premiums range from $225 to $603 per month. Running on an unusual team structure, the clinic pairs doctors with full-time "health coaches" who follow up on diet and medications, often helping patients avoid costly hospital stays. Because they operate more like a co-op than a for-profit, they are able to put all the profits back in to the company, to provide even better services. About 2,300 members have signed up for clinics, while others see doctors through plans such as Blue-Cross Blue Shield.

Horowitz operates more like an entrepreneur than an old-time union organizer. She identified the gaping hole of no health insurance and found investors to back up her plan. And she knows she brings more independence to workers who feel trapped in jobs that offer benefits. One such person is Jo-Ann Mort, who left corporate America to start her own fund-raising firm. "I was scared to go out on my own because I was worried I couldn't find affordable insurance," she said. "Sara made that possible."

SOURCES: Lydia DePillis, "Freelancing Can be the Future," *The Plain Dealer*, February 8, 2015, 3; Greenhouse, "Going It Alone, Together," *New York Times*, March 24, 2013, B1 and B4.

as a routine practice. Others find that short breaks to meditate for a few minutes several times a day are just as effective.[84] Any time during the day when you're feeling overwhelmed, you can close your eyes, focus on an image or a phrase that you find calming, and breathe deeply. Meditation can be an important part of an overall healthy lifestyle, such as eating right, getting enough rest, and exercising regularly, that helps you better cope with stress.

- *Find work–life balance.* A lack of work–life balance was the number one predictor of high levels of unhealthy stress, according to a 2012 report by the Kenexa High Performance Institute.[85] Innovative organizations offer options to help people lead more balanced lives. But you, as an individual, are also responsible for finding work–life balance. A survey by the Society for Human Resource Management found that 70 percent of employees said that they work beyond scheduled time and on weekends, but more than half of those admitted that it is because of *self-imposed pressure.* People who live balanced lives typically accomplish more than those who push themselves. For example, when 37Signals goes to a 32-hour workweek from May through October, managers say better work often gets done in four days than in five.[86]

What Managers and Organizations Can Do   Helping employees manage stress can sometimes be as simple as encouraging people to take regular breaks and vacations. Consider that more than a third of U.S. employees surveyed by the Families and Work Institute don't take their full allotment of vacation time.[87] Here are some proactive approaches that managers can take to combat the growing stress level in today's workplace:

- *Create a psychologically healthy workplace.* The number-one way to lessen employee stress is to create a healthy corporate culture that makes people feel valued.[88] This includes making sure that people don't have unreasonable workloads, providing opportunities for growth and advancement, and offering suitable salaries and benefits. It also means setting an example for employees to live balanced lives. Paul English, cofounder and chief technology officer of the travel search engine Kayak, says that the company's philosophy is to "work really hard for 40 to 45 hours a week, but we believe in people having strong personal lives."[89] English sometimes takes his children on business trips so that they can have new experiences together. At night, he reads murder mysteries or books about global health rather than reading about business or technology.

- *Make sure that people have some fun at work.* Particularly for jobs that have a high degree of task-related stress, allowing people to blow off steam by having fun can make all the difference in the stress level. At one Tampa-based software company help desk, Zane Bond is the "go-to guy for angry callers," but the stress doesn't get to him. One reason is that he loves solving problems. Another is that he has fun with his team members, breaking out the foam-dart guns and launching into battle with the soundtrack from *Top Gun* playing in the background.[90]

Managers should always remember that employees are *human* resources, with human needs. By acknowledging the personal aspects of employees' lives, these various initiatives communicate that managers and the organization care about employees. In addition, managers' attitudes make a tremendous difference in whether employees are stressed out and unhappy or relaxed, energetic, and productive.

REMEMBER THIS

- **Stress** is a physiological and emotional response to stimuli that place physical or psychological demands on an individual and create uncertainty and lack of personal control when important outcomes are at stake.
- Stress can sometimes be a positive force, but too much stress is harmful to individuals and the organizations where they work.
- The behavior pattern referred to as **Type A behavior** is characterized by extreme competitiveness, impatience, aggressiveness, and devotion to work.
- **Type B behavior** is a behavior pattern that reflects few of the Type A characteristics and includes a more balanced, relaxed approach to life.
- Type A managers can be powerful forces for innovation and change, but they can also create great stress for themselves and others.

- Work stress can be caused by both task demands and interpersonal demands.
- **Role ambiguity** refers to uncertainty about what behaviors are expected of a person in a particular role.
- **Role conflict** refers to incompatible demands of different roles, such as the demands of a manager's superiors conflicting with those of the manager's subordinates.
- Individuals can apply a variety of techniques to alleviate the ill effects of stress, and managers can implement initiatives in the workplace to help solve the problem of skyrocketing workplace stress.

CHAPTER **10**   **DISCUSSION QUESTIONS**

1. Why is self-awareness important for being a good manager? Can you think of some specific negative consequences that might result from a manager with low self-awareness?

2. As a manager, how might you deal with an employee who is always displaying negative emotions that affect the rest of the team? How might you use an understanding of attributions and emotional contagion to help you decide what to do?

3. What are some specific tips that you would give a new manager for building trust with subordinates? With other managers?

4. The chapter suggests that optimism is an important characteristic for a manager, yet some employees complain that optimistic managers cause them significant stress because they expect their subordinates to meet unreasonable goals or expectations. How might an employee deal with a perpetually optimistic manager?

5. Studies have suggested that extroverts contribute less to teams and are poor listeners, yet other studies suggest that they are more likely to earn six-figure incomes, even in today's collaborative, team-oriented workplaces. Discuss why you think this might be the case.

6. Surveys by the Conference Board show that job satisfaction has declined from 61 percent of people surveyed in 1987 to 45 percent in 2009, and one workplace analyst has said a high level of dissatisfaction is "the new normal." What are some factors that might explain this decline in satisfaction levels? Do you think it is possible for managers to reverse the trend? Discuss.

7. Which of the four components of emotional intelligence do you consider most important to an effective manager in today's world? Why?

8. How might understanding whether an employee has an internal or an external locus of control help a manager better communicate with, motivate, and lead the employee?

9. How do you think a system for self-management such as the five-step system described in this chapter could benefit you as a student? What parts of the system seem particularly useful to you? Explain.

10. Why do you think workplace stress is skyrocketing? Do you think it is a trend that will continue? Explain the reasons for your answer. Do you think it is the responsibility of managers and organizations to help employees manage stress? Why or why not?

SKILLS SELF-LEARNING

Personality Assessment: Jung's Typology[91]

For each of the following items, circle either a or b. In some cases, both a and b may apply to you. You should decide which is more like you, even if it is only slightly more true.

4. I would rather:
   a. Solve a new and complicated problem
   b. Work on something that I have done before

5. I like to:
   a. Work alone in a quiet place
   b. Be where "the action" is

6. I want a boss who:
   a. Establishes and applies criteria in decisions
   b. Considers individual needs and makes exceptions

7. When I work on a project, I:
   a. Like to finish it and get some closure
   b. Often leave it open for possible change

8. When making a decision, the most important considerations are:
   a. Rational thoughts, ideas, and data
   b. People's feelings and values

9. On a project, I tend to:
   a. Think it over and over before deciding how to proceed
   b. Start working on it right away, thinking about it as I go along

10. When working on a project, I prefer to:
    a. Maintain as much control as possible
    b. Explore various options

11. In my work, I prefer to:
    a. Work on several projects at a time, and learn as much as possible about each one
    b. Have one project that is challenging and keeps me busy

12. I often:
    a. Make lists and plans whenever I start something and may hate to alter my plans significantly
    b. Avoid plans and just let things progress as I work on them

13. When discussing a problem with colleagues, it is easy for me:
    a. To see "the big picture"
    b. To grasp the specifics of the situation

14. When the phone rings in my office or at home, I usually:
    a. Consider it an interruption
    b. Don't mind answering it

15. The word that describes me better is:
    a. Analytical
    b. Empathetic

16. When I am working on an assignment, I tend to:
    a. Work steadily and consistently
    b. Work in bursts of energy with "down time" in between

17. When I listen to someone talk on a subject, I usually try to:
    a. Relate it to my own experience and see whether it fits
    b. Assess and analyze the message

18. When I come up with new ideas, I generally:
    a. "Go for it"
    b. Like to contemplate the ideas some more

19. When working on a project, I prefer to:
    a. Narrow the scope so it is clearly defined
    b. Broaden the scope to include related aspects

20. When I read something, I usually:
    a. Confine my thoughts to what is written there
    b. Read between the lines and relate the words to other ideas

21. When I have to make a decision in a hurry, I often:
    a. Feel uncomfortable and wish I had more information
    b. Am able to do so with available data

22. In a meeting, I tend to:
    a. Continue formulating my ideas as I talk about them
    b. Speak out only after I have carefully thought the issue through

23. In work, I prefer spending a great deal of time on issues of:
    a. Ideas
    b. People

24. In meetings, I am most often annoyed with people who:
    a. Come up with many sketchy ideas
    b. Lengthen the meeting with many practical details

25. I tend to be:
    a. A morning person
    b. A night owl

26. My style in preparing for a meeting is:
    a. To be willing to go in and be responsive
    b. To be fully prepared and sketch an outline of the meeting

27. In meetings, I would prefer for people to:
    a. Display a fuller range of emotions
    b. Be more task-oriented

28. I would rather work for an organization where:
    a. My job was intellectually stimulating
    b. I was committed to its goals and mission

29. On weekends, I tend to:
    a. Plan what I will do
    b. Just see what happens and decide as I go along

30. I am more:
    a. Outgoing
    b. Contemplative

31. I would rather work for a boss who is:
    a. Full of new ideas
    b. Practical

In the following, choose the word in each pair that appeals to you more:

32. a. Social   b. Theoretical

33. a. Ingenuity   b. Practicality

34. a. Organized   b. Adaptable

35. a. Active   b. Concentration

Scoring and Interpretation

Count one point for each of the following items that you circled in the inventory.

	Score for I (Introversion)	Score for E (Extroversion)	Score for S (Sensing)	Score for N (Intuition)
	2a	2b	1b	1a
	6a	6b	10b	10a
	11a	11b	13a	13b
	15b	15a	16a	16b
	19b	19a	17a	17b
	22a	22b	21a	21b
	27b	27a	28b	28a
	32b	32a	30b	30a
Total	_____	_____	_____	_____

Circle the one with more points:
I or E
(If tied on I/E, don't count #11)

Circle the one with more points:
S or N
(If tied on S/N, don't count #16)

	Score for T (Thinking)	Score for F (Feeling)	Score for J (Judging)	Score for P (Perceiving)
	3a	3b	4a	4b
	5a	5b	7a	7b
	12a	12b	8b	8a
	14b	14a	9a	9b
	20a	20b	18b	18a
	24b	24a	23b	23a
	25a	25b	26a	26b
	29b	29a	31a	31b
Total	_____	_____	_____	_____

Circle the one with more points:
T or F
(If tied on T/F, don't count #24)

Circle the one with more points:
J or P
(If tied on J/P, don't count #23)

Your score is: I or E _____ S or N _____ T or F _____ J or P _____
Your type is _____ (example: INTJ, ESFP, etc.)

Characteristics Frequently Associated with Each Type

The scores above measure variables similar to the MBTI™ assessment, based on the work of psychologist Carl Jung. The MBTI™ assessment, which was described in the chapter text, identifies four dimensions and 16 different "types." The dominant characteristics associated with each type are described next. Remember that no one is a pure type; however, each individual has preferences for introversion versus extroversion, sensing versus intuition, thinking versus feeling, and judging versus perceiving. Read the description of your type as determined by your scores in the survey. Do you believe the description fits your personality?

Characteristics for Each Type

ISTJ: Organizer, trustworthy, responsible; good trustee or inspector

ISFJ: Quiet, conscientious, devoted, handles detail; good conservator

INFJ: Perseveres, inspirational, quiet, caring for others; good counselor

INTJ: Independent thinker, skeptical, theory, competence; good scientist

ISTP: Cool, observant, easygoing; good craftsperson

ISFP: Warm, sensitive, team player, avoids conflict; good artist

INFP: Idealistic, strong values, likes learning; good at noble service

INTP: Designer, logical, conceptual, likes challenges; good architect

ESTP: Spontaneous, gregarious; good at problem solving and promoting

ESFP: Sociable, generous, makes things fun; good entertainer

ENFP: Imaginative, enthusiastic, starts projects; good champion

ENTP: Resourceful, stimulating, dislikes routine, tests limits; good inventor

ESTJ: Order, structure, practical; good administrator or supervisor

ESFJ: People skills, harmonizer, popular, does things for people; good host

ENFJ: Charismatic, persuasive, fluent presenter, sociable, active; good teacher

ENTJ: Visionary planner, takes charge, hearty speaker; natural leader

GROUP LEARNING

Attribution Theory and Personality Role Play[92]

Step 1. Read the following background information: You are the new distribution manager for French Grains Bakery. Five drivers who deliver French Grains baked goods to grocery stores in the metropolitan area report to you. The drivers are expected to complete a Delivery Report to keep track of actual deliveries and any changes that occur. The Delivery Report is a key element in inventory control and provides the data for the company's invoicing of grocery stores. Errors become excessive when drivers fail to complete the report each day, especially when store managers request additional or different breads and baked goods when the driver arrives. As a result, French Grains may not be paid for several loaves of bread a day for each mistake in the Delivery Report. The result is lost revenue and poor inventory control.

One of the drivers accounts for about 60 percent of the errors in the Delivery Reports. This driver is a nice person and is generally reliable, but he is sometimes late for work. His major problem is that he falls behind in his paperwork. A second driver accounts for about 30 percent of the errors, and a third driver for about 10 percent of the errors. The other two drivers turn in virtually error-free Delivery Reports.

Step 2. Divide into groups of four to six students. As a group, discuss why you think one driver makes so many mistakes… List the reasons here:

1.

2.

3.

4.

Then, one person volunteer to play the role of the new distribution manager and another person play the role of the driver who accounts for 60 percent of the errors in the Delivery Reports.

Step 3. The new distribution manager should act the role as if his or her personality is high on "thinking" and low on "feeling," (on the MBTI™) or as if he or she is high on "authoritarianism." You have called the driver into your office to talk to him about doing a more complete and accurate job with the Delivery Report. Make some notes about how you will go about correcting this problem as a thinking-oriented or authoritarian leader. Exactly what will you say, and how will you get the driver to listen and change his behavior?

_____

_____

_____

Step 4. Now, start the role play between the distribution manager and the driver. Other group members should act as observers.

Step 5. After the role play is completed, the observers should give feedback on what worked and did not work with respect to the thinking or authoritarian personality style of giving feedback. How effective was it?

_____

_____

Step 6. Repeat steps 3 through 5, with other students volunteering to be the distribution manager and driver. This time, the manager should act as if his or her personality is strongly "feeling" or nonauthoritarian. Was this personality style more or less effective for correcting the problem?

Step 7. (Optional) The instructor can ask students to volunteer to play the role of the distribution manager and the driver in front of the class. Different students might take turns playing the role of distribution manager, emphasizing a different personality trait each time. The instructor can ask other students for feedback on the leader's effectiveness and about which approach seems more effective for correcting this situation and why.

Step 8. The instructor will lead a discussion on attribution theory and personality types and how these relate to effective work behaviors.

ACTION LEARNING

1. On your own complete the table that follows, making assessments of your family members according to the Myers-Briggs Type Indicator. Include some notes on why you have chosen each type for that particular person.

2. Talk over these assessments with at least one person in your family and try to listen to that other person's opinions, changing any of your own assessments as you think is necessary.

3. In class in groups of three or four, share your results and talk about why you think each person is a certain type and if you changed any assessments after the discussion with a family member. Also talk about how the combination of personality types has impacted your family.

4. Your instructor may choose to have you write a paper on your assessments.

	Introvert or extrovert?	Sensing or intuition?	Thinking or feeling?	Perceptive or judging?
Mother				
Father				
Sibling				
Sibling				
Other				
Other				
Other				

ETHICAL DILEMMA

Should I Fudge the Numbers?[93]

Sara MacIntosh recently joined MicroPhone, a large telecommunications company, to take over the implementation of a massive customer service training project. The program was created by Kristin Cole, head of HR and Sara's new boss. According to the grapevine, Kristin is hoping this project alone will give her the "star quality" that she needs to earn a coveted promotion. Industry competition is heating up, and MicroPhone's strategy calls for being the best at customer service, which means having the most highly trained people in the industry, especially those who work directly with customers. Kristin's new training program includes an average of one full week of intense customer service training for each of 3,000 people and has a price tag of about $40 million.

Kristin put together a team of overworked staffers to develop the training program, but she needed someone well qualified and dedicated to manage and implement the project. Sara, with eight years of experience, a long list of accomplishments, and advanced degrees in finance and organizational behavior, seemed perfect for the job.

During a thorough review of the proposal, Sara discovered some assumptions built into the formulas that raised red flags. She approached Dan Sotal, the team's coordinator, about her concerns, but the more Dan tried to explain how the financial projections were derived, the more Sara realized that Kristin's proposal was seriously flawed. No matter how she tried to work them out, the most that could be squeezed out of the $40 million budget was 20 hours of training per person, not the 40 hours everyone expected for such a high price tag.

Sara knew that although the proposal had been largely developed before she came on board, it would bear her signature. As she carefully described the problems with the proposal to Kristin and outlined the potentially devastating consequences, Kristin impatiently tapped her pencil. Finally, she stood up, leaned forward, and interrupted Sara, quietly saying, "Sara, make the numbers work so that it adds up to 40 hours and stays within the $40 million budget."

Sara glanced up and replied, "I don't think it can be done unless we either change the number of employees who are to be trained or the cost figure…."

Kristin's smile froze on her face as she again interrupted. "I don't think you understand what I'm saying. We have too much at stake here. *Make the previous numbers work.*" Stunned, Sara belatedly began to realize that Kristin was ordering her to fudge the numbers. She felt an anxiety attack coming on as she wondered what she should do.

What Would You Do?

1. Make the previous numbers work. Kristin and the entire team have put massive amounts of time into the project, and they all expect you to be a team player. You don't want to let them down. Besides, this project is a great opportunity for you in a highly visible position.

2. Stick to your principles and refuse to fudge the numbers. Tell Kristin that you will work overtime to help develop an alternative proposal that stays within the budget by providing more training to employees who work directly with customers and fewer training hours for those who don't have direct customer contact.

3. Go to the team and tell them what you've been asked to do. If they refuse to support you, threaten to reveal the true numbers to the CEO and board members.

CASE FOR CRITICAL ANALYSIS

A Nice Manager

The management promotion process at Chisum Industries was a benchmark for providing lateral moves, as well as promotion to the next level within the company. With offices, plants, and warehouses located in seven Texas cities, opportunities for the best and brightest at Chisum were extensive for middle management employees. The process invited candidates to explore their goals, strengths, and weaknesses, and to recount real-life scenarios and accomplishments. The selection team also visited the work sites of candidates for on-the-job observations and talks with fellow workers before bringing the final candidates to Dallas for interviews. The process offered personal insight and growth opportunities to all candidates for promotion. In March 2011, top management, including Marcus Chisum, Karl Jacobson, Mitch Ivey, Wayne Hughes, and Barbara Kennedy, were midway through a meeting to consider which of four middle management candidates to promote to the top position in the San Antonio office.

Marcus: "Who do we have next?"

Barbara: "Harry Creighton."

Scanning the group, Marcus saw a few nods and a shrug.

Marcus: "Feedback?"

Karl and Wayne, simultaneously: "Great guy."

Karl: "We all know that Harry came into a situation in which that particular location was suffering a drop in performance. Morale was low, and there were rumors of layoffs. He came in and calmed employee fears and has done a good job of raising performance levels."

Wayne: "He has a great relationship with employees. As we went around and talked to people, it was obvious that he has developed a level of trust and a vision that workers buy into."

Barbara: "The word that kept coming up among the workers was 'nice.'"

As was his habit during meetings, Mitch leaned back in his chair, tapping his pencil on the table. Initially annoyed by the habit, the team had gotten used to the sound over time.

Marcus: "Mitch, your initial reaction to his name was a shrug. What are you thinking?"

Mitch: "Just wondering if *nice* is what we're looking for here."

The remark was met with laughter.

Mitch: "Tell me, how does a manager achieve an across-the-board reputation as a *nice* guy? I've worked for and with a number of managers during my life. I respected them, thought many of them were fair and up-front in their treatment of us, thought some were jerks who should be canned …"

Marcus: "I hope I don't fall into that last category." (Laughter)

Mitch: "I don't recall any consensus about a manager being *nice*."

Karl: "Several people mentioned that Harry always has their back."

Barbara: "I got the impression that Harry covers for them."

Marcus: "Meaning what?"

Wayne: "Meaning, giving them some slack when it comes to things like overlooking their weaknesses, a little sloppiness with deadlines or taking time off."

Barbara: "Several mentioned that he's always willing to … let me look at my notes … '*Always willing to step in and help out.*' The phrase came up more than a few times and when I pressed them, they didn't elaborate. But I wondered …"

Karl: "… Is he managing or taking on some of their responsibilities?"

Barbara: "Exactly."

Mitch: "It's bothering me that he comes across as the parent who does his kid's project for the science fair."

Wayne: "I don't think it's that bad, but when you look at him in comparison with the other candidates, it makes me question whether he can take on the tough part of top management. There is nothing distinctive about him or his style."

Karl: "There's no *edge* here. No sense of boundaries. Does he want to manage employees or be popular with them? Can he say 'No' and mean it?"

Barbara: "Does Harry have the capability to walk that fine line that separates leaders; that distinguishes respect versus popularity or encouragement and support over *stepping in and helping out*?"

Marcus: "So, we see some good things about Harry. He has a lot of potential. But we also see that he has not yet reached a level where we can entrust him with this top management position. Our task here then, is to move on with the selection process, but over the next weeks, I would like for us to consider ways to help Harry reach that potential for future opportunities."

Questions

1. What does *nice* mean to you? Is being considered nice a good trait for managers to have or the kiss of death?

2. Is *nice* related to any concepts in the chapter, such as agreeableness, conscientiousness, or emotional intelligence? Discuss.

3. If Harry is passed over for promotion, what feedback and advice should he be given about how to improve his management skills for possible future promotion?

ON THE JOB VIDEO CASES

Mike Boyle Strength & Conditioning: Understanding Individual Behavior

Questions

1. Does Mike Boyle appear to be self-aware? How does his level of self-awareness affect the way he runs his business?

2. As you watch the video, focus on Marco's comments about himself and Mike's comments on Marco. Then use the four components of emotional intelligence to evaluate Marco as an employee and explain whether you think he *is* or *is not* emotionally intelligent.

3. Listen to Mike Boyle describe some of the characteristics and behaviors he requires of his employees, and then compare these to the Big Five personality traits. Pretend you are Mike Boyle and write out how valuable you think each of these traits is in the workplace. Rank them in order of importance, according to Boyle.

ENDNOTES

1. Claire Cain Miller, "For Incoming I.B.M. Chief, Self-Confidence Is Rewarded," *The New York Times*, October 27, 2011, www.nytimes.com/2011/10/28/business/for-incoming-ibm-chief-self-confidence-rewarded.html (accessed October 28, 2011).

2. "There's Life (and a Living) After Rejection," *The Independent on Sunday*, January 6, 2008; Amy Ellis Nutt, "Harry Potter's Disappearing Act," *Newhouse News Service* (April 23, 2007): 1; and Tom Muha, "Achieving Happiness: Setbacks Can Make Us Stronger," *The Capital*, May 31, 2009.

3. Muha, "Achieving Happiness"; and Melinda Beck, "If at First You Don't Succeed, You're in Excellent Company," *The Wall Street Journal*, April 29, 2008.

4. M. E. Gist, "Self-Efficacy: Implications for Organizational Behavior and Human Resource Management," *Academy of Management Review* (July 1987): 47; and Arthur Bandura, "Self-efficacy," in V. S. Ramachaudran, ed., *Encyclopedia of Human Behavior*, vol. 4 (New York: Academic Press, 1994): pp. 71–81.

5. Reported in William W. George et al., "Discovering Your Authentic Leadership," *Harvard Business Review* (February 2007): 129–138.

6. Bill George, "Leadership Skills: It Starts with Self-Awareness," *Leadership Excellence* (June 2011): 13; Tricia Bisoux, "What Makes Leaders Great" (interviews with leadership experts), *BizEd* (September–October 2005): 40–45; Warren Bennis, *Why Leaders Can't Lead* (San Francisco: Jossey-Bass, 1989); Daniel Goleman, "What Makes a Leader?" *Harvard Business Review* (November–December 1998): 93ff; and Richard E. Boyatzis, *The Competent Manager: A Model for Effective Performance* (New York: Wiley, 1982).

7. Employee quoted in Stratford Sherman, "How Tomorrow's Best Leaders Are Learning Their Stuff," *Fortune* (November 27, 1995): 90–102.

8. Charlotte Beers, interviewed by Adam Bryant, "The Best Scorecard Is the One You Keep for Yourself," *The New York Times*, March 31, 2012, www.nytimes.com/2012/04/01/business/charlotte-beers-on-the-importance-of-self-assessment.html?pagewanted=all (accessed April 1, 2012).

9. Thanks to Scott Williams, "Self-Awareness and Personal Development," *LeaderLetter* Web site, www.wright.edu/~scott.williams/LeaderLetter/selfawareness.htm (accessed August 21, 2007), for this image.

10. Steven Snyder, "Leadership Struggle: It's an Art to Be Mastered," *Leadership Excellence* (January 2013): 11; and Ira Chaleff, "Avoid Fatal Crashes: Leaders and Their Blind Spots," *Leadership Excellence* (May 2012): 13.

11. Adam Bryant, "Francisco D'Souza of Cognizant, on Finding Company Heroes" (Corner Office column), *The New York Times*, September 1, 2013, BU2.

12. C. Fletcher and C. Baldry, "A Study of Individual Differences and Self-Awareness in the Context of Multi-Source Feedback," *Journal of Occupational and Organizational Behavior* 73, no. 3 (2000): 303–319.

13. Ellen McGirt, "Do You Pass the Leadership Test?" *Fast Company* (December 2012–January 2013): 63–67.

14. George, "Leadership Skills"; and Beers, "The Best Scorecard Is the One You Keep for Yourself."

15. Kevin Baxter, "Landon Donovan Rediscovered His Love of Soccer When He Left It," *The Los Angeles Times*, September 5, 2013, http://articles.latimes.com/2013/sep/05/sports/la-sp-landon-donovan-20130906 (accessed October 16, 2013); Paul Chant, "Is This Guy Mutts Nuts … Or a Dog of Awe? Answer June 12, D-Day for Donovan," *The People* (May 30, 2010): 7; Jere Longman, "Donovan Pushes Ahead, Looking Inside," *The New York Times*, May 19, 2010; Nancy Armour, "Top U.S. Soccer Star Finds Peace," *Journal-Gazette*, June 25, 2010; and Ives Galarcep, "World Cup 2014: Bitter Landon Donovan Criticizes U.S. Coach Klinsmann," *Sporting News*, July 3, 2014, http://www.sportingnews.com/soccer/story/2014-07-03/world-cup-2014-landon-donovan-jurgen-klinsmann-la-galaxy-mls (accessed August 6, 2014).

16. Jerry Krueger and Emily Killham, "At Work, Feeling Good Matters," *Gallup Management Journal*, December 8, 2005, http://gmj.gallup.com/content/20311/work-feeling-good-matters.aspx (accessed September 17, 2010).

17. M. T. Iaffaldano and P. M. Muchinsky, "Job Satisfaction and Job Performance: A Meta-Analysis," *Psychological Bulletin* (March 1985): 251–273; C. Ostroff, "The Relationship Between Satisfaction, Attitudes, and Performance: An Organizational-Level Analysis," *Journal of Applied Psychology* (December 1992): 963–974; and M. M. Petty, G. W. McGee, and J. W. Cavender, "A Meta-Analysis of the Relationship between Individual Job Satisfaction and Individual Performance," *Academy of Management Review* (October 1984): 712–721.

18. Conference Board survey, reported in "Job Satisfaction in U.S. Hits All-Time Low," *News for You* (February 17, 2010): 4.

19. Tony Schwartz, "The Greatest Sources of Satisfaction in the Workplace Are Internal and Emotional," *Fast Company* (November 2000): 398–402.

20. Reported in Victor Lipman, "The Foundational Importance of Trust in Management," *Forbes*, October 7, 2013, http://www.forbes.com/sites/victorlipman/2013/10/07/the-foundational-importance-of-trust-in-management/ (accessed October 17, 2013).

21. "Closing the Engagement Gap: A Road Map for Driving Superior Business Performance," *Towers Perrin Global Workforce Study 2007–2008,* www.towersperrin.com/tp/getwebcachedoc?webc=HRS/USA/2008/200803/GWS_Global_Report20072008_31208.pdf (accessed September 20, 2010).

22. Example in Rick Wartzman, "Trust: Effective Managers Make It a Priority," *Bloomberg BusinessWeek*, October 16, 2009, http://www.businessweek.com/managing/content/oct2009/ca20091019_333718.htm (accessed October 17, 2013).

23. Lipman, "The Foundational Importance of Trust in Management"; and Wartzman, "Trust: Effective Managers Make It a Priority."

24. Leadership IQ survey, reported in "Many Employees Don't Trust Their Boss," *Machine Design* (September 2007): 2.

25. Quoted in Paul Harris, "Leadership: Role Models Earn Trust and Profits," *T&D* (March 2010): 47.

26. This is a very brief introduction to the subject of attributions and their role in organizations. For a recent overview of the research on attributional theory and a special issue devoted to the topic, see Marie Dasborough, Paul Harvey, and Mark J. Martinko, "An Introduction to Attributional Influences in Organizations," *Group & Organization Management* 36, no. 4 (2011): 419–426.

27. "Poll: Most Organizations Don't Use Personality Tests," *HR Magazine* 57, no. 2 (February 2012): 88; and Stephen T. Watson, "Job Hunting in the Virtual Age: Recruiters Can Be Overwhelmed by the Flood of Resumes," *Buffalo News*, August 19, 2012, D1.

28. See J. M. Digman, "Personality Structure: Emergence of the Five-Factor Model," *Annual Review of Psychology* 41 (1990): 417–440; M. R. Barrick and M. K. Mount, "Autonomy as a Moderator of the Relationships Between the Big Five Personality Dimensions and Job Performance," *Journal of Applied Psychology* (February 1993): 111–118; and J. S. Wiggins and A. L. Pincus, "Personality: Structure and Assessment," *Annual Review of Psychology* 43 (1992): 473–504.

29. Patricia Sellers, "Marissa Mayer: Ready to Rumble at Yahoo," *Fortune* (October 29, 2012): 118–128; Ginka Toegel and Jean-Louis Barsoux, "How to Become a Better Leader," *MIT Sloan Management Review* (Spring 2012): 51–60; and Nancy Ancowitz, "Success Isn't Only for the Extroverts," *The New York Times*, November 1, 2009, BU8.

30. Del Jones, "Not All Successful CEOs Are Extroverts," *USA TODAY*, June 6, 2006, www.usatoday.com/money/companies/management/2006-06-06-shy-ceo-usat_x.htm (accessed September 20, 2010).

31. Susan Cain, "Hire Introverts," *The Atlantic* (July–August 2012), p. 68; Adam M. Grant, Francesca Gino, and David A. Hofmann, "The Hidden Advantages of Quiet Bosses," *Harvard Business Review* (December 2010), p. 28; Susan Cain, "Must Great Leaders Be Gregarious?" *The New York Times*, September 16, 2012, SR-8; and Bryan Walsh, "The Upside of Being an Introvert (and Why Extroverts Are Overrated)," *Time* (February 6, 2012): 40–45

32. Sellers, "Marissa Mayer: Ready to Rumble at Yahoo."

33. Reported in Daisy Grewal, "When Nice Guys Finish First," *Scientific American Mind* (July–August 2012): 62–65.

34. Reported in Christopher Palmeri, "Putting Managers to the Test," *BusinessWeek* (November 20, 2006): 82.

35. Research reported in J. J. McCorvey, "Research Corner: Feeling Guilty? Good. Why Guilt Makes You a Better Leader," *Inc.* (July–August 2012): 26; and Rachel Emma Silverman, "Plagued by Guilt? You May Be Management Material," *The Wall Street Journal*, May 29, 2012, http://blogs.wsj.com/atwork/2012/05/29/plagued-by-guilt-you-may-be-management-material/ (accessed June 3, 2012).

36. Julian B. Rotter, "Generalized Expectancies for Internal versus External Control of Reinforcement," *Psychological Monographs* 80, no. 609 (1966); and J. B. Rotter, "Internal Versus External Control of Reinforcement: A Case History," *American Psychologist* 45, no. 4 (April 1990): 489–493.

37. See P. E. Spector, "Behavior in Organizations as a Function of Employees' Locus of Control," *Psychological Bulletin* (May 1982): 482–497.

38. T. W. Adorno et al., *The Authoritarian Personality* (New York: Harper & Row, 1950).

39. Niccolò Machiavelli, *The Prince*, trans. George Bull (Middlesex: Penguin, 1961).

40. Richard Christie and Florence Geis, *Studies in Machiavellianism* (New York: Academic Press, 1970).

41. R. G. Vleeming, "Machiavellianism: A Preliminary Review," *Psychological Reports* (February 1979): 295–310.

42. Christie and Geis, *Studies in Machiavellianism*.

43. Carl Jung, *Psychological Types* (London: Routledge and Kegan Paul, 1923).

44. Mary H. McCaulley, "Research on the MBTI and Leadership: Taking the Critical First Step," keynote address, The Myers-Briggs Type Indicator and Leadership: An International Research Conference (January 12–14, 1994).

45. Jennifer Overbo, "Using Myers-Briggs Personality Type to Create a Culture Adapted to the New Century," *T+D* (February 2010): 70–72.

46. Reported in Lillian Cunningham, "Does It Pay to Know Your Type?" *Washington Post*, December 14, 2012, http://articles.washingtonpost.com/2012-12-14/national/35847528_1_personality-types-myers-briggs-type-indicator-financial-success (accessed March 20, 2013).

47. Reported in Lisa Takeuchi Cullen, "SATs for J-O-B-S," *Time* (April 3, 2006): 89.

48. Michael Kinsman, "Businesses Can Suffer If Workers' Emotions Not Dealt With" (an interview with Mel Fugate), *San Diego Union-Tribune*, December 17, 2006; and Mel Fugate, Angelo J. Kinicki, and Gregory E. Prussia, "Employee Coping with Organizational Change: An Examination of Alternative Theoretical Perspectives and Models," *Personnel Psychology* 61, no. 1 (Spring 2008): 1–36.

49. "Emotion," *The Free Dictionary*, www.thefreedictionary.com/Emotions (accessed June 15, 2010); and "Motivation and Emotion," *Psychology 101* (AllPsych Online), http://allpsych.com/psychology101/emotion.html (accessed June 15, 2010).

50. E. Hatfield, J. T. Cacioppo, and R. L. Rapson, *Emotional Contagion* (New York: Cambridge University Press, 1994).

51. Reported in Robert I. Sutton, "Are You Being a Jerk? Again?" *BusinessWeek* (August 25, 2008): 52.

52. Research by Noah Eisenkraft and Hillary Anger Elfenbein, reported in Nicole Branan, "The 'Me' Effect," *Scientific American Mind* (November–December 2010): 14–15; Noah Eisenkraft and Hillary Anger Elfenbein, "The Way You Make Me Feel," *Psychological Science* 21 (April 2010): 505–510; Robert I. Sutton, "How Bad Apples Infect the Tree," *The New York Times*, November 28, 2010, BU.8; and Roy Baumeister et al., "Bad Is Stronger Than Good," *Review of General Psychology* 5, no. 4 (2001): 323–370.

53. Krueger and Killham, "At Work, Feeling Good Matters."

54. Daniel Goleman, "Leadership That Gets Results," *Harvard Business Review* (March–April 2000): 79–90; Daniel Goleman, "Emotional Mastery: Seek to Excel in Four Dimensions," *Leadership Excellence* (June 2011): 12–13; and Daniel Goleman, *Emotional Intelligence: Why It Can Matter More Than IQ* (New York: Bantam Books, 1995).

55. Alan Farnham, "Are You Smart Enough to Keep Your Job?" *Fortune* (January 15, 1996): 34–47.

56. Hendrie Weisinger, *Emotional Intelligence at Work* (San Francisco: Jossey-Bass, 2000); D. C. McClelland, "Identifying Competencies with Behavioral-Event Interviews," *Psychological Science* (Spring 1999): 331–339; Goleman, "Leadership That Gets Results"; D. Goleman, *Working with Emotional Intelligence* (New York: Bantam Books, 1999); and Lorie Parch, "Testing … 1,2,3," *Working Woman* (October 1997): 74–78.

57. Michael Wolff, "Tim Armstrong's Tantrum Reveals the Anomaly That Is AOL," *The Guardian* August 19, 2013, http://www.theguardian.com/commentisfree/2013/aug/19/tim-armstrong-tantrum-patch-aol (accessed October 18, 2013); and Leslie Kaufman, "AOL Chief Apologized over Firing of Worker," *The New York Times*, August 14, 2013, B3.

58. Reported in Cari Tuna, "Lawyers and Employers Take the Fight to 'Workplace Bullies'" (Theory & Practice column), *The Wall Street Journal*, August 4, 2008.

59. These examples and statistics are from Sam Hananel, "Workplace Bullying Gets Higher Profile as Movement Grows to Limit Worker Abuse," Associated Press, at *Yahoo News*, March 1, 2013, http://news.yahoo.com/growing-push-halt-workplace-bullying-091201526.html (accessed October 18, 2013).

60. This section on self-management is based heavily on David Allen, *Getting Things Done: The Art of Stress-Free Productivity* (New York: Viking Penguin, 2001).

61. Reported in "One of These Days," *The Wall Street Journal*, March 11, 1997, A1.

62. Based on Allen, *Getting Things Done*; and Francis Heylighen and Clément Vidal, "Getting Things Done: The Science Behind Stress-Free Productivity, *Long Range Planning* 41 (2008): 585–605.

63. T. A. Beehr and R. S. Bhagat, *Human Stress and Cognition in Organizations: An Integrated Perspective* (New York: Wiley, 1985); and Bruce Cryer, Rollin McCraty, and Doc Childre, "Pull the Plug on Stress," *Harvard Business Review* (July 2003): 102–107.

64. Anita Bruzzese, "Wall Street Woes, Election Add to Workplace Stress," *Gannett News Service* (September 29, 2008).

65. "Desk Rage Rising," *Office Solutions* (January 2009): 9; and Carol Hymowitz, "Bosses Have to Learn How to Confront Troubled Employees," *The Wall Street Journal*, April 23, 2007.

66. Sam Hananel, "Workplace Bullying Gets Higher Profile."

67. Discussed in Alice Park, "The Two Faces of Anxiety," *Time* (December 5, 2011): 54–65; and Melinda Beck, "Anxiety Can Bring Out the Best," *The Wall Street Journal*, June 18, 2012, http://online.wsj.com/article/SB10001424052702303836404577474451463041994.html (accessed June 20, 2012).

68. "Are You Working Too Hard? A Conversation with Mind-Body Researcher Herbert Benson," *Harvard Business Review* (November 2005): 53–58; and R. M. Yerkes and J. D. Dodson, "The Relation of Strength of Stimulus to Rapidity of Habit Formation," *Journal of Comparative Neurology and Psychology* 18 (1908): 459–482.

69. Mathias V. Schmidt and Lars Schwabe, "Splintered by Stress," *Scientific American Mind* (September–October 2011): 22–29.

70. Reported in Brian Nadel, "The Price of Pressure," special advertising feature, *Fortune* (December 11, 2006): 143–146.

71. Health and Safety Authority survey, reported in Joe Humphreys, "Stress Will Be Main Cause of Workplace Illness by 2020," *Irish Times*, July 27, 2005.

72. Don Mills, "Running on High Octane or Burning Out Big Time? Stress Flunkies," *National Post*, April 8, 2006.

73. M. Friedman and R. Rosenman, *Type A Behavior and Your Heart* (New York: Knopf, 1974).

74. David Sacks, "The Way I Work: Yammer," *Inc.* (November 2011): 123–124.

75. American Psychological Association, *Stress in America 2009*, APA.org, 2009, www.apa.org/news/press/releases/stress-exec-summary.pdf (accessed September 5, 2012).

76. Mills, "Running on High Octane or Burning Out Big Time?"; Vani Doraisamy, "Young Techies Swell the Ranks of the Depressed," *The Hindu*, October 11, 2005.

77. Charles Duhigg and David Barboza, "In China, Human Costs Are Built into an iPad," *The New York Times*, January 25, 2012, www.nytimes.com/2012/01/26/business/ieconomy-apples-ipad-and-the-human-costs-for-workers-in-china.html?pagewanted=all (accessed January 26, 2012); and Nick Wingfield and Charles Duhigg, "Apple Asks Outside Groups to Inspect Factories," *The New York Times*, February 13, 2012, http://bits.blogs.nytimes.com/2012/02/13/apple-announces-independent-factory-inspections/ (accessed February 13, 2012).

78. Quoted in Elizabeth Bernstein, "When a Co-Worker Is Stressed Out," *The Wall Street Journal*, August 26, 2008.

79. Reported in Sue Shellenbarger, "Health & Fitness: How to Keep Your Cool in Angry Times," *The Wall Street Journal Asia*, September 27, 2010, 11.

80. "APA Survey Finds Feeling Valued at Work Linked to Well-Being and Performance," American Psychological Association, March 12, 2012, www.apa.org/news/press/releases/2012/03/well-being.aspx (accessed September 5, 2012).

81. Reported in Ruth Mantell, "How to Lower Your Workplace Stress," *The Wall Street Journal*, January 15, 2012, http://online.wsj.com/news/articles/SB10001424052970204257504577152502470874464 (accessed October 18, 2013).

82. Robert Epstein, "Fight the Frazzled Mind," *Scientific American Mind* (September–October 2011): 30–35.

83. Sheldon Cohen and Thomas Ashby Wills, "Stress, Social Support, and the Buffering Hypothesis," *Psychological Bulletin* 85, no. 2 (1985): 310–357.

84. Eilene Zimmerman, "When Stress Flirts with Burnout," *The New York Times*, January 17, 2010; and Joanna Barsh, J. Mogelof, and C. Webb, "How Centered Leaders Achieve Extraordinary Results," *McKinsey Quarterly*, October 2010, www.mckinseyquarterly.com/How_centered_leaders_achieve_extraordinary_results_2678 (accessed January 16, 2011).

85. Reported in Ann Pace, "Stressed Out?" *T+D* (October 2012): 14.

86. Jason Fried, "Be More Productive. Take Time Off." *The New York Times*, August 18, 2012, http://www.nytimes.com/2012/08/19/opinion/sunday/be-more-productive-shorten-the-workweek.html?_r=0 (accessed October 18, 2013).

87. Rosabeth Moss Kanter, "Balancing Work and Life," *Knight-Ridder Tribune News Service*, April 8, 2005.

88. "APA Survey Finds Feeling Valued at Work Linked to Well-Being and Performance."

89. "The Way I Work: Paul English, Kayak," *Inc.* (February 2010): 98–101.

90. Shellenbarger, "Health & Fitness: How to Keep Your Cool in Angry Times."

91. From Dorothy Marcic, *Organizational Behavior*, 4th ed. (Mason, OH: South-Western, Cengage Learning, 1995). Reproduced by permission.

92. Based on K. J. Keleman, J. E. Garcia, and K. J. Lovelace, *Management Incidents: Role Plays for Management Development* (Dubuque, IA: Kendall-Hunt Publishing Company, 1990): 69–72.

93. Adapted from Doug Wallace, "Fudge the Numbers or Leave," *Business Ethics* (May–June 1996): 58–59. Copyright © 1996 by New Mountain Media LLC. Reproduced with permission of New Mountain Media LLC.

CHAPTER

11

Leadership

CHAPTER OUTLINE

LEARNING OUTCOMES

After studying this chapter, you should be able to:

11.1 Define leadership and explain its importance for organizations.

11.2 Describe the leadership trends emerging in today's organizations, including Level 5 leadership, servant leadership, and authentic leadership.

11.3 Discuss how women's style of leading is typically different from men's.

11.4 Identify personal characteristics associated with effective leaders.

11.5 Define task-oriented behavior and people-oriented behavior and explain how these categories are used to evaluate and adapt leadership style.

11.6 Describe the situational model of leadership and its application to subordinate participation.

11.7 Discuss how leadership fits the organizational situation and how organizational characteristics can substitute for leadership behaviors.

11.8 Describe transformational leadership and when it should be used.

11.9 Explain how followership is related to effective leadership.

11.10 Identify sources of leader power and the tactics that leaders use to influence others.

R U Ready 2 B a Manager?

Delivered

Before reading this chapter, please circle either "Mostly True" or "Mostly False" for each of the five questions below.

1 I am able to get people enthused about an idea and to take action.

Mostly True	Mostly False

[page 470]

2 I think a leader who is humble will not gain the respect of subordinates. Servant leadership is an oxymoron.

Mostly True	Mostly False

[page 474]

3 Leaders need to be strong and hard-nosed and I'm not sure women are up to that part of the job.

Mostly True	Mostly False

[page 477]

4 When I am working with a leader, I make sure I bring my critical thinking skills so that I am not merely a passive follower.

Mostly True	Mostly False

[page 494]

5 When I am working with a group, I am able to get things done through the strength of the relationships and my expertise, rather than relying on authoritarian methods.

Mostly True	Mostly False

[page 499]

An interesting thing happened when Daniel Snyder, owner of the Washington Redskins, stopped meddling in the decisions of his football coaches—the team started winning. For many of Snyder's 14 years as owner of the team, he had a reputation as a meddlesome, overbearing boss who got in the way of people doing their jobs. The problem was that Snyder wanted to be involved in every detail of the team, even making big decisions on player acquisition himself. Snyder has a natural "telling" style that didn't go over well with highly skilled, well-trained coaches and players who wanted to get on with doing their work. But Snyder has proven that leaders can change. "He's stepped back from it," one insider says. "And he's having more fun because of it." In 2012, the Redskins won their first NFC East division title since 1999, Snyder's first season as owner. "I think he deserves a lot of credit," said former general manager Charley Casserly, whom Snyder fired in 1999. "He's allowed them to do their jobs. They've turned the franchise around and made it a winner again."[1]

In the previous chapter, we explored differences in personality, perception, and emotions that affect behavior. Some of the most important personality differences for the organization's success are those of its leaders because leader behaviors play a critical role in shaping employee performance. Some leaders take a heavily task-oriented approach, as Daniel Snyder did with the Washington Redskins, whereas others use a more people-oriented style. Yet as the opening example shows, many leaders can also change their style. In this chapter, we define leadership and explore how managers develop leadership qualities. We look at some important leadership approaches for contemporary organizations, as well as examine trait, behavioral, and contingency theories of leadership effectiveness, discuss charismatic and transformational leadership, explore the role of followership, and consider how leaders use power and influence to get things done. Chapters 11 through 12 will look in detail at many of the functions of leadership, including employee motivation, communication, and encouraging teamwork.

11.1 The Nature of Leadership

Chris Zane

CONCEPT CONNECTION Chris Zane, founder and owner of Zane's Cycles in Branford, Connecticut, is an expert at turning first-time customers into lifetime customers. In fact, he wrote the book on it—*Reinventing the Wheel*. The book is a reflection of his enduring goal, which is to provide the ultimate shopping experience that makes customers feel great about his products and services. Zane actually started his business at age 16 with a $23,000 loan from his grandfather. Under his **leadership**, Zane's Cycles now posts about $21 million in annual sales.

In most situations, a team, military unit, department, or volunteer group is only as good as its leader. Yet there are as many variations among leaders as there are among other individuals, and many different styles of leadership can be effective.

So, what does it mean to be a leader? Among all the ideas and writings about leadership, three aspects stand out—people, influence, and goals. Leadership occurs among people, involves the use of influence, and is used to attain goals.[2] *Influence* means that the relationship among people is not passive. Moreover, influence is designed to achieve some end or goal. Thus, **leadership**, as defined here, is the ability to influence people toward the attainment of goals. This definition captures the idea that leaders are involved with other people in the achievement of goals. Leadership is reciprocal, occurring *among* people.[3] Leadership is a "people" activity, distinct from administrative paperwork or problem-solving activities. Throughout this text, we have looked at various organizations that are experimenting with bosslessness. But every team and organization needs leadership. As described in the "Director's Toolkit," being a "leader" can be more powerful than being a "boss."

Task versus People Orientation

Instructions: Responding to the statements below can help you diagnose your approach to dealing with others when you are in a leadership role. If you have been a leader at work with people reporting to you, think back to that experience. Or you can think about how you usually behave as a formal or informal leader in a group to get an assignment completed. Please answer honestly about how frequently you display each behavior.

	Mostly True	Mostly False
1. I intentionally try to make people's work on the job more pleasant.	_____	_____
2. I focus more on execution than on being pleasant with people.	_____	_____
3. I go out of my way to help others.	_____	_____
4. I personally hold people accountable for their performance.	_____	_____
5. I work hard to maintain a friendly atmosphere on the team.	_____	_____
6. I clearly tell people what I expect of them.	_____	_____
7. I think a lot about people's personal welfare.	_____	_____
8. I check up on people to know how they are doing.	_____	_____
9. I am concerned more with relationships than with results.	_____	_____
10. I assign people to specific roles and tasks.	_____	_____
11. I focus more on being pleasant with people than on execution of tasks.	_____	_____
12. I am concerned more with results than with people's feelings.	_____	_____

Scoring and Interpretation: Give yourself 2 points for each Mostly True and 1 point for each Mostly False.

People Orientation: Sum your points for the odd-numbered questions: _____.
Task Orientation: Sum your points for the even-numbered questions: _____.
Your People Orientation score reveals your orientation toward people and relationships, which will be described in the chapter. A score of 10 or higher suggests that you may be "high" on people behavior. A score of 9 or below suggests that you may be "low" on people orientation. Your Task Orientation score reveals your orientation toward tasks and outcomes. A score of 10 or higher suggests that you may be "high" on task-oriented behavior. A score of 9 or below suggests that you may be "low" on task orientation.

What is your primary leadership orientation? Which of the following best represents your leadership style (check one)? Look at Exhibit 11.7 on page 486 to see the quadrant in which you fit.

_____Low Task, Low People = Delegating style
_____Low Task, High People = Participating style
_____High Task, Low People = Telling style
_____High Task, High People = Selling style
Does your quadrant seem correct based on your experience? Compare your scores to the scores of other students.

REMEMBER THIS

- The attitudes and behaviors of leaders shape the conditions that determine how well employees can do their jobs; thus, leaders play a tremendous role in the organization's success.

- **Leadership** is the ability to influence people toward the attainment of organizational goals.
- Many different styles of leadership can be effective.

Director's Toolkit

Bossless Does Not Mean Leaderless

Conventional management states that when managing a company, it needs to be highly ordered, with well-defined roles, rules, and regulations, and led by a strong boss. This has always been the standard in the U.S. military. But what if bosslessness and self-organization give rise to an effective order far more powerful than what traditional management might carry out?

The story of Captain Michael Abrashoff and his command of the USS Benfold is legendary inside and outside the Navy. Within months, he transformed a crew of demoralized sailors into confident and inspired problem solvers eager to take the initiative. To do this, Captain Abrashoff had to change his traditional management style to a more "bossless" leadership style. Some of Captain Abrashoff's methods for becoming less of a boss and more of a leader include the following:

- **Lead by example.** Real leadership is done by example. Whenever he could not get the results he wanted, Captain Abrashoff asked himself three questions: Did I clearly articulate the goals? Did I give people enough time and resources to accomplish the task? Did I give them enough training? He discovered that many times, he was as much a part of the problem as his people were.

- **Communicate purpose and meaning.** Give employees a compelling vision of their work and a good reason to believe that it is important. Tell people personally what's in it for them. Abrashoff found that the more people knew what the goals were, the better buy-in he got—and the better results they achieved together.

- **Create a climate of trust.** The best way to get a ship—or any organization—to improve dramatically is to give the troops all the responsibility they can handle and then stand back.

- **Look for results, not salutes.** You need to have people in your organization who can tap you on your shoulder and say, "Is this the best way?" or "Slow down," or "Think about this." When managers announce decisions after little or no consultation, and when they make it clear that their orders aren't to be questioned, then conditions are ripe for disaster.

- **Take calculated risks.** An organization that aims to stay alive and strong should make sure to praise and promote risk takers, even when they fail once in a while. Show me someone who has never made a mistake, and I will show you someone who is not doing anything to improve your organization. If all you give are orders, then all you will get are order takers.

- **Generate unity.** Abrashoff states that organizations can always hire smart people, but he found what works better are staff members who work together and support one another. Treating people with dignity and respect is not only morally right, but also highly practical and productive.

SOURCES: D. Michael Abrashoff, "Retention Through Redemption," *Harvard Business Review* (February 2001): 136–141; D. Michael Abrashoff, *It's Your Ship: Management Techniques from the Best Damn Ship in the Navy* (New York: Business Plus, 2002); and Mike Abrashoff, "The Bossless, Not Leaderless Office," Leadership Blog, *GLS Worldwide*, June 25, 2013, http://www.glsworld.com/thought-leadership/leadership-blog/2013/06/the-bossless-not-leaderless-office/ (accessed November 23, 2013).

11.2 Contemporary Leadership

The concept of leadership evolves as the needs of organizations change. That is, the environmental context in which leadership is practiced influences which approach might be most effective, as well as what kinds of leaders are most admired by society. The technology, economic conditions, labor conditions, and social and cultural mores of the times all play a role. A significant influence on leadership styles in recent years is the turbulence and uncertainty of the environment. Ethical and economic difficulties, corporate governance concerns, globalization, changes in technology, new ways of working, shifting employee expectations, and significant social transitions have contributed to a shift in how we think about and practice leadership. Four approaches that are in tune with leadership for today's turbulent times are Level 5 leadership, servant leadership, authentic leadership, and interactive leadership, which has been associated with women's style of leading.

11.2a Level 5 Leadership

A study conducted by Jim Collins and his research associates identified the critical importance of what Collins calls *Level 5 leadership* in transforming companies from merely good to truly great organizations.[4] As described in his book *Good to Great: Why Some Companies Make the Leap ... and Others Don't*, Level 5 leadership refers to the highest level in a hierarchy of manager capabilities, as illustrated in Exhibit 11.1.

EXHIBIT 11.1 Level 5 Hierarchy

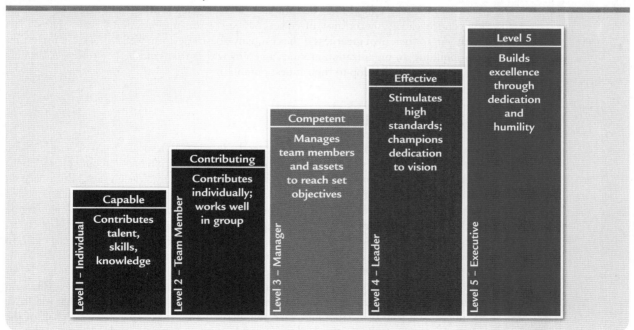

SOURCE: Based on Jim Collins, *Good to Great: Why Some Companies Make the Leap ... and Others Don't* (New York: HarperCollins, 2001), p. 20.

As reflected in the exhibit, a key characteristic of Level 5 leaders is an almost complete lack of ego (humility) coupled with a fierce resolve to do what is best for the organization (will). **Humility** means being unpretentious and modest rather than arrogant and prideful. In contrast to the view of great leaders as larger-than-life personalities with strong egos and big ambitions, Level 5 leaders often seem shy and self-effacing. Although they accept full responsibility for mistakes, poor results, or failures, Level 5 leaders give credit for successes to other people. Level 5 leaders build organizations based on solid values that go far beyond just making money, with an unwavering resolve to do whatever is needed to make the company successful over the long term.[5]

An example of a leader who demonstrates Level 5 leadership qualities is Sir Terry Leahy, who recently retired after more than a decade leading Britain's Tesco chain of supermarkets. That's a long and successful tenure for a leader that most people know little about. Leahy didn't court personal publicity, much to the chagrin of journalists, and he put his energies into promoting Tesco and its employees rather than himself.[6] Or consider Qi Lu of Microsoft, who grew up in a rural village in China with no electricity or running water. Today, he is executive vice president of Microsoft's Applications and Services Group. How did he get there? Not from personal ambition, say former colleagues at Yahoo. "He shunned the limelight," said Tim Cadogan, now CEO of OpenX, "but he was considered one of the stars." Lu rose through the ranks at Yahoo, and he got the job at Microsoft based not on aggressiveness and pursuit of personal advancement, but rather because of his sheer intellectual abilities and his commitment to go above and beyond the call of duty to accomplish organizational goals. Lu feels a strong sense of duty and loyalty, pouring his heart and soul into the mission rather than spending his energies promoting himself.[7]

Level 5 leaders like Sir Terry Leahy and Qi Lu are extremely ambitious for their companies rather than for themselves. This attitude becomes highly evident in the area of succession planning. Level 5 leaders develop a solid corps of leaders throughout the organization so that when they leave, the company can continue to thrive and grow even stronger. Egocentric leaders, by contrast, often set their successors up for failure because it will be a testament to their own greatness if the company doesn't perform well without them. Rather than building an organization around "a genius with a thousand helpers," Level 5 leaders want everyone to develop to their fullest potential.

11.2b Servant Leadership

When Jack Welch, longtime CEO of General Electric (GE), speaks to MBA students, he reminds them that "any time you are managing people, your job is not about you, it's about them. It starts out about you as … an individual in a company," Welch says. "But once you get a leadership job, it moves very quickly to being about them."[8] Some leaders operate from the assumption that work exists for the development of the worker as much as the worker exists to do the work.[9] The concept of servant leadership, first described by Robert Greenleaf in 1970, has gained renewed interest in recent years as companies recover from ethical scandals and compete to attract and retain the best human talent.[10]

A **servant leader** transcends self-interest to serve others, the organization, and society.[11] Marilyn Carlson Nelson, former chairman and CEO of the Carlson Companies (Radisson Hotels, TGI Fridays, Regent Seven Seas Cruises), says being a true leader means that you "have to subordinate your own emotions, your own desires, even make decisions on behalf of the whole that might conflict with what you would do on an individual basis."[12] A stunning example of this occurred in the spring of 2009, when a U.S.-flagged cargo ship, the Maersk Alabama, was seized and raided by Somali pirates. Captain Richard Phillips ordered crew members of the unarmed ship not to fight and gave himself up as a hostage to free the ship and crew. The story of the captain's dilemma and rescue is told in a 2013 movie, Captain Phillips, starring Tom

Hanks. Contrast his behavior with that of Captain Francesco Schettino, who allegedly abandoned his ship while passengers were still aboard after the luxury cruise liner Costa Concordia hit a rock and sank off the coast of Italy in 2012, killing at least 30 people. Schettino has been charged with manslaughter, shipwreck, and abandoning ship.[13]

In organizations, servant leaders operate on two levels: for the fulfillment of their subordinates' goals and needs and for the realization of the larger purpose or mission of their organization. Servant leaders give things away—power, ideas, information, recognition, credit for accomplishments, even money. Servant leaders often work in the nonprofit world because it offers a natural way to apply their leadership drive and skills to serve others. But servant leaders also succeed in business. In 2013, for the second year in a row, Lenovo CEO Yang Yuanqing shared $3.25 million of his $4.23 million bonus with hourly manufacturing workers to recognize their role in the company's success.[14] Fred Keller has built a $250 million plastics manufacturing company, Cascade Engineering, by continuously asking one question: *What good can we do?* Keller started the business 40 years ago with six employees. Today, it has 1,000 employees in 15 business divisions. Keller has made social responsibility a cornerstone of the business. The company offers jobs to welfare recipients. Keller has also donated large amounts to various philanthropic causes, both as an individual and through Cascade.[15]

Go to the "Ethical Dilemma" on page 506, which pertains to leadership for turbulent times.

11.2c Authentic Leadership

Another popular concept in leadership today is the idea of **authentic leadership**, which refers to individuals who know and understand themselves, who espouse and act consistent with higher-order ethical values, and who empower and inspire others with their openness and authenticity.[16] To be authentic means being *real*, staying true to one's values and beliefs, and acting based on one's true self rather than emulating what others do. Authentic leaders inspire trust and commitment because they respect diverse viewpoints, encourage collaboration, and help others learn, grow, and develop as leaders.

Exhibit 11.2 outlines the key characteristics of authentic leaders, and each is discussed below.[17]

- Authentic leaders pursue their purpose with passion. Leaders who lead without a purpose can fall prey to greed and the desires of the ego. When leaders demonstrate a high level of passion and commitment to a purpose, they inspire commitment from followers.

- Authentic leaders practice solid values. Authentic leaders have values that are shaped by their personal beliefs, and they stay true to them even under pressure. People come to know what the leader stands for, which inspires trust.

- Authentic leaders lead with their hearts as well as their heads. All leaders sometimes have to make tough choices, but authentic leaders maintain a compassion for others as well as the courage to make difficult decisions.

- Authentic leaders establish connected relationships. Authentic leaders build positive and enduring relationships, which makes followers want to do their best. In addition, authentic leaders surround themselves with good people and work to help others grow and develop.

- Authentic leaders demonstrate self-discipline. A high degree of self-control and self-discipline keeps leaders from taking excessive or unethical risks that could harm others and the organization. When authentic leaders make mistakes, they openly admit them.

EXHIBIT 11.2   Components of Authentic Leadership

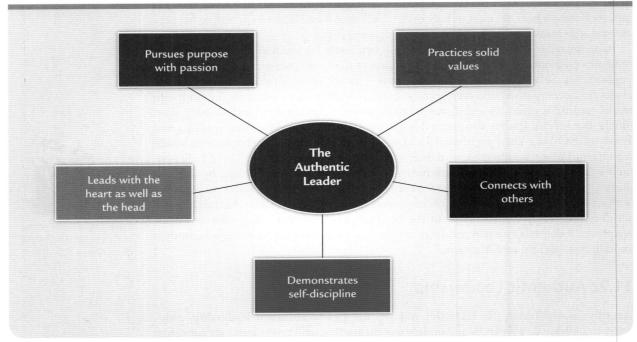

SOURCE: Based on Bill George, *Authentic Leadership: Rediscovering the Secrets to Lasting Value* (San Francisco: Jossey-Bass, 2003).

Spotlight on Skills

Admiral Vernon E. Clark, U.S. Chief of Naval Operations, 2000–2005

Admiral Vernon E. Clark, who retired in July 2005 after a 37-year career in the U.S. Navy, was the second longest-serving U.S. Chief of Naval Operations (CNO). The job of the CNO is to advise the president on the conduct of war.

When Clark was named CNO in July 2000, the Navy was losing too many good sailors who didn't want to reenlist. For Clark, getting and keeping good sailors who could protect the national security was a top priority, and all his decisions were based on connecting with and valuing the people on the front lines. When Navy officials proposed budget cuts in training and development, Clark rebelled. Instead he *increased* the training budget, strongly supported an increase in pay for sailors, and established the Naval Education and Training Command to increase training. Clark also revised the performance appraisal system to provide constructive feedback for people at all levels. Clark made it a priority to blur the lines between enlisted sailors and officers and revised the job assignment process so that people didn't get forced into jobs and locations they didn't want. Always more concerned about doing things right than *being* right, Clark encouraged everyone to challenge assumptions, ask questions, and express conflicting views.

Thanks to Admiral Clark's emphasis on treating sailors right, first-term reenlistment soared from 38 to 56.7 percent within his first 18 months as CNO. Moreover, as the Navy retained more sailors, its ability to respond more quickly to protect the nation increased.[18]

One leader who demonstrates many of the characteristics of authentic leadership is Vernon Clark, who served as U.S. Chief of Naval Operations (CNO) from 2000 until his retirement in 2005.

An authentic leader like Vernon Clark places high value on personal relationships, supporting followers, being courageous, and standing up for what one believes. Thus, this type of leader is much more likely to make decisions that may not always be popular, but that he believes are right. Clark also engaged people by emphasizing each individual's personal role. "What we do matters," he told them. "We do it because it's important and we are people of service. We are committed to something larger than ourselves: the protection of America's interests around the world and democracy."[19]

"True leadership is a fire in the mind.... It is a strength of purpose and belief in a cause that reaches out to others, touches their hearts, and makes them eager to follow."

—Robert M. Gates, former U.S. secretary of defense

11.2d Gender Differences

Some of the general characteristics associated with Level 5 leaders and authentic leaders are also hallmarks of interactive leadership, which has been found to be associated with female leaders. **Interactive leadership** means that the leader favors a consensual and collaborative process, and influence derives from relationships rather than position power and formal authority.[20]

Although both men and women can practice interactive leadership, research indicates that women's style of leadership is typically different from that of most men and is particularly suited to today's organizations.[21] When leadership development firm Zenger Folkman surveyed more than 7,200 businesspeople in 2011 about leaders in their organizations, women were rated as better overall leaders.[22] Using data from actual performance evaluations, one study found that when rated by peers, subordinates, and bosses, female managers scored significantly higher than men on abilities such as motivating others, fostering communication, and listening.[23] Another study of leaders and their followers in businesses, universities, and government agencies found that women were rated higher on social and emotional skills, which are crucial for interactive leadership.[24] Indeed, a review of more than 7,000 360-degree performance evaluations discovered that women outshone men in almost every leadership dimension measured, even some considered typically masculine qualities, such as driving for results. The exception was that women were typically rated lower on developing a strategic perspective, which some researchers believe hinders female managers' career advancement despite their exceptional ratings in other leadership dimensions.[25] Exhibit 11.3 shows results for six of the 16 dimensions measured by the study.

One good example of an interactive leader is Cindy Szadokierski, who started as a reservations agent for United Airlines and today is vice president in charge of operations for United's largest hub at O'Hare International Airport. As she oversees 4,000 employees and 600 flights a day, her favorite times are her weekly afternoon walkabouts on the O'Hare ramp and weekly morning strolls through the terminal, where she can connect with employees and customers. Pete McDonald, chief operating officer of United's parent, UAL Corporation, says that there

Jin Lee/Bloomberg/Getty Images

CONCEPT CONNECTION The 2008 financial collapse put Debra Cafaro's leadership skills to the test. The CEO of Ventas Inc. saw the housing crisis approaching and insisted the Louisville-based health care real estate investment trust build cash reserves. Although she wanted to project calmness and certainty when the economic downturn hit, Cafaro says that "in order to be authentic, I also had to acknowledge, 'I'm scared, too.'" Throughout the crisis, Cafaro operated as an **interactive leader**, one who, in her words, makes sure "we're working together, collaborating—marching in the same direction." She succeeded. Ventas not only survived the recession but is flourishing.

EXHIBIT 11.3   Gender Differences in Leadership Behaviors

Leadership Ability	Who Does It Best?	
Develops Others		(Women rated higher)
Drives for Results		(Women rated higher)
Inspires and Motivates Others		(Women rated higher)
Innovates		(Women and men rated about equally)
Builds Relationships		(Women rated higher)
Technical or Professional Expertise		(Women and men rated about equally)

SOURCE: Data from Zenger Folkman, Inc., reported in Jack Zenger and Joseph Folkman, "Are Women Better Leaders than Men?" HBR Blog Network, *Harvard Business Review*, March 15, 2012, http://blogs.hbr.org/cs/2012/03/a_study_in_leadership_women_do.html (accessed September 12, 2012).

were serious operations problems at O'Hare, so they put "the most communicative person" in the job. Szadokierski's approach to leadership is more about collaboration than command and control.[26]

Men can be interactive leaders as well, as illustrated by the example of Pat McGovern, founder and chairman of IDG, a technology publishing and research firm that owns magazines such as *CIO, PC World,* and *Computerworld.* McGovern believes that having personal contact with employees and letting them know that they're appreciated is a primary responsibility of leaders.[27] The characteristics associated with interactive leadership are emerging as valuable qualities for both male and female leaders in today's workplace. John Gerzema, author of *The Athena Doctrine* and executive chairman of Young & Rubicam's BAV Consulting division, asked 32,000 people to classify 125 traits as masculine, feminine, or neutral, and another 125 to rate the importance of the traits to effective leadership. The results showed that traits considered feminine and often associated with interactive leadership, such as empathy, personal humility, inclusiveness, vulnerability, generosity, patience, and flexibility, topped the list of qualities most desirable for leaders.[28]

REMEMBER THIS

- A significant influence on leadership styles in recent years is the turbulence and uncertainty of the environment.

- One effective approach in today's environment is Level 5 leadership, which is characterized by an almost complete lack of ego (humility), coupled with a fierce resolve to do what is best for the organization (will).

- **Humility** means being unpretentious and modest rather than arrogant and prideful.

- A **servant leader** is a leader who serves others by working to fulfill followers' needs and goals, as well as to achieve the organization's larger mission.

- **Authentic leadership** refers to leadership by individuals who know and understand themselves, who espouse and act consistent with higher-order ethical values, and who empower and inspire others with their openness and authenticity.

- Women leaders typically score significantly higher than men on abilities such as motivating others, building relationships, and developing others—skills that are based on humility and authenticity and are particularly suited to today's organizations.

- **Interactive leadership** is a leadership style characterized by values such as inclusion, collaboration, relationship building, and caring.

- Although interactive leadership is associated with women's style of leading, both men and women can be effective interactive leaders.

11.3 From Management to Leadership

Hundreds of books and articles have been written in recent years about the differences between management and leadership. Good management is essential in organizations, yet managers have to be leaders too, because distinctive qualities are associated with management and leadership that provide different strengths for the organization. A good way to think of the distinction between management and leadership is that management organizes the production and supply of fish to people, whereas leadership teaches and motivates people to fish. Organizations need both types of skills.[29]

As shown in Exhibit 11.4, management and leadership reflect two different sets of qualities and skills that frequently overlap within a single individual. A person might have more of one set of qualities than the other, but ideally, a manager develops a balance of both manager and leader qualities.[30] A primary distinction between management and leadership is that management promotes stability and order within the existing organizational structure and systems. This ensures that suppliers are paid, customers invoiced, products and services produced on time, and so forth. Leadership, on the other hand, promotes vision and change. Leadership means questioning the status quo and being willing to take reasonable risks so that outdated, unproductive, or socially irresponsible norms can be replaced to meet new challenges.

EXHIBIT 11.4 Leader and Manager Qualities

Manager Qualities   Leader Qualities

Focus on the Organization

Rational
Maintains stability
Assigns tasks
Organizes
Analyzes
Position power

Focus on People

Visionary
Promotes change
Defines purpose
Nurtures
Innovates
Personal power

SOURCES: Based on "What Is the Difference Between Management and Leadership?" *The Wall Street Journal Online*, http://guides.wsj.com/management/developing-a-leadership-style/what-is-the-difference-between-management-and-leadership (accessed June 28, 2009); and Genevieve Capowski, "Anatomy of a Leader: Where Are the Leaders of Tomorrow?" *Management Review* (March 1994): 12.

For example, when Google's founders needed more structured management at their growing company, they hired Eric Schmidt as CEO in 2001 to provide operational expertise and oversight. Schmidt was not a heavy take-charge manager, which suited the founders just fine, but coming from a corporate background, Schmidt knew how to plan and organize and keep things focused. More important, it turned out that Schmidt also had leadership qualities that fit well with Google's need for innovation and change to keep the company thriving. His leadership principles can be summarized in the following five precepts:

1. Get to know your employees.

2. Create new ways to reward and promote high performers.

3. Let employees own the problems that you want them to solve.

4. Allow people to function outside the hierarchy.

5. Have employees' performance reviewed by someone whom they respect for their objectivity.[31]

When he was CEO, Schmidt used to make a list of his best employees so that he could interact with them personally and encourage them to implement their innovative ideas and to protect them from unwanted interference by other managers. He made employees the owners of their work by allowing them a great deal of latitude in how they accomplished goals. He believed in structure, but he also allowed people to work outside the company hierarchy when necessary to solve problems and be creative.[32] Schmidt used a combination of skillful management and good leadership to take Google to the next stage of growth.

Leadership cannot replace management; it should be in addition to management. Good management is needed to help the organization meet current commitments, while good leadership is needed to move the organization into the future. Leadership's power comes from being built on the foundation of a well-managed organization.

REMEMBER THIS

- Leadership and management reflect two different sets of qualities and skills that provide different benefits for the organization.
- Management promotes stability and efficient organizing to meet current commitments, whereas leadership often inspires engagement and organizational change to meet new conditions.

- Both leadership and management are important to organizations, and people can learn to be good leaders as well as good managers.
- When he was hired as CEO of Google, Eric Schmidt applied both skilled management and good leadership to take the startup to the next stage of growth.

11.4 Leadership Traits

Early efforts to understand leadership success focused on the leader's traits. **Traits** are the distinguishing personal characteristics of a leader, such as intelligence, honesty, self-confidence, and even appearance. The early research looked at leaders who had achieved a level of greatness, and hence was referred to as the "great man" approach. The idea was relatively simple: Find out what made these people great, and select future leaders who already exhibited the same traits or could learn to develop them. Generally, early research found only a weak relationship between personal traits and leader success.[33]

In recent years, interest in examining leadership traits has reemerged. In addition to personality traits, physical, social, and work-related characteristics of leaders have been studied.[34] Exhibit 11.5 summarizes the physical, social, and personal leadership characteristics that have received the greatest research support. However, these characteristics do not stand alone. The appropriateness of a trait or set of traits depends on the leadership situation.

Effective leaders typically possess varied traits, and no single leader can have a complete set of characteristics that is appropriate for handling any problem, challenge, or opportunity that comes along. In addition, traits that are typically considered positive can sometimes have negative consequences, and traits sometimes considered negative can have positive consequences. For example, optimism is a highly desirable trait for a leader. Studies have shown that optimism is the single characteristic most common to top executives.[35] Leaders need to be able to see possibilities where others see problems and to instill in others a sense of hope for a better future. However, optimism can also lull leaders into laziness and overconfidence, causing them to miss danger signals and underestimate risks. The 2007–2008 crisis in the financial services industry can be blamed partly on leaders who grew overconfident and led their organizations astray. Optimism has to be paired with "reality testing" and conscientiousness, another trait common to successful leaders, as shown in Exhibit 11.5.[36]

> "The good news: these [leadership] traits are not genetic. It's not as if you have to be tall or left-handed. These qualities are developed through attitude, habit, and discipline—factors that are within your control."
>
> —Adam Bryant, senior editor for features at *The New York Times*, in the "Corner Office" column

EXHIBIT 11.5 Personal Characteristics of Leaders

Physical Characteristics	Personality	Work-Related Characteristics
Energy Physical stamina	Self-confidence Honesty and integrity Optimism Desire to lead Independence	Achievement drive, desire to excel Conscientiousness in pursuit of goals Persistence against obstacles, tenacity
Intelligence and Ability	**Social Characteristics**	**Social Background**
Intelligence, cognitive ability Knowledge Judgment, decisiveness	Sociability, interpersonal skills Cooperativeness Ability to enlist cooperation Tact, diplomacy	Education Mobility

SOURCES: Based on Bernard M. Bass, *Bass & Stogdill's Handbook of Leadership: Theory, Research, and Managerial Applications*, 3rd ed. (New York: Free Press, 1990), pp. 80–81; and S. A. Kirkpatrick and E. A. Locke, "Leadership: Do Traits Matter?" *Academy of Management Executive* 5, no. 2 (1991): 48–60.

Therefore, rather than just understanding their *traits*, the best leaders recognize and hone their *strengths*.[37] **Strengths** are natural talents and abilities that have been supported and reinforced with learned knowledge and skills and provide each individual with his or her best tools for accomplishment and satisfaction.[38] Every manager has a limited capacity; those who become good leaders are the ones who tap into their key strengths that can make a difference. Effective leadership isn't about having the "right" traits, but rather about finding the strengths that one can best exemplify and apply as a leader.

REMEMBER THIS

- **Traits** are distinguishing personal characteristics, such as intelligence, self-confidence, energy, and independence.

- **Strengths** are natural talents and abilities that have been supported and reinforced with learned knowledge and skills.

11.5 Behavioral Approaches

The inability to define effective leadership based solely on traits led to an interest in looking at the behavior of leaders and how it might contribute to leadership success or failure. Two basic leadership behaviors identified as important for leadership are attention to tasks and attention to people.

11.5a Task versus People

Two types of behavior that have been identified as applicable to effective leadership in a variety of situations and time periods are *task-oriented behavior* and *people-oriented behavior*.[39] Although they are not the only important leadership behaviors, concern for tasks and concern for people must be shown at some reasonable level. Thus, many approaches to understanding leadership use these *metacategories*, or broadly defined behavior categories, as a basis for study and comparison.

Important early research programs on leadership were conducted at The Ohio State University and the University of Michigan.[40] Ohio State researchers identified two major behaviors they called consideration and initiating structure. **Consideration** falls in the category of people-oriented behavior and is the extent to which the leader is mindful of subordinates, respects their ideas and feelings, and establishes mutual trust. **Initiating structure** is the degree of task behavior; that is, the extent to which the leader is task-oriented and directs subordinate work activities toward goal attainment. Studies suggest that effective leaders may be high on consideration and low on initiating structure or low on consideration and high on initiating structure, depending on the situation.[41]

Research at the University of Michigan at about the same time also considered task- and people-oriented behaviors by comparing the behavior of effective and ineffective supervisors.[42] The most effective supervisors were those who established high performance goals and displayed supportive behavior toward subordinates. They were referred to as *employee-centered leaders*. The less effective leaders were called *job-centered leaders*; they tended to be less concerned with goal achievement and human needs in favor of meeting schedules, keeping costs low, and achieving production efficiency. Comedian Louis C.K. is the leader of his entertainment company. He combined a concern for people (in this case his audience and venue owners) with task (using an innovative model for deterring piracy and also maneuvering around the giant ticketing companies), which led him to new levels of success, as described in this chapter's Director's Toolkit box.

As a new manager, realize that both task-oriented behavior and people-oriented behavior are important, although some situations call for a greater degree of one over the other. Review your responses to the opening questionnaire to measure your degree of task orientation and people orientation.

Director's Toolkit

Louis C.K.

As a young man, Louis C.K. worked at a car mechanic and had disastrous results in his first attempts at stand-up. He kept trying because he wanted his mother to watch higher-quality television than what was available, and he felt *he* could do better. Working at small clubs for years, he learned his craft and got hired as a writer for David Letterman, Conan O'Brien, Chris Rock, and Dana Carvey. He's found fame by showing the insides of passivity: "I have a list of beliefs and I live by none of them." But perhaps Louis C.K.'s greatest legacy to entertainment might be his leadership on how he runs the business side of his work.

He's done at least three leaderful things: First, with his own work, he was inspired by George Carlin and decided to start fresh each year with his jokes, something almost unheard of in comedy.

Second, he had a deep desire to reach his fans in innovative ways, so in 2011 he released his special, *Live at the Beacon Theater* and sold it exclusively on his own website for $5, hoping to be a role model and create the kind of relationship with his audience that would deter copying and piracy. He earned over $1 million in sales. He followed this up with another stand-up special in 2015,

which he also sold on his website. And third, right after the video release, he organized a national tour without using any of the major ticketing companies. Not wanting to fight with these companies, or venues, that often have exclusive arrangements, Louis had to come up with a new model. It was tricky, he said, because of contracts that keep out anyone who won't play by the ticket company's rules. "They pay them [the venues] not to work with others," and might pay a club $30,000 a year not to work with outsiders such as Louis. So he tried a different tactic. "We didn't attack their territory. We went to places they didn't care about."

Louis's advice: work hard. People complain about all the deals and attention he gets, he says, how unfair it is. But he says he wasn't born with it. "It was a horrible process to get to this. It took me my whole life." And he credits other comics such as Larry David, Jerry Seinfeld, Garry Shandling, who proved you could be a little weird and still make money.

SOURCES: "And In Other Developments on the Small Screen," *USA Today*, January 19, 2015, D3; David Itzkoff, "The Joke's on Him," *New York Times*, April 7, 2013, C1 and C20.

REMEMBER THIS

- Two basic leadership behaviors identified as important for leadership are attention to tasks and attention to people.
- **Consideration** is the term used by researchers at The Ohio State University to describe the extent to which a leader is sensitive to subordinates, respects their ideas and feelings, and establishes mutual trust.
- **Initiating structure** is the term that describes the extent to which a leader is task-oriented and directs subordinates' work activities toward goal accomplishment.

- Researchers at the University of Michigan used the terms *employee-centered leaders* and *job-centered leaders* to describe the same two basic leadership behaviors.
- The **Leadership Grid**® is a two-dimensional leadership model that measures the leader's concern for people and concern for production to categorize the leader in one of five different leadership styles.

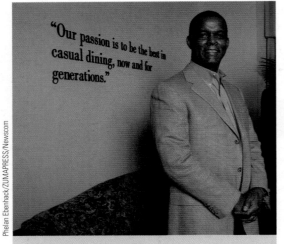

"Our passion is to be the best in casual dining, now and for generations."

Phelan Ebenhack/ZUMAPRESS/Newscom

CONCEPT CONNECTION How has Clarence Otis, Jr.'s leadership style changed since he became CEO of Darden Restaurants? His experience has driven home the importance of **team management**. Otis has found that "it's less and less about getting the work done, and more and more about building the team." His team includes 180,000 employees working in the largest full-service restaurant operation in the United States. Darden's new headquarters was designed to facilitate teamwork among its brands—especially Olive Garden, Red Lobster, and Longhorn Steakhouse—by bringing approximately 1,500 executives and support staff previously scattered in separate buildings under one roof for the first time.

11.5b The Leadership Grid

Building on the work of the Ohio State and Michigan studies, Robert R. Blake and Jane S. Mouton of the University of Texas proposed a two-dimensional theory called the Managerial Grid®, which was later restated by Robert R. Blake and Anne Adams McCanse as the Leadership Grid®.[43] The model and five of its major management styles are depicted in Exhibit 11.6. Each axis on the grid is a nine-point scale, with 1 meaning low concern and 9 meaning high concern.

Team management (9, 9) often is considered the most effective style and is recommended for leaders because organization members work together to accomplish tasks. *Country club management* (1, 9) occurs when the primary emphasis is given to people rather than to work outputs. *Authority-compliance management* (9, 1) occurs when efficiency in operations is the dominant orientation. *Middle-of-the-road management* (5, 5) reflects a moderate amount of concern for both people and production. *Impoverished management* (1, 1) means the absence of a management philosophy; managers exert little effort toward interpersonal relationships or work accomplishment.

11.6 Contingency Approaches

Denise Morrison, CEO of Campbell Soup Company, is a strong proponent of empowerment and employee engagement. She has been referred to as "tough on the issues but tender on people." Morrison is known to be patient and supportive, even though she can make difficult operational decisions. On the other hand, Pamela Forbes Lieberman, former president and CEO of

EXHIBIT 11.6 The Leadership Grid Figure

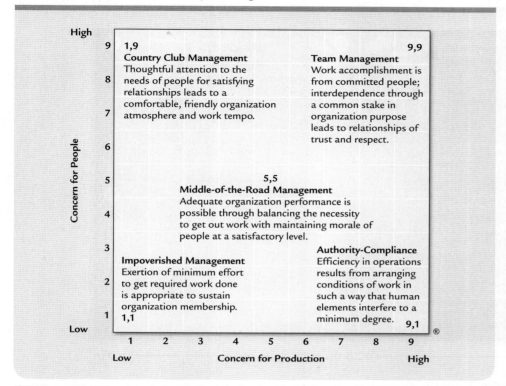

SOURCE: The Leadership Grid figure, Paternalism figure, and Opportunism figure from Robert R. Blake and Anne Adams McCanse, *Leadership Dilemmas—Grid Solutions* (formerly *The Managerial Grid* by Robert R. Blake and Jane S. Mouton) (Houston: Gulf Publishing Company, 1991), Grid figure, p. 29; Paternalism figure, p. 30; Opportunism figure, p. 31. Copyright © 1991 by Blake and Mouton, and Scientific Methods, Inc. Reproduced by permission of the owners.

TruServ Corporation (now known as True Value Company), was once called "the dragon lady" by employees at a former job. She embraced the name and even hung a watercolor of a fire-breathing dragon on her office wall to let people know that she didn't mind being known as a hard-nosed manager. No laid-back approach for Lieberman.[44]

How can two people with widely different styles both be effective leaders? The answer lies in understanding **contingency approaches** to leadership, which explore how the organizational situation influences leader effectiveness. Contingency approaches include the situational model based on the work of Paul Hersey and Kenneth Blanchard, the leadership model developed by Fred Fiedler and his associates, and the substitutes-for-leadership concept.

11.6a The Situational Model of Leadership

The situational model of leadership, which originated with Hersey and Blanchard, is an interesting extension of the behavioral theories summarized in the leadership grid (see Exhibit 11.6). This approach focuses a great deal of attention on the characteristics of followers in determining appropriate leadership behavior. The point of the situational model is that subordinates vary in readiness, which is determined by the degree of willingness and ability that a subordinate demonstrates while performing a specific task. *Willingness* refers to a combination of confidence, commitment, and motivation, and a follower may be high or low on any of the three variables. *Ability* refers to the amount of knowledge, experience, and demonstrated skill that a subordinate brings to the task. Effective leaders adapt their

EXHIBIT 11.7 Hersey and Blanchard's Situational Model of Leadership

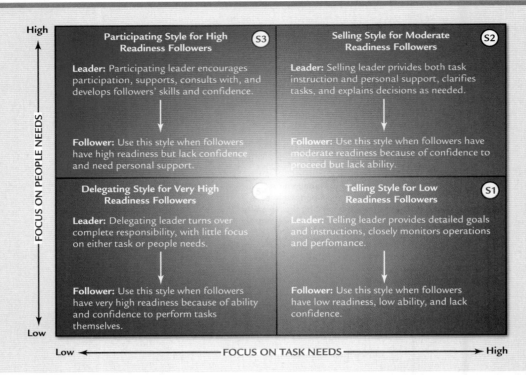

SOURCE: Based on Gary Yukl, Angela Gordon, and Tom Taber, "A Hierarchical Taxonomy of Leadership Behavior: Integrating a Half Century of Behavior Research," *Journal of Leadership and Organizational Studies* 9, no. 1 (2002): 15–32; and Paul Hersey, Kenneth Blanchard, and Dewey Johnson, *Management of Organizational Behavior: Utilizing Human Resources*, 7th ed. (Upper Saddle River, NJ: Prentice Hall, 1996).

style according to the readiness level of the people they are managing. People low in readiness—because of little ability or training or insecurity—need a different leadership style than those who are high in readiness and have good ability, skills, confidence, and willingness to work.[45]

According to the situational model, a leader can adopt one of four leadership styles, as shown in Exhibit 11.7. The *telling style (S1)* is a highly dictating style and involves giving explicit directions about how tasks should be accomplished. The *selling style (S2)* is one where the leader explains decisions and gives subordinates a chance to ask questions and gain clarity and understanding about work tasks. The *participating style (S3)* is one where the leader shares ideas with subordinates, gives them a chance to participate, and facilitates decision making. The fourth style, the *delegating style (S4)*, provides little direction and little support because the leader turns over responsibility for decisions and their implementation to subordinates.

Exhibit 11.7 summarizes the situational relationship between leader style and follower readiness. The S1 telling style has the highest probability of successfully influencing low-readiness followers who are unable or unwilling—because of poor ability and skills, lack of experience, or insecurity—to take responsibility for their own task behavior. The leader is specific, telling people exactly what to do, how to do it, and when. The S2 selling and S3 participating styles work for followers at moderate-to-high readiness levels. For example, followers might lack some education and experience for the job but have high confidence, interest, and willingness to learn. As shown in the exhibit, the S2 selling style is effective in this situation because it involves giving direction, but it also includes seeking input from others and clarifying tasks rather than simply instructing that they be performed. When followers have the necessary skills and experience but are somewhat insecure in their abilities or lack high willingness, the S3 participating style enables the leader to guide followers' development and act as a resource for advice and assistance. When followers demonstrate very high readiness (that is, they have high levels of education, experience, and readiness to accept responsibility for their own task behavior), the S4 delegating style can effectively be used. Because of the high readiness level of followers, the leader can delegate responsibility for decisions and their implementation to subordinates who have the skills, abilities, and positive attitudes to follow through. The leader provides a general goal and sufficient authority to do the task as followers see fit.

To apply the situational model, the leader diagnoses the readiness level of followers and adopts the appropriate style—telling, selling, participating, or delegating. For example, Jo Newton, an impulse import category leadership manager at Mars Incorporated's Slough office near London, uses primarily a participating style. Most members of Newton's team are at moderate to high readiness levels, so Newton advises them of the results that the company wants and then steps back, providing guidance and support as needed. "I like people to come up with their own way of doing things….," she says. "I like to support people, as opposed to directing them to do things."[46] A leader taking over a new team of inexperienced or uncertain members would likely have to provide more direction with either a telling or selling style. On the other hand, Warren Buffett uses a primarily delegating style. The 80-year-old CEO of Berkshire Hathaway is considered one of the world's best managers, but he isn't closely involved in the day-to-day management of all the businesses that Berkshire owns. He trusts the managers of the various units, who are highly skilled professionals able and willing to take responsibility for their own task behavior.[47] A delegating leader style is not always appropriate, but all managers need to be able to delegate some tasks and decisions for the organization to work smoothly.

11.6b Fiedler's Contingency Theory

Whereas the situational model focused on the characteristics of followers, Fiedler and his associates looked at some other elements of the organizational situation to assess when one leadership style is more effective than another.[48] The starting point for Fiedler's theory is the extent to which the leader's style is task-oriented or relationship (people)-oriented. Fiedler considered a person's leadership style to be relatively fixed and difficult to change; therefore, the basic idea is to match the leader's style with the situation most favorable for his or her effectiveness. By diagnosing leadership style and the organizational situation, the correct fit can be arranged.

Situation: Favorable or Unfavorable? The suitability of a person's leadership style is determined by whether the situation is favorable or unfavorable to the leader. The favorability of a leadership situation can be analyzed in terms of three elements: the quality of relationships between leader and followers, the degree of task structure, and the extent to which the leader has formal authority over followers.[49]

As illustrated in the lower portion of Exhibit 11.8, a situation would be considered *highly favorable* to the leader when leader–member relationships are positive, tasks are highly structured, and the leader has formal authority over followers. In this situation, followers trust, respect, and have confidence in the leader. The group's tasks are clearly defined, involve specific procedures, and have clear, explicit goals. In addition, the leader has formal authority to direct and evaluate followers, along with the power to reward or punish. In a highly unfavorable situation, followers have little respect for or confidence and trust in the

EXHIBIT 11.8   How Leader Style Fits the Situation

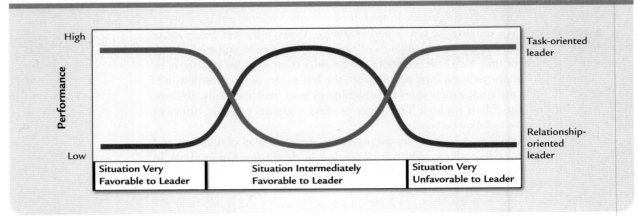

SOURCE: Based on Fred E. Fiedler, "The Effects of Leadership Training and Experience: A Contingency Model Interpretation," *Administrative Science Quarterly* 17 (1972): 455.

leader. Tasks are vague and ill-defined and lack clear-cut procedures and guidelines. The leader has little formal authority to direct subordinates and does not have the power to issue rewards or punishments.

Matching Leader Style to the Situation   When Fiedler examined the relationships among leadership style and situational favorability, he found the pattern shown in the upper portion of Exhibit 11.8. Task-oriented leaders are more effective when the situation is either highly favorable or highly unfavorable. Relationship-oriented leaders are more effective in situations of moderate favorability.

The task-oriented leader excels in the favorable situation because everyone gets along, the task is clear, and the leader has power; all that is needed is for someone to lead the charge and provide direction. Similarly, if the situation is highly unfavorable to the leader, a great deal of structure and task direction is needed. A strong leader will define task structure and establish strong authority. Because leader–member relations are poor anyway, a strong task orientation will make no difference in the leader's popularity. Sergio Marchionne has used strong task-oriented leadership in an unfavorable situation at Chrysler.

Marchionne's tough, task-oriented approach is suitable for the difficult situation at Chrysler. On the other hand, Ohio Republican John Boehner has not done so well as House Speaker during several recent political struggles, including the partial U.S. government shutdown over Obamacare. Part of the reason, some say, is that Boehner just isn't "intimidating" enough. Republicans are more divided than ever, and one observer said that Boehner's future success would depend on his ability to "lead more and listen less." Boehner typically uses a relatively laid-back, people-oriented style. "I can't think of any time he's been heavy-handed with me," said Representative Charlie Dent of Pennsylvania. Many both inside and outside the Republican Party believe that a strong, task-oriented leader is needed to keep the unruly House from turning into "an ungovernable quagmire."[50]

Researchers at the University of Chicago who looked at CEOs in turnaround situations—where companies typically have high debt loads and a need to improve results in a hurry—found that tough-minded, task-focused characteristics such as analytical skills, a focus on efficiency, and setting high standards were more valuable leader qualities than were relationship skills such as good communication, listening, and teamwork.[51]

The relationship-oriented leader performs better in situations of intermediate favorability because human relations skills are important in achieving high group performance.

Spotlight on Skills

Sergio Marchionne, Chrysler Group LLC

The fate of the smallest of the big three U.S. automakers rests in the hands of Italian-born Sergio Marchionne, who rescued Fiat from the brink of collapse a few years ago with his close attention to detail. Marchionne is a strong, task-oriented leader. Rather than settling into the top-floor executive suite at Chrysler's headquarters in Auburn Hills, Michigan, Marchionne chose an office in the fourth-floor engineering center. He carries six smartphones and keeps tabs on the smallest details, down to a faulty door handle on the new Dodge Charger. "If you really want to run the business," he says, "you need to get involved at this level."

Marchionne came into a highly unfavorable situation at Chrysler. Like General Motors (GM), Chrysler had to be rescued by a federal bailout several years ago, and Marchionne took charge just after the company emerged from bankruptcy and Fiat assumed part-ownership. Sales were slumping, Chrysler's image was tarnished,

morale and motivation were low, costs were high, and operational problems plagued the company. Marchionne became known at Fiat for working long hours seven days a week, and he told his top executives at Chrysler to plan on doing the same for the foreseeable future. He meets with managers regularly and gives them specific orders for what he wants to see accomplished. Managers who were committed to staying stuck in the old way of doing things were fired.

Marchionne's task-oriented leadership is having a positive effect. Chrysler's auto sales are improving, and operational problems have been brought under control. In addition, Marchionne's hard-hitting approach has brought a refreshing energy into the organization, giving employees a greater sense of hope and motivation.[52]

In these situations, the leader may be moderately well liked, have some power, and supervise jobs that contain some ambiguity. A leader with good interpersonal skills can create a positive group atmosphere that will improve relationships, clarify task structure, and establish position power.

A leader, then, needs to know two things to use Fiedler's contingency theory. First, the leader should know whether he or she has a relationship- or task-oriented style. Second, the leader should diagnose the situation and determine whether leader–member relations, task structure, and position power are favorable or unfavorable.

Fiedler believed fitting leader style to the situation can yield big dividends in profits and efficiency.[53] On the other hand, the model has also been criticized.[54] For one thing, some researchers have challenged the idea that leaders cannot adjust their styles as situational characteristics change. Despite criticisms, Fiedler's model has continued to influence leadership studies. Fiedler's research called attention to the importance of finding the correct fit between leadership style and situation.

11.6c Situational Substitutes for Leadership

The contingency leadership approaches considered so far focus on the leader's style, the subordinates' nature, and the situation's characteristics. The final contingency approach suggests that situational variables can be so powerful that they actually substitute for or neutralize the need for leadership.[55] This approach outlines those organizational settings in which a leadership style is unimportant or unnecessary.

Exhibit 11.9 shows the situational variables that tend to substitute for or neutralize leadership characteristics. A substitute for leadership makes the leadership style unnecessary or redundant. For example, highly professional subordinates who know how to do their tasks do not need a leader who initiates structure for them and tells them what to do. A neutralizer counteracts the leadership style and prevents the leader from displaying certain behaviors. For example, if a leader has absolutely no position power or is physically removed from subordinates, the leader's ability to give directions to subordinates is greatly reduced.

Situational variables in Exhibit 11.9 include characteristics of the group, the task, and the organization itself. When followers are highly professional and experienced, both leadership styles are less important. People do not need much direction or consideration. With respect to task characteristics, highly structured tasks substitute for a task-oriented style and a satisfying task substitutes for a people-oriented style. With respect to the organization itself, group cohesiveness substitutes for both leader styles. Formalized rules and procedures substitute for leader task orientation. Physical separation of leader and subordinate neutralizes both leadership styles.

The value of the situations described in Exhibit 11.9 is that they help leaders avoid leadership overkill. Leaders should adopt a style with which to complement the organizational situation. Consider the work situation for bank tellers. A bank teller performs highly structured tasks, follows clearly written rules and procedures, and has little flexibility in terms of how to do the work. The head teller should not adopt a task-oriented style because the organization already provides structure and direction. The head teller should concentrate on a people-oriented style to provide a more pleasant work environment. In other organizations, if group cohesiveness or intrinsic satisfaction meets employees' social needs, the leader is free to concentrate on task-oriented behaviors. The leader can adopt a style complementary to the organizational situation to ensure that both the task needs and people needs of the work group will be met.

EXHIBIT 11.9   Substitutes and Neutralizers for Leadership

Variable		Task-Oriented Leadership	People-Oriented Leadership
Organizational variables	Group cohesiveness	Substitutes for	Substitutes for
	Formalization	Substitutes for	No effect on
	Inflexibility	Neutralizes	No effect on
	Low position power	Neutralizes	Neutralizes
	Physical separation	Neutralizes	Neutralizes
Task characteristics	Highly structured task	Substitutes for	No effect on
	Automatic feedback	Substitutes for	No effect on
	Intrinsic satisfaction	No effect on	Substitutes for
Group characteristics	Professionalism	Substitutes for	Substitutes for
	Training/experience	Substitutes for	No effect on

REMEMBER THIS

- A **contingency approach** is a model of leadership that describes the relationship between leadership styles and specific situations.

- One contingency approach is the **situational model**, which links the leader's behavioral style with the readiness level of followers.

- In general, a task-oriented leader style fits a low-readiness follower, and a relationship leader style fits a higher-readiness follower.

- In Fiedler's contingency theory, the suitability of a leader's style is determined by whether the situation is considered favorable or unfavorable to the leader.

- Task-oriented leaders are considered to perform better in either highly favorable or highly unfavorable situations.

- Relationship-oriented leaders are considered to perform better in situations of intermediate favorability.

- A **substitute for leadership** is a situational variable that makes a leadership style redundant or unnecessary.

- A **neutralizer** is a situational variable that counteracts a leadership style and prevents the leader from displaying certain behaviors.

11.7 Charismatic and Transformational Leadership

Research has also looked at how leadership can inspire and motivate people beyond their normal levels of performance. Some leadership approaches are more effective than others for bringing about high levels of commitment and enthusiasm. Two types with a substantial impact are charismatic and transformational.

11.7a Charismatic Leadership

Charisma has been referred to as "a fire that ignites followers' energy and commitment, producing results above and beyond the call of duty."[56] The **charismatic** leader has the ability to inspire and motivate people to do more than they would normally do, despite obstacles and personal sacrifice. Followers are willing to put aside their own interests for the sake of the team, department, or organization. The impact of charismatic leaders normally comes from (1) stating a lofty vision of an imagined future that employees identify with, (2) displaying an ability to understand and empathize with followers, and (3) empowering and trusting subordinates to accomplish results.[57] Charismatic leaders tend to be less predictable because they create an atmosphere of change, and they may be obsessed by visionary ideas that excite, stimulate, and drive other people to work hard.

One of the best-known charismatic leaders in the business world in recent years was Apple's late cofounder and CEO, Steve Jobs. Jobs commanded a rock-star-like following. The tale of how he dropped out of college, cofounded Apple, got fired from his own company, returned years later to save it, and then transformed it by creating a whole new business with the iPod and iPhone is the stuff of legend. Yet Jobs could be immature, impatient, and downright cruel at times. His demanding leadership could undermine performance as well as inspire it. Despite this, many people—even some he mistreated—admired and respected (some have even said *worshiped*) Steve Jobs. They tell their "Steve-Jobs-yelled-in-my-face" stories with pride. His energizing personality and his refusal to "sell out" made people want to be around him and want to be *like* him.[58]

As the example of Steve Jobs illustrates, there can be both positive and negative aspects of charisma. Other charismatic leaders include Mother Teresa, David Koresh, Sam Walton, Alexander the Great, Oprah Winfrey, Martin Luther King, Jr., and Osama bin Laden. Charisma can be used for positive outcomes that benefit the group, but it can also be used for self-serving purposes that lead to the deception, manipulation, and exploitation (and even deaths) of others. When charismatic leaders respond to organizational problems in terms of the needs of the entire group rather than their own emotional needs, they can have a powerful, positive influence on organizational performance.[59] As with the Level 5 and authentic leadership approaches that we discussed earlier in the chapter, *humility* typically plays an important part in distinguishing whether a charismatic leader will work to benefit primarily the larger organization or use his or her gifts for ego-building and personal gain.[60]

Charismatic leaders are skilled in the art of *visionary leadership*. A vision is an attractive, ideal future that is credible yet not readily attainable. Vision is an important component of both charismatic and transformational leadership. Visionary leaders speak to the hearts of employees, letting them be part of something bigger than themselves. Where others see obstacles or failures, they see possibility and hope.

Charismatic leaders typically have a strong vision for the future, almost an obsession, and they can motivate others to help realize it.[61] These leaders have an emotional impact on subordinates because they strongly believe in the vision and can communicate it to others in a way that makes the vision real, personal, and meaningful.

11.7b Transformational versus Transactional Leadership

Transformational leaders are similar to charismatic leaders, but they are distinguished by their special ability to bring about innovation and change by recognizing followers' needs and concerns, providing meaning, challenging people to look at old problems in new ways, and acting as role models for the new values and behaviors. Transformational leaders inspire followers not just to believe in the leader personally, but to believe in their own potential to imagine and create a better future for the organization. Transformational leaders create significant change in both followers and the organization.[62]

Transformational leadership can be better understood in comparison to *transactional leadership*.[63] **Transactional leaders** clarify the role and task requirements of subordinates, initiate structure, provide appropriate rewards, and try to be considerate and meet the social

Green Power

In the Hands of a Matador

It was, by any standard, a bold move. Taking the leadership reins in 2004 as CEO and president of Spain-based **Acciona**, one of Europe's most profitable real estate and construction businesses, José Manuel Entrecanales envisioned a future in which businesses would balance economic gain with environmental standards. Entrecanales convinced his board to address climate change and promote renewable energy development. The company wasted no time making a public announcement of its long-term sustainability plans and undertaking new strategies led by a Sustainability Committee. Over the next six years, Acciona managers made investments in sustainability, including wind generators. By 2009, Acciona had risen to third in the world in wind energy production. In less than a decade, Acciona has established a green reputation, and it was the leadership of Entrecanales, with the precise timing and calculated moves of a great matador, that envisioned the new spheres of action.

SOURCES: Daniel Arenas, Jeremie Fosse, and Matthew Murphy, "Acciona: A Process of Transformation Towards Sustainability," *Journal of Management Development* 30, no. 10 (2011): 1027–1048; and Patricia McCormick, "A Brave Matador Explains the Bullfight," *Sports Illustrated*, March 11, 1963, http://sportsillustrated.cnn.com/vault/article/magazine/MAG1074594/2/index.htm (accessed August 4, 2012).

needs of subordinates. The transactional leader's ability to satisfy subordinates may improve productivity. Transactional leaders excel at management functions. They are hardworking, tolerant, and fair-minded. They take pride in keeping things running smoothly and efficiently. Transactional leaders often stress the impersonal aspects of performance, such as plans, schedules, and budgets. They have a sense of commitment to the organization and conform to organizational norms and values. Transactional leadership is important to all organizations, but leading change requires a different approach.

Transformational leaders have the ability to lead changes in the organization's mission, strategy, structure, and culture, as well as to promote innovation in products and technologies. Transformational leaders do not rely solely on tangible rules and incentives to control specific transactions with followers. They focus on intangible qualities, such as vision, shared values, and ideas, to build relationships, give larger meaning to diverse activities, and find common ground to enlist followers in the change process.[64] For example, Michelle Rhee, former chancellor of the District of Columbia public schools, acted as a transformational leader to revamp one of the most expensive, worst-performing school systems in the country.

Rhee has continued to act as a transformational leader after leaving D.C. Her current organization, StudentsFirst, has a mission "to ensure great teachers, access to great schools, and effective use of public dollars" across the United States. "Some people think she is a transformative leader, and some people think she is a controversial figure, but everyone agrees she gets people talking," said one organizer of a recent conference in Michigan.[65]

Studies show that transformational leadership has a positive impact on follower development and follower performance.[66] Moreover, transformational leadership skills can be learned and are not ingrained personality characteristics. However, some personality traits

Spotlight on Skills

Michelle Rhee, StudentsFirst

Michelle Rhee, former chancellor of Washington, D.C., public schools and founder of StudentsFirst, is one of the most controversial figures in U.S. education—but love her or hate her, you can't say that she's afraid of change. A daughter of Korean immigrants, Rhee wanted to quit halfway through her first year in Teach for America, an organization that sends new college graduates into some of the toughest schools in the United States, but her father made her go back and finish the job. That's where she first embarked on a personal mission to change the system for the country's poorest students. Rhee noticed that students responded to teachers who pushed them hard and kept them interested.

A couple of decades later, Rhee had the chance to put some of her ideas into action on a large scale as she tried to revamp one of the most expensive, worst-performing school systems in the country. As chancellor of the D.C. public schools, Rhee attacked the dysfunctional culture that rewarded teachers for seniority rather than performance, revised systems and structures to

slash bureaucracy, held school principals accountable for improving student performance, and focused people on a mission of putting the best interests of students first.

Her vision of making D.C. schools "the highest-performing urban school district in the nation" brought new energy and movement to a long-stagnant system. "We have a system that does wrong by poor kids of color," Rhee said. "If we're going to live up to our promise as a country … that has got to stop." Rhee becomes angry when people say that "teachers cannot make up for what parents and students will not do," emphasizing that each teacher *can* make a difference. She didn't hesitate to cut administrative positions that weren't contributing value, fire teachers and principals who didn't meet performance standards, and close underperforming schools. She instituted new procedures to handsomely reward high-performing teachers and give principals more control over hiring, promoting, and firing. New evaluation procedures put people on alert that low performance and complacency would not be tolerated.[67]

may make it easier for a leader to display transformational leadership behaviors. For example, studies of transformational leadership have found that the trait of agreeableness, as discussed in the previous chapter, is often associated with transformational leaders.[68] In addition, transformational leaders are typically emotionally stable and positively engaged with the world around them, and they have a strong ability to recognize and understand others' emotions.[69] These characteristics are not surprising, considering that these leaders accomplish change by building networks of positive relationships.

REMEMBER THIS

- A **charismatic leader** is a leader who has the ability to inspire and motivate people to transcend their expected performance, even to the point of personal sacrifice.
- Both charismatic and transformational leaders provide followers with an inspiring **vision**, an attractive, ideal future that is credible, yet not readily attainable.

- A **transformational leader** is distinguished by a special ability to bring about innovation and change by creating an inspiring vision, shaping values, building relationships, and providing meaning for followers.
- A **transactional leader** clarifies subordinates' roles and task requirements, initiates structure, provides rewards, and displays consideration for followers.

11.8 Followership

No discussion of leadership is complete without a consideration of followership. Indeed, despite the focus on leadership, everybody in an organization is both a follower and a leader.[70] Leadership matters, but without effective followers, no organization can survive. People have different expectations of what constitutes a good follower versus a good leader, as illustrated by the results of studies asking people to rank the desired characteristics of leaders and followers. The top five qualities desired in each are as follows:[71]

Leader	Follower
Honest	Honest
Competent	Competent
Forward-looking	Dependable
Inspiring	Cooperative
Intelligent	Loyal

There may be some differences, but overall, many of the qualities that define a good follower are the same qualities as those possessed by a good leader. Leaders can develop an understanding of their followers and create the conditions that help them be most effective.[72]

One model of followership is illustrated in Exhibit 11.10. Robert E. Kelley conducted extensive interviews with managers and their subordinates and came up with five *follower styles*, which are categorized according to two dimensions, as shown in the exhibit.[73]

EXHIBIT 11.10 Styles of Followership

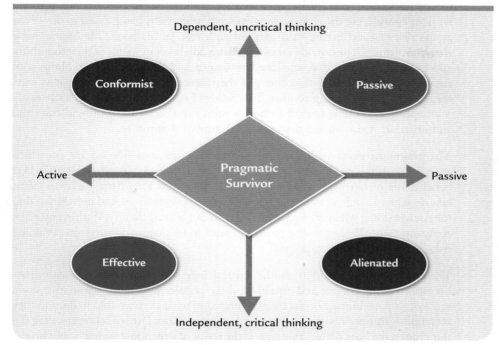

SOURCE: Based on Robert E. Kelley, *The Power of Followership* (New York: Doubleday, 1992).

The first dimension is the quality of independent, **critical thinking** versus dependent, **uncritical thinking**. Independent, critical thinkers are mindful of the effects of their own and others' behavior on achieving organizational goals. They can weigh the impact of their boss's and their own decisions and offer constructive criticism, creativity, and innovation. Conversely, a dependent, uncritical thinker does not consider possibilities beyond what he or she is told, does not contribute to the cultivation of the organization, and accepts the supervisor's ideas without thinking.

The second dimension of follower style is active versus passive behavior. An active follower participates fully in the organization, engages in behavior that is beyond the limits of the job, demonstrates a sense of ownership, and initiates problem solving and decision making. A passive follower, by contrast, is characterized by a need for constant supervision and prodding by superiors. Passivity is often regarded as laziness; a passive person does nothing that is not required and avoids added responsibility.

The extent to which an individual is active or passive and is an independent, critical thinker or a dependent, uncritical thinker determines whether the person will be an alienated follower, a passive follower, a conformist, a pragmatic survivor, or an effective follower, as illustrated in Exhibit 11.10:

- The **alienated follower** is a passive, yet independent, critical thinker. Alienated employees are often effective followers who have experienced setbacks and obstacles—perhaps promises broken by their superiors. Thus, they are capable, but they focus exclusively on the shortcomings of their bosses. Often cynical, alienated followers are able to think independently, but they do not participate in developing solutions to the problems or deficiencies that they see. These people waste valuable time complaining about their boss without offering constructive feedback.

- The **conformist** participates actively in a relationship with the boss but doesn't use critical-thinking skills. In other words, a conformist participates willingly, but without considering the consequences of what he or she is being asked to do—even at the risk of contributing to a harmful endeavor. In his book *The Foreclosure of America*, former Countrywide executive Adam Michaelson writes of the groupthink and blind conformity that squelched resistance and led people to go along with company actions even if they thought they were wrong.[74] A conformist is concerned only with avoiding conflict. This follower style might reflect an individual's overdependent attitude toward authority, yet it can also result from rigid rules and authoritarian environments that create a culture of conformity.

- The **pragmatic survivor** has qualities of all four extremes—depending on which style fits with the prevalent situation. This type of person uses whatever style best benefits his or her own position and minimizes risk. Pragmatic survivors often emerge when an organization is going through desperate times, and individuals find themselves doing whatever is needed to get through the difficulty. Within any given company, some 25–35 percent of people tend to be pragmatic survivors, avoiding risks and fostering the status quo.[75]

- The **passive follower** exhibits neither critical, independent thinking nor active participation. Being passive and uncritical, these people show neither initiative nor a sense of responsibility. Their activity is limited to what they are told to do, and they accomplish things only with a great deal of supervision. Passive followers leave the thinking to the boss. Often, this style is the result of a micromanaging boss who encourages passive behavior. People learn that to show initiative, accept responsibility, or think creatively is not rewarded, and may even be punished by the boss, so they grow increasingly passive.

- The **effective follower** is both a critical, independent thinker and active in the organization. Effective followers behave the same toward everyone, regardless of their position in the organization. They develop an equitable relationship with their leaders and do not try to avoid risk or conflict. These people are capable of self-management, they discern strengths and weaknesses in themselves and their bosses, they are committed to something bigger than themselves, and they work toward competency, solutions, and positive impact.

Are you an effective follower, or do you tend to be alienated, passive, conforming, or a pragmatic survivor? Answer the questions in the "New Manager Self-Test" on page 497 to find out.

One example of an effective follower is Laurie Stein, general counsel of Clorox. When a company brings in an outside CEO, one expert estimates that managers have a 30–40 percent chance of being fired. But not effective followers like Laurie Stein. Before Donald Knauss even took the CEO job, Stein did extensive research on him to help her figure out how to work with him most effectively. She began looking for how she could best serve Knauss and the organization as it embarked on a new path. Even if she disagreed with any strategic changes that he wanted to make, Stein believed that it was her job to support them. Since Stein had previously worked in China, she volunteered to informally advise colleagues about revamping the company's strategy in that country. Knauss appreciated Stein's proactive approach. "She will help anyone who asks for help," he says. Within months of taking the CEO job, Knauss had broadened Stein's duties and power.[76]

Effective followers recognize that they have power in their relationships with superiors; thus, they have the courage to manage upward, to initiate change, and even to put themselves at risk or in conflict with the boss if they believe that it serves the best interest of the team or organization.

NEW MANAGER Self-Test

What Is Your Follower Style?

Instructions: For each of the following statements, think of a specific situation in which you worked for a boss in an organization. Then answer whether each item below is Mostly True or Mostly False for you.

	Mostly True	Mostly False
1. I often commented to my manager on the broader importance of data or events.	_____	_____
2. I thought carefully and then expressed my opinion about critical issues.	_____	_____
3. I frequently suggested ways of improving my and others' ways of doing things.	_____	_____
4. I challenged my manager to think about an old problem in a new way.	_____	_____
5. Rather than wait to be told, I would figure out the critical activities for achieving my unit's goals.	_____	_____
6. I independently thought up and championed new ideas to my boss.	_____	_____
7. I tried to solve the tough problems rather than expect my manager to do it.	_____	_____
8. I played devil's advocate if needed to demonstrate the upside and downside of initiatives.	_____	_____
9. My work fulfilled a higher personal goal for me.	_____	_____
10. I was enthusiastic about my job.	_____	_____
11. I understood my manager's goals and worked hard to meet them.	_____	_____
12. The work that I did was significant to me.	_____	_____
13. I felt emotionally engaged throughout a typical day.	_____	_____
14. I had the opportunity to do what I do best each day.	_____	_____
15. I understood how my role contributed to the company's success.	_____	_____
16. I was willing to put in a great deal of effort beyond what is normally expected.	_____	_____

Scoring and Interpretation: Sum 1 point for each Mostly True answer for questions 1–8 for your score on Critical Thinking: _____. Sum 1 point for each Mostly True answer for questions 9–16 for your Active Engagement Score: _____. Based on whether your scores are high (6–8), medium (4–5), or low (0–3), identify your followership style next.

Followership Style	Critical Thinking Score	Active Engagement Score
Effective	High	High
Alienated	High	Low
Conformist	Low	High
Pragmatist	Medium	Medium
Passive	Low	Low

Read the descriptions of follower styles in the text. How do you feel about your followership style? What might you do to be more effective as a follower?

SOURCE: Based on Douglas R. May, Richard L. Gilson, and Lynn M. Harter, "The Psychological Conditions of Meaningfulness, Safety, and Availability and the Engagement of the Human Spirit at Work," *Journal of Occupational and Organizational Psychology* 77 (March 2004): 11–38; Robert E. Kelley, *The Power of Followership: How to Create Leaders People Want to Follow and Followers Who Lead Themselves* (New York: Doubleday, 1992); and Towers Perrin HR Services, "Working Today: Understanding What Drives Employee Engagement: The 2003 Towers Perrin Talent Report," http://www.towersperrin.com/tp/getwebcachedoc?webc=hrs/usa/2003/200309/talent_2003.pdf (accessed February 20, 2012).

REMEMBER THIS

- Leaders can accomplish nothing without effective followers.
- **Critical thinking** means thinking independently and being mindful of the effect of one's behavior on achieving goals.
- **Uncritical thinking** means failing to consider the possibilities beyond what one is told and accepting others' ideas without thinking.
- An **effective follower** is a critical, independent thinker who actively participates in the organization.

- An **alienated follower** is a person who is an independent, critical thinker but is passive in the organization.
- A **conformist** is a follower who participates actively in the organization but does not use critical thinking skills.
- A **passive follower** is one who exhibits neither critical independent thinking nor active participation.
- A follower who has qualities of all four follower styles, depending on which fits the prevalent situation, is called a **pragmatic survivor**.

11.9 **Power and Influence**

Both followers and leaders use power and influence to get things done in organizations. Sometimes the terms *power* and *influence* are used synonymously, but there are distinctions between the two. **Power** is the potential ability to influence the behavior of others.[77] **Influence** is the effect that a person's actions have on the attitudes, values, beliefs, or behavior of others. Whereas power is the capacity to cause a change in a person, influence may be thought of as the degree of actual change.

Most discussions of power include five types that are available to leaders,[78] and these can be categorized as either *hard power* or *soft power*. Hard power is power that stems largely from a person's position of authority and includes legitimate, reward, and coercive power. Soft power includes expert power and referent power, which are based on personal characteristics and interpersonal relationships more than on a position of authority.

11.9a Hard Position Power

The traditional manager's power comes from the organization (hard power). The manager's position gives him or her the ability to reward or punish subordinates to influence their behavior. Legitimate power, reward power, and coercive power are all forms of position power used by managers to change employee behavior.

CONCEPT CONNECTION At Google, Inc., managers encourage employees to take advantage of the many **rewards** that the company offers, including on-site dry cleaning, haircutting, and massage therapy services. These may sound like overly generous rewards, but they are actually smart management. The less time that employees spend on taking care of common personal tasks, the more time and energy they can devote to keeping this technology giant on top.

Lynn Johnson/National Geographic Image Collection/Alamy

Legitimate Power Power coming from a formal management position in an organization and the authority granted to it is called **legitimate power**. Once a person has been selected as a supervisor, most employees understand that they are obligated to follow his or her direction with respect to work activities. Subordinates accept this source of power as legitimate, which is why they comply.

Reward Power Another kind of power, **reward power**, stems from the authority to bestow rewards on other people. Managers may have access to formal rewards, such as pay increases or promotions. They also have at their disposal rewards such as praise, attention, and recognition. Managers can use rewards to influence subordinates' behavior.

Coercive Power The opposite of reward power is **coercive power**. It refers to the authority to punish or recommend punishment. Managers have coercive power when they have the right to fire or demote employees, criticize them, or withhold pay increases. If an employee does not perform as expected, the manager has the coercive power to reprimand him, put a negative letter in his file, deny him a raise, and hurt his chances for a promotion.

11.9b Personal Soft Power

Effective leaders don't rely solely on the hard power of their formal position to influence others. Jeffrey Immelt, CEO of GE, considers himself a failure if he exercises his formal authority more than seven or eight times a year. The rest of the time, he is using softer means to persuade and influence others and to resolve conflicting ideas and opinions.[79] In contrast to the external sources of position power, personal power most often comes from internal sources, such as an individual's special knowledge or personal characteristics. Personal power is the primary tool of the leader, and it is becoming increasingly important as more businesses are run by teams of workers who are less tolerant of authoritarian management.[80] Michelle Davis, who works as a middle manager at Fair Isaac Corporation (FICO), says that relying on soft power can be frustrating, but it is a crucial part of the job.[81] Two types of personal power are expert power and referent power.

Spotlight on Skills

Detroit Lions

Forget everything you've heard about tough, bullying coaches being the most effective. Jim Caldwell runs the Detroit Lions with poetry, proverbs, and quotations from Nelson Mandela to Joe Torre. And some days he recites in Finnish. He does not curse or get angry, and believes if he cannot get his point across without swearing, it is *his* fault. With such unusual tactics for an NFL coach, Caldwell has turned the Lions from an team known for committing dumb penalties, to one tied with the Green Bay Packers atop the NFL.

Caldwell reads a lot and started one session with the players using the Finnish word, *sisu*, which roughly means the burden of responsibility and the ability to carry it out. *Sisu*, he said, should define who the players are and what they want to achieve. All this might sound like new agey trite, but Caldwell came to Detroit with instant credibility, having won Super Bowls as assistant coach in both Baltimore and Indianapolis. He started by getting the

players to focus on their loftier sides, on their skills, and to leave the bad-boy image behind. He invited them in small groups to dinner and asked about their families. The players were shocked, but in a good way. As Cornerback Rashean Mathis said, "In 12 years, that's the first time I've been to dinner with my head coach."

It takes more than a nice guy, though. Caldwell is known for his offensive expertise, and he detailed every speech and every meeting of every single coach he's ever worked for. At practices, Caldwell reviews decisive moments in the NFL during the past week, focusing on poor time management, avoidable penalties, and he simulates potential game situations. And he reminds the players, "Opportunities multiply when they are seized."

SOURCE: Ben Shpigel, "Thanks to a Cerebral Influence, the Lions Find Enlightenment," *New York Times*, December 21, 2014, SP1–3.

Expert Power   Power resulting from a person's special knowledge or skill regarding the tasks being performed is referred to as **expert power**. When someone is a true expert, others go along with recommendations because of his or her superior knowledge. Both followers and leaders can possess expert power. For example, some managers lead teams in which members have expertise that the leader lacks. Some leaders at top management levels may lack expert power because subordinates know more about technical details than they do.

Referent Power   **Referent power** comes from an individual's personal characteristics that command others' identification, respect, and admiration so that they wish to emulate that individual. Referent power does not depend on a formal title or position. When employees admire a supervisor because of the way that she deals with them, the influence is based on referent power. Referent power is most visible in the area of charismatic leadership. In social and religious movements, we often see charismatic leaders who emerge and gain a tremendous following based solely on their personal power. One leader who exemplifies both expert and referent power is Detroit Lions coach Jim Caldwell, as shown in the Spotlight on Skills box.

11.9c Other Sources of Power

There are additional sources of power that are not linked to a particular person or position, but rather to the role that an individual plays in the overall functioning of the organization. These important sources include personal effort, relationships with others, and information.

Personal Effort   People who show initiative, work beyond what is expected of them, take on undesirable but important projects, and show interest in learning about the organization and industry often gain power as a result. Stephen Holmes says that he began his journey toward the CEO's office at Wyndham Worldwide because of personal effort. As a young internal auditor at a private-equity firm in the early 1980s, Holmes was spending his evenings trying to learn a new spreadsheet program. Noted investor Henry Silverman noticed him night after night and, intrigued by the young auditor's efforts, stopped by to see what he was doing. Silverman asked Holmes to move with him to future companies, including Blackstone, HMS, and eventually Wyndham. "I was a kid," Holmes says, "[but he] put me into positions that no one else my age was getting to do."[82]

Network of Relationships People who are enmeshed in a network of relationships have greater power. A leader or employee with many relationships knows what's going on in the organization and industry, whereas one who has few interpersonal connections is often in the dark about important activities or changes. Networks of relationships are crucial in the political arena for instance. Abraham Lincoln is considered by historians to be one of the greatest U.S. presidents partly because he built relationships and listened carefully to a broad range of people both inside and outside of his immediate circle when the nation was so bitterly divided over the Civil War. He included people who didn't agree with him and were critical of his goals and plans.[83] As for President Barack Obama, the jury is still out on how his presidency will be evaluated. However, Obama has been criticized for failing to develop relationships with even his biggest donors and leaving the relationship-building with Democrats on Capitol Hill and others to Vice President Joe Biden. Obama is widely viewed as a loner who prefers policy to people and consults primarily with a close circle of advisers.[84]

Information Information is a primary business resource, and people who have access to information and control over how and to whom it is distributed are typically powerful. To some extent, access to information is determined by a person's position in the organization. Top managers typically have access to more information than middle managers, who in turn have access to more information than lower-level supervisors or front-line employees.

Both leaders and followers can tap into these additional sources of power. Leaders succeed when they take the time to build relationships both inside and outside the organization and to talk informally about important projects and priorities. Jack Griffin was forced out as CEO of Time Inc. after less than six months on the job, largely because he failed to develop positive relationships. Griffin tried to use the hard power of his position to make needed changes at *Time* without building the soft-power connections needed to implement the changes. Board members began to realize that Griffin had become so unpopular that the company was likely to lose valuable employees if he stayed on as CEO.[85]

11.9d Interpersonal Influence Tactics

Leaders often use a combination of influence strategies, and people who are perceived as having greater power and influence typically are those who use a wider variety of tactics. One survey of a few hundred leaders identified more than 4,000 different techniques that these people used to influence others.[86]

However, these tactics fall into basic categories that rely on understanding the principles that cause people to change their behavior and attitudes. Exhibit 11.11 lists six principles for asserting influence. Notice that most of these involve the use of personal power rather than relying solely on position power or the use of rewards and punishments.[87]

1. Use rational persuasion. The most frequently used influence strategy is to apply facts, data, and logical argument to persuade others that a proposed idea, request, or decision is appropriate. Using rational persuasion can often be highly effective because most people have faith in facts and analysis.[88] Rational persuasion is most successful when a leader has technical knowledge and expertise related to the issue

EXHIBIT 11.11 Six Interpersonal Influence Tactics for Leaders

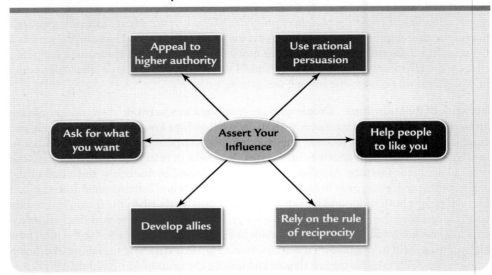

at hand (expert power), although referent power is also used. That is, in addition to facts and figures, people have to believe in the leader's credibility.

2. Help people to like you. People would rather say yes to someone they like than to someone they don't. Effective leaders strive to create goodwill and favorable impressions. When a leader shows consideration and respect, treats people fairly, and demonstrates trust in others, people are more likely to want to help and support this person by doing what he or she asks. In addition, most people like a leader who makes them feel good about themselves, so leaders should never underestimate the power of praise.

3. Rely on the rule of reciprocity. Leaders can influence others through the exchange of benefits and favors. Leaders share what they have—whether it is time, resources, services, or emotional support. The feeling among people is nearly universal that others should be paid back for what they do, in one form or another. This unwritten "rule of reciprocity" means that leaders who do favors for others can expect that others will do favors for them in return.[89]

4. Develop allies. Effective leaders develop networks of allies—people who can help the leader accomplish his or her goals. Leaders talk with followers and others outside formal meetings to understand their needs and concerns, as well as to explain problems and describe the leader's point of view. They strive to reach a meeting of minds with others about the best approach to a problem or decision.[90]

5. Ask for what you want. Another way to influence others is to make a direct and personal request. Leaders have to be explicit about what they want or they aren't likely to get it. An explicit proposal is sometimes accepted simply because others have no better alternative. Also, a clear proposal or alternative will often receive support if other options are less well defined.

6. Appeal to higher authority. Sometimes, to get things done, leaders have to use their formal authority, as well as gain the support of people at higher levels to back them

up. However, research has found that the key to successful use of formal authority is to be knowledgeable, credible, and trustworthy—that is, to demonstrate expert and referent power as well as legitimate power. Managers who become known for their expertise, who are honest and straightforward with others, and who inspire trust can exert greater influence than those who simply issue orders.[91]

Research indicates that people rate leaders as "more effective" when they are perceived to use a variety of influence tactics. But not all managers use influence in the same way. Studies have found that leaders in human resources, for example, tend to use softer, more subtle approaches, such as building goodwill, using favors, and developing allies, whereas those in finance are inclined to use harder, more direct tactics, such as formal authority and assertiveness.[92]

REMEMBER THIS

- **Power** is the potential ability to influence the behavior of others.
- All leaders use power to influence people and accomplish organizational goals.
- **Influence** is the effect that a person's actions have on the attitudes, values, beliefs, or behavior of others.
- **Legitimate power** is power that stems from a manager's formal position in an organization and the authority granted by that position.
- **Reward power** results from the authority to bestow rewards.
- **Coercive power** stems from the authority to punish or recommend punishment.

- **Expert power** is power that results from a leader's special knowledge or skill in the tasks performed by subordinates.
- **Referent power** results from characteristics that command subordinates' identification with, respect and admiration for, and desire to emulate the leader.
- Both leaders and followers can tap into other sources of power, including personal effort, networks of relationships, and access to or control over information.
- Leaders use a wide range of interpersonal influence tactics, and people who use a wider variety of tactics are typically perceived as having greater power.

CHAPTER **11** DISCUSSION QUESTIONS

1. Suggest some personal traits that you believe would be useful to a business leader today. Are these traits more valuable in some situations than in others? How do you think traits differ from strengths?

2. In a study asking what people wanted from leaders versus followers, people ranked *maturity* number 8 for followers, but number 15 for leaders. What might account for people wanting a higher maturity level from followers?

3. If a male manager changes his behaviors to incorporate elements of interactive leadership more common to female managers, can he still be an "authentic" leader? Discuss.

4. Studies of women leaders suggest that many of them view power differently than men do and prefer a collaborative, relationship-oriented use of power. If this is the case, what does it suggest about women leaders' abilities to accomplish goals? What does it suggest about women's ability to rise to higher organizational levels? Discuss.

5. What skills and abilities does a manager need to lead effectively in a virtual environment? Do you believe a leader with a consideration style or an initiating-structure style would be more successful as a virtual leader? Explain your answer.

6. What is transformational leadership? Give examples of organizational situations that would call for transformational, transactional, or charismatic leadership.

7. How does Level 5 leadership differ from the concept of servant leadership? Do you believe that anyone has the potential to become a Level 5 leader? Discuss.

8. Why do you think that so little attention is given to followership compared to leadership in organizations? Discuss how the role of an effective follower is similar to the role of a leader.

9. Do you think leadership is more important or less important in today's flatter, team-based organizations? Are some leadership styles better suited to such organizations as opposed to traditional hierarchical organizations? Explain.

10. Consider the leadership position of a senior partner in a law firm. What task, subordinate, and organizational factors might serve as substitutes for leadership in this situation?

SELF-LEARNING

What Is the Impact of Leadership?[93]

What are your beliefs and understandings about how top leaders influence organizational performance?

To learn about your beliefs, please answer whether each item below is Mostly True or Mostly False based on your personal beliefs.

	Mostly True	Mostly False
1. The quality of leadership is the most important influence on the performance of an organization.		
2. People in top-level leadership positions have the power to make or break an organization.		
3. Most activities in an organization have little to do with the decisions or activities of the top leaders.		
4. Even in a bad economy, a good leader can prevent a company from doing poorly.		
5. A company cannot do well unless it has high-quality leadership at the top.		
6. High-quality versus low-quality leadership has a bigger impact on a firm's performance than does the business environment.		
7. Poor organizational performance is often due to factors beyond the control of even the best leaders.		
8. Eventually, bad leadership at the top will trigger poor organizational performance.		
9. Leaders typically should not be held responsible for a firm's poor performance.		

Interpretation: This scale is about the "romance" of leadership, which is the romantic view that leaders are very responsible for organizational performance as opposed to other factors such as economic conditions. Company performance is difficult to control and is an outcome of complex forces. Attributing too much responsibility to leaders is a simplification shaped more by our own mental construction than by the reality and complexity of organizational performance. Top leaders are not heroes, but they are important as one of several key factors that can shape organizational performance.

Scoring: Give yourself 1 point for each item 1, 2, 4, 5, 6, and 8 marked as Mostly True and each item 3, 7, and 9 marked as Mostly False. A score of 7 or higher suggests a belief in the romance of leadership—that leaders have more control over performance

outcomes than is actually the case. If you scored 3 or less, you may underestimate the impact of top leaders—a somewhat skeptical view. A score of 4 to 6 suggests a balanced view of leadership.

In Class: Sit with a student partner and explain your scores to each other. What are your beliefs about leadership? What is the basis for your beliefs? The instructor can ask for a show of hands concerning the number of high, medium, and low scores on the questionnaire. Discuss the following questions: Do you believe that presidents, top executives, and heads of nonprofit organizations act alone and hence are largely responsible for performance? What is the evidence for this belief? What other forces will affect an organization? What is a realistic view of top leader influence in a large organization?

GROUP LEARNING

Assumptions about Leaders

Individually complete the sentences below.

1. A leader must always…

2. Leaders should never…

3. The best leader I ever had did…

4. The worst leader I ever had did…

5. When I am doing a good job as a leader, I…

6. I am afraid of leaders who…

7. I would follow a leader who…

8. I am repelled by leaders who…

9. Some people think they are good leaders, but they are not because they…

10. I want to be the kind of leader who…

In groups of four to six, discuss the following:

A. What did you learn about your own assumptions about leadership?

B. Trace those assumptions back to theories on leadership in this chapter.

C. What were common themes in your group?

ACTION LEARNING

1. Find three people who have had bosses or CEOs who were either charismatic or transformational.

2. Ask them to describe what the leader was like, what were the values, the behaviors?

3. Ask them to contrast those charismatic or transformational leaders with an ineffective boss or CEO they worked with.

4. What were the differences in behavior? How did the behavior of the ineffective leaders impact the organization?

5. Ask them to give a few sentences on how they would compare the transformational or charismatic leader to the ineffective one.

6. Your instructor may ask you to write a paper on this subject or bring this information to class and be prepared to discuss it.

7. What did you learn about transformational and charismatic leadership from this assignment? Did it agree with what the textbook described?

ETHICAL DILEMMA

Too Much of a Good Thing?

Not long ago, Jessica Armstrong, vice president of administration for Delaware Valley Chemical Inc., a New Jersey–based multinational company, made a point of stopping by department head Darius Harris's office and lavishly praising him for his volunteer work with an after-school program for disadvantaged children in a nearby urban neighborhood. Now she was about to summon him to her office so she could take him to task for his dedication to the same volunteer work.

It was Carolyn Clark, Harris's secretary, who'd alerted her to the problem. "Darius told the community center he'd take responsibility for a fund-raising mass mailing. And then he asked me to edit the letter he'd drafted, make all the copies, stuff the envelopes, and get it into the mail—most of this on my own time," she reported, still obviously indignant. "When I told him, 'I'm sorry, but that's not my job,' he looked me straight in the eye and asked when I'd like to schedule my upcoming performance appraisal."

Several of Harris's subordinates also volunteered with the program. After chatting with them, Armstrong concluded most were volunteering out of a desire to stay on the boss's good side. It was time to talk to Harris.

"Oh, come on," responded Harris impatiently when Armstrong confronted him. "Yes, I asked for her help as a personal favor to me. But I only brought up the appraisal because I was going out of town, and we needed to set some time aside to do the evaluation." Harris went on to talk about how important working for the after-school program was to him personally. "I grew up in that neighborhood, and if it hadn't been for the people at the center, I wouldn't be here today," he said. Besides, even if he had pressured employees to help out—and he wasn't saying he had—didn't all the emphasis the company was putting on employee volunteerism make it okay to use employees' time and company resources?

After Harris left, Armstrong thought about the conversation. There was no question that Delaware Valley actively encouraged employee volunteerism—and not just because it was the right thing to do. The chemical company had suffered a couple of unfortunate accidental spills in its recent past that caused environmental damage and sparked community anger.

Volunteering had the potential to help employees acquire new skills, create a sense of camaraderie, and play a role in recruiting and retaining talented people. But most of all, it gave a badly needed boost to the company's public image. Recently, Delaware Valley took every opportunity to publicize its employees' extracurricular community work on its Web site and in company publications. And the company created the annual Delaware Prize, which granted cash awards ranging from $1,000 to $5,000 to outstanding volunteers.

So now that Armstrong had talked with everyone concerned, just what was she going to do about the dispute between Darius Harris and Carolyn Clark?

What Would You Do?

1. Tell Carolyn Clark that employee volunteerism is important to the company and that while her performance evaluation will not be affected by her decision, she should consider helping Harris because it is an opportunity to help a worthy community project.

2. Tell Darius Harris that the employee volunteer program is just that: a volunteer program. Even though the company sees volunteerism as an important piece of its campaign to repair its tarnished image, employees must be free to choose whether to volunteer. He should not ask for the help of his direct employees with the after-school program.

3. Discipline Darius Harris for coercing his subordinates to spend their own time on his volunteer work at the community after-school program. This action will send a signal that coercing employees is a clear violation of leadership authority.

CASE FOR CRITICAL ANALYSIS

"What's Wrong with the Team?"

What's wrong with the team? What's wrong with the team? Nichole Dyer's words repeated over and over in Henry Rankin's head as he boarded the plane from Los Angeles to Chicago.

Rankin is responsible for the technical implementation of the new customer relationship management (CRM) software being installed for the sales offices in both cities. The software is badly needed to improve follow-up sales for his company, Reflex Systems. Reflex sells exercise equipment to high schools and colleges, as well as to small to mid-sized businesses for recreation centers, through a national force of 310 salespeople. The company's low prices have won a lot of sales; however, follow-up service is uneven, and the new CRM system promises to resolve those problems with historical data, inquiries, reminders, and updates going to sales reps daily. The CEO of Reflex has ordered the CRM system installed with all possible haste.

Rankin pulled a yellow pad and pen from the side pocket of his carry-on bag and tossed them on the seat beside the window, stashed the bag in the overhead compartment, and sat down as other passengers filed past. In an effort to shut out his thoughts, he closed his eyes and concentrated on the muffled voices and low whooshing sound of the air vents. He wrote "What's wrong with the team?" three times and began drawing arrows to circles bearing the names of his team members: Barry Livingston and Max Wojohowski in L.A., and Bob Finley, Lynne Johnston, and Sally Phillips in Chicago.

He marked through Sally's name. She had jumped ship recently, taking her less-than-stellar but still-much-needed talents with her to another company. It was on a previous L.A.-to-Chicago flight that Sally had pumped him for feedback on her future with Reflex. She had informed him that she had another job offer. She admitted it was for less money, but she was feeling under pressure as a member of the team and she wanted more "quality of life." Rankin told Sally bluntly that her technical expertise, on which he placed top importance, was slightly below her peers, so future promotion was less likely despite her impressive people and team skills.

He wrote "quality of life," circled it, and then crossed it out and wrote "what the hell?" "Why should she get quality of life?" he mused. "I've barely seen my wife and kids since this project started." Rankin's team was under a great deal of pressure, and he had needed Sally to stick it out. He told her so, but the plane had barely touched down when she went directly to the office and quit, leaving the team shorthanded and too close to deadline to add another body.

What's wrong with the team? Rankin furiously scribbled as his thoughts raced:

(1) *The deadline is ridiculously short.* Dyer had scheduled a 10-week completion deadline for the new CRM software, including installation and training for both cities.

He suddenly stopped writing and drew a rider and horse, then returned to his list.

(2) *I feel like some frazzled pony-express rider running back and forth across the country, trying to develop, build, set-up and work the kinks out of a new system that everyone at Reflex is eager to see NOW.*

He was interrupted by the flight attendant. "Would you care for a drink, sir?"

"Yes. Make it a scotch and water. And be light on the water."

Rankin took his drink and continued to write.

(3) *Thank God for L.A.* From the outset, Barry and Max had worked feverishly while avoiding the whining and complaining that seemed to overwhelm members of the Chicago team. The atmosphere was different. Although the project moved forward, meeting deadlines, there appeared to be less stress. The L.A. guys focused tirelessly on work, with no families to consider, alternating intense work with joking around. *Those are my kind of people*, he thought.

(4) *But there is Chicago*, he wrote. Earlier in the day, Sam Matheny from sales had e-mailed, and then called, Rankin to tell him that the two remaining members of the Chicago team appeared to be alternating between bickering and avoiding one another. Apparently, this had been going on for some time. "What's with that?" Rankin wondered. "And why did Sam know and I didn't?" So that morning, before his flight, Rankin had to make time

to call and text both Finley and Johnston. Finley admitted that he had overreacted to Johnston.

"Look, man. I'm tired and stressed out," Finley said. "We've been working nonstop. My wife is not happy."

"Just get along until this project is completed," Rankin ordered.

"When will *that* be?" Finley asked before hanging up.

Rankin thought about Nichole Dyer's persistent complaints to him that the team appeared to have a lack of passion, and she admonished him to "get your people to understand the urgency of this project." Her complaints only added to his own stress level. He had long considered himself the front-runner for Dyer's job when she retired in two years. But had his team ruined that opportunity? The sense of urgency could be measured now in the level of stress and the long hours that they had all endured. He admitted his

team members were unenthusiastic, but they seemed committed.

Rankin wondered, "Is it too late to turn around and restore the level of teamwork?" He tore off the sheet from the pad, crumpled it in his hand, and stared out the window.

Questions

1. How would you characterize Rankin's leadership style? What approach do you think is correct for this situation? Why?

2. What would you do now if you were Rankin? How might you awaken more enthusiasm in your team for completing this project on time? Suggest specific steps.

3. How would you suggest that Rankin modify his leadership style if he wants to succeed Dyer in two years? Be specific.

ON THE JOB
VIDEO CASES

Camp Bow Wow: Leadership

Questions

1. Does Camp Bow Wow CEO Heidi Ganahl possess qualities associated with contemporary leadership?

2. In what way is Ganahl's leadership charismatic and visionary? Give examples.

3. Where does Ganahl's leadership fall on the Leadership Grid discussed in this chapter and illustrated in Exhibit 11.6? Explain.

ENDNOTES

1. Mark Maske, "Daniel Snyder, Washington Redskins Owner, Adopts Hands-Off Role—and Team Wins," *The Washington Post*, January 4, 2013, http://articles.washingtonpost.com/2013-01-04/sports/36209112_1_daniel-snyder-washington-redskins-redskins-park (accessed March 15, 2013).

2. Gary Yukl, "Managerial Leadership: A Review of Theory and Research," *Journal of Management* 15 (1989): 251–289.

3. James M. Kouzes and Barry Z. Posner, "The Credibility Factor: What Followers Expect from Their Leaders," *Management Review* (January 1990): 29–33.

4. Jim Collins, "Level 5 Leadership: The Triumph of Humility and Fierce Resolve," *Harvard Business Review* (January 2001): 67–76; Jim Collins, "Good to Great," *Fast Company* (October 2001): 90–104; A. J. Vogl, "Onward and Upward" (an interview with Jim Collins), *Across the Board* (September–October 2001): 29–34; and Jerry Useem, "Conquering Vertical Limits," *Fortune* (February 19, 2001): 84–96.

5. Jim Collins, "Enduring Greatness," *Leadership Excellence* (January 2011): 8.

6. As described in Stefan Stern, "A New Leadership Blueprint," *Management Today* (October 1, 2010): 38.

7. Miguel Helft, "A Hired Gun for Microsoft, in Dogged Pursuit of Google," *The New York Times*, August 31, 2009, www.nytimes.com/2009/08/31/technology/internet/31search.html (accessed August 31, 2009); and Brian R. Fitzgerald, "Who Will Be the Next Microsoft CEO? *The Wall Street Journal*, August 23, 2013, http://blogs.wsj.com/digits/2013/08/23/who-will-be-the-next-microsoft-ceo/ (accessed October 21, 2013).

8. Quoted in William J. Holstein, "The View's Still Great from the Corner Office," *The New York Times*, May 8, 2005.

9. Richard L. Daft and Robert H. Lengel, *Fusion Leadership: Unlocking the Subtle Forces That Change People and Organizations* (San Francisco: Berrett-Koehler, 1998).

10. Leigh Buchanan, "In Praise of Selflessness: Why the Best Leaders Are Servants," *Inc.* (May 2007): 33–35.

11. Robert K. Greenleaf, *Servant Leadership: A Journey into the Nature of Legitimate Power and Greatness* (Mahwah, NJ: Paulist Press, 1977).

12. "Not Her Father's Chief Executive" (an interview with Marilyn Carlson Nelson), *U.S. News & World Report* (October 30, 2006): 64–65.

13. "*Maersk Alabama* Crew Recalls Pirate Attack," *USA Today*, April 16, 2009, www.usatoday.com/news/nation/2009-04-16-pirates_N.htm (accessed April 30, 2009); Stacy Meichtry, Arian Campo-Flores, and Leslie Scism, "Cruise Company Blames Captain," *The Wall Street Journal*, January 17, 2012, http://online.wsj.com/article/SB10001424052970203735304577165290656739300.html (accessed January 20, 2012); and "Death Toll of Italy's Costa Concordia Wreck Rises to 30," *Philippine Star*, March 23, 2012, www.philstar.com/article.aspx?articleid=790169&publicationsubcategoryid=200 (accessed September 14, 2012).

14. Jena McGregor, "Lenovo CEO Hands over His Bonus to Hourly Workers—Again," *Washington Post*, September 5, 2013, http://www.washingtonpost.com/blogs/on-leadership/wp/2013/09/05/lenovo-ceo-hands-over-his-bonus-to-hourly-workers-again/ (accessed October 21, 2013).

15. Adam Bluestein, "Start a Company. Change the World," *Inc.* (May 2011): 71–80.

16. Bill George et al., "Discovering Your Authentic Leadership," *Harvard Business Review* (February 2007): 129–138; and Bill George, *Authentic Leadership: Rediscovering the Secrets to Lasting Value* (San Francisco: Jossey-Bass, 2003). For a recent review of the literature on authentic leadership, see William L. Gardner et al., "Authentic Leadership: A Review of the Literature and Research Agenda," *The Leadership Quarterly* 22 (2011): 1120–1145.

17. Bill George, *Authentic Leadership: Rediscovering the Secrets to Lasting Value* (San Francisco: Jossey-Bass, 2003); and Bill George, "Truly Authentic Leadership," Special Report: America's Best Leaders, *U.S. News & World Report*, October 22, 2006, www.usnews.com/usnews/news/articles/061022/30authentic.htm (accessed October 5, 2010).

18. Example from Michael Lee Stallard, "Great Leaders Connect: Using Their Vision, Values, and Voice," *Leadership Excellence* (August 2012): 19.

19. Vernon Clark, quoted in Michael Lee Stallard and Jason Pankau, "To Boost Performance, Connect with the Core," *Leader to Leader* (Summer 2010): 51–57.

20. Judy B. Rosener, *America's Competitive Secret: Utilizing Women as a Management Strategy* (New York: Oxford University Press, 1995), pp. 129–135.

21. Alice H. Eagly and Linda L. Carli, "The Female Leadership Advantage: An Evaluation of the Evidence," *Leadership Quarterly* 14 (2003): 807–834; Rosener, *America's Competitive Secret*; Judy B. Rosener, "Ways Women Lead," *Harvard Business Review* (November–December 1990): 119–125; Sally Helgesen, *The Female Advantage: Women's Ways of Leadership* (New York: Currency/Doubleday, 1990); Bernard M. Bass and Bruce J. Avolio, "Shatter the Glass Ceiling: Women May Make Better Managers," *Human Resource Management* 33, no. 4 (Winter 1994): 549–560; and Carol Kinsey Goman, "What Men Can Learn from Women about Leadership in the 21st Century," *Washington Post*, August 10, 2011, www.washingtonpost.com/national/on-leadership/what-men-can-learn-from-women-about-leadership/2011/08/10/gIQA4J9n6I_story.html (accessed September 12, 2012).

22. Reported in Leigh Buchanan, "Between Venus and Mars," *Inc.* (June 2013): 64–74, 130.

23. Rochelle Sharpe, "As Leaders, Women Rule," *BusinessWeek* (November 20, 2000): 75–84.

24. Kevin S. Groves, "Gender Differences in Social and Emotional Skills and Charismatic Leadership," *Journal of Leadership and Organizational Studies* 11, no. 3 (2005): 30ff.

25. Jack Zenger and Joseph Folkman, "Are Women Better Leaders Than Men?" HBR Blog Network, *Harvard Business Review,* March 15, 2012, http://blogs.hbr.org/cs/2012/03/a_study_in_leadership_women_do.html (accessed September 12, 2012); and Herminia Ibarra and Otilia Obodaru, "Women and the Vision Thing," *Harvard Business Review* (January 2009): 62–70.

26. Susan Carey, "More Women Take Flight in Airline Operations," *The Wall Street Journal,* August 14, 2007, B1; and Ann Therese Palmer, "Teacher Learns All About Airline; United VP Began as Reservations Clerk, Rose Through Ranks," *Chicago Tribune,* December 24, 2006, 3.

27. Leigh Buchanan, "Pat McGovern … For Knowing the Power of Respect," segment in "25 Entrepreneurs We Love," *Inc.* (April 2004): 110–147.

28. Reported in Buchanan, "Between Venus and Mars."

29. This analogy is from Gordon P. Rabey, "Leadership Is Response: A Paper for Discussion," *Industrial and Commercial Training* 42, no. 2 (2010): 87–92.

30. This discussion is based on Philip A. Dover and Udo Dierk, "The Ambidextrous Organization: Integrating Managers, Entrepreneurs, and Leaders," *Journal of Business Strategy* 31, no. 5 (2010): 49–58; Gary Yukl and Richard Lepsinger, "Why Integrating the Leading and Managing Roles Is Essential for Organizational Effectiveness," *Organizational Dynamics* 34, no. 4 (2005): 361–375; and Henry Mintzberg, *Managing* (San Francisco: Berrett-Kohler Publishers, 2009).

31. Mathew J. Manimala and Kishinchand Poornima Wasdani, "Distributed Leadership at Google: Lessons from the Billion-Dollar Brand," *Ivey Business Journal,* May–June 2013, http://iveybusinessjournal.com/topics/leadership/distributed-leadership-at-google-lessons-from-the-billion-dollar-brand#.UmalkSbD91s (accessed October 22, 2013).

32. As described in Manimala and Wasdani, "Distributed Leadership at Google."

33. G. A. Yukl, *Leadership in Organizations* (Englewood Cliffs, NJ: Prentice Hall, 1981); and S. C. Kohs and K. W. Irle, "Prophesying Army Promotion," *Journal of Applied Psychology* 4 (1920): 73–87.

34. R. Albanese and D. D. Van Fleet, *Organizational Behavior: A Managerial Viewpoint* (Hinsdale, IL: The Dryden Press, 1983); and S. A. Kirkpatrick and E. A. Locke, "Leadership: Do Traits Matter?" *Academy of Management Executive* 5, no. 2 (1991): 48–60.

35. A summary of various studies and surveys is reported in Del Jones, "Optimism Puts Rose-Colored Tint in Glasses of Top Execs," *USA Today,* December 15, 2005.

36. Annie Murphy Paul, "The Uses and Abuses of Optimism (and Pessimism)," *Psychology Today* (November–December 2011): 56–63.

37. Tom Rath and Barry Conchie, *Strengths Based Leadership* (Gallup Press, 2009); Marcus Buckingham and Donald O. Clifton, *Now, Discover Your Strengths* (New York: Free Press, 2001), p. 12.

38. Buckingham and Clifton, *Now, Discover Your Strengths.*

39. Gary Yukl, Angela Gordon, and Tom Taber, "A Hierarchical Taxonomy of Leadership Behavior: Integrating a Half-Century of Behavior Research," *Journal of Leadership and Organizational Studies* 9, no. 1 (2002): 13–32.

40. C. A. Schriesheim and B. J. Bird, "Contributions of the Ohio State Studies to the Field of Leadership," *Journal of Management* 5 (1979): 135–145; C. L. Shartle, "Early Years of the Ohio State University Leadership Studies," *Journal of Management* 5 (1979): 126–134; and R. Likert, "From Production- and Employee-Centeredness to Systems 1–4," *Journal of Management* 5 (1979): 147–156.

41. P. C. Nystrom, "Managers and the High-High Leader Myth," *Academy of Management Journal* 21 (1978): 325–331; and L. L. Larson, J. G. Hunt, and Richard N. Osborn, "The Great High-High Leader Behavior Myth: A Lesson from Occam's Razor," *Academy of Management Journal* 19 (1976): 628–641.

42. Likert, "From Production- and Employee-Centeredness to Systems 1–4."

43. Robert R. Blake and Jane S. Mouton, *The Managerial Grid III* (Houston: Gulf, 1985).

44. Diane Brady and Matthew Boyle, "Campbell's Recipe for a CEO Yields Denise Morrison," *Bloomberg BusinessWeek,* June 23, 2011, http://www.businessweek.com/magazine/content/11_27/b4235060614059.htm (accessed March 12, 2013); and Jo Napolitano, "Private Sector; No, She Doesn't Breathe Fire," *The New York Times,* September 1, 2002, http://www.nytimes.com/2002/09/01/business/private-sector-no-she-doesn-t-breathe-fire.html (accessed October 23, 2013).

45. This discussion is based on Paul Hersey and Ken Blanchard, "Revisiting the Life-Cycle Theory of Leadership," in "Great Ideas Revisited," *Training & Development* (January 1996): 42–47; Kenneth H. Blanchard and Paul Hersey, "Life-Cycle Theory of Leadership," in "Great Ideas Revisited," *Training & Development* (January 1996): 42–47; Paul Hersey, "Situational Leaders: Use the Model in Your Work," *Leadership Excellence* (February 2009): 12; and Paul Hersey and Kenneth H. Blanchard, *Management of Organizational Behavior: Utilizing Human Resources,* 4th ed. (Englewood Cliffs, NJ: Prentice Hall, 1982). The concept of *readiness* comes from Hersey, "Situational Leaders."

46. Jennifer Robison, "Many Paths to Engagement: How Very Different Management Styles Get the Same Great Results at Mars Incorporated," *Gallup Management Journal,* January 10, 2008, http://gmj.gallup.com/content/103513/Many-Paths-Engagement.aspx (accessed July 31, 2010).

47. Andrew Ross Sorkin, "Warren Buffett, Delegator in Chief," *The New York Times,* April 23, 2011, http://www.nytimes.com/2011/04/24/weekinreview/24buffett.html (accessed September 14, 2012).

48. Fred E. Fiedler, "Assumed Similarity Measures as Predictors of Team Effectiveness," *Journal of Abnormal and Social Psychology* 49 (1954): 381–388; F. E. Fiedler, *Leader Attitudes and Group Effectiveness* (Urbana, IL: University of Illinois Press, 1958); and F. E. Fiedler, *A Theory of Leadership Effectiveness* (New York: McGraw-Hill, 1967).

49. Fred E. Fiedler and M. M. Chemers, *Leadership and Effective Management* (Glenview, IL: Scott, Foresman, 1974).

50. Mark Silva, "Boehner's Struggle Within Own Party Wounds House Leader," *Bloomberg*, October 17, 2013, http://www.bloomberg.com/news/2013-10-16/boehner-s-struggle-within-own-party-wounds-house-leader.html (accessed October 23, 2013); and Paul Kane and David A. Fahrenthold, "Boehner's Laid-Back Approach Is Considered Boon, Bane for House Republicans," *Washington Post*, June 29, 2013, http://articles.washingtonpost.com/2013-06-29/politics/40269981_1_house-republicans-immigration-legislation-house-speaker (accessed June 30, 2013).

51. Reported in George Anders, "Theory & Practice: Tough CEOs Often Most Successful, a Study Finds," *The Wall Street Journal*, November 19, 2007.

52. Neal E. Boudette, "Fiat CEO Sets New Tone at Chrysler," *The Wall Street Journal*, June 21, 2009, http://online.wsj.com/article/SB124537403628329989.html (accessed September 14, 2012); Jeff Bennett and Neal E. Boudette, "Boss Sweats Details of Chrysler Revival," *The Wall Street Journal*, January 31, 2011, A1; and Kate Linebaugh and Jeff Bennett, "Marchionne Upends Chrysler's Ways," *The Wall Street Journal*, January 12, 2010, http://online.wsj.com/article/SB10001424052748703652104574652364158366106.html (accessed September 14, 2012).

53. Fred E. Fiedler, "Engineer the Job to Fit the Manager," *Harvard Business Review* 43 (1965): 115–122; and F. E. Fiedler, M. M. Chemers, and L. Mahar, *Improving Leadership Effectiveness: The Leader Match Concept* (New York: Wiley, 1976).

54. R. Singh, "Leadership Style and Reward Allocation: Does Least Preferred Coworker Scale Measure Tasks and Relation Orientation?" *Organizational Behavior and Human Performance* 27 (1983): 178–197; and D. Hosking, "A Critical Evaluation of Fiedler's Contingency Hypotheses," *Progress in Applied Psychology* 1 (1981): 103–154.

55. S. Kerr and J. M. Jermier, "Substitutes for Leadership: Their Meaning and Measurement," *Organizational Behavior and Human Performance* 22 (1978): 375–403; and Jon P. Howell and Peter W. Dorfman, "Leadership and Substitutes for Leadership among Professional and Nonprofessional Workers," *Journal of Applied Behavioral Science* 22 (1986): 29–46.

56. Katherine J. Klein and Robert J. House, "On Fire: Charismatic Leadership and Levels of Analysis," *Leadership Quarterly* 6, no. 2 (1995): 183–198.

57. Jay A. Conger and Rabindra N. Kanungo, "Toward a Behavioral Theory of Charismatic Leadership in Organizational Settings," *Academy of Management Review* 12 (1987): 637–647; Jaepil Choi, "A Motivational Theory of Charismatic Leadership: Envisioning, Empathy, and Empowerment," *Journal of Leadership and Organizational Studies* 13, no. 1 (2006): 24ff; and William L. Gardner and Bruce J. Avolio, "The Charismatic Relationship: A Dramaturgical Perspective," *Academy of Management Review* 23, no. 1 (1998): 32–58.

58. Jon Katzenbach, "The Steve Jobs Way," *Strategy + Business* (Summer 2012), www.strategy-business.com/article/00109?gko=d331b (accessed June 11, 2012); Steve Moore, "Not Bad for a Hippie Dropout," *Management Today* (March 2009): 27; Leslie Kwoh and Emma Silverman, "Bio as Bible: Managers Imitate Steve Jobs," *The Wall Street Journal* (March 31, 2012), B1; and Miguel Helft and Claire Cain Miller, "A Deep Bench of Leadership at Apple," *The New York Times*, January 17, 2011, www.nytimes.com/2011/01/18/technology/18cook.html?_r=0 (accessed January 18, 2011).

59. Robert J. House and Jane M. Howell, "Personality and Charismatic Leadership," *Leadership Quarterly* 3, no. 2 (1992): 81–108; and Jennifer O'Connor et al., "Charismatic Leaders and Destructiveness: A Historiometric Study," *Leadership Quarterly* 6, no. 4 (1995): 529–555.

60. Rob Nielsen, Jennifer A. Marrone, and Holly S. Slay, "A New Look at Humility: Exploring the Humility Concept and Its Role in Socialized Charismatic Leadership," *Journal of Leadership and Organizational Studies* 17, no. 1 (February 2010): 33–44.

61. Robert J. House, "Research Contrasting the Behavior and Effects of Reputed Charismatic vs. Reputed Non-Charismatic Leaders," paper presented as part of a symposium, "Charismatic Leadership: Theory and Evidence," Academy of Management, San Diego, 1985.

62. Bernard M. Bass, "Theory of Transformational Leadership Redux," *Leadership Quarterly* 6, no. 4 (1995): 463–478; Noel M. Tichy and Mary Anne Devanna, *The Transformational Leader* (New York: John Wiley & Sons, 1986); James C. Sarros, Brian K. Cooper, and Joseph C. Santora, "Building a Climate for Innovation Through Transformational Leadership and Organizational Culture," *Journal of Leadership and Organizational Studies* 15, no. 2 (November 2008): 145–158; and P. D. Harms and Marcus Crede, "Emotional Intelligence and Transformational and Transactional Leadership: A Meta-Analysis," *Journal of Leadership and Organizational Studies* 17, no. 1 (February 2010): 5–17.

63. The terms *transactional* and *transformational* come from James M. Burns, *Leadership* (New York: Harper & Row, 1978); and Bernard M. Bass, "Leadership: Good, Better, Best," *Organizational Dynamics* 13 (Winter 1985): 26–40.

64. Daft and Lengel, *Fusion Leadership*.

65. Jonathan Oosting, "StudentsFirst's Michelle Rhee Returns to Michigan as Education Reform Group Makes Mark," *MLive*, May 26, 2013, http://www.mlive.com/politics/index.ssf/2013/05/studentsfirst_spotlight_michel.html (accessed June 11, 2013).

66. Gang Wang et al., "Transformational Leadership and Performance Across Criteria and Levels: A Meta-Analytic Review of 25 Years of Research," *Group & Organization Management* 36, no. 2 (2011): 223–270; Taly Dvir et al., "Impact of Transformational Leadership on Follower Development and Performance: A Field Experiment," *Academy of Management Journal* 45, no. 4 (2002): 735–744.

67. Naomi Schaefer Riley, "Seeing Through the School Daze; Michelle Rhee Fired 241 Teachers, 36 Principals, and 22 Assistant Principals After Taking over the District's Schools," *The Wall Street Journal*, February 19, 2013, A13; Michelle Rhee and Adrian Fenty, "Review—The Education Manifesto—Michelle Rhee and Adrian Fenty on What They Learned While Pushing to Reform D.C.'s Failing Public Schools," *The Wall Street Journal*, October 30, 2010, C1; Jeff Chu, "The Iron Chancellor," *Fast Company* (September 2008): 112–143; Amanda Ripley, "Can She Save Our Schools?" *Time* (December 8, 2008): 36–44; and William McGurn, "Giving Lousy Teachers the Boot; Michelle Rhee Does the Once Unthinkable in Washington," *The Wall Street Journal*, July 27, 2010.

68. Robert S. Rubin, David C. Munz, and William H. Bommer, "Leading from Within: The Effects of Emotion Recognition and Personality on Transformational Leadership Behavior," *Academy of Management Journal* 48, no. 5 (2005): 845–858; and Timothy A. Judge and Joyce E. Bono, "Five-Factor Model of Personality and Transformational Leadership," *Journal of Applied Psychology* 85, no. 5 (October 2000): 751ff.

69. Rubin, Munz, and Bommer, "Leading from Within."

70. The discussion of followership is based in part on John S. McCallum, "Followership: The Other Side of Leadership," *Ivey Business Journal*, September–October 2013, http://iveybusinessjournal.com/topics/leadership/followership-the-other-side-of-leadership#.UmfUoybD91s (accessed October 23, 2013);Warren Bennis, "Art of Followership: Followers Engage in an Interdependent Dance," *Leadership Excellence* (January 2010): 3–4; and Robert E. Kelley, "In Praise of Followers," *Harvard Business Review* (November–December 1988): 142–148.

71. Augustine O. Agho, "Perspectives of Senior-Level Executives on Effective Followership and Leadership," *Journal of Leadership and Organizational Studies* 16, no. 2 (November 2009): 159–166; and James M. Kouzes and Barry Z. Posner, *The Leadership Challenge: How to Get Extraordinary Things Done in Organizations* (San Francisco: Jossey-Bass, 1990).

72. Barbara Kellerman, "What Every Leader Needs to Know About Followers," *Harvard Business Review* (December 2007): 84–91.

73. Robert E. Kelley, *The Power of Followership* (New York: Doubleday, 1992).

74. Discussed in Michael G. Winston, "Say *No* to Yes Men," *Leadership Excellence* (November 2010): 15.

75. Kelley, *The Power of Followership*, pp. 117–118.

76. Joann S. Lublin, "How to Prove You're a Keeper to a New CEO," *The Wall Street Journal*, March 8, 2013, B8.

77. Henry Mintzberg, *Power In and Around Organizations* (Englewood Cliffs, NJ:Englewood Cliffs, NJ: Prentice Hall, 1983); and Jeffrey Pfeffer, *Power in Organizations* (Marshfield, MA: Pitman, 1981).

78. John R. P. French, Jr., and Bertram Raven, "The Bases of Social Power," in D. Cartwright and A. F. Zander, eds., *Group Dynamics* (Evanston, IL: Row Peterson, 1960), pp. 607–623.

79. Reported in Vadim Liberman, "Mario Moussa Wants You to Win Your Next Argument" (Questioning Authority column), *Conference Board Review* (November–December 2007): 25–26.

80. Jay A. Conger, "The Necessary Art of Persuasion," *Harvard Business Review* (May–June 1998): 84–95.

81. Melissa Korn, "What It's Like Being a Middle Manager Today," *The Wall Street Journal*, August 6, 2013, B1.

82. Roger Yu, "Co-Workers Praise Wyndham CEO's Welcoming Demeanor," *USA TODAY*, November 22, 2010, www.usatoday.com/money/companies/management/profile/2010-11-22-wyndhamceo22_ST_N.htm (accessed September 14, 2012).

83. Nancy F. Koehn, "Lincoln's School of Management," *The New York Times*, January 26, 2013; Hitendra Wadhwa, "Lessons in Leadership: How Lincoln Became America's Greatest President," *Inc.com*, February 12, 2012, http://www.inc.com/hitendra-wadhwa/lessons-in-leadership-how-abraham-lincoln-became-americas-greatest-president.html (accessed March 4, 2013); and Gil Troy and Karl Moore, "Leading from the Centre: What CEOs Can Learn from U.S. Presidents," *Ivey Business Journal*, September–October, 2010, http://www.iveybusinessjournal.com/topics/leadership/leading-from-the-centre-what-ceos-can-learn-from-u-s-presidents (accessed May 21, 2013).

84. Scott Wilson, "Obama, the Loner President," *Washington Post*, October 7, 2011, http://articles.washingtonpost.com/2011-10-07/opinions/35280751_1_president-obama-politics-obama-administration (accessed October 8, 2011); and Peter Nicholas, "Obama's Insular White House Worries His Allies," *Los Angeles Times*, December 24, 2010, http://articles.latimes.com/2010/dec/24/nation/la-na-obama-insular-presidency-20101225 (accessed December 25, 2010).

85. Jeremy W. Peters, "Time Inc. Chief Executive Jack Griffin Out," *The New York Times*, February 17, 2011, http://mediadecoder.blogs.nytimes.com/2011/02/17/time-inc-chief-executive-jack-griffin-out/ (accessed February 18, 2011).

86. D. Kipnis et al., "Patterns of Managerial Influence: Shotgun Managers, Tacticians, and Politicians," *Organizational Dynamics* (Winter 1984): 58–67.

87. These tactics are based on "The Uses (and Abuses) of Influence (Spotlight: Interview with Robert Cialdini)," *Harvard Business Review* (July–August 2013): 76–81; Kipnis et al., "Patterns of Managerial Influence"; and Robert B. Cialdini, "Harnessing the Science of Persuasion," *Harvard Business Review* (October 2001): 72–79.

88. Ibid.; and Jeffrey Pfeffer, *Managing with Power: Politics and Influence in Organizations* (Boston: Harvard Business School Press, 1992), Chapter 13.

89. Cialdini, "Harnessing the Science of Persuasion."

90. V. Dallas Merrell, *Huddling: The Informal Way to Management Success* (New York: AMACOM, 1979).

91. Robert B. Cialdini, *Influence: Science and Practice*, 4th ed. (Boston: Pearson Allyn & Bacon, 2000).

92. Harvey G. Enns and Dean B. McFarlin, "When Executives Influence Peers, Does Function Matter?" *Human Resource Management* 4, no. 2 (Summer 2003): 125–142.

93. Adapted from Birgit Schyns, James R. Meindl, and Marcel A. Croon, "The Romance of Leadership Scale: Cross-Cultural Testing and Refinement," *Leadership* 3, no. 1 (2007): 29–46.

CHAPTER
12

Motivating Employees

CHAPTER OUTLINE

LEARNING OUTCOMES

After studying this chapter, you should be able to:

12.1 Define motivation and explain the difference between intrinsic and extrinsic rewards.

12.2 Identify and describe content theories of motivation based on employee needs.

12.3 Identify and explain process theories of motivation.

12.4 Describe the reinforcement perspective and social learning theory and how they can be used to motivate employees.

12.5 Discuss major approaches to job design and how job design influences motivation.

12.6 Explain how empowerment heightens employee motivation.

12.7 Identify three elements of employee engagement and describe some ways that managers can create a work environment that promotes engagement.

12.8 Describe how managers give people a sense of making progress toward meaningful goals to build a thriving workforce and create a high-performing organization.

•••••○ 📶   100% 🔋

‹ Messages

R U Ready 2 B a Manager?

Delivered

Before reading this chapter, please circle either "Mostly True" or "Mostly False" for each of the five questions below.

1 Everyone knows that people are mostly motivated by money at work.

| Mostly True | Mostly False |

[page 518]

2 The need for power seems to dominate every workplace I've seen.

| Mostly True | Mostly False |

[page 526]

3 I wish I worked somewhere that they encourage people to set goals and then get feedback on how well I achieved those targets.

| Mostly True | Mostly False |

[page 528]

4 I like learning new skills and behaviors when I have a positive role model, someone I work with who does with ease the skills I am trying to learn.

| Mostly True | Mostly False |

[page 536]

5 I'd find it very motivating for me if I were empowered to do a more difficult job; this would include having information on the company's performance, to be given enough power to carry out the assignment and then to be rewarded on my performance.

| Mostly True | Mostly False |

[page 541]

When people get a job at Mars Incorporated, the third-largest private company in the United States, they rarely leave. An interview by *Fortune* magazine after the company was named to its "The 100 Best Companies to Work For" list for the first time in 2013 revealed some interesting tidbits that might explain why. Compensation at Mars, maker of candy such as M&Ms and Snickers and pet food such as Pedigree and Whiskas, is very good compared to similar companies. Many employees get bonuses from 10 to 100 percent of their salaries if their team performs well. Vending machines dispense free candy all day long, and employees in the pet food division can take their dogs to work. Employees have to punch a time clock and their pay gets docked if they are late—but the policy applies just as much to top executives as it does to the lowest-level worker.

NEW MANAGER Self-Test

What Motivates You?

Instructions: Think of a specific recent work or study task on which you worked alone. How important were each of the following as a reason for doing that activity?

	Mostly True	Mostly False
1. I received a reward for doing it.	_____	_____
2. I was supposed to do the activity.	_____	_____
3. It was something I felt that I had to do.	_____	_____
4. I avoided the negative consequences that would happen if I didn't do it.	_____	_____
5. I think the task was interesting.	_____	_____
6. I enjoyed doing the task.	_____	_____
7. I acquired new knowledge or skill.	_____	_____
8. I became fully immersed in the task.	_____	_____

Scoring and Interpretation: Give yourself 1 point for each Mostly True answer for questions 1–4 and write your score here: E = _____. Then give yourself 1 point for each Mostly True answer for questions 5–8 and write your score here: I = _____. Your "E" score represents your *extrinsic* motivation for that task, and your "I" score indicates your *intrinsic* motivation for that task. Each type of motivation is described in the next few pages of this chapter. Managers and organizations often use extrinsic motivation techniques, but intrinsic motivation is more satisfying for most people. Which score was higher for you? Do you think you would prefer intrinsic or extrinsic rewards in your career?

Many people at Mars get a mentor to learn a new skill. Executives often get mentored by younger employees who introduce them to using social media. Development doesn't stop at the factory gates, either. People can take paid time off to volunteer for community activities such as cleaning parks, planting gardens, or assisting at medical clinics. A highly competitive program selects 80 or so people each year to spend up to six weeks working with Mars-related partners (such as growers of cocoa beans) in remote areas of other countries.[1]

Managers in other companies are discovering that creating an environment where people feel valued and feel that they have opportunities for growth and development is one key to high employee motivation, which is an essential ingredient for organizational success. Most people begin a new job with energy and enthusiasm, but employees can lose their drive if managers fail in their role as motivators. Yet motivation is a challenge for many managers because motivation arises from within employees and may differ for each person. Some people are motivated primarily by money, others are motivated to perform well because managers make them feel appreciated for doing a good job, and still others find their primary motivation in the challenge of solving complex problems or making a contribution to society. With such diverse motivations among individuals, how do managers find the right way to motivate people toward common organizational goals?

This chapter reviews several approaches to employee motivation. First, we define motivation and the types of rewards that managers use. Then, we examine several models that describe the employee needs and processes associated with motivation. We also look at the use of reinforcement for motivation, explain social learning theory, and examine how job design—changing the structure of the work itself—can affect employee satisfaction and productivity. We discuss how managers build a thriving workplace by giving people a sense of making progress toward meaningful goals and helping people feel engaged and empowered at work.

12.1 Individual Needs and Motivation

Most of us get up in the morning, go to school or work, and behave in ways that are predictably our own. All these behaviors are motivated by something, but most of us don't think of why we do the things we do. **Motivation** refers to the forces either within or external to a person that arouse enthusiasm and persistence to pursue a certain course of action. Employee motivation affects productivity, and part of the manager's job is to channel motivation toward the accomplishment of organizational goals.[2] Studies have found that high employee motivation goes hand in hand with high organizational performance and profits.[3] It is the responsibility of managers to find the right combination of motivational techniques and rewards to satisfy employees' needs and simultaneously encourage great work performance. A simple model of human motivation is illustrated in Exhibit 12.1. People have *needs*—such as for recognition, achievement, or monetary gain—that translate into an internal tension that motivates specific behaviors with which to fulfill various needs. To the extent that the behavior is successful, the person is rewarded because the need is satisfied. The reward also informs the person that the behavior was appropriate and can be used again in the future.

EXHIBIT 12.1   A Simple Model of Motivation

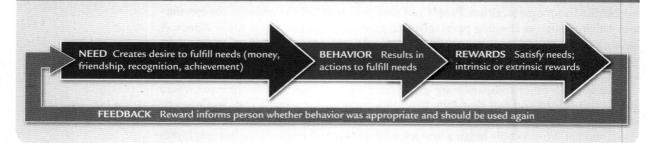

NEED Creates desire to fulfill needs (money, friendship, recognition, achievement)

BEHAVIOR Results in actions to fulfill needs

REWARDS Satisfy needs; intrinsic or extrinsic rewards

FEEDBACK Reward informs person whether behavior was appropriate and should be used again

12.2 Intrinsic and Extrinsic Rewards

Managers who understand the motives that compel people to initiate, alter, or continue a desired behavior are more successful as motivators. Exhibit 12.2 illustrates four categories of motives based on two criteria. The vertical dimension contrasts intrinsic versus extrinsic rewards. The horizontal dimension contrasts behaviors that are driven by fear or pain versus those driven by growth or pleasure.

Intrinsic rewards are the satisfactions that a person receives in the process of performing a particular action. The completion of a complex task may bestow a pleasant feeling of accomplishment, or solving a problem that benefits others may fulfill a personal mission. For example, employees at Salesforce.com, which provides cloud computing services to organizations such as Bank of America, Cisco, Google, and the Japanese government, are motivated by being on the "cutting edge" of reinventing how companies handle ordinary but critical tasks like sales, customer relations, and internal communications.[4]

EXHIBIT 12.2   Four Categories of Motives Managers Can Use

Extrinsic

1.
Negative Approach
Threats and punishments

3.
Positive Approach
Rewards such as pay raises, bonuses, praise

Intrinsic

2.
Negative Approach
Tap into self-doubts

4.
Positive Approach
Help people enjoy their work, get sense of accomplishment

Pain/Fear   **Pleasure/Growth**

SOURCE: Based on Bruce H. Jackson, "Influence Behavior; Become a Master Motivator," *Leadership Excellence* (April 2010): 14.

Extrinsic rewards are given by another person, typically a manager, and include promotions, praise, and pay increases. They originate externally, as a result of pleasing others. At the Alta Gracia factory in the Dominican Republic, owned by Knights Apparel, employees are motivated by the extrinsic reward of high pay because they need money to support their families and can't make nearly as much anywhere else.[5]

Effective managers want people to receive both extrinsic and intrinsic rewards to meet their needs. Google, for example, which is built on the philosophy of creating the "happiest, most productive workplace in the world," provides some of the most amazing extrinsic rewards in corporate America—free breakfast, lunch, and dinner; subsidized massages; free yoga and Pilates classes; fitness centers; free snacks, beverages, and candy all day. The headquarters includes play areas, cafes, coffee bars, and cozy conversation areas, as well as conference rooms and offices, many with desks that engineers were allowed to design for themselves. Yet the strongest employee motivation seems to come from the sense of community and support that these lavish perks create rather than from the perks themselves. Google analyzes data on everything to see how people are interacting because creativity requires "serendipitous interaction. For this to happen, you need to shape a community," says Ben Waber, the author of *People Analytics*. "It's the antithesis of the old factory model, where people were just cogs in a machine."[6] The perks help keep people happy, but the sense of meaning and engagement that people get from their work keeps them motivated day in and day out.

CONCEPT CONNECTION The Container Store has the motto that one great person equals three good people. Here, a storage system designer works with a couple to design an Elfa custom storage plan. Getting hired is quite competitive at this retailer, which has been on *Fortune* magazine's list of 100 Best Companies to Work for in America year after year since 2000. Employees get **intrinsic rewards** from knowing that they were selected to work for this winning company. The Container Store also puts its money where its motto is—providing the **extrinsic rewards** of higher-than-average retail pay and other benefits.

The four quadrants represent four differing approaches for motivating people.[7] Quadrants 1 and 2 are both negative approaches to motivating. Quadrant 1 uses negative, extrinsic methods, such as threats or punishments, to get people to perform as desired. For example, some companies have found that penalizing employees for smoking or being overweight by charging extra for health insurance is an effective way to change behaviors and lower company health care costs. The practice is growing, with leaders citing behavioral science research showing that people typically respond more strongly to a potential loss (such as a financial penalty for not losing weight), referred to as *loss aversion*, than to an expected gain (such as a financial reward for losing weight). At Michelin North America, overweight employees paid up to $1,000 more for health care coverage starting in 2014. Participation in the health-risk assessment program at Mohawk Industries increased 97 percent after leaders began penalizing employees $100 if they didn't participate. Previously, the company offered rewards for participation, but enrollment rates remained low, which sparked the shift to penalties.[8] Quadrant 2 methods attempt to motivate people by tapping into their self-doubts or anxieties. For example, a manager might motivate people to work hard by emphasizing the weak economy and high unemployment rate. Quadrant 1 and 2 methods can indeed be effective, as fear is a powerful motivator.[9] However, using fear to motivate people in organizations almost always has negative consequences for employee development and long-term performance.

Quadrants 3 and 4 are positive motivational approaches. Quadrant 3 methods attempt to influence behavior by using extrinsic rewards that create pleasure. At Hilcorp Energy, for example, managers offered employees the chance to earn a bonus of $50,000 each if they help the organization meet its growth goal.[10] Many managers are finding that small, unexpected rewards, such as gift cards, water bottles, or pizza vouchers, are highly effective extrinsic motivators. When people aren't expecting a reward, it can have a disproportionate psychological impact.[11] This positive motivational approach is useful but limited. External rewards are important, but they can lose their power as motivational tools over time. The most effective managers also emphasize Quadrant 4 techniques that tap into deep-seated employee energy and commitment by helping people get intrinsic rewards from their work. For example, in a bossless workplace where no one is telling people what to do and keeping tabs on whether they do it, managers need people who can act based on their own motivation. The "Director's Toolkit" describes motivation techniques managers use in a bossless environment.

Director's Toolkit

Motivating in a Bossless Environment

As companies flatten their hierarchies and eliminate managers, motivated employees become especially important. In a truly bossless organization, no one is taking attendance or monitoring work. People and teams act on their own. An organization that wants to go bossless should consider the following motivation methods:

- **Don't hide information.** At Menlo Innovations, information concerning motivational factors is so open that a new employee is likely to feel exposed. A chart displays the names, titles, and pay grades of all employees. In response to a question about what it felt like to have his salary visible to colleagues, an employee responded, "It's liberating."

- **Rely on intrinsic rewards.** People at the Web design firm DreamHost understand that the way employees are motivated is changing. "Twenty years ago, it was about higher pay. Now it's more about finding your work meaningful and interesting," said CEO Simon Anderson. Chris Rufer, founder of tomato-processor Morning Star, describes his company as deeply humane, something that buoys the spirits of workers because relationships among members are deep and substantive.

- **Let people own the goal.** At Morning Star, goals, not supervisors, are used for motivation. A tomato sorter pledges to sort a predetermined amount of tomatoes a day, for example. A person responsible for helping evaporate the water out of tomato pulp signs an agreement to evaporate a specific number of gallons of water every week. With a clear goal, people are left alone to do their work.

- **Reward the team.** In a bossless environment, achievement is usually tied to the team, so individual work means nothing until it fits into a larger

project that requires the assistance of peers. Individual rewards are replaced by shared achievement. Friendliness and helpfulness matter more than personal ladder-climbing and reward-seeking. At Menlo Innovations and other bossless companies, peer teams make hiring decisions as well as deciding promotions, layoffs, and firings.

- **Hire attitude over aptitude.** Hiring workers who are self-starters and team players can be vital to making a boss-free system work. Technical wizards who are jerks will poison the culture. Cissy Pau of Clear HR Consulting says employees "need to know what to do, how to do it, when to do it."

- **Reinvent management.** Thomas Davenport, coauthor of Manager Redefined, says that managers have to learn to motivate in a different way. "Nobody comes to work in the 21st century world and says, 'Please manage me.' They say, 'Create an environment where I can be successful.'" Managers must learn to see themselves as working among equals rather than being above others. Their new job is to support the people around them, remove obstacles, and encourage better work, which is similar to "servant leadership," as described in Chapter 11.

SOURCES: Matthew Shaer, "The Boss Stops Here," New York Magazine (June 24–July 1, 2013): 25–34; Knowledge@Wharton, "Going Boss-Free: Utopia or 'Lord of the Flies'?" August 1, 2012, http://www.theglobeandmail.com/report-on-business/small-business/sb-managing/human-resources/the-bossless-office-motivational-experience-or-invitation-to-anarchy/article4601671/; Shelley White, "The Bossless Office: Motivational Experience or Invitation to Anarchy?" October 11, 2012, http://www.theglobeandmail.com/report-on-business/small-business/sb-managing/human-resources/the-bossless-office-motivational-experience-or-invitation-to-anarchy/article4601671/; and Ilya Pozin, "Want Happier Employees? Get Rid of the Bosses," Inc., June 18, 2012, http://www.inc.com/ilya-pozin/want-happier-employees-get-rid-of-the-bosses.html.

At Morrison Management Specialists, which provides food, nutrition, and dining services to the health care and senior living industries, managers provide training sessions under the title of "Our Great Partnership" and strive to help people see how their jobs make a difference in the lives of elderly or ill people. A "People First" recognition program gives employees a chance to recognize one another for exceptional service.[12]

REMEMBER THIS

- **Motivation** is the arousal of enthusiasm and persistence to pursue a certain course of action.
- All behaviors are motivated by something, such as the desire to fulfill needs for money, recognition, friendship, or a sense of accomplishment.
- **Intrinsic rewards** are the feelings of satisfaction that a person receives in the process of performing a particular action.
- **Extrinsic rewards** are given by another person, such as a manager, and include pay increases, promotions, and praise.

- People can be driven to act by fear, but good managers avoid the use of fear tactics to motivate people because this approach damages employee commitment and performance in the long run.
- In addition to providing appropriate extrinsic rewards, effective managers try to help people achieve intrinsic rewards from their work.

12.3 Content Perspectives on Motivation

Content theories emphasize the needs that motivate people. At any point in time, people have a variety of needs. These needs translate into an internal drive that motivates specific behaviors in an attempt to fulfill the needs. In other words, our needs are like a hidden catalog of the things that we want and will work to get. To the extent that managers understand employees' needs, they can design reward systems to meet them and direct employees' energies and priorities toward attaining organizational goals.

12.3a The Hierarchy of Needs

Probably the most famous content theory was developed by Abraham Maslow.[13] Maslow's **hierarchy of needs theory** proposes that people are motivated by multiple needs and that these needs exist in a hierarchical order, as illustrated in Exhibit 12.3.

Maslow identified five general types of motivating needs, listed in order of ascendance:

1. *Physiological needs.* These most basic human physical needs include food, water, and oxygen. In the organizational setting, they are reflected in the needs for adequate heat, air, and base salary to ensure survival.

2. *Safety needs.* These needs include a safe and secure physical and emotional environment and freedom from threats—that is, for freedom from violence and for an orderly society. In the workplace, safety needs reflect the needs for safe jobs, fringe

EXHIBIT 12.3 Maslow's Hierarchy of Needs

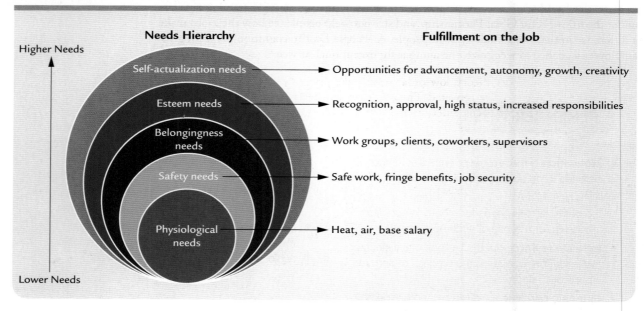

Needs Hierarchy | Fulfillment on the Job

Higher Needs

Self-actualization needs → Opportunities for advancement, autonomy, growth, creativity

Esteem needs → Recognition, approval, high status, increased responsibilities

Belongingness needs → Work groups, clients, coworkers, supervisors

Safety needs → Safe work, fringe benefits, job security

Physiological needs → Heat, air, base salary

Lower Needs

benefits, and job security. Because of the weak economy and high unemployment in recent years, safety needs have taken priority for many people. A recent job satisfaction survey indicated that job security was the most important element of job satisfaction, with good benefits being second most important.[14] When managers at Burgerville, a regional restaurant chain based in Vancouver, Washington, began paying at least 90 percent of health insurance premiums for hourly employees who worked at least 20 hours a week, turnover plunged, employees began working harder to get more hours (which are assigned based on performance), service improved, and sales increased.[15]

3. **Belongingness needs.** These needs reflect the desire to be accepted by one's peers, have friendships, be part of a group, and be loved. In the organization, these needs influence the desire for good relationships with coworkers, participation in a work group, and a positive relationship with supervisors. In some Chinese factories, leaders have gone beyond financial incentives to try to meet belongingness and esteem needs of employees with work contests, *American Idol*–type singing contests, karaoke rooms, dinners with managers, and more communications about the greater purpose of employees' contributions.[16]

4. **Esteem needs.** These needs relate to the desire for a positive self-image and to receive attention, recognition, and appreciation from others. Within organizations, esteem needs reflect a motivation for recognition, an increase in responsibility, high status, and credit for contributions to the organization. One example comes from Intuit, where Jennifer Lepird spent weeks working long, grueling hours on a big acquisition deal. After the deal closed, Lepird was delighted to get a thank-you note from her manager, along with a small gift certificate, because it met her need to feel appreciated. "The fact that somebody took the time to recognize the effort made the long hours just melt away," she says.[17]

5. **Self-actualization needs.** These needs include the need for self-fulfillment, which is the highest need category. They concern developing one's full potential, increasing one's competence, and becoming a better person. Self-actualization needs can be met in the organization by providing people with opportunities to grow, be creative, and acquire training for challenging assignments and advancement.

According to Maslow's theory, low-order needs take priority—they must be satisfied before higher-order needs are activated. The needs are satisfied in sequence: Physiological needs come before safety needs, safety needs before belongingness needs, and so on. A person desiring physical safety will devote his or her efforts to securing a safer environment and will not be concerned with esteem needs or self-actualization needs. Once a need is satisfied, it declines in importance, and the next higher need is activated.

A study of employees in the manufacturing department of a major health care company in the United Kingdom provides some support for Maslow's theory. Most line workers said that they worked at the company primarily because of the good pay, benefits, and job security. Thus, employees' lower-level physiological and safety needs were being met. When questioned about their motivation, employees indicated the importance of positive social relationships with both peers and supervisors (belongingness needs) and a desire for greater respect and recognition from management (esteem needs).[18]

As a new manager, recognize that some people are motivated primarily to satisfy lower-level physiological and safety needs, while others want to satisfy higher-level needs. Learn which lower- and higher-level needs motivate you by completing the "Self-Learning" on page 546.

12.3b ERG Theory

Clayton Alderfer proposed a modification of Maslow's theory in an effort to simplify it and respond to criticisms of its lack of empirical verification.[19] His **ERG theory** identified three categories of needs:

1. **Existence needs.** The needs for physical well-being

2. **Relatedness needs.** The needs for satisfactory relationships with others

3. **Growth needs.** The needs that focus on the development of human potential and the desire for personal growth and increased competence

The ERG model and Maslow's needs hierarchy are similar because both are in hierarchical form and presume that individuals move up the hierarchy one step at a time. However, Alderfer reduced the number of need categories to three and proposed that movement up the hierarchy is more complex, reflecting a frustration-regression principle: Namely, that failure to meet a high-order need may trigger a regression to an already fulfilled lower-order need. Thus, a worker who cannot fulfill a need for personal growth may revert to a lower-order need and redirect his or her efforts toward making a lot of money. The ERG model therefore is less rigid than Maslow's needs hierarchy, suggesting that individuals may move down as well as up the hierarchy, depending on their ability to satisfy needs. Needs hierarchy theories explain why organizations find ways to recognize employees, encourage their participation in decision making, and give them opportunities to make significant contributions to the organization and society.

George Doyle/Stockbyte/Getty Images

CONCEPT CONNECTION Gen-Yers, who according to their managers report for work with self-esteem to spare, often proceed directly from **existence needs** to **growth needs**. Once they're satisfied that they're receiving fair pay, what younger employees want most is training. In fact, recent studies found that respondents chose training from a list of benefits three times more often than a cash bonus. There's a practical reason for this interest in personal growth. Gen-Yers know they need to acquire skills that will make them attractive job candidates. Unlike many of their elders, they don't expect to work for a single employer throughout their careers.

Spotlight on Skills

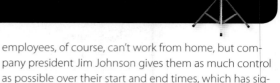

Johnson Storage & Moving

Employees in low-wage hourly jobs don't often get white-collar perks, but some managers are trying a fresh and unlikely approach—letting hourly workers do some jobs at home, set their own schedules, or otherwise have more control over their work lives.

At Johnson Storage & Moving, based in Centennial, Colorado, and operating in five states, administrative workers, call center staff, and dispatchers have been able to work remotely or to work hours of their own choosing for more than 16 years. Among the employees taking advantage of the flexible policy, there has been almost no turnover in that time span. Movers and warehouse employees, of course, can't work from home, but company president Jim Johnson gives them as much control as possible over their start and end times, which has significantly reduced no-shows, tardiness, and turnover.

Managers in other companies are also giving manual workers more flexibility. Turck Inc., a manufacturer of automation equipment in Plymouth, Minnesota, is evaluating a plan to let people do some jobs from home. "We have a lot of products where literally you just need to sit there and put a label on," says production supervisor Dee Comeau. "Honestly, it can be done anywhere."[20]

Many companies are finding that creating a humane work environment that allows people to achieve a balance between work and personal life is also a great high-level motivator.

Some companies go even further with job flexibility. At J. A. Coulter & Associates, an insurance and investment advisory firm in New Richmond, Wisconsin, employees can come and go as they please, without telling anyone where they are going or why, so long as they get their jobs done. Shannon Mehls, who works as an assistant to one of Coulter's senior investment advisors, says employees now feel like "mini-entrepreneurs," managing their own schedules and focusing on results instead of just putting in 40 hours and getting a paycheck.[21] Although not all managers would be comfortable working in an environment where employees come and go as they please, there is some evidence that people who have greater control over their work schedules are significantly less likely to suffer job burnout and are more highly committed to their employers.[22]

In the recent economic downturn, some companies found flexible options a great way to cut payroll costs while retaining and motivating valued employees. Accounting firm KPMG tried a program called Flexible Futures, which offered employees in its British operations several options: (1) go to a four-day workweek and take a 20 percent pay cut; (2) choose a mini-sabbatical at 30 percent base pay; (3) opt for a combination of these; or (4) stay with their current employment arrangement. Over 80 percent of employees chose one of the flexible options. Other companies have implemented similar programs with great success.[23]

12.3c A Two-Factor Approach to Motivation

Frederick Herzberg developed another popular theory of motivation called the *two-factor theory*.[24] Herzberg interviewed hundreds of workers about times when they were highly motivated to work and other times when they were dissatisfied and unmotivated. His findings suggested that the work characteristics associated with dissatisfaction were quite different from those pertaining to satisfaction, which prompted the notion that two factors influence work motivation.

EXHIBIT 12.4   Herzberg's Two-Factor Theory

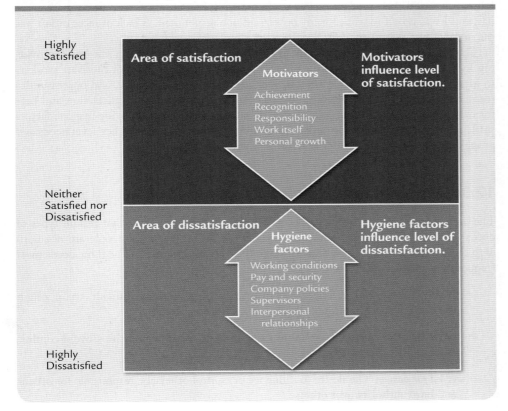

The two-factor theory is illustrated in Exhibit 12.4. The center of the scale is neutral, meaning that workers are neither satisfied nor dissatisfied. Herzberg believed that two entirely separate dimensions contribute to an employee's behavior at work. The first, called **hygiene factors**, involves the presence or absence of job dissatisfiers, such as working conditions, pay, company policies, and interpersonal relationships. When **hygiene factors** are poor, work is dissatisfying. However, good hygiene factors simply remove the dissatisfaction; they do not in themselves cause people to become highly satisfied and motivated in their work.

The second set of factors does influence job satisfaction. **Motivators** focus on high-level needs and include achievement, recognition, responsibility, and opportunity for growth. Herzberg believed that when motivators are absent, workers are neutral toward work, but when motivators are present, workers are highly motivated and satisfied. Thus, hygiene factors and motivators represent two distinct factors that influence motivation. Hygiene factors work only in the area of dissatisfaction. Unsafe working conditions or a noisy work environment will cause people to be dissatisfied, but their correction will not lead to a high level of motivation and satisfaction. Motivators such as challenge, responsibility, and recognition must be in place before employees will be highly motivated to excel at their work.

There is a growing realization among managers of the importance of employee recognition, perhaps because tough economic conditions have made it more difficult for them to reward people with large pay increases. The most recent Globoforce MoodTracker Survey report indicates that 82 percent of employees surveyed say that being recognized for their efforts increased their motivation. "It made me work harder, want to come to work every day, and I was proud to work for my boss," said one respondent. A lack of recognition was the number two reason cited for leaving a job among job seekers.[25]

The implication of the two-factor theory for managers is clear. On one hand, providing hygiene factors will eliminate employee dissatisfaction but will not motivate workers to high achievement levels. On the other hand, recognition, challenge, and opportunities for personal growth are powerful motivators and will promote high satisfaction and performance. The manager's role is to remove dissatisfiers—that is, to provide hygiene factors sufficient to meet basic needs—and then to use motivators to meet higher-level needs and propel employees toward greater achievement and satisfaction.

12.3d Acquired Needs

The *acquired needs theory*, developed by David McClelland, proposes that certain types of needs are acquired during the individual's lifetime. In other words, people are not born with these needs but may learn them through their life experiences.[26] The three needs most frequently studied are these:

- *Need for achievement.* The desire to accomplish something difficult, attain a high standard of success, master complex tasks, and surpass others

- *Need for affiliation.* The desire to form close personal relationships, avoid conflict, and establish warm friendships

- *Need for power.* The desire to influence or control others, be responsible for others, and have authority over others

Early life experiences typically determine whether people acquire these needs. If children are encouraged to do things for themselves and receive reinforcement, they will acquire a need to achieve. If they are reinforced for forming warm human relationships, they will develop a need for affiliation. If they get satisfaction from controlling others, they will acquire a need for power.

For more than 20 years, McClelland studied human needs and their implications for management. People with a high need for *achievement* are frequently entrepreneurs. People who have a high need for *affiliation* are successful integrators, whose job is to coordinate the work of several departments in an organization. Integrators include brand managers and project managers who must have excellent people skills. A high need for power often is associated with successful attainment of top levels in the organizational hierarchy.[27] For example, McClelland studied managers at AT&T for 16 years and found that those with a high need for power were more likely to follow a path of continued promotion over time. More than half of the employees at the top levels had a high need for power. In contrast, managers with a high need for achievement but a low need for power tended to peak earlier in their careers and at a lower level. The reason is that achievement needs can be met through the task itself, but power needs can be met only by ascending to a level at which a person has power over others.

In summary, content theories focus on people's underlying needs and label those particular needs that motivate behavior. The hierarchy of needs theory, the ERG theory, the two-factor theory, and the acquired needs theory all help managers understand what motivates people. In this way, managers can design work to meet needs and hence elicit appropriate and successful work behaviors.

Do you have a greater need for achievement, affiliation, or power? Complete the "New Manager Self-Test" on page 527 to learn more about which needs motivate you.

NEW MANAGER Self-Test

Need for Achievement, Affiliation, and Power

Instructions: This questionnaire asks you to describe situations that you like. For each item below, give the number "3" to the phrase that best describes you, "2" to the item that is next best, and "1" for the item that is least like you.

1. _____ a. I like to do my best in whatever I undertake.

   _____ b. I like to form new friendships.

   _____ c. I like to tell other people how to do their jobs.

2. _____ a. I like to be able to say that I have done a difficult job well.

   _____ b. I like to have strong attachments with my friends.

   _____ c. I like to take on responsibilities and obligations.

3. _____ a. I like to accomplish tasks that require skill and effort.

   _____ b. I like to share things with my friends.

   _____ c. I like to be called upon to settle arguments and disputes between others.

4. _____ a. I like to be successful in things I undertake.

   _____ b. I like to do things for my friends.

_____ c. I like to be able to persuade others to do what I want to do.

5. _____ a. I like to seek satisfaction from accomplishing a difficult task.

   _____ b. I like to meet new people.

   _____ c. I like to be regarded by others as a leader.

6. _____ a. I would like to be a recognized authority in my career field.

   _____ b. I like to participate in groups in which the members have warm and friendly feelings toward one another.

   _____ c. When in a group, I like to make the decisions about what we are going to do.

7. _____ a. I like to confront the difficult challenges of the job.

   _____ b. I like to make as many friends as I can.

   _____ c. I would like to be a powerful executive or politician.

Scoring and Interpretation: Compute your scores as follows:

Need for achievement = 1a + 2a + 3a + 4a + 5a + 6a + 7a = _____

Need for affiliation = 1b + 2b + 3b + 4b + 5b + 6b + 7b = _____

Need for power = 1c + 2c + 3c + 4c + 5c + 6c + 7c = _____

David McClelland's research found that some human needs are learned during early life experiences, and the three that he studied are personal need for achievement, affiliation, and power. *Achievement* means the need to excel. *Affiliation* means the need for harmonious relationships. *Power* means the need to direct and influence others. One of the three needs is typically stronger than the others in most people. The higher your score on a need, the stronger it is and the more it will guide your behavior. What do the relative strengths of the three needs mean to you? If you can align your career to use and satisfy your stronger needs, you are more likely to be successful.

SOURCES: Based on Joel B. Bennett, "Power and Influence as Distinct Personality Traits: Development and Validation of a Psychometric Measure," *Journal of Research in Personality* 22 (1988): 361–394; and Yongmei Liu, Jun Liu, and Longzeng Wu, "Are You Willing and Able? Roles of Motivation, Power, and Politics in Career Growth," *Journal of Management* 36, no. 6 (2010): 1432–1460.

REMEMBER THIS

- **Content theories** emphasize the needs that motivate people.
- The most well-known content theory is Maslow's **hierarchy of needs theory**, which proposes that people are motivated by five categories of needs—physiological, safety, belongingness, esteem, and self-actualization—that exist in a hierarchical order.
- **ERG theory** is a modification of the needs hierarchy and proposes three categories of needs: existence, relatedness, and growth.
- The **frustration-regression principle** is the idea that failure to meet a high-order need may cause a regression to an already satisfied lower-order need; thus, people may move down as well as up the needs hierarchy.
- Giving people more control over their work schedules and opportunities to contribute ideas are two ways that managers meet people's higher-level needs.

- Johnson Storage & Moving lets hourly administrative personnel work remotely or work hours of their own choosing and gives movers and warehouse workers control over their start and end times.
- One element of Herzberg's two-factor theory, **hygiene factors**, focuses on lower-level needs and involves the presence or absence of job dissatisfiers, including working conditions, pay, and company policies.
- Herzberg's second factor, **motivators**, influences job satisfaction based on fulfilling higher-level needs such as achievement, recognition, responsibility, and opportunities for personal growth.
- The acquired needs theory proposes that certain types of needs, including the need for achievement, need for affiliation, and need for power, are acquired during an individual's lifetime of experiences.

12.4 Process Perspectives on Motivation

Process theories explain how people select behavioral actions to meet their needs and determine whether their choices were successful. Important perspectives in this area include goal-setting, equity theory, and expectancy theory.

12.4a Goal Setting

Recall from Chapter 5 our discussion of the importance and purposes of goals. Numerous studies have shown that specific, challenging targets significantly enhance people's motivation and performance levels.[28] You have probably noticed in your own life that you are more motivated when you have a specific goal, such as making an A on a final exam, losing 10 pounds before spring break, or earning enough money during the summer to buy a used car.

Goal-setting theory, described by Edwin Locke and Gary Latham, proposes that managers can increase motivation and enhance performance by setting specific, challenging goals, and then helping people track their progress toward goal achievement by providing timely feedback. Exhibit 12.5 illustrates key components of goal-setting theory.[29]

- *Goal specificity* refers to the degree to which goals are concrete and unambiguous. Specific goals, such as "Visit one new customer each day" or "Sell $1,000 worth of merchandise a week," are more motivating than vague goals, such as "Keep in touch with new customers" or "Increase merchandise sales." A lack of clear, specific goals is cited as a major cause of the failure of pay-for-performance incentive plans in many organizations.[30] Vague goals can be frustrating for employees.

EXHIBIT 12.5   Criteria for Motivational Goals

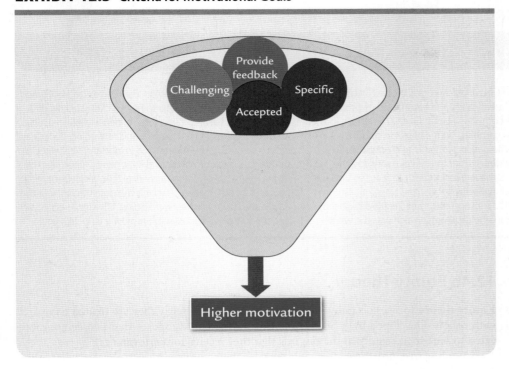

- In terms of *goal difficulty*, hard goals are more motivating than easy ones. Easy goals provide little challenge for employees and don't require them to increase their output. Highly ambitious but achievable goals ask people to stretch their abilities and provide a basis for greater feelings of accomplishment and personal effectiveness. A study in Germany found that, over a three-year period, only employees who perceived their goals as difficult reported increases in positive emotions and feelings of job satisfaction and success.[31]

- *Goal acceptance* means that employees have to "buy into" the goals and be committed to them. Having people participate in setting goals is a good way to increase acceptance and commitment.

- Finally, the component of *feedback* means that people get information about how well they are doing in progressing toward goal achievement. It is important for managers to provide performance feedback on a regular, ongoing basis. However, self-feedback, where people are able to monitor their own progress toward a goal, has been found to be an even stronger motivator than external feedback.[32]

Why does goal setting increase motivation? For one thing, it enables people to focus their energies in the right direction. People know what to work toward, so they can direct their efforts toward the most important activities to accomplish the goals. Goals also energize behavior because people feel compelled to develop plans and strategies that keep them focused on achieving the targets. Specific, difficult goals provide a challenge and encourage people to put forth high levels of effort. In addition, when goals are achieved, pride and satisfaction increase, contributing to higher motivation and morale.[33] The following example illustrates the motivational power of goal setting.

"If you look at the modern workplace, I would say it's one of the most feedback-deprived places in American civilization."

—Daniel Pink, journalist and author of *Drive: The Surprising Truth About What Motivates Us*

Spotlight on Skills

Advanced Circuits

When Advanced Circuits of Aurora, Colorado, was having trouble with frequent stops and restarts on its production line, costing the company about $50,000 a month, former CEO Ron Huston came up with a plan. He bought a junk car, placed it in the parking lot, and told employees they could take a sledgehammer to the car every day the production line didn't have a restart. Employees set a goal of flattening the car in 90 days.

Everybody had fun, and they met the 90-day goal by solving production-line problems, which was the whole point of the exercise for Huston. Huston realized how motivating it could be for people to have a clear, specific goal, especially if achieving it was fun. He began setting goals for other aspects of the business and rewarding people when the goals were met. Just as important, he steered performance toward goals and kept people energized by giving everyone ongoing numerical feedback about their progress. People began checking the data throughout the day to see how well they were doing. "The more goals we get, the better it is for us," said employee Barb Frevert.[34]

12.4b Equity Theory

Equity theory focuses on individuals' perceptions of how fairly they are treated compared with others. Developed by J. Stacy Adams, equity theory proposes that people are motivated to seek social equity in the rewards that they receive for performance.[35]

According to equity theory, if people perceive their compensation as equal to what others receive for similar contributions, they will believe that their treatment is fair and equitable. People evaluate equity by a ratio of inputs to outcomes. Inputs to a job include education, experience, effort, and ability. Outcomes from a job include pay, recognition, benefits, and promotions. The input-to-outcome ratio may be compared to that of another person in the work group or to a perceived group average. A state of **equity** exists whenever the ratio of one person's outcomes to inputs equals the ratio of another's outcomes to inputs.

Inequity occurs when the input-to-outcome ratios are out of balance, such as when a new, inexperienced employee receives the same salary as a person with a high level of education or experience. Interestingly, perceived inequity also occurs in the other direction. Thus, if an employee discovers that he or she is making more money than other people who contribute the same inputs to the company, the employee may feel the need to correct the inequity by working harder or getting more education. Scientific studies indicate that the human brain seems programmed to dislike inequity, even when we benefit from it. Moreover, people get less satisfaction from money they receive without having to earn it than they do from money they work to receive.[36] Perceived inequity creates tensions within individuals that motivate them to bring equity into balance.[37]

The most common methods for reducing a perceived inequity are the following:

- *Change work effort.* A person may choose to increase or decrease his or her inputs to the organization. Individuals who believe that they are underpaid may reduce their level of effort or increase their absenteeism. Overpaid people may increase their effort on the job.

- *Change outcomes.* A person may change his or her outcomes. An underpaid person may request a salary increase or a bigger office. A union may try to improve wages and working conditions to be consistent with a comparable union whose members make more money.

- **Change perceptions.** Research suggests that people may change perceptions of equity if they are unable to change inputs or outcomes. They may increase the status attached to their jobs artificially or distort others' perceived rewards to bring equity into balance.

- **Leave the job.** People who feel inequitably treated may decide to leave their jobs rather than suffer the inequity of being underpaid or overpaid. In their new jobs, they expect to find a more favorable balance of rewards. For example, Brian Bader left his technical support job at Apple when he learned that he was twice as productive as the lowest-performing members of the team but earned only 20 percent more.[38]

The implication of equity theory for managers is that employees indeed evaluate the perceived equity of their rewards compared to others'. Many big law firms are reducing the compensation of 10–30 percent of their partners each year in order to free up money to hire and reward "star performers," rejecting the traditional practice of paying partners relatively similar amounts. The change fits with the strategy of rewarding people who generate more business, but it is having a damaging effect on the morale and motivation of other partners, who perceive the new compensation scheme as inequitable.[39] Inequitable pay puts pressure on employees that is sometimes almost too great to bear. They attempt to change their work habits, try to change the system, or leave the job.[40] Equity theory explains why Hostess Inc. employees got riled up when the failing company paid its executives high bonuses, as shown in this chapter's Business Blooper.

Interesting changes are occurring in some workplaces as a result of changing attitudes of younger employees, as described in the following example.

CONCEPT CONNECTION Many of today's top companies are using sales software and apps to significantly improve their salespeople's job performance. Products like Salesforce and NetSuite give sales managers and salespeople a means of working together to set specific, measurable sales targets, or **goals**, that everyone can agree upon and accept. And because these online tools allow salespeople to track their progress online, they get instantaneous **feedback** on their efforts, which is often extremely motivating.

© Syda Productions/Shutterstock.com

Business Blooper

Twinkies

Twinkies took a dive in 2012 when its manufacturer, Hostess Brands Inc., went out of business. Despite federal laws prohibiting bonuses during the bankruptcy process, Hostess executives helped themselves to big raises. The executives did not seem to be thinking about the impact this would have on the workforce. Union representatives cried foul and led a strike. Poisoned relationships between management and labor did not help the ailing company, which was liquidated in December 2012. Over 18,000 people lost their jobs. And the world was

left—at least for the time being—Twinkie-less. That is, until turnaround billionaire—once the owner of Pabst Brewing Co.—bought Hostess and reintroduced Twinkies to an appreciative world in 2013, calling it "The sweetest comeback in the history of ever."

SOURCE: Darrell Hofheinz, "Billionaire Pays $7.4 Million for Midtown House—the Buyer, C. Dean Metropoulos, Saved Twinkie Last Year," *Palm Beach Daily News*, December 20, 2014, A1; Mike Spector and Tom McGinty, "In Trouble and Paying Out," *Wall Street Journal*, December 4, 2012, C1.

Spotlight on Skills

SumAll

"There's a culture of transparency in my generation," says 25-year-old Dustin Zick. When Zick was ready to leave his job as a social media specialist at BuySeasons Inc., he asked a few coworkers about their salaries so that he would have some idea of how to negotiate pay at his next job. The taboo against comparing salaries is fading among young employees who are accustomed to documenting their private lives on social media. Some don't understand why companies don't just tell everybody what everyone else is making anyway.

Dane Atkinson of SumAll agrees. Atkinson and his cofounders started the data-analytics company as an open enterprise. Hiring and promotion decisions, performance appraisal data, pay scales, and individual employees' pay rates are shared with everyone in the company. The owners say that it creates trust and keeps people from worrying about inequity. Peer Insight, a Washington, D.C.–based innovation-consulting company, also shares salaries, bonuses, and performance appraisals among the firm's dozen or so employees. Others, though, say too much openness creates more problems. Slava Akhmechet, CEO and cofounder of database firm RethinkDB, experimented with open pay, but he ran into problems when he needed to hire new technical employees in a tight labor market. Akhmechet found that he needed to offer the newcomers higher salaries than current employees were making. Longtime employees began demanding more pay, and in some cases, motivation, performance, and commitment declined significantly if the demands were not met because people felt treated unfairly. Akhmechet eventually shelved the open salary model.[41]

Employees and managers who support transparency argue that it ensures that everyone is paid fairly and reduces discrimination. Others say that perceived inequity will always be a problem in organizations, and that keeping some things under wraps is better for all concerned.

12.4c Expectancy Theory

Expectancy theory suggests that motivation depends on individuals' expectations about their ability to perform tasks and receive desired rewards. Expectancy theory is associated with the work of Victor Vroom, although a number of scholars have made contributions in this area.[42]

Expectancy theory is concerned not with identifying types of needs, but with the thinking process that individuals use to achieve rewards. For example, one interesting study of expectancy theory looked at patrol officer drug arrests in the midwestern United States. The research found that officers who produced the most drug arrests were more likely to have perceived that such arrests were a management priority and were rewarded by their organization, received specialized training to hone their skills related to drug interdiction, and perceived that they had sufficient time and resources to investigate suspected drug activity properly.[43] Walmart is using expectancy theory by tying some senior executive compensation to an overhaul of its corporate compliance program (executives' compliance with antibribery laws and other policies for international behavior). By tying rewards directly to achieving specific compliance goals, top leaders are demonstrating that the compliance overhaul is a priority.[44]

Expectancy theory is based on the relationship among the individual's *effort*, the individual's *performance*, and the desirability of *outcomes* associated with high performance. These

EXHIBIT 12.6 Major Elements of Expectancy Theory

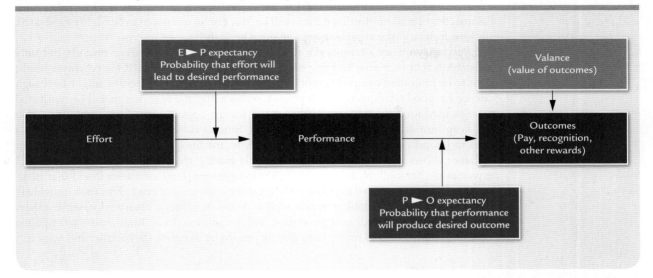

elements and the relationships among them are illustrated in Exhibit 12.6. The keys to expectancy theory are the expectancies for the relationships among effort, performance, and the value of the outcomes to the individual.

E → P expectancy involves determining whether putting effort into a task will lead to high performance. For this expectancy to be high, the individual must have the ability, previous experience, and necessary equipment, tools, and opportunity to perform. Let's consider a simple sales example. If Paloma, a salesperson at the Diamond Gift Shop, believes that increased selling effort will lead to higher personal sales, we can say that she has a high E → P expectancy. However, if Paloma believes that she has neither the ability nor the opportunity to achieve high performance, the expectancy will be low, and so will be her motivation.

P → O expectancy involves determining whether successful performance will lead to the desired outcome or reward. If the P → O expectancy is high, the individual will be more highly motivated. If the expectancy is that high performance will not produce the desired outcome, motivation will be lower. If Paloma believes that higher personal sales will lead to a pay increase, we can say that she has a high P → O expectancy. She might be aware that raises are coming up for consideration and talk with her supervisor or other employees to see if increased sales will help her earn a better raise. If not, she will be less motivated to work hard.

Valence is the value of outcomes, or attraction to outcomes, for the individual. If the outcomes that are available from great effort and good performance are not valued by employees, motivation will be low. Likewise, if outcomes have a high value, motivation

CONCEPT CONNECTION According to **expectancy theory**, a reward that effectively motivates one individual doesn't necessarily work for another. So how can employers create attractive rewards that motivate all their employees, especially when economic conditions necessitate cuts in salary and benefits budgets? Many managers are turning to gift cards. One advantage is that they can be issued in virtually any denomination. But even more important, many gift cards allow the recipient to tailor a reward to his or her individual preference. A person can choose to splurge on some small luxury or use the card for essentials such as groceries.

will be higher. If Paloma places a high value on the pay raise, valence is high, and she will have a high motivational force. On the other hand, if the money has low valence for Paloma, the overall motivational force will be low. For an employee to be highly motivated, all three factors in the expectancy model must be high.[45]

Expectancy theory attempts not to define specific types of needs or rewards, but only to establish that they exist and may be different for every individual. One employee might want to be promoted to a position of increased responsibility, and another might have high valence for good relationships with peers. Consequently, the first person will be motivated to work hard for a promotion and the second for the opportunity of a team position that will keep him or her associated with a group. Studies substantiate the idea that rewards need to be individualized to be motivating. A recent finding from the U.S. Department of Labor shows that the top reason for people leaving their jobs is that they "don't feel appreciated." Yet Gallup's analysis of 10,000 workgroups in 30 industries found that making people feel appreciated depends on finding the right kind of reward for each individual. Some people prefer tangible rewards such as bonuses, gifts, or luxury trips, while others place high value on words of appreciation and recognition. In addition, some want public recognition, while others prefer to be quietly praised by someone they admire and respect.[46]

REMEMBER THIS

- **Process theories**, including goal-setting theory, equity theory, and expectancy theory, explain how people select behaviors with which to meet their needs and determine whether their choices were successful.
- **Goal-setting theory** proposes that specific, challenging goals increase motivation and performance when the goals are accepted by subordinates and these subordinates receive feedback to indicate their progress toward goal achievement.
- **Equity theory** focuses on individuals' perceptions of how fairly they are treated relative to others.
- Managers at SumAll use an open-pay model so that people know what everyone else makes, arguing that it reduces stress over potential inequity.

- A situation of **equity** exists when the ratio of one person's outcomes to inputs equals that of another's.
- **Expectancy theory** proposes that motivation depends on individuals' expectations about their ability to perform tasks and receive desired rewards.
- A person's **E → P expectancy** is the expectancy that putting effort into a given task will lead to high performance.
- **P → O expectancy** is the expectancy that high performance of a task will lead to the desired outcome.
- **Valence** is the value of outcomes (rewards) to the individual.

12.5 Reinforcement Perspective on Motivation

The reinforcement approach to employee motivation sidesteps the issues of employee needs and thinking processes described in the content and process theories. **Reinforcement theory** simply looks at the relationship between behavior and its consequences. It focuses on changing or modifying employees' on-the-job behavior through the appropriate use of immediate rewards and punishments.

12.5a Direct Reinforcement

Behavior modification is the name given to the set of techniques by which reinforcement theory is used to modify human behavior.[47] The basic assumption underlying behavior modification is the **law of effect**, which states that behavior that is positively reinforced tends to be repeated, and behavior that is not reinforced tends not to be repeated. **Reinforcement** is defined as anything that causes a certain behavior to be repeated or inhibited. For example, Whole Foods gives employees a 30 percent discount on store purchases if they meet certain criteria for healthy habits, such as maintaining low cholesterol and blood pressure or quitting smoking. With health insurance costs on the rise, many companies are searching for ways to reinforce behaviors that create healthier employees.[48] The four reinforcement tools are positive reinforcement, avoidance learning, punishment, and extinction, as summarized in Exhibit 12.7 and described next:

- **Positive reinforcement** is the administration of a pleasant and rewarding consequence following a desired behavior. Research shows that positive reinforcement does help motivate desired behaviors. Moreover, nonfinancial reinforcements such as positive feedback, social recognition, and attention are just as effective as financial incentives.[49] Studies of children indicate that those praised for trying hard and taking risks tend to enjoy challenges and find greater success over the long term. A recent study of employees at a fine-dining restaurant found that when leaders provided clear task guidelines and clear feedback on how well people were performing the tasks, motivation and performance improved. Cleaning and sanitizing of tables, chairs, floors, and restrooms increased by 63 percent, and restocking of side stations increased by 48 percent.[50] Supervisor attention and feedback provide a psychological boost to motivation that has nothing to do with financial rewards.

EXHIBIT 12.7   Changing Behavior with Reinforcement

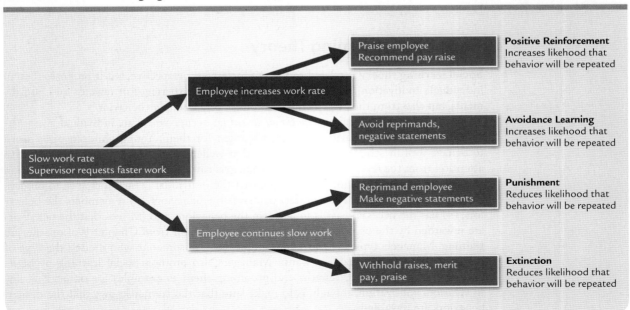

SOURCE: Based on Richard L. Daft and Richard M. Steers, *Organizations: A Micro/Macro Approach* (Glenview, IL: Scott, Foresman, 1986), p. 109.

- **Avoidance learning** is the removal of an unpleasant consequence once a behavior is improved, thereby encouraging and strengthening the desired behavior. Avoidance learning is sometimes called *negative reinforcement*. The idea is that people will change a specific behavior to avoid the undesired result that the behavior provokes. As a simple example, a supervisor who constantly reminds or nags an employee who is goofing off on the factory floor and stops the nagging when the employee stops goofing off is applying avoidance learning.

- **Punishment** is the imposition of unpleasant outcomes on an employee. Punishment typically occurs following undesirable behavior. An example of punishment was when the board of J. C. Penney cut former CEO Ron Johnson's pay almost 97 percent (to $1.9 million) after the retailer lost more than $4 billion in sales. Unfortunately, the punishment didn't help Johnson turn things around, and he was ousted after only 17 months on the job.[51] The use of punishment in organizations is controversial and often criticized because it fails to indicate the correct behavior. However, almost all managers report that they find it necessary to occasionally impose forms of punishment ranging from verbal reprimands to employee suspensions or firings.[52]

- **Extinction** is the withholding of a positive reward. Whereas with punishment, the supervisor imposes an unpleasant outcome such as a reprimand, extinction involves withholding praise or other positive outcomes. With extinction, undesirable behavior is essentially ignored. The idea is that behavior that is not positively reinforced will gradually disappear. A *New York Times* reporter wrote a humorous article about how she learned to stop nagging and instead use reinforcement theory to shape her husband's behavior after studying how professionals train animals.[53] When her husband did something she liked, such as throw a dirty shirt in the hamper, she would use *positive reinforcement,* thanking him or giving him a hug and a kiss. Undesirable behaviors, such as throwing dirty clothes on the floor, on the other hand, were simply ignored, applying the principle of *extinction*.

12.5b Social Learning Theory

Social learning theory is related to the reinforcement perspective, but it proposes that an individual's motivation can result not just from direct experience of rewards and punishments, but also from the person's observations of other people's behavior.[54]

Vicarious learning, or *observational learning*, occurs when an individual sees others perform certain behaviors and get rewarded for them. Young children often learn to behave well in school because they see that well-behaved children get more positive attention from the teacher, for example. Managers can enhance an individual's motivation to perform desired behaviors by ensuring that the individual (1) has a chance to observe the desirable behaviors, (2) accurately perceives the behaviors, (3) remembers the behaviors, (4) has the necessary skills to perform the behaviors, and (5) sees that the behaviors are rewarded by the organization.[55] Recall the discussion from Chapter 9 of on-the-job training. Managers typically pair a new employee with someone who models the type of behavior that the organization wants. Managers also promote social learning by highlighting top performers' strengths and grooming them as examples for others.[56] A key to vicarious motivation, though, is to make sure that the learner knows that the desired behaviors are rewarded.

REMEMBER THIS

- **Reinforcement theory** is based on the relationship between a given behavior and its consequences.
- **Behavior modification** refers to the set of techniques by which reinforcement theory is used to modify human behavior.
- The **law of effect** asserts that positively reinforced behavior tends to be repeated, and unreinforced or negatively reinforced behavior tends to be inhibited.
- **Reinforcement** is anything that causes a certain behavior to be repeated or inhibited.
- **Positive reinforcement** is the administration of a pleasant and rewarding consequence following a desired behavior.
- Managers apply **avoidance learning**, called negative reinforcement, when they remove an unpleasant consequence once a behavior is improved.
- **Punishment** refers to the imposition of an unpleasant outcome following an undesirable behavior.
- **Extinction** refers to withholding positive rewards and essentially ignoring undesirable behavior.
- **Social learning theory** proposes that an individual's motivation can result not just from direct experience of rewards and punishments, but also from thoughts, beliefs, and observations of other people's behavior.
- **Vicarious learning** occurs when an individual sees others perform certain behaviors and get rewarded for them.

12.6 Job Design for Motivation

A *job* in an organization is a unit of work that a single employee is responsible for performing. A job could include writing tickets for parking violators in New York City, performing magnetic resonance imaging (MRI) at Salt Lake Regional Medical Center, or doing long-range planning for Netflix. Jobs are an important consideration for motivation because performing their components may provide rewards that meet employees' needs. Managers need to know what aspects of a job provide motivation as well as how to compensate for routine tasks that have little inherent satisfaction. **Job design** is the application of motivational theories to the structure of work for improving productivity and satisfaction.

12.6a Job Enrichment

Recall from Chapter 1 the principles of scientific management, in which tasks are designed to be simple, repetitive, and standardized. This contributes to efficiency, but simplified jobs aren't typically effective as a motivational technique because they can be boring and routine. Thus, managers in many companies are redesigning simplified jobs into jobs that provide greater variety and satisfaction. One technique, called *job rotation*, is to move employees systematically from one job to another to provide variety and stimulation. Another approach is to combine a series of small tasks into one new, broader job so that people perform a variety of activities, which is referred to as *job enlargement*.

Andy Sacks/Jupiter Images

CONCEPT CONNECTION In the past, an employee might have been assigned to complete just one step in the overall assembly of a new vehicle, car after car after car. A second worker would do the next step, and so forth. In manufacturing plants where **job enrichment** is practiced, however, one employee might be asked to complete a whole series of steps in the assembly process. Not only does the variety make the work more interesting and engaging, it also helps the employee feel more responsible and invested in his or her work.

Overall, the trend is toward **job enrichment**, which means incorporating high-level motivators into the work, including responsibility, recognition, and opportunities for growth, learning, and achievement. In an enriched job, employees have control over the resources necessary for performing tasks, make decisions on how to do the work, experience personal growth, and set their own work pace. Research shows that when jobs are designed to be controlled more by employees than by managers, people typically feel a greater sense of involvement, commitment, and motivation, which in turn contributes to higher morale, lower turnover, and stronger organizational performance.[57]

12.6b Job Characteristics Model

One significant approach to job design is the job characteristics model developed by Richard Hackman and Greg Oldham.[58] Hackman and Oldham's research concerned **work redesign**, which is defined as altering jobs to increase both the quality of employees' work experience and their productivity. Hackman and Oldham's research into the design of hundreds of jobs yielded the **job characteristics model**, which is illustrated in Exhibit 12.8. The model consists of three major parts: core job dimensions, critical psychological states, and employee growth-need strength.

EXHIBIT 12.8 The Job Characteristics Model

SOURCE: Adapted from J. Richard Hackman and G. R. Oldham, "Motivation Through the Design of Work: Test of a Theory," *Organizational Behavior and Human Performance* 16 (1976): 256.

Core Job Dimensions   Hackman and Oldham identified five dimensions that determine a job's motivational potential:

- *Skill variety.* This is the number of diverse activities that compose a job and the number of skills used to perform it. A routine, repetitive assembly-line job is low in variety, whereas an applied research position that involves working on new problems every day is high in variety.

- *Task identity.* This is the degree to which an employee performs a total job with a recognizable beginning and ending. A chef who prepares an entire meal has more task identity than a worker on a cafeteria line who ladles mashed potatoes.

- *Task significance.* This is the degree to which the job is perceived as important and having an impact on the company or consumers. People who distribute penicillin and other medical supplies during times of emergencies would feel that they have significant jobs.

- *Autonomy.* This is the degree to which the worker has freedom, discretion, and self-determination in planning and carrying out tasks. A house painter can determine how to paint the house; a paint sprayer on an assembly line has little autonomy.

- *Feedback.* This is the extent to which doing the job provides feedback to the employee about his or her performance. Jobs vary in their ability to let workers see the outcomes of their efforts. A football coach knows whether the team won or lost, but a basic research scientist may have to wait years to learn whether her research project was successful.

The job characteristics model says that the more these five core characteristics can be designed into the job, the more the employees will be motivated and the higher will be the employees' performance, quality of work, and satisfaction.

Critical Psychological States   The model posits that core job dimensions are more rewarding when individuals experience three psychological states in response to job design. In Exhibit 12.8, skill variety, task identity, and task significance tend to influence the employee's psychological state of *experienced meaningfulness of work.* The work itself is satisfying and provides intrinsic rewards for the worker. The job characteristic of autonomy influences the worker's *experienced responsibility.* The job characteristic of feedback provides the worker with *knowledge of actual results.* The employee thus knows how he or she is doing and can change work performance to increase desired outcomes.

Personal and Work Outcomes   The impact of the five job characteristics on the psychological states of experienced meaningfulness, responsibility, and knowledge of actual results leads to the personal and work outcomes of high work motivation, high work performance, high satisfaction, and low absenteeism and turnover.

Employee Growth-Need Strength   The final component of the job characteristics model is called *employee growth-need strength,* which means that people have different needs for growth and development. If a person wants to satisfy low-level needs, such as safety and belongingness, the job characteristics model has less effect. When a person has a high need for growth and development, including the desire for personal challenge, achievement, and challenging work, the model is especially effective. People with a high need to grow and expand their abilities respond favorably to the application of the model and to improvements in core job dimensions.

One interesting finding concerns the cross-cultural differences in the impact of job characteristics. Intrinsic factors such as autonomy, challenge, achievement, and recognition can be highly motivating in countries such as the United States. However, they may contribute little to motivation and satisfaction in a country such as Nigeria and might even lead to *demotivation*. A recent study indicates that the link between intrinsic characteristics and job motivation and satisfaction is weaker in economically disadvantaged countries with poor governmental social welfare systems, as well as in countries that value high power distance, as defined in Chapter 3.[59] Thus, the job characteristics model would be expected to be less effective in these countries.

REMEMBER THIS

- Jobs are an important consideration for motivation because performing their components may provide intrinsic rewards that meet employees' needs.

- **Job design** refers to applying motivational theories to the structure of work to improve motivation, productivity, and satisfaction.

- Most companies are moving away from simplified jobs and are using job rotation, job enlargement, and job enrichment to provide employees with greater variety, stimulation, and satisfaction.

- **Job enrichment** refers to incorporating high-level motivators, such as achievement, recognition, and opportunities for growth, into the work.

- **Work redesign** means altering jobs to increase both the quality of employees' work experience and their productivity.

- The **job characteristics model** is a model of job design that considers core job dimensions, individuals' critical psychological states, and employee growth-need strength.

12.7 Innovative Ideas for Motivating

Go to the "Ethical Dilemma" on pages 548-549, which pertains to the use of incentive compensation as a motivational tool.

Organizations are increasingly using various types of incentive compensation as a way to motivate employees to higher levels of performance. For example, when Elise Lelon, owner of the leadership consulting firm The You Business, couldn't give pay raises because of budget pressures, she created a generous lump-sum bonus program tied to the amount of revenue that employees generated for the firm. "It gets their juices flowing and it helps the business grow," Lelon says.[60] Exhibit 12.9 summarizes several popular methods of incentive pay.

Variable compensation and forms of "at risk" pay such as bonus plans are key motivational tools that are becoming more common than fixed salaries at many companies. However, unless they are carefully designed, incentive plans can backfire, as evidenced by problems in the mortgage and finance industries, where some people resorted to overly aggressive and even unethical behavior to earn huge bonuses. Numerous companies, including financial firms such as Morgan Stanley, Credit Suisse, and Goldman Sachs, as well as other organizations such as Home Depot, Verizon, and Aflac, are revising their compensation plans to make sure that incentives reward the desired behaviors.[61] Unfortunately, many managers are still encouraging the wrong kinds of behavior by rewarding people who behave unethically to get more business, signaling to employees that profits are more important than integrity. The most recent National Business Ethics Survey from the Ethics Resource Center indicates that 45 percent of people have witnessed ethical misconduct at work, and

EXHIBIT 12.9 New Motivational Compensation Programs

Program	Purpose
Pay for performance	Rewards individual employees in proportion to their performance contributions. Also called *merit pay.*
Gain sharing	Rewards all employees and managers within a business unit when predetermined performance targets are met. Encourages teamwork.
Employee stock ownership plan (ESOP)	Gives employees part ownership of the organization, enabling them to share in improved profit performance.
Lump-sum bonuses	Rewards employees with a one-time cash payment based on performance.
Pay for knowledge	Links employee salary with the number of task skills acquired. Workers are motivated to learn the skills for many jobs, thus increasing company flexibility and efficiency.
Flexible work schedule and arrangements	*Flextime* allows workers to set their own hours. *Job sharing* allows two or more part-time workers to jointly cover one job. *Telecommuting*, sometimes called *flex-place*, allows employees to work from home or an alternative workplace.
Team-based compensation	Rewards employees for behavior and activities that benefit the team, such as cooperation, listening, and empowering others.
Lifestyle awards	Rewards employees for meeting ambitious goals with luxury items, such as tickets to big-name sporting events or exotic travel.

13 percent say that they have felt pressure to bend the rules or even break the law to earn rewards—an increase of 5 percentage points from the previous survey in 2010.[62]

Incentive programs can be effective if they are used appropriately and combined with motivational ideas that also provide people with intrinsic rewards and meet higher-level needs. The most effective motivational programs typically involve much more than money or other external rewards in order to create an environment in which people thrive. Three important approaches are empowerment, engagement, and making progress, as described in the following sections.

12.7a Empowering People to Meet Higher Needs

One significant way that managers can meet higher motivational needs is to shift power down from the top of the organization and share it with employees to enable them to achieve goals. **Empowerment** is power sharing, the delegation of power and authority to subordinates in an organization.[63] Increasing employee power heightens motivation for task accomplishment because people improve their own effectiveness, choosing how to do a task and using their creativity.[64] At Ritz-Carlton hotels, employees have up to $1,000 to use at their discretion to create a great customer experience. When homes in the area near the Ritz in Laguna Niguel, California, were evacuated due to risk of fires, the hotel made an exception to its "no pets" rule. One employee anticipated the need for pet food and drove to the nearest grocery for dog and cat food, making life a little easier for harried guests who were temporarily homeless.[65] Empowering employees involves giving them four elements that enable them to act more freely to accomplish their jobs: information, knowledge, power, and rewards.[66]

1. ***Employees receive information about company performance***. In companies where employees are fully empowered, all employees have access to all financial and operational information.

2. ***Employees have knowledge and skills to contribute to company goals.*** Companies use training programs and other development tools to help people acquire the knowledge and skills that they need to contribute to organizational performance.

3. ***Employees have the power to make substantive decisions.*** Empowered employees have the authority to influence work procedures and organizational performance directly, such as through quality circles or self-directed work teams.

4. ***Employees are rewarded based on company performance.*** Organizations that empower workers often reward them based on the results shown in the company's bottom line. Organizations may also use other motivational compensation programs described in Exhibit 12.9 to tie employee efforts to company performance.

> *"I think a lot of times it's not money that's the primary motivation factor; it's the passion for your job and the professional and personal satisfaction that you get out of doing what you do that motivates you."*
>
> —Martin Yan, Chinese chef, author, and host of cooking shows, including *Yan Can Cook* and *Martin Yan's China*

The following example from Hilcorp Energy illustrates the four elements of empowerment.

At companies such as Hilcorp Energy empowerment means giving employees almost complete freedom and power to make decisions and exercise initiative and imagination. However, organizations empower workers to varying degrees, from a situation where managers encourage employee ideas but retain final authority for decisions to a condition of full empowerment such as that at Hilcorp. Research shows that empowerment typically increases employee satisfaction, motivation, and productivity.[67]

Spotlight on Skills

Hilcorp Energy

Hilcorp Energy, based in Houston, Texas, is the nation's fourth-largest private producer of onshore crude oil and natural gas. But Hilcorp is different from most energy companies. Hilcorp takes over holes abandoned by the big energy companies—and produces about 25 million barrels of oil and gas a year from them.

Hilcorp is different from most other energy companies in its approach to managing people, too. Managers attribute the company's success to the people on the front lines. All associates have access to all financial and operating information. Because managers put decision-making power in the hands of people on the front lines, those people need to have full information to make good choices.

"You want to know how we're doing? How your slice of the pie is performing? We share the good news and the bad," said a senior financial analyst. "We owe that to every employee whose work generates the numbers we report."

Associates at Hilcorp are always interested in how well the company is doing because they are rewarded based on company performance. Associates can earn bonuses of up to 60 percent of their annual salaries based on meeting performance goals. At Hilcorp, employees truly do feel like owners. "Since we pull together, not competing against each other, and we all have skin in the game, it's amazing what we can accomplish," said founder Jeff Hildebrand.[68]

12.7b Giving Meaning to Work Through Engagement

Employee engagement means that people enjoy their jobs and are satisfied with their work conditions, contribute enthusiastically to meeting team and organizational goals, and feel a sense of belonging and commitment to the organization. Alarmingly, recent surveys show that only 30 percent of employees in the United States are engaged and inspired at work, and 18 percent are actively *disengaged.*[69] Fully engaged employees care deeply about the organization and actively seek ways to serve the mission.[70] Active disengagement means that people are actively undermining their organization's success.

How do managers engage employees? Exhibit 12.10 illustrates the three elements that create employee engagement: a sense of meaningfulness, a sense of connection, and a sense of growth.[71] When managers organize the workplace in such a way as to create these feelings, employee engagement grows, leading to high motivation and high organizational performance.

- *People feel that they are working toward something important.* When employees have a chance to accomplish something that provides real value, they feel a sense of *meaningfulness.* Good managers help people understand the purpose of their work, which contributes to feelings of pride and dignity. Kenexa, the leading human resources (HR) services company in the United States (recently purchased by IBM), uses psychologists and other scientists to study what motivates employees. One finding is that turnover is significantly lower among people who feel pride in their company and its mission than among those who don't.[72] Academy Award winning director James Cameron helps employees feel connected to their work, and to the higher goal of making a good movie, by planning daily and detailed meetings solving all and every problem they are up against, as shown in this chapter's Director's Toolkit.

- *People feel connected to the company, to one another, and to their managers.* In a survey asking people what factors contribute to their engagement, 79 percent of people said "good relationships with coworkers" drove engagement to a high or very high extent. Even more (91 percent) pointed to good relationships with their immediate supervisor as highly important.[73] The behavior of managers makes the biggest difference in whether or not people feel engaged at work.[74] Managers promote engagement when they listen to employees, genuinely care about their concerns, and help them develop positive relationships with colleagues.

EXHIBIT 12.10 Employee Engagement Model

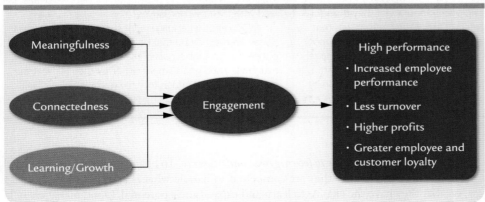

SOURCE: Based on Fig. 1, "Integrative Model of Employee Engagement," in J. Lee Whittington and Timothy J. Galpin, "The Engagement Factor: Building a High-Commitment Organization in a Low-Commitment World," *Journal of Business Strategy* 32, no. 5 (2010): 14–24.

Director's Toolkit

James Cameron

As one of the most successful director's in the world, James Cameron has proved his ability to create block-busters with *The Terminator, Titanic,* and *Avatar,* among others. And you don't bring in billions of dollars in ticket sales without knowing how to keep people motivated.

In his younger days, Cameron admits to putting people under a lot of pressure and seeing how they perform, but he now realizes how easy it is to go from "auteur" to "diva," and get sunk in the process. He's modified that procedure, which he calls "total radical transparency," to where it's more long-term productive. Everyone working on one aspect of a project—for example, designing a vehicle for a film—sits around a table from 8:15 each morning. And he does mean 8:15 *precisely.* Each person would air any problems or concerns they were having. No offline conversations about the issues. Everything came to the group to hammer out. And then the group would

solve the problems. People thought he was crazy, but after two weeks, members started acting like a real team, and they appreciated the opportunity to bring every problem to the group.

After a project is completed, Cameron continues this group communication strategy. When *Avatar* was done, he brought the team back to do an after-action review, with each department writing an analytical paper on what went right, what went wrong, and what could be better next time. Ideas resulted on software and technology improvements, which will make the next film more efficient and cost-effective. Even the director of one of the world's top-grossing films, *Titanic,* needs to be concerned about costs. And keeping people motivated.

SOURCE: Josh Rottenberg, "The Second You Think You're an Auteur, You're Sunk," *Fast Company*, September 2014, 30–32.

Spotlight on Skills

Prudential UK and Europe

Like other companies in the financial services industry, Prudential UK and Europe (Pru UK) is operating in a highly turbulent environment that has been wracked further by the global economic crisis and scandals in the financial industry.

Cathy Lewis, Pru UK's director of HR, CEO Rob Devey, and other top executives decided to focus on improving employee engagement. The first step was a survey to gather data from employees about what they thought would make a difference. One of the findings was that line managers were not living up to the ideal of empowerment. Top executives redefined roles for line managers and had to reassign some who couldn't make the shift. "It was quite painful," said customer services director Tracy Harris, but it allowed top executives to let managers run

their own departments as if they were their own small businesses. Senior managers have begun writing weekly blogs, including notes about people who have made significant contributions or received awards. "It's a little thing, but our people love it," Lewis says. One reason is that it encourages and enables close connections among employees. "These actions," says Devey, "are about showing you care and giving permission for people to take the lead with their own initiatives."

When another engagement survey was conducted a year later, it showed that both engagement (whether people felt enough a part of the organization to "go the extra mile") and enablement (whether they felt that they had the resources and autonomy to do their jobs well) had strongly increased.[75]

- ***People have the chance to learn, grow, and advance.*** To be fully engaged, people need not only to feel that they are competent to handle what is asked of them, but also that they have the chance to learn and expand their potential. Good managers help employees understand their own unique set of talents, skills, interests, attitudes, and needs; put people in jobs where they can make their best contribution and receive intrinsic rewards every day; and make sure that people have what they need to perform well. In addition, they give people the chance to work on challenging projects, offer high-quality training and learning programs, and provide opportunities for advancement within the organization.

Studies have identified a correlation between employee engagement and company performance, including less turnover, greater profitability, and stronger employee and customer loyalty, as illustrated in Exhibit 12.10.[76]

Managers can use strategies to facilitate engagement and improve performance. Consider the following example from Prudential UK and Europe, which provides life insurance and pensions for around 7 million customers.

Although the results of the follow-up survey at Pru UK were overwhelmingly positive and "a source of pride," leaders say that doesn't mean their job is done. "Keep asking, keep talking," says Lewis. It is "the people in the organization who know what will make the difference."[77]

12.7c The Making Progress Principle

Sometimes what makes the biggest difference is a relatively "small" thing. Recent research points to the importance of *making progress toward goals* as a key to high motivation. The **making progress principle** is the idea that the single most important factor that can boost motivation, positive emotions, and perceptions during a workday is making progress toward meaningful goals.[78] People are most motivated when they have the opportunity to experience achievement. Providing feedback on how well people are progressing and giving them a way to track their progress toward goals provides a renewable energy that fuels motivation. Knowing that they are making everyday progress, even in small steps, can make all the difference in how motivated people feel to continue pursuing a course of action.

REMEMBER THIS

- Variable compensation and "at-risk" pay have become key motivational tools, although these practices have been criticized in recent years for rewarding the wrong types of behavior.

- Employee empowerment and engagement are recent motivational trends that focus less on extrinsic rewards and more on creating a work environment that enables people to achieve intrinsic rewards and meet higher-level needs.

- **Empowerment** is the delegation of power and authority to subordinates in an organization.

- Empowering employees involves giving them information, knowledge, power, and rewards.

- **Engagement** is an emotional and mental state in which employees enjoy their work, contribute enthusiastically to meeting goals, and feel a sense of belonging and commitment to the organization.

- Managers create an environment that promotes engagement by providing employees with a sense of meaning, a sense of connection, and a sense of competence and growth.

- The behavior of managers is the biggest factor in determining whether people feel motivated and engaged at work.

- The **making progress principle** is the idea that the single most important factor that can boost motivation, positive emotions, and perceptions during a workday is making progress toward meaningful goals.

CHAPTER **12** **DISCUSSION QUESTIONS**

1. Why do you think that making progress ranks as the most important factor contributing to motivation, according to recent studies? How can managers provide a sense of progress for employees working on long-range projects that might not show results for months or even years?

2. Psychologists have identified three pathways to happiness: pleasure, engagement, and meaning. Do you think that it is the manager's responsibility to help people find these elements in their work? Discuss.

3. Assume that you are a front-line manager at a call center. Try to come up with a specific motivational idea that fits into each of the four quadrants in Exhibit 12.2: Positive Extrinsic; Positive Intrinsic; Negative Extrinsic; Negative Intrinsic.

4. In response to security threats in today's world, the U.S. government has federalized airport security workers. Many argued that simply making screeners federal workers would not solve the root problem: Bored, low-paid, and poorly trained security workers have little motivation to be vigilant. How might these employees be motivated to provide the security that travel threats now demand?

5. Using Hackman and Oldham's core job dimensions, compare and contrast the jobs of these two state employees: (1) Jared, who spends much of his time researching and debating energy policy to make recommendations that will eventually be presented to the state legislature and (2) Anise, who spends her days planting and caring for the flower gardens and grounds surrounding the state capitol building.

6. If an experienced executive assistant discovered that she made the same amount of money as a newly hired janitor, how do you think she would react? What inputs and outcomes might she evaluate to make this comparison?

7. A survey of teachers found that two of the most important rewards were the belief that their work was important and a feeling of accomplishment. According to Maslow's theory, what needs do these rewards meet?

8. Use Herzberg's two-factor theory to explain why motivation seems to be high and turnover low at Mars, based on the information provided in the chapter-opening example.

9. Why do you think empowerment increases motivation? Do you see any ways in which a manager's empowerment efforts might contribute to demotivation among employees? Discuss.

10. A recent Gallup survey shows that highly educated workers are significantly less likely to be engaged than are those with a high school diploma or less. What might be some reasons for this lower level of engagement among more-educated employees?

SELF-LEARNING

What Motivates You?[79]

Indicate how important each characteristic is to you. Answer according to your feelings about the most recent job you had or about the job you currently hold. Circle the number on the scale that represents your feeling—ranging from 1 (very unimportant) to 7 (very important).

4. The feeling of self-esteem that a person gets from being in that job

   1   2   3   4   5   6   7

5. The opportunity for personal growth and development in that job

   1   2   3   4   5   6   7

6. The prestige of the job inside the company (i.e., regard received from others in the company)

   1   2   3   4   5   6   7

7. The opportunity for independent thought and action in that job

   1   2   3   4   5   6   7

8. The feeling of security in that job

    1   2   3   4   5   6   7

9. The feeling of self-fulfillment a person gets from being in that position (i.e., the feeling of being able to use one's own unique capabilities, realizing one's potential)

    1   2   3   4   5   6   7

10. The prestige of the job outside the company (i.e., the regard received from others not in the company)

    1   2   3   4   5   6   7

11. The feeling of worthwhile accomplishment in that job

    1   2   3   4   5   6   7

12. The opportunity in that job to give help to other people

    1   2   3   4   5   6   7

13. The opportunity in that job for participation in the setting of goals

    1   2   3   4   5   6   7

14. The opportunity in that job for participation in the determination of methods and procedures

    1   2   3   4   5   6   7

15. The authority connected with the job

    1   2   3   4   5   6   7

16. The opportunity to develop close friendships in the job

    1   2   3   4   5   6   7

Scoring and Interpretation

Score the exercise as follows to determine what motivates you:

Rating for question 5 = _____.

Divide by 1 = _____ security.

Rating for questions 9 and 13 = _____.

Divide by 2 = _____ social.

Rating for questions 1, 3, and 7 = _____.

Divide by 3 = _____ esteem.

Rating for questions 4, 10, 11, and 12 = _____.

Divide by 4 = _____ autonomy.

Rating for questions 2, 6, and 8 = _____.

Divide by 3 = _____ self-actualization.

Your instructor has national norm scores for presidents, vice presidents, and upper-middle-level, lower-middle-level, and lower-level managers with which you can compare your mean importance scores. How do your scores compare with the scores of managers working in organizations?

GROUP LEARNING

Work vs. Play

1. Form groups of three to four members. Answer this question: What drives you to expend energy on a play activity? For leisure, why do you choose the activities you do? (Don't discuss the particular activities, but rather *why* you choose them.) Select one of your group members as presenter.

2. Each group presents its main points to the class. The instructor will draw on the board a table, similar to the one below, based on information from the class presentations.

Activities	Outcome #1	Outcome #2	Outcome #3	Outcome #4	Outcome #5	Outcome #6
Example: #1 Soccer	High-energy	Team-bonding	Fitness			
#2						
#3						
#4						

3. Questions for class discussion:

   a. How can you build some of these motives for play into a work environment?

   b. What prevents you from making work more intrinsically motivating, as play is?

   c. Which motivation theories are relevant here?

Adapted from Phil Anderson, University of St. Thomas, Minneapolis.

ACTION LEARNING

Interview four people who've had at least three jobs (maybe part-time) in their lives.

1. Ask them which jobs did they like the best, which did they work the hardest. Why did they like that job and why did they work harder? Fill out table below:

Name of person	Job #1		Job #2		Job #3	
	What they liked about the job	What didn't like about the job	Liked	Didn't like	Liked	Didn't like
1.						
2.						
3.						
4.						

2. Try to find patterns, in the answers of the four people. Compare your outcomes to the motivation theories in this chapter. Which theories are validated or contradicted based on your interviews? Did you see patterns of working hard and how much they like the job, or particular tasks? Any patterns in motivation?

3. Your instructor may ask you to write a report on your findings, or meet in small groups to discuss patterns amongst all the interviewees. You would then be asked to either present your findings in class and/or write a group report.

ETHICAL DILEMMA

To Renege or Not to Renege?[80]

Federico Garcia, vice president of sales for Puget Sound Building Materials, a company based in Tacoma, Washington, wasn't all that surprised by what company president Michael Otto and CFO James Wilson had to say during their meeting that morning.

Last year, launching a major expansion made sense to everyone at Puget, a well-established company that provided building materials, as well as manufacturing and installation services, to residential builders in the Washington and Oregon markets. Puget looked at the record new housing starts and decided that it was time to move into the California and Arizona markets, especially concentrating on San Diego and Phoenix, two of the hottest housing markets in the country. Federico carefully hired promising new sales representatives and offered them hefty bonuses if they reached the goals set for the new territory over the following 12 months. All the representatives had performed well, and three of them had exceeded Puget's goal—and then some. The incentive system he'd put in place had worked well. The sales reps were expecting handsome bonuses for their hard work.

Early on, however, it became all too clear that Puget had seriously underestimated the time that it would take them to build new business relationships and the costs associated with the expansion, a mistake that was already eating into profit margins. Even more distressing were the most recent figures for new housing starts, which were heading in the wrong direction. As Michael said, "Granted, it's too early to tell if this is just a pause or the start of a real long-term downturn. But I'm worried. If things get worse, Puget could be in real trouble."

James looked at Federico and said, "Our lawyers built enough contingency clauses into the sales reps' contracts that we're not really obligated to pay those bonuses you promised. What would you think about not paying them?" Federico turned to the president, who said, "Why don't you think about it, and get back to us with a recommendation?"

Federico felt torn. On the one hand, he knew that the CFO was correct. Puget wasn't, strictly speaking, under any legal obligation to pay out the bonuses, and the eroding profit margins were a genuine cause for concern. The president clearly did not want to pay the bonuses. But Federico had created a first-rate sales force that had done exactly what he'd asked them to do. He prided himself on being a man of his word—someone others could trust. Could he go back on his promises?

What Would You Do?

1. Recommend to the president that a meeting be arranged with the sales representatives entitled to a bonus and tell them that their checks were going to be delayed until Puget's financial picture clarified. The sales reps would be told that the company had a legal right to delay payment and that it may not be able to pay the bonuses if its financial situation continues to deteriorate.

2. Recommend a meeting with the sales representatives entitled to a bonus and tell them that the company's deteriorating financial situation triggers one of the contingency clauses in their contract, so the company won't be issuing their bonus checks. Puget will just have to deal with the negative impact on sales rep motivation.

3. Recommend strongly to the president that Puget pay the bonuses as promised. The legal contracts and financial situation don't matter. Be prepared to resign if the bonuses are not paid as you promised. Your word and a motivated sales team mean everything to you.

CASE FOR CRITICAL ANALYSIS

Lauren's Balancing Act

DeMarco's Department Store manager Lauren Brewster's "wow" moment came when she observed a Chicago restaurant staff's gushing treatment of an international celebrity.

"Everyone dreams of that kind of star treatment," Lauren told her assistant, Jack Klein. "Think about it. People brag about their bank or the local bar where 'everybody knows your name,' or enjoy showing off a favorite restaurant where the hostess always remembers their favorite table."

DeMarco's, like other upscale department stores, suffered the double whammy of a slumping economy and increased competition from discount retailers and online shopping. How could the store, the "box," compete, retain its old customers, and build a strong future customer base?

"We've always known that it's all about customer service," Lauren said. "But what's so great about grabbing a giant plastic shopping cart and slogging through some giant warehouse in your shorts and flip-flops, and then joining the herd at the checkout? That is not a shopping *experience*."

"And what *isn't* great about being treated like Oprah from the moment you hit the door until the sales associate swipes your card and hands over something lovely that you just purchased?" Jack asked.

Lauren's idea was that store customers receive that personal, upscale, "you're somebody special here" treatment at DeMarco's. Sales associates would raise their own professional level, regard customers as worthy of personalized service, and build their own clientele. As added incentive, the entire DeMarco's sales team was changed over from hourly pay to straight commission. "Your pay is built through your own initiative and individualized service that makes customers return to you again and again," Lauren instructed the sales force at the outset of the experiment. The idea intrigued Corporate, which approved a two-year experiment.

As expected, the new plan created a minor exodus among those who wanted the assurance of a "regular paycheck." But as the program moved through its first year, both store and corporate management was pleased with the overall results. Marketing pushed the new image of elite, personalized customer service, and statements such as "Katherine at DeMarco's helped me select this outfit," or "Damien always lets me know when something new arrives at DeMarco's that he thinks is perfect for me" became the typical boast of savvy shoppers.

Now, two years into the experiment, Corporate urged Lauren to submit a full assessment of the program as a potential model for implementation throughout the department store chain. Sales numbers vouched for the overall success, particularly over the last two quarters of the second year. Certain associates, including Katherine Knowles in designer dresses and Damien Fotopolous in women's shoes, showed significant gains as a result of straight commissions, and sales associates and customers responded favorably overall, urging a continuation of the program. Reliance on commissions inspired these and other sales associates to treat their individual department as if it were their own small business, becoming experts on nuances of merchandise, exploring designs and trends, finding ways to promote their expertise, and building an impressive number of loyal customers.

The satisfaction level of customers was apparent in the numbers—not only sales numbers, but in repeat business, customer referrals to friends, and customer comment cards, all of which had been tracked since the beginning of the program.

The downside of the experiment was that while some associates soared, others either veered toward an aggressive, pushy sales style or became intimidated by coworkers and teetered, monthly, on the verge of being replaced because they weren't making sales. The once-proud tradition of cooperation among sales staff was, in many instances, being eaten away by relentless competition. Work assignments away from the sales floor were resented. In addition, the managers and

sales associates of certain departments, such as women's accessories, complained of lower wages because, as one sales associate pointed out, "My commission on a $50 belt is nothing compared to Katherine's commission on a $2,800 designer dress." Resentment was mounting among those who witnessed the extravagant wages of a few.

"If we change this program, if we keep straight commission for some and return to hourly pay for others, how does that fit with our new image?" Lauren said to Jack. "How does it deal with the difference in pay scale? How does it assure us that the attitudes of our sales team and the culture of this store will not return to what we were before—just another store?"

Questions

1. What do you see as the advantages and disadvantages of the incentive system that DeMarco's is using for sales associates? What impact do you think it's having on the DeMarco's culture? Explain.

2. Do you think the complaints of lower-paid sales associates are legitimate? Why? How do you suggest that Lauren respond to these complaints, such as the gripe that the system offers few opportunities for large commissions in some departments?

3. Have the successes of sales associates such as Katherine or Damien created a situation in which customers' loyalty to particular salespeople is stronger than their loyalty to the store? For example, if a successful associate leaves DeMarco's, might the customer leave also?

ON THE JOB
VIDEO CASES

Mike Boyle Strength & Conditioning: Motivating Employees

Questions

1. In the video, Mike Boyle talks about establishing a work environment that motivates employees to do great work. List two or three specific ways Boyle has created this type of environment in his gyms, and explain how these actions empower the employees.

2. Cofounder Bob Hanson says that education is an important part of their approach to management. How does education relate to employee motivation and job enrichment?

3. The two trainers featured in the video seem very satisfied with their jobs. Use Maslow's hierarchy of needs to explain why you think they feel the way they do.

ENDNOTES

1. David A. Kaplan, "Inside Mars," *Fortune* (February 4, 2013): 72–82.

2. Richard M. Steers and Lyman W. Porter, eds., *Motivation and Work Behavior,* 3rd ed. (New York: McGraw-Hill, 1983); Don Hellriegel, John W. Slocum, Jr., and Richard W. Woodman, *Organizational Behavior,* 7th ed. (St. Paul, MN: West, 1995), p. 170; and Jerry L. Gray and Frederick A. Starke, *Organizational Behavior: Concepts and Applications,* 4th ed. (New York: Macmillan, 1988), pp. 104–105.

3. See Linda Grant, "Happy Workers, High Returns," *Fortune* (January 12, 1998): 81; Elizabeth J. Hawk and Garrett J. Sheridan, "The Right Stuff," *Management Review* (June 1999): 43–48; Michael West and Malcolm Patterson, "Profitable Personnel," *People Management* (January 8, 1998): 28–31; Anne Fisher, "Why Passion Pays," *FSB* (September 2002): 58; and Curt Coffman and Gabriel Gonzalez-Molina, *Follow This Path: How the World's Great Organizations Drive Growth by Unleashing Human Potential* (New York: Warner Books, 2002).

4. David A. Kaplan, "Salesforce's Happy Workforce," *Fortune* (February 6, 2012): 100–112.

5. Steven Greenhouse, "A Factory Defies Stereotypes, but Can It Thrive?" *The New York Times,* July 18, 2010, BU1.

6. James B. Stewart, "Looking for a Lesson in Google's Lavish Perks," *The New York Times,* March 15, 2013, http://www.nytimes.com/2013/03/16/business/at-google-a-place-to-work-and-play.html?_r=0 (accessed October 29, 2013).

7. Based on Bruce H. Jackson, "Influence Behavior; Become a Master Motivator," *Leadership Excellence* (April 2010): 14.

8. Leslie Kwoh, "Shape Up or Pay Up: Firms Put in New Health Penalties," *The Wall Street Journal,* April 6, 2013, A1.

9. Ashley Halsey III, "Fines Lower Drivers' Use of Cellphones," *Washington Post,* July 10, 2011, www.washingtonpost.com/local/fines-lower-drivers-use-of-cellphones/2011/07/08/gIQAMvX67H_story.html (accessed July 11, 2011).

10. Jack Stack, "Hilcorp Energy Shares the Wealth," *The New York Times,* July 6, 2010, http://boss.blogs.nytimes.com/2010/07/06/hilcorp-energy-shares-the-wealth/ (accessed July 7, 2010).

11. Susie Cranston and Scott Keller, "Increasing the 'Meaning Quotient' of Work," *McKinsey Quarterly,* January 2013, http://www.mckinseyquarterly.com/Increasing_the_meaning_quotient_of_work_3055 (accessed April 17, 2013).

12. This example is from Maureen Soyars and Justin Brusino, "Essentials of Engagement: Contributions, Connections, Growth," *T+D* (March 2009): 62–65.

13. Abraham F. Maslow, "A Theory of Human Motivation," *Psychological Review* 50 (1943): 370–396.

14. Barbara Bowes, "More Than Money: Make Your Employees Feel Secure, Satisfied in Job," *Winnipeg Free Press,* July 24, 2010, I.1.

15. Sarah E. Needleman, "Burger Chain's Health-Care Recipe," *The Wall Street Journal,* August 31, 2009.

16. Kathy Chu, "China Factories Try Karaoke, Speed Dating, to Keep Workers," *The Wall Street Journal,* May 2, 2013, http://online.wsj.com/article/SB1000142412788732323798104578452634075519230.html?KEYWORDS=kathy+Chu (accessed May 13, 2013).

17. Telis Demos, "The Way We Work: Motivate Without Spending Millions," *Fortune* (April 12, 2010): 37–38.

18. Sarah Pass, "On the Line," *People Management* (September 15, 2005): 38.

19. Clayton Alderfer, *Existence, Relatedness, and Growth* (New York: Free Press, 1972).

20. Rachel Emma Silverman, "For Manual Jobs, White-Collar Perks," *The Wall Street Journal,* October 3, 2011, B8.

21. Scott Westcott, "Beyond Flextime; Trashing the Work Week," *Inc.* (August 2008): 30–31.

22. Studies and surveys reported in Karol Rose, "Work–Life Effectiveness," special advertising section, *Fortune* (September 29, 2003): S1–S17.

23. Sylvia Ann Hewlett, "Making Flex Time a Win-Win," *The New York Times,* December 19, 2009.

24. Frederick Herzberg, "One More Time: How Do You Motivate Employees?" *Harvard Business Review* (January 2003): 87–96.

25. "Workforce MoodTracker Summer 2013 Report: Empowering Employees to Improve Employee Performance" (Southborough, MA: Globoforce, 2013), http://go.globoforce.com/rs/globoforce/images/Summer2013Moodtracker.pdf (accessed October 28, 2013); and "Workforce MoodTracker Fall 2012 Report: Revealing Key Practices for Effective Recognition," (Southborough, MA: Globoforce, 2012), http://www.globoforce.com/resources/research-reports/mood-tracker-fall-2012-revealing-key-practices-for-effective-recognition/ (accessed October 28, 2013).

26. David C. McClelland, *Human Motivation* (Glenview, IL: Scott, Foresman, 1985).

27. David C. McClelland, "The Two Faces of Power," in *Organizational Psychology,* ed. D. A. Colb, I. M. Rubin, and J. M. McIntyre (Englewood Cliffs, NJ: Prentice Hall, 1971), pp. 73–86.

28. See Gary P. Latham and Edwin A. Locke, "Enhancing the Benefits and Overcoming the Pitfalls of Goal Setting," *Organizational Dynamics* 35, no. 4 (2006): 332–338; Edwin A. Locke and Gary P. Latham, "Building a Practically Useful Theory of Goal Setting and Task Motivation: A 35-Year Odyssey," *American Psychologist* 57, no. 9 (September 2002): 705ff; Gary P. Latham and Edwin A. Locke, "Self-Regulation Through Goal Setting," *Organizational Behavior and Human Decision Processes* 50, no. 2 (December 1991): 212–247; G. P. Latham and G. H. Seijts, "The Effects of Proximal and Distal Goals on Performance of a Moderately Complex Task," *Journal of Organizational Behavior* 20, no. 4 (1999): 421–428; P. C. Earley, T. Connolly, and G. Ekegren, "Goals, Strategy Development, and Task Performance: Some Limits on the Efficacy of Goal Setting," *Journal of Applied Psychology* 74 (1989): 24–33; E. A. Locke, "Toward a Theory of Task Motivation and Incentives," *Organizational Behavior and Human Performance* 3 (1968): 157–189; Gerard H. Seijts, Ree M. Meertens, and Gerjo Kok, "The Effects of Task Importance and Publicness on the Relation Between Goal Difficulty and Performance," *Canadian Journal of Behavioural Science* 29, no. 1 (1997): 54ff. See Gerard H. Seijts and Gary P. Latham, "Knowing When to Set Learning versus Performance Goals," *Organizational Dynamics* 41 (2012): 1–6, for a discussion of the importance of learning goals versus performance goals in turbulent environments.

29. Locke and Latham, "Building a Practically Useful Theory of Goal Setting and Task Motivation."

30. Edwin A. Locke, "Linking Goals to Monetary Incentives," *Academy of Management Executive* 18, no. 4 (2005): 130–133.

31. Latham and Locke, "Enhancing the Benefits and Overcoming the Pitfalls of Goal Setting."

32. J. M. Ivancevich and J. T. McMahon, "The Effects of Goal Setting, External Feedback, and Self-Generated Feedback on Outcome Variables: A Field Experiment," *Academy of Management Journal* 25, no. 2 (June 1982): 359–372; G. P. Latham and E. A. Locke, "Self-Regulation Through Goal Setting," *Organizational Behavior and Human Decision Processes* 50, no. 2 (1991): 212–247.

33. Gary P. Latham, "The Motivational Benefits of Goal-Setting," *Academy of Management Executive* 18, no. 4 (2004): 126–129.

34. Julie Sloane, "The Number Cruncher," in Ellyn Spragins, "The Best Bosses," *Fortune Small Business* (October 2004): 39–57; and Maggie Rauch, "Great Expectations," *Incentive* (December 2004): 18–19.

35. J. Stacy Adams, "Injustice in Social Exchange," in *Advances in Experimental Social Psychology*, 2nd ed., ed. L. Berkowitz (New York: Academic Press, 1965); and J. Stacy Adams, "Toward an Understanding of Inequity," *Journal of Abnormal and Social Psychology* (November 1963): 422–436.

36. Elizabeth Weise, "Our Brains Dislike Inequality, Even When It's In Our Favor," *USA Today*, February 25, 2010, http://content.usatoday.com/communities/sciencefair/post/2010/02/our-brains-dont-like-inequality-even-when-its-in-our-favor/1 (accessed March 21, 2011); Daniel Yee, "Brain Prefers Working over Money for Nothing," *Cincinnati Post*, May 14, 2004.

37. Ray V. Montagno, "The Effects of Comparison to Others and Primary Experience on Responses to Task Design," *Academy of Management Journal* 28 (1985): 491–498; and Robert P. Vecchio, "Predicting Worker Performance in Inequitable Settings," *Academy of Management Review* 7 (1982): 103–110.

38. Lauren Weber and Rachel Emma Silverman, "Workers Share Their Salary Secrets," *The Wall Street Journal*, April 27, 2013, B1.

39. Nathan Koppel and Vanessa O'Connell, "Pay Gap Widens at Big Law Firms as Partners Chase Star Attorneys," *The Wall Street Journal*, February 8, 2011, http://online.wsj.com/article/SB1000142405274870457010457612423278006700 2.html (accessed February 8, 2011).

40. James E. Martin and Melanie M. Peterson, "Two-Tier Wage Structures: Implications for Equity Theory," *Academy of Management Journal* 30 (1987): 297–315.

41. Weber and Silverman, "Workers Share Their Salary Secrets"; and Rachel Emma Silverman, "Psst . . . This Is What Your Co-Worker Is Paid," *The Wall Street Journal*, January 30, 2013, B6.

42. Victor H. Vroom, *Work and Motivation* (New York: Wiley, 1964); B. S. Gorgopoulos, G. M. Mahoney, and N. Jones, "A Path-Goal Approach to Productivity," *Journal of Applied Psychology* 41 (1957): 345–353; and E. E. Lawler III, *Pay and Organizational Effectiveness: A Psychological View* (New York: McGraw-Hill, 1981).

43. Richard R. Johnson, "Explaining Patrol Officer Drug Arrest Activity Through Expectancy Theory," *Policing* 32, no. 1 (2009): 6ff.

44. Shelly Banjo, "Wal-Mart Will Tie Executive Pay to Compliance Overhaul," *The Wall Street Journal*, April 22, 2013, B8.

45. Richard L. Daft and Richard M. Steers, *Organizations: A Micro/Macro Approach* (Glenview, IL: Scott, Foresman, 1986).

46. Studies reported in Tom Rath, "The Best Way to Recognize Employees," *Gallup Management Journal* (December 9, 2004): 1–5; and Erin White, "Theory & Practice: Praise from Peers Goes a Long Way—Recognition Programs Help Companies Retain Workers as Pay Raises Get Smaller," *The Wall Street Journal*, December 19, 2005.

47. Alexander D. Stajkovic and Fred Luthans, "A Meta-Analysis of the Effects of Organizational Behavior Modification on Task Performance, 1975–95," *Academy of Management Journal* (October 1997): 1122–1149; H. Richlin, *Modern Behaviorism* (San Francisco: Freeman, 1970); and B. F. Skinner, *Science and Human Behavior* (New York: Macmillan, 1953).

48. "100 Best Companies to Work For: Whole Foods Market," *Fortune* (May 23, 2011): 30; "Employees Earn Cash for Exercising More," *The Wall Street Journal*, June 2, 2010, D3.

49. Stajkovic and Luthans, "A Meta-Analysis of the Effects of Organizational Behavior Modification on Task Performance," and Fred Luthans and Alexander D. Stajkovic, "Reinforce for Performance: The Need to Go Beyond Pay and Even Rewards," *Academy of Management Executive* 13, no. 2 (1999): 49–57.

50. Michael Alison Chandler, "In Schools, Self-Esteem Boosting Is Losing Favor to Rigor, Finer-Tuned Praise," *The Washington Post*, January 15, 2012, www.washingtonpost.com/local/education/in-schools-self-esteem-boosting-is-losing-favor-to-rigor-finer-tuned-praise/2012/01/11/gIQAXFnF1P_story.html (accessed January 16, 2012); and Anthony DeRiso and Timothy D. Ludwig, "An Investigation of Response Generalization across Cleaning and Restocking Behaviors in the Context of Performance Feedback," *Journal of Organizational Behavior Management* 32 (2012): 141–151.

51. Stephanie Clifford, "J.C. Penney Slashes Pay of Its Chief," *The New York Times*, April 2, 2013, http://www.nytimes.com/2013/04/03/business/jc-penney-slashes-pay-for-chief.html?_r=0 (accessed October 28, 2013); and Stephanie Clifford, "J.C. Penney Ousts Chief of 17 Months," *The New York Times*, April 9, 2013, B1.

52. Kenneth D. Butterfield and Linda Klebe Treviño, "Punishment from the Manager's Perspective: A Grounded Investigation and Inductive Model," *Academy of Management Journal* 39, no. 6 (December 1996): 1479–1512; and Andrea Casey, "Voices from the Firing Line: Managers Discuss Punishment in the Workplace," *Academy of Management Executive* 11, no. 3 (1997): 93–94.

53. Amy Sutherland, "What Shamu Taught Me About a Happy Marriage," *The New York Times*, June 25, 2006, www.nytimes.com/2006/06/25/fashion/25love.html?ex=1175659200&en=4c3d257c4d16e70d&ei=5070 (accessed April 2, 2007).

54. Arthur Bandura, *Social Learning Theory* (Englewood Cliffs, NJ: Prentice Hall, 1977); and T. R. V. Davis and F. Luthans, "A Social Learning Approach to Organizational Behavior," *Academy of Management Review* 5 (1980): 281–290.

55. Bandura, *Social Learning Theory*; and Davis and Luthans, "A Social Learning Approach to Organizational Behavior."

56. Ilya Pozin, "The Takeaway: Three Things That Motivate Employees More Than Money," *Inc.* (February 2012): 6.

57. Christine M. Riordan, Robert J. Vandenberg, and Hettie A. Richardson, "Employee Involvement Climate and Organizational Effectiveness," *Human Resource Management* 44, no. 4 (Winter 2005): 471–488.

58. J. Richard Hackman and Greg R. Oldham, *Work Redesign* (Reading, MA: Addison-Wesley, 1980); and J. Richard Hackman and Greg Oldham, "Motivation Through the Design of Work: Test of a Theory," *Organizational Behavior and Human Performance* 16 (1976): 250–279.

59. Xu Huang and Evert Van de Vliert, "Where Intrinsic Job Satisfaction Fails to Work: National Moderators of Intrinsic Motivation," *Journal of Organizational Behavior* 24 (2003): 157–179.

60. Sarah E. Needleman, "Business Owners Try to Motivate Employees; As Recession Lingers, Managers Hold Meetings and Change Hiring Practices to Alleviate Workers' Stress," *The Wall Street Journal*, January 14, 2010.

61. Aaron Lucchetti, "Morgan Stanley to Overhaul Pay Plan," *The Wall Street Journal*, December 29, 2009; Graham Bowley, "Credit Suisse Overhauls Compensation," *The New York Times*, October 21, 2009; Liam Pleven and Susanne Craig, "Deal Fees Under Fire Amid Mortgage Crisis; Guaranteed Rewards of Bankers, Middlemen Are in the Spotlight," *The Wall Street Journal*, January 17, 2008; Phred Dvorak, "Companies Seek Shareholder Input on Pay Practices," *The Wall Street Journal*, April 6, 2009; and Carol Hymowitz, "Pay Gap Fuels Worker Woes," *The Wall Street Journal*, April 28, 2008.

62. Reported in Sarah Fister Gale, "Keeping Your Nose Clean: A Look at Ethics in the Workplace," *Workforce.com*, September 6, 2012, www.workforce.com/article/20120906/NEWS02/120909987/keeping-your-nose-clean-a-look-at-ethics-in-the-workplace (accessed October 29, 2013).

63. Edwin P. Hollander and Lynn R. Offermann, "Power and Leadership in Organizations," *American Psychologist* 45 (February 1990): 179–189.

64. Jay A. Conger and Rabindra N. Kanungo, "The Empowerment Process: Integrating Theory and Practice," *Academy of Management Review* 13 (1988): 471–482.

65. John Izzo, "Step-Up Initiative: Create a Culture of Initiators," *Leadership Excellence* (June 2012): 13.

66. David E. Bowen and Edward E. Lawler III, "The Empowerment of Service Workers: What, Why, How, and When," *Sloan Management Review* (Spring 1992): 31–39; and Ray W. Coye and James A. Belohav, "An Exploratory Analysis of Employee Participation," *Group and Organization Management* 20, no. 1 (March 1995): 4–17.

67. Golnaz Sadri, "Empowerment for the Bottom Line," *Industrial Management* (May–June 2011): 8–13; and Robert C. Ford and Myron D. Fottler, "Empowerment: A Matter of Degree," *Academy of Management Executive* 9, no. 3 (1995): 21–31.

68. Stack, "Hilcorp Energy Shares the Wealth."

69. Gallup data reported in Kelli B. Grant, "Americans Hate Their Jobs, Even with the Perks," *USA Today*, June 30, 2013, http://www.usatoday.com/story/money/business/2013/06/30/americans-hate-jobs-office-perks/2457089/ (accessed October 29, 2013).

70. This definition is based on Mercer Human Resource Consulting's Employee Engagement Model, as described in Paul Sanchez and Dan McCauley, "Measuring and Managing Engagement in a Cross-Cultural Workforce: New Insights for Global Companies," *Global Business and Organizational Excellence* (November–December 2006): 41–50.

71. This section is based on Soyars and Brusino, "Essentials of Engagement"; Kenneth W. Thomas, "The Four Intrinsic Rewards That Drive Employee Engagement," *Ivey Business Journal,* November–December 2009, www.iveybusinessjournal.com/article.asp?intArticle_id=867 (accessed November 24, 2009); and Cristina de Mello e Souza Wildermuth and Patrick David Pauken, "A Perfect Match: Decoding Employee Engagement—Part II: Engaging Jobs and Individuals," *Industrial and Commercial Training* 40, no. 4 (2008): 206–210.

72. Kate Rockwood, "The Employee Whisperer," *Fast Company* (November 2008): 72–73.

73. Soyars and Brusino, "Essentials of Engagement."

74. Theresa M. Welbourne, "Employee Engagement: Beyond the Fad and into the Executive Suite," *Leader to Leader* (Spring 2007): 45–51.

75. Anna Scott, "Dear Prudence," *People Management* (January 2012): 36–39.

76. See J. K. Harter, F. L. Schmidt, and T. L. Hayes, "Business-Unit-Level Relationship Between Employee Satisfaction, Employee Engagement, and Business Outcomes: A Meta-Analysis," *Journal of Applied Psychology* 87, no. 2 (2002): 268–279; Coffman and Gonzalez, *Follow This Path*; M. Buckingham and C. Coffman, *First, Break All the Rules: What the World's Greatest Managers Do Differently* (New York: Simon & Schuster, 1999); A. M. Saks, "Antecedents and Consequences of Employee Engagement," *Journal of Managerial Psychology* 21, no. 7 (2006): 600–619; and Nikki Blacksmith and Jim Harter, "Majority of American Workers Not Engaged in Their Jobs," Gallup.com, October 28, 2011, www.gallup.com/poll/150383/majority-american-workers-not-engaged-jobs.aspx (accessed September 24, 2012).

77. Ibid.

78. This definition and discussion is based on Teresa M. Amabile and Steven J. Kramer, "The Power of Small Wins," *Harvard Business Review* (May 2011): 71–80; and Teresa M. Amabile and Steven J. Kramer, "What Really Motivates Workers: Understanding the Power of Progress," *Harvard Business Review* (January–February 2010): 44–45.

79. Lyman W. Porter, *Organizational Patterns of Managerial Job Attitudes* (New York: American Foundation for Management Research, 1964), pp. 17, 19.

80. Based on Doug Wallace, "The Company Simply Refused to Pay," *Business Ethics* (March–April 2000): 80; and Adam Shell, "Overheated Housing Market Is Cooling," *USA Today*, November 2, 2005, http://usatoday30.usatoday.com/money/economy/housing/2005-11-01-real-estate-usat_x.htm?csp=34 (accessed May 22, 2014).

CHAPTER
13

Managing Communication

CHAPTER OUTLINE

LEARNING OUTCOMES

After studying this chapter, you should be able to:

13.1 Explain why communication is essential for effective management.

13.2 Describe the model of communication.

13.3 Explain how an open communication climate and the choice of a communication channel influence the quality of communication.

13.4 Clarify how communicating with candor, asking questions, listening, and nonverbal communication affect communication between a manager and an employee.

13.5 Describe the manager's role in using social media to improve organizational communication.

13.6 Explain the role of personal communication channels, including networks and the grapevine, in enhancing organizational communication.

13.7 Compare and contrast formal and informal organizational communications.

13.8 Summarize strategies for managing communication during a crisis.

R U Ready 2 B a Manager?

Delivered

Before reading this chapter, please circle either "Mostly True" or "Mostly False" for each of the five following questions.

1 If someone does not understand what I am saying, it is important for me to make sure I am using an effective means of communication for that particular person.

Mostly True	Mostly False

[page 561]

2 When I have a message to deliver with emotional content, I know better than to send it via e-mail. Face to face is the best, or if that's not possible, then telephone.

Mostly True	Mostly False

[page 564]

3 If I hope to persuade people, I know that I have to communicate with them often and easily.

Mostly True	Mostly False

[page 565]

4 I could learn a lot about good communication from listening to women interact.

Mostly True	Mostly False

[page 562]

5 When someone else is talking, I focus on what the person is saying, as well as trying to find the underlying meaning, rather than just prepare for my next air time.

Mostly True	Mostly False

[page 568]

In her 20 years with Metro Guide Publishing in Halifax, Nova Scotia, Patty Baxter had never known the phones to be so quiet. A leading publisher of glossy magazines in tourism, arts and culture, entertainment, business, lifestyle, and several other categories, Metro's offices were usually humming with sales calls. Advertising sales were way down, and fortunately, Baxter discovered the reason before they fell off the cliff. It turned out that

NEW MANAGER Self-Test

Do You Focus on What Others Say?[1]

Instructions: Think about how you communicate with other people during a typical day at work or school. Answer the following statements based on whether they are Mostly True or Mostly False for you. There are no right or wrong answers, so answer honestly.

	Mostly True	Mostly False
1. I am extremely attentive to what others say.		
2. I deliberately show people that I am listening to them.		
3. I really enjoy listening very carefully to people.		
4. My mind does not wander when someone is talking.		
5. I often restate what the person said and ask if I got it right.		
6. I usually think about a response while a person is still talking.		
7. I often ask people to clarify what they mean.		
8. I ask questions in every conversation.		
9. I am genuinely curious in conversations about what other people think.		
10. During a conversation, I frequently probe for deeper information.		
11. I inquire about others' points of view on topics.		

Scoring and Interpretation: Focusing on what others say is comprised of two aspects—listening and asking questions. For your Listening score, sum 1 point for each Mostly True answer to items 1–5, plus 1 point for a Mostly False answer to question 6. Listening score = _____. For your Asking Questions score, sum 1 point for each Mostly True answer to items 7–11. Asking Questions score = _____. Managers face many distractions, which makes it hard to pay attention when someone is speaking. Listening attentiveness prevents many communication mistakes. In addition, effective managers learn the habit of inquiry, which means to ask questions to learn more about something or to confirm their understanding. A score of 4 or more on either scale suggests that you are pretty good on that aspect of communication. A combined score of 8 or higher on the two scales suggests that you have excellent focus on what others are saying.

the young sales staff members were e-mailing clients and potential clients with their sales pitches rather than telephoning them. For these young people, who grew up texting and chatting online, calling someone without e-mailing first was strange, if not downright rude, suggesting as it did in their minds that they were prioritizing their needs over the client's. Time for a lesson in business sales communications, Baxter decided. E-mail, texting, and online chatting is fine for some purposes, she pointed out, but it won't cut it in professions like sales, where personal rapport is crucial. Establishing a personal relationship is a key part of making a sale, and that requires the warmth of a voice, if not a handshake. Baxter also hired Mary Jane Copps, a phone-use consultant, who was at first skeptical that she could actually make a living doing such a thing. Now Copps is in high demand because many young employees have "phone aversion." At Metro Guide, training includes role playing that simulates sales calls to build confidence so the sales reps feel that they will be able to "say the right words, in the right order, in the right amount of time," and that they will be able to listen with empathy and ask the right kinds of questions. Employees now keep track of how they contact clients and how they follow up with them to make sure that they are building the personal connections that will keep those advertising sales growing.[2]

Knowing how to communicate effectively is a vital part of every manager's job. Good managers know which channels of communication to use for different types of messages, as well as why aspects of communication such as listening, asking questions, and giving candid feedback are so important to organizational success. The most successful organizations are the ones whose managers keep the lines of communication open. They have the courage to talk about what employees want to hear and explain difficult decisions, especially during tough economic times. In fact, one study shows that companies with highly effective communication had 47 percent higher total returns to shareholders between 2004 and 2009, compared to companies with less effective communication practices.[3]

Not only does effective communication lead to better bottom-line results, but much of a manager's time is spent communicating as well. Managers spend at least 80 percent of every working day in direct communication with others. In other words, 48 minutes of every hour are spent in meetings, on the telephone, communicating online, or talking informally while walking around. The other 20 percent of a typical manager's time is spent doing desk work, most of which is also communication in the form of reading and writing.[4]

This chapter explains why managers should make effective communication a priority. First, we examine communication as a crucial part of the manager's job and describe a model of the communication process. Next, we consider how the interpersonal aspects of communication, including open communication climates, communication channels, persuasion, communicating with candor, asking questions, and listening, affect managers' ability to communicate. Then we look at the workplace as a whole and consider the role of social media, personal communication networks, formal communications, and the importance of crisis communication.

13.1 Communication Is the Manager's Job

Exhibit 13.1 illustrates the crucial role of managers as communication champions. Managers gather important information from both inside and outside the organization and then distribute appropriate information to others who need it. Managers' communication is *purpose-directed*, in that it directs everyone's attention toward the vision, values, and desired goals of the team or organization and influences people to act in a way to achieve the goals. Managers facilitate *strategic conversations* by using open communication, actively listening to others, asking questions, and using feedback for learning and change. **Strategic conversation** refers to people talking across boundaries and hierarchical levels about the team or organization's

EXHIBIT 13.1 The Manager as Communication Champion

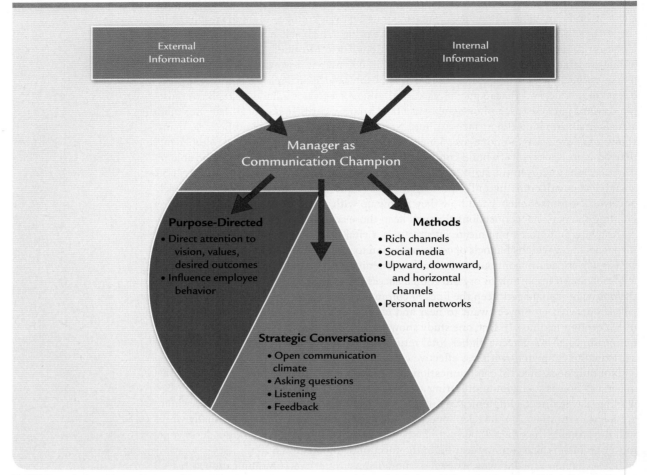

External Information

Internal Information

Manager as Communication Champion

Purpose-Directed
- Direct attention to vision, values, desired outcomes
- Influence employee behavior

Methods
- Rich channels
- Social media
- Upward, downward, and horizontal channels
- Personal networks

Strategic Conversations
- Open communication climate
- Asking questions
- Listening
- Feedback

SOURCES: Adapted from Henry Mintzberg, *The Nature of Managerial Work* (New York: Harper and Row, 1973); and Richard L. Daft, *The Leadership Experience*, 3rd ed. (Mason, OH: South-Western, 2005), p. 346.

vision, critical strategic themes, and the values that help achieve important goals.[5] At Procter & Gamble (P&G), for instance, CEO A. G. Lafley created a process that opened a strategic conversation between top management and leaders in the business units to discuss five themes: What is your vision? Where will you play? How will you win? What capabilities must be in place? What management systems are needed? Rather than formal presentations by top leaders, strategy meetings became informal dialogues among small teams of people from all levels. The goal was to create strategic thinkers throughout the organization.[6]

Managers use different *methods* to communicate, depending on the purpose of the communication and the audience. After disappointing sales results, Virginia Rometty, CEO of IBM, posted a video on the company's internal Web site to get the word out to hundreds of thousands of employees in 170 countries that IBM must move faster and do better at letting clients know the value that IBM can bring to them. Her "think fast, move faster" speech was part reprimand and part pep talk. "Our fundamentals are strong and our future is in our own hands," Rometty said. "I know we will confront this honestly and with urgency, and moments like this are when IBMers rise to the occasion."[7]

Online communication, including social media, which will be discussed later in this chapter, is growing in popularity. In fact, 65 percent of managers surveyed say that they expect to use social media more next year to communicate with employees.[8]

13.1a What Is Communication?

Most of us think of spoken or written language when we think about communication, but words are only a small part of human communication. Managers are observed carefully by employees, so it's important to remember that everything a manager does *and* says will communicate something. In addition, communication is a two-way street that includes asking questions, seeking feedback, paying attention to nonverbal communication of others, and listening actively. **Communication** is the process by which information is exchanged and understood by two or more people, usually with the intent to influence or motivate behavior.

Surveys of managers show that they consider communication their most critical skill and one of their top responsibilities.[9] Most managers realize, however, that they need to improve their communication effectiveness. Fewer than half of responding managers bother to tailor their messages to employees, customers, or suppliers. Even fewer seek feedback from employees or customers because they fear hearing bad news. Without feedback, though, managers can't respond adequately to problems or opportunities, and their plans and decisions may be out of alignment with employee perceptions and interests.[10] In another recent survey by AMA Enterprise, nearly 40 percent of employees said that they feel out of the loop and don't know what is going on at their companies. Only a measly 9 percent reported knowing what is going on most of the time.[11]

CONCEPT CONNECTION Michael Newcombe has climbed the corporate ladder of the prestigious Four Seasons Hotel chain successfully due to his exceptional management capabilities, including his **communication skills**. Newcombe firmly believes in routinely talking with all his workers at all levels in order to understand their changing needs and to prevent problems before they occur. His personal interest in every employee also makes people feel valued and invested in the organization.

13.1b A Model of Communication

Being a good communicator starts with appreciating how complex communication is and understanding the key elements of the communication process, as illustrated in Exhibit 13.2 and described in the following text.

Many people think communication is simple and natural. After all, we communicate every day without even thinking about it. In reality, though, human communication is quite complex and fraught with opportunities for misunderstanding. Communication is not just sending information, but sharing information in a planned way. A manager who has the ability to deliver rousing speeches or write brilliant commentary, but who doesn't know how to listen, is not an effective communicator. Honoring this distinction between *sharing* and *proclaiming* is crucial for successful management.

Knowing what communication entails helps you appreciate the complexity of it. As shown in Exhibit 13.2, a manager who wants to communicate with an employee **encodes** a thought or idea by selecting symbols (such as words) with which to compose a message. The **message** is the tangible formulation of the thought or idea sent to the employee, and the **channel** is the medium by which the message is sent. The channel might be a telephone call, an e-mail message, a formal report, or a face-to-face conversation. The employee **decodes** the symbols to interpret the meaning of the message. **Feedback** occurs when the employee responds to a manager's communication with a return message. As illustrated in the exhibit, the nature of effective communication is cyclical, in that a sender and receiver may exchange messages several times to achieve a mutual understanding.

Encoding and decoding sometimes can cause communication errors. Have you heard someone say, "But that's not what I meant!" or wasted time and energy on misunderstood instructions? Individual differences, knowledge, values, attitudes, and background act as

EXHIBIT 13.2 A Model of Communication

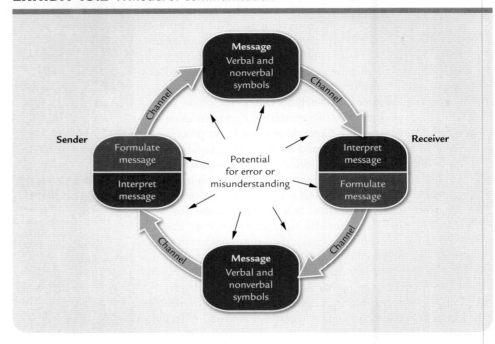

filters and may create "noise" when translating from symbols to meanings. We've all likely experienced communication breakdowns because people can misinterpret a message easily. Feedback enables a manager to determine whether the employee correctly interpreted the message. The potential for communication errors is why feedback is so important. Without feedback, the communication cycle is incomplete. Effective communication involves both the transference and the mutual understanding of information.[12]

REMEMBER THIS

- The manager's role as communication champion means to engage in purpose-driven strategic conversations via multiple channels.

- Social media is a method of communication that is growing in popularity as an effective way to communicate information within an organization.

- **Strategic conversation** refers to dialogue across boundaries and hierarchical levels about the team or organization's vision, critical strategic themes, and the values that help achieve important goals.

- **Communication** is the process by which information is exchanged and understood by two or more people.

- The sender **encodes** the idea by selecting symbols with which to compose a message and selecting a communication channel; the receiver **decodes** the symbols to interpret the meaning of the message.

- The **message** is the tangible formulation of an idea to be sent to the employee.

- The term **channel** refers to the medium by which a message is sent, such as a phone call, blog, or text message.

- **Feedback** occurs when the receiver responds to the sender's communication with a return message.

13.2 Communicating among People

Quicken Loans CEO Bill Emerson holds two-hour lunch meetings with groups of 15 employees at a time to fill them in on what is happening with the company and the mortgage industry, ask about their problems and concerns, and solicit ideas and opinions about how the company operates. Emerson depended heavily on middle- and lower-level managers for maintaining a strong communication climate while he wrestled with business problems during the worst of the recent financial crisis, but he knows that his visible commitment is essential to keep effective organizational conversations going.[13] Even in 1928, when Paul Galvin founded Motorola, he recognized the importance of being a communication champion. His son Bob said that his father did much of his important work in the company cafeteria. "He would always make a point of eating with employees at lunchtime," Bob Galvin said. "He'd ask them lots of questions about operations, customers, and how to improve quality."[14]

To act as communication champions and achieve the best possible outcomes, managers must understand how factors such as open communication climates, communication channels, the ability to persuade, communicating with candor, asking questions, listening, and nonverbal behavior all work to enhance or detract from communication. Managers should also consider how gender affects communication. The "Director's Toolkit" explores how gender differences influence the effectiveness of communication between men and women.

13.2a Open Communication Climate

A survey of U.S. employees reveals that people genuinely want open and honest communication from their managers, including the bad news as well as the good.[15] This created a dilemma for Tom Szaky, CEO of TerraCycle, a waste-recycling business, because he was hesitant to share bad news with his employees. He didn't want them worrying about something that didn't affect their jobs and becoming distracted and unproductive as a result. "The problem with hiding information," Szaky said, "was that when challenges came up, I felt pretty much alone on them, and the staff was left guessing what was happening. Predictably, the lack of information fueled rumors and damaged morale." Today, Szaky encourages transparency and promotes open, honest communication. Employees see everything in great detail, even the bad news. This new climate has fostered a feeling of ownership and trust. It also brings issues to the forefront faster than ever before.[16]

Open communication means sharing all types of information throughout the organization, across functional and hierarchical boundaries. People throughout the organization need to see the big picture, understand the decisions that managers make, and know how their work contributes to the success of the company. Particularly in times of change, if people don't hear what's happening from managers, they rely on rumors and will often assume the worst.[17] In an open communication environment, people know where they stand and what rules they need to play by. Open communication helps people accept, understand, and commit to

AP Images/Wade Payne

CONCEPT CONNECTION Research has shown that a culture of **open communication** offers many benefits to an organization and its employees, including higher productivity, better decision making, and lower turnover rates. Experts say that, even in the largest organizations, face-to-face communication is still the best means of being open and honest. Staff meetings or larger "town hall" meetings like this one emphasize the importance of the information being shared more so than any form of written communication, such as e-mail.

Director's Toolkit

Gender Differences in Communication

To improve the effectiveness of workplace communication, managers should be aware of various factors that influence how people communicate. For example, according to Marianne Legato, founder of the Partnership for Gender-Specific Medicine at New York's Columbia University, there is evidence that men's and women's brains process language differently, which leads to real differences in communication. In addition, learned behaviors associated with being male or female influence communication patterns. Deborah Tannen, author of *You Just Don't Understand: Women and Men in Conversation*, has spent three decades studying gender differences in communication. Grasping the following different communication styles of men and women can help managers maximize every employee's talents and encourage both men and women to contribute more fully to the organization.

- **Purposes of conversations.** Men's conversations tend to focus on hierarchy—competition for relative power. To men, talk is primarily a means to preserve independence and negotiate and maintain status in a hierarchy. Men tend to use verbal language to exhibit knowledge and skill, such as by telling stories, joking, or passing on information. For most women, although certainly not all, conversation is primarily a language of rapport, a way to establish connections and negotiate relationships. Women use their unique conversational style to show involvement, connection, and participation, such as by seeking similarities and matching experiences with others.

- **Decision-making styles.** When women make decisions, they tend to process and think of options out loud. Men process internally until they come up with a solution. Men can sometimes misunderstand women's verbal brainstorming and assume that a woman is seeking approval rather than just thinking aloud.

- **Success in collaborative environments.** A report from McKinsey & Company, "Leadership through the Crisis and After," notes that the kinds of behaviors that executives say will help their companies through the economic crisis are most often practiced by female managers. Women typically score higher than men on abilities such as motivating others, fostering communication, and listening, abilities that are more important than ever when organizations are going through tough times.

- **Interpretation of nonverbal messages.** About 70 percent of communication occurs nonverbally, but men and women interpret nonverbal communication differently. Women believe that good listening skills involve making eye contact and demonstrating understanding by nodding. To men, listening can take place with minimum eye contact and almost no nonverbal feedback. Further, when a man nods, it means that he agrees. When a woman nods, it means that she is listening. Women tend to be better at interpreting nonverbal communication. They are able to assess coalitions and alliances just by noting who is making eye contact during critical points in a meeting.

Interestingly, some male managers may be shifting to a more female-oriented communication style in today's challenging economic environment because women's approach to leadership and communication may be more suited to inspiring employees and helping people pull together toward goals during difficult times.

SOURCES: Based on Deborah Tannen, "He Said, She Said," *Scientific American Mind* (May–June 2010): 55–59; Carol Kinsey Goman, "Men and Women and Workplace Communication," *Business Analyst Times*, May 26, 2009, www.batimes.com/articles/men-and-women-and-workplace-communication.html (accessed September 20, 2012); and Elizabeth Bernstein, "She Talks a Lot, He Listens a Little," *The Wall Street Journal*, November 16, 2010, http://online.wsj.com/news/articles/SB10001424052748704658204575610921238173714 (accessed October 30, 2013).

goals. People can see how their actions interact with and affect others in the organization. When people have access to complete information, they are more likely to come up with creative solutions to problems and make decisions that are good for the company.

Unfortunately, when the employees in the survey mentioned here were asked to evaluate how well their managers were doing in providing open and honest communication, the average score, on a scale of zero to 100, was 69.[18] Managers can build an open communication climate by breaking down conventional hierarchical and department boundaries that may be barriers to communication. They can take care to communicate honestly with subordinates, keep people posted when things change in either a positive or negative direction, and help people see the financial impact of their decisions and actions.[19]

EXHIBIT 13.3 **Communication Networks**

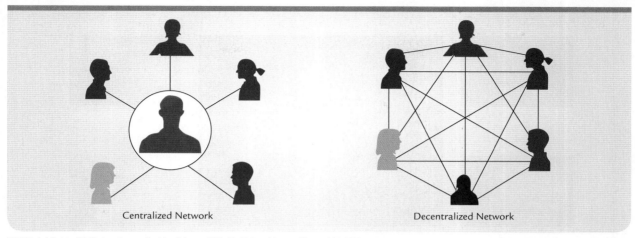

Centralized Network   Decentralized Network

SOURCE: Joel Spolsky, "A Little Less Conversation," *Inc.* (February 2010): 28–29. From Mansueto Ventures LLC, 2010.

To achieve the advantages of open communication, managers should use the type of communication network that maximizes employee performance and job satisfaction. Research into employee communication has focused on two characteristics of effective communication: the extent to which team communications are centralized and the nature of the team's task.[20] The relationship between these characteristics is illustrated in Exhibit 13.3. In a **centralized network**, team members must communicate through one individual to solve problems or make decisions. Centralized communication can be effective for large teams because it limits the number of people involved in decision making. The result is a faster decision that involves fewer people.[21] In a **decentralized network**, individuals can communicate freely with other team members. Members process information equally among themselves until all agree on a decision.[22] Decentralized communication is best for complex, difficult work environments where teams need a free flow of communication in all directions.[23]

13.2b Communication Channels

Managers have a choice of many channels through which to communicate. A manager may discuss a problem face to face, make a telephone call, use text messaging, send an e-mail, write a memo or letter, or use social media, depending on the nature of the message. Research has attempted to explain how managers select communication channels to enhance communication effectiveness.[24] One approach to selecting an effective communication channel is to interpret the emotions of the person who will be receiving the message and then select the channel that will result in the best outcome. Scientists have shown that managers can understand how a person is feeling by studying important clues: facial expressions, gestures, body posture, and tone of voice. A smirk, a furrowed brow, or sagging body posture are strong indicators of a person's emotions.[25]

Another factor that shapes a manager's selection of a communication channel is the type and amount of information to be communicated. Research has shown that channels differ in their capacity to convey data. Just as a pipeline's physical characteristics limit the kind and amount of liquid that can be pumped through it, a communication channel's physical characteristics limit the kind and amount of information that can be conveyed through it. The channels available to managers can be classified into a hierarchy based on information richness.

EXHIBIT 13.4   A Continuum of Channel Richness

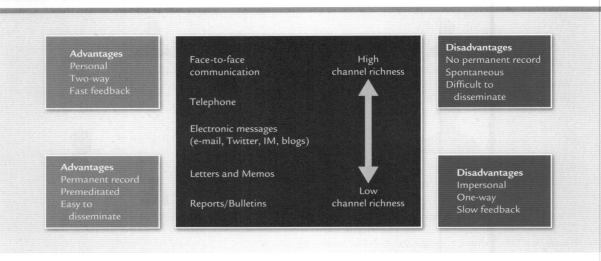

The Hierarchy of Channel Richness   **Channel richness** is the amount of information that can be transmitted during a communication episode. The hierarchy of channel richness is illustrated in Exhibit 13.4. The capacity of an information channel is influenced by three characteristics: (1) the ability to handle multiple cues simultaneously; (2) the ability to facilitate rapid, two-way feedback; and (3) the ability to establish a personal focus for the communication. Face-to-face discussion is the richest medium because it permits direct experience, multiple information cues, immediate feedback, and personal focus. Because of its richness, it is the best channel when communicating to people who are exhibiting strong emotions, such as anxiety, fear, or defensiveness. Face-to-face discussions facilitate the assimilation of broad cues and deep, emotional understanding of the situation. Telephone conversations are next in the richness hierarchy. Although eye contact, posture, and other body language cues are missing, the human voice still can carry a tremendous amount of emotional information.

Electronic communication, such e-mail, instant messaging, and text messaging, is increasingly being used for messages that were once handled face to face or by telephone. However, in a survey by researchers at The Ohio State University, most respondents said that they preferred the telephone or face-to-face conversation for communicating difficult news, giving advice, or expressing affection.[26] Because e-mail messages lack both visual and verbal cues and don't allow for interaction and feedback, messages can sometimes be misunderstood. Using e-mail to discuss disputes, for example, can lead to escalation rather than resolution of conflict.[27] Too often, managers use e-mail or text messaging to avoid the emotional discomfort of a real-time conversation, hiding behind their computers to send rebukes or criticisms that they would never deliver in person. "Because we can't see their hurt, it doesn't matter as much," says business consultant Margie Warrell. She advises managers to never use e-mail in the following circumstances:

- *When you are angry.* As our anger increases, so does our inability to communicate effectively. Wait at least two hours to cool off before sending an e-mail message. Then you will be more able to choose the most constructive way to convey that you are upset.

- *When your message may be misunderstood.* Meet in person with someone who may be defensive about certain issues. A face-to-face conversation ensures that the other person hears your message in the most positive way.

- **When you are cancelling or apologizing.** To cancel an engagement, pick up the phone and call instead of e-mailing, to demonstrate that you care about the relationship. When an apology is called for, meet in person so that you can ask and receive forgiveness, which goes a long way toward restoring a damaged relationship.

- **When you are rebuking or criticizing.** While it is never easy to deliver negative feedback, it is better to communicate rebukes or criticisms in person so that you can read visual cues and address any issues that the other person might raise.[28]

- Still lower on the hierarchy of channel richness are written letters and memos. Written communication can be personally focused, but it conveys only the cues written on paper and is slower to provide feedback. Impersonal written media, including flyers, bulletins, and standard computer reports, are the lowest in richness. These channels are not focused on a single receiver, use limited information cues, and do not permit feedback.

Selecting the Appropriate Channel   It is important for managers to understand that each communication channel has advantages and disadvantages and that each can be an effective means of communication in the appropriate circumstances.[29] Channel selection depends on whether the message is routine or nonroutine. *Nonroutine messages* typically are ambiguous, concern novel events, and involve great potential for misunderstanding. They often are characterized by time pressure and surprise. Managers can communicate nonroutine messages effectively by selecting rich channels. *Routine* messages are simple and straightforward. They convey data or statistics or simply put into words what managers already agree on and understand. Routine messages can be efficiently communicated through a channel lower in richness, such as a memo, e-mail, text message, or Twitter. Written communications should be used when the communication is official and a permanent record is required.[30]

The key is to select a channel to fit the message. During a major acquisition, one firm decided to send top executives to all major work sites of the acquired company, where most of the workers met the managers in person, heard about their plans for the company, and had a chance to ask questions. The results were well worth the time and expense of the personal, face-to-face meetings because the acquired workforce saw their new managers as understanding, open, and willing to listen.[31] Communicating their nonroutine message about the acquisition in person prevented damaging rumors and misunderstandings. The choice of a communication channel can also convey a symbolic meaning to the receiver; in a sense, the medium becomes the message. The firm's decision to communicate face to face with the acquired workforce signaled to employees that managers cared about them as individuals.

13.2c Communicating to Persuade and Influence Others

Communication is not just for conveying information, but also for persuading and influencing people. Although communication skills have always been important to managers, the ability to persuade and influence others is even more critical today. The command-and-control mind-set of managers telling workers what to do and how to do it is gone. Key points for practicing the art of persuasion include the following:[32]

- **Establish credibility.** A manager's credibility is based on knowledge, expertise, and interpersonal skills. By demonstrating a consistent ability to make well-informed, sound decisions, managers inspire employees to have more confidence in the manager's leadership abilities.

- **Build goals on common ground.** To be persuasive, managers should describe the benefits that employees will experience by embracing a new policy or fulfilling a request. An example is the manager who wanted to persuade fast food franchisees

> *"Electric communication will never be a substitute for the face of someone who with their soul encourages another person to be brave and true."*
>
> —Charles Dickens (1812–1870), English novelist

to support new pricing discounts desired by headquarters. The manager didn't just explain that headquarters wanted the policies implemented; he cited research showing that the revised pricing would increase franchisees' profits.[33] When the franchisees saw how they would benefit personally, they were eager to adopt the new policies. If a manager can't find common advantages, this is typically a signal that goals and plans need to be adjusted.

- *Connect emotionally.* The most effective persuaders are good listeners who establish an emotional connection with others and balance their competence and credibility with warmth and understanding.[34] They learn to understand others' emotions and needs and adjust their approach to match the audience's ability to receive their message. In addition, by looking at how people have interpreted and responded to past events, a manager can get a better grasp on how they might react to new ideas and proposals that the manager wants them to adopt.

- *Use multiple media to send important messages.* When a message is highly important, leaders often use *redundant communications*, sending the same message using different channels. For example, one leader explained a request to an employee in person, then immediately composed a follow-up e-mail to the same employee that summarized the request in writing. For companywide changes, leaders might hold small group sessions to talk with employees about a new policy, post an article in the newsletter, and use social media to make sure that everyone gets the information. By saying the same thing more than once via multiple channels, leaders add weight to the message and keep the issue at the top of employees' minds.[35]

To persuade and influence, managers have to communicate frequently and easily with others. Yet some people find interpersonal communication experiences unrewarding or difficult and thus tend to avoid situations where communication is required. The term **communication apprehension** describes this avoidance behavior and is defined as "an individual's level of fear or anxiety associated with either real or anticipated communication." With training and practice, managers can overcome their communication apprehension and become more effective communicators.

13.2d Communicating with Candor

To influence and persuade, managers also have to be frank and straightforward about what they want and need from others. Communicating with candor means being direct, honest, and clear about what employees need to do to meet objectives, while also expressing respect for others and not making people feel slighted, controlled, or exploited. Unfortunately, communicating with candor is a problem for many managers. Jack Welch, speaker, author, and former CEO of General Electric (GE), says that when he asks groups of managers how many of them have received candid performance appraisals, only about 10 percent of people raise their hands. When he asks how many have given candid appraisals to their employees, the results aren't much better.[36]

Communicating with candor is a confident, positive approach that lets others know exactly where you stand and what you're asking of them. The appropriate use of candid communication acknowledges the other person's perspective and opinion, yet is very specific about what the manager wants and why. Some valuable techniques for communicating with candor include the following:[37]

- *Use "I statements."* To communicate with candor, you should keep the focus on the specific perception that you have, how it makes you feel, and the effect that it is having on you, rather than accusing or blaming the other person. Suppose that you share office space with a sloppy colleague. Rather than saying, "You drive me crazy by leaving food wrappers scattered all over the place," you might say, "I'm finding it really hard to get our work done with all this clutter on the work table."

- **Stick to facts rather than judgments.** Don't tell your colleague that she's a disgusting slob; just let her know that the clutter she's leaving on the table is interfering with your ability to do your work.

- **Be clear, specific, and direct in your requests.** Say "I'd like for you to keep the work-table clean because we both have to use it to get our work done," rather than "Why don't you clean up the mess you leave around here?"

Communicating with candor is an important part of creating an open communication climate. When managers communicate with candor, they encourage others to do the same. Sheryl Sandberg, COO of Facebook and author of the controversial book *Lean In*, is known as a straight talker who believes in soliciting candid feedback broadly. Several years ago, after an interview with Tom Brokaw, Sandberg felt that she had stumbled through some of her answers. After the interview, she asked Brokaw how she could have done better. He seemed surprised by the question and said that in his entire career, she was only the second person to have asked him for feedback.[38] In an organization where candid communication is the norm, everything works faster and better. When everyone feels free to open up and speak frankly, more people get involved in organizational conversations, which leads to more ideas and faster learning. In addition, candor means that ideas get debated, adapted, and acted upon more quickly. Candid communication leads to genuine ongoing conversations and limits common problems such as meaningless meetings, workplace incivility, or rancorous silence.

At Taunton Press, a special-interest publishing company, the lack of candor led to endless meetings and decreased productivity. In a small, close-knit company like Taunton, people naturally don't want to offend one another. Yet over time, the culture of "terminal niceness" that evolved sabotaged teamwork. Executives hired consultants from Fierce Inc. to help Taunton leaders and employees see that healthy relationships include both confrontation and appreciation. Over time, Taunton transformed to a culture of candor, collaboration, and accountability.[39]

Becoming an effective communicator may require you to overcome your fears and anxiety when communicating. Go to the "Self-Learning" on pages 583 to assess your communication apprehension in a variety of communication settings.

13.2e Asking Questions

The traditional top-down, command-and-control approach to organizational communication is no longer viable in today's global, technologically sophisticated workplace. This traditional model is giving way to a more dynamic form of communication that is characterized by *organizational conversations*, which involve a give-and-take exchange of information.[40] To have successful organizational conversations, managers need to learn to ask questions. Most managers do 80 percent telling and 20 percent asking, while it should be the other way around. Glenn Kelman, CEO of online real estate site Redfin, says "the most important thing you can do as an executive is to just ask the most basic question, which is, 'What should Redfin be doing better?'" Kelman says people will automatically respond that everything is great, but if you keep asking and show that you're sincere, they'll eventually come forward with thoughts and ideas for how to make things better.[41] Asking questions can benefit both managers and employees in numerous ways:[42]

- **Asking questions builds trust and openness between managers and employees.** Managers who ask questions encourage their employees to share ideas and offer feedback. Duke Energy's president and CEO, James E. Rogers, holds listening sessions with groups of 90–100 employees, where he asks questions and offers responses. By engaging with employees in a format that resembles ordinary person-to-person conversation, Rogers is developing a culture built on trust and authenticity.[43]

- ***Asking questions builds critical thinking skills.*** In one survey, 99 percent of top managers said critical thinking skills at all levels are crucial to the success of their organizations.[44] Asking questions stimulates critical, independent thinking, encourages people to use their creativity, and leads to deeper, more lasting learning.

- ***Questions stimulate the mind and give people a chance to make a difference.*** When a manager asks a question of someone, it puts the individual on alert in a way that making a statement does not. If a plant foreman says, "We have to increase production to fill this order," workers can listen to him and try to speed things up, or continue working as they have been. If, instead, the foreman asks employees, "What can we do to make sure we fill this order on time?" people can't ignore him; they have to start looking for solutions. Thus, asking questions gets people to accept responsibility for solving their own problems.

Asking questions is an important dimension of the organizational conversation. Just as important is listening to the answers.

13.2f Listening

Of all the competencies critical to successful managerial communication, listening is at the top of the list. Yet listening seems to be a rare skill among managers, and the inability to listen is one of the key reasons that managers fail. In fact, a startling 67 percent of new managers fail within 18 months, and it's because they don't listen.[45]

Listening involves the skill of grasping both facts and feelings to interpret a message's genuine meaning. Only then can the manager provide the appropriate response. Listening requires attention, energy, and skill. Although about 75 percent of effective communication is listening, most people spend only 30–40 percent of their time listening, which leads to many communication errors.[46] One of the secrets of highly successful salespeople is that they spend 60–70 percent of a sales call letting the customer talk.[47] However, listening involves much more than just not talking. Many people do not know how to listen effectively. They concentrate on formulating what they are going to say next rather than on what is being said to them. *Harvard Business Review on Effective Communication* cites research indicating that within 48 hours, most people retain only 25 percent of what they've heard.[48]

Spotlight on Skills

Amgen Inc.

Kevin Sharer admits that he was a terrible listener for much of his career. He didn't mean to be; he just wanted to get ahead in life and believed to do so meant that he had to convince others of his point of view. Then, one day, he heard Sam Palmisano, who guided IBM to record growth and profits before he turned over the CEO position to Virginia Rometty in 2012, talk about why his work in Japan was so important to his leadership development. "Because I learned to listen," Palmisano said. "I learned to listen by having only one objective: *comprehension*.... I wasn't listening to critique or object or convince."

It was an epiphany for Sharer, who realized that being a good leader is less about convincing others of your point of view and more about respecting and getting the best out of people—and that requires really listening to them. A leader operates in a complex ecosystem, Sharer says, and has to employ strategic listening to get all the signals that give a full picture of what is going on. "You've got to seek out these signals actively and use every possible means to receive them," he says. Sharer began regularly visiting and genuinely listening to people throughout the company. He admits that it wasn't easy. "You have to change," he says, "and you have to *want* to change.... There has to be a certain humility to listen well."[49]

Most managers now recognize that important information flows from the bottom-up, not the top-down, and managers had better be tuned in.[50] Some organizations use innovative techniques for finding out what's on employees' and customers' minds. Done correctly, listening is a vital link in the communication process, shown in the model of communication in Exhibit 13.2. Kevin Sharer, recently retired CEO of Amgen, calls it "strategic listening."

Listening, Sharer believes, is the greatest sign of respect that you can give someone. "Eventually, executives who don't listen lose the support of their teams and colleagues. And once you've lost that support, it's almost impossible to get it back."[51]

Managers at many companies are also tapping into the interactive nature of blogs and social media to stay in touch with employees and customers. *Blogs*, running Web logs that allow people to post opinions, ideas, and information, provide a low-cost, always-fresh, real-time link between organizations and customers, employees, the media, and investors.[52] One estimate is that 28 percent of *Fortune* 500 companies have a public blog to keep in touch with stakeholders.[53] Blogs give managers another way to get valuable feedback.

What constitutes good listening? Exhibit 13.5 gives 10 keys to effective listening and illustrates a number of ways to distinguish a bad listener from a good listener. A good listener finds areas of interest, is flexible, works hard at listening, and uses thought speed to mentally summarize, weigh, and anticipate what the speaker says. Good listening means shifting from thinking about self to empathizing with the other person, which requires a high degree of emotional intelligence, as described in Chapter 10.

EXHIBIT 13.5 Ten Keys to Effective Listening

Key	Poor Listener	Good Listener
1. Listen actively	Minimally involved; unfocused	Shows interest; nods; asks questions; paraphrases what is said
2. Keep an open mind	Pays attention only to ideas that conform to own opinions	Looks for opportunities and new learning
3. Resist distractions	Is easily distracted	Fights distractions; tolerates bad habits; knows how to concentrate
4. Capitalize on the fact that thought is faster than speech	Tends to daydream with slow speakers	Challenges assumptions, anticipates; summarizes; listens between lines to tone of voice
5. Seek understanding	Feigns agreement to bring the conversation to an end	Searches for common ground and new understanding
6. Judge content, not delivery	Tunes out if delivery is poor	Judges content; skips over delivery errors
7. Hold one's fire	Spouts solutions before understanding the problem or question	Does not judge or respond until comprehension is complete
8. Listen for ideas	Listens for facts	Listens to central themes
9. Work at listening	No energy output; passive and laid back	Works hard; exhibits active body state, eye contact
10. Show respect	Interrupts; talks over the other person when trying to get a point across	Learns to keep quiet and let the other person do most of the talking

SOURCES: Based on "A Field Guide to Identifying Bad Listeners," *McKinsey Quarterly*, Issue 2 (2012): 112; Bernard T. Ferrari, "The Executive's Guide to Better Listening," *McKinsey Quarterly*, Issue 2 (2012): 50–60; John Keyser, "Active Listening Leads to Business Success," *T+D* (July 2013): 26–28; Diann Daniel, "Seven Deadly Sins of (Not) Listening," *CIO*, September 7, 2004, www.cio.com/article/134801/Seven_Deadly_Sins_of_Not_Listening_ (accessed December 7, 2012); Philip Morgan and Kent Baker, "Building a Professional Image: Improving Listening Behavior," *Supervisory Management* (November 1985): 34–38; and Sherman K. Okun, "How to Be a Better Listener," *Nation's Business* (August 1975): 62.

CONCEPT CONNECTION Messages are conveyed not only by what is said, but by how it is said and the facial expressions and body language of the people involved. Face-to-face communication is the richest **communication channel** because it facilitates these **nonverbal cues** and allows for immediate feedback. Important issues should be discussed face to face.

13.2g Nonverbal Communication

Managers should be aware that their body language—facial expressions, gestures, touch, and use of space—can communicate a range of messages, from enthusiasm, warmth, and confidence to arrogance, indifference, displeasure, and condescension.[54] For example, a manager who consistently delivers his or her verbal messages with a scowling expression or a sarcastic look will likely not develop positive interpersonal relationships, no matter how positive the verbal messages are.[55] **Nonverbal communication** refers to messages sent through human actions and behavior rather than through words.[56] Managers should take care to align their facial expressions and body language to support an intended message. When nonverbal signals contradict a manager's words, people become confused and may discount what is being said and believe the body language instead. Managers are watched, and their behavior, appearance, actions, and attitudes are symbolic of what they value and expect of others.

Most of us have heard the saying "Actions speak louder than words." Indeed, we communicate without words all the time, whether we realize it or not. Interesting new research shows that posture and body position has a tremendous impact both on how people are perceived as well as how they actually perform.[57] Katy Keim, chief marketing officer of Lithium, used to step back from listeners during presentations or conversations, resting her weight on her back foot with her hands clasped in front of her. She was often surprised when people asked if she was nervous. After working with a coach and watching herself on video, she realized that her posture "was slightly standoffish" and didn't project the strength that she wanted to show to clients.[58] Research from Harvard Business School and Columbia Business School shows that merely holding your body in a "high-power pose" for a few minutes in private—such as standing tall with shoulders pulled back, widening your stance, or leaning forward over a desk with hands planted firmly on the surface—leads to higher levels of testosterone and lower levels of stress. That is, these powerful body poses seem to boost as well as project confidence and assertiveness. Most people are totally unaware of the signals that they send through their body language, and breaking old habits that project defensiveness, nervousness, or a lack of confidence, such as slumping, folding one's arms across the chest, and waving the hands when talking, can take concentrated effort and practice.

Most managers are astonished to learn that words themselves often carry little meaning. A significant portion of the shared understanding from communication comes from the nonverbal messages of facial expression, voice, mannerisms, posture, and dress. One researcher found three sources of communication cues during face-to-face communication: the *verbal*, which are the actual spoken words; the *vocal*, which include the pitch, tone, and timbre of a person's voice; and *facial expressions*. According to this study, the relative weights of these three factors in message interpretation are as follows: verbal impact, 7 percent; vocal impact, 38 percent; and facial impact, 55 percent.[59] To some extent, we are all natural *face readers*, but at the same time, facial expressions can be misinterpreted, suggesting that managers need to ask questions to make sure that they're getting the right message. Managers can hone their skills at reading facial expressions and improve their ability to connect with and influence followers. Studies indicate that managers who seem responsive to the unspoken emotions of employees are more effective and successful in the workplace.[60]

REMEMBER THIS

- **Open communication** means sharing all types of information throughout the organization and across functional and hierarchical boundaries.
- A **centralized network** is a communication structure in which team members communicate through a single individual to solve problems or make decisions.
- A **decentralized network** is a communication structure in which team members freely communicate with one another and arrive at decisions together.
- **Channel richness** is the amount of information that can be transmitted during a communication episode.
- Although communication skills have always been important to managers, the ability to persuade and influence others is even more critical today.
- **Communication apprehension** is an individual's level of fear or anxiety associated with interpersonal communication.

- Communicating with candor means being direct, honest, and clear about what employees need to do to meet objectives, while also expressing respect for others and not making people feel slighted, controlled, or exploited.
- To encourage a give-and-take exchange of information between managers and employees, managers need to learn to ask questions.
- **Listening** involves the skill of grasping both facts and feelings to interpret a message's genuine meaning.
- **Nonverbal communication** means communicating through actions, gestures, facial expressions, and behavior rather than through words.
- Practicing powerful body poses seem to boost as well as project confidence and assertiveness.

13.3 Workplace Communication

Another aspect of management communication concerns the organization as a whole. Four elements of workplace communication for managers to master are (1) using social media to improve internal and external communication; (2) using informal, personal communication channels; (3) establishing formal communication channels; and (4) developing strategies for crisis communication.

13.3a Social Media

Social media refers to a group of Internet-based applications that allow the creation and exchange of user-generated content. The term *social media* covers a broad range of applications, including wikis, blogs, microblogs (e.g., Twitter and China's Sina Weibo), content communities (e.g., YouTube), social networking sites (e.g., Facebook), and virtual social worlds (e.g., Second Life).[61] Various forms of social media are reinventing how people in organizations communicate among themselves and with customers and other stakeholders. Dallas-based 7-Eleven Inc. has about 2,000 field consultants who use Yammer to share knowledge and learn best practices for how to help franchise owners improve their businesses.[62] Starbucks asks customers for ideas on a social media portion of its Web site and then lets people vote on them, turning criticism into better products. Managers at Aquasana, a home water filtration company, mine the social media interactions of its competitors' customers to find out what people like and don't like and create marketing campaigns that win business.[63]

© Racorn/Shutterstock.com

Companies are embracing social media in a big way. Forrester Research says that sales of software to run corporate social networks will grow 61 percent a year and be a $6.4-billion business by 2016.[64] So far, social media hasn't boosted U.S. productivity significantly, but economists such as MIT's Erik Brynjolfsson say that it takes about five years for a new technology to show its full impact on companies that use it. Social media has been used for only two or three years in most companies, largely for communicating with customers and enhancing employee collaboration.[65]

Listening to Customers   Managers in companies from small entrepreneurial firms and nonprofit agencies to huge corporations are using social media to listen to customers. Dr. Pepper, for example, uses social media to listen to customers by building an 8.5-million-strong fan base on Facebook. These loyal followers who "like" the soft drink help the brand hone its marketing message. The company sends out two messages daily on its Facebook fan page and then monitors the fans' reactions. Using tools from Facebook, Dr. Pepper measures how many times a message is viewed, how many times it is shared with other Facebook users, and what responses it gets. These data help managers adjust their brand messaging. "We mine data to understand what is appreciated, and what is not," says Robert Stone, director of interactive media services for Dr. Pepper Snapple Group Inc. "It helps us shape what we are."[66] The huge health care provider Kaiser Permanente has used social media tools so effectively to listen to customers and improve service that positive media mentions of the organization have increased close to 500 percent over the past five years.[67]

CONCEPT CONNECTION   Home decor retailer Pottery Barn has been acknowledged as a leader in the use of **social media** for listening to and communicating with customers. The organization has representatives dedicated to monitoring the company Facebook page, for example, so that customer questions and complaints are addressed right away—often within minutes of the initial posting. Pottery Barn also follows the current etiquette for social media by focusing on sharing information rather than seizing the opportunity to "hard-sell" its products.

Communicating to Customers   Managers also use social media to communicate corporate news quickly to customers. Domino's relied on the popularity of online communities to calm jittery customers after a damaging prank video showing two employees defacing pizzas and sandwiches was uploaded to YouTube. Domino's managers chose to respond with a viral video of their own. The company president apologized and thanked the online community for bringing the issue to his attention. He announced that the wrongdoers would be prosecuted and outlined the steps that Domino's was taking to ensure that the episode would never happen again. By engaging in an online conversation about the crisis, Domino's demonstrated concern for its customers and squelched further rumors and fears.[68] An opposite example is Target Canada, which was unable to communicate effectively to customers, as shown in this chapter's Business Blooper.

Engaging Employees   Using social media can enable people to connect with one another easily across organizational and geographical boundaries based on professional relationships, shared interests, problems, or other criteria. Interacting through public sites and corporate networks gives employees opportunities to participate in an online community, sharing personal and professional information and photos, and producing and sharing all sorts of ideas and opinions. By 2013, social media had become not just a means for connection and collaboration, but also an effective employee engagement tool for companies such as GE.[69] GE introduced an internal social network called GE Colab in January 2012, and it has been an astounding success, thanks partly to the efforts of Ron Utterbeck, CIO for GE Corporate, who first introduced it to GE's "power users" to encourage high levels of activity. "Our social

"Don't think of social media as just another check box on your list of things to do. . . . It's not just about putting information out there, but listening and engaging in conversation."

—Lasandra Brill, senior manager of global social media, Cisco

Business Blooper

Target Canada

After losing more than $2 billion, going bankrupt and letting 17,000 go, Target Canada shut its operations permanently in January of 2014. It was a two-year experiment that was hampered by the company's inability to communicate adequately with customers about two things: First was the data breach at the height of the 2013 shopping season, and second was the struggle to differentiate Target Canada from other Big Box stores. Even though Canadian retails tourists were frequent in U.S.

stores, somehow the droves did not show up to the 133 stores in Canada. Analysts blamed the appointment of management who had no international experience. Target's new CEO, Brian Cornell, was lauded by the business community for finally pulling the plug on a "lost cause."

SOURCE: Ian Austen and Hiroko Tabuchi, "Red Ink Runs Out in Canada," *New York Times*, January 16, 2014, B1–B4.

Spotlight on Skills

Tupperware Nordic

Tupperware may seem "old school," but it is cutting edge when it comes to using social media to engage people and build community. Steve Ove Fenne, former managing director at Tupperware Nordic, used social media to create a high level of employee engagement by building a connected community based on authenticity, pride, attachment, and fun.

To support authenticity, Fenne began building positive connections with distributors and consultants in the real world and then made sure that messages delivered through social media were consistent with actions in the real world. Previously, individuals operating distribution warehouses and sales consultants were almost never invited to headquarters. Fenne didn't just invite them— he literally rolled out a long red carpet as a symbolic

gesture. He began regularly visiting all major centers of activity to establish personal relationships. He followed up with blogs, e-mails, podcasts, and other messages on social media. He also personally read every message sent to him by consultants, rather than assigning the job to others, and would respond with one-liners such as "WOW! We are so proud of you" (adding the person's first name). When his time was limited, he posted messages on his social media page explaining the situation and reaffirming his support of and pride in each and every consultant.

By using social media to build a community, Fenne helped people who were often working in isolation feel more attached to one another and to the company as a whole.[70]

media metrics focus largely on engagement [of both employees and customers] because that's where we connect with people and build the bond of emotional equity," said Linda Boff, GE's executive director of global digital marketing.[71] Another company that effectively uses social media for engagement is the Northern European branch of Tupperware, Tupperware Nordic.

13.3b Personal Communication Channels

Personal communication channels coexist with formal channels within an organization but may skip hierarchical levels, cutting across vertical chains of command to connect virtually anyone in the organization. In most organizations, these informal channels are the primary way that information spreads and work gets accomplished. Three important types of personal communication channels are *personal networks*, the *grapevine*, and *written communication*.

Developing Personal Communication Networks   Personal networking refers to the acquisition and cultivation of personal relationships that cross departmental, hierarchical, and even organizational boundaries.[72] Successful managers consciously develop personal communication networks and encourage others to do so. Consider Nick Chen, who loved his job as a software engineer designing programs for mobile phones. The work was rewarding, the pay was good, and the working conditions were excellent. "The best part of being a software engineer," said Nick, "is working with a team of professionals who are excited about finding the next breakthrough in mobile technology." Nick's team had recently designed a chipset that would revolutionize the way that people communicate with their mobile phones. Nick's managers recognized his contributions with a year-end bonus, so he was feeling confident about his future with the company. However, Nick had become eager for more responsibility, so he began looking for a management position. During his one-hour commute to work every morning, he used LinkedIn to strengthen his professional network and explore job openings in the mobile technology industry. His efforts paid off. One morning, while updating his profile, Nick got a message from a former colleague who had recently taken a position at Qualcomm in San Diego. She recommended that Nick apply for a new position as product manager for the Android smartphone. Eager to learn more, Nick became one of the company's

Spotlight on Skills

Theater Resources Unlimited

Even though Bob Ost was an award-winning playwright, he was having a difficult time getting his work produced. He thought the secret to success was to find producers, so he found three small theater companies in New York City, hoping at least one of them could help him. The problem was those companies were also struggling to raise money and put up their shows. When he invited people from those three companies to come to his apartment to discuss their mutual problems and explore solutions, suddenly others wanted to attend and he ended up with 30 people in his small living room. At the end of the evening, people indicated they wanted to come for another meeting and that turned into several more, before Ost realized he needed to create an organization with a name, Theater Resources Unlimited (TRU), which he soon made into a not-for-profit. Ost became an entrepreneur.

There was so much interest in the type of networking TRU offered that within two years, Ost starting scaling back his job as an advertising executive and in the past few years has devoted himself full-time to TRU. A turning point for him on the importance of networking was watching the movie *Working Girl*, where secretary Melanie Griffith listens to people at her brokerage firm, sees an article about a radio network up for sale and another article about a company that wants to enter the media

business. She sees the makings of a major business deal. Ost realized he is skilled in matching people up, or putting them together like pieces of a puzzle, as he likes to say. His advice for people who want to get themselves out there more: Networking is a slow process, not a quick fix. It's about building relationships and being genuinely interested in the other person. The worst thing to do when a writer meets a producer is to immediately ask, "Can you produce my play?" Instead, get to know the person, take interest in what the producer is doing, and perhaps even offering to help.

The strength of Ost's ideas are shown in the growth of TRU, which went from 30 initial participants to almost 500 paid members, including producers, playwrights, actors, and other assorted theater folks. As a service to members, TRU hosts monthly panel discussions on such topics as "Producing Your Own Work," "Getting Financing," as well as audition clinics, workshops on developing a "pitch" for one's play, Writer–Producer Speed Date sessions and labs for Writer–Director communications. Attendance at events tops 2,000 per year. Not bad for someone who went from new playwright scribe to nonprofit steward, who leveraged his skills in putting people together with ideas.

SOURCE: Personal communication, Bob Ost, April 2015.

LinkedIn followers, and he found out that Qualcomm had earned a strong reputation as a great place to work and had been named to *Fortune* magazine's list of "100 Best Companies to Work For" 14 years in a row. Nick quickly updated his résumé and applied for the position.[73] An aspiring theatrical producer, Bob Ost started an organization to formally network, and discovered other theater people also were hungry for this service, as described next.

Personal networking, enhanced through social and professional networking sites like LinkedIn, is an important skill for managers because it enables them to get things done more smoothly and rapidly than they could do in isolation. People who have more contacts have greater influence in the organization and get more accomplished. Exhibit 13.6 illustrates a communication network within an organization. Some people are central to the network while others play only a peripheral role. The key is that relationships are built across functional and hierarchical boundaries. For example, in Exhibit 13.6, Sharon has a well-developed personal communication network, sharing information and assistance with many people across the marketing, manufacturing, and engineering departments. Contrast Sharon's contacts with those of Mike or Jasmine, who are on the periphery of the network. Who do you think is more likely to have greater access to resources and more influence in the organization? Here are a few tips from one expert networker for building a personal communication network:[74]

Jetta Productions/Iconica/Getty Images

CONCEPT CONNECTION There are many opportunities for **personal networking**, both in the real world and online. Professional and trade associations, for example, often host after-work events where professionals from the same industry can meet and get to know one another. A city's chamber of commerce may also sponsor networking events that span industries and business types. And of course, Web sites like LinkedIn provide excellent networking opportunities online. A savvy businessperson will pursue many of these options simultaneously in an ongoing manner.

EXHIBIT 13.6   An Organizational Communication Network

As a new manager, it is essential to nurture a personal communication network. Complete the "New Manager Self-Test" on page 577 to see if you have the skills for effective networking.

- *Build it before you need it.* Smart managers don't wait until they need something to start building a network of personal relationships—by then, it's too late. Instead, they show genuine interest in others and develop honest connections.

- *Never eat lunch alone.* Master networkers make an effort to connect with as many people as possible, and they keep their social as well as business conference and event calendars full. Tim Gutwald created a service called Network Shuffle that randomly assigns members a new connection once a month to make sure that people's networks are constantly expanding.[75]

- *Make it win-win.* Successful networking isn't just about getting what *you* want; it's also about making sure that other people in the network get what *they* want.

- *Focus on diversity.* The broader your base of contacts, the broader your range of influence. Build connections with people from as many different areas of interest as possible (both within and outside the organization).

Most of us know from personal experience that "who you know" sometimes counts for more than what you know. More than 200 years ago, Joseph Priestly, a young amateur scientist and minister, was performing experiments in isolation in a makeshift laboratory in the English countryside. Priestly was very intelligent, but he was isolated from other scientists until he traveled to London to attend a meeting of the Club of Honest Whigs, where a wide range of thinkers convened to talk about science, theology, politics, and other topics. The brainchild of Benjamin Franklin, the club was an early networking group that gave Priestly the chance to build a network of relationships and collaborations. He went on to have an illustrious scientific and writing career, famously discovering the existence of oxygen.[76] Like Priestly, by cultivating a broad network of contacts, managers can extend their influence significantly and accomplish greater results.

The Grapevine   Because 90 percent of employees engage in gossip, every manager eventually will have to contend with its effects in the workplace.[77] Although the word *gossip* has a negative connotation, it may actually be good for a company, especially during times of significant organizational change, such as layoffs or downsizing. In fact, gossip can be an invaluable tool for managers. Gossip provides an efficient channel to communicate information because it will move more rapidly than through a formal channel. Another advantage of gossip is that managers who tap into the gossip network may find it a useful "early warning system" that helps them learn about internal situations or events that might need their attention. Plus, gossip is one way employees relieve feelings of tension and anxiety, especially during periods of change. Another benefit is that gossip may give marginalized employees an opportunity to have a voice within the organization.[78]

Gossip typically travels along the **grapevine**, an informal, person-to-person communication network that is not officially sanctioned by the organization.[79] The grapevine links employees in all directions, ranging from the CEO through middle management, support staff, and line employees. The grapevine will always exist in an organization, but it can become a dominant force when formal channels are closed. In such cases, the grapevine is actually a service because the information that it provides helps makes sense of an unclear or uncertain situation. Employees use grapevine rumors to fill in information gaps and clarify management decisions. One estimate is that as much as 70 percent of all communication in a firm is carried through its grapevine.[80] The grapevine tends to be more active during periods of change, excitement, anxiety, and sagging economic conditions. Managers often keep silent during times of change because they don't want to mislead employees by giving out incomplete information.[81] However, when people don't hear about what is going

NEW MANAGER Self-Test

Are You Building a Personal Network?

Instructions: How much effort do you put into developing connections with other people? Personal networks may help a new manager in the workplace. To learn something about your networking skills, answer the questions that follow. Please indicate whether each item is Mostly True or Mostly False for you in school or at work.

	Mostly True	Mostly False
1. I learn early on about changes going on in the organization and how they might affect me or my position.		
2. I network as much to help other people solve problems as to help myself.		
3. I am fascinated by other people and what they do.		
4. I frequently use lunches to meet and network with new people.		
5. I regularly participate in charitable causes.		
6. I maintain a list of friends and colleagues to whom I send holiday greeting cards.		
7. I maintain contact with people from previous organizations and school groups.		
8. I actively give information to subordinates, peers, and my boss.		

Scoring and Interpretation: Give yourself one point for each item marked as Mostly True. A score of 6 or higher suggests that you engage in active networking and have a solid foundation on which to begin your career as a new manager. When you create a personal network, you become well connected so that you can get things done through a variety of relationships. Having sources of information and support helps a new manager gain career traction. If you scored 3 or less, you may want to focus more on building relationships if you are serious about a career as a manager. People with active networks tend to be more effective managers and have broader impact on the organization.

on from managers, the grapevine goes into overdrive. A survey by professional employment services firm Randstad found that about half of all employees reported first hearing of major company changes through the grapevine.[82]

Surprising aspects of the grapevine are its accuracy and its relevance to the organization. About 80 percent of grapevine communications pertain to business-related topics rather than personal gossip. Moreover, from 70 to 90 percent of the details passed through a grapevine are accurate.[83] Managers should be aware that almost five of every six important messages are carried to some extent by the grapevine rather than through official channels. In a survey of 22,000 shift workers in varied industries, 55 percent said that they get most of their information via the grapevine.[84] Smart managers understand the company's grapevine. "If a leader has his ear to the ground, gossip can be a way for him to get a sense of what his employees are thinking or feeling," says Mitch Kusy, an organizational consultant, psychologist, and professor at Antioch University.[85] In all cases, but particularly in times of crisis, executives need to manage communications effectively so that the grapevine is not the only source of information.[86]

Written Communication   "With the fast pace of today's electronic communications, one might think that the value of fundamental writing skills has diminished in the workplace," said Joseph M. Tucci, president and CEO of EMC Corporation. "Actually, the need to write clearly and quickly has never been more important than in today's highly competitive, technology-driven global economy."[87]

Managers who are unable to communicate in writing will limit their opportunities for advancement. "Writing is both a 'marker' of high-skill, high-wage, professional work and a 'gatekeeper' with clear equity implications," says Bob Kerrey, president of The New School in New York and chair of the National Commission on Writing. Managers can improve their writing skills by following these guidelines:[88]

- *Respect the reader.* The reader's time is valuable; don't waste it with a rambling, confusing memo or e-mail that has to be read several times to make sense of it. Pay attention to your grammar and spelling. Sloppy writing indicates that you think your time is more important than that of your readers. You'll lose their interest—and their respect.

- *Know your point and get to it.* What is the key piece of information that you want the reader to remember? Many people just sit and write, without clarifying in their own mind what it is they're trying to say. To write effectively, know what your central point is and write to support it.

- *Write clearly rather than impressively.* Don't use pretentious or inflated language, and avoid jargon. The goal of good writing for business is to be understood the first time through. State your message as simply and as clearly as possible.

- *Get a second opinion.* When the communication is very important, such as a formal memo to the department or organization, ask someone you consider to be a good writer to read it before you send it. Don't be too proud to take their advice. In all cases, read and revise the memo or e-mail a second and third time before you hit the Send button.

A former manager of communication services at consulting firm Arthur D. Little Inc. has estimated that around 30 percent of all business memos and e-mails are written simply to get clarification about an earlier written communication that didn't make sense to the reader.[89] By following these guidelines, you can get your message across the first time.

REMEMBER THIS

- Four elements of workplace communication are using social media, using personal communication channels, establishing formal communication channels, and developing strategies for crisis communication.

- The term **social media** refers to a group of Internet-based applications that allow the creation and sharing of user-generated content.

- Companies are using social media for enabling employees to communicate among themselves and with managers, communicating with customers and other outsiders, and building employee engagement.
- **Personal communication channels** exist outside formally authorized workplace channels and include personal networks, the grapevine, and written communication.
- **Personal networking** refers to acquiring and cultivating personal relationships that cross departmental, hierarchical, and even organizational boundaries.
- Benjamin Franklin established the Club of Honest Whigs in London more than 200 years ago as a networking group where a wide range of thinkers from various walks of life could establish relationships with others and advance their professional and personal interests.
- The **grapevine** carries workplace gossip, a dominant force in workplace communication when official channels are not functioning effectively.

13.3c Formal Communication Channels

Formal communication channels are those that flow within the chain of command or task responsibility defined by the organization. The three formal channels and the types of information conveyed in each are illustrated in Exhibit 13.7.[90] Downward and upward communications are the primary forms of communication used in most traditional, vertically organized companies. However, many of today's organizations emphasize horizontal communication, with people continuously sharing information across departments and levels. Electronic communication methods such as e-mail and social media, as described previously, have made it easier than ever for information to flow in all directions.

The most familiar and obvious flow of formal communication, **downward communication,** consists of the messages and information sent from top management to subordinates in a downward direction. Managers can communicate downward to employees in many ways. Some of the most common are through speeches, videos, blogs, social media, and

EXHIBIT 13.7 Downward, Upward, and Horizontal Communication in Organizations

CONCEPT CONNECTION   When the Mayo Clinic formulated a strategic plan for the world-famous medical center in 2007, the communications department experimented with a new way to facilitate **upward and downward communications**. They created "Let's Talk," an internal blog that allowed managers to use videos and blog posts to explain the plan. The clinic's employees found the blog to be so useful that it continues to be used years later as an ongoing, open communication channel. The Mayo Clinic has since added numerous external blogs to facilitate greater **horizontal communication** with customers and other stakeholders as well.

company intranets. When Red Robin Gourmet Burgers introduced its new line of Tavern Burgers, top executives decided to use an internal social network to communicate the recipe and cooking methods to company managers. Instead of mailing out spiral-bound books, Red Robin successfully used social media as a method to train managers and encourage freewheeling discussions and feedback.[91]

It is impossible for managers to communicate with employees about everything that goes on in the organization, so they have to make choices about the important information to communicate.[92] Typical topics encompassed by downward communication include goals and strategies, job instructions and rationale, procedures, policies and practices, performance feedback, and motivation and indoctrination. For example, some managers use Twitter as a preferred channel of downward communication for time-sensitive job instructions. With a limit of 140 characters, reading and replying to a tweet is a lot faster than other forms of communication.[93]

Many U.S. managers could do a better job of effective downward communication. As we reported earlier in this chapter, the results of one survey show that employees want open and honest communication about both the good and the bad aspects of the organization's performance. But when asked to rate their company's communication effectiveness on a scale of 0–100, the survey respondents' average score was 69. In addition, a study of 1,500 managers, mostly at first and second management levels, found that 84 percent of these leaders perceive communication as one of their most important tasks, yet only 38 percent believe that they have adequate communication skills.[94]

Formal **upward communication** includes messages that flow from the lower to the higher levels of the organization's hierarchy. Most organizations take pains to build in healthy channels for upward communication. Employees need to air grievances, report progress, and provide feedback on management initiatives. Coupling a healthy flow of upward and downward communication ensures that the communication circuit between managers and employees is complete.[95] Smart managers make a serious effort to facilitate upward communication. For example, Mike Hall, CEO of Borrego Solar Systems, found an effective way to encourage his introverted engineers to speak up and submit ideas for improving the business. To get his staff to offer feedback and suggestions, Hall organized an internal contest that he called the Innovation Challenge. All employees were encouraged to submit ideas about improving the business using the company intranet. Once all of the ideas were submitted, employees voted for their favorite idea, and the winner won $500 in cash. Nearly all of Borrego's employees participated in the contest. "We've been able to generate a lot of great ideas by tapping everyone's brains," Hall says.[96] Typical areas of information communicated upward include problems and exceptions that need management's attention, ideas and suggestions for improvement, performance reports, grievances and disputes, and financial and accounting information.

Horizontal communication is the lateral or diagonal exchange of messages among peers or coworkers. It may occur within or across departments. The purpose of horizontal communication is not only to inform, but also to request support and coordinate activities.

Recall from Chapter 7 that many organizations build in horizontal communication in the form of task forces, committees, or even a matrix or horizontal structure to encourage

You can polish your professional listening skills by completing the "Self-Learning Instrument" on page 583.

coordination. At Chicago's Northwestern Memorial Hospital, two doctors created a horizontal task force to reduce the incidence of hospital-borne infections. The infection epidemic that kills nearly 100,000 people a year is growing worse worldwide, but Northwestern reversed the trend by breaking down communication barriers. Infectious-disease specialists Lance Peterson and Gary Noskin launched a regular Monday-morning meeting involving doctors and nurses, lab technicians, pharmacists, computer technicians, admissions representatives, and even the maintenance staff. The enhanced communication paid off. Over a three-year period, Northwestern's rate of hospital-borne infections plunged 22 percent and was roughly half the national average.[97]

13.3d Crisis Communication

A manager's skill at communicating becomes even more crucial during times of rapid change, uncertainty, or crisis. Over the past few years, the sheer number and scope of crises have made communication a more demanding job for managers. Unfortunately, many managers have shown themselves to be not up to the challenge. At the Long Island Power Authority (LIPA), for example, Superstorm Sandy revealed a lack of attention to crisis communication. The deadly 2012 storm was massive, and utilities across the Northeast came under criticism for delays in restoring power, but recovery seemed slowest on Long Island. After the storm, phones went unanswered at authority offices, and even if someone answered, that person had little information to provide distressed customers. There seemed to be no crisis communication plan in place. "The upper management couldn't communicate with the middle management," said Frank Petrone, the chief executive of the Town of Huntington and a former official with the Federal Emergency Management Agency (FEMA). "The middle management couldn't communicate with the crews."[98]

As a manager, your ability to communicate effectively during a crisis will determine how effectively the organization survives the upheaval. Consider the mistakes made by the captain of the *Costa Concordia*, who ran his ship aground in January 2012, causing a disaster that claimed 32 lives. The ship capsized off the coast of the Tuscan island of Giglio after Captain Francesco Schettino allegedly took it off course as part of a stunt, accidentally running it aground. Schettino is accused of manslaughter and abandoning ship before all the passengers had been evacuated. Schettino is said to have contributed to the crisis by failing to respond for 45 minutes after the crew told him that the ship was flooding and its motors were dead. He issued the "abandon ship order" nearly an hour after the ship had run aground—too late to save many lives. Schettino also failed to step forward, accept responsibility, and explain what happened during the days following the disaster.[99]

Four primary skills for managers to follow when communicating in a crisis are outlined next. As you read them, consider how (in)effective Captain Schettino was in communicating during and after the cruise ship crisis.[100]

- *Stay calm, listen hard.* Good crisis communicators don't allow themselves to be overwhelmed by the situation. Calmness and listening become more important than ever. Managers also learn to tailor their communications to reflect hope and optimism as they acknowledge current difficulties.

- *Be visible.* Many managers underestimate just how important their presence is during a crisis.[101] A manager's job is to step out immediately, both to reassure employees and respond to public concerns. Face-to-face communication with employees is crucial for letting people know that managers care about them and what they're going through.

- *Get the awful truth out.*[102] Effective managers gather as much information as they can, do their best to determine the facts, and tell the truth to employees and the public as soon as possible. Getting the truth out quickly prevents harmful rumors and misunderstandings.

- *Communicate a vision for the future.* People need to feel that they have something to work for and look forward to. Moments of crisis present opportunities for managers to communicate a vision of a better future and unite people toward common goals.

- Former U.S. Army Major Giovanni Feroce brought a formal system to Alex and Ari's upward communication, as described in this chapter's Executive Edge box.

Alex and Ani

Imagine a Cranston, Rhode Island, jewelry company headed up by two completely different people: a creative free spirit and by a former U.S. Army major. Thus, you have Alex and Ani, the up-and-coming multimillion dollar firm. Founder and chief creative officer Carolyn Rafaelian took over a small family business and brought Major Giovanni Feroce on as CEO, causing a shift in the culture from relaxed to focused and hard-working. Most of the previous 23 employees were friends of Rafaelian, whom she hired with little concern for skills. A year after Feroce became CEO in 2010, 21 of those had left, mostly voluntarily.

Feroce brought vision, discipline and a new team spirit that changed the company's culture. Twice a week, including first thing Monday morning, executive staff meet around a large table and present sitreps (situational reports), which are updates on operations similar to what is used in the U.S. Army. Members are expected to contribute and then act on any instructions. But unlike the Army, the table is embedded with crystals, meant to deflect negative energy and to be part of emotional healing. It is this unusual hybrid of New Age values with military discipline that might account for Alex and Ani's exploded growth between 2010 and 2014: from 23 to 1,100 employees and from $4.5 million in sales to $230 million. While Rafaelian insists that what the company actually sells is positive energy, Feroce, who left in 2014 to revitalize a watch company, reminded everyone he was a conservative and interested in the well-being of the company. He oversaw the opening of 57 boutiques across the country, making sure its products are sold in Bloomingdale's and Nordstroms, as well as airports and hospitals. His former partner Rafaelian is happy with the growth and is especially proud they can provide local tooling companies to make her jewelry of chains, bracelets, stones, and crystals. "Manufacturing is alchemy," she says. "It's magic."

SOURCE: Kate Bramson, "Feroce Has Designs on Rebooting Classic Brand," *The Providence Journal*, July 7, 2014, 1; Leigh Buchanan, "The Disciplined and the Divine," *Inc.*, April 2013, 78–84.

REMEMBER THIS

- A communication channel that flows within the chain of command is called a **formal communication channel**.

- **Downward communication** refers to messages sent from top management down to subordinates; **upward communication** includes messages that flow from the lower to the higher levels in the organization's hierarchy.

- **Horizontal communication** is the lateral or diagonal exchange of messages among peers or coworkers and includes team communication.

- During a communication crisis, a manager should stay calm and listen carefully, reassure employees and the public, tell the truth, and communicate a vision for the future.

CHAPTER 13 DISCUSSION QUESTIONS

1. What are the characteristics of an open communication climate? Describe the organizational benefits of managers cultivating an open communication climate.

2. Describe the elements of the communication model in Exhibit 13.2. Give an example of each part of the model as it exists in the classroom during communication between teacher and students.

3. Lana Lowery, a regional manager for a 100-person inside-sales team, notices that its best performer is struggling. Her sales are down 20 percent from a year ago, and she frequently arrives late for work, looking upset. Lowery needs to find out why her performance is suffering. What advice would you give Lowery for communicating with this employee? Which communication channel should she use? What would be the relative importance of candor, listening, and asking questions? Explain.

4. One small business owner said that he had to teach his young employees what a "dial tone" was. Do you have phone aversion? Do you think it is possible to build a solid business relationship with customers using only text messaging, e-mail, and social media?

5. Some senior managers believe they should rely on written information and computer reports because these yield more accurate data than do face-to-face communications. Do you agree? Why or why not?

6. During times of significant organizational change, such as downsizing and layoffs, the grapevine becomes more active as anxious employees share organizational news and rumors. As a manager, what communication strategies would you employ during a time of uncertainty in the workplace? What are the advantages and disadvantages of gossip during a time of uncertainty?

7. Assume that you manage a small online business that sells herbal supplements. Without your knowledge, a disgruntled employee has posted damaging information about your company to the company's public blog, including false information about dangerous ingredients in your best-selling supplement. What specific steps would you take to minimize the impact of this crisis?

8. If you were asked to design a training program to help managers become better communicators, what would you include in the program?

9. Suppose that you manage an employee who is spending too much time using social media at work. The result is that he has missed three important deadlines in one week. You are planning a face-to-face conversation to address this performance problem, and your goal is to communicate with candor. Using "I" statements as described in this chapter, how would you begin this conversation?

10. Describe specific ways that you might incorporate Twitter into an organization's crisis communication plan for customers. How about for employees?

SELF-LEARNING

Personal Assessment of Communication Apprehension[103]

The following questions are about your feelings toward communication with other people. Indicate the degree to which each statement applies to you by marking (5) Agree Strongly, (4) Agree, (3) Undecided, (2) Disagree, or (1) Disagree Strongly. There are no right or wrong answers. Many of the statements are similar to other statements. Do not be concerned about their similarities. Work quickly, recording just your first impressions.

Disagree Strongly 1 2 3 4 5 Agree Strongly

4. When talking in a small group of acquaintances, I am tense and nervous.

   1   2   3 4 5

5. When presenting a talk to a group of strangers, I am tense and nervous.

   1   2   3 4 5

6. When conversing with a friend or colleague, I am calm and relaxed.

    1   2   3   4   5

7. When talking in a large meeting of acquaintances, I am calm and relaxed.

    1   2   3   4   5

8. When presenting a talk to a group of friends or colleagues, I am tense and nervous.

    1   2   3   4   5

9. When conversing with an acquaintance or colleague, I am calm and relaxed.

    1   2   3   4   5

10. When talking in a large meeting of strangers, I am tense and nervous.

    1   2   3   4   5

11. When talking in a small group of strangers, I am tense and nervous.

    1   2   3   4   5

12. When talking in a small group of friends and colleagues, I am calm and relaxed.

    1   2   3   4   5

13. When presenting a talk to a group of acquaintances, I am calm and relaxed.

    1   2   3   4   5

14. When I am conversing with a stranger, I am calm and relaxed.

    1   2   3   4   5

15. When talking in a large meeting of friends, I am tense and nervous.

    1   2   3   4   5

16. When presenting a talk to a group of strangers, I am calm and relaxed.

    1   2   3   4   5

17. When conversing with a friend or colleague, I am tense and nervous.

    1   2   3   4   5

18. When talking in a large meeting of acquaintances, I am tense and nervous.

    1   2   3   4   5

19. When talking in a small group of acquaintances, I am calm and relaxed.

    1   2   3   4   5

20. When talking in a small group of strangers, I am calm and relaxed.

    1   2   3   4   5

21. When presenting a talk to a group of friends, I am calm and relaxed.

    1   2   3   4   5

22. When conversing with an acquaintance or colleague, I am tense and nervous.

    1   2   3   4   5

23. When talking in a large meeting of strangers, I am calm and relaxed.

    1   2   3   4   5

24. When presenting a talk to a group of acquaintances, I am tense and nervous.

    1   2   3   4   5

25. When conversing with a stranger, I am tense and nervous.

    1   2   3   4   5

26. When talking in a large meeting of friends or colleagues, I am calm and relaxed.

    1   2   3   4   5

27. When talking in a small group of friends or colleagues, I am tense and nervous.

    1   2   3   4   5

Scoring and Interpretation

This questionnaire includes the computation of four subscores and one total score. Subscores relate to communication apprehension in four common situations—public speaking, meetings, group discussions, and interpersonal conversations. To compute your scores, add or subtract your scores for each item as indicated next.

Subscore/Scoring Formula

For each subscore, start with 18 points, and then add the scores for the plus (+) items and subtract the scores for the minus (−) items.

Public Speaking

18 + scores for items 2, 5, and 21; − scores for items 10, 13, and 18. Score = _____

Meetings

18 + scores for items 7, 12, and 15; − scores for items 4, 20, and 23. Score = _____

Group Discussions

18 + scores for items 1, 8, and 24; − scores for items 9, 16, and 17. Score = _____

Interpersonal Conversations

18 + scores for items 14, 19, and 22; − scores for items 3, 6, and 11. Score = _____

Total Score

Sum the four subscores to get the Total Score _____

This personal assessment provides an indication of how much apprehension (fear or anxiety) you feel in a variety of communication settings. Total scores may range from 24 to 120. Scores above 72 indicate that you are more apprehensive about communication than the average person. Scores above 85 indicate a high level of communication apprehension. Scores below 59 indicate a low level of apprehension. These extreme scores (below 59 and above 85) are generally outside the norm. They suggest that the degree of apprehension that you may experience in any given communication situation may not be associated with a realistic response to that situation.

Scores on the subscales can range from a low of 6 to a high of 30. Any score above 18 indicates some degree of apprehension. If you score above 18 for the public speaking context, you are like the overwhelming majority of people.

To be an effective communication champion, you should work to overcome your communication anxiety. Interpersonal conversations create the least apprehension for most people, followed by group discussions, larger meetings, and finally public speaking. Compare your scores with another student's. What aspect of communication creates the most apprehension for you? How do you plan to improve it?

GROUP LEARNING

Not Listening Exercise

1. In small groups, identify one person as the speaker for each round. That person will talk about something important to them or something that happened recently that had a great impact.

2. Round one: ABC round. Listeners mark down on a paper the number of times the speaker uses words that start in A, B, or C.

3. Round two: self-directed. Listeners try to direct attention to themselves. For example, if someone is talking about their planned trip to Europe, someone else may jump in with, "Oh, I went to Europe last year."

4. Round four: not listening. When the person is speaking, be as unattentive as possible. If they ask if you are listening, always say "yes." You must stay in your seat.

Not Listening Behaviors

Following is the list of things often done that are part of poor listening habits:

1. *Not paying attention* or being distracted.

2. *Pseudo-listening.* Pretending to be listening but thinking of other things.

3. Listening but *not really hearing.* Getting the words but not the real meaning.

4. *Rehearsing.* Going over in your mind what you will say next.

5. *Interrupting.* Not giving the other person the chance to finish.

6. *Hearing only what you expect.* Sometimes listeners think they already know the other person's position and don't really see what is being said.

7. *Defensiveness.* Expecting to be attacked and getting ready to explain your position.

8. *Listen for disagreement.* Only looking for something to argue about. **Good Listening Skills**.

Becoming conscious of the poor listening habits and working to change can help anyone become a better listener. Following is the list of good listening skills.

1. *Pay attention.* Even if the person is dull or cantankerous, make an effort to really listen for all the points.

2. *Listen for the whole message.* Look for deeper meanings in the message and for consistency with verbal and nonverbal cues.

3. *Listening before evaluating.* Ask questions to get further clarification before making up your mind what the speaker is saying.

4. *Paraphrasing.* Try to reword the message (not merely parroting back words in a different order) to avoid misinterpretations.

SOURCE: Adapted from Joe Seltzer in Marcic and Seltzer, *Organizational Behavior: Experiences and Cases* (Cincinnati: Southwestern Publishing, 1998).

ACTION LEARNING

1. Form into pairs. You will be studying organizational communications at your university (or another company, which one of you may or may not work at).

2. Go to pages 579–580 in this textbook, the section on "Formal Communication Channels," especially referring to the sections on downward communication and upward communication. Become familiar with the two lists of communication channels in both upward and downward communication.

3. Go to the university website (or the company) and find the places relevant to faculty and students. Look for examples of upward and downward communication. Write them down.

4. What is the purpose of each of these communications? What, in reality, do you expect the actual consequence of each communication to be?

5. The instructor may ask you to either bring your findings to class for a discussion or to hand in a written report.

ETHICAL DILEMMA

On Trial[104]

When Werner and Thompson, a Los Angeles business and financial management firm, offered Iranian-born Firoz Bahmania a position as an accountant assistant one spring day in 2007, Bahmani felt a sense of genuine relief, but his relief was short-lived.

With his degree in accounting from a top-notch American university, he knew he was more than a little overqualified for the job. But time after time, he'd been rejected for suitable positions. His language difficulties were the reason most often given for his unsuccessful candidacy. Although the young man had grown up speaking both Farsi and French in his native land, he'd begun to pick up English only shortly before his arrival in the United States a few years ago. Impressed by his educational credentials and his quiet, courtly manner, managing partner Beatrice Werner overlooked his heavy accent and actively recruited him for the position, the only one available at the time. During his interview, she assured him that he would advance in time.

It was clear to Beatrice that Firoz was committed to succeeding at all costs. But it soon also became apparent that Firoz and his immediate supervisor, Cathy Putnam, were at odds. Cathy was a seasoned account manager who had just transferred to Los Angeles from the New York office. Saddled with an enormous workload, she had let Firoz know right from the start, speaking in her rapid-fire Brooklyn accent, that he'd need to get up to speed as quickly as possible.

Shortly before Cathy was to give Firoz his three-month probationary review, she came to Beatrice, expressed her frustration with Firoz's performance, and suggested that he be let go. "His bank reconciliations and financial report preparations are first-rate," Cathy admitted, "but his communication skills leave a lot to be desired. In the first place, I simply don't have the time to keep repeating the same directions over and over again when I'm trying to teach him his responsibilities. Then there's the fact that public contact is part of his written job description. Typically, he puts off making phone calls to dispute credit card charges or ask a client's staff for the information he needs. When he does finally pick up the phone . . . well, let's just say I've had more than one client mention how hard it is to understand what he's trying to say. Some of them are getting pretty exasperated."

"You know, some firms feel it's their corporate responsibility to help foreign-born employees learn English," Beatrice began. "Maybe we should help him find an English-as-a-second-language course and pay for it."

"With all due respect, I don't think that's our job," Cathy replied, with barely concealed irritation. "If you come to the United States, you should learn our language. That's what my mom's parents did when they came over from Italy. They certainly didn't expect anyone to hold their hands. Besides," she added, almost inaudibly, "Firoz's lucky we let him into this country."

Beatrice had mixed feelings. On one hand, she recognized that Werner and Thompson had every right to expect someone in Firoz's position to be capable of carrying out his public contact duties. Perhaps she had made a mistake in hiring him. But as the daughter of German immigrants herself, she knew firsthand both how daunting language and cultural barriers can be and that they can be overcome in time. Perhaps in part because of her family background, she had a passionate commitment to the firm's stated goals of creating a diverse workforce and a caring, supportive

culture. Besides, she felt a personal sense of obligation to help a hard-working, promising employee realize his potential. What will she advise Cathy to do now that Firoz's probationary period is drawing to a close?

What Would You Do?

1. Agree with Cathy Putnam. Despite your personal feelings, accept that Firoz Bahmani is not capable of carrying out the accountant assistant's responsibilities. Make the break now, and give him his notice on the grounds that he cannot carry out one of the key stated job requirements. Advise him that a position that primarily involves paperwork would be a better fit for him if he doesn't improve his speaking skills.

2. Place Firoz with a more sympathetic account manager who is open to finding ways to help him improve his English and has the time to help him develop his assertiveness and telephone skills. Send Cathy Putnam to diversity awareness training.

3. Create a new position at the firm that will allow Firoz to do the reports and reconciliations for several account managers, freeing the account assistants to concentrate on public contact work. Make it clear that he will have little chance of future promotion unless his English improves markedly.

CASE FOR CRITICAL ANALYSIS

E-mail Adventure

The toy industry is highly competitive and can be as cutthroat as any pirate adventure. *Yo-ho-ho!* Snooping, corporate espionage, and efforts to keep emerging ideas under wraps are all part of life in the toy industry. A certain level of managerial paranoia is expected. But when the private e-mail of an industry CEO was discovered and began making the rounds, it unleashed a firestorm and brought disastrous results on company morale, unwanted media attention, and public embarrassment.

Howard Tannenbaum is the longtime CEO of a major toy company. Over the past few years, his

company worked to develop a new product line, called Brainchild, that all concerned believed would be a blockbuster. The passion of Tannenbaum, this new line of toys was so top secret that portions of the line were created and produced piecemeal among the various divisions. In the beginning, it was all very hush-hush. But as the line moved closer to completion, with the expected Christmas season launch date more than a year away, press and industry rumors gained momentum.

At 8:00 a.m. on a June morning, Barry Paine, Tannenbaum's attorney and longtime friend and confidante, arrived at his office, opened his e-mail, and saw a flagged message from Howard:

Barry:

We have a disaster in the making here. Looks like I'm going to have to come down hard on all of my managers. Somebody will go—perhaps several people—before this situation is over. They're obviously getting EXTREMELY slack on design security. I won't say now how I discovered the breach or what was stolen with regard to the new product designs, but suffice it to say that at this point, EVERYONE is suspect. Needless to say, I am FURIOUS! When I find out who it is—and it could be anyone—believe me, heads will roll!!! I'll call you later this morning. WE NEED TO MEET. Thanks for letting me vent. Now, I can compose the REAL e-mail to managers.

Howard

Later that same morning, managers throughout the company received the following:

TO ALL MANAGERS:

We have a situation here in which product design information on the new line, information that should have been under the HIGHEST SECURITY, has been breached. Let me make it clear that each of you is responsible for investigating your division and finding the source of the leak. Please be thorough in your investigation and be TOTALLY HONEST with me in presenting your findings in this matter. Someone will pay for this. THIS IS TOP PRIORITY!

Howard Tannenbaum, CEO

Many recipients of the e-mail felt personally attacked and threatened. Before day's end, e-mail, phone calls, and rumors were flying. By the following day, Tannenbaum felt pressured into trying to defuse the anger by issuing a second, apologetic e-mail. However, events were already spiraling out of hand, as somehow the contents of the original e-mail to Barry

Paine began circulating throughout management and beyond—to employees and at least one member of the press, who dubbed the debacle *Toy-Gate*. The perception of a CEO and a company out of control increased, and the stock price took a minor hit.

"The first e-mail left me stunned," one longtime manager said. "But when I saw the e-mail to Paine about how Howard *really* felt and the level of contempt he showed for all of us, making us *all* appear incompetent and dishonest—that, for me, is the last straw. Even if I stay, it has destroyed my relationship with Howard forever."

Now Tannenbaum sat, head in hands, in Paine's office. "Barry, I was simply trying to find the truth."

Paine walked over to a bookshelf and pulled an old, well-used volume. "Do you remember your Sophocles from school, Howard? In one Greek tragedy, Oedipus the King and his persistent search for truth in the murder of his predecessor, King Laius, followed a path that abandoned reason and led to his own undoing. My friend, in your case, it's not the search for truth, but it's the path you take—what you say, how you say it, and to whom you say it—that is important."

"OK—what do you think I should do next?"

Questions

1. What is the underlying communication mistake in this case? Why do you think Howard Tannenbaum sent those e-mails?

2. How do you think Tannenbaum should have communicated his concerns about the information link? Why?

3. What should Tannenbaum do now to try to recover from the negative impact of his e-mails? Suggest specific steps.

ON THE JOB
VIDEO CASES

Intermountain Healthcare: Managing Communication

Questions

1. Intermountain Healthcare is a very large organization with thousands of employees. List at least four methods it uses to communicate with employees. Why do you think this organization feels the need to use so many different methods to communicate?

2. In the video, Fritz Grohn says that communicating with patients as they are being released from the hospital is not always successful at first. Use this situation (a nurse discharging a patient from the hospital after a surgery or illness) to describe the communication model, and explain where the communication breaks down and why. How do Intermountain's employees overcome this problem to successfully complete the communication process with patients?

3. How is Intermountain using technology to improve internal communication? Include at least two examples described in the video in your answer.

ENDNOTES

1. Based in part on William B. Snavely and John D. McNeill, "Communicator Style and Social Style: Testing a Theoretical Interface," *Journal of Leadership and Organizational Studies* 14, no. 1 (February 2008): 219–232.

2. Anita Hofschneider, "That Thing with the Buttons and Receiver? Pick It Up," *The Wall Street Journal*, August 28, 2013, D1.

3. "Capitalizing on Effective Communication: How Courage, Innovation, and Discipline Drive Business Results in Challenging Times," Communication ROI Study Report by Watson, Wyatt, Worldwide, 2009/2010, www.towerswatson.com/DownloadMedia.aspx?media={70A3EAFB-0BDE-4359-B8FF-38FEC2E43853} (accessed September 5, 2012).

4. Henry Mintzberg, *The Nature of Managerial Work* (New York: Harper & Row, 1973).

5. Phillip G. Clampitt, Laurey Berk, and M. Lee Williams, "Leaders as Strategic Communicators," *Ivey Business Journal* (May–June 2002): 51–55.

6. A. G. Lafley and Roger Martin, "Instituting a Company-Wide Strategic Conversation at Procter & Gamble," *Strategy & Leadership* 41, no. 4 (2013): 4–9.

7. Spencer E. Ante, "IBM's Chief to Employees: Think Fast, Move Faster," *The Wall Street Journal*, April 25, 2013, B1.

8. Communication ROI Study Report.

9. Eric Berkman, "Skills," *CIO* (March 1, 2002): 78–82; Louise van der Does and Stephen J. Caldeira, "Effective Leaders Champion Communication Skills," *Nation's Restaurant News* (March 27, 2006): 20; and Byron Reimus, "Ready, Aim, Communicate," *Management Review* (July 1996): 485–503.

10. Reimus, "Ready, Aim, Communicate"; and Dennis Tourish, "Critical Upward Communication: Ten Commandments for Improving Strategy and Decision Making," *Long Range Planning* 38 (2005): 485–503.

11. AMA Enterprise, a division of American Management Association, reported in "Employees Are Clueless about What's Going on at Work," *T+D* (June 2012): 23.

12. Bernard M. Bass, *Bass & Stogdill's Handbook of Leadership*, 3rd ed. (New York: Free Press, 1990).

13. Dana Mattioli, "As Crisis Eases, CEOs Give Staff Some TLC," *The Wall Street Journal*, April 5, 2010, http://online.wsj.com/article/SB1000142405270230345070457515985064 7117086.html (accessed September 21, 2012).

14. Reported in Andrew Sobel, "Leading with Questions: Ask, Don't Tell," *Leader to Leader* (Winter 2013): 24–29.

15. Reported in van der Does and Caldeira, "Effective Leaders Champion Communication Skills."

16. Tom Szaky, "How Much Information Do You Share with Employees?" *The New York Times*, September 8, 2011, http://boss.blogs.nytimes.com/author/tom-szaky/page/2/ (accessed September 5, 2012).

17. Quint Studer, "Case for Transparency," *Leadership Excellence*, (April 2010): 19.

18. Van der Does and Caldeira, "Effective Leaders Champion Communication Skills."

19. Studer, "Case for Transparency."

20. E. M. Rogers and R. A. Rogers, *Communication in Organizations* (New York: Free Press, 1976); and A. Bavelas and D. Barrett, "An Experimental Approach to Organization Communication," *Personnel* 27 (1951): 366–371.

21. Joel Spolsky, "A Little Less Conversation," *Inc.* (February, 2010): 28–29.

22. This discussion is based on Richard L. Daft and Richard M. Steers, *Organizations: A Micro/Macro Approach* (New York: Harper Collins, 1986).

23. Richard L. Daft and Norman B. Macintosh, "A Tentative Exploration into the Amount and Equivocality of Information Processing in Organizational Work Units," *Administrative Science Quarterly* 26 (1981): 207–224.

24. Robert H. Lengel and Richard L. Daft, "The Selection of Communication Media as an Executive Skill," *Academy of Management Executive* 2 (August 1988): 225–232; Richard L. Daft and Robert H. Lengel, "Organizational Information Requirements, Media Richness, and Structural Design," *Managerial Science* 32 (May 1986): 554–572; and Jane Webster and Linda Klebe Treviño, "Rational and Social Theories as Complementary Explanations of Communication Media Choices: Two Policy-Capturing Studies," *Academy of Management Journal* 38, no. 6 (1995): 1544–1572.

25. Janina Seubert and Christina Regenbogen, "I Know How You Feel," *Scientific American Mind* (March/April 2012): 54–58.

26. Research reported in "E-mail Can't Mimic Phone Calls," *Johnson City Press*, September 17, 2000.

27. Raymond A. and Steven C. Currall, "E-Mail Escalation: Dispute Exacerbating Elements of Electronic Communication," http://papers.ssrn.com/sol3/papers.cfm?abstract_id=459429 (accessed September 21, 2010); Lauren Keller Johnson, "Does E-Mail Escalate Conflict?" *MIT Sloan Management Review* (Fall 2002): 14–15; and Alison Stein Wellner, "Lost in Translation," *Inc.* (September 2005): 37–38.

28. Margie Warrell, "Hiding Behind E-mail? Four Times You Should Never Use E-mail," *Forbes*, www.forbes.com/sites/margiewarrell/2012/08/27/do-you-hide-behind-email/ (accessed September 10, 2012).

29. Ronald E. Rice, "Task Analyzability, Use of New Media, and Effectiveness: A Multi-Site Exploration of Media Richness," *Organizational Science* 3, no. 4 (November 1992): 475–500; and M. Lynne Markus, "Electronic Mail as the Medium of Managerial Choice," *Organizational Science* 5, no. 4 (November 1994): 502–527.

30. Richard L. Daft, Robert H. Lengel, and Linda Klebe Treviño, "Message Equivocality, Media Selection and Manager Performance: Implication for Information Systems," *MIS Quarterly* 11 (1987): 355–368.

31. Mary Young and James E. Post, "Managing to Communicate, Communicating to Manage: How Leading Companies Communicate with Employees," *Organizational Dynamics* (Summer 1993): 31–43.

32. This section is based on Jay A. Conger, "The Necessary Art of Persuasion," *Harvard Business Review* (May–June 1998): 84–95.

33. Ibid.

34. Amy J. C. Cuddy, Matthew Kohut, and John Neffinger, "Connect, Then Lead," *Harvard Business Review* (July–August 2013): 3–9; and Kevin Daum, "7 Things *Really* Persuasive People Do," *Inc.com*, August 2, 2013, http://www.inc.com/kevin-daum/7-things-really-persuasive-people-do.html (accessed October 31, 2013).

35. Paul M. Leonardi, Tsedal B. Neeley, and Elizabeth M. Gerber, "How Managers Use Multiple Media: Discrepant Events, Power, and Timing in Redundant Communication," *Organization Science* 23, no. 1 (January–February 2012): 98–117.

36. This discussion is based in part on Jack Welch with Suzy Welch, *Winning* (New York: HarperBusiness, 2005), Chapter 2.

37. These are based on E. Raudsepp, "Are You Properly Assertive?" *Supervision* (June 1992); and M. J. Smith, *When I Say No, I Feel Guilty* (New York: Bantam Books, 1975).

38. Sheryl Sandberg, *Lean In: Women, Work, and the Will to Lead* (New York: Alfred A. Knopf, 2013), p. 81.

39. Halley Bock, "Fierce Communication," *T+D* (November 2012): 80.

40. Boris Groysberg and Michael Slind, "Leadership Is a Conversation," *Harvard Business Review* (June 2012): 75–84.

41. Adam Bryant, "Be Yourself, Even If You're a Little Goofy" (Corner Office column, an interview with Redfin's Glenn Kelman), *The New York Times*, August 25, 2013, BU2.

42. Many of these benefits are based on "The Power of Questions," *Leader to Leader* (Spring 2005): 59–60; Quinn Spitzer and Ron Evans, "The New Business Leader: Socrates with a Baton," *Strategy & Leadership* (September–October 1997): 32–38; and Gary B. Cohen, "Just Ask Leadership: Why Great Managers Always Ask the Right Questions," *Ivey Business Journal*, July–August 2010, www.iveybusinessjournal.com/topics/leadership/just-ask-leadership-why-great-managers-always-ask-the-right-questions (accessed March 7, 2011).

43. Groysberg and Slind, "Leadership Is a Conversation."

44. Reported in Spitzer and Evans, "The New Business Leader: Socrates with a Baton."

45. Kevin Cashman, "Powerful Pause: Listening Is Leadership," *Leadership Excellence* (January 2012): 5.

46. M. P. Nichols, *The Lost Art of Listening* (New York: Guilford Publishing, 1995).

47. "Benchmarking the Sales Function," a report based on a study of 100 salespeople from small, medium, and large businesses, conducted by the Ron Volper Group, White Plains, New York, as reported in "Nine Habits of Highly Effective Salespeople," *Inc.com*, June 1, 1997, www.inc.com/articles/1997/06/12054.html (accessed September 23, 2010).

48. Discussed in John Keyser, "Active Listening Leads to Business Success," *T+D* (July 2013): 26–28.

49. "Why I'm a Listener: Amgen CEO Kevin Sharer" (interview), *The McKinsey Quarterly*, Issue 2 (April 2012): 61–65.

50. C. Glenn Pearce, "Doing Something About Your Listening Ability," *Supervisory Management* (March 1989): 29–34; and Tom Peters, "Learning to Listen," *Hyatt Magazine* (Spring 1988): 16–21.

51. Ibid.

52. Debbie Weil, *The Corporate Blogging Book* (New York: Penguin Group, 2006), p. 3.

53. Reported in Arik Hanson, "5 Inspiring Corporate Blogs to Emulate," *Ragan.com*, April 9, 2013, http://www.ragan.com/Main/Articles/5_inspiring_corporate_blogs_to_emulate_46503.aspx (accessed October 31, 2013).

54. This discussion is based in part on Carol Kinsey Goman, "Body Language: Mastering the Silent Language of Leadership" (The Leadership Playlist column), *Washington Post Online*, July 17, 2009, http://views.washingtonpost.com/leadership/leadership_playlist/2009/07/body-language-mastering-the-silent-language-of-leadership.html (accessed July 17, 2009).

55. "Management Tip of the Day: Leaders, Stop These Behaviors Now," *Harvard Business Review*, August 30, 2013, http://hbr.org/tip/2013/08/30/leaders-stop-these-behaviors-now (accessed October 31, 2013).

56. Goman, "Body Language"; and I. Thomas Sheppard, "Silent Signals," *Supervisory Management* (March 1986): 31–33.

57. This research is reported in Carol Kinsey Goman, "10 Simple and Powerful Body Language Tips for 2013," *Forbes*, January 7, 2013, http://www.forbes.com/sites/carolkinseygoman/2013/01/07/10-simple-and-powerful-body-language-tips-for-2013/ (accessed November 4, 2013); and Sue Shellenbarger, "How 'Power Poses' Can Help Your Career," *The Wall Street Journal*, August 20, 2013, http://online.wsj.com/news/articles/SB10001424127887323608504579022942032641408 (accessed November 4, 2013).

58. Shellenbarger, "How 'Power Poses' Can Help Your Career."

59. Albert Mehrabian, *Silent Messages* (Belmont, CA: Wadsworth, 1971); and Albert Mehrabian, "Communicating Without Words," *Psychology Today* (September 1968): 53–55.

60. Meridith Levinson, "How to Be a Mind Reader," *CIO* (December 1, 2004): 72–76; Mac Fulfer, "Non-Verbal Communication: How to Read What's Plain as the Nose …," *Journal of Organizational Excellence* (Spring 2001): 19–27; and Paul Ekman, *Emotions Revealed: Recognizing Faces and Feelings to Improve Communication and Emotional Life* (New York: Time Books, 2003).

61. Andreas M. Kaplan and Michael Haenlein, "Social Media: Back to the Roots and Back to the Future," *Journal of Systems and Information Technology* 14, no. 2 (2012): 101–104.

62. Shayndi Raice, "Social Networking Heads to the Office," *The Wall Street Journal*, April 2, 2012, http://online.wsj.com/article/SB10001424052702304459804577285354046601614.html (accessed September 18, 2012).

63. Scott Martin, "Small-Business Customer Service Tools: Social Media, Surveys," *USA Today*, August 26, 2012, http://usatoday30.usatoday.com/money/smallbusiness/story/2012-08-26/efficient-small-business-online-ecommerce/57291490/1 (accessed November 1, 2013).

64. Tim Mullaney, "Social Media Is Reinventing How Business Is Done," *USA Today*, August 31, 2012, www.usatoday.com/money/economy/story/2012-05-14/social-media-economy-companies/55029088/1 (accessed September 5, 2012).

65. Ibid.

66. Geoffrey A. Fowler, "Are You Talking to Me?" *The Wall Street Journal*, April 25, 2011, http://online.wsj.com/article/SB10001424052748704116404576263083970961862.html (accessed September 18, 2012).

67. Vince Golla, interviewed by David Kiron, "Social Business at Kaiser Permanente: Using Social Tools to Improve Customer Service, Research, and Internal Collaboration," *MIT Sloan Management Review*, March 6, 2012, http://sloanreview.mit.edu/article/kaiser-permanente-using-social-tools-to-improve-customer-service-research-and-internal-collaboration/ (accessed November 1, 2013).

68. Richard S. Levick, "Domino's Discovers Social Media," *BusinessWeek*, April 21, 2009, www.businessweek.com/print/managing/content/apr2009/ca20090421_555468.htm (accessed April 21, 2009).

69. Ron Utterbeck, interviewed by Robert Berkman, "GE's Colab Brings Good Things to the Company," *MIT Sloan Management Review*, November 2012, http://sloanreview.mit.edu/article/ges-colab-brings-good-things-to-the-company/ (accessed November 1, 2013); Meenu Bhatnagar, "General Electric: Engaging Employees through Social Media," Case Study 413-103-1, Amity Research Centers, Bangalore, India, Distributed by The Case Centre, 2013; and Giselle Abramovich, "Inside General Electric's Digital Strategy" (an interview with GE's Linda Boff), *Digiday*, May 21, 2012, http://digiday.com/brands/inside-general-electrics-digital-strategy/ (accessed November 1, 2013).

70. The Tupperware example is discussed in Huy and Shipilov, "The Key to Social Media Success within Organizations."

71. Quoted in Abramovich, "Inside General Electric's Digital Strategy." The relationship between internal social media and emotional capital is in Quy Huy and Andrew Shipilov, "The Key to Social Media Success Within Organizations," *MIT Sloan Management Review* (Fall 2012), http://sloanreview.mit.edu/article/the-key-to-social-media-success-within-organizations/ (accessed November 1, 2013).

72. This discussion of informal networks is based on Rob Cross, Nitin Nohria, and Andrew Parker, "Six Myths about Informal Networks," *MIT Sloan Management Review* (Spring 2002): 67–75; and Rob Cross and Laurence Prusak, "The People Who Make Organizations Go—or Stop," *Harvard Business Review* (June 2002): 105–112.

73. Careercast.com Web site, www.careercast.com/jobs-rated/10-best-jobs-2012 (accessed September 21, 2012); George Anders, "LinkedIn's Edge: The 7 Habits of a Well-Run Social Network," *Forbes*, August 3, 2012, www.forbes.com/sites/georgeanders/2012/08/03/linkedins-edge-the-7-habits-of-a-well-run-social-network/ (accessed September 3, 2012); CNNmoney.com Web site, http://money.cnn.com/magazines/fortune/best-companies/2012/full_list/.

74. Tahl Raz, "The 10 Secrets of a Master Networker," *Inc.* (January 2003).

75. Laura Vanderkam, "What Successful People Do during Lunch," *Fast Company* July 29, 2013, http://www.fastcompany.com/3014909/how-to-be-a-success-at-everything/what-successful-people-do-during-lunch (accessed November 1, 2013).

76. Reid Hoffman and Ben Casnocha, "The Start-up of You," *Leader to Leader* (Spring 2013): 41–45. Adapted from their book, *The Start-up of You: Adapt to the Future, Invest in Yourself, and Transform Your Career* (New York: Crown Business, 2012).

77. Travis J. Grosser et al., "Hearing It through the Grapevine: Positive and Negative Workplace Gossip," *Organizational Dynamics* 41 (2012): 52–61.

78. Grant Michelson, Ad van Iterson, and Kathryn Waddington, "Gossip in Organizations: Contexts, Consequences, and Controversies," *Group & Organizational Management* 35, no. 4 (2010): 371–390.

79. Keith Davis and John W. Newstrom, *Human Behavior at Work: Organizational Behavior*, 7th ed. (New York: McGraw-Hill, 1985).

80. Suzanne M. Crampton, John W. Hodge, and Jitendra M. Mishra, "The Informal Communication Network: Factors Influencing Grapevine Activity," *Public Personnel Management* 27, no. 4 (Winter 1998): 569–584.

81. N. DiFonzo and P. Bordia, "A Tale of Two Corporations: Managing Uncertainty during Organizational Change," *Human Resource Management* 37, 3–4 (1998): 295–303.

82. Survey results reported in Jared Sandberg, "Ruthless Rumors and the Managers Who Enable Them," *The Wall Street Journal*, October 29, 2003.

83. Donald B. Simmons, "The Nature of the Organizational Grapevine," *Supervisory Management* (November 1985): 39–42; and Davis and Newstrom, *Human Behavior at Work*.

84. Barbara Ettorre, "Hellooo. Anybody Listening?" *Management Review* (November 1997): 9.

85. Eilene Zimmerman, "Gossip Is Information by Another Name," *The New York Times*, February 3, 2008, www.nytimes.com/2008/02/03/jobs/03career.html?scp=1&sq=Gossip%20Is%20Information%20by%20Another%20Name&st=cse (accessed February 3, 2008).

86. Lisa A. Burke and Jessica Morris Wise, "The Effective Care, Handling, and Pruning of the Office Grapevine," *Business Horizons* (May–June 2003): 71–74; "They Hear It through the Grapevine," cited in Michael Warshaw, "The Good Guy's Guide to Office Politics," *Fast Company* (April–May 1998): 157–178; and Carol Hildebrand, "Mapping the Invisible Workplace," *CIO Enterprise*, Section 2 (July 15, 1998): 18–20.

87. National Commission on Writing, "Writing Skills Necessary for Employment, Says Big Business," September 14, 2004, www.writingcommission.org/pr/writing_for_employ.html (accessed April 8, 2008).

88. Based on Michael Fitzgerald, "How to Write a Memorable Memo," *CIO* (October 15, 2005): 85–87; and Jonathan Hershberg, "It's Not Just What You Say," *Training* (May 2005): 50.

89. Mary Anne Donovan, "E-Mail Exposes the Literacy Gap," *Workforce* (November 2002): 15.

90. Daft and Steers, *Organizations*; and Daniel Katz and Robert Kahn, *The Social Psychology of Organizations*, 2nd ed. (New York: Wiley, 1978).

91. Mullaney, "Social Media Is Reinventing How Business Is Done."

92. Phillip G. Clampitt, Robert J. DeKoch, and Thomas Cashman, "A Strategy for Communicating about Uncertainty," *Academy of Management Executive* 14, no. 4 (2000): 41–57.

93. Alexandra Samuel, "Better Leadership through Social Media," *The Wall Street Journal*, April 2, 2012, http://online.wsj.com/article/SB10001424052970203753704577255531558650636.html (accessed September 12, 2012).

94. Reported in van der Does and Caldeira, "Effective Leaders Champion Communication Skills."

95. Michael J. Glauser, "Upward Information Flow in Organizations: Review and Conceptual Analysis," *Human Relations* 37 (1984): 613–643; and "Upward/Downward Communication: Critical Information Channels," *Small Business Report* (October 1985): 85–88.

96. Darren Dahl, "Pipe up, People! Rounding up Staff," *Inc.* (February 2010): 80–81.

97. Thomas Petzinger, "A Hospital Applies Teamwork to Thwart an Insidious Enemy," *The Wall Street Journal*, May 8, 1998.

98. Danny Hakim, Patrick McGeehan, and Michael Moss, "Suffering on L.I. as Power Agency Shows Its Flaws," *The New York Times*, November 14, 2012, A1.

99. Stacy Meichtry, Arian Camp-Flores, and Leslie Scism, "Cruise Company Blames Captain," *The Wall Street Journal*, January 17, 2012, http://online.wsj.com/article/SB10001424052970203735304577165290656739300.html (accessed September 19, 2012).

100. This section is based on Leslie Wayne and Leslie Kaufman, "Leadership, Put to a New Test," *The New York Times*, September 16, 2001; Ian I. Mitroff, "Crisis Leadership," *Executive Excellence* (August 2001): 19; Jerry Useem, "What It Takes," *Fortune* (November 12, 2001): 126–132; Andy Bowen, "Crisis Procedures That Stand the Test of Time," *Public Relations Tactics* (August 2001): 16; and Matthew Boyle, "Nothing Really Matters," *Fortune* (October 15, 2001): 261–264.

101. Stephen Bernhut, "Leadership, with Michael Useem" (interview), *Ivey Business Journal* (January–February 2002): 42–43.

102. Mitroff, "Crisis Leadership."

103. J. C. McCroskey, "Measures of Communication-Bound Anxiety," *Speech Monographs* 37 (1970): 269–277; J. C. McCroskey and V. P. Richmond, "Validity of the PRCA as an Index of Oral Communication Apprehension," *Communication Monographs* 45 (1978): 192–203; J. C. McCroskey and V. P. Richmond, "The Impact of Communication Apprehension on Individuals in Organizations," *Communication Quarterly* 27 (1979): 55–61; and J. C. McCroskey, *An Introduction to Rhetorical Communication* (Englewood Cliffs, NJ: Prentice Hall, 1982).

104. Mary Gillis, "Iranian Americans," *Multicultural America*, www.everyculture.com/multi/Ha-La/Iranian-Americans.html (accessed September 19, 2006); and Charlene Marmer Solomon, "Managing Today's Immigrants," *Personnel Journal* 72, no. 3 (February 1993): 56–65.

CHAPTER

14 Leading Teams

CHAPTER OUTLINE

LEARNING OUTCOMES

After studying this chapter, you should be able to:

14.1 Explain contributions that teams make and how managers can make teams more effective.

14.2 Identify the types of teams in organizations.

14.3 Summarize some of the problems and challenges of teamwork.

14.4 Identify ways in which team size and diversity of membership affect team performance.

14.5 Identify roles within teams and the type of role that you could play to help a team be effective.

14.6 Explain the general stages of team development.

14.7 Explain the concepts of team cohesiveness and team norms and their relationship to team performance.

14.8 Identify the causes of conflict within and among teams and explain how to reduce conflict.

14.9 Describe the different characteristics and consequences of task conflict versus relationship conflict.

●●●●○ 🛜   100% ▰

‹ Messages

R U Ready 2 B a Manager?

Delivered

Before reading this chapter, please circle either "Mostly True" or "Mostly False" for each of the five questions below.

1 I am energized when I work in a productive team.

| Mostly True | Mostly False |

[page 598]

2 I find it difficult to have honest discussions with "free riders" on my team.

| Mostly True | Mostly False |

[page 604]

3 I work to create accountability, because I know its lack is hazardous to effective teams.

| Mostly True | Mostly False |

[page 605]

4 When I join a new team, I spend time observing the norms of this group before I take any actions or make comments.

| Mostly True | Mostly False |

[page 615]

5 I know that some conflict is good in a team, to prevent "groupthink," and I am able to help resolve conflicts by assertively and collaboratively addressing the issues.

| Mostly True | Mostly False |

[page 620]

What went wrong aboard Asiana Flight 214? The Boeing 777 crashed at San Francisco International Airport on July 6, 2013, killing three passengers and injuring many more. The pilots and the airline have said that a key device that controlled the aircraft's speed might have malfunctioned. Others suggest that it might have been pilot error. National Transportation Safety Board (NTSB) investigators are still sorting out what happened. Nevertheless, it remains true that airline accidents are far fewer and far less deadly today than they were decades ago. Part of that comes from better engineering, but part of it also comes from better teamwork, says Patrick Smith, a commercial pilot who writes a blog called "Ask the Pilot" and recently wrote a book titled *Cockpit Confidential: Everything You Need to Know About Air Travel: Questions, Answers, and Reflections*. "You no longer have

NEW MANAGER Self-Test

How Do You like to Work?[1]

Instructions: Your approach to your job or schoolwork may indicate whether you thrive on a team. Answer the questions that follow about your work preferences. Please answer whether each item in the following list is Mostly True or Mostly False for you.

	Mostly True	Mostly False
1. I prefer to work on a team rather than do individual tasks.		
2. Given a choice, I try to work by myself rather than face the hassles of group work.		
3. I enjoy the personal interaction when working with others.		
4. I prefer to do my own work and let others do theirs.		
5. I get more satisfaction from a group victory than an individual victory.		
6. Teamwork is not worthwhile when people do not do their share.		
7. I feel good when I work with others, even when we disagree.		
8. I prefer to rely on myself rather than others to do an assignment.		

Scoring and Interpretation: Give yourself one point for each odd-numbered item that you marked Mostly True and one point for each even-numbered item that you marked Mostly False. As a new manager, you will be both part of a team and work alone. These items measure your preference for group work. Teamwork can be both frustrating and motivating. If you scored 2 or fewer, you definitely prefer individual work. A score of 7 or more suggests that you prefer working in teams. A score of 3–6 indicates comfort working alone and in a team. A new manager needs to do both.

that strict hierarchical culture in the cockpit, where the captain was king and everyone blindly followed his orders," Smith says. Crew training today for most airlines is team-oriented, with everyone working together to ensure safety. Pilots don't rely just on their own instincts and abilities; instead, they draw knowledge from the cabin crew, people on the ground, dispatchers, meteorologists, and others.[2] Perhaps the most awe-inspiring example of flawless teamwork in the airline industry was the landing of U.S. Airways Flight 1549 on the Hudson River in January 2009. Captain Chesley "Sully" Sullenberger says that he knew he wanted to be a pilot at the age of five, and he spent the rest of his life in the pursuit of excellence in his chosen field. After 40 years of pursuing excellence, there couldn't have been anyone better prepared to be in control. Yet Sullenberger's passion for learning also meant that he was a proponent of continuous training for every member of a flight crew, and he instilled in his crew members a commitment to teamwork and safety. Sullenberger gave credit to every member of the team for the safe landing of Flight 1549.[3]

Many people get their first management experience in a team setting, and you probably will have to work on a team sometimes as a new manager. Many companies have discovered that teams have real advantages, but it can be tough to work in a team. You may have already experienced the challenges of teamwork as a student, where you've had to give up some of your independence and rely on a team to perform well in order to earn a good grade.

Good teams can produce amazing results, but teams aren't always successful. In a survey of manufacturing organizations, about 80 percent of respondents reported using some kind of team, but only 14 percent of those companies rated their teaming efforts as highly effective. Just over half of the respondents said their efforts were only "somewhat effective," and 15 percent considered their efforts not effective at all.[4]

This chapter focuses on teams and their applications within organizations. We define what a team is, look at the contributions that teams can make, and define various types of teams. Then we discuss the dilemma of teamwork and present a model of work team effectiveness, explore the stages of team development, and examine how characteristics such as size, cohesiveness, diversity, and norms influence team effectiveness. The chapter also looks at the roles that individuals play on teams, discusses techniques for managing team conflict, and describes how negotiation can facilitate cooperation and teamwork. Teams are a central aspect of organizational life, and the ability to manage them is a vital component of manager and organization success.

14.1 The Value of Teams

Why aren't organizations just collections of individuals going their own way and doing their own thing? Clearly, teamwork provides benefits or companies wouldn't continue to use this structural mechanism. One illustration of the value of teamwork comes from the military, where forward surgical teams made up of U.S. Navy surgeons, nurses, anesthesiologists, and technicians operated for the first time ever in combat during Operation Iraqi Freedom. These teams were scattered over Iraq and were able to move to new locations and be set up within an hour. With a goal of saving the lives of the 15–20 percent of wounded soldiers and civilians who would die unless they received critical care within 24 hours, members of these teams smoothly coordinated their activities to accomplish a vital shared mission.[5]

Although their missions might not involve life or death, all organizations are made of various individuals and groups that have to work together and coordinate their activities to accomplish objectives. Much work in organizations is *interdependent*, which means that individuals and departments rely on other individuals and departments for information or resources to accomplish their work. When tasks are highly interdependent, a team can be the best approach to ensuring the level of coordination, information sharing, and exchange of materials necessary for successful task accomplishment.

14.1a What Is a Team?

A **team** is a unit of two or more people who interact and coordinate their work to accomplish a common goal to which they are committed and hold themselves mutually accountable.[6] The definition of a team has three components. First, two or more people are required. Second, people in a team interact regularly. People who do not interact (for example, people standing in line at a lunch counter or riding in an elevator) do not compose a team. Third, people in a team share a performance goal, whether it is to design a new tablet, build an engine, or complete a class project.

Putting together a *team* and building *teamwork* aren't the same thing, as the coach of the Miami Heat basketball team learned. In the spring of 2010, LeBron James, Dwyane Wade, and Chris Bosh were the top scorers on their respective basketball teams. The next year, they were all playing for the Miami Heat. With that kind of talent, the team should have been tough for anyone to beat, but the Heat opened with a humiliating loss and stumbled through the early weeks of the season. Star players who were used to being in charge at crunch time found themselves working at cross purposes. Discussing the Heat's loss to the New York Knicks, former Chicago Bulls player Steve Kerr said, "It was a total meltdown. It was, 'I'm so talented, I'll take over.' They looked awful."[7]

Individual stars don't necessarily make a great team, in sports or in business. The Heat turned things around by incorporating the elements of effective teamwork, as shown in Exhibit 14.1. Teamwork requires bringing together the right set of personalities, specialties, and skills; clearly defining roles and responsibilities; focusing everyone on a well-defined mission; establishing clear channels of communication and information sharing so that team members communicate their objectives and needs in all directions; and getting everyone to sublimate their individual egos and pull together in the same direction. Trust is a

Green Power

The Team's the Thing

Managers at **Subaru Indiana Automotive (SIA)** put the company's desire to reduce, reuse, and recycle waste squarely on the line with television ads boasting "zero-landfill." SIA was not hedging, maintaining that "zero means zero," and managers placed confidence in every member of every team in every manufacturing process to hit the target. And the teams proved to be up to the challenge. For example, shop floor initiatives within the stamping unit led to partnering agreements with suppliers for more precise steel sheeting that reduced 100 pounds of steel per vehicle. Teams initiated efforts to use plant water flow to drive mini-hydraulic electric generators, and the company's Green Payback Curve recycled a variety of waste products. Assembly-line lights were turned down during breaks and shift changes to decrease the company's carbon footprint. Respect for and confidence in its teams has made SIA a recognized leader of sustainability in manufacturing.

SOURCES: Brad Kenney, "The Zero Effect: How to Green Your Facility," *Industry Week* (July 2008): 36–41; and Dean M. Schroeder and Alan G. Robinson, "Green Is Free: Creating Sustainable Competitive Advantage Through Green Excellence," *Organizational Dynamics* 39, no. 4 (2010): 345–352.

EXHIBIT 14.1   Requirements of Teamwork

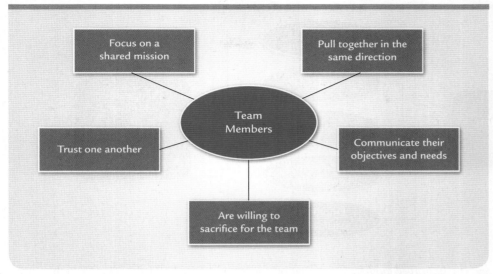

Focus on a shared mission

Pull together in the same direction

Team Members

Trust one another

Communicate their objectives and needs

Are willing to sacrifice for the team

SOURCES: Based on Rick Wartzman, "Microsoft's New Mission: To Create Real Teamwork, Not Just Teams," *Time*, July 17, 2013, http://business.time.com/2013/07/17/microsofts-new-mission-to-create-real-teamwork-not-just-teams/ (accessed July 19, 2013); and Chuck Salter, "What LeBron James and the Miami Heat Teach Us About Teamwork," *Fast Company*, April 2011, http://www.fastcompany.com/magazine/155/the-worlds-greatest-chemistry-experiment.html (accessed April 25, 2011).

crucial aspect of teamwork. People have to be willing to collaborate and sometimes sacrifice their individual objectives for the sake of the larger goal, which requires that they believe that others are willing to do the same thing.

David Novak, CEO of Yum Brands (including KFC, Pizza Hut, and Taco Bell), has built the world's largest restaurant company based on teamwork. Since Yum was spun off from PepsiCo in 1997, its stock has returned 16.5 percent compounded annually, versus the S&P 500's 3.9 percent over that same period. When he was first put in charge of running KFC, the U.S. division hadn't met its profit target for ages. Headquarters blamed the franchisees; the franchisees blamed headquarters. Novak embarked on a team-building crusade that is still going on today. KFC resumed growing, and its profits nearly doubled in three years. "What really made the difference," Novak says, "was the idea that if we trusted each other, we could work together to make something happen that was bigger than our individual capabilities."[8]

> *"Individual commitment to a group effort—that is what makes a team work, a company work, a society work, a civilization work."*
>
> —Vince Lombardi (1913–1970), NFL football coach

14.1b Contributions of Teams

Effective teams can provide many advantages, as illustrated in Exhibit 14.2. These contributions of teams lead to stronger competitive advantage and higher overall organizational performance.

- *Creativity and innovation:* Because teams include people with diverse skills, strengths, experiences, and perspectives, they contribute to a higher level of creativity and innovation in the organization.[9] One factor that has been overlooked in the success of Apple, for instance, is that Steve Jobs built a top management team of superb technologists, marketers, designers, and others who kept the company's innovative juices flowing. Most of Jobs's top management team worked with him for a decade or more.[10]

EXHIBIT 14.2   Five Contributions Teams Make

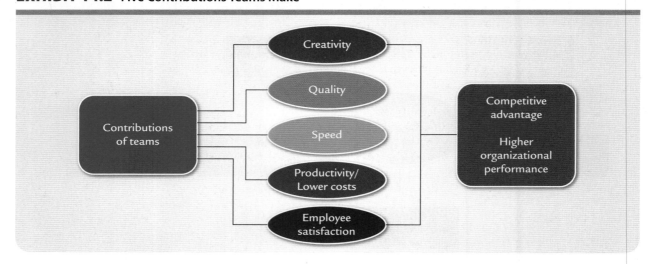

- **Improved quality:** One criterion for organizational effectiveness is whether products and services meet customer requirements for quality. Perhaps nowhere is this more essential than in health care. The days when a lone physician could master all the skills, keep all the information in his or her head, and manage everything required to treat a patient are long gone. Organizations that provide the highest quality of patient care are those in which teams of closely coordinated professionals provide an integrated system of care.[11]

- **Speed of response:** Tightly integrated teams can maneuver incredibly fast. Apple again provides an example. Apple's close-knit team has changed pricing as late as 48 hours before the launch of a new product, which would be inconceivable at most companies.[12] In addition, teams can speed product development (as we discussed in Chapter 7), respond more quickly to changing customer needs, and solve cross-departmental problems more quickly.

A self-organizing team of Toys R Us customers forced the company into a speedy response, as shown in this chapter's Business Blooper.

Business Blooper

Toys R Us and Breaking Bad Dolls

Toys R Us came out with a new action figure. In 2014, it introduced "Breaking Bad" dolls, including a bag of meth and a detachable sack of cash, and it had these figures next to children's toys. Public reaction was swift, and here's where teams played a role. A Florida woman became "team leader" and started a petition that quickly got 9,000 signatures. Social media went crazy. But then Aaron Paul—who played the drug maker and dealer, Jesse, on the show, fought back and wondered why Toys R Us wasn't also considering taking Barbie off the shelves. "Why can you sell guns and not Walt and Jesse?" he asked. Paul backed a counterpetition started by a California man to keep the action figures and he got 30,000 signatures.

Toys R Us responded by pulling the Breaking Bad dolls. A company spokesman said, "let's just say, the action figures have taken an 'indefinite sabbatical.'" Dr. Patrali Chatterjee of Monclair State University said the company made the right decision, that they had to figure out who were the most important stakeholders. "The company decided that parents of young kids are very important to them—they cannot afford to antagonize their core customer group."

SOURCE: Meg Fry, Toys R Us in Social Media Uproar, NJBIZ, Nov. 3, 2014, p. 3.

- *Higher productivity and lower costs:* Effective teams can unleash enormous energy from employees. **Social facilitation** refers to the tendency for the presence of others to enhance one's performance. Simply being around others has an energizing effect.[13] In addition, the blend of perspectives enables creative ideas to percolate. At Boeing, innovation teams made up of engineers, mechanics, and other workers have come up with time-saving ideas that have boosted production of the 737 jet to 35 a month (up from 31), and the goal is to be producing 42 a month by the end of 2014.[14]

- *Enhanced motivation and satisfaction:* As described in Chapter 12, people have needs for belongingness and affiliation. Working in teams can meet these needs and create greater camaraderie across the organization. Teams also reduce boredom, increase people's feelings of dignity and self-worth, and give people a chance to develop new skills. Individuals who work in an effective team cope better with stress, enjoy their jobs more, and have a higher level of motivation and commitment to the organization.

14.1c Types of Teams

Organizations use many types of teams to achieve the advantages discussed in the previous section. Two common types of teams in organizations are functional and cross-functional, as illustrated in Exhibit 14.3. Organizations also use self-managed teams to increase employee participation.

Functional Teams   A **functional team** is composed of a manager and his or her subordinates in the formal chain of command. Sometimes called a *command team,* the functional team in some cases may include three or four levels of hierarchy within a functional department. Typically, the team includes a single department in an organization. A financial

EXHIBIT 14.3 **Functional and Cross-Functional Teams in an Organization**

President

Project control   Finance   Engineering   Production   Marketing

- - - - Cross-functional team for L21 modification project
——— Functional engineering team

analysis department, a quality control department, an engineering department, and a human resource department are all functional teams. Each is created by the organization to attain specific goals through members' joint activities and interactions.

Cross-Functional Teams   A **cross-functional team** is composed of employees from about the same hierarchical level, but from different areas of expertise. One type of cross-functional team is a *task force*, which is a group of employees from different departments formed to deal with a specific activity and existing only until the task is completed. For example, an aerospace company created a task force to solve the problem of an unexpected loss of key parts needed to keep aircraft assembly going.

The Critical Path Part Team at Southwestern Aerospace illustrates many of the advantages of teams discussed previously—particularly innovation and speed. Another type of cross-functional team, the *special-purpose team*, is created outside the formal organization structure to undertake a project of special importance or creativity.[15] Sometimes called a *project team*, a special-purpose team still is part of the formal organization structure, but members perceive themselves as a separate entity. Special-purpose teams are often created for developing a new product or service. In 2008, Ford Motor Company created a special-purpose team to solve a problem that could determine whether the organization survived the turmoil in the automotive industry. Managers knew that without parts, nothing else that they could do to save the company would matter. With many of the industry's suppliers on the brink of bankruptcy, Tony Brown, Ford's vice president of global purchasing, suggested creating a special-purpose team to monitor parts manufacturers, prevent supply chain disruptions, and speed up Ford's plan to narrow its base of suppliers. CEO Alan Mulally quickly agreed, and Project Quark (named after the family dog in the movie

Spotlight on Skills

Southwestern Aerospace Inc.

Southwestern Aerospace Inc. (not the company's real name) got some of the worst news that a manufacturer can get—one of the aluminum heat-treat suppliers had lost its lease and would soon be shutting down. The loss of this specialized heat-treat capacity was devastating because there was no equivalent in the region. The bottom line was that Southwestern would soon be faced with running out of the parts it needed to continue manufacturing aircraft.

Southwestern's response was to form a cross-functional task force called the Critical Path Part Team, made up of 12 subject matter experts from across the company and its suppliers. The team identified 18 parts that would be affected by the closing of the aluminum heat-treat supplier and determined that 14 of them could be acquired from another local supplier. The team's challenge was to find manufacturing capacity for the remaining four parts—fuselage skins—that were crucial for aircraft assembly.

During creative brainstorming sessions, team members generated spontaneous ideas and eventually came up with six options for solving the problem, to be evaluated based on cost, time, and feasibility. Quick action was essential, as was maintaining the confidence of customers, who were kept informed of progress throughout the team's work. The project was technically challenging, and the team members were geographically separated across three states. The team overcame the geographic obstacle by establishing a comprehensive communications plan. Management then approved a plan to test the feasibility of Option 6 (redesigning the existing process), which was one of the most technologically challenging but most economical options. In the end, thanks to superb cross-functional teamwork, Southwestern implemented a program that ensured that production was maintained and all financial and quality objectives were met. The team responsible for meeting this massive challenge was honored with an International Team Excellence silver-level award from the American Society for Quality in 2011.[16]

Honey, I Shrunk the Kids) came into being. The team included people from all of Ford's divisions and functional departments—manufacturing, human resources (HR), engineering, finance, information technology (IT), legal, and others. The team created a risk profile for each supplier, and the team narrowed the list to 850 critical suppliers that Ford wanted to keep. Making sure that these companies survived was Project Quark's top priority.[17] This special-purpose team played a critical role in helping Ford prevent a supply breakdown—and ultimately in helping Alan Mulally and other managers revive the company.

Self-Managed Teams   The third common type of team used in organizations is designed to increase the participation of workers in decision making and the conduct of their jobs, with the goal of improving performance. **Self-managed teams** typically consist of five to 20 multiskilled workers who rotate jobs to produce an entire product or service or at least one complete aspect or portion of a product or service (e.g., engine assembly or insurance claim processing). At the Chicago-based software firm 37Signals, for example, customer service is run by a self-managed team that handles everything associated with providing service and support. Customer service, support, and satisfaction have improved since the company started using a self-managed team. "We've measured the difference, and we know it works," says cofounder Jason Fried. Today, 37Signals is run almost entirely by self-managed teams.[18]

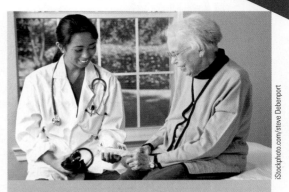

CONCEPT CONNECTION   In recent years, hundreds of hospitals have been forming palliative care **teams** to address the unique needs of patients with terminal illnesses. These teams consist of doctors, nurses, social workers, and various types of spiritual advisors, who work together to treat each patient holistically—physically, mentally, emotionally, and spiritually. Dr. Diane Meier, a leader in the palliative care trend, notes, "Patients [typically] see a different person for every single part of their body or every problem. The patient as a whole person gets lost." Hospitals are adopting these teams because they improve the quality of care provided to patients just when they need it most.

Self-managed teams are related to the trend toward the boss-less organization. The central idea is that the teams themselves, rather than managers or supervisors, take responsibility for their work, make decisions, monitor their own performance, and alter their work behavior as needed to solve problems, meet goals, and adapt to changing conditions.[19] At Ciplex, a Web design and marketing company, founder Ilya Pozin did away with all the bosses and reorganized the whole company into self-managed teams who have full freedom to accomplish their goals. Pozin says that employees are happier and more productive since he smashed the hierarchy.[20]

A self-managed team is a permanent team that typically includes the following elements:

- The team includes employees with several skills and functions, and its combined skills are sufficient to perform a major organizational task. For example, in a manufacturing plant, a team may include members from the foundry, machining, grinding, fabrication, and sales departments, with members cross-trained to perform one another's jobs. The team eliminates barriers among departments, enabling excellent coordination to produce a product or service.

- The team is given access to the resources, such as information, equipment, machinery, and supplies, needed to perform the complete task.

- The team is empowered with decision-making authority, which means that members have the freedom to select new members, solve problems, spend money, monitor results, and plan for the future. Self-managed teams can enable employees to feel challenged, find their work meaningful, and develop a stronger sense of identity with the organization.

REMEMBER THIS

- A **team** is a unit of two or more people who interact and coordinate their work to accomplish a goal to which they are committed and hold themselves mutually accountable.

- Organizations as diverse as Ford Motor Company, Apple, and the U.S. Navy use teams to perform tasks that are highly interdependent and require a high level of coordination.

- Teams provide distinct advantages in the areas of innovation, quality, speed, productivity, and employee satisfaction.

- **Social facilitation** is the tendency for the presence of other people to influence an individual's motivation and performance.

- A **functional team** is composed of a manager and his or her subordinates in the formal chain of command.

- A **cross-functional team** is made up of employees from about the same hierarchical level, but from different areas of expertise.

- Cross-functional teams include task forces and special-purpose teams.

- A task force is a group of employees from different departments who deal with a specific activity and exist as a team only until the task is completed.

- A **special-purpose team** is a team created outside the formal structure to undertake a project of special importance, such as developing a new product.

- A **self-managed team** consists of multiskilled employees who rotate jobs to produce an entire product or service, often led by an elected team member.

- Self-managed teams are related to the trend toward bosslessness because team members take responsibility for their work, make decisions, monitor their own performance, and alter their work behavior as needed to solve problems and meet goals.

14.2 The Personal Dilemma of Teamwork

When David Ferrucci was trying to recruit scientists to participate on a team at IBM to build a computer smart enough to beat grand champions at the game of *Jeopardy!*, he learned firsthand that teamwork presents a dilemma for many people. To be sure, building "Watson" was an unusual project, and its results would be put to the test in a televised "human versus machine" competition. If it failed, it would be a public fiasco that would hurt the credibility of everyone involved. And if it succeeded, the hero would be the team, not any individual team member. Many of the scientists that Ferrucci approached preferred to work on their individual projects, where the success would be theirs alone. Eventually, however, he pulled together a core team of people willing to take the risk. "It was a proud moment, frankly, just to have the courage as a team to move forward," Ferrucci says.[21] In organizations all over the world, some people love the idea of teamwork, others hate it, and many people have both positive and negative emotions about being part of a team. There are three primary reasons that teams present a dilemma for many people:

- *We have to give up our independence.* When people become part of a team, their success depends on the team's success; therefore, they must depend on how well other people perform, not just on their own individual initiative and actions. Most people are comfortable with the idea of making sacrifices to achieve their own individual success, yet teamwork demands that they make sacrifices for *group* success.[22] The idea is that each person should put the team first, even if it hurts the individual at times. A recent study suggests that Americans have become increasingly focused on the individual over the group since 1960, reflecting "a sea change in American culture toward more individualism."[23] Some cultures, such as Japan, have had greater success with teams because traditional Japanese culture values the group over the individual.

- *We have to put up with free riders.* Teams are sometimes made up of people who have different work ethics. The term **free rider** refers to a team member who attains benefits from team membership but does not actively participate in and contribute to the team's work. You might have experienced this frustration in a student project team, where one member put little effort into the group project but benefited from the hard work of others when grades were handed out. Free riding is sometimes called *social loafing* because some members do not exert equal effort.[24]

- *Teams are sometimes dysfunctional.* Some companies have had great success with teams, but there are also numerous examples of how teams in organizations fail spectacularly.[25] "The best groups will be better than their individual members, and the worst groups will be worse than the worst individual," says organizational psychologist Robert Sutton.[26] A great deal of research and team experience over the past few decades has produced significant insights into what causes teams to succeed or fail. The evidence shows that the way teams are managed plays the most critical role in determining how well they function.[27] Exhibit 14.4 lists five dysfunctions that are common in teams and describes the contrasting desirable characteristics that effective team leaders develop.

The "Action Learning" on page 626 gives you a chance to evaluate and discuss various team member behaviors.

EXHIBIT 14.4 Five Common Dysfunctions of Teams

Dysfunction	Effective Team Characteristics
Lack of trust—People don't feel safe to reveal mistakes, share concerns, or express ideas.	**Trust**—Members trust one another on a deep emotional level; feel comfortable being vulnerable with one another.
Fear of conflict—People go along with others for the sake of harmony; don't express conflicting opinions.	**Healthy conflict**—Members feel comfortable disagreeing and challenging one another in the interest of finding the best solution.
Lack of commitment—If people are afraid to express their true opinions, it's difficult to gain their true commitment to decisions.	**Commitment**—Because all ideas are put on the table, people can achieve genuine buy-in around important goals and decisions.
Avoidance of accountability—People don't accept responsibility for outcomes; engage in finger-pointing when things go wrong.	**Accountability**—Members hold one another accountable rather than relying on managers as the source of accountability.
Inattention to results—Members put personal ambition or the needs of their individual departments ahead of collective results.	**Results orientation**—Individual members set aside personal agendas; focus on what's best for the team. Collective results define success.

SOURCES: Based on Patrick Lencioni, *The Five Dysfunctions of a Team* (New York: John Wiley & Sons, 2002); and P. Lencioni, "Dissolve Dysfunction: Begin Building Your Dream Team," *Leadership Excellence* (October 2009): 20.

REMEMBER THIS

- Teams present a dilemma for most people because individual success depends on how well others perform, there are common dysfunctions that afflict teams, and there is a potential for free riders.

- A **free rider** is a person who benefits from team membership but does not make a proportionate contribution to the team's work.

- Five common dysfunctions of teams are lack of trust, fear of conflict, lack of commitment, avoidance of accountability, and inattention to results.

14.3 Model of Team Effectiveness

Smoothly functioning teams don't just happen. Stanford sociologist Elizabeth Cohen studied group work among young schoolchildren and found that only when teachers took the time to define roles, establish norms, and set goals did the groups function effectively as a team.[28] In organizations, effective teams are built by managers who take specific actions to help people come together and perform well as a team.

Some of the factors associated with team effectiveness are illustrated in Exhibit 14.5. Work team effectiveness is based on three outcomes—productive output, personal satisfaction, and the capacity to adapt and learn.[29] *Satisfaction* pertains to the team's ability to meet the personal needs of its members, and hence maintain their membership and commitment. *Productive output* pertains to performance and the quality and quantity of task outputs as defined by team goals. *Capacity to adapt and learn* refers to the ability of teams to bring greater knowledge and skills to job tasks and enhance the potential of the organization to respond to new threats or opportunities in the environment.

The model of team effectiveness in Exhibit 14.5 provides a structure for this chapter. The factors that influence team effectiveness begin with the organizational context.[30] The

EXHIBIT 14.5 Work Team Effectiveness Model

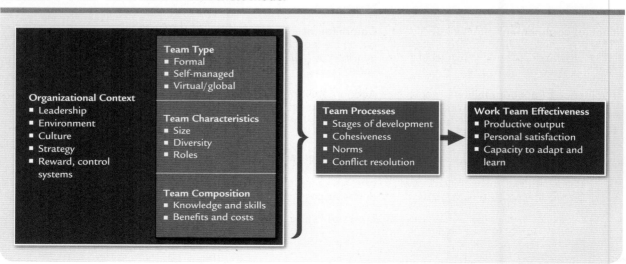

organizational context in which the team operates is described throughout this book and includes such matters as overall leadership, strategy, environment, culture, and systems for controlling and rewarding employees. Within that context, managers define teams. Important team characteristics are the type of team and team composition. Managers must decide when to create permanent self-managed teams and when to use a temporary task force or special-purpose team. The diversity of the team in terms of task-related knowledge and skills can have a tremendous impact on team processes and effectiveness. In addition, diversity in terms of gender and race affects a team's performance.[31] Team size and roles also are important.

These team characteristics influence processes that are internal to the team, which, in turn, affect output, satisfaction, and the team's contribution to organizational adaptability. Good team leaders understand and manage stages of team development, cohesiveness, norms, and conflict to build an effective team. These processes are influenced by team and organizational characteristics and by the ability of members and leaders to direct these processes in a positive manner. Another requirement of the team leader is to know how to run a good meeting. The "Director's Toolkit" gives some tips for running a dynamic, productive meeting.

Go to the "Self-Learning" on page 626, which pertains to effective versus ineffective teams.

14.4 Virtual Teams

An exciting new approach to teamwork has resulted from advances in IT, shifting employee expectations, and the globalization of business. A **virtual team** is a group made up of geographically or organizationally dispersed members who are linked primarily through advanced information and telecommunications technologies.[32] A virtual team can be local, national, or global, with members coming from one firm or many.

A survey of employees at multinational corporations found that 80 percent of respondents belong to virtual teams.[33] In a virtual team, members use groupware, e-mail, instant messaging, telephone and text messaging, wikis and blogs, videoconferencing, and other technology tools to collaborate and perform their work, although they also might meet face to face at times. Although some virtual teams are made up of only organizational members, virtual teams often include contingent workers, members of partner organizations, customers, suppliers, consultants, or other outsiders. Many virtual teams are also global teams. A **global team** is a cross-border team made up of members of different nationalities whose activities span multiple countries.[34]

One of the primary advantages of virtual teams is the ability to assemble the most talented group of people to complete a complex project, solve a particular problem, or exploit a specific strategic opportunity. The diverse mix of people can fuel creativity and innovation. On a practical level, organizations can save employees time and cut travel expenses when people meet in virtual rather than physical space. IBM reported that it saved more than $50 million in travel-related expenses in one recent year by using virtual teams.[35]

However, virtual teams also present unique challenges, particularly in terms of building rapport and trust. Exhibit 14.6 lists some critical areas that managers should address when leading virtual teams. Each of these areas is discussed in more detail in the following list:[36]

Mark Leong/Redux

 CONCEPT CONNECTION   To update Lotus Symphony, a package of PC software applications, IBM assigned the project to teams in Beijing, China; Austin, Texas; Raleigh, North Carolina; and Böblingen, Germany. Leading the project, the Beijing group—shown here with Michael Karasick (center), who runs the Beijing lab, and lead developer Yue Ma (right)—navigated the **global team** through the programming challenges. To help bridge the distance gap, IBM uses Beehive, a corporate social network similar to Facebook, where employees create profiles, list their interests, and post photos.

EXHIBIT 14.6 What Effective Virtual Team Leaders Do

Practice	How It's Done
Use virtual technology to build relationships	• Bring attention to and appreciate diverse skills and opinions. • Use technology to enhance communication and trust. • Ensure timely responses online. • Manage online socialization.
Shape culture through virtual technology	• Create a psychologically safe virtual culture. • Share members' special experience and strengths. • Engage members from cultures that may discourage people from sharing their ideas.
Monitor progress and rewards	• Scrutinize electronic communication patterns. • Post targets and scorecards in virtual work space. • Reward people through online ceremonies and recognition.

SOURCES: Based on Table 1, "Practices of Effective Virtual Team Leaders," in Arvind Malhotra, Ann Majchrzak, and Benson Rosen, "Leading Virtual Teams," *Academy of Management Perspectives* 21, no. 1 (February 2007): 60–69; and Table 2, "'Best Practices' Solutions for Overcoming Barriers to Knowledge Sharing in Virtual Teams," in Benson Rosen, Stacie Furst, and Richard Blackburn, "Overcoming Barriers to Knowledge Sharing in Virtual Teams," *Organizational Dynamics* 36, no. 3 (2007): 259–273.

• ***Use virtual technology to build trust and relationships for effective teamwork.*** Leaders first select people who have the right mix of technical, interpersonal, and communication skills to work in a virtual environment, and then make sure that they have opportunities to know one another and establish trusting relationships. Encouraging online social networking, where people can share photos and personal biographies, is one key to virtual team success. One study suggests that higher levels of online communication increase team cohesiveness and trust.[37] Leaders also build trust by making everyone's roles, responsibilities, and authority clear from the beginning, by shaping norms of full disclosure and respectful interaction, and by providing a way for everyone to stay up to date. In a study of which technologies make virtual teams successful, researchers found that round-the-clock virtual workspaces, where team members can access the latest versions of files, keep track of deadlines and timelines, monitor one another's progress, and carry on discussions between formal meetings, got top marks.[38]

• ***Shape culture through virtual technology to reinforce productive norms.*** This involves creating a virtual environment in which people feel safe to express concerns, admit mistakes, share ideas, acknowledge fears, or ask for help. Leaders reinforce a norm of sharing all forms of knowledge, and they encourage people to express "off-the-wall" ideas and ask for help when it's needed. Team leaders set the example by their own behavior. Leaders also make sure that they bring diversity issues into the open and educate members early on regarding possible cultural differences that could cause communication problems or misunderstandings in a virtual environment. Leaders address conflicts immediately because virtual conflicts can escalate quickly.

• ***Monitor progress and reward members to keep the team progressing toward its goals.*** Leaders stay on top of the project's development and make sure that everyone knows how the team is progressing toward meeting its goals. Posting targets, measurements, and milestones in the virtual workspace can make progress explicit. Leaders also provide regular feedback, and they reward both individual and team accomplishments

Director's Toolkit

How to Run a Great Meeting

A survey in the United States and Britain found that people spend an average of 5.6 hours a week in meetings, yet 69 percent of respondents considered most of that time wasted. Meetings can be excellent avenues to solving problems, sharing information, and achieving shared goals, but good meetings don't just happen. Here are some tips on how to make meetings worthwhile and productive.

Prepare in Advance
Advance preparation is the single most important tool for running an efficient, productive meeting:

- **Define the purpose.** Is the meeting's purpose to share information, draw on participants' expertise and skills, elicit their commitment to a project, or coordinate the efforts required to accomplish a specific task? The leader needs to be clear about what the purpose is. If a meeting isn't essential, don't have it.

- **Invite the right people.** Meetings fail when too many, too few, or the wrong people are involved. Don't let the meeting get too big, but make sure everyone with a contribution to make or a stake in the topic is represented.

- **Prepare an agenda and identify the expected outcome.** Distributing a simple list of the topics to be discussed lets people know what to expect. If the meeting is for exploration only, say so. A lack of decision making can be frustrating if participants expect action to be taken.

Bring out the Best during the Meeting
During the meeting, certain techniques will bring out the best in people and ensure a productive session:

- **Start on time, state the purpose, and review the agenda.** Starting on time has symbolic value: It tells people that the topic is important and that the leader values their time. Begin by stating the meeting's explicit purpose and clarifying what should be accomplished by its conclusion.

- **Establish ground rules.** Banning the use of cell phones, tablets, and laptops in meetings can make sure that people aren't distracted. Other rules concern how people should interact, such as emphasizing equal participation and respectful listening.

- **Create involvement.** Good leaders draw out the silent and control the talkative so that the meeting isn't dominated by one or two assertive people. In addition, they encourage a free flow of ideas, provoke discussion with open-ended questions, and make sure that everyone feels heard.

- **Keep it moving.** For virtual meetings, it can be a good idea to begin with a "warm-up" of informal, non-work-related conversation. Otherwise, allowing people to waste time by getting into discussions of issues not on the agenda is a primary reason that people hate meetings. Move the meeting along as needed to meet time constraints.

Attend to the End as Much as the Beginning
Review and follow-up is important to summarize and implement agreed-upon points:

- **End with a call to action.** Summarize the discussion, review any decisions made, and make sure that each person understands his or her assignment.

- **Follow up swiftly.** Send a short e-mail or memo to summarize the meeting's key accomplishments, outline agreed-upon activities, and suggest schedules for implementation.

SOURCES: Based on Antony Jay, *How to Run a Meeting* (Boston: Harvard Business Review Classics, 2009); Beth Bratkovic, "Running an Effective Meeting," *Government Finance Review* (April 2007): 58–60; Phred Dvorak, "Corporate Meetings Go Through a Makeover," *The Wall Street Journal*, March 6, 2006; Richard Axelrod et al., "Creating Dynamic, Energy-Producing Meetings," *Leader to Leader* (Spring 2005): 53–58; Howard M. Guttman, "Leading Meetings 101: Transform Them from Dull to Dynamic," *Leadership Excellence* (July 2009): 18; and Darleen DeRosa, "Hello, Is Anybody Out There? Six Steps to High-Impact V-Meetings," *T+D* (August 2011): 28–29.

through avenues such as virtual award ceremonies and recognition at virtual meetings. They are liberal with praise and congratulations, but criticism or reprimands are handled individually, rather than in the virtual "presence" of the team.

As the use of virtual teams grows, there is growing understanding of what makes them successful. At Spring Company, a large consumer goods company with a virtual team of engineers working in the United States and India, leaders took care to help the team develop rapport at the beginning of the project.

Spotlight on Skills

Spring Company

When top executives at Spring Company decided to move some aspects of supply chain process development to one of the company's Indian facilities, one of their key concerns was making sure that the engineers in the United States and the ones in India came together quickly around a shared mission and a focus on key performance goals, putting the success of the team ahead of individual interests.

Company managers, team leaders, and consultants held a series of team-building activities, during which team members together created a shared vision, developed specific team norms and agreements, built virtual relationships, clarified roles and responsibilities, and established expectations for the team's work. Cultural education and exercises on virtual communication were also a part of the process. By the end of the team-building activities, members were laughing together and eager to get on with their work. A follow-up by webinar and phone found that the team was on track toward meeting its goals; moreover, everyone was still having a good time working together.[39]

The time spent building rapport and trust paid off in smooth team interactions for the Spring Company virtual team. Many experts suggest that leaders bring people together face to face at the beginning of a project so that people can begin building trusting relationships. Others also suggest that managers solicit volunteers as much as possible for virtual teams, and interviews with virtual team members and leaders support the idea that members who truly want to work as a virtual team are more effective.[40] In a study of 52 virtual teams in 15 leading multinational companies, London Business School researchers found that Nokia's teams were among the most effective, even though they were made up of people working in several different countries, across time zones and cultures. What makes Nokia's teams so successful? One key is that many of Nokia's virtual teams consist of people who volunteered for the task. The company also tries to make sure that some members of a team have worked together before, providing a base for trusting relationships.[41]

Global teams, such as the ones at Nokia and Spring Company, present even greater challenges for team leaders, who have to bridge gaps of time, distance, and culture. Different cultural attitudes can affect work pacing, team communications, decision making, the perception of deadlines, and other issues, and provide rich soil for misunderstandings and conflict. No wonder when the executive council of *CIO* magazine asked global chief information officers (CIOs) to rank their greatest challenges, managing virtual global teams ranked as the most pressing issue.[42]

REMEMBER THIS

- A **virtual team** is a team made of members who are geographically or organizationally dispersed, rarely meet face to face, and interact to accomplish their work primarily using advanced information and telecommunications technologies.

- A **global team** is a group made of employees who come from, and whose activities span, multiple countries.

- Virtual teams provide many advantages, but they also present new challenges for leaders, who must learn to build trusting relationships in a virtual environment.

14.5 Team Characteristics

After deciding the type of team to use, the next issue of concern to managers is designing the team for greatest effectiveness. Team characteristics of particular concern are size, diversity, and member roles.

14.5a Size

More than 30 years ago, psychologist Ivan Steiner examined what happened each time the size of a team increased, and he proposed that a team's performance and productivity peaked when it had about five members—a quite small number. He found that adding members beyond five caused a decrease in motivation, an increase in coordination problems, and a general decline in performance.[43] Since then, numerous studies have found that smaller teams perform better, although most researchers say that it's impossible to specify an optimal team size. One investigation of team size based on data from 58 software development teams found that the best-performing teams ranged in size from three to six members.[44]

Teams need to be large enough to incorporate the diverse skills needed to complete a task, enable members to express good and bad feelings, and aggressively solve problems. However, they also should be small enough to permit members to feel an intimate part of the team and to communicate effectively and efficiently. The ability of people to identify with the team is an important determinant of high performance.[45] At Amazon.com, CEO Jeff Bezos established a "two-pizza rule." If a team gets so large that members can't be fed with two pizzas, it should be split into smaller teams.[46] In general, as a team increases in size, it becomes harder for each member to interact with and influence the others. Subgroups often form in larger teams, and conflicts among them can occur. Turnover and absenteeism are higher because members feel less like an important part of the team.[47] Although the Internet and advanced technologies are enabling larger groups of people to work more effectively in virtual teams, studies show that members of smaller virtual teams participate more actively, are more committed to the team, are more focused on team goals, and have higher levels of rapport than larger virtual teams.[48]

14.5b Diversity

Because teams require a variety of skills, knowledge, and experience, it seems likely that heterogeneous teams would be more effective than homogeneous ones. In general, research supports this idea, showing that diverse teams produce more innovative solutions to problems.[49] Diversity in terms of functional area and skills, thinking styles, and personal characteristics is often a source of creativity. In addition, diversity may contribute to a healthy level of disagreement that leads to better decision making.

Research studies have confirmed that both functional diversity and demographic diversity can have a positive impact on work

Richard T Gagnon/Getty Images Sport/Getty Images

CONCEPT CONNECTION At 6-foot-9, professional hockey player Zdeno Chara is a commanding presence, but as the captain of the Boston Bruins, he is all about making team members feel like equals who all contribute to the group's success. As the **socioemotional leader**, Chara has established certain boundaries that help **harmonize** the team. For example, team members cannot refer to new players as "rookies," nor are they allowed to engage in any kind of harmful bullying behavior that can be common on sports teams. And with this **diverse** team filled with players from a number of countries, Chara insists that all team meetings and conversations be conducted in English. Under his supportive leadership, the Bruins have advanced to the Stanley Cup finals several times in the last few seasons.

team performance.[50] For example, recent research suggests that gender diversity, particularly with more women than men on a team, leads to better performance.[51] Ethnic, national, and racial diversity sometimes can hinder team interaction and performance in the short term, but with effective leadership, the problems fade over time.[52]

14.5c Member Roles

For a team to be successful over the long run, it must be structured in a way that both maintains its members' social well-being and accomplishes its task. To understand the importance of members fulfilling various roles on a team, consider the 33 miners who were trapped underground after a copper mine collapsed in San José, Chile, in August 2010. With little food, scant water, dusty conditions, and frayed nerves, the situation could have led to chaos. However, the miners organized into several teams in charge of critical activities such as communication with rescue workers, transport of supplies from above ground, rationing and distribution of food, managing health concerns, and securing the mine to prevent further collapses. Some team members were clearly focused on helping the trapped miners meet their needs for physical survival; some focused on helping people coordinate their activities; and still others focused on the group's psychological and social needs, helping people maintain hope and a sense of solidarity as the ordeal stretched to a harrowing 69 days. Experts agree that teamwork and leadership were key to the miners' survival.[53]

With successful teams, the requirements for task performance and social satisfaction are met by the emergence of two types of roles: task specialist and socioemotional.[54]

People who play a **task specialist role** spend time and energy helping the team reach its goal. They often display the following behaviors:

- *Initiate ideas.* Propose new solutions to team problems

- *Give opinions.* Offer judgments on task solutions; give candid feedback on others' suggestions

- *Seek information.* Ask for task-relevant facts

- Summarize. Relate various ideas to the problem at hand; pull ideas together into a brief overview

- Energize. Stimulate the team into action when interest drops[55]

People who adopt a **socioemotional role** support team members' emotional needs and help strengthen the social entity. They display the following behaviors:

- *Encourage.* Are warm and receptive to others' ideas; praise and encourage others to draw forth their contributions

- *Harmonize.* Reconcile group conflicts; help disagreeing parties reach agreement

- *Reduce tension.* Tell jokes or diffuse emotions in other ways when the group atmosphere is tense

- *Follow.* Go along with the team; agree to other team members' ideas

- *Compromise.* Shift own opinions to maintain team harmony[56]

Teams with mostly socioemotional roles can be satisfying, but they also can be unproductive. At the other extreme, a team made up primarily of task specialists will tend to have a singular focus on task accomplishment. This team will be effective for a short period of time but will not be satisfying for members over the long run. Effective teams have people in both task specialist and socioemotional roles. A well-balanced team will do best over the long term because it will be personally satisfying for team members, as well as permitting the accomplishment of team tasks.

Complete the "New Manager Self-Test" to see how you contribute as a team member.

What Team Role Do You Play?

Instructions: Think about how you communicate and contribute during teamwork sessions at school or work. Indicate whether the statements that follow are Mostly True or Mostly False for your behavior on a team. There are no right or wrong answers, so answer honestly.

	Mostly True	Mostly False
1. I often speak out in the interest of getting the best solution.		
2. I typically try to help disagreeing members reach agreement.		
3. I typically push the team to get things done.		
4. I make comments that are sometimes playful or humorous.		
5. I tend to bring up or ask others for facts relevant to a solution.		
6. I am especially warm and complementary toward others' ideas.		
7. I can sometimes upset people by pushing for the rational solution.		
8. I praise and encourage others for their work on the team.		
9. I make suggestions that are logical and rational.		
10. I give team members appreciation and support for a job well done.		

Scoring and Interpretation: Your behavior on a team may reflect either a task-specialist role or a socioemotional role. For your score as a task specialist, sum 1 point for each Mostly True answer to the odd-numbered items. Task Specialist score = _____. For your score as playing a socioemotional role, sum 1 point for each Mostly True answer to the even-numbered items. Socioemotional score = _____. Both task-specialist and socioemotional roles are necessary for team success. Do you tend to naturally focus more on achieving the team's task or on meeting the social needs of members? A score of 4 or more on either scale suggests you are pretty strong on that team member role. If one score is three points higher than the other, you likely specialize in the higher-scoring role during team sessions.

REMEMBER THIS

- Issues of particular concern to managers for team effectiveness are selecting the right type of team for the task, balancing the team's size and diversity, and ensuring that both task and social needs are met.

- Small teams are typically more productive and more satisfying to their members than are large teams.

- Jeff Bezos established a "two-pizza rule" at Amazon.com: If a team gets so large that members can't be fed with two pizzas, it is split into smaller teams.

- The **task specialist role** is a team role in which an individual devotes personal time and energy to helping the team accomplish its activities and reach its goal.

- The **socioemotional role** is a team role in which an individual provides support for team members' emotional needs and helps strengthen social unity.

14.6 Team Processes

Now we turn our attention to internal team processes. Team processes pertain to those dynamics that change over time and can be influenced by team leaders. In this section, we discuss stages of development, cohesiveness, and norms. The fourth type of team process, conflict, will be covered in the next section.

14.6a Stages of Team Development

After a team has been created, it develops by passing through distinct stages. New teams are different from mature teams. Recall a time when you were a member of a new team, such as a fraternity or sorority pledge class, a committee, or a small team formed to do a class assignment. Over time, the team changed. In the beginning, team members had to get to know one another, establish roles and norms, divide the labor, and clarify the team's task. In this way, each member became part of a smoothly operating team. The challenge for leaders is to understand the stages of development and take action that will lead to smooth functioning.

Research findings suggest that team development is not random, but evolves over definitive stages. One useful model for describing these stages is shown in Exhibit 14.7. Each stage confronts team leaders and members with unique problems and challenges.[57]

Forming   The **forming** stage of development is a period of orientation and getting acquainted. Members break the ice and test one another for friendship possibilities and task orientation. Uncertainty is high during this stage, and members usually accept whatever power or authority is offered by either formal or informal leaders. During this initial stage, members are concerned about things such as "What is expected of me?" "What behavior is acceptable?" and "Will I fit in?" During the forming stage, the team leader should provide time for members to get acquainted with one another and encourage them to engage in informal social discussions.

Storming   During the **storming** stage, individual personalities emerge. People become more assertive in clarifying their roles and what is expected of them. This stage is marked by conflict and disagreement. People may disagree over their perceptions of the team's goals

EXHIBIT 14.7 Five Stages of Team Development

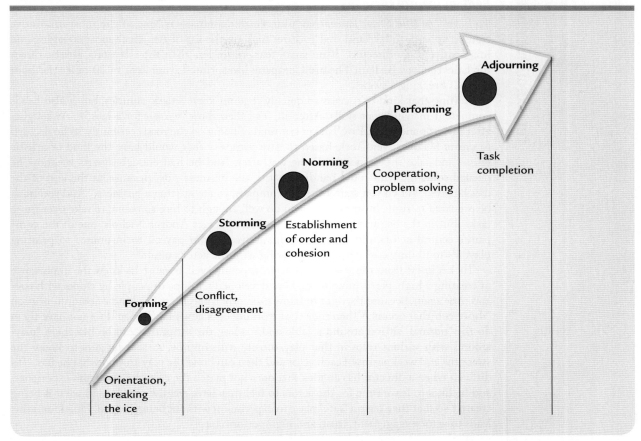

SOURCES: Based on the stages of small group development in Bruce W. Tuckman, "Developmental Sequence in Small Groups," *Psychological Bulletin* 63 (1965): 384–399; and B. W. Tuckman and M. A. Jensen, "Stages of Small Group Development Revisited," *Group and Organizational Studies* 2 (1977): 419–427.

or how to achieve them. Members may jockey for position, and coalitions or subgroups based on common interests may form. Unless teams can successfully move beyond this stage, they may get bogged down and never achieve high performance. A recent experiment with student teams confirms the idea that teams that get stuck in the storming stage perform significantly less well than teams that progress to future stages of development.[58] During the storming stage, the team leader should encourage participation by each team member. Members should propose ideas, disagree with one another, and work through the uncertainties and conflicting perceptions about team tasks and goals. The expression of emotions, even negative ones, helps to build camaraderie and a shared understanding of goals and tasks.[59]

Norming   During the **norming** stage, conflict is resolved and team harmony and unity emerge. Consensus develops on who has the power, who the leaders are, and what the various members' roles are. Members come to accept and understand one another. Differences are resolved, and members develop a sense of team cohesion. During the norming stage, the team leader should emphasize unity within the team and help to clarify team norms and values. Creating a new way of operating a theater company, along with new norms, was Eric Tucker's goal, when he started Bedlam Theatre Company with Andrus Nichols, as shown below in this chapter's Executive Edge.

Bedlam Theatre Company

To have *The Wall Street Journal* say your theater company is "one of the most innovative troupes at work today," and that you are "high on the list of America's most engaging and imaginative stage directors" is no small feat. Yet in less than three seasons, artistic director Eric Tucker's Bedlam Theatre Company has sprinted from zero to 30 miles per hour without breaking a sweat.

Getting that kind of success so quickly requires keen artistic abilities, but it also needs competent management skills. After all, it's called show *business* for a reason. As sought-after director and actor, Eric Tucker got tired of being on the road constantly, so he decided to create his own New York–based theatre company that would have the kind of artistic vision and take the sorts of risks he was after. And he had enough smarts to know he needed someone who could handle most of the business side. Because, at the end of the day, he says, "When you start a theatre company, you're starting a business." And you must be prepared to run a business until you do well enough to hire someone to take over those tasks. But in the beginning, he and his business partner Andrus Nichols, one of the company's central actors, did everything themselves—from payroll to insurance to printing playbills to finding costumes to negotiating with the actor's union.

Tucker knew from the start he had to treat people well, because he knew the importance of creating a high-performing team. He's developed a troupe of people he works with over and over again, because they get to know each other, and there is a kind of communication "short-cut" that occurs. When they start working on a new play, Tucker does not have them do the "normal" sitting around a table and reading the script. Instead he has them "play" around with various roles in that play, mostly with improv, so that he gets to know the strengths and weaknesses of each actor and then can build the play around what he has. "It's difficult when a director has an idea that does not match the cast," he says from experience, and he likes to leave time for the actors to feel they have creative freedom in what is being created, so that they have a "safe" place to experiment without being judged. He's found this leads to actor engagement, trust, and high performance.

Working as a team is not only for the artistic side, but also the organizational. People who start theatre companies often don't know this, he says, but you never stop fund-raising. That means constant interaction with people, developing bonds and alliances, working toward common goals—all things teams do. "Your whole life is about finding money and asking people for money." And because of his good team skills, Bedlam makes resourceful use of that money.

SOURCES: Eric Tucker, Personal communication, April 2015; Terry Teachout, Two Stagings, 'Twelfth Night,' *Wall Street Journal Online*, April 3, 2015 (accessed April 14, 2015), http://search.proquest.com.proxy.library.vanderbilt.edu/pqcentral/docview/1668438525/C81F6334E2ED47FBPQ/4?accountid=14816).

Performing   During the performing stage, the major emphasis is on problem solving and accomplishing the assigned task. Members are committed to the team's mission. They are coordinated with one another and handle disagreements in a mature way. They confront and resolve problems in the interest of task accomplishment. They interact frequently and direct their discussions and influence toward achieving team goals. During this stage, the leader should concentrate on managing high task performance. Both socioemotional and task specialist roles contribute to the team's functioning.

Adjourning   The adjourning stage occurs in committees and teams that have a limited task to perform and are disbanded afterward. During this stage, the emphasis is on wrapping up and gearing down. Task performance is no longer a top priority. Members may feel heightened emotionality, strong cohesiveness, and depression or regret over the team's

Spotlight on Skills

McDevitt Street Bovis

Rather than the typical construction project characterized by conflicts, frantic scheduling, and poor communication, McDevitt Street Bovis wants its collection of contractors, designers, suppliers, and other partners to function as a true team, putting the success of the project ahead of their own individual interests.

The team-building process at Bovis is designed to take teams to the performing stage as quickly as possible by giving everyone an opportunity to get to know one another, explore the ground rules, and clarify roles, responsibilities, and expectations. The team is first divided into separate groups that may have competing objectives—such as the clients in one group, suppliers in another, engineers and architects in a third, and so forth—and asked to come up with a list of their goals for the project. Although interests sometimes vary widely in purely accounting terms, common themes almost always emerge. By talking about conflicting goals and interests, as well as what all the groups share, facilitators help the team gradually come together around a common purpose and begin to develop shared values that will guide the project. After jointly writing a mission statement for the team, each party says what it expects from the others, so that roles and responsibilities can be clarified. The intensive team-building session helps take members quickly through the forming and storming stages of development. "We prevent conflicts from happening," says facilitator Monica Bennett. Leaders at McDevitt Street Bovis believe that building better teams builds better buildings.[60]

disbanding. At this point, the leader may wish to signify the team's disbanding with a ritual or ceremony, perhaps giving out plaques and awards to members to signify closure and completeness.

These five stages typically occur in sequence, but in teams that are under time pressure, they may occur quite rapidly. The stages may also be accelerated for virtual teams. For example, at McDevitt Street Bovis, a large construction management firm, bringing people together for a couple of days of team building helps teams move rapidly through the forming and storming stages.

14.6b Building a Cohesive Team

Another important aspect of the team process is cohesiveness. **Team cohesiveness** is defined as the extent to which members are attracted to the team and motivated to remain in it.[61] Members of highly cohesive teams are committed to team activities, attend meetings, and are happy when the team succeeds. Members of less cohesive teams are less concerned about the team's welfare. High cohesiveness is normally considered an attractive feature of teams.

Determinants of Team Cohesiveness   Several characteristics of team structure and context influence cohesiveness. First is *team interaction*. When team members have frequent contact, they get to know one another, consider themselves a unit, and become more committed to the team.[62] Second is the concept of *shared goals*. If team members agree on purpose and direction, they will be more cohesive. Third is *personal attraction to the team*, meaning that members have similar attitudes and values and enjoy being together.

Two factors in the team's context also influence cohesiveness. The first is the *presence of competition*. When a team is in moderate competition with other teams, its cohesiveness

Director's Toolkit

TEDxPfizerMumbai

TEDx is everywhere, and for good reason. They offer smart people with similar goals coming together to share new ideas and solutions. But TEDxPfizerMumbai seems to be especially adept at bringing intelligence, goal setting, and culture in one place and getting superior results. How do they get ahead of a pack already working at warp speed?

Raghuveer Surupa put in a proposal to do a TEDx at the PfizerMumbai, and once he got the CEO's approval, he sent out requests to department heads to recommend employees who could possibly be core team members. Team members were ultimately self-selected and were people with self-motivated goals. The planning team organized itself so that members chose tasks, and they had open decision making and brainstorming sessions, with a free-flowing process from brainstorming to execution. They met regularly, with one of their goals to become more cohesive and more productive.

Early on they decided to **choose a diverse set of speakers** for the event that would help the participant

employees to enhance their abilities to demonstrate and develop certain necessary traits in the pharmaceutical environment, such as being collaborative, flexible, entrepreneurial, customer-obsessed and focused. Speakers were then curated **to deliver their ideas with special emphasis on these traits**. And intentionally long breaks were built in, to allow maximum interactions between attendees and speakers.

By working as a high-functioning, self-organizing team, they were able to bring success and motivate employees to be more high-functioning. After the TEDx events, employees reported their daily work problems seemed less overwhelming and more manageable, they were more willing to take on difficult projects, and they found more meaning in their work. As a result, the **TEDxPfizerMumbai is currently being replicated in other South Asian countries as well**. This is a real application of TED's motto, "Ideas worth spreading."

SOURCE: Raghuveer Surupa, personal communication, March–April 2015.

increases as it strives to win. Finally, *team success* and the favorable evaluation of the team by outsiders add to cohesiveness. When a team succeeds in its task and others in the organization recognize the success, members feel good, and their commitment to the team will be high. Such was the case of the planning team for the TEDxPfizerMumbai meeting in 2014, as shown the Director's Toolkit next.

Consequences of Team Cohesiveness   The outcome of team cohesiveness can fall into two categories—morale and productivity. As a general rule, morale is higher in cohesive teams because of increased communication among members, a friendly team climate, maintenance of membership because of commitment to the team, loyalty, and member participation in team decisions and activities. High cohesiveness has almost uniformly good effects on the satisfaction and morale of team members.[63]

With respect to the productivity of the team as a whole, research findings suggest that teams in which members share strong feelings of connectedness and generally positive interactions tend to perform better.[64] Thus, a friendly, positive team environment contributes to productivity, as well as member satisfaction. Among call center teams at Bank of America, for example, productivity rose 10 percent when leaders scheduled more face-to-face interaction time outside of formal meetings. Simply interacting with others in a positive way has an energizing effect. Alex "Sandy" Pentland, a professor at the Massachusetts Institute of Technology (MIT), and his colleagues at MIT's Human Dynamics Laboratory studied teams across diverse industries to identify what gives some teams the energy, creativity, and shared commitment that leads to high productivity. They found positive patterns of communication to be the most important predictor of a team's success—as significant as individual intelligence, personality, skill, and the substance of discussions combined.[65]

Other research indicates that the degree of productivity in cohesive teams may depend on the relationship between management and the work team. One study surveyed more than 200 work teams and correlated job performance with their cohesiveness.[66] Highly cohesive teams were more productive when team members felt management support and less productive when they sensed management hostility and negativism.

14.6c Establishing Team Norms

A **team norm** is an informal standard of conduct that is shared by team members and guides their behavior.[67] Norms are valuable because they provide a frame of reference for what is expected and acceptable.

Norms begin to develop in the first interactions among members of a new team. Exhibit 14.8 illustrates four common ways in which norms develop.[68] Sometimes the first behaviors that occur in a team set a precedent. For example, at one company, a team leader began his first meeting by raising an issue and then "leading" team members until he got the solution he wanted. The pattern became ingrained so quickly into an unproductive team norm that members dubbed meetings the "Guess What I Think" game.[69] Other influences on team norms include critical events in the team's history, as well as behaviors, attitudes, and norms that members bring with them from outside the team.

Team leaders play an important role in shaping norms that will help the team be effective. For example, research shows that when leaders have high expectations for collaborative problem solving, teams develop strong collaborative norms.[70] Making explicit statements about desired team behaviors is a powerful way that leaders influence norms. When he was CEO of Ameritech, Bill Weiss established a norm of cooperation and mutual support among his top leadership team by telling them bluntly that if he caught anyone trying to undermine the others, the guilty party would be fired.[71]

EXHIBIT 14.8 Four Ways Team Norms Develop

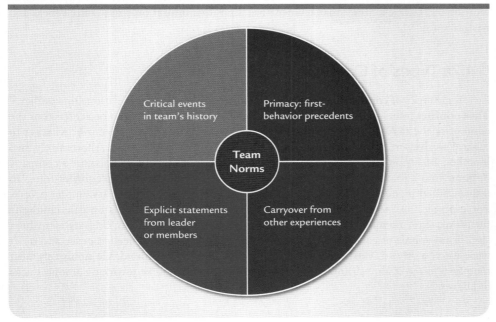

REMEMBER THIS

REMEMBER THIS

- The **forming** stage of team development is a period of orientation and getting acquainted.

- **Storming** is the stage of team development in which individual personalities and roles emerge, along with resulting conflicts.

- **Norming** refers to the stage of development in which conflicts are resolved and team harmony and unity emerge.

- The **performing** stage is the stage in which members focus on problem solving and accomplishing the team's assigned task.

- **Adjourning** is the stage during which members of temporary teams prepare for the team's disbanding.

- **Team cohesiveness** refers to the extent to which team members are attracted to the team and motivated to remain a part of it.

- Morale is almost always higher in cohesive teams, and cohesiveness can also contribute to higher productivity.

- A **team norm** is an informal standard of conduct that is shared by team members and guides their behavior.

14.7 Managing Team Conflict

"In great teams, conflict becomes productive. The free flow of ideas and feelings is critical for creative thinking, for discovering new solutions no one individual would have come to on his own."

—Peter Senge, author of
The Fifth Discipline: The Art and Practice of the Learning Organization

The final characteristic of team process is conflict. Conflict can arise among members within a team or between one team and another. **Conflict** refers to an antagonistic interaction in which one party attempts to block the intentions or goals of another.[72] Whenever people work together in teams, some conflict is inevitable. Bringing conflicts into the open and effectively resolving them is one of the team leader's most challenging yet most important jobs. Effective conflict management has a positive impact on team cohesiveness and performance.[73]

14.7a Types of Conflict

Two basic types of conflict that occur in teams are task conflict and relationship conflict.[74] **Task conflict** refers to disagreements among people about the goals to be achieved or the content of the tasks to be performed. Two shop foremen might disagree over whether to replace a valve, or let it run despite the unusual noise that it is making. Alternatively, two members of a top management team might disagree about whether to acquire a company or enter into a joint venture as a way to expand globally. **Relationship conflict** refers to interpersonal incompatibility that creates tension and personal animosity among people. For example, in one team at a company that manufactures and sells upscale children's furniture, team members found their differing perspectives and working styles to be a significant source of conflict during crunch times. Members who needed peace and quiet were irked at those who wanted music playing in the background. Compulsively neat members found it almost impossible to work with those who liked working among stacks of clutter.[75]

In general, research suggests that task conflict can be beneficial because it leads to better decision making and problem solving. On the other hand, relationship conflict is typically associated with negative consequences for team effectiveness.[76] One study of top management teams, for example, found that task conflict was associated with higher decision quality, greater commitment, and more decision acceptance, while the presence of relationship conflict significantly reduced those same outcomes.[77]

14.7b Balancing Conflict and Cooperation

There is evidence that mild conflict can be beneficial to teams.[78] A healthy level of conflict helps to prevent *groupthink* (as discussed in Chapter 6), in which people are so committed to a cohesive team that they are reluctant to express contrary opinions. When people in work teams go along simply for the sake of harmony, problems typically result. Thus, a degree of conflict leads to better decision making because multiple viewpoints are expressed.

However, conflict that is too strong, focused on personal rather than work issues, or not managed appropriately can be damaging to the team's morale and productivity. Too much conflict can be destructive, tear relationships apart, and interfere with the healthy exchange of ideas and information.[79] Team leaders have to find the right balance between conflict and cooperation, as illustrated in Exhibit 14.9. Too little conflict can decrease team performance because the team doesn't benefit from a mix of opinions and ideas—even disagreements—that might lead to better solutions or prevent the team from making mistakes. At the other end of the spectrum, too much conflict outweighs the team's cooperative efforts and leads to a decrease in employee satisfaction and commitment, hurting team performance. A moderate amount of conflict, when it is managed appropriately, typically results in the highest levels of team performance.

Go to the "Ethical Dilemma" on page 627, which pertains to team cohesiveness and conflict.

EXHIBIT 14.9 Balancing Conflict and Cooperation

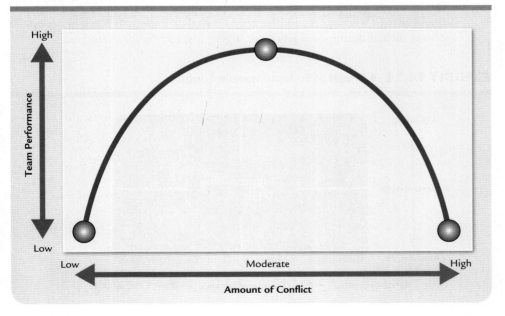

14.7c Causes of Conflict

Several factors can lead to conflict.[80] One of the primary causes is competition over resources, such as money, information, or supplies. When individuals or teams must compete for scarce or declining resources, conflict is almost inevitable. In addition, conflict often occurs simply because people are pursuing differing goals. Goal differences are natural in organizations. Individual salespeople's targets may put them in conflict with one another or with the sales manager. Moreover, the sales department's goals might conflict with those of manufacturing, and so forth.

Conflict may also arise from communication breakdowns. Poor communication can occur in any team, but virtual and global teams are particularly prone to communication breakdowns. In one virtual team developing a custom polymer for a Japanese manufacturer, the marketing team member in the United States was frustrated by a Japanese team member's failure to provide her with the manufacturer's marketing strategy. The Japanese team member, in turn, thought that her teammate was overbearing and unsupportive. She knew that the manufacturer hadn't yet developed a clear marketing strategy, and that pushing for more information could damage the relationship by causing the customer to "lose face."[81] Trust issues can be a major source of conflict in virtual teams if members feel that they are being left out of important communication interactions.[82] In addition, the lack of nonverbal cues in virtual interactions leads to more misunderstandings.

14.7d Styles to Handle Conflict

Teams as well as individuals develop specific styles for dealing with conflict, based on the desire to satisfy their own concern versus the other party's concern. A model that describes five styles of handling conflict is shown in Exhibit 14.10. The two major dimensions are the extent to which an individual is assertive versus unassertive and cooperative versus uncooperative in his or her approach to conflict:[83]

- The *dominating style* (my way) reflects assertiveness to get one's own way and should be used when quick, decisive action is vital on important issues or unpopular actions, such as during emergencies or urgent cost cutting requirements.

EXHIBIT 14.10 A Model of Styles to Handle Conflict

SOURCES: Adapted from Kenneth Thomas, "Conflict and Conflict Management," in *Handbook of Industrial and Organizational Behavior*, ed. M. D. Dunnette (New York: John Wiley, 1976), p. 900; and Nan Peck, "Conflict 101: Styles of Fighting," North Virginia Community College Web site, September 20, 2005, www.nvcc.edu/home/npeck/conflicthome/conflict/Conflict101/conflictstyles.htm (accessed April 13, 2011).

- The *compromising style* (halfway) reflects a moderate amount of both assertiveness and cooperativeness. It is appropriate when the goals on both sides are equally important, when opponents have equal power and both sides want to split the difference, or when people need to arrive at temporary or expedient solutions under time pressure.

- The *accommodating style* (your way) reflects a high degree of cooperativeness, which works best when people realize that they are wrong, when an issue is more important to others than to oneself, when building social credits for use in later discussions, and when maintaining harmony is especially important.

- The *collaborating style* (our way) reflects a high degree of both assertiveness and cooperativeness. The collaborating style enables both parties to win, although it may require substantial bargaining and negotiation. The collaborating style is important when both sets of concerns are too important to be compromised, when insights from different people need to be merged into an overall solution, and when the commitment of both sides is needed for a consensus.

- The *avoiding style* (no way) reflects neither assertiveness nor cooperativeness. It is appropriate when an issue is trivial, when there is no chance of winning, when a delay to gather more information is needed, or when a disruption would be costly.

An example of the collaborating style could be seen during the 2008 Summer Olympics in Beijing. When building the Beijing National Aquatics Center (typically called the "Water Cube"), two architectural firms—one Chinese and the other Australian—developed designs that were totally different. Although this created some tension, instead of fighting for their own ideas, the two sides came up with a totally new concept that excited everyone. The resulting award-winning building is spectacular.[84] Each of the five styles is appropriate in certain cases, and effective team members and leaders vary their styles to fit the specific situation.

14.7e Negotiation

One distinctive type of conflict management is **negotiation**, whereby people engage in give-and-take discussions and consider various alternatives to reach a joint decision that is acceptable to both parties. Negotiation is used when a conflict is formalized, such as between a union and management.

Types of Negotiation Conflicting parties may embark on negotiation from different perspectives and with different intentions, reflecting either an *integrative* approach or a *distributive* approach.

Integrative negotiation is based on a win-win assumption, in that all parties want to come up with a creative solution that can benefit both sides. Rather than viewing the conflict as a win-lose

AP Images/Keystone, Laurent Gillieron

CONCEPT CONNECTION Just who's running the Large Hadron Collider (LHC) project, an international, $6-billion particle accelerator designed to simulate the universe's birth by producing high-energy proton collisions? The answer: everyone. Built at the European Organization of Nuclear Research (known for short as CERN), near Geneva, LHC involves 10,000 scientists and engineers working in hundreds of institutions. Because participants recognize that they need everyone's cooperation to succeed, they've adopted a **collaborative style of handling conflicts**. Each research group is a democratic collective; those collectives appoint members to negotiate with other groups. "The top guy," notes CERN's "top guy," Director-General Rolf-Dieter Heuer, "can only convince the other guys to do what he wants them to do."

situation, people look at the issues from multiple angles, consider trade-offs, and try to "expand the pie" rather than divide it. With integrative negotiation, conflicts are managed through cooperation and compromise, which fosters trust and positive long-term relationships. **Distributive negotiation**, on the other hand, assumes that the size of the "pie" is fixed, and each party attempts to get as much of it as they can. One side wants to win, which means the other side must lose. With this win-lose approach, distributive negotiation is competitive and adversarial, rather than collaborative, and does not typically lead to positive long-term relationships.[85]

Most experts emphasize the value of integrative negotiation for today's collaborative business environment. That is, the key to effectiveness is to see negotiation not as a zero-sum game, but as a process for reaching a creative solution that benefits everyone.[86]

Rules for Reaching a Win-Win Solution   Achieving a win-win solution through integrative negotiation is based on four key strategies:[87]

- *Separate the people from the problem.* For successful integrative negotiation, people stay focused on the problem and the source of conflict, rather than attacking or attempting to discredit each other.

- *Focus on underlying interests, not current demands.* Demands are what each person wants from the negotiation, whereas underlying interests represent the "why" behind the demands. Consider two sisters arguing over the last orange in the fruit bowl. Each insists that she should get the orange and refuses to give up (demands). If one sister had asked the other *why* she wanted the orange, the sisters would have discovered that one wanted to eat it, and the other wanted the peel to use for a project (interests). By focusing on interests, the sisters would have been able to arrive at a solution that gave each what she wanted.[88] *Demands* create yes-or-no obstacles to effective negotiation, whereas *interests* present problems that can be solved creatively.

- *Listen and ask questions.* A good strategy for most negotiations is to listen and ask questions. You can learn more about your opponent's position, their constraints, and their needs by being quiet or asking questions. Smart negotiators want to learn the other side's constraints so that they can help overcome them. Don't dismiss the opposing party's limitation as unreasonable or think "That's your problem." You can take it on as your own problem and try to come up with a solution for your opponent so that you can get closer to an agreement.

- *Insist that results be based on objective standards.* Each party in a negotiation has its own interests and naturally would like to maximize its outcomes. Successful negotiation requires focusing on objective criteria and maintaining standards of fairness rather than using subjective judgments about the best solution.

REMEMBER THIS

- **Conflict** refers to antagonistic interaction in which one party attempts to block the intentions or goals of another.
- Some conflict, particularly task conflict, can be beneficial to teams.
- **Task conflict** is conflict that results from disagreements about the goals to be achieved or the content of the tasks to be performed.
- **Relationship conflict** results from interpersonal incompatibility that creates tension and personal animosity among people.

- Causes of conflict include competition over resources, goal differences, and communication breakdowns.

- Teams and individuals use a variety of styles for dealing with conflict, including the dominating style, the avoiding style, the compromising style, the accommodating style, and the collaborating style, and each can be effective under certain circumstances.

- **Negotiation** is a conflict management strategy whereby people engage in give-and-take discussions and consider various alternatives to reach a joint decision that is acceptable to both parties.

- **Integrative negotiation** is a collaborative approach that is based on a win-win assumption, whereby the parties want to come up with a creative solution that benefits both sides of the conflict.

- **Distributive negotiation** is a competitive and adversarial approach in which each party strives to get as much as it can, usually at the expense of the other party.

CHAPTER **14** **DISCUSSION QUESTIONS**

1. One company had 40 percent of its workers and 20 percent of its managers resign during the first year after it reorganized from a vertical hierarchy into teams. What might account for this dramatic turnover? How might managers ensure a smooth transition to teams?

2. Have you experienced any of the five contributions of teams shown in Exhibit 14.2 with a team that you have participated in? Describe your experience and why you think that the team was able to make that specific contribution.

3. Suppose that you are the leader of a team that has just been created to develop a new registration process at your college or university. How can you use an understanding of the stages of team development to improve your team's effectiveness?

4. Research on team interactions described in the chapter indicates that when people eat lunch at 12-person tables, they are more productive and collaborative than when they eat at 4-person tables, even if they aren't eating with their own team members. What do you think would explain this finding?

5. Imagine yourself as a potential member of a team responsible for designing a new package for a breakfast cereal. Do you think interpersonal skills would be equally important if the team is organized face to face versus a virtual team? Why or why not? Might different types of interpersonal skills be required for the two types of teams? Be specific.

6. If you were the leader of a special-purpose team developing a new computer game and conflicts arose related to power and status differences among team members, what would you do? Which of the styles to handle conflict described in the chapter do you think might be most effective? Explain your answer.

7. Experts say that for teams to function well, members have to get to know one another in some depth. What specifically would you do to facilitate this in a co-located team? What about in a global, virtual team?

8. Some people argue that the presence of an outside threat correlates with a high degree of team cohesion. Would you agree or disagree? Explain your answer.

9. Discuss how the dilemma of teamwork vs. individual work might be intensified in a virtual team. What dilemmas do you encounter when you have to do class assignments as part of a team? Discuss.

10. If you were the leader of a newly formed team, what might you do to make sure that the team developed norms of high performance?

SELF-LEARNING

This and That: Best Team—Worst Team[89]

Think of two teams of which you were a member—the best and the worst in terms of personal satisfaction and team performance. These teams could come from any area in your experience—for example, athletic team, student club, class team, work team, project team, church committee, or volunteer organization. List here the specific behaviors of the teams that made them the best and worst for you.

Best team behaviors: _____

_____

Worst team behaviors: _____

_____

In class: (1) Sit in a small group of three to five students. Each student should tell the brief story of his or her best and worst team experiences. (2) After all the stories are heard, one team member writes on a flipchart (or blackboard) two headings—"More of This" and "Less of That." Under "This," write team member suggestions for positive behaviors that make for effective teamwork. Under "That," write team member suggestions for negative behaviors that prevent effective teamwork. (3) After brainstorming items, each group condenses each list to five key behaviors that the group considers most important. (4) After the lists are finalized, students can walk around the classroom and review all lists. (5) Discuss answers to the following questions, either in your group or as a class.

4. What are the most important behaviors for This and for That?

5. What factors influence the presence of This or That behaviors on a team?

6. What personal changes would you need to make as a team member to demonstrate more of This?

7. What personal changes would you need to make as a team member to demonstrate less of That?

8. How might a team leader be able to attain more of This on a team and less of That?

GROUP LEARNING

Teams on TV

1. Form into groups of three to five members. As a group, choose a TV show where teams are central to the plot. Examples include: *The Office, Community, Parks & Recreation, Law & Order (any of them), CSI, 30 Rock*, etc. Make sure the instructor agrees with your choice of TV show.

2. Watch several TV shows, or several episodes of one TV show (make sure group members watch the same shows) and study team behavior. Use the Team Member Roles on pages [29–30] of this textbook and also the Stages of Team Development on pages [33–34]. Take notes on which characters perform which role(s) and what stages of development the group is in during a particular show.

3. As a group, come to an agreement on which roles and stages were present in those shows.

4. Your instructor will tell you whether to prepare either a group presentation or group paper on your findings.

5. What did you learn about teams from this assignment? Were there some surprises?

ACTION LEARNING

Team Feedback Exercise

Step 1. Divide into groups of three to four students. Think back to recent experiences working in a team, either at work or school. Write down your answers to the following questions.

What behaviors by other team members did you most appreciate?

_____

_____

What behaviors of other team members did you least appreciate?

_____

_____

What do you think the team members appreciated about you?

_____

_____

What actions of yours might the team members have appreciated least?

_____

_____

Step 2. Take turns sharing your answers with other members of your group. Make notes about common themes for answers to each of the previous questions. What is the single most important theme for each of the answers above?

Step 3. What are the implications of the answers for you as a member of a future team? How might you change your behavior to make a larger contribution to a team?

ETHICAL DILEMMA

One for All and All for One?[90]

Melinda Asbel watched as three of her classmates filed out of the conference room. Then she turned back to the large wooden table and faced her fellow members (a student and three faculty members) of the university's judiciary committee.

The three students—Joe Eastridge, Brad Hamil, and Lisa Baghetti—had just concluded their appeal against a plagiarism conviction stemming from a group project for an international marketing course. Melinda, who happened to be in the class with the students on trial, remembered the day that the professor, Hank Zierden, had asked Joe, Brad, and Lisa, along with the group's leader, Paul Colgan, to stay after class. She happened to walk by the classroom a half hour later to see four glum students emerge. Even though Paul had a chagrined expression on his face, Joe was the one who looked completely shattered. It didn't take long for word to spread along the ever-active grapevine that Paul had admitted to plagiarizing his part of the group paper.

At the hearing, the students recounted how they'd quickly and unanimously settled on Paul to lead the group. He was by far the most able student among them, someone who managed to maintain a stellar GPA even while handling a full course load and holding down a part-time job. After the group worked together for weeks analyzing the problem and devising a marketing plan, Paul assigned a section of the final paper to each member. With the pressure of all those end-of-the-semester deadlines bearing down on them, everyone was delighted when Paul volunteered to write the company and industry background, the section that typically took the most time

to produce. Paul gathered in everyone's contributions, assembled them into a paper, and handed the final draft to the other members. They each gave it a quick read. They liked what they saw and thought they had a good chance for an A.

Unfortunately, as Paul readily admitted when Professor Zierden confronted them, he had pulled the section that he'd contributed directly off the Internet. Pointing out the written policy that he had distributed at the beginning of the semester, which stated that each group member was equally responsible for the final product, the professor gave all four students a zero for the project. The group project and presentation counted for 30 percent of the course grade.

Joe, Brad, and Lisa maintained that they were completely unaware that Paul had cheated. "It just never occurred to us Paul would ever need to cheat," Brad said. They were innocent bystanders, the students argued. Why should they be penalized? Besides, the consequences weren't going to fall on each of them equally. Although Paul was suffering the embarrassment of public exposure, the failing group project grade would only put a dent in his solid GPA. Joe, on the other hand, was already on academic probation. A zero probably meant that he wouldn't make the 2.5 GPA that he needed to stay in the business program.

At least one of the faculty members of the judiciary committee supported Professor Zierden's actions. "We're assigning more and more group projects because increasingly that's the way these students are going to find themselves working when they get real jobs in the real world," he said. "And the fact of the matter is that if someone obtains information illegally while on the job, it's going to put the whole corporation at risk for being sued, or worse."

Even though she could see merit to both sides, Melinda was going to have to choose. If you were Melinda, how would you vote?

What Would You Do?

1. Vote to exonerate the three group project members who didn't cheat. You're convinced that they had no reason to suspect Paul Colgan of dishonesty. Exonerating them is the right thing to do.

2. Vote in support of Hank Zierden's decision to hold each individual member accountable for the entire project. The professor clearly stated his policy at the beginning of the semester, and the students should have been more vigilant. The committee should not undercut a professor's explicit policy.

3. Vote to reduce each of the three students' penalties. Instead of a zero, each student will receive only half of the possible total points for the project, which would be an F. You're still holding students responsible for the group project, but not imposing catastrophic punishment. This compromise both undercuts the professor's policy and punishes "innocent" team members to some extent, but not as severely.

CASE FOR CRITICAL ANALYSIS

Are We a Team?

Hi. My name is Jenny McConnell. I am the newly appointed CIO of a medium-sized technology company. Our company recruits top graduates from schools of business and engineering. Talent, intellect, creativity—it's all there. If you lined up this crowd for a group photo, credentials in hand, the "wow" factor would be there.

Our company is spread over a dozen states, mostly in the Northwest. The talent pool is amazing across the board, both in IT and in the rest of the company. But when the CEO hired me, he said that we are performing nowhere near our potential. On the surface, the company is doing fine. But we should be a *Fortune* 500 organization. With this much talent, we should be growing at a much faster rate. The CEO also said that I was inheriting "a super team with disappointing performance." His task for me was to pull the IT stars into a cohesive team that would meet company needs for new IT systems and services much faster and more effectively.

Without making our superstars feel that they were being critiqued and second-guessed, or indicating "there's a real problem here," I wanted to gather as much information and feedback as possible from the 14 team members (regional CIOs and department heads) who report to me. I held one-on-one meetings in order to give a voice to each person, allowing each individual to provide an honest assessment of the team as well as areas for improvement and a vision for the future of team efforts.

I was surprised by the consistency of remarks and opinions. For example, a picture emerged of the previous CIO, who was obviously awed by the talent level of team members. Comments such as "Bob pretty much let us do what we wanted" and "Bob would start the meeting and then just fade into the background, as if he found us intimidating" were typical. The most disturbing comment, "Bob always agreed with *me*," was expressed by most of the team members at some point in our conversation. It was as if the regional heads believed that the CIO wanted them to succeed by doing as they thought best for themselves.

I queried members about the level of cooperation during meetings and uncovered areas of concern, including the complaint that others at the table were constantly checking their iPads and smartphones during meetings. One department head told me, "You could turn off the sound while watching one of our meetings, and just by the body language and level of attention, tell who is aligned with whom and who wishes the speaker would just shut up. It would be comical if it weren't so distressing."

Such remarks were indicative of a lack of trust and respect and a breakdown of genuine communication. One team member told me, "I recently encountered a problem that a department head from another region had successfully solved, but the information was never shared, so here I am reinventing the wheel and wasting valuable time." It was apparent that these so-called high performers were territorial, and that the "each division for itself" attitude was becoming a cultural norm that, unchecked, was slowing our response to line departments and customers.

I was also struck by the similarity of the regional IT leaders in their backgrounds, comments, and attitudes, which presented a whole new dilemma: How do we create diversity, jump-start ideas, and reignite passion? This looks like a group of individualists who don't know how to play as a team. I don't want to diminish the individual talent, but I am concerned by the lack of cohesion. I need to find a way to help people think less about themselves and more about sharing work and information and achieving collective results for the good of the company.

Team building is an art, anchored by trust and communication, and committed to mutual success.

What I'm seeing looks like team dysfunction to me. Now I have to determine the steps necessary to build a cohesive, visionary team.

Questions

1. What type of team does the new CIO have? What do you see as the key problem with the team?

2. How do you think that the team evolved to this low level of cooperation and cohesiveness?

3. What suggestions do you have for the CIO to help her turn this collection of individual regional and department heads into a top-performing team? Explain.

ON THE JOB
VIDEO CASES

Tough Mudder: Leading Teams

Questions

1. Alex Patterson notes that our educational system is often focused on individual achievement, but when we go out into the work world as adults, almost all of us are required to work in teams. In what ways does this early focus on individual work make it difficult for us to work in teams? What should an individual do to become a good team member, according to Patterson?

2. These Tough Mudder employees appear to be members of a highly cohesive team. What are some of the qualities described in the video that indicate strong cohesiveness? Include at least two specific examples in your answer.

3. Patterson describes the benefits and challenges of working in an open-plan, collaborative workspace. Do you think you would enjoy working in this type of team-centric environment? Explain *why* or *why not* in your answer.

ENDNOTES

1. Based on Eric M. Stark, Jason D. Shaw, and Michelle K. Duffy, "Preference for Group Work, Winning Orientation, and Social Loafing Behavior in Groups," *Group & Organization Management* 32, no. 6 (December 2007): 699–723.

2. Emily Brennan, "A Pilot's Views on Flight Safety" (an interview with Patrick Smith), *The New York Times*, July 17, 2013, http://www.nytimes.com/2013/07/21/travel/a-pilots-views-on-flight-safety.html (accessed July 21, 2013); Patrick Smith, *Cockpit Confidential: Everything You Need to Know about Air Travel: Questions, Answers, and Reflections* (Naperville, IL: Sourcebooks, Inc., 2013).

3. Betsy Myers, *Take the Lead: Motivate, Inspire, and Bring Out the Best in Yourself and Everyone around You* (New York: Atria, 2011).

4. Industry Week/Manufacturing Performance Institute's Census of Manufacturers for 2004, reported in Traci Purdum, "Teaming, Take 2," *Industry Week* (May 2005): 41–43.

5. "'Golden Hour' Crucial Time for Surgeons on Front Line," *Johnson City Press*, April 1, 2003.

6. Carl E. Larson and Frank M. J. LaFasto, *TeamWork* (Newbury Park, CA: Sage, 1989); J. R. Katzenbach and D. K. Smith, *The Wisdom of Teams* (Boston: Harvard Business School Press, 1993); and Dawn R. Utley and Stephanie E. Brown, "Establishing Characteristic Differences between Team and Working Group Behaviors," *Institute of Industrial Engineers Annual Conference Proceedings* (2010): 1–6.

7. Chuck Salter, "What LeBron James and the Miami Heat Teach Us about Teamwork," *Fast Company*, April 2011, http://www.fastcompany.com/magazine/155/the-worlds-greatest-chemistry-experiment.html (accessed April 25, 2011).

8. Geoff Colvin, "Great Job! Or How Yum Brands Uses Recognition to Build Teams and Get Results," *Fortune* (August 12, 2013): 62–66.

9. Some of the advantages in this section are discussed in "The Rewards of Teaming" sidebar in Amy C. Edmondson, "Teamwork on the Fly," *Harvard Business Review* (April 2012): 72–80.

10. Geoff Colvin, "First: Team Players Trump All-Stars," *Fortune* (May 21, 2012): 46–47.

11. See the excellent discussion in Atul Gawande, "Cowboys and Pit Crews," 2011 Harvard Medical School commencement address, *The New Yorker* (May 26, 2011), www.newyorker.com/online/blogs/newsdesk/2011/05/atul-gawande-harvard-medical-school-commencement-address.html (accessed September 26, 2012).

12. Colvin, "First: Team Players Trump All-Stars."

13. R. B. Zajonc, "Social Facilitation," *Science* 145 (1969): 269–274.

14. David Kesmodel, "Boeing Teams Speed up 737 Output," *The Wall Street Journal Online*, February 7, 2012, http://online.wsj.com/article/SB10001424052970203436904577155204034907744.html (accessed September 25, 2012)

15. Susanne G. Scott and Walter O. Einstein, "Strategic Performance Appraisal in Team-Based Organizations: One Size Does Not Fit All," *Academy of Management Executive* 15, no. 2 (2001): 107–116.

16. This is based on a true story of an anonymous company reported in Ronald A. Gill, "Quality-Oriented Teamwork Resolves Aerospace Manufacturer's Critical Path Tooling Crisis," *Global Business and Organizational Excellence* (September–October 2012): 34–41.

17. Bryce G. Hoffman, "Inside Ford's Fight to Avoid Disaster," *The Wall Street Journal*, March 9, 2012, B1.

18. Jason Fried, "Get Real: When the Only Way Up Is Out," *Inc.* (April 2011): 35–36.

19. The discussion of self-managed teams is based on Ruth Wageman, "Critical Success Factors for Creating Superb Self-Managing Teams," *Organizational Dynamics* (Summer 1997): 49–61; James H. Shonk, *Team-Based Organizations* (Homewood, IL: Business One Irwin, 1992); and Thomas Owens, "The Self-Managing Work Team," *Small Business Report* (February 1991): 53–65.

20. Lindsay Blakely, "The Right Man for the Job (Sometimes)," *Inc.*, July 2, 2012, http://www.inc.com/30under30/lindsay-blakely/ilya-pozin-founder-of-ciplex.html (accessed November 5, 2013); and Ilya Pozin, "Want Happier Employees? Get Rid of the Bosses," *Inc.*, June 18, 2012, http://www.inc.com/ilya-pozin/want-happier-employees-get-rid-of-the-bosses.html/1 (accessed October 2, 2013).

21. David A. Ferrucci, "Building the Team that Built Watson," *The New York Times*, January 7, 2012, www.nytimes.com/2012/01/08/jobs/building-the-watson-team-of-scientists.html?_r=0 (accessed October 1, 2012).

22. Study by G. Clotaire Rapaille, reported in Karen Bernowski, "What Makes American Teams Tick?" *Quality Progress* 28, no. 1 (January 1995): 39–42.

23. Study by Jean Twenge and colleagues, reported in Sharon Jayson, "What's on Americans' Minds? Increasingly, 'Me,'" *USA Today*, July 10, 2012, http://usatoday30.usatoday.com/LIFE/usaedition/2012-07-11-Individualism--Twenge----_ST_U.htm (accessed October 2, 2012).

24. Avan Jassawalla, Hemant Sashittal, and Avinash Malshe, "Students' Perceptions of Social Loafing: Its Antecedents and Consequences in Undergraduate Business Classroom Teams," *Academy of Management Learning and Education* 8, no. 1 (2009): 42–54; and Robert Albanese and David D. Van Fleet, "Rational Behavior in Groups: The Free-Riding Tendency," *Academy of Management Review* 10 (1985): 244–255.

25. See David H. Freedman, "The Idiocy of Crowds" ("What's Next" column), *Inc.* (September 2006): 61–62.

26. Quoted in Jason Zweig, "The Intelligent Investor: How Group Decisions End Up Wrong-Footed," *The Wall Street Journal*, April 25, 2009.

27. "Why Some Teams Succeed (and So Many Don't)," *Harvard Management Update* (October 2006): 3–4; Frederick P. Morgeson, D. Scott DeRue, and Elizabeth P. Karam, "Leadership in Teams: A Functional Approach to Understanding Leadership Structure and Processes," *Journal of Management* 36, no. 1 (January 2010): 5–39; and Patrick Lencioni, "Dissolve Dysfunction: Begin Building Your Dream Team," *Leadership Excellence* (October 2009): 20.

28. Reported in Jerry Useem, "What's That Spell? Teamwork!" *Fortune* (June 12, 2006): 65–66.

29. Eric Sundstrom, Kenneth P. DeMeuse, and David Futtrell, "Work Teams," *American Psychologist* 45 (February 1990): 120–133; María Isabel Delgado Piña, Ana María Romero Martínez, and Luis Gómez Martínez, "Teams in Organizations: A Review on Team Effectiveness," *Team Performance Management* 14, no. 1–2 (2008): 7–21; and Morgeson, DeRue, and Karam, "Leadership in Teams."

30. Deborah L. Gladstein, "Groups in Context: A Model of Task Group Effectiveness," *Administrative Science Quarterly* 29 (1984): 499–517. For an overview of research on team effectiveness, see John Mathieu et al., "Team Effectiveness 1997–2007: A Review of Recent Advancements and a Glimpse into the Future," *Journal of Management* 34, no. 3 (June 2008): 410–476.

31. Sujin K. Horwitz and Irwin B. Horwitz, "The Effects of Team Diversity on Team Outcomes: A Meta-Analytic Review of Team Demography," *Journal of Management* 33, no. 6 (December 2007): 987–1015; and Dora C. Lau and J. Keith Murnighan, "Demographic Diversity and Faultlines: The Compositional Dynamics of Organizational Groups," *Academy of Management Review* 23, no. 2 (1998): 325–340.

32. The discussion of virtual teams is based on Andrea Lekushoff, "Lifestyle-Driven Virtual Teams: A New Paradigm for Professional Services Firms," *Ivey Business Journal* (September–October 2012): 24–27; Phillip L. Hunsaker and Johanna S. Hunsaker, "Virtual Teams: A Leader's Guide," *Team Performance Management* 14, no. 1–2 (2008): 86ff; Chris Kimble, "Building Effective Virtual Teams: How to Overcome the Problems of Trust and Identity in Virtual Teams," *Global Business and Organizational Excellence* (January–February 2011): 6–15; Wayne F. Cascio and Stan Shurygailo, "E-Leadership and Virtual Teams," *Organizational Dynamics* 31, no. 4 (2002): 362–376; Anthony M. Townsend, Samuel M. DeMarie, and Anthony R. Hendrickson, "Virtual Teams: Technology and the Workplace of the Future," *Academy of Management Executive* 12, no. 3 (August 1998): 17–29; and Deborah L. Duarte and Nancy Tennant Snyder, *Mastering Virtual Teams* (San Francisco: Jossey-Bass, 1999).

33. Survey by RW3CultureWizard, reported in Golnaz Sadri and John Condia, "Managing the Virtual World," *Industrial Management* (January–February 2012): 21–25.

34. Vijay Govindarajan and Anil K. Gupta, "Building an Effective Global Business Team," *MIT Sloan Management Review* 42, no. 4 (Summer 2001): 63–71.

35. Jessica Lipnack and Jeffrey Stamps, "Virtual Teams: The New Way to Work," *Strategy & Leadership* (January–February 1999): 14–19; and Sadri and Condia, "Managing the Virtual World."

36. This discussion is based on Lekushoff, "Lifestyle-Driven Virtual Teams"; Arvind Malhotra, Ann Majchrzak, and Benson Rosen, "Leading Virtual Teams," *Academy of Management Perspectives* 21, no. 1 (February 2007): 60–69; Benson Rosen, Stacie Furst, and Richard Blackburn, "Overcoming Barriers to Knowledge Sharing in Virtual Teams," *Organizational Dynamics* 36, no. 3 (2007): 259–273; Marshall Goldsmith, "Crossing the Cultural Chasm," *BusinessWeek Online*, May 31, 2007, www.businessweek.com/careers/content/may2007/ca20070530_521679.htm (accessed August 24, 2007); and Bradley L. Kirkman et al., "Five Challenges to Virtual Team Success: Lessons from Sabre, Inc.," *Academy of Management Executive* 16, no. 3 (2002): 67–79.

37. Darl G. Kolb, Greg Prussia, and Joline Francoeur, "Connectivity and Leadership: The Influence of Online Activity on Closeness and Effectiveness," *Journal of Leadership and Organizational Studies* 15, no. 4 (May 2009): 342–352.

38. Ann Majchrzak et al., "Can Absence Make a Team Grow Stronger?" *Harvard Business Review* 82, no. 5 (May 2004): 131.

39. This is based on a true story of an anonymous company reported in Vicki Fuller Hudson, "From Divided to Ignited to United," *Industrial Management* (May–June 2010): 17–20.

40. Lynda Gratton, "Working Together … When Apart," *The Wall Street Journal*, June 18, 2007; and Kirkman et al., "Five Challenges to Virtual Team Success."

41. Pete Engardio, "A Guide for Multinationals: One of the Greatest Challenges for a Multinational Is Learning How to Build a Productive Global Team," *BusinessWeek* (August 20, 2007): 48–51; and Gratton, "Working Together … When Apart."

42. Reported in Richard Pastore, "Global Team Management: It's a Small World After All," *CIO*, January 23, 2008, www.cio.com/article/174750/Global_Team_Management_It_s_a_Small_World_After_All (accessed May 20, 2008).

43. Reported in Jia Lynn Yang, "The Power of Number 4.6," part of a special series, "Secrets of Greatness: Teamwork," *Fortune* (June 12, 2006): 122.

44. Martin Hoegl, "Smaller Teams–Better Teamwork: How to Keep Project Teams Small," *Business Horizons* 48 (2005): 209–214.

45. Stephanie T. Solansky, "Team Identification: A Determining Factor of Performance," *Journal of Managerial Psychology* 26, no. 3 (2011): 247–258.

46. Reported in Yang, "The Power of Number 4.6."

47. For research findings on group size, see Erin Bradner, Gloria Mark, and Tammie D. Hertel, "Team Size and Technology Fit: Participation, Awareness, and Rapport in Distributed Teams," *IEEE Transactions on Professional Communication* 48, no. 1 (March 2005): 68–77; M. E. Shaw, *Group Dynamics*, 3rd ed. (New York: McGraw-Hill, 1981); G. Manners, "Another Look at Group Size, Group Problem-Solving, and Member Consensus," *Academy of Management Journal* 18 (1975): 715–724; and Martin Hoegl, "Smaller Teams–Better Teamwork."

48. Bradner, Mark, and Hertel, "Team Size and Technology Fit: Participation, Awareness, and Rapport in Distributed Teams"; Sadri and Condia, "Managing the Virtual World."

49. Warren E. Watson, Kamalesh Kumar, and Larry K. Michaelsen, "Cultural Diversity's Impact on Interaction Process and Performance: Comparing Homogeneous and Diverse Task Groups," *Academy of Management Journal* 36 (1993): 590–602; Gail Robinson and Kathleen Dechant, "Building a Business Case for Diversity," *Academy of Management Executive* 11, no. 3 (1997): 21–31; and David A. Thomas and Robin J. Ely, "Making Differences Matter: A New Paradigm for Managing Diversity," *Harvard Business Review* (September–October 1996): 79–90.

50. D. van Knippenberg and M. C. Schippers, "Work Group Diversity," *Annual Review of Psychology* 58 (2007): 515–541; J. N. Cummings, "Work Groups: Structural Diversity and Knowledge Sharing in a Global Organization," *Management*

Science 50, no, 3 (2004): 352–364; J. Stuart Bunderson and Kathleen M. Sutcliffe, "Comparing Alternative Conceptualizations of Functional Diversity in Management Teams: Process and Performance Effects," *Academy of Management Journal* 45, no. 5 (2002): 875–893; and Marc Orlitzky and John D. Benjamin, "The Effects of Sex Composition on Small Group Performance in a Business School Case Competition," *Academy of Management Learning and Education* 2, no. 2 (2003): 128–138.

51. Anita Woolley and Thomas Malone, "Defend Your Research: What Makes a Team Smarter? More Women," *Harvard Business Review* (June 2011), http://hbr.org/2011/06/defend-your-research-what-makes-a-team-smarter-more-women/ar/1 (accessed October 1, 2012).

52. Watson et al. "Cultural Diversity's Impact on Interaction Process and Performance"; and D. C. Hambrick et al., "When Groups Consist of Multiple Nationalities: Towards a New Understanding of the Implications," *Organization Studies* 19, no. 2 (1998): 181–205.

53. Matt Moffett, "Trapped Miners Kept Focus, Shared Tuna—Foiled Escape, Bid to Organize Marked First Two Weeks Underground in Chile," *The Wall Street Journal*, August 25, 2010; and "Lessons on Leadership and Teamwork—From 700 Meters below the Earth's Surface," Universia Knowledge @ Wharton, September 22, 2010, www.wharton.universia.net/index.cfm?fa=view Article&id=1943&language=english (accessed September 29, 2010).

54. R. M. Belbin, *Team Roles at Work* (Oxford, UK: Butterworth Heinemann, 1983); Tony Manning, R. Parker, and G. Pogson, "A Revised Model of Team Roles and Some Research Findings," *Industrial and Commercial Training* 38, no. 6 (2006): 287–296; George Prince, "Recognizing Genuine Teamwork," *Supervisory Management* (April 1989): 25–36; K. D. Benne and P. Sheats, "Functional Roles of Group Members," *Journal of Social Issues* 4 (1948): 41–49; and R. F. Bales, *SYMLOG Case Study Kit* (New York: Free Press, 1980).

55. Robert A. Baron, *Behavior in Organizations*, 2nd ed. (Boston: Allyn & Bacon, 1986).

56. Ibid.

57. Bruce W. Tuckman and Mary Ann C. Jensen, "Stages of Small-Group Development Revisited," *Group and Organizational Studies* 2 (1977): 419–427; and Bruce W. Tuckman, "Developmental Sequences in Small Groups," *Psychological Bulletin* 63 (1965): 384–399. See also Linda N. Jewell and H. Joseph Reitz, *Group Effectiveness in Organizations* (Glenview, IL: Scott Foresman, 1981).

58. Oluremi B. Ayoko, Alison M. Konrad, and Maree V. Boyle, "Online Work: Managing Conflict and Emotions for Performance in Virtual Teams," *European Management Journal* 30 (2012): 156–174.

59. Ibid.

60. Thomas Petzinger Jr., "Bovis Team Helps Builders Construct a Solid Foundation" *The Wall Street Journal*, March 21, 1997.

61. Shaw, *Group Dynamics*.

62. Daniel C. Feldman and Hugh J. Arnold, *Managing Individual and Group Behavior in Organizations* (New York: McGraw-Hill, 1983).

63. Amanuel G. Tekleab, Narda R. Quigley, and Paul E. Tesluk, "A Longitudinal Study of Team Conflict, Conflict Management, Cohesion, and Team Effectiveness," *Group & Organization Management* 34, no. 2 (April 2009): 170–205; Dorwin Cartwright and Alvin Zander, *Group Dynamics: Research and Theory*, 3rd ed. (New York: Harper & Row, 1968); and Elliot Aronson, *The Social Animal* (San Francisco: W. H. Freeman, 1976).

64. Vishal K. Gupta, Rui Huang, and Suman Niranjan, "A Longitudinal Examination of the Relationship between Team Leadership and Performance," *Journal of Leadership and Organizational Studies* 17, no. 4 (2010): 335–350; and Marcial Losada and Emily Heaphy, "The Role of Positivity and Connectivity in the Performance of Business Teams," *American Behavioral Scientist* 47, no. 6 (February 2004): 740–765.

65. Bank of America example from Rachel Emma Silverman, "Tracking Sensors Invade the Workplace; Devices on Workers, Furniture Offer Clues for Boosting Productivity," *The Wall Street Journal*, March 7, 2013, http://online.wsj.com/article/SB1000142412788732403480457834430342 9080678.html (accessed May 3, 2013); and Alex "Sandy" Pentland, "The New Science of Building Great Teams," *Harvard Business Review* (April 2012): 61–70.

66. Stanley E. Seashore, *Group Cohesiveness in the Industrial Work Group* (Ann Arbor, MI: Institute for Social Research, 1954).

67. J. Richard Hackman, "Group Influences on Individuals," in *Handbook of Industrial and Organizational Psychology*, ed. M. Dunnette (Chicago:Chicago: Rand McNally, 1976).

68. These are based on Daniel C. Feldman, "The Development and Enforcement of Group Norms," *Academy of Management Review* 9 (1984): 47–53.

69. Jeanne M. Wilson et al., *Leadership Trapeze: Strategies for Leadership in Team-Based Organizations* (San Francisco: Jossey-Bass, 1994), p. 12.

70. Simon Taggar and Robert Ellis, "The Role of Leaders in Shaping Formal Team Norms," *The Leadership Quarterly* 18 (2007): 105–120.

71. Geoffrey Colvin, "Why Dream Teams Fail," *Fortune* (June 12, 2006): 87–92.

72. Stephen P. Robbins, *Managing Organizational Conflict: A Nontraditional Approach* (Englewood Cliffs, NJ: Prentice Hall, 1974).

73. Tekleab, Quigley, and Tesluk, "A Longitudinal Study of Team Conflict, Conflict Management, Cohesion, and Team Effectiveness."

74. Based on K. A. Jehn, "A Multimethod Examination of the Benefits and Determinants of Intragroup Conflict," *Administrative Science Quarterly* 40 (1995): 256–282; and K. A. Jehn, "A Qualitative Analysis of Conflict Types and Dimensions in Organizational Groups," *Administrative Science Quarterly* 42 (1997): 530–557.

75. Linda A. Hill, "A Note for Analyzing Work Groups," *Harvard Business School Cases*, August 28, 1995; revised April 3, 1998, Product # 9-496-026, ordered at http://hbr.org/search/linda+a+hill/4294934969/.

76. A. Amason, "Distinguishing the Effects of Functional and Dysfunctional Conflict on Strategic Decision Making:

Resolving a Paradox for Top Management Teams," *Academy of Management Journal* 39, no. 1 (1996): 123–148; Jehn, "A Multimethod Examination of the Benefits and Determinants of Intragroup Conflict"; and K. A. Jehn and E. A. Mannix, "The Dynamic Nature of Conflict: A Longitudinal Study of Intragroup Conflict and Group Performance," *Academy of Management Journal* 44 (2001): 238–251.

77. Amason, "Distinguishing the Effects of Functional and Dysfunctional Conflict on Strategic Decision Making."

78. Dean Tjosvold et al., "Conflict Values and Team Relationships: Conflict's Contribution to Team Effectiveness and Citizenship in China," *Journal of Organizational Behavior* 24 (2003): 69–88; C. De Dreu and E. Van de Vliert, *Using Conflict in Organizations* (Beverly Hills, CA: Sage, 1997); and Kathleen M. Eisenhardt, Jean L. Kahwajy, and L. J. Bourgeois III, "Conflict and Strategic Choice: How Top Management Teams Disagree," *California Management Review* 39, no. 2 (Winter 1997): 42–62.

79. Kenneth G. Koehler, "Effective Team Management," *Small Business Report* (July 19, 1989): 14–16; and Dean Tjosvold, "Making Conflict Productive," *Personnel Administrator* 29 (June 1984): 121.

80. This discussion is based in part on Richard L. Daft, *Organization Theory and Design* (St. Paul, MN: West, 1992), Chapter 13; and Paul M. Terry, "Conflict Management," *Journal of Leadership Studies* 3, no. 2 (1996): 3–21.

81. Edmondson, "Teamwork on the Fly."

82. Yuhyung Shin, "Conflict Resolution in Virtual Teams," *Organizational Dynamics* 34, no. 4 (2005): 331–345.

83. This discussion is based on K. W. Thomas, "Towards Multidimensional Values in Teaching: The Example of Conflict Behaviors," *Academy of Management Review* 2 (1977): 487.

84. Edmondson, "Teamwork on the Fly."

85. "Negotiation Types," The Negotiation Experts, June 9, 2010, www.negotiations.com/articles/negotiation-types/ (accessed September 28, 2010).

86. Rob Walker, "Take It or Leave It: The Only Guide to Negotiating You Will Ever Need," *Inc.* (August 2003): 75–82.

87. Based on Roger Fisher and William Ury, *Getting to Yes: Negotiating Agreement Without Giving In* (New York: Penguin, 1983); Walker, "Take It or Leave It"; Robb Mandelbaum, "How to Negotiate Effectively," *Inc.*, November 1, 2010, www.inc.com/magazine/20101101/how-to-negotiate-effectively.html (accessed April 12, 2011); and Deepak Malhotra and Max H. Bazerman, "Investigative Negotiation," *Harvard Business Review* (September 2007): 72–78.

88. This familiar story has been reported in many publications, including "The Six Best Questions to Ask Your Customers," Marketing and Distribution Company Limited, www.madisco.bz/articles/The%20Six%20Best%20 Questions%20to%20Ask%20Your%20Customers.pdf (accessed September 28, 2010).

89. Based on James W. Kinneer, "This and That: Improving Team Performance," in *The 1997 Annual: Volume 2, Consulting* (San Francisco: Pfeiffer, 1997), pp. 55–58.

90. Based on Ellen R. Stapleton, "College to Expand Policy on Plagiarism," *The Ithacan Online*, April 12, 2001, www.ithaca.edu/ithacan/articles/0104/12/news/0college_to_e.htm (accessed April 12, 2001).

PART 5: INTEGRATIVE CASE

Part 5: Leading

Range Resources: Leading Ethically, Communicating Openly

"Natural gas has been a godsend to this area. It has helped farmers see a return on all the hard work they have put into their land just to keep it," says Bev Romanetti, a Pennsylvania cattle farmer. "I have found that Range Resources wants to be responsible; they want to do the right things, they want to protect our environment, and they want to do right by us," remarks Albie Rinehart, a retired schoolteacher from Greene County, Pennsylvania. "I personally know a lot of the people who work for Range Resources—it's like dealing with your neighbors," states Buzz Meddings, a firefighter from Washington County, Pennsylvania.

Citizens of rural Pennsylvania are the people most affected by natural gas exploration in the eastern region of the United States. They are farmers, firefighters, teachers, single moms, restaurant owners, and volunteers. They are hardy. They are the salt of the earth. More important, they are the face of natural gas development in the Keystone State, and they provide the voices through which the Texas-based energy company Range Resources communicates its message of good corporate citizenship to the public. At the company's public outreach site, MyRangeResources.com, everyday people offer video testimonials about the economic and social benefits that Range brings to local communities, whether in terms of jobs, new development, or concern for the natural environment. The site, which functions as part of Range's communications strategy, is an information clearinghouse for all things related to natural gas exploration.

Since discovering the second-largest natural gas field in the world in 2004, Range has used open communication to build trust among the stakeholders most affected by the development of natural gas resources. While natural gas is recognized as a clean energy solution to America's energy needs, citizens still want to know that natural gas exploration is safe for communities and good for the environment.

As explained at MyRangeResources.com, Range makes safety a central component of its natural gas production. To extract methane from rock formations deep down in the Earth, engineers guide a 5-inch-diameter drill straight down more than a mile and then turn it horizontally to penetrate shale rock thousands of feet in all directions. This horizontal drilling method is a groundbreaking advancement that allows drillers to capture far more methane than the old vertical-only method, which requires many more wells to get a fraction of the output. Once Range's drill arrives at its destination 6,500 feet below the Earth's surface, electric charges produce cracks in the rock from which methane gas escapes. To enlarge these fractures for maximum gas recovery, millions of gallons of water and sand are pumped to the area under extreme pressure, expanding the cracks and freeing even more gas to flow back up to the well head at the surface. For environmental safety, Range houses its drill in a 24-inch-diameter casing comprised of five layers of steel and concrete, isolating the entire production process from contact with surrounding land and water.

In its desire to leave as small an environmental footprint as possible, Range has pioneered a way to recycle the millions of gallons of water used in the drilling process. "One thing we've done from an environmental point of view is we now recycle 100 percent of our water in our development areas in Pennsylvania. In fact, we're recycling nearly all of our fluid, which is a real breakthrough for the industry," says Jeffrey Ventura, president and CEO of Range Resources. "Back when we began that process, a lot of people felt that it couldn't be done, that it was physically impossible. Lo and behold, not only did we do it successfully, but now we're doing it large-scale." Ventura, the leader credited with Range's decision to explore the Marcellus Shale gas formation in Pennsylvania, says water recycling is a major innovation in natural gas production. "Just like the Marcellus Shale was a breakthrough," Ventura says, "on the environmental side, water recycling was a real breakthrough."

To keep stakeholders informed about safety, Range has also led the industry in the disclosure of core production processes, especially the use of liquids for drilling and fracturing. "In the middle of 2010, there was a lot of concern nationwide about what's in frack fluid, and Range was the first company in the industry to say exactly what's in our frack fluid," Ventura says. "We post it on our website and we supply it to the state for every Marcellus Shale well that we're drilling. It's 99.9 percent water, and the 0.1 percent are common everyday household chemicals." Range's open communication with the public has earned the respect of environmental groups as well as the U.S. Environmental Protection Agency (EPA), which in 2012 announced that natural gas production was safe for drinking water at its test site in Dimock Township, Pennsylvania.

Consumers who want to keep informed on the latest safety news can also visit RangeResponsibility.com, a new information hub for the company's corporate social responsibility efforts. The site, which features an up-to-date *Corporate Social Responsibility Report*, is part of the company's goal to "be good stewards for shareholders while doing the same thing for the environment and the communities where we live and work." The online communications effort is bolstered by daily Twitter updates and monthly videos posted on YouTube.

Safety, open communication, and leadership—these are the qualities that have made Range Resources a vanguard of America's natural gas boom and a pioneer of sustainable energy development. "I'm proud of what our technical team has done on the environmental side and the communications side," says Ventura of his company's contribution to America's clean energy future.

Questions

1. Range Resources CEO Jeffrey Ventura emphasizes public safety, environmental concern, and open communication with stakeholders. Which of the four contemporary leadership approaches do you think best describes Ventura? Explain.

2. Managers at Range Resources use communication to develop a climate of trust and openness. Why is this especially important for energy companies, and what specific actions can managers take to enhance this communication approach?

3. How might Range's leadership, communication, and values affect employees' organizational commitment? Explain.

SOURCES: Based on My Range Resources Video Interview Series, Range Resources, www.myrangeresources.com (accessed July 20, 2012); Jeffrey Ventura (president and chief executive officer of Range Resources), interview by Rodney Waller, "Range Up Close: Range's Technical Team," Range Resources corporate site, 2010, online video, www.rangeresources.com/Media-Center/Featured-Stories.aspx (accessed July 20, 2012); Jack Z. Smith, "New CEO Taking Helm as Range Continues Push into Marcellus," *Star-Telegram*, December 17, 2011, www.star-telegram.com/2011/12/17/3601200/new-ceo-taking-helm-as-range-continues.html (accessed July 19, 2012); Jeffrey Ventura, "Letter from our CEO," Range Resources corporate Web site, http://rangeresponsibility.com/letter-from-our-ceo (accessed January 10, 2014); Rick Stouffer, "Range Resources Recycles All Waste Water from Washington Drilling," *Pittsburgh Tribune-Review*, October 19, 2009, http://triblive.com/x/pittsburghtrib/business/s_648781.html (accessed July 20, 2012); Natural Gas Company Reveals Fracking Chemical Composition," NewsWorks, July 16, 2012, www.newsworks.org/index.php/local/healthscience/5361-natural-gas-company-reveals-fracking-chemical-composition (accessed July 19, 2012); Range Resources, "Hydraulic Fracturing: Marcellus," Range Resources corporate site, www.rangeresources.com/rangeresources/files/6f/6ff33c64-5acf-4270-95c7-9e991b963771.pdf (accessed July 19, 2012); Laura Legere, "EPA to Stop Dimock Water Deliveries," *Scranton Times-Tribune*, July 26, 2012, http://thetimes-tribune.com/news/gas-drilling/epa-to-stop-dimock-water-deliveries-1.1348393 (accessed July 26, 2012); Timothy Gardner, "Dimock, PA Water Deemed Safe By EPA," Reuters, May 11, 2012, www.huffingtonpost.com/2012/05/11/dimock-pa-water-safe-epa_n_1510035.html (accessed July 19, 2012).

CHAPTER

15

Managing Quality and Performance

CHAPTER OUTLINE

After studying this chapter, you should be able to:

15.1 Define organizational control and explain why it is a key management function.

15.2 Explain the four steps in the control process.

15.3 Describe the benefits of using a balanced scorecard to track the performance and control of the organization.

15.4 Contrast the hierarchical and decentralized methods of control.

15.5 Explain the benefits of open-book management.

15.6 Describe the concept of total quality management (TQM) and major TQM techniques, including quality circles, benchmarking, Six Sigma principles, quality partnering, and continuous improvement.

15.7 Discuss the use of financial statements, financial analysis, and budgeting as management controls.

15.8 Identify current trends in quality and financial control, including ISO 9000 and corporate governance, and their impact on organizations.

•••••○ 📶   100% ▬

< Messages

> ## R U Ready 2 B a Manager?
>
> Delivered

Before reading this chapter, please circle either "Mostly True" or "Mostly False" for each of the five questions below.

1 I enjoy keeping track of my own or my team's progress and like to keep statistics on how well we are doing.

Mostly True   Mostly False

[page 641]

2 In my own life, I judge my success not only by how much money I do or can earn, but also by how much I learn and the quality of my relationships.

Mostly True   Mostly False

[page 644]

3 I set goals for myself each week and then look and see how well I met my own goals.

Mostly True   Mostly False

[page 641]

4 I have a budget for myself and know this is a tool to help me make better decisions about how to use my resources.

Mostly True   Mostly False

[page 657]

5 When I'm working on a project, I try to find someone who's done something similar and been very successful and I try to learn from that person how I can be even more effective.

Mostly True   Mostly False

[page 653]

Imagine taking a beloved family member to a hospital or clinic to receive an injection of pain medication, only to have the person contract fungal meningitis, a rare but potentially deadly disease. That's exactly what happened for many families during the fall of 2012,

Improvement Attitude

Instructions: Respond to each statement that follows based on how you think and act in a typical situation of work accomplishment at school or on the job. Mark whether each statement is Mostly True or Mostly False for you. There are no right or wrong answers, so answer honestly.

	Mostly True	Mostly False
1. I spend time developing new ways of approaching old problems.		
2. So long as things are done correctly and efficiently, I prefer not to take on the hassle of changing them.		
3. I believe the effort to improve something should be rewarded, even if the final outcome is disappointing.		
4. A single change that improves things 30 percent is much better than 30 improvements of 1 percent each.		
5. I frequently compliment other people on changes that they have made.		
6. I let people know in a variety of ways that I need to be on my own to do my job efficiently.		
7. I am typically involved in several improvement projects at one time.		
8. I try to be a good listener and to be patient with what people say, except when it is a stupid idea.		
9. I am frequently proposing unconventional techniques and ideas to improve things.		
10. I usually do not take the risk of proposing an idea that might fail.		

Scoring and Interpretation: Score one point for each Mostly True answer to the odd-numbered items and one point for each Mostly False answer to the even-numbered items. Total score = _____

In organizations, continuous improvement in quality sometimes competes with managerial desires for production efficiency. Efficiency can be maximized by eliminating changes and quality improvements. Continuous improvement, however, is an attitude that productivity can always get better, and each employee can take responsibility to improve it. This attitude is appropriate for quality-conscious managers. Introducing frequent small changes that may temporarily reduce efficiency is the best path to continuous improvement. A score of 7 or higher indicates that you may take personal responsibility for improving activities on which you work. A score of 3 or lower indicates that you may prefer stable and efficient work. A score of 4–6 suggests that you are balanced between efficiency and continuous improvement.

when tainted spinal steroid injections from the New England Compounding Center caused one of the worst public health drug disasters since the 1930s. As many as 14,000 patients across 19 states were exposed to fungal meningitis, with 438 becoming ill and at least 32 dying. A federal inspection found mold and bacteria growing on surfaces, greenish-yellow residue on sterilization equipment, and air conditioning equipment that was shut off at night despite the importance of controlling temperature and humidity. Although U.S. Food and Drug Administration (FDA) inspectors found numerous instances of violations of federal standards, they also noted that surfaces in the clean rooms were contaminated with levels of bacteria or mold exceeding levels at which the company's own procedures called for remedial measures, yet there was no evidence that the company ever took such measures. Company managers, the Massachusetts Board of Pharmacy, and FDA officials all came under scrutiny in the wake of this breakdown of quality control.[1]

What a tragic illustration of the need for quality and behavioral control. Control is a serious responsibility for every manager. It might not always be a matter of life or death, but as a manager, you will use a variety of measures to monitor employee behavior and keep track of the organization's performance and finances. Many of these measures will involve control issues, including controlling work processes, regulating employee behavior, maintaining quality standards, setting up basic systems for allocating financial resources, developing human resources, analyzing financial performance, and evaluating overall profitability.

This chapter introduces basic mechanisms for controlling an organization. We begin by defining organizational control and summarizing the four steps in the control process. Then we discuss the use of the balanced scorecard to measure performance and examine the changing philosophy of control. We discuss today's approach to total quality management (TQM) and consider methods for controlling financial performance, including the use of budgets and financial statements. The final sections look at trends such as International Organization for Standardization (ISO) certification and corporate governance.

15.1 **The Meaning of Control**

Before New York City buildings are demolished or renovated, licensed inspectors are required to inspect them for the presence of lead or asbestos. Both substances can cause severe, long-term health problems, including cancer. If either is found, it must be either removed or contained using an expensive and time-consuming process. Given the serious health risks associated with these two substances, you could assume that the inspection process would be carefully regulated and controlled. Yet many law enforcement officials and industry experts say that New York City's inspection system is highly corrupt. As evidence, licensed safety inspector Saverio F. Todaro recently made a stunning confession in federal court. He revealed that although he had submitted clean asbestos and lead test results for over 200 buildings and apartments, he had not performed a single one of the tests. Although shocking, the Department of Environmental Protection (DEP) claims that these crimes occur frequently and easily because of a lack of controls. The DEP audits only a tiny fraction of the roughly 28,400 projects that inspectors like Todaro certify each year as safe. "We can always look for new ways to improve our process," said a spokesman for the mayor. "DEP is going to start increasing audits, which is the right step to ensure inspections are being completed properly."[2]

CONCEPT CONNECTION The state of California has deep concerns about paint solvents, concrete slurry, and other pollutants entering the water supply through work done at construction sites. Thus, the state government now offers training programs for contractors and others in the construction industry to learn how to improve **organizational control**. In addition to using filters that keep the water supply clean, effective control means ensuring that builders comply with new state regulations.

The "Group Learning" on page 668 will give you a chance to practice developing a control system that includes rules to guide behavior and statistics for measuring performance.

Organizational control refers to the systematic process of regulating organizational activities to make them consistent with the expectations established in plans, targets, and standards of performance. In a classic article on the control function, Douglas S. Sherwin summarizes the concept as follows: "The essence of control is action which adjusts operations to predetermined standards, and its basis is information in the hands of managers."[3] Thus, effectively controlling an organization requires information about performance standards and actual performance, as well as actions taken to correct any deviations from the standards.

Managers must decide what information is essential, how they will obtain that information, and how they can and should respond to it. Having the correct data is essential. Managers decide which standards, measurements, and metrics are needed to monitor and control the organization effectively and set up systems for obtaining that information. If a hospital, for example, carefully monitors and controls its health care services, patients should receive safe, high-quality health care. A pay-for-performance system built into President Barack Obama's health care overhaul for Medicare payments to hospitals has prompted some hospitals to initiate broader initiatives that tie doctors' pay to patient outcomes and quality measures. New York City's Health and Hospitals Corporation, which runs the city's 11 public hospitals, for example, will monitor 13 performance indicators that are believed to be correlated with better quality care, including how quickly emergency room patients go from triage to beds, whether doctors get to the operating room on time, how well patients say their doctors communicate with them, and so forth. If the plan is approved, doctors' raises would be tied to how well they perform on the benchmarks. One doctor warned that when a similar system was implemented in England, quality improved on all the benchmarks, but many of the things that were not measured seemed to decline in quality.[4] The "Director's Toolkit" describes auto-analytics, an innovative reporting system for individuals that can provide information that may help people control their own personal and professional growth.

REMEMBER THIS

- **Organizational control** is the systematic process through which managers regulate organizational activities to meet planned goals and standards of performance.

- Most organizations measure and control performance using quantitative financial measures.

15.2 **Feedback Control Model**

Teams of researchers asked managers in thousands of organizations questions designed to determine how well they were implementing various management control practices, such as establishing standards and targets and measuring performance data, and they found that better control is strongly correlated with better organizational productivity and performance.[5] A feedback control model can help managers meet strategic goals by monitoring and regulating the organization's activities and using feedback to determine whether performance meets established standards.

15.2a Four Steps of Feedback Control

Managers set up control systems that consist of the four key steps illustrated in Exhibit 15.1: establish standards, measure performance, compare performance to standards, and make corrections as necessary.

Establish Standards of Performance   Within the organization's overall strategic plan, managers define goals for organizational departments in specific, operational terms that include a *standard of performance* against which to compare organizational activities. At H&M retail stores, for example, sales floor employees are guided by the standard that clothes should always be "easy to find, easy to buy." Pants, sweaters, and shirts are stacked neatly, with perfect folds; size stickers are placed with precision; and hangers are lined up uniformly. All that precision turns to chaos as soon as the doors open for business, of course, but employees are trained to restore order whenever they have moments to do so. "One thing to keep in mind," said Edwin Mercedes, a store visual manager who is responsible for the look of several stores in the eastern United States, "is standards. We want perfect folds." Garments are replenished on the racks or shelves as soon as they are depleted, and they should never, ever be allowed to lie on the floor. Basic standards for customer service are also followed precisely.[6]

Tracking such measures as customer service, product quality, or order accuracy is an important supplement to traditional financial and operational performance measurement, but many companies have a hard time identifying and defining nonfinancial measurements. To evaluate and reward employees effectively for the achievement of standards, managers need clear standards that reflect activities that contribute to the organization's overall strategy in a significant way. Standards should be defined clearly and precisely so that employees know what they need to do and can determine whether their activities are on target.[7]

Measure Actual Performance   Most organizations prepare formal reports of quantitative performance measurements that managers review daily, weekly, or monthly. Managers should take care, however, that they are not generating reports just because they have data

EXHIBIT 15.1   Feedback Control Model

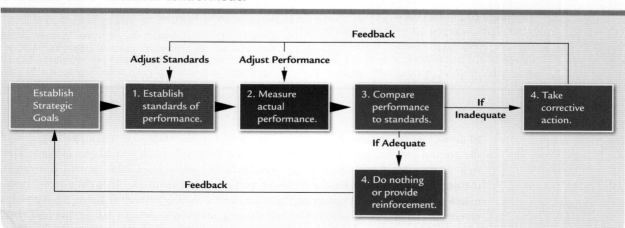

Director's Toolkit

Quantify Yourself

Imagine becoming better at your job and more satisfied with your life by tracking information that reveals exactly how you spend your day. For 22 years, entrepreneur and scientist Stephen Wolfram did just that. He mapped data about his time spent in meetings, e-mail usage, and the number of keystrokes he logged so that he could analyze how he spent his time. Wolfram was able to identify work habits that squelched his creativity and stymied his productivity. So he started planning changes that would help him become more productive and happier.

New devices such as computer software and smartphone apps help people gather and analyze data about what they do at work so they can use it to do their jobs better. This interest in self-awareness is part of a growing discipline called auto-analytics, which is the practice of voluntarily collecting and analyzing data about oneself in order to improve. It consists of the following:

- **Tracking screen time.** While it may be unsettling to have our managers watching what's on our computer screens, it's much more acceptable when we do the watching. New technology called knowledge workload tracking records how you use your computer, such as measuring how long you have an open window, how often you switch between windows, and how long you're idle. The software turns all the measurements into charts so that you can see where you're spending your time and how you can improve your productivity. One computer programmer thought that his online chats were eating into his programming time, so he analyzed how much time he spent chatting during certain periods, and then looked at how much code he wrote during those times. Surprisingly, he found that talking online with colleagues actually improved his productivity.

- **Measuring cognitive tasks.** Another set of tracking tools can help you gather data as you perform cognitive tasks, such as client research on your smartphone or statistical analysis in Microsoft Excel. Although it is notoriously difficult to measure

knowledge work, a tool such as MeetGrinder can measure the time and money spent doing any activity. Bob Evans, a Google engineer, used it to explore the relationship between his attention and productivity. "As engineers, we load up our heads with all these variables, the intellectual pieces of the systems we are building. If we get distracted, we lose that thread in our heads," he said. MeetGrinder revealed to him that he needs about four straight hours to get anything challenging done, so he tackles those projects when he has that kind of time, not on days that are interrupted with meetings and phone calls.

- **Improving health.** Exercise, amount of sleep, and the stress levels of knowledge workers have been shown to affect productivity, creativity, and job performance. Employees can choose from a variety of mobile apps and wearable sensors that collect valuable data about their physical health. Sacha Chua wanted to better understand how her sleep schedule affected her professional priorities, so she monitored her bedtimes, wake-up times, and amount of sleep over several weeks using a tracker called Sleep On It. She changed her routine and started waking up at 5:40 a.m. instead of 8:30 a.m. She gave up late-night activities like browsing the Web and started going to bed earlier. With these adjustments, she discovered that her work productivity soared. The data from Sleep On It gave Chua measurable information that allowed her to establish priorities on what really mattered to her.

Tools used for auto-analytics will continue to become more sophisticated. The data that they reveal will provide the hard evidence we sometimes need to adjust the way we use our time and nurture our minds and bodies to have more success in work and life.

SOURCES: Based on H. James Wilson, "Employees, Measure Yourselves," *The Wall Street Journal*, April 2, 2012, http://online.wsj.com/article/SB1000142405297020452020 4577249691204802060.html#articleTabs%3Darticle (accessed September 28, 2012); and H. James Wilson, "You, by the Numbers," *Harvard Business Review* (September, 2012): 2–5.

---

to do so.[8] These measurements should be related to the standards set in the first step of the control process, and the reports should be designed to help managers evaluate how well the organization is meeting its standards. For example, if sales growth is a target, the organization should have a means of gathering and reporting sales data. If the organization has identified appropriate measurements, regular review of these reports helps managers stay aware of whether or not the organization is doing what it should. Grady Memorial Hospital in Atlanta measures patient satisfaction based in part on the results of a government-mandated patient satisfaction survey that has been administered since 2006. Hospitals that receive Medicare payments must administer at least 100 patient surveys over a period of a year, and Grady's administrators use the results combined with other metrics to evaluate overall patient care.[9]

Compare Performance to Standards The third step in the control process is comparing actual activities to performance standards. When managers read computer reports or walk through the plant, they identify whether actual performance meets, exceeds, or falls short of standards. Typically, performance reports simplify such comparisons by placing the performance standards for the reporting period alongside the actual performance for the same period and by computing the variance—that is, the difference between each actual amount and the associated standard. To correct the problems that most require attention, managers focus on variances.

When performance deviates from a standard, managers must interpret the deviation. They are expected to dig beneath the surface and find the cause of the problem. Assume that a grocer established a goal of increasing seafood sales by 10 percent during the month of July, but sales increased by only 8 percent. Managers must investigate the reasons behind the shortfall. They may discover that recent price increases for shrimp and three late shipments of salmon from Canada caused weaker sales during July, for instance. Managers should take an inquiring approach to deviations to gain a broad understanding of factors that influence performance. Effective management control involves subjective judgment and employee discussions, as well as objective analysis of performance data.

CONCEPT CONNECTION When it comes to pharmaceutical drugs, accuracy is essential—human lives are at stake. Researchers like this one follow precise procedures to ensure that test results are both objective and accurate and that the testing processes meet research goals. Pharmaceutical firms establish standards of performance to measure research activities and results. For example, many companies set a standard for how many compounds should move forward at each stage of the drug development process.

Ryan McVay/Photodisc/Getty Images

Spotlight on Skills

FreshDirect

With more than 45,000 deliveries per week, FreshDirect is known for its farm-fresh produce, custom-butchered meat, seafood, and bakery-fresh pastries and breads. It may be surprising that this successful organization stumbled through a series of missteps during its early days. Although FreshDirect was very successful attracting first-time customers with coupons and incentives, the majority of these customers dropped the service after placing one or two orders because of poor customer service. "We broke too many eggs," said Richard S. Braddock, who was CEO in 2008. "We showed up with thawed ice cream. We bruised produce. We delivered late. We missed boxes."

Managers decided to create a system of continuous feedback, a real-time database that would follow every step—and misstep—of each business day, so that minor problems could be corrected before they erupted into big problems. FreshDirect developed performance standards designed to strengthen customer service and build loyal customers. For example, managers introduced a rating system to measure the quality of its produce and seafood. Every morning, managers and buyers rank their products from one star (below average) to five (never better) and share that information with customers so that they can simulate the in-store shopping experience and decide what to purchase. Other standards of performance included tracking on-time deliveries and the number of errors per order. FreshDirect has a warehouse on Long Island where workers are responsible for butchering, baking, and food preparation. Warehouse managers analyze numerous reports that track plant operations, including inventory levels, quality assurance, and freshness. Managers also monitor real-time data that show the popularity of certain products in specific delivery zones and time slots.

Take Corrective Action   The final step in the feedback control model is to determine what changes, if any, are needed. An example comes from FreshDirect, a premium online grocer in New York City, which used a feedback control model to improve the quality of its products and customer service.

Analyzing performance data also showed other problems: FreshDirect was falling short of its revenue goals, and customers were complaining about sold-out items, limited delivery options, and mistakes in orders. The CEO took corrective action by remaking the company with a stronger focus on customer service. He upgraded the company's Web site to provide a customized online experience. Now, the Web site can analyze order patterns, remind customers of their favorite products, and suggest other items that they might like.[10]

15.2b The Balanced Scorecard

A current approach to organizational control is to take a balanced perspective on company performance, integrating various dimensions of control that focus on markets and customers, as well as employees and financials.[11] Managers recognize that relying exclusively on financial measures can result in short-term, dysfunctional behavior. Nonfinancial measures provide a healthy supplement to the traditional financial measures, and companies are investing significant sums in developing more balanced measurement systems as a result.[12] The **balanced scorecard** is a comprehensive management control system that balances traditional financial measures with operational measures relating to a company's critical success factors.[13]

A balanced scorecard contains four major perspectives, as illustrated in Exhibit 15.2: financial performance, customer service, internal business processes, and the organization's capacity for learning and growth.[14] Within these four areas, managers identify key performance metrics the organization will track:

- *Financial performance.* The *financial performance* perspective reflects a concern that the organization's activities contribute to improving short- and long-term financial performance. It includes traditional measures such as net income and return on investment.

- *Customer service.* *Customer service* indicators measure information such as how customers view the organization and customer retention and satisfaction. These data may be collected in many forms, including testimonials from customers describing superlative service or from customer surveys.[15] The Internal Revenue Service (IRS) has been embroiled in a controversy that shows poor attention to customer service. As a part of the government that many people already loathe, the IRS opened itself to scathing attack by selecting certain groups applying for tax-exempt status for extra scrutiny. The initial impression was that the IRS was targeting only conservative "tea party" organizations, but subsequent investigation revealed they were looking at both left- and right-leaning groups. The scandal has particularly tarnished the image of the IRS's tax-exempt unit, which has been described as "a bureaucratic mess, with some employees ignorant about tax laws, defiant of their supervisors, and blind to the appearance of impropriety."[16]

- *Internal business processes.* *Business process* indicators focus on production and operating statistics. For an airline, business process indicators may include on-time arrivals and adherence to safety guidelines. An event at Reagan National Airport in Washington, D.C., reflected weak adherence to safety standards, for instance. When a lone air traffic controller at this airport fell asleep while on duty and failed

EXHIBIT 15.2 The Balanced Scorecard

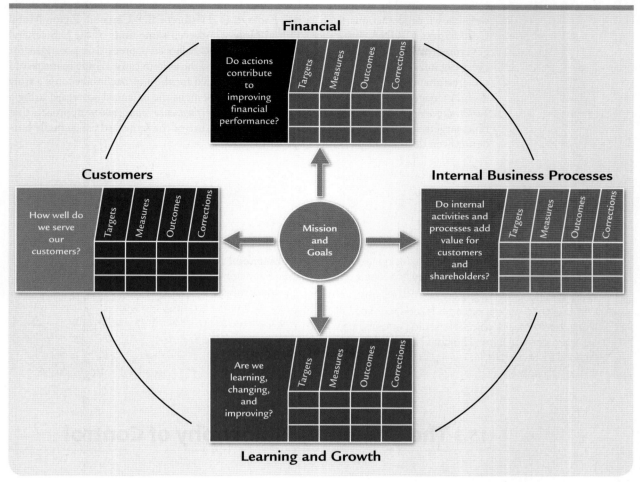

SOURCES: Based on Robert S. Kaplan and David P. Norton, "Using the Balanced Scorecard as a Strategic Management System," Harvard Business Review (January–February 1996): 75–85; and Chee W. Chow, Kamal M. Haddad, and James E. Williamson, "Applying the Balanced Scorecard to Small Companies," Management Accounting 79, no. 2 (August 1997): 21–27.

to respond to repeated radio transmissions, two pilots waiting to land jets carrying a total of 160 people decided to land without clearance, violating Federal Aviation Administration (FAA) safety regulations and damaging the reputations of both airlines involved, as well as the airport.[17]

- **Potential for learning and growth.** The final component of the balanced scorecard looks at the organization's *potential for learning and growth*, focusing on how well resources and human capital are being managed for the company's future. Metrics may include things such as employee retention and the introduction of new products. The components of the scorecard are designed in an integrative manner, as illustrated in Exhibit 15.2.

Managers record, analyze, and discuss these various metrics to determine how well the organization is achieving its strategic goals. The balanced scorecard is an effective tool for managing and improving performance, but only if it is clearly linked to a well-defined organizational strategy and goals.[18] At its best, use of the scorecard cascades down from the

"Not everything that counts can be counted, and not everything that can be counted counts."

—Albert Einstein, theoretical physicist

top levels of the organization so that everyone becomes involved in thinking about and discussing strategy. The scorecard has become the core management control system for many well-known organizations, such as Bell Emergis (a division of Bell Canada), Exxon Mobil Corporation, CIGNA (insurance), Hilton Hotels, and even some units of the U.S. federal government.[19] As with all management systems, the balanced scorecard is not right for every organization in every situation. The simplicity of the system causes some managers to underestimate the time and commitment that is needed for the approach to become a truly useful management control system. If managers implement the balanced scorecard using a *performance measurement* orientation rather than a *performance management* approach that links targets and measurements to corporate strategy, use of the scorecard can actually hinder or even decrease organizational performance.[20]

REMEMBER THIS

- The feedback control model involves using feedback to determine whether performance meets established standards.

- Well-designed control systems include four key steps: establish standards, measure performance, compare performance to standards, and make corrections as necessary.

- A **balanced scorecard** is a comprehensive management control system that balances traditional financial measures with measures of customer service, internal business processes, and the organization's capacity for learning and growth.

15.3 The Changing Philosophy of Control

Managers' approach to control is changing in many of today's organizations. In connection with the shift to employee participation and empowerment, many companies are adopting a *decentralized* rather than a *hierarchical* control process. Hierarchical control and decentralized control represent different philosophies of corporate culture, which was discussed in Chapter 2. Most organizations display some aspects of both hierarchical and decentralized control, but managers generally emphasize one or the other, depending on the organizational culture and their own beliefs about control.

15.3a Hierarchical versus Decentralized Approaches

Hierarchical control involves monitoring and influencing employee behavior through extensive use of rules, policies, hierarchy of authority, written documentation, reward systems, and other formal mechanisms.[21] In contrast, decentralized control relies on cultural values, traditions, shared beliefs, and trust to foster compliance with organizational goals. Managers operate on the assumption that employees are trustworthy and willing to perform effectively without extensive rules and close supervision. Pharrell Williams has learned it's better to run his business with decentralization, as described in this chapter's Executive Edge.

Pharrell Williams Inc.

You might have seen Pharrell Williams winning awards on the Grammies, or listened to one of his many hit songs, but maybe you didn't know what an astute businessman he is. The 40-year-old musician with the hat has a number-one album, 17 top-10 hits, and three Grammy Awards. He began to write and produce early in his career and recently has produced for Jay-Z and Miely Cyrus, as well as written for the movie *Despicable Me*. He's also doing fashion labels, a cloud-based musical platform (UJAM), a YouTube Channel (iOTHER) and a nonprofit for empowering needy kids.

How does he get more done in a week than most do in a year? He surrounds himself with smart people. Currently, he has 10 employees, eight of whom are female. "I would go crazy with an office full of dudes," he says. "What am I going to talk about? Football? I don't know anything about sports."

What he does know is how to collaborate, which includes being humble, in order to be productive. Other people have noted how he constantly gives credit to his staff. And because he doesn't get stressed out, he can be more productive, too. He likes to do what he calls "Tapping In," which means being open to peripheral ideas that can lead to innovation, and he does the opposite of multitasking, preferring more like fixation.

In decision making, he uses his mind and his emotions. He notes successful apparel companies put taste first, which is his goal, as well, to have the aesthetic match the business acumen. His company Bionic Yarn, which is about sustainability and profitability, follows that principle and is now profitable, after only three years in operation. He originally started the company because Rush Limbaugh shamed him and his desire to save the earth. But Williams is unashamedly happy to be called "involved."

Does he believe in luck? Not anymore, since he's seen what hard work it takes to be productive—and successful. But anyone can figure out how to solve problems. "That's always an option," he says.

SOURCE: Mary Kaye Schilling, "Get Busy: Pharrell's Productivity Secrets," *Fast Company*, December 2013/January 2014, 96–100, 104, 158.

Exhibit 15.3 contrasts the use of hierarchical and decentralized methods of control. Hierarchical methods define explicit rules, policies, and procedures for employee behavior. Control relies on centralized authority, the formal hierarchy, and close personal supervision. Responsibility for quality control rests with quality control inspectors and supervisors rather than with employees. Job descriptions generally are specific and task-related, and managers define minimal standards for acceptable employee performance. In exchange for meeting the standards, individual employees are given extrinsic rewards such as wages, benefits, and possibly promotions up the hierarchy. Employees rarely participate in the control process, with any participation being formalized through mechanisms such as grievance procedures. With hierarchical control, the organizational culture is somewhat rigid, and managers do not consider culture a useful means of controlling employees and the organization. Technology often is used to control the flow and pace of work or to monitor employees, such as by measuring the number of minutes that employees spend on phone calls or how many keystrokes they make at the computer.

The hierarchical approach to control is strongly evident in many Japanese companies. Japanese culture reflects an obsession with rules and a penchant for bureaucracy that can excel at turning chaos to order. For example, after the devastating 2011 earthquake and tsunami, the Japanese efficiently organized evacuation centers for families who lost homes during the disaster. Self-governing committees managed these temporary shelters and laid out, in painstaking detail, the daily responsibilities of the residents. People were assigned

TAKE Action!

Will you take a hierarchical or a decentralized approach to control as a new manager? Answering the questions in the "New Manager Self-Test" on page 649 will give you an idea of your attitude toward organizational control.

HOT TOPIC

EXHIBIT 15.3   Hierarchical and Decentralized Methods of Control

	Hierarchical Control	Decentralized Control
Basic assumptions	• People are incapable of self-discipline and cannot be trusted. They need to be monitored and controlled closely.	• People work best when they are fully committed to the organization.
Actions	• Uses detailed rules and procedures; formal control systems. • Uses top-down authority, formal hierarchy, position power, quality control inspectors. • Relies on task-related job descriptions. • Emphasizes extrinsic rewards (pay, benefits, status). • Features rigid organizational culture; distrust of cultural norms as means of control.	• Features limited use of rules; relies on values, group and self-control, selection, and socialization. • Relies on flexible authority, flat structure, expert power; everyone monitors quality. • Relies on results-based job descriptions; emphasizes goals to be achieved. • Emphasizes extrinsic and intrinsic rewards (meaningful work, opportunities for growth). • Features adaptive culture; culture recognized as means for uniting individual, team, and organizational goals for overall control.
Consequences	• Employees follow instructions and do just what they are told. • Employees feel a sense of indifference toward work. • Employee absenteeism and turnover is high.	• Employees take initiative and seek responsibility. • Employees are actively engaged and committed to their work. • Employee turnover is low.

SOURCES: Based on Naresh Khatri et al., "Medical Errors and Quality of Care: From Control to Commitment," California Management Review 48, no. 3 (Spring 2006): 118; Richard E. Walton, "From Control to Commitment in the Workplace," Harvard Business Review (March–April 1985): 76–84; and Don Hellriegel, Susan E. Jackson, and John W. Slocum, Jr., Management, 8th ed. (Cincinnati, Ohio: South-Western, 1999), p. 663.

specific tasks, including sorting the garbage, washing the bathrooms, and cleaning fresh-water tanks. "The Japanese people are the type to feel more reassured the more rules are in place," said Shintara Goto, a tsunami survivor. This hierarchical method of managing the temporary evacuation centers helped survivors find routine and responsibility, which could play a big role in reducing the long-term psychological and physical toll of this natural disaster.[22]

Decentralized control is based on values and assumptions that are almost opposite to those of hierarchical control. Rules and procedures are used only when necessary. Managers rely instead on shared goals and values to control employee behavior. The organization places great emphasis on the selection and socialization of employees to ensure that workers have the appropriate values needed to influence behavior toward meeting company goals. No organization can control employees 100 percent of the time, and self-discipline and self-control are what keep workers performing their jobs up to standard. Empowerment of employees, effective socialization, and training all can contribute to internal standards that provide self-control. Nick Sarillo, who owns two Nick's Pizza & Pub shops in Illinois, says his management style is "trust and track," which means giving people the tools and information they need, telling them the result they need to achieve, and then letting them get there in their own way. At the same time, Sarillo keeps track of results so that the company stays on solid ground. He uses open-book management, which will be described in the next section, so that everyone in the company has information about how the company is doing.[23]

What Is Your Attitude Toward Organizational Regulation and Control?

Instructions: Managers have to control people for organizations to survive, yet this control should be the right amount and type. Companies are often less democratic than the society of which they are a part. Honestly consider your beliefs about the regulation of other people and indicate whether each item that follows is Mostly True or Mostly False for you.

	Mostly True	Mostly False
1. I believe that people should be guided more by feelings and less by rules.		
2. I think employees should be on time to work and to meetings.		
3. I believe efficiency and speed are not as important as letting everyone have his or her say when making a decision.		
4. I think employees should conform to company policies.		
5. I let my significant other make the decision and have his or her way most of the time.		
6. I like to tell other people what to do.		
7. I am more patient with the least capable people.		
8. I like to have things running "just so."		

Scoring and Interpretation: Give yourself one point for each Mostly True answer to the odd-numbered questions and one point for each Mostly False answer to the even-numbered questions. A score of 6 or above suggests that you prefer decentralized control for other people in an organization. A score of 3 or less suggests a preference for more control and bureaucracy in a company. Enthusiastic new managers may exercise too much of their new control and get a negative backlash. However, too little control may mean less accountability and productivity. The challenge for new managers is to strike the right balance for the job and people involved.

SOURCES: Adapted from J. J. Ray, "Do Authoritarians Hold Authoritarian Attitudes?" Human Relations 29 (1976): 307–325.

With decentralized control, power is more dispersed and is based on knowledge and experience as much as position. The organizational structure is flat and horizontal, as discussed in Chapter 7, with flexible authority and teams of workers solving problems and making improvements. Everyone is involved in quality control on an ongoing basis. Job descriptions generally are results-based, with an emphasis more on the outcomes to be achieved than on the specific tasks to be performed. Managers use not only extrinsic rewards such as pay, but the intrinsic rewards of meaningful work and the opportunity to learn and grow. Technology is used to empower employees by giving them the information they need to make effective

Spotlight on Skills

Campbell Soup Company

Campbell Soup Company, which controls 60 percent of the U.S. soup market, is piling up profits by implementing cost-saving ideas suggested by its employees. At the plant in Maxton, North Carolina, factory workers huddle every morning with managers to find ways to save the company money. These employees are part of a decentralized culture where both managers and workers share the company's goals and collaborate on ways to improve efficiency. The daily worker–manager huddles are about "getting everybody involved," says "Big John" Filmore, a longtime plant veteran. "Instead of being told what to do, we get to tell people about our problems," he said.

When challenged to find efficiency in the new Swanson broth line, which processes 260 million pounds of raw ingredients per year, operators and mechanics devised a numbering system for each gasket to speed repairs of the processing equipment. They cut windows into the metal covers over conveyor belts so they could identify signs of wear. They color-coded valve handles to avoid confusion in the settings. With employee-driven changes like these, Campbell says that operating efficiency at the Maxton plant has climbed to 85 percent of what its managers say is the maximum possible, up from 75 percent three years ago. That pays off, as a 1 percent gain in plant efficiency adds $3 million to operating profits.

Campbell's latest challenge is reinventing how the company makes soup. In the past, each soup had its own recipe. Now many soups will share a common base, such as chicken broth, and will be adapted by adding different types of meats and vegetables. Employees at all levels of the organization will help plan and implement the new processes. "We have to collaborate at the highest levels of the organization right down to the plant floor," says Dave Biegger, Campbell's vice president for North America supply chain.[24]

decisions, work together, and solve problems. People are rewarded for team and organizational success as well as their individual performance, and the emphasis is on equity among employees. Employees participate in a wide range of areas, including setting goals, determining standards of performance, governing quality, and designing control systems.

With decentralized control, the culture is adaptive, and managers recognize the importance of organizational culture for uniting individual, team, and organizational goals for greater overall control. Ideally, with decentralized control, employees will pool their areas of expertise to arrive at procedures that are better than managers could come up with working alone. Campbell Soup is using decentralized control by enlisting its workers to help squeeze efficiency out of its plants.

15.3b Open-Book Management

One important aspect of decentralized control in many organizations is open-book management. An organization that promotes information sharing and teamwork admits employees throughout the organization into the loop of financial control and responsibility to encourage active participation and commitment to goals. **Open-book management** allows employees to see for themselves—through charts, computer printouts, meetings, and so forth—the financial condition of the company. Second, open-book management shows the individual employee how his or her job fits into the big picture and affects the financial future of the organization. Finally, open-book management ties employee rewards to the company's overall success. With training in interpreting the financial data, employees can see the interdependence and importance of each function. If they are rewarded according to performance, they become motivated to take responsibility for their entire team or function, rather than merely their individual jobs.[25]

The goal of open-book management is to get every employee thinking and acting like a business owner. To get employees to think like owners, management provides them with the same information owners have: what money is coming in and where it is going. Open-book management helps employees appreciate why efficiency is important to the organization's success as well as their own. Laura Ortmann, who owns Ginger Bay Salon and Spa in St. Louis, Missouri, with her husband, discovered that her hairstylists and massage therapists became more motivated to reach their own performance goals once she trained them to understand the company's financial goals. Individual and company goals were recorded prominently on a scoreboard in the break room and listed each employee's daily sales results and whether goals were met. "Behavior changed overnight," said Ortmann. "No one wants their name next to a low number." By helping her employees see how their efforts affected the financial success of the company, Ortmann increased their motivation. "I love the numbers, and I love knowing how I'm doing," says nail technician Terri Kavanaugh.[26]

Managers in some countries have more trouble running an open-book company because prevailing attitudes and standards encourage confidentiality (even secrecy) concerning financial results. Many businesspeople in countries such as China, Russia, and India, for example, are not accustomed to disclosing financial details publicly, which can present problems for multinational companies operating there.[27] Exhibit 15.4 lists a portion of a

EXHIBIT 15.4 International Opacity Index: Which Countries Have the Most Secretive Economies?

Country	2009 Opacity Score
Nigeria	55
Venezuela	48
Saudi Arabia	45
Chinaw	42
India	41
Indonesia	40
Russia	40
Mexico	37
Taiwan	32
South Korea	29
South Africa	24
Japan	25
United States	22
Canada	20
Germany	17
Ireland	15
Singapore	14
Hong Kong	12
Finland	9

The higher the opacity score, the more secretive the national economy, meaning that prevailing attitudes and standards discourage openness regarding financial results and other data.

SOURCE: Joel Kurtzman and Glenn Yago, "Opacity Index, 2009: Measuring Global Risks," published by Milken Institute (April 2009), www. kurtzmangroup.com/pdf/InstituteOpacityIndex_Apr8.pdf (accessed October 4, 2012).

recent Opacity Index, which offers some indication of the degree to which various countries are open regarding economic matters. The higher the rating, the more opaque, or hidden, the economy of that country. In the partial index for 2009 in Exhibit 15.4, Nigeria has the highest opacity rating at 55, and Finland the lowest at 9. The United States has an opacity rating of 22. In countries with higher ratings, financial figures are typically closely guarded, and managers may be discouraged from sharing information with employees and the public. Globalization is beginning to have an impact on economic opacity in various countries by encouraging a convergence toward global accounting standards that support more accurate collection, recording, and reporting of financial information. Thus, most countries have improved their ratings over the past few years.

REMEMBER THIS

- The philosophy of control has shifted to reflect changes in leadership methods.
- **Hierarchical control** involves monitoring and influencing employee behavior through extensive use of rules, policies, hierarchy of authority, written documentation, reward systems, and other formal mechanisms.
- With **decentralized control**, the organization fosters compliance with organizational goals through the use of organizational culture, group norms, and a focus on goals rather than rules and procedures.
- Campbell Soup uses decentralized control at its plant in Maxton, North Carolina, to encourage employees to cut costs and increase efficiency.
- **Open-book management** allows employees to see for themselves the financial condition of the organization and encourages them to think and act like business owners.

15.4 Total Quality Management

Another popular approach based on a decentralized control philosophy is total quality management (TQM), an organization-wide effort to infuse quality into every activity in a company through continuous improvement. Managing quality is a concern for every organization. Consider the problems that Boeing has had with the new 787 Dreamliner. The new aircraft has been hailed as one of the most innovative planes in years because it is made from composites (a first for the industry), is 20 percent more fuel-efficient, and has 20 percent fewer emissions. But the Dreamliner has been plagued with quality problems from the beginning. In January 2013, a battery caught fire aboard an All Nippon Airways flight. That, combined with other problems, including fuel leaks, a cracked cockpit window, wiring problems, and overheating batteries, prompted the FAA to ground the entire fleet of 787s for four months. Not long after the Dreamliner was allowed to fly again, a fire broke out on a 787 parked at London's Heathrow Airport. Then, in mid-October, a fuselage panel fell from a 787 operated by Air India while it was in mid-flight from Delhi to Bangalore. Although the incident posed no safety risk to passengers, it was yet another black eye for Boeing's high-tech jet, which has suffered more quality problems in two years than most planes ever do.[28]

TQM became attractive to U.S. managers in the 1980s because it had been implemented successfully by Japanese companies, such as Toyota, Canon, and Honda, which were gaining market share and an international reputation for high quality. The Japanese system was based on the work of such U.S. researchers and consultants as W. Edwards Deming, Joseph Juran, and Armand Feigenbaum, whose ideas attracted U.S. executives after the methods were tested overseas.[29] The TQM philosophy focuses on teamwork, increasing customer satisfaction, and lowering costs. Organizations implement TQM by encouraging managers and employees to collaborate across functions and departments, as well as with customers and suppliers, to identify areas for improvement, no matter how small. Each quality improvement is a step toward perfection and meeting a goal of zero defects. Quality control becomes part of the day-to-day business of every employee rather than being assigned to specialized departments.

15.4a TQM Techniques

The implementation of TQM involves the use of many techniques, including quality circles, benchmarking, Six Sigma principles, quality partnering, and continuous improvement.

Quality Circles   A quality circle is a group of six to 12 volunteer-employees who meet regularly to discuss and solve problems that affect the quality of their work.[30] At a set time during the workweek, the members of the quality circle meet, identify problems, and try to find solutions. Circle members are free to collect data and take surveys. Many companies train people in team building, problem solving, and statistical quality control. The reason for using quality circles is to push decision making to an organization level at which recommendations can be made by the people who do the job and know it better than anyone else. At Carrier Collierville, a manufacturer of residential air conditioners and heat pumps, a quality circle attacked a leak issue at braze joints on a heat pump component. Changes made to the work area resulted in a 50 percent reduction in leaks and associated repair costs.[31]

Benchmarking   Introduced by Xerox in 1979, benchmarking is now a major TQM component. Benchmarking is defined as "the continuous process of measuring products, services, and practices against the toughest competitors or those companies recognized as industry leaders to identify areas for improvement."[32] Organizations may also use benchmarking for generating new business ideas, assessing market demand, or identifying best practices within an industry. A five-step benchmarking process is shown in Exhibit 15.5.[33]

EXHIBIT 15.5   A Five-Step Benchmarking Process

SOURCE: Based on Deven Shah and Brian H. Kleiner, "Benchmarking for Quality," Industrial Management (March–April 2011): 22–25.

The first step involves planning the benchmarking study, which includes identifying the objectives of the study and the characteristics of a product or service that significantly influence customer satisfaction. The second step involves identifying the source of the information to be collected. For example, the sources of data for a Sherwin-Williams benchmarking study may include national independent lab studies or studies published in *Consumer Reports* magazine. Once the source of information is identified, data is then collected. Xerox collected information on the order fulfillment techniques of L. L. Bean, the Freeport, Maine, mail-order firm, and learned ways to reduce warehouse costs by 10 percent. The fourth step includes analyzing the benchmarking data that has been collected and recommending areas of improvement. The fifth step includes implementing recommendations and then monitoring them through continuous benchmarking.

Six Sigma   Six Sigma quality principles were first introduced by Motorola in the 1980s and were later popularized by General Electric (GE), where former CEO Jack Welch praised Six Sigma for quality and efficiency gains that saved the company billions of dollars. Based on the Greek letter *sigma*, which statisticians use to measure how far something deviates from perfection, Six Sigma is a highly ambitious quality standard that specifies a goal of no more than 3.4 defects per million parts. That essentially means being defect-free 99.9997 percent of the time.[34] However, Six Sigma has deviated from its precise definition to become a generic term for a quality-control approach that takes nothing for granted and emphasizes a disciplined and relentless pursuit of higher quality and lower costs. Like other aspects of TQM, Six Sigma is not just for manufacturing organizations. Service firms have reaped significant benefits from Six Sigma and other TQM techniques. Cardinal Health, a distributor of health care products, is a critical link in the health care supply chain and handles one-fourth of all medications prescribed every day. Cardinal embarked on a Lean Six Sigma initiative that has led to a 30 percent drop in the order error rate over a three-year period. Cardinal has now extended the scope of its Six Sigma efforts to its supply chain partners with a goal of achieving zero errors, zero waste, and zero lost revenue.[35]

Six Sigma is based on a five-step methodology referred to as *DMAIC*, pronounced "deMay-ick" (standing for Define, Measure, Analyze, Improve, and Control), which provides a structured way for organizations to approach and solve problems.[36] Effectively implementing Six Sigma requires a major commitment from top management because Six Sigma involves widespread change throughout the organization. At Honeywell, for example, all employees are expected to understand Six Sigma fundamentals. Six Sigma provides a common language among employees, complements efforts to cut unnecessary costs from the organization, and supports efforts to "get it right the first time." Honeywell explains its dedication to Six Sigma and what it means to reach this high level of performance with these examples:

- If your water heater operated at Four Sigma (not Six), you would be without hot water for more than 54 hours each year. At Six Sigma, you would be without hot water for less than two minutes a year.

- If your smartphone operated at Four Sigma, you would be without service for more than four hours a month. At Six Sigma, it would be about nine seconds a month.

- A Four Sigma process will typically result in one defective package of products for every three truckloads shipped. A Six Sigma process means one defective package for every 5,350 truckloads.[37]

Exhibit 15.6 lists some additional statistics that illustrate why Six Sigma is important for both manufacturing and service organizations.

Green Power

The Honeybee Style

The honeybee is known for its hard work and wise use of natural resources, as well as for living in a cooperative, interconnected community. Likewise, Munich-based **BMW** recognizes that true sustainability involves the protection and wise use of not only the environment, but of every resource used to provide quality vehicles for consumers. Dating back to the 1970s, BMW's approach to sustainable growth can be seen throughout its well-controlled production process. Self-managed teams oversee rigorous quality control measurement of sustainability, building for BMW an A+ international sustainability rating. A total of 23 interconnected "honeybee" practices address everything from ethical behavior and social responsibility to quality and innovation. The results include the recycling of production waste and the reuse of scrap from BMW's new carbon-fiber car bodies.

SOURCE: Gayle C. Avery and Harald Bergsteiner, "How BMW Successfully Practices Sustainable Leadership Principles," Strategy & Leadership 39, no. 6 (2011): 11–18.

EXHIBIT 15.6   The Importance of Quality Improvement Programs

99 Percent Amounts to:	Six Sigma Amounts to:
117,000 pieces of lost first-class mail per hour	1 piece of lost first-class mail every two hours
800,000 mishandled personal checks each day	3 mishandled checks each day
23,087 defective computers shipped each month	8 defective computers shipped each month
7.2 hours per month without electricity	9 seconds per month without electricity

SOURCE: Based on data from Statistical Abstract of the United States, U.S. Postal Service, as reported in Tracy Mayor, "Six Sigma Comes to IT: Targeting Perfection," CIO (December 1, 2003): 62–70.

Quality Partnering   One of the drawbacks of a traditional quality control program is that people from the quality control department are often seen as "outsiders" to the business groups that they serve. Because they don't always have a strong knowledge of the processes that they are studying, their work may be viewed with suspicion or as an interruption to the normal work routine. The risk here is that quality control is seen as separate from everyday work. Another drawback of the traditional model is that quality control is usually conducted after a product is completed or a service delivered—the time when it's most expensive to make corrections.

A new approach called **quality partnering** involves assigning dedicated personnel within a particular functional area of the business. In this approach, the quality control personnel work alongside others within a functional area identifying opportunities for quality improvements throughout the work process. This integrated, partnering approach to quality makes it possible to detect and address defects early in the product life cycle, when they can be corrected most easily. Another advantage of this approach is that quality partners are viewed as "insiders" and peers who are readily accepted into the work group.[38]

Spotlight on Skills

La-Z-Boy Tennessee

"If we were doing business the same way we did in 2005," said La-Z-Boy's continuous improvement manager David Robinson, "somebody else would be here because we would already be closed. We are $50 million a year better now than we were."

The U.S. furniture industry has been decimated by foreign competition, but a dedication to cost efficiency and continuous improvement has enabled La-Z-Boy to flourish. Robinson points out that 23 of the facility's managers and engineers have been trained in Six Sigma, and cross-functional teams have completed 24 kaizen events focused on safety, quality, and productivity. A significant process improvement at the Dayton facility is the Flawless Launch Program, which assigns a production engineer to make sure that quality and manufacturability is designed into all new products. "Before the product ever makes it to manufacturing, she has been on the front end of the design," Robinson says of the current production engineer. That way, the company knows the tooling and equipment that will be needed to produce the product repeatedly, at low cost, and relatively error-free. As an example, he points to the plant's first attempt to manufacture an electric lift chair. It had about a 40 percent failure rate in the field. After reintroducing it using the flawless launch process, Robinson reports, "We now have a fraction of 1 percent failure in the field."[39]

As a new manager, will you support TQM by taking personal responsibility for improving the tasks and activities that you work on? Refer to your responses on the questionnaire at the beginning of the chapter to get some feedback on your attitude toward continuous improvement.

Continuous Improvement   In North America, crash programs and designs traditionally have been the preferred method of innovation. Managers measure the expected benefits of a change and favor the ideas with the biggest payoffs. In contrast, Japanese companies have realized extraordinary success from making a series of mostly small improvements. This approach, called **continuous improvement**, or *kaizen*, is the implementation of a large number of small, incremental improvements in all areas of the organization on an ongoing basis. In a successful TQM program, all employees learn that they are expected to contribute by initiating changes in their own job activities. The basic philosophy is that improving things a little bit at a time, all the time, has the highest probability of success. Innovations can start simple, and employees can build on their success in this unending process. A commitment to continuous improvement has allowed La-Z-Boy in Dayton, Tennessee, to thrive even during the recent recession.

15.4b TQM Success Factors

Despite its promise, TQM does not always work. A few firms have had disappointing results. In particular, Six Sigma principles might not be appropriate for all organizational problems, and some companies have expended tremendous energy and resources for little payoff.[40] Many contingency factors (listed in Exhibit 15.7) can influence the success of a TQM program. For example, quality circles are most beneficial when employees have challenging jobs; participation in a quality circle can contribute to productivity because it enables employees to pool their knowledge and solve interesting problems. TQM also tends to be most successful when it enriches jobs and improves employee motivation. In addition, when participating in the TQM program improves workers' problem-solving skills, productivity is likely to increase. Finally, a TQM program has the greatest chance of success in a corporate culture that values quality and stresses continuous improvement.

EXHIBIT 15.7   Quality Program Success Factors

Positive Factors	Negative Factors
• Tasks make great skill demands on employees. • TQM serves to enrich jobs and motivate employees. • Problem-solving skills are improved for all employees. • Participation and teamwork are used to tackle significant problems. • Continuous improvement is a way of life.	• Management expectations are unrealistically high. • Middle managers are dissatisfied about loss of authority. • Workers are dissatisfied with other aspects of organizational life. • Union leaders are left out of quality control discussions. • Managers wait for big, dramatic innovations.

REMEMBER THIS

- **Total quality management (TQM)** is an organization-wide effort to infuse quality into every activity in a company through continuous improvement.

- The TQM philosophy focuses on teamwork, increasing customer satisfaction, and lowering costs.

- **Quality circles** offer one technique for implementing TQM and include groups of six to 12 volunteer employees who meet regularly to discuss and solve problems affecting the quality of their work.

- Another option for tracking quality is **benchmarking**, the continuous process of measuring products, services, and practices against major competitors or industry leaders.

- **Six Sigma** is a quality control approach that emphasizes a relentless pursuit of higher quality and lower costs.

- **Quality partnering** involves assigning dedicated personnel within a particular functional area of the business to identify opportunities for improvement throughout the work process.

- **Continuous improvement**, or *kaizen,* is the implementation of a large number of small, incremental improvements in all areas of the organization on an ongoing basis.

15.5 Budgetary Control

Debbie Dusenberry was following her dream as a successful entrepreneur. She had opened a beautifully designed store called Curious Sofa and filled its expansive showroom with antiques, offbeat furniture, accessories, and gifts. She had a dedicated staff and sales reaching $800,000 per year. She had borrowed a lot of money and was planning to expand her inventory. Business was growing fast. But Dusenberry was typical of many small business owners who are long on drive and passion but short on financial experience. Caught up in the excitement of growing sales, she was unaware that excessive costs in staffing, inventory, and freight were hurting her profitability. She was operating without a budget and not keeping track of all her expenses. When sales dropped during the economic recession, the glaring weaknesses in her financial system were exposed. Scared and exasperated, Dusenberry began thinking about how she could save her business and realized she needed a new system that would help her monitor and manage her costs. Her first step was to create a budget.[41]

Budgetary control, one of the most commonly used methods of managerial control, is the process of setting targets for an organization's expenditures, monitoring results and comparing them to the budget, and making changes as needed. As a control device, budgets are reports that list planned and actual expenditures for cash, assets, raw materials, salaries, and other resources. In addition, budget reports usually list the variance between the budgeted and actual amounts for each item.

A budget is created for every division or department within an organization, no matter how small, as long as it performs a distinct project, program, or function. The fundamental unit of analysis for a budget control system is called a responsibility center. A **responsibility center** is defined as any organizational department or unit under the supervision of a single person who is responsible for its activity.[42] A three-person appliance sales office in Watertown, New York, is a responsibility center, as is a quality control department, a marketing department, and an entire refrigerator manufacturing plant. The manager of each unit has budget responsibility. Top managers use budgets for the company as a whole, and middle managers traditionally focus on the budget performance of their department or division. Budgets that managers typically use include expense budgets, revenue budgets, cash budgets, and capital budgets.

15.5a Expense Budget

An expense budget includes anticipated and actual expenses for each responsibility center and for the total organization. An expense budget may show all types of expenses, or it may focus on a particular category, such as materials or research and development expenses. When actual expenses exceed budgeted amounts, the difference signals the need for managers to identify possible problems and take corrective action if needed. The difference may arise from inefficiency, or expenses may be higher because the organization's sales are growing faster than anticipated. Conversely, expenses below budget may signal exceptional efficiency or possibly the failure to meet some other standards, such as a desired level of sales or quality of service. Either way, expense budgets help identify the need for further investigation but do not substitute for it.

Go to the "Self-Learning" on pages 667–668, which pertains to budgetary control.

15.5b Revenue Budget

A revenue budget lists forecasted and actual revenues of the organization. In general, revenues below the budgeted amount signal a need to investigate the problem to see whether the organization can improve revenues. In contrast, revenues above budget would require determining whether the organization can obtain the necessary resources to meet the higher-than-expected demand for its products or services. Managers then formulate action plans to correct the budget variance.

Cash Budget   The cash budget estimates receipts and expenditures of money on a daily or weekly basis to ensure that an organization has sufficient cash to meet its obligations. The cash budget shows the level of funds flowing through the organization and the nature of cash disbursements. If the cash budget shows that the firm has more cash than necessary to meet short-term needs, the company can arrange to invest the excess to earn interest income. In contrast, if the cash budget shows a payroll expenditure of $20,000 coming at the end of the week but only $10,000 in the bank, the organization must borrow cash to meet the payroll.

Capital Budget   The capital budget lists planned investments in major assets such as buildings, heavy machinery, or complex information technology systems, often involving expenditures over more than a year. Capital expenditures not only have a large impact on future expenses, but they also are investments designed to enhance profits. Therefore, a capital budget is necessary to plan the impact of these expenditures on cash flow and profitability. Controlling involves not only monitoring the amount of capital expenditures, but also evaluating whether the assumptions made about the return on the investments are holding true. Managers can evaluate whether continuing investment in particular projects is advisable, as well as whether their procedures for making capital expenditure decisions are adequate. Some companies, including Boeing, Merck, Shell, United Technologies, and Whirlpool, evaluate capital projects at several stages to determine whether they are still in line with the company's strategy.[43]

15.5c Zero-Based Budget

Zero-based budgeting is an approach to planning and decision making that requires a complete justification for every line item in a budget instead of carrying forward a prior budget and applying a percentage change. A zero-based budget begins with a starting point of $0, and every dollar added to the budget is reflected by an actual, documented need.[44] Shell, the oil and gas industry giant, implemented a zero-based budget to drive significant financial performance improvements. Facing unpredictable oil and gas demand and an uncertain global economy, CFO Gerard Paulides believed that a cost reduction strategy was as important to Shell's business as oil and gas production and hydrocarbon maturation. "We dove in deeply, stripping all business areas down to zero and then going back through the exercise of building them back up." Paulides and other executives looked at the minimum resources required to run each part of the business, which Paulides referred to as the *must-haves*. "All other activities are essentially discretionary and optional, or in the zero-based framework, *nice to have*," said Paulides.[45] This approach to budgeting helped Shell shave excessive and unnecessary costs from its yearly expenditures.

Budgeting is an important part of organizational planning and control. Many traditional companies use **top-down budgeting**, which means that the budgeted amounts for the coming year are literally imposed on middle- and lower-level managers.[46] These managers set departmental budget targets in accordance with overall company revenues and expenditures specified by top executives. Although the top-down process provides some advantages, the movement toward employee empowerment, participation, and learning means that many organizations are adopting **bottom-up budgeting**, a process in which lower-level managers anticipate their departments' resource needs and pass them up to top management for approval.[47] Companies of all kinds are increasingly involving line managers in the budgeting process. At the San Diego Zoo, scientists, animal keepers, and other line managers use software and templates to plan their department's budget needs because, as CFO Paula Brock says, "Nobody knows that side of the business better than they do."[48] Each of the 145 zoo departments also does a monthly budget close and reforecast so that resources can be redirected as needed to achieve goals within budget constraints. Thanks to the bottom-up process, for example, the zoo was able to redirect resources quickly to protect its valuable exotic bird collection from an outbreak of a highly infectious bird disease without significantly damaging the rest of the organization's budget.[49]

REMEMBER THIS

- Budgetary control, one of the most commonly used forms of managerial control, is the process of setting targets for an organization's expenditures, monitoring results and comparing them to the budget, and making changes as needed.
- A **responsibility center** is any organizational department or unit under the supervision of a single person who is responsible for its activity.
- An **expense budget** outlines the anticipated and actual expenses for a responsibility center.
- A **revenue budget** lists forecasted and actual revenues of the organization.
- The **cash budget** estimates receipts and expenditures of money on a daily or weekly basis to ensure that an organization has sufficient cash to meet its obligations.

- A budget that plans and reports investments in major assets to be depreciated over several years is called a **capital budget**.
- **Zero-based budgeting** is an approach to planning and decision making that starts at zero and requires a complete justification for every line item in a budget, instead of carrying forward a prior budget and applying a percentage change.
- Many companies use **top-down budgeting**, which means that the budgeted amounts for the coming year are literally imposed on middle- and lower-level managers.
- On the other hand, **bottom-up budgeting** involves lower-level managers anticipating their department's budget needs and passing them up to top management for approval.

15.6 Financial Control

"Numbers run companies," claims Norm Brodsky, a veteran entrepreneur and writer for *Inc.* magazine.[50] In every organization, managers need to watch how well the organization is performing financially by watching the numbers. For example, Nick Sarillo grew up in the pizza business—his father owned a pizzeria in Carpentersville, Illinois—so he already knew a lot about running the business when he opened the first Nick's Pizza & Pub in Crystal Lake, Illinois, in 1995. It was so successful that he opened a second in 2005. By 2007, annual revenues had grown to $7 million. But like many small business owners, Sarillo was naïve about the financial side of the business. When he asked an adviser for help, he was told that he had borrowed too much money during good times; as the economy turned, he almost lost his business because he hadn't paid attention to the debt ratio. Only an impassioned online plea to his customers, which enabled Sarillo to bring in more business and get current with all his vendors, and the willingness of the bank to defer the principal payments on his mortgage for a year saved his company. Sarillo says that things still aren't easy, but he's now paying close attention to the financial statements. As mentioned previously, he has instituted open-book management and taught all employees to read the financial statements so that they also know how the company is performing.[51] Not only do the numbers tell whether the organization is on sound financial footing, but they also can be useful indicators of other kinds of performance problems. For example, a sales decline may signal problems with products, customer service, or sales force effectiveness.

Business Blooper

American Apparel

CEOs are supposed to take their fiduciary responsibility seriously, so one wonders what happened with Dov Charney and American Apparel. An internal investigation revealed professional and personal misconduct, including allowing the posting of nude photos of an employee online, using company funds for family expenses, and so on. There had been problems and allegations for years, including a recent Securities and Exchange Commission (SEC) investigation, so the Board finally fired Charney in December 2014. But Charney is not taking it lying down, in jean or otherwise. He's sued the company for

$35 million in damages in March 2015. The company is not happy, having recently spent $10.4 million in its own investigation of Charney, in addition to the $7 million in severance and settlements with disgruntled employees. Not to mention the losses the company itself experienced from 2010 through 2014, which totaled $340 million. That's a lot of fiduciary responsibility that evidently was not given adequate attention.

SOURCE: L. Shan Li, "Fired CEO Seeks Damages from America Apparel," *Los Angeles Times*, March 28, 2015, p. C1.

What about when managers don't exert financial controls? Read this chapter's business Blooper to how American Apparel's CEO caused multiple problems.

15.6a Financial Statements

Financial statements provide the basic information used for financial control of an organization. Two major financial statements—the balance sheet and the income statement—are the starting points for financial control.

Think of the balance sheet as a thermometer that provides a reading on the health of the business at the moment you take its temperature.[52] The **balance sheet** shows the firm's financial position with respect to assets and liabilities at a specific point in time. An example of a balance sheet is presented in Exhibit 15.8. The balance sheet provides three types

EXHIBIT 15.8 Balance Sheet

New Creations Landscaping Consolidated Balance Sheet December 31, 2015					
Assets			**Liabilities and Owners' Equity**		
Current assets			Current liabilities		
Cash	$ 25,000		Accounts payable	$200,000	
Accounts receivable	75,000		Accrued expenses	20,000	
Inventory	500,000		Income taxes payable	30,000	
Total current assets		$ 600,000	Total current liabilities		$ 250,000
Fixed assets			Long-term liabilities		
Land	250,000		Mortgages payable	350,000	
Buildings and fixtures	1,000,000		Bonds outstanding	250,000	
			Total long-term liabilities		$ 600,000
Less depreciation	200,000		Owners' equity		
Total fixed assets		$1,050,000	Common stock	540,000	
			Retained earnings	260,000	
			Total owners' equity		$ 800,000
Total assets		$1,650,000	Total liabilities and net worth		$1,650,000

EXHIBIT 15.9 Income Statement

New Creations Landscaping Income Statement For the Year Ended December 31, 2015		
Gross sales	$3,100,000	
Less sales returns	200,000	
Net sales		$2,900,000
Less expenses and cost of goods sold:		
Cost of goods sold	2,110,000	
Depreciation	60,000	
Sales expenses	200,000	
Administrative expenses	90,000	2,460,000
Operating profit		$ 440,000
Other income		$ 20,000
Gross income		$ 460,000
Less interest expense	80,000	
Income before taxes		380,000
Less taxes	165,000	
Net income		$ 215,000

of information: assets, liabilities, and owners' equity. *Assets* are what the company owns, and they include *current assets* (those that can be converted into cash in a short time period) and *fixed assets* (such as buildings and equipment that are long term in nature). *Liabilities* are the firm's debts, including both *current debt* (obligations that will be paid by the company in the near future) and *long-term debt* (obligations payable over a long period of time). *Owners' equity* is the difference between assets and liabilities and is the company's net worth in stock and retained earnings.

The **income statement**, sometimes called a *profit-and-loss statement* or *P&L* for short, summarizes the firm's financial performance for a given time interval, usually one year. A sample income statement is shown in Exhibit 15.9. Some organizations calculate the income statement at three-month intervals during the year to see whether they are on target for sales and profits. The income statement shows revenues coming into the organization from all sources and subtracts all expenses, including cost of goods sold, interest, taxes, and depreciation. The *bottom line* indicates the net income—profit or loss—for the given time period.

During the economic recession, companies cut discretionary spending, such as travel expenses, to improve the bottom line, and managers are pushing to keep those expenses from creeping back up. If managers keep costs low where they can, they can spend scarce dollars on higher-priority areas, such as salary increases for staff or research and development. To avoid a cost creep in travel expenses, Deloitte reminds employees of company travel policies when managers see costs rising. Employees are discouraged from traveling to meetings that are expected to last less than eight hours and to use video and Web conferencing whenever possible as an alternative to travel.[53]

The following example describes how one successful franchise owner uses a financial control system to manage one of the most profitable 7-Eleven stores in Manhattan.

15.6b Financial Analysis: Interpreting the Numbers

A manager needs to be able to evaluate financial reports that compare the organization's performance with earlier data or industry norms. These comparisons enable the manager to see whether the organization is improving and whether it is competitive with others in the industry. The most common financial analysis focuses on ratios, statistics that express the

Spotlight on Skills

7-Eleven

Norman Jemal, an enthusiastic and gregarious 7-Eleven franchise owner in Manhattan, loves crunching the numbers with field consultant Kunta Natapraya. Together, they study the sales data and profit margins for the thousands of snack foods that Jemal sells in his three profitable stores. Some claim that Jemal's success is because his stores are located on busy Manhattan streets. High vehicle and pedestrian traffic produce lots of potential customers. But Jemal's success also comes from his knack for analyzing financial data to spot the most profitable products in his inventory and maximizing profits through efficient ordering.

When faced with reordering decisions, Jemal uses 7-Eleven's proprietary Retail Information System (RIS), which helps him analyze sales and profitability data for each product in his inventory. For example, when corporate 7-Eleven announced it was rolling out a sugar-free Slurpee Lite and an empanada, Jemal needed to make room for both by eliminating an existing product. Using RIS, he studied the profitability of each snack product and discovered that the spicy beef patty was lagging in sales and profitability, so he removed it from the stores' inventory to make room for the new products.

7-Eleven focuses on its core competence of figuring out what to sell to rushed customers and how to sell it to them. "Other franchises pitch their name," Jemal says. "7-Eleven, which I think has a great name, pitched their [RIS] system." That system is part of a carefully designed financial control model that also includes regular audits. A good audit performance will go a long way toward determining if 7-Eleven allows Jemal to open more stores. He says he'd like to open 20 more.[54]

relationships between performance indicators such as profits and assets, sales, and inventory. Ratios are stated as a fraction or proportion; Exhibit 15.10 summarizes some financial ratios, which are measures of an organization's liquidity, activity, profitability, and leverage. These ratios are among the most common, but many measures are used. Managers decide which ratios reveal the most important relationships for their business.

Liquidity Ratios   The **liquidity ratio** indicates an organization's ability to meet its current debt obligations. For example, the *current ratio* (current assets divided by current liabilities) tells whether the company has sufficient assets to convert into cash to pay off its debts, if needed. If a hypothetical company, Oceanographics, Inc., has current assets of $600,000 and current liabilities of $250,000, the current ratio is 2.4, meaning it has sufficient funds to pay off immediate debts 2.4 times. This level for the current ratio

EXHIBIT 15.10 Common Financial Ratios

Liquidity Ratios	**Current assets/Current liabilities**
Current ratio	Cash + Accounts receivable/Current liabilities
Quick ratio	
Activity Ratios	**Total sales/Average inventory**
Inventory turnover	Purchase orders/Customer inquiries
Conversion ratio	
Profitability Ratios	**Net income/Sales**
Profit margin on sales	Gross income/Sales
Gross margin	Net income/Total assets
Return on assets (ROA)	
Leverage Ratios	**Total debt/Total assets**
Debt ratio	

CONCEPT CONNECTION   Can you imagine a world without milk? If milk's **profitability ratio** doesn't recover soon, dairy farmers may opt out of producing it. Analysts say that milk is profitable only when its ratio is 3.0 or higher, but milk's ratio has been hovering around 2.0 in recent years. This is due to the high cost of feed for dairy cows, which is mainly corn, and given that the drought of 2012 killed off a huge percentage of the corn crop, the price of corn is expected to remain high.

is normally considered a satisfactory margin of safety. Another liquidity ratio is the *quick ratio*, which is typically expressed as cash plus accounts receivable divided by current liabilities. The quick ratio is a popular metric to pair with the current ratio to gauge liquidity. "If a business does not have decent liquidity, then one unexpected expense could severely hurt it," said Brad Schaefer, an analyst with Sageworks Inc., a financial information company.[55]

Activity Ratios   The **activity ratio** measures internal performance with respect to key activities defined by management. For example, *inventory turnover* is calculated by dividing total sales by average inventory. This ratio tells how many times the inventory is used up to meet the total sales figure. If inventory sits too long, money is wasted. Dell Inc. achieved a strategic advantage by minimizing its inventory costs. Dividing Dell's annual sales by its small inventory generates an inventory turnover rate of 35.7.[56]

Another type of activity ratio, the *conversion ratio*, is purchase orders divided by customer inquiries. This ratio is an indicator of a company's effectiveness in converting inquiries into sales. For example, if Cisco Systems moves from a 26.5 to a 28.2 conversion ratio, more of its inquiries are turned into sales, indicating better sales activity.

Profitability Ratios   Managers analyze a company's profits by studying **profitability ratios**, which state profits relative to a source of profits, such as sales or assets. When Alan Mulally became CEO of Ford Motor Company in 2008, he emphatically stressed the importance of profitability. At that time, Ford was a sick company, losing $83 million a day, and the stock price had plummeted to $1.01. Mulally initiated Ford's remarkable turnaround by fostering a new culture of accountability that emphasized the use of consistent metrics to gauge performance. Mulally expected each department head to know and report on how his or her department was performing. His emphasis on data-driven management permanently changed the culture at Ford. In 2010, Ford posted a profit of $6.6 billion, the most money that the company had made in more than a decade.[57]

One important profitability ratio is the *profit margin on sales*, which is calculated as net income divided by sales. Similarly, *gross margin* is the gross (before-tax) profit divided by total sales. Another profitability measure is *return on assets (ROA)*, which is a percentage representing what a company earned from its assets, computed as net income divided by total assets. ROA is a valuable yardstick for comparing a company's ability to generate earnings with other investment opportunities. In basic terms, the company should be able to earn more by using its assets to operate the business than it could by putting the same investment in the bank.

Leverage Ratios   *Leverage* refers to funding activities with borrowed money. A company can use leverage to make its assets produce more than they could on their own. However, too much borrowing can put the organization at risk for being unable to keep up with repayment of its debt. Managers therefore track their *debt ratio*, or total debt divided by total assets, to make sure that it does not exceed a level that they consider acceptable. Lenders may consider a company with a debt ratio above 1.0 to be a poor credit risk.

REMEMBER THIS

- Financial statements provide the basic information used for financial control of an organization.
- The **balance sheet** shows the firm's financial position with respect to assets and liabilities at a specific point in time.
- The **income statement** summarizes the firm's financial performance for a given time interval.
- The most common financial analysis focuses on the use of ratios—statistics that express the relationships between performance indicators such as profits and assets, sales, and inventory.
- The **liquidity ratio** indicates the organization's ability to meet its current debt obligations.
- The **activity ratio** measures the organization's internal performance with respect to key activities defined by management.
- The **profitability ratio** describes the firm's profits relative to a source of profits, such as sales or assets.

15.7 Trends in Quality and Financial Control

Many companies are responding to changing economic realities and global competition by reassessing organizational management and processes—including control mechanisms. Two major trends are international quality standards and increased corporate governance.

15.7a International Quality Standards

One impetus for TQM in the United States is the increasing significance of the global economy. Many countries have adopted a universal benchmark for quality management practices, ISO 9000 standards, which represent an international consensus of what constitutes effective quality management as outlined by the International Organization for Standardization (ISO) in Geneva, Switzerland.[58] Hundreds of thousands of organizations in 157 countries, including the United States, have been certified against ISO 9000 standards to demonstrate their commitment to quality. Europe continues to lead in the total number of certifications, but the greatest number of new certifications in recent years has been in the United States. One of the more interesting organizations to become ISO certified was the Phoenix, Arizona, police department's Records and Information Bureau. In today's environment, where the credibility of law enforcement agencies has been called

Agencja Fotograficzna Caro/Ruffer/Alamy

CONCEPT CONNECTION In order to become **ISO 9000–certified**, companies have to work with an independent registrar that will audit the company's practices and procedures according to the certification guidelines. U.S.-based Heartlab, Inc., for example, worked with the ISO to earn its certification. Heartlab makes medical information management systems that store data about heart patients.

into question, the bureau wanted to make a clear statement about its commitment to the high quality and accuracy of information provided to law enforcement personnel and the public.[59] ISO certification has become the recognized standard for evaluating and comparing companies on a global basis, and more U.S. companies are feeling the pressure to participate to remain competitive in international markets. In addition, many countries and companies require ISO certification before they will do business with an organization.

15.7b Corporate Governance

Many organizations have moved toward increased control from the top in terms of corporate governance. Traditionally defined as the ways in which an organization safeguards the interests of shareholders, the term *corporate governance* has been expanded to refer to the framework of systems, rules, and practices by which an organization ensures accountability, fairness, and transparency in its relationships with all stakeholders, including investors, employees, customers, and the general public.[60]

Concerns over corporate governance came to the forefront some years ago in light of the failure of top executives and corporate directors to provide adequate oversight and control at failed companies such as Enron, HealthSouth, Adelphia Communications, and WorldCom. In some cases, financial reporting systems were manipulated to produce false results and hide internal failures. In response, the U.S. government enacted the Sarbanes-Oxley Act of 2002, often referred to as SOX, which requires several types of reforms, including better internal monitoring to reduce the risk of fraud, certification of financial reports by top leaders, improved measures for external auditing, and enhanced public financial disclosure. The initial cost of implementing the SOX reforms may run as high as $5 million to $10 million for a small business once it has gone public. (Private firms do not have to meet the same accounting and compliance regulations imposed by SOX.) To ease the significant burden on small, emerging growth firms, the JOBS Act (an acronym for Jumpstart Our Business Startups) allows some small companies to avoid the internal control requirements of SOX and the associated costs for up to five years. The statute defines an eligible firm as one with less than $1 billion in annual gross revenue. The JOBS Act is a boon to small companies because it lowers the costs associated with outside auditor review requirements for internal controls.[61]

With the failure of large firms such as Lehman Brothers and Bear Stearns in 2008, corporate governance again became a hot topic. Lax oversight likely contributed both to the failure of these firms and to a worldwide economic crisis. "I don't think there's any question that a dramatic failure of corporate governance was a central issue of the crisis," said Phil Angelides, chairman of the Financial Crisis Inquiry Commission appointed by the U.S. Congress. Global regulators from 27 countries recently imposed new rules and restraints on financial institutions designed to limit risk taking and increase oversight.[62] In addition, the SEC now requires that companies justify their board structure in proxy statements to ensure that boards are designed in a way to provide needed oversight of management actions.[63]

As a new manager, find a balance between oversight and control on the one hand and mutual trust and respect on the other. Go to the "Ethical Dilemma" on pages 669–670, which pertains to new workplace control issues.

REMEMBER THIS

- As global business expands, many companies have adopted a universal benchmark for quality management practices, including **ISO 9000 standards**, which represent an international consensus of what constitutes effective quality management as outlined by the International Organization for Standardization (ISO).

- Many organizations are moving toward increased control from the top in terms of **corporate governance**, which refers to the framework of systems, rules, and practices by which an organization ensures accountability, fairness, and transparency in the firm's relationships with stakeholders.

CHAPTER 15   DISCUSSION QUESTIONS

1. You have been hired to manage a 20-person staff for Nightlight Travels, a travel agency in Las Vegas. For five years, sales have been hammered by the global recession, and staff morale has plummeted as star employees have left for positions in more secure industries. Key customer relationships have been damaged by the sloppy and unprofessional work habits of the remaining staff members. Your first responsibility as new manager is to create next year's budget for all planned expenditures. But first you must decide if you will adopt a hierarchical approach or a decentralized approach to control. Which one would you choose, and why?

2. You're a manager who employs a participative control approach. You've concluded that corrective action is necessary to improve customer satisfaction, but first you need to convince your employees that the problem exists. What kind of evidence do you think employees will find more compelling: quantitative measurements or anecdotes from your interactions with customers? Explain your answer.

3. Describe the advantages of using a balanced scorecard to measure and control organizational performance. Suppose that you created a balanced scorecard for Walmart. What specific customer service measures would you include?

4. In zero-based budgeting, every account starts at $0, and every dollar added to the budget is reflected by an actual, documented need. Identify the possible advantages of zero-based budgeting.

5. Most companies have policies that regulate employees' personal use of work computers during work hours. Some even monitor employee e-mails and track the Web sites that have been visited. Do you consider this type of surveillance an invasion of privacy? What are the advantages of restricting employee use of the Internet and e-mail at work?

6. Think of a class that you've taken in the past. What standards of performance did your professor establish? How was your actual performance measured? How was your performance compared to the standards? Do you think the standards and methods of measurement were fair? Were they appropriate to your assigned work? Why or why not?

7. Some critics argue that Six Sigma is a collection of superficial changes that often result in doing a superb job of building the wrong product or offering the wrong service. Do you agree or disagree? Explain.

8. What types of analysis can managers perform to help them diagnose a company's financial condition? How might a review of financial statements help managers diagnose other kinds of performance problems as well?

9. Why is benchmarking an important component of TQM programs? Do you believe a company could have a successful TQM program without using benchmarking?

10. What is ISO certification? Why would a global company like GE want ISO certification?

SELF-LEARNING

Is Your Budget in Control?

By the time you are in college, you are in charge of at least some of your own finances. How well you manage your personal budget may indicate how well you will manage your company's budget on the job. Respond to the following statements to evaluate your own budgeting habits. If the statement doesn't apply directly to you, respond the way you think that you would behave in a similar situation.

	Yes	No
1. I spend all my money as soon as I get it.	___	___
2. At the beginning of each week (or month, or term), I write down all my fixed expenses.	___	___
3. I never seem to have any money left over at the end of the week (or month).	___	___

	Yes	No

4. I pay all my expenses, but I never seem to have any money left over for fun. ___ ___

5. I am not putting any money away in savings right now; I'll wait until after I graduate from college. ___ ___

6. I can't pay all my bills. ___ ___

7. I have a credit card, but I pay the balance in full each month. ___ ___

8. I take cash advances on my credit card. ___ ___

9. I know how much I can spend on eating out, movies, and other entertainment each week. ___ ___

10. I pay cash for everything. ___ ___

11. When I buy something, I look for value and determine the best buy. ___ ___

	Yes	No

12. I lend money to friends whenever they ask, even if it leaves me short of cash. ___ ___

13. I never borrow money from friends. ___ ___

14. I am putting aside money each month to save for something that I really need. ___ ___

Scoring and Interpretation

Yes responses to statements 2, 9, 10, 13, and 14 point to the most disciplined budgeting habits; *Yes* responses to 4, 5, 7, and 11 reveal adequate budgeting habits; *Yes* responses to 1, 3, 6, 8, and 12 indicate the poorest budgeting habits. If you have answered honestly, chances are you'll have a combination of all three. Look to see where you can improve your budgeting behaviors.

GROUP LEARNING

Create a Group Control System

Step 1. Form into groups of three to five students. Each group will assume that another student group has been given an assignment of writing a major paper that will involve research by individual group members that will be integrated into the final paper. Each group member has to do his or her part.

Step 2. Your assignment is to develop a list of rules and identify some statistics by which to control the behavior of members in that group. Brainstorm and discuss potential rules to govern member behavior and consequences for breaking those rules.

Step 3. First, select the five rules that you think are most important for governing group member behavior. Consider the following situations that rules might cover: arriving late for a meeting; missing a meeting; failing to complete a work assignment; disagreements about desired quality of work; how to resolve conflicts about paper content; differences in participation, such as one person doing all the talking and someone else talking hardly at all; how to handle meetings that start late; the use of an agenda and handling deviations from the agenda; and any other situation that your group thinks a rule should cover. that your group thinks a rule should cover.

Rules you determine are important	List statistics that could be developed to measure the behavior and group outcomes	How will you know if the group is following the rule and performing as expected?
1.		
2.		
3.		
4.		
5.		

Step 4. Now consider what statistics could be developed to measure the behavior and outcome of the group pertaining to those five rules. What kinds of things could be counted to understand how the group is performing and whether members are following the rules?

Step 5. Discuss the following questions: Why are rules important as a means of control? What

are the advantages and disadvantages of having many rules (hierarchical control) versus few rules (decentralized control) for a student group? How can statistics help a group ensure appropriate behavior and a high-quality product?

Step 6. Be prepared to present your conclusions to the class.

ACTION LEARNING

Schoolwork standards

4. Interview four students besides yourself, students not taking this same course right now. Make sure two of them are top grade-earners and two are about average. Tell the students you will keep their information confidential, that you will only be reporting results in a paper you will write, that you will not divulge any names. And then stick to that promise.

5. Ask them questions about how they study, how much they read, how do they manage to work on an finish a project or paper, how they feel about grades, etc.

6. Determine if they use any of the control mechanisms described in this chapter: Feedback Control, Financial or budgetary control.

7. Have they developed standards for their work? Do they compare the actual performance to the standard? What happens when the performance is less than expected, for example, they don't get as high a grade?

8. Write a report for your instructor, comparing the top students to the others. Make sure you don't mention the students' names in your report, but you keep it anonymous.

9. Your instructor may lead a class discussion on the findings. Again, do not mention anyone's names. If you want to talk about your own experiences as a student, that would be fine.

ETHICAL DILEMMA

The Wages of Sin?[64]

Chris Dykstra, responsible for loss prevention at Westwind Electronics, took a deep breath before he launched into making his case for the changes that he was proposing to the company's shoplifting policy. He knew that convincing Ross Chenoweth was going to be a hard sell. Ross, the president and CEO, was the son of the founder of the local, still-family-owned consumer electronics chain based in Phoenix, Arizona. He'd inherited not only the company, but also his father's strict moral code.

"I think it's time to follow the lead of other stores," Chris began. He pointed out that most other retailers didn't bother calling the police and pressing charges unless the thief had shoplifted merchandise worth more than $50 to $100. In contrast, Westwind currently had a zero-tolerance policy toward theft that Ross's father had put in place when he started the business. Chris wanted

to replace that policy with one that prosecuted only individuals between 18 and 65 who had stolen more than $20 worth of goods, and who had a previous history of theft at Westwind. In the case of first-time culprits under 18 or over 65, he argued for letting them off with a strict warning, regardless of the value of their ill-gotten goods. Repeat offenders would be arrested.

"Frankly, the local police are getting pretty tired of having to come to our stores every time a teenager sticks a CD in his jacket pocket," Chris pointed out. "And besides, we just can't afford the costs associated with prosecuting everyone." Every time he pressed charges against a shoplifter who'd made off with a $10 item, Westwind lost money. The company had to engage a lawyer and pay employees overtime for their court appearances. In addition, Chris was looking at hiring more security guards to keep up with the workload. Westwind was already in a losing battle at the moment with mass retailers who were competing all too successfully on price, so passing on the costs of its zero-tolerance policy to customers wasn't really an option. "Let's concentrate on catching dishonest employees and those organized-theft rings. They're the ones who are really hurting us," Chris concluded.

There was a long pause after Chris finished his carefully prepared speech. Ross thought about his recently deceased father, both an astute businessman and a person for whom honesty was a key guiding principle. If he were sitting here today, he'd no doubt say that theft was theft—that setting a minimum was tantamount to saying that stealing was acceptable, just as long as you don't steal too much. He looked at Chris. "You know, we've both got teenagers. Is this really a message you want to send out, especially to kids? You know as well as I do that there's nothing they like better than testing limits. It's almost an invitation to see if you can beat the system." But then Ross faltered as he found himself glancing at the latest financial figures on his desk—another in a string of quarterly losses. If Westwind went under, a lot of employees would be looking for another way to make a living. In his heart, he believed in his father's high moral standards, but he had to ask himself: Just how moral could Westwind afford to be?

What Would You Do?

1. Continue Westwind's zero-tolerance policy toward shoplifting. It's the right thing to do—and it will pay off in the end in higher profitability because the chain's reputation for being tough on crime will reduce overall losses from theft.

2. Adopt Chris Dykstra's proposed changes and show more leniency to first-time offenders. It is a more cost-effective approach to the problem than the current policy, plus it stays close to your father's original intent.

3. Adopt Chris Dykstra's proposed changes, but with a higher limit than the proposed $20 amount (say, $50 or $100), but which is still less than the cost of prosecution. In addition, make sure that the policy isn't publicized. That way, you'll reduce costs even more and still benefit from your reputation for prosecuting all shoplifters.

CASE FOR CRITICAL ANALYSIS

Five Stars

Cousins Jeri Lynn DeBose, Tish Hoover, and Josephine (Joey) Parks looked forward to meeting up during the Christmas holidays to compare notes on the results of midyear teacher evaluations.

All were public school teachers in districts scattered over the state. In the pressured search for new levels of teacher accountability demanded by legislators, the state department of education joined 16 other states in implementing a new teacher evaluation system. The goal is to hold teachers accountable for student learning progress in the classroom. Under the guidance of the National Council for Teacher Quality, criteria varies by state, but in most cases, 40 percent of each teacher's accountability score would be based on the principal's evaluation and ranking based on personal observation, 30 percent would be based on personal observation by a master teacher from outside the district, and the other 30 percent would be based on student test score gains. The state department of education would set a performance goal for each school district, and the principal would set a performance goal for each teacher. In preparation, the state conducted intensive training sessions for principals and designated master teachers who would conduct the evaluations based on four class observations per teacher. Officials used standardized achievement tests to derive value-added scores that measure student learning over the year.

Teacher ratings were 1–5, with 1 being the lowest and 5 representing near perfection. The publication of the first year's evaluations stirred interest and controversy, particularly among teachers who worried about the possible long-term effects on job retention and tenure.

Now, with the first-year evaluations in hand, the three cousins pored over their experiences. The three represented different types of school systems within the state. Jeri Lynn worked for a metropolitan system in the state capital. The system included many low-income students whose first language was not English, and several schools within the system were teetering on the brink of state takeover if improvement in student scores didn't materialize this school year. Tish worked in a county system dominated by upper-income residents, and Joey taught in the rural community in which all three grew up. The rural community had high unemployment, and a low percentage of graduates went on to college. As a result, the cousins came to the table with differing teaching experiences.

"The numbers are all over the place," Jeri Lynn remarked as she studied the pages.

"The whole system is flawed and they need to make changes," Joey said. "It's too subjective. The principal and master teacher observations are subjective because there are personal factors that affect a true outcome."

"Yeah, look at the numbers from your upper-income district," Jeri Lynn said to Tish. "How can 60 percent of the teachers score 5s?"

Tish chuckled. "Yeah, lucky us. Our schools are overflowing with children from wealthy families. These are the kids who will apply to Ivy League schools. I can tell you that the principals are going to avoid confrontation on all fronts. No principal is going to give any indication that their students are receiving an education that's less than perfect, and that means cramming the rankings with 5s. They claim a higher level of motivation for students, and thus the selection of an elite team of educators. So with those pressures, I don't think we get personal feedback that is accurate."

"At the other end of the spectrum, we have my rural district," Joey said. "The big problem is that the principals know everyone and have longstanding relationships with everyone in the county, so I think scores are based on personal history. We could almost predict who would get high or low scores *before* the observations. For principals, it can go back as far as 'his daddy and my daddy hated each other in high school, and now I get to evaluate his daughter.'"

"I think that in many cases, principals feel pressure to align scores with state expectations. The state *expected* my district to have high scores and *expected* rural schools such as yours to be lower," Tish said.

"But isn't that partially offset by lower goals for the rural school districts?" responded Joey.

"The key to the accountability system is the principal in each school," Jeri Lynn suggested. "With several of the schools in Metro teetering on the edge of state takeover by the end of the year, we had lots of strict principals who wanted to hold our feet to the fire with lower scores."

"I thought the whole idea was to provide the teachers with feedback so that we would know the areas where we need improvement," Tish said.

"The principals were supposed to conduct two observations in the fall and two more in the spring," Jeri Lynn said. "I think that's asking too much of them when they already have so much on their plates. I think a lot of them are skimping on their visits. I know I only had one observation last semester, and I'm sure Mr. Talley just faked the second set of numbers. The master teachers make only two observations a year, which may be more objective but counts for less."

"I'm wondering, too, how a principal measures performance in a course area outside his area of expertise, such as math," Joey said. "If the guy has a phobia about math, anything the teacher says or does is going to look brilliant—thus a 5."

Tish and Jeri Lynn looked at each other and laughed. "Maybe we picked the wrong subjects," Tish said.

"My question is one of perception," Jeri Lynn said. "A large percentage of my students are ELL. That affects their scores. How do you measure a 3 in my situation against a 5 for Tish? At the end of the school year, little Carlos is thrilled that his reading in English has improved, but there's no Big Bang here. It's a slow steady improvement that may not actually show up in big strides for a couple of years."

"So the question is *how do they create a system that is fair?*" Tish asked.

"*And accurate,*" added Jeri Lynn.

Questions

1. What do you see as the major strengths and flaws in the feedback control system used in the schools in this scenario? What changes do you recommend to overcome the flaws?

2. Is a 1–5 grading system by principals and master teachers a valuable part of a feedback control system for teachers? Why?

3. How might the state control the accuracy of principals who are conducting teacher evaluations? Explain.

ON THE JOB
VIDEO CASES

Barcelona Restaurant Group: Managing Quality and Performance

Questions

1. How do managers at Barcelona control the company's financial performance?

2. What is the "balanced scorecard" approach to measuring corporate performance, and in what ways does Barcelona use this approach?

3. List the four steps of the feedback control model and describe an instance where Barcelona followed this process to improve its performance.

ENDNOTES

1. Sabrina Tavernise and Andrew Pollack, "F.D.A. Details Contamination at Pharmacy," *The New York Times*, October 26, 2012, http://www.nytimes.com/2012/10/27/health/fda-finds-unsanitary-conditions-at-new-england-compounding-center.html?_r=0 (accessed October 26, 2012); "Meningitis Outbreak Toll: 438 Cases, 32 Deaths," *ABC News* http://abcnews.go.com/Health/meningitis-outbreak-toll-438-cases-32-deaths/comments?type=story&id=17682688 (accessed November 9, 2012); and Timothy W. Martin, Thomas M. Burton, and Jennifer Corbett Dooren, "Outbreak Spurs Calls for New Controls," *The Wall Street Journal*, October 9, 2012, A1.

2. Willaim K. Rashbau, "Inspector Says He Faked Data in New York Building Tests," *The New York Times*, April 26, 2010, www.nytimes.com/2010/04/27/nyregion/27inspect.html?pagewanted=all&_r=0 (accessed October 2, 2012).

3. Douglas S. Sherwin, "The Meaning of Control," *Dunn's Business Review* (January 1956).

4. Anemona Hartocollis, "New York Ties Doctors' Pay to Care Issues," *The New York Times*, January 12, 2013, A1.

5. Nicholas Bloom, Raffaella Sadun, and Jon Van Reenen, "Does Management Really Work?" *Harvard Business Review* (November 2012): 76–81.

6. Eric Wilson, "No. 279 Puts on Its Game Face," *The New York Times*, November 22, 2012, E1.

7. Richard E. Crandall, "Keys to Better Performance Measurement," *Industrial Management* (January–February 2002): 19–24; Christopher D. Ittner and David F. Larcker, "Coming up Short on Nonfinancial Performance Measurement," *Harvard Business Review* (November 2003): 88–95.

8. Jamie Flinchbaugh, "Don't Waste Your Metrics," *Industry Week* (June 2012): 10.

9. Janet Adamy, "U.S. Ties Hospital Payments to Making Patients Happy," *The Wall Street Journal*, October 15, 2012, A1.

10. Jessica Bruder, "Can FreshDirect Survive a Crisis and Reinvent Itself?" *The New York Times,* August 11, 2010, www.nytimes.com/2010/08/12/business/smallbusiness/12sbiz.html?pagewanted=all&_r=0 (accessed September 28, 2012).

11. This discussion is based on a review of the balanced scorecard in Richard L. Daft, *Organization Theory and Design*, 7th ed. (Cincinnati, OH: South-Western, 2001), pp. 300–301.

12. Andy Neely and Mohammed Al Najjar, "Management Learning, Not Management Control: The True Role of Performance Measurement," *California Management Review* 48, no. 3 (Spring 2006): 101–114.

13. Robert Kaplan and David Norton, "The Balanced Scorecard: Measures That Drive Performance," *Harvard Business Review* (January–February 1992): 71–79; Chee W. Chow, Kamal M. Haddad, and James E. Williamson, "Applying the Balanced Scorecard to Small Companies," *Management Accounting* 79, no. 2 (August 1997): 21–27; and Meena Chavan, "The Balanced Scorecard: A New Challenge," *Journal of Management Development* 28, no. 5 (2009): 393–406.

14. Based on Kaplan and Norton, "The Balanced Scorecard"; Chow, Haddad, and Williamson, "Applying the Balanced Scorecard"; and Cathy Lazere, "All Together Now," *CFO* (February 1998): 28–36.

15. Karen S. Cravens, Elizabeth Goad Oliver, and Jeanine S. Stewart, "Can a Positive Approach to Performance Evaluation Help Accomplish Your Goals?" *Business Horizons* 53 (2010): 269–279.

16. Juliet Eilperin and Zachary A. Goldfarb, "IG Report: 'Inappropriate Criteria' Stalled IRS Approvals of Conservative Groups," *Washington Post*, May 14, 2013, http://articles.washingtonpost.com/2013-05-14/politics/39248137_1_watchdog-report-tea-party-conservative-groups (accessed May 15, 2013).

17. Andy Pasztor, "Decisions by Pilots to Land Criticized," *The Wall Street Journal*, March 28, 2011, http://online.wsj.com/article/SB10001424052748703576204576227111819017454.html (accessed October 11, 2012).

18. Geert J. M. Braam and Edwin J. Nijssen, "Performance Effects of Using the Balanced Scorecard: A Note on the Dutch Experience," *Long Range Planning* 37 (2004): 335–349; Kaplan and Norton, "The Balanced Scorecard"; and Cam Scholey, "Strategy Maps: A Step-by-Step Guide to Measuring, Managing, and Communicating the Plan," *Journal of Business Strategy* 26, no. 3 (2005): 12–19.

19. Nils-Göran Olve et al., "Twelve Years Later: Understanding and Realizing the Value of Balanced Scorecards," *Ivey Business Journal Online*, May–June 2004, www.iveybusinessjournal.com/article.asp?intArticle_ID=487 (accessed October 4, 2010); Eric M. Olson and Stanley F. Slater, "The Balanced Scorecard, Competitive Strategy, and Performance," *Business Horizons* (May–June 2002): 11–16; Eric Berkman, "How to Use the Balanced Scorecard," *CIO* (May 15, 2002): 93–100; and Brigitte W. Schay et al., "Using Standardized Outcome Measures in the Federal Government," *Human Resource Management* 41, no. 3 (Fall 2002): 355–368.

20. Braam and Nijssen, "Performance Effects of Using the Balanced Scorecard."

21. William G. Ouchi, "Markets, Bureaucracies, and Clans," *Administrative Science Quarterly* 25 (1980): 129–141; and B. R. Baligia and Alfred M. Jaeger, "Multinational Corporations: Control Systems and Delegation Issues," *Journal of International Business Studies* (Fall 1984): 25–40.

22. Daisuke Wakabayashi and Toko Sekiguchi, "Disaster in Japan: Evacuees Set Rules to Create Sense of Normalcy," *The Wall Street Journal*, March 26, 2011, http://online.wsj.com/article/SB1000142405274870378400457620382991112672.html (accessed October 3, 2012).

23. Ian Mount, "A Pizzeria Owner Learns the Value of Watching the Books," *The New York Times*, October 25, 2012, B8.

24. Craig Torres and Anthony Feld, "Campbell's Quest for Productivity," *Bloomberg BusinessWeek* (November 29–December 5, 2010): 15–16.

25. Perry Pascarella, "Open the Books to Unleash Your People," *Management Review* (May 1998): 58–60.

26. Leigh Buchanan, "Learning from the Best," *Inc.* (June 2010): 85–86.

27. Mel Mandell, "Accounting Challenges Overseas," *World Trade* (December 1, 2001): 48–50.

28. Nancy Trejos, "Boeing Faces More Dreamliner Problems," *USA Today*, September 26, 2013, http://www.usatoday.com/story/todayinthesky/2013/09/26/norwegian-air-polish-lot-boeing-dreamliner/2878019/ (accessed November 13, 2013); "Boeing 787 Dreamliner: A Timeline of Problems," *The Telegraph*, July 28, 2013, http://www.telegraph.co.uk/travel/travelnews/10207415/ (accessed November 13, 2013); and Alwyn Scott, "Fuselage Panel Falls from Boeing 787 Dreamliner In Flight," Reuters, October 15, 2013, http://www.reuters.com/article/2013/10/16/us-boeing-dreamliner-idUSBRE99F02X20131016 (accessed November 13, 2013).

29. A. V. Feigenbaum, *Total Quality Control: Engineering and Management* (New York: McGraw-Hill, 1961); John Lorinc, "Dr. Deming's Traveling Quality Show," *Canadian Business* (September 1990): 38–42; Mary Walton, *The Deming Management Method* (New York: Dodd-Meade & Co., 1986); and J. M. Juran and Frank M. Gryna, eds., *Juran's Quality Control Handbook,* 4th ed. (New York: McGraw-Hill, 1988).

30. Edward E. Lawler III and Susan A. Mohrman, "Quality Circles After the Fad," *Harvard Business Review* (January–February 1985): 65–71; and Philip C. Thompson, *Quality Circles: How to Make Them Work in America* (New York: AMACOM, 1982).

31. Jill Jusko, "Meeting the Efficiency Challenge," *Industry Week* (January 2012): 28.

32. D. J. Ford, "Benchmarking HRD," *Training & Development* (July 1993): 37–41.

33. Deven Shah and Brian H. Kleiner, "Benchmarking for Quality," *Industrial Management* (March/April 2011): 22–25.

34. Tracy Mayor, "Six Sigma Comes to IT: Targeting Perfection," *CIO* (December 1, 2003): 62–70; Hal Plotkin, "Six Sigma: What It Is and How to Use It," *Harvard Management Update* (June 1999): 3–4; Tom Rancour and Mike McCracken, "Applying Six Sigma Methods for Breakthrough Safety Performance," *Professional Safety* 45, no. 10 (October 2000): 29–32; G. Hasek, "Merger Marries Quality Efforts," *Industry Week* (August 21, 2000): 89–92; and Lee Clifford, "Why You Can Safely Ignore Six Sigma," *Fortune* (January 22, 2001): 140.

35. Dave Blanchard, "Lean Six Sigma Keeps Cardinal's Supply Chain Healthy," *Industry Week* (October 2012): 54.

36. Dick Smith and Jerry Blakeslee, "The New Strategic Six Sigma," *Training & Development* (September 2002): 45–52; Michael Hammer and Jeff Goding, "Putting Six Sigma in Perspective," *Quality* (October 2001): 58–62; and Mayor, "Six Sigma Comes to IT."

37. Jack Bouck, "Creating a Customer-Focused Culture: The Honeywell Experience," *Industrial Management*, (November/December 2007): 11.

38. This discussion is based on Eileen Newman Rubin, "A Partnered Approach to QA Increases Efficiency Through Early Problem Detection," *Global Business and Organizational Excellence* (May–June 2012): 28–37.

39. Steve Minter, "La-Z-Boy Never Rests on Continuous Improvement," *Industry Week* (January 2013): 25.

40. Clifford, "Why You Can Safely Ignore Six Sigma"; and Hammer and Goding, "Putting Six Sigma in Perspective."

41. Jay Goltz, "The Dusenberry Diary: When Passion Meets Math," *The New York Times*, June 23, 2009, http://boss.blogs.nytimes.com/2009/06/23/the-dusenberry-diary-when-passion-meets-math/ (accessed October 2, 2012).

42. Sumantra Ghoshal, *Strategic Control* (St. Paul, MN: West, 1986), Chapter 4; and Robert N. Anthony, John Dearden, and Norton M. Bedford, *Management Control Systems*, 5th ed. (Homewood, IL: Irwin, 1984).

43. John A. Boquist, Todd T. Milbourn, and Anjan V. Thakor, "How Do You Win the Capital Allocation Game?" *Sloan Management Review* (Winter 1998): 59–71.

44. Jason Gillikin, "What Is Zero-Based Budgeting and How Is It Used by an Organization?" *Houston Chronicle*, http://smallbusiness.chron.com/zerobased-budgeting-used-organization-22586.html (accessed October 3, 2012).

45. Gerard Paulides, "Resetting the Cost Structure at Shell," *Strategy + Business* 65 (Winter 2011): 1–4.

46. Anthony, Dearden, and Bedford, *Management Control Systems*.

47. Participation in budget setting is described in a number of studies, including Neil C. Churchill, "Budget Choice: Planning Versus Control," *Harvard Business Review* (July–August 1984): 150–164; Peter Brownell, "Leadership Style, Budgetary Participation, and Managerial Behavior," *Accounting Organizations and Society* 8 (1983): 307–321; and Paul J. Carruth and Thurrell O. McClandon, "How Supervisors React to 'Meeting the Budget' Pressure," *Management Accounting* 66 (November 1984): 50–54.

48. Tim Reason, "Budgeting in the Real World," *CFO* (July 2005): 43–48.

49. Ibid.

50. Norm Brodsky, "Balance-Sheet Blues," *Inc.* (October 2011): 34.

51. Mount, "A Pizzeria Owner Learns the Value of Watching the Books."

52. This analogy is from Brodsky, "Balance-Sheet Blues."

53. Dana Mattioli, "CEOs Fight to Prevent Discretionary Spending from Creeping Back Up," *The Wall Street Journal*, January 1, 1998, http://online.wsj.com/article/SB10001424 05274870360900457535490154556456.html (accessed December 11, 2012).

54. Willy Staley, "How 7-Eleven Plans to Put the Bodega Out of Business," *New York* (May 14, 2012): 38–41, 87–88.

55. Mary Ellen Biery, "Five Metrics You Should Know," *Washington Post*, May 25, 2012, www.washingtonpost.com/blogs/on-small-business/post/5-financial-metrics-you-should-know/2012/05/25/gJQAuDSjpU_blog.html (accessed October 9, 2012).

56. Lawrence M. Fisher, "Inside Dell Computer Corporation: Managing Working Capital," *Strategy + Business* 10, (First Quarter 1998): 68–75; and Randy Myers, "Cash Crop: The 2000 Working Capital Survey," *CFO* (August 2000): 59–69.

57. Nancy F. Koehn, "The Driver in Ford's Amazing Race," *The New York Times*, March 31, 2012, www.nytimes.com/2012/04/01/business/american-icon-examines-fords-rebound-review.html?pagewanted=all&_r=0 (accessed September 28, 2012).

58. Syed Hasan Jaffrey, "ISO 9001 Made Easy," *Quality Progress* 37, no. 5 (May 2004): 104; Frank C. Barnes, "ISO 9000 Myth and Reality: A Reasonable Approach to ISO 9000," *SAM Advanced Management Journal* (Spring 1998): 23–30; and Thomas H. Stevenson and Frank C. Barnes, "Fourteen Years of ISO 9000: Impact, Criticisms, Costs, and Benefits," *Business Horizons* (May–June 2001): 45–51.

59. David Amari, Don James, and Cathy Marley, "ISO 9001 Takes On a New Role—Crime Fighter," *Quality Progress* 37, no. 5 (May 2004): 57ff.

60. "*Corporate Governance,*" Business Dictionary Web site, www.businessdictionary.com/definition/corporate-governance.html (accessed September 16, 2010); "*Words to Understand: Corporate Governance Models,*" Gruppo Hera Italy Web site, http://eng.gruppohera.it/group/hera_ondemand/words_understand/page23.html (accessed September 16, 2010); and "Corporate Governance Issues in 2009," *The Corporate Eye*, March 10, 2009, www.corporate-eye.com/blog/2009/03/corporate-governance-issues-2009 (accessed September 16, 2010).

61. Peter J. Henning, "At Large and Small Companies, Internal Controls Matter," *The New York Times*, April 5, 2012, http://dealbook.nytimes.com/2012/04/05/at-large-and-small-companies-internal-controls-matter/ (accessed October 8, 2012).

62. Damian Paletta and David Enrich, "Banks Get New Restraints," *The Wall Street Journal*, September 13, 2010.

63. Joann S. Lublin, "Lead Directors Gain Clout to Counterbalance Strong CEOs," *The Wall Street Journal*, September 13, 2010.

64. Based on Michael Barbaro, "Some Leeway for the Small Shoplifter," *The New York Times*, July 13, 2006.

PART 6: INTEGRATIVE CASE

Part Six: Controlling

Range Resources Leads Great Shale Gas Rush amidst Global Recession

When Range Resources began drilling a vertical test well between the towns of Westland and Hickory, Pennsylvania, in 2004, the Texas exploration-and-production (E&P) company had no idea what it would discover. The sedimentary layers of gray shale rock lying more than a mile beneath the Appalachian Basin had been thought to hold a relatively modest 1.9 trillion cubic feet of natural gas. But when Range's Renz well No.1 instantly tapped a large methane reserve, the company's technical team realized that they were onto something big. As geological experts descended on the rocky area known as the Marcellus Formation, the public soon learned that the shale might contain as much as 516 trillion cubic feet of natural gas, making it one of the largest natural gas reserves in the world. The Great Shale Gas Rush had begun.

Since the drilling of the Renz well in 2004, leaders in industry and government have called the Marcellus discovery "a game changer" and a potential savior of the U.S. economy. Range Resources, with its 1.4 million acres of drilling territory in the region, is one of only a handful of exploration companies positioned to turn that hope into reality. In 2008, Range's technical teams extracted 30 million cubic feet of natural gas per day from the Marcellus Formation. By 2012, production had jumped to 400 million cubic feet of gas per day, and by the end of 2013, that number more than doubled to an astounding 960 million cubic feet per day. Looking ahead, Range executives expect crews to capture more than 1 billion cubic feet of natural gas daily.

"Our technical team is one of the best in the industry," says Jeffrey Ventura, Range's president and CEO. "They not only discovered the Marcellus and ramped production up, but we were the first company to drill a horizontal Devonian shale well in Pennsylvania, which is the shale right on top of the Marcellus, and we were the first to drill a horizontal well in the Utica, which is below the Marcellus. So we have a great technical team and a great acreage position."

According to Range's top executives, the discovery of the Marcellus led the company to adopt a 10-year growth outlook based on high production and a low-cost operating structure. "Our low-cost structure gives us a huge competitive advantage," says Roger Manny, Range's chief financial officer (CFO). "In the commodity business, all of us are selling our products for about the same price. So being able to do it at a lower cost really gives you a big edge." Manny adds that controlling costs improves Range's cash flow and gives the company discretionary cash to explore and drill more wells.

Range's financial managers have various tools to monitor performance and control costs. "Our balance sheet is the first element of that strategy," says Manny. "It's a simple balance sheet that consists of senior bank debt, ten-year subordinated notes, and common equity. So having a simple strong balance sheet is the core to our financial strategy." While financial statements help measure the company's financial health over time, a strong cash position helps the company battle turbulence in the economy. Because of the topsy-turvy nature of the global recession, Range manages its massive land acreage portfolio in a way that provides added liquidity—the ability to sell assets in a pinch to pay off debts. "Another feature of our financial strategy is having liquidity to absorb shocks in the market," Manny states.

At Range, keeping a lid on expenses is not just the job of company accountants—it's everyone's job. "Maintaining a low-cost structure is not so much what we do, but who we are," Manny says. "It's part of our culture." Range encourages employees to make cost-cutting a part of their regular duties, and it rewards them with equity in the company. "Equity ownership creates a unique bond among employees and also between the employees and shareholders," says Manny, "because, after all, they themselves are shareholders." Range's CFO believes that companies perform best when everyone has skin in the game. "I think the fact that everybody owns equity in the company makes them more willing to be vigilant about costs. And that's a big contributor to the long-term cost performance of the company," Manny states.

Range's money management philosophy has paid off. Over the past ten years, Range Resources has been one of the top three E&P companies on the New York Stock Exchange (NYSE). In addition, the company has delivered nearly a decade of sequential annual growth with some of the lowest finding and development costs in the industry—all this during a global recession that has torpedoed top corporations. "Clearly, 2009 was one of the most difficult periods in time in terms of running a business in America," says Range executive chairman John Pinkerton, reflecting on the economic downturn. "A number of companies simply didn't make it, a lot of companies had to totally restructure their business, and other companies issued a lot of equity and diluted their shareholders. The good news is that none of that happened at Range; we ended that year with less debt than we started, and we didn't have to issue any equity to prop up our balance sheet."

Despite the broad weakness of the economy going into 2014, Ventura predicts continued growth at Range for the foreseeable future. "Our sizable position in the Marcellus Shale gives us confidence that we can deliver similar growth of 20 percent to 25 percent for many years," he said. "We believe this strong growth, coupled with high returns, low cost, and low reinvestment risk, will allow Range to drive substantial growth per share for our shareholders for years to come."

Ultimately, effective financial control frees Range to do what it does best: develop America's clean energy future. Says Pinkerton: "I think the most exciting thing when you look at Range going forward is some of the assets we have, in particular the Marcellus. It could be one of the largest gas fields in the United States, and maybe the world. To be involved with that is fabulous, and it's going to help drive our growth."

Questions

1. Managers at Range Resources say that maintaining a low-cost structure is the job of every employee, and they make cost control part of the company culture. Is this indicative of a hierarchical or a decentralized philosophy of control? Explain.

2. What is liquidity, and how can Range's managers know if they have enough of it to keep the company's finances on track?

3. Short-term thinking can be disastrous for a business. What indications are there to show that financial managers at Range Resources take a long-term approach to financial performance and control?

SOURCES: Based on Christopher Helman, "Range Resources Is King of the Marcellus Shale," *Forbes*, July 22, 2010, www.forbes.com/forbes/2010/0809/companies-energy-range-resources-bp-gas-blowout-beneficiary.html (accessed July 14, 2012); Range Resources, "Range Third Quarter Production Reaches Record Level," press release, October 17, 2013, www.businesswire.com/news/home/20131017005255/en/Range-Quarter-Production-Reaches-Record-Level (accessed January 13, 2014); Roger Manny (executive vice president and chief financial officer of Range Resources), interview by Rodney Waller, "Range Up Close: Corporate Overview," Range Resources corporate site, 2010, online video, www.rangeresources.com/Media-Center/Videos/Corporate-Overview.aspx (accessed July 15, 2012); Jeffrey Ventura (president and chief executive officer of Range Resources), interview by Rodney Waller, "Range Up Close: Competitive Advantage," Range Resources corporate site, 2010, online video, www.rangeresources.com/Media-Center/Featured-Stories.aspx (accessed July 15, 2012); John Pinkerton (executive chairman of Range Resources), interview by Rodney Waller, "Range Up Close: Corporate Overview," Range Resources corporate site, 2010, online video, www.rangeresources.com/Media-Center/Videos/Corporate-Overview.aspx (accessed July 15, 2012); Elwin Green, "Natural Gas Locked in the Marcellus Shale Has Companies Rushing to Cash in on Possibilities," *Pittsburgh Post-Gazette*, March 16, 2012, www.post-gazette.com/stories/business/news/natural-gas-locked-in-the-marcellus-shale-has-companies-rushing-to-cash-in-on-possibilities-370058/ (accessed July 10, 2012); and Martin Neil Baily and Philip K. Verleger Jr, "Could Cheap Gas Save the Economy?" CNN Money, June 27, 2012, http://money.cnn.com/2012/06/27/news/economy/shale-gas/ (accessed July 15, 2012).

Glossary

360-degree feedback A recent trend in performance appraisal is called 360-degree feedback, a process that uses multiple raters, including self rating, as a way to increase awareness of strengths and weaknesses and guide employee development.

Accountability Accountability means that people with authority and responsibility are subject to reporting and justifying task outcomes to those above them in the chain of command.

Achievement culture The achievement culture is suited to organizations concerned with serving specific customers in the external environment, but without the intense need for flexibility and rapid change. This results-oriented culture values competitiveness, aggressiveness, personal initiative, cost cutting, and willingness to work long and hard to achieve results.

Acqui-hiring When established companies such as Facebook, Google, Yahoo, LinkedIn, and Salesforce.com buy early-stage start-ups, often shutting them down, simply to acquire their engineering talent.

Activity ratio The activity ratio measures the organization's internal performance with respect to key activities defined by management.

Adaptability culture The adaptability culture emerges in an environment that requires fast response and high-risk decision making. Managers encourage values that support the company's ability to rapidly detect, interpret, and translate signals from the environment into new behaviors.

Adjourning The adjourning stage occurs in committees and teams that have a limited task to perform and are disbanded afterward. During this stage, the emphasis is on wrapping up and gearing down.

Administrative model The administrative model is descriptive, an approach that describes how managers actually make

decisions, rather than how they should make decisions according to a theoretical model.

Administrative principles approach Another major subfield within the classical perspective that focuses on the total organization rather than the productivity of the individual worker. The major contributor to this approach was Henri Fayol (1841–1925), a French mining engineer.

Affirmative action Affirmative action requires that an employer take positive steps to guarantee equal employment opportunities for people within protected groups.

After-action review A technique adopted from the U.S. Army, the after-action review is a disciplined procedure whereby managers review the results of decisions to evaluate what worked, what didn't, and how to do things better.

Age discrimination Age discrimination has made a difficult situation even more trying for older workers looking for jobs in the recent economic downturn.

Alienated follower The alienated follower is a passive, yet independent, critical thinker. Alienated employees are often effective followers who have experienced setbacks and obstacles, perhaps promises broken by their superiors.

Ambidextrous approach An ambidextrous approach means incorporating structures and processes that are appropriate for both the creative impulse and the systematic implementation of innovations.

Ambiguity Ambiguity means that the goals to be achieved or the problem to be solved is unclear, alternatives are difficult to define, and information about outcomes is unavailable.

Application form The application form is a selection device that collects information about the applicant's education, previous work experience, and other background characteristics.

Attributions Attributions are judgments about what caused a person's behavior—something about the person or something about the situation. People make attributions as an attempt to understand why others behave as they do.

Authentic leadership Authentic leadership refers to leadership by individuals who know and understand themselves, who espouse and act consistent with higher order ethical values, and who empower and inspire others with their openness and authenticity.

Authoritarianism Authoritarianism is the belief that power and status differences should exist within an organization.

Authority Authority is the formal and legitimate right of a manager to make decisions, issue orders, and allocate resources to achieve organizationally desired outcomes.

Avoidance learning Avoidance learning is the removal of an unpleasant consequence once a behavior is improved, thereby encouraging and strengthening the desired behavior. Managers apply avoidance learning, called negative reinforcement, when they remove an unpleasant consequence once a behavior is improved.

Balance sheet Shows the firm's financial position with respect to assets and liabilities at a specific point in time.

Balanced scorecard A comprehensive management control system that balances traditional financial measures with measures of customer service, internal business processes, and the organization's capacity for learning and growth.

Behavior modification Behavior modification is the name given to the set of techniques by which reinforcement theory is used to modify human behavior.

Behavioral sciences approach The behavioral sciences approach draws from psychology, sociology, and other social sciences to develop theories about human behavior and interaction in an organizational setting.

Behaviorally anchored rating scale (BARS) One way to overcome evaluation errors is to use a behaviorally anchored rating scale (BARS), which is a performance evaluation technique that relates an employee's performance to specific job-related incidents.

Benchmarking Benchmarking is defined as the continuous process of measuring products, services, and practices against the toughest competitors or those companies recognized as industry leaders to identify areas for improvement.

Big data analytics Technologies, skills, and processes for searching and examining massive, complex sets of data that traditional data processing applications cannot handle to uncover hidden patterns and correlations.

Big Five personality factors The Big Five personality factors describe an individual's extroversion, agreeableness, conscientiousness, emotional stability, and openness to experience.

Bottom of the pyramid (BOP) concept The bottom of the pyramid (BOP) concept proposes that corporations can alleviate poverty and other social ills, as well as make significant profits, by selling to the world's poor.

Bottom-up approach Innovative companies use a bottom-up approach, which means encouraging the flow of ideas from lower levels and making sure they get heard and acted upon by top executives.

Bottom-up budgeting Bottom-up budgeting involves lower-level managers anticipating their department's budget needs and passing them up to top management for approval.

Boundary-spanning roles Boundary-spanning roles link to and coordinate the organization with key elements in the external environment. Boundary spanners serve two purposes for the organization: They detect and process information about changes in the environment, and they represent the organization's interests to the environment.

Bounded rationality Bounded rationality means that people have limits, or boundaries, on how rational they can be.

Brainstorming Brainstorming uses a face-to-face interactive group to spontaneously suggest a wide range of alternatives for decision making.

Bureaucratic organizations approach A systematic approach developed in Europe that looked at the organization as a whole, a subfield within the classical perspective. Max Weber (1864–1920), a German theorist, introduced most of the concepts on bureaucratic organizations.

Capital budget A budget that plans and reports investments in major assets to be depreciated over several years is called a capital budget.

Cash budget The cash budget estimates receipts and expenditures of money on a daily or weekly basis to ensure that an organization has sufficient cash to meet its obligations.

Centralization Centralization means that decision authority is located near top organization levels.

Centralized network A centralized network is a communication structure in which team members communicate through a single individual to solve problems or make decisions.

Ceremonies Managers hold ceremonies, planned activities at special events, to reinforce company values.

Certainty Certainty means that all the information the decision maker needs is fully available.

Chain of command The chain of command is an unbroken line of authority that links all employees in an organization and shows who reports to whom.

Change agent The change agent is an OD specialist who performs a systematic diagnosis of the organization and identifies work-related problems by gathering and analyzing data through personal interviews, questionnaires, and observations of meetings.

Changing Changing, the second stage of organization development, occurs when individuals experiment with new behavior and learn new skills to be used in the workplace. This process is sometimes known as *intervention*, during which the change agent implements a specific plan for training managers and employees.

Channel The term channel refers to the medium by which a message is sent, such as a phone call, blog, or text message.

Channel richness Channel richness is the amount of information that can be transmitted during a communication episode.

Charismatic leader A charismatic leader is a leader who has the ability to inspire and motivate people to transcend their expected performance, even to the point of personal sacrifice.

Chief ethics officer Some organizations have ethics offices headed by a chief ethics officer, a manager who oversees all aspects of ethics and legal compliance.

Classical model The classical model of decision making is based on rational economic assumptions and manager beliefs about what ideal decision making should be.

Classical perspective This perspective contains three subfields, each with a slightly different emphasis: scientific management, bureaucratic organizations, and administrative principles.

Coalition A coalition is an informal alliance among managers who support a specific goal.

Code of ethics A code of ethics is a formal statement of the company's values concerning ethics and social issues; it communicates to employees what the company stands for. Codes of ethics tend to exist in two types: principle-based statements and policy-based statements.

Coercive power Coercive power stems from the authority to punish or recommend punishment.

Collaboration Collaboration means a joint effort between people from two or more departments to produce outcomes that meet a common goal or shared purpose and that are typically greater than what any of the individuals or departments could achieve working alone.

Collectivism Collectivism means a preference for a tightly knit social framework in which individuals look after one another and organizations protect their members' interests.

Communication Communication is the process by which information is exchanged and understood by two or more people.

Communication apprehension Communication apprehension is an individual's level of fear or anxiety associated with interpersonal communication.

Compensation Compensation refers to all monetary payments and all nonmonetary goods or benefits used to reward employees.

Compensatory justice Compensatory justice argues that individuals should be compensated for the cost of their injuries by the party responsible.

Competitive advantage Competitive advantage refers to what sets the organization apart from others and provides it with a distinctive edge for meeting customer or client needs in the marketplace.

Competitors Organizations in the same industry or type of business that provide goods or services to the same set of customers are referred to as competitors.

Conceptual skills The cognitive ability to see the organization as a whole and the relationships among its parts.

Conflict Conflict refers to antagonistic interaction in which one party attempts to block the intentions or goals of another.

Conformist The conformist participates actively in a relationship with the boss but doesn't use critical thinking skills. In other words, a conformist typically carries out any and all orders, regardless of the nature of the request.

Consideration Consideration is the term used by researchers at The Ohio State University to describe the extent to which a leader is sensitive to subordinates, respects their ideas and feelings, and establishes mutual trust.

Consistency culture Consistency culture uses an internal focus and a consistency orientation for a stable environment. Following the rules and being thrifty are valued, and the culture supports and rewards a methodical, rational, orderly way of doing things.

Content theories Content theories emphasize the needs that motivate people.

Contingency approaches Contingency approaches to leadership explore how the organizational situation influences leader effectiveness. Contingency approaches include the situational model based on the work of Hersey and Blanchard, the leadership model developed by Fiedler and his associates, and the substitutes-for-leadership concept.

Contingency plans Contingency plans define company responses to be taken in the case of emergencies, setbacks, or unexpected conditions. To develop contingency plans, managers identify important factors in the environment, such as possible economic downturns, declining

markets, increases in cost of supplies, new technological developments, or safety accidents.

Contingency view Contingency means that one thing depends on other things and a manager's response to a situation depends on identifying key contingencies in an organizational situation.

Contingent workers Contingent workers are people who work for an organization, but not on a permanent or full-time basis.

Continuous improvement Continuous improvement, or *kaizen,* is the implementation of a large number of small, incremental improvements in all areas of the organization on an ongoing basis.

Continuous process production In continuous process production, the entire workflow is mechanized in a sophisticated and complex form of production technology. Because the process runs continuously, it has no starting and stopping.

Coordination Coordination refers to the managerial task of adjusting and synchronizing the diverse activities among different individuals and departments.

Core competence A company's core competence is something that the organization does especially well in comparison to its competitors.

Corporate governance Corporate governance refers to the framework of systems, rules, and practices by which an organization ensures accountability, fairness, and transparency in its relationships with all stakeholders, including investors, employees, customers, and the general public.

Corporate social responsibility (CSR) The formal definition of corporate social responsibility (CSR) is management's obligation to make choices and take actions that will contribute to the welfare and interests of society, not just the organization.

Corporate university A corporate university is an in-house training and education facility that offers broad-based learning opportunities for employees—and frequently for customers, suppliers, and strategic partners as well—throughout their careers.

Cost leadership strategy A strategy with which managers aggressively seek efficient facilities, cut costs, and use tight cost controls to be more efficient than others in the industry.

Creativity Creativity is the generation of novel ideas that may meet perceived needs or respond to opportunities for the organization.

Critical thinking Independent critical thinkers are mindful of the effects of their own and others' behavior on achieving organizational goals. They can weigh the impact of their boss's and their own decisions and offer constructive criticism, creativity, and innovation.

Cross-functional team A cross-functional team is composed of employees from about the same hierarchical level, but from different areas of expertise.

Crowdsourcing Crowdsourcing, an open innovation approach used by many companies, taps into ideas from around the world and lets thousands or hundreds of thousands of people participate in the innovation process, usually via the Internet.

Cultural intelligence (CQ) The ability to use reasoning and observation skills to interpret unfamiliar gestures and situations and devise appropriate behavioral responses.

Cultural leader A cultural leader defines and uses signals and symbols to influence corporate culture.

Culture Culture is the set of key values, beliefs, understandings, and norms shared by members of an organization.

Culture change Culture change pertains to the organization as a whole, such as when a company shifts its basic mind-set.

Customers Those people and organizations in the environment that acquire goods or services from the organization are customers.

Customer relationship management (CRM) Customer relationship management (CRM) is a model for managing a company's interactions with current and future customers.

Decentralization Decentralization means that decision authority is pushed down to lower organization levels.

Decentralized control With decentralized control, the organization fosters compliance with organizational goals through the use of organizational culture, group norms, and a focus on goals rather than rules and procedures.

Decentralized network A decentralized network is a communication structure in which team members freely communicate with one another and arrive at decisions together.

Decentralized planning Planning involving everyone in an organization. Planning experts work with managers in major divisions or departments to develop their own goals and plans.

Decision A decision is a choice made from available alternatives.

Decision making Decision making is the process of identifying problems and opportunities and then resolving them.

Decision Styles Differences among people with respect to how they perceive problems and make choices.

Delegation Delegation is the process managers use to transfer authority and responsibility to positions below them in the hierarchy.

Departmentalization Another fundamental characteristic of organization structure is departmentalization, which is the basis for grouping positions into departments and departments into the total organization.

Descriptive The administrative model is descriptive, an approach that describes how managers actually make decisions, rather than how they should make decisions according to a theoretical model.

Devil's advocate A devil's advocate is a person who is assigned the role of challenging the assumptions and assertions made by the group to prevent premature consensus.

Diagnosis Diagnosis is the step in the decision-making process in which managers analyze underlying causal factors associated with the decision situation.

Differentiation strategy A strategy with which managers seek to distinguish the organization's products and services from those of others in the industry.

Direct investing Direct investing is a market entry strategy in which the organization is directly involved in managing its production facilities in a foreign country.

Discretionary responsibility Discretionary responsibility is purely voluntary and is guided by a company's desire to make social contributions not mandated by economics, law, or ethics. Discretionary activities include generous philanthropic contributions that offer no payback to the company and are not expected.

Discrimination Discrimination occurs when hiring and promotion decisions are made based on criteria that are not job-relevant; for example, refusing to hire a black applicant for a job he is qualified to fill and paying a woman a lower wage than a man for the same work are discriminatory acts.

Disruptive innovation Disruptive innovation refers to innovations in products, services, or processes that radically change competition in an industry, such as the advent of streaming video or e-books.

Distributive justice Distributive justice requires that different treatment of people not be based on arbitrary characteristics. For example, men and women should not receive different salaries if they have the same qualifications and are performing the same job.

Distributive negotiation Distributive negotiation, on the other hand, assumes that the size of the "pie" is fixed, and each party attempts to get as much of it as they can.

Diverse inclusive workforce A definition that recognizes diversity includes many areas including how people approach work, interact at work and derive satisfaction from work as well as who they are in the workplace.

Diversity Decades ago, many companies defined diversity in terms of race, gender, age, lifestyle, and disability. That focus helped create awareness, change mindsets, and create new opportunities for many. Today, companies are embracing a more inclusive definition of diversity that recognizes a spectrum of differences that influence how employees approach work, interact with each other, derive satisfaction from their work, and define who they are as people in the workplace.

Diversity dividend The benefits from workplace diversity which include better use of employee talent, increased understanding of the marketplace, enhanced breadth of understanding in leadership positions, increased quality of team problem solving, reduced costs associated with high turnover, absenteeism, and lawsuits.

Diversity of perspective Diversity of perspective is achieved when a manager creates a heterogeneous team made up of individuals with diverse backgrounds and skill sets. By tapping into the strengths of diversity, teams are more likely to experience the following: higher efficiency, better quality, less duplication of effort among team members, and increased innovation and creativity.

Divisional structure The divisional structure groups employees and departments based on similar organizational outputs (products or services), such that each division has a mix of functional skills and tasks.

Downward communication Downward communication refers to the messages and information sent from top management to subordinates in a downward direction. Managers can communicate downward to employees in many ways. Some of the most common are through speeches, videos, blogs, podcasts, and company intranets.

E → P expectancy A person's E → P expectancy is the expectancy that putting effort into a given task will lead to high performance.

Economic development Economic development differs widely among the countries and regions of the world. Countries can be categorized as either *developing* or *developed*.

Economic dimension The economic dimension represents the general economic health of the country or region in which the organization operates. Consumer purchasing power, the unemployment rate, and interest rates are part of an organization's economic environment.

Effective follower The effective follower is both a critical, independent thinker and active in the organization. Effective followers behave the same toward everyone, regardless of their position in the organization.

Effectiveness The degree to which the organization achieves a stated goal.

Efficiency The amount of resources—raw materials, money, and people—used to produce a desired volume of output.

Electronic brainstorming Electronic brainstorming, sometimes called *brainwriting*, brings people together in an interactive group over a computer network.

Emotion An emotion is a mental state that arises spontaneously rather than through conscious effort and is often accompanied by physiological changes.

Employer brand An employer brand is similar to a product brand except that rather than promoting a specific product, its aim is to make the organization seem like a highly desirable place to work.

Employment tests Tests given to employees to evaluate their abilities; can include cognitive ability tests, physical ability tests, personality inventories, and other assessments.

Empowerment A management practice of sharing information, rewards, and power with employees, facilitating rather than controlling employees, so that they can take initiative and make decisions to solve problems and improve service and performance.

Encodes/decodes The sender encodes the idea by selecting symbols with which to compose a message and selecting a communication channel; the receiver decodes the symbols to interpret the meaning of the message.

Engagement Employee engagement means that people enjoy their jobs and are satisfied with their work conditions, contribute enthusiastically to meeting team and organizational goals, and feel a sense of belonging and commitment to the organization.

Equity A situation of equity exists when the ratio of one person's outcomes to inputs equals that of another's.

Equity theory Equity theory focuses on individuals' perceptions of how fairly they are treated relative to others.

ERG theory ERG theory is a modification of the needs hierarchy and proposes three categories of needs: existence, relatedness, and growth.

Escalating commitment Escalating commitment is the tendency for managers and organizations to invest time and money in a solution even when there is strong evidence that it is not appropriate.

Ethical dilemma Includes the technological, economic, political/legal, and sociocultural dimensions that affect a firm's external environment.

Ethics Ethics is the code of moral principles and values that governs the behaviors of a person or group with respect to what is right or wrong.

Ethics committee An ethics committee is a group of executives (and sometimes lower-level employees as well) appointed to oversee company ethics.

Managerial ethics Managerial ethics are a set of standards that dictate the conduct of a manager operating within a workplace.

Ethnocentrism Ethnocentrism is the belief that one's own group is inherently superior to other groups.

Ethnorelativism Ethnorelativism is the belief that groups and subcultures are inherently equal.

Euro The euro is a single European currency that has replaced the currencies of sixteen EU member nations.

Evidence-based decision making Evidence-based decision making is founded on a commitment to examining potential biases, seeking and examining evidence with rigor, and making informed and intelligent decisions based on the best available facts and evidence.

Exit interview An exit interview is an interview conducted with departing employees to determine why they are leaving the company.

Expectancy theory Expectancy theory proposes that motivation depends on individuals' expectations about their ability to perform tasks and receive desired rewards.

Expense budget An expense budget outlines the anticipated and actual expenses for a responsibility center.

Expert power Expert power is power that results from a leader's special knowledge or skill in the tasks performed by subordinates.

Exploration phase Exploration involves designing the organization to encourage creativity and the initiation of new ideas.

Exporting Exporting is a market entry strategy in which a company maintains production facilities within its home country and transfers products for sale in foreign countries.

Extinction Extinction is the withholding of a positive reward. Whereas with punishment, the supervisor imposes an unpleasant outcome such as a reprimand, extinction involves withholding praise or other positive outcomes.

Extrinsic rewards Extrinsic rewards are given by another person, typically a manager, and include promotions, praise, and pay increases. They originate externally, as a result of pleasing others.

Feedback Feedback occurs when the receiver responds to the sender's communication with a return message.

Femininity Femininity reflects the values of relationships, cooperation, group decision making, and quality of life.

Flat structure A flat structure is characterized by an overall broad span of management and relatively few hierarchical levels.

Focus strategy A strategy where managers use either a differentiation or a cost leadership approach, but they concentrate on a specific regional market or buyer group.

Force-field analysis Force-field analysis is a technique for determining which forces drive a proposed change and which forces restrain it.

Formal communication channels Formal communication channels are those that flow within the chain of command or task responsibility defined by the organization.

Forming The forming stage of development is a period of orientation and getting acquainted. Members break the ice and test one another for friendship possibilities and task orientation.

Franchising Franchising is a form of licensing in which a company provides its foreign franchisees with a complete package of materials and services.

Free rider The term free rider refers to a team member who attains benefits from team membership but does not actively participate in and contribute to the team's work.

Frustration-regression principle The frustration-regression principle is the idea that failure to meet a high-order need may cause a regression to an already satisfied lower-order need; thus, people may move down as well as up the needs hierarchy.

Functional structure In a functional structure, also called a *U-form (unitary structure),* activities are grouped together by common function from the bottom to the top of the organization.

Functional team A functional team is composed of a manager and his or her subordinates in the formal chain of command.

Fundamental attribution error When evaluating others, we tend to underestimate the influence of external factors and overestimate the influence of internal factors. This tendency is called the fundamental attribution error.

General environment The general environment affects organizations indirectly. It includes social, economic, legal-political, international, natural, and technological factors that influence all organizations about equally.

Glass ceiling The glass ceiling is an invisible barrier that exists for women and minorities that limits their upward mobility in organizations. They can look up through the ceiling and see top management, but prevailing attitudes and stereotypes are invisible obstacles to their own advancement.

Global mindset The ability of managers to appreciate and influence individuals, groups, organizations, and systems that represent different social, cultural, political, institutional, intellectual, and psychological characteristics.

Global outsourcing Global outsourcing, also called *offshoring,* means engaging in the international division of labor so that work activities can be done in countries with the cheapest sources of labor and supplies.

Global team A global team is a cross-border team made up of members of different nationalities whose activities span multiple countries.

Globalization The integration and interdependence of economic, technological, socio-cultural, and political systems across diverse geographic regions.

Goal A goal is a desired future circumstance or condition that the organization attempts to realize.

Goal-setting theory Goal-setting theory proposes that specific, challenging goals increase motivation and performance when the goals are accepted by subordinates and these subordinates receive feedback to indicate their progress toward goal achievement.

Grapevine Gossip typically travels along the grapevine, an informal, person-to-person communication network that is not officially sanctioned by the organization.

Greenfield venture The most risky type of direct investment is the greenfield venture, in which a company builds a subsidiary from scratch in a foreign country.

Groupthink Groupthink refers to the tendency of people in groups to suppress contrary opinions.

Halo effect The halo effect occurs when the perceiver develops an overall impression of a person or situation based on one characteristic, either favorable or unfavorable. In other words, a halo blinds the perceiver to other characteristics that should be used in generating a more complete assessment.

Hawthorne effect Observation that employee motivation is affected as much or more by recognition and show of concern, as it is by improvements in their work conditions. Observed by the US productivity researcher George Elton Mayo (1810–1949), during 1927 to 1933 at the Hawthorne (Illinois) plant of Western Electric.

Hawthorne studies Observation that employee motivation is affected as much or more by recognition and show of concern, as it is by improvements in their work conditions. Observed by the US productivity researcher George Elton Mayo (1810–1949), during 1927 to 1933 at the Hawthorne (Illinois) plant of Western Electric.

Hero A hero is a figure who exemplifies the deeds, character, and attributes of a strong culture. Heroes are role models for employees to follow.

Hierarchical control Hierarchical control involves monitoring and influencing employee behavior through extensive use of rules, policies, hierarchy of authority, written documentation, reward systems, and other formal mechanisms.

Hierarchy of needs theory The most well known content theory is Maslow's hierarchy of needs theory, which proposes that people are motivated by five categories of needs—physiological, safety, belongingness, esteem, and self-actualization—that exist in a hierarchical order.

High-context culture In a high-context culture, people are sensitive to circumstances surrounding social exchanges.

High-performance culture High-performance culture is a culture that (1) is based on a solid organizational mission or purpose, (2) embodies shared adaptive values that guide decisions and business practices, and (3) encourages individual employee ownership of both bottom-line results and the organization's cultural backbone.

Horizontal communication Horizontal communication is the lateral or diagonal exchange of messages among peers or coworkers. It may occur within or across departments. The purpose of horizontal communication is not only to inform but also to request support and coordinate activities.

Horizontal linkage model Using a horizontal linkage model means that several departments, such as marketing, research, and manufacturing, work closely together to develop new products.

Human capital Human capital refers to the economic value of the combined knowledge, experience, skills, and capabilities of employees.

Human relations The study of how people interact with one another.

Human relations movement The human relations movement was based on the idea that truly effective control comes from within the individual worker rather than from strict, authoritarian control.

Human resource management Human resource management (HRM) refers to the design and application of formal systems in an organization to ensure the effective and efficient use of human talent to accomplish organizational goals.

Human resource planning Human resource planning refers to the forecasting of human resource needs and the projected matching of individuals with anticipated job vacancies.

Human resources perspective The human resources perspective maintained an interest in worker participation and considerate leadership but shifted the emphasis to consider the daily tasks that people perform. The human resources perspective combines prescriptions for design of job tasks with theories of motivation.

Humanistic perspective Emphasizes the importance of understanding human behaviors, needs, and attitudes in the workplace, as well as social interactions and group processes. There are three primary subfields based on the humanistic perspective: the human relations movement, the human resources perspective, and the behavioral sciences approach.

Humility Humility means being unpretentious and modest rather than arrogant and prideful.

Hygiene factors One element of Herzberg's two-factor theory, hygiene factors, focuses on lower-level needs and involves the presence or absence of job dissatisfiers, including working conditions, pay, and company policies.

Idea champion The formal definition of an idea champion is a person who sees the need for and champions productive change within the organization.

Idea incubator An idea incubator is an organizational program that provides a safe harbor where employees can generate and develop ideas without interference from company bureaucracy or politics.

Implementation Implementation involves using managerial, administrative, and persuasive abilities to translate the chosen alternative into action.

Inclusion Inclusion is the degree to which an employee feels like an esteemed member of a group in which his or her uniqueness is highly appreciated.

Income statement The income statement, sometimes called a *profit-and-loss statement* or *P&L* for short, summarizes the firm's financial performance for a given time interval, usually one year.

Individualism Individualism reflects a value for a loosely knit social framework in which individuals are expected to take care of themselves.

Individualism approach The individualism approach contends that acts are moral when they promote the individual's best long-term interests.

Influence Influence is the effect that a person's actions have on the attitudes, values, beliefs, or behavior of others.

Informal organization The informal organization occurs in all formal organizations and includes cliques, informal networks, and naturally occurring social groupings.

Infrastructure The physical facilities such as highways, airports, utilities, and telephone lines that support economic activities.

Initiating structure Initiating structure is the term that describes the extent to which a leader is task oriented and directs subordinates' work activities toward goal accomplishment.

Innovation by acquisition A strategy to obtain innovation by buying other companies, recognizing that the cutting edge of innovation often happens with young, small, entrepreneurial companies rather than inside the walls of established firms.

Integrative negotiation Integrative negotiation is based on a win-win assumption, in that all parties want to come up with a creative solution that can benefit both sides.

Inter organizational partnerships Inter organizational partnerships reduce boundaries and increase collaboration with other organizations.

Interactive leadership Interactive leadership is a leadership style characterized by values such as inclusion, collaboration, relationship building, and caring.

Internal coordination Innovation often requires internal coordination because it takes the combined expertise of a number of different team players, each with their own areas of specialization, to come up with a single creative, yet realistic, solution.

Internal environment The organization also has an internal environment, which includes the elements within the organization's boundaries. The internal environment is composed of current employees, management, and especially corporate culture, which defines employee behavior in the internal environment and how well the organization will adapt to the external environment.

Internal locus of control Having the belief that one's own actions strongly influence what happens to oneself and feeling in control of one's own fate.

International dimension The international dimension of the external environment includes events originating in foreign countries, as well as new opportunities for U.S. companies in other countries.

International management International management is the management of business operations conducted in more than one country.

Internship An internship is an arrangement whereby an intern, usually a high school or college student, exchanges free or low-cost labor for the opportunity to explore whether a particular career is appealing or to gain valuable work experience in a particular field.

Intrinsic rewards Intrinsic rewards are the satisfactions that a person receives in the process of performing a particular action.

Intuition Intuition represents a quick apprehension of a decision situation based on past experience but without conscious thought. Intuitive decision making is not arbitrary or irrational because it is based on years of practice and hands-on experience.

Involvement culture The involvement culture emphasizes an internal focus on the involvement and participation of employees to adapt rapidly to changing needs from the environment. This culture places high value on meeting the needs of employees, and the organization may be characterized by a caring, family-like atmosphere.

ISO 9000 standards Many countries have adopted a universal benchmark for quality management practices, ISO 9000 standards, which represent an international consensus of what constitutes effective quality management as outlined by the International Organization for Standardization (ISO).

Job analysis Job analysis is a systematic process of gathering and interpreting information about the essential duties, tasks, and responsibilities of a job, as well as about the context within which the job is performed.

Job characteristics model The job characteristics model is a model of job design that considers core job dimensions, individuals' critical psychological states, and employee growth-need strength.

Job description A job description is a clear and concise summary of the specific tasks, duties, and responsibilities of a particular position in an organization.

Job design Job design is the application of motivational theories to the structure of work for improving productivity and satisfaction.

Job enrichment Job enrichment refers to incorporating high-level motivators, such as achievement, recognition, and opportunities for growth, into the work.

Job evaluation Job evaluation is the process of determining the value of jobs within an organization through an examination of job content.

Job satisfaction A positive attitude toward one's job is called job satisfaction.

Job specification A job specification outlines the knowledge, skills, education, physical abilities, and other characteristics needed to perform a specific job adequately.

Joint venture In a joint venture, a company shares costs and risks with another firm, typically in the host country, to develop new products, build a manufacturing facility, or set up a sales and distribution network.

Justice approach The justice approach holds that moral decisions must be based on standards of equity, fairness, and impartiality.

Key performance indicators (KPIs) Tools used to assess what is important to an organization and how well the organization is progressing toward attaining its strategic goal, so that managers can establish lower-level goals that drive performance toward the overall strategic objective.

Labor market The labor market represents people in the environment who can be hired to work for the organization.

Large-group intervention Large-group intervention is an OD approach that brings together people from different parts of the organization (and often including outside stakeholders) to discuss problems or opportunities and plan for change.

Law of effect The basic assumption underlying behavior modification is the law of effect, which states that behavior that is positively reinforced tends to be repeated, and behavior that is not reinforced tends not to be repeated.

Leadership grid The Leadership Grid is a two-dimensional leadership model that measures the leader's concern for people and concern for production to categorize the leader in one of five different leadership styles.

Leadership Leadership is the ability to influence people toward the attainment of organizational goals.

Legal responsibility Legal responsibility defines what society deems as important with respect to appropriate corporate behavior.

Legal-political dimension The legal-political dimension includes government regulations at the local, state, and federal levels, as well as political activities designed to influence company behavior.

Legitimate power Legitimate power is power that stems from a manager's formal position in an organization and the authority granted by that position.

Licensing With licensing, a corporation (the licensor) in one country makes certain resources available to companies in another country (the licensee). These resources include technology, managerial skills, and patent or trademark rights.

Line authority Line authority means that people in management positions have formal authority to direct and control immediate subordinates.

Liquidity ratio The liquidity ratio indicates an organization's ability to meet its current debt obligations.

Listening Listening involves the skill of grasping both facts and feelings to interpret a message's genuine meaning.

Long-term orientation The long-term orientation, found in China and other Asian countries, includes a greater concern for the future and highly values thrift and perseverance.

Low-context culture In a low-context culture, people use communication primarily to exchange facts and information; meaning is derived primarily from words; business transactions are more important than building relationships and trust; and individual welfare and achievement are more important than the group.

Machiavellianism Machiavellianism refers to a tendency to direct one's behavior toward the acquisition of power and the manipulation of other people for personal gain.

Making progress principle The making progress principle is the idea that the single most important factor that can boost motivation, positive emotions, and perceptions during a workday is making progress toward meaningful goals.

Manage stress Many companies help employees manage stress by offering discounts to local gyms, although a fairly recent workplace trend enables employees to work out while they work. Treadmill desks have shelves where employees can park their laptops and plug in their mobile phones so they can review documents, do online research, and hold meetings as they rack up the miles.

Management The attainment of organizational goals in an effective and efficient manner through planning, organizing, leading, and controlling organizational resources. This definition includes two important ideas: (1) the four functions of planning, organizing, leading, and controlling, and (2) the attainment of organizational goals in an effective and efficient manner.

Management by means (MBM) Management by means (MBM) focuses attention on the methods and processes used to achieve goals.

Management by objectives (MBO) Management by objectives (MBO) is a method whereby managers and employees define goals for every department, project, and person and use them to monitor subsequent performance.

Management science Management science, also referred to as the quantitative perspective, provided a way to address those problems. This view is distinguished for its application of mathematics, statistics, and other quantitative techniques to management decision making and problem solving.

Managing diversity Managing diversity, a key management skill in today's global economy, means creating a climate in which the potential advantages of diversity for organizational or group performance are maximized, while the potential disadvantages are minimized.

Market entry strategies Market entry strategies are various tactics that managers use to enter foreign markets.

Masculinity Masculinity stands for preference for achievement, heroism, assertiveness, work centrality (with resultant high stress), and material success.

Mass production Mass production technology is distinguished by standardized production runs. A large volume of products is produced, and all customers receive the same product.

Matching model Underlying the organization's effort to attract employees is a matching model. With the matching model, the organization and the individual attempt to match the needs, interests, and values that they offer each other.

Matrix approach The matrix approach uses both functional and divisional chains of command simultaneously, in the same part of the organization.

Matrix boss A matrix boss is a functional or product supervisor responsible for one side of the matrix.

Merger A merger occurs when two or more organizations combine to become one.

Message The message is the tangible formulation of an idea to be sent to the employee.

Mission The mission describes the organization's values, aspirations, and reason for being. A well-defined mission is the basis for development of all subsequent goals and plans.

Mission statement The formal mission statement is a broadly stated definition of purpose that distinguishes the organization from others of a similar type.

Monoculture A culture that accepts only one way of doing things and one set of values and beliefs is called a monoculture.

Moral-rights approach The moral-rights approach asserts that human beings have fundamental rights and liberties that cannot be taken away by an individual's decision. Thus, an ethically correct decision is one that best maintains the rights of those affected by it.

Motivation Motivation is the arousal of enthusiasm and persistence to pursue a certain course of action.

Motivators Herzberg's second factor, motivators, influences job satisfaction based on fulfilling higher-level needs such as achievement, recognition, responsibility, and opportunities for personal growth.

Multinational corporation (MNC) Although the term has no precise definition, a multinational corporation (MNC) typically receives more than 25 percent of its total sales revenues from operations outside the parent's home country.

Myers-Briggs Type Indicator (MBTI) The MBTI™ assessment measures a person's preferences for introversion versus extroversion, sensation versus intuition, thinking versus feeling, and judging versus perceiving.

Natural dimension The natural dimension includes all elements that occur naturally on Earth, including plants, animals, rocks, and resources such as air, water, and climate.

Need for change A need for change is a disparity between existing and desired performance levels.

Negotiation One distinctive type of conflict management is negotiation, whereby people engage in give-and-take discussions and consider various alternatives to reach a joint decision that is acceptable to both parties.

Neutralizer A neutralizer is a situational variable that counteracts a leadership style and prevents the leader from displaying certain behaviors.

New-venture fund Provides resources from which individuals and groups can draw to develop new ideas, products, or businesses.

New-venture team A new-venture team is a unit separate from the rest of the organization that is responsible for developing and initiating a major innovation. New venture teams give free rein to members' creativity because their separate facilities and location unleash people from the restrictions imposed by organizational rules and procedures.

Nondirective interview A conversation where the interviewer asks broad, open-ended questions and permits the applicant to talk freely with minimal interruption, in an attempt to bring to light information, attitudes, and behavioral characteristics that might be concealed when answering structured questions.

Nonprogrammed decision A nonprogrammed decision is one made in response to a situation that is unique, is poorly defined and largely unstructured, and has important consequences for the organization.

Nonverbal communication Nonverbal communication means communicating through actions, gestures, facial expressions, and behavior rather than through words.

Normative The classical model of decision making is considered to be normative, which means it defines how a decision maker *should* make decisions.

Norming During the norming stage, conflict is resolved, and team harmony and unity emerge.

On-the-job training (OJT) In on-the-job training (OJT), an experienced employee is asked to take a new employee "under his or her wing" and show the newcomer how to perform job duties.

Open communication Open communication means sharing all types of information throughout the organization and across functional and hierarchical boundaries.

Open innovation Open innovation extends the search for and commercialization of innovative ideas beyond the boundaries of the organization.

Open-book management Open-book management allows employees to see for themselves—through charts, computer printouts, meetings, and so forth—the financial condition of the company.

Operational goals The results expected from departments, work groups, and individuals are the operational goals.

Opportunity An opportunity exists when managers see potential accomplishment that exceeds specified current goals.

Organization A social entity that is goal directed and deliberately structured.

Organization chart The characteristics of vertical structure are portrayed in the organization chart, which is the visual representation of an organization's structure.

Organization development Organization development (OD) is a planned, systematic process of change that uses behavioral science knowledge and techniques to improve an organization's health and effectiveness through its ability to adapt to the environment, improve internal relationships, and increase learning and problem-solving capabilities.

Organization structure Organization structure is the framework in which the organization defines how tasks are divided, resources are deployed, and departments are coordinated.

Organizational change Organizational change is defined as the adoption of a new idea or behavior by an organization.

Organizational commitment Organizational commitment refers to loyalty to and engagement with one's work organization.

Organizational control Organizational control is the systematic process through which managers regulate organizational activities to meet planned goals and standards of performance.

Organizational ecosystem An organizational ecosystem includes organizations in all the sectors of the task and general environments that provide the resource and information transactions, flows, and linkages necessary for an organization to thrive.

Organizational effectiveness The degree to which the organization achieves a stated goal, or succeeds in accomplishing what it tries to do.

Organizational environment The external organizational environment includes all elements existing outside the boundary of the organization that have the potential to affect the organization.

Organizational Planning A process where managers develop the overall plan for the organization, translate the plan into action, lay out operational factors, execute the plan, and then monitor and learn from it.

Organizational virtuousness A principle in which an organization pursues a positive human impact, moral goodness, and unconditional society betterment for its own sake.

Organizing Organizing refers to the deployment of organizational resources to achieve strategic goals.

Overconfidence When people overestimate their ability to predict uncertain outcomes.

P → O expectancy P → O expectancy is the expectancy that high performance of a task will lead to the desired outcome.

Panel interview An interview in which the candidate meets with several interviewers who take turns asking questions.

Passive follower The passive follower exhibits neither critical, independent thinking nor active participation. Being passive and uncritical, these people show neither initiative nor a sense of responsibility.

Pay-for-performance Pay-for-performance, also called *incentive pay*, means tying at least a portion of compensation to employee effort and performance.

People change People change concerns just a few employees, such as sending a handful of middle managers to a training course to improve their leadership skills.

Perception Perception is the cognitive process that people use to make sense out of the environment by selecting, organizing, and interpreting information from the environment.

Perceptual distortions Perceptual distortions are errors in perceptual judgment that arise from inaccuracies in any part of the perception process.

Performance The attainment of organizational goals by using resources in an efficient and effective manner.

Performance appraisal Performance appraisal refers to observing and assessing employee performance, recording the assessment, and providing feedback to the employee.

Performing During the performing stage, the major emphasis is on problem solving and accomplishing the assigned task. Members are committed to the team's mission.

Permanent team A permanent team is a group of employees from all functional areas permanently assigned to focus on a specific task or activity.

Personal communication channels Personal communication channels exist outside the formally authorized channels. These informal communications coexist with formal channels but may skip hierarchical levels, cutting across vertical chains of command to connect virtually anyone in the organization.

Personal networking Personal networking refers to the acquisition and cultivation of personal relationships that cross departmental, hierarchical, and even organizational boundaries.

Personality An individual's personality is the set of characteristics that underlie a relatively stable pattern of behavior in response to ideas, objects, or people in the environment.

Personality testing A method by which a person answers a series of questions about his/her beliefs, attitudes, work habits, and how he/she might handle situations, in order to identify some of his/her interests and motivations.

Plan A plan is a blueprint for goal achievement and specifies the necessary resource allocations, schedules, tasks, and other actions.

Planning The concept of planning usually incorporates both ideas; it means determining the organization's goals and defining the means for achieving them.

Pluralism Pluralism means that an organization accommodates several subcultures. Movement toward pluralism seeks to integrate fully into the organization the employees who otherwise would feel isolated and ignored.

Point-counterpoint Point-counterpoint is a way to encourage constructive conflict by breaking a decision-making group into two subgroups and assigns them different, often competing, responsibilities.

Political instability Events such as riots, revolutions, or government upheavals that can affect the operations of an international company.

Political risk Political risk is the risk of loss of assets, earning power, or managerial control due to politically based events or actions by host governments.

Positive reinforcement Positive reinforcement is the administration of a pleasant and rewarding consequence following a desired behavior, such as praise for an employee who arrives on time or does a little extra work. Research shows that positive reinforcement does help motivate desired behaviors.

Post conventional or principled level At the post conventional, or principled level, individuals are guided by an internal set of values based on universal principles of justice and right and will even disobey rules or laws that violate these principles.

Power Power is the potential ability to influence the behavior of others.

Power distance The degree to which people accept inequality in power among institutions, organizations, and people.

Practical approach The practical approach sidesteps debates about what is right, good, or just and bases decisions on prevailing standards of the profession and the larger society, taking the interests of all stakeholders into account.

Pragmatic survivor The pragmatic survivor has qualities of all four extremes—depending on which style fits with the prevalent situation. This type of person uses whatever style best benefits his or her own position and minimizes risk.

Prejudice Prejudice is the tendency to view people who are different as being deficient.

Problem A problem occurs when organizational accomplishment is less than established goals.

Procedural justice Procedural justice requires that rules be administered fairly. Rules should be clearly stated and consistently and impartially enforced.

Process theories Process theories, including goal-setting theory, equity theory, and expectancy theory, explain how people select behaviors with which to meet their needs and determine whether their choices were successful.

Product change A product change is a change in the organization's product or service outputs.

Profitability ratio The profitability ratio describes the firm's profits relative to a source of profits, such as sales or assets.

Programmed decisions Programmed decisions involve situations that have occurred often enough to enable decision rules to be developed and applied in the future. Programmed decisions are made in response to recurring organizational problems.

Project manager A project manager is a person who is responsible for coordinating the activities of several departments for the completion of a specific project.

Punishment Punishment is the imposition of unpleasant outcomes on an employee, typically occurring after undesirable behavior.

Quality circle A quality circle is a group of six to twelve volunteer employees who meet regularly to discuss and solve problems affecting the quality of their work.

Quality partnering Quality partnering involves assigning dedicated personnel within a particular functional area of the business to identify opportunities for improvement throughout the work process.

Quantitative techniques The use of mathematics, statistics, and computer technology to facilitate management decision making.

Quants Refers to financial managers and others who make decisions based primarily on complex quantitative analysis.

Quasirationality Combining intuitive and analytical thought.

Queen bee syndrome Refers to a female boss who not only has no interest in fostering the careers of other women, but might even actively undermine them.

Realistic job preview (RJP) Managers use realistic job previews in recruiting to give applicants all pertinent and realistic information, both positive and negative, about a job and the organization.

Recruiting Recruiting is defined as "activities or practices that define the characteristics of applicants to whom selection procedures are ultimately applied."

Reengineering Reengineering refers to the radical redesign of business processes to achieve dramatic improvements in cost, quality, service, and speed.

Referent power Referent power results from characteristics that command subordinates' identification with, respect and admiration for, and desire to emulate the leader.

Refreezing Refreezing, the third stage of organization development, occurs when individuals acquire new attitudes or values and are rewarded for them by the organization. The impact of new behaviors is evaluated and reinforced.

Reinforcement Reinforcement is defined as anything that causes a certain behavior to be repeated or inhibited.

Reinforcement theory Reinforcement theory simply looks at the relationship between behavior and its consequences. It focuses on changing or modifying employees' on-the-job behavior through the appropriate use of immediate rewards and punishments.

Relational coordinator Relational coordination refers to "frequent, timely, problem-solving communication carried out through [employee] relationships of shared goals, shared knowledge, and mutual respect."

Relationship conflict Relationship conflict refers to interpersonal incompatibility that creates tension and personal animosity among people.

Responsibility Responsibility is the flip side of the authority coin; it refers to the duty to perform the task or activity that one has been assigned.

Responsibility center A responsibility center is any organizational department or unit under the supervision of a single person who is responsible for its activity.

Responsibility Responsibility is the flip side of the authority coin; it refers to the duty to perform the task or activity that one has been assigned.

Revenue budget A revenue budget lists forecasted and actual revenues of the organization.

Reverse innovation Creating innovative, low-cost products for emerging markets and then quickly and inexpensively repackaging them for sale in developed countries.

Reward power Reward power results from the authority to bestow rewards.

Rightsizing Rightsizing refers to reducing the company's workforce intentionally to the point where the number of employees is deemed to be right for the company's current situation.

Risk Risk means that a decision has clear-cut goals and good information is available, but the future outcomes associated with each alternative are subject to chance.

Risk propensity Risk propensity is the willingness to undertake risk with the opportunity of gaining an increased payoff.

Role A set of expectations for a manager's behavior.

Role ambiguity Role ambiguity refers to uncertainty about what behaviors are expected of a person in a particular role.

Role conflict Role conflict refers to incompatible demands of different roles, such as the demands of a manager's superiors conflicting with those of the manager's subordinates.

Satisficing Satisficing means that decision makers choose the first solution alternative that satisfies minimal decision criteria. Rather than pursuing all alternatives to identify the single solution that will maximize economic returns, managers will opt for the first solution that appears to solve the problem, even if better solutions are presumed to exist.

Scenario building An extension of contingency planning is a forecasting technique known as scenario building.

Scientific management Scientifically determined jobs and management practices as the way to improve efficiency and labor productivity.

Selection In the selection process, employers assess applicants' characteristics in an attempt to determine the "fit" between the job and applicant characteristics.

Self-awareness Self-awareness means being aware of the internal aspects of one's nature, such as personality traits, beliefs, emotions, attitudes, and perceptions, and appreciating how your patterns affect other people.

Self-confidence Self-confidence refers to general assurance in one's own ideas, judgment, and capabilities.

Self-efficacy Self-efficacy is an individual's strong belief that he or she can accomplish a specific task or outcome successfully.

Self-managed teams Self-managed teams typically consist of five to twenty multi-skilled workers who rotate jobs to produce an entire product or service or at least one complete aspect or portion of a product or service (e.g., engine assembly or insurance claim processing).

Self-management Self-management is the ability to engage in self-regulating thoughts and behavior to accomplish all your tasks and handle difficult or challenging situations.

Self-serving bias The self-serving bias is the tendency to overestimate the contribution of internal factors to one's successes and the contribution of external factors to one's failures.

Servant leader A servant leader is a leader who serves others by working to fulfill followers' needs and goals, as well as to achieve the organization's larger mission.

Service technology Service technology is characterized by intangible outputs and direct contact between employees and customers.

Short-term orientation A short-term orientation, found in Russia and West Africa, is more concerned with the past and the present and places a high value on tradition and meeting social obligations.

Situational model The situational model of leadership, which originated with Hersey and Blanchard, is an interesting extension of the behavioral theories summarized in the leadership grid. This approach focuses a great deal of attention on the characteristics of followers in determining appropriate leadership behavior.

Six sigma Six Sigma is a quality control approach that emphasizes a relentless pursuit of higher quality and lower costs.

Skunkworks A skunkworks is one variation of a new-venture team, a separate small, informal, highly autonomous, and often secretive group that focuses on breakthrough ideas for a business.

Slogan A slogan is a phrase or sentence that succinctly expresses a key corporate value. Many companies use a slogan or saying to convey special meaning to employees.

Small-batch production Small-batch production firms produce goods in batches of one or a few products designed to customer specification.

Social facilitation Social facilitation is the tendency for the presence of other people to influence an individual's motivation and performance.

Social learning Social learning means to learn informally from others by using social media tools, including mobile technologies, social networking, wikis and blogs, virtual games, and so forth.

Social learning theory Social learning theory is related to the reinforcement perspective, but it proposes that an individual's motivation can result not just from direct experience of rewards and punishments but also from the person's observations of other people's behavior.

Social media Social media is a group of Internet-based applications that allow the creation and exchange of user-generated content.

Social media programs Social media programs include company online community pages, social media sites such as Facebook or LinkedIn, microblogging platforms such as Twitter and China's Weibo, and company online forums.

Sociocultural dimension The sociocultural dimension of the general environment represents the demographic characteristics as well as the norms, customs, and values of the general population. Important sociocultural characteristics are geographical distribution and population density, age, and education levels.

Socioemotional role The socioemotional role is a team role in which an individual provides support for team members' emotional needs and helps strengthen social unity.

Span of management The span of management is the number of employees reporting to a supervisor.

Special-purpose team Another type of cross-functional team, the special purpose team, is created outside the formal organization structure to undertake a project of special importance or creativity.

Staff authority Staff authority includes the right to advise, recommend, and counsel in the staff specialists' area of expertise. Staff authority is a communication relationship; staff specialists advise managers in technical areas.

Stakeholder A stakeholder is any group or person within or outside the organization that has some type of investment or interest in the organization's performance and is affected by the organization's actions (employees, customers, shareholders, and so forth).

Stakeholder mapping There is growing interest in a technique called stakeholder mapping, which basically provides a systematic way to identify the expectations, needs, importance, and relative power of various stakeholders, which may change over time.

Stereotype A rigid, exaggerated, irrational belief associated with a particular group of people is called a stereotype.

Stereotype threat Stereotype threat occurs when a person who, when engaged in a task, is aware of a stereotype about his or her identity group suggesting that he or she will not perform well on that task.

Stereotyping One common perceptual error is stereotyping, the tendency to assign an individual to a group or broad category (e.g., female, black, elderly; or male, white, disabled) and then to attribute widely held generalizations about the group to the individual.

Storming During the storming stage, individual personalities emerge. People become more assertive in clarifying their roles and what is expected of them. This stage is marked by conflict and disagreement.

Story A story is a narrative based on true events and is repeated frequently and shared among organizational employees.

Strategic conversation Strategic conversation refers to dialogue across boundaries and hierarchical levels about the team or organization's vision, critical strategic themes, and the values that help achieve important goals.

Strategic goals Strategic goals, sometimes called *official goals*, are broad statements describing where the organization wants to be in the future.

Strategic issues Strategic issues are "events or forces either inside or outside an organization that are likely to alter its ability to achieve its objectives."

Strategic management Strategic management refers to the set of decisions and actions used to formulate and execute strategies that will provide a competitively superior fit between the organization and its environment so as to achieve organizational goals.

Strategic plans Strategic plans define the action steps by which the company intends to attain strategic goals. The strategic plan is the blueprint that defines the organizational activities and resource allocations—in the form of cash, personnel, space, and facilities—required for meeting these targets.

Strategy The plan of action that describes resource allocation and activities for dealing with the environment, achieving a competitive advantage, and attaining the organization's goals.

Strategy execution Strategy execution is the stage of strategic management that involves the use of managerial and organizational tools to direct resources toward achieving strategic outcomes.

Strategy formulation The stage of strategic management that involves the use of managerial and organizational tools to direct resources toward achieving strategic outcomes.

Strengths Strengths are natural talents and abilities that have been supported and reinforced with learned knowledge and skills.

Stress Stress is a physiological and emotional response to stimuli that place physical or psychological demands on an individual and create uncertainty and lack of personal control when important outcomes are at stake.

Stretch goals Stretch goals are reasonable yet highly ambitious goals that are so clear, compelling, and imaginative that they fire up employees and engender excellence. Stretch goals are typically so far beyond the current levels that people have to be innovative to find ways to reach them.

Structured interviews Interviews that use a set of standardized questions that are asked of every applicant so comparisons can be made easily.

Substitute for leadership A substitute for leadership is a situational variable that makes a leadership style redundant or unnecessary.

Subsystems Parts of a system that depend on one another for their functioning.

Suppliers Suppliers provide the raw materials that the organization uses to produce its output.

Supply chain management Supply chain management refers to managing the sequence of suppliers and purchasers, covering all stages of processing from obtaining raw materials to distributing finished goods to consumers.

Survey feedback With survey feedback, OD change agents survey employees to gather their opinions regarding corporate values, leadership, participation, cohesiveness, and other aspects of the organization, then meet with small groups to share the results and brainstorm solutions to problems identified by the results.

Sustainability Sustainability refers to economic development that generates wealth and meets the needs of the current generation while preserving the environment and society so future generations can meet their needs as well.

SWOT analysis SWOT analysis includes a careful assessment of strengths, weaknesses, opportunities, and threats that affect organizational performance.

Symbol A symbol is an object, act, or event that conveys meaning to others.

Synergy The concept of synergy says that the whole is greater than the sum of its parts. The organization must be managed as a whole.

System A set of interrelated parts that function as a whole to achieve a common purpose.

Systems thinking Systems thinking is the ability to see both the distinct elements of a system or situation and the complex and changing interaction among those elements.

Tactical goals After strategic goals are formulated, the next step is to define tactical goals, which are the results that major divisions and departments within the organization intend to achieve.

Tactical plans Tactical plans are designed to help execute the major strategic plans and to accomplish a specific part of the company's strategy.

Tall structure A tall structure is characterized by an overall narrow span of management and a relatively large number of hierarchical levels.

Task conflict Task conflict refers to disagreements among people about the goals to be achieved or the content of the tasks to be performed.

Task environment The task environment is closer to the organization and includes the sectors that conduct day-to-day transactions with the organization and directly influence its basic operations and performance. It is generally considered to include competitors, suppliers, customers, and the labor market.

Task force A task force is a temporary team or committee designed to solve a problem involving several departments.

Task specialist role The task specialist role is a team role in which an individual devotes personal time and energy to helping the team accomplish its activities and reach its goal.

Team A team is a unit of two or more people who interact and coordinate their work to accomplish a common goal to which they are committed and hold themselves mutually accountable.

Team building Team building is an OD intervention that enhances cohesiveness by helping groups of people learn to work together as a team.

Team cohesiveness Team cohesiveness is defined as the extent to which members are attracted to the team and motivated to remain in it.

Team management A management style that is often considered the most effective style and is recommended for leaders because organization members work together to accomplish tasks.

Team norm A team norm is an informal standard of conduct that is shared by team members and guides their behavior.

Team-based structure A team-based structure is one in which the entire organization is made up of horizontal teams that coordinate their activities and work directly with customers to accomplish organizational goals.

Technical complexity The difference among the three manufacturing technologies is called technical complexity. Technical complexity is the degree to which machinery is involved in the production to the exclusion of people.

Technical skills The understanding and proficiency in the performance of specific tasks.

Technological dimension The technological dimension of the general environment includes scientific and technological advancements in a specific industry, as well as in society at large.

Technology change A technology change is a change in the organization's production process—how the organization does its work. Technology changes are designed to make the production of a product or service more efficient.

Top leader In a matrix structure, the top leader oversees both the product and the functional chains of command and is responsible for the entire matrix.

Top-down budgeting Many companies use top-down budgeting, which means that the budgeted amounts for the coming year are literally imposed on middle- and lower-level managers.

Total quality management (TQM) Total quality management focuses on managing the total organization to deliver better quality to customers, moved to the forefront in helping U.S. managers deal with global competition. The approach infuses high-quality values throughout every activity within a company, with frontline workers intimately involved in the process. Four significant elements of quality management are employee involvement, focus on the customer, benchmarking, and continuous improvement.

Traits Traits are distinguishing personal characteristics, such as intelligence, self confidence, energy, and independence.

Transactional leader A transactional leader clarifies subordinates' roles and task requirements, initiates structure, provides rewards, and displays consideration for followers.

Transformational leader A transformational leader is distinguished by a special ability to bring about innovation and change by creating an inspiring vision, shaping values, building relationships, and providing meaning for followers.

Triple bottom line The term triple bottom line refers to measuring an organization's social performance, its environmental performance, and its financial performance. This is sometimes called the three Ps: People, Planet, and Profit.

Two-boss employees In a matrix structure, a person who reports to two supervisors simultaneously.

Type A behavior The behavior pattern referred to as Type A behavior is characterized by extreme competitiveness, impatience, aggressiveness, and devotion to work.

Type B behavior Type B behavior is a behavior pattern that reflects few of the Type A characteristics and includes a more balanced, relaxed approach to life.

Uncertainty Uncertainty means that managers know which goals they wish to achieve, but information about alternatives and future events is incomplete.

Uncertainty avoidance Characterized by people's intolerance for uncertainty and ambiguity and resulting support for beliefs that promise certainty and conformity.

Uncritical thinking A dependent, uncritical thinker does not consider possibilities beyond what he or she is told, does not contribute to the cultivation of the organization, and accepts the supervisor's ideas without thinking.

Unfreezing The first stage of the theory of organizational development, unfreezing, makes people throughout the organization aware of problems and the need for change.

Upward communication Formal upward communication includes messages that flow from the lower to the higher levels of the organization's hierarchy.

Utilitarian approach The utilitarian approach, espoused by the nineteenth century philosophers Jeremy Bentham and John Stuart Mill, holds that moral behavior produces the greatest good for the greatest number.

Valence Valence is the value of outcomes (rewards) to the individual.

Vicarious learning Vicarious learning, or *observational learning*, occurs when an individual sees others perform certain behaviors and get rewarded for them.

Virtual network approach A method of departmentalization that extends the idea of horizontal coordination and collaboration beyond the boundaries of the organization.

Virtual network structure With a virtual network structure, the organization subcontracts most of its major functions to separate companies and coordinates their activities from a small headquarters organization.

Virtual team A virtual team is a group made up of geographically or organizationally dispersed members who are linked primarily through advanced information and telecommunications technologies.

Vision An attractive, ideal future that is credible yet not readily attainable.

Wage and salary surveys Wage and salary surveys show what other organizations pay incumbents in jobs that match a sample of key jobs selected by the organization.

Whistle-blowing Employee disclosure of illegal, unethical, or illegitimate practices on the employer's part is called whistle-blowing.

Wholly owned foreign affiliate A wholly owned foreign affiliate is a foreign subsidiary over which an organization has complete control.

Work redesign Work redesign means altering jobs to increase both the quality of employees' work experience and their productivity.

Work specialization Work specialization, sometimes called *division of labor*, is the degree to which organizational tasks are subdivided into separate jobs.

Zero-based budgeting Zero-based budgeting is an approach to planning and decision making that requires a complete justification for every line item in a budget, instead of carrying forward a prior budget and applying a percentage change.

Name Index

Company Index